22624

REFERENCE

ef
T
00
C8
985

Current
biography yearbook

P9-CIU-827

Current biography yearbook.
Ref CT100.C8                    60528

SOUTH PUGET SOUND COMM. COLLEG

8856011538560115385601

# Current Biography Yearbook

# 1985

LIBRARY-MEDIA CENTER
SOUTH PUGET SOUND COMMUNITY COLLEGE
2011 MOTTMAN ROAD, S.W.
OLYMPIA, WA 98502

# Current Biography Yearbook
## 1985

EDITOR
Charles Moritz

ASSOCIATE EDITORS
Henry Sloan
Kieran Dugan
Judith Graham
Mary E. Kiffer

ASSISTANT EDITOR
Margaret Brodhead

LIBRARY-MEDIA CENTER
SOUTH PUGET SOUND COMMUNITY COLLEGE
2011 MOTTMAN ROAD, S.W.
OLYMPIA, WA 98502

THE H. W. WILSON COMPANY

NEW YORK

FORTY-SIXTH ANNUAL CUMULATION—1985

PRINTED IN THE UNITED STATES OF AMERICA

*International Standard Serial No. (0084-9499)*

*Library of Congress Catalog Card No. (40-27432)*

Copyright © 1985, 1986 by The H. W. Wilson Company. All rights reserved. No part of this work may be reproduced or copied in any form or by any means, including but not restricted to graphic, electronic, and mechanical—for example, photocopying, recording, taping, or information and retrieval systems—without the express written permission of the publisher, except that a reviewer may quote and a magazine or newspaper may print brief passages as part of a review written specifically for inclusion in that magazine or newspaper.

22624

# PREFACE

The aim of *Current Biography Yearbook 1985,* like that of the preceding volumes in this series of annual dictionaries of contemporary biography, now in its fifth decade of publication, is to provide the reference librarian, the student, or any researcher with brief, objective, accurate, and well-documented biographical articles about living leaders in all fields of human accomplishment the world over. Whenever feasible, obituary notices appear for persons whose biographies have been published in *Current Biography,* and every attempt is made to pick up obituaries that have inadvertently been omitted in previous years.

*Current Biography Yearbook 1985* carries on the policy of including new and updated biographical sketches that supersede earlier, outdated articles. Sketches have been made as accurate and objective as possible through careful researching by *Current Biography* writers in newspapers, magazines, authoritative reference books, and news releases of both government and private agencies. Immediately after they are published in the eleven monthly issues, articles are submitted to biographees to give them an opportunity to suggest corrections in time for publication of the *Current Biography Yearbook.* To take account of major changes in the careers of biographees, sketches have also been revised before they are included in the yearbook. With the exception of occasional interviews, the questionnaire filled out by the biographee remains the main source of direct information.

Some persons who are not professional authors but who have written books are included under *Nonfiction* in addition to their vocational fields. The annual bestowal of Nobel Prizes has added articles to the volume. The pages immediately following contain *Explanations; Key to Reference Abbreviations; Key to Pronunciation;* and *Key to Abbreviations.* The indexes at the end of the volume are *Biographical References; Periodicals and Newspapers Consulted; Classification by Profession;* and *Cumulated Index—1981-1985.* The newly published *Current Biography Cumulated Index 1940-1985* cumulates and supersedes all previous indexes, and the reader will need to consult only that index in order to locate a name.

For their assistance in preparing *Current Biography Yearbook 1985,* I should like to thank the associate and assistant editors.

Charles Moritz

# Explanations

Authorities for biographees' full names, with some exceptions, are the bibliographical publications of The Wilson Company. When a biographee prefers a certain name form, that is indicated in the heading of the article: for example, Niemöller, (Friedrich Gustav Emil) Martin means that he is usually referred to as Martin Niemöller. When a professional name is used in the heading, as, for example, Anne Bancroft, the real name (in this case Annemarie Italiano) appears in the article itself.

The heading of each article includes the pronunciation of the name if it is unusual, date of birth (if obtainable), and occupation. The article is supplemented by a list of references to sources of biographical information, in two alphabets: (1) newspapers and periodicals and (2) books. (See the section *Biographical References*, found in the rear of this volume.)

# Key to Reference Abbreviations

References to some newspapers and periodicals are listed in abbreviated form; for example, "Sat Eve Post 217:14 S 30 '44 por" means *Saturday Evening Post*, volume 217, page 14, September 30, 1944, with portrait. (For full names, see the section *Periodicals and Newspapers Consulted*, found in the rear of this volume.)

| | | |
|---|---|---|
| January—Ja | July—Jl | Journal—J |
| February—F | August—Ag | Magazine—Mag |
| March—Mr | September—S | Monthly—Mo |
| April—Ap | October—O | Portrait—por |
| May—My | November—N | Weekly—W |
| June—Je | December—D | Review—R |

# Key to Pronunciation

| | | | | | |
|---|---|---|---|---|---|
| ā | āle | ō | ōld | ü | Pronounced approximately as ē, with rounded lips: French u, as in *menu* (mə-nü); German ü, as in *grün* |
| â | câre | ô | ôrb | | |
| a | add | o | odd | | |
| ä | ärm | oi | oil | | |
| | | o͞o | ooze | | |
| ē | ēve | o͝o | foot | | |
| e | end | ou | out | ə | the schwa, an unstressed vowel representing the sound that is spelled |
| | | | | | a as in sofa |
| g | go | | | | e as in fitted |
| | | | | | i as in edible |
| î | îce | *th* | *then* | | o as in melon |
| i | ill | th | thin | | u as in circus |
| ᴋ | German *ch* as in *ich* (iᴋ) | | | | |
| | | ū | cūbe | zh | azure |
| ɴ | Not pronounced, but indicates the nasal tone of the preceding vowel, as in the French *bon* (bôɴ) | û | ûrn; French eu, as in *jeu* zhû), German ö, oe, as in *schön* (shûn), *Goethe* (gû´te) | ´ = | main accent |
| | | | | ˝ = | secondary accent |
| | | u | tub | | |

# Key to Abbreviations

| | | | |
|---|---|---|---|
| AAAA | Amateur Athletic Association of America | ECA | Economic Cooperation Administration |
| AAU | Amateur Athletic Union | ECOSOC | Economic and Social Council |
| AAUP | American Association of University Professors | EDC | Economic Defense Community |
| ABA | American Bar Association | EEC | European Economic Community |
| ABC | American Broadcasting Company | EEOC | Equal Employment Opportunity Commission |
| ACA | Americans for Constitutional Action | ERA | Equal Rights Amendment |
| ACLU | American Civil Liberties Union | E.R.A. | Earned Run Average |
| ACTWU | Amalgamated Clothing and Textile Workers Union | ESA | Economic Stabilization Administration |
| ADA | Americans for Democratic Action | | |
| AEC | Atomic Energy Commission | FAO | Food and Agriculture Organization |
| AFL | American Football League | FBI | Federal Bureau of Investigation |
| AFL-CIO | American Federation of Labor and Congress of Industrial Organizations | FCC | Federal Communications Commission |
| ALA | American Library Association | FEPC | Fair Employment Practice Committee |
| AMA | American Medical Association | FHA | Federal Housing Administration |
| AP | Associated Press | FOA | Foreign Operations Administration |
| ASCAP | American Society of Composers, Authors and Publishers | FPC | Federal Power Commission |
| | | FSA | Federal Security Agency |
| ASNE | American Society of Newspaper Editors | FTC | Federal Trade Commission |
| | | GATT | General Agreement on Tariffs and Trade |
| B.A. | Bachelor of Arts | G.B.E. | Knight or Dame, Grand Cross Order of the British Empire |
| BBC | British Broadcasting Corporation | | |
| B.D. | Bachelor of Divinity | G.C.B. | Knight or Dame, Grand Cross of the Bath |
| B.L.S. | Bachelor of Library Science | | |
| B.S. | Bachelor of Science | GOP | Grand Old Party (Republican) |
| CAA | Civil Aeronautics Administration | | |
| CAB | Civil Aeronautics Board | HHS | Department of Health and Human Services |
| C.B. | Companion of the Bath | | |
| CBC | Canadian Broadcasting Corporation | H.M. | His Majesty; Her Majesty |
| C.B.E. | Commander of (the Order of) the British Empire | HUD | Department of Housing and Urban Development |
| CBS | Columbia Broadcasting System | | |
| C.E. | Civil Engineer | IBM | International Business Machines Corporation |
| CEA | Council of Economic Advisers | | |
| CED | Committee for Economic Development | ICBM | Intercontinental Ballistic Missile |
| | | ICC | Interstate Commerce Commission |
| CENTO | Central Treaty Organization | ICFTU | International Confederation of Free Trade Unions |
| CIA | Central Intelligence Agency | | |
| C.M.G. | Companion of (the Order of) St. Michael and St. George | IGY | International Geophysical Year |
| | | ILA | International Longshoremen's Association |
| CNN | Cable Network News | | |
| Com. | Commodore | ILGWU | International Ladies' Garment Workers Union |
| CORE | Congress of Racial Equality | | |
| | | ILO | International Labor Organization |
| DAR | Daughters of the American Revolution | IMF | International Monetary Fund |
| | | INS | International News Service |
| D.C.L. | Doctor of Civil Law | IRA | Irish Republican Army |
| D.D. | Doctor of Divinity | | |
| D.Eng. | Doctor of Engineering | J.D. | Doctor of Jurisprudence |
| D.F.C. | Distinguished Flying Cross | | |
| D.J. | Doctor of Jurisprudence | K.B.E. | Knight of (the Order of) the British Empire |
| D.Litt. | Doctor of Literature | | |
| D.Mus. | Doctor of Music | K.C. | King's Counsel |
| D.Pol.Sc. | Doctor of Political Science | K.C.B. | Knight Commander of the Bath |
| D.S.C. | Distinguished Service Cross | KGB | Committee of State Security (Soviet secret police) |
| D.Sc. | Doctor of Science | | |
| D.S.M. | Distinguished Service Medal | | |
| D.S.O. | Distinguished Service Order | L.H.D. | Doctor of Humane Letters |

| | | | | |
|---|---|---|---|---|
| Litt.D. | Doctor of Letters | | Q.C. | Queen's Counsel |
| LL.B. | Bachelor of Laws | | | |
| LL.D. | Doctor of Laws | | RAF | Royal Air Force |
| | | | RCA | Radio Corporation of America |
| M.A. | Master of Arts | | REA | Rural Electrification Administration |
| M.B.A. | Master of Business Administration | | RFC | Reconstruction Finance Corporation |
| MBS | Mutual Broadcasting System | | RKO | Radio-Keith-Orpheum |
| M.C.E. | Master of Civil Engineering | | ROTC | Reserve Officers' Training Corps |
| M.D. | Doctor of Medicine | | | |
| M.E. | Master of Engineering | | SAC | Strategic Air Command |
| METO | Middle East Treaty Organization | | SALT | Strategic Arms Limitation Talks |
| MGM | Metro-Goldwyn-Mayer | | S.J. | Society of Jesus (Jesuit) |
| M.Lit. | Master of Literature | | SCAP | Supreme Command for the Allied Powers |
| M.P. | Member of Parliament | | | |
| MPPDA | Motion Picture Producers and Distributors of America | | SEATO | Southeast Asia Treaty Organization |
| | | | SEC | Securities and Exchange Commission |
| MRP | Mouvement Républicain Populaire | | | |
| MSA | Mutual Security Agency | | SHAEF | Supreme Headquarters, Allied Expeditionary Force |
| M.Sc. | Master of Science | | | |
| Msgr. | Monsignor, Monseigneur | | SHAPE | Supreme Headquarters, Allied Powers Europe |
| | | | S.J.D. | Doctor of Juridical Science |
| NAACP | National Association for the Advancement of Colored People | | SLA | Special Libraries Association |
| | | | S.T.B. | Bachelor of Sacred Theology |
| NAB | National Association of Broadcasters | | S.T.D. | Doctor of Sacred Theology |
| NAM | National Association of Manufacturers | | TVA | Tennessee Valley Authority |
| NASA | National Aeronautics and Space Administration | | UAR | United Arab Republic |
| | | | UAW | United Automobile, Aircraft, and Agricultural Implement Workers of America |
| NATO | North Atlantic Treaty Organization | | | |
| NBC | National Broadcasting Company | | | |
| NCAA | National Collegiate Athletic Association | | UK | United Kingdom |
| | | | UMWA | United Mine Workers of America |
| NEA | National Education Association | | UN | United Nations |
| NFL | National Football League | | UNESCO | United Nations Educational, Scientific, and Cultural Organization |
| NLRB | National Labor Relations Board | | | |
| NMU | National Maritime Union | | UNICEF | United Nations Children's Fund |
| NOW | National Organization for Women | | UNRRA | United Nations Relief and Rehabilitation Administration |
| NRA | National Recovery Administration | | | |
| NRPB | National Resources Planning Board | | UPI | United Press and International News Service |
| NYA | National Youth Administration | | | |
| | | | USFL | United States Football League |
| OAS | Organization of American States | | USO | United Service Organizations |
| O.B.E. | Officer of (the Order of) the British Empire | | USSR | Union of Soviet Socialist Republics |
| | | | USWA | United Steel Workers of America |
| OCD | Office of Civilian Defense | | | |
| OEEC | Organization for European Economic Cooperation | | VA | Veterans Administration |
| | | | VFW | Veterans of Foreign Wars |
| OMB | Office of Management and Budget | | | |
| OPA | Office of Price Administration | | WFTU | World Federation of Trade Unions |
| OPEC | Organization of Petroleum Exporting Countries | | WHO | World Health Organization |
| | | | WPA | Work Projects Administration |
| PBS | Public Broadcasting Service | | YMCA | Young Men's Christian Association |
| PEN | Poets, Playwrights, Editors, Essayists and Novelists (International Association) | | YMHA | Young Men's Hebrew Association |
| | | | YWCA | Young Women's Christian Association |
| Ph.B. | Bachelor of Philosophy | | | |
| Ph.D. | Doctor of Philosophy | | YWHA | Young Women's Hebrew Association |
| PLO | Palestine Liberation Organization | | | |
| PWA | Public Works Administration | | | |

# Current
# Biography
# Yearbook
# 1985

## Adelman, Kenneth L(ee)

*June 9, 1946– Director of the United States Arms
Control and Disarmament Agency. Address: b.
U.S. Arms Control and Disarmament Agency,
320 21st St., N.W., Washington, D.C. 20451*

President Ronald Reagan made one of his most
controversial appointments when in January 1983
he nominated Kenneth L. Adelman to become director of the semiautonomous Arms Control and
Disarmament Agency, which since 1961 has had
responsibility for developing arms control initiatives and overseeing related negotiations. Adelman
had been dealing with problems in international
relations as a student, researcher, and government
official for the previous decade and a half and was
serving as deputy permanent representative of the
United States to the United Nations at the time of
his nomination to the ACDA post. His relative
youth and limited experience, as well as his reputation as an acerbic advocate of conservative
views, created substantial opposition to the appointment, which was approved in the Senate only
after bitter debate. Although Adelman is nominally
the principal adviser on arms control to the president and the secretary of state, his actual influence
seems, like that of his predecessors, to be limited.

Kenneth Lee Adelman, the fourth of the six children of Harry Adelman, an attorney, and Corinne
(Unger) Adelman, was born on June 9, 1946 in Chicago and grew up in the city's South Shore neighborhood. He swam competitively as a high-school
student, and after his graduation he entered Grinnell College in Iowa to engage in that sport under
the tutelage of a coach whom he admired. While
there, he set a conference record in the butterfly
event, became captain of the swimming team, and
earned a B.A. degree in philosophy and religion in
1967.

After leaving Grinnell, Adelman volunteered
for the Marine Corps but was rejected because of
chronic eczema. He then went to Washington,
D.C., where he worked for the Department of
Commerce from 1968 to 1970 and obtained an M.A.
degree in political science from Georgetown University in 1969. He moved to the Office of Economic Opportunity in 1970, and during his two years
there he served as special assistant to the director
of Volunteers in Service to America (VISTA) and
as assistant to the director of congressional relations. At OEO he met his future wife, Carol Craigle,
who had been on the staff of Representative Donald Rumsfeld when President Richard Nixon appointed him director of the OEO.

In the fall of 1972 Adelman accompanied his
wife to Zaire, where she worked as a public-health

specialist for the State Department's Agency for International Development (AID). During their two-
and-a-half years in Zaire, Adelman collected African art, wrote articles for the *Washington Post* and
*Foreign Affairs*, and perfected his French to the
point that he was able to serve as Muhammad Ali's
translator when the boxer came to Zaire in 1974 to
fight George Foreman for the world heavyweight
title. Adelman also served as chief liaison officer
for the Zaire River expedition, which commemo-
rated the 100th anniversary of Sir Henry Morton
Stanley's exploration of that waterway.

Adelman spent most of his time in Zaire, however, in doing research for his dissertation, "The Influence of Religion on National Integration in
Zaire," in which he concluded that Catholicism,
Protestantism, and the traditional religions of the
Bantu people had all hindered the substitution of
national for parochial loyalties. Only Kimbangu-
ism—an indigenous Zairian offshoot of Christianity, founded by Simon Kimbangu—had shown any
potential for becoming a national religion, but it remained primarily the religion of the Bokongo element of the population. Adelman's work earned
him a Ph.D. degree in political theory from Georgetown University in 1975.

The Adelmans returned to the United States in
the spring of 1975 to await the birth of their first
child. They had intended to go next to Bangkok,
Thailand, where he planned to teach philosophy
and religion and she had been assigned to another
AID post. But developments in neighboring Indo-

china dissuaded them from moving to that troubled region. After working briefly in AID's congressional liaison office in Washington in 1975-76, Adelman became special assistant to Donald Rumsfeld, who had been appointed Secretary of Defense by President Gerald R. Ford.

With the beginning of President Jimmy Carter's administration in early 1977, Adelman left government service to become a senior political scientist with the Strategic Studies Center of the Stanford Research Institute in Arlington, Virginia, a defense-oriented think tank, now known as SRI International. He spent most of his time working as a specialist in African affairs and wrote a number of articles about that continent. During that time he also taught evening classes on Shakespeare at Georgetown University and gave lectures in African studies at the Catholic University of America.

In 1980, under the auspices of the Strategic Studies Center, Adelman published *African Realities* (Crane, Russak Co.), a book that dealt at length with the region's relevance for American security and its place in East-West relations. He emphasized what he saw as a grave Soviet threat in Africa, warned that Americans must encourage the development of democracy and capitalism on that continent, and called for greater understanding of its people.

In 1977 Adelman's article "The Black Man's Burden" appeared in the fall issue of *Foreign Affairs*. That tough-minded essay on the lack of democracy among black-ruled nations of Africa caught the attention of Richard Allen, who later became President Ronald Reagan's national security adviser. Allen introduced Adelman to the inner circle of neoconservatives who eventually played a significant role in the Reagan administration. Adelman became a member of the executive board of the Committee on the Present Danger, which criticized the strategic arms limitation talks (SALT) conducted by the Carter administration. When Reagan began his campaign for the presidency, Adelman provided him with position papers and appeared on his list of foreign-policy advisers.

After Reagan's election in November 1980, Adelman served on the president-elect's transition team, where he became identified with the more moderate wing of the victorious Republican coalition. He was offered posts as assistant secretary of state for Latin American affairs, as deputy director of the Arms Control and Disarmament Agency, and as a member of the staff of the National Security Council, but he insisted that he was not interested in a position with the administration. Following Reagan's inauguration Adelman returned to the SRI. He finally changed his mind, however, when in April 1981 one of his former professors from Georgetown, Jeane Kirkpatrick, asked him for the second time to join her at the United Nations, where she had taken the post of United States ambassador. Adelman accepted the post of deputy permanent representative with the rank of ambassador extraordinary and plenipotentiary.

As the second-ranking member of the United States mission, Adelman headed the American delegation to the UN second special session on disarmament. At the UN he proved himself to be a vigorous defender of the United States position and an outspoken critic of the Soviet bloc and of what he considered to be the hypocrisy of Third World diplomacy. Among other things, he accused the USSR and its allies of using banned chemical and biological weapons in Afghanistan and Southeast Asia. One western diplomat described his speeches as containing "some of the most ferocious language heard around here since the cold war," and another observer equated Adelman's dealings with representatives of Third World nations with the behavior of a "junior Mafia don." Adelman's relationship with Jeane Kirkpatrick was said to have become strained after *Harper's* (July 1981) published his article about President Julius Nyerere of Tanzania, in which he attacked what he perceived to be the "royal incompetence" of the man thought by some in the West to be "the conscience of Africa."

On January 12, 1983 President Reagan nominated Adelman as director of the ACDA, to replace Eugene V. Rostow, who had been at odds with the White House on several issues. Some commentators predicted that Adelman would prove more of a "team player" than Rostow and would be able to move more adroitly among competing interests in the White House, the State Department, and the Defense Department. Conservatives did not immediately adopt Adelman, an ally of Rumsfeld and other moderates, as one of their own; but they found him an acceptable alternative to some other possible nominees. Many centrists and liberals, however, found the appointment "mind-boggling." "He bubbles over with ideas," said one of Adelman's colleagues at the UN, "and many of them are bad."

Resistance to Adelman had become embattled by the time the nomination reached the Committee on Foreign Relations of the Senate. Only a modest percentage of Adelman's prolific output of more than 100 magazine and newspaper articles dealt with arms control, and in those he was sharply critical of negotiations conducted under the Carter administration. Some observers, while conceding that he presented a reasonable argument when he contended in his articles that Carter had exaggerated the promises of the SALT II treaty, observed that Adelman's extravagant language raised serious doubts about his commitment to the idea of arms control negotiations.

At Adelman's first appearance before the Foreign Relations Committee, on January 27, 1983, Democratic Senator Alan Cranston of California suggested that President Reagan, who had previously appointed James Watt as Secretary of the Interior, was once again placing in a sensitive post a person out of sympathy with the mission of his office. With great effect Cranston quoted from an SRI study in which Adelman and a coauthor had argued that the United States would gain some advantages if South Africa developed nuclear weapons. Adelman was dismayed and pointed out that the bulk of the study had concentrated on the disadvantages of such a move. Overall, however, the nominee's performance did considerable harm to his own cause. He answered "I don't know" or "I hadn't thought about that" to some twenty questions on such key topics as the possibilities of winning or limiting nuclear wars, and the clumsy phrasing of many of his responses made Adelman seem uninformed.

On February 3, 1983, following two briefing sessions in which advisers bombarded him with practice questions, Adelman made his second appearance before the Foreign Relations Committee and conceded that he had been "overly cautious" at the previous hearing. Republican Senator Charles H. Percy of Illinois, a supporter of the nomination, described Adelman's second performance as "extremely satisfactory," and even opponents of the appointment were nonplussed. Paul E. Tsongas, the Massachusetts Democrat, asked: "Who is the real Ken Adelman, last week's or this week's?"

When the Foreign Relations Committee gathered on February 16, 1983, an announcement by Maryland's Republican Senator Charles McC. Mathias Jr. that he opposed Adelman's confirmation indicated that opponents of the nomination had the votes to recommend rejection. The senators, however, were not inclined to confront the president unnecessarily and voted to delay their decision for another week. The intention of some was to allow Reagan time to withdraw the nomination, but the president remained staunchly behind his candidate.

In an unusual step, Senator Cranston subsequently asked for a third hearing on the Adelman appointment, to draw attention to an article by Ken Auletta in the New York *Daily News* in May 1981, based on a telephone interview with Adelman, whom he quoted as describing arms negotiations as a "sham" to be pursued primarily for "political reasons." At the hearing, on February 24, Auletta confirmed what he had written, but the committee's examination of his notes showed that Adelman had also endorsed "real reductions" in nuclear weaponry.

On February 24, 1983 the Foreign Relations Committee, by a vote of nine to eight, recommended that the Senate reject Adelman's nomination as director of ACDA. The committee members agreed, however, by a margin of fourteen to three, to allow the nomination to be brought before the full Senate. Nevertheless, the rejection was a sharp blow to the administration.

Adelman's opponents gained time to fortify their case against him, and on March 17, 1983 the committee issued its report on the matter. In the portion that reflected the majority's opinion, Adelman was described as unqualified because his "interest in arms control was . . . more general than specific, his familiarity with a broad range of arms control issues low, his background in . . . negotiations

shallow, his approach political rather than substantive." On March 23 the committee also made public four documents sent to or passed on by Adelman, in which personnel at ACDA were criticized. The effect of the revelation was to heighten fears of an impending purge at the agency if Adelman's appointment were confirmed, and to erode further the credibility of the nominee.

By the time the Senate took up the Adelman nomination on April 14, 1983, opponents had not gained enough votes to block it. Reagan and other high-level officials had lobbied strongly in Adelman's behalf, and a majority of the Republican-dominated body was unwilling to deny the president his choice for such an important post. When the tally was finally made, eight Democrats and forty-nine Republicans voted to confirm Adelman, while four Republicans and thirty-eight Democrats voted to reject him. The margin of fifty-seven to forty-two was the closest since Earl L. Butz was confirmed as Nixon's secretary of agriculture in 1971 and marked only the seventh time in twenty-four years that forty or more senators voted against a presidential nominee.

As director of the ACDA, Adelman has been a forceful proponent of President Reagan's policies. In an article in the *New York Times* (October 6, 1984), he argued that recent improvements in the American economy and in the nation's defensive posture had improved the prospects for arms control. In another *Times* article (March 10, 1985), Adelman defended the Strategic Defense Initiative to develop space-based weapons that would destroy missiles fired at the United States. He described the program, known as "Star Wars," as a contribution to arms control in that it would mark a significant move away from reliance on the threat of nuclear counterattack as the guarantor of peace.

On occasion during his tenure at ACDA, Adelman's statements have stirred up controversy. In an unclassified letter to Senator Charles H. Percy, made public in June 1983, Adelman suggested that the United States would forgo deployment of 100 of the new MX missiles if the Soviet Union agreed to scrap most of its arsenal of over 800 medium and heavy land-based missiles. Former ACDA directors immediately criticized Adelman's proposal. Eugene V. Rostow commented unfavorably on the tactic of using a public letter to clarify the American negotiating position. President Carter's ACDA directors, Paul C. Warnke and George C. Seignious, respectively termed Adelman's remarks an unwise effort to make the Soviets "cry 'uncle'" and labeled it "preposterous." And Nixon's ADCA director, Gerard C. Smith, described the plan as "totally impractical."

A further source of embarrassment for the Reagan administration was an article by Adelman in *Foreign Affairs* (Winter 1984–85), in which he pointed out the grave difficulties in verifying compliance with the terms of treaties. He suggested that instead of pursuing formalized pacts, the superpowers might try an approach in which reciprocal acts of restraint would evolve into a system of "arms control without agreements." Whatever the merits of the suggestion, the timing of the article caused concern, since it appeared just weeks before Secretary of State George P. Shultz was to meet with Soviet Foreign Minister Andrei A. Gromyko to discuss the resumption of arms limitation talks, broken off in 1983. In the minds of some observers, Adelman's remarks raised doubts about the sincerity of the Reagan administration's commitment to serious negotiations. Furthermore, President Reagan's appointment in December 1984 of Paul H. Nitze as special adviser to the Secretary of State on arms control was interpreted by some as a "bureaucratic and diplomatic demotion" for Adelman.

On the other hand, sympathetic analysts have noted that Adelman has given the members of his staff three times the number of tasks that Rostow assigned them. Adelman himself has claimed that ideas proposed by him have influenced the president's initiatives regarding a ban on chemical weapons and a call for "umbrella talks" covering the gamut of the nuclear arsenal from intermediate and intercontinental missiles to space-based weapons.

Described by Carla Hall in the *Washington Post* (June 2, 1983) as "short, well-built, and just shy of being a little stocky," Kenneth L. Adelman has a round face, a mustache, and curly light brown hair flecked with gray. On August 29, 1971 he was married to Carol Craigle, who has been working for her Ph.D. degree at Johns Hopkins University. Adelman, who is Jewish, and his wife, who is Protestant, have agreed to bring up their two daughters, Jessica and Jocelyn, in Judaism.

Although sometimes considered cocky and combative, Adelman is also friendly and gregarious. One of his critics, Senator Paul E. Tsongas, once described him as "the kind of guy you'd want as a next-door neighbor." In a display of self-deprecating humor, Adelman has decorated his office walls with originals of newspaper and magazine cartoons dealing with his struggle for confirmation. As a graduate student, he started a Sherlock Holmes club in Washington, D.C. Now, according to his wife, "his hobby is his work," and he oftens spends his evenings, at his home in Arlington, Virginia, reading professional journals.

References: Atlan 252:31+ Jl '83 pors; N Y Times A p8 Ja 13 '83, A p13 Ap 15 '83; Time 121:18 Ja 24 '83 por; Washington Post E p1+ Je 2 '83 por; Who's Who in America, 1984-85

---

## Adler, Stella

Feb. 10, 1902– Actress; director; teacher.
Address: b. The Stella Adler Conservatory of Acting, 130 W. 56th St., New York City, N.Y. 10019

"The theatre—acting, creating, interpreting—means total involvement, the totality of heart, mind, and spirit," Stella Adler once remarked. As an actress, director, and teacher, Miss Adler has been totally involved in the theatre for just under eighty years. Since making her stage debut, in 1906, she has appeared in nearly 200 productions in the United States and abroad, most notably for the Group Theatre, the Depression-era experimental company whose actors and directors drew their inspiration from the ideals of Konstantin Stanislavsky. Considered by many American theatre professionals to be the finest teacher of acting in the country, Stella Adler equates the craft of acting with life itself. As she explained in an interview in 1968, acting is "the total development of a human being into the most he can be and in as many directions as he can possibly take." Among those actors who have studied at the Stella Adler Conservatory of Acting since its establishment in 1949 are Marlon Brando, Eddie Albert, Warren Beatty, and Robert De Niro.

The youngest daughter of Jacob Pavlovitch and Sara (Levitzky) Adler, Stella Adler was born in New York City, New York on February 10, 1902. Her Russian-immigrant parents were the preemi-

Jose R. Lopez/New York Times

nent tragedians of the Yiddish stage in the United States. According to most theatre historians, it was largely because of the efforts of the Adlers' Independent Yiddish Art Company, a classical repertory troupe, that the Yiddish American theatre flourished in the early decades of the twentieth century. All of her siblings—most notably, Luther—became actors. "In my family, immediately you could barely walk, you were put on the stage," she told one interviewer. "All the children were."

Stella Adler made her own stage debut in 1906, in her father's production of Broken Hearts at the Grand Street Theatre in New York. The following year, she took the part of one of the young princes in Richard III. For the next ten years, she was in great demand, playing both girls' and boys' roles in a wide variety of classical and contemporary works for her parents' Yiddish-speaking group and for other theatrical companies. Because she spent so much of her time rehearsing and performing, her formal education was necessarily less extensive than that of her playmates—a fact that at the time caused her, by her own admission, considerable anguish and humiliation. In retrospect, however, she has come to see her years of observing the performances of great artists, her solid grounding in Shakespeare and in the European classics, and, perhaps most important, her onstage experience as the best possible training for her chosen craft.

In 1919 Stella Adler made her first appearance in London, as Naomi in Elisha Ben Avia at the Pavilion Theatre, Mile End. On her return to New York a year later, she accepted featured roles in several commercial productions, among them the part of Butterfly in the fantasy The World We Live In, an unexpected hit of the 1922–23 theatrical season. Following a coast-to-coast tour on the Orpheum vaudeville circuit, the young actress enrolled at the newly established American Laboratory Theatre school, which was founded in 1925 by Richard Boleslavsky and Maria Ouspenskaya, former members of the famed Moscow Art Theatre, then widely acknowledged to be the best repertory company in the world. There, Miss Adler studied diction, voice production, movement and dance, theatre history, and art and music appreciation, took part in countless scene workshops, and played important parts in major American Laboratory Theatre productions, including Beatrice in Much Ado About Nothing. It was there, too, that she was introduced to Stanislavsky's revolutionary acting technique. "It was marvelous training," she said years later, as quoted by Foster Hirsch in his book A Method to Their Madness (1984). "It was thorough and complete, well-rounded and systematic, at an unmatchable level."

In addition to performing with the American Laboratory Theatre, in the late 1920s Miss Adler played two seasons at the Living Place Theatre with the renowned Yiddish actors Bertha Kalich and Jacob Ben Ami and headed a repertory company on an international tour of Latin America and Western Europe. Returning to New York in 1930, she took on a series of leading parts in Yiddish Art Theatre productions of The God of Vengeance, The Lower Depths, Liliom, The Witch of Castile, and Jew Süss, among other plays. Between 1927 and 1931, she enacted more than 100 roles, many of them character parts.

Welcoming the opportunity to perfect her craft within the security of a permanent company, Stella Adler decided, in the spring of 1931, to join the fledgling Group Theatre. Founded by former Theatre Guild associates Harold Clurman, Lee Strasberg, and Cheryl Crawford, the Group Theatre aimed to offer an alternative to the commercial stage by establishing an ensemble of players, directors, designers, and writers committed to the creation of a theatre where, in Clurman's words, "plays could be seen as artistic wholes." To achieve that artistic unity, Strasberg devised a technique for training the actors based on the Stanislavsky "system" that he, like Miss Adler, had learned at the American Laboratory Theatre.

At a summer retreat in Brookfield Center, Connecticut, Stella Adler and twenty-seven other hand-picked performers—among them Franchot Tone, Morris Carnovsky, Robert Lewis, and Clifford Odets—who were to become the nucleus of the Group Theatre prepared for their first New York season under Strasberg's direction. Strasberg's unorthodox rehearsal methods included extensive improvisational work, in which the actors were asked to do extemporaneous scenes based on situations analogous to those in the play being rehearsed, and exercises in what he called "affective memory," or the memory of an emotion that an actor had felt in the past.

The Group Theatre's first effort was Paul Connelly's Chekhovian period piece The House of Connelly, which opened on Broadway under the auspices of the Theatre Guild on September 23, 1931. Dealing with the rejuvenation of a fading aristocratic Southern family by the infusion of new blood and new ideas, the play won unqualified raves from the critics, who hailed the Group's finely coordinated ensemble playing as "too beautifully imagined and modulated to concentrate on personal achievements," to quote the New York Times's resident critic, Brooks Atkinson. Miss Adler played a principal role—that of the ineffectual Geraldine Connelly—in The House of Connelly, but in keeping with the Group's "no-star" policy, she happily accepted a bit part in the company's follow-up production, 1931, Paul and Claire Sifton's provocative analysis of the plight of the jobless during the early years of the depression. The troupe completed its first New York season with Maxwell Anderson's literate but lifeless historical drama Night Over Taos, in which Stella Adler portrayed the hot-blooded and revengeful Doña Josepha.

She found more to her liking the part of a loyal secretary cast aside by an ambitious lover in Success Story, John Howard Lawson's scathing critique of the advertising business, which opened the Group Theatre's second Broadway season. As the spiritually tortured Sarah Glassman, she turned in a performance so fully realized—especially in the last scene, where she keens over her dead lover's body—that many working actors dropped by the theatre nightly just to catch those final moments. "Anyone who witnessed that acting feat of Stella's might well wonder when he would see the like again," Robert Lewis recalled in his book Slings and Arrows (1984).

Over the next few years, Stella Adler played leading roles in several Group Theatre productions, including Myra Bonney, the exploited wife in Dawn Powell's venomous comedy *Big Night*; Gwyn Ballantyne in John Howard Lawson's drawing-room drama *Gentlewoman*; and the notorious actress Adah Isaacs Menken in *Gold Eagle Guy*, Melvin Levy's gaudy melodrama. But it was her portrayal of Bessie Berger, the harassed matriarch in *Awake and Sing*, Clifford Odets' look at the struggles of a financially strapped Jewish family, that most impressed the critics. Determined to avoid the tired stereotype, she lightened the overbearing nature of her character with grace and humor and, according to Robert Lewis, "set a standard for Jewish mother parts that has not been approached since."

The most experienced of the Group Theatre's actors, Stella Adler had never fully approved of Lee Strasberg's idiosyncratic interpretation of Stanislavsky's so-called "method." She especially objected to his relentless emphasis on affective memory exercises, which made acting increasingly painful for her. "The emphasis was a sick one," she explained years later, as quoted in the *Educational Theatre Journal* (December 1976). "You couldn't be on the stage thinking of your own personal life. It was just schizophrenic." Frustrated and disillusioned, she took a leave of absence from the company in 1934 and embarked on an extensive European trip. While in Paris, she was introduced to Stanislavsky himself by Olga Knipper, a celebrated actress with the Moscow Art Theatre and the widow of Anton Chekhov. For the next several months, she studied daily with the master, working on specific scenes and on various aspects of his technique. As she told Laurence Kitchin in an interview for the London *Times* (June 24, 1961), Stanislavsky taught her that "the source of acting is imagination and that the key to its problems is truth, truth *in the circumstances of the play*."

On her return to the Group Theatre in August 1934, Miss Adler made a formal report, complete with a chart illustrating all the elements—external and internal—that go into the art of acting, on Stanislavsky's technique to the company. According to several Group members, among them Sanford Meisner, Phoebe Brand, Margaret Barker, and Robert Lewis, her report had "an enormously salutary effect," to use Lewis' words, on the actors. From then on, the Group's directors placed less emphasis on resurrecting the actors' personal emotional experiences and concentrated instead on helping the actors to discover the emotional experiences of their characters. Openly challenging Strasberg's authority, Miss Adler shortly began to give acting classes herself. One of her first pupils was Margaret Barker, whom she coached for a principal role in the Group's production of *Case of Clyde Griffiths*, Erwin Piscator's version of Theodore Dreiser's novel *An American Tragedy*. "In a half hour working with Stella Adler on that play I knew more about it than from all the rehearsals," Miss Barker said later, as quoted in *A Method to Their Madness*.

Stella Adler made her last stage appearance with the Group Theatre in December 1935, as the indomitable Clara in *Paradise Lost*, Odets' ambitious but ultimately disappointing play about the confused, middle-class Gordon family. When, in January 1937, the increasingly beleaguered and strife-ridden company called off its scheduled productions for the remainder of the season, she left for Hollywood "simply to make a break," as she explained it. Later that year, under the name Stella Ardler, the actress made her motion picture debut in the lighthearted Paramount comedy *Love on Toast*. Her subsequent screen credits include *Shadow of the Thin Man* (MGM, 1941) and *My Girl Tisa* (United Artists, 1948).

Because of her "allegiance" to the company's basic approach to theatre, Stella Adler returned periodically to the Group Theatre until its dissolution in 1941, mainly to direct. Among other things, she staged the critically acclaimed touring production of Odets' *Golden Boy* that stunned audiences in London and Paris in the winter of 1938–39. Looking back on her "frustrating" and occasionally "miserable" years with the Group Theatre in an interview for the *Educational Theatre Journal*, Miss Adler deplored above all the dearth of good roles for women in what was essentially, in her view, "a man's theatre . . . aimed at plays for men." But even though she acknowledged that her time and talent "could have been better used, especially with a larger scope in the repertory," she nonetheless credited the company with calling forth in her the "idealism" that has since shaped her career. "I knew that I had it in me to be more creative, had much more to give to people, had much more to say about my own life . . . ," she explained. "It was the Group Theatre that gave me my life."

After a short period as an associate producer for MGM, Miss Adler returned to the Broadway stage in May 1943 to portray Catherine Carnrick, the sluttish wife in Max Reinhardt's spectacular staging of *Sons and Soldiers*, Irwin Shaw's pretentious fantasy about a woman's vision of the future. The following year, as the central figure in Claiborne Foster's one-dimensional character study *Pretty Little Parlour*, she pulled out all the stops to make the rapacious Clothilde Hilyard seem larger-than-life. Her portrayal of Zinaida, the volcanic lion tamer in the Theatre Guild's 1946 revival of Leonid Andreyev's mystical melodrama *He Who Gets Slapped* was equally flamboyant and, according to some critics, overblown. Miss Adler last appeared on stage in London in 1961, when she played Madame Rosepettle, the overprotective mother whose eccentricities comprise the plot of Arthur Kopit's zany black comedy *Oh, Dad, Poor Dad, Mamma's Hung You in the Closet and I'm Feeling So Sad*.

As a commercial theatrical director, Stella Adler staged in New York City productions of *Manhattan Nocturne*, Roy Walling's anemic psychological drama, in 1943; the musical *Polonaise*, in 1945; *Sunday Breakfast*, a taut domestic drama by Emery Rubio and Miriam Balf, in 1952; and a revival of the Paul Green-Kurt Weill antiwar musical

*Johnny Johnson*, in 1956. Of those, only *Polonaise*, a historical extravaganza set to the music of Frédéric Chopin, enjoyed a respectable run, but as more than one critic pointed out, Stella Adler's skill as a director was perhaps best measured by the finely drawn characterizations she coaxed from her actors, especially from newcomers, such as Terry Holmes and Eddie Dowling, the young stars of *Manhattan Nocturne*.

Concurrently with her twin careers as an actress and director, Miss Adler began, in the early 1940s, to teach acting at Erwin Piscator's Dramatic Workshop at the New School for Social Research in New York City. She left the faculty of the New School in 1949 to establish the Stella Adler Theatre Studio as a place for serious young actors to work, study, and, perhaps most important, perform. Drawing on her own experience, she formulated an ambitious curriculum specifically designed to provide each student with a "practical acting technique" that would, in her words, not only help him to "extend his range," but also enable him to "develop his craft and independence" in the theatre. "The ultimate aim of the training," she explained in the published syllabus, "is to create an actor who can be responsible for his artistic development and achievement."

To that end, Miss Adler devised a comprehensive two-year program of classes in acting, speech and voice production, Shakespeare, make-up, movement, and sight-reading, among other things, and workshops in play analysis, characterization, scene preparation, and acting styles. The basic course work was supplemented by frequent performances of scenes and plays for an invited audience of theatre professionals. As the school expanded over the years, she added to the curriculum courses for advanced students and professionals, including classes in rehearsal technique, mime, stage direction, playwriting, and theatre history. By 1960 the faculty of the Stella Adler Conservatory of Acting, as the school was renamed, numbered more than a dozen, but she herself continued to teach principles of acting characterization and script analysis.

In her acting classes, Stella Adler teaches the "more externalized" technique that she learned from Stanislavsky. Instead of the extensive memory exercises favored by Lee Strasberg in his workshops for professional actors at the Actors Studio, she trains her students to build characters through the evidence provided in the text, embellished by their imaginations and their knowledge of the historical period rather than their personal experiences. "You must get away from the real thing because the real thing will limit your acting and cripple you . . . ," she told one beginning class of student actors, as quoted by Rue Faris Drew in the *New York Times* (August 15, 1976). "*Don't* use your conscious past. Use your creative imagination to *create* a past that belongs to your character. I don't want you to be stuck with your own life. It's too little."

Believing that a teacher's job is to "agitate" as well as to "inspire," Stella Adler is a stern, even brutal taskmistress. She demands from her students "maximum, not minimum" efforts, and to get them, she will encourage, wheedle, scold, and occasionally explode. "I'm rough," she admitted to Miss Drew, "but that's my way of being kind. My ability to bring out [the students'] talent is somewhere deep inside me, and I must do whatever I need to pull it out." More often than not, she demonstrates the effect she wants, moving seemingly effortlessly from Desdemona to Nina to Blanche du Bois in a single scene-study class. As Foster Hirsch reported in *A Method to Their Madness*, her classroom performances are surely among the "most energetic" in New York: "For two hours, sharing personal anecdotes, theatrical reminiscences, and bits of philosophy . . . , she never stops radiating: the acting teacher as bravura actress." In addition to teaching regularly at her own school, Miss Adler served as adjunct professor of acting at Yale University's School of Drama in 1966–67, and she currently heads the undergraduate drama department at New York University.

Because she feels acting is "too complex" to be explained in a few minutes' time, Stella Adler seldom grants interviews. On those rare occasions, she candidly discusses her disenchantment with the highly commercialized Broadway stage, with the growing cult of the director, and with the "completely shapeless" American style of acting. "The American actor has no sense of himself, of being part of a profession, a tradition of acting styles," she told a reporter for the *New York Theatre Review* (February 1978). "He comes, I think, unequipped for any other style except what we call thoughtless, naturalistic behavior on the stage"—largely because, in her view, he tends to "approach a role too much from the inside." But at the same time, she went on, he has within him "a sizable inner truth," and once he understands the "Greek sense of what a human being is" and learns how "to balance the inner and the outer," the American actor "has the potential of becoming an actor unparalleled."

A tall, well-proportioned woman who appears to be several decades younger than her chronological age, Stella Adler has honey-blond hair and large, watchful gray-green eyes. "There is no mistaking that she is an actress: the pride of her bearing and the keenness of her observations express it," Stephen Fife observed in the *Village Voice* (March 13, 1978) after meeting her for the first time. "If she were a character in a Greek play," he added, "her flaw would be hubris." Since the death of her third husband, Mitchell Wilson, the physicist and novelist, in 1973, Miss Adler has lived alone in a spacious apartment on Manhattan's Upper East Side that she has decorated in the style of the Italian Renaissance. Her earlier marriages, to Horace Eleascheff and Harold Clurman, ended in divorce. She has one daughter, Ellen, from her first marriage and several grandchildren.

References: Educational Theatre J 28:506+ D 76;
N Y Post p13 My 20 '67 por; N Y Times D p5+
Ag 15 '76 pors; N Y Times Mag p32+ O 7 '79
pors; N Y World Journal Tribune mag Ja 8 '67
pors; Yale/Theatre 8:30+ Spring '77 pors;
Clurman, Harold. The Fervent Years (1945);
Kitchin, Laurence. Mid-century Drama (1962)

## Ariyoshi, George R(yoichi)

Mar. 12, 1926– Governor of Hawaii. Address: b.
Executive Chambers, State Capitol, Honolulu,
HI 96813; h. Washington Place, Honolulu, HI
96813

The first American of Japanese ancestry to become
a state governor, George R. Ariyoshi of Hawaii regards limiting population growth and diversifying
an economy that has been overdependent on tourism as pivotal to the future of the fiftieth state.
Since first taking office in 1974, the three-term governor has focused much of his attention on the
problems of overcrowding and environmental
damage that have accompanied Hawaii's rapid
economic expansion during its first twenty-five
years of statehood and is perhaps best known for
his controversial policy of selective, "preferred
growth" that he hopes will help solve Hawaii's economic and demographic dilemmas.

Born over a soybean-curd shop in Honolulu on
March 12, 1926 to Ryozo Ariyoshi, a former sumo
wrestler from Fukuoka Prefecture, Japan, and Mit-
sue (Yoshikawa) Ariyoshi, a native of Kumamoto,
Japan, George Ryoichi Ariyoshi grew up in the
downtown and Kalihi sections of Honolulu. When
he immigrated to Hawaii, Ryozo Ariyoshi first

worked as a stevedore, but he later owned and operated a dry-cleaning shop. Although before World
War II Americans of Japanese ancestry (known in
Hawaii as "AJAs") had only limited opportunities
for advancement within the Caucasian-dominated
social and political structure of Hawaii, the Ariyoshis encouraged their son in his ambitious career
goals. "When I was still a kid," George Ariyoshi recalled in Time (October 20, 1975), "I told my father
I wanted to be a lawyer. He said, 'Go to it. You can
have the shirt off my back.'"

On graduating from Honolulu's McKinley High
School as senior class president in 1944, Ariyoshi
served as an interpreter with the United States
Army's Military Intelligence Service in occupied
Japan in 1945 and 1946. After his discharge, he enrolled in the University of Hawaii in 1947 but soon
transferred to Michigan State University, from
which he received his B.A. degree in history and
political science in 1949. Three years later, he realized his childhood dream when he obtained his
law degree from the University of Michigan Law
School, and in 1953 he entered private practice in
Honolulu as a criminal lawyer.

While continuing to practise law, Ariyoshi entered politics in 1954 when at the urging of John A.
Burns, the chairman of the Hawaiian Democratic
party, he made a successful bid for a seat in the territorial house of representatives. The election of
Ariyoshi and other Japanese-Americans was a
clear sign of the emergence of that group as a political power in the hitherto Caucasian-controlled Republican government of the territory. The
improved status of Japanese-Americans in Hawaii
largely derived from their military efforts in World
War II. Although the United States had at first refused their services, when the government let the
AJAs enlist in 1942 they acquitted themselves with
honor. For example, the 7,500 Japanese-Americans
who volunteered to fight in Europe in the all-Nisei
(segregated) 442d Infantry Regimental Command
Team, fully half of whose troops were killed or
wounded in combat, became, according to the
Almanac of American Politics 1986, "the most decorated and perhaps most celebrated American military unit in World War II." Having proved their
loyalty and courage, they were gradually accepted
into the mainstream of society, and with the aid of
the GI Bill a Japanese-American professional class
emerged. Finally, in 1952 they won the naturalization and American citizenship rights previously
denied them.

Burns and other Democrats had helped the Japanese-Americans while they had been interned
during the war and had fought for the admission of
AJAs into the military. As a result of having won
the support of that group, of other ethnic minorities, and of the labor unions, the Democratic party
emerged in 1954 as the chief political power in the
territory. Since the election of John A. Burns as
governor in 1962, the Democrats have retained that
office and controlled the statehouse. Moreover, the
Japanese-Americans quickly established themselves as the dominant force within that party. By

1974, that minority held half the seats in the state legislature and three of the four seats allotted to Hawaii in the United States Congress.

At the end of his four-year term in the territorial house of representatives, Ariyoshi was elected to the territorial senate in 1958 and remained in the senate after Hawaii was admitted to the Union as the fiftieth state in 1959, serving as chairman of the Ways and Means Committee in 1964, as senate majority leader in 1965–66, and as majority floor leader in 1969–70. Continuing his legal practice over that period, he was elected vice-president of the Hawaii Bar Association in 1968 and president in 1969. Ariyoshi was also appointed a director of three major Hawaiian corporations: the First Hawaiian Bank (1962), the Honolulu Gas Company (1964), and the Hawaiian Insurance and Guaranty Company (1966).

Invited by Governor Burns to run for election as his lieutenant governor, Ariyoshi gave up his law practice and resigned his corporate directorships to devote himself full-time to the 1970 gubernatorial campaign. After scoring a victory over former lieutenant governor Thomas P. Gill in the Democratic primary, Burns and Ariyoshi defeated the Republican ticket, led by Judge Samuel P. King, in the general election with about 55 percent of the vote. As Hawaii's junior executive, Ariyoshi identified himself closely with the expansive development goals of Governor Burns. Although Gill and other Hawaiians favored controlled development of the islands and strict environmental safeguards, Burns tried to entice an array of mainland and foreign investors, primarily in the booming tourist industry, by marketing the new state's "aloha spirit," and his program was a major reason for Hawaii's strong economic growth, which averaged almost 7 percent annually in the 1960s. Burns also advocated a much expanded international role for Hawaii, especially through closer cultural and commercial ties with the countries of Asia and the Pacific Basin, a view that Ariyoshi shared and later adopted as a key part of his own gubernatorial program.

Stricken with cancer, Burns turned over day-to-day administration to Ariyoshi as acting governor in October 1973. The following August, Ariyoshi announced his intention to seek the Democratic nomination for governor in the October primary. In an interview with Curtis J. Sitomer for the *Christian Science Monitor* (August 22, 1974), he outlined his economic views, stressing the need for agricultural diversification from sugar and pineapples toward greater self-sufficiency on the islands. In the early 1970s, Hawaii imported four times as many goods and foodstuffs as it exported, and as a result the islands had been particularly hard hit by rising inflation rates. He theorized that an improved balance of trade and expansion into new agricultural pursuits might lessen the impact of inflation and lower the 8 percent unemployment rate that resulted from cutbacks in pineapple production and other problems. In keeping with that proposal, he encouraged foreign investors in Hawaii to move away from the tourist industry and toward more agricultural enterprises.

In the primary, Ariyoshi faced stiff competition from Honolulu mayor Frank F. Fasi, former lieutenant governor Thomas P. Gill, and the state senate president, David C. McClung. With Burns no longer on the scene in his role as broker of the diverse ethnic groups that make up Hawaii's Democratic party coalition, simmering ethnic tensions came to a boil during the campaign. Resentment of Japanese-American political dominance and accusations of racism reached a crescendo when Ariyoshi's campaign manager, Robert C. Oshiro, made an open appeal to a group of AJA World War II veterans to elect a Japanese-American governor. Ariyoshi's campaign was further hampered by his failure to obtain the unqualified public endorsement of Burns, who had been a longtime political ally of McClung, but he managed to win the nomination in a tight race. Ariyoshi garnered 36 percent of the vote to gain a four-point lead over Fasi, whose support was concentrated in Honolulu among native Hawaiians, Filipinos, and other minorities. Gill captured 30 percent of the vote, mostly from educators and environmentalists, with his plan for controlled growth and environmental protection, and McClung came away with a mere 2 percent. Backed by the public-employee unions and other groups, Ariyoshi easily defeated the Republican Randolph A. Crossley, the wealthy chief executive officer of Hawaii Corporation, in the November general election with 55 percent of the vote to become the first Japanese-American governor in the United States.

Although he had supported Burns's prodevelopment programs, Ariyoshi was forced soon after his election as governor to deal with the legacy of the boom years that Hawaii had enjoyed during his predecessor's administrations: excessive population growth, urban encroachment on agricultural lands, and industrial overdevelopment. As a first step in addressing those problems, the Hawaii legislature passed funding in 1976 for a Commission on Population and the Hawaiian Future to report to the governor on matters concerning population and planning in Hawaii. In its 1977 report the commission made clear that at the current rate of immigration from the mainland United States and abroad the population would increase from 850,000 in 1977 to 1.35 million by the year 2000, which would impose serious strains on the job market, government benefits and services, and the urban infrastructure.

As a result of such findings, Ariyoshi persuaded the legislature to pass a bill establishing a one-year residency requirement for most state and county jobs. The job-protection proposal, which Hawaii's public-employee unions strongly supported, was viewed by its backers as especially important because of the slowed economy and unemployment rates of 9.8 percent in 1976 and 8 percent in 1977. When the new law was challenged in federal district court and pronounced unconstitutional by Judge Samuel P. King, the governor then lobbied for a constitutional amendment to permit states to set residency requirements for welfare (the costs of which had more than tripled in Hawaii from 1970 to 1976), public employment, and housing. Following Ariyoshi's lead, the legislature passed more stringent requirements for welfare payments, which were expected to eliminate more than 1,100 people from the welfare rolls and save the state more than $3 million annually. Ariyoshi also appointed forty experts from various fields to a Growth Management Task Force to prepare for the 1978 legislative session proposals addressing the growth problem. Among other initiatives, the task force called for a revision of federal immigration laws to encourage a more equitable distribution among the states of foreign immigrants—in 1977 aliens made up 8 percent of Hawaii's population, the highest proportion in the Union—and for federal aid to support them.

The governor's "preferred growth" policy led some critics to accuse him of giving Hawaii an anti-business image. Ariyoshi denied that charge, insisting that his purpose was to protect the "fragile beauty" of Hawaii and to "seek the kind of growth for [the] economy, in tourism, agriculture and other commerce which will not encourage [im]migration, but rather will provide jobs" for the citizens of the state. In 1978 he established the Committee for Hawaii as the Regional Center of the Pacific in order to find effective ways to convince more multinational companies to establish regional centers in the Hawaiian islands.

To strengthen the economy, Ariyoshi has also proposed several ways to lessen the state's dependence on tourism (4.2 million people visited Hawaii in 1982 and seven million are expected in 1990), ease congestion on Oahu island, and reduce Hawaii's dependence on imports. His suggestions include redistributing tourist and industrial facilities to the less developed "neighbor islands," developing manganese nodule mining and ocean thermal-energy conversion, and also promoting aquaculture. The governor has also targeted increased production of luxury export crops, such as macadamia nuts, guavas, and papayas, to take up some of the slack from declining sugar and pineapple exports. Ariyoshi acknowledges, however, that the billions of dollars brought into the state each year through tourism, which surpassed federal defense spending as the state's leading industry in the 1970s, will remain Hawaii's economic mainstay for the foreseeable future. Ariyoshi also favored the Hawaiian Land Reform Act of 1967 that would allow the state to use the power of eminent domain to break up large estates and transfer the land ownership to the tenants, to the considerable benefit of Hawaii's middle class. (By one estimate, twenty-two persons owned 72.5 percent of the land on Oahu.) Although the act was ruled unconstitutional by the U.S. Ninth Circuit Court of Appeals, in May 1984 the United States Supreme Court overturned the lower court decision.

Ariyoshi's growth strategy came under early and vigorous attack from Honolulu mayor Frank Fasi, who emerged as the governor's principal political rival. Fasi lambasted Ariyoshi's residency require-

ment proposals as unconstitutional and refused to put them into effect in Honolulu when they became law. Relations between the two men reached their nadir in late 1976 when Ariyoshi appointed Grant Cooper, a lawyer from Los Angeles, as special prosecutor to investigate allegations that Fasi and Harry C. C. Chung, his campaign finance manager, had conspired to collect $500,000 in bribes from Hal J. Hansen, a Honolulu builder, in exchange for the construction contract for the $50-million Kukui Plaza, a city-subsidized apartment building. The mayor denounced the investigation as an attempt to destroy him politically and to prevent him from challenging Ariyoshi in the 1978 gubernatorial race. Although the governor denied any such motivation and insisted he had no role in the investigation, a number of observers detected significant political overtones in the case. A grand jury indicted Fasi for conspiracy to accept bribes in March 1977, but the case against him crumbled when Hansen, the key prosecution witness, refused to testify against Fasi after he himself was indicted in connection with the Kukui Plaza project, on the ground that it might jeopardize his own defense. Instead, he filed a $25-million suit against Ariyoshi, alleging that state officials had urged him to commit perjury in his testimony against the mayor. The charges against Fasi were dismissed on December 27, 1977, and the entire episode ultimately strengthened Fasi's popular support.

The bribery case added bitterness to the 1978 primary campaign, in which Fasi was considered the early front-runner. The heated contest again drew charges of racism; Ariyoshi's opponents denounced his plans to slow population growth as motivated by a desire to maintain Japanese-American dominance by preserving the existing ethnic and political equations. (Most newcomers from the mainland were white Republicans.) The governor's supporters countered that Fasi was running an overtly anti-AJA campaign. The mayor stepped up his criticism of Ariyoshi's economic strategy, declaring that a "closed door policy" would be economically disastrous for Hawaii and increase unemployment, and he promised to eliminate the 4-percent state sales tax and to improve public-school education. On the opposite side, environmentalists, though they supported many of Ariyoshi's controlled-growth policies, questioned his sincerity, noting that he drew heavily on developers and builders for campaign contributions.

Again, Ariyoshi rallied to pull off a very close contest, edging out Fasi for the nomination by a narrow margin of 3,612 votes, and went on to defeat Republican John R. Leopold in November by a vote of 153,593 to 124,610. His controlled-growth position, which, according to polls, had wide support in the state, was considered a critical factor in his victory, but he once more ignited past controversy when he proposed in his inaugural address that Hawaii be allowed to limit mainland immigration. Since the proposal was considered racist by some and stood little chance of ever winning congressional support, Ariyoshi let the matter drop.

Two labor disputes in 1979 marred Ariyoshi's second term. A four-day strike over wages by most of Hawaii's 1,800 police officers ended on July 19, but when the 7,700 members of the United Public Workers Union, an affiliate of the American Federation of State, County, and Municipal Employees (AFSCME), went on strike for higher wages on October 26, the dispute was not so easily resolved. The walkout by custodial workers shut down the public schools, all of which are administered by the state Department of Education rather than by county boards, and strikes by other public employees disrupted garbage collection and other vital services. The four-week strike, the longest yet under Hawaii's 1970 collective bargaining law, turned acrimonious when Ariyoshi adopted a hard-line position. When he obtained court injunctions against the strikers, they countered by posting waterfront picket lines that dock workers refused to cross, thus briefly tying up Hawaii's vital maritime trade. The contract settlement in November, which would increase the average worker's salary by 23.8 percent by July 1981, was favorable to the state, but Ariyoshi's supporters feared that the dispute would cost him the political support of the unionized workers, traditional partisans of Ariyoshi and a key constituency of the Democratic coalition.

In July 1982, in the midst of his campaign for a third term, the governor faced another major problem when the civil-rights division of the United States Department of Justice began investigating conditions in Hawaii's state-run prisons. A shakedown of prisoners at Oahu Community Correctional Center the previous December had drawn charges of brutality from six inmates and prompted the probe under a law authorizing federal suits in behalf of prisoners suffering civil-rights violations. When the state refused investigators access to state facilities until they made known exactly what they were searching for, the Justice Department filed a lawsuit, the first brought under the Civil Rights of Institutionalized Persons Act of 1980, that charged that two Hawaiian state prisons—the Oahu Community Correctional Center and the Halawa High Security Facility—subjected prisoners to cruel and unusual punishment. The charges included illegal segregation of prisoners, censorship of mail, inadequate protection of prisoners from assault by other inmates, and the excessive use of tranquilizing drugs on inmates. Ariyoshi, four other state officials, and the state government were named as the defendants. Since, according to the governor's own investigating committee report, only "two isolated cases in which excessive force was clearly employed" during the 1981 shakedown could be proved, the state planned to contest every allegation in court.

In the 1982 gubernatorial election George Ariyoshi and Frank Fasi met as leading rivals for the third time. Fasi, who had been defeated in 1980 in his bid for a fourth term as Honolulu mayor by Ariyoshi protégée Eileen Anderson, chose to bypass the Democratic primary and run for governor as an independent, in part to save his campaign funds for the general-election battle. After defeating a surprisingly strong challenge from Lieutenant Governor Jean King in the primary, the governor mounted an expensive, high-powered campaign against Fasi, whose support was strongest among middle-income white voters on Oahu, and his Republican opponent, State Senator D. G. Anderson, whose campaign attracted mostly upper-income voters in Honolulu and on the Windward Coast. But once again backed by the AJAs and the labor unions, Ariyoshi triumphed with 45 percent of the vote. In a close race for second, Fasi drew 29 percent of the vote, outstripping Anderson by a three-point margin. Since the Hawaiian state constitution limits a governor to three terms, Ariyoshi must leave that office in 1986.

During his eleven years as governor of Hawaii, Ariyoshi has chaired such important meetings as the Western Governor's Conference in 1977-78 and served as president of the Pacific Basin Development Council in 1980-81. He has received several honorary doctor of law degrees, an honorary doctorate in the humanities, and distinguished alumni awards from the University of Hawaii and Michigan State University.

George R. Ariyoshi, a tall, craggy-faced, soft-spoken man who enjoys swimming and golf, married the former Jean Miya Hayashi, a third-generation Japanese-American, on February 5, 1955. They have three children—Lynn Miye, who is at present studying in Japan, Todd Ryozo, and Donn Ryoji—all of whom helped the governor in his recent political campaigns. The Ariyoshis reside with their four dogs at Washington House, the oldest home in Hawaii and the governor's official residence. The governor is affiliated with the United Church of Christ.

References: Almanac of American Politics 1986; Who's Who in America, 1984–85; Who's Who in American Politics, 1983–84

---

## Bacon, Francis

Oct. 28, 1909– English painter. Address: b. c/o Marlborough Fine Art, 6 Albemarle St., London WIX 3HF, England

NOTE: This biography supersedes the article that appeared in Current Biography in 1957.

Together with the sculptor Henry Moore, with whom he is paired in critical esteem, the painter Francis Bacon has brought England a distinction in the visual arts that rivals since World War II its achievements in the literary and performing arts. His appeal is global: Susan Sontag finds that "Bacon seems particularly supra-national, almost ideally European." On the occasion, however, of a major retrospective exhibition of forty years of Ba-

*Francis Bacon*

con's work, held at London's Tate Gallery in the spring and summer of 1985, Lord Gowrie, Britain's Arts Minister, pointed out in the London *Sunday Times Magazine,* "Bacon's paintings are documentaries of nervous stress. They may be staged contemporarily but they are always performed—and this is perhaps the most English thing about them—with awareness of historical precedent and the shapes of tradition." While following tradition as a figure painter, Bacon is controversial and idiosyncratic in combining the techniques of old masters with such diverse other means as random brush strokes to project directly from the canvas to the nervous system his existential images of horror, despair, and the loss of love and other forms of death. The beauty and polish of his painting contrast with the sometimes savage rawness of his subject matter as he seeks "to unlock the valves of feeling," "to unlock the barrels of sensation," in fulfillment of what he sees as the artist's purpose.

Francis Bacon was born on October 28, 1909 in Dublin, Ireland to English parents, Edward Anthony Mortimer and Christine Winifred (Firth) Bacon, who had four other children. He is a collateral descendant of the Elizabethan philosopher and essayist Francis Bacon. At the outbreak of World War I his father temporarily left his work in Ireland as a breeder and trainer of racehorses to serve in the War Office in London. He afterward shuffled his family between England and Ireland, frequently changing addresses and accustoming his asthmatic son to a nomadic lifestyle. Having been a student for less than a year at a boarding school in Cheltenham, England, Francis Bacon had very little formal education and apparently no instruction in art.

A boyhood spent for the most part in Ireland left identifiable emotional, thematic, and formal traces in Bacon's painting. Violence and the threat of violence were everyday experiences for a child of English parentage during the heyday of the nationalist Sinn Fein movement. He often stayed at the country house of his grandmother, among whose several successive husbands was a commissioner of police, the target of considerable sniping. Once when asked in an interview about the omnipresent circles in his pictures, he recalled his grandmother's enormous house, where "all the rooms were oval." From his father he seems to have acquired his predisposition for gambling, or trusting to chance. On the whole he did not get along with the elder Bacon, who banished him at sixteen from the family home, reportedly because of his sexual indulgences with the grooms in the racehorse stables.

Free to drift about, Bacon went to London in 1925, but after a year or so gave up his office job to move along to Berlin, the decadent, unruly capital of the Weimar Republic. His visit, though brief, remained memorable because of the tension and emotional violence he sensed in the city. Paris, where he also spent some time in the late 1920s and saw a Picasso exhibition, among others, made an even more enduring impression on Bacon, who, self-taught, was working on drawings and watercolors and was soon to advance to oil painting. On his return to London later in the decade, he set up his own studio and worked for a time, as he had abroad, in interior decorating and design, probably producing the sort of rugs and tubular furniture in the modern idiom that later appeared in some of his pictures.

Bacon attracted little attention at the first showing of his paintings, in 1930 at the Bacon Studio, in a joint exhibition with his friend the Australian painter Roy de Maistre. Soon afterward, however, he did come to public notice with the reproduction of his semiabstract *Crucifixion* in Herbert Read's *Art Now* of 1933. The theme of crucifixion, which is recurrent in the work of Bacon, a nonbeliever, sometimes alludes to Christ's Crucifixion to the extent that an elevated image may be suggestive of a cross. But, as John Russell explained in his critical study *Francis Bacon* (1979), "'A crucifixion' [in Bacon's painting] is not a descriptive title, and still less is it a reference to an actual event. It is, rather, a generic name for an environment in which bodily harm is done to one or more persons and one or more persons gather to watch."

Such was the environment that distressed Bacon throughout World War II, during which his asthma disqualified him for army service and limited his contributions to the Civil Defense Corps. He painted obsessively in the war years, but destroyed much of his work. A group of paintings that survived was shown at the Lefevre Gallery in London in April 1945, shortly before the end of the war. Among them was the triptych *Three Studies for Figures at the Base of a Crucifixion* (1944), which heralded, in the words of a critic for *Art News and Review,* "a new, original talent." Bacon's gloating spectators, whom he also thought of as the Eumenides, are fantastically deformed and mutilated creatures, inspired in part by some Picasso drawings of the 1920s. Agonized and agonizing, they embody unspeakable depravity.

Other paintings of the mid-1940s point more directly to the course Bacon would take in developing his singular technique and style. One of several surrealistic studies of figures in lurid settings, whose garish colors reflect the influence of Graham Sutherland, is *Painting 1946*, which Alfred Barr acquired for the Museum of Modern Art in New York in 1948. The monumental picture, executed in the old masters' manner, includes elements of Bacon's startling stock-in-trade nightmarish imagery: an open umbrella (which has reappeared intermittently over the years), a mouth in an almost faceless head, and carcasses—in this instance slabs of beef hung in a cruciform. Carcasses fascinate Bacon, as he explained in one of a series of interviews with David Sylvester, because to a painter "there is great beauty in the colour of meat." His idea that human beings are "potential carcasses" accounts for the connection he repeatedly makes between meat and crucifixion, very obviously so in *Three Studies for a Crucifixion* (1962). "If I go into a butcher's shop I always think it's surprising that I wasn't there instead of the animal," he told Sylvester.

A partly concealed head beneath an umbrella in *Figure Study II* (1945-46) has a wide open mouth, as does one of the hideous heads in *Three Studies for Figures at the Base of a Crucifixion*. Borrowing from the image of the blood-splattered, screaming nurse in Sergei Eisenstein's film *The Battleship Potemkin* (1925), Bacon often used the open, rounded mouth to paint the human cry. But the open mouth did not necessarily indicate a scream, and even when it did, his interest was not confined to conveying pain. He had been aesthetically obsessed by the hand-colored illustrations in a book on diseases of the mouth that he purchased in Paris in the 1930s.

With the prevalence of open mouths in the group of *Heads* and other canvases exhibited in his one-man show in 1949 at London's Hanover Gallery, Bacon's reputation as a painter of the horrific became more firmly established. The mouth open in an anguished cry contributed to the range of facial expressions in the several series of popes that Bacon began in 1949 and continued to paint and exhibit in the 1950s; one of the series is, in fact, known as "The Screaming Popes." The papal portraits are variations of Velázquez' *Portrait of Innocent X*, which Bacon knew from photographs and considered to be among the world's most beautiful masterpieces. In his 1953 study after Velázquez' painting, a pope of unmatched authority and power becomes a man screaming hysterically and wearing a white lace-trimmed skirt suggestive of infantilism or transvestism. As that picture exemplifies, the surprise and shock elements in Bacon's work depend considerably on his bold conjunction of new or taboo subject matter and the old European formal tradition.

Probably as much as any other canvases, Bacon's series of popes illustrates his practice of superimposing upon the original meaning of available, or ready-made, images his own individual, existential sense of reality. Even the paintings of African scenes and animals inspired by his travels in South Africa and Kenya in 1952 depend upon photographs as well as his own observations. He used Vincent van Gogh's *The Painter on the Road to Tarascon* in much the same way that he had used Velázquez' pope, though less effectively, in a series of variations that dominated his one-man show at the Hanover Gallery in 1957.

Early in his career, moreover, Bacon had been impressed by the pictures of Eadweard Muybridge, the Victorian pioneer of photography of animals and human beings in motion. The sequential aspect of Muybridge's documentary studies may have given him the idea of working in series. Muybridge's photographs served directly as a point of departure for some of Bacon's figural paintings, either of a single figure or of two figures coupled in a sexually ambiguous embrace, or in a wrestling match, as in *Two Figures* (1953) and *Two Figures in the Grass* (1954). Bacon's ability to retain a resemblance from his source while transforming its emotional impact is particularly evident in *After Muybridge—Woman Emptying a Bowl of Water and Paralytic Child on All Fours* (1965), with its grim and violent combination of purple, orange, and red colors.

For a while during the 1960s, Bacon, an admirer of Michelangelo, mulled over the idea of presenting the human figure in sculpture. The carved-out and molded forms that he envisaged at that time eventually appeared not in sculpture but in his paintings. The sculptural, or plastic, treatment of the nude figure, already evident in *Three Figures in a Room* (1964), for example, became more pronounced in *Three Studies of the Male Back* (1970), *Lying Figure in a Mirror* (1971), *Triptych—March 1974*, and many other paintings. Commenting on the exhibition in 1975 at the Metropolitan Museum of Art, "Francis Bacon: Recent Paintings 1968-1974," Robert Hughes wrote in *Time* (April 7, 1975), "With the recent triptychs and other paintings, his ambition to reinstate the human figure as a primary subject of art has been to some degree fulfilled. No other living artist can paint flesh at this pitch of intensity, in this extremity of rage, loss and voluptuousness, or with this command over pigment."

In scores of his early pictures Bacon surrounded his figures, and heads, with wirelike lines that made them appear to be trapped in aloneness in glass boxes. The enclosures also asserted the figures as a focal point, serving a purpose more often achieved in his later paintings by various compositional devices and even, as seen in *Triptych—May-June 1973*, by the use of arrows. A window shade pulled down sets the mood of a typical Bacon setting, of which Hughes wrote in *The Shock of the New* (1980), "The closed rooms and unidentifiable furniture, nasty in texture and colour, lit by a single unshaded bulb, are an arena for violence; in them, sex becomes a doglike grappling and all emotions are equally subsumed in rage and its hangover, the sense of isolation."

As the subjects for his portraits, paintings of heads or of figures, Bacon often chooses himself and his close friends. The model of his first named portrait, painted in 1951, was the painter Lucian Freud, who joined Bacon and Ben Nicholson in representing Great Britain at the 1954 Venice Biennale. Some of Bacon's later paintings of Freud include other figures, *Portrait of George Dyer and Lucian Freud* (1967) and *Three Portraits— Triptych George Dyer, Self-Portrait, Lucian Freud* (1973), for example. The latter work is one of Bacon's so-called "black" triptychs, painted between August 1972 and June 1973, of which Dyer is the unifying element. *Triptych—May-June 1973*, the concluding triptych in the series, is a dramatic confrontation with the fact of Dyer's death, by suicide, in Paris in October 1971, just before the opening of Bacon's major retrospective in that city. "Very simply stated," Hugh M. Davies related in *Art in America* (March 1975), "the three panels— reading from right to left—depict a naked man vomiting into the bathroom sink, then crossing the room, then dying on the toilet."

Another friend whose savaged visage appears often in Bacon's work, especially during the 1960s, is Isabel Rawsthorne. In addition to head portraits of her, he has executed several notable figural canvases, including *Isabel Rawsthorne in a Street in Soho* (1967), which Russell regards as "one of his finest of all paintings." "Who can I tear to pieces, if not my friends?" Russell has quoted Bacon as saying. " . . . If they were not my friends, I could not do such violence." Painting not from life, but from memory reinforced by photographs, Bacon makes his subjects recognizable as individual persons, but he distorts their features, as a candid camera might do, in a way that intensifies the reality of human character—its flaws, its fugitive quality— and replaces literalness, which he finds boring, with vitality and immediacy.

Distortion, or contortion, in Bacon's pictures sometimes occurs by his superimposing one image on another or by deliberate blurring of paint and sometimes by chance. A gambler and a frequenter of Monte Carlo casinos, he takes risks in the manipulation of the extremely fluid medium of oil paint and turns to his advantage accidents that may result in a "truer," more poignant image. For that reason he does not work from sketches. Even though he may on occasion throw a handful of paint on the canvas, he dislikes sloppiness and is convinced that art must be disciplined. "I want a very ordered image but I want it to come about by chance," he explained to Sylvester. When luck fails him, he destroys the canvas.

Arguing that great art is "recording" and "reporting," Bacon rejects abstract and abstract expressionist art as decoration concerned only with aesthetic values. But he dislikes narration and illustration because he believes that by engaging the intellect they interfere with the direct impact of paint on the nervous system. To avoid storytelling, he insists that the panels of his triptychs be framed separately. The dramatic situation, nevertheless, in such a work as *Triptych—May-June 1973* does invite narrative interpretation, however ambiguous, as do the literary allusions of *Triptych (Inspired by T. S. Eliot's Poem "Sweeney Agonistes")* (1967) and *Painting 1978*, which borrows from Eliot's *The Wasteland* the image of turning a key in the lock of an imprisoning door.

Some of Bacon's admirers feel that in his seventies he is painting as powerfully as ever. In a review for the *New York Times* (May 4, 1984) of Bacon's show of his recent work at New York's Marlborough Gallery, for example, Russell pointed to signs of continuing development: "He is as inventive as ever. Not only has he a whole new slew of images, . . . but after nearly half a century of painting in oils, he began not long ago to use both oils and pastels in the same picture." Bacon's striving to refine his technique, however, may paradoxically also have provoked negative criticism. Without commenting on their justification, Franz Schulze summarized in *Artnews* (November 1976) arguments against Bacon: "These arguments, which have come more from American than from European critics, hold that there is an excess of rhetoric in Bacon's work, a slickness, a horrific sort of bombast. It is evident especially in the man's paint technique, in his formal handling, which the anti-Baconians contend is all too often glib and superficial, thus not nearly so charged with genuine existential fury or angst or whatever, as his champions claim." The American critic Hilton Kramer, who shares the skepticism regarding Bacon, noted in the *New York Times* (March 30, 1975) that although he had influenced painters in other countries around the world, he had not discernibly affected American art. But he suggested that the upswing of a conservatism in art fashions would be likely to favor Bacon's reception in the United States. The Solomon R. Guggenheim Museum included in "Painterly Visions, 1940-84," its 1985 summer exhibition, Bacon's *Arab and Child*, an oil on canvas executed in 1956. Commenting on that work in the *New York Times* (July 5, 1985), Michael Brenson noted: "When we see the figures and paint handling in . . . 'Arab and Child,' whatever edge there was in many of the oil-on-velvet paintings in Julian Schnabel's most recent exhibition disappears."

Francis Bacon has an open and unaggressive manner and, according to one interviewer, "a wry wit and Shakespearian delivery." Reflecting on his life, he was quoted in *Time* (April 7, 1975) as saying, "I've led a very hypnotic and curious one— being homosexual I have lived with the most marvelously disastrous people." He spends part of his time in Paris, where he has a rented apartment, but does most of his work in London, at his South Kensington home and studio amid layers of congenial clutter—old photographs, empty paint tubes, rags, discarded brushes. His preference for painting in early morning light imposes a certain discipline on a lifestyle that to a large extent is shaped by his love of gambling and cultivated taste in food and wine. After meeting him at his recent Tate Gallery show, journalists for the London *Times* observed, "He is dressed with a dapper, studied carelessness. . . . His ageless bearing is dwarfed by that remarkable head; it resembles nothing so much as an owl's—feathers puffed out chuffily; eyes hooded and with an uncanny ability to pursue and trap in their roving gaze."

References: Art in Am 63:62+ Mr '75 por; Flash Art p8+ My '83 por; Horizon 13:79+ Autumn '71; London Sunday Times p46+ My 19 '85 por; London Times p10 My 20 '85 pors; N Y Times C p44 Mr 20 '75 pors; Sat R 8:36+ S '81 por; Time 105:54+ Ap 7 '75 por; Vogue 165:136 Mr '75; Washington Post B p1+ Mr 21 '75 pors; Contemporary Artists (1983); Russell, John. Francis Bacon (1979); Sylvester, David. Interviews with Francis Bacon (1975); Who's Who, 1985–86; Who's Who in the World, 1984–85; World Artists 1950–1980 (1984)

## Barnet, Will

*May 25, 1911– Painter; printmaker. Address: National Arts Club, 15 Gramercy Park, New York City, N.Y. 10003*

Highly respected as a painter, printmaker, and dedicated teacher, the American artist Will Barnet has resolutely developed his own style, which he terms Abstract Reality. That style has set him apart from any of his contemporaries. Unswayed by the succession of stylistic "isms" in fashion in the New York art world in which he has worked for something over fifty years, Barnet has never become widely popular or subject to the kind of publicity and promotion tendered to many of his peers. But he has exerted a steady influence on several generations of students, and starting with the 1970s, has won the increasing acclaim of critics and collectors.

Born in Beverly, Massachusetts on May 25, 1911, Will Barnet is the youngest of four children of East-ern European immigrants, Noah and Sarah (Toahnich) Barnet. Because his two sisters and a brother were much older than he, and because his father worked long hours as a machinist, Barnet's childhood was a lonely one, but his solitude was relieved by a special closeness to his mother, by his love of drawing and painting, and by long walks along the Beverly waterfront. His observations of shore and ocean played an important role in his work many years later. Another formative influence was the time he spent reading as a child in the Beverly Public Library, particularly after he discovered its collection of books on art and art history.

In 1927, before even finishing high school, Barnet talked his reluctant parents into allowing him to go to the School of the Museum of Fine Arts, in Boston. Although he has acknowledged his indebtedness to his favorite teacher, Philip L. Hale, an impressionist who had studied with Monet, and has expressed his gratitude for the opportunity to copy paintings in the museum, he eventually rebelled against the school's strict academicism and its apathy toward modern trends. In 1930, therefore, he applied for and won a scholarship to the Art Students League in New York City.

Foremost among the artists of the past with whom Will Barnet felt a marked affinity was the nineteenth-century French lithographer Honoré Daumier. With Daumier's example in mind, and with the intent of mastering a craft in order to earn a livelihood, he began by studying lithography, etching, and woodcutting, and in 1934, the year in which he finished his course of study, he became the Art Students League's official printmaker. At that time the streets of New York were populated with victims of the Great Depression, who provided him with subjects for the first definable body of his work, a series of lithographs done between 1932 and 1942. Among them was *Idle Hands* (1935), a study of the bowed head of an unemployed laborer. "I had sympathy for the suffering of people . . . but I was not bitter or acid in my feeling," Barnet once recalled in referring to those works, and despite the fact that during that era of social realism he worked briefly for the Graphic Art Division of the WPA Federal Arts Project, his own art remained apolitical.

SOUTH PUGET SOUND LIBRARY

When, in 1936, Barnet was made an instructor in graphics at the Art Students League, he became the youngest teacher ever appointed to the staff, and about ten years later he began to teach painting there as well. By the mid-1930s, too, he was beginning to be exhibited: his first one-man show was held at the 8th Street Playhouse in 1935, and his representation in a group print show at the Downtown Gallery in 1934 marked the start of a sequence, virtually unbroken right up to the present, of annual group exhibitions.

Working in a studio in his apartment, Will Barnet now turned to depictions of his wife and children. From the time when as a child he first set up a small workroom in the cellar of his parents' house, he has always located his studios in his living quarters: cramped railroad flats in the early, economically pinched days, or in the spacious brownstone of his later, more affluent years. Members of his family have been his constant inspiration, along with the household cats and birds that have become the hallmarks of his figurative painting. Part of the attraction of cats, Barnet has explained, is the analogy of their forms to the soft undulations of a woman's body.

One of the abiding characteristics of Barnet's art is its concentration on figures of women and the concomitant almost total absence of men or of landscape and still life. Whether represented with or without children, women seem to symbolize to him comfort, strength, patience, endurance, and hope. Inevitably, a number of American art critics have explained that facet of Barnet's work in terms of his childhood loneliness and reliance on his mother for solace, comfort, and inspiration.

The novelist James T. Farrell, who wrote the introduction to a 1950 monograph on Will Barnet's paintings, commented on his friend's intense interest in the unposed everyday activities of the people around him. In observing those activities, Barnet made a number of sketches before deciding on one that might be developed into a painting or a print. Often the print might be later transformed into a painting or, at a further stage in his career, the oil might precede a more complex treatment in some graphic medium. The 1939 woodcut *Under the Table*, for example, is repeated in the 1945 painting *Child's View*. By now, the artist had largely eliminated modeling in favor of a linear two-dimensional style. Those compositions of his son Peter at play thus emphasize the child's-eye vantage point and so convey a delightfully intimate sense of a child's own world.

By the late 1940s, as Barnet explains, he had "eliminated realistic space and substituted a painting space based purely on the rectangle: the vertical and horizontal expansion of forms." Thus, one of the best-known paintings of that period, the glowingly colored *Soft-Boiled Eggs* (1946) had started out as a picture of a family birthday party. Realizing that representing a birthday cake on the table would create an unwanted three-dimensionality, Barnet hit upon the idea of depicting their breakfast eggs as set out before his wife

and sons, since those shapes fitted perfectly into the flat horizontality of plane he wished to emphasize.

During the next fifteen years or so, Barnet's work became more and more abstract, but despite his affiliation with the American Abstract Artists group, he did not go the way of many of his contemporaries and never wholly abandoned his basic interest in the human form. Although Barnet worked to convey mood and emotion, his approach is the antithesis of abstract expressionism or action painting. His cool, slow deliberation of line reflects his patient, unhurried painting technique, and he has always used oils, never the quicker drying acrylics. Concentrating on one area at a time, he applies his colors heavily, in layers, removing the excess while still wet, using a clean brush for each color. By means of that meticulous method he achieves what he calls a "canvas that breathes" and a special vibrancy of color. He may spend two to three years or even more on one painting. Denying that he is interested in technique for its own sake, he explains that "living with a painting is almost as exciting as finishing it. It becomes more than just seeing an idea, saying it and leaving it."

In one of his early abstract paintings, *Summer Family* (1948), the figures of Barnet's wife and sons and the animals and birds around them in their new summer place in Connecticut have become a grouping of entangled shapes, abstract but still somewhat figurative. Thin vertical rectangles serve both as references to the trees among which the figures stand and also as a way of compartmentalizing and at the same time unifying the elements of the composition. That mode of organization and the interweaving of human and animal shapes Barnet owes to another influence, the art of Africans and Native Americans. Since his boyhood visits to the Peabody Museum in Salem, Massachusetts, he has always been fascinated by African and American Indian art.

In 1953 Barnet traveled to Europe for the first time, and in the following year returned, briefly, to figurative representation, as in his monumental *Baltic Madonna*, a black and white woodcut. In contrast, there is the celebrated 1955 abstract *Janus and the White Vertebra*, which makes a strong, elegantly patterned allusion to the human torso, at once cleft and supported by the solid white vertebral line that divides the body and the composition into halves.

The summers of 1958 and 1959, which Will Barnet spent teaching at the University of Minnesota in Duluth, resulted in some wholly abstract landscapes, *Big Duluth* and *Little Duluth* (both 1959–60), inspired by the sunlit water and shore of Lake Superior. Another severely abstract painting, *Singular Image* (1959; color woodcut, 1964), is based on the play of strong geometric forms, interlocking verticals and horizontals. The print scholar Una Johnson contends that the forms were influenced by Native American totemic symbols, as was *Compression—Spokane* (1964; also done in an aquatint version, 1967), painted while Barnet taught at Washington State University in the summer of 1963.

In 1961, just when abstract art was at its height in the United States, Barnet began to turn back to a figurative style. Heralded by such works as *Mother and Child* and *Gray Horizontal* (both portraits of his second wife and their young daughter seated on a sofa), his new Abstract Reality began to emerge: sharp-edged forms reduced to a carefully articulated, decorative pattern; flat planes; space almost completely compressed; colors applied without modulation or suggestion of texture. The similarity to Japanese prints is striking, understandable in light of Barnet's affinity for the woodcut.

A group of portraits of people outside Barnet's immediate family circle, mainly of friends in academic life or in the arts, illustrates the development of that style. An abstract "likeness" of his friend, the artist Henry Pearson (1966–67) is virtually devoid of extraneous, explanatory detail. Both form and face are starkly silhouetted against a featureless background. Gradually, Barnet elaborated on his theory that a portrait should be an "idea of a person in its most intense and essential aspect," and he now placed his subjects in their accustomed settings, making more explicit their status and interests. Thus in 1966 a profile of the formally attired director of the Solomon R. Guggenheim Museum, Thomas M. Messer, is set against a fragment of a painting by one of his favorite artists, Edvard Munch.

Several critics have drawn attention to the fact that those paintings echo the conventions of eighteenth- and early nineteenth-century portraits by itinerant American artists. The comparison is apt, for Barnet had in fact become thoroughly familiar with such works during his earliest visits to the Museum of Fine Arts in Boston. With some modification and softening, he continued the tradition as late as 1982, with his double portrait, *Artist and Scholar. Homage to Léger, with K. K.* (also 1982) not only portrays the critic Katherine Kuh, catching her in one of her characteristic gestures, fingering her necklace, but as in the Messer portrait, positions her in front of a section of a painting by one of her favorite artists, Fernand Léger.

In the late 1960s and early 1970s a number of Barnet's paintings recorded the interior of his home, which was then a stately brownstone on Manhattan's Upper West Side. Stairs, bannisters, and doorways, meticulously detailed, provide a somewhat oppressive, confining setting for the figures of his wife or daughter, but Barnet has characteristically softened the mood by introducing a figure of a cat somewhere, almost as part of the woodwork. A new allegorical quality becomes apparent in other work. *Silent Seasons* (1967) is a quartet of paintings, each showing Barnet's daughter profiled against a window, leaning over a table, across from a pet parrot. Subtle changes in pose or in decorative features, and more distinct shifts in color harmonies, indicate the phases of the year. The series is a quiet evocation of an intensely private, perhaps lonely, childhood world.

That inwardness increases in the next phase of Barnet's career, which he commenced in 1972 when he began to paint his Woman and the Sea series. Although originally inspired by the sight of his wife, standing on the porch of their Maine summerhouse, gazing out at the ocean, those paintings are not representational in any way but are essentially a continuation of his search for simplification of visual statement in order to convey a mood—a sense of a mysterious quest, disquieting but not overtly ominous. Critics have discerned not only a link with New England transcendental philosophy but allusions to the fortitude of New England women, wives and mothers of men who made their hazardous living on the sea. Again, Barnet's childhood loneliness, and the scenes he grew up with, are mirrored in them.

From that concern with the inner life, dream and symbol have come to play a dominant role in the artist's latest, somewhat ambiguous compositions, including works such as *Circe* (1979) or *Hera* (1980), in which a female form is posed in flat relief against horizon and sky, feeding large crow-like birds roosting among leafless trees. They seem to be private meditations, incorporating his favorite repertoire of figures, but at the same time they also appear to be references to universal myths.

Will Barnet has been married twice, first in 1935, to Mary Sinclair, a student of painting at the Art Students League. She and their three sons, Peter (now also an artist), Richard, and Todd, became the focus of his earlier prints and paintings. In 1953, after his divorce, he married Elena Ciurlys, a dancer. Her form and face, with her distinctively slanted blue-green eyes, and representations of their daughter Ona (born in 1954) dominated his work from then on.

Although introspective and familial, Barnet has social horizons, as a lifelong teacher, that stretch very far. He is warm and friendly, if at first somewhat reticent. Barnet has been on the staff of the Art Students League for almost half a century, a professor at the Cooper Union Art School from 1945 to 1978, and an instructor at the Pennsylvania Academy of Fine Arts in Philadelphia since 1967. Other teaching appointments include years at Yale University as visiting critic (1952 and 1953) and a post as visiting professor at Cornell (1968–69). When interviewed in 1981, he acknowledged that teaching still inspired him because of the opportunity for contact with young artists.

Will Barnet's achievements as artist and teacher have been recognized by election to the American Academy and Institute of Arts and Letters in 1983 and by membership in the national Academy of Design; in 1976 he became a fellow of the Royal Society of Arts, London. His paintings and prints are to be seen in all the major museums of the United States, and the latest of several retrospectives of his work was mounted by the Currier Gallery of Art, in Manchester, New Hampshire, before touring the United States and Canada in 1984.

A vigorous septuagenarian, Will Barnet does not differ very much from the figure he projected of himself in a 1966 self-portrait. His six-foot frame is still relatively lean, and though his white hair is thinning so that his high forehead dominates the somewhat plain face, his bespectacled blue eyes still fix the viewer calmly, directly, and seriously. He continues to hold firm convictions, among them a belief that artists must have a thorough knowledge both of technique and of artistic tradition. Now living in a gracious studio-home at the National Arts Club on New York's Gramercy Park, he works surrounded by a collection of art objects and a library of books that are mute testimony to his own dedication to that tradition.

References: Artnews 81:94+ '82 por; Doty, Robert. Will Barnet (1984); Who's Who in America, 1984–85; Who's Who in American Art, 16th ed (1984)

## Bartlett, Jennifer

Mar. 14, 1941– Artist. Address: c/o Paula Cooper Gallery, 155 Wooster St., New York City, N.Y. 10012

Hailed for the past decade as one of the brightest young creative talents in the United States, the artist Jennifer Bartlett is engaged in an analysis of visual experience that involves an almost obsessive recording of the same image from different perspectives and in different styles and media. Respected by art critics for her dazzling command of technique and for what the New York Times's John Russell has called her "ferocious and gleeful intelligence," she is at the same time regarded as good copy by trendy, personality-oriented magazines and newspapers.

A descendant of Tilly Losch, the famed Austrian dancer, choreographer, actress, and painter, Jennifer Bartlett was born Jennifer Losch in Long Beach, California on March 14, 1941. Since she grew up in the laid-back ambience of the southern California coast, it is not surprising that water as a sportive environment has been a constant motif in her work. Her father was a pipeline engineer, and her mother had been a fashion illustrator before Jennifer, the oldest of her four children, was born.

Jennifer Bartlett wanted to be an artist even as a child, and though unable to draw faithful renditions of objects, she created fanciful drawings, full of action and drama, that won her praise from her teachers. Throughout elementary and high school, her passions were drawing and reading. In 1959 she entered Mills College in Oakland, California and received her undergraduate degree from there in 1963. At that prestigious women's college, renowned for its superior music and art faculties, Jennifer Bartlett began to do abstract painting in a style that owed much to the work of Arshile Gorky. Her first one-woman show, held at Mills College in her senior year, won her acceptance to the Yale University School of Art and Architecture, where she took her B.F.A. degree in 1964 and an M.F.A. degree in the following year. There her teachers were Jack Tworkov, James Rosenquist, Al Held, and Jim Dine, and her peers included such now well-established figures as Jonathan Borofsky, Nancy Graves, and Richard Serra. Although she became one of the significant number of talented young women artists who achieved recognition during the late 1960s and into the 1970s, she still had to contend with overt sexism while at Yale. Her way of distancing herself literally from her male fellow students and of coping with her repressed anger was to build huge stretchers for her splashy abstract canvases.

After completing her graduate work, Jennifer Bartlett began teaching art at the University of Connecticut in Storrs. Meanwhile she commuted constantly to New York City, but she eventually reversed that pattern by moving to a small loft in what is now Manhattan's SoHo district. Through Borofsky and former schoolmates from California she got to know other young New York artists and became exposed to the ferment of styles and attitudes characteristic of that period. Stimulated by all that experimentation, Jennifer Bartlett began her own, starting with a form of process art involving plastic bowls that she subjected to various treatments and then installed on her studio floor. She also began a series of minimalist or conceptualist drawings consisting of colored dots arranged mathematically within squares of graph paper. Also in the conceptual mode, she started to write. Her Cleopatra, a long, ruminative essay on a miscellany of topics, was published in 1971, after which she began a manuscript on which she has been working intermittently ever since. Somewhat facetiously titled History of the Universe: A Novel, it was scheduled for publication, with her own photographic montage illustrations, in October 1985.

It was around 1970 that Jennifer Bartlett decided to find her own unique style and content by adopting a more labor-effective method than working on huge canvases. Inspired by New York City subway station signs, she developed the idea of painting on one-foot-square steel plates covered with baked enamel, which she used as modules for her compositions. A silk-screened grid, reminiscent of the graph paper she had been using for drawing, was superimposed on the plates. For paints she used Testor's enamels, sold in hobby shops in small, recappable bottles. The idea and the process met her requirements perfectly: an easily handled surface to work on and a lack of the usual studio mess that her fastidious nature abhors. By placing dots of the vivid enamel colors on the grids, she achieved varied and schematized clusters. Her first New York show, which was held in 1970 at Alan Saret's SoHo studio-gallery, exhibited several hundred of those plates. By 1972, in her next exhibition, at the Reese Palley Gallery, she arranged the plates in series, with one large painting formed of sixty individual squares showing recognizable images of a house, done in a range of colors that suggested the times of day and seasons of the year. Adumbrations of the work that was to make her famous in 1976 were to be found in that exhibition.

In the meantime, Jennifer Bartlett had left her teaching at Storrs, Connecticut and in 1972 joined the faculty of the School of Visual Arts in New York. No longer having to commute gave her more time for painting and joining in several group exhibitions, and it allowed her to work on her novel-in-progress, which by now included candid, circumstantial descriptions of all those close to her and of such newly acquired friends as the gallery owner Paula Cooper. Although at first wary of taking her on, Paula Cooper gradually gave in to the artist's obvious desire to be represented by her. "Jennifer usually gets what she wants," Paula Cooper has pointed out, and in the spring of 1974 her gallery showed the first of many Bartlett exhibitions. That debut was devoted to a group of paintings using only dots of black and red arranged on the background grid according to her arcane conceptual system—"mathematics' goofy side," as the critic Calvin Tomkins wryly termed it in his New Yorker profile of Jennifer Bartlett (April 15, 1985). By the time a group show was held at the Paula Cooper Gallery in the autumn of 1974, that schematism was beginning to disappear, and several of her steel plates were painted with loose brush strokes that obliterated the grid.

During the summer of 1975, while taking care of the house and garden of friends in Southampton, Long Island, Jennifer Bartlett unfortunately let their garden dry up while she worked steadily on a steel-plate painting that "had everything in it," both figurative and nonfigurative images. Its four archetypal figures are a house, tree, mountain, and ocean; its abstract elements are the square, circle, and triangle; and its drawing is freehand, ruled, and dotted. She devoted some sections to lines or to icy, brilliant tones of enamel paint. The whole is organized like a conversation or an orchestral composition, with themes and subthemes introduced, then dropped, only to be taken up again later in different forms. The work's grand finale is a sequence of 126 plates devoted to the ocean that she painted in fifty-four shades of blue.

Completed in Jennifer Bartlett's New York loft by the winter of that year and ultimately consisting of 988 plates, the work remained untitled until an architect friend christened it Rhapsody. Installed in May 1976 in the Paula Cooper Gallery, Rhapsody occupied some 153 feet of wall space to a height of over seven feet and immediately created an enormous sensation. In a much quoted review in the New York Times (May 16, 1976), John Russell pronounced it "the most ambitious single work of new art" that had come his way since he started to live in New York and went on to describe how it "enlarged our notions of time, and of memory, and of change, and of painting itself." Almost immediately, Rhapsody was sold to a private collector for $45,000, but first it was shown in a number of museums across the United States.

What followed was a series of "house paintings" that repeated Rhapsody's simple house-image in a repertory of modern styles that ranged from impressionism to Jackson Pollock. Since the paintings take their titles from the addresses of people significant to Jennifer Bartlett, they are in a sense their portraits. Thus White Street, using all the available range of Testor colors, refers to the "contained chaos" that she associates with her close friend, the artist Elizabeth Murray. Graceland Mansion, consisting of five paintings in five different styles, pays tribute to its former owner, Elvis Presley. From Graceland Mansion, Jennifer Bartlett developed one of her best-known print sequences, a virtuoso display of her mastery of the graphic arts, in which each of the five parts is done in a separate technique: aquatint, drypoint, silk screen, woodcut, and lithography. Typifying her drive to achieve all-inclusiveness, her prints combine or juxtapose reworkings of the same theme in different media. Her graphic work was represented in a 1980 Museum of Modern Art show, "Printed Art: A View of Two Decades."

In 1979 Jennifer Bartlett received a commission from the General Services Administration to do a work for the Richard B. Russell Federal Building in Atlanta, Georgia. Somewhat confused about the city's proximity to the coast, she chose as her subject swimmers in different ocean environments as they encounter icebergs, whirlpools, eels, seaweed, or boats. Swimmers Atlanta, as the project came to be called, consists of nine paintings in a medley of formats, textures, colors, types of brushstroke, representational and abstract images, and moods. Half of each painting is made up of individual enamel-on-steel plates, while the other half consists of oils on canvas. One half, according to Jennifer Bartlett's preliminary notes for the series, is sad and turbulent; the other is happy and calm. The "swimmer" is represented by a featureless, flesh-colored ellipse, and the surrounding waters are painted in a variety of tones. The installation for *Swimmers Atlanta*, in a very long and narrow lobby, mixes paintings that vary in size from an intimate two feet square to a towering eighteen feet square, thus inviting the viewer to move, imaginatively at least, backward and forward in space.

By now Jennifer Bartlett was living and working in an enormous new loft in SoHo, elegantly designed for her in Art Deco style, where she busied herself with several projects simultaneously. There her paintings, such as her *At the Lake* series, began to be more realistic in manner, and since then, often using photographs as an image bank, she has become increasingly concerned with figures and with painterly evocations of landscape or waterscape.

As a respite from her hectic pace, Jennifer Bartlett agreed in 1979 to exchange houses with the English writer Piers Paul Read, by going to stay at his villa in Nice, on the French Riviera, but it proved to be a dismal site and a dreary stay. Her original plan had been to travel, visit museums, and write. Finding writing was impossible, she turned to drawing, and with the help of her sister Julie, a commercial artist, set herself finally to learn shading, perspective, and other rendering techniques. Her sketches of "the awful little garden" at the villa in Nice developed, over the next fifteen months, into a suite of 200 drawings in pencil, pen, brush and ink, Conté crayon, charcoal, watercolor, pastel, and gouache. Some of the later studies, completed after she returned to New York, were worked up from photographs or done from memory. The dried-up garden pool, the kitschy little statue of a urinating cherub, and the moribund cypress trees in the background are seen almost cinematically, from every angle and sight level, in various lightings and are represented in her usual abundance of stylistic treatment, from abstract to meticulously realistic. *In the Garden*, which has been described by Calvin Tomkins as a remarkable work of self-discovery and ultimately a revelation about the process of drawing itself, was exhibited in 1981 at the Paula Cooper Gallery and was handsomely reproduced in a monograph in 1982, with an introduction by John Russell. The peculiar sense of unease and imbalance that pervades the drawings has been transferred to the eight large paintings to which they gave rise in 1983.

Since her Atlanta federal building project, Jennifer Bartlett has done four other major commissioned paintings. When, in 1981, she was called on to decorate the dining room of the London home of the art collectors Charles and Doris Saatchi, she produced a multimedia work that linked the environments of garden and interior space. In a witty allusion to the fact-gathering process, for the Institute for Scientific Information in Philadelphia she painted 270 steel plates so distributed throughout the building that a process of synthesis is required to register their cumulative image. She has executed two thirty-foot murals for the staff dining room of Philip Johnson's new AT&T building in New York, and an outdoor/indoor installation for the Volvo Corporation's headquarters in Göteborg, Sweden, where her free-standing sculptured objects on the grounds are echoed in smaller objects or painted images inside.

Such created "objects that have walked out of [the] paintings," as John Russell once described them in the *New York Times* (May 19, 1985), have figured prominently in Jennifer Bartlett's most recent work and now require her to hire assistants. One of those paintings-with-objects, for example, represents the Luxembourg Gardens in Paris, with full-scale model sailboats with tartan sails, just like the ones on the canvas, sitting on the floor beneath the painting. Some critics have characterized that trend as excessively decorative, but Jennifer Bartlett, contending that all painting is to some extent decoration, does not contemplate abandoning that manner or any other that appeals to her.

The list of one-woman and group shows of Jennifer Bartlett's work in museums and galleries worldwide is impressive, including her representation in the 1977 Documenta in Kassel, Germany and at the 1980 Venice Biennale. In addition, her work is now owned by, among others, the Museum of Modern Art, the Metropolitan Museum of Art, and the Whitney Museum of American Art, in New York City; the Art Gallery of South Australia, Adelaide; the Rhode Island School of Design, in Providence; the Yale University Art Gallery; and the Walker Art Center in Minneapolis, where in the spring of 1985 a major retrospective of her drawings and paintings was mounted. That show, documented in a comprehensive catalogue, was scheduled to travel cross-country, including a stop at the Brooklyn Museum in November. Jennifer Bartlett received the Harris Prize of the Art Institute of Chicago in 1976 and a creative arts award from Brandeis University and an award from the American Academy and Institute of Arts and Letters, both in 1983.

An elegant, attractive woman with large mobile features, vivid blue eyes, and a distinctive cap of dark hair, Jennifer Bartlett has been a commanding presence since her early school days. Her reputation for confrontational dialogue has been confirmed by Elizabeth Murray, who recalls her as "sort of a brat." That outspoken manner has always been combined, however, with self-deprecating humor, and some interviewers have speculated that her very openness to different styles and ways of seeing betrays a certain lack of self-assuredness. In any case, she is reluctant to discuss her work, preferring to talk about movies, books, or even money. As for money, she believes it "can buy you two things, and that's all—silence and mobility." She has acknowledged that she has developed "a very happy relationship with luxury."

Jennifer Bartlett was first married in 1964 to Edward Bartlett, who came East with her to enter Yale Medical School. They were divorced in 1972. In 1980 she met the German film actor Mathieu Carrière in New York, and she married him three years later. Jetting back and forth between Europe and the United States on the Concorde, she spends half the year in New York City and the other half with her husband in their Paris apartment. Bored at first by life away from the vibrancy of the New York art world, she has lately become more enthusiastic about the Paris scene. Both she and her dealer, Paula Cooper, agree that she is still in the process of finding her own style and that the French capital may well inspire her to find new ways to exploit what she acknowledges to be her "infinite capacity for work."

References: Artnews 82:72+ Nov '83 por; New Yorker 61:50+ Ap 15 '85; Vanity Fair 48:81+ Ap '85 por; Contemporary Artists 2d ed (1983); Who's Who in America, 1984–85; Who's Who in American Art, 16th ed (1984); Who's Who of American Women, 1985–86

© Thomas Victor

## Beattie, Ann

Sept. 8, 1947– Writer. b. c/o Random House, Inc., 201 E. 50th St., New York City, N.Y. 10022

In the eleven years since her first story was published in the New Yorker, thirty-eight-year-old Ann Beattie has earned a reputation as a prodigiously gifted fiction writer. Since her work is largely populated by men and women who grew up in the 1960s, she has sometimes been labeled a "cult" author, but, as Margaret Atwood has pointed out, the "shifting and dubious no man's land known as interpersonal relationships," rather than any sociological emphasis or nostalgic yearnings, forms the core of Ann Beattie's fiction. In spite of their material success, her characters, now up-and-coming New Yorkers or New England suburban-

ites, are haunted by a sense of not having it all. What is usually missing is a genuinely loving connection with another person. Her troubled, passive characters rarely achieve such a relationship in her stories, and in spite of the gleams of humor with which she laces her work, her ambiguous endings intimate that that may indeed be impossible. Nevertheless, Ann Beattie is not putting forth in her oeuvre any philosophy of life. "I don't think I have an overall view of things to express," she asserts.

The only child of James A. Beattie, an administrator in the Department of Health, Education and Welfare, and Charlotte (Crosby) Beattie, Ann Beattie was born in Washington, D.C., on September 8, 1947 and was raised in suburbs of the capital. Even as a child, she was "an artsy little thing" who enjoyed painting and writing, in addition to reading. In 1966 she enrolled at the American University in the District of Columbia to study English literature. She completed the requirements for her baccalaureate degree in only three years, but in spite of the demands of her accelerated schedule she found time to edit the university's literary magazine. She was also one of several college women chosen in 1968 to be a guest editor of Mademoiselle magazine.

On graduating in 1969, Ann Beattie accepted an assistantship at the University of Connecticut and entered its graduate English program to study eighteenth-century literature. She received her M.A. degree the following year and immediately began working toward her doctorate. Soon bored with her studies, she resumed writing her own stories "in some kind of attempt to care about literature again." Encouraged by her friend J. D. O'Hara, who teaches literature at the university, she submitted her work to several "little" magazines. The Western Humanities Review and Texas Quarterly, among other journals, published some of her stories, but the turning point in her early career came when the redoubtable New Yorker, after rejecting about twenty of her pieces, printed "A Platonic Relationship" in its April 8, 1974 issue and published two more of her stories later that year. Realizing then that her writing talent offered a means of escape from the grind of graduate school, she left the University of Connecticut shortly before she would have completed the requirements for her Ph.D. degree. "Writing was just sort of a process of elimination," she admitted to Maggie Lewis of the Christian Science Monitor (October 23, 1979). "I don't have tremendous skills in a tremendous number of areas. I never really set out to be a writer. I just sort of backed into it."

While serving as a visiting writer and lecturer at the University of Virginia at Charlottesville from 1975 to 1977, Ann Beattie concentrated on writing short stories with the precise descriptions, realistic dialogue, and ambiguous conclusions that were becoming her hallmarks. "It was really [J. D.] O'Hara," she explained in a 1982 interview published in Literary Review (Winter 1984), "who, in literally taking the scissors to my pages, suggested that more elliptical endings to my stories might be advantageous." Ernest Hemingway's works also influenced her writing: her short sentences and emotionless tone are clear reflections of his clipped style, and, like him, she prefers "to bury things too obviously symbolic." "I write in those flat simple sentences because that's the way I think," she explained to Bob Miner of the *Village Voice* (August 9, 1976). "I don't mean to do it as a technique. It might just be that I am incapable of breaking through to the complexities underlying all that sort of simple statement you find in my work."

Over the next several years her stories continued to appear regularly in print, chiefly in the *New Yorker*, which had successfully negotiated for the right of first refusal on her work. In 1976 Doubleday simultaneously issued *Distortions*, her first collection of short stories, and *Chilly Scenes of Winter*, her first novel, which became a Book-of-the-Month Club alternate selection. Written in only three weeks, *Chilly Scenes of Winter* focused on the obsession of Charles, its principal character, with regaining Laura, a former lover who left him to return to her husband and family. Virtually paralyzed by his desperation for their reunion, he passively waits for her return. The novel's lack of action reflects that stasis, which is underlined by the unadorned, almost monotonic, prose style. Nevertheless, most critics agreed that Ann Beattie's use of both dialogue and the accretion of telling details to develop her characters—whom John Updike described in the *New Yorker* (November 29, 1976) as "exquisitely modulated studies in vacancy"—and her compassionate but humorous treatment of Charles's plight carried the story forward and rendered *Chilly Scenes of Winter* a remarkably successful first novel. Ann Beattie had a bit part in *Head Over Heels* (Triple Play/United Artists, 1979), a film of the novel written and directed by Joan Micklin Silver and starring John Heard and Mary Beth Hurt. The movie flopped, but when re-released in 1982 with a new ending and the original title restored, it enjoyed a somewhat longer run.

Since *Chilly Scenes of Winter* and many of her earlier short stories were peopled by characters who had grown up in the 1960s and now found themselves muddling uneasily through the 1970s, Ann Beattie was labeled with increasing frequency as the chronicler of the coming-of-age of the counterculture. While acknowledging that her characters are of that generation, she is quick to point out that they are not representative and that such a view is "a horribly reductive approach to [her] work." More often her stories explore a person's sense of emptiness and unhappiness, a longing he cannot articulate even to himself, and the adverse effect that inability to communicate has on his relationships.

But even that reading, Miss Beattie cautioned in the *Literary Review*, "tends to generalize a great deal" since the scope of her fiction is very wide. *Distortions* is a case in point. In the nineteen stories in that collection, most of which had previously appeared in the *New Yorker* or other magazines, her characters are usually bizarre. Among them are a woman who no longer speaks to her husband but arises each night to mail him a letter; a man who begins seeing sunsets at midnight; and a disturbed child who purposely drowns himself and several other children by setting the boat they are in afire. Interviewed by Jay Parini for *Horizon* (December 1982), Ann Beattie described the composition of those stories: "In those days, I would write the most fanciful thing I could, like imagining an obese woman who was marrying for the fourth time . . . or spacemen who come to earth to take pornographic pictures. It was fun."

Although reviewers acknowledged that the collection was original and often witty, many complained that her stories nonetheless lacked substance. However, even Anatole Broyard, who was dissatisfied with both *Chilly Scenes of Winter* and *Distortions*, shared the majority's opinion that "Ann Beattie is, potentially, a good writer." "In spite of a style that virtually eliminates personality," he concluded in the *New York Times* (August 24, 1976), "she still manages to haunt the reader with her work. The things her characters say and do are rather like the inexplicable noises very old houses make in the middle of the night. You wake up in alarm when you hear them—what can *that* be?—then reason asserts itself and you go uneasily back to sleep."

On leaving the University of Virginia in 1977, Ann Beattie accepted a Briggs Copeland lectureship at Harvard University. However, soon feeling overworked and ignored by the English department and distracted from her own writing by the demands of her students, she left at the end of the academic year. Supported in part by a $10,000 Guggenheim fellowship she received in 1977, she then rented a house on four acres of land in Redding, Connecticut and returned to writing full time. The result was *Secrets and Surprises* (Random House, 1979), a collection of fifteen short stories, most of which had first appeared in the *New Yorker*. Turning away from the grotesqueries of *Distortions*—a collection that one critic labeled a "salute to Diane Arbus"—Ann Beattie created in these stories believably human characters who suffer from an unshakable anomie.

Unable to form loving relationships, the characters in *Secrets and Surprises* share instead a thing or an animal, which is their only real bond, and a very tenuous one at best. In "Vintage Thunderbird" a couple's relationship dissolves when the woman sells her prized car; two people are brought together in "Distant Music" by their concern for an abandoned puppy named Sam, but, when the young man moves away, Sam, suddenly turned vicious, has to be put to sleep; and the fame of their artist-fathers forms the only link between the protagonists in "La Petite Danseuse de Quatorze Ans." Although the characters are intensely self-conscious, their self-awareness and the occasional insights it yields offer no solutions, and neither do the stories' uneasy endings. Responding to those readers who find such inconclusiveness a weak point in her fiction, Ann Beattie maintained in the *Literary Review* interview (Winter 1984) that "what matters is that [the characters are] getting through life and they're unhappy and there's something missing. If I knew what it *was* that was missing, I'd write about it, I'd write for Hallmark cards." "I certainly don't feel," she added, "that it's the obligation of *any artist* to supply answers." Voicing the critical consensus in the *Washington Post's Book World* (January 7, 1979), Terence Winch, who admitted that some of the stories were deficient, nevertheless concluded that "the five or six solid successes are works of vivid honesty and insight that confirm Beattie's reputation as one of our best young writers." Her well-received adaptation of "Weekend," one of the stories in the collection, for the *American Playhouse* series was aired by PBS on April 20, 1982.

Her impressive literary output notwithstanding, Ann Beattie has always had writer's block and a very erratic work schedule. What finally drives her to the typewriter is a "physiological feeling," a kind of compulsion. "It's not totally amorphous," she explained in *Literary Review* (Winter 1984). "There is something in the back of my mind: it's a name, it's a sentence, it's a sense of remembering what it is like to be in the dead of winter and wanting to go to the beach in the summer, some vague notion like that. It's never more than that." But that feeling does not always result in successful fiction: in the summer of 1979, just seven weeks before a deadline from her publisher, she scrapped the 400-page novel she was working on because she could not find an appropriate ending. To make matters worse, her troubled six-year marriage to David Gates, a musician whom she had met while both were graduate students at the University of Connecticut, was disintegrating, and she was suffering from an infection that required massive doses of antibiotics. "I wanted to block out my life, to forget it," she recalled in *Horizon* (December 1982). "So I sat down at my typewriter for eighteen hours a day and after a month or so I had another novel."

Seeing a peach tree outside her window, she imagined someone sitting in it. "Then it occurred to me," she recounted in *Literary Review*, "that if somebody was up high in a tree, it would probably be a child, and if it were a child it was likely that there would be a family surrounding him." With only those rudimentary ideas, she rapidly produced *Falling in Place* (Random House, 1980). It is set in the summer of 1979: Skylab is falling, Blondie's recording "Heart of Glass" is climbing the charts, and John Knapp, a frustrated ad man from Connecticut, is having an affair with a woman young enough to be his daughter. Meanwhile, Knapp's family life is steadily deteriorating: dissatisfied with their marriage but unwilling to get a divorce, his wife broods; the relationship of their children—Mary, suffering the usual traumas of adolescence, and John Joel, a fat, unhappy youngster—grows increasingly antagonistic. The family's problems are not improved by John Joel's friendship with Parker, an obese, hateful boy whose idea

of fun is pricking pin holes in his mother's diaphragm and reading sadomasochistic comic books. Typical Beattie characters, they passively mull over their problems, unsuccessfully looking for solutions, until the tragic climax creates a climate where, as Peter Collier described it in the *Chicago Tribune* (April 27, 1980), "love is momentarily permitted, rather than being affirmed, and not as the result of any soul searching that takes place. It is rather the case . . . that after a while 'things just fall in place.'"

While very much in the mold of her earlier compositions, *Falling in Place* has, nonetheless, some important differences. Including a climactic event was in itself an innovation, and Richard Locke discerned in that work, which he praised in the *New York Times Book Review* (May 11, 1980) as "the most impressive American novel of the season," a "new urgency to the characters' feelings" that helped produce an effect he compared to "going from gray television to full-color movies." Robert Towers and a minority of other critics, however, found the novel skillfully written but ultimately disappointing. "So much passivity, aimlessness, and narcissism," Towers noted in the *New York Review of Books* (May 15, 1980), "is easier to take in small doses—in Ann Beattie's short stories for instance—than in a novel of this length."

The response to the sixteen stories in *The Burning House* (Random House, 1982) was more uniformly enthusiastic and reinforced the general agreement that Ann Beattie's literary intentions are best realized in short fiction. The characters are typically in the midst of a dissolving relationship, but the loosing of the traditional bonds results not in a feeling of liberation but in a frightening sense of being suspended in space. The author offered no humorous touches to lighten the depressing mood as she had in the past, and her emotionless treatment of both the mundane and the terrifying gave the stories a nightmarish tone. Jonathan Yardley of the *Washington Post's Book World* (September 19, 1982) chided Miss Beattie for essentially reworking, albeit very skillfully, the characters and themes of her earlier stories, but the reviewer for *Publishers Weekly* (July 28, 1982), entranced by the "grisaille, sharply observed" world presented in *The Burning House*, joined the majority of critics in extolling the collection as a "stunning" achievement.

Following her divorce from David Gates, Ann Beattie lived in New York City. Driven out of her apartment there by escalating rent and a number of mice, she spent the summer of 1984 in the Green Mountains of Vermont. Happy in her new surroundings, she decided to attempt a comedic novel, and, working between midnight and 4 A.M. from June 22 to July 31, she produced *Love Always* (Random House, 1985), which was offered as a Book-of-the-Month Club alternate selection. Most of its characters work for *Country Daze*, a slick and fashionably irreverent magazine whose subscribers and the targets of its cynical humor are affluent young Americans very much like the editorial staffers themselves. The magazine's success, according to its editor, Hildon, is "proof positive that the entire country was coked-out." Hildon has been having an on-again-off-again affair for fifteen years with Lucy, who, as "Cindi Coeur," writes both the answers and the questions for the magazine's patently ludicrous advice-to-the-lovelorn column. With the arrival from Hollywood of Nicole, Lucy's precocious fourteen-year-old niece, their lives become almost as convoluted as those of the characters in *Passionate Intensity*, the second-rate soap opera in which Nicole stars. While *Love Always* is almost slapstick in parts, after an unexpected death the mood darkens as the author gives deeper insights into the characters, especially Lucy and Nicole, who then grow more three dimensional and human.

"My idea," Ann Beattie explained in an interview with Nancy Connors for the *Cleveland Plain Dealer* (June 23, 1985), "was that no person is any one thing. Who you are at noon is different from who you'll be at midnight." The novel's sudden change in tone left most critics cold. While conceding that "the jump-cuts from mockery to insight to sentiment may be intended as a demonstration of Beattie's belief in human nature's many-sidedness . . . ," Josh Rubins, writing in the *New York Review of Books* (July 18, 1985), shared the majority's opinion that "the attempt to invest [her characters] with emotional heft registers only as mawkish gimmick."

Frequently on the road, Ann Beattie often gives readings of her works or lectures, and during the fall semesters of 1980 and 1982 she returned to the University of Virginia to teach. She has received several honors for her writings, including an award in literature from the American Academy and Institute of Arts and Letters (1980) and a Distinguished Alumnae award from American University (1980). In 1985, *Spectacles*, her first children's book, helped to inaugurate *Goblin Tales*, the Workman Publishing Company's supernatural fiction series for young readers. Currently she is working on a nonfiction study—another first for her—of the painter Alex Katz. Her professional memberships include the Authors Guild and PEN.

A lean woman with hazel eyes and long, light-brown hair framing her heart-shaped face, Ann Beattie admits to a single "genuine affectation"—very long fingernails that she polishes in bright colors. She recently moved to her own home, a renovated house in Charlottesville, Virginia. Since she and her characters are of the same generation, she was asked during the *Literary Review* interview if in writing her stories she ever discovers something about herself. "Yes," she conceded, "but always only in retrospect. I don't ever sit down thinking that. I just *do it*, the way I get my groceries."

References: *Horizon* 25:22+ D '82 por; *Literary R* 27:165+ Winter '84 por; *N Y Times Bk R* p1+ My 11 '80 pors; *People* 13:67+ Je 16 '80 pors; *Washington Post* B p1+ S 13 '76 por;

*Contemporary Authors* vols 81–84 (1979); *Dictionary of Literary Biography* (1982)

## Behrens, Hildegard

Feb. 9, 1937– Soprano. Address: b. c/o Columbia Artists Management Inc., 165 W. 57th St., New York City, N.Y. 10019

In the fourteen years that have passed since she made her European operatic debut, German-born Hildegard Behrens has established herself as a dramatic soprano of the highest calibre and as one of the most accomplished actresses on the lyric stage. Although she has been acclaimed by audiences from the Bayreuth Festspielhaus in West Germany to New York's Metropolitan Opera House as the leading Wagnerian soprano of the day, she continues to broaden her already variegated repertoire, winning ovations for her performances in taxing roles that range from Leonore in Beethoven's *Fidelio* to Marie in Alban Berg's *Wozzeck*. Her many admirers among critics and opera buffs alike maintain that resplendent though she is today, Hildegard Behrens has yet to realize her full potential.

Hildegard Behrens was born on February 9, 1937 in the small northern German town of Varel, in Oldenburg, not far from Bremen, to parents who were physicians. As the youngest of six children, Hildegard at first tagged along with her older brothers and sisters, meekly accepting their rules and opinions. But, as she related to Thomas P. Lanier in *Opera News* (February 2, 1980): "Suddenly I surprised them by making up my own play rules. My opinions were my own, right or wrong, and this gave me a wonderful sense of freedom, a lasting feeling that I need never be threatened by anyone, regardless of titles, power, whatever."

All of the Behrens brood studied violin and piano, and one of the soprano's brothers is now a professor of piano in West Germany. Miss Behrens' family did not anticipate great musical achievements from her, however. Nevertheless, when she was at the University of Freiburg studying law (she was convinced that there were enough doctors in the family), she joined the school chorus and found that she enjoyed it immensely. Still, it was not until after she had completed three years of law school that her interest in singing grew so great that she decided to take lessons. As she explained to Thomas P. Lanier in *Opera News*, the more she studied, the more she loved singing, and the more indifferent she became to law. Although she passed her law exam, she worked part-time as a' substitute teacher to support herself while continuing her vocal studies for the next six years at the Freiburg Conservatory, despite the well-meant advice of her voice teacher Ines Leuwen, who at first thought that she had "a beautiful voice but no talent" and counseled her to give up singing. Some of the teachers for whom she auditioned judged her to be both an alto and a soprano; however, she finally chose the latter register.

At the suggestion of one of her professors, Miss Behrens auditioned for the Deutsche Oper am Rhein in Düsseldorf, which accepted her for its opera studio and engaged her for *comprimario* (secondary) roles in its opera house. During her first year there, she made a guest appearance in the small city of Osnabrück as the Countess Almaviva in Mozart's *The Marriage of Figaro* on February 2, 1971, an event that she looks back upon as her formal operatic debut. That appearance led to twenty performances of the same role that season, including five in a single week. Since her studies and chores with the opera studio continued during that period, Miss Behrens had to commute by train from her engagements to Düsseldorf and then back again for each evening's performance. Although that hectic schedule left her little time for rest, she savored the experience, perhaps because she feels that she is at her best under stress.

Although at the time of her debut in *The Marriage of Figaro* Miss Behrens was almost thirty-four, she is convinced that her late start in opera has been beneficial. "I consider my career to have had a fantastic logic, . . . " she explained in an interview with John Rockwell for the *New York Times* (December 10, 1983). "I realize that all that time I spent at the conservatory allowed me to evolve as a musician. It was like playing a role out in my mind, before I actually did it. Even today, I can *think* through a part, and my throat will subconsciously assume all the correct positions without my actually having to sing."

Since leaving music school, Hildegard Behrens has had only one vocal coach—an American tenor named Jerome Lo Monaco, a colleague in Düsseldorf with whom she studied for two seasons.

It was he who persuaded her to make fuller use of her chest voice, a practice proscribed at school, so that now she takes the chest voice as high as possible and the head voice as low as she can manage. "I will be thankful to him for this the rest of my life," she said during the *Opera News* interview. "Now I believe in using the chest voice, even in Mozart, especially as Fiordiligi [in *Così fan Tutte*]. She overreacts to almost everything, and this is a funny way of showing that, with these vehement low tones."

Steadily adding to her repertory such roles as those of Agathe in Von Weber's *Der Freischütz*, Elsa in Wagner's *Lohengrin*, and Giorgetta in Puccini's *Il Tabarro*, Hildegard Behrens ignored the cautious counsel of studio colleagues who advised her to acquire provincial experience first. Instead, she joined the Düsseldorf Opera ensemble in 1972 and proceeded to appear in major European opera houses in the early 1970s. Putting Lo Monaco's instruction to the test, she sang the role of Fiordiligi in Frankfurt in September 1974 and again, under the baton of Christoph von Dohnányi, in September 1975, and in Prague in the late 1970s. She also essayed the part of Victoria in Milks Kelemen's *Belagerungszustand* (Conditions Under Occupation) on March 10, 1973 at the Düsseldorf Opera and sang "with great vocal and dramatic intensity" (according to Hildegard Weber in the May 1974 issue of *Opera*) the title role in Leoš Janáček's *Katya Kabanova*, produced by Volker Schlöndorff at the Frankfurt Opera in January 1974. Once again at the Düsseldorf Opera in May 1974, she was acclaimed for her appearance as Marie in Alban Berg's somber *Wozzeck*.

But it was with her triumphant debut at the Zurich Opera in October 1975 that Hildegard Behrens first came to international attention. In a review for the British publication *Opera* (March 1976), Heinz Kern rhapsodized that her premiere performance as Leonore in Beethoven's *Fidelio* "caused a minor sensation. Her powerful voice and completely unforced tone mastered this taxing soprano role with seemingly effortless accomplishment. . . . She also possesses such outstanding dramatic talent, that it almost places her among the ranks of the great tragediennes." Reprising that role for her debut at the Royal Opera at Covent Garden on April 14, 1976, she drew even more enthusiastic notices. "This is the kind of voice we had long been waiting for—youthful-sounding, large, true, not necessarily intrinsically beautiful, but without any of the Viennese 'schmaltz' we sometimes get . . . ," Harold Rosenthal wrote in *Opera* (June 1976). "There is a searing intensity and sincerity in everything she does on stage. She combines the feminity and warmth of Sena Jurinac and Gré Brouwenstijn with the intensity of Martha Mödl, and is surely destined for a truly great career."

Hildegard Behrens has since repeated her interpretation of Leonore at some of the most celebrated opera houses in the world, including the Paris Opéra, the Palais Garnier (Paris), the Budapest State Opera, the Metropolitan Opera, and the Munich Opera, and at the festivals of Salzburg and Tanglewood. "*Fidelio* is the opera I have done the most productions of, and the more I invest in it, the more I love it, . . . " she informed Thomas Lanier. "Maybe, when all is said and done, it is my favorite opera." In 1980 she recorded *Fidelio* for London Records with Sir Georg Solti and the Chicago Symphony Orchestra.

In spite of her success in *Fidelio*, Hildegard Behrens regards her debut in the title role of Richard Strauss's *Salome*, which is based on Oscar Wilde's version of the Biblical story of the beheading of John the Baptist, as "[her] real breakthrough into the international opera scene." While attending a rehearsal for a May 1974 production of *Wozzeck* in Düsseldorf, Herbert von Karajan was so impressed by her voice that he decided she would be ideal for the title role in *Salome*, an opera he had long wanted to record. That project came to fruition in 1976 with an Angel recording featuring Hildegard Behrens and the Vienna Philharmonic under the baton of von Karajan.

In 1977 Hildegard Behrens made her highly praised stage debut as Salome, under the direction of von Karajan, at the Salzburg Festival in a performance that was broadcast worldwide. For her interpretation of that role at Covent Garden on January 2, 1979, with Zubin Mehta on the podium, she again won critical accolades. In his review for *Opera* (March 1979), Harold Rosenthal marveled that her "performance was not only magnificently sung with her voice sounding beautiful and fresh and as steady as a rock, but also acted in the most convincing manner. One saw every thought that went through Salome's mind mirrored in her face and actions."

In addition to recording *Salome* with von Karajan and making her debuts at the National Theatre in Prague in the title role of Leoš Janáček's *Katya Kabanova* and at Covent Garden, in 1976 Hildegard Behrens appeared for the first time at the Metropolitan Opera in New York, singing the role of the adulterous Giorgetta in Puccini's *Il Tabarro*, the melodramatic opening segment of his *Trittico*. According to Hubert Saal in *Newsweek* (October 23, 1978), Miss Behrens "slipped almost unheralded" into that production on October 15, 1976 and "departed almost unnoticed," but she was far from unheralded or unnoticed when she made her return engagement at the Met in its 1978–79 season as Leonore in *Fidelio*. Saal termed her performance a "triumph . . . the high point of an already uncommonly good season in New York." Saal added that she "has the heroic presence of Flagstad, the passion of Sills, and the power of Nilsson. By the end of her opening performance, anyone who wasn't standing was probably too weak from excitement."

That same vocal stamina and intense acting were evident in her performance as Electra in Mozart's *opera seria Idomeneo* at the Met in January 1983. She "stole the show," according to a critic for the *New York Times*, from an all-star cast that included the Italian tenor Luciano Pavarotti, mezzo-

soprano Frederica Von Stade, and the Rumanian lyric soprano Ileana Cotrubas. In commenting on her powerhouse style and commanding stage presence, Miss Behrens told Thomas P. Lanier that "nowadays there is a lot of puritanism in opera. People listen to these light voices that have no hormones and think this singing is so cultivated, but I think it's fishy—and in almost all operas, not just Mozart. But with Mozart especially the problem is that people think of him and his time as powdered wigs and perfume. They don't think this was a man who had his own inferno, his own complexes." Miss Behrens has enjoyed equal success at the Met as Marie in *Wozzeck* and as Donna Anna in Mozart's *Don Giovanni*, but her performance in the title role in the Met's new production of Puccini's *Tosca* in March and April of 1985 was less warmly received.

Expanding her repertory in Richard Strauss on her return to Europe after making her Met debut, Hildegard Behrens groomed herself for the demanding role of the Empress in *Die Frau ohne Schatten*. She sang the Empress for the first time in 1979 in Düsseldorf and repeated the role when she made her Paris Opéra debut at the opening of the 1980–81 season under Christoph von Dohnányi. At the Salzburg Festival on July 28, 1979 she sang for the first time the title role in Strauss's *Ariadne auf Naxos*, which was conducted by Karl Böhm. In his review for *Opera* (Autumn 1979), Horst Koegler applauded her "stunning achievement" in that performance. She "looked almost destitute in her austere black dress, like a woman worn out by suffering, very tired, very vulnerable," Koegler noted, "but her voice belied her from her very first 'Wo war ich?,' gradually warming up, expanding all the time, sending glorious soprano waves into space and filling it with the most luscious sounds until it exploded in pure ecstasy."

Returning to the stage of the Zurich Opera where she had triumphed in her first portrayal of Leonore, Hildegard Behrens equaled that achievement on September 8, 1977 when she appeared for the first time as the young romantic Senta, who sacrifices her life to save the accursed Dutch sea captain in Richard Wagner's *Der Fliegende Holländer*. She reprised that role to critical enthusiasm in a 1980 production at the Paris Opéra and, though hindered by a cold, in her debut at the Deutsche Oper in 1981. Other characters in her Wagnerian repertoire include Elsa in *Lohengrin*, Eva in *Der Meistersinger von Nürnberg*, Elisabeth in *Tannhäuser*, and Sieglinde in *Die Walküre*. It was her first appearance in July 1983 at the Bayreuth Festival, where she sang Brünnhilde in Sir Peter Hall's controversial production of Wagner's cycle *Der Ring des Nibelungen*, conducted by Sir Georg Solti, that established her as the consummate Wagnerian soprano. Reviewing her performance in *Die Walküre* for the *New York Times* (July 28, 1983), Donal Henahan hailed her as "probably the most sensitive and intelligent Brünnhilde active today" and praised her "exciting vocal force and purity." Apparently most critics and aficionados shared that view (though the production itself was viewed as a fiasco), for at the conclusion of *Götterdämmerung*, the last of the four operas that constitute the "Ring," Henahan reported in the *New York Times* (August 1, 1983) that Hildegard Behrens "was deafeningly cheered for her vocally true and intelligent portrayal of Brünnhilde" and "emerged as the new darling of Bayreuth." "She may not have the endless column of dramatic-soprano sound that has been the hallmark of great Brünnhildes of the past," Henahan conceded, "but in this house, at least, she is all but perfect." She returned in the summer of 1984 to Bayreuth for a repetition of the "Ring," this time conducted by Peter Schneider, and again earned a rapturous response for her Brünnhilde.

With her spectacular performance on December 5, 1983 as the Irish princess Isolde in *Tristan und Isolde*, under the baton of James Levine at the Metropolitan Opera, Hildegard Behrens proved to skeptics that her resounding success at the considerably smaller Bayreuth Festspielhaus—known for its flattering acoustics—was solidly based. Donal Henahan elevated her to the rank of the "new Wagnerian queen" of the Met in his *New York Times* review of December 7, and the critic for *Opera News* commended not only her vocalism but her "extraordinary presence, passionate involvement, [and] near-mystic sensuality." Unlike some operatic stars who have magnificent voices but only mediocre acting ability, Hildegard Behrens has consistently been lauded for both her vocal production and her subtle impersonations of the characters in her repertoire. Reviewing her appearance in Munich in March 1981 as the title character in *Rusalka*, Anton Dvořák's tale of a naiad's fateful marriage to a mortal man, the critic for *Opera* (July 1981) admired her "gentle, sinuous performance of the sprite-become-woman, one who never lets us forget that her original element was water. In moments of the most intensive, silent grief [Miss Behrens] could almost sing an aria with her body, with sheer physical movement." But in spite of her already impressive dramatic achievements, Hildegard Behrens is still not content. "I'm trying to expand my emotional panorama, from the most tender to the most violent," she told John Rockwell in a *New York Times* interview (December 10, 1983). "I take my ideas of interpretation from the complexity of my life-experiences."

Hildegard Behrens' eclectic and wide-ranging repertoire also includes Santuzza in Pietro Mascagni's *Cavalleria Rusticana*, as well as Jenufa in Leoš Janáček's opera of the same name, Marenka in Bedrich Smetana's *The Bartered Bride*, and Musetta in Puccini's *La Bohème*. She has also sung Arnold Schoenberg's monodrama, *Erwartung*, and in June 1984, with soprano Jessye Norman and rock star David Bowie, was to have performed three roles in Robert Wilson's *Civil Wars* at the Los Angeles Olympic Arts Festival, but the production was canceled. She has also fulfilled many symphonic engagements with the Boston Symphony, the New York Philharmonic, the Chicago Symphony, and the Philadelphia Orchestra. Miss Behrens was one of the soloists in the Verdi *Requiem* with the Cleveland Orchestra at Carnegie Hall as part of a farewell concert tribute to its former conductor Lorin Maazel. In addition, she has made two recordings with the Bavarian Symphony, von Weber's *Der Freischütz* and Wagner's *Tristan und Isolde*, and early in 1985 her interpretations of Ravel's "Shéhérezade" and of Berlioz' song cycle "Les nuits d'été" were released. When, on April 25, 1985, at Carnegie Hall, she gave her first song recital in the United States, she received only mixed notices.

In June 1979 Hildegard Behrens moved to Paris but by the early 1980s, according to John Rockwell of the *New York Times* (December 10, 1983), "if any theater is her 'home' now, it is the Met." She lives in a Chelsea loft in lower Manhattan with Seth Schneidman, an American filmmaker, their preschool-age daughter, and her teenaged son Philip, whose father is a musician she knew during her student days. Since the soprano, who has never married, refuses to be away from home any more than is absolutely necessary, she turns down many engagements, limiting her schedule to about fifty performances a year. She appreciates both "the luxury of being very choosy" and the premium quality of most of her contracts, which ensures a high publicity profile to her appearances. In the *Opera News* interview, she declared that she is curious, eager to enrich her experience, and pleased to be considered a "today" person. Interviewers find her relaxed but determined, honest, affable, and "laid-back." Defying the stereotype of the temperamental diva, Hildegard Behrens "radiates a sense of security," according to Hubert Saal in *Newsweek* (October 23, 1978). "I'm happy," she told Saal. "I don't get nervous onstage. What's the worst that could happen? I'll fail. That would be a pity, that's all. In my life I've not done one thing I regret—or one thing I would want to repeat. I want to develop. I want to go on."

References: N Y Times p13 D 10 '83 por; Newsweek 92:128 O 23 '78 pors; Opera N 44:10+ F 2 '80 pors; Who's Who in America, 1984-85; Who's Who in Opera, 1976

---

## Bennett, William J(ohn)

*July 31, 1943– United States Secretary of Education. Address: b. Department of Education, 400 Maryland Ave. SW, Washington, D.C. 20202*

William J. Bennett, who was sworn in as United States Secretary of Education on February 6, 1985, has been a figure of controversy ever since he came to national prominence in 1981 as chairman of the National Endowment for the Humanities. An independent thinker who defies easy classification, Bennett has described himself as a disaf-

*William J. Bennett*

fected Democrat sympathetic to "neoconservative" causes and as an enthusiastic supporter of the education policies of President Ronald Reagan. Despite his credentials as an accomplished scholar, teacher, and academic administrator, Bennett alienated influential members of Congress, the education establishment, and the liberal press shortly after taking office, with his outspoken remarks in favor of the administration's proposed cuts in student aid. Sharply departing from the low-key manner of his predecessor, T. H. Bell, Bennett has continued to generate sensational headlines, eliciting both praise and censure for his strongly held and bluntly articulated views.

Born on July 31, 1943 into a middle-class Roman Catholic family in Brooklyn, New York, William John Bennett spent his early years in Flatbush, the stamping ground of the old Brooklyn Dodgers baseball team. A self-styled "streetwise" youth, he attended Public School 92 and Holy Cross boys' school in Flatbush, and he has suggested that his strict Jesuit education may have contributed to his stubbornness of character. As a teenager, he moved with his family to Washington, D.C., where he graduated from Gonzaga High School.

Bennett's first memorable contact with the classics was through a comic-book version of Homer's *Iliad*, in his words, an "epic of war, jealousy, and friendship," and "just the thing for bellicose young boys," that was given to him by a friend when he was nine. A pantheon of fictional and nonfictional heroes inspired his youth, the mythical superheroes of Homer mingling in his imagination with Abraham Lincoln, Roy Campanella, the biblical Queen Esther, and Gary Cooper as Marshal Will Kane in the film *High Noon*. Through such figures the young Bennett learned of "a certain nobility, . . . a hitching up of one's own purposes to larger purposes."

The need of the young for moral inspiration and guidance became one of Bennett's predominant concerns. "Children need to know what deserves to be emulated and loved and nurtured, but knowing these things is not transmitted by their genes," he has observed. "These things must pass through education, from generation to generation." Another major factor in the development of character, according to Bennett, is competitive sports, and he remembers the moral influence of his high school football coach, who taught "toughness without callousness."

At Williams College in Williamstown, Massachusetts, Bennett studied philosophy and was an interior lineman on the football team. As his former professor John Chandler, now the president of Williams, has recalled, "He came to play football and found he had a mind as well." With only limited financial support available from his parents, Bennett worked his way through college and graduate school, getting by on scholarships, part-time and summer jobs, and loans that left him for a time $12,000 in debt, but he looked back on those experiences as "part of growing up." After obtaining his B.A. degree at Williams in 1965, Bennett went on to the University of Texas for graduate work, and on completing his dissertation on the theory of the social contract, he received his Ph.D. degree in philosophy there in 1970. Among his other academic credentials is a J.D. degree from Harvard Law School, granted him in 1971.

Among the teaching positions that Bennett held during his years as a graduate student was that of assistant professor of religion and philosophy, in 1967-68, at the University of Southern Mississippi—where, he later recalled, he was regarded as "very liberal" for advocating a "colorblind society." At Harvard, he served as a resident advisor from 1969 to 1971 and as a tutor in a social sciences program in 1970-71. Martin Peretz, the editor-in-chief of the *New Republic*, who administered the Harvard program at the time, has recalled that Bennett had "the teacher's gift and the scholar's temperament."

From Harvard, Bennett went to Boston University as a teacher and administrator. After a year as associate dean of liberal arts, he served from 1972 to 1976 as assistant to the president, John R. Silber—one of the candidates whom he later edged out for the nomination as education secretary. Serving in addition as an assistant professor of philosophy at Boston University, from 1971 to 1976, Bennett developed a reputation for being "thought-provoking, tough, and stimulating." His experiences in the academic world left him with a somewhat jaundiced view of the education establishment and convinced him that "the percentage of knaves and fools in higher education is as great as it is elsewhere." He believes, with Martin Buber, that "all education is the education of character" and that a teacher is not merely a "skills facilitator," but is engaged in "the architecture of the human soul." In 1973 Bennett headed a teacher workshop project on the question of authority in American high schools, sponsored by the National Humanities Faculty, an agency promoting improvements in humanities education, and in 1974 he was associate chairman of its Bicentennial study "The American Covenant: The Moral Uses of Power."

In May 1976 Bennett became executive director of the National Humanities Center in North Carolina, an agency that he and the Columbia University philosopher Charles Frankel founded to foster advanced study in the humanities. After Frankel was killed by intruders in his upstate New York home in the spring of 1979, Bennett succeeded him as president and director. His work at the center further enabled him to advance his belief in the necessity of the humanities, which, he has emphasized, "bring together the perennial questions of human life." During his years in North Carolina, Bennett continued to teach philosophy, at North Carolina State University in Raleigh and at the University of North Carolina in Chapel Hill. He also contributed articles to such periodicals as *Commentary, The Public Interest, Change,* and *Newsweek,* often presenting right-of-center views on contemporary issues.

In collaboration with journalist Terry Eastland, Bennett wrote *Counting by Race: Equality from the Founding Fathers to Bakke and Weber* (Basic Books, 1979), tracing the concept of equality in American thought from the "moral equality" of individuals envisioned by Thomas Jefferson to the "numerical equality" between groups sought through contemporary affirmative action programs. Arguing that the backers of the 1964 Civil Rights Act in no way intended it to serve as an invitation to practice "reverse discrimination," Bennett and Eastland went on to show how subsequent Supreme Court rulings gradually tended to establish the legitimacy of such discrimination and concluded with the principle, advanced by Alexander Bickel, that any form of "discrimination on the basis of race is illegal, immoral, and unconstitutional, inherently wrong, and destructive of democratic society." Reviews of the book were generally favorable, though several critics suggested that the coauthors had oversimplified the legal, historical, and social complexities of the issue.

Moral education was another subject on which Bennett concentrated his attention in his articles during the late 1970s and early 1980s. He was especially critical of programs like the "values clarification" exercises developed by Sidney B. Simon of the University of Massachusetts and the "cognitive moral development" approach devised by Lawrence Kohlberg of Harvard. In Bennett's view, such programs—which recognize "the child's right to freedom from indoctrination" and which view the child "not as a pupil but as a 'moral philosopher' in his own right"—err most in their "unwillingness to argue for certain reasonable standards of right and wrong." Such programs also mislead, Bennett maintained, in claiming to be faithful to the Socratic tradition which, he argued, offers no comfort to "values educators" who insist that teachers must remain ethically neutral. Bennett also deplored what he saw as the underlying *ethos* of most current sex education programs, to advocate sexual gratification divorced from any larger context. The only caveat appears to be to avoid venereal disease and pregnancy, while abstinence is rarely recommended.

In December 1981 President Ronald Reagan appointed Bennett to the chairmanship of the National Endowment for the Humanities, to replace Joseph Duffey, an appointee of Jimmy Carter. Having sat on the boards of the "neoconservative" Committee for the Free World and the Institute for Educational Affairs, Bennett had the strong support of influential neoconservatives like Irving Kristol. He had also worked closely with the Heritage Foundation, one of the leading right-wing think tanks, helping to draft the arts and humanities section of its 1981 presidential agenda, "Mandate for Leadership," which included the recommendation that the NEH shun the funding of "faddishly innovative" programs.

During his three-year tenure at NEH, Bennett largely reversed the liberal course charted by his predecessor and substantially trimmed its budget. Claiming to return NEH to a strict interpretation of the "humanities" as defined in the 1965 law establishing the endowment, he reorganized divisions, eliminating the categories under which many liberal projects had previously been funded. He publicly criticized three documentary films—*From the Ashes . . . Nicaragua Today, Women under Siege,* and *Four Corners: A National Sacrifice Area?*—which had received funding from the endowment under Duffey and maintained that the projects, "veering toward political harangue rather than scholarship," failed to meet the agency's funding criteria.

Programs that Bennett promoted at NEH included summer humanities seminars for high school teachers; challenge grants for thirteen of the nation's major independent research libraries; and plans to improve state-based humanities programs. He also helped to prepare educational programs to commemorate the forthcoming bicentennial of the United States constitution.

Bennett's final major undertaking at NEH was the preparation of a study entitled "To Reclaim a Legacy: A Report on the Humanities in Higher Education," issued in November 1984. Based on the findings of a study group comprising leading educators, the report deplored the decline of the humanities in American education and the "collective loss of nerve and faith on the part of both faculty and academic administrators during the late 1960s and early 1970s" that induced them to capitulate to student demands for a "greater role in setting their own educational agendas." The report acknowledged that the American college curriculum "must take the non-Western world into account" but insisted that "the core . . . should be the civilization of the West." It concluded with a quote from Walter Lippmann: "What enables men to know more than their ancestors is that they start with a knowledge of what their ancestors have already learned. . . . A society can be progressive only if it conserves its tradition."

While the report was, on the whole, well received, some liberal critics maintained that Bennett failed to address adequately the political, economic, and social conditions affecting the decline of education in the humanities. Leo Botstein, the president of Bard College, commented in the *New Republic* (February 11, 1985): "We are addressing an American college population that increasingly will come from homes and heritages that have remarkably little autobiographical continuity with Bennett's great tradition of Western civilization. To find new ways to introduce the great tradition and make it 'relevant' is not necessarily to violate it."

At a meeting of the American Historical Association in December 1984, Bennett's strict interpretation of the humanities was sharply criticized by Professor Mary Beth Norton of Cornell University, who charged that the endowment, under Bennett, was abandoning programs in black, ethnic, and women's studies and that Bennett's idea of the past was that of "a Western white man's past." In a similarly critical vein, John S. Friedman and Eric Nadler in the *Nation* (April 14, 1984) had accused Bennett of "transforming the endowment into an ideological pork barrel," with a marked bias in favor of "ultraconservative" institutions and individuals. But according to the rightist *National Review* (March 8, 1985), Bennett "performed with unshakable integrity" as the head of NEH.

In November 1984 T. H. Bell announced his resignation as secretary of education, reportedly under right-wing pressure. That month, at the urging of the White House, Bennett met privately with right-wing leaders, who screened him on his views. When it appeared that Bennett would be nominated as education secretary, the Reverend Jerry Falwell wrote an article in his *Moral Majority Report,* headlined "Finally, A Friend in Education." On the other hand, Bennett came under attack from such liberal organizations as People for the American Way for his "courtship of the far right" and his relationship with "theo-political extremists."

Although President Reagan had indicated that he would have preferred to abolish the education department if Congress would allow it, on January 10, 1985 he formally nominated Bennett to succeed T. H. Bell as education secretary. In response to the nomination, President Mary Futrell of the National Education Association criticized Bennett's "less than exemplary record on civil rights," referring to his refusal to comply with the Equal Employment Opportunity Commission's race- and gender-based affirmative action goals for hiring personnel at the NEH. Questioned about his refusal at the Senate Labor and Human Resources Committee confirmation hearing, Bennett affirmed his belief in a "colorblind society." Because of his formidable credentials as a scholar and educator, Bennett won unanimous confirmation from the ninety-three senators present on February 6, 1985 and was sworn in as secretary of education on the same day.

In his first press conference as education secretary, on February 11, 1985, Bennett unequivocally supported the administration's proposed reductions in government-subsidized student loans, asserting that some people should not go to college and that many educational institutions were mismanaged or "ripped off" their students. His remark that the budget cuts might "require of some students divestiture of certain sorts—stereo divestiture, automobile divestiture, three-weeks-at-the-beach divestiture" was seized upon by the press and the academic community in what Bennett later referred to as a "media mugging."

Bennett again became embroiled in controversy in April 1985, when his choice of two special assistants, Eileen Marie Gardner and Lawrence A. Uzzell, was challenged by Senator Lowell Weicker, head of the Senate appropriations subcommittee for education. The two appointees were widely criticized for having questioned the entire federal role in education, and Dr. Gardner's published views attacking special education for the handicapped were particularly condemned. After initially defending both aides, Bennett, to the dismay of right-wing spokesmen, capitulated to congressional and public pressure, accepting their resignations and issuing a statement repudiating Dr. Gardner's views on the handicapped as "insensitive and repugnant."

Bennett believes that the secretary of education should work "for the American people," not "for the education establishment." Final responsibility for education, he has asserted, should rest not with the federal government but with parents, teachers, and local authorities. He also supports education vouchers and tuition tax credits to give parents greater options in the choice of their children's schooling, and he has spoken out for merit pay to reward effective teachers—views that brought him criticism from American Federation of Teachers president Albert Shanker. Bilingual education, in his view, should aim at "getting people into the mainstream."

On the issue of school prayer, Bennett supports a constitutional amendment under which the federal government would neither prohibit nor require prayer in school. He strongly criticized a United States Supreme Court five-to-four decision, in July 1985, withholding public funds for remedial-education programs in church-related schools, and charged that the court displayed a "fastidious disdain for religion." American values, he asserted, are "intimately interwined" with the "Judeo-Christian tradition."

Bennett regards as his main goals the promotion of curriculum reform, with an emphasis on moral content and "development of character"; renewal and elevation of the teaching profession; and more effective monitoring of educational quality, through an overhaul of federal data collection and evaluation. "This department has no function more important than the production of high quality research and accurate information about the condition of all levels of American education," Bennett said at a news conference in July 1985, in which he outlined plans for a reorganization of the education department's research functions.

Early in the 1985 fall term, Bennett assumed the duties of a substitute teacher of social studies at schools in Washington, D.C., Louisiana, Missouri, Idaho, California, New Hampshire, and North Carolina and won high marks for his pedagogical skills. Addressing the Eagle Forum Leadership Conference, a "new right" education lobby in the nation's capital, in September 1985, he asserted that students should be taught "patriotism, self-discipline, thrift, honesty," and "respect for elders," and that teachers should emphasize the "moral superiority" of the United States over the Soviet Union.

A burly, "rumpled-looking" man, six feet two inches tall and weighing 220 pounds, with short, wiry hair graying at the temples, Bennett has a youthful, rugged appearance, deep-set eyes, a heavy, furrowed brow, a down-turned mouth, and a strong chin that often give him a pugnacious expression. He has been described by the press as "contentious" and "intense," a "figure of considerable nervous energy and impatience." When asked in an interview in the Chronicle of Higher Education (February 27, 1985) about his "combative tone," Bennett replied: "The notion that I am combative may be just a weakness of press categories. That is, you are either for gobble-dygook or you're combative. . . . I was trained as a philosopher . . . under the Socratic dictum that for good conversation three things are necessary—intelligence, candor, and good will. I always speak with good will, that is, with the hope of arriving at a conclusion that we can all share. . . . "

A bachelor until the age of thirty-nine, William J. Bennett married Mary Elayne Glover on May 29, 1982. They have one son, John, born in 1984, and live in Washington, D.C. In recent years, Bennett's preferred leisure-time activities have included summer mountain-climbing in the Colorado Rockies, softball, and the study of ancient Greek—so that he can "read the Iliad as Homer wrote it."

References: Christian Sci Mon p3+ Mr 12 '85 por; N Y Times B p6 Ja 11 '85; Time 125:49 My 20 '85 por; Wilson Lib Bul 57:56+ S '82 por; Directory of American Scholars (1982); Who's Who in America, 1984–85

## Berri, Nabih
(ber´ē näb´ē)

1938(?)– Lebanese government official; Muslim political leader. Address: Ministry of Justice, Beirut, Lebanon

The Beirut TWA hostage crisis of June 1985 catapulted to international recognition Nabih Berri, the leader of Amal, the chief organization representing Shiite Muslims in Lebanon and the strongest military force in the country. After Shiite extremists hijacked Trans World Airlines flight 847 out of Athens, Berri, with his mainstream Shiite followers, took protective custody of the American passenger-hostages and eventually mediated their release. During seventeen tense days of negotiation, Berri, who has headed Amal since 1980, proved himself to be the most powerful factional chieftain in war-torn Lebanon. Although virtually unknown in the West before the hijacking drama, he has been a major power broker in Lebanon's splintered political life since February 1984, when his Amal militia overpowered the forces loyal to President Amin Gemayel, a Maronite Christian favored by the United States, in the battle for control of West Beirut.

Berri, now the multi-portfolioed minister of justice, reconstruction, water and electricity, and southern Lebanon in Lebanon's "national unity" government, has been a harsh critic of what he considers to be Israel's American-backed ravaging of Lebanon, the motivation for the TWA hijacking. Compared to the hijackers and their cohorts, he

may be a moderate, but he is also a pragmatist. Although he would prefer to separate faith from state and politics, he has been increasingly radicalized by the militancy for Islamization among his following. Some observers consider it ironic that Berri has strong ties to the United States, in the form of an American ex-wife and six children, among other relatives, in Dearborn, Michigan, where he lived periodically in the 1970s and which he visits annually.

Unlike his rivals for Muslim leadership in Lebanon, who are hereditary warlords, Nabih Berri is a self-made politician from the upper middle class. The grandson of two sheiks, he was born in 1938 into an expatriate Lebanese merchant family in Freetown, Sierra Leone, West Africa, where his father, Hajj Mustapha Berri, prospered as a trader. When he was still a child his parents returned with him to their home village of Tibneen in southern Lebanon.

"He was a dynamic student, a very good leader and a passionate person," Nasib Fawaz, a friend of Berri's from childhood, has recollected. "He enjoyed literature, sports, and had lots of friends." Berri studied law at the Lebanese University of Beirut—where he was president of the student union and a member of Baath, a secular pan-Arab political party, rival branches of which now rule Syria and Iraq—and at the University of Paris. He worked in the business his father still maintained in West Africa before opening his own law practice in Beirut. Visiting the United States, he took part in the civil-rights march on Washington in 1963, according to his son-in-law, Imad Fadlallah. In later visits, he perfected his reading knowledge of English by reading newspapers and magazines in the Dearborn Public Library.

In Lebanon, Berri's energy was increasingly diverted from his practice of law into his involvement in the turbulent politics of his country, particularly the Shiites' struggle for equality. Constituting more than a third of the total population of 2.6 million, the Shiites were (and are) the largest faction in Lebanon. They were also the most oppressed, kept at the bottom of the economic and political ladder by the Christians and the Sunnis.

The second-class status of the Shiites was institutionalized in the informal "national covenant" with which Lebanon began its existence as an independent republic in the 1940s. Formed from five former districts of the Turkish Empire following World War I and administered as a French mandate from 1920, the country became legally independent in 1941 and fully so with the withdrawal of French troops five years later. Because of its strong position as a Mediterranean commercial power (going back to Phoenician days) and despite sporadic disturbances (including an uprising precipitated by the expulsion of Arab critics of Lebanon's pro-Western policies from the government and suppressed with the help of United States Marines in 1958), Lebanon enjoyed an enviable standard of living among developing nations for three decades following its independence, and its capital, Beirut, was the showcase city of the Middle East.

Lebanon's relative tranquility in those years was bolstered by the unwritten national covenant of 1943, which held Arab nationalism in check. That pact, now blatantly anachronistic, supposedly reflected the balance of religious groups within the country at the time of its formulation. The agreement provided for a sharing of executive and legislative power in the ratio of six Christians to five

Muslims (who now make up about two-thirds of the population). It guaranteed that the president would be a Maronite Christian and the vice-president a Sunni Muslim. Other groups, including the Shiites and the less numerous Druze (sometimes spelled Druse or Druses) were relegated to minor governmental posts. The Druze are an Islam-related esoteric sect based in the mountains of Lebanon and adjoining countries, especially Syria. Despite their small numbers (a total of some 350,-000, including those in Jordan, Israel, and Syria), their militancy under the leadership of the Jumblatt family brought them an increased share of the governmental power in Lebanon in the 1960s. In the majority numerically, the Shiites remained in a condition that Berri compared in some ways to that of the blacks in South Africa.

The situation began to change in the early 1970s, when the general Muslim desire for self-determination was strengthened by population growth and rising political consciousness. The Shiites in particular were inspired by the leadership of Imam Musa Sadr, a charismatic Iranian-born cleric who organized them into the Movement of the Deprived in 1974 with the backing of Colonel Muammar Qaddafi, the ruler of Libya. Musa Sadr had been cooperating with another Qaddafi client, Yasir Arafat, whose Palestine Liberation Organization guerrillas were using southern Lebanon as a base for attacking Israel, but he began to withdraw his support for Arafat when the PLO turned the south into an occupied land. As more and more Shiites, caught in the Israeli-PLO crossfire, were driven from their homes and land, Musa Sadr realized that his political organization needed a military wing. Accordingly, in 1975 he formed Amal, a name that means "hope" in Arabic and also an acronym for Lebanese Defense Organization in Arabic. Nabih Berri, who had joined the Imam's political movement in 1974 and was a member of its politburo, was put in charge of the militia, whose name would ultimately supersede that of the political organization.

Meanwhile, clashes between left-wing Muslim groups led by the Druze chieftain Kamal Jumblatt and right-wing Christian groups led by the Gemayel family escalated into civil war in 1975. In their confrontation with the Christians, the Muslim activists turned to the long-silent Shiite community for support. Concerned about the Shiites being driven from the southern suburbs of Beirut as well as from southern Lebanon, the Amal formed an alliance with the Druze, who were clearing the mountains southeast of Beirut of Christian militia.

Musa Sadr mysteriously disappeared in 1978 on a trip to Libya, where his followers believe Qaddafi killed or kidnapped him for allegedly misusing Libyan financial aid. Musa Sadr's disappearance set off a bitter power struggle within Amal that lasted two years. After defeating opposition from Shiite elders, who felt the movement should be led by a holy man, Berri emerged as the new head of Amal in 1980. A religious hard core within Amal, refusing to believe that Musa Sadr is dead without conclusive evidence of that fact, to this day accepts Berri only as the Imam's surrogate. Berri's insecurity as a Shiite leader was compounded by repercussions from the Iranian revolution of 1979, in which Islamic religious and political authority was united under the fundamentalist Shiite leadership of the Ayatollah Ruhollah Khomeini.

Berri took advantage of the continued fighting between Christians and Muslims to expand Amal's political and military presence. A major break came in the summer of 1982, when Israel invaded Lebanon to crush the PLO. Amal at that point gave support to the PLO, and when the latter had to evacuate Beirut, they left Berri's militia with a large cache of arms. That largesse of materiel enabled the Amal organization to turn the southern suburbs of Beirut into a Shiite stronghold.

From that stronghold, Berri tried to win concessions from the American-backed government of Amin Gemayel, initially with little success. Under pressure from both leftists and religious fundamentalists within his movement, he hardened his opposition to the government, and clashes between Amal and Christian forces became more and more frequent. Berri's hand was strengthened enormously by a deed he did not condone, the suicide bombing in October 1983 of the American Marine barracks in Beirut, an act approved if not planned by Hezbollah ("Party of God"), a fundamentalist, pro-Iranian Shiite splinter group headed spiritually by Sheikh Muhammad Hussein Fadlallah. The bombing, which killed 241 Marines, destroyed the viability of the American military presence on which the Gemayel government was totally dependent for its credibility.

After the withdrawal of its surviving military personnel from Lebanon, the United States took an alternative course, trying to build President Gemayel's dominantly Christian Lebanese army into an effective force. Berri shattered that effort in February 1984. Early in the month, the Lebanese army shelled the Shiite southern suburbs of Beirut, forcing 170,000 to flee and causing extensive damage. When, a few days later, the government announced its intention to move the army into Muslim West Beirut, Berri retaliated. He ordered the Shiite soldiers of the army's sixth brigade to lay down their arms, and when they did so the Amal and Druze militia overpowered the remaining government forces. With that victory, Berri's decisive role in the future of Lebanon was clinched.

In April 1985 Berri's Amal forces drove the Mourabitou, the Sunni militia, from the streets of West Beirut. The following month Amal began raiding Palestinian refugee camps south of Beirut in an attempt to empty pockets of PLO guerrillas threatening to reestablish a military presence in Lebanon. Both actions were backed by the government of Syria (although that government eventually brokered a ceasefire in the anti-PLO campaign) and opposed by Muslim fundamentalists advocating Arab solidarity at all costs. Earlier, Berri and his militia had been instrumental in freeing an American and a Frenchman kidnapped by Muslim extremists.

On April 30, 1984 Prime Minister-elect Rashid Karami, a Sunni Muslim trying to form a "national unity" cabinet, offered Berri the portfolios of justice and water and electricity. Berri rejected the offer, on the grounds that the "national rank" of Muslims opposed to President Gemayel had not been consulted adequately and had been given posts that were "unconnected with political decison-making." He agreed to join the government seven days later, after the additional positions of minister of reconstruction and for southern Lebanon were accorded him. As a cabinet member, Berri participated in negotiations to rid Lebanon of the Israeli occupation, at the same time that his Amal militia was using firepower to that end.

In withdrawing from southern Lebanon in April 1985, the Israeli forces took with them some 1,100 Lebanese civilians, mostly Shiites, who were then placed in a military prison in Atlit, Israel. The transfer of the prisoners to Israel raised a storm of domestic and international criticism, because the 1949 Geneva Convention prohibits the transfer of civilians captured by occupying forces to the territory of the occupying power, "regardless of motive," as a spokesman for the United States Department of State pointed out.

The illegal detention of the civilian Shiites in Israel was apparently the final straw for many militant Shiite fundamentalists, and the release of the detainees was the chief demand of the hijackers (allegedly members of Hezbollah) of Trans World Airlines flight 847 out of Athens on June 14, 1985. (At that point, 731 Shiites remained in the jail at Atlit.) After shuttling across the Mediterranean, between Beirut and Algiers, twice, dropping off passengers at each stop, the commandeered jet ended up at the airport in Beirut with thirty-nine hostages aboard, all American. Writing in the *Christian Science Monitor* (June 25, 1985), Jim Muir tried to explain the thinking of the hijackers to Americans, who tended to view the hijacking as an act of barbarism committed against innocents: "A fact little appreciated by most Americans, but made clear to this reporter from many encounters on the ground in the past three years, is that ordinary Lebanese—and the Shiites in particular—hold the United States directly responsible for the suffering inflicted on them by the Israeli invasion of 1982 and the subsequent occupation. This is because of Washington's massive military and economic aid to Israel, and the political permissiveness which many Lebanese saw as conferring on the U.S. a degree of responsibility almost beyond that of Israel itself."

The hijackers killed one passenger, a United States navy diver, and threatened to kill more if their demands were not met. Because he feared that further deaths would bring down severe reprisals on the Shiites and discredit his own movement, and because no one else was ready or able to do so, Berri reluctantly came forward to protect the hostages and mediate the crisis. On June 16 Amal militiamen boarded the hijacked plane and worked out a plan for joint custody of the hostages.

Amal removed the majority of the passengers to its own safe houses in West Beirut; the hijackers did the same with the remainder; and the two parties shared control of the plane and its pilot and crew, who stayed on board throughout the crisis.

Given the implacability of the America-hating Shiite extremists and the refusal of both Washington and Tel Aviv to make any public concessions to the hijackers, the task of negotiating in behalf of the hostages was as delicate as it was onerous. For more than two weeks Berri tirelessly consulted not only with American, Israeli, and Muslim authorities (including those in Iran), but also with the International Red Cross and governments around the world who might help, including those of France, Switzerland, the Soviet Union, and, above all, Syria, the dominant regional power.

Syrian President Hafez al-Assad, having no desire to see a Shiite theocracy established in neighboring Lebanon, was, as always, interested in shoring up Berri's precarious political position, and he also apparently did not relish the prospect of American military retaliation in the Middle East. According to reports, Assad secretly met with Berri and told him to negotiate in earnest with the Americans, in exchange for Syrian help in controlling the Lebanese extremists. Finally, Assad himself became involved in the negotiations, speaking with, among others, President Ronald Reagan of the United States. Informally guaranteed that the Shiite detainees would be released by Israel subsequent to the freeing of the American hostages, Assad brought about the release of the Americans on June 30, 1985. The Israelis, who had already begun releasing the Shiite detainees in small groups according to a plan they said had nothing to do with ransom, completed the whole process on September 10, 1985.

Berri and his American wife, Lila, who is an interpreter for the Dearborn police department, were divorced in 1984. Since divorce is not necessary in Muslim tradition, he married his present wife, Randa Assi, a Lebanese, in 1982. By his second wife he has a daughter, Amal. When Berri visits his older children in Dearborn each year he gets his American green card, or residency permit, validated.

A leading Lebanese Christian politician has described Nabih Berri as "a nice man, a modern man, someone I can deal with." Berri is urbane and mild in manner and neat in appearance, and he speaks in a soft precise voice. He is a chain smoker. With his family, he lives in a heavily guarded fourth-floor apartment in the Mazraa district of West Beirut. According to his wife, his favorite relaxation is watching movies—including Charles Bronson and John Wayne vehicles—on his video machine. Although secular in his politics, he is personally a devout Muslim, and his wife wears a veil at his request.

References: Macleans 98:16+ Jl 1 '85 por; N Y Times A p1+ Je 18 '85 por; Time 123:40 F 20 '84 por, 125:22 Jl 1 '85 por; U S News 99:28 Jl 1 '85 por; Wall St J p31 Je 26 '85 por

## Betancur (Cuartas), Belisario
(bā´ tän´ kōōr bā´ lē sä´ ryō)

1923– President of Colombia. Address: b. Office of the President, Bogotá, Colombia; Conservative Party Headquarters, Bogotá, Colombia

The populist Conservative party leader Belisario Betancur, president of the Republic of Colombia since 1982, has made the negotiation of peace the "transcendental goal" of his remarkable administration, perhaps the most respected democratic regime in Latin America. Domestically, Betancur has forged tentative ceasefires with leftist guerrillas and begun a "national dialogue" that, if successful, will bring to an end three decades of political violence. Regionally, he is a founder of the Contadora group (Colombia, Mexico, Venezuela, and Panama), which is trying to mediate peace in Central America. Internationally, he has brought Colombia into the Movement of Nonaligned Nations and has warned the creditor nations that "the solution to Latin America's debt crisis is an essential ingredient for world peace." Unlike its neighbors, Colombia has been punctual in meeting the payments on its foreign debt, thanks to strict economic measures imposed by Betancur.

Betancur is widely admired in Latin America, and Richard Stone, President Reagan's special envoy in Central America, has hailed him as "a key man of peace" there, although the Reagan administration has not been happy with his refusal to accept the mindset that places leftist insurgency in the context of an East-West power struggle. American drug enforcement officers, on the other hand, very much appreciate Betancur's cooperation in the war on narcotraficantes, a cooperation unique among Latin leaders.

Betancur's unusual popular rapport (which has been somewhat weakened by resentment against his economic austerity measures) is partly explained by the fact that he comes not from the privileged classes but from the peasantry. The second son among twenty-two children of semiliterate parents, Belisario Betancur Cuartas was born in the town of Amaga in the department of Antioquia, Colombia in 1923. His father drove mule cargoes in Amaga until a railroad was built, rendering the mule trade obsolete. Growing up in poverty, Betancur was ten years old before he owned his first pair of shoes. After striking out on his own in the city of Medellín, eighteen miles from Amaga, he often, by his own account, "stared poverty in the face, slept on park benches, and [took] any kind of work to survive." According to at least one source, he was jailed many times in his younger years.

Betancur worked his way through Bolivar Pontifical University, the Catholic university in Medellín, where he received a law degree in 1947. In Medellín, he was assistant editor of the newspaper *La Defensa*. From Medellín he moved to Bogotá, the capital of Colombia, where he edited the daily *El Siglo* and taught constitutional law and was dean of the law school at the National University. Apace with the development of his journalistic and academic careers, he rose gradually to leadership in the Conservative party. Historically, the Conservatives are rooted in the agrarian aristocracy, and their chief rivals, the Liberals, in the more commercialized and industrialized sector of the electorate, but factionalism is rife in both parties and there is no great difference between the dominant Liberal and Conservative factions. Following a plebiscite, those dominant factions formed a National Front in 1958 in an effort to bring to an end an undeclared civil war, known popularly as "la Violencia," which had cost an estimated 150,000 or more lives over the previous ten years. The Liberal-Conservative coalition ruled for sixteen years in accordance with a "parity" formula. Under that arrangement, the presidency alternated every four years between the popularly elected candidates of each party; the cabinets were bipartisan; and Liberals and Conservatives had equal representation in the House of Representatives, the Senate, the departmental assemblies, and the municipal councils.

After serving two terms in the House of Representatives, Betancur was elected to the Senate in 1958. In bipartisan cabinets, he was minister of education in 1960 and minister of labor in 1962 and 1963. In 1970, a Conservative presidential year in the National Front arrangement, he ran for president as a dissident and finished far behind Misael Pastrana Borrero, the regular Conservative candidate, the victor, and Gustavo Rojas Pinilla, the dissident runner-up. Misael Pastrana was the last National Front coalition president.

Betancur served as Colombia's ambassador to Spain and representative to the Arab nations in 1974. In a second try for the presidency, he lost by a slim margin to Julio César Turbay Ayala, the Liberal candidate, in 1978. He again ran for president in 1982, on pledges to reduce unemployment and the inflation rate, which was then 30 percent, and to stimulate industrial growth with tax incentives and direct foreign credits for businesses. Although the Liberals won a majority of congressional seats in March 1982, Betancur drew enough Liberal support in the presidential election on May 31, 1982 to win a decisive 47 percent of the seven million votes cast. His Liberal rivals, Alfonso López Michelsen and Luis Carlos Galán, took 40 percent and 12 percent, respectively, and Garardo Molina, who led an alliance of Communists and Socialists, captured the remainder.

President Betancur immediately introduced a new style to Colombian politics. At his inauguration on August 7, 1982 he departed from tradition both by wearing a business suit rather than a cutaway and by appearing on the steps of the Supreme Court building to address a gathering of thousands. In addition, he opened the presidential palace to the public on Sundays; banished high-status Mercedes-Benzes from his motor pool; ordered his chauffeur to silence the horn on the presidential limousine and to obey downtown traffic signals; abolished the practice of appropriating prime-time television hours for coverage of presidential addresses and ceremonial activities; and named women to every post of deputy minister in the government.

One of President Betancur's highest priorities was an initiative to end the armed struggle between government forces and several leftist guerrilla groups that had cost 20,000 lives over the previous thirty years. From the beginning, he referred to the guerrillas as "brothers"; stressed the economic and social causes of their armed rebellion rather than the alleged influence of Cuba or the Soviet Union; and preached the possibility and practicality of a "democratic peace" as the alternative to a situation in which the military would never wipe out all the guerrillas and the rebels would never win power without participating in legal political life.

In the months following his election, Betancur pardoned hundreds of imprisoned rebels; declared an unconditional amnesty that persuaded at least another 1,000 guerrillas (of a total of some 6,000) to lay down (without giving up) their arms; met secretly in Spain with some of the guerrilla leaders; and appointed a forty-member peace commission, including representatives of the Communist party and other legal Marxist groups, to begin negotiating with the insurgents. Progress in the negotiations was slow, and it suffered a setback on November 22, 1983, when five guerrillas from the Cuban-oriented National Liberation Army kidnapped the president's brother Jaime, a law professor in Bogotá. Jaime Betancur was released unharmed on December 7, 1983, after Fidel Castro, Cuba's revolutionary leader, denounced the kidnapping as an "unrevolutionary act."

In January 1984 the minister of defense, General Fernando Landazabel Reyes, and several army commanders opposed to Betancur's efforts at reconciliation with the armed rebels resigned, but the peace initiative had such wide popular support that the military and right-wing establishments generally gave it their reluctant acquiescence. During 1984 the initiative finally began to bear fruit. In May the peace commission reached a ceasefire agreement with the largest of the insurgent groups, the Soviet-line Fuerzas Armadas Revolucionarias de Colombia (FARC), or the Colombian Armed Revolutionary Forces, which had originated in the 1950s as a militant offshoot of the left wing of the Liberal party. (FARC is now formally constituted as a political party.) The following August the commission reached similar agreements with the next largest group, the urban guerrillas known as the M-19 or April 19 Movement, and two smaller rebel bands, the Trotskyite Workers' Self-Defense Force and the Maoist Popular Liberation Army. Only two significant groups, the National Liberation Army and the Ricardo Franco command, which had split from FARC, remained unwilling to negotiate. The temporary ceasefires became the basis for the "national dialogue" that began formally on November 1, 1984. In its series of talks with the insurgents, the government has pledged to enact a number of laws and presidential decrees to effect political and social reform.

The government's effort to reach an understanding with the guerrillas was complicated by its simultaneous war against the Colombian drug traffic, because there were some ties between the insurgents and the *narcotraficantes*. Rebel leaders themselves admitted to taking "war taxes" from the drug manufacturers, and FARC troops were reported to be providing protection for the cocaine factories in the southern jungle site known as Tranquilandia. The crackdown on the *narcotraficantes* began cautiously, with the knowledge that the leverage exerted on the economics and politics of a developing nation by a $2-billion-a-year business would not be easy to neutralize. On March 10, 1984 Colombian security forces made the biggest drug raid in world history, seizing 13.8 tons of cocaine base and refined cocaine at Tranquilandia. The crackdown did not go into high gear, however, until Minister of Justice Rodrigo Lara Bonilla, who had been publicly linking some politicians, rich citizens, and soccer team managers to the drug-trafficking rings, was assassinated by gunmen on a Bogotá street on April 30, 1984. Following the assassination, Betancur declared a nationwide state of siege that, among other things, gave the security forces the authority to make arrests without warrants, and he reversed his previous stand against extraditing drug smugglers wanted in the United States, where well more than half of the cocaine and marijuana consumed is Colombian in origin. "As a law professor I taught for more than forty years that we have the right to be judged by our own laws in our own country," he explained. "But we are fighting with scarce resources against an international mafia that is threatening the very security of the Colombian state." At the same time, he pointed out that the success of Colombia's efforts would depend in part on the willingness of North Americans and Europeans to reduce their consumption of drugs and to stop exporting the base chemicals needed for their manufacture.

In retaliation, drug ring hit men began assassinating security officers and other officials involved in the war on drugs at the rate of almost one a day. Betancur and some of his ministers were threatened, but the president refused to discuss the threats lest it "alarm the country." The *narcotraficantes* also served notice that they would murder five Americans for every one of their number extradited to the United States.

Many of the drug ring leaders fled to Panama soon after the anti-drug war went all-out. Attorney General Carlos Jiminez Gómez, who had opposed an extradition treaty with the United States, held a secret meeting (apparently arranged by Alfonso López Michelsen, the former Liberal president of Colombia) with seven of them in Panama during May 1984, and two months later he publicly revealed that they had offered to "return to the legal and constitutional arena" in return for an amnesty. Jiminez's motives were widely questioned in the media and by political and Roman Catholic church leaders, and the reported offer by the head *narcotraficantes* drew no response from President Betancur except an expression of his happiness, in Jiminez's paraphrase, "that anyone would want to return to legitimate life."

Regionally, Betancur worked against American efforts to isolate Marxist Cuba and Nicaragua from the Organization of American States, and he joined with the presidents of Mexico, Venezuela, and Panama in forming the Contadora Group, named for the island off Panama where the foreign ministers of the four countries first met to discuss the group's aim of working toward the negotiation of peace in Central America, especially in Nicaragua and El Salvador. In September 1984 the Contadora negotiators approved a draft treaty calculated to insure free, internationally inspected elections, the withdrawal of foreign military forces, and the halting of outside support for guerrilla movements. Nicaragua surprised all sides by announcing it was prepared to sign the treaty. At that point the United States, which was supporting "freedom fighters" making incursions into Nicaragua, suddenly began mounting objections to the treaty.

Colombia's economic growth rate, previously running better than 5 percent annually, took a downturn in 1982, partly because of depressed coffee prices. Faced with a growing government deficit, President Betancur in his first months in office suspended or reduced the implementation of his plans for such social programs as public housing and began gradually to impose harsh economic measures and to curb imports in order to preserve dwindling foreign currency reserves. As a result, Colombia, though hurt by the international recession and the rising interest rates imposed by American banks, was not inundated by the tide of debt moratoriums that swept Latin America. As of June

1983, the country had $4 billion in reserves and a foreign debt of $8 billion—small in comparison with the external debts of such countries as Argentina and Venezuela, which were well into eleven figures, and those of Brazil and Mexico, which were approaching twelve figures.

At the General Assembly of the United Nations in October 1983 Betancur drew a standing ovation with an eloquent address in which he called for a fairer distribution of the world's wealth, denounced terrorism, and warned of the danger posed to all mankind by the superpowers' pursuit of "their own, sometimes warped interest." In June 1984, when Latin America's total debt burden stood at $350 billion, ministers from eleven debtor countries met in Cartagena, Colombia, where Betancur welcomed them with a rousing, chilling speech in which he compared Latin America's financial plight with the conditions that wrecked the international economy in the 1930s and led to World War II. The Cartagena conference concluded with the issuing of seventeen proposals, including an extension of loan-payment deadlines, a commitment to hold interest rates at a level equal to that paid by the United States on its debt, and the establishment of a relation between the payments due from a nation and its ability to export. Although the suggestions, if implemented, would cost creditors money, Betancur's contribution to their overall

moderation enhanced his standing with the United States government and banking community, which has feared that the debtor nations might disavow their financial obligations or seek to reduce them through collective action.

Belisario Betancur is married and has three children. At the beginning of his presidency, he often made solitary excursions among the citizenry without the company of aides or the protection of bodyguards, chatting with his constituents at fast-food counters and, on at least one occasion, going to the emergency room of a hospital posing as an ill *campesino* to find out what kind of treatment the sick poor were getting. With his declaration of war against the *narcotraficantes*, those days of easy democratizing ended. The threats against his life have been numerous, and his family has been forced to seek refuge abroad. Following the presidential election in 1986, Betancur will step down from the presidency in accordance with the Colombian constitution, which prohibits a president from serving more than one term in succession.

*References: Colombia Today vol 17 issue 3 '82 pors; Toronto Globe and Mail p9 Ag 13 '83 por; Wall St J p10 D 24 '84 por; International Who's Who, 1984–85; International Year Book and Statesmen's Who's Who, 1985; Who's Who in the World, 1984–85*

## Borofsky, Jonathan

*1942– Artist. Address: b. c/o Paula Cooper Gallery, 155 Wooster St., New York City, N.Y. 10012*

The excitement he generates in the international art world of the mid-1980s marks a very different state of affairs for the postmodernist artist Jonathan Borofsky from the bleak time twenty years earlier, when he spent day after day alone in his studio, compulsively counting as a means of controlling and centering his thoughts. Then suddenly he began to draw and to paint again, with his customary vigor and wit.

Jonathan Borofsky was one of the leaders in the trend away from the cool intellectuality of the minimal and conceptual art of the 1970s to the more spontaneous, emotive art sometimes labeled neo-expressionism that typifies those painters who came of age in the turbulent 1960s. From his youthful experiments with dripping paint in the manner of Jackson Pollock, and later with the styles that succeeded abstract expressionism, he turned to wholly figurative work. All media interest Borofsky, who translates the same image from drawing into lithograph, or into quasi-sculptural form made up of a hardware-store array of such components as rheostats, light bulbs, videos, and tape cassettes. Assemblages of those images on paper or on canvas and of objects that he either found or created

make up the installations for which he is now famous.

Jonathan Borofsky was born in Boston, Massachusetts in 1942 and raised in its nearby suburbs. His father, who taught piano and organ, and his mother, a painter who had been trained as an architect, encouraged their only child to become an artist. Throughout his childhood Borofsky took painting lessons. Among his interests as a teenager were singing and sports, and he now compares functioning in the art world or working to assemble one of his installations to athletic competition. Many of his art forms refer to sports as vehicles of escape from oppression: running, skating, tightrope-walking, flying through the air.

In 1964 Borofsky received a B.F.A. degree from Carnegie-Mellon University in Pittsburgh, Pennsylvania and did graduate work that summer at the Ecole de Fontainebleau, in France. In 1966 he obtained his M.F.A. degree from Yale University's School of Art and Architecture, where Jack Tworkov was chairman and where his fellow students included such now well-known artists as Jennifer Bartlett and Richard Serra. Borofsky then went to New York City and set up a loft studio in lower Manhattan.

For a while, in reaction to the city's blatant commercialism, Borofsky fashioned a series of deliberately ugly parodies of mundane objects, such as lamps. When that soon came to an end, he surrendered himself to meditation, filling 450 pages of a notebook with cosmic thoughts, an activity that might be termed a form of conceptual art. By 1968 he had isolated himself in his studio, and as a way of escaping the incessant jumble of thought ("chattering," he later called it), began to write down numbers in the squares of sheets of graph paper. Intending to go on counting from one to infinity, he sometimes spent as many as eight hours at a stretch at this. Eventually he began to scribble stick figures on his sheets of numbers, and then one day in 1972 decided to do a painting of one of those drawings. To that first painting, a tree with a head sprouting from it, he added the number he had then reached, 843,956. Thus, he says, "I had both a recognizable image and a conceptual ordering in time." Since then, the corners of all his works have borne numbers, which have now reached almost 3 million. Although he has spent less time counting, since 1974, he feels it imparts a unity to the varied forms of his creativity, and is still "the purest statement" that he can make.

A computer printout that Borofsky had made of his numerical sequence was chosen by the influential critic Lucy Lippard for display in a traveling show of conceptual art in 1969. Through other acquaintances in the art world he obtained a post at New York's School of Visual Arts, where he taught from 1969 to 1977. In 1973, at the invitation of the artist Sol LeWitt, Borofsky exhibited his Counting Piece, a stack of his number-filled graph sheets, at the Artists Space Gallery. That constantly growing work has remained a fixture of his installations exhibited since that time.

From then on, too, perhaps because he was involved in group therapy, dreams became the nucleus of Borofsky's work. Despite his years of academic training, his dream imagery is recorded in naive, childlike, often cartoonlike black-and-white drawings. Executed with magic marker, pen-

cil, or ballpoint pen, they are usually accompanied by handwritten notes, sometimes deliberately misspelled and invariably beginning with the words "I dreamed I . . . " They allude to childhood memories, often to fears of persecution and to such ways of escaping it as flying around a room or roller skating away from a Hitler-like pursuer. A set of those drawings was reproduced in the Winter 1981 number of The Paris Review.

One of them, "I dreamed I found a red ruby," has taken many forms as a complex metaphor for his own heart and the search for perfection. In a 1980 show, a ruby fashioned of translucent resin sat atop his Counting Piece, which by then was a three-foot-high stack enclosed in Plexiglas. The conceptual part of him, he thus signaled, was joined with the spiritual. Borofsky's images have also gained greater impact and are reaching larger audiences as silkscreen prints, lithographs, etchings, and cutouts from sheets of aluminum.

Encouraged by the example of Sol LeWitt, in 1974 Borofsky also began to draw directly on the walls of his studio. As the wall drawings became larger and began to spill over onto adjoining walls, the ceiling, or the floor, he began to experiment with an opaque projector so that he could beam enlargements of his small drawings on those surfaces. Once he had found the most satisfactory position, he could trace the blown-up image in a matter of hours, and could carry the small originals around in a briefcase to fulfill commissions on the walls of private collectors or galleries and museums. Out of those experiments was born his later multimedia piece Man with a Briefcase, in which a figure, dressed in hat and businessman's suit, is, like all of his work, at once self-referent and universal in making its comment on contemporary life and values. The wall drawings are in fact by their very nature an attack on the rampant commercialism of today's art market, since works affixed to a wall have no potential resale value. Whether they stay or are obliterated, they must be appreciated for their own sake. Paradox is at the center of all of Borofsky's creations. Each of his pieces is a tangible object in the ephemeral, site-specific installations they compose. Depending on their juxtapositions and on the audiences viewing them, they will give out different messages at different times.

When Paula Cooper, one of the pioneer gallery owners in New York's SoHo district, visited Borofsky's studio in 1975, she was so impressed by what she termed his "strange and metaphysical" works that she immediately arranged for his first solo exhibition. The entire contents of his studio, cluttered like the human mind itself, as one observer noted, were transferred to the Paula Cooper Gallery just as she had found them, strewn on the floor and pinned to the walls. In 1977 Borofsky left New York City to live and teach in California, though he continues to like the stimulation of occasional visits to New York. Until 1980 he taught at the avantgarde California Institute of the Arts in Valencia, maintaining a studio on the coast at Venice, California, a community of writers and artists.

In the course of the ten years that have elapsed since his first Paula Cooper Gallery show, certain images keep turning up so repeatedly in Borofsky's exhibitions that in their various guises they may be said to have become the artist's "archetypes." The *Hammering Men* and *Chattering Men*, the *Running Man* and the *Man with a Briefcase*, a head with rabbit ears, *Molecule Man*, and a dancing clown are the artist's personal totems. Paradoxically, however, they are essentially anonymous, with their anonymity reinforced by Borofsky's use of numbers as a signature. An example of that, and also of the way Borofsky's art takes on layers of meaning, is his 1980 self-portrait, a photograph scribbled over with numbers that almost efface the image in the same way that the holes drilled through the figure of *Molecule Man*, a pasteboard cutout of Borofsky's own body, dematerialize it. At the same time, he is making an allusion to the numbers tattooed on prisoners in Nazi concentration camps.

"Part carnival, part seminar," is how the *New York Times* art critic John Russell once described a Borofsky installation in 1980. The artist himself compares the intensity of those showings, with their simultaneity of visual image and sound effects, to what happens "as you walk down the street . . . bombarded by sounds . . . your thoughts about the day . . . politics. . . . " Some critics have described those "events" as being similar to the "happenings" staged in the 1960s. In any event, Borofsky now thinks of the whole room or gallery space as a painting that can be activated by the placement of his drawings and objects. Enveloped in the multidimensional space the artist has created, the viewer becomes its fourth dimension.

Among those installations, a highly acclaimed show at the Paula Cooper Gallery in 1983 furthered Borofsky's reputation enormously. Paintings and drawings were hung in corners or turned upside down, while others were suspended from the ceiling or done directly on the walls in charcoal or acrylic. Papers littered the floor; blue neon-lighted hoops floated in the air. A sad-faced hermaphroditic clown in a tutu and with a ballet slipper on one foot whirled about to the taped accompaniment of Borofsky's voice singing "I'll Do It My Way." The juxtaposition of an enlargement of an El Salvadoran postage stamp and a painted version of a Maidenform brassiere advertisement seemed to some critics to make a political comment. The Maidenform model coolly saunters past a lineup of faceless United States Army generals, whose lack of concern alludes to the obliteration of the significance of the Central American situation by the constant bombardment of messages from the media. The inanity of those messages and of contemporary thought was echoed by the incessant "chatter-chatter-chatter" emanating from the mechanized wooden *Chattering Men* figures throughout the gallery. Five *Hammering Men*, wooden cutouts sixteen feet tall (based on an encyclopedia drawing of a shoemaker), kept up their motorized pounding to underscore the meaning-less din. Another piece, with a more overt political message, was a ping-pong table on which people were invited to play. In addition to making a reference to Borofsky's lifelong love of sports, it alluded to the military budgets of the United States and the Soviet Union on either side. Similarly, in the 1981 Whitney Biennial, Borofsky had exhibited drawings inscribed with those monstrously swollen defense budget figures, giving them ironic emphasis by placing sacks of grain on the floor beneath them.

One of the great surprises in the American art world came in 1984 when the Philadelphia Museum of Art opened its august doors to a Borofsky installation that amounted to a major retrospective. Over an imposing interior staircase floated a gigantic *Flying Man* in neoprene. Among all the core figurative repertoire were *Counting Piece*, now grown to four feet, and *Age Piece*, done in 1972-73. An assemblage that recapitulated Borofsky's development up to that point, it begins with a still life painted in oils when he was eight, and includes such examples of his student works as abstract sculpture in welded steel and plaster cutouts of tree forms. From Philadelphia the show moved to New York's Whitney Museum of American Art, and then in the spring of 1985 began a tour of the country's museums scheduled to end in Washington, D.C., at the Corcoran Gallery of Art in 1986.

The list of Borofsky's one-man and group shows since 1969 is impressive both numerically and geographically. He has been widely exhibited in the United States and abroad beginning with 1976. One of his sculptures, a head surmounted by a book, one eye a light bulb, hung from a ceiling at the 1980 Venice Biennale. There was a retrospective show of his drawings at the Basel (Switzerland) Kunsthalle in 1983, and in the same year he painted, with obvious political intent, a *Running Man* figure on the Berlin Wall, just outside the international "Zeitgeist" exhibition where his *Briefcase Man* hovered over the central glass dome of the Martin-Gropius-Bau. He had installations at London's Institute for Contemporary Arts in 1981; at the Museum Boymans–van Beuningen, Rotterdam, in 1982; and at the Israel Museum in Jerusalem in 1984.

Although Borofsky conceives of his shows as "one whole work made up of individual parts," he is now willing to sell those components to private collectors or to museums, at impressive prices. According to his dealer, Paula Cooper, there has been an "hysterical" demand for his work. Examples are owned by such public institutions as the Whitney, the Museum of Modern Art, and the Los Angeles County Museum of Art. By 1980 the artist had earned enough so that he could resign from teaching, but most of his money has to be plowed back into the costs of producing his art pieces as they have become increasingly automated and sound-equipped, now requiring the help of three assistants.

For all the publicity that surrounds Borofsky these days, he remains a private and reticent person. A bibliography of articles about him and catalogues of his exhibitions covers several pages, but despite the fact that he is the object of intense public interest, professional art journals and magazines like *Vogue* and *Vanity Fair* concentrate on his art rather than on his personality.

Tall and athletic, Borofsky has a long thin face that is animated by his engaging smile and dark eyes. Drawn back from his high forehead, his wiry black hair, now somewhat graying, is worn long, contained in a pony tail reminiscent of the styles of the 1960s. Although amiable and easygoing, he is also energetic and restless. Now a world traveler, like his "briefcase man," he spends much time arranging his farflung exhibitions. Since he is seldom at home, he has kept his creature comforts in the Venice studio purposely few: he sleeps on a mattress atop a row of storage cabinets, and the other furnishings are some chairs and a television set. Never much of a reader, except for doses of Wittgenstein, Einstein, Freud, and Jung back in his counting days, he watches television as a preferred diversion. But he also revels in the outdoor space of another studio home in the mountains just north of Los Angeles. He has never married.

"All is one" is a Borofsky mantra. First attracted to it when he saw it written in Persian characters, he has included the phrase in different forms in many of his drawings and prints, and given his energetic inventiveness, its implications for his future are enormous. He is currently interested in exploring music, returning to his teenage interest, and an elaborate high fidelity recording system dominates his Venice quarters, along with various devices he calls his "noisemakers." Music, he explains, quiets the mind, enabling one to tune in to the self.

References: N Y Daily News p9 F 20 '81 por; Philadelphia Inquirer mag p24+ O 7 '84 por; Contemporary Artists 2d ed (1983); Philadelphia Museum of Art and Whitney Museum of American Art, pubs. Jonathan Borofsky (1984); Who's Who in America, 1984–85; Who's Who in American Art (1984)

---

## Boy George

*June 14, 1961– Singer; songwriter. Address: b. c/o Epic Records, 51 W. 52d St., New York City, N.Y. 10022*

The interracial quartet Culture Club, possibly the most artistically significant and certainly the most commercially successful of the latest wave of British rock-theatre bands, is fronted by the flamboyant vocalist and songwriter Boy George, the current pop culture's androgynous Peter Pan. Aside from his music, George's bizarre cosmetic and sartorial style, obscuring both gender and ethnicity and therefore outraging many in the older generation, has had a strong influence on adolescents as well as fashion designers on both sides of the Atlantic.

Behind Boy George's painted, wigged, and baggy-smocked facade is a sense of humor and one of the most dulcet crooning voices in popular music today. That gripping voice began making an international impact in 1982 with Culture Club's first hit single, "Do You Really Want to Hurt Me?," a melancholy Motown-style ballad with a reggae beat, and it became established internationally the following year with the blockbuster "Karma Chameleon," a playful and charming blue-eyed-soul song with bluegrass elements. By the time Culture Club released its third album, *Waking Up With the House on Fire* (1984), with its outstanding, Philadelphia soul-styled track "Mistake No. 3," Boy George had become a millionaire, in faster time (eighteen months) than the Beatles, Elton John, and Rod Stewart before him.

The third of six children in a working-class Catholic family of Irish descent, George Alan O'Dowd was born on June 14, 1961 to Jeremiah and Diana O'Dowd. With his four brothers and his sister, he grew up in Bexleyheath and Eltham in outer London. His mother is a cleaning woman in a home for the elderly, and his father is a construction worker, sometime independent builder, and coach at a local boxing club, where George's brother Gerald became a champion.

The cross-cultural ideal that Boy George brings to Culture Club ("to make people tolerant of things" that are divergent but "not harmful") is rooted in his early rearing. "I was brought up to be democratic, to love all people and not to be bigoted," he told Lynn Van Matre of the *Chicago Tribune* (April 22, 1984). "I was also taught to be optimistic, but not stupid. My father had some very bad business experiences when I was younger. There was barely enough money to go around, and times were very hard. We learned that you can't take things for granted. Sometimes something that seems perfect may not turn out that way. So I've made a deliberate effort to stay on the ground."

As a child, George was, by his own description, "a total pop fan." The first record he remembers buying was "Alexander Beetle," by Melanie, of which he can still sing a few bars. "I never really had heroes to the extent that some people follow me around . . . ," he has said. "But I had a few people I admired. Marc Bolan [the late glitter rocker] was one of them, and a lot of old jazz singers [were others]." Later, obviously, he was influenced by such Motown groups as the Four Tops and Gladys Knight and the Pips and such reggae singers as Johnny Nash. He disdained the Sex Pistols as "a bad version of the Rolling Stones," and he "never liked punk" because he likes "quality."

According to his father, George "began to dress outrageously at fifteen and suffered considerably," but he "refused to give in." Expelled from school, he moved into London to pursue the outré on his own. His parents "never liked it all," he admitted, as quoted by Roger Wolmuth in *People* (April 23, 1984), but when he "lived in the squats [abandoned housing]" his father helped him "a lot," slipping in and filling "the cupboards with food."

In London, George took odd jobs, including short stints as a window dresser and as a costume and makeup man at the Royal Shakespeare Company, before finding steady work as a manager of the Foundry, a clothing shop. Sue Clowes, a young art-school graduate who shared management duties with him, was "a bit scared of him" because he was "such an over-the-top character." Evenings, George frequented the gay, glitter-rock, and new wave clubs, insinuating himself into the combined, inbred London fashion-music scene (where image is everything) with his freakish makeup and getups, including nun, geisha girl, spike-locked punk, mauve-haired teddy boy, and turbaned harem girl with heavy-metal neckwear. Emulating the late Marc Bolan, he affected a glacial aloofness when he went out on the town. "He [Bolan] was an ace face, one of the people that people talked about," George pointed out in an interview with Richard Harrington of the *Washington Post* (November 13, 1984). "He was the supreme mod, which is what I was to my scene, the one who was most over the top. I was the one who always managed to get my face in the paper."

George's underground celebrity as a flamboyant, wildly cross-dressing "Blitz kid" led to modeling assignments for British Airways and a major bank, in whose ads he appeared as a cute punk rocker. Chiefly on the strength of his offbeat appearance, he was hired by the pop impresario Malcolm McLaren, the former manager of the Sex Pistols, to front briefly for the New Wave group Bow Wow Wow under the name "Lieutenant Lash."

As Lieutenant Lash, George surprised audiences with the sweetness of his crooning as well as his stage panache, and he caught the attention of Mikey Craig, a young black bass player, who approached him about forming a band of their own that would represent a mixture of cultural influences. They recruited the Jewish drummer and idea man Jon Moss, formerly with the Clash, and the white Anglo-Saxon Protestant guitarist and keyboardist Roy Hay, and Culture Club was formed. With the understanding that all members would share in the credits and royalties, the band began composing its own songs, in a process that continues to this day: George, who plays no instruments and cannot write music, usually sings into a tape recorder, and his colleagues polish the result; sometimes, the band comes up with the tune and then George writes the lyrics. The group's catchy, synthesizer-enhanced songs are influenced by American, Latin, and third-world musical styles, but they are not deliberate copies of those styles.

In Culture Club's early days, as now, the essence of Boy George's image was in his femme-fatale face, with its plucked, penciled eyebrows, mascaraed and shadowed eyes, pancaked and blushed skin, and tart-bright lipstick. In the beginning the hair he displayed, in a succession of rainbow colors, including orange, was apparently his own. For a long time, he wore it in brightly ribboned, Rastafarian-style braids, topped by an Hasidic hat. The rest of his costume usually consisted of colorful scarves, a loosely flowing kimono over leggings, and ballet slippers.

Culture Club progressed slowly until Virgin Records gambled on the group in the United Kingdom and Epic Records followed suit in the United States. The band's first album, *Kissing to Be Clever* (1982), went platinum in the U.K. and gold in the U.S. and sold more than seven million copies worldwide. The biggest hit on the album was "Do You Really Want to Hurt Me?," a reggae-inflected lament with a simple melody and a swaying beat that George has said he wrote with his former roommate, Kirk Brandon of the group Spear of Destiny, in mind. As Bill Barol observed in *Newsweek* (May 16, 1983), "'Do You Really Want to Hurt Me?' wafted onto the American charts like a warm tropical breeze . . . the kind of pop song that just drifted into the mind and clung there. . . . The voice . . . was the real grabber. Warm, urgent, thrilling, it instantly recalled the perfect falsetto of soul great Smokey Robinson." In the spring of 1983 "Do You Really Want to Hurt Me?" was still in the Top 40 in the United States, and a new single, the lush "Time (Clock of the Heart)" was entering the Top 20. "Church of the Poison Mind" was high in the U.K. charts, and later in 1983 that single became Culture Club's fourth straight Top-10 single in the United States.

The group's first American tour, beginning in the summer of 1983, led some critics to judge Culture Club to be a superior singles band, disappointing in live performance. "Boy George may be a top-flight soul crooner, but he's no Jackie Wilson onstage; his manner in concert is gawky and awkward," Bill Barol observed in his *Newsweek* article. "What's more, George sets an artistic agenda that the band can't as yet fulfill. 'The aim is to be creatively fluid,' he says, 'to make everything we do a little different. We want to be a bridge between white rock and black soul.' But outside the recording studio, in which the sound of the group can be carefully manipulated, emotionally charged tunes like 'White Boys Can't Control It' and 'I'm Afraid of Me' sound only ragged and diffuse."

Appearing on the *Tonight Show* on the NBC network on November 30, 1983, Boy George sidestepped guest host Joan Rivers' questions about sexual preference to explain that he had been using heavy makeup since he was fifteen because he had "no wish to look like a piece of paper . . . to look ordinary." "I'm not like normal rock stars . . . ," he said. "I didn't conjure up this image for the stage. I'm not like Kiss or David Bowie. I never have excuses about the way I look. . . . You don't get Boy George saying, 'OK, I've created a persona, and he's the freak and I'm normal.' I am the freak. . . . Basically, I do it because I think my dial [face] is hideous without makeup. We live in a society where people are basically imperfect. I'm one of those people. Like Sheena Easton, I make the best of myself." He pointed out to Miss Rivers, "England didn't begin to accept me as a person until we got successful over here. . . . Everyone's attitude was, 'He's got a good voice, but he's still a clown.'" Reviewing the television show for the *Los Angeles Times*, Robert Hilburn described Boy George as wearing an outfit "made from a bedspread," with "more bright colors than a jumbo box of crayons," as flashing a smile "as disarming as a new-born pup," and as being "an articulate, even endearing conversationalist."

The slow, sweet songs on Culture Club's second album, *Color by Numbers* (1983), were inspired by the experiences Boy George had "facing up to success and facing up to having money and all the things that happen to you and the way people behave toward you when you become successful." He told Lynn Van Matre of the *Chicago Tribune*: "The greatest thing in the whole world is to love somebody and have them love you in return, but you can become so isolated and so much of a recluse that you begin to think that you're so important that nobody else matters."

*Color by Numbers* tied with the reconvened art-rock group Yes's *90125* for the most commercially successful English pop album of late 1983 and early 1984. It entered the U.K. charts at number one, and within five months it racked up international sales of $3.6 million. Among the cuts on the album were "Black Money," which views love as a currency far more precious than the coin of the realm; the melancholy "Victims," in which the singer ends the day without a lover in his arms; and the number-one international hit "Karma Chameleon," a teasing mixture of rhythm-and-blues and old-timey country music containing the lines, "I'm a man without conviction / I'm a man who doesn't know / How to sell a contradiction / You come and go, you come and go." (Jimmy Jones and Otis Blackwell have brought suit against Culture Club for allegedly plagiarizing their 1959 song "Handy Man" in writing "Karma Chameleon.")

The best songs on *Color by Numbers*, in the opinion of Stephen Holden, were those describing "Boy George's vulnerable fantasy world, in which 'dreams are made of emotion.'" "With their West Indian-inflected settings and vocal arrangements in which Boy George and the white soul singer Helen Terry engage in heated gospel-styled call and response," Holden wrote in the *New York Times* (January 15, 1984), "the songs offer a highly tuneful pastiche."

The only remark that the sometimes sharp-tongued George says he would like to retract was the one he made when Culture Club was awarded the Grammy in the best new artist category in February 1984. Appearing live via satellite from London, George told the Grammy Awards audience: "Thank You, America. You've got taste, style, and you know a good drag queen when you see one." He later explained that he made the remark in cynical anger over a combination of two facts. One was the exclusion of the three other members of Culture Club, who had spent a whole day preparing for the event, from appearing on the screen with him. The other was "this transvestite thing, these comments about me being a transvestite." "I am very much a man," he explained to Lynn Van Matre of the *Chicago Tribune*. "What most people don't realize is that the whole thing of people wearing costumes has been going on for centuries. It's very pathetic and hypocritical, when you think about it, the way people go on and on about people dressing up. If you look at a priest, his robes are very much like a dress, very eccentric, but people never question *that*."

In the spring of 1984 Culture Club followed up a second North America tour with a cable television concert, taped at the Hammersmith Odeon in London the previous December and shown on Home Box Office in the United States beginning on May 6, 1984. Wayne Robbins reported in *Newsday* that the tour included "scenes of Beatle-mania-style hysteria in Montreal" and that many in the audience at the televised concert were dressed similarly to Boy George, "like Amish farmers reincarnated as Lana Turner." Pamela Sommers of the *Washington Post* analyzed Boy George's influence on young people in England and elsewhere—fans, or "posers," who follow his "philosophy" to the letter, "choosing glamor over any sort of political involvement." She pointed out that on video he comes across as "the innocent imp, the fey rag doll" who admittedly "lives to dress." "Smiling wanly, he bobs and dips, looping his limp fingers through space," Miss Sommers observed. "At times he laughs coyly, placing his hand over his ruby-red mouth, then points ever so ineffectually. Boy George does not threaten, does not challenge, does not—despite his unconventional getup—exude any sort of sexual allure."

Culture Club returned to the United States in the autumn of 1984 for a tour timed to coincide with the American release of their third album, *Waking Up With the House on Fire*. The title of the LP, according to Boy George, was a reference to the "naked" feeling that comes with sudden fame, the realization that "there isn't anywhere in the world I can go where I'm not known." In a New York *Daily News* (November 18, 1984) interview with Fred Schruers he pointed out that much of the album, is "sort of cynical," about "the way that people treat you before and after you're successful."

The lead-off track of *Waking Up With the House on Fire* was "Dangerous Man," inspired by the lives and deaths of Martin Luther King Jr., John Lennon, and Brian Epstein, the Beatles' manager. The other cuts included "Mannequin"; the jazz-flavored "Crime Time"; the outstanding ballad "Mistake No. 3"; "Dive In," a song with a Caribbean beat about the universality of the need for love, heterosexual or homosexual, and of the singer's waking up "feeling victimized"; and "The Medal Song," with its line "Life will never be the same," inspired by *Frances*, the harrowing film biography of the late, emotionally ravaged Hollywood star Frances Farmer. The most personal of the songs was "Unfortunate Thing," about George's childhood and later stages in his life. The least autobiographical was "The War Song," a social statement to the effect that a country's warlike behavior can be traced to the attitudes of individuals who love to play war. The $125,000 video of "The War Song" showed children playing the adult war roles, making the bombs, carrying stretchers, and so on.

Reviewing *Waking Up With the House on Fire* in the New York *Daily News* (October 21, 1984), David Hinckley judged it to be "easily the band's most ambitious album, with more complex orchestration" than its predecessors. "Something else is equally clear," Hinckley wrote. "Behind the new polish, the core of the band has not shifted one centimeter since the beginning. What makes this music work is lyrical hooks, catchy pop beats with a Caribbean flavor, and, most of all, one of the most melodic, pleasant and distinct lead voices in pop music today. This fact may get lost in the babbling about his hair, clothes, and eating habits, but Boy George has the sort of voice for which pop singers sell the souls of grandmothers."

Boy George avoids most of his old night haunts, which he describes as "meat markets," and he visits his parents almost every week. As soon as he could afford to do so, he moved from a flat he shared with a young man and a young woman in the St. John's Wood section of London to a studio in Chelsea, and he recently moved again, into a house he bought in North London. Among the belongings he has carried with him from residence to residence are his collections of dolls, stuffed animals, crucifixes, and antique books. In his personal music listening he has lately been struck by a surprisingly disparate assortment of albums: recordings of the operas *Carmen* and *Madame Butterfly*, Joni Mitchell's *Court and Spark*, and, above all, Pink Floyd's *Dark Side of the Moon*, which has "got every noise [he] ever wanted to make."

The singer and songwriter is six feet tall and, having gained twenty pounds, a little plumper of face than he was when Culture Club was formed. His wardrobe is now more tasteful—typified by dark blazers and pants and white shirts—and his natural hair is short and stylishly punkish. The essence of his image remains his carefully cosmeticized face, which has been ubiquitous in the press, appearing not only in the tabloids and gossip columns but gracing, for example, the cover of the glossy British women's magazine *Cosmopolitan* and illustrating eight pages of beauty advice in the high-caliber American fashion magazine *Harper's Bazaar*. "What I am trying to do . . . outside of Culture Club, by appearing in women's magazines, doing beauty shots, is prove that beauty is an absolute con," he pointed out in his interview with Fred Schruers for the New York *Daily News*. "It is basically a matter of air-brushing, good lighting, and the way you carry yourself. The most important thing to work on is your personality, because we're all gonna get ugly."

References: N Y Daily News p12+ N 18 '84 por, p4 Ja 27 '85 pors; N Y Times p23 Ja 15 '84 por; Chicago Tribune XIII p14+ Ap 22 '84 pors; People 20:86+ Ag 1 '83 por, 21:93+ Ap 23 '84 pors, 21:44+ Je 18 '84 pors; Washington Post B p1+ N 13 '84 por; Brompton, Sally. Chameleon: The Boy George Story (1985); Cohen, Scott. Boy George (1984)

## Braudel, Fernand (Paul)

*Aug. 24, 1902– French historian. Address: b. c/o Maison des sciences de l'Homme, 54 blvd. Raspail, 75270 Paris, France; h. 59 rue Brillat-Savarin, 75013 Paris, France*

In the opinion of many historians, Fernand Braudel, who is the acknowledged doyen of the large and influential *Annales* school of historiography, enjoys the distinction of being the greatest living practitioner of his craft. Because of the scope, grandeur, and readability of his now classic work, *The Mediterranean and the Mediterranean World in the Age of Philip II* (1949), and his monumental trilogy, *Civilization and Capitalism, 15th–18th Century* (1979), Braudel has often been compared with such historians as Arnold Toynbee, Oswald Spengler, and even Edward Gibbon. A former professor at the Collège de France, Braudel has also had a marked influence on a whole generation of French historians as editorial director of the journal *Annales: Economies, Sociétés, Civilisations*; as president of the Sixth Section of the Ecole Pratique des Hautes Etudes; as the founder and chief administrator of the Maison des Sciences de l'Homme; and as director of the Centre des Re-

*Fernand Braudel*

cherches Historiques. As Peter Scott noted in the London *Times's Higher Education Supplement* (December 9, 1977) in a typical appraisal of the French historian's career, Braudel is "a powerful, even venerable symbol of a whole approach to history. . . . He is a great institution-builder who has shaped in a decisive way the development not only of history but of all the social sciences in France during the past generation."

A native of the region of northeastern France known as Lorraine, Fernand Braudel was born on August 24, 1902 in his paternal grandmother's "simple peasant house" in the village of Luméville, in the department of the Meuse. He is the son of Charles Braudel, a teacher who later became a school headmaster, and Louise (Falet) Braudel. The historian has credited his familiarity with French rural life, which he acquired during frequent visits with his grandmother, with having profoundly influenced his development as a historian. "Things that others had to learn from books I knew all along from firsthand experience," he has recalled. " . . . I was in the beginning and I remain now a historian of peasant stock."

From 1913 to 1920, Fernand Braudel studied at the Lycée Voltaire in Paris, where he excelled in mathematics and history, took "a lot of Latin and a little Greek," and wrote poetry in his spare time. After giving up the idea of becoming a doctor because of his father's opposition to a medical career, he decided at eighteen to enroll in the Sorbonne as a student of history. With only a few exceptions, Braudel's courses at the Sorbonne were heavily weighted with the minutiae of political and diplomatic history. His teachers were, in his own words, "indifferent to the discoveries of geography, little concerned . . . with economic and social problems; slightly disdainful towards the achievements

of civilization, religion, and also of literature and the arts. . . . [They] regarded it beneath a historian's dignity to look beyond the diplomatic files, to real life, fertile and promising."

After receiving his advanced teaching diploma, the *agrégation,* Braudel became a teacher of history in colonial Algeria, where he taught for nearly a decade at *lycées* in the cities of Constantine and Algiers. During the years 1925–26, he served with French forces occupying the Rhineland, which gave him the opportunity to "learn to know and then to love Germany," despite the anti-German sentiments he had developed while growing up near the German border. Eventually he became disenchanted with German nationalism. After resuming his teaching duties, he published his first scholarly paper, "The Spaniards and North Africa," which was based on research in the Spanish national archives at Simancas.

Braudel's extensive travels throughout North Africa had afforded him an intimate view of the Mediterranean region "as seen from the opposite shore, upside down," and since he was teaching in Algeria, he decided to write his thesis on the Mediterranean policy of Philip II of Spain (1556–98). He projected it as a conventional work of diplomatic history based on archival materials at Simancas, but as he roamed about the Mediterranean region during the years 1927–1933, using an antiquated movie camera given to him by an American cameraman to photograph thousands of virtually inaccessible documents, he radically altered the scope of his thesis. "Little by little, I grew doubtful about the subject of my labors," he later explained. "Philip II . . . attracted me less and less, and the Mediterranean more and more."

From 1932 to 1935, Fernand Braudel taught at the Lycée Condorcet and at the Lycée Henri-IV in Paris. He then accepted a chance invitation to teach a course in the history of civilization at the newly founded Universidade de São Paulo in Brazil, where he spent three "marvelous years" reading the "kilometers of microfilm" that he had collected with his camera and where, he has said, he became what he is today. In 1937 he returned to France to take up a position as a *directeur d'études* at the Ecole des Hautes Etudes in Paris. He also became a member of the editorial board of the journal *Annales d'histoire économique et sociale* (later renamed *Annales: Economies, Sociétés, Civilisations*), which had been founded in 1929 by Marc Bloch and Lucien Febvre in an attempt to revolutionize French historiography. Braudel was deeply influenced by the views of both men and especially by Febvre, with whom he formed a close friendship and whose views on the relationship between history and geography had a profound impact on him.

After the outbreak of World War II, Braudel served briefly as an army lieutenant on the Rhine frontier. Captured by the Germans in 1940, he was eventually sent to a special prison camp in Lübeck, Germany because of what he has called his "Lorrainer's rebelliousness." While in captivity, he kept up his morale by teaching other prisoners, by occasionally playing pranks on the German guards, and by working on his thesis. Because of his prodigious memory, he was able to write the first draft of the 600,000-word work without any notes or documents at his disposal. Completed portions of the manuscript, written in school exercise books, were sent clandestinely to Febvre, whose advice and encouragement helped Braudel to overcome his nagging doubts about whether he would ever finish the project. In 1947 Braudel was granted the degree of *docteur ès lettres* by the Sorbonne, and his thesis was published in 1949 with the title *La Méditerranée et le Monde Méditerranéan À l'Epoque de Philippe II* (Armand Colin; *The Mediterranean and the Mediterranean World in the Age of Philip II*, Harper, 1972–73).

Almost immediately, *The Mediterranean and the Mediterranean World in the Age of Philip II* was hailed as a sterling example of the "total history" advocated by Bloch and Febvre when they established the journal *Annales d'histoire économique et sociale*. The members of the *Annales* school, as the group associated with the journal became known, tended to reject as inadequate *l'histoire événementielle*, the straightforward chronicle of events that is characteristic of political, diplomatic, and military history. They hoped to supplant the "great men and great events" view that typified history as taught at the Sorbonne with a more scientific approach. The historian would draw on the insights and methods of disciplines such as geography, economics, linguistics, psychology, sociology, anthropology, and demography in order to reconstruct a more accurate picture of what life in the past was really like for the average person.

As Lawrence Stone pointed out in his seminal work *The Past and the Present* (Routledge and Kegan Paul, 1981), *The Mediterranean and the Mediterranean World in the Age of Philip II* "is significant for two reasons. First, it stresses very heavily geography, ecology, and demography as the constraining factors which set limits on all human action. Second, it frees itself entirely from any national perspective and ranges around the Mediterranean basin, seeing the great clash of Ottoman Islam and Latin Christianity that culminated in the Battle of Lepanto in 1571 as a global whole, without any attempt to take sides." Instead of beginning with Philip II's reign, which is not even covered until the last part of his book, Braudel starts out with an almost lyrical account of the "human geography" of the Mediterranean region—its mountains and plains, coastlines and islands, climate, and trade routes. He then addresses such topics as trade and transport, the role of precious metals in the Mediterranean economy, class tensions, and types of warfare before focusing on the events leading up to the Battle of Lepanto, which is usually thought of as one of the great turning points in European history. Braudel continually goes out of his way to remind the reader that such events are mere "surface disturbances, crests of

foam that the tides of history carry on their strong backs," and that the policies of statesmen such as Philip II are of only marginal importance when viewed against the backdrop of the vast geographic, economic, and social forces that represent "the deeper realities of history."

The most original, as well as the most controversial, aspect of the book is Braudel's now famous conception of three different levels of historical time—the *longue durée* (long term), which Braudel defines as a history "of man in his relationship to the environment, . . . of constant repetition, ever-recurring cycles"; the *moyenne durée* (medium term), the "slow but perceptible rhythms" of economic and social trends that last for several decades; and the *courte durée* (short term), which corresponds to the history of events. The three levels are presented consecutively in an attempt "to encompass the history of the Mediterranean in its complex totality." His tripartite framework has been criticized by some historians on the ground that Braudel never makes entirely clear the interrelationship among the three types of historical phenomena. As Eric Christiansen expressed it in *The Spectator* (June 23, 1984), "Each third of the work remains an 'essay in general explanation' connecting with the others in any way the reader chooses, without merging or even locking."

Despite such criticisms, *The Mediterranean and the Mediterranean World in the Age of Philip II* has received perhaps more acclaim than any other historical work published in the twentieth century, with the possible exception of Toynbee's *A Study of History*. It has been accorded the status of a classic ever since the publication in the early 1970s of a two-volume English translation, based on the revised and expanded French edition published in 1966. "As an intellectual and scholarly tour de force it is almost unequaled," J. H. Plumb asserted in a review of the first volume that appeared in the *New York Times Book Review* (December 31, 1972), and John Bossy registered the opinion in *Encounter* (April 1973) that he considered it the "best history book ever written." Writing in the *New York Times Book Review* (May 18, 1975), Richard Mowery Andrews called Braudel's study of the Mediterranean "probably the most significant historical work to appear since World War II . . . both the crowning achievement of postwar French historiography and the fullest revelation of its intentions." And John Kenyon found in the *Observer* (October 22, 1972) that trying to write a brief estimate of Braudel's work was like trying to review Gibbon's *Decline and Fall of the Roman Empire*. "If Gibbon had been born in the twentieth century, this is the book he would have written," Kenyon observed.

A more immediate effect of the publication of Braudel's masterpiece was his elevation to a position of leadership among the members of the *Annales* school. In collaboration with Lucien Febvre, Braudel played a major role in establishing the world-famous Sixth Section of the Ecole Pratique des Hautes Etudes and in setting up a Centre des

Recherches Historiques under its auspices. He succeeded Febvre in the prestigious chair of the history of modern civilization at the Collège de France in 1950 and, on Febvre's death in 1956, was appointed to succeed his former mentor both as president of the Sixth Section and as editorial director of the Annales school's "house organ," Annales: Economies, Sociétés, Civilisations. During Braudel's tenure in those two key posts, from both of which he resigned in the aftermath of the French student uprisings of May and June 1968, the Annales school became the world's most productive and creative group of historians. After retiring from active teaching status in 1972, Braudel continued to serve as the chief administrator of the Maison des Sciences de l'Homme, an institution that he founded in the early 1960s to coordinate the work of the Sixth Section and other research centers devoted to the study of the "sciences of man."

Nowhere is Braudel's belief in the inexorability of longterm historical forces more apparent than in his second major work, Civilisation Matérielle, Economie et Capitalisme, XVe–XVIIIe Siècle (Civilization and Capitalism, 15th–18th Century), an economic and social history of the preindustrial world that was published in its final form in 1979. The 1,750-page work consists of three volumes: Les Structures du Quotidien: Le Possible et l'Impossible (Armand Colin, 1979) (The Structures of Everyday Life: The Limits of the Possible, Harper, 1981); Les Jeux de l'Echange (Armand Colin, 1979) (The Wheels of Commerce, Harper, 1982); and Le Temps du Monde (Armand Colin, 1979) (The Perspective of the World, Harper, 1984). In those volumes, Braudel tries to chart the growth of early capitalism and to explain the reasons why capitalism took root and flourished in Europe, paving the way for European domination of the world.

According to Braudel, most historians have tended to oversimplify the early economic history of modern Europe by equating capitalism with the cataclysmic upheaval of the Industrial Revolution and by limiting their studies to the "so-called market economy." In The Structures of Everyday Life, which is the least technical and the most accessible to the lay reader of the three volumes, he explores "the shadowy zone, often hard to see for lack of adequate historical documents, lying underneath the market economy." A sustained theme of the book, which focuses on such topics as food and drink, the history of fashion, modes of transport, and forms of currency, is the squalor, poverty, and desperation of the average man's life in the period between the end of the Middle Ages and the coming of the Industrial Revolution. In the second volume, The Wheels of Commerce, which was awarded the 1983 Los Angeles Times book award for history, Braudel concentrates on the "mechanisms of exchange"—shops, fairs, trading companies, and small businesses—that were beginning to undermine the stagnant agricultural economy described in The Structures of Everyday Life. He also advances the controversial thesis that the first capitalists were not industrialists but international bankers and traders, essentially parasitic speculators whose vast financial empires endowed them with enormous power and influence.

The Perspective of the World chronicles the dramatic rise of European capitalism to world power beginning with the age of the great city-states (Venice, Antwerp, Genoa, and Amsterdam) and concluding with an attempt to explain the phenomenon of the Industrial Revolution. "For Braudel," Keith Thomas commented in an appraisal of The Perspective of the World that appeared in the New York Review of Books (November 22, 1984), "the instruments of aggression and domination during these centuries were not states and armies, but banks and trading companies. . . . The triumph of European capitalism and the industrialization of the West ahead of the rest of the world are thus the logical culmination of Braudel's story."

Although Civilization and Capitalism is in many respects an even more ambitious work than The Mediterranean and the Mediterranean World in the Age of Philip II, Braudel's method of combining bold theoretical speculation with a seemingly inexhaustible profusion of detail has not been immune from criticism. In reviewing The Perspective of the World, Keith Thomas observed that "Braudel's style is musing, conversational, and often indecisive," that "there is a lack of rigor about the argument," and that the book "does not always measure up to normal scholarly standards." He found that Civilization and Capitalism was "not as impressive or original a work as The Mediterranean and the Mediterranean World in the Age of Philip II," but nevertheless concluded that "it has many splendid qualities and its conceptual framework deserves serious discussion." Eric R. Wolf noted in the New York Times Book Review (November 11, 1984): "This is a great book by a great historian. But it is not history for everyone. Mr. Braudel's writings are infused with a moral passion, but it is a passion for Olympian knowledge, not for the recognition of a moral purpose in human affairs. . . . [He] has compassion for his fellow humans, but not much concern for their emotions and motivations; he offers cold comfort to those who think people can take charge of their own destinies."

Besides his two major works, to which he has devoted almost a half a century of research, Braudel is the author of scholarly articles, many of which have been collected in book form and published under the title Ecrits sur l'Histoire (Flammarion, 1969) (On History, University of Chicago Press, 1980). In April 1976 the French historian gave a series of lectures at Johns Hopkins University that have been published as Afterthoughts on Material Civilization and Capitalism (Johns Hopkins University Press, 1977). Braudel has contributed to the Encyclopédie Française, the Encyclopedia Americana, and The Cambridge Economic History of Europe. He was coeditor with Ernst Labrousse of a massive scholarly undertaking by the Annales school, the eight-volume Histoire Economique et Sociale de la France (Presses Universitaires de France, 1970–82).

Fernand Braudel holds honorary doctorates from Oxford, Cambridge, Edinburgh, Geneva, Brussels, Cologne, Madrid, Warsaw, São Paulo, Yale, Chicago, Montreal, and many other universities throughout the world. He has been decorated as a *commandeur* of the French Legion of Honor. The somewhat belated but nonetheless significant impact of Braudel's achievements on American scholarship culminated in 1977 with the establishment of a Fernand Braudel Center for the Study of Economies, Historical Systems, and Civilizations at the State University of New York at Binghamton.

Considered a master stylist by those who read him in the original French, Braudel tends to write a chapter quickly and then rewrite it as many as twenty times before he is satisfied. He often reads his work aloud to his wife, the former Paule Pradel,

for her guidance in matters of rhythm and style. The Braudels, who have been married since September 14, 1933, have two daughters, Marie-Pierre and Françoise. Although Braudel is fully retired from his teaching and administrative duties, he has by no means curtailed his scholarly activities and is currently working on a three-volume history of France, partly because he feels that he had neglected that subject earlier in his career.

References: *Journal of Modern History* 44:448+ D '72; *Time* 109:77+ My 23 '77 por; *World Press Review* 32:30+ Mr '85 por; *International Encyclopedia of the Social Sciences* vol 18 (1979); *International Who's Who, 1985–86*; *Who's Who in France, 1983–84*; *World Authors 1970–1975* (1980)

## Buchanan, Patrick J(oseph)

*Nov. 2, 1938– White House official. Address: b. The White House, 1600 Pennsylvania Ave., Washington, D.C. 20500; h. 1017 Savile Lane, McLean, Va. 22101*

When Patrick J. Buchanan took the post of director of communications for the White House at the start of Ronald Reagan's second term, conservative activists rejoiced. The well-known columnist and radio and television commentator, who previously had served as a special assistant to President Richard M. Nixon, became the first acknowledged member from their ranks to gain a position on Reagan's senior staff. Their hopes ran high that Buchanan would be able to divert Reagan from the

compromising approach that moderate advisers had persuaded him to follow during his first four years in office and would redirect his attention to the full agenda favored by right-wing Republicans. Whether or not Buchanan would succeed in such an effort remains in doubt but, in the opinion of some observers, his first few months at the White House were marked by an increased stridency in the president's tone and by more frequent confrontations between the executive and the legislature.

Patrick Joseph Buchanan was born in Washington, D.C., on November 2, 1938 to William Baldwin Buchanan and his wife, Catherine E. (Crum) Buchanan. The third of the family's nine children, he grew up with his six brothers and two sisters in a six-bedroom house in Chevy Chase, Maryland. His father, a certified public accountant, exposed his children to the dominant political conservatism of the 1950s. As a youngster, Buchanan followed the Korean war in newspaper maps, read conservative columnists Westbrook Pegler and George Sokolsky, and watched televised coverage of Senator Joseph McCarthy's investigations of Communist influence in government. "My views, my values, my beliefs were shaped by being a member of an Irish-Catholic conservative family of nine children," Buchanan has said. "The church taught, and I think, correctly, that the great ideological enemy of Christianity and Catholicism was Communism."

Buchanan received his primary education at the local Catholic elementary school and proceeded to the Jesuit Gonzaga College High School in downtown Washington, where he was valedictorian of his class and won a scholarship to Georgetown University. There he majored in English and philosophy and came under the influence of the writings of St. Thomas Aquinas, Eric Hoffer, and William F. Buckley Jr. As a commuter, he took part in few campus activities. In his senior year Buchanan became involved in a fracas with police officers after a minor traffic accident in the Georgetown district, which left him with a broken hand, a $25 fine, and a one-year suspension from school. Despite that setback, he returned to Georgetown and graduated *cum laude,* ranking third in the class of 1961.

Supported by a scholarship, Buchanan enrolled at Columbia University's School of Journalism. On completion of his master's degree in 1962, Buchanan, whose goal it was to become a conservative columnist, ironically was turned down for a job on the *National Review.* He also failed to gain a berth with the much more liberal *Washington Post.* He finally signed on with the smaller, more conservatively oriented *St. Louis Globe-Democrat.* After working only two months as a reporter, Buchanan was able to make an important career move when a retirement opened a spot on the paper's editorial staff. He won the appointment and served as an editorial writer until 1964, when he became the assistant editorial editor.

By late 1965, after working for three years on the editorial page, Buchanan was ready for a change. Moreover, he was having differences with the publisher of the *Globe-Democrat,* which in 1964 had refused to endorse the presidential bid of the Republican party's conservative nominee, Senator Barry Goldwater of Arizona. Having campaigned in St. Louis in behalf of Goldwater, Buchanan was eager to become more directly involved in politics. He therefore gladly accepted when Don Hesse, the cartoonist for the *Globe-Democrat,* invited him to his home in December 1965 for a party to be attended by Richard M. Nixon. Convinced that Nixon offered the only real hope of a conservative victory in 1968, Buchanan told the former vice-president that he wanted to "get aboard early" if the Republicans' 1960 nominee decided to try again. A few weeks later, Buchanan went to Nixon's law office in New York City and, after a three-hour interview, persuaded the would-be candidate to hire him.

In January 1966 Buchanan settled into an office at Nixon's law firm as executive assistant, factotum, and researcher. Paid by the Republican national election fund, he helped Nixon to prepare for his trips to the Middle East and Africa in 1967. Buchanan was the first to bring to Nixon's attention Spiro Agnew, who eventually emerged as the Republican vice-presidential candidate, and served as Nixon's press secretary through the 1968 primary campaigns, but he made his main contribution as a speechwriter on such immediate campaign issues as law and order.

Although disappointed when the victorious Nixon hired John Ehrlichman and H. R. Haldeman as his chief White House aides after the general election, Buchanan agreed to become a special assistant. Ranking just below the top administrative tier, the post involved Buchanan as the spokesman for rock-ribbed conservatism in a speechwriting triumvirate with the moderate Raymond K. Price Jr. and the centrist William Safire. Buchanan's main responsibility, however, was the preparation of the "President's Daily Briefing Book," which summarized what the media were saying about the world and the Nixon administration. Although marked "Eyes Only for the President," it actually reached about fifty members of the White House staff. The few outsiders who ever saw a copy varied widely in their reports about it, ranging from high marks for its objectivity to charges that it was riddled with inaccuracies of fact and interpretation.

During the Nixon years, Buchanan made his greatest public impact as a media critic. Observers believed that it was he who wrote the stinging attack that Agnew delivered before the Midwest Regional Republican Committee in Des Moines, Iowa in November 1969. In it the vice-president charged that television's power over public opinion was in the hands of a "small and unelected elite" of producers, newsmen, and commentators who, "to a man," reflected the "geographical and intellectual confines of Washington, D.C., or New York City." Buchanan's principal targets were usually the television networks, which, in his opinion, constituted a much greater problem than the print media. "They've got control of essentially three giant complexes which enable individuals to send comment at an instant's notice into 100 million homes," he argued. "And there are only three of them and so they have obligations that, say, *The New Republic* doesn't have." Buchanan believed that the situation in television would be better if, as in radio, there were approximately fifty networks. But, aware of the difficulties in challenging licenses and passing antitrust legislation, he believed that public pressure was more likely to bring about the desired objective.

Buchanan kept up his attack on the television networks in a brief book entitled *The New Majority,* which was privately published by the Girard Bank of Philadelphia in 1973 and distributed to 25,000 subscribers as part of a series on major issues and problems. In it, Buchanan repeated the theme that Nixon enjoyed the support of a "new majority" made up of Middle Americans espousing traditional values, while an antigovernment, liberal elite continued to exercise undue influence through its control of the educational institutions, research foundations, and, especially, television. He urged better balance in news commentaries, the recruitment of less liberal newsmen and commentators, the assignment of other than overtly hostile reporters to cover an administration, the avoidance of "advocacy journalism," and the insistence by local stations on objective news and balanced commentaries.

There is no indication that Buchanan ever knew anything about political abuses associated with the Nixon administration. In 1971 he declined, as a waste of his time and abilities, to conduct an investigation aimed at discrediting Daniel Ellsberg, who gave the so-called "Pentagon Papers" to the *New York Times.* Such an attack, he argued, though gratifying, would be of no political value to the president. And in carrying out an assignment to write scenarios of the strategies likely to be followed by leading Democratic aspirants in 1972, Buchanan not only had no access to information from spies planted in the opposition's ranks but also failed to write one for Senator George McGovern, the eventual nominee, whom he did not consider a serious contender.

Named special consultant to the president after the 1972 election, Buchanan defended himself ably when he appeared before Senator Sam Ervin's select committee on presidential campaign activities in September 1973. He was not accused of any wrongdoing, and his five hours of testimony made him the administration's most effective witness. Buchanan began by attacking the Watergate committee's staff for conducting a "covert campaign of vilification" against him and more than held his own throughout the session. Admitting that some actions taken in behalf of Nixon's candidacy, including the Watergate wiretapping, were illegal or crossed the boundaries of propriety, he equated much of what was done with the "hardball" tactics and pranks he considered normal in American politics. Denying that the 1972 election was stolen, Buchanan asserted that "the president of the United States did not achieve the greatest landslide of any minority candidate in history because of Watergate and dirty tricks—but in spite of them."

Through the final months of the Nixon administration, Buchanan remained steadfastly loyal, and when the president finally resigned in August 1974, he stayed on to serve his successor, Gerald R. Ford. Ready to return to private life, in January 1975 he reached an agreement to write a thrice-weekly column of political and social commentary that would be distributed by Special Features, a subsidiary of the the the New York Times Company. Three years later he switched to the Chicago Tribune–New York News Syndicate, gradually expanding the number of papers that carried his column from 30 to 138. In 1978 he introduced on NBC radio a brief commentary program called *Confrontation*, in which he exchanged views on controversial topics with Tom Braden, a liberal columnist. The two men added a Saturday morning talk show and then branched out into television with *After Hours*, which was broadcast originally on a local Washington station and later, under the name *Crossfire*, by Ted Turner's Cable News Network. In 1982 Buchanan also became a panelist on a Washington television talk show known as the *McLaughlin Group*.

As a private citizen, Buchanan continued to be a scourge of liberals and Democrats. His second book, *Conservative Votes, Liberal Victories* (Quadrangle, 1975), renewed his assault on the media, which he blamed for sustaining civil rights disturbances, for undermining support for the war in Vietnam, and for making the Democratic party a formidable opponent. In his syndicated columns and on radio and television he excoriated doctors who perform abortions as "butchers," lashed out at the women's movement as "feminist idiocy," and in *Rolling Stone* (June 15, 1978) dismissed Jimmy Carter as a failed president without an undergirding political philosophy or an ability to communicate.

There are two different versions as to how Donald Regan, who replaced James A. Baker as White House chief of staff at the beginning of the second Reagan administration, came to pick Buchanan to be director of communications. According to columnists Rowland Evans and Robert Novak in the *Washington Post* (February 3, 1985), Regan came across Buchanan's name on a list of potential appointees that he had asked Joseph Coors, the beer baron and conservative activist, to submit. But, according to the *New Republic* (May 13, 1985) and to *New York* magazine (June 10, 1985), the speechwriter Kenneth Khachigian and Buchanan's sister Bay, who had served as treasurer of the United States while Regan was Secretary of the Treasury, were the first to bring the conservative columnist to the attention of the new chief of staff. In either case, Regan immediately warmed to Buchanan because he found him to be "feisty" and "Irish." Regan had no trouble in persuading the president, who was a fan of Buchanan's appearances on the *McLaughlin Group*, and the appointment was announced on February 5, 1985.

Accepting the appointment as director of communications, which pays $75,100 a year, entailed considerable financial loss for Buchanan, who reported earnings of $400,000 in 1984 from lectures, writing, and broadcasting. He did not find the choice difficult. Comparing his dilemma with that of the Americans who flocked to Washington to help create Roosevelt's New Deal, Buchanan asked: "What young journalist writing in the thirties would not have given his right arm to have been in there, when a lot of the great initiatives were taken? I don't see how you can turn it down." William F. Buckley Jr. commented in his *National Review* that Buchanan is basically an activist, who could not let the opportunity to translate his words into action slip past. Buchanan concurred in that judgment. "I've been working in the conservative movement for twenty-five years," he said. "I don't want it said of me . . . that when I had my chance I didn't go in because I had too many outside activities."

Although hard-line conservatives rejoiced at Buchanan's appointment, their jubilation was not universally shared. A number of reporters, like Sam Donaldson of ABC-TV, read an unwelcome irony into the appointment as a director of communications of a person with Buchanan's antimedia reputation. There was even some grumbling within the Reagan camp. Michael K. Deaver, a moderate getting ready to leave the White House post of deputy chief of staff, discouraged the selection, while David Gergen, a former director of communications for Reagan, predicted that Buchanan would make the administration seem "more combative and confrontational." Others predicted that Buchanan, by accentuating rather than muting Reagan's instincts, could destroy the balanced approach that made the president's first term a success.

Gauging the extent of Buchanan's influence became a popular pastime during his first months on the job. Observers noted that he was one of the few aides to have an office on the first floor of the West Wing of the White House, near those of both the president and the chief of staff. They also contended that the decision to keep the Office of Public Liaison under Buchanan's control represented a major victory, though the *New Republic* (May 13, 1985) reported that Buchanan had been more than willing to turn over two-thirds of the positions involved to Edward J. Rollins, the White House political boss. Commentators credit Buchanan with responsibility for Reagan's description of the Nicaraguan "contras" as "the moral equal of our Founding Fathers" and they maintain that he influenced the president's decisions to veto a farm bailout bill, to ignore an incident in which South Korean functionaries pushed Americans accompanying a dissident on his return to Seoul, and to visit a military cemetery in Bitburg, Germany, despite the discovery there of the graves of Waffen SS troops.

But Reagan has not accepted all of Buchanan's suggestions. When Buchanan urged him to speak on television about Nicaragua on the eve of the House of Representatives' vote on the ill-fated $14 million military aid package, the president followed the counsel of advisers who told him that silence would save embarrassment when the measure went down to inevitable defeat, and despite Buchanan's objections, he agreed to reduce the increase in defense spending originally proposed by the administration. Finally, other aides softened a tough anti-Communist speech that Buchanan had prepared for Reagan to deliver before the European Parliament during the president's visit in May 1985 to the continent. Buchanan remarked that, in his current position, "you get the right to make your arguments as well and as persuasively as you can. When I lose those fights, I have an obligation to remain loyal to the people on this staff and in this government—even those I disagree with."

In his first months at the White House, Buchanan survived a series of sharp attacks, the most serious of which stemmed from the Bitburg episode. During that crisis some commentators recalled that Buchanan, as a columnist, had been a foe of the Justice Department's Office of Special Investigations, which tracks down Nazi war criminals in the United States, and had opposed stripping American citizenship from staunchly anti-Communist East European émigrés accused of war crimes on the basis of evidence provided by the Soviets. NBC news reported that Buchanan repeatedly jotted the phrase "succumbing to the pressure of the Jews" at a meeting in which Jewish leaders asked Reagan not to go to the Bitburg cemetery. Buchanan dismissed the charge as "utterly ridiculous," and Kenneth Bialkin, the national chairman of the Anti-Defamation League, who had been sitting beside him at the meeting, denied that the director had penned the words "of the Jews." When Donald Regan was asked whether he still had confidence in Buchanan, his response was, "Oh, certainly."

Overall, Buchanan's stature appears to be growing. He admits to having "some influence, some ideas," and the departure of Michael K. Deaver in May 1985 for a public-relations job removed one of his main foes. After three months of silence, Buchanan began to grant press interviews, and, in recent weeks, he has taken the initiative in speaking out on issues. In particular, Buchanan has strongly endorsed the president's tax reform proposal, calling it "a tax plan for Main Street" that will help "traditional" families and bring "working-class Americans, Hispanics, blacks, [and] Catholics" into the Republican fold. When Mario Cuomo, the Democratic governor of New York, criticized its implications for nontraditional families and argued that its elimination of tax deductions for state and local taxes contradicted the president's own belief that federal functions should be transferred to those levels of government, Buchanan set off a furor by assailing New York as a high-tax "neo-socialist" state government seeking to "redistribute the wealth."

Standing six feet tall and weighing a trim 170 pounds, Patrick J. Buchanan has pink cheeks, brown eyes, and black hair that is still untouched by grey. He speaks in a flat voice with a hint of a Southern accent. Since May 8, 1971 he has been married to Shelley Ann Scarney, who was a receptionist in the Nixon White House. He is a member of the University Club in Washington, and his principal diversion is watching movies. Buchanan numbers among his friends people of various political persuasions, including influential Democrats, and his radio and television colleague, Tom Braden, states that "he's the only hard right-winger I know who gets a kick out of life."

When interviewed in his tiny White House office by Robert W. Merry of the *Wall Street Journal* (June 20, 1985), Buchanan explained: "I'm here because Reagan's my man, and this is my cause. The goal is to help make Ronald Reagan a great president, so that when he leaves here people will say this was the silver age of the conservative revolution."

References: *New York* 18:48+ Je 10 '85 pors; N Y *Times Mag* p9+ Ag 20 '72 pors; *Newsweek* 105:26+ My 27 '85 pors; *Washington Post* A p9 S 26 '73 por; *Washington Post Potomac Mag* p12+ D 9 '73 pors; *Who's Who in America*, 1984–85

---

# Byrne, David

May 14, 1952– Musician and performer.
Address: b. Index Music, c/o Overland, 1775
Broadway, New York City, N.Y. 10019

With the release of their first album, *Talking Heads: 77*, the members of a quartet of former art students found themselves in the vanguard of the "new wave" musical movement. The emergence of

*David Byrne*

Talking Heads from the underground New York rock scene in 1977 coincided with that of other influential downtown Manhattan bands—the Patti Smith Group, Television, Blondie, and the Ramones—and it took place amid the excitement generated by such London-based "punks" as Elvis Costello, the Clash, and the Sex Pistols.

By 1985 most of those punk groups had either broken up or faded from view. Not so the Talking Heads, which was celebrating its tenth anniversary as a still evolving, art-rocking musical aggregation that had once proclaimed its ambition to be nothing less than "to change the face of music." But the members of Talking Heads have accomplished more than mere survival in an increasingly slick entertainment industry that is attuned to the sound of the cash register. They have expanded the boundaries of contemporary popular music by achieving a synthesis of Afro-American and traditional rock styles. And David Byrne, the group's acknowledged leader and creative cynosure of media attention, has been compared to Bob Dylan in that he is, as one journalist wrote, "the major musical voice of an epoch, [who] has written lyrics that have the power of poetry and . . . has sung them in a unique style that, lying somewhere between a hiccup and a cry, perfectly reflects a tense and anxious age."

The members of the Talking Heads have rejected the punk visual glamour of Blondie, the hip nihilism of the Sex Pistols, and the glib espousal of the ideology of third-world liberation of the Clash in favor of an image of heightened normalcy. Their art-school and upper-middle-class backgrounds and their cleancut, WASP good looks have earned them the tag of "Preppie," though David Byrne's origins complicate that characterization. He was born in Scotland on May 14, 1952 to Thomas and Emily (Brown) Byrne, who immigrated to Canada before he was three, and before the birth of a daughter, their only other child. In 1958 the family resettled in Landsdowne, Maryland, just outside of Baltimore, where the father worked as an electrical engineer for Westinghouse. As David Byrne told Christopher Connelly of *Rolling Stone* (October 27, 1983), he grew up in "a lower-middle-class area, although the high school was probably upper lower class."

It was in the mid-1960s that David Byrne learned to play guitar. Although his musical abilities were rudimentary—even today, his guitar playing is distinctive, but by no means virtuosic—in junior high school he formed a rock band, Revelation, whose repertoire consisted largely of covers of Motown songs and top-ten hits by British groups like the Beatles, the Rolling Stones, and the Kinks. What Byrne found compelling in the popular music of the 1960s was its overall sound or "feel," because, as he told Bill Flanagan in an interview for the journal *Music & Sound Output* (February 1985), "The words were, for the most part, pretty stupid."

As a teenager, Byrne combined his fascination with the textures of pure sound with his abiding interest in technical gadgetry by composing experimental music on an inexpensive tape recorder, which his father, an electronics wizard, helped him to adapt to perform such sophisticated functions as double track recording and tape loops. Using the tape machine to record "songs" composed of primitive, homemade sound effects, Byrne produced aural collages that foreshadowed his later, state-of-the-art studio collaborations with Brian Eno, the heralded avant-garde coproducer of three Talking Heads albums.

When Revelation broke up in the late 1960s, Byrne put together a solo act for the college coffeehouse circuit. Audiences expected an earnest folk-oriented singer and songwriter with a quiet political message. Instead they were treated to a performance of no-holds-barred rock 'n' roll, including a version of "Summertime Blues," a 1950s anthem of teen frustration, that Byrne sang to his own accompaniment on the ukelele. On his graduation from high school in 1970, Byrne toyed with the idea of pursuing his interest in science and mathematics at a technical school, but instead enrolled at the Rhode Island School of Design, a prestigious art school in Providence.

At Rhode Island School of Design, Byrne felt out of place, because so many of his fellow students were, as he told Christopher Connelly, "rich kids, [who had been] brought up with a very different sensibility" from his own. Another source of alienation seems to have been that his quirky individualism was out of synchronization with the values of the 1960s counterculture that continued to prevail among the college elite of the early 1970s. Indeed, Byrne's firsthand experience of the political militancy of the later 1960s had been limited to attendance at a couple of antiwar rallies, which he found unexciting. "At one," he recalled in the interview with Connelly, "the National Guard came in and was shooting tear gas. And the kids would throw tear gas back. I thought that was kind of neat, but that's about all."

At the end of the academic year, Byrne dropped out of classes at the Rhode Island School of Design and returned to Baltimore for another year of art training at a local school. Dropping out again, he traveled around the country, and in 1973, after his application for readmission to the Rhode Island School of Design had been rejected, he began dividing his time between Providence and New York City. The early 1970s witnessed the heyday of performance and conceptual art and of minimalism in painting, sculpture, and avant-garde musical theatre, and Byrne affiliated himself with the experimental art scene that was flourishing in the SoHo district of lower Manhattan. At SoHo's Mercer Arts Center and at small clubs in Providence, Byrne mounted performances that teetered so precariously between satire and whimsicality that audiences often failed to perceive their humor. In one of Byrne's pieces, for example, he shaved off his beard while a collaborator played "Pennies from Heaven" on an accordion, and a woman at center stage flashed cue cards written in Russian. He also passed out questionnaires on UFOs to nonplussed coffeehouse patrons, and for another antic performance gave dramatic readings of transcripts from television game shows. "The Price Is Right, I think," Byrne explained, deadpan, to Connelly. "'Come on down!' I thought it was poetry, in a way."

Byrne entertained no illusions about the limited appeal of those pieces. Wanting to reach a larger audience, and impatient with the hermetic world of experimental art, he turned again to music. Late in 1973 he teamed up with drummer Chris Frantz, a painting student from the Rhode Island School of Design and the son of an army general, to form the Artistics, an unabashedly amateur five-piece band whose on-stage idiosyncrasies prompted fans and detractors alike to dub them "The Autistics."

When graduation from the Rhode Island School of Design scattered the members of the Artistics in mid-1974, Byrne and Frantz moved to lower Manhattan, where they conducted fruitless auditions for new band members. For Byrne could find no musicians capable of reproducing the new sound that was beginning to crystallize inside his head: lean, funk-influenced rock rhythms that were to become fused with his own cerebral reinvention of 1960s soul music. But when Frantz persuaded Byrne to teach Martina Weymouth, a former design major at the Rhode Island School of Design whose socially prominent father had been a navy admiral, to play bass guitar, Talking Heads was born. The name came from the media term for close-up head shots of participants on television talk shows.

In June 1975, after six months of intensive rehearsal, Talking Heads made its debut at CBGB's, a seedy "underground" nightclub on the Bowery that served as the birthplace of punk and new wave. There, and later at the Mudd Club, the Heads and other raucous new groups developed the styles that were to resuscitate the moribund rock scene. Byrne recalled that bland period of the reign of Middle of the Road sound in a *Washington Post* interview (February 10, 1985): "There were a few [underground New York bands] starting at the time who thought there was a big gap in the music we were hearing over the radio and on the records, that there was not much being made for us, that spoke to what we were feeling. . . . So we felt we had to do it ourselves. If other people across the country felt that as well, they might like it, even if it wasn't as slick as some of the other stuff. It was going to feel more real to them."

Talking Heads became a quartet in 1977 with the addition of Jerry Harrison, a dropout from the Harvard School of Architecture who had played in the innovative Boston-based band called Jonathan Richman and the Modern Lovers. Harrison filled out the sound with his backup singing and rhythm playing on keyboards and guitar. That year, on the Sire label, Talking Heads released their first album—the relatively spare and brittle-sounding *Talking Heads: 77*—to panegyrics from the rock intelligentsia, including the *New York Times* critic John Rockwell, who admired its "minimalism and rigorous structuralism." It was followed by *More Songs About Buildings and Food* (Sire, 1978), whose richer textures were considerably indebted to the band's coproducer, Brian Eno, who had earned a cult following for his mastery of studio-production techniques. In 1979 Talking Heads released *Fear of Music* (Sire), perhaps the apotheosis of the 1970s sound of the original quartet.

In those years the Talking Heads were praised for their innovative formalism. In a Byrne composition, as John Rockwell explained in the *New York Times* (August 18, 1979), "music in general and rock in particular is abstracted into clear, direct, exact structural units. . . . But if this is a formalist group, that hardly means it lacks emotion. . . . In fact, what formalist groups do is strip music of false emotionality and allow true emotions to be conveyed all the more directly." Because Byrne abstracted elements from the Afro-funk rhythms of James Brown and George Clinton, the rock 'n' roll of Elvis Presley and the Beatles, and gospel-influenced soul music, Talking Heads developed a captivating instrumental sound, vividly described by Rockwell in his book *All-American Music: Composition in the Late Twentieth Century* (1983): "Like all rock, it was rhythmically simple (or primally satisfying) in its underpinning of solid common time. But it was also precise and delicate, marked by incessant repetition in the bass line, a clipped tightness in the drumming, and scratchy, coloristic chording from the guitar." Moreover, its rocking beat made it danceable.

Unlike anything ever heard in rock 'n' roll, Byrne's lyrics are as simply structured in terse verbal units as the dialogue in a Samuel Beckett play. The dissociated product of a fractured sensibility, his compositions pulse with urban tensions in unsentimental, Pinteresque fables of contemporary life that chillingly evoke extreme states of mind. In "Psycho Killer" (1977), for example, Byrne slips into the soul of a David Berkowitz type of madman, and in "Life During Wartime" (1979) his paranoid persona is that of a humorless apparatchik in a band of would-be urban guerrillas. His sense of humor can be as coolly iconoclastic as Marcel Duchamp's, and because it is often countermanded by music that is either ethereal or throbbingly anxious, its point is often missed by listeners.

As riveting as the band's music was the quality of "repressed hysteria," to use Pauline Kael's phrase, that Byrne evinced on stage. Gaunt and ascetic-looking, poised as tight as a knot before the microphone, his shoulders tense and hunched, staring straight ahead with his Buster Keaton eyes, he could seem as solemn as a Calvinist preacher or as dazed as "someone who has spent the last half-hour whirling around in a spin dryer," to quote an observer writing for the *Village Voice*. Although Byrne's shellshocked performance style was born, as Rockwell has pointed out, "of terrified nervousness," it earned him what Christopher Connelly called a "somber-wacko tag [that] has proved hard to shuck." That image was reinforced by Byrne's superficial resemblance to the Anthony Perkins of the film *Psycho*, and by such quintessential early compositions as "Psycho Killer" and "No Compassion" (1977), in which he informs a clinging lover or friend: "In a world where people have problems . . . Compassion is a virtue, but I don't have the time . . . What are you, in love with your problems? . . . Don't expect me to explain your indecision . . . Go talk to your analyst, isn't that what he's paid for?"

The release of the ornately textured album *Remain in Light* (Sire, 1980) transformed Talking Heads into an ecstatically joyous nine-member stage ensemble and triggered what Connelly has described as their "explosion into megafunk." Through his reading of the musicologist John Miller Chernoff's book *African Rhythm and African Sensibility* (1979), Byrne became fascinated by the social meanings of polyrhythms, the complex, discrete but interlocking, drumming patterns which, in the dance music of West African tribal cultures, both symbolize and promote "the welding of a complex of individuals and social forces into a unified community," as Robert Palmer wrote in the *New York Times* (September 20, 1981).

Inspired by that communal model, David Byrne and Brian Eno created the unique *Remain in Light* sound from a fusion of American funk and West African rhythms, which they then blended with fresh pop melodies. Byrne's lyrics, too, changed to accommodate the spiritual, emotionally charged music, becoming more oblique and impressionistic, with an emphasis on meter and euphony rather than on literal meaning. In his desire to have the words augment the roiling, multilayered rhythms, Byrne achieved an incantatory effect by appropriating imagery from radio sermons by evangelical preachers and inserting it in vaguely hortatory songs such as "Houses in Motion," "Once in a

Lifetime," and "The Great Curve." "What it's about," he said of his band's new music, as quoted in the *Chicago Tribune* (November 30, 1980), "is using multiple rhythms to make people go out of themselves and . . . into a sort of a trance—not a meditative trance state, but sort of an ecstatic trance. It has . . . to do with a feeling of community and forgetting oneself. . . . In our earlier music, that might happen occasionally, but it still had more to do with Western music that's ego—and personality—centered."

For the concert tour that followed *Remain in Light*, Talking Heads added five musicians so that the sound of Eno's elaborate studio overdubs could be reproduced on stage. Since the augmentation consisted of two black men, one white guitarist, and two black women vocalists, the Talking Heads became integrated, both racially and sexually. While touring in England, Tina Weymouth publicly voiced the group's resentments over what was seen as the obtrusive influence of Eno, now an unofficial fifth band member, and Byrne's increasingly Olympian and peremptory manner. "They're like two fourteen-year-old-boys making an impression on each other," she complained to a British journalist. "I can see them when they're eighty years old and alone. There'll be David Bowie, David Byrne, and Brian Eno, and they'll just talk to each other."

For the next year, amid rumors that Talking Heads were soon to split up, Byrne busied himself with outside endeavors. He produced the album *Mesopotamia* for the B-52's, a new-wave band from Georgia; released an African-influenced album with Eno whose title, *My Life in the Bush of Ghosts* (Sire, 1981), was taken from a 1954 novel by the Nigerian writer Amos Tutuola; and, drawing again on African sources for inspiration, composed the music for the choreographer Twyla Tharp's *The Catherine Wheel*, a critically acclaimed production that had its premiere on Broadway in the fall of 1981.

The other Talking Heads, however, also undertook independent projects. Jerry Harrison released a well-received album, *The Red and the Black* (Sire, 1981), and Chris Frantz and Tina Weymouth, who had married in 1977, formed a group called Tom-Tom Club. Released by *Sire* late in 1981, their giddily delightful first LP, *Tom-Tom Club*, quickly sold more than 600,000 copies, almost twice as many as *Fear of Music*, then the best-selling Talking Heads album. Those successes, as Connelly put it, "reestablished the balance of power in the band," and in 1982 the four Heads came together, without Eno, to select tracks for *The Name of This Band is Talking Heads* (Sire, 1982), a two-disc LP of live performances that both documents the Heads' artistic evolution and serves as a kind of compilation of their "greatest hits."

Through assembling the tracks for that record, the group concluded that, as Byrne told an interviewer for *High Fidelity* (September 1983), the Heads' many changes had wrought a loss of "some of the simplicity, some of the feeling of a band playing." It is that combination of austerity and passion that animates *Speaking in Tongues* (Sire, 1983), the first Heads studio record on which Eno had played no part since 1977. *Speaking in Tongues* also became their first album to reach the top ten on LP charts, and its hit single, "Burning Down the House," was their first to rise into the national top five. In his *High Fidelity* review Sam Sutherland called the album "quietly brilliant. . . . The songs [by this] truly original and now influential group . . . perpetuate the percolating rhythms and rich, extended vamps of the [*Remain in Light*] ensemble performances, but they are astutely edited and better focused melodically."

To build on the popularity of *Speaking in Tongues*, Byrne enthusiastically accepted the noted movie director Jonathan Demme's offer to film three Talking Heads concerts at the Hollywood Pantages Theatre in December 1983. In a series of concerts in the summer of 1982, and again the following year, the loose-limbed Byrne had brought stunned audiences to their feet with his sinuous shimmying and dancing, and that, along with the exhilarating playing of the band in its nine-piece mega-Heads configuration, contributes to the celebratory feeling of *Stop Making Sense* (Cinecom International, 1984), the result of Byrne's collaboration with Demme. In the *New Yorker* (November 26, 1984) Pauline Kael called the film "a dose of happiness from beginning to end." Byrne, she wrote, is "a stupefying performer who gives the group its modernism. . . . He's an idea man, an aesthetician who works in the modernist mode of scary, catatonic irony." She also observed that, unlike many rock bands, in Talking Heads "there's no glitter, no sleaze. . . . And there's more vitality and fervor and rhythmic dance than there is with groups that whip themselves through the motions of sexual arousal and frenzy, and try to set the theatre ablaze." In a *High Fidelity* (December 1984) review of the soundtrack LP *Stop Making Sense* (Sire, 1984), which consists of nine of the sixteen numbers performed in the film, Joyce Millman reported that it is "as good as live albums get. . . . In nearly every case, these live takes outsparkle their originals."

As Byrne's emphasis has shifted from writing first-person narratives to stringing together fragments of evocative phrases that often seem to be non sequiturs, his method of composition has changed as well. Whereas he used to tailor his music to fit previously written lyrics, he now weaves words and melodies around song structures that have evolved out of group jam sessions. Increasingly frustrated by the limitations imposed on him by rock-song conventions, in 1984 Byrne composed nonelectronic musical sequences, most of them for horns backed by a minimum of percussion and some accompanied by his narrations, for *Civil Wars: A Tree is Best Measured When It's Cut Down*, an epic, twelve-hour, as-yet-unfinished theatre production by the avant-garde director-writer Robert Wilson. *Music for the Knee Plays*

(ECM, 1985), as the pieces were called because they formed the entr'actes or "joints" between the main action of *Civil Wars*, takes the inspiration for its grave simplicity from the funeral dirges of New Orleans brass bands. To satisfy his need for visual artistic expression, Byrne has designed album covers, directed the acclaimed "Burning Down the House" video, and devised the sophisticated lighting and slide projections that provide backdrops to the band's teeming stage show. Byrne is currently collaborating with the playwright Beth Henley on the script for "True Stories," a Talking Heads movie that he will direct. He has completed the filming of "Surviving a Family Tree," teleplay directed by Jonathan Demme and starring himself and Rosanna Arquette, which has been scheduled to be shown on PBS in late 1985.

On their album *Little Creatures* (Sire), released in the summer of 1985, the Talking Heads collaborated to produce several appealing melodies that sounded to reviewers like innovative pop anthems marked by occasional flashes of pessimism. Two hit songs from the album were "And She Was," about a woman who levitates and then voyages through the universe, and "Road to Nowhere," a paean to nihilism. *Little Creatures* became the group's second LP to make the Top Ten charts.

The titles of recent Talking Heads ventures—*Speaking in Tongues*, a phrase in Pentecostal religious sects for the nonrational utterances accompanying states of intense spiritual rapture, and *Stop Making Sense*, whose provenance is a line in the song "Girlfriend is Better" (1983) that equates wisdom with not always letting the head rule the heart—suggest that Byrne's once clinical vision of contemporary life has been transformed. In the 1970s Byrne rejected all forms of belief that were not grounded in logic or fact, but in recent years he has "discovered that there are subtle forces in human beings that, for want of a better word, would have to be called spiritual or religious," as he explained in *Maclean's* (June 13, 1983). "I believe," he said, "there are things that are difficult to measure with scientific instruments."

David Byrne has monkishly short dark hair that, on stage, he often wears slicked back in the style of a 1920s matinee idol, and in *Stop Making Sense* he looks taller than his five feet, ten inches because of the way he "contorts his Tommy Tune legs and Tony Perkins shoulders," to quote a writer for *Newsday* (October 19, 1984). Byrne lives in a large loft in SoHo, in an area of pricey boutiques, tony art galleries, and hordes of tourists that he finds "a little too trendy" for his taste. Although he admits to having been too absorbed in his work to commit himself to a traditional relationship, since 1982 his name has been linked romantically to that of Bonnie Lutz, a former model and fashion designer of Japanese and German-American descent.

References: *Artforum* p90+ My '85 pors; *Chicago Tribune* IV p13 N 30 '80, XII p14 Ag 28 '83 pors; *Guardian* p11 D 10 '79 por; *Hi Fi* 34:66+ D '84 por; *Maclean's* 96:42+ Je 13 '83 por; *N Y Daily*

News F 18 '81 por, p20 0 14 '84 pors; N Y Times
C p21 O 22 '81 por, C p29 N 18 '81 por, p22 Ag
23 '82, C p26 Je 22 '83, C p25 0 10 '84 por; N Y
Times Mag p54+ My 5 '85 pors; Reese, Krista.
The Name of This Book is Talking Heads (1982)

## Chillida, Eduardo

(chē lyē´də ā dwä´dō)

*Jan. 10, 1924- Spanish sculptor. Address: "Villa
Paz," Alto de Maracruz, San Sebastián, Spain*

"Like the animal in its shell, I am the architect of
living space," Eduardo Chillida, Spain's foremost
living sculptor, has said in describing himself.
Trained first as an architect, Chillida views sculpture as a kind of architecture that has been freed
from practical considerations, a way of making
space visible by means of the forms that surround
or dissect it. "I am not concerned," he has explained, "with the space which lies outside the
form, but with the space actually created by the
shapes, which dwells in them, their hidden core."
In that, his approach completely differs from the
usual concept of sculpture as a means of creating
volumes or forms within space.

Some critics have called Chillida's abstract
sculpture cubist-inspired, like the work of his
countrymen, the Catalonians Julio González and
Pablo Picasso, and he is also considered to have
been influenced by the linearism of Russian con-
structivism. Ultimately, however, his style, though
not radically innovative, is unique; and the creative energy behind his search for space is very
much the product of his Basque heritage. Spiritually and physically, his work is the product of the
harsh mountain spaces and terrain of the Basque
country, worked in materials hewn from the earth,
shaped by age-old artisan techniques. Nevertheless, Chillida's work transcends geographic and
aesthetic boundaries, so much so that it is honored
and collected throughout Europe and the United
States, perhaps because the tension between its
passionate lyrical form and austere media give it a
mysterious force that has a wide appeal.

Born Eduardo Chillida Juantegui on January 10,
1924, in the provincial capital and resort town of
San Sebastián in the Spanish Basque country, the
artist comes from a family that loves music and art.
After completing his studies at the Colegio Marian-
istas in San Sebastián in 1942, he enrolled at the
University of Madrid to study architecture, but left
in 1947. Although his father would have preferred
Eduardo to finish the degree, he supported his
son's decision to take private art lessons instead. In
1948, in any case, Chillida left Madrid for Paris,
where he began to work in sculpture and became
acquainted with Julio González and other artists.
On his return to Spain in 1950, he settled in Her-
nani, not far from San Sebastián, and in 1959
moved back to his birthplace.

Eduardo Chillida's first projects were nudes, executed in plaster. Among them were a female figure done in 1948 and a male torso, reworked in
stone in 1949, that was exhibited in the 1949 Salon
de Mai at the Musée d'Art Moderne in Paris in
what was his first exhibition. The following year he
took part in "Les Mains Eblouies," a showing of
postwar art at the Galerie Maeght. It was not until
he came back to Spain that Chillida began to turn
from the figurative to an abstract style, and, discouraged at finding the possibilities of his previous
work exhausted, made an abrupt decision to do a
work in iron. Since he had never used metal before, he set himself to learn from a local blacksmith
all the tough, demanding labor of the forge, from
stoking a fire and handling a bellows to pounding
the malleable metal to achieve the desired form.
His future course was decided by his respect for
the medium itself and for the craft involved in forg-
ing it. "A piece of iron is an idea in itself, a powerful and unyielding object," Chillida has said. "I
must gain complete mastery over it, and force it to
take on the tension which I feel within myself."

One of Chillida's earliest notable works in iron
was *Ilarik* (1951), a simple abstract geometrical
shape, twenty-nine inches high, which was clearly
inspired by Basque grave slabs. Atop its shaft, two
right-angled bars meet one another in a tight interlocking. From then on, his art, in the words of
*Newsweek* critic Mark Stevens (December 31,
1979), "often quarreled respectfully with the right
angle." For the next few years, however, Chillida
worked in a very different, open manner, doing a
number of horizontally aligned works. Among
them are the 1952–53 *Wind Comb*, the first in a series of similarly titled pieces, with its thin, ribbon-
like strands of iron that undulate like grasses in a
wind, and *From Within* (1953), which is now
owned by the Solomon R. Guggenheim Museum in

New York City. Despite his earlier successful exhibitions, Chillida refrained from showing any of those now famous pieces until 1954, when the Galeria Clan in Madrid gave him his first solo show. That year he was also represented by ten sculptures at the Triennale in Milan, in which he received an honorable mention, and was commissioned to do four iron doors, in relief, for the basilica in the Basque town of Aranzazu. In 1955 further recognition came in the form of an invitation to exhibit at the "Eisenplastik" show in the Kunsthalle in Bern, Switzerland and a commission to create for a park in San Sebastián a monument honoring the memory of Sir Alexander Fleming, the discoverer of penicillin. Sculpture intended for public places would, over the years, occupy an important place in Chillida's oeuvre. The relationship of a work of art to other art, to the surrounding landscape, and to its viewers is vital, he believes, for "sculpture should always face and be attentive to everything around it which moves and enlivens it."

Works endowed with such significant titles as *Resounding Spaces I* and *Music of the Constellations* (both 1954), *The Tremor of Iron* (a series of three, 1955–57), and *Place of Silences* (1958) allude to Chillida's comparison of sculptural volumes that cannot exist without space to musical sound that fills the void of silence. In particular, he is fascinated with a kinship between metallic vibrations and the harsh music of the Basques, and the clangorous beauty of the Basque language. In a discussion with the critic Pierre Volboudt, Chillida eloquently reflected on the Basque word *irrintzina*, "which rumbles and roars; it is a cry which shepherds sing to each other from miles away . . . which has come down to us from an age filled with the . . . howling of the wind in mountain gorges and the voice of waves clashing against the reefs of the Cantabrian coast. . . . Doesn't it make you think of iron ringing on the anvil . . . ?" That linking of concepts he made manifest in his *Silent Music* (1955), a constellation of iron forms suggesting both a trident and a harp.

Those early works in forged iron—executed from 1952 to 1956—are characterized by jagged shafts that forcefully curve or angle out into space to form a kind of hollow-centered cage. Possibly indirectly influenced by Julio González, they have also been compared to calligraphic symbols or ancient Cantabrian rock drawings. By about 1962 Chillida had developed another style, in which rhythmic continuity of line is often broken sharply and turns back on itself, becoming taut yet remaining supple, and space is squeezed into the form, acting as its negative image.

In the years between 1954 and 1966 Chillida worked on a series of seventeen pieces, entitled the "Anvil of Dreams," in which he used wood for the first time as a base from which the metal forms rise up in explosive, rhythmic curves. As he went on, he began to use wood as a medium in itself, and again his sensitive handling of the material reflects his respect for natural substances. Thus, as is his practice with forged metal that shows traces of the

hammer (the "wounds to which it owes its form," as Chillida puts it), he allows the thick, heavy planks he usually employs to keep their rough surfaces, knotholes, and marks of axe and hammer.

Chillida executed his first wooden sculptures in 1959, and noteworthy among his earliest work in that medium are the first three "Abesti Gogora" ("Rough Chant") pieces. Done from 1960 to 1964, they echo the subtle stylistic changes in his metal work. Thus, *Abesti Gogora I* (1960–61), now in the Museum of Fine Arts in Houston, Texas, is worked on the horizontal plane; the second in the series (1962) is a vertical shape, seemingly raised and supported by the air around it; and the third piece (1962–64) is a construction of tightly interlocked asymmetrical blocks, affording only tiny glimpses into its hidden and secret core of space.

Adding steel to his repertoire of materials, Chillida fashioned the "Rumor of Limits" series, consisting of five pieces in iron and two in steel, between 1956 and 1959. Since the 1960s he has worked primarily in steel, with occasional ventures into clay, porcelain, alabaster, marble, concrete, and granite. He incises his simple cubes of marble with tracings in black lead that recall the characteristic linear patterns of his drawings and prints. His works in alabaster, including his 1965 "Praise of Light" series, are directly inspired by his travels, in about 1963, in Greece, where he became reacquainted with classical sculpture and found himself intrigued by the ancients' fascination with the play of light within and on stone surfaces. *Abesti Gogora V*, a fifty-ton sculpture hewn from rose-colored granite quarried in Galicia, stands in the garden of the Houston Museum of Fine Arts. Commissioned as a memorial to the museum's benefactors, Jesse and Mary Jones, it was completed and set in place in 1966, in conjunction with Chillida's first retrospective exhibition in the United States. In its outdoor setting, the play of light and shadow appears to articulate and set into motion the three massive blocks of which the work is composed.

Other sculptures by Chillida that enhance important public spaces include the 1966 steel *Wind Comb IV* in the UNESCO building in Paris. Probably the most dramatic and fitting setting for any of his works is the coast off San Sebastián where three monumental steel Wind Combs are attached to the rocks above the sea. Considered perhaps his greatest sculptures to date, they seem to unite the elemental forces of sea, mountains, and air; and as the wind vibrates off the curved metal forms, Chillida's quest for equivalences between natural and geometric forms, between space and sound, is triumphantly solved.

Proceeding by intuition, Chillida allows his work to develop slowly, create itself in its own way, spiral back on itself, and go on again. "That's why I have so often harked back to a spiral in my sculptures," he has explained. And that is also why he never does models or preliminary sketches, though drawing has always been of great importance to him, and it is possible to see parallels between his many drawings and prints and his sculptures. Typically, Chillida's works in brush and black ink consist of simple, broad lines that either flow searchingly across large expanses of white paper, or interlock like puzzle pieces separated by only the narrowest of white spaces. The different linear forces behind both types of abstract configurations relate directly to his manners of handling metal: the open forms or the interlock forms.

Both modes of drawing have been translated into Chillida's etchings, lithographs, and woodcuts, which some critics have compared to Japanese calligraphy because of their complete absence of spatial illusion. His work in graphic media has been exhibited frequently, for example in a one-man show at the Basel Kunstmuseum in 1969 and in group print shows in Venice in 1972 and in Japan in 1974. Chillida has also worked in collage, usually preparing his own delicately tinted black and brown papers that give a sense of difference in texture to the abstract designs arranged on the white ground paper.

A number of Chillida's collages were used as illustrations for a special edition of Martin Heidegger's *Die Kunst und der Raum* (Art and Space), which was published in 1969 in Switzerland, where Chillida met the German ontological philosopher with whose metaphysical ideas his own are in such sympathy. Other books Chillida has illustrated include *Meditationen in Kastilien* (Meditations in Castille) by Max Holzer, which was published in Switzerland in 1968; a volume of work by the Spanish poet Jorge Guillén, published in Paris in 1973; and an edition of Aeschylus, published in Madrid in 1978.

Eduardo Chillida has been accorded honors and awards throughout the world. He won the grand prize in sculpture at the 1958 Venice Biennale and came to the United States that year to accept the Graham Foundation Award in Chicago. He received the Kandinsky Prize in 1960 and the Wilhelm Lehmbruck Sculpture Prize in 1966. In 1976 he was awarded an engraving prize from the Japanese Ministry of Culture, and in 1979, along with the American painter Willem de Kooning, he shared the Andrew W. Mellon Prize of the Carnegie Institute in Pittsburgh. In 1971 he held a visiting professorship at Harvard University.

Chillida's work may be seen in such public collections as the Wilhelm-Lehmbruck-Museum in Duisburg, Germany; the Kunstmuseum in Basel and the Kunsthaus in Zurich; London's Tate Gallery; and, in the United States, the Museum of Modern Art and the Guggenheim Museum in New York City, the Art Institute of Chicago, and the Museum of Fine Arts in Houston.

Apart from his 1966 show in Houston, Chillida's really important introduction to the American public took place more than a decade later, at the 1979 Carnegie International in Pittsburgh, the most comprehensive exhibition of his work held anywhere up to that time. In the spring of 1980 another retrospective, consisting of sixty-eight sculptures and forty-one works on paper, from 1951 to 1980,

was held at the Guggenheim, accompanied by an extensive catalogue with an introductory text by the Mexican poet and critic Octavio Paz. Included in the show was the dangling steel bauble called *Homage to Calder* (1979), a playful tribute to an artist Chillida knew and much admires. Another feature was the monumental reinforced concrete *Meeting Place IV* (1973-74), suspended from a scaffold outside the museum. A small exhibition at the Guggenheim in the spring of 1985 included a 1966 steel construction, *Iru Burni* (Three Irons), one of his pieces that constrict space in a tight labyrinth of metal blocks. Following the show, it was acquired for the museum's permanent collection.

The stability of Eduardo Chillida's own life would seem to be reflected in the balanced harmonies of his art. Married in 1950 to Pili de Belzunce, a French Basque, he is the father of five children. San Sebastián is still his home. Unlike Spain's writers, its artists were allowed to work virtually unchallenged under the Franco regime, and the Spanish public remained generally indifferent to Chillida until his second one-man show in Madrid, in 1972. The Basque claim to political and linguistic autonomy is a cause that Chillida, although not an activist, earnestly espouses.

Of medium height, slender, with a thin, ascetic face, Eduardo Chillida appears to be the prototype of the Spanish gentleman. His manner bears that out: courteous and gentle in speech, he is introspective in his approach to his work. But at the same time he is intense in his manner of working, and expansive when discussing his methods and intentions. For many years he has been recording his aesthetic theories, particularly about the relevance of space to art, and there is some speculation that his notebooks will eventually be published. In the meantime, as he made clear in an interview for the *Christian Science Monitor* (February 5, 1980), he works "in order to understand. . . . My art is a part of my understanding. I expect to work, or, better, always to question because never is one's knowledge enough: in the known there is still hidden the not-known."

*References: Bénézit, E., ed. Dictionnaire des peintres, sculpteurs et graveurs (1976); Contemporary Artists 2d ed (1983); International Who's Who, 1984-85; Marks, Claude. World Artists 1950-1980 (1984); Volboudt, Pierre. Chillida (1967); Who's Who in the World, 1984-85*

## Churchill, Caryl

*Sept. 3, 1938- British playwright. Address: b. c/o Margaret Ramsey, 14A Goodwin Ct., St. Martin's Lane, London WC2N 4LL, England*

Caryl Churchill is one of the few women to earn a place among the group of left-wing, intellectual

*Caryl Churchill*

playwrights who have dominated British theatre since the early 1970s. Like her colleagues David Hare, Trevor Griffiths, and Edward Bond, she examines the state of contemporary society, particularly contemporary British society, but from the viewpoint of a committed socialist and feminist. Having learned her craft as a writer of provocative and strikingly original radio and television dramas, she brings to her stage plays the same imaginative flights of fancy and theatrical daring. Her Obie Award–winning plays *Cloud Nine*, a wry critique of sexual compartmentalization, and *Top Girls*, about the personal costs of sexual equality, are as celebrated for their unconventional stagecraft, including intentionally overlapping dialogue and cross-gender casting, as for their probing social analyses. Productions of Miss Churchill's works have been mounted in nearly a dozen countries, among them Germany, Brazil, and Japan, as well as in Britain and the United States.

Caryl Churchill was born on September 3, 1938 in London, England, the only child of Robert Churchill, a political cartoonist for the London *Daily Mail*, and his wife, a former fashion model. She is, in her words, "infinitely distantly" related to Sir Winston Churchill. She began writing stories when she was little more than a toddler and, by the time she was eight, knew that she wanted to become a writer. In the late 1940s the Churchills immigrated to Canada, settling in Montreal, where Caryl completed her elementary education at the Trafalgar School.

In 1956 Caryl Churchill returned to England to attend Oxford University. While an undergraduate in English literature at Lady Margaret Hall, Oxford, her first play, the one-act *Downstairs*, was produced by Oriel College students for the National Union of Students Drama Festival. Two years

later, in 1960, *Having a Wonderful Time*, her satiric verse play, was staged by the Oxford Players. After seeing that production, a critic for the British trade publication *Stage* remarked in his review of August 11, 1960, "It is contemporary and original, well constructed and well characterised, and excels in conveying the stresses of modern life upon modern youth without self-consciousness or tub-thumping. The author uses words with appreciation and economy, a rare virtue among comparatively inexperienced writers."

After taking her B.A. degree in 1960, Caryl Churchill left Oxford, "very seriously intending to write," as she recalls. At the time, however, she was also, by her own admission, "very unadventurous." "I was an intellectually 'good girl,'" she explained, as quoted in *Other Stages* (December 3, 1981). "I went to university, read my books, had my friends, and got married." In the ten years immediately following her marriage, in 1961, to David Harter, a London barrister, she devoted most of her time to rearing their three sons, but she nonetheless managed to write some thirty-odd plays, most of them one-act radio dramas because, with three young children, "[her] attention span was short." Among her radio credits in the 1960s and early 1970s were *Lovesick, Identical Twins, Abortive, Perfect Happiness, Schreber's Nervous Illness*, and *Not, Not, Not, Not, Not Enough Oxygen*. As she told John Hall, who interviewed her for a *Guardian* (December 12, 1972) profile, some of those works, particularly the earlier ones, like *Abortive* and *Identical Twins*, were "depressed plays about depression and a way of coping with depression, which were related to [her] own experience."

With the rise of "fringe" theatre in the 1970s, Caryl Churchill increasingly found outlets for stage presentations of her plays in neighborhood playhouses, pub-theatres, and subsidized theatres. In 1972 the Royal Court, London's leading alternative theatre, mounted a production of her tragic farce, *Owners*, in its small, experimental Upstairs theatre. A blistering attack on the ways in which rampant materialism perverts human relationships, *Owners* focuses on Marion, a rapacious and iron-willed property developer who expropriates the lives as well as the property of virtually everyone she knows. Critics were admittedly baffled by the play's "seemingly unconnected scenes" and "insufficiently integrated" plot strands, among other things, but almost to a man, they marked Caryl Churchill down as a playwright to watch. A short-lived Off-Broadway production of *Owners*, in 1973, was dismissed by New York critics as a "curiosity."

Largely on the strength of *Owners*, Caryl Churchill was named to a year's appointment as resident playwright of the Royal Court Theatre in 1974, the first woman to be chosen for the position. For her debut as house dramatist, she offered the unsettling *Objections to Sex and Violence*, an examination of the interrelatedness of sexuality, violence, and power that opened on January 2, 1975. Set on a rocky, litter-strewn strip of beach, the play looks at different responses to various forms of aggression and carnality through the eyes of an ill-assorted group of holiday-makers, including a bickering middle-aged couple, a lonely old woman returning to the scene of an idyllic youthful affair, a psychically bruised divorcée and her docile lover, and an enigmatic female terrorist. In their commentaries on the production, many reviewers noted that *Objections to Sex and Violence* seemed to be more a series of polemical debates than a play. That minor reservation aside, the majority found much to admire in the punctilious acting and in Caryl Churchill's Pinteresque sense of obscurity. Later in the year, the Royal Court Theatre Upstairs gave two special performances of her futuristic parable *Moving Clocks Go Slow*.

It was in *Objections to Sex and Violence* that Caryl Churchill introduced feminist ideology into her work. She explored female oppression in one of its most extreme forms—witch-hunting—in her one-act play *Vinegar Tom*, which she created in 1976 for and with the feminist touring troupe Monstrous Regiment. (The group takes its name from a contemporary slur on the accession of Queen Elizabeth I: "God save us from the monstrous regiment of women.") In the course of her research, Caryl Churchill came to the conclusion that "witches" were merely convenient scapegoats in times of social stress. Although *Vinegar Tom* is set in seventeenth-century England, Miss Churchill, in an attempt to stress its parallels in the present, interrupted the action from time to time with contemporary songs—a device some critics thought diminished the dramatic tension of what was otherwise a powerful and unnerving work.

Like *Vinegar Tom*, and written concurrently with it, Caryl Churchill's complex and epic drama, *Light Shining in Buckinghamshire*, examines the suppression of the poor and the powerless in the seventeenth century and, by extension, also in the twentieth. The play, which interweaves historical and fictional characters and events, traces the development of a short-lived uprising by several extremist religious sects in the late 1640s, but it is, as Donald Campbell observed in *Plays and Players* (November 1976), "a genuine study of revolution itself, any revolution," and it suggests that there may be "a direct correlation between the efficiency of a revolution and the nature of the society that creates it."

Crucial to an appreciation of *Light Shining in Buckinghamshire* is Caryl Churchill's belief in a collective vision of history. To underline that concept and, at the same time, demonstrate the collective nature of the play, which she had created in collaboration with the actors of the Joint Stock Company, a theatre cooperative, she had the players switch and share roles. First presented at the Edinburgh Festival in August 1976, *Light Shining in Buckinghamshire* opened the following month at the Royal Court's studio theatre to overwhelmingly favorable reviews, with David Zane Mairowitz going so far as to call it "one of the finest pieces of English playwriting for years."

*Light Shining in Buckinghamshire* owed much of its impact to its spare and understated text. Caryl Churchill's uncommon awareness of the dramatic power of understatement was perhaps never more evident than in *Traps*, an elliptically structured puzzle about communal living that was staged at the Royal Court Upstairs in January 1977. Audiences and critics alike were willing to overlook its baffling plot, which one critic described as "R. D. Laing's *Knots* revisited," and its lackluster characters, finding more than enough compensation in its "crisp," "sinewy" dialogue and in the playwright's creative deployment of stagecraft.

Almost since the beginning of her career, Caryl Churchill has written with a poet's ear for the spoken word, but she also writes with a vigilant eye on the action, and it is that rare ability to write for actors that makes her plays so eminently watchable. Some of her best work has emerged from developmental workshops, such as those that led to her Obie-winning *Cloud Nine*. The seed for that complex satirization of sex-role confusion was planted during a freewheeling discussion of contemporary sexuality with members of the Joint Stock Company and nurtured over several weeks of textual improvisation sessions. "What surprised us was our realization that we had all been brought up in an atmosphere of conventional, Victorian morality," the playwright told Bernard Weiner in an interview for the *San Francisco Chronicle* (September 27, 1983). "This got us to talking about the parallels between the way colonizers treat the colonized and the way men tended to treat women in our own society."

To illustrate those parallels, Miss Churchill set the first act of *Cloud Nine* in an African colonial outpost in Victorian times and her second act in the present, but she deliberately aged her characters only twenty-five years. "I meant to show the way people move away from the rigid ways of the past and open themselves to the new ways," she explained to Weiner. Moreover, by having a white actor play a native houseboy, a man play a passive and unfulfilled wife, and a woman take the part of a sensitive schoolboy, she not only pointed out the similarities between colonial and sexual oppression, but also demonstrated the artificiality of conventional sex roles.

The Joint Stock Company's production of *Cloud Nine* opened for a limited run at the Royal Court on March 29, 1979. A box-office hit, it returned to the Royal Court repertory, with a new cast, in September 1980, when for a short time it played alongside a studio production of *Three More Sleepless Nights*, Caryl Churchill's dispassionate study of the different forms that noncommunication between men and women can take. An American production of *Cloud Nine* opened in May 1981 at the Lucille Lortel Theatre Off Broadway, where it settled in for a two-year, sold-out engagement. Although British critics appreciated *Cloud Nine*'s "gentle playfulness" and "genuinely funny" approach to what was essentially, as Irving Wardle has pointed out, "an exercise on the theme of ghosts," they were on the whole more restrained in their praise than their American counterparts. The enthusiasm of American reviewers may have been at least partly generated by the exuberant direction of Tommy Tune, the Tony Award–winning choreographer and musical-comedy director. Afraid that American audiences would fail to understand the low-key British humor, he treated *Cloud Nine* as, in his words, "one gigantic, never-ending musical number."

Caryl Churchill continued her scrutiny of the ways in which entrenched moral imperatives of a male-dominated society profoundly affect women's lives in *Top Girls*, a realistic probing of the psyche of Marlene, an ambitious career woman who climbs the corporate ladder. *Top Girls* opens with a dazzling fantasy scene—a dinner party attended by an odd assortment of legendary "top girls," including a thirteenth-century Japanese courtesan, the indomitable Victorian traveler Isabella Bird, and the legendary Pope Joan, who, disguised as a man, was widely believed during medieval times to have been a pope in the mid-ninth century. They have assembled at a fashionable restaurant to celebrate Marlene's appointment as managing director of the Top Girls employment agency. The rest of the play is divided between scenes in Marlene's London office, where she is surrounded by a coterie of equally callous assistants, and at her family home in a working-class neighborhood in East Anglia, where she has left her retarded, illegitimate daughter in the care of her sister in order to devote herself to her career. "I wanted it to set off, with all those historical women celebrating Marlene's achievement, to look as if it were going to be a celebration of women achieving things," she explained to Lynne Truss in an interview for *Plays and Players* (January 1984), "and then put the other perspective on it, to show that just to achieve the same things that man had achieved in capitalist society wouldn't be a good object."

Commissioned by the Royal Court, *Top Girls* opened on the theatre's main stage on September 1, 1982 under the direction of Max Stafford-Clark, the artistic director of the English Stage Company, the Royal Court's resident troupe. An immediate critical and commercial success, the production transferred later in the year to the Public Theatre in New York City, in exchange for the Public's production of *Buried Inside Extra*, then returned to London in February 1983 to complete its engagement at the Court while an American cast continued the New York run. Despite its "startling technique" and "dazzling writing," the majority of New York reviewers agreed with Frank Rich that *Top Girls* was not in the same league as *Cloud Nine*. "The playwright seems to beg her complicated issue by showing us only her monstrous heroine at one extreme and, at the other, the victimized women that the Marlenes of this world exploit and betray," Rich contended in the *New York Times* of December 29, 1982. "The absence of the middle range—of women who achieve without imitating power-crazed men and denying their own humanity—is an artificial polemical contrivance that cuts the play off at the heart." A few English critics were similarly dismayed by what they thought were *Top Girls'* predictable and simplistic arguments, but most of them lined up behind the *Guardian's* Michael Billington, who maintained in his opening night review that "this is the best British play ever from a woman dramatist."

In *Fen,* her third collaboration with the Joint Stock Company, Caryl Churchill looked at Marlene's opposites, at those women condemned by birth or circumstances to lives of grinding poverty. Most of the women in *Fen* are tenant farm workers who eke out a precarious living in the desolate marshlands of East Anglia by picking potatoes, finding solace from their backbreaking labor only in alcohol, tranquilizers, and random, guilt-ridden love affairs. Derived from on-the-scene conversations between a group of Joint Stock actors and the citizens of a fen village and developed in workshops over a period of weeks, *Fen* documents the bleakness of frustrated lives, in a series of loosely linked vignettes.

First presented by the Joint Stock Company at the Almeida, a fringe playhouse in north London, in February 1983, *Fen* traveled to the United States two months later for an Off-Broadway engagement as part of Britain's "Salute to New York" festival. It was later revived at the Royal Court Theatre in July 1983 and, with an American cast, at the Public Theatre in New York in March 1984. More than any of Miss Churchill's other plays, *Fen* seems to draw strength from its stunning physical set, for the fog-shrouded, furrowed potato field bordered by the blank walls of the women's cheerless homes is, as Michael Billington noted, an "apt metaphor" for enslavement not only to the land but also to the oppressive and dehumanizing traditions of the past. Well received in each of its incarnations, *Fen* won for Caryl Churchill the sixth annual Susan Smith Blackburn Prize, which is awarded annually to a woman playwright for "a work of outstanding quality in the English-speaking theatre."

Long interested in what she has called the "soft" methods of social control, Miss Churchill focused on changing attitudes to crime and punishment in nineteenth-century France in her kaleidoscopic *Softcops,* which Howard Davies mounted as a studio production for the Royal Shakespeare Company in January 1984. Over the course of the play, members of the all-male cast gradually come to represent various approaches to crime prevention and law enforcement, from public execution to solitary confinement to a "garden of laws." A curious blend of music hall routine, *tableau vivant*, and "illustrated lecture," to use Giles Gordon's term, *Softcops* reflects the ideas outlined by the Marxist philosopher Michel Foucault in his book *Surveiller et punir (Discipline and Punish)*. As Sheridan Morley, among other critics, noted in his review for *Punch* (January 18, 1984), somewhere along the line, Foucault's theories appeared to have taken over, leaving Caryl Churchill with "a lot of random notes for a *New Society* article about penal reform but nothing that could remotely be called a play."

Caryl Churchill is a slender woman with short, thick, dark blond hair and hazel eyes. Reticent to the point of self-effacement, she seldom grants interviews, and when she does she usually confines the discussion to her work. "I believe in the magic of theatre," she has said, as quoted in the *New York Times* (January 9, 1983), "but I think it's important to realize that there is nothing magical about the work behind it. . . . I spend ages researching my plays and sitting alone writing them." She enjoys seeing actors "bending and shaping" her material and has observed that "this is a very

good, optimistic time for women, which is why many plays written by women are simply more interesting than those written by men." Miss Churchill lives with her husband, who gave up his lucrative practice as a barrister in 1972 to run a community legal-aid center, and their three sons in an early Victorian house in Islington, a newly gentrified residential area in north London.

*References: Guardian* p9 Ja 2 '75 por, p10 D 12 '72 por; *N Y Times* II p1+ Ja 9 '83 por; *Plays and Players* p40+ Mr '73 por, p8+ Ja '84 por; *Contemporary Authors* vol 102 (1981); *Contemporary Dramatists* (1977); *Who's Who in the Theatre* (1981)

---

© 1985 Fred W. McDarragh

## Cleveland, James

*Dec. 5, 1931– Gospel singer; composer; clergyman. Address: b. c/o Ed Smith, Gospel Artists Association, Box 4632, Detroit, Mich. 48243*

"The focal point of my life," the Reverend James Cleveland told David Jackson in the course of an interview for the *Village Voice* (April 19, 1979), "is music. I love it. I have respect for rock music, jazz, but I love gospel music. I never tire of it. I never tire of writing it, of performing it myself. An artist has to be in love with what he or she does." James Cleveland's love has carried him from his practice on an imaginary piano as a child in Chicago to his current reputation as "the king of gospel music." The scores of albums he has recorded for Savoy Records have sold millions of copies, and his hun-

dreds of compositions are solidly entrenched in the contemporary gospel repertory, including "Grace Is Sufficient," "He's Using Me," and "The Man, Jesus."

Such diverse performers as Aretha Franklin, Jessy Dixon, and Billy Preston have acknowledged Cleveland as a major influence on their style, but during the 1960s, when his "Without A Song" almost became a hit in Detroit, he declined the tempting opportunity to cross over to a popular audience. Instead, in 1968 he founded the Gospel Music Workshop of America for the purpose of bringing together and training younger singers from all over the United States and around the world. The Workshop's annual convention now attracts over 15,000 aspiring musicians.

James Cleveland was born on December 5, 1931 on Chicago's South Side, the only son among the three children of Ben Cleveland, who in the midst of the Great Depression worked for the WPA, and his wife. He grew up in what he has since described as "the gospel atmosphere," at first through the influence of his grandmother, who was a devout member of the Pilgrim Baptist Church. There the chorus director was Thomas A. Dorsey, a former blues musician and composer who cofounded the National Convention of Gospel Choirs and Choruses and established the first music publishing house devoted exclusively to the work of black gospel composers. His approach to the performance and composition of gospel music, incorporating elements of blues, jazz, and work songs, became the focal point for a whole generation of gospel musicians and brought him recognition as "the father of gospel music." Cleveland recalled during an interview for *Ebony* (November 1968): "It was Mr. Dorsey who gave me my first chance to sing in public. I was sort of a mascot for the choir, and I'd sing louder than anybody else. Mr. Dorsey heard me and put me up on a box to sing a song called 'He's All I Need.' Oh, I was about eight years old then. . . . " Cleveland joined the church's junior choir and began teaching himself the piano. At home he practiced on imaginary keys until he was a teenager and the family bought him a small upright piano.

One of Cleveland's earliest idols on the piano was Roberta Martin, a pioneering figure in Chicago's gospel music community, who, by working with Dorsey's National Convention of Gospel Choirs and Choruses, became a major influence on the generations of singers and pianists who followed her. Learning her songs, Cleveland absorbed the work of the Roberta Martin Singers, the group she founded in 1936 and led for three decades. He developed his early singing style under the influence of its members, most notably Myrtle Scott, Eugene Smith, and Robert Anderson, and he studied gospel piano with the group's organist, ("Little") Lucy Smith, and informally with Roberta Martin herself.

Mahalia Jackson also cast her spell on the impressionable Cleveland. "I grew up completely fascinated by Mahalia Jackson," he recalled for *Ebony*. "I was Mahalia's paperboy, and I'd go over to her apartment on Indiana Avenue and leave her paper and then put my ear to the door to try to hear her singing. If she wasn't at home, I'd go over to her beauty shop—she used to be a hairdresser, you know—and just sit around there and listen to her hum songs while she was straightening hair."

Encouraged by Roberta Martin, who also owned a flourishing gospel music publishing house, Cleveland started composing while still a teenager. He began singing with a group called the Thorn Gospel Crusaders, made up of teenagers from his own neighborhood, and soon attracted attention from the city's leading gospel musicians when the group started performing his own songs. One of his earliest compositions, "Grace Is Sufficient," which was presented at a 1948 Baptist Convention, so impressed Roberta Martin that she began publishing his work at a flat fee of $40 for each song. She herself later performed "Grace Is Sufficient" at the National Baptist Convention in 1955.

James Cleveland's early professional career remained closely tied to both Roberta Martin and her singers. Shortly after his success with "Grace Is Sufficient," he joined two former members of the Roberta Martin Singers, Bessie Folk and Norsalus McKissick, who had formed their own group, the Gospelaires, as pianist and occasional third lead. Cleveland made his recording debut at the age of nineteen with the Gospelaires, when he sang "Oh, What A Time" on a disc for the Apollo label that was issued in 1950. During the early 1950s he also toured with Mahalia Jackson.

But Cleveland's first major break came with the Caravans, originally an all-female ensemble that was founded in 1953 in Chicago by the contralto Albertina Walker, the former lead singer of Robert Anderson's group. He joined the Caravans a year after its inception, serving as singer, songwriter, and arranger of gospel standards. His interpretation of "Old Time Religion," according to David Jackson in the *Village Voice*, was "guaranteed to turn out the church," and Albertina Walker assured Jackson that "James's arrangements simply make you sing."

It was sometime, however, before Cleveland emerged as a singer, and when the Caravans made their first recordings for the Chicago-based States label, he was still presiding at the piano. His once soaring boy soprano voice had matured into a gruff, rasping baritone that reminded some listeners of Louis Armstrong, a price he paid for his earlier enthusiasm for singing. As Cleveland explained to the interviewer for *Ebony*: "I had a beautiful boy soprano voice. Later on, I sang so hard that I strained my voice. That's why it sounds like a foghorn now." But by 1955 Cleveland had begun to surmount his vocal problems, and it was with him as lead singer that the Caravans recorded their first big hits, "The Solid Rock" and "Old Time Religion." On a tour with the Caravans in 1956 he was also prominently featured as a composer as well as an arranger.

During the late 1950s James Cleveland briefly left the Caravans to join the Gospel All Stars, with whom he recorded "Lord Remember Me" and a devotional adaptation of Ray Charles's hit, "Hallelujah, I Love Her So," retitled as "That's Why I Love Him So." After that, he rejoined the Caravans for a short time before leaving to form his own group, the Gospel Chimes. Organized by Cleveland in Chicago in 1959 with a membership of Dorothy Norwood, Imogene Greene, Lee Charles Neely, Claude Timmons, and Jessy Dixon, the Gospel Chimes was the first of his gospel groups, important not only as a vehicle for him to present his own style of singing and approach to arrangements and composition but also as an influence over other performers. Perhaps the most notable among them was Jessy Dixon, the future founder and leader of the Jessy Dixon Singers, who acquired his first professional experience as a member of the Gospel Chimes and who modeled his own singing style upon Cleveland's.

In 1960 James Cleveland moved to Detroit, Michigan to become musical director of the New Bethel Baptist Church with the Reverend C. L. Franklin. His work with several of Detroit's other choirs soon brought him into contact with the Reverend Charles Crain and the Reverend Leslie Bush at the Prayer Tabernacle, where he became minister of music. It was with that church's 100-voice choir, the Voices of Tabernacle, that he recorded a song called "The Love of God" for Cameron Murphy's Detroit-based Hob label. Originally composed for Johnnie Taylor, "The Love of God" became a hit and brought him to the attention of Herman Lubinsky, owner of the gospel label Savoy Records, with headquarters in New Jersey. Although the Voices of Tabernacle were already under contract to Hob, James Cleveland was not, so that Lubinsky was free to approach him with an offer during an engagement at the Apollo Theater in Harlem, in 1960. At first somewhat wary of Lubinsky's interest, Cleveland really wanted to ally himself with the firm of Veejay Records, which at that time was a large and prospering company. But Lubinsky's persistence eventually persuaded Cleveland to sign with Savoy Records, a decision that represented a turning point in his career.

During the 1950s and early 1960s Cleveland was busily involved in what he has called "paying his dues," since his successes, whether with the Caravans, the Gospelaires, the Gospel Chimes, or with the leadership of the choir of a particular church, were rewarded only with psychic income. Most of his recognition was confined to Chicago or Detroit, and there was "no money at all," in his words, to go with it. While Sam Cooke, who had been perhaps the most promising male gospel singer of his generation, turned to secular music during the late 1950s and made millions, Cleveland preached as a licensed minister in the Church of God in Christ. The contract with Savoy did not immediately make Cleveland a wealthy star, but it did provide him with the means to stop paying dues during the 1960s and start collecting them back by enabling him to reach a national audience.

In 1963 Savoy released a live performance recording of James Cleveland with the Angelic Choir of Nutley, New Jersey, entitled *Peace Be Still* that earned him the honorific epithets of "King James," "the king of gospel music," and "the crown prince of gospel" from a host of new admirers. *Peace Be Still* remained on the gospel charts for more than fifteen years, selling over 750,000 copies in its first decade of release and well over a million copies as of 1985. His tour obligations in the United States grew to a point where he had to make his bookings a year in advance. During 1966 he and his James Cleveland Singers played a two-week engagement at the Olympia Theater in Paris, followed by command performances in Monaco before Prince Rainier and Princess Grace.

In 1963, the same year in which *Peace Be Still* was released, Cleveland, by then a minister, moved to Los Angeles to become the pastor of the New Greater Harvest Baptist Church. Recruiting from among the best young singers then available, he founded the James Cleveland singers, the gospel group with which he built his international career over the following decades. Because the sales of their albums ran as high as 70,000 copies, Cleveland achieved a degree of independence almost unheard of in gospel music up until that time. Unlike most gospel singers, who are paid against specific sales royalties, Cleveland has collected a guaranteed annual salary from Savoy Records under the terms of a contract that requires him to record four albums every year.

Within five years of the release of *Peace Be Still*, James Cleveland was the highest paid performer in gospel music, with an income as of 1968 rumored to be well into six figures. Commenting on his records for Savoy, one of its executives, Fred Mendelsohn, was quoted in *Ebony*: "Everything he records will sell. Even his new releases sell more than we can expect from the complete sale of any of our other artists." Cleveland's other top-selling albums, for which he holds gold record awards, include *I'll Do His Will*; *Lord, Do It*; *I Stood On The Banks*; *Lord Help Me*; and *Jesus Is The Best Thing*.

At the same time that Cleveland was making his ascent in the world of gospel music, two musicians

whom he had once trained became celebrities. Aretha Franklin, the daughter of the Reverend C. L. Franklin, to whom Cleveland had given lessons in gospel singing when she was nine years old, became the leading female "soul" singer of the late 1960s, and Billy Preston, who was organ accompanist with the James Cleveland Singers during their first year, achieved stardom as a collaborator with the Beatles, which led to his own solo career during the 1970s. But for all of his own success, Cleveland remained committed to gospel music and continued to be relatively little known beyond its ranks of enthusiasts. *Peace Be Still's* one million sales were made almost exclusively to a black audience, and when a Detroit disc jockey turned his "Without A Song" into a pop hit, there was no follow-up effort to hold the attention of the new and wider audience that the song had achieved.

In 1968 James Cleveland convened the Gospel Music Workshop of America, which was, in many respects, a much more ambitious extension of the convention that Thomas A. Dorsey organized in Chicago in 1932. "There is no basic difference between the Gospel Music Workshop and Reverend Dorsey's group," Cleveland explained to a *Village Voice* reporter in 1979. "They dealt with solo singers, choirs, and choruses, but it was more of a fellowship showcase, where they would get together once a year and show off their individual talents. They did not have the workshop aspect of teaching." More than 3,000 delegates from twenty-three states attended the first convention in Detroit. More recent meetings have attracted over 15,000 of the convention's 25,000 members from as far away as Hamburg, West Germany. The organization's ranks contain thousands of amateur singers who are also doctors, lawyers, construction workers, domestics, and students, whose ages range from fifteen to twenty-five years.

That accent on youth is central to the convention's purpose, according to Cleveland, its founder and president. "The kids that are coming up with gospel," he told the *Village Voice*, "don't know the pioneers, because there have not been chronicles written on the history of gospel. Many of the pioneers of gospel are still living, so we try to acquaint people with the living and those that have passed on. I wanted to get the best exponents of gospel music in every area—the best pianist, the best organist, the best director, the best songwriter—to come together and share their knowledge." In 1969 James Cleveland founded the Southern California Community Choir, and other workshop chapters, in their turn, started their own choral groups. One of the most successful was the Northern California Community Choir, which evolved into the Edwin Hawkins Singers, who became famous for their international hit, "Oh Happy Day." Hundreds of community choirs eventually emerged out of the workshop's activities.

Recognition from outside the ranks of gospel music enthusiasts began to be accorded to James Cleveland during the 1970s. In addition to his gold record awards, he received the National Association of Negro Musicians award in 1975, the NAACP Image Award the following year, and an honorary doctorate from Temple Bible College. A musical institution by his mid-40s, Cleveland used his prestige to help to introduce new soloists and choral groups, both on records and in the concert hall, and his jazz-influenced pianism, innovative voicings, and rocking cadences are among the most recognizable attributes of gospel music. He has set for himself future goals for his music and faith, including his dream of a spiritual retreat called Gospeland, which would include a hotel, restaurant, amusement park, shopping area, housing, six auditoriums, and a music school.

The Reverend James Cleveland lives in Los Angeles, where he founded his Cornerstone Institutional Baptist Church in 1970. Now one of the largest congregations in the city, it moved in the spring of 1983 into a new $2 million, 1,250-seat building. Cleveland lives in a spacious house in the black upper-middle-class suburb of View Park, decorated in colors as bright and "happy" as he can make them, in compensation for the drabness of his parents' Chicago flat, where he was born. He has provided his family, including his grandmother, Mrs. Annie Hicks, and his two sisters, with homes of their own. His daughter LaShone, born in 1966, lives with her mother, who is now Mrs. Jean Ervin. Cleveland's hobbies and diversions include a financial interest in a soul-food restaurant in Los Angeles, where he occasionally drops in to lend a hand to the cooking.

Despite a recent heart attack, Cleveland sang "God, Do It for Me" to a throng of thousands assembled at Grant's Tomb on Riverside Drive in New York City on August 11, 1985 in celebration of Harlem Week. His doctors had advised against it, but as he explained, "For something like this, I just had to be there."

References: Ebony 24:74+ N '68, 40:148+ D '84; Village Voice p73+ Ap 16 '79; Washington Post B p1+ Ag 21 '78; Biographical Dictionary of Afro-American and African Musicians (1982); Gospel Music Encyclopedia (1979); Who's Who in America, 1984–85

## Colville, (David) Alex(ander)

*Aug. 24, 1920– Canadian painter. Address: 408 Main St., Wolfville, Nova Scotia, B0P 1X0, Canada*

During the decades following World War II when international tastes and markets favored abstract expressionism and other nonrepresentational art trends, the Canadian realist painter Alex Colville devoted himself to satisfying what he saw as "the hunger of people for images they can recognize." His capturing of a Canadian ethos in figurative paintings and prints of people, places, and animals of the Maritime Provinces eventually won him financial success, popularity among Canadians, and an impressive reputation in England and Germany, but he remains for art critics a controversial painter of whom the final appraisal has yet to be made. Meanwhile, the art world's recent revival of interest in realism coincides with two major shows of Colville's work: a retrospective that opened at the Art Gallery of Ontario in the summer of 1983 and traveled across Canada and to Germany and, simultaneously, an exhibition of prints that toured Canada and several European countries.

The second of two sons, David Alexander Colville was born on August 24, 1920 in Toronto, Canada to David Harrower Colville, who had emigrated from Fifeshire, Scotland a decade earlier, and Frances (Gault) Colville, an Ontarian. His brother, Robert Colville, was five years older. When Alex was seven, the family moved to St. Catharines, Ontario, but stayed only two years before settling in Amherst, Nova Scotia. His father worked as a laborer in steel construction and was, with his agrarian background, temperamentally ill-adapted to an industrial job, though he managed to advance to a supervisory position in his company's plant in Amherst. A onetime milliner with a knack for business, Mrs. Colville owned and operated a clothing store in the town. The family's faith was Roman Catholic, but Alex was not sent to church schools. "Although he made no open declaration," David Burnett wrote in his essay for the catalogue of the retrospective show, "Colville early on denied for himself the value of organized religion."

A prolonged recuperation from pneumonia in 1929 had a lasting impact on Colville's life. Because of his inability or disinclination to play with other children, he turned inward, developing an interest in books that led in his adult years to extensive reading in French, English, and American literature, including the work of Jean-Paul Sartre, Albert Camus, André Malraux, Joseph Conrad, John Dos Passos, Saul Bellow, and John Updike. Also during his convalescense he spent much time drawing. His subjects were cars, boats, and other familiar objects of his environment, the celebration of which eventually became a hallmark of his work. In his paintings they take on a symbolic significance while retaining their objective validity.

For three years, while in high school in Amherst, Colville attended weekly art classes in neighboring Sackville, New Brunswick. Through his teacher, Sarah Hart, he met Stanley Royle, a British postimpressionist landscape painter and the director of the School of Fine and Applied Arts at Mount Allison University in Sackville. Recognizing the merit in Colville's student efforts, Royle obtained a scholarship in art for him at Mount Allison. Colville then opted to reject the scholarship he had earlier won to Dalhousie University, where he had intended to study law. Any misgivings he may have felt about his choice of a career seem to have been dispelled by the time he received his Bachelor of Fine Arts degree from Mount Allison in 1942. He reaffirmed his identity as a painter in a self-portrait of that year that depicted him wearing an artist's smock, standing before a canvas on an easel, and holding a palette and paint brushes. Recalling his decision for art, he explained to James Purdie of the Toronto Globe and Mail (November 26, 1977), "I wasn't driven to art by any inner compulsions or torments. I was just like an apprentice carpenter. I began learning the trade by painting landscapes in the style of my teacher."

Colville's service as a war artist in the Canadian Army during World War II abruptly changed the course of his apprenticeship. Sent overseas in 1944, he spent nearly two years recording events of the war in southern France, England, the Netherlands, and Germany. Throughout his European tour, which he has wryly referred to as his "Guggenheim fellowship in art," his daily routine was to make on-the-scene drawings and watercolor sketches from which he would later develop interpretative, as well as reportorial, oil paintings. One of his canvases, dated 1945, is entitled Bodies in a Grave, Belsen.

Before leaving Europe at the end of the war, Colville spent two days at the Louvre in Paris. The masterpieces that he saw there, and in later years at other great museums, gave him a standard to which he could aspire. "I was never trying to be an A. Y. Jackson," he told Gillian MacKay in an interview for Maclean's (August 1, 1983), "but rather a Vermeer, a Manet, or a Piero della Francesca. I always thought I was in that league." (A. Y. Jackson was a member of the Group of Seven painters, pioneers of a Canadian national art movement mainly during the 1920s.)

In 1946, after he had completed his service as a war artist in Ottawa, Colville joined the faculty of Mount Allison University. Having married Rhoda Wright of Wolfville on August 5, 1942, he had a growing family to support, and it was not until 1963 that he felt financially able to resign from the university and devote all his time to painting. During his early years of teaching, isolated from avant-garde postwar art movements but not unaware of them, he developed his own philosophy of art and style of painting. In a lecture that he gave in 1951 at the New Brunswick Museum in Saint John, he rejected the currently fashionable persuasion of "art for art's sake" in favor of representational art with a message: "I regard art not as a means of soliloquizing, but as a means of communicating."

Far from subscribing to the gestural spontaneity of the action painters within abstract expressionism, then in vogue, Colville began in 1950 to base the design of each picture on an intricate and carefully calculated geometric substructure that controlled the position of figures and objects, perspective, and proportion. Among his predecessors in the use of such a framework were the ancient Egyptian artists, whose work he had admired in the Louvre, Piero della Francesca and other early Italian Renaissance painters, and, as Helen Dow pointed out in Art Journal (Summer 1965), the French impressionist Georges Seurat, whose pointillistic technique Colville also followed in his own fastidious blending of colors by thousands of tiny brush strokes. For some of his paintings he may make as many as thirty preliminary studies.

Several art critics have called attention to the pictures of Edward Hopper, Ben Shahn, Grant Wood, and other figurative painters at work in the United States during the pre-World War II era as a major force in shaping Colville as an artist. The British critic Robert Melville, reviewing an exhibition of Colville's work at London's Marlborough Fine Art Gallery, argued in the New Statesman (January 23, 1970) with those who perceive the painter as "a completely Canadian phenomenon, totally without predecessors." On the contrary, Melville went on to say, "I see no strong line of demarcation between Canada and the U.S., and think of him as America's most distinguished realist painter since Edward Hopper" in a tradition dating back to George Caleb Bingham.

The more specific label of "magic realist" that Colville has attracted is in accord with his conviction, expressed in his 1951 lecture, that one of the qualities essential to an artist is "the sense of mystery." In his ability to evoke a mood of loneliness and atmosphere of stillness, he has been compared to the American magic realists George Tooker and Andrew Wyeth. The term "magic realism" also covers the link between some of Colville's work and elements of surrealism in the paintings of Paul Delvaux, René Magritte, and Giorgio de Chirico, particularly as regards the sense of unease and foreboding that they arouse.

One of Colville's pictures that approaches surrealism is Nude and Dummy (1950), which Gillian

MacKay and others consider to be his first success-ful painting. A departure from the Maritimes out-door scenes that had been engaging him, *Nude and Dummy* has an interior setting, an attic room in which a nude facing a window gazes back over her shoulder at a dressmaker's dummy. The picture's deep Renaissance perspective calls to mind de Chirico, some of whose "metaphysical interiors" included dressmaker's mannequins. Colville's nude, for which his wife was the model, is more particularized, less impersonal, than his usual sim-plified female forms of the early 1950s, such as those in *Coastal Figure* (1951) and *Seated Nude* (1951), which indicate a familiarity with the sculp-ture of Henry Moore. *Nude and Dummy*, more-over, with its explorative use of a geometric network, is an early instance of the artist's concern with figures in settings, or "spatial environments," to use his term.

Surrealistic overtones are discernible also in Colville's *Horse and Train* (1954), in which a black horse running down a railroad track at night is about to collide with an oncoming train. He took the theme of his painting from two lines of a poem by the South African writer Roy Campbell: "Against a regiment I oppose a brain/And a dark horse against an armoured train." The import is tragic, for, as Helen Dow explained in *Art Journal*, "In the painting, as in the context of the poem, the horse symbolically represents the artist, man as creator." One of Colville's best-known paintings, *Horse and Train* was reproduced on the cover of *Night Vision*, the 1973 top-selling album of the Ca-nadian pop musician Bruce Cockburn.

The juxtaposition of irrelative images abounds in Colville's work, but the disparity is seldom so startling as that of his horse and train. And unlike surrealists, he does not propose farfetched or im-possible relationships. It is, rather, by eliciting dra-ma and an unexpected significance from commonplace situations that he explores the ques-tions that he believes to be the proper province of the artist: "Who are we? What are we like? What do we do?" The answers, which are not likely to be final, are proffered in terms of imaginative com-posites of actual details, the precise depiction of which, as Burnett quoted him, is necessary to his process of "authenticating" images that originate as "a kind of fantasy." Referring to the pop artists, who flourished in the 1960s, he once observed to Helen Dow, "I think I preceded them in many ways, in the use of cars and trucks and such ordi-nary things conceived in terms of absolute reality."

*Pacific* (1967), painted when Colville was a visit-ing artist at the University of California at Santa Cruz in 1967-68, and *The River Spree* (1971) and *Berlin Bus* (1978), which were inspired by his six-month stay in Germany in 1971 as a visiting artist in the Berliner Künstlerprogramm, are among his few major works that do not derive mainly from the world around his home in the Maritimes. (The man, however, in *Pacific* is undoubtedly the artist and the dog in *The River Spree*, a family pet.) With an occasional exception, such as *Snowstorm* (1971),

a scene of deserted expanses, his landscapes and seascapes include persons (*New Moon*, 1980; *Swimmer*, 1982), or animals (*Cow and Calf*, 1969), or both (*Dog, Boy and St. John River*, 1958; *Woman, Dog, and Canoe*, 1982).

Birds, particularly crows, and domestic animals are among Colville's favorite subjects. "I have vi-cariously experienced the lives of numerous animals," he wrote in the introduction to the ca-talogue of his retrospective. Elsewhere he has said that he feels that "without animals everything is incomplete" and that he regards them "as being in-capable of evil." The sense of completeness for him that animals lend especially to home life is reflect-ed in *Dog, Boy and School Bus* (1960), *My Father With His Dog* (1968), *Cat and Artist* (1979), and many other pictures. The family cat with tail up-right strolls indifferently past a nude woman stand-ing on her head in *Headstand* (1982), but in the frequently reproduced *Refrigerator* (1977), when a nude couple raid the refrigerator for a late-night snack, their three well-fed cats eagerly join them for a handout.

Some of Colville's finest studies of animals, such as *Hound in Field* (1958) and *Moon and Cow* (1963), reveal his sensitivity to the harmony be-tween animals and a natural environment. In the latter painting, for example, the color pattern and contour of the cow are echoed in the land and sky, recalling Henry Moore's enunciation of the formal relationship between the human figure and land-scape. Commissioned in 1965 by the Canadian gov-ernment, after a nationwide competition, to design the commemorative coins for Canada's Centennial Year (1967), Colville symbolized his country through its wildlife, in widely acclaimed images of a pigeon, rabbit, mackerel, wildcat, wolf, and the Canada goose.

Like his several other treatments of husband-and-wife communication, *Refrigerator* is among Colville's more cheerful paintings. Gillian Mac-Kay, however, who finds the artist's "view" to be "essentially tragic," noted in *Maclean's* that even that work "is charged with an ambivalent mood of celebration and lament for a precious moment that must pass." Colville's pictures often have an unset-tling effect, sometimes because of the inclusion of puzzling objects or details, like the guns in *Pacific* and *Target Pistol and Man* (1980) or the bandaged arm of the service-station attendant in *Truck Stop* (1966). Subtleties in color and lighting evoke recur-ring melancholy and eeriness, with particular ef-fectiveness in *Night Walk* (1981), for example. Colville also heightens tension and expectation through his skillfully employed technique of freez-ing time and space, as in *Hound in Field, Family and Rain Storm* (1955), and dozens of other pic-tures. To increase its enigmatic quality, Colville may frame his picture in such a way as to cut off part of his figure—a device that, like his suspension of movement, was later exploited by the photoreal-ists.

For the past twenty years Colville has used acrylic paint, in place of oil or casein tempera, on sanded gesso-prepared wood board, rather than canvas. His layered overpainting on a smooth surface permits a sharp focus, as compared with his softer-edged serigraphs. He works painstakingly, sometimes spending three or more months on a single painting. Independent and craftsmanlike, he pulls his prints by hand and makes his own frames for his paintings and the crates for their shipment. His dealers are Fischer Fine Art Ltd. of London, England and the Mira Godard Gallery of Toronto.

Reviewing Colville's 1983 exhibition at the Art Gallery of Ontario for *Art in America* (April 1984), Ross Skoggard devoted part of his critique to the controversy surrounding the evaluation of his contribution to contemporary art. "Colville has not yet been properly assessed in his own country," Skoggard wrote. " . . . He is both admired for his workmanlike technique and denounced as a provincial embarrassment by the segment of the Canadian art world that takes its cue from international art magazines." John Bentley Mays maintained in the Toronto *Globe and Mail* (July 23, 1983), "Its widespread popularity and potential as a crowd-pleaser apart, Colville's art is worthy of inclusion in a small, didactic group show of realists from Canada's Atlantic region; nothing more." But the cover story in *Maclean's* (August 1, 1983), generated by the retrospective, included among its favorable assessments that of the British critic Terence Mullaly, who had earlier hailed Colville as "the most important realist in the Western world."

The selection of Colville in 1975 to design the commemorative medal for Governor General and Mrs. Jules Léger is one of many tributes paid to him. He served for a time on the visiting committee of the National Gallery of Canada, on the board of the National Museum of Canada, and, from 1966 to 1972, on the Canada Council, which awarded him the Molson Prize in 1975. Seven Canadian universities have conferred honorary degrees on him, including Acadia University, of which he was appointed chancellor in 1981. He was decorated an Officer of the Order of Canada in 1967 and a Companion in 1982.

Since 1973, when he moved from Sackville, Colville has been living in Wolfville, in a large stucco house built and once occupied by his wife's father, a well-to-do contractor. Alex and Rhoda Colville have three sons, Graham, John, and Charles, and a daughter, Ann. They appear from time to time in Colville's pictures, as do, more often, the artist and his wife. But the only self-portrait of direct confrontation in his mature work is that of *Target Pistol and Man*, which presents him as a trim, aging, solemn man with a furrowed forehead, penetrating blue eyes, and close-cropped graying blond hair. A documentary about Colville that was screened at the Festival of Festivals in Toronto in 1984 shows him to be a lover of order in his lifestyle as well as in his art. He is a politically concerned conservative whose admission to Mays in a Toronto *Globe and Mail* interview, "I do have a fear of chaos, and a strong sense of the fragility of civilization," goes far toward accounting for the disquieting presentiment that invades his visions of peace, contentment, and beauty.

References: Art J 24:318+ Summer '65; Macleans 96:42+ Ag 1 '83 por; Toronto Globe and Mail p33 N 26 '77 por, ET p1 Jl 23 '83 por; Contemporary Artists (1983); Who's Who in America, 1984-85

## Conti, Tom

Nov. 22, 1941– British actor and director.
Address: b. c/o Chatto and Linnit, Prince of Wales Theatre, Coventry St., London W1V 7FE, England

Tom Conti has been an actor virtually all of his adult life, but it was not until 1973—after fifteen "not terribly illustrious," to use his words, years in the business—that a part in Christopher Hampton's *Savages* enabled him to quit singing in restaurants for a living, and not until 1976 that his casting as Adam Morris in the much praised British television series *Glittering Prizes* brought him widespread recognition. Since then, Conti's acting gifts, which include a resonant voice, a broad emotional range, a mobile, expressive face, and a razor-sharp wit, have earned him international acclaim and his choice of a variety of roles. Among the more notable parts he has played are the lascivious Norman in the British television trilogy *The Norman Conquests*, the paralyzed sculptor in the stage play *Whose Life Is It Anyway?*, for which he received "best actor" awards from the Society of West End Theatre in London and the League of New York Theaters and Producers, and the besotted Scottish poet Gowan McGland in the film *Reuben, Reuben*.

Tom Conti was born in Paisley in western Scotland on November 22, 1941, the only child of Mary (McGoldrick) Conti, a native of Paisley, and her husband, Alfonso Conti, an Italian immigrant. Both of his parents worked as hairdressers. As a dark-haired Catholic growing up in the fair-haired, Presbyterian community of Ralston, Tom Conti "felt definitely an outsider, and not particularly wanted," as he told Alan Wallach in an interview for Newsday (August 19, 1979). His sense of alienation was heightened by the harrowing stories his father told about his life as an internee on the Isle of Man, where he was briefly detained as an undesirable alien during the early days of World War II. Perhaps in an effort to fill the lonely hours, Conti began taking piano lessons when he was just four years old. According to Hugh McIlvanney, who interviewed him for the London Observer (April 29, 1979), by the time he was six, he was "threatening to be a genuine prodigy." After his graduation from the Hamilton Park School in nearby Glasgow, Conti enrolled at the Royal Scottish Academy of Music and Drama, also in Glasgow. He had intended to become a professional musician, but one day, on a whim, he auditioned for the drama department. From that moment, he was hooked. While he concedes that acting school gave him a solid foundation in the classics of the English theatre, Conti has repeatedly insisted that his instructors did not teach him how to act. "Nobody can do that," he explained to Robert Berkvist of the New York Times (April 22, 1979). "If you have the instinct, you'll develop a memory for it, somehow. You become a sponge, soaking up character. You don't have any control over it."

Conti served a traditional apprenticeship in repertory at the Glasgow Citizens' Theatre, making his first stage appearance, as Willie, a minor character in Joe Corrie's The Roving Boy, a play about the young Robert Burns, in February 1959. Over the next dozen years, he took what jobs he could find in repertory theatres "here and there" and in television, most notably Mother of Men, in 1959, but he "spent a lot of time being unemployed." To pay the bills, he played flamenco guitar in restaurants and worked part-time as a tour guide. Looking back on those lean years, he told Joyce Wadler in a conversation for a New York Daily News (April 15, 1979) profile, "I do think an artist needs a little bit of hardship. Not starving in a garret, but enough pain to make him realize the pain of other people."

In the fall of 1972 Conti finally achieved a measure of critical success in two plays: Cecil P. Taylor's The Black and White Minstrels, which was produced at the Traverse Theatre Club in Edinburgh in September under the direction of Michael Rudman; and David Mercer's Let's Murder Vivaldi, a production of the King's Head Theatre Club, in north London. In The Black and White Minstrels, a wicked comedy about contemporary social radicalism, Conti portrayed Harry Vine, the boisterous "bedroom philosopher," to use Jeremy Kingston's term, in a ménage à quatre of Glaswegian leftists.

A little more than a month later, he played the part of Ben, the young architect who seems to thrive on violent confrontations with his live-in girlfriend in Robert Gillespie's staging of Let's Murder Vivaldi, Mercer's clinical dissection of intimate relationships. His performance, along with those of his three fellow actors, was praised as "brilliant" and "memorable" by reviewers.

The turning point in Conti's career, in his own view, came when he landed the part of Carlos, the intellectual Brazilian terrorist in Savages, Christopher Hampton's impassioned attack on political and social corruption, which opened at the Royal Court Theatre in London in April 1973 and eventually transferred to the West End. Directed by Robert Kidd, Savages starred Paul Scofield as the kidnapped British diplomat whom Carlos engages in a lengthy ideological debate before executing him. Among the mostly favorable notices was that of the British reviewer for Variety (April 25, 1973), who singled out Conti as a "standout in support" whose "study of his character is admirable in every fluent detail."

Conti's impressive performance in Savages won him the assignment of playing Charles Bovary in the BBC's adaptation of Gustave Flaubert's Madame Bovary, which was seen in the United States in October 1976 on PBS's Masterpiece Theatre, as well as his first film role, as Andrea in Joseph Losey's Galileo (American Film Theatre, 1975), an overlong and uninspired version of the Bertolt Brecht play. Conti then landed a leading role in Flame (VPS/Goodtimes, 1975), about the marketing of a fictional troupe of rock musicians that starred the popular group Slade. His characterization of the group's slick, cynical promoter was judged by Derek Malcolm, the Guardian's film critic, to be "well-nigh perfect."

Continuing his stage work, Conti reprised the role of Harry Vine in a production of The Black and White Minstrels at the Hampstead Theatre Club in January 1974. Later in the year, at the same theatre, he played Enrico Zamati, a frenetic Italian peddling a harebrained scheme to sell sexy underwear to Arabs in Mike Stott's comedy Other People. He returned to the Hampstead Theatre Club in May 1976 to enact the title character in an anonymous eighteenth-century English translation of Molière's Don Juan. Two months later, at the Aldwych Theatre in London's West End, his sly, mischievous, and outrageously seductive Dick Dudgeon in the Royal Shakespeare Company's acclaimed production of George Bernard Shaw's The Devil's Disciple delighted audiences and critics alike.

It was not stage or film, however, but television that finally brought Tom Conti stardom when, in 1976, he played Adam Morris, the middle-class, Jewish outsider among a group of upper-class Cambridge University students in the six-part BBC-TV series The Glittering Prizes, which traced the characters' lives from the 1950s to the mid-1970s. Conti's interpretation of the brilliant, savagely funny Adam, who outwits the rules of the game of social climbing by becoming a famous screenwriter, came in for nearly as much critical admiration as Frederick Raphael's literate script. For his contribution, he was named Britain's "best TV actor" in 1976. *The Glittering Prizes* was broadcast in the United States on public television in January 1978 and again in November 1980, at which time the *New York Times* television critic John J. O'Connor observed that, as Adam Morris, Conti was "far more versatile and dazzling than he was in the constrained lead of Broadway's *Who's Life Is It Anyway?*

Even more applause attended Conti's next television venture, in which he portrayed the irrepressible, skirt-chasing title character in Alan Ayckbourn's comic trilogy *The Norman Conquests*. In a part that called on him to exhibit "a considerable degree of outrageous, articulate, and manipulative charm," as Diana Loercher, the television critic for the *Christian Science Monitor*, expressed it in her review of June 9, 1978, Conti used "his soulful, dark eyes and shaggy appearance to give Norman an added dimension of pseudosensitivity and warmth. Picture a basset hound with a sense of humor and a devious nature." Largely because of Conti's engaging performance, *The Norman Conquests*, which was aired in the United States in June 1978 by PBS's *Great Performances*, became one of the most popular dramatic series in the history of public television.

Some time elapsed before Conti came upon a vehicle to equal *The Glittering Prizes* or *The Norman Conquests*. In the interim, he played identical twin brothers, one of whom disappears from a sailboat during an eclipse of the moon, in the suspense film *Eclipse* (EMI International, 1977), a supporting role in *Full Circle* (Fester Productions, 1977), an occult thriller starring Mia Farrow, and a sympathetic doctor in *The Duellists* (Paramount, 1977), Ridley Scott's visually dazzling motion picture based on a Joseph Conrad short story about a long-running feud between two of Napoleon's cavalry officers. Conti was only slightly more fortunate on the stage, where his roles included Frederick the Great in the Cambridge Theatre Company's staging of Romulus Linney's turgid historical drama *The Sorrows of Frederick*.

Conti finally came into his own again when he created at the Mermaid Theatre in London the role for which he perhaps is best known—that of Ken Harrison in *Whose Life Is It Anyway?* Paralyzed after his spinal cord is severed in a car accident, Harrison, a former sculptor unwilling to live out his days shackled to a life-support system, pleads for the right to exercise control over his own existence and die on his own terms. "I've always felt that people have had that right—the right to chuck it all when the only answer to life's problems is death . . . ," Conti told Robert Berkvist in an interview for a *New York Times* (April 22, 1979) profile. "This play isn't about [euthanasia], but about suicide; it's a *choice*. If your death is not going to hurt somebody else, I don't think anybody has a right to deny it to you. Especially to ask a person to remain

alive against their will and go through torment is an act bordering on savagery."

Originally scripted for television, *Whose Life Is It Anyway?* was the first professional effort of Brian Clark. According to Hugh McIlvanney, Conti and Michael Lindsay-Hogg, the director, helped to give the play its final theatrical shape, not only by reinterpreting it for the stage but also by revising speeches, excising some lines and bits of stage business, and adding dialogue, in particular a few jokes that the actor invented both to fill awkward pauses and to underscore the irreverent defiance of his character. The role was the most demanding of Conti's career, for as he explained to Robert Berkvist, he had to "go limp, switching off everything below the neck," and rely only on his face and voice to convey Harrison's passionate intelligence, humor, and creative energy as he argues his case before the hospital staff and the audience.

After playing to capacity houses for three months at the Mermaid Theatre, *Whose Life Is It Anyway?* moved, in June 1978, to the Savoy Theatre in the West End, where it settled in for a long run. Conti eventually repeated the role of Harrison on Broadway, but first he had to endure a series of hearings before the Actors Equity Council, in which the play's New York producers responded to Equity's argument that he would have to yield the part to an American because he did not fit the union's definition of an "international star." Conti won his case only after producer Emanuel Azenberg, the New York drama critic Clive Barnes, and Robert Lantz, a talent agent, testified in his behalf at a special arbitration meeting. That Conti's supporters were justified in their defense of the actor was borne out by the rapturous opening night notices. Three months later, critics were still awestruck by the dexterity of his performance. "The man's range is so great that he can outdistance those around him without making any use at all of their showier equipment: arms, legs, torsos . . . ," Walter Kerr wrote in the *New York Times* (July 1, 1979). "A grand tour of the emotions without a finger lifted."

In the fall of 1979, Conti left the cast of *Whose Life Is It Anyway?* to direct the Broadway production of Frank D. Gilroy's new play, *Last Licks*. The three-character drama revolves around a confrontation between a recently widowed father and his middle-aged son over whether the father should go to a nursing home or hire a housekeeper. The situation is further complicated when the father's ex-mistress applies for the job. Panned by critics as a contrived and "talky" psychological drama, *Last Licks* closed after only twenty-five performances at the Longacre Theatre. Conti, however, in his first directorial assignment, was commended for having "done creditably with virtually impossible material," in the opinion of the reviewer for *Variety* (November 21, 1979).

Immediately after his return to England in December 1979, Conti set to work directing the Oxford Playhouse Company in *Before the Party*, Rodney Ackland's adaptation of a W. Somerset

Maugham story about a respectable family thrown into upheaval when the oldest daughter confesses that she murdered her husband. After a short pre-West End tour, the play opened at the Queen's Theatre in London in March 1980 to generally favorable reviews. The actor subsequently directed a short-lived West End production of *Last Licks*, retitled *The Housekeeper*, at the Apollo Theatre in February 1982 and, later in the same year, the British premiere of Christopher Durang's satiric look at neurotic New Yorkers, *Beyond Therapy*, at the Gate at the Latchmere, a dinner theatre in South London. Perhaps because he is an actor himself, Conti is able to coax unusually strong performances from his casts, even in mediocre vehicles. "Acting is like walking a tightrope, with Niagara below you and the wire stretching ahead," he explained to Robert Berkvist in the *New York Times* interview. "It's the director's job to make sure nothing causes turbulence when you're out there in the middle. He should be constantly underneath with the safety net, correcting any signs of imbalance."

Conti himself was back onstage in September 1980, starring in the London version of the Broadway hit *They're Playing Our Song*, a musical comedy about the stormy relationship between an egocentric composer and his free-spirited lyricist. Both he and his costar, Gemma Craven, were warmly applauded by the critics, Conti for his way with one-liners and his "mischievously ironic style," if not for his singing voice, which the London *Sunday Telegraph*'s Francis King compared to "James Stewart doing his bit at a wartime Stage Door Canteen." Conti remained with the long-running show until the summer of 1981 and returned to it briefly in March 1982 to fill in for his injured successor. Equally congenial was the part of playwright Jason Carmichael in Bernard Slade's stylish *Romantic Comedy*, which began a respectable run at London's Apollo Theatre in the spring of 1983. Two years later, the actor assumed a leading role in *Two Into One*, Ray Cooney's popular sex farce.

The motion picture *Reuben, Reuben* (Twentieth Century-Fox, 1983) added further luster to Conti's reputation. An adaptation of a 1964 novel by Peter De Vries, the film was scripted by one of Hollywood's most experienced writers, Julius J. Epstein, and directed by Robert Ellis Miller, but it was still seen as a personal tour de force for Conti. Among those reviewers enchanted by the actor's portrayal of a scruffy, womanizing Scottish poet was *Time* magazine's Richard Corliss. "This delightful English actor uses all his honed tools—the dimples, the fluty voice, the hermit-crab walk, the little-boy eyes—to steal every scene just by being in it," Corliss wrote in his appraisal of January 2, 1984. "Petty and poetic, desperate and delightful, Conti's Gowan is the funniest portrayal of a down-on-his-art genius since Alec Guinness's Gulley Jimson in *The Horse's Mouth*." The performance earned him an Academy Award nomination for best actor of the year.

Conti's other recent screen credits include *Merry Christmas, Mr. Lawrence* (Universal, 1983), in which he took the part of a British officer struggling to preserve his sanity and dignity in a Japanese prisoner-of-war camp during World War II, and *American Dreamer* (Warner Brothers, 1984), a romantic adventure about a vacationing American housewife and a rumpled English playboy caught up in international intrigue. In April 1984 Conti costarred with Liza Minnelli in a whimisical adaptation of "The Princess and The Pea" for *Faerie Tale Theater*, a children's series on the cable television service Showtime.

A man of short stature and slight build, Tom Conti has a long, broad-nosed face, large, expressive brown eyes, and thick black hair. Because he believes that audiences become distracted if they know too much about a performer, he rarely grants interviews. "The more people get to know about you, then the more difficult it is to convince them that you're Richard III or Joe Blokes, the bus driver," he explained recently, as quoted in the *Aquarian* (September 7, 1983). "So it's better actually just to keep a low profile as far as the job is concerned."

Married for nearly twenty years to the actress Kara Wilson, Conti laughs at the notion that his personal life bears any resemblance to the womanizing characters he so frequently plays. His daring is all in his work, in which he is a relentless experimenter. "The most exciting thing," he once told a reporter for *Time*, "is to be on the razor's edge and not cut your feet." Conti lives with his wife and their daughter, Nina, in the Hampstead section of London.

References: Esquire 103:112+ Ap '85 por; London Observer p33 Ap 29 '79 por; London Times p11 Je 9 '78 por; N Y Daily News Leisure p13 Je 11 '78 por, Leisure p3 Ap 15 '79 por; N Y Post p35 N 16 '79 por; N Y Times II p1+ Ap 22 '79 por; Newsday p20+ Ag 19 '79 por; People 11:126+ Je 18 '79 pors; Time 113:57 Ap 30 '79 pors; Who's Who, 1985-86; Who's Who in the Theatre (1981)

---

## Crenshaw, Ben

*Jan. 11, 1952– Professional golfer. Address: b. c/o United States Golf Association, Liberty Corners Rd., Far Hills, N.J. 07931*

Although some professional golfers have won more major tournaments and others have collected more in winnings, Ben Crenshaw remains after twelve years one of the most popular and talented players on the grueling PGA circuit. In spite of his roller-coaster career, his all-American looks, charisma, and grace under pressure have made him a gallery favorite from his days at the University of Texas, where he was heralded as the next Jack Nicklaus, to the 1984 Masters Tournament, where he ended

Ben Crenshaw

a decade of frustration to capture his first major-championship title.

Ben Daniel Crenshaw was born on January 11, 1952 in Austin, Texas to Pearl (Johnson) Crenshaw, an elementary school teacher from Tazewell, Virginia, and Charles Edward Crenshaw 4th, an attorney who had worked as an assistant to State Attorney General Price Daniel. The Crenshaws gave Ben his middle name in honor of Daniel, who later became a United States senator and governor of Texas. Ben Crenshaw has two siblings: Bonnie, who is ten years his senior, and Charles Edward 5th, who is one year older. Members of the family treasured Pearl Crenshaw, and her death of a heart attack in 1974, during Ben's second year on the Professional Golfers Association (PGA) tour, traumatized them.

A scratch golfer himself, Charlie Crenshaw introduced his son to the game at the Country Club of Austin. "I got exposed to golf by riding around in a cart while dad played," he told Louis Sabin in an interview for the *Washington Post's Parade* magazine (June 2, 1974). "When I finally got to play regularly, all my dad said was I'd have to learn how to play the right way, and by the rules." Ben learned those lessons quickly, winning his first tournament—the Casis Elementary Invitation—in the fourth grade with a score of 96. Continuing to improve, he shot a 74 for eighteen holes when he was ten and three years later qualified for the state junior tournament—a major event in Texas—with an impressive score of 69. Perhaps overly confident, he then neglected golf in order to spend more time with his girlfriend, but after failing to make the cut for the next year's state junior tournament he applied himself more diligently to his game. At fifteen he won that championship, a feat he repeated in 1968, as well as the first of three consecutive

Austin City championships, and in 1968 he took his first national title when he outperformed the field at the Jaycees Junior Championship.

"I was so lucky in having the competition to play against. There is no substitute for that," he admitted to Herbert Warren Wind in the *New Yorker* (June 10, 1985). "When you grow up with a Tom Kite in the same town, and you play against him from the age of ten on, it's bound to help." While in high school he also played other future professionals, including Bruce Lietzke and Bill Rogers. Nevertheless, Harvey Penick, the house pro at the Country Club of Austin and a well-known instructor for over four decades, was even more influential in shaping and improving his game. Crenshaw never took formal lessons from Penick, but he had always turned to him whenever he had a problem with his game that he could not work out himself. "He stressed the natural moves—what was natural for me," Crenshaw recalled in the *New Yorker* (May 13, 1974). "He never tried to change any particular part of my swing. He doesn't believe in too much analysis. Sometimes he'd just ask me what my shots were doing—if they were going left or right—and then he'd say, 'Go right ahead. Keep playing.'"

At Austin High School, Crenshaw did not limit his activities to golf: he broadjumped and played guard in basketball, quarterback in football, and catcher in baseball. But golf continued to exert the strongest pull on him, and throughout high school he played up to thirty-six holes a day, ten months a year. His hard work paid off when he was a senior. Although an attack of bursitis kept him from competing in the U.S. Amateur Open, he finished thirty-second in the field at his first U.S. Open—ahead of such seasoned professionals as Gary Player, Arnold Palmer, and Jack Nicklaus—and tied John Mahaffey for the low amateur medal. After that stunning performance, Lee Trevino, with whom Crenshaw had been paired for a round in that tournament, termed him "the best eighteen-year-old golfer [he had] ever seen." Crenshaw then went on to win eighteen of the nineteen tournaments he entered that year.

Awarded a golf scholarship, Crenshaw entered the University of Texas in 1971 with the intention of majoring in business administration. His presence and performance served as a catalyst for his Longhorn teammates at the four-day National Collegiate Athletic Association (NCAA) Tournament at the Tucson National Golf Club. Playing a whirlwind round of golf on the final day, he led his team past a University of Florida squad that seemed to wilt under the Longhorns' pressure, and he captured the individual title—the first freshman ever to do so—with a record fifteen-under-par 273 for the tournament. He went on that year to win five other championships, to place fifth at the U.S. Amateur Open, and to tie for twenty-seventh at the U.S. Open against stiff professional competition. For his accomplishments, he was named to the 1971 All-America collegiate golf team.

Impressed by his abilities, critics of the game classed him with Arnold Palmer and Jack Nicklaus. Unlike most golfers, Crenshaw draws the club back past parallel, but his smooth downswing and strong legs combine to give him great distance on his drives. The ease with which he routinely sinks difficult putts or saves balls in traps or hazards also seemed to warrant comparing him with the masters of the sport. Crenshaw justified the critics' high praise at the 1972 NCAA tournament at Cape Coral, Florida, where he sank a thirty-foot putt on the final hole to share the first-place prize with his teammate and archrival, Tom Kite. In addition to capturing ten more championship titles in 1972, including the Trans-Mississippi Amateur and the Porter Cup, Crenshaw scored a 288 at the U.S. Amateur Open to tie Mark Hayes for second place and was named to the U.S. World Amateur Cup team. He fared almost as well against the pros, placing nineteenth and winning low-amateur honors at his first Masters Tournament and fighting to an amazing tie for third at the Heritage Classic in South Carolina that fall.

Crenshaw's academic performance was less impressive, however. "I think it'll take me eight years to get my degree," he admitted to Barry McDermott in *Sports Illustrated* (July 3, 1972). "All through college, I've never had anything on my mind except golf. I can't get interested in anything else." Nevertheless, he hesitated to join the pro tour before finishing his studies because he wanted a college degree in case his golfing skills failed him. But after clinching his third NCAA title at Springwater, Oklahoma, on June 23, 1973, and winning ten other championships that year, Crenshaw could no longer resist the temptation to turn professional. In mid-August 1973 he entered the mandatory PGA Players School competition and, three days later, overwhelmed the field with a twelve-stroke lead during the 144-hole qualifier to receive his approved player's card.

Few players in the history of golf have made a more auspicious debut than Ben Crenshaw. In his first appearance in a professional tournament, the seventy-two-hole, $125,000 San Antonio-Texas Open in November 1973, he played with the poise of a veteran. On the last day, after shrugging off a watery bogey on the Woodlake Golf Course's ninth hole and twice extricating himself from ties with George Archer and Orville Moody, he coolly finished the tournament with a fourteen-under-par 270 to capture the $25,000 first prize.

Just three weeks later, Crenshaw injected new life into the eight-round, $500,000 World Open in Pinehurst, North Carolina. He made his presence felt in the sixth round, shooting a seven-under-par 64 in a blustering wind—one of the best rounds, according to experts, played in fifty years on that demanding and often-tested course. That score brought him from a distant twenty-fifth into serious contention with a tie for second place. Although he maintained a nip-and-tuck battle with Miller Barber on the final day, a bad swing at a tee shot on the par-five sixteenth hole resulted in a bogey and he lost by one stroke. In his account of the tournament for *Sports Illustrated* (November 26, 1973),

Dan Jenkins described the rookie as "a thrilling personality with devastating talent and potential," a view that Miller Barber shared. "He's the best that's come along since Nicklaus," Barber said. "He's gonna be the new gunner. I knew when I beat him that I'd done beat somebody."

In just six weeks on the tour, Crenshaw captured $76,749 in prize money. His seemingly effortless game and easy-going manner earned the respect of the other pros, and his boyish good looks attracted a faithful following of young women groupies dubbed "Ben's Bunnies" or "Ben's Wrens." But trying too hard to fulfill others' expectations after his spectacular start as a pro, he faltered, finishing twenty-fourth at the Masters and missing the cut at the U.S. Open. Although he took two second-place prizes and finished in the top ten three other times in 1974, he again failed to make the thirty-six hole cut at the U.S. Open and, according to Herbert Warren Wind in the *New Yorker* (May 13, 1974), played "perhaps his least solid golf of the past four years." His most impressive showing in 1975, at the U.S. Open at Medinah, Illinois, resulted in a tie with three other players for third when, after making a heartbreaking shot into the water on the seventeenth hole, he missed the playoff with Lou Graham and John Mahaffey by one stroke. The ranks of Ben's Wrens thinned, and the media focused less frequently on the PGA's highly touted golden boy. His confidence badly shaken, Crenshaw considered leaving the tour.

With some help from Bob Toski, a professional golf instructor, Crenshaw began to regain his confidence and with it his magic. "He made some minor changes in my swing," Crenshaw told Bob Sherrill in an interview for *People* (April 12, 1976), "but mainly he worked on my mental attitude. I was about five inches from becoming an outstanding golfer—that's the distance between my left ear and my right one." Once again fighting his way to the top, he finally nabbed his second professional win at the Bing Crosby Pro-Am Open in Pebble Beach, California on January 25 with a seven-under-par 281, defeating Jack Nicklaus, the leader going into the fourth round, by ten strokes.

The very next week, Crenshaw netted $46,000 and his second straight tournament at the Hawaiian Open in Honolulu. His four-round total of 270 (eighteen under par) broke the Waialae Country Club's course record and reestablished him as one of the game's brightest young stars. Later that year, Crenshaw captured the first-place purse at the $150,000 Ohio King's Island Open and went on to take his first European title with a victory at the Irish Open at Portmarnock. At the end of 1976, after adding a second-place finish at the Masters to his honors, he ranked second only to Nicklaus on the PGA's annual money list.

Although victories at the three major tournaments on the PGA tour—the U.S. Open, the Masters Tournament, and the British Open—continued to elude him over the next five years, Crenshaw added a number of championships to his name, including the $200,000 Colonial National Invitational in 1977, the Phoenix Open and the National Team Championship (with George Burns) in 1979, and the Anheuser-Busch Classic and the Walt Disney World Team Championship in 1980. In addition, at the Bing Crosby Pro-Am in 1978 and 1981 and at the Western Open and PGA Championship in 1979, among other tourneys, he came agonizingly close to victory, only to take second place after losing a hole in the sudden-death playoff. As a result of his consistent game, from 1976 to 1981 he often earned over $200,000, and never less than $100,000, on the tour.

Perhaps Crenshaw's most disappointing near-misses during those years occurred in the British Open. As an ardent golf historian, he had read everything he could about the many classic matches fought out on the famous golf links of the British Isles, especially accounts of the 1926 British Open, in which the legendary golfer Bobby Jones, whom Crenshaw idolizes, took the title in his first attempt. Quickly advancing from twenty-eighth place at his first British Open in 1974, he took third in the Open at Turnberry three years later and finished in a four-way tie for second behind Jack Nicklaus at St. Andrews in 1978. His special reverence for the British Open only intensified his anguish in 1979: he was in strong contention until he duffed the seventy-first hole with a double-bogey six to lose the match to the Spaniard Severiano Ballesteros. In 1980 he ended his tournament in third place with a four-round total of 277, six shots behind a victorious Tom Watson.

In spite of those frustrations, Crenshaw returns to the British Isles almost every year to play in the British Open; to explore the lesser-known courses in England and Scotland, his detailed knowledge of which, according to Herbert Warren Wind, "bowls over British golf authorities"; or occasionally to guide tourists around the more famous courses while recounting, stroke by stroke, some memorable holes played at celebrated matches. He explained his love for the British golf links in the *Chicago Tribune* (July 18, 1982): "Back home, our courses are built with bulldozers, with smooth fairways and sculptured contours. Here the links courses were created by the interaction of rain, wind, snow, tides, erosion, even sheep and burrowing animals. Here, it's man against the elements, golf in its natural state."

In 1982, after taking the Mexico Open and tying for second at the PGA Championship at Royal Melbourne, Australia, Ben Crenshaw once again went into a slump, missing the cut for the PGA Championship at Southern Hills and dropping to eighty-third on the 1982 money list. With his confidence in his swing shattered, he left the tour in August to reassess his game. "People were telling me all kinds of things and trying to help," he told Sarah Pileggi in *Sports Illustrated* (May 14, 1984). "But by then it was going in one ear and out the other. . . . I was a basket case." With the help of Charlie Crenshaw, Harvey Penick, and his former college roommate Brent Buckman, Ben Crenshaw realized that in trying to make his unorthodox swing conform to

the classic model he had abandoned the form that was most natural for him. Once he stopped analyzing his swing and allowed his instinct and muscles to work for him, he was able to concentrate on his aim and to hit the ball unerringly again. With his faith in himself renewed, he returned to the tour to tie Tom Kite for second at the 1983 Masters Tournament in April and to win the Byron Nelson Classic at Irving, Texas a few weeks later.

As one of the best and most personable players of his generation never to have won a major title, Crenshaw had the entire golfing world behind him at the 1984 Masters as he took a one-stroke lead with a first-round 67 and then dropped two shots behind Tom Kite's nine-under-par 207 over the next thirty-six holes. In spite of the enormous pressure, Crenshaw continued to play smoothly during the fourth round. With a ten-foot putt for a birdie on the ninth hole, he moved into the back side with a three-under-par 33 to take a one-stroke lead over Kite and a two-stroke lead over Larry Nelson.

When Crenshaw sank a seemingly impossible sixty-foot putt on the tenth hole his opponents were visibly shaken. Using an iron on the twelfth tee, Nelson splashed into the creek to take a double bogey. Moments later, after Crenshaw birdied the twelfth, Kite also found the water with a seven-iron: he holed out with a triple bogey that shattered his hopes for victory. Playing conservatively, Crenshaw hit safe tee shots to the fat part of the green on the thirteenth hole for par and on the fifteenth for a birdie rather than gambling on his woods or irons for a more spectacular eagle and took par on the fourteenth hole with a fifteen-foot second putt. Although a bogey on the seventeenth narrowed his lead to two strokes over Tom Watson, who had finished the round, Crenshaw insured his victory with a perfect three-wood shot into the eighteenth fairway and a five iron onto the green, twenty feet from the cup. He holed out with two putts for par to take the title by two strokes with a final score of 277 (eleven under par). For winning that tournament, his first major victory in his eleven years on the tour, he received not only the highly prized green blazer awarded to all Masters champions but also a $108,000 first-place purse.

Soon after that long-awaited victory, Crenshaw seemed to lose his touch once again. By June 1985, he had failed to make the cut for eight tournaments and fallen to 133d on the money list. "My golf game is much like my emotions—ups and downs and long, deep, dark spells," he admitted in *Sports Illustrated* (May 14, 1984). "But that's kind of the way I am. That's my personality."

Sandy-haired, blue-eyed Ben Crenshaw, who stands five feet nine inches tall and weighs about 165 pounds, has an easy-going manner both on and off the golf links that has earned him the nickname of "Gentle Ben." Since his divorce in October 1984 from Polly Speno, whom he wed on June 29, 1975, he has remained single. A dedicated student of golf history and of golf-course architecture, he is one of the best-known members of the Golf Collectors' Society. In addition to the miniature clubs, golf painting and sculpture, and memorabilia that he has acquired over the years, he owns about 400 golf books, many of them rare editions printed in Britain at the turn of the century. He has also written extensively about the game and contributed an introduction to a United States Golf Association 1982 special edition of Sir Walter Simpson's classic *The Art of Golf*. He would like to become a golf course architect when he retires, and currently he is helping Byron Nelson to design at the Las Colinas Country Club in Texas a new course, scheduled to

open in the spring of 1986, for the Byron Nelson Golf Classic. A life-long bird-watching enthusiast with a special fondness for birds of prey, he is the PGA's only lifetime member of the National Audubon Society.

References: *New Yorker* 50:102+ My 13 '74, 60:72+ My 28 '84, 61:102+ Je 10 '85; *Sports Illus* 40:32+ F 11 '74 pors, 60:42+ My 14 '84 pors, 62:66+ Je 3 '85 pors; Hobbs, Michael. *50 Masters of Golf* (1984); *Who's Who in America*, 1984-85

## Davis, Al(len)

*July 4, 1929– Football executive. Address: b. Los Angeles Raiders, 332 Center St., El Segundo, Calif. 90245*

An ever-controversial rebel, Al Davis is the managing general partner and "total boss" of the fabled Los Angeles Raiders. Often abrasive and sometimes devious, Davis has not hesitated to buck the powerful National Football League and Commissioner Pete Rozelle to achieve his goals. In 1982 he transferred his team from Oakland to Los Angeles in defiance of the league's rules, a move upheld after years of court battles. Long known as "the Genius," and as an innovative strategist and hard worker, Al Davis acquired his football smarts in a turbulent career as head coach, general manager, league commissioner, and part-owner that began in 1963 when he set about refashioning the Oakland Raiders in his image. Brawling their way to the top record in professional sports—217 wins, 11 ties, and 87 losses in twenty winning seasons—the

Raiders have won the world championship three times, in Super Bowls XI, XV, and XVIII.

Alluding to the contradictory images that Davis presents to football pundits, Al Stump noted in *Los Angeles* magazine (November 1984) that "whatever Davis really is—powermonger, mad genius, super egoist, brilliant strategist, renegade opportunist, skilled motivator—he's got one big thing going for him. Everybody loves a winner. And how can you help but love someone whose only goal is 'Just Win, Baby, Win'?"

Allen Davis was born in Brockton, Massachusetts on July 4, 1929 to Rose (Kirschenbaum) Davis and Louis Davis, the well-to-do proprietor of a clothing store and other enterprises. When "Al" Davis was five, his family moved to the Crown Heights section of Brooklyn, where he attended P.S. 189, Winthrop Junior High, and Erasmus Hall High School. His sports idols were men in positions of power such as George Weiss, a general manager of the Yankees, and Branch Rickey, an owner of the Brooklyn Dodgers, perhaps because, as he related to writer Michael Janofsky of the *New York Times* (September 2, 1984), his own dream was "to build the finest organization in sports." "And some day, in some way, I would be in control," he added. "I'd have the greatest players, the greatest coaches. We'd play the greatest games. . . . I wanted it to be the ultimate."

After spending a year at Syracuse University, in 1947 Davis attended Wittenberg College in Springfield, Ohio for a semester on an athletic scholarship. Still dissatisfied, he then transferred to Hartwick College in Oneonta, New York, but after only two weeks there he returned to Syracuse University, where he obtained an A.B. degree in English in 1950. Although only a mediocre athlete himself, he already believed that he could motivate others "to do things well . . . [and also] dominate them and make them do it."

Sidestepping a career in the family business, in the fall of 1950 Al Davis fast-talked Edward Stanczyk into hiring him as a football line coach under John Cerny at Adelphi College in Garden City, Long Island; in addition, he doubled as baseball coach, the youngest head baseball coach ever hired by an American college. As Stanczyk told Robert Lindsey in an interview for the *New York Times Magazine* (December 13, 1981), even at twenty Davis was making his mark as an innovator: "He was a great fundamentalist who knew how to block and tackle; he was the first coach I know who advocated a four-man line. He tried to sell it, but nobody would accept it; now everybody does." When he was drafted into the United States Army in 1952 and assigned to special services at Fort Belvoir, Virginia, Davis became the first private ever to serve as the head coach of a military team, and one who quickly built an impressive football team that lost only two games during his two-year tenure. But his alleged underhanded methods for securing professional and college stars who had been drafted nearly triggered a congressional investigation into the coddling of athletes. Nevertheless, after Davis' discharge in 1954 his recruiting abilities helped him to land a job as one of the forty player-personnel scouts for Weeb Ewbank, then the coach of the Baltimore Colts, and in 1955-56 he was hired as a line coach and chief recruiter for The Citadel.

Several of his best recruits left The Citadel with Davis when, in 1957, he accepted a post as line coach for the University of Southern California (USC), whose football team, then on probation for recruiting violations, had lost all but one of its ten games that year. Describing himself as "wild-eyed about tactics and strategy," Davis credits the USC Trojans' head coach Don Clark, "a great fundamentalist" who also started at USC in 1957, with giving him invaluable insights into technical football—"an area that [he] wasn't totally interested in." Among his own contributions to the Trojans, Davis persuaded the reluctant head coach to implement his new blocking system called "Go-Go-with-Oomph," which Al Stump described in the Los Angeles magazine article as "a kind of hit-'em-and-then-hit-'em-again double block." That offensive maneuver helped the Trojans to rebound and chalk up a 8-2-0 won-lost record in 1959. Sports analysts also give Davis the credit for providing the team with many of the players who carried the Trojans to victory in the 1962 national championship. In 1959 Davis was placed in charge of the Trojans' defense, and when Clark retired at the end of that season, he recommended two of his assistants—Davis and John McKay—as promising candidates for head coach, but officials of USC, whose probation had ended the year before, shied away from the controversial defensive coach and chose McKay.

A disappointed Davis returned to professional football in a much more important position when he signed on as offensive end coach for the Los Angeles Chargers in 1960, the first year of play for the new American Football League (AFL). Although the AFL recruiters faced stiff competition for talent from the established National Football League (NFL), "baby-sitting" promising college stars who were also sought after by the NFL proved to be Davis' forte. As Don Kowet wrote in The Rich Who Own Sports (1977): "He would spirit a prospect away in the dead of night, book him into a hotel in some forgotten backwater and talk until the prospect was dizzy enough to have signed his own

death warrant." In Sports Illustrated (November 4, 1963) Walter Bingham contended that three of Davis' recruits—end Lance Alworth, tackle Ron Mix, and back Paul Lowe—were pivotal in leading the Chargers to the top of the AFL in 1963, and Davis also helped the Chargers to transform their passing game into one of the best in the league. In 1962 head coach Sid Gillman made his now famous appraisal of his young assistant: "There isn't a doubt in Al Davis' mind that right now he's the smartest guy in the game. He isn't, but he will be pretty damned soon."

Davis' reputation for abrasive aggressiveness led to his appointment, on January 15, 1963, as both head coach and general manager of the AFL Oakland Raiders, a virtually stillborn franchise that had lost thirty-three of its first forty-two games. As Wayne Valley, one of the team's owners, recalled, "We needed someone who wanted to win so badly, he would do anything." After turning down the owners' first two offers, Davis only accepted the position when he was given absolute control of the team. Overhauling the roster, he retained such stalwarts as All-League center Jim Otto and quarterbacks Cotton Davidson and Tom Flores, acquired free agent Art Powell as a wide receiver, and traded three players to the Buffalo Bills for Archie Matsos, a middle linebacker. On the field, he inaugurated "pressure football," a painstakingly mapped offense centered on the long pass and new defensive formulations, including the "bump and run," in which cornerbacks and safeties throw one hard block or "bump" at receivers before covering them on their downfield patterns.

Al Davis, the youngest person ever to be the head coach and general manager of a professional football team, worked hard to transform the Raiders' image. He changed the team colors to black and silver, assigned it the motto "Pride and Poise," and chose as its logo a helmeted pirate with a patch over one eye and crossed swords behind him. An avid reader of military history, Davis ran his training camp in paramilitary fashion and took elaborate security precautions to prevent opposing teams from discovering his stratagems. He made a point of not saddling his players with dress, hair, or drinking codes. "We're in a . . . war for 20 weeks a season. We come to kick butts, not to show off our good manners," he explained in Los Angeles magazine (November 1984). "Our way is to put fear in the opponent, baby, and outscore him. Nothing else."

After earning only a .214 winning percentage under three different coaches in their first three seasons, under Davis' guidance the Raiders posted ten wins against only four losses in 1963 and lost the Division championship by only one game. Al Davis was named Coach of the Year by the Associated Press, United Press International, Sports Illustrated, The Sporting News, and his fellow coaches; he was also designated the Outstanding Young Man of the Year by Oakland's Junior Chamber of Commerce. After the Raiders' first winning season, the momentum slowed as the Raiders went 5-7-2 in 1964 and 8-5-1 in 1965.

While the Raiders were maturing into a team to be reckoned with, the fledgling AFL, founded in 1959 by Dallas billionaire Lamar Hunt, was in the midst of a cutthroat bidding war for college recruits with the forty-seven-year-old National Football League and its commissioner, Pete Rozelle. Unhappy with the performance of Joe Foss, their own commissioner, the AFL owners hired Al Davis to replace him on April 8, 1966. Putting his recruiting talents to the test once again, the new commissioner set out to weaken the NFL clubs by signing their disgruntled star quarterbacks. His strategy proved successful, for within only eight weeks, after Davis had signed several top players for the league, including John Brodie and Roman Gabriel, the NFL owners acceded to a merger. Made public on June 8, the epochal pact called for a common draft of graduating college players, the creation of the Super Bowl championship game, and AFL indemnity payments of around $25 million to the NFL over a twenty-year period. However, the provision for a unified schedule would not be implemented until 1970, after the multimillion-dollar television contracts of each league had expired.

The AFL acquired immediate prestige, but Al Davis was frustrated both by the terms of the merger, which were unfavorable to the AFL, and by his being passed over for the post of commissioner of the unified league in favor of Rozelle. Although he could have remained as head of the AFL, Davis returned to the Oakland Raiders as the managing general partner with a 10 percent share of the club. Meanwhile he continued to collect an annual salary of about $60,000 for his uncompleted five-year term as commissioner. John Rauch, an assistant coach for the Raiders and a former star quarterback at the University of Georgia, took over as head coach and Scotty Stirling became general manager.

Proving that he was still the driving force behind the Raiders, Davis persuaded officials of the city of Oakland to replace Youell Field, the 12,000-seat, wooden-bleacher ballpark where the team had been playing, with a new stadium, and the Oakland–Alameda County Coliseum, seating 54,-000 fans, opened on September 18, 1966. In 1967, the team's second season in that stadium, the Raiders compiled the best record in AFL history, 13-1, thanks to the thirty touchdown passes thrown by quarterback Daryle Lamonica, whom Davis had acquired in a shrewd trade with the Buffalo Bills. Led by Lamonica, on December 31 the team blasted Houston, 40-7, to capture the AFL championship, but the Raiders' first season in the playoffs ended disappointingly when the Green Bay Packers flattened them, 33-14, in the Super Bowl in Miami on January 15, 1968. After winning twelve of their fourteen games the next year, the Raiders toppled the visiting Kansas City team to gain the Western Division Playoff by a score of 41-6 but succumbed to the New York Jets, 27-23, in the AFL championship game on December 29, 1968 at Shea Stadium.

Adept at perceiving the potential in other teams' "discards"—including quarterback George Blanda, defensive end and tackle John Matuszak, and linebacker Bob Nelson—Davis at first relied less heavily on the draft than on carefully calculated trades and acquisitions of free agents to build his team. For example, he realized spectacular performances from running back Billy Cannon and tight end Hewritt Dixon, whom others considered mediocre players, simply by switching their positions. In an interview for Scholastic Coach (August 1982), he admitted that when scouting he always looked for a certain type of player: "I wanted speed and ability, of course, but I was partial to big people. In the middle 50's, it was 6-2, 210-lb. people who could run. That's now equivalent to 6-4, 230-lb. people who can run. The Raiders have always been a big team—and a tough team." They are so "tough," in fact, that critics have characterized them as "a gang of alley thugs in cleats" and Pittsburgh Steelers' coach Chuck Noll labeled them "a criminal element" after they injured one of his players.

Al Davis' detractors maintain that he relies on such dirty tricks as watering the field before Raiders' home games to slow their opponent and bugging visiting teams' locker rooms to get an inside edge for his squad. According to Al Stump in Los Angeles magazine (November 1984), his "reputation as a spook, a shadowy saboteur who'd do anything to win . . . spread throughout the league to the point of paranoia." Bob Bestor, a former Raiders business manager, contended in Look (November 18, 1969) that Davis tried to instill fear in his staff because he "thinks people perform better if they're afraid." In the same article Davis agreed with that assessment: "People in an organization have to have the feeling that there's someone there who, if they don't move in the right direction, will chop." It is alleged that Davis, unafraid to take on even the club's owners, used underhanded means to gain a majority share of the organization, to oust Wayne Valley (a principal owner), and to secure himself a handsome contract at a time when Valley intended to fire him. But most of Davis' players are loyal to him, perhaps because their salaries are among the highest in the league, and they often get unexpected raises for exceptional performances.

Under John Madden, who succeeded Rauch as head coach in 1969, the Raiders remained among the best teams in the league, having by 1977 clinched nine American Football Conference (AFC) Western Division championships in ten years. (After the 1970 merger, the NFL was divided into the American and National Football Conferences.) In 1977 the Raiders sweetened their record by overwhelming the Minnesota Vikings, 32-14, in Super Bowl XI at Pasadena's Rose Bowl to win their first World Championship title. Davis was named NFL Executive of the Year, but he was also ousted by Commissioner Pete Rozelle from the NFL's Competition Committee, which recommends playing conditions and rule changes to the owners. "We'd just had the Players Association settlement in which a lot of powers were taken away from Pete," Davis explained in *Sport* (January 1981). "He thought I had been a little too willing to give up some of his powers to the league management council. I guess it was his way of getting back at me."

In spite of wrangles with NFL management, the Raiders continued their winning tradition. In 1980 under Tom Flores, who became head coach in 1979, the team tied for first in its division and entered the playoffs for the eleventh time since 1967, largely because quarterback Jim Plunkett had been added to the roster in 1978. Davis signed the Heismann Trophy-winning player after the San Francisco 49ers had let him go when, following about a half dozen spectacular pro seasons, his arm and talent seemed to have failed him. After sitting out one season for intensive coaching, Plunkett led the Raiders to Super Bowl XV in New Orleans, where they defeated the Philadelphia Eagles, 27-10, becoming the first Wild Card team since the merger to win the World Championship. Four years later, Plunkett and the Raiders captured their third Super Bowl crown with a victory over the Washington Redskins by the largest margin in that game's history: 38-9. By 1984 the Raiders had accrued the highest winning percentage—over .700—of any team in professional sports for the years 1963 to 1983, the period of Al Davis' reign.

The team's 1980 Super Bowl achievement was clouded, however, by lawsuits over the Raiders' proposed move to Los Angeles, and the champions dropped to 7-9 in 1981—their first losing season in sixteen years. Despite a decade of sellout seasons in Oakland, Davis was unable to persuade the city to make major improvements, including luxury boxes, in the stadium. Insisting that he could not maintain the Raiders' winning record without additional profits to enable him to offer competitive salaries in the 1980s, Davis signed a memorandum of agreement with the Los Angeles Coliseum on March 1, 1980, but the NFL would not budge on its rule requiring three-quarters of the owners to approve a franchise relocation. When Davis defiantly moved the Raiders' offices to Los Angeles that month, a court injunction promptly drove his forces back to Oakland. The city also instituted an eminent domain suit to retain the Raiders. After lengthy litigation, the franchise became legally free to relocate on May 7, 1982, when a United States Federal District Court jury unanimously ruled for the Raiders and against the NFL on antitrust and bad faith counts. Two months later, Davis announced that he had signed a ten-year pact, with five successive three-year renewal options, with the Los Angeles Coliseum Commission, and on August 29 the Los Angeles Raiders played their first home preseason game in the 92,516-seat Los Angeles Memorial Coliseum, defeating the Green Bay Packers, 24-3. In spite of the NFL's legal appeals, the courts upheld the awards of $35 million to the Raiders and nearly $15 million to the Los Angeles Coliseum in compensatory damages, and the antitrust rulings against the NFL were allowed to stand when on November 5, 1984 the United States Supreme Court refused to review the case.

Variously labeled "the Sphinx" for his refusal to give interviews to Los Angeles sports writers, the "Outlaw King" for the brash behavior of himself and his players, and "the Fonz of Football" for his well-known 1950s-style ducktail haircut, Al Davis presents something of an enigma. According to Mark Heisler of the *Los Angeles Times* (January 20, 1984), among his friends "his compassion and generosity are legend. He conceals his warmer impulses, so the intrigue part is what shows." A blue-eyed blond, Davis, who stands six feet tall and weighs 188 pounds, usually wears flashy clothes in the black and silver colors he chose for the Raiders. A multimillionaire, he owns a home in the Piedmont area of the Oakland Hills and a luxurious condominium in Marina del Rey, where he lives during the playing season. He and Carol Segall, whom he married on July 11, 1954, have one son, Mark, the namesake of General Mark Clark, the former president of The Citadel. Davis' obsession has always been football. He was quoted in *People* (January 26, 1981) as saying: "It's tunnel vision, a tunnel life. I'm not really part of society."

References: *Look* 33:50+ N 18 '69 por; *Los Angeles* 29:218+ N '84 pors; *N Y Times Mag* p97+ D 13 '81 por; *People* 15:24+ Ja 26 '81 pors; *Sat Eve Post* 247:36+ N '75 por; *Scholastic Coach* 52:37+ Ag '82 por; *Sports Illus* 19:27+ N 4 '63 pors, 41:28+ D 2 '74 por; Kowet, Don. *The Rich Who Own Sports* (1977); *Who's Who in America*, 1984-85

---

## De Mille, Agnes

*Sept. 18, 1905- Dancer; choreographer. Address: b. c/o Harold Ober Associates, 40 E. 49th St., New York City, N.Y. 10017*

NOTE: This biography supersedes the article that appeared in *Current Biography* in 1943.

With the creation of her trailblazing dance-dramas for the 1943 Rodgers and Hammerstein Broadway hit *Oklahoma!*, the choreographer Agnes de Mille permanently changed the look of the American musical. No longer an irrelevant interlude, a dance number became an integral part of the action, and as essential to the story line as dialogue. Miss de Mille, who learned to sketch a character in a few movements and pithy gestures (much "as Daumier outlined a face," she once said) during her years as a concert dancer, used that skill to great dramatic effect in such ballets as *Rodeo* and *Fall River Legend*, and in her dances for almost a score of Broadway musicals. Although comfortable in a variety of styles, Agnes de Mille is best known for using folk forms in a new and theatrically striking

*Agnes De Mille*

gan taking a weekly class at the Theodore Koslov School of Imperial Russian Ballet in Los Angeles.

Following her graduation from the Hollywood School for Girls, Miss de Mille, in keeping with her father's wish that she become a writer, enrolled at the University of California at Los Angeles with a major in English. During her sophomore year she appeared in a benefit variety show for the student victims of a campus fire. As she recalled in *Dance to the Piper* (Little, Brown, 1952), the first volume of her memoirs, she performed a short dance about "French *bergerettes* in the manner of Watteau." Later, she created skits and ballets—"mostly to Chopin, . . . about Beauty and how one should be ready to die for it"—for student rallies and campus assemblies.

After earning her B.A. degree, *cum laude,* Miss de Mille decided to become a dancer. Aware of her deficiencies as a classical technician, she prepared a recital of what she has called "character studies"—a young ballerina with stagefright, an Elizabethan girl watching a parade, a hardy pioneer woman—set to popular or folk songs. "My pieces were not properly dances at all," she wrote in *Dance to the Piper.* "They were realistic character sketches, dramatic rather than choreographic in form. What dancing there was derived from authentic folk or old-fashioned theatrical steps which I used as decoration and accouterment exactly like costumes, or lights, or music."

Encouraged by the response to her amateur appearances in California, she decided to try her luck in New York City. When she made her bow as a concert dancer there in January 1928, John Martin, the *New York Times's* dance critic, pronounced her "undoubtedly one of the brightest stars now rising above our native horizon." As he explained in a follow-up review, on March 4, 1928, he was especially impressed by the "rare and intuitive understanding of human beings that is the heart and soul of her work." Like Charlie Chaplin, he went on, "she sees tragedy through a lens of comedy" and "leaves you with the same sort of wistful laughter on your lips and the same sort of lump in your throat."

Over the next several years, Agnes de Mille accepted professional engagements with theatrical stock companies, variety shows, private parties, and even "third-rate nightclubs." "All I balked at was jigging on the sidewalk with a tambourine," she recalled in *Dance to the Piper.* Her first choreographic assignment came in 1929, when she arranged the dances for Christopher Morley's short-lived but much discussed revival of the melodrama *The Black Crook* in Hoboken, New Jersey.

Late in 1932 Agnes de Mille sailed for Europe, where she gamely mounted several well-received solo concerts in Paris, Brussels, and London "without management, public relations, patronage, or money," as she put it. Her London appearances led to a job with Charles B. Cochrane, who hired her to stage the dances for his production of Cole Porter's *Nymph Errant* starring Gertrude Lawrence, and an invitation from Marie Rambert, the

way. "I'm really like a playwright," she declared in a recent interview for *Ballet News.* "That is my real value as choreographer. I tell a story, and I tell it well."

Miss de Mille comes by her theatrical flair naturally. Both her father, William Churchill de Mille, and her paternal grandfather, Henry de Mille, were successful playwrights, and her uncle, Cecil B. de Mille, was a pioneering filmmaker. Her father went on to become a motion-picture producer and director; her mother, Anna (George) de Mille, devoted much of her time to campaigning in behalf of the single-tax theory originated by Miss de Mille's maternal grandfather, the political economist Henry George. Born into that "family of compulsive achievers," to use her phrase, in New York City on September 18, 1905, Agnes George de Mille, the older of two children, was by her own account "a spoiled, egocentric, wealthy girl." In New York and, after 1914, in Hollywood, California, she enjoyed the prerogatives of the privileged upper class: trips to the theatre, summers at a country house in upstate New York, and an endless stream of eminent visitors, including the dancers Ruth St. Denis and Ted Shawn, for whom the girl danced auditions.

As she told Patricia O'Haire in an interview for the *New York Sunday News* (May 15, 1983), Agnes de Mille wanted to be a dancer "from the moment [she] heard music," but she "really caught the virus" when she attended a performance by Anna Pavlova. At first, her parents refused to allow her to take dancing lessons, mainly because William de Mille disapproved of a theatrical career for his daughter. Undaunted, Agnes read dance history, studied photographs of famous dancers, and kept scrapbooks of ballet performances. Finally, when she was thirteen, her father relented, and she be-

founder of the newly formed Ballet Rambert, to give a series of recitals at the company's Mercury Theatre and to study at the company school. Under Madame Rambert's tutelage, Miss de Mille acquired a "passable," to use her word, classical technique; more important, under Antony Tudor's, she came to understand "the principles behind the technique." By that time an accomplished dramatic dancer, she appeared in a number of works choreographed by company members, including the world premiere of Tudor's dance of lamentation, *Dark Elegies*.

Like her fellow dancer-choreographers at the Mercury Theatre, Miss de Mille found her ingenuity tested by the theatre's lilliputian stage dimensions and the company's inadequate budget. Turning those disadvantages to her benefit, she developed an economical vocabulary of movements and gestures, a feeling for visual variety, and a sense of dramatic structure to create what a critic for the London *Daily Telegraph* (January 6, 1937) called "short stories in movement." Her intellectual approach to choreography was as evident in the stylized "dumb show" she devised for Leslie Howard's 1936 Broadway production of *Hamlet* and in the formal court dances she created for MGM's opulent film version of *Romeo and Juliet* (1937) as it was in the individualistic, distinctively American pieces she created for the experimental Dance Theatre, the company she and a few like-minded Rambert colleagues formed in London in 1937.

When the Dance Theatre, unable to secure bookings, disbanded in mid-1938, Miss de Mille returned to the United States. Settling in New York City, she taught ballet classes to support herself while she continued to experiment with the American folk themes and styles that were to become her trademarks. In 1939 she was invited to join the newly organized Ballet Theatre (now known as the American Ballet Theatre) as resident choreographer. Over the next five years, she devised for the company three of her best-known works: *Black Ritual* (Milhaud), a primitive Haitian ceremonial rite for a cast of sixteen black dancers; *Three Virgins and a Devil* (Respighi), a comedy ballet that Walter Terry described as "pure medieval allegory" executed in "pure Harpo Marx" style; and *Tally-Ho* (Gluck), a stylish theatre piece about eighteenth-century French court life. Agnes de Mille herself danced the roles of the self-righteous Fanatical One and the bored Wife in the world premieres of, respectively, *Three Virgins and a Devil* in 1941 and *Tally-Ho* in 1944.

The turning point in Agnes de Mille's choreographic career, however, was *Rodeo* (Copland), a piece of Americana that she created for the touring Ballet Russe de Monte Carlo. Drawing on skills she had developed as a concert dancer, she dreamed up a scenario about a tomboyish cowgirl who triumphs over the jokes of the ranch hands and the sneers of the local beauties and wins the "Champeen Roper." With Miss de Mille as the Cowgirl, *Rodeo* had its premiere in New York City on October 16, 1942 to twenty-two curtain calls and critical acclaim. Although dance historians agree that *Rodeo* owed much of its original success to Miss de Mille's exuberant portrayal of the ugly-duckling Cowgirl, the ballet, now in the repertories of international dance companies, has held up remarkably well without becoming dated.

Captivated by *Rodeo*, lyricist Oscar Hammerstein 2d and composer Richard Rodgers asked Agnes de Mille to stage the dances for their first collaborative effort, the musical *Oklahoma!* Adapted from *Green Grow the Lilacs*, Lynn Riggs's play set in Indian territory around the turn of the century, the project seemed tailor-made for the choreographer. "It had the kind of materials I wanted to use—the Anglo-American tradition, the square dances, the running sets—all the native dances I was using in ballet but which hadn't been done on Broadway," Miss de Mille explained years later, as quoted in *Cue* magazine (December 21, 1979).

Working closely with Rodgers and Hammerstein, she contributed to *Oklahoma!* a series of dances that not only enhanced appreciation of the music but also strengthened the story line and enriched characterizations by exploring the inner longings of its protagonists. The famous dream-ballet sequence, for example, exposed the repressed sexuality of its wholesome heroine, Laurey, in a nightmarish fantasy revealing her fascination with the sinister Jud as well as her desire for Curly, the amiable cowhand. When *Oklahoma!* opened on Broadway in the spring of 1943, New York drama critics acclaimed Miss de Mille's dances as "supreme esthetic delights." *Oklahoma!*, which enjoyed an initial Broadway run of more than five years, is a staple on the strawhat circuit, and it has been revived in New York a half-dozen times, most recently in 1979. Agnes de Mille supervised the staging and the choreography of that latest New York reincarnation and of the 1955 film version.

Because of the phenomenal success of *Oklahoma!*, Agnes de Mille had "first refusal of every good show" on Broadway throughout the 1940s. Among her choreographic stage credits for that period are the fantasy *One Touch of Venus* (1943), with music by Kurt Weill and a book by S. J. Perelman and Ogden Nash; *Bloomer Girl* (1944), the Harold Arlen-E. Y. Harburg musical set in 1861 and dealing with women's rights and black aspirations for freedom; Rodgers and Hammerstein's *Carousel* (1945), an adaptation of Ferenc Molnár's *Liliom*, about the devotion of a shy young woman to a shiftless carnival barker; and *Brigadoon* (1947), Alan Jay Lerner and Frederick Loewe's tale of an enchanted Scottish village that comes to life for one day every one hundred years. For *Brigadoon*, Miss de Mille researched the native dances of Scotland and incorporated some of their precise steps and formal patterns into her otherwise free and imaginative creations, the most striking being the frenzied "sword dance."

Not long after *Brigadoon* opened in March 1947, Rodgers and Hammerstein hired Agnes de Mille to choreograph and direct *Allegro*, their experimental musical that had to do with the troubled life of a dedicated small-town physician. It was the first time that the direction of a large-scale Broadway production had been entrusted to a choreographer. Hampered by a fragmented script and a pallid score, *Allegro* was the least successful of the trio's collaborations, but Miss de Mille impressed critics by triumphing over her material. Inadequate books and unmemorable scores also hobbled her later directorial efforts—Cole Porter's musical fable *Out of This World* (1950) and *Come Summer* (1971), a picaresque tale about a philosophical peddler that she has dismissed as "a colossal failure."

Agnes de Mille fared much better in her straight choreographic assignments: *Gentlemen Prefer Blondes*, the 1949 smash hit, with music by Jule Styne and a book by Joseph Fields and Anita Loos, that made a star out of Carol Channing; Lerner and Loewe's *Paint Your Wagon* (1951), a rambunctious musical set during the California gold rush; and *The Girl in Pink Tights* (1954), an old-fashioned Sigmund Romberg romance featuring the French ballerina Jeanmaire. Her stage credits as a choreographer also include *Goldilocks* (1958), a spoof of silent-filmmaking written and directed by the drama critic Walter Kerr, with music by Leroy Anderson; *Juno* (1959), Joseph Stein and Marc Blitzstein's short-lived musical version of Sean O'Casey's tragicomedy *Juno and the Paycock*; *Kwamina* (1961), an attempt to dramatize in story and song the collision between past and present in a West African colony on the eve of its independence; and *110 in the Shade* (1963), a musical adaptation, by Tom Jones and Harvey Schmidt, of N. Richard Nash's novel *The Rainmaker*. Although it was only moderately successful at the box office, Agnes de Mille considers *Paint Your Wagon* to be her finest, most integrated work for the Broadway stage. But it was the primitive vigor and explosive force of the ceremonial dances she created for *Kwamina* that won her a Tony Award for best choreography.

Concurrently with her Broadway career, Agnes de Mille continued to fashion pieces for Ballet Theatre, among them the grisly dance-drama *Fall River Legend* (Morton Gould); *The Harvest According* (Virgil Thompson), a life-cycle dance in which she fused ballet, modern dance, and folk techniques; the satirical morality play *The Rib of Eve* (Morton Gould); *The Four Marys* (Trude Rittmann), a "dance cantata," to use Miss de Mille's term, about a doomed interracial love affair in the Old South; *The Wind in the Mountains* (Lawrence Rosenthal), a generous serving of apple-pie Americana reminiscent of *Rodeo* and *Oklahoma!*; and *A Rose for Miss Emily* (Alan Hovhaness), adapted from a short story by William Faulkner.

Of those works, the acknowledged masterpiece is *Fall River Legend*, based on the celebrated case of Lizzie Borden, who was accused of hacking her father and stepmother to death in 1892. The jury acquitted Miss Borden, but the choreographer, after an exhaustive investigation of the facts, found her guilty as charged, and *Fall River* relates her story in a series of flashbacks as she stands at the foot of the gallows awaiting execution. The Accused (as the Lizzie Borden character is called) relives her happiness as a child, her grief at her mother's untimely death, her loneliness as a young woman, and her increasing despair as her villainous stepmother thwarts her budding romance with a kindly minister. But *Fall River Legend* is more than an apologia; according to Agnes de Mille, in a program note for the ballet's 1948 premiere, it is a psychological exploration of "the passions that lead to a violent resolution of the oppressions and turmoils that can beset an ordinary life."

In the *Chicago Tribune* (July 24, 1978), Deborah Jowitt, the dance critic and historian, paid tribute to Agnes de Mille's "astute sense of human behavior" as revealed in gesture, physical bearing, and action patterns. That sense is perhaps nowhere more apparent than in *Fall River Legend*. Each of its central characters has a distinguished choreographic vocabulary: stiff movements for the black-clothed Stepmother; open gestures for the understanding Pastor; and emotionally charged lifts and falls for the Accused. The role of the Accused challenges even the most experienced of dramatic ballerinas. Among those who have essayed it with distinction are Nora Kaye, Alicia Alonso, Sallie Wilson, Cynthia Gregory, and Virginia Johnson.

In addition to choreographing for Ballet Theatre, Agnes de Mille created pieces for other leading dance companies, including the Boston Ballet, the Royal Winnipeg Ballet, and the Harkness Ballet. Among her commissions are *The Bitter Weird*, an adaptation of Scottish folk dances set to melodies from *Brigadoon*; the backstage satire *Golden Age* (Genevieve Pitot, after Rossini); *The Rehearsal*, an illustrated guide, with commentary, to choreography; and the lyrical *Summer* (Schubert), which she later revised into a small suite of dances called *Inconsequentials*.

Agnes de Mille had long lamented the lack of an intrinsically American national dance company to preserve and present in authentic form the native and popular dances of the United States. In 1973 she founded the Heritage Dance Theatre at the North Carolina School of the Arts, where she is a charter trustee. With financial support from the National Endowment for the Arts and some private foundations, the company, comprised largely of dancers from the School of the Arts, set off on the first of several national tours in late 1973. Its eclectic program of folk and historical dances arranged by Miss de Mille and ballets reflecting American themes by Miss de Mille, Katherine Dunham, and Anna Sokolow was enthusiastically received by audiences, though critics were somewhat restrained in their praise.

Shortly before a scheduled performance by the Heritage Dance Theatre at Hunter College in New York City in May 1975, Agnes de Mille suffered a massive cerebral hemorrhage that left her right side partially paralyzed. As she has recounted in *Reprieve* (Doubleday, 1981), her moving account of her illness and recovery, she gradually learned to write with her left hand and to walk with the aid of a cane. Just fourteen months after her stroke, she stood on the stage of the New York State Theatre in the Lincoln Center for the Performing Arts complex, acknowledging the ovation that greeted the American Ballet Theatre's world premiere of her Bicentennial celebration piece, *Texas Fourth*. A year later, she was herself performing again, as the narrator of the Joffrey Ballet's production of her lecture-demonstration *Conversations About the Dance*, which Walter Kerr has described simply as "an encounter with wisdom." A televised version was broadcast by the Public Broadcasting Service in January 1980.

Standing five feet two inches tall, Agnes de Mille is a stocky woman with steely, ice-blue eyes and white hair, usually worn pulled back into a bun. According to Clive Barnes, she has a "knowingly imperious glance" and the voice of "a Yankee democrat, with a dry and devastating sense of the ridiculous." Despite her disability, she still does a series of simple barre exercises daily. Otherwise, she told an interviewer for *Ballet News* (September 1983), "I just sit here, and everyone treats me like some holy relic." Miss de Mille shares her book-lined apartment in New York's Greenwich Village with her husband, Walter F. Prude, a retired artists' agent whom she married on June 14, 1943. They have one son, Jonathan, a history professor.

Miss de Mille has published articles on a wide variety of subjects in popular periodicals, and she has written more than a dozen books, including—in addition to those mentioned above—the autobiographies *And Promenade Home* (Little, Brown, 1956), *Speak To Me, Dance With Me* (Atlantic-Little, Brown, 1973), and *Where the Wings Grow* (Doubleday, 1978); *To a Young Dancer* (Atlantic-Little, Brown, 1962), a handbook for dance students; *Lizzie Borden: A Dance of Death* (Atlantic-Little, Brown, 1968); and the illustrated choreographic histories *The Book of the Dance* (Golden Press, 1964), *Dance in America* (Harper, 1971), and *America Dances* (Macmillan, 1981).

An outspoken proponent of increased federal aid to the performing arts, she has served on the National Advisory Council of the Performing Arts and the Committee for the National Endowment for the Arts. For years she has been closely affiliated with the Henry George School of Social Science founded to further the teachings of her grandfather. Among her many honorary degrees and awards are the Handel Medallion, New York City's highest award for achievement in the arts, in 1976, the Arnold Gingrich Memorial Award from the Arts and Business Council in 1979; the Kennedy Center Career Achievement Award in 1980; and the Elizabeth Blackwell Award honoring outstanding women in the arts and sciences in 1982.

References: *Ballet N* 5:11+ S '83 pors; *Dance* 31:14+ Mr '57 por, 45:47+ O '71 pors; *Dance Observer* 1:1+ O/N '34; *Horizon* 23:29+ S '80 pors; *N Y Post* p15 D 12 '74 por; *N Y Sunday News Leisure* p3+ My 15 '83 pors; *N Y Times Mag* p14+ D 19 '43 pors; *New Yorker* 22:32+ S 14 '48; *People* 16:71+ S 21 '81 pors; *Theatre Arts* 45:14+ O '61 por; *Contemporary Authors* vols 65-68 (1977); *Who's Who in America*, 1984-85; *Who's Who in Theatre* (1981)

---

## Demme, Jonathan

(dem´ ē)

1944- Motion-picture director. *Address:* b. c/o Arnold Stiefel, William Morris Agency, 151 El Camino Dr., Beverly Hills, Calif. 90212; c/o Lee Winkler, Global Business Management, 9000 Sunset Blvd., Suite 1115, Beverly Hills, Calif. 90069

In the opinion of John Simon, a critic not given to hyperbole, the director Jonathan Demme is "probably the most gifted young filmmaker to come out of the stable of Roger Corman." Demme, a master stylist, learned his craft turning out for Corman's New World Pictures such quick, cheap B movies as *Caged Heat* (1974) and *Crazy Mama* (1975), exploitation films that soon drew a cult following. Among the "serious" folk comedies he has since directed are *Citizens Band* (1977), *Melvin and Howard* (1980), and *Swing Shift* (1984), charming slices of Americana rich in commonplace detail, relaxed and uncondescending in their humor, and oblique in their social commentary. None of his films have been hits, but several have enjoyed *succès d'estime*. "Very few directors have had Demme's delicate intuitive feel for the ragged texture of life out of the mainstream," Hal Hinson wrote in the *Washington Post* (April 22, 1984); "for the way we talk and separate and make love; for the look of lunch counters, bathrooms, and gas stations. Demme suffuses the people in his films with a warm acceptance, but he stands back as well, looking on with appreciation and detachment. This balance gives his films a floating, bemused quality that never seems sticky or cloying, a sense of events seen in their proper proportions." Others have hailed Demme for "combining the keen satiric perceptions of a Preston Sturges with a masculine tenderness for the feelings of ordinary people" and for "bringing the heartiness and sensitivity of a home-grown Jean Renoir into latter-day American film comedy."

Jonathan Demme was born in 1944 in Baldwin, Long Island, New York. He grew up in Rockville Center, Long Island, where he completed elementary school, and Miami, Florida, where he went to high school. His father worked as a publicist for airlines and for the Fontainebleau Hotel in Miami and as editor of the aviation magazine *Wings*. As a high-school student Demme earned pocket money ushering at a movie theatre, and after graduating he worked in a kennel and an animal hospital. At first aspiring to become a veterinarian, he studied with that goal in mind at the University of Miami briefly, until he realized that he "couldn't hack" the required science courses. "After I failed chemistry," he recollected when Hal Hinson interviewed him for the *Washington Post* (April 22, 1984), "I realized that there was no movie critic on the *Florida Alligator*, the college newspaper there, so to feed my moviegoing habit I offered my services. After the semester was over I went back to the animal hospital, and also became the movie critic for a biweekly shopping guide [the *Coral Gables Times*]."

Demme told Hinson that he got into filmmaking "by pure luck," with "no motivation whatsoever." The first major "fortuitous" step was his introduction, through his father, to the producer Joseph E. Levine, the founder and president of Embassy Pictures Corporation, when Levine was vacationing in Miami. After a brief stint in the United States Air Force, in 1966, Demme worked in Embassy Pictures' publicity department in New York City for two years. During that period he also sold films for Pathé Contemporary's theatrical division, wrote movie reviews for *Film Daily* and rock music reviews for *Fusion*, and made his first motion picture, an amateur 16mm experimental short titled *Good Morning, Steve*. In 1969 he moved to England to work with Al Viola, who had set up an office in London for promoting American investment in British films. Al Viola's enterprise quickly fizzled, but Demme remained in London, producing television commercials for an American company there.

The American documentary and feature-film director Irwin Allen, who was on location in England making *Sudden Terror* (National General, 1970), originally titled *Eyewitness*, asked Demme to put together a contemporary score for the film. Rounding up several rock groups for the purpose,

Demme did so, and earned his first feature-picture credit, as music coordinator. Shortly thereafter he met Roger Corman, who was in Ireland directing *Von Richthofen and Brown* (United Artists, 1971) and needed a unit publicist, which Demme became. Corman, who had been producing as well as directing for years, stopped directing altogether with the completion of *Von Richthofen and Brown* and the founding of his own film production and distribution company, New World Pictures. Needing scripts for his new company, Corman asked Demme to try his hand at one. With the help of Joe Viola, Al's brother, then a director of television commercials, Demme, borrowing the premise of *Rashomon*, wrote *Angels, Hard as They Come* (New World, 1971), a motorcycle-gang movie in which the central violent action (a rape and fight) is seen from four widely differing points of view. The film, shot in and around Los Angeles, was produced by Demme and directed by Viola on a shoe-string budget of $125,000.

After the completion of *Angels, Hard as They Come*, Corman sent Viola and Demme to the Philippines to make *The Hot Box* (New World, 1972), a film, in Demme's words, "about nurses who become captured by a revolutionary band in a small deprived nation." The two collaborated in the writing of *The Hot Box*, Viola directed it, and Demme was producer and second-unit director, responsible for battle scenes and shots establishing location—his first directing credit.

Demme made his full directorial debut with *Caged Heat* (New World, 1974), a $160,000 melodrama, written by him, about imprisoned vixens who battle each other and the insanely dictatorial woman warden. The perverse Freudianism of the film, with its female characters enacting scene after scene of symbolic castration, was lightened by a sense of humor, by a naturalistic style, and by professionally restrained and paced camera work. "The most important thing Roger did for me was to sit down with me right before I directed *Caged Heat* and run down just how to do a job of moviemaking," Demme recounted to Michael Sragow in an interview for *American Film* (January-February 1984). "He hit everything: Have something interesting in the foreground of the shot; have something interesting happening in the background of the shot; try to find good motivation to move the camera, because it's more stimulating to the eyes; if you're shooting the scene in a small room where you can't move the camera, try to get different angles, because cuts equal movement; respect the characters and try to like them, and translate that into the audience liking and respecting the characters. To me, those are the fundamentals."

When Shirley Clark had a falling-out with Corman, Demme replaced her, before shooting began, as director of *Crazy Mama* (New World, 1975), a comedy about an eccentric matriarchal family (Cloris Leachman, Ann Sothern, *et al*) driven to crime by economic oppression. As James Monaco observed in his book *American Film Now* (1979), it is in *Crazy Mama* that Demme shows "for the first time . . . the strong sense of community that marks his work." Roger Corman was executive producer of *Fighting Mad* (Twentieth Century-Fox, 1976), which Demme wrote as well as directed. That picture stars Peter Fonda as Tom Hunter, the city-bred nemesis of a strip-mining tycoon (Philip Carey) who has murdered Hunter's father and brother to get their ranch land. Leslie Halliwell in his *Film Guide* (1984) dismissed *Fighting Mad* as just "another vigilante western in modern dress," failing to point out that the violence in the film is counterpointed with a series of quiet, lyrical montages establishing and invoking the ties to land and family that justify Hunter's wrath. In *Fighting Mad* one can begin to see, as Hal Hinson points out, Demme's "fondness for off-beat American kitsch life styles."

The screenplay for *Fighting Mad* was the last that Demme would write, at least for the time being. "Writing was a way of getting to direct," he explained to Michael Sragow, "and I soon realized I was a much better director than I was a writer." Paul Brickman provided the original screenplay (which was rewritten under Demme's supervision) for *Citizens Band* (Paramount, 1977), an episodic, cross-plotted comedy about small-town Sun Belt CB radio maniacs whose ids come alive in the personae they assume on the airwaves—with the prominent exception of the broadcaster whose "handle" is "Spider" (Paul Le Mat), a radio vigilante who operates on the super-ego level, as a Good Samaritan. Directing *Citizens Band* at the request of producer Freddie Fields, Demme interpreted Brickman's script with a personal sensibility more overt than that which had come through his own scripts for Corman, infusing the rollicking plot with wit, intelligence, and affection for the characters. Exhibited regionally, outside New York, in the spring of 1977, *Citizens Band* failed to attract even the drive-in audiences to which it was assumed to appeal. Withdrawn from exhibition for five months, the film re-emerged under a new title, *Handle with Care*, in October 1977 at the New York Film Festival, where it was warmly received. Following the festival, the picture again failed at box offices, although it enjoyed substantial runs in Boston and Washington, D.C. "In this case," Vincent Canby wrote in the *New York Times* (November 6, 1977), "I'm convinced it was the public that flopped." Other critics described *Citizens Band/Handle With Care* as "a grown-up *American Graffiti*" and "a Middle American *Midsummer Night's Dream*," "too subtle for the open-air crowd, but not sufficiently angst-ridden for art houses."

Temporarily bereft of motion-picture opportunities following the commercial failure of *Citizens Band*, Demme directed "Murder in Aspic," a 1978 episode in the television whodunit series *Columbo*, the star of which, Peter Falk, had liked *Citizens Band*. Among other admirers of *Citizens Band* were two producers at United Artists, Mike Taylor and Dan Wigutow. At their invitation, Demme returned to the big screen as the director of *Last*

*Embrace* (United Artists, 1979), a murky romantic thriller adapted from Murray Teigh Bloom's suspense novel *The Thirteenth Man*, about a disoriented American secret agent, played by Roy Scheider in the movie, who finds himself simultaneously cut off from the protection of his agency and the recipient of mysterious death threats. The screenplay was written by David Shaber, with uncredited assists from Demme, and the dreamlike, nervously mobile but precise photography was directed by Tak Fujimoto, a favorite and effective collaborator of Demme's. Some reviewers panned *Last Embrace* as a "preposterous" melodrama, "filled with false leads" and filmed in the style of "a fatigued Hitchcock." But the critical consensus was that the film's stylistic panache redeemed its deficiencies of plot.

When Jonathan Demme first read in a newspaper about the so-called "Mormon will" through which the legendary billionaire Howard Hughes, an eccentric recluse, allegedly left $156 million to Utah gas-station attendant Melvin Dummar, "the idea of such a thing," he told Seth Cagin of the *Soho Weekly News* (September 24, 1980), "really turned [him] on." The will's validity was rejected in court, but producer Don Phillips acquired Dummar's story and sold it to Universal Pictures. That story began one evening in January 1968 when Dummar, driving through the Nevada desert in his pickup truck, gave a lift to a gruff and grizzled old coot injured in a motorcycle spill. Although the wild-eyed and disreputable-looking fellow whom he drove to Las Vegas claimed to be Howard Hughes, Dummar did not realize he was telling the truth until April 1976, when Hughes died and the disputed will came to light. The screenplay Bo Goldman wrote for Universal in consultation with the director Mike Nichols opened with the strange desert encounter between the two men from opposite ends of the economic ladder and their drive to Las Vegas, during which Dummar gets a reluctant Hughes to join in the singing of an atrocious song he proudly composed, "Santa's Souped-Up Sleigh." Then the scenario concentrated on fleshing out the following eight-and-a-half years in the Sisyphean life of Dummar, a good-natured blue-collar loser in pursuit of the American consumerist dream, moving from one job failure, marital crisis, and property repossession to another with no diminution of his optimism. When Mike Nichols bowed out of the project in 1978, before shooting began, Thom Mount, executive vice-president in charge of production at Universal, asked Demme to take over. After reading Bo Goldman's script, "the most beautiful screenplay" he had ever read, Demme agreed, with alacrity, to direct *Melvin and Howard*.

Demme persuaded Paul Le Mat, whose dissatisfaction with scripts had driven him out of movies and into boxing, to return to the screen as Melvin Dummar; Jason Robards Jr. was assigned the cameo Hughes role; Mary Steenburgen was cast as Dummar's first wife, Lynda; and Tak Fujimoto took direction of the cinematography. Filmed in Nevada, Utah, and California at a cost of $7.5 million, *Melvin and Howard* was previewed for East Coast exhibitors in June 1980. Most of the exhibitors failed fully to appreciate Goldman and Demme's unstrained and subtle comic vision of lower Middle American culture and values as personified, touchingly, with respect as well as affection, in the good old boy Melvin Dummar. The reaction of the exhibitors made Universal executives so "nervous" (their word) that they postponed releasing the movie.

*Melvin and Howard* finally had its world premiere at the Venice Film Festival in August 1980 and its American premiere at the New York Film Festival the following month, winning admiring audiences at both. Following the New York festival, the film went into limited distribution, receiving everywhere it played praise for its lyrical and relaxed style, density of detail, and oblique and uncondescending satirical insights into the quality of a working-class life buoyed in near-poverty by the pathetic illusion of an imminent jackpot. "Demme and . . . Goldman have entered the soul of American blue-collar suckerdom and brought us close enough to see that the people on the screen are us," Pauline Kael observed in the *New Yorker* (October 13, 1980). David Denby of *New York* magazine (November 3, 1980) called Demme a "true populist" filmmaker, "funny without malice," making us "understand what the crazy, paranoid, fanatically embittered old tycoon might have seen in Melvin (and in Lynda, had he met her)—not innocence exactly, but a quality of American hopefulness that once fired his own bizarre and implacable ambitions." The film made Gene Siskel of the *Chicago Tribune* (February 13, 1981) "smile from start to finish" and John Simon of *National Review* (June 12, 1981) "laugh and cry simultaneously, which makes rainbows in your eyes." *Melvin and Howard* was named best picture of the year by the National Society of Film Critics; for his direction, Demme won a New York Film Critics award; and scenarist Bo Goldman and supporting actress Mary Steenburgen won Academy Awards. The nationwide distribution of *Melvin and Howard* in 1981 earned Universal the respectable but still disappointing sum of $2 million.

Following the completion of *Melvin and Howard*, Jonathan Demme went through another fallow period, during which he helped photograph Adam Brooks's independent film *Ghost Sisters*, withdrew from the rock documentary *Urgh! A Music War* (Filmways, 1982) after a dispute with producer Michael White, and directed the lovely Public Broadcasting Service teleplay *Who Am I This Time?*, based on a short story by Kurt Vonnegut Jr. The hour-long teleplay, about a painfully withdrawn young man (Christopher Walken) and an aggressive young woman (Susan Sarandon) who develops a strategy for piercing his defenses and winning his heart, was first broadcast in PBS's American Playhouse drama series on February 2, 1982. Also for PBS, Demme in 1984 directed *Surviving a Family Tree*, a half-hour pilot for a proposed comedy series.

The "Rob Morton" who is listed as scenarist in the credits for *Swing Shift* (Warner Brothers, 1984) is a pseudonym. The film originated in a screenplay by Nancy Dowd about the women who entered the "home front" work force en masse when their men went off to fight World War II. The scenario, rewritten by Bo Goldman, made the Hollywood rounds for several years without winning the backing of a major studio but meanwhile gaining at least two fans: the director Jonathan Demme and the actress and producer Goldie Hawn. Demme and Miss Hawn began preparatory work on *Swing Shift* at United Artists in 1981, after Paramount Pictures dropped the project. United Artists in its turn decided that the projected cost of making the movie was too high a gamble. After another rewrite, by Ron Nyswaner, the cost was brought down from $20 million to $14 million, and Miss Hawn used her influence at Warner Brothers to get that studio to finance the production.

Nancy Dowd's original screenplay was political, stressing the manipulation of women, who were induced to take over "men's jobs" as riveters and welders in factories during the war and then summarily sent back to their kitchens, checkout counters, and waitress stations when the war was over. Demme, whose grandmother had worked in a wartime defense plant and who was enamored of the subject and the period, made a quite different picture, "a salute," in his words, to women who "rose to the challenge," represented in the movie by two workers on an aircraft assembly line, Kay (Goldie Hawn) and Hazel (Christine Lahti). The film, photographed by Tak Fujimoto, was completed to Demme's satisfaction in December 1983, but Goldie Hawn demanded extra footage to enhance her role and brought in Robert Towne to write additional scenes. A half hour of new footage was shot, but Demme used only two minutes of it in the version of the film he presented to Warner Brothers in January 1984. Exercising her clout as producer, Miss Hawn then had the film reedited. Demme was "deeply disappointed" with the result, in which his emphasis on the friendship between the women characters was reduced in favor of male-female romance, especially the adulterous affair between Kay and Lucky (Kurt Russell). "Every movie has a key line for me," Demme told Michael Sragow. "In *Melvin and Howard* it is when Melvin tells his lawyer, 'I'm never going to receive that money. I know that. But Howard Hughes sang Melvin Dummar's song.' In *Swing Shift*, there's a moment when the women are partying after they've all been fired, and one of them says, 'Well, we showed 'em, didn't we?'" The consensus of reviewers was that the movie perfectly evoked the ambience of the wartime home front despite a "distracted," "diffuse," "cooked-to-death" scenario. "The good things here," Jack Kroll wrote in *Newsweek* (April 23, 1984), "are the sweet humanist touch of director Jonathan Demme and the warm, no-frills acting of his cast."

Demme, who confesses to a lifelong "obsessive interest in rock and roll," had been a fan of the

Talking Heads, the "new wave" band headed by David Byrne, since 1977, when the band released its first album. With Jordan Cronenweth supervising the photography, Demme filmed three performances by the Talking Heads at the Hollywood Pantages Theatre in December 1983 and edited the footage, minus interviews and most cutaways, into *Stop Making Sense*, a Cinecom International film released by Island Alive productions in October 1984. Janet Maslin of the *New York Times* (October 19, 1984) described the movie as "a rock concert film that looks and sounds like no other," thanks to the pioneering use of "extraordinarily clear" 24-track digital recording and to a visual style "as coolly iconoclastic as the Talking Heads itself." Other reviewers hailed it as "an exhilarating celebration" and as "a continuous rock experience that keeps building, becoming ever more intense and euphoric."

"There's nothing I'd rather do than direct," Demme has said, "because directing combines three of my favorite things in life: people, imagery, and sound—not just music, but the sounds of life." As a director, he sees himself not as a promoter of personal themes but as an interpreter of scripts "that reflect real life—which is not exactly comedy and not exactly drama, but a blend of both." "I

don't want to do a series
ies . . . ," he told Hal Hins
of being an 'anybody-esqu
I like real tough pictures
*Chain Saw Massacre. . . .*1
story. Just so I am gripped b

Jonathan Demme has bee
viewers as an "enthusiastic'
who often "speaks in excli
dresses casually, in clothes boi
at second-hand and vintage cli
scribes himself as "basically a
person" who doesn't "function
attention is coming" his way. W
he lives in a hotel on Central P
wife, the Australian-born direct
who has served as second-unit d
his films. Demme's recreations,
tening to rock music, include di.
and bird watching.

*References: American Film* 9:44+
*N Y Daily News* p19+ S 26 '80 po
p41 My 13 '79 por, C p10 O 24 '80
11 '83; *Washington Post* F p1+ Ap
*International Dictionary of Films* (
*Filmmaking* (1984); Quinlan, David
*Guide to Film Directors* (1983)

## DeVries, William C(astle)

*Dec. 19, 1943– Surgeon. Address: b. c/o Humana Heart Institute International, Humana Hospital-Audubon, 1 Audubon Plaza Dr., Louisville, Ky. 40217*

On December 2, 1982 Dr. William C. DeVries and a surgical team at the University of Utah Medical Center replaced the dysfunctioning heart of Barney Clark with the Jarvik-7, a plastic-and-aluminum substitute, the first permanent artificial heart ever implanted in the chest of a living human patient. Clark lived for 112 days following the epoch-making operation, attended by DeVries and his colleagues. A potential option for patients who would otherwise die from cardiovascular disease, the artificial heart does not carry the risk of foreign-tissue rejection.

DeVries, who is the principal investigator for the Symbion artificial-heart program approved by the Food and Drug Administration and the only surgeon authorized to implant an artificial heart into a human being, is a protégé of Dr. Willem Kolff, the pioneer of biomedical engineering, or "spare parts medicine." DeVries served as chairman of the division of cardiovascular and thoracic surgery at the University of Utah from 1979 until 1984, when he joined the Humana Heart Institute International in Louisville, Kentucky. At Humana, DeVries continued to perform the artificial-heart implant operation on cardiac patients whose conditions seemed

otherwise hopeless. As of late October 1985, twi
those patients, William J. Schroeder and Murraj
Haydon, were still surviving with the Jarvik-7 ai
ficial heart.

William Castle DeVries was born on Decemb(
19, 1943 in Brooklyn, New York, to Henrick D(
Vries, a physician serving with the United State

Navy in
few mo
William
Lucille
of Utah
childre
as a N
manua
effacir
about
taking
ability
sewin
stepfa
ness.
In (
ceive
Ogd(
ketb
letic
Uni
tere
evir
and
rec(
the
I
ha
far
W
sis
he
ge
th
at
a
fi
h
f
a

World War II, who was killed in action a ▊ths after his son's birth. Shortly afterward, ▊ DeVries was taken by his mother, Kathryn ▊ (Castle) DeVries, a nurse, to her home state ▊, where she remarried and bore eight more ▊n. DeVries, who was reared in Ogden, Utah ▊ Iormon, was a mechanically-minded and ▊lly dextrous boy, though, according to a self-▊g tale he told Denise Grady for her article ▊ him in Discover (February 1983), his skill in ▊ clocks apart was not accompanied by an ▊ to reconstruct them. His early jobs included ▊g saddles at a local saddlery and helping his ▊ther in his heating and air conditioning busi-

▊spite of his prankish inclinations, DeVries re-▊d high grades at Ben Lomond High School in ▊n and excelled as a member of the school bas-▊ll team and as a track-and-field star. His ath-▊ prowess earned him a scholarship at the ▊ersity of Utah, in Salt Lake City, which he en-▊d in 1962. As a premedical student, DeVries ▊ced for a time considerable interest in botany ▊ in molecular and genetic biology. In 1966 he ▊ived his B.S. degree cum laude and enrolled in ▊ University of Utah College of Medicine.

▊During his first year of medical school, DeVries ▊pened to be present at a lecture given by the ▊ed Dutch-born Dr. Willem Kolff, who during ▊rld War II built the first successful kidney dialy-▊ machine and later developed one of the early ▊art-lung machines, which make open-heart sur-▊ry possible. In 1967, after a number of years with ▊ Cleveland Clinic, Kolff moved his base of oper-▊ions to the University of Utah. His focal project ▊ the time was the development of a workable arti-▊cial heart, a long-term endeavor that had engaged ▊is interest since the mid-1950s and was still far ▊om completion.

Fascinated by Dr. Kolff's presentation, DeVries ▊sked him for a position on his research team. As ▊DeVries recalls the incident, after he told Kolff his ▊name the senior physician said, "That's a good ▊Dutch name. You're hired." As a research associate ▊ for Kolff, DeVries performed experimental surgery ▊ on the various animals that became the first recipi-▊ents of the artificial heart. In an interview for Allen ▊ B. Weisse's book Conversations in Medicine ▊ (1984), Kolff remembered DeVries' precocity. "He ▊ was still a medical student in Utah . . . but wrote ▊ a paper on 'Consumption Coagulation Shock and ▊ the Heart,' a problem we found in animals with ar-▊ tificial hearts," Kolff recalled. "This became a clas-▊ sic after publication in 1970."

On obtaining his M.D. degree from the Univer-▊ sity of Utah College of Medicine in 1970, DeVries ▊ chose to specialize in surgery. Hardly an agonizing ▊ decision, it reflected DeVries' mechanical abilities ▊ and his desire to put his knowledge and skills to ▊ practical use. "I think I'd be bored to death in clini-▊ cal practice," he told Denise Grady in the Discover ▊ interview. "A surgeon can do more. An internist ▊ can diagnose acute appendicitis, say, but then his ▊ part of the job is done. A surgeon can go in and fix

it." Following his internship, in 1970-71, at the Duke University Medical Center in Durham, North Carolina, DeVries served as resident in cardiovascular and thoracic surgery there from 1971 until 1979.

Returning to Salt Lake City in 1979 to renew his commitment to research on the artificial heart, DeVries was appointed assistant professor of surgery at the University of Utah and chairman of its division of cardiovascular and thoracic surgery, as well as chief of thoracic surgery at the Salt Lake Veterans Administration Medical Center. Meanwhile, Kolff's team had made considerable advances on the artificial-heart project. Of special importance was Dr. Robert K. Jarvik's design and construction of a heart replacement made of polyurethane and aluminum, which is lightweight, durable, and generally efficient. The Jarvik-7, as the first definitive model was called, replaced only the ventricles, or lower pumping chambers, of the natural heart and was powered by compressed air from an electrical unit located outside the patient's body. Convinced that the device could be implanted successfully in a human patient, DeVries was told by Dr. Kolff to "go ahead and do it."

To prepare for human implantation, DeVries first installed Jarvik's artificial hearts in animals, which survived for increasing spans of time, and he also practised the preliminary phases of the operation on cadavers. But before he could implant the artificial heart in living human beings, he had to undergo the long and arduous process of obtaining the required permission for the operation from the Food and Drug Administration. After rejecting the first application from the Utah doctors, the FDA approved a protocol in September 1981, allowing the artificial heart to be implanted in patients whose hearts had failed during an operation and who could not survive except on a heart-lung machine. Those strictures were eased somewhat in June 1982, when new protocols gave permission for the implant in cases of end-stage progressive heart disease that were otherwise inoperable. Following FDA approval, heart patients began presenting themselves to a review board at the University of Utah Medical Center, a panel of six members—including DeVries and two cardiologists, a psychiatrist, a nurse, and a social worker—whose decisions were required to be unanimous.

The patient finally chosen for the first artificial-heart implant was Barney Clark, a sixty-one-year-old retired dentist, suffering from the final stages of idiopathic, or primary, cardiomyopathy, a disease in which the heart muscle degenerates and ultimately fails. According to DeVries, Clark "was too old for a transplant, there were no drugs that would help; the only thing that he could look forward to was dying." On December 1, 1982 Clark began suffering from ventricular tachycardia, an ominously regular but excessively rapid heart rhythm that led DeVries and his colleagues to rush their patient into surgery that same night, hours earlier than originally planned.

During the course of the operation, which took seven-and-a-half hours to complete, DeVries was aided by a team of fourteen doctors, nurses, and technicians. After opening Clark's chest, he placed the patient on a heart-lung machine. He then surgically cut away the left and right ventricles of Clark's diseased and swollen heart. To the upper chambers, or atria, and to the aorta and the pulmonary artery, DeVries sewed on "cuffs" made of Dacron mesh. The artificial heart was attached to these cuffs in "snap-fit" fashion, with the separate ventricles held together by Velcro fabric fasteners.

When that arrangement worked successfully, as it did after DeVries replaced a dysfunctioning artificial ventricle, the operation was basically complete. Each plastic ventricle contained a disk valve to control the flow of blood from the natural atrium. The blood in the right ventricle was pumped into the lungs via the pulmonary artery and, once oxygenated, returned to the left ventricle to be pumped to the arterial system via the aorta. The major mechanical feature that made Barney Clark's heart unique was that it was connected by two plastic tubes, one-quarter inch in diameter and six feet long, to an electrical air compressor unit outside of his body. The Jarvik-7 heart was working within Barney Clark about four-and-a-half hours after the first incision was made, and three hours later the operation was complete.

As a technical feat of no small proportions that was interesting to the public at large, the operation on Barney Clark was widely reported in the news media, which also kept a close watch on postoperative developments. But in the wake of that barrage of publicity, DeVries remained largely out of reach of the press. He and his principal associate in the case, Dr. Lyle Joyce, alternated overnight stays at the hospital in order to maintain constant vigil over their patient. Although Clark's new heart continued to beat, medical complications set in almost immediately. Two days after the original operation Clark required further surgery to close tiny air leaks in his lungs. Shortly after that problem had been corrected, Clark suffered convulsions that caused DeVries to wonder whether his patient might have suffered a massive cerebral hemorrhage. In an interview in the New York Times (April 12, 1983), DeVries remembered that episode as the most agonizing of his crises. He asked himself, he recalled, "Was Dr. Clark's head dead? Was his artificial heart working and everything else dead? Had I created a vegetable or a Frankenstein monster, something way out of control?" Fortunately, Clark had not suffered a stroke, and DeVries' decision to attach him temporarily to a respirator was the proper course.

A third operation on Clark became necessary on December 14 to replace a broken mitral valve in the artificial heart. A few days later, Clark was for the first time able to stand, with help. Soon afterward, he managed to walk a few steps and to ingest some soft food by mouth. But, though doctors continued to hold out the possibility that Clark would recover more fully, a multiform decline set in over the next three months. Clark suffered from complications of kidney and lung problems that had antedated the heart operation, and his psychological condition also declined. He eventually became disoriented and confused, especially during a period when severe nosebleeds made him extremely uncomfortable. In early March 1983, attacks of nausea and vomiting led to pneumonia and other infections which, in effect, signaled impending multiple organ failure and death. On March 23, 1983, 112 days after the artificial heart was implanted, Barney Clark died. According to DeVries, "his colon failed. Then his kidneys failed. . . . Then his lungs failed. Then his brain failed, and lastly, when the key was turned off, his heart failed."

Expressing disappointment that Barney Clark had been unable to leave the hospital after the operation, DeVries also revealed to Lawrence Altman of the New York Times (April 12, 1983) that he had established a close relationship with Clark and his wife, Una Loy, and that he and other members of the surgical team had taken the unusual step of attending their patient's funeral. From a clinical angle, DeVries and his colleagues began to sift the Barney Clark case for its important future implications. With Lyle Joyce and others involved in the case, he published the paper, "Response of the Human Body to the First Permanent Implant of the Jarvik-7 Total Artificial Heart" in the 1983 edition of Transactions, the yearly volume of proceedings of the American Society for Artificial Internal Organs. Among other findings, the authors observed that the case of Barney Clark had shown that the artificial heart would fit in the chest of an adult male without causing obstructions, that ideally, life could be sustained over a long term without causing infections or other side effects, and that a patient could tolerate the noise and bulk of the external power plant.

Although DeVries had been prepared to perform another implant of the Jarvik-7 heart within a week after Clark's death, other forces at work thwarted his enthusiasm. Objections to the artificial heart on philosophical and religious as well as practical grounds had emerged from the Clark case. Some critics, such as Professor George Annas of Boston University, suggested that the artificial-heart operation had made Barney Clark a "slave to the technology," citing the poor quality of his life while he was tethered to an unwieldy air compressor. Others questioned the worthiness of the project on the basis of its costs. The Food and Drug Administration, reevaluating the protocol of the implants, waited over a year before granting its permission for a second implant in mid-1984. According to DeVries, some seventy-seven possible candidates for an artificial heart had died in the meantime, and each operation still had to be approved by the University of Utah's institutional review board on a case-by-case basis.

On July 31, 1984 DeVries announced that he was leaving the University of Utah and his Salt Lake City medical posts for a new position. "I don't like to see people die while I wait for the red tape," he explained to reporters at a press conference, referring to the long delays he had experienced at Utah. DeVries declared his intention to become associated with the Humana Heart Institute International, an adjunct of Humana Hospital-Audubon in Louisville, Kentucky, effective October 1, 1984, and to take with him from Utah a substantial portion of the artificial-heart program. He also said that he would enter private practice in partnership with Dr. Allan M. Lansing, the chief heart surgeon at Humana.

According to the *Wall Street Journal* (August 1, 1984), Humana, one of the largest privately operated hospital chains in the United States, is also "a zealous and well-heeled backer of the artificial-heart program." It had agreed, moreover, to pay the expenses of hospitalization for as many as 100 patients undergoing the artificial-heart implant at a cost estimated at $25 million. "We won't have to worry whether a patient can pay or not," DeVries said after taking on his duties at Humana. "That was something that bothered me very much." DeVries received FDA approval, on November 8, 1984, to perform six additional artificial-heart implants.

The second implantation of the Jarvik-7 heart—an updated version equipped with a compact portable drive mechanism—was performed by Dr. DeVries, at Humana, on November 25, 1984, in a six-and-a-half-hour operation on William J. Schroeder, a fifty-two-year-old cardiac patient with a long history of serious heart disease. After additional surgery was required to stop excessive bleeding, the patient was reported on the day following the operation to be in still critical but stable condition. Despite complications, including a stroke that impaired his memory and speech, by early April 1985 Schroeder's condition had sufficiently improved to enable him to leave Humana and move to a nearby specially furnished "transition apartment." Readmitted to the hospital in May, following a second stroke, Schroeder was making slow progress in the weeks that followed toward restoration of his physical and mental functions.

Meanwhile, on February 17, 1985 Murray P. Haydon, a retired auto worker, aged fifty-eight, became the third Jarvik-7 heart recipient in a three-and-a-half hour operation by DeVries that was described as "perfect." Although he later suffered internal bleeding and a stroke, as well as anemia and kidney problems, by mid-1985 Haydon appeared to be making a "dramatic recovery," according to physicians at Humana.

A fourth implantation of the Jarvik-7—in which DeVries was not directly involved—was performed on April 9, 1985 on Leif Stenberg by Dr. Bjarne K. H. Sembe at the Karolinske Thoracic Clinic in Stockholm, Sweden, apparently without major complications. The fifth recipient of the Jarvik-7, and the fourth to be operated on by DeVries, was Jack C. Burcham, a terminally ill sixty-two-year-old former railroad engineer, who underwent the operation on April 14, 1985 but died ten days later, following internal bleeding as well as respiratory and kidney failure. Despite setbacks, DeVries has indicated that he would move ahead with the artificial-heart implants.

Some commentators, noting the restricted quality of life that artificial-heart recipients can expect and the huge expense of each implantation and postoperative care, question the benefits of continuing the procedure at this time. But many in the medical community believe that complications will ease as more operations are performed. In the words of one surgeon from Stanford, California, "This is not the time to say stop."

DeVries has written some fifty articles and papers for medical and scientific publications and has received a number of awards and honors, including the 1970 Wintrobe award. A director and principal stockholder of Symbion, Inc., the company established by Kolff and Jarvik to produce the artificial heart, DeVries has indicated that he may resign his directorship and divest himself of his stock if necessary, to avoid possible conflict of interest.

On June 12, 1965 William C. DeVries married Karen Olsen, a fellow student at the University of Utah who became a high-school teacher of mathematics. They have seven children: John, Adrie, Kathrine, Andrew, Janna, William, and Diana. Six feet five inches tall, DeVries was described in an article in the *Deseret News* (December 2, 1982) as "gangly and with a shock of straw-colored hair that he constantly fingers out of his eyes." Formerly fond of such high-risk activities as sky diving and rock climbing, DeVries was persuaded by his wife to give up those pursuits, and he now confines his leisure-time pursuits to skiing, racquetball, volleyball, and coaching and playing basketball. He enjoys reading verse, especially the works of Robert Service, and he listens to classical or country music while operating. DeVries and his wife make stained-glass windows of their own design.

DeVries' sensitivity, empathy, and friendliness with his patients belie the stereotypical view of surgeons as being cold and unfeeling. But in the operating room, he rules as a genial despot. "I'm the captain of the ship," he assured Denise Grady in the interview for *Discover*. "I'm in complete control of my environment. There are no distractions, I can ignore the telephone, play the music I want to hear, tell other people what to do." Within that context, DeVries revealed his self-confidence and his hopes for the value of his work to Frank W. Martin of *People* magazine (July 19, 1982) when he said, "I do the best surgery anybody can do," and added, "You're taking a person who feels rotten, who is at death's doorstep, and you're giving him life. What could be more satisfying?"

References: *Chicago Tribune* I p14+ D 2 '82 por; *Discover* 4:22+ F '83 pors; *Louisville Courier-Journal* p1+ Jl 31 '84 por, p1+ Ag 12 '84 por; *Newsweek* 100:70+ D 13 '82 pors; *N Y Times* C p1+ Ap 12 '83; *Who's Who in America*, 1984-85

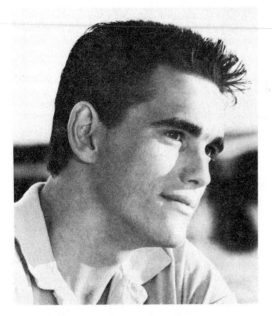

## Dillon, Matt

*Feb. 18, 1964– Motion-picture actor. Address: b. c/o Vic Ramos, 49 W. 9th St., New York City, N.Y. 10011*

Matt Dillon, who made his screen debut at age fifteen as the ill-fated suburban juvenile gang leader in *Over the Edge* (1979), established himself as teenage America's favorite heartthrob in the roles of the summer-camp kid who deflowers the willing Kristy McNichol character in *Little Darlings* (1980) and the Chicago high-school bully in *My Bodyguard* (1980). Following a slight departure from type as a poor farm youth in love above his class in *Liar's Moon* (1982), Dillon portrayed alienated and rebellious adolescents feeling trapped by life but unable to articulate that feeling in *Tex* (1982), *The Outsiders* (1983), and *Rumble Fish* (1983), all based on S. E. Hinton's "young adult" novels about good-hearted bad boys coming of age in the American heartland. After undergoing six years of near-stereotyping as a sullen, monosyllabic delinquent, Dillon made a memorable comic hero of the title character in director-writer Garry Marshall's affectionate slice of 1960s nostalgia, *The Flamingo Kid* (1984). Writing in *Vanity Fair* (August 1985), John Duka observed that out of the whole current crop of stripling male movie actors "Dillon alone, with his pseudo-macho swagger purposefully designed to conceal his shyness, his pale black-Irish luminescence, could someday fill the boots left by Gary Cooper . . . once described by Carl Sandburg as 'one of the most beloved illiterates this country has ever known.'"

Matt Dillon was born on February 18, 1964 in the New York City suburb of New Rochelle, in Westchester County, the second of six children of Paul Dillon, a sales manager for a packaging company, and Mary Ellen Dillon. He was named Matt not, as some have supposed, after Marshal Matt Dillon, the protagonist of the old television western series *Gunsmoke*, but, rather, after an uncle. A great-uncle, Alex Raymond, created the comic strips *Flash Gordon* and *Jungle Jim*, and Alex's brother Jim was among the succession of cartoonists who have drawn the strip *Blondie*, created by Chic Young. Matt's younger brother Kevin may also have a motion-picture career ahead of him; his first movie role is in *Heaven Help Us* (1985).

Growing up in the Westchester town of Mamaroneck, five miles northeast of New Rochelle, Dillon, along with the rest of the family, attended Mass every Sunday in the local Roman Catholic church. As an elementary-school student, he played Benjamin Franklin in a fourth-grade play, and in the sixth grade he won a presidential physical-fitness award for the 600-yard dash. At Hommocks Junior High School in Larchmont, midway between New Rochelle and Mamaroneck, he was "a tough guy," according to a fellow student, and he himself admits going through "a weird phase" when he was "a wise guy" and "used to get into fights." Recalling that stage of early adolescence in an interview with Lewis Archibald for the *Aquarian* (September 29–October 6, 1982), he said that, although he "liked to learn," he "wasn't a great fan of formal education" and that he "hung around with all the lowest guys in the class." "I had no identity," he told Archibald. "I didn't know what I wanted to do."

Dillon's uncertainty about his future came to an abrupt end one day in 1978 when he was spotted in a Hommocks Junior High School hallway by two women he thought to be "some sort of new hall monitors or something." In fact, they were representatives of Vic Ramos, a casting agent who was looking for "non-actors, realistic types" for *Over the Edge*, a motion picture about rampaging suburban youth that Jonathan Kaplan was preparing to direct for Orion Pictures.

When Dillon auditioned for *Over the Edge*, it took Ramos "maybe thirty seconds to realize that Matt had everything . . . it took to be a major star." For his part, Dillon swaggered through the audition with insouciance, intending "to wise off at all these movie people," but by the time he became a finalist for the second lead, a juvenile gang leader named Richie, he was eager for the role. "This guy is just like me," he later explained. "He's neat." With Dillon cast as Richie, *Over the Edge* was shot on location in Colorado, except for some scenes and some dubbing that were added in Hollywood. On his first day in the film capital, Dillon was mistaken for a runaway by police and briefly detained.

The screenplay for *Over the Edge*, written by Charlie Haas and Tim Hunter, was based on events that had actually occurred several years before in Foster City, a condominium complex built on landfill in San Francisco Bay, which in the movie becomes New Granada, a half-finished condo development somewhere in California or the Southwest. The parents who have bought into New

Granada are mostly middle-class refugees from large cities seeking better lives for their families and a return on their investment. To the children, however, the parents are the victims of a real-estate scam and New Granada is an antiseptic limbo, with no community roots, no shopping mall, roads leading nowhere, and recreation confined to a Quonset hut. Their attitude is best personified in Carl (Michael Kramer), the central figure in the movie, a basically decent fifteen-year-old, alienated but long-suffering. Not so Richie, the worldly-wise, insolent Dillon character, the provocateur who sparks the teenagers' anomie into gang vandalism. The delinquency escalates, and it reaches its climax when, after Richie is shot dead by a bungling New Granada policeman, Carl leads a riot in which the high school and its adjacent parking lot are laid waste.

Completed in 1979, *Over the Edge* was handled warily by its distributor, Warner Brothers, because of a backlash against teen gang films following disturbances incited in a few theatres by the 1979 Paramount release *The Warriors*, an extremely violent youth exploitation picture. After some regional showings, *Over the Edge* was withdrawn from theatrical distribution, and for almost two years it was seen only on cable television. It finally had its New York City premiere at the venturesome Public Theater in December 1981 and went into limited general distribution the following month. Reviewers observed that *Over the Edge* operated on two levels, combining conventions of the grade-B teen-movie genre with sociological insights, especially into the relationship between alienation and violent anarchy. As David Denby observed in *New York* (January 18, 1982), *Over the Edge* is "an exploitation movie that gets at social truths and middle-class nightmares far more effectively" than most "responsible" films. After describing Dillon's delivery as "little more than a breathy snarl," Denby went on to say, "Acting technique may come later; in 1978 he had the sensual command to play a graceful young hood on instinct alone."

Ronald F. Maxwell directed the comedy *Little Darlings* (Paramount, 1980), an exercise in titillation over pubescent sexual initiation, set in a summer camp. Two of the fifteen-year-old girl campers, Ferris (Tatum O'Neal) and Angel (Kristy McNichol) are bullied by peer pressure into a contest over who will lose her virginity first. Angel does, to a surly young stud named Randy, played by Dillon, who, in the words of David Ansen of *Newsweek* (March 4, 1980), "mixes a tough-kid manner with his androgynous prettiness in a role that requires more posturing than performing." The McNichol character emerges from her deflowering sadder but wiser, bringing the film to its cautionary close. While too simpleminded for prurient adults, *Little Darlings* was deemed too smutty for children (because of its theme and context and not its depictions of sex, which are discreet), and for that reason it was given a restricted rating, which denied it much of the juvenile audience that

would most have appreciated it. Despite that handicap and negative notices ("blatantly sexploitative," "distasteful," "astonishingly offensive"), the picture was a box-office hit, grossing $16.7 million in the United States and Canada.

In his supporting role in *Little Darlings*, Dillon, as some reviewers noted, came across as much more of a sex object than the female title characters. Soon after the movie's release the advertising for it caught up with that fact, promoting Dillon as "America's newest sensation." His reputation as a teen "idol" was reinforced by a publicity campaign orchestrated by Vic Ramos, who had become his manager. Ramos flooded such juvenile magazines as *Tiger Beat, Sixteen*, and *Teen World* with pinup photographs of his client, and a Matt Dillon fan club was formed. Soon Dillon was receiving hundreds of letters a day (the count is now up to 1,000 a day); teenyboppers were hanging around his locker at Mamaroneck High School (which he was by then attending) and sitting in parked cars on the street in front of his house, lying in wait for him; and his harried family had to get an unlisted telephone number.

With sensitivity and affection for its young characters, Alan Ormsby wrote and Tony Bill directed *My Bodyguard* (Twentieth Century-Fox, 1980), an unpretentious film several cuts above the average coming-of-age flick. In that ingratiating sleeper of the summer and fall of 1982, Dillon managed to imbue the supporting role of the school bully with some appeal and to show, as Norma McLain Stoop pointed out in *After Dark* (October 1980), "that even the worst kid on the block is a human being."

Dillon departed from the young hood stereotype in *Liar's Moon* (Crown International, 1982), the sweet, sentimental story of a poor farm boy (Dillon) and a rich girl (Cindy Fisher) overcoming the obstacles to their love in a small Texas town circa 1949. In the 1982 Public Broadcasting Service teleplay *The Great American Fourth of July and Other Disasters*, one of Jean Shepherd's fictionalized recollections of growing up in the Midwest a generation ago, Dillon radiated what John J. O'Connor of the *New York Times* (March 16, 1982) called "a boyish goofiness" in the role of the young hero, Ralph Parker.

Through Dillon and other young fans of the best-selling "young adult" novelist Susan Eloise Hinton, known to her readers as S. E. Hinton, the scenarist and director Tim Hunter became acquainted with her realistically set and emotionally empathetic stories about boys growing up manic-depressive, or at least volatile and brooding, in the American heartland. She began creating her fictional characters, loosely based on some of her gang-oriented high-school classmates, when she was herself still a teen in Oklahoma, in the mid-1960s. "I was just looking for something for Matt," Hunter told Joseph Gelmis of *Newsday* (October 10, 1982). "I thought Susie Hinton's stuff might just fit the bill. She's popular with 'Y.A.' because she hits the mark without preaching. She incorporates the real stuff—about problems with parents and how hard it is to grow up—in a wider perspective."

In collaboration with Charlie Haas and consultation with Susan Hinton, Hunter wrote *Tex* (Buena Vista, 1982), based on her novel of the same name, and that film became his first feature as a director. *Tex* is about the love-hate relationship between two brothers growing up on the Oklahoma plains poor and parentless. (The mother is dead and the improvident father is forever away on the rodeo circuit.) The title character (Dillon) is a happy-go-lucky fifteen-year-old prankster who hates school and loves his horse, Rowdy. His level-headed older brother and surrogate father, Mason (Jim Metzler), in trying to make ends meet, sells Rowdy off. Tex's bereavement over the loss of Rowdy diminishes in the course of a plot dense with such problems as class stigma, drugs, alcohol, sex, confrontations with cops and robbers, and the discovery of a skeleton in the family closet. Despite those problems, and the sense of fatalism that pervades Susan Hinton's fiction, the movie is not joyless, and its ending is upbeat.

"Hunter's major contribution as a director," Pauline Kael wrote in her review of *Tex* in the *New Yorker* (October 4, 1982), "is that he allows Dillon's mysteriously effortless charm to shine, and Dillon, who has a gift for expressing confused and submerged shifts of feeling, makes us see that *Tex* is developing into a more definite—and stronger—boy." In *Time* (October 11, 1982), Richard Schickel wrote of Dillon as Tex: "He's the kind of youngster who blends the antic and the stormy and makes it come out pure lopsided charm. No one has more accurately captured the mercurial quality of adolescence than he has, with anger, rebelliousness, gallantry, goofiness all tumbled together to create a confused, wholly believable vulnerability."

While making *Tex*, Matt Dillon developed a close relationship with Susan Hinton, who taught him how to ride a horse and became a sort of second mother to him. At her request, the director Francis Ford Coppola cast Dillon as Dallas, a tough, older member of a gang of mixed-up lower-class Tulsa boys besieged by upper-class young ruffians in *The Outsiders* (Warner Brothers, 1983), adapted by scenarist Kathleen Knutsen Rowell from Miss Hinton's novel of the same name. Working with Dillon, Coppola saw him "really turning into a man," and predicted that "from this year on, he'll be one of the exciting, young leading men that we have to think of."

*The Outsiders* did well enough at the box office, but many critics faulted Coppola and his screenwriter for losing Susan Hinton's offhand humor, tenderness, and casual pace in their translation of her novel and for turning the wistfulness of the book into portentous mush. Among them was David Denby of *New York* (April 4, 1983), who considered *The Outsiders* "an overblown, inauthentic movie" in which "the younger boys act with complete sincerity, and . . . sink to the level of the script." For Denby, Dillon, having "honed his punk mannerisms into a consistently amusing style," provided "the only moments of pleasure for adults."

Coppola followed up *The Outsiders* with another motion picture based on a Hinton novel, *Rumble Fish* (Universal, 1983), a feverish, dream-like story of sibling devotion. Written by Coppola in collaboration with Miss Hinton, that idiosyncratic production was the director's most personal film to date, dedicated to his own older brother. Shot in Tulsa, the visually bizarre, often surreal movie was stunningly photographed by Stephen H. Borum in black and white, except for shots of a pet-shop tank cruelly confining the red and blue marine creatures that give the film its title, two Siamese goldfish of a breed so bellicose that they cannot coexist even with their own reflections—apparently representing the martyrdom of American teenagers, black and white, living in internal spiritual exile. The film's spastic plot is given a semblance of continuity by the main characters, the two sons of an alcoholic father (Dennis Hopper). One is the twenty-one-year-old "Motorcycle Kid" (Mickey Rourke), a once charismatic but now burned out veteran of gang wars. The other is seventeen-year-old Rusty-James (Dillon), who still hero-worships his deranged older brother and finally, battered and bloody, succeeds in realizing the Motorcycle Kid's dream of liberating the creatures in the pet shop, especially its fighting fish. The film did poorly commercially, and critics excoriated what they considered Coppola's stylistic self-indulgence, which in their view resulted in a mélange of overblown imagery. Among the more positive notices were those of Jack Kroll of *Newsweek* (November 7, 1983), who regarded *Rumble Fish* as "a brilliant tone poem" creating "a myth about spiritual failure," and Janet Maslin of the *New York Times* (October 7, 1983), for whom the film remained interesting "as an actors' showcase . . . long after its visual affectations" had "worn thin." The measure of Dillon's performance, Miss Maslin observed, "is in the way Rusty-James changes in his brother's presence," shedding "his swaggering facade" and suggesting "weakness and uncertainty just when those things are needed."

Garry Marshall, who created and was executive producer of the nostalgic television situation comedies *Happy Days* and *Laverne and Shirley*, co-wrote and directed the sentimental comedy/drama *The Flamingo Kid* (Twentieth Century–Fox, 1984), described by Marshall as being "about the last innocent summer of Matt Dillon, and also the last innocent summer of our country—just around the corner was Kennedy's death [and] all that noisy music from England." While not as broadly humorous as Marshall's television work, the film, set in a Long Island beach club called El Flamingo in the summer of 1963, was refreshingly lighter than Dillon's previous screen vehicles. In the title role of Jeffrey Willis, Dillon is a working-class youth from Brooklyn, just out of high school, who becomes a cabana boy at the beach club, where he is bedazzled by the high life of its nouveau riche patrons and begins to question the values instilled in him by his family. In particular, under the influence of a fast-talking auto dealer named Phil Brody (Richard Crenna), he almost decides to reject his plumber father's dream of sending him to college—until he sees the hollowness of the fast-bucks future that Brody represents.

Dillon approached the comedy in *The Flamingo Kid* with some trepidation, but by "not trying to be funny but simply to play things as honestly as possible," he carried it off with impressive timing. "Matt has finally come of age himself, being less brooding and more audible," Hank Gallo observed in the New York *Daily News* (December 21, 1984), and David Ansen of *Newsweek* (December 31, 1984) expressed a common critical sentiment when he wrote, "This is not the off-putting Dillon of recent movies. . . . He's far more appealing as an awkward rube than a preening stud."

Early in 1985 Dillon was in Paris making "Target," an action adventure picture in which he plays the son of a former CIA agent (Gene Hackman) whose wife (Gayle Hunnicutt) is kidnapped by the KGB. According to Jeff Silverman in the *Chicago Tribune* (March 17, 1985), Arthur Penn, the director of "Target," describes Dillon as "a southpaw." "Like lefthanded pitchers, he's a little crazy, a little wild, a little wonderful, a little unexpected. You never know what he is going to throw. [But] he tends to come up with it [the right pitch] sooner or later." Silverman saw Dillon on the brink of developing into "young-leading-man maturity." "His charisma is unquestioned. His skills are improving. Hackman says he has the rare ability to project both innocence and vulnerability when he's right on screen."

Matt Dillon has raven hair and deep-set hazel eyes surmounted by heavy dark eyebrows, and his generic All-American-boy visage is personalized by a slightly crooked mouth that curls when he smiles or—in his tough-guy roles—snarls. "The first twenty minutes with Matt are a little uncomfortable," Garry Marshall has observed. "That's because he's shy. But when you get to know him, he's terrific." Marshall has described Dillon to interviewers as "a very nice boy—no drugs, no booze" and as "a professional" whose "whole career is keyed to being an actor" and who "probably dislikes this screaming and yelling [of fans] more than anyone [Marshall has] ever worked with."

In his relaxed way, Dillon does not let the adulation go to his head or interfere with "a normal life." He still manages to achieve a somewhat incognito public persona ("sometimes sunglasses work," but basically "it's an attitude") that allows him to "take the subways, still . . . sometimes" and enjoy "the simple things in life," such as "certain parts of the evening outdoors, walking around the streets." "I go out dancing . . . ," he told Lawrence Eisenberg in an interview for the New York *Sunday News Magazine* (December 16, 1984), "go to films, get together with friends, go to a Knicks [basketball] game." He also follows the football Giants and likes rock music (he has taken singing as well as acting lessons in recent years, and is thinking of taking saxophone lessons). On his return from making "Target" in Paris, he said, he planned to

move out of his parents' home in Mamaroneck and into his own apartment in Manhattan.

References: *Newsday* II p3+ Mr 14 '82 por; *People* 14:60+ S 29 '82 pors; *Rolling Stone* p14+ N 25 '82 pors; *Seventeen* 39:70+ Jl '80 pors

## Dohnányi, Christoph von
(doĸ-nän´ yē)

*Sept. 8, 1929- Conductor; music director.*
*Address: b. The Cleveland Orchestra, Severance Hall, Cleveland, O. 44106*

When Christoph von Dohnányi, the conductor of the Hamburg State Opera, was named music director of the Cleveland Orchestra in 1982 (effective 1984), some chauvinistic critics expressed resentment over the choice going to a foreigner whose international reputation was not yet, in their opinion, commensurate with that of the Cleveland symphony and its precise, clear "chamber music" sound, one of the best balanced in the world. Without meddling with that sound, Dohnányi has confounded his critics, making the Cleveland Orchestra, in the words of John Rhein, the music critic of the *Chicago Tribune*, "in every important respect like the patrician ensemble one remembers from the [George] Szell years [1946–70], but also a warmer and rather more mellow instrument."

Grounded in classicism, Dohnányi is disciplined but not doctrinaire, a mainstream, intellectual modernist, boldly programming contemporary works as well as bringing fresh insights into old warhorses. A no-nonsense conductor with a sharp ear for textures and balances, he is intense at the podium, leading crisply and economically but with more motion than the legendary Szell used to, coaxing his musicians and, often, urging them on with elegant sweeps of his arms. Although meticulous and demanding, he does not trap his players into metronomic rigidity but instead encourages a vibrant sound in which "beating time is less and less important." "The main thing," he has explained, "is that the orchestra is so secure about what we all together want that by listening together we can make music—style, phrasing, et cetera—instead of beating bars."

Christoph von Dohnányi was born in Berlin, Germany on September 8, 1929 to Johann-Georg von Dohnányi, commonly called Hans, a jurist who worked in banking law before obtaining posts in the German Ministry of Justice and the Abwehr counterespionage agency, and Christine (Bonhoeffer) von Dohnányi. Christoph has an older brother, Klaus, a lawyer and Social Democratic politician who is currently the mayor of Hamburg. The lineage on both sides of the family was illustrious. On the father's side, Dohnányi's forebears were Hungarian aristocrats and his grandfather was the composer and pianist Ernst von Dohnányi, also known as Ernö. On the mother's, the German psychiatrist Karl Bonhoeffer, a leading dissident from the theories of Freud and Jung, was his grandfather, and Dietrich Bonhoeffer, the German Protestant theologian martyred by the Nazis, was an uncle. Like Dietrich Bonhoeffer, Hans von Dohnányi was executed for his complicity in a plot to assassinate Adolph Hitler. "How much Dietrich Bonhoeffer meant to the world I did not know then," Christoph von Dohnányi told Paul Ingrassia of the Wall Street Journal (October 10, 1984). "I wasn't even fifteen; I played chess and soccer with him. But even as children we had a very strong feeling about being on the right side."

Before war and politics disrupted their lives, the members of the Dohnányi family regularly played chamber music together. Christoph began studying the piano when he was five, and he was soon trying his hand at composing as well. Growing up, he attended rehearsals and concerts of the Berlin Philharmonic under Wilhelm Furtwängler. Although he would nowadays fault some of Furtwängler's interpretative excesses, particularly in Beethoven, he counts that conductor among his formative models. Another was Hans Rosbaud, a teacher at the Musikhochschule in Munich, where Dohnányi became a student in 1948, after dropping out of law studies at the University of Munich. His other early conducting models included Fritz Busch, Sir Thomas Beecham, Bruno Walter, and Victor de Sabata.

Dohnányi won the Richard Strauss Prize for composition and conducting at the Musikhochschule in 1951, his final year at the Munich school. Later in the same year he came to the United States to study piano and composition under his grandfather at Florida State College in Tallahassee, where the elder Dohnányi had settled after leaving Europe. From his grandfather, a protégé of Brahms,

he imbibed a deep love and understanding of lyrical music. Before returning to Germany in the autumn of 1952, he attended the summer institute at Tanglewood in Lenox, Massachusetts, the home of the Berkshire Music Festival, where the young Leonard Bernstein was on the conducting faculty.

Georg Solti, who had studied with Dohnányi's grandfather, gave the grandson his professional start in the 1953–54 opera season. After a five-year apprenticeship as coach and conductor under Solti at the Frankfurt Opera, Dohnányi honed his conducting and managing skills as music director of the opera companies in Lübeck (1957–63) and Kassel (1963–66). In addition, he was the chief conductor of the West German Radio Symphony Orchestra in Cologne (1964–69), and as a guest maestro he conducted the world premieres of Hans Werner Henze's operas Der junge Lord (Berlin, 1965) and Die Bassariden (Salzburg, 1966) and made his first podium appearances in London, Bayreuth, Vienna, Milan, and Rome. Conducting the BBC Symphony Orchestra in London, he gave Bruckner's Sixth Symphony in A what Edward Greenfield of the Guardian (December 8, 1966) called "an unusual freshness," injecting with "the passion of youth" a work too often treated by others as that "of an old man." "Dohnányi made one remember that Bruckner . . . was in an important sense always a young composer," Greenfield wrote, "a man whose overriding quality was his child-like simplicity."

From 1968 to 1977 Dohnányi was the general music director and opera director of the Frankfurt Opera. Among his productions there were Alban Berg's Wozzeck and Lulu, Mozart's Le Nozze di Figaro, and new productions of Schoenberg's Moses und Aron, Cherubini's Medea, and Richard Strauss's Elektra. His only notable failure was a revolutionary production of Götterdämmerung, the last part of Richard Wagner's Ring cycle, the first performance of which drew a tumult of disapproval from audience and critics. He was forced to revise the production, and he finally withdrew it. In guest appearances away from Frankfurt, Dohnányi made his American debut with the Chicago Lyric Opera in 1969, conducting Wagner's Der Fliegende Holländer; returned to the Lyric several times in the early 1970s, conducting, among other operas, Strauss's Der Rosenkavalier and Mozart's Così Fan Tutte; and conducted Verdi's Falstaff at the Metropolitan Opera in New York City in 1972 and Strauss's Salome at Covent Garden in London in 1974.

During his tenure as artistic director and principal conductor of the Hamburg State Opera, from 1977 to 1982, Dohnányi spent ten weeks on the road each year, conducting operas at La Scala in Milan, at other opera houses from Paris to Tokyo, and at the major European festivals. In addition, he guest-led symphony orchestras in London, Vienna, Berlin, Amsterdam, Prague, and elsewhere. Particularly memorable, and controversial, was his leading of the Vienna Philharmonic in the first Viennese performance of Charles Ives's Symphony

No. 4. At home, he embarked on his most ambitious project when he brought producer Götz Friedrich and stage designer Jürgen Rose to Hamburg to help him begin mounting a production of Wagner's *Der Ring des Nibelungen*. Following the staging of the first two parts of the *Ring* cycle, a writer in *Scala* (No. 4, 1981) reported that "there was not only praise, [but] some of the audience found the daring ideas that were put before them to be rather strange."

Dohnányi's imaginative programming won him a host of admirers in Hamburg, but his efforts to raise performance standards also made him some enemies, who accused him, according to Michael Walsh in *Time* (November 19, 1984), of being a martinet, critical of "the smallest mistake." He took the accusations philosophically, realizing that "to have difficulties is just part of the job" and that "50 percent of the people will always be against you." Other problems made him restive, however. One was the outmoded state of the technical facilities in the opera house. Another, worse, was the unreasonable freedom enjoyed by German opera musicians, who, within minimum attendance limits, may pick and choose their schedules and substitute as they wish between rehearsals and performances, detracting from musical consistency and making difficult the attraction of high-caliber guest conductors. All along, Dohnányi was planning at some point to switch from opera to a symphonic repertory, and his decision to leave Hamburg was clinched by his brother's election as mayor of the city, a circumstance that threatened to muddy with the appearance of nepotism the negotiations for government subsidies for the opera house.

Meanwhile, Lorin Maazel, George Szell's successor as the music director of the Cleveland Orchestra, was preparing to leave that post at the end of the 1981–82 season in order to assume direction of the Vienna State Opera. (Dohnányi had vied for the Vienna position, but ambivalently, because he did "not wish to become the plaything of Viennese politics." Maazel himself would angrily resign after two years in Vienna.) When Dohnányi, at Maazel's invitation, guest-led the Cleveland Orchestra on December 3 and 5, 1981, the orchestra members as well as the audiences responded favorably to his musicianship, especially his concern for shading and balance, and for Dohnányi the experience was "love at first sight." After a careful search, the orchestra's ad hoc committee on artistic direction selected him as Maazel's successor, effective September 1984.

In the two-and-a-half-year interim between Dohnányi's appointment and his formal assumption of duties, the Cleveland Orchestra was led by various other conductors as well as, on many occasions, by Dohnányi himself. An orchestra staff member described his rehearsals on those occasions as "models of organization and efficiency." His first appearance with the Cleveland Orchestra after his appointment was at a benefit concert on February 6, 1983 that drew "the most excited audience" the assistant head usher at Severance Hall, the orchestra's home, had seen in six years of ushering. On that occasion Dohnányi's wife, the lyric soprano Anja Silja, sang Schoenberg's Six Lieder, opus 8, to thunderous applause. Local critics, who felt that standards had been let slip during the final years of Maazel's tenure, were pleased to see in Dohnányi a strict taskmaster, "woodshedding" passages over and over until he was satisfied with the result.

Following Dohnányi's fourth performing visit, Frank Hruby observed in *High Fidelity/Musical America* (February 1984) that he "simply astounded" the Cleveland listeners with his direction of Schubert's "Unfinished" Symphony, which his predecessors had made into a Cleveland Orchestra tour de force "of polish, discipline, and virtuosic balance." "Here was a performance which found delightfully new ways to please—by perfectly applied sensitivity, by the rediscovery of true pianissimo, by providing breathing space between motives, phrases, and sections," Hruby wrote. "The sympathetically accompanied Mozart and Reicha did nothing to dispel the mood of serious yet nonponderous music-making. But of course there remained the *Eroica,* which under Dohnányi's hands was rugged, heroic, square, and almost rough-cut."

"Although [personally] warm and accessible . . . ," James Badal observed in *Symphony Magazine* (June/July 1984), "on the podium Dohnányi is all business. . . . At his best he has proven himself capable of delivering performances of startling power that display a strongly individualistic profile while remaining remarkably free of self-indulgent excesses. . . . On an off day, however, he is neat and correct, more efficient than exciting." Badal noted a similarity to George Szell in Dohnányi's "predilection for firm accents, careful balances, precise attacks, and strong rhythmic thrust." On the other hand, Badal pointed out, Dohnányi "opts for a darker, weightier orchestral sonority; and in the intensely lyrical and flexible phrasing he brought to Schubert's Eighth Symphony one can, perhaps, hear echoes of the sounds Dohnányi heard over forty years ago in the old Berlin Philharmonic." According to Badal, the conductor, loath to cram, "prefers to set aside blocks of time for specific projects, such as *Ariadne auf Naxos* and *Katya Kabanova* (with Silja) this past fall in San Francisco and the recent highly successful series of *Wozzeck* performances at Covent Garden."

Dohnányi's longest stint at the Cleveland podium before he formally took over was a two-week engagement at Tanglewood, where the Cleveland Orchestra substituted for the Boston Symphony (the resident Tanglewood orchestra, which was touring Europe) in the summer of 1984. On that occasion John Rockwell of the *New York Times* (August 27, 1984) was particularly struck by the "fierce strength" that Dohnányi and the orchestra caught in Carl Ruggles' symphonic suite *Men and Mountains* and by the conductor's "thoughtful," "involving," and "daring" approach to Dvořák's Symphony in G, opus 88. Departing from the custom of treating that Dvořák symphony as a bracing romp through the Czech countryside, Dohnányi, without ignoring the folk elements, interpreted the work as a serious Brahms-style symphony and thus reminded the audience that it was composed in the Germanic idiom that prevailed in the late nineteenth century. Following the Tanglewood engagement, Dohnányi went to Germany to conduct the Berlin Philharmonic in the world premiere of the Soviet composer Alfred Schnittke's Violin Concerto No. 4, with soloist Gidon Kremer.

In Dohnányi's inaugural season as music director, 1984-85, the Cleveland schedule included some lesser known as well as standard works of composers ranging from Brahms, J. C. Bach, Haydn, Lalo, and Tchaikovsky to Wuorinen, Ruggles, Messiaen, Lutoslawski, and Schnittke. Dohnányi opened the season on September 23, 1984, conducting a program that included a passionate interpretation of Alban Berg's twelve-tone Violin Concerto, with soloist Itzhak Perlman. That concert was telecast live to Europe and taped for later American viewing over the Public Broadcasting Service.

In October 1984 Dohnányi and the Cleveland Orchestra made a two-week tour of some dozen cities in the Midwest and the East, accumulating notices as ecstatic as those it had been receiving in Cleveland. "From the opening adagio of Mozart's Symphony No. 38 in D (Prague)," Ray Cooklis wrote in the Cincinnati Enquirer, "it seemed evident that here was an orchestra with an extra dimension of unity." For John Guinn of the Detroit Free Press, Beethoven's "Grosse Fugue" and Schumann's Second Symphony "came very close to perfection." Writing in the New York Times, Tim Page reported that the orchestra sounded "luxuriant, well-rehearsed, and full of energy" and that Dohnányi conducted Dvořák's Symphony No. 9 in E-minor (New World) "as if he genuinely loved it and was determined to milk some new secrets from this most exploited of scores." Another Times critic, Donal Henahan, considered the pairing of Strauss's tone poem Also sprach Zarathustra and Schoenberg's unfinished oratorio Die Jakobsleiter (in its New York premiere) to be "inspired."

Regarding the Cleveland Orchestra's New World performance in Boston on October 15, 1984, Richard Dyer of the Boston Globe observed that Dohnányi "avoided eccentricities and exaggeration, but let nothing get by him." "He is a master of transition," Dyer wrote, "so that every change in idea, color, rhythm, and episode was both prepared for and followed up naturally, precisely, magically." Dyer thought that it was "too early to say that Cleveland is again the leading American orchestra, as it was in the '60s," but that "it could well be that the reflex response of 'Chicago' when great orchestras are discussed will have to change."

Back at Severance Hall, the Cleveland Orchestra performed the United States premiere of Schnittke's Violin Concerto No. 4 on February 7, 8, and 9, 1985, with Gidon Kremer as soloist. Three months later the orchestra again visited New York

City, giving concerts at Carnegie and Avery Fisher halls that included Bartók's Divertimento for String Orchestra, Janacek's "Taras Bulba," Brahms's Piano Concerto No. 1 in D minor (with Alfred Brendel as soloist), Beethoven's Eroica, Schoenberg's Six Lieder (with the conductor's wife, Anja Silja, as soloist), Haydn's Symphony No. 64, and Renard, Stravinsky's ballet-burlesque for dancers and singers. Writing in the New York Times, Donal Henahan observed that Dohnányi's "ardent collaboration mated perfectly with the pianist's ambitious conception" in the Brahms concerto and that Dohnányi and the Cleveland strings gave the Bartók divertimento "an unusually relaxed, pliant performance."

Henahan's Times colleague Bernard Holland, reviewing the Beethoven and Haydn performances, credited Dohnányi with submitting "performing ego in the service of style" and making his players "forget about how good they are technically and think mainly about music." Played without mannerism or extraneous gesture, the familiar pieces sounded "fresh and strong" to Holland. "What a splendid orchestra this is," he wrote, "and how well suited to its new director." Keeping his hand in opera, Dohnányi produced and directed Mozart's Die Zauberflöte (The Magic Flute) at the Blossom Music Center, the Cleveland Orchestra's summer home, on August 30 and September 1, 1985. It was the first fully staged opera to be presented at the seventeen-year-old center, and it will not be the last if Dohnányi is able to fulfill his plans for future summers.

Maestro Dohnányi has made a number of recordings on the London label, among them the five Mendelssohn symphonies with the Vienna Philharmonic. "For most music lovers in the United States," Thor Eckert Jr. wrote in the Christian Science Monitor (September 19, 1984), "the first important encounter with the name of Christoph von Dohnányi probably came with an early digital recording of rare beauty and elegance of Mendelssohn's Fourth Symphony." That digital recording, one of the first cut in Europe, was a best-seller for many weeks on the Billboard magazine classical record charts. Other Dohnányi discs with the Vienna Philharmonic include works by Strauss, Schoenberg, and Berg. His version of the Berg opera Wozzeck was nominated for a Grammy Award as the best opera recording of 1982. Under new contracts, with the Cleveland Orchestra Dohnányi will record for Decca/London and TELARC.

Christoph von Dohnányi and his wife, the opera singer Anja Silja, live in the Cleveland suburb of Shaker Heights with their three children, Julia, Benedikt, and Olga. Dohnányi also has two children from a previous marriage, to the German actress Renate Zillessen, which ended in divorce. The conductor is a voluble conversationalist, and he enjoys reading and walking. His Cleveland schedule permits him to spend a generous portion of each year traveling to guest-conducting engagements in Europe.

Dohnányi told John Rockwell of the *New York Times* (October 14, 1984) how he views his relationship to his musicians: "Conductors today have to convince an orchestra by their technique, their musicianship. Music is not a democracy; music is the meaning of one person." He added: "You see it in the Cleveland Orchestra: they have a desire for a strong person, but that person has to give his life to them and to music, and only then will they follow."

References: *Chicago Sun-Times* p23+ O 7 '84 por; *Christian Sci Mon* p25+ S 19 '84 por; *Musical America* p6+ S '84 pors; *N Y Times* p22 Mr 13 '82 por; *Opera News* 35:24 O 31 '70 por; *Scala No. 4* p27+ '81 pors; *International Who's Who, 1985-86; Slonimsky, Nicholas. Baker's Biographical Dictionary of Musicians* (1978)

## Duras, Marguerite
(dü-rä´)

*Apr. 4, 1914– Writer; filmmaker. Address: b. 5 rue St.-Benoit, 75006 Paris, France*

One of the most original and controversial figures to have emerged on the French cultural scene since World War II, Marguerite Duras resists easy classification. Her prose is cinematic, her films, literary, and her plays, nontheatrical from a traditional point of view. She has gone so far as to subtitle a seminal work, *India Song*, "text, theatre, film." It is instructive that "text" comes first. As Miss Duras told Carlos Clarens in an interview for *Sight and Sound* (Winter 1975-76), "I didn't come to the cinema from nothing, I came from writing. . . . Literature comprises everything. Everything. The text

contains the image, the performances, the readers, the spectators, everything."

In Marguerite Duras's world, memory and desire, eroticism and death, love and solitude blend, and yearnings, places, and characters from the author's life and literary works recur, as if in a cycle of eternal return. It is a return to the self. Miss Duras once described the act of writing as communication with that part of herself she calls her "writer-being." "It [the writer-being] recounts the story of my life . . . ," she said, as quoted in *Marguerite Duras* (1972). "It modifies what was lived yesterday because of what was lived today, it classifies, closes certain chapters, opens others, leaves them open, waiting for what will be lived tomorrow." How this happens, she insisted, "escapes all attempts at analysis."

Marguerite Duras was born Marguerite Donnadieu on April 4, 1914, in Gia Dinh, a small town just north of Saigon in what was then known as French Indochina, the daughter of Henri and Marie (Legrand) Donnadieu. (She took her pen name, Duras, from a village in central France where her family once owned property.) Her father was a mathematics professor; her mother, a teacher in a native village school. After her husband's death, in about 1918, Marie Donnadieu, with her three small children—Marguerite and her two older brothers, Pierre and Paul—in tow, returned to the Dordogne region of France. Recalling that period in her life for a *Guardian* (September 7, 1968) profile, Miss Duras told Lee Langley, "My mother was very distracted [absentminded] and she forgot to send me to school. For two years I ran wild; it was probably the time in my life I came closest to complete happiness. At eight, I still couldn't read or write."

A few years later, having failed to make a life for herself and her family in France, Mme. Donnadieu decided to go back to Indochina. Intending to become a rice farmer, she used most of her savings to purchase, sight unseen, a parcel of land near the Thai border. "It was salt," Miss Duras told Langley. "Just salt. We were ruined . . . . I was twelve and I remember it very clearly—the injustice, the unfairness of it, abominable." Despite the financial hardship to her family, Mme. Donnadieu managed to scrape together enough money to send Marguerite to the prestigious Lycée de Saigon. Following her graduation, in 1932, Miss Duras traveled to France, where she enrolled at the University of Paris to study law, politics, and mathematics.

From 1935 to 1941 Marguerite Duras worked as a secretary at the Ministry of Colonial Affairs in Paris. According to some sources, she was active in the Resistance movement during World War II and, at one point, was deported to Germany. She was at that time a member of the French Communist party, but she eventually left the organization "over a question of culture." "We were told one day we should burn [Jean-Paul] Sartre's books," she explained to Lee Langley, "so I said 'vive la liberté' and left. And I wasn't even an admirer of Sartre! But the intrusion of political commitment into literary creation is, for me, the beginning of a moral position which is incompatible with literature."

Marguerite Duras began her literary career in the mid-1940s, with the publication of *Les Impudents* (The Impudent Ones, Plon, 1943) and *La Vie tranquille* (The Quiet Life, Gallimard, 1944). Neither critical nor popular successes, those two otherwise unremarkable novels introduced a theme that the author was to return to again and again—namely, the "interplay between love and destruction," as Erica M. Eisinger observed in an analysis of Marguerite Duras's fiction for the scholarly quarterly *Contemporary Literature* (Autumn 1974).

The critic Germaine Brée identified another recurrent theme in Miss Duras's third novel, *Un Barrage contre le Pacifique* (Gallimard, 1950), which was published in an English translation in the United States as *The Sea Wall* (Pellegrini & Cudahy, 1952) and in Britain as *A Sea of Troubles* (Methuen, 1953). Even the title suggested to Germaine Brée "a dogged, unequal battle" against such universal and occasionally overwhelming human problems as loneliness, boredom, despair, and what she called "the pain of all involvements." At least partly autobiographical, *Un Barrage contre le Pacifique* is the story of an impoverished white colonial family's struggle to survive in Southeast Asia. Widely admired in France for its energy and its precise observation of detail, the novel was adapted for the screen in 1959 by Réné Clément, and it later served as the basis for the BBC television production *A Dam Against the Ocean*.

The "pain of all involvements" and the futility of trying to assuage loneliness through love are central to *Le Marin de Gibraltar* (Gallimard, 1952; *The Sailor from Gibraltar*, Grove, 1966), in which a blossoming relationship is frustrated by the woman's yearning for her former lover, the "sailor" of the title, and to *Les Petits Chevaux de Tarquinia* (Gallimard, 1953; *The Little Horses of Tarquinia*, J. Calder, 1960), a spare, detached account of a doomed holiday love affair that illustrates some of the obstacles to human communication and heralds Miss Duras's shift to more abstract and stylized narrative forms. *Le Square* (Gallimard, 1954; *The Square*, Grove, 1959), for example, tells its tale of a chance encounter between a young servant girl and an elderly peddler almost entirely in dialogue. Marguerite Duras's brilliant exposure of the two characters' souls through their desultory conversation turned what might have been an empty exercise in style into "a drama of redemption through language, a secular confession of loneliness and uncertainty," as Geoffrey A. Wolff remarked in his review of the English translation of the novel for the *Washington Post* (December 9, 1965).

Marguerite Duras ingeniously constructed her novel *Moderato cantabile* (Minuit, 1958; Grove, 1959) according to a musical technique suggested by the Diabelli sonatina that the heroine's child is learning to play as the story opens. The lyrical mood of the music lesson is shattered by a brutal murder in the café below and the mother's obsessive curiosity about the killer and his victim. Anne Desbaresdes, the central character, is the archetypical Duras heroine: a brooding, emotional young woman who, neglected by her husband and trapped in bourgeois routine, dreams of escape and of a love "strong as death." Described by one reviewer as a "contemporary *Madame Bovary*," the novel enjoyed considerable success with the critics and with the reading public. Peter Brook's film version, with a screenplay by Miss Duras, Brook, and Gérard Jarlot, was the official French entry at the Cannes International Film Festival in 1960, where Jeanne Moreau was named best actress for her portrayal of Anne.

Although Marguerite Duras has repeatedly rejected the label *nouveau romancier* or "new novelist," she is often included among those writers—Nathalie Sarraute, Michel Butor, and Alain Robbe-Grillet, to name a few—who in the 1950s revolutionized the French novel. But if Miss Duras shares their refusal to be bound by literary "rules," she lacks their strong theoretical bent. Moreover, her inspiration is visceral rather than cerebral, her concerns social rather than intellectual, and her prose passionate—even hallucinatory—rather than rational. Nevertheless, throughout the 1950s and for much of the 1960s, Marguerite Duras continued to explore and develop the stylistic and structural devices usually associated with the *nouveau roman* in such novels as *Dix heures et demi du soir en été* (Gallimard, 1960; *Ten-thirty on a Summer Night*, Grove, 1963), about the impact of a violent crime on a group of "respectably repressed" French tourists vacationing in Spain; *L'Après-midi de Monsieur Andesmas* (Gallimard, 1960; *The Afternoon of Monsieur Andesmas*, Calder, 1964), in which the real protagonist is time itself; *Le Vice-consul* (Gallimard, 1967; *The Vice-consul*, Hamish Hamilton, 1968), a Kafkaesque mystery set in India; and *Le Ravissement de Lol V. Stein* (Gallimard, 1964; *The Ravishing of Lol Stein*, Grove, 1966; *The Rapture of Lol V. Stein*, Hamish Hamilton, 1967).

Perhaps the most technically brilliant of those novels is *Le Ravissement de Lol V. Stein*, a detached, ambiguous account of a woman's descent into madness after being rejected by her fiancé, told from her former lover's point of view. "With her remarkable objective style, full of strange contrasts, sudden insights, and haunting images, [Miss Duras] shoots vertical shafts down into the dark morass of human love," Peter Buitenhuis observed in his assessment for the *New York Times Book Review* (February 19, 1967). "She may not come up with any answers, but she does display to the reader's eye strange cut gems of the imagination that stay with him after the shape of the events themselves has begun to dissolve."

Marguerite Duras's extraordinary visual sense and ear for dialogue make her novels ideal candidates for stage and screen adaptation. Recognizing the cinematic elements in her work, Alan Resnais, the motion-picture director, asked Miss Duras to write an original screenplay for a proposed film about the atomic bombing of Hiroshima. Her sparse, lyrical scenario became the basis for *Hiroshima, mon Amour* [Zenith International, 1959), the story of a brief, bittersweet love affair between a French film actress on location in Hiroshima and a Japanese architect in which each tries unsuccessfully to exorcise the other's wartime traumas. Acclaimed at the 1959 Cannes International Film Festival, *Hiroshima, mon Amour* went on to win several international prizes in cinema, including the New York Film Critics Award for best foreign film of 1960.

Marguerite Duras also scripted, among others, the motion pictures *10:30 P.M. Summer* (Lopert, 1966), adapted from her novel of the same name, *Les Rideaux blancs* (The White Curtains, 1966), and *Ce que savait Morgan* (What Morgan Knew, 1974). The deliberately artificial and literary dialogue that she wrote, in collaboration with Gérard Jarlot, for *Une aussi longue absence* (A Long Absence), about a café owner who becomes convinced that a tramp suffering from amnesia is her missing husband, helped earn that film the Grand Prix at the Cannes Film Festival in 1961.

In the mid-1960s, shortly after she completed work on her novel *Le Vice-consul*, Marguerite Duras decided to try her hand as a motion picture director. "I didn't feel like starting to write something else immediately . . . ," she explained to Lee Langley in the *Guardian* interview. "What interested me was the physical aspect of [filmmaking]. . . . It really is the antidote to literature." For her first project, she chose to make a screen version of her play *La Musica*, a bleak tale about a recently divorced couple who meet by chance in a gloomy hotel and discover their mutual understanding too late. To assist her, she hired Paul Seban, an experienced television director. When *La Musica* was finally screened in the United States in 1970, some four years after its European release, Vincent Canby, writing in the *New York Times* (September 15, 1970), dismissed the film as "intellectually chic moviemaking of the sort that is quite entertaining while it is going on but practically ceases to exist, even as a memory, when it's over."

In an interview for *Cahiers du Cinéma* (November 1969), Miss Duras said that in translating her novel *Détruire, dit-elle* (Minuit, 1969: *Destroy, She Said*, Grove, 1970) to the screen she wanted the camera to have the same viewpoint as the reader of the book. For that reason, she filmed *Détruire, dit-elle*, an intellectual exploration of the boundaries of sanity, mostly in long-held, almost static shots. (There are only 136 shots in *Détruire*, as opposed to 500 to 600 in the average Hollywood movie.) Some film critics complained about its insubstantial plot, intentionally bland characters, and what one called "somnambulistic dialogue," but John Russell Taylor, who appraised it for the British quarterly *Sight and Sound* (Winter 1969–70), thought that it transferred to the screen "with uncanny precision the special world of Marguerite Duras the writer: as in her novels, the outer form may be prose, but the inner life is pure poetry."

According to William F. Van Wert, who analyzed her work as a director in *Film Quarterly* (Fall 1979), Marguerite Duras refined her cinematic technique over the years by gradually exchanging "concrete references for symbolic ones" and by restricting the camera to "long, repetitive takes" and "fixed frames" that were, in his view, "both boring and fascinating, flattened out and trance-inducing." She began to experiment with sound, too. For example, in *India Song* (1975), a compelling story of lost love, murder, and suicide told in fragments of images and bits and pieces of dialogue, the characters the viewer sees do not speak and those he hears do not appear. Similar experiments with sound distinguished *Nathalie Granger* (1972), her "most minimal" film in the view of many critics, and *La Femme du Ganges* (Woman of the Ganges, 1973), among others.

In making her films, Marguerite Duras has always emphasized the primacy of text and atmosphere over camera technique and technological wizardry. With *Le Camion* (The Truck), she pushed her theories to the limit by eliminating "such middlemen," in her words, as the director and the actors in order to preserve "textual obscurity." *Le Camion* records a script-reading session, in which Miss Duras herself reads to the prospective leading player (Gérard Depardieu) the scenario for a motion picture about a truck driver and a mysterious female hitch-hiker. When the film was first shown at the Cannes Film Festival in 1977, the audience shouted insults at the screen, but reviewers generally found it to be as haunting and "perversely transfixing" as it was annoying—"a class-act monkeyshine made with absolutely confident artistry," according to Pauline Kael, who evaluated *Le Camion* for the *New Yorker* (September 26, 1977).

Throughout her career, Marguerite Duras has been fascinated by what she has called "the multiple work of art," the text that can be, successively, a novel, a play, or a film, or, occasionally, all three. *Des Journées entières dans les arbres* (Days in the Trees), perhaps her most famous play, began its life as the title piece in a collection of short stories published by Gallimard in 1954. Consisting almost entirely of dialogue, it examines futility and loneliness through the relationship of an aged, domineering mother and her shiftless son. Some ten years later she adapted her story for the stage. Directed by Jean-Louis Barrault and starring Madeleine Renaud, it was an unqualified hit in Paris, where it enjoyed an unusually long run. Equally successful productions of the English-language version, *Days in the Trees*, were mounted by the Royal Shakespeare Company, with Dame Peggy Ashcroft in the leading role, in London in 1966 and at the Circle in the Square Theatre, with Mildred Dunnock, in New York City in 1970.

Marguerite Duras's first play, *Les Viaducs de la Seine-et-Oise* (The Viaducts of Seine-et-Oise), a psychological analysis of the reasons behind a grisly crime as revealed during the interrogation of the confessed murderess and her accomplice-husband, reappeared in 1967 as the structurally austere novel *L'Amante anglaise* (Gallimard; *The English Lover*, Grove, 1968). Among the stage versions of the story are *The Viaduct*, produced in 1967 at the Yvonne Arnaud Theatre in Guildford, England, with Dame Sybil Thorndike in the leading role; *L'Amante anglaise*, mounted at the Théâtre National Populaire in Paris in 1969; *A Place Without Doors*, produced in 1970 at the Long Wharf Theatre in New Haven, Connecticut and starring Mildred Dunnock; and *The Lovers of Viorne*, staged at London's Royal Court Theatre in 1971, with Dame Peggy Ashcroft enacting the central character. Miss Duras's list of original stage credits also includes *Un Homme est venue me voir* (*A Man Came to See Me*, 1968), *Suzanna Andler* (1969), *Aurélia Steiner, Aurélia Steiner, Aurélia Steiner* (1979), *L'Homme assis dans le couloir* (*The Man Seated in the Corridor*, 1980), and *La Maladie de la mort* (*The Sickness of Death*, 1983).

In 1984, at the age of seventy, Marguerite Duras scored the greatest triumph of her long and productive career with the publication of *L'Amant* (Minuit), an idiosyncratic, at least partly autobiographical novel about an adolescent girl's first love affair. Universally praised in France, where it won the Prix Goncourt, the country's most prestigious literary prize, *L'Amant* sold more than 700,000 copies in hardcover, and the book was greeted with similar enthusiasm by American critics on its publication, as *The Lover*, in the United States by Pantheon books in 1985. Writing in the *New York Times Book Review* (June 23, 1985), Diane Johnson went so far as to call it a "perfect" novel with "a felicitous and masterly balance between formalism and powerful emotional effect." All its critical accolades notwithstanding, *The Lover* failed to generate much interest among the American book-buying public and dropped off the national bestseller list after only a few weeks.

When Lee Langley interviewed Marguerite Duras in 1968, he described her as "small-boned, pale, with the olive and brown coloring of a Courbet portrait." She still wears her unruly, now gray, hair cropped close to her head, and her narrow brown eyes are still alert, but her round face with its delicate, slightly Eurasian features has been "laid waste," as she put it, by time and alcoholism. In 1982 she voluntarily checked into the detoxification program at the American Hospital in Neuilly-sur-Seine. Unusually frank in interviews, she has willingly discussed her nightmarish experiences at the hospital with reporters, but she has been less forthcoming about other aspects of her private life, including her marital status. According to some sources, she has been briefly married twice: to the writer Robert Antelme and to Dionys Moscolo, the political philosopher and critic who is the father of her only son, Jean. Other sources say she has never married, and she herself assured Lee Langley that she was "against marriage," which she defined as "the best situation yet invented for killing love."

Marguerite Duras owns an apartment on the Left Bank in Paris, but she is more often at her farm house in Neauphle-le-Château, which she shares with Yanne Andrea, a writer. In her spare time, she reads. Although her taste in literature is eclectic, ranging from Pepys to Hemingway, she has what she has called a "true affinity" for the poets and playwrights of late seventeenth-century France, especially Ronsard and Racine.

*References: Guardian* p6 S 7 '68; *New Repub* 193:26+ S 9 '85; *People* 23:47+ S 2 '85 pors; *Sat R* 11:12 My/Je '85 por; *Contemporary Authors* 1st rev vols 25-28 (1971); *Contemporary Foreign Language Writers* (1985); *McGraw-Hill Encyclopedia of World Drama* (1984); *World Authors 1950-1970* (1975)

## Durrell, Gerald (Malcolm)
(dûr′ el)

*Jan. 7, 1925– English naturalist; writer. Address: Jersey Zoo Park, "Les Augrès Manor," Trinity, Jersey, Channel Islands*

"I cling desperately to the one thing I have—a rapport with animals," Gerald Durrell once told a Manchester *Guardian* interviewer as he talked about his lifelong mission of wild animal conservation. All forms of wildlife, whether slithering, crawling, walking, swimming, or flying, are lovely and endearing to Durrell—some more so than others, but "no creature is horrible." Dedicated to the preservation and propagation of rare wild animals endangered by man's encroachment on their habitats, in 1963 Durrell founded the Jersey Wildlife Preservation Trust to operate the model captive-breeding zoo that he had earlier created, the first and most fully developed zoo of its kind.

During his struggle to help pay the debt that he believes humanity owes for the joy of living in so marvelous a world of animals, Durrell's most persistent obstacle has been lack of sufficient funds. Since 1953, when he published *The Overloaded Ark,* he has met that constant demand for money with an outpouring of generally lucrative books, some thirty in all. Capitalizing on a fluid, easygoing, anecdotal style that seems inborn, he has written about his childhood and family relationships, his far-flung journeys on animal collecting and rescue expeditions, encounters with all sorts of people and other animals, the birth and growth of his zoological park, wildlife husbandry, and more. Today's hard-working "Noah," as he is often called, intertwines his various subjects and nearly always unifies them by the theme of conservation.

Gerald Malcolm Durrell was born on January 7, 1925 in Jamshedpur, India to Lawrence Samuel and Louisa Florence (Dixie) Durrell. His father, an Anglo-Irish civil engineer, built some of India's major railroads and bridges. There were three other children in the family, the oldest of whom is Lawrence Durrell, the distinguished poet and novelist, best known for *The Alexandria Quartet.* Gerald Durrell has said that his other brother and his sister, both older than he is, also had considerable talent, Leslie Durrell in painting and Margot Durrell in dress designing and interior decorating, as well as writing, but that they did not make an effort to develop their potential fully. According to his mother, the first word that Gerald spoke clearly was *zoo.* At the age of two he insisted that his ayah take him every day to the local "zoo of sorts." One of his most memorable early experiences was his discovery of two slugs in a ditch along a mountain road in India.

When Gerald was still in infancy, his father died. The family left India for England in 1928 and lived from time to time in London and Bournemouth, but Gerald grew up mainly on the Continent, obtaining his education from private tutors in Greece, France, Italy, and Switzerland. His most important early years were the five that he spent on Corfu just before the outbreak of World War II. He has recalled his "truly happy and sunlit childhood" in three books: *My Family and Other Animals* (Hart-Davis; Viking, 1956); *Birds, Beasts and Relatives* (Collins; Viking, 1969); and *The Garden of the Gods* (Collins, 1978; American title *Fauna and Family,* Simon and Schuster, 1979). The first chapter of his autobiographical *Fillets of Plaice* (Collins; Viking, 1971) is also devoted to an escapade on Corfu.

In his humorous, nostalgic recounting of life on the then relatively unspoilt Greek island, Durrell blends anecdotes about the foibles and antics of his colorful family with his observations of Corfu's natural history and his experiences as a collector of its many exotic forms of wildlife, pursuits in which he had the guidance of the Greek scientist Theodore Stephanides. Except perhaps for his mother, the family hopefully dismissed Gerald's self-acquired passion for animals as a phase that he would outgrow. The house seemed a "death-trap" to his brother Larry, who exploded over finding a scorpion and her infants in his match box, snakes in the bathtub, and other ubiquitous pets just "waiting to pounce." Nevertheless, repeatedly throughout *My Family and Other Animals* the boy rushes home to show his latest specimen to his family, feeling that he "would burst with suppressed joy" if he did not share his discoveries with them.

Although Lawrence Durrell can take no credit for his brother's achievements as a naturalist, he did have a positive influence on one aspect of his career. Thirteen years older, he served as something of a father figure to Gerald, whom he urged to spend time reading and later encouraged to write. The extensiveness of Gerald Durrell's reading is evident from the literary allusions in his books and his impressive range of quotations from classical and modern authors.

Forced by the inevitability of war to return to England, the Durrells lived during part of 1939 in London, where Gerald found a job in a pet shop. The family apartment was too small for him to add to the collection, including birds, dogs, and a marmoset, that he had brought from Corfu. But his work in the pet shop and his visits to the London zoo helped to satisfy his desire to be with many different kinds of animals. At the end of the war, in 1945, he eagerly accepted a position as a student keeper at Whipsnade in Bedfordshire, the Zoological Society of London's country zoo for the breeding and preservation of animals.

Durrell's entertaining account of his education at the Whipsnade Zoological Park in *Beasts in My Belfry* (Collins, 1973; American title *A Bevy of Beasts,* Simon and Schuster, 1973) makes clear his determination to have his apprenticeship serve his ambition to be someday the keeper of his own zoo. Beyond making friends with the animals and mastering the chores of feeding, grooming, and cage cleaning, he kept a detailed record of his observations of their behavior and compared his own findings with information in books about wild animals and zoos that he read incessantly. One special area of his research, which began with his working closely with the rare Père David deer, involved keeping a count of animals throughout the world that were threatened with extinction. "It was then, really," he wrote, "that I conceived the idea that should I ever acquire a zoo of my own, its main function in life would be . . . to act as a reservoir and sanctuary for these harried creatures."

After slightly more than a year at Whipsnade, Durrell gave up his job as odd-beast boy to go on an animal-collecting expedition. He was able to finance the venture, in fulfillment of a long-held ambition, with an inheritance of three thousand pounds that came to him on his twenty-first birthday. During his first zoological trip, in 1947–48, to the rain forests of the British Cameroons in Africa, he and a companion collected over a hundred crates of mammals, reptiles, and birds for English zoos. In 1948–49 he returned to the Cameroons, this time to collect in the grasslands of Bafut, and the following year he journeyed to British Guiana in South America in search of anacondas, squirrel monkeys, pipa toads, curassows, anteaters, and specimens of other rare and curious animals.

Far more rewarding in adventure than in monetary gain, the three expeditions left Durrell virtually penniless, partly because he refused to follow the practice of some animal collectors of jamming too many animals into a cage and then raising the price to compensate for the creatures who perished as a result of the squeeze. It was Lawrence Durrell, his own literary reputation then in ascent, who suggested a solution to his brother's financial problems, urging him to write books about his experiences as a wild animal collector in faraway lands so that he could fund future expeditions.

With his first book, *The Overloaded Ark* (Faber; Viking, 1953), the story of his 1947–48 trip to the British Cameroons, Durrell hit the jackpot. His account of the Cameroons revisited, *The Bafut Beagles* (Hart-Davis; Viking, 1954), proved to be equally popular, as did *Three Singles to Adventure* (Hart-Davis, 1954; American title *Three Tickets to Adventure*, Viking, 1955), which tells of his trip to British Guiana. English and American reviewers of the three books liked Durrell's refreshing straightforwardness, his joviality, and his inquisitiveness and enthusiasm toward the flora and fauna of remote places, which he described in fascinating detail. As if to account for the apparent ease with which he was able to reach a variety of readers, Maurice Richardson noted in the *New Statesman and Nation* (September 5, 1953), "Mr. Durrell has a lot of natural, unsugared charm, a pervasive mercifully unobstreperous personality."

When Durrell returned to South America in 1953 on a collecting expedition in Argentina and the Gran Chaco of Paraguay, he was accompanied by his wife, the former Jacqueline Sonia Rasen, whom he had married in 1951. She has a role in his book about that tour, *The Drunken Forest* (Hart-Davis; Viking, 1956), and also in his narrative of his 1957 Cameroons expedition, *A Zoo in My Luggage* (Hart-Davis; Viking, 1960). The latter work, like *The Bafut Beagles*, features Durrell's warmhearted friend the Fon of Bafut, ruler of the grasslands principality, who was blessed with a multitude of children from two-score wives.

The purpose of Durrell's third visit to the Cameroons, and also of his 1958–59 expedition in Patagonia and other parts of Argentina, which he related in *The Whispering Land* (Hart-Davis, 1961; Viking, 1962), had been to gather animals not for other people's zoos, but for his own. It had always been painful for him to part with the reptiles, birds, and mammals that he had cared for after capture and then had to turn over to zookeepers at the end of a voyage. He worried, moreover, about the possible maltreatment and exploitation of the animals and about the tendency of zoos generally to neglect their conservation function. Because of the success of his early books he was convinced that he could borrow money on the strength of his future books and he persuaded his British publisher, Rupert

Hart-Davis, to guarantee a large enough loan for him to establish a nonprofit scientific zoo.

If given his first choice, Durrell would have located his zoo in Bournemouth or some other town on the south coast of England, but he found the "fumbling bureaucracy" of local councils so discouraging that eventually, in 1958, he decided in favor of a thirty-five-acre site on the Channel Island of Jersey, which had the advantage of a mild climate. On the estate, furthermore, was an ideal headquarters for his undertaking, a seventeenth-century mansion named "Les Augrès Manor."

Since 1963, with Durrell as honorary chairman, the zoological park has been operated by the Jersey Wildlife Preservation Trust, whose objectives are: "1. To promote interest in wildlife conservation throughout the world. 2. To build up under controlled conditions breeding colonies of various species of animals that were threatened with extinction in the wild state. 3. To organize special expeditions to rescue seriously threatened species. 4. By studying the biology of those species, to amass and correlate data which would help toward protecting those endangered animals in the wild state." While on a lecture tour of the United States in 1973 under the auspices of SAFE (Save Animals from Extinction), of which he is a founder, Durrell established the Wildlife Preservation Trust International, with headquarters in Philadelphia, an affiliate organization of the Jersey trust. By the late 1970s Durrell's undertaking had some 15,000 member-subscribers worldwide. At the entrance to the park, Jersey's principal tourist attraction, more than 200,000 visitors annually pass by the zoo's replica of the dodo bird, a cautionary symbol of extinction. Among the hundreds of rare mammals, birds, and reptiles bred at the zoo are pygmy hedgehog tenerecs, white-eared pheasants, and Jamaican boas.

In his usual sprightly style Durrell wrote about his early struggles, setbacks, and triumphs in trying to fulfill his dream of keeping a zoo of his own in *Menagerie Manor* (Hart-Davis, 1964; Viking, 1965). More serious in approach, but not without humor, is his account in *The Stationary Ark* (Collins; Simon and Schuster, 1976) of his pioneering efforts and achievements in regard to the zoo's practice of conservation, scientific research, and specialized training programs. He also summarized the remaining goals of the Jersey trust.

After the Jersey park had become a smoothly run enterprise, Durrell continued to make round-the-world expeditions, both to rescue imperiled species for his breeding program and to find material for his books. In *Two in the Bush* (Collins; Viking, 1966) he chronicled a six-month trip through New Zealand, Australia, and Malaya to investigate wildlife conservation efforts and to help in filming rare animals for a BBC-TV series. *Catch Me a Colobus* (Collins; Viking, 1972) deals with the techniques and risks involved in breeding rare animals like the Colobus monkey and with his search in Sierra Leone and Mexico for various endangered species. The title creatures of *Golden Bats and*

Pink Pigeons (Collins; Simon and Schuster, 1977) were among the objects of Durrell's rescue operations during the 1970s in Mauritius, Rodriques, and Round Island in the Indian Ocean. He described his return to those islands in 1981, along with his visit to Madagascar, in his beautifully illustrated Ark on the Move (Coward-McCann, 1983).

One of the purposes of Durrell's 1981 visit to the Indian Ocean islands was to film a BBC-TV series, Ark on the Move, showing his breeding successes, rescue endeavors, and conservation undertakings in cooperation with governments throughout the world. Among his earlier films for television were Animal People-Menagerie Manor (1967) and The Stationary Ark (1976). He is also the author of the script for Elephant Country, a 1971 NBC-TV production. His radio talks have been collected in Encounters With Animals (Hart-Davis, 1958).

Durrell has written a half-dozen or more books for children—including The Donkey Rustlers (Collins; Viking, 1968) and The Talking Parcel (Collins, 1974; Lippincott, 1975)—most of which, like his adult books, convey his love of animals and concern for wildlife conservation. He has also produced two amusing novels, Rosie Is My Relative (Collins; Viking, 1968), a fantasy about a dipsomaniac elephant, and The Mockery Bird (Simon and Schuster, 1982), whose setting is the mythical island of Zenkali.

Turning out books is for Durrell "a terrible chore," he once disclosed in an interview for the Christian Science Monitor (November 28, 1979), going on to say, "I try to get it over with as quickly as possible. Larry writes for posterity, but I write for money—it provides me with the wherewithal to do the things I really like doing, which is rushing off to Mexico to catch volcano rabbits." While finding signs of haste now and then in his writing and of overreaching on occasion in attempts to sustain hilarity, most reviewers have praised his lucid and engaging way with words. "Durrell's surest touch is the lyric one," Silence Buck Bellows commented in the Christian Science Monitor (September 11, 1969). "He has a rare gift for capturing a fleeting moment and preserving it lastingly in the clear amber of his prose."

In 1979 Gerald Durrell's marriage to Jacqueline Durrell ended in divorce. Later in that year he married Lee Wilson McGeorge, an American zoologist who had recently obtained her doctorate. She collaborated with her husband on The Amateur Naturalist: A Practical Guide to the Natural World (Knopf, 1983), a well-received, handsomely designed introduction to field biology. Durrell is a burly six-footer with blue eyes and a whitening beard. His "exuberant life-style," as it was described in People, accommodates his fondness for rich food and ample drink. When not off on wildlife expeditions or lecture tours, Durrell divides his residence between "Les Augrès Manor" and a home near Nîmes in the south of France.

References: Discover 5:42+ D '84 pors; Manchester Guardian p10 N 10 '71 por; N Y Daily News p64 S 19 '73; N Y Times F p3+ Je 24 '73 por; People 17:119+ Mr 15 '82 pors; Washington Post L p1+ S 16 '73 por; Contemporary Authors new rev vol 4 (1981); Durrell, Gerald. My Family and Other Animals (1956), Birds, Beasts and Relatives (1969), Fillets of Plaice (1971), Beasts in My Belfry (1973), The Garden of the Gods (1978); International Who's Who, 1985–86; Who's Who, 1985–86; World Authors 1950–1970 (1975)

## Eco, Umberto

Jan. 5, 1932– Italian writer; semiotician; university professor. Address: b. University of Bologna, Via Guerrazzi 20, Bologna, Italy; h. Via Melzi d'Eril 23, Milan, Italy

Among semioticians Umberto Eco, professor of semiotics at the University of Bologna, has long been known internationally for his original theoretical contributions to the study of signs, which claims all cultural phenomena as its province. Much of his work, such as A Theory of Semiotics (1976), has been in the development of a methodology, but he has also demonstrated the practical application of his theories in scores of newspaper and magazine articles and literary essays. Recently, extending the uses of semiotics to fiction, he reached a worldwide popular audience with The Name of the Rose, published in Italy in 1980 and in the United States in 1983. His best-selling first novel is a murder mystery set in a medieval monastery, a blending of imagination and scholarship that lures its readers, partly by means of an adroit manipulation of the clichés of detective fiction, or elements of a mechanical structure, into a dazzling re-creation of life and thought in the Middle Ages. Almost all of Eco's books in Italian have been published by the Milanese firm of Bompiani, of which he is a consulting editor.

Umberto Eco was born to Giulio and Giovanna (Bisio) Eco on January 5, 1932 in Alessandria, a medieval fortress city in northwest Italy's Piedmont region. His father was employed as an office worker for a manufacturer of iron bathtubs. In an interview with Herbert Mitgang of the New York Times Book Review (July 17, 1983), Umberto Eco talked about the "exciting time" of his boyhood during World War II, when the occupying German Army fought Allied forces in Italy: "I lived in the countryside and learned to escape the bombs when I was barely 13." His familiarity with American culture began in those years, as he recalled, because "American literature was read as an anti-Fascist statement. . . . American jazz was also a statement of resistance and defiance."

It was, however, the medieval world that fascinated Eco as a student of philosophy at the University of Turin, which awarded him his doctorate in 1954. He wrote his thesis on a phase of the work of St. Thomas Aquinas, Il problema estètico in san Tommaso (The Aesthetic Problem in St. Thomas, Edizioni di Filosofia, 1956), and followed it with Sviluppo dell'Estètica Medioevale (The Development of Medieval Aesthetics, 1959). Although a variety of other interests made increased demands on his attention after a time, he yielded again, in 1972, to what he has called "this taste and this passion" for the Middle Ages with a lengthy scholarly analysis of the commentary of Beatus of Liébana, an eighth-century saint, on the Book of Revelation and of the eleventh-century illuminations of that commentary. His research into the medieval view of the Apocalypse turned out to be a particularly useful part of the thirty-year study of the Middle Ages that Eco lavished on The Name of the Rose.

After earning his doctorate, Eco became necessarily engaged in the contemporary scene because he took a job helping to prepare cultural programs in the Milan office of the RAI, the newly established Italian state television network. His on-the-spot experience from 1954 to 1959 with a developing form of public entertainment contributed much to his comprehension of the mass media, a major subject of his later books and essays. Throughout his career, Eco has combined his research and writing with teaching. His early faculty positions were assistant lecturer in aesthetics from 1956 to 1963 and lecturer in 1963–64 at the University of Turin and lecturer in the department of architecture at the University of Milan in 1964–65. For about seventeen years beginning in 1959, he was also employed as a nonfiction editor for the Bompiani publishing house. One of his first books for Bompiani, Storia figurata delle invenzioni dalla selce scheggiata al volo spaziali, which he edited with G. Zorzoli in 1961, was published by Macmillan in 1963 as The Picture History of Inventions from Plough to Polaris.

"I think that the duty of a scholar is not only to do scientific research but also to communicate with people through various media about the most important issues of social life from the point of view of his own discipline," Eco wrote in a statement for Contemporary Authors (1979). Through his commitment to involvement in present-day problems he became associated with a group of writers concerned with social change known as the Gruppo 63, who formed an avant-garde literary movement that flourished in Italy during the late 1950s and most of the 1960s. As David Robey pointed out in his essay on Eco in Writers and Society in Contemporary Italy (1984), Eco's seminal study in aesthetics, and his first book on a contemporary subject, Opera aperta (The Open Work, 1962), served as "a theoretical manifesto" for the Gruppo 63.

To reach a truer perception of the world or representation of modern experience than those of traditional art, Eco argued in Opera aperta, the avant-garde artist uses an "open," or indeterminate, form that encourages the creative collaboration of recipients of the work. The serial music of Anton von Webern, the mobiles of Alexander Calder, the novels of Franz Kafka, Symbolist poetry, and abstract painting are examples of innovative open structural forms that deliberately heighten degrees of ambiguity and increase multiplicity of interpretation. But freedom is qualified: the disorder produced by violation of conventional idiom must be controlled by the "organic fusion of multiple elements" and interpretation must be directed by the artist's intention, a purpose intrinsic to the form of the work.

The exemplary open work that receives the greatest attention in Opera aperta is James Joyce's Finnegans Wake, in which form and content merge as a contravention of established language practices conveys a sense of anarchy. Eco felt a special affinity for Joyce, he told Adele Freedman in a interview for the Toronto Globe and Mail (June 21, 1983): "The fact he was using and manoeuvering medieval elements drew me to work on him substantially—the way he recycled medieval influences." Eco's loss of faith as a Catholic, which resulted from his study of medieval philosophy for his doctoral thesis, strengthened his link with Joyce, who also had abandoned a Thomist vision of order and centrality. Only the first edition of Opera aperta included the analysis that established Eco as a Joyce scholar. It was published as a separate treatise in 1966 under the title of Le poetiche di Joyce: dalla "Summa" al "Finnegans Wake" (The Poetics of Joyce: from the "Summa" to "Finnegans Wake").

Later editions, in 1972 and 1976, of Opera aperta did, however, add an essay that Eco had written in the early 1960s for the journal Il Menabò, "Del modo di formare come impego sulla realtà" (On the Manner of Giving Form as a Committed Way of Acting on Reality). He emphasized that the open formal structure itself, regardless of content, is an instrument for social change because it creates an awareness of the present-day "crisis" and envisages the possibility of exchanging worn-out conventional relationships for new, more satisfactory ones.

A concern for social betterment also underlies Eco's approach to issues relating to mass culture and the mass media. In *Apocalittici e integrati* (Apocalyptic and Integrated [Individuals], 1964), he stood midway between intellectuals who deplored and those who approved the effect of the media on contemporary society, urging the study of the various means of communication with the purpose of finding out how to improve their cultural impact. His examination of comic strips like Superman, the lyrics of popular songs, best-selling books like Ian Fleming's James Bond novels, and television programs showed that they have a tendency to duplicate a view of life and attitude toward society already held by the complacent spectator. He objected not to occasional escapist amusement but to an exclusive diet of the kind of entertainment that neither provokes social criticism nor points to the possibilities for needed reform.

From 1966 to 1969 Eco was professor of visual communications at the University of Florence. One of the books that he wrote during that period, *Appunti per una semiologia delle communicazioni visive* (Notes for a Semiology of Visual Communications, 1967), marked his turn of attention to the expanding discipline of semiotics, an interest that grew out of his work in aesthetics and mass communications. During the year 1970–71 he taught semiotics at the Milan Polytechnic and in 1971 became professor of semiotics at the University of Bologna. That university, where he still lectures, three days a week, was the first to establish a chair in semiotics, and Eco was the first to occupy it. He made his major contributions to semiotics in *La struttura assente* (The Absent Structure, 1968), *Le Forme del contenuto* (Forms of Content, 1971), *A Theory of Semiotics* (Indiana Univ. Press, 1976), *The Role of the Reader: Explorations in the Semiotics of Texts* (Indiana Univ. Press, 1979), *Lector in fabula* (The Reader in the Tale, 1979), and *Semiotics and the Philosophy of Language* (Indiana Univ. Press, 1984). Both the last-named work and *A Theory of Semiotics* were written originally in English and have been published in Italy in Italian translation. With two other semioticians, V.V. Ivanov and Monica Rector, Eco collaborated on *Carnival!*, which was published in England by Mouton in 1985. Eco sees the carnival as the product of a comic viewpoint of the world when it is "turned upside down," as a kind of "natural theater in which animals and animal-like beings take over the power and become the masters."

As the study of signs, semiotics is concerned with communication in all its forms—words, pictures, music, gestures, clothing, architecture—and therefore with all aspects of culture. Eco's theory of semiotics, which proposes a unified approach or methodology applicable to all modes of communication, builds to some extent on the thinking of French scholars of structural linguistics—Ferdinand de Saussure and Roland Barthes,

among others—in stressing the interrelationship of elements, or units, within a structure, system, or entity. Eco postulates a process of communication, entailing a theory of "sign production," which depends upon a system of signification, entailing a theory of codes. As a bridge between "units of expression," verbal or otherwise, and "units of content," codes make it possible for signs to have meaning. To arrive at meaning, the interpreter consults a vast cultural "encyclopedia."

In his chapter "Dictionary vs. Encyclopedia" in *Semiotics and the Philosophy of Language*, Eco likened "the universe of semiosis, that is, the universe of human culture," to a rhizome labyrinth, explaining, in part, that "it is structured according to a *network of interpretants* [and] it is virtually *infinite* because it takes into account multiple interpretations realized by different cultures: a given expression can be interpreted as many times, and in as many ways, as it has been actually interpreted in a given cultural framework; it is infinite because every discourse about the encyclopedia casts in doubt the previous structure of the encyclopedia itself." As John Sturrock pointed out in his review of the book in the *New York Times Book Review* (June 13, 1984), Eco's observations make clear that differences in interpretation are inevitable and that the realization of that fact through semiotics can lead to acknowledging and coping with causes for misunderstanding. But, to quote Sturrock's summary of Eco's argument, "to try to formulate a logic for [the universe of meaning], as semanticists have long craved to do, is hopeless because no logical model will account for the indescribable and idiosyncratic complexity of its networks of sense." Although not a science, semiotics can nevertheless be used in a rational way—in criticizing art, literature, and films, for example, and in recognizing how admen and politicians can finagle codes.

Interpreting signs often involves inference, or supposition based partly on probability, as does solving a mystery. One of the subjects of Eco's lectures in the late 1970s concerned the connection between the theories of the American pioneer in semiotics, Charles Sanders Peirce, about the abductive process of reasoning and the conjectural thinking that occurs in Voltaire's *Zadig* and Arthur Conan Doyle's Sherlock Holmes stories. From his lectures Eco developed the essay "Horns, Hooves, Insteps: Some Hypotheses on Three Types of Abduction," which appears in *The Sign of Three: Dupin, Holmes, Peirce* (Indiana Univ. Press, 1983), a collection of essays on induction, deduction, and abduction in literary crime detection that he edited with Thomas A. Sebeok. Eco's interest in the theme of the book was closely related to his work on *Il nome della rosa* (1980; *The Name of the Rose*, Harcourt, 1983; translated by William Weaver).

Sebeok has said that *The Name of the Rose* "is a completely semiotic book." Its intellectual challenge begins with the title itself, taken from the Latin verse that ends the novel: "stat rosa pristina nomine, nomina nuda tenemus," which translates approximately, "the rose of an earlier time stands only as a name, we hold names alone." Attributing the quotation to the twelfth-century Benedictine Bernard of Morlay, Eco insists in *Postille a "Il nome della rosa"*(1983; *Postscript to "The Name of the Rose"*, Harcourt, 1984) that an author must not interpret his title. Nor does he make any concessions to the average modern reader in a book replete with other, sometimes lengthy, Latin passages; detailed accounts of social upheavals, papal and secular power struggles, scholastic disputes, and the contents of medieval encyclopedias and monastic libraries; and descriptions of the architectural, sculptural, and pictorial achievements of the era.

The "digressions" that make up Eco's reconstruction of the Late Middle Ages are skillfully woven into a suspense story centering on the criminal investigation of Brother William of Baskerville, a Franciscan from England and a friend of the empiricists Roger Bacon and William of Occam. Brother William's Dr. Watson is an eighteen-year-old novice Benedictine, Adso of Melk, who at the age of eighty narrates what happened during one week back in November 1327 when he and William were visiting a wealthy Benedictine abbey in Italy. Sent to the monastery to mediate a discussion between representatives of the Avignon Pope John XXII and leaders of the Franciscan order regarding their theological differences, William becomes engaged in finding the perpetrator of the macabre murders of, eventually, seven monks. He traces the cause for the killings to a secret book hidden in the abbey's forbidden labyrinthian library, "the greatest library in Christendom." But his discovery of the book and the identity of the man behind the murders precipitates the devastation by fire of the library and then the entire abbey.

A disconsolate Brother William, whose solution to the mystery was the result partly of accident rather than wholly of reasoning, reflects, "I have never doubted the truth of signs, Adso; they are the only things man has with which to orient himself in the world. What I did not understand was the relation among signs. . . . I behaved stubbornly, pursuing a semblance of order, when I should have known well that there is no order in the universe"—a conclusion that Eco himself has reached repeatedly in his work. But far from being a grim book, *The Name of the Rose* is a vigorous plea for reason, tolerance, and intellectual freedom. In trying to account for the wide appeal of the novel, reviewers have pointed to many analogies between the early fourteenth century and the late twentieth century. "I hope readers see the roots, that everything that existed then—from banks and the inflationary spiral to the burning of libraries—exists today," Eco said in his interview with Mitgang. "We are always approaching the time of the anti-Christ. In the nuclear age, we are never far from the Dark Ages."

The Name of the Rose won Italy's two top literary awards, the Premio Strega and the Premio Viareggio, and the Prix Medici in France; was a best-seller in France, Germany, and Sweden, as well as Italy; and has been translated into seventeen languages. When, in the summer of 1983, the American edition topped the *New York Times* fiction best-seller list, its paperback rights were sold to Warner Books for $550,000. The French director Jean-Jacques Arnaud is expected to make a film version of the novel.

By his own example, especially in his journalistic writing, Eco has often demonstrated one of the lessons of *The Name of the Rose*—the effectiveness of humor. His articles for the weekly *L'Espresso* and other newspapers and for more intellectual periodicals, like *Quindici* and the London *Times Literary Supplement*, deal with topical political, economic, and cultural events, frequently in practical explication of his semiotic theories. Many of his articles have been collected in *Diario minimo* (Minimum Diary; Mondadori, 1963), *Il costume di casa* (Domestic Customs, 1973), *Dalla periferia dell'impero* (From the Borders of the Empire, 1977), and *Sette anni di desiderio: Chronache 1977-1983* (Seven Years of Desire: Chronicles 1977-1983, 1984).

One of the periodicals to which Eco contributes is the semiotic review *VS*, which he founded in 1971 and has since then edited. He organized the first congress in Milan of the International Association for Semiotic Studies, of which he was secretary-general. He is also an honorary trustee of the James Joyce Foundation. Besides lecturing in European countries, he has been a visiting professor in the United States at New York University (1969-70 and 1976), Northwestern University (1972), Yale University (1977, 1980, and 1981), and Columbia University (1978).

At Bompiani in 1960, Umberto Eco met Renate Ramge, a German-born graphic artist who now teaches. They were married on September 24, 1962 and have two grown children, Stefano and Carlotta. The family lives in a large apartment in Milan and spends summers at a centuries-old manor house in the village of Montecerignone, near San Marino. Eco is a bearded, robust man whose wit, exuberance, and obliging manner delight his press interviewers. Bart Testa described him in the Toronto *Globe and Mail* (July 18, 1984) giving a lecture at the University of Toronto on the film *Casablanca*: "With his round figure dancing around the podium, his gruff voice speaking musically accented English, Eco was living up to his reputation as the Pavarotti of the lecture circuit." For a long time he has been thinking of writing a book on the philosophy of laughter.

*References:* N Y Times Bk R p31 Jl 17 '83 por; People 20:40+ Ag 29 '83 pors; Toronto Globe and Mail p13 Je 21 '83 por, p14 Jl 18 '84 por; Vanity Fair 47:112 Je '84 por; Washington Post F p1+ O 9 '83 por, C p4 My 29 '84; Caesar, Michael, and Hainsworth, Peter, eds. Writers and Society in Contemporary Italy (1984); Contemporary Authors vols 77-80 (1979); Eco, Umberto. Postscript to The Name of the Rose (1984); International Who's Who, 1985-86

## Eliade, Mircea
(el ē äd´)

Mar. 9, 1907– Religious scholar; writer. Address:
b. c/o University of Chicago, Divinity School,
1025 E. 58th St., Chicago, Ill. 60637

An encyclopedic syncretist who is best known in
the United States for his books *The Myth of the
Eternal Return* (1959) and *The Sacred and the
Profane* (1959), the eminent Romanian-born scholar Mircea Eliade has taught religious history and
ethnology throughout Europe and, since 1956, at
the University of Chicago. His rich but less familiar
body of fiction complements his hundreds of articles and more than two score of scholarly books by
using literature as a forum to expound the dialecti-
cal parallels of the sacred and the profane. Beginning with his adventurous journey to India in the
late 1920s, Eliade has continued to study the nature
of religious symbolism and to identify recurrent
patterns of ritual in a "new humanism" that acknowledges a common creative enterprise to be
found in all societies.

Although Eliade views "profane" human life as
limited by historical time, physical space, and mortality, he believes that the sacred and eternal dimension enters the world by means of those very
restrictions: indeed, he writes that "if the fantastic
or the supernatural is somehow accessible to us, we
cannot encounter it *except* [as] camouflaged in the
banal." In order to reach the spiritual plane that
transcends history, man has to experience to the
full the crises, pleasures, and penalties that accompany his temporal existence. Although modern
man cannot escape from secular and scientific consciousness, he needs a knowledge of ancient perceptions about cosmic order and timeless forms in
order to survive. By virtually inventing the contem-

porary study of comparative religion, Eliade has
added immeasurably to the understanding of
"man's cognitive relationship to the universe," to
quote the French philosopher Paul Ricoeur.
Among his honorary doctorates are those from
Yale and Loyola universities, the Universidad Nacional de la Plata in Argentina, and the Sorbonne
at the University of Paris.

Mircea Eliade was born in the Romanian capital, Bucharest, on March 9, 1907, the son of
Gheorghe, a captain in the Romanian army, and
Ioana (Stoenescu) Eliade. The father had changed
his original family name, Ieremia, to Eliade in hon-
or of the Romanian writer Eliade-Rădulescu. Mircea's brother, Nicholaie, was a year older, and he
had a sister, Cornelia, four years younger. The family apparently led a comfortable way of life, disrupted only by several moves required by
Gheorghe Eliade's military assignments, first to the
town of Rimnicu-Sărat, then to Cernavodă near the
Black Sea, and, soon after the outbreak of World
War I in 1914, back to Bucharest.

As he recalls in his *Autobiography, Volume I:
1907–1937, Journey East, Journey West* (Harper &
Row, 1981), Mircea Eliade's childhood was marked
by a relentless intellectual curiosity that was leav-
ened by his instinct for rebellion. Because he was
nearsighted, his parents forbade him to read for
recreation, lest he further impair his vision, and so
he quenched his thirst in secret and at random with
cheap novels, mysteries, psalm books, or anything
else that fell into his hands. He
showed some talent for the piano, and his boy's soprano voice raised his father's hopes that he would
become a great musician. When he could not hide
away with a book, Mircea enjoyed comradeship in
the streets with young "ruffians and urchins from
every lower-class neighborhood in town." The occupying Austro-German troops requisitioned the
family home after Romania surrendered in 1916.
Although Eliade remembers the officers billeted
with them as cosmopolitan gentlemen, the material
hardships of occupation and the sight of zeppelins
dropping bombs over the city fed his early experiments as a writer, in which he attempted an emotional war story of conquering the enemy.

After completing the primary grades, Eliade entered the Lycée Spiru-Haret in Bucharest in 1917,
where his childish fondness for all kinds of animals matured into a fascination for the natural sciences. As he was initiated into the "secrets of that
mysterious force . . . called 'Nature,'" he later recalled, " . . . everything acquired meaning and
purpose." Soon he installed in the basement and
attic of his home an insectarium, a terrarium, a
mineralogical exhibit, and later, when he learned
chemistry, a laboratory. At twelve he was filling
notebooks with scientific theories, résumés of
books, fantasy stories, and diary entries; his first
published article, on "The Enemy of the
Silkworm," appeared in a popular science periodical when he was fourteen and was followed by a
long series of his "Entomological Conversations."
While serving as editor in chief of the lycée review,

*Vlastarul*, Eliade developed segments of his journal, which he called "Romanul adolescentului miop" (A Nearsighted Romanian Youth), into articles documenting the experience of the new postwar generation, and he began several unpublished novels of cosmic scope. A manifestly brilliant but "frustrated and anarchic" student, by his own admission, he failed several lycée courses because he passionately studied everything except what his teachers insisted upon. "It seemed to me," he wrote in the *Autobiography*, "that I was entirely different from all my classmates, that I was predestined to remain on the fringes of society, . . . and that I would be forced to find a new path for myself."

The direction of that path asserted itself by the time Eliade entered the University of Bucharest in 1925, when he turned from the sciences to philosophy, alchemy, Oriental studies, and primitive religions and often slept as little as four-and-a-half hours a night to maintain his rigorous study schedule. His articles on those subjects appeared in many journals, and he served for a time on the editorial board of *Revista Universitară*. Fully immersed in student life, he nevertheless hoped to surpass his personal cultural condition and one day "solve all the 'secrets' of religions, of history, and of man's destiny on earth." He visited Orientalist scholars in Rome while on a student trip and haunted the Asiatic libraries in Geneva during two months as a League of Nations fellow there, meanwhile coming to believe that the Western gospel of progress could not respond to the modern generation's hunger for a more personal religious experience of the divine. In 1928 he completed his master's degree with a dissertation on Italian Renaissance philosophy from Marsilio Ficino to Giordano Bruno.

"India fascinated me," Eliade acknowledged in his *Autobiography*; "it drew me like a mystery through which I seemed to foresee my destiny. It was necessary that I tear myself away from everything and everyone, at any cost, to go there." On a scholarship from the Maharajah of Kassimbazar he traveled to Calcutta in the fall of 1928—as perhaps the first contemporary Romanian to do so—for doctoral studies in yoga under Surendranath Dasgupta, the renowned Indian philosopher and religious historian. Lodging at an Anglo-Indian boarding house, Eliade spent about two years mining the riches to be found at the Imperial Library, the Asiatic Society, and in classes at the University of Calcutta, meanwhile pursuing his interests in east Asian ethnology and such languages as Pali, Sanskrit, Dravidian, and Bengali. But when he moved into Dasgupta's home as his research assistant, his scholarly concentrations were interrupted by a brief but intense love affair with Dasgupta's daughter, a liaison of which the family disapproved. Eliade soon quit the house and within weeks took up residence at an ashram, or religious colony, in Rishikesh in the Himalayan region, under the tutelage of Swami Shivananda. Living for about six months in an unfurnished hut, he struggled to come to spiritual and intellectual terms with yoga's dual aspects—the stark discipline of asceticism and the transformative *eros* of tantric sexual practice. Although his Indian sojourn convinced Eliade of the unified "cosmic religiosity" displayed by all archaic traditions, at the same time he realized the futility of prematurely renouncing his own world of Romanian language and culture.

Returning to Bucharest on Christmas Eve, 1931, after serving for several months as an auxiliary in the Romanian army's antiaircraft division Eliade played a prominent role in the cultural ferment taking place among the nation's young intellectuals. His doctoral dissertation on yogic techniques and philosophies was accepted in 1933, and he then took an assistant professorship in philosophy in the University of Bucharest's Faculty of Letters, earning a reputation for his lively and vibrant lectures. Meanwhile he gave talks to and held symposia for the general public, often sponsored by a group he helped to form, Criterion, which was dedicated to broad cultural revival.

Appearing at the same time as his continual stream of short articles were Eliade's several volumes of Indian commentaries, among them *Intr'o mănăstire din Himalaya* (In a Himalayan Monastery, Bucharest, 1932), *India* (Bucharest, 1934), based on a series of radio talks, *Alchimia Asiatică* (Asiatic Alchemy, Bucharest, 1934), and *Şantier* (Work in Progress, Bucharest, 1935), his reminiscences, in the form of a journal, of Indian social trends. In 1938 he founded *Zalmoxis*, a journal of Orientalism and other religious studies. Eliade's marriage in about 1933 to Nina Mareş, a divorced secretary several years his senior, led friends to predict that his brilliant career would mire in trivial and bourgeois concerns, but he understood his choice to be part of his "destiny." "Precisely because my marriage to Nina seemed, *apparently*, to be a disaster," he later wrote, "it must, if I believed in the dialectics and mystery of camouflage, mean exactly the opposite."

Eliade's fictional works of the 1930s explored the conflict between ascetic and voluptuous modes of life, as well as points of contact between private and transcendent experience. The professor who travels to India to study its art in *Isabel şi Apele Diavolului* (Isabel and the Devil's Waters, Bucharest, 1930) reveals his obsession with sin and spiritual sterility in his pansexual adventures. *Maitreyi* (Bucharest, 1933), Eliade's semi-autobiographical novel of his doomed Indian love affair, is concerned with the passion, drama, and suffering that mark the way to transhistorical serenity. He examined nihilism and the struggle for authenticity among Romania's postwar bourgeoisie in *Intoarcerea din Rai* (Return from Paradise, Bucharest, 1934) and its two-volume sequel, *Huliganii* (The Hooligans, Bucharest, 1935), while *Nuntă in Cer* (Marriage in Heaven, Bucharest, 1938) is about an artist and a businessman who both love, and lose, the same woman.

While not all of Eliade's novels were considered artistically successful, the boundless imagination displayed in his writings seemed guaranteed to arouse public interest and to fuel occasional controversy. Long interested in the mythic, dreamlike literary narratives of modernists like James Joyce, Eliade first entered the genre of *littérature fantastique* with *Lumina ce se stinge* (The Light That Fails, Bucharest, 1934), most of which he wrote in Calcutta, using tantric elements and the notion of the "magic deed" in telling the effects of a mysterious fire. In *Domnişoara Christina* (Mademoiselle Christina, Bucharest, 1936) he adapted the Gothic genre to an erotic tale of possession. Another erotic fantasy, *Şarpele* (The Snake, Bucharest, 1937), disguises the eternal juxtaposition of the sacred and the profane within a novella of middle-class manners. "A favorite technique of mine," Eliade wrote in the introduction to his *Two Tales of the Occult* (Herder and Herder, 1970), a translation of two of his early stories, "aims at the imperceptible yet gradual transmutation of a commonplace setting into a new 'world,'" where the categories of "reality" and "fiction" are hidden within each other and intermingled. That literary device mirrors the concept, so central to his scholarship, that the intervention of the sacred in the world "is always camouflaged in a series of 'historical' forms, manifestations that *apparently* are in no way different from millions of other cosmic or historic manifestations." So daring were Eliade's writings in that period that some readers found them "pornographic."

Eliade believed that the cultural rebirth of Romania, with its ties to East and West and its ancient folk heritage, could contribute to a new twentieth-century humanism, but the events of World War II halted that trend indefinitely. When, in April 1940, he was called to London as cultural attaché to the Royal Romanian Legation, he left Bucharest "with empty hands," feeling that "if Romania was to disappear, [his] past no longer had any meaning." In 1941 he was transferred to the legation in Lisbon, where he managed to continue his scholarly pursuits. After the Allied victory, Eliade became visiting professor at the Ecole des Hautes Etudes of the Sorbonne at the University of Paris, in September 1945. Despite the difficulties of starting a new career in a foreign country and a foreign language, he chose to remain permanently exiled from his beloved country, which had come under Soviet control.

International recognition was accorded Eliade on the publication of his now classic texts *Traité d'histoire des religions* (Payot, 1949; *Patterns in Comparative Religion*, Sheed and Ward, 1958) and *Le Mythe de l'éternel retour* (Gallimard, 1949; *The Myth of the Eternal Return*, Pantheon, 1955). Those studies, which are Eliade's inquiries into mankind's religious experience of time, history, and three-dimensional space, survey the myths and rituals whereby archaic societies invested the chaos of daily experience with cosmic significance. Concepts of a primordial golden age; veneration of an *axis mundi*, or world center, connected to heaven; the consecration of cities, temples, or holy objects; and the ceremonial observation of nature's cyclic rhythms are all symbolic instances of the *hierophany*, Eliade's term for the manifestation of the sacred in the profane realm. For aboriginal and ancient peoples, "all the varieties of being [attained] existence only in an area dominantly sacred," mundane history was periodically nullified, and all acts were patterned on a divinely ordained model. In contrast to that "eternal return," Eliade suggests, modern historicism posits a freely innovated linear progress in time, possibly leaving mankind vulnerable to the pressure and terror of a history without meaning.

It was as an honored visiting professor that Eliade traveled, beginning in 1950, to universities throughout Scandinavia and Western Europe. His lectures at the University of Rome and the Italian Institute of the Middle and Far East were collected, along with a number of articles, into *Le Chamanisme* (Payot, 1951; *Shamanism: Archaic Techniques of Ecstasy*, Routledge, Pantheon, 1964), which detailed the practices, mythologies, and ritual accessories used by traditional shamans in North and Central Asia and other regions. He found that, far from being degraded witch doctors, those important figures, who combined the functions of magician, priest, and theologian, defended the "psychic integrity" of their communities by reaffirming the mythical time of direct communication with God in their ecstatic, trance-induced ascents into heaven or descents into hell.

Three years later Eliade produced *Le Yoga* (Payot; *Yoga: Immortality and Freedom*, Routledge, Pantheon, 1958), his masterly interpretation of that ancient spiritual philosophy, which has met with continuing acclaim. According to Eliade, yogic practice, in its comprehension of the temporal and historical finitude that condition human life, can inform the modern existentialist search for authenticity. Both the ascetic yogi and, paradoxically, the adherent of tantric sexual rituals refine physical matter—as in the alchemists' transmutations—in order to liberate the consciousness from its constraints while, at the same time, accepting the necessity of limitations in all forms of worldly being.

In all his works, Eliade insists that the sacred is an irreducible and fundamental dimension of human existence that belongs to man as *homo religiosus* and demands investigation separate from dissections by sociology, anthropology, or psychology. The hierophany must be understood as revealing the real continuity between human and cosmic structures; he writes that, by virtue of religious symbols "man does not feel himself 'isolated' in the cosmos, but he 'opens out' to a world which . . . proves 'familiar.'" He elaborated that framework in *Images et symboles* (Gallimard, 1952; *Images and Symbols: Studies in Religious Symbolism*, Harvill, Sheed and Ward, 1961), a revision of previous studies about "families" of symbols—such as "the center," knots that bind, shells from the sea, and other evocations of time and eternity—showing that the mundane object, no matter how humble, may be transformed into *autre chose*, a holy "something else" unveiling aspects of ultimate reality that are otherwise inaccessible. *Mythes, Rêves et Mystères* (Gallimard, 1957; *Myths, Dreams and Mysteries*, Harvill, Harper, 1960) used a wealth of ethnographic detail to discuss the import of such archaic beliefs for Western thought, and in *Das Heilige und das Profane* (Ruwohlt, 1957; *The Sacred and the Profane: The Nature of Religion*, Harper, 1959) he dealt with the sacralization of such mundane activities as eating, sexual congress, planting, and building by which time and space are translated into epiphanies that revivify the cosmos, society, and the individual.

In 1956 Eliade was invited to the University of Chicago to deliver its Haskell Lectures in religion, which were published in 1958 as *Birth and Rebirth: The Religious Meaning of Initiation in Human Culture* (Harvill, Harper). Named professor of history of religions in 1957, he taught classes in yoga, shamanism, and the morphology of religion, enjoying, as he wrote in *No Souvenirs: Journal, 1957-1969* (Gallimard, 1973; Harper, 1977; Routledge, 1978), the university's academic freedom and its creative interdisciplinary teaching system. In 1962 Eliade became Sewell L. Avery Distinguished Service Professor in the Divinity School and professor in the Committee on Social Thought. Among the important books he has produced since that time are *Mephistopheles and the Androgyne: Studies in Religious Myth and Symbol* (Gallimard, 1962; Sheed and Ward, 1965; *The Two and the One*, Harvill, 1965), about the resolution of duality in psychology and history; *The Quest: History and Meaning in Religions* (Univ. of Chicago Press, 1969), describing the contemporary search for the sacred; and two volumes of *The History of Religious Ideas* (Payot, 1976, 1978; Univ. of Chicago Press, 1978, 1981), spanning the paleolithic and Christian eras. His *Autobiography* was originally published in Romanian under the title *Amintiri: I. Mansarda* (Madrid, 1966).

In 1978 the University of Notre Dame published in English translation Eliade's literary masterpiece, *The Forbidden Forest* (*La forêt interdite*, Gallimard, 1955). Cast in the mold of the "magic realism" of postmodern Latin American fiction, that epic novel of shifting identities and archetypal time relates the initiatory quest of Stefan, the Romanian hero, who lives through the "nightmare of history" in the rise of fascism and the postwar Soviet occupation of his country. The book's theme of mythic tragedy, suggesting that modernity must be lived through before it can be transcended, is considered to be a key expression of Eliade's philosophical creativity, found in a novel ranked by some critics with Dostoevsky or Proust.

While teaching in Bucharest, Eliade edited several volumes of works by his countrymen Nae Ionescu, a philosopher who was his professor and friend, and the polymathic historian B. P. Hasdeu. With Joseph M. Kitagawa, he edited *History of Religions: Essays in Methodology* (Univ. of Chicago Press, 1959), and in 1961 he was made senior editor of the journal *History of Religions*. The anthology *Myths, Rites, Symbols: A Mircea Eliade Reader* was published by Harper in 1976.

At seventy-eight, with whitened hair and beard and lined features, Mircea Eliade has lost little of the handsomeness of his youth. Since January 9, 1950 he has been married to Georgette Christinel Cottescu, a Romanian emigré whom he met in France. His first wife, Nina Mareş, died while they were in Portugal during the war years. Eliade is now an emeritus professor at the University of Chicago, and his writings have been translated into more than a dozen languages. Among other projects, he is editor in chief of a proposed sixteen-volume encyclopedia of religion to be published by Macmillan. His lifelong habit of voracious reading still sustains him, and he occasionally enjoys a murder story for entertainment. Eliade does not own a car and never drives because he considers himself "too absentminded and nearsighted" to be trusted behind the wheel. He spends part of each year in Paris.

Commenting on contemporary trends in an interview for the journal *Encounter* (March 1980), Eliade approved "the new freedom of each to seek his own path" in yoga, Zen Buddhism, the natural lifestyles of hippies, and other forms, as "the roundabout way whereby we shall someday be restored to our own spiritual and religious beginnings." He seems to have been guided in his career by his conviction that religious scholarship, complemented by creative hermeneutics, "changes people." "It is more than a process of investigation," he has said. "It is also a spiritual technique which can change the very fabric of existence."

References: *Encounter* 54:21+ Mr '80; *Newsweek* 106:63 Jl 15 '85 por; *World Lit Today* 52:558+ Autumn '78; *Contemporary Authors* vols 65-68 (1977); *Contemporary Literary Criticism* vol 19 (1977); Eliade, Mircea. *Autobiography: Volume I* (1981), *No Souvenirs* (1977); *International Who's Who, 1985-86*; *Makers of Modern Culture* (1981); *Thinkers of the Twentieth Century* (1983); *Who's Who in America, 1984-85*; *World Authors 1950-1970* (1975) por

---

## Evans, Harold (Matthew)

June 28, 1928- Journalist; editor. Address: b. U.S. News & World Report, 2400 N St., N.W., Washington, D.C. 20037

In the eyes of his peers, Harold Evans is, "quite possibly, the best all-around newspaper editor in the world," to quote Tom Buckley of the *New York Times*. A staunch advocate of freedom of the press, Evans won international recognition and a clutch of journalism's most prestigious awards, notably for the controversial investigative features he oversaw during his fourteen years at the helm of the London *Sunday Times*. As overall director of the newspaper's famous "Insight" team, he instigated

*Harold Evans*

After his graduation in 1943, Evans signed up for shorthand and typing courses at Loreburn Business College and at the Brookdale Park Technical Evening School, both in Manchester, hoping that those skills would give him a head start in his chosen career of journalism. His resolve paid off the following year, when he landed a job as a general assignment reporter for the *Ashton-under-Lyne Reporter*, a Lancashire weekly. As he explained to David Remnick in an interview for a *Washington Post* (November 21, 1984) profile, Evans "covered the inquests, the courts and just walked around the streets picking up local news" until he was called up by the Royal Air Force in 1946. Assigned to duty as a clerk on an RAF base, the enterprising Evans used his free time to launch a camp newspaper, the *Empire Flying School Review*. Its first issue, which featured pictures of various airplanes on the front page, was a flop, but Evans quickly recovered. "The next month," he told David Remnick, "I had a photograph of [the actress] Diana Dors on the cover, naked except for a fur muff. It was a complete sellout." An avid sportsman, Evans also took time out from his duties to take part in the English Open Table Tennis Championships in 1946 and the Royal Air Force Athletics Finals in 1948.

Discharged from the RAF with the rank of corporal in 1949, Evans immediately enrolled at the University of Durham on a government veteran's grant. There, in addition to studying economics and political science, he edited the college newspaper and captained the University College Athletic Club. Shortly after taking his B.A. degree, with honors, in 1952, Evans secured a position as copy desk editor with the daily *Manchester Evening News*. By 1954 he had moved up to covering regional politics and to writing daily editorials. As the recipient of a Harkness Fellowship from the Commonwealth Fund of New York in 1956, he spent the next two years in the United States studying foreign policy at the University of Chicago and at Stanford University. On his return to the *Manchester Evening News* in 1958, he was promoted to assistant editor, a post he held until he assumed, in 1961, the editorship of the Darlington-based *Northern Echo*, a morning newspaper that he has since described as "the miners' daily."

Following in the footsteps of his idol and predecessor at the helm of the *Northern Echo*, W. T. Stead, a zealous, public-spirited Victorian journalist who once observed that editing a newspaper was "a marvelous opportunity for attacking the devil" (a maxim that Evans kept framed on a bookcase in his office), Evans soon inaugurated the crusading investigative series that were to become the hallmark of his editorial career. Perhaps the best-known of the *Echo*'s crusades was its "Man On Our Conscience" campaign. It called for an official inquiry into the case of Timothy Evans, who in 1950 had been wrongfully convicted and hanged as a mass murderer largely on the testimony of John Christie, the man later found to be guilty of the crimes. Realizing that "there are occasions when it is no use publishing the truth once," as he wrote in

major probes of, among other things, the Kim Philby spy scandal and the Thalidomide drug tragedy, successfully challenging Britain's restrictive press laws at the risk of a jail sentence. Under his courageous and innovative leadership in the late 1960s and 1970s, the *Sunday Times* became the largest and most profitable of the British "quality" newspapers. Evans' success at editing the *Sunday Times* was followed by a stormy, one-year editorship of the venerable daily London *Times*, culminating in a dispute with the newspaper's owner, the Australian press magnate Rupert Murdoch, over editorial independence that resulted in Evans' forced resignation in March 1982. Since October 1984, Evans has been the editorial director of *U.S. News & World Report*, a task he combines with book publishing as the editor in chief of the Atlantic Monthly Press.

Harold Matthew Evans was born on June 28, 1928 in Manchester, England, the oldest of the four sons of Frederick Albert Evans and his wife, Mary Hannah (Haselum) Evans. Of his younger brothers, Frederick is an ordained priest and a publisher's representative; Peter Brian is an insurance manager in Canada; and John is in the British foreign service. Determined to obtain for her children the formal education that she and her husband lacked, Mary Evans opened a small grocery shop in their front room in the late 1930s. The business prospered, providing a supplement to Frederick Evans' steady salary as a railroad engineer. Their combined regular incomes, though modest, were unusual in their depressed Manchester neighborhood and earned Harold the sobriquet "Posh Evans" from his classmates at St. Mary's Road Central School, where he was school captain, editor of the school magazine, and a member of the football team.

his autobiography *Good Times, Bad Times* (Atheneum, 1984), Evans printed a daily article about the case for months. His persistence eventually aroused national interest in Timothy Evans' case, culminating in a parliamentary inquiry and a posthumous royal pardon. The widely read series also contributed to a groundswell of public support for the abolition of England's death penalty. During his years at the *Northern Echo*, Evans completed work on his master's thesis on foreign policy reporting, and he received his M.A. degree from the University of Durham in 1966.

Impressed by Evans' direction of the "Man On Our Conscience" campaign, C. D. Hamilton, the editor of the London *Sunday Times*, hired him as his chief assistant in 1966. Rising to the post of managing editor within weeks, Evans took over as editor of Britain's most prestigious weekly newspaper the following year, after Hamilton was named chairman and editor in chief of Times Newspapers, the managing company for both the *Sunday Times* and the *Times* under the ownership of the Thomson Organization. Determined to transform the staid, predictably conservative *Sunday Times* into the best investigative newspaper in Britain, he immediately built up and reorganized its "Insight" team, whose staff of three reporters had mainly been used for short background features, and directed it to start in-depth, investigative reporting. Eighteen reporters were assigned to Insight's intensive 1967 investigation of the Soviet "mole" Kim Philby, which was launched just two months after Evans became editor. Their exhaustive research revealed that Philby had been a high-level operative in the vaunted MI 6, the British secret intelligence service, as head of the department's anti-Soviet operations and as its chief liaison officer with the CIA. The *Sunday Times's* investigative series outraged and embarrassed the British intelligence establishment by challenging its official line, set forth at the time of his defection to Moscow in 1963, that Philby was merely a low-level diplomat. Some government leaders went so far as to charge that, in publishing the series, Evans had "aided the enemy" and jeopardized national security.

Subsequent *Sunday Times* campaigns were occasionally met with court injunctions as well as indignation, for Evans repeatedly ran up against the countless statutes restricting press disclosures, among them the Official Secrets Act and the often broadly interpreted laws of confidence, contempt of court, and parliamentary privilege. Evans' controversial serialization, in 1975, of the late Richard H. S. Crossman's diaries documenting what the former Labour minister of housing and local government viewed as a breakdown of Cabinet government in favour of an "invisible government," to use his term, of permanent civil servants, landed the *Sunday Times* in court for having allegedly violated the law of confidence. The court's ruling upheld the applicability of the law of confidence to government, but set a favorable precedent for the press by permitting the diaries' publication on the ground that it would not inhibit the free discussion of issues in the sitting Cabinet. Parliament later ruled against regulating ministerial memoirs by statute.

Evans' thorniest legal battle—and, in the eyes of many, his greatest success—involved the *Sunday Times's* eight-year campaign to publish the Insight probe into the manufacture and distribution of Thalidomide, a tranquilizer widely prescribed in the late 1950s and early 1960s, that had since been found to cause debilitating birth defects. Motivated by an admitted desire to win higher damage settlements for the severely deformed victims and their families in pending court cases against the drug's manufacturer, Distillers Ltd., and by what he saw as a duty to "shed light on how the disaster had occurred," Evans deliberately challenged Britain's statute of civil contempt prohibiting the publication of articles that might be prejudicial to pending lawsuits. Risking heavy fines for his newspaper, a big loss of advertising revenues, and a possible jail sentence for himself, he mounted a public-pressure campaign against Distillers Ltd. that eventually resulted in the drug manufacturer's agreeing, in 1973, to a £20-million out-of-court settlement—a figure ten times higher than its original offer. Later in the same year, after an appeals court upheld the court-ordered suppression of a documented Insight investigative piece that faulted Distillers for failing to undertake reproductive studies before marketing Thalidomide, Evans took the unprecedented step of making a complaint before the European Commission of Human Rights on the ground of a violation of free speech. At least partly in response to Evans' bold step, in 1976 the British Attorney-General lifted the injunction, and Evans at last published the long-suppressed article. The following year, he won additional vindication when the European Commission ruled that the British civil contempt law violated the European Convention on Human Rights, to which Britain had been a signatory. Largely because of the *Sunday Times's* initiative, Parliament considerably liberalized the civil contempt regulation in 1982.

Evans recouped some of the enormous costs of the *Sunday Times's* major investigations by publishing many of the Insight team's reports in book form. Among those which became best sellers were *Philby; the Spy Who Betrayed a Generation* (1968), *Suffer the Children; the Story of Thalidomide* (1979), and *Destination Disaster* (1976), an analysis of the design defects that led to the crash of a wide-bodied DC-10 passenger aircraft near Paris in 1974. As of 1981, of the more than 250 libel suits filed against the *Sunday Times* as a result of the zeal of Evans' investigative reporters, in only one instance was the newspaper found guilty, and even in that case, the amount of damages assessed—reportedly about $12,000—was negligible.

Superlative investigative reporting was perhaps the most important factor accounting for the steady growth in the circulation of the *Sunday Times* under the editorship of Harold Evans, but his other innovations undoubtedly also played a part. Evans, who during the 1970s wrote a five-volume series on editing and newspaper design, changed the typography of the *Sunday Times* and radically revamped its page layout to make it more eye-catching and more readable. He added more photographs, maps, and diagrams to help his readers understand complex stories, and he hired the best journalists he could find. By 1980 the *Sunday Times* was widely regarded as a "model of excellence" by which other papers were judged, according to Tom Buckley of the *New York Times*. "Its news reporting, interpretive columns, and criticisms are written with an intelligent skepticism, sophistication, and wit that are seldom encountered in the press," Buckley wrote in an article for *Quest* (December 1980). In recognition of his contribution, his peers named Evans Campaigning Journalist of the Year in 1967, Journalist of the Year in 1973, and International Editor of the Year in 1976. He was also awarded the European Gold Medal of the Institute of Journalists.

Evans and the other members of the staff of the *Sunday Times* found themselves idle in November 1978, when mounting production losses caused by a running pressroom dispute over union-manning levels led management to suspend publication. The frustrating suspension, which lasted a full year, failed to resolve the issue, and over the next few months, sporadic labor disputes lost the *Sunday Times* an additional four million copies. Its ongoing and seemingly intractable labor problems, coupled with the chronic unprofitability of its sister publication, the daily London *Times*, prompted the Thomson Organization to put both papers on the selling block late in 1980. Evans and William Rees-Mogg, the editor of the *Times*, formed separate consortiums of journalists to purchase their respective papers, but Lord Thomson, the chairman of the Thomson Organization, eventually sold them both to Rupert Murdoch, the Australian press baron, not only because he admired Murdoch's record in subduing the unions but also because he wanted the two papers to remain under one owner.

As a condition of the sale, Murdoch, whose conservative views were reflected in a tabloid empire spanning three continents, was required to submit a written assurance of editorial independence. Moreover, he was made answerable to Parliament for keeping his side of the bargain. Under the terms of the agreement, the editors of the two papers could appeal to an independent national board of directors in the event of any editorial interference from the owner. The parliamentary guarantees undoubtedly contributed to Evans' decision to accept Murdoch's offer of the editorship of the daily London *Times* in February 1981. In so doing, he became only the second non-Oxbridge man in the two-hundred-year history of that august newspaper to hold the position. Excited by the prospect of modernizing the hidebound *Times*, Evans quickly set about rejuvenating the newspaper's layout and design, much as he had done with the *Sunday Times*. He also launched a regular Friday arts guide, reintroduced "light" editorials, and, in spite

of an uproar from longtime readers, replaced the traditional classified advertisements on the back page with the "Times Information Service," a fact-packed potpourri of news and announcements that soon became a popular feature.

Although his staff responded to most of his innovations with enthusiasm, some of the old guard resisted Evans' efforts to step up the paper's coverage of fast-breaking news events, arguing that thoughtful analyses after the dust had settled were more in keeping with the *Times's* reputation as Britain's "newspaper of record." But his experiments paid off in a gradual increase in the number of readers. In the first eight months of Evans' tenure, the average daily circulation jumped from 272,000 to 303,-000.

At first Murdoch supported Evans in his experiments, but after a six-month honeymoon the owner began to vent his growing irritation over his editor's failure to champion Prime Minister Margaret Thatcher's monetarist economic policies and to uphold the conservative line on other national and international issues. In his *Good Times, Bad Times* Evans recounted several of Murdoch's attempts to meddle with the newspaper's editorial and news content, in apparent violation of the parliamentary guarantees. Those attempts ranged from a suggestion that the *Times* run a daily bingo game to a refusal to provide an overall editorial budget, which severely curtailed Evans' freedom as an editor by undermining his ability to plan the news mix and assign major features. While they disagreed with Murdoch's tactics, a few former Timesmen, among them Henry Fairlie and Nicholas Hirst, found some truth in his criticisms of Evans' alleged indecisiveness, poor administration, and lack of a consistent editorial viewpoint.

After a bitter battle to retain his post—a battle marked by intrigue and infighting among members of the *Times* staff, including the defection to Murdoch of deputy editor Charles Douglas-Home—Evans finally agreed to resign in March 1982, under a reported cash settlement of $450,000. Recognizing the futility of effectively using the parliamentary guarantees against the manifold powers of a determined tycoon, and griefstricken by the recent death of his father, Evans refused to press his case before the national directors. His resignation came only weeks after he was named Editor of the Year by Granada Television Ltd.

Following his highly publicized departure from the *Times*, Evans returned briefly to teaching, as a Poynter Fellow at Yale University and, later, as a visiting professor at the Poynter Institute for Media Studies at the University of South Florida in St. Petersburg. He had previously taught in India, Malaya, Korea, and the Philippines as a visiting lecturer for the International Press Institute in the 1960s and at London University in the academic year of 1978-79. Evans also served as executive producer of the six-part documentary series *How We Learned to Ski*, which was broadcast by independent television stations in Britain in 1983. His earlier television credits, stretching back to the

1950s, include appearances on the current affairs programs *What The Papers Say, Pictures on a Page,* and *Face the Press.*

In May 1984 Evans accepted an offer from Mortimer B. Zuckerman, the chairman of the *Atlantic* magazine, to become editor in chief of the Atlantic Monthly Press, the Boston-based book publishing division of the *Atlantic.* Five months later, Zuckerman named Evans editorial director of his publication *U.S. News & World Report,* giving him broad responsibility for evaluating and redesigning the weekly newsmagazine's editorial content, staffing, and design.

Harold Evans and Tina Brown, the editor in chief of the recently revived *Vanity Fair* magazine, were married on August 19, 1981. He has three grown children, Ruth, Katherine, and Michael, from an earlier marriage to the former Enid Parker that ended in divorce in 1978. Five feet eight inches in height, Evans has the trim, athletic build that is to be expected of a man who numbers skiing, running, swimming, and taking long walks among his favorite recreations. Reading and listening to classical music are his more sedentary pursuits.

The Evanses often invite to dinner such celebrated writers, journalists, and politicians as Tom Stoppard, Michael Frayn, Benjamin C. Bradlee, Sally Quinn, and Dr. Henry A. Kissinger, whose memoirs Evans edited for publication. An admirer of the United States, which he regards as a more dynamic and open society than Great Britain, Evans has applied for permanent American residence. He divides his work week between offices in Manhattan and Washington, D.C.

References: *New Statesman* 90:106+ Jl 25 '75; *Newsweek* 99:78 Mr 29 '82 por; *Quest* 4:41+ D '80 pors; *Time* 117:59 Mr 2 '81 por; *Washington Post* D p1+ N 21 '84 por; *Contemporary Authors* vols 41–44 (1974); *International Who's Who, 1985–86; Who's Who, 1985–86*

---

## Fabius, Laurent

(fä-būs´ lō-rän)

*Aug. 20, 1946– Prime Minister of France.*
*Address: b. Hôtel Matignon, 57, rue de Varennes; h. 15 place du Panthéon, Paris*

With his popularity in mid-term decline and his country in need of economic and social change, François Mitterand, the Socialist president of France, in July 1984 made a dramatic shift in his government, committing it fully and openly to a long-building move from left to center. Accepting the resignation of Prime Minister Pierre Mauroy, a bluff populist welfare-statesman from the northern working class whose administration had been marked by disastrous experiments in nationalization and reflation, Mitterand installed at the head of a reshuffled cabinet his young protégé and confidant ("the one who best represents my ideas") Laurent Fabius, a bright, cool Parisian technocrat, the personification of pragmatic "modernization." As director of the budget and minister of industry in the Mauroy administration, Fabius had played a major role in planning Mitterand's strategy for abandoning the policy of state-controlled economic "expansion" and introducing "rigor." Now, as a prime minister trying to regear France socially and economically for the post–labor-intensive, high-tech future, he espouses a policy that has been variously categorized as "liberalism" and "supply-side socialism." Fabius envisions the state as playing a helpful but not dominant role in an economy where private enterprise will have the initiative. "My wish is to make things more efficient," he has explained. "The left has achieved a lot through legislation, but the state can't do everything. It can't stand in for business."

The scion of a wealthy, conservative Catholic family of Jewish extraction, Laurent Fabius was born in Paris on August 20, 1946 to André Fabius, a prominent antiques dealer, and Louise (Mortimer) Fabius. A brilliant student, he was educated in Paris at the Lycée Janson-de-Sailly, the Lycée Louis-le-Grand, the Ecole Normale Supérieure, the Insitut d'Etudes Politiques, and, finally, the prestigious Ecole Nationale d'Administration, which prepares the cream of France's intellectual elite for careers in management. He began his career as a civil servant in the Council of State, and he was recruited into the Socialist party by Georges Dayan, a close friend of François Mitterand, in 1974, three years after Mitterand, a late and ambiguous convert to the left, took over the party's leadership.

To foreigners, the name of the French Socialist party can be misleading. Founded in 1905 by Jean Jaurès (1859–1914), an idealistic Marxist revisionist, the party began in anticapitalist orthodoxy, committed to the achievement of world peace, social democracy, and economic equality through peaceful revolution. Its membership swelled with the influx of those who broke from Marxism when the French Communist party was established in 1921, but that membership tended to be Republican-nationalistic and viscerally anti-Communist, with a largely theoretical attraction to socialist principles. The party's history thereafter was marked by moderation, compromise, and occasional swings to the right at home and, abroad, by an empathy for the third world that seldom rose above the sentimental. It became more elitist than egalitarian, drawing its leadership from the bourgeoisie and academia and maintaining only weak ties with the French labor movement, which the Communists tended to dominate, except among Catholic workers in the north. Splintered and moribund when Mitterand took over, it was gradually transformed into the strongest party in France through Mitterand's strategy of "unity of the left," or alliance with the Communists and lesser left-wing parties.

In 1975 the Hachette publishing house issued Fabius' book La France Inégale. The following year Fabius became economic adviser to Mitterand, who was then the opposition leader, and later he became his chief of staff. He joined the Socialist party steering committee in 1977, and the following year he became the party's first secretary and press spokesman. In electoral politics, Fabius' base was Grand-Quevilly, a working-class suburb of Rouen, where he became a member of the municipal council and deputy mayor in 1977. From that base he became deputy for Seine-Maritime in the National Assembly in 1978. He won re-election to the Assembly in 1981 but gave up his seat when, having managed Mitterand's successful campaign for the presidency in the same year, he was rewarded with the post of budget director, a sub-cabinet position within the Ministry of Finance.

President Mitterand's first prime minister was Pierre Mauroy, a stalwart Socialist with a northern Catholic trade-union background. Mauroy's administration bucked the austerity trend prevalent in Western countries and committed itself to a vigorous policy of "reflation," hoping to jolt France out of economic recession by vigorous state intervention and a combination of government and worker spending at the expense of the wealthy and big business. During Mauroy's first year as prime minister, the government nationalized five major industries and thirty-nine banks, raised the minimum wage by 10 percent, increased welfare payments by 25 percent, and created 50,000 state jobs.

In helping to implement Mauroy's expansionist economic program, Fabius generally worked inconspicuously, under finance minister Jacques Lu-

cien Delors, but he established his independence with his aggressive taxation and currency policies. He introduced a punitive wealth tax (the first ever imposed in France), stringent controls to curb widespread tax fraud, a 30-percent tax on company expense accounts, and high taxes on corporate profits. He also waged an all-out war against currency smuggling, put an end to anonymity in gold transactions (the most common means of hoarding in France), and, by using French customs agents, obtained the names and amounts of previously secret Swiss bank accounts belonging to French citizens. He also tried, but failed, to introduce taxes on works of art, domestic servants, babysitters, and au-pair girls.

While scourging the rich, Fabius continued openly to flaunt his own great personal wealth, driving a pink Porsche to work, show-riding horses, and generally projecting the image of a bon vivant. His lifestyle did little to endear him to the French lower classes, and the upper classes, livid over his tax policies and the rhetoric that went along with them, branded him a "hypocrite" as well as "a traitor to his class." Following ugly confrontations with upper-class peers in two exclusive restaurants (he was booed out of the first and was refused service in the second) one night in the spring of 1982, he took his unpopularity to heart, lowered his profile, and perfected the gravity of manner that he had been cultivating, according to an admiring associate, "to get over the handicap of his youth."

At the same time, Fabius was reassessing the Socialist economic program in the light of an inflation rate reaching 12 percent, a trade deficit growing to 90 billion francs, and a franc suffering its third devaluation. After intensive consultations with Pierre Bérégevoy, the minister of social affairs, and others, he persuaded President Mitterand to change economic course, away from reflation and toward austerity. In March 1983 Mitterand did so, approving deep spending cuts and across-the-board tax increases.

The minister of industry, Jean Pierre Chevènement, a hard-line left-winger, resigned in protest over the new economic program, and Mitterand appointed Fabius to succeed him. As minister, Fabius began restructuring French industry, away from labor intensity and toward high technology. Defying the sacrosanctity of keeping employment up through state support of inefficient or obsolescent industries, he withdrew subsidies from nationalized steel, coal, and ship-building and began developing incentives for industrial modernization by private enterprise in cooperation with the government.

While big business was pleased with the change of course, the unions, the Communists, and the left-wingers in the Socialist party were not. The new austerity program resulted in dozens of plant closures and over 400,000 layoffs. Riots broke out in the steel districts of Lorraine, and in Paris thousands of workers took to the streets in protest. By the early summer of 1984, Mitterand's popularity had plummeted, with only 35 percent of the French voters expressing confidence in him. In June 1984 the Socialist coalition won only 32 percent of the vote in the elections for the European Parliament. Later in the same month, Mitterand introduced a bill to extend state control over the nation's private schools, hoping to mollify leftist discontent with the economy; instead, the bill infuriated the right, which mounted the largest public gathering since the liberation of Paris in 1944. Hastily withdrawing the school bill, Mitterand proposed in its place a constitutional amendment allowing public referendums on such issues.

Unable to accept Mitterand's capitulation on the school issue, Prime Minister Mauroy resigned on July 17, 1984. Mauroy's resignation gave Mitterand the opportunity for a bold move to revive his flagging political fortunes. Surprising all observers, he immediately named as Mauroy's successor Laurent Fabius, who thus became the youngest French chief minister since the Duke Decazes (1780–1860), who, as minister of police and the interior, ran domestic policy from 1815 to 1820. The appointment represented a gamble that the displeasure of the left (the four Communist ministers in the Cabinet resigned) would be more than offset by the appeal to the right and center of Fabius' new, hard-headed "realism" and that the Fabius administration would help win voters back to the Socialist cause before the 1986 parliamentary elections. As John Vinocur observed in the New York Times (July 18, 1984), Fabius' appointment was a "political choice aimed at bringing vigor, freshness, and an untarnished record to a government worn out by economic difficulties and unfavorable election results."

In the months following his appointment, Fabius has again and again driven home the hard message that France has no choice but "modernization or decline." Fabius' plan for the industrial modernization of France borrowed some of the lessons of American business, but it was based in larger measure on the model of Japan, where government and management cooperated in anticipating the waning of labor-intensive industry and in preparing a sophisticated work force for high technology through "preventive retraining," an antidote to transitional unemployment. According to his plan, French children would be kept in school longer for advanced technological training, displaced labor-intensive workers would be put into retraining programs, and the unemployables would be consigned to community tasks. Among his other "fronts" against inflation were greater flexibility of working hours and the extension of work in the public interest. Fabius has promised the eventual abolition of the surtax on higher incomes, with the result, he hopes, that investment in private industry will be stimulated. The revenue lost in taxes would be made up in such camouflaged levies as the increase of state transport and utility prices to "realistic" levels.

In the spring of 1985 the government announced its plan for a system of proportional representation. The announcement was greeted with outrage on all sides and even within segments of the Socialist party, and a poll taken shortly thereafter showed that only 41 percent of the French voters had confidence in Mitterand. In the same poll, 55 percent said they had confidence in Fabius, although most added that they disagreed with many of his policies.

Socialist hopes of retaining a majority in the March 1986 parliamentary elections were considerably diminished, if not dashed, by "l'affaire Greenpeace," the scandal triggered by the scuttling of the ship Rainbow Warrior by French agents in Auckland, New Zealand harbor in July 1985. The explosion of two bombs attached to the hull of the ship—which the environmental group Greenpeace was preparing for a protest voyage into the French nuclear-testing area in the South Pacific—partially sank the vessel and killed a photographer on board. After an official French inquiry was widely dismissed as a whitewash, Fabius in the course of one of his regular television interviews in September guardedly admitted the French government's culpability in the affair. While blaming the "bad decision" on his former defense minister and the recently dismissed head of Direction Générale de la Sécurité Extérieure, the French central intelligence agency, he did not make clear how high in the government the ultimate responsibility went.

Laurent Fabius has large brown eyes, a prematurely balding pate, and the most fashionable wardrobe in the French cabinet. Reserved in manner, he strikes some critics as "aloof" and even "arrogant," but those who know him well report that he is invariably "charming" and "relaxed," and in a poll announced in August 1985 the readers of a leading French women's magazine rated him the sexiest man in France. Fabius' placidity in the midst of the busiest of schedules is a conscious habit, a concomitant of his self-discipline and organization. He absorbs information quickly, retains it prodigiously, and speaks eloquently without notes.

Fabius and the former Françoise Castro were married in 1981 and have two sons, Vincent and Thomas. Trained as a sociologist, Madame Fabius is a Socialist party activist, editor of the party's journal, and a member of the communications ministry, a position in which she advises President Mitterand on the government's and the party's image among intellectuals. Soon after her husband's appointment as prime minister, Madame Fabius told a reporter, "Perhaps he will no longer be able to take care of the children as he has been doing every morning before leaving for the office." The prime minister now usually tools about in a modest two-horsepower Citröen, rather than the pink Porsche of his high-life days, but he is still a show equestrien. He also continues to go out to the movies on Sunday afternoons. According to some reports, he gave up smoking and the drinking of alcoholic beverages at the time of his personality transformation in 1982.

References: London Observer p7 Jl 22 '84; London Sunday Times p8 Jl 22 '84 por; Manchester Guardian Weekly p10 Jl 29 '84 por, p8 S 30 '84 pors; N Y Times A p6 Jl 18 '84; *International Who's Who, 1985–86; Who's Who in France, 1984–85*

## Flutie, Doug

*Oct. 23, 1962– Football player. Address: b. New Jersey Generals, 3 Empire Blvd., South Hackensack, N.J. 07606*

The college senior most assiduously pursued by the professional United States Football League after the 1984 season was the Heisman Trophy winner Doug Flutie, the improbably short (under five feet ten inches) quarterback whose passing arm and improvisational genius carried Boston College to the national spotlight. In his four seasons with the B.C. Eagles, the nimble and brainy Flutie set new National Collegiate Athletic Association Division 1-A records for yards gained passing (10,579) and in total offense (11,317), and he crowned his college career with a spectacular senior season, the high point of which was a last-second game-winning pass against Miami that clinched his reputation as a daring and imaginative gridiron miracle worker. As Alabama coach Ray Perkins observed during that season, Flutie's special magic is not in running or even in passing but in "his ability to make a play out of nothing." Acquired by the USFL's New Jersey Generals for a then record amount (a little more than $1 million a year) in February 1985, Flutie was adjusting well to the Generals' conservative running game until he broke his left collarbone, on June 1. When the Generals merged with the Houston Gamblers two months later, Donald J. Trump, the owner of the Generals, announced that Jim

Kelly would be the new team's quarterback and that he, Trump, would try to trade Flutie.

Douglas Richard Flutie was born in Manchester, Maryland on October 23, 1962 to Richard and Joan Flutie. He has an older brother, Bill, a younger brother, Darren, and a younger sister, Denise. The Flutie children grew up successively in Manchester, in Melbourne Beach, Florida, and in Natick, Massachusetts. Their father, a high-tech engineer who also played the organ, envisioned a family band, but his three sons were more interested in sports than in music. Not permitted to play football by his own father (who had been injured playing), Richard bought the *Sports Illustrated* teaching series and coached his sons himself. The boys played on sandlots, in their front yard, and even in the house. As Bill has recalled, "Doug always had to be playing. He used to make up games. . . . Hall football. Cup baseball. Crush a snow-cone cup, hit it with your hand and go around the bases." A precocious strategist, Doug was a Pop Warner League quarterback from the age of nine. His aggressiveness and determination to win were inculcated by his father and intensified by competition with his older brother. Joan Flutie told Gary Binford of *Newsday* (October 7, 1984): "Doug always felt inferior to Bill. Bill was always big, Doug was always little. . . . He wanted to be better than Bill or on a level with Bill." Watching Doug was "always a thrill," according to his mother, even if he "wasn't doing something as right" as Bill.

At Natick High School, Flutie earned eight varsity letters. In basketball, probably his favorite sport, he played point guard and was a Bay State All Star. On the baseball team, he pitched and played shortstop. Making the varsity football team (then quarterbacked by his brother Bill) as a five-foot-eight, 150-pound sophomore, he began the 1978 season as a defensive back and became quarterback two games later, when his brother moved to the position of wide receiver. Pacing Natick to three consecutive 8-2 seasons, he made the *Boston Globe* All-Scholastic team twice. In the June 1981 Shriners Classic High School All-Star game, he led the South to a 21-16 upset of the North.

Because of his height, diminutive for a quarterback, Flutie did not impress college recruiters. The only NCAA Division 1-A scholarship offered him came from Boston College (the only Division 1-A team in New England), and it did so ambivalently. Coach Ed Chlebeck, who originally made the offer, withdrew it. After Chlebeck was fired, Jack Bicknell, the new coach, was urged by his assistant, Barry Gallup, a friend of Tom Lamb, the Natick High School coach, to reconsider Flutie's case. After viewing footage of Flutie in action (scrambling, dropping back, playing defensive back, driving the Natick team down the field, and kicking a winning field goal), Bicknell decided in the affirmative. "We knew we had a talented athlete," Gallup later said, "but we weren't sure where he should play."

Listed as a flanker at the beginning of his freshman season, in 1981, Flutie was marking time as a fourth-string quarterback and thinking of asking for a switch to wide receiver. His break came in the fourth quarter of the fourth game of the season, when Boston College trailed Penn State 38-0. With the three quarterbacks in front of Flutie either injured or unable to advance, Bicknell, reasoning "Why not?," decided to "go with the kid." Turning the tide was out of the question, but Flutie got the ball moving, completing eight of eighteen passes for 135 yards and a touchdown. "It was like somebody hit a switch and the tempo picked up," Bicknell marveled. "Never, ever, ever could we imagine what we had."

Flutie made his debut as a starter in the next game, a loss to Navy, which was followed by, first, a trouncing of Army in which he passed for 244 yards and three touchdowns, and then, a narrow loss to Pittsburgh in which he played the second-best statistical passing game in Boston College history against the best defense in the country. After the Pittsburgh game, Coach Bicknell said of Flutie: "You look at him, look at his poise for being so young, look at the things he does and just hope we don't ruin him. He believes in everything he does. He's flipping the ball around, doing some real goofy things . . . and they work. You watch him and just hope you don't coach all that out of him."

Flutie had lucked into the ideal offense for him, a sophisticated, mostly aerial attack that allowed him both to drop back and to improvise under the aegis of a non-coercive coach with a receptive attitude. In the last half of the 1981 season he passed the B.C. Eagles to victories over the University of Massachusetts, Rutgers, and Holy Cross, losing only to Syracuse. He ended the season with 105 completions in 192 attempts for 1,652 yards and ten touchdowns, the ninth best record in the country.

Flutie's status as the Eagles' regular starter became official at the beginning of his sophomore season, in 1982. That season, when the National Collegiate Athletic Association ranked the B.C. schedule the fifth toughest in the nation, Flutie broke B.C.'s single-season passing records. In the opening game, a win over Texas A & M, he, typically, threw three touchdown passes following last-minute changes in strategy by him at the line of scrimmage. His best game that season was a loss to Penn State in which he passed for 520 yards, a career high, a B.C. record, and the best single-game mark in college football that year. Meriting a bowl bid for the first time in forty years, the Eagles lost to Auburn in the Tangerine Bowl, where Flutie was voted the outstanding player. His passing statistics for the year were 184 completions in 363 attempts for 3,048 yards.

As a junior, Flutie led the Eagles to nine wins in twelve starts and the Lambert Trophy for best team in the East. Among the victories were their first win over Penn State and a narrow besting of Temple, of which Coach Bicknell said: "Doug Flutie doesn't always do what he's supposed to do. Thank God." The media attention attracted by Flutie was bringing unaccustomed income to Boston College, chiefly in the form of television rights. The 1983 Alabama-B.C. game (a B.C. win), for example, pre-empted the popular show *Love Boat* on the ABC network. Flutie was selected the most valuable player in the thrilling Liberty Bowl game, fought on a frozen field, in which Boston College bowed to Notre Dame, 19-18. His 1983 passing totals, including the Liberty Bowl statistics, were 194 completions in 381 attempts for 3,011 yards and twenty touchdowns. Academically, he changed his major from computer science to speech communications in his junior year. An easy learner, good at last-minute cramming, he had a National Football Foundation scholarship.

In his senior year, when the Eagles went 9-2 in the regular season, Flutie's most memorable games were a comeback upset of Alabama, again televised on prime-time national television; a win over North Carolina in which he threw six TD passes from the pocket; a loss to Penn State in which he threw for 447 yards, an NCAA record for career yards against one opponent (1,455 in thirteen quarters against Penn State); a victory over Army in which he brought his career total of yards gained passing to 9,695, shattering the NCAA record of Ben Bennett; the legendary game in which he outdueled Miami's All-American quarterback Bernie Kosar, beating the Hurricanes 47-45 on a desperation forty-eight-yard heave with no time remaining; and the final regular-season game, a trouncing of Holy Cross, in which Flutie was thrilled to throw his first touchdown pass, a thirty-yarder, to his brother Darren, a B.C. freshman. His season totals in passing, all B.C. records, were 233 completions in 386 attempts for 3,454 yards.

Later on the day of the Holy Cross game, December 1, 1984, the announcement was made that Flutie had been voted the winner of the Heisman Trophy in balloting by 1,050 sports media representatives. He was the first quarterback since 1971 to win the trophy, symbolic of the best college football player in the country. Other honors included the Maxwell Club Trophy, the *Sporting News* College Football Player of the Year citation, a first-string berth on the consensus 1984 All-America team, and a Rhodes scholarship nomination. His college career was capped, Flutie felt, by Boston College's first post-season bowl victory, a Cotton Bowl win over Houston that gave the Eagles a number-five ranking among NCAA Division 1-A teams. On that occasion, having an off day, he handed off to his running backs, gladly letting his teammates share belatedly in the glory he had monopolized for four years. Financially, the bowl game made Boston College richer by $2 million, bringing to more than $7 million the amount of money from television and ticket sales that went into the B.C. general fund since Flutie's freshman year. Flutie's final collegiate appearances were in the Hula Bowl in Hawaii, on January 5, 1985, and the Japan Bowl in Yokohama, a week later.

Although Coach Bicknell maintained that Flutie had "broken down the physical stereotype for his position," the old, established teams of the National Football League deemed his height a liability, according to published reports. The upstart, faltering United States Football League, however, courted the much-publicized Flutie as a possible savior. Choosing not to wait for the NFL pro draft of college players on April 30, Flutie on February 4, 1985, signed a then record five-year contract, estimated between $5 and $7 million, with Donald Trump, the owner of the New Jersey Generals of the USFL.

To his surprise, Flutie was rushed into the starting position on his first day as a professional, February 6, 1985, when veteran quarterback Brian Sipe was suddenly traded by Trump to the Jacksonville Bulls. Without a breather after his grinding final college season and with only five days of practice, the twenty-two-year-old Generals rookie made an inauspicious professional debut in an exhibition game against the Orlando Renegades on February 15, 1985. In his first regular-season pro game, a 38-28 loss to the Birmingham Stallions on February 24, Flutie was uncomfortably confined in the pocket that New Jersey coach Walt Michaels favored for his quarterbacks until the fourth quarter, when, scrambling, he rallied the Generals from a 31-7 deficit. Animating the offense with his rollout passes early in the next game, he led the Generals to a 28-10 wipeout of the Orlando Renegades. The Generals would not have won game three (35-24), against the Los Angeles Express and quarterback Steve Young, had not a fiercely motivated Flutie gone into action in the last quarter. "He came up with some strange kinds of throws," said Coach Michaels, a defense-oriented conservative who was becoming more flexible. "I don't know where he got them from but I'll take [them]."

Flutie's magic again rallied the Generals to a comeback win (28-24) against Tampa Bay. His rollouts and bootlegs were usually employed in combination with the running threat posed by halfback Herschel Walker, and during much of the spring of 1985 Flutie's role became secondary to that of Walker, but he came through with more dramatic finishes against the Baltimore Stars on May 12 and the Tampa Bay Bandits on May 26. The season ended abruptly for him on June 1, when his left collarbone was fractured on impact with Reggie White, the 305-pound defensive tackle of the Memphis Showboats.

After fifteen games, Flutie ranked eleventh among the USFL's fifteen quarterbacks. He had completed 134 of 281 passes for 2,109 yards and thirteen TDs, with fourteen interceptions, and his 465 yards rushing made him the Generals' third-leading ground gainer. His presence in the USFL had a strong impact on league attendance, and his wildly creative, unpredictable play-making was a key factor in the success of the Generals, who went 11-7 and made the playoffs. Feeling that his collarbone had healed sufficiently, he asked Coach Michaels to start him in the playoff game against the Baltimore Stars on July 1, but Michaels, fearing a re-injury, refused. With John Reeves playing quarterback, the Generals lost to the Stars, 20-17.

When the merger of the Generals and the Houston Gamblers was announced on August 1, 1985, Donald Trump told reporters that he had telephoned Flutie to inform him of the merger and of the decisions to go with Gambler Jim Kelly as quarterback of the new team and to try to trade him, Flutie. "He's had some games that were good and some that were bad," Trump said of Flutie, as quoted by Jim Smith in *Newsday* (August 3, 1985). "But he's been an amazing phenomenon. A lot of people are interested in Doug. . . . Maybe we'll keep him." Smith quoted Flutie as saying that he was "a little disappointed" to be leaving the New York City area but hopeful that "some good will come out of it," such as finding himself "back in Boston." Flutie's agent, Bob Woolf, said that if the quarterback did not connect with a Boston-based team, and if the USFL should fold, he would seek to sign with a National Football League team. The Los Angeles Rams, who picked Flutie in the eleventh round of the April 1985 draft, have the NFL rights to him.

Doug Flutie is five feet nine and three-quarter inches tall and weighs about 175 pounds. Some commentators suggest that his relatively short stature would handicap him if he should move into NFL play. The whole offensive strategy would need to be specially structured to compensate for his size, according to the Giants coach Bill Parcells, and another NFL strategist has noted that Flutie might have trouble spotting open passing lanes while the league's fast, tall rushers bear down upon him. But with straightforward confidence he discounts those doubts: "I'm a winner. I deserve a shot."

The cleancut Flutie has been described by sports writers as "angel faced," "bright," "charming," and "decent," a man whose "true best friends" are his parents. "My way of living," Flutie himself has said, "is being home with a pizza and cola and watching football on TV." A teetotaler as well as a non-smoker, he has made public appearances in behalf of the Massachusetts-based organization GUARDD (Governor and Universities Against Drunk Driving).

After five years of courtship, Flutie married Laurie Fortier, a secretary, his girlfriend since high school, in St. Patrick's Roman Catholic church in Natick on August 10, 1985. The couple plans to live in a house Flutie is buying a few miles outside of Natick. Before becoming a millionaire, Flutie owned one sports jacket, one suit, and no car. His chief extravagance now is a garnet red (B.C.'s color) Porsche. His recreations include movies, chess, golf, and listening to rock music, especially the recordings of the group Van Halen. In cuisine, he likes Italian food and dislikes sea food. Flutie's immediate plans are to do college football commentary on television and to complete the work for his B.A. degree. He has a Hall of Fame scholar-athlete grant for postgraduate study if he chooses to go beyond the B.A. Among his business ventures is a restaurant called Flutie's at South Street Seaport in New York City.

References: *Los Angeles Times* III p1+ D 30 '84 pors; *N Y Times* V p1+ Ag 28 '83 pors, V p1+ N

11 '84 pors, I p16 D 3 '84 por, p29+ D 31 '84 pors; Newsday S p16+ O 7 '84 pors; Newsweek 104:67 D 3 '84 por, 105:78 F 18 '85 por; Sport 17:69+ N '83 por, 76:57+ My '85 por; Sporting News 198:2+ N 12 '84 pors; Sports Ill 59:38+ S 26 '83 pors, 61:22+ D 3 '84 pors, 62:20+ F 4 '85 pors; Thomsen, Ian. Flutie! (1985)

## Fossey, Dian

*1932– Primatologist. Address: b. c/o Houghton Mifflin Company, 2 Park St., Boston, Mass. 02108*

The world's leading authority on the mountain gorilla, Dian Fossey devoted thirteen years, from 1967 to 1980, to the study of that endangered species in its only known habitat: six extinct volcanoes in the Virungas Mountains in east central Africa. Despite intense solitude, personal discomfort, and other hardships, Miss Fossey—whom the natives called *Nyiramachabelli*, "the old lady who lives in the forest without a man"—amassed a wealth of detail on every aspect of the gorillas' lives and recorded behavioral phenomena that had never before been witnessed. She has published her findings in several articles and in her book, *Gorillas in the Mist* (1983). Having developed an affectionate rapport with the primate, Miss Fossey has become an ardent conservationist in her continuing attempt to protect the dwindling number of "the greatest of the great apes."

Dian Fossey was born in 1932 in San Francisco. Even as a small child, she was fond of animals, but her parents would not allow her to keep any pets but goldfish. She has said that the death of her fa-

vorite, Goldie, whom she had owned for six years, was the first trauma in her life. After graduating from high school, she enrolled in the preveterinary medicine program at the University of California at Davis, but eventually transferred to San Jose State College to study occupational therapy, where she received her B.A. degree in 1954. As an undergraduate, she became a prize-winning equestrienne, and after completing her clinical training at four California hospitals in 1956 she moved to Kentucky, a state known for its horses, to work as director of the occupational therapy department at the Kosair Crippled Children's Hospital in Louisville.

But a longing to study gorillas in their native habitats kept intruding upon Dian Fossey's contentment with her career. "I had this great urge, this *need* to go to Africa," she explained to Peter Gorner in an interview for the *Chicago Tribune* (October 3, 1983). "I had it the day I was born. Some may call it destiny. My parents and friends called it dismaying. I call it fortuitous." Aware, as she later wrote, that "dreams seldom materialize on their own," she took out a three-year bank loan for $8,000 to finance a seven-week safari, in 1963, to the places she most wanted to see. Her first stop was the Olduvai Gorge in Tanzania, where Louis S. B. Leakey and his wife, Mary, were engaged in their long-term search for hominid fossils. The charismatic Louis Leakey, who had encouraged Jane Goodall in her work with chimpanzees at the Gombe Stream Research Centre in Tanzania, was equally intrigued with Dian Fossey's plans to visit the mountain gorillas.

Just how determined Dian Fossey was to achieve that goal she proved when, only two weeks after shattering her ankle in a fall at one of the fossil digs, she left the Leakey camp, hobbling with the aid of a walking stick, to make her way to Zaire (known until 1971 as the Democratic Republic of the Congo) for her eagerly anticipated meeting with the great ape. Describing her first encounter with the mountain gorilla, she later wrote: "Sound preceded sight. Odor preceded sound in the form of an overwhelming musky-barnyard, humanlike scent. The air was suddenly rent by a high-pitched series of screams followed by the rhythmic rondo of sharp *pok-pok* chestbeats from a great silverback male. . . . Immediately I was struck by the physical magnificence of the huge jet-black bodies blended against the green palette wash of the thick forest foliage."

Excited and captivated by the mountain gorillas she had seen, Dian Fossey nevertheless returned to the United States and resumed her work with handicapped children. But when, in 1966, Dr. Leakey visited her in Louisville to persuade her to study the mountain gorilla on a long-term basis, she readily assented. To prove her enthusiasm, she acted on Leakey's advice to have her appendix removed as a prophylactic measure. Only later did she find out that his suggestion had been a facetious attempt to test her resolve.

Thanks to the efforts of the American naturalist Carl Ethan Akeley, the first preserve for the mountain gorilla had been established in the Belgian Congo in the 1920s, but both poachers and natives desperate for farmland continually encroached on the gorilla's already circumscribed habitat. Political differences further hindered research and conservation efforts since the gorilla's tiny range is divided among parks in three separate but adjacent nations in east central Africa: Zaire's Parc National des Virungas, Rwanda's Parc National des Volcans, and Uganda's Kigezi Gorilla Sanctuary. Louis Leakey realized, as Miss Fossey recalled, that as a result of those problems, the mountain gorilla, which had not been recognized as a separate species until 1902, "might possibly be doomed to extinction in the same century in which it had been discovered."

Leakey was especially eager that the animal's behavior be documented for its own sake as well as for what it might reveal about the behavior of its distant relative, primitive man. Because of its intense shyness and its range within dense, high-altitude montane rain forests, in-field gorilla research was extremely difficult, and no serious studies of the primate had been undertaken until 1959 when the renowned American zoologist George B. Schaller observed the mountain gorilla in the wild. Dian Fossey's interest in the largest of the great apes (mature males weigh about four hundred pounds and stand about six feet tall) had been fueled by Schaller's studies, and to a large extent her work was built upon the foundation he had laid.

By late 1966, Dian Fossey was back in Africa and ready to begin her project, which was initially funded by the Wilkie Brothers' Foundation and the National Geographic Society. (Later, the L. S. B. Leakey Foundation also supported her work.) After paying a brief visit to Jane Goodall in Tanzania to learn the best methods for fieldwork and data collection, she struck out on her own. Early in 1967 she set up her first campsite and work station at Kabara, a site in the Parc National des Virungas where Akeley had been buried and where Schaller had conducted his pioneering studies of the gorilla a few years before.

Observation of the gorillas presented a considerable challenge. Although they feed and travel in close-knit groups, they flee from strangers, so that at first Dian Fossey had to conceal herself at a distance to watch them. She gradually initiated open contacts by copying the gorillas' behavior, learning by trial and error the best means of "habituating" the gorillas to a stranger in their midst. "For a number of months," she recalled in her article for *Science Digest* (August 1983), "I imitated the gorillas' chestbeats by slapping my hands against my thighs in studious mimicry of their rhythm. The sound was an instant success in gaining the gorillas' attention. . . . I thought I was very clever but did not realize that I was conveying the wrong information. Chestbeating is the gorillas' signal for excitement or alarm, certainly the wrong message for me to have sent as appeasement!"

Knuckle-walking, announcing her approach by making contentment vocalizations, pretending to eat the gorillas' favorite foods, and imitating their grooming practices proved much more effective. Her innovative method of field research ultimately succeeded in piquing the gorillas' strong natural curiosity and thereby gained their acceptance of her presence. Within a relatively short time, she was able to observe regularly three groups of gorillas whose ranges were near her camp.

Political unrest in Zaire ended her studies at Kabara after only seven months. On July 10, 1967 armed guards escorted her from her campsite and kept her in custody for about two weeks. Doubting that her confinement would soon end without action on her part, she used a ruse to persuade her military captors to accompany her to Uganda. Once across the border, she escaped from her drunken guards, who had stopped at pubs en route, and took refuge in the Travellers' Rest Hotel, operated by Walter Baumgärtel, who had befriended her during her first trip to Africa and often aided researchers and tourists.

Although the message was relayed to Miss Fossey that if she returned to Zaire she would be shot on sight, she resumed her research, this time in the tiny country of Rwanda. With diplomatic intervention in her behalf by Dr. Leakey and renewed support from Leighton Wilkie, on September 24, 1967 she established the Karisoke Research Centre, named after two nearby mountains in the Parc National des Volcans.

Renewing her fieldwork, she studied some fifty-one gorillas living in four relatively stable groups within reasonable proximity of the camp. Each of those families was a cohesive unit dominated by a silverback (a sexually mature male more than fifteen years old), whose hegemony was supported by a blackback (a sexually immature male between eight and thirteen years old). The silverback's harem generally consisted of four or more females who usually remained with him permanently, together with their offspring. Dian Fossey tracked the animals daily, discovering that they were vegetarians who rested about 40 percent of the time in their ground nests and traveled about 400 meters each day. She also eventually identified some fifteen different sounds that the gorillas made in various distinctive contexts: they chuckled during the play session, grunted like pigs to scold too rambunctious juveniles or to warn off threatening adults within their group, made "belch vocalizations" when content, and gave their legendary growl and roar when they sensed danger.

Despite their "King Kong" image, she found the gorillas to be pacific, only charging at humans or at other animals when threatened or approached without warning. However, what Dian Fossey found most impressive about the mountain gorillas were their strong family ties and altruism. They tenderly nurse members of the group who are hurt or ill, carefully cleaning their wounds and slowing the traveling pace of the group to accommodate them, and an entire family will fight to the death to prevent even one infant from being harmed or captured.

Nevertheless, those "gentle giants," as Miss Fossey called them, would occasionally attack members of their own group, and she also discovered strong evidence of infanticide. Six of the thirty-eight gorillas born during the thirteen years of her study had apparently been intentionally killed by grown males. She speculated that, grisly though the practice might seem, it represented an instinctive reproductive strategy. A female with a young offspring who left her group or was taken by a rival silverback could not become pregnant again until about four years after the young gorilla's birth. If the baby died, she would return to estrous more quickly and her new silverback mate could then breed with her, perpetuating his own genetic line. In an interview with Sara Ann Friedman for Geo (November 1982), Dian Fossey suggested that the declining ratio of females to males among the surviving gorillas, as well as their reduced range due to human encroachment, might account for the high incidence of infanticide.

After several years of working only with her native trackers and other African tribesmen who maintained the camp and replenished supplies, Dian Fossey somewhat reluctantly decided she needed research assistance. Although many of the student volunteers who came to Karisoke found the activity physically exhausting or else suffered from the effects of long-term isolation, which she terms the "astronaut blues," a few offered valuable help in developing a parasitology project, which involved the microscopic examination of gorilla dung, and in autopsy work. In 1981 the students also helped Miss Fossey to conduct a much-needed census of the mountain gorilla population. The results turned out to be alarming: in the twenty-two years since Schaller's census, the number of gorillas had dropped by almost 50 percent, to 242, a finding that gave added impetus to her continuing conservation efforts. Students and some natives joined her in regular poacher patrols to confiscate weapons and destroy traps, set for other animals, that too often snared a gorilla. She also did her utmost to frustrate European trophy hunters and those hired to capture gorillas for foreign zoos.

In 1978, following the slaughter of Digit, one of her most beloved silverbacks, Dian Fossey decided to publicize the problem. The gorilla's death was announced on the CBS evening news program, and she set up a Digit Fund to raise money for anti-poacher patrols and equipment. However, six months later, despite increased patrols, poachers killed two other gorillas and thus effectively decimated one of the groups that she had been studying. Rumors reached the outside world that her intense grief over the deaths of the gorillas had resulted in a nervous breakdown. But, as she told Peter Gorner in the Chicago Tribune interview, "I didn't go bonkers over the killings. Sure, I cried a lot. The place began to reek of death." "I survived because I've locked it away," she added. "There's a great part of me that's totally gone."

The natives' genuine, ever-increasing need for land presented a more perplexing conservation problem. In Rwanda, the most densely populated country in Africa, the average person has only about two acres for farming and cattle grazing. As a result, the government gradually reduced the Parc National des Volcans by over 4,000 acres to accommodate its people. That encroachment alone could, according to Miss Fossey, account for a 60 percent drop in the mountain gorilla population. Although she realized the tribesmen's straits, she drove out cattle grazing on parkland and had some success in persuading the natives to respect the boundaries of the game reserve.

Around 1970, Dian Fossey temporarily left Africa for Great Britain, where she studied for a doctorate at Cambridge University. In 1974 she received her Ph.D. in zoology from Cambridge with her dissertation, The Behaviour of the Mountain Gorilla. After spending thirteen years in the field, she was once again forced to leave the Karisoke Research Centre, this time out of concern for her health. "I was a walking skeleton," she explained to Peter Gorner. "Up where I lived, you can't get calcium. So your bones eventually break, and your teeth rot and fall out. I needed to leave for a while." She returned to the United States in 1980 to accept a visiting associate professorship at Cornell University, but before long she was dividing her time between her academic responsibilities and her duties as project coordinator at the Karisoke Research Centre.

While teaching, Dian Fossey also completed Gorillas in the Mist, which was published in 1983 by Houghton Mifflin. In that volume, parts of which had been previously published in magazines and scientific journals, she chronicled the main aspects of her studies of the various groups of gorillas, spanning three generations. She described the natural demise of gorilla families, explained how a new family formed and developed stability over time, and gave poignant accounts of the slayings of gorillas by poachers and of her anti-poaching activities. Generally anecdotal rather than highly technical, her book also included appendixes that summarized many of the scientific aspects of her work at the Karisoke Research Centre.

Gorillas in the Mist received generally positive reviews in the mass media. Katherine Bouton praised it warmly in the New York Times Book Review (September 4, 1983): "Miss Fossey's research is invaluable . . . her dedication unremitting, her subject matter of unquestionable ecological importance." However, a minority of critics thought that in attempting to appeal to a popular audience, Dian Fossey had lessened the book's scientific worth, citing, for example, her anthropomorphic descriptions of the gorillas' behavior. But in Newsweek (August 29, 1983), Gene Lyons declared that "if the love that animates every page of 'Gorillas in the Mist' occasionally offends scientific purists, it is bound to delight almost everyone else."

Dian Fossey, whom Nan Robertson described in the *New York Times* (May 1, 1981) as a "brawny six-footer with a shock of black hair and coltish movements who somewhat resembles Julia Child," belongs to the Explorer's Club, one of the few female members of that organization, often lectures for the L. S. B. Leakey Foundation, and has been featured on several wildlife television specials. At the time *Gorillas in the Mist* was published, her teaching responsibilities at Cornell had ended, and she admitted that she was eager to once again live in Africa, not only because she is "more comfortable with gorillas than with people" but also because she loves the natural splendor and solitude of Rwanda. "Anywhere you look," she explained to Peter Gorner, "there is beauty."

References: *Chicago Tribune* p15+ O 3 '83 por; *Geo* p10+ N '82 por; *N Y Times* B p4 My 1 '81 por; Fossey, Dian. Gorillas in the Mist (1983)

## Frayn, Michael

Sept. 8, 1933– British writer. Address: b. c/o *Elaine Greene, Ltd., 31 Newington Green, London N16 9PU, England*

The British writer Michael Frayn is known on the American side of the Atlantic chiefly as the author of the long-running Broadway hit *Noises Off,* a send-up of a British sex farce. In his homeland, however, Frayn's reputation rests on a much broader base. An award-winning journalist and best-selling novelist before he turned to playwriting in 1970, Frayn has been called England's "most versatile man of letters," but it is as a playwright

that he has had the most impact. Robert Cushman, the veteran British drama critic, classes Frayn's cerebral whimsy with the works of Alan Ayckbourn and Tom Stoppard. "Frayn's wordplay is less effervescent than Tom Stoppard's," Cushman wrote in the London *Observer* (August 22, 1976), "but even more acute; his view of the middle classes betterhumoured than Alan Ayckbourn's . . . , but his satire even more accurate." "Comedy is about the grimness of the world," Frayn himself explained in a recent interview. "It's one way of looking at pain and difficulty."

Michael Frayn was born on September 8, 1933 at Mill Hill in North London, England, the son of Violet Alice (Lawson) Frayn and Thomas Allen Frayn, a sales representative for an asbestos manufacturing firm. Shortly thereafter, the Frayns moved to Ewell, just south of London in central Surrey. When his wife died a few years later, Thomas Frayn, unable to pay both the wages of a housekeeper and school fees, removed his son from the private school where he had begun his education and enrolled him instead in the directgrant Kingston Grammar school. A sensitive child, Michael Frayn adjusted to all the changes in his life with difficulty, and his academic performance was poor, but he covered up his insecurities by developing his sense of humor and soon became the class wag.

Before continuing his education at the university level, Frayn completed his two years of national service—then mandatory—as a corpsman in the Royal Artillery and Intelligence Corps, during which time he learned to speak fluent Russian. Following his discharge in 1954, he enrolled at Emmanuel College, the University of Cambridge. At first, he studied French and Russian, but he eventually switched his major to moral sciences, or philosophy. In his spare time, he wrote a regular column for the university newspaper, and he contributed several pieces to one of the annual May Week shows presented by Footlights, Cambridge's revue club. After that, he said, as quoted in the *New York Times* (December 11, 1983), "I turned my back on the theatre, except for making fun of it."

On taking his B.A. degree in 1957, Frayn joined the staff of the *Guardian,* a liberal newspaper based in Manchester, for a six-month trial period as a general-assignment reporter. He remained in that job for two years, covering such newsworthy events as Prime Minister Harold Macmillan's first official visit to the Soviet Union, then went to London to write "Miscellany," the *Guardian's* thriceweekly column of social commentary. It was as the author of "Miscellany" that Frayn began to acquire a national reputation as a satirist of contemporary mores. His column often featured "interviews" with such fictional characters as Christopher and Lavinia Crumble, a trendy childless couple, Rollo Swavely, "the well-known public relations consultant," and Christopher Smoothe, the "Minister for Chance and Speculation." Some of Frayn's columns were later collected in the books

The Day of the Dog (Collins, 1962; Doubleday, 1963), The Book of Fub (Collins, 1963), and Never Put Off to Gomorrah . . . (Pantheon, 1964).

Finding that three deadlines a week left him little time for other writing, Frayn left the Guardian in 1962 and signed on as a columnist with the weekly London Observer, a post he held until 1968. (A collection of his Observer columns was published by William Collins Sons & Company, Ltd. in 1967 under the title At Bay in Gear Street.) During his tenure on the Observer staff, he wrote two television plays—Jamie on a Flying Visit and Birthday—and four of his five novels. Although he resigned from the Observer in 1968, Frayn has continued to contribute features on foreign countries to that newspaper, including his perceptive series of articles about Cuba that earned him a 1970 National Press Award from the International Publishing Corporation for "distinguished" reporting.

Frayn's first novel, The Tin Men (Collins, 1965; Little, Brown, 1965), a whimsical account of the efforts of computer wizards at the William Morris Institute of Automation to prepare for an upcoming royal visit, won him a Somerset Maugham travel award of £500. His second, The Russian Interpreter (Collins, 1966; Viking, 1966), which was based partly on his army experience, secured him the prestigious Hawthornden Prize. It was, however, Frayn's third effort at fiction that finally brought him to the attention of American readers. Towards the End of the Morning (Collins, 1967; Against Entropy, Viking, 1967) has as its setting a particularly dull department of a provincial newspaper whose staff members, all in their mid-thirties, are approaching "the end of their lives' mornings." Its slender plot provided Frayn with just enough opportunities to "lean over and chip set pieces from the passing backgrounds," as Josh Greenfeld put it in his admiring appraisal of the novel for the New York Times Book Review (July 16, 1967). Greenfeld added that Frayn "possesses to a high degree the essential humorist's knack: he knows how to cross over the bounds of reality without extending credulity to the breaking point."

A Very Private Life (Collins, 1968), Frayn's fourth novel in as many years, represented something of a departure for him. Partly inspired by his recent visit to the United States, which included a traversal of the affluent bedroom suburbs of Connecticut, A Very Private Life is a morality tale about a future world in which the upper classes live a life of comfort and isolation in hermetically sealed boxes, perceiving the outside world only through the technological magic of "holovision." Stephen Wall, who reviewed the book for the London Observer (September 29, 1968), thought that it was "a logical projection into the future of our present increasing skill at shutting out uncomfortable realities." Although he found fault with the novel as "an instrument of narrative," Wall nonetheless felt that A Very Private Life was "a further demonstration of Michael Frayn's unrivaled position as the most sympathetic of our contemporary moralists."

In 1970 the American producer Alexander H. Cohen commissioned Frayn to write a two-character skit for a revue called Mixed Doubles that he was producing in London. Frayn complied, but Cohen turned down his effort reportedly because it called for a baby's diaper to be changed onstage. "Riled," to use his word, by what he regarded as Cohen's hypocrisy, Frayn responded by devising three more two-handed one-act plays along the same lines for a dramatic evening of his own. Frayn's quartet of comic marital sketches, entitled The Two of Us and starring Lynn Redgrave and Richard Briers, opened in July 1970 at the Garrick Theatre in London. For the most part, critics found The Two of Us to be diverting but disappointingly slight. Its lukewarm critical reception notwithstanding, The Two of Us enjoyed a respectable run of nearly 200 performances.

Buoyed by his commercial success, Frayn followed up with The Sandboy, a seriocomic piece concerning the making of a television documentary about a day in the life of Phil Schaffer, a celebrated city planner. Schaffer's hope of presenting a good image on television is shattered by the repeated intrusions of his next-door neighbors, an aggressively unhappy and demanding couple whose misfortunes symbolize for Schaffer the precariousness of his own position. Produced at the Greenwich Theatre in the fall of 1971 under the direction of Robert Chetwyn, The Sandboy failed to attract critical or audience approval despite the superb comic performance of Joe Melia in the role of Phil. Most reviewers agreed with Irving Wardle that the play's structure, particularly the pretense that the audience constituted the television crew, was "notoriously unworkable." But even if one overlooked "the continuous implausibility of the whole situation," Wardle concluded in his review for the New York Times (September 18, 1971), "what comes across is not an exposure of intellectual gamesmanship but an unappealingly reactionary illustration of the modern liberal's incapacity to deal with his social inferiors."

Frayn's next effort, Alphabetical Order, was considerably more successful. Set in the cuttings library of a moribund provincial newspaper, the play's plot turns on the impact a zealous and compulsively organized young woman assistant has on the library's long-established and comfortable chaos. Michael Rudman's production of Alphabetical Order for the Hampstead Theatre Club transferred in mid-1975 to the Mayfair Theatre in the West End, where it played to enthusiastic audiences for months. British critics unanimously acclaimed Frayn's witty and well-crafted play, the London Evening Standard going so far as to name it Best Comedy of the Year. Their American counterparts, however, were considerably less impressed when Alphabetical Order was staged at the Long Wharf Theater in New Haven, Connecticut in October 1976. Their chief complaint was perhaps best expressed by Walter Kerr, writing in the New York Times (October 17, 1976). Although he, like many of his colleagues, found some admirable qualities in the play, the "event as a whole" remained, in his view, "unsatisfying," primarily because the playwright seemed unable to fuse his various components, which Kerr identified as "comedy," "seriousness," and "symbolism," into "a single dominant chord." Only the British-born New York Times critic Clive Barnes, who conceded in his opening night review for the Times (October 14, 1976) that Alphabetical Order was a peculiarly "English delight," was unstinting in his praise, calling it "the best play to be written about newspapers since Front Page."

While stage plays were beginning to occupy more and more of Frayn's time, he continued to write novels, teleplays, essays, and even a book of philosophy. Like A Very Private Life, Sweet Dreams (Collins, 1973; Viking, 1973), his fifth novel, explores an imaginary world—this one the fantasy of a thirty-seven-year-old architect who daydreams his way into a Utopian "Heavenly City"—and at the same time satirizes current fashions and attitudes. Frayn's television credits for the mid-1970s include the six-part BBC-2 comedy series Making Faces, in which Eleanor Bron portrayed in succession the six different personae of an intellectual Englishwoman, several documentaries, among them Imagine a City Called Berlin and Vienna: the Mask of Gold, in which he analyzed cities through their cultures, and the program on Australia in the series Great Railway Journeys of the World. But perhaps his most unusual creation was Constructions (Wildwood House, 1974), which Russell Davies described in the London Observer (July 18, 1976) as "an extraordinary book of numbered perceptions about the nature of perception: a kind of philosophy which has infuriated academic thinkers, while delighting many readers for whom rigor takes second place to piquancy."

Frayn's investigation of perception served as the basis for Clouds, an offbeat comedy about a press junket to Cuba, in which he points out, among other things, that an individual's perception of reality shifts and changes as often as the shapes of clouds and is as insubstantial as they are, depending as it does on such variables as mood and viewpoint. Some two years after its 1976 premiere, under Michael Rudman's direction, at the Hampstead Theatre Club, Clouds opened at the Duke of York's Theatre in the West End, where, with Tom Courtenay and Felicity Kendal in the leading roles, it settled in for a long run. Frayn and Rudman teamed up again for what was to be the playwright's biggest hit to that date: Donkeys' Years, a vintage English farce about a college reunion that turns into a bacchanalia. Starring Peter Barkworth and Penelope Keith, the play, which made its West End bow at London's Globe Theatre in July 1976, ran for eighteen months and earned Frayn his first Society of West End Theatre Award for best comedy of the year. While it had its moments, Liberty Hall, a "philosophical farce," to use James Fenton's term, that turned on the improbable premise that the Russian Revolution of 1917 occurred not in the Soviet Union but in the United Kingdom, failed to find its audience.

Frayn often sets his novels and plays in the workplace because, as he explained to an interviewer for the Washington Post (October 16, 1983), he believes that "we reveal a lot of ourselves on the job." In Make and Break, he focused on the competitive world of international business. The protagonist is the ruthless chief executive of a firm that manufactures moveable room dividers; the set, a changeable array of partitions representing the company's marketing display at an international trade fair; and the theme, the destructive effect of the lust for power on men's lives. After favorable notices helped pack the Lyric Hammersmith for a month, Make and Break transferred, in May 1980, to the more centrally located Haymarket Theatre. With three British "best comedy of the year" awards to its credit, Make and Break seemed destined for a New York run, but its pre-Broadway tryout at the John F. Kennedy Center for the Performing Arts in Washington, D.C., in 1982, was a flop, largely because of the miscasting of Peter Falk as the wheeling and dealing businessman.

Frayn finally achieved critical and commercial success in the United States with Noises Off, his hilarious "farce within a farce" about a third-rate repertory company touring the English provinces in a production of the tacky sex comedy "Nothing On." Winner of both the Evening Standard and the Society of West End Theatre "best comedy" awards, Noises Off transferred shortly after its February 1982 opening at the Lyric Hammersmith to the Savoy Theatre, where it passed the 1,000th-performance mark.

The American production of Noises Off, which like its British forerunner was directed by Michael Blakemore, premiered at the Brooks Atkinson Theatre on Broadway in December 1983 to rapturous reviews. "I doubt whether Frayn has written anything else as funny, but, then, very few people have," wrote New York magazine's usually acerbic John Simon in a review which, like that of virtually every other New York Broadway critic, was larded with superlatives. Simon observed: "In Noises Off we have the pleasure of seeing a once thriving but lately moribund genre come alive again to shake us with laughter and even, improbably, shake us up into a little peripheral thought. I call that exciting." Noises Off has since been produced in Australia, New Zealand, South Africa, Canada, France, Belgium, and Scandinavia.

The plot of Benefactors, Frayn's most recent London hit, is somewhat reminiscent of that of The Sandboy. A sardonic comedy, told in flashback, about an architect and his socially conscious wife whose lives are profoundly changed by a neurotic neighboring couple, Benefactors evoked, in Frank Rich's mind, "Chekhov, Othello, and The Master Builder," yet it remained "an original, not to mention demanding achievement that is well beyond the ambitions of most contemporary dramatists." In reviewing Benefactors for the New York Times (July 23, 1984), Rich especially admired the "classical elegance" of its architecture: "The author unravels his characters with an invisible hand—as if he were slowly yanking apart a huge tapestry by steadily pulling a tiny stray thread at its edge." *Benefactors* won both the Society of West End Theatre and *Evening Standard* awards as the best play of 1984.

In addition to writing his original works for the stage, Frayn has translated several French and Russian classics, including Anton Chekhov's *The Cherry Orchard* and Leo Tolstoy's *The Fruits of Enlightenment,* which were produced by the National Theatre in 1978 and 1979, respectively. Most recently, he "extensively reworked," as he put it, Chekhov's first, unnamed play (usually known as "Platonov," after its hero), which has generally been dismissed as "unstageable" since it was discovered some sixty years ago. Treating Chekhov's rambling manuscript "as if it were the rough draft of one of [his] own plays," Frayn drastically cut the script, reorganized its chronology, eliminated subplots, wrote new lines, reduced the number of characters, and even introduced two new ones. Frayn took his title, *Wild Honey,* for the play from an original line that seemed to him to suggest "both the wayward sweetness of forbidden sexual attraction and the intense feeling of summer that pervades the play." In a program note he explained that he did not intend to make an "academic contribution" to Chekhovian scholarship or a "pious tribute" to Chekhov himself, but to create a "text for production." That he succeeded became evident in the ovations accorded the play, featuring Ian McKellen, by the SRO audiences at the National Theatre, where it reigned as the acknowledged hit of the 1984 season. In the following year, Frayn's lucid and "empathetically straight" (to quote the London *Observer's* Michael Ratcliffe) translation of Chekhov's *The Three Sisters* was a box-office success at the Royal Exchange Theatre in Manchester.

Interviewers often comment that while they are prepared for Michael Frayn's keen intelligence and quick wit, his gentleness and quiet manner come as a surprise. Lean and bespectacled, with a sharp-featured face and thinning hair, he bears a striking resemblance to his friend, the playwright Peter Nichols, and among the many examples of life imitating farce that seem to abound in Frayn's life is the fact that he is often congratulated as the author on the opening nights of Nichols' plays. He lives with his wife, Gillian (Palmer) Frayn, whom he married on February 18, 1960, and their three daughters, in a house outside London.

*References: Guardian p6 O 1 '68 por; London Observer p8 Jl 18 '76, p44 Ap 27 '80 por; Sunday Times Ja 27 '80 por; N Y Times II p1+ D 11 '83; Plays and Players p8+ D '84 por; Washington Post G p1+ O 16 '83 por; Contemporary Authors vols 5-6 (1963); Contemporary Dramatists (1977); Who's Who, 1985-86; Who's Who in the Theatre (1981)*

## Futter, Ellen V(ictoria)

(fut´ er)

*Sept. 21, 1949- College president. Address: b. Office of the President, 606 W. 120th St., New York City, N.Y. 10027*

Although coeducation has been a fact of life at most American colleges and universities for decades, it is still a controversial issue at Barnard College, the prestigious women's college situated across the street from Columbia University in New York City. Personally committed to the notion of women's education, Ellen Futter, the ninth president of Barnard College and the first alumna to head the school in more than thirty years, recently succeeded in renewing Barnard's image as a strong, independent institution offering women a unique academic environment in which they might flourish as well as the advantages of a close affiliation with a leading research university. Not least among her achievements is the distinction of being, at the time of her initial appointment, in 1980, the youngest chief executive of a major American college.

Ellen Victoria Futter was born in New York City, New York on September 21, 1949, the daughter of Victor Futter, a lawyer and a top-level executive with the Allied Chemical Corporation, and

Joan Babette (Feinberg) Futter. Not long after their daughter's birth, the Futters moved to Port Washington, Long Island, where Ellen attended the local public schools. In high school, she was active in

student politics, serving as a class officer and as a member of the student council, and she captained the girls' tennis team.

Following her graduation from high school in 1967, Ellen Futter enrolled at the University of Wisconsin in Madison, but she found it hard to adjust to the impersonal environment of the huge Midwestern institution. "I never felt the college reached me as an individual," she told Georgia Dullea in an interview for a *New York Times Magazine* (December 2, 1984) profile, "and I never spoke to any of my professors outside of class." Before her junior year, Miss Futter transferred to Barnard College. Thriving in the close-knit academic community, she was elected to Phi Beta Kappa and, in her senior year, was chosen to be a student representative on the college's board of trustees.

Undecided about a career, Miss Futter applied to law schools and to several universities with graduate programs in English, American studies, or journalism. After spending a summer working for *Newsweek* magazine, however, she realized that she was, in her words, "more of a doer than an observer," and upon taking her A.B. degree, *magna cum laude,* in 1971, she entered Columbia University's School of Law. She received her J.D. degree in 1974. A few months later, she passed the New York State Bar exam and joined the staff of Milbank, Tweed, Hadley and McCloy, the Wall Street corporate law firm, as an associate attorney.

In July 1980, Miss Futter took a year's leave of absence from her job to accept a temporary appointment as the acting president of Barnard College. She succeeded Dr. Jacquelyn A. Mattfeld, who had resigned two months earlier, reportedly under pressure from the trustees, who were said to be dissatisfied with the way she was handling the ongoing negotiations with Columbia University officials regarding the future nature of Barnard's affiliation with the larger institution.

Miss Futter's experience in negotiating as a corporate lawyer and her "familiarity with the college," as she put it, were decisive factors in her selection to the post. "I'm a problem-solver by nature," she told Dena Kleiman of the *New York Times* (July 28, 1980). "I listen carefully, articulate effectively. And as a young professional woman, I represent what Barnard is all about. . . . I make no pretense about being an academic. I have the skills to do the job."

Founded in 1889 by Frederick A. P. Barnard, then the president of Columbia, because Columbia refused to admit women, Barnard College has its own board of trustees, endowment, administration, faculty, and physical plant, although it has always relied heavily on Columbia for libraries and research facilities. In the face of increasing pressure from Columbia's administrators, who hoped to merge Barnard with Columbia College, the university's all-male undergraduate liberal arts school, Dr. Mattfeld fought to preserve Barnard's independence. In the interview with Dena Kleiman, Miss Futter stated that she, too, was committed to an "independent" Barnard, with "an autonomous

faculty," but she also insisted on maintaining an "affiliated role" with Columbia. "It is an exciting, unique relationship," she told Miss Kleiman, "but the relationship needs to be clarified."

Under the terms of a 1973 covenant between the two institutions, Barnard, rather than surrender its autonomy, accepted a measure of coeducation in which Barnard and Columbia students shared some facilities and cross-registered for courses. For a few years, the coeducational scheme seemed to satisfy both parties, but by the end of the decade, faculty and students from the two schools were publicly challenging the agreement. Columbia's professors and administrators questioned the wisdom of an admissions policy that excluded women, contending that such a policy threatened to lower the academic quality of Columbia's applicant pool in the 1980s. Barnard faculty members complained about the provision in the agreement that gave Columbia a majority on the ad hoc committees that voted on Barnard's tenure appointments. In their view, highly qualified Barnard teachers were regularly passed over because their particular areas of expertise did not fit in with the needs of the research-oriented university.

Within days of her taking office as acting president of Barnard College, Ellen Futter opened discussions with the president of Columbia University, Michael I. Sovern, who had been her dean at law school. Maintaining that single-sex undergraduate education was "anachronistic," Sovern put forward a formula for what he called "de facto coeducation." Under this proposal, the two schools were to remain single-sex institutions, but there was to be more academic and social mixing of the students in classrooms, dining halls, and dormitories. Although she viewed Sovern's offer to change the composition of the ad hoc tenure committees as a step in the right direction, Miss Futter had some doubts about the package as a whole. While negotiations proceeded, she began to strengthen Barnard's bargaining position by reorganizing a faltering $20 million capital-fund drive and by purchasing a nearby apartment building to ease the college's housing shortage.

In recognition of Miss Futter's considerable skills as an administrator, Barnard's board of trustees, acting upon the recommendation of a thirteen-member search committee comprised of trustees, faculty members, students, and alumni, named her president of the college on May 6, 1981. "Ellen was a mover and a doer . . . ," Helene L. Kaplan, the chairman of the board of trustees, said, as reported in the December 2, 1984 edition of the *New York Times.* "That's why we chose her." Within weeks, the ongoing debate over Barnard's relationship with Columbia intensified, as Sovern announced Columbia College's intention to begin admitting women undergraduates as early as the fall 1983 term unless Barnard agreed, in his words, to "as much coeducation in the classroom as there is in the rest of the Ivy League." Undaunted, Miss Futter stood her ground. As she told a reporter for the *New York Times* (May 27, 1981), "Barnard fully intends to go forward as an undergraduate liberal arts college for women."

Miss Futter elaborated on her vision of Barnard's future as an independent women's college in her inaugural address, on November 22, 1981: "While we shall do everything in our power to reach agreement with Columbia and to preserve a relationship which we value greatly, let this day mark . . . the end of our psychological preoccupation with the Barnard-Columbia relationship. Let us return to focusing on what is the fundamental business for Barnard College—providing a first-rate liberal arts education."

Shortly thereafter, Ellen Futter and Michael Sovern finally came to terms regarding the future relationship between their respective colleges. Under the conditions of a seven-year pact that the two presidents signed in January 1982, Columbia College began to admit women students and Barnard remained an independent women's college. Although the agreement generally preserved Barnard's close ties to the university, Miss Futter had managed to win more control over faculty matters, including the granting of tenure. The main stumbling block to a more traditional coeducational arrangement with Columbia "was simply the notion that there had to be a formula approach to the definition of coeducation," Miss Futter told Gene I. Maeroff, who interviewed her for the New York Times (May 11, 1982). "The formula would have operated in such a way that we would wind up with too many of our students compelled to take classes at Columbia. It was that sense of both compulsion and numbers that left us uncomfortable." Freed after "ten years of uncertainty" from the "specter of merger" with Columbia, she went on, "the future of Barnard is clear: we are healthy, we are thriving, and we are not about to be absorbed."

With the time-consuming coeducation negotiations behind her, Miss Futter turned her attention to other areas, such as fund raising, admissions policy, and a review of the curriculum. To meet the challenge of open competition with Columbia College for the best women applicants in the country, she engaged the services of a top-flight public relations firm to promote Barnard as an institution that is especially responsive to the concerns of women. "Barnard has a tradition of successful women," she explained to Gene Maeroff in outlining Barnard's advantages over Columbia. "In the last decade, of all the women who have gone on to receive a Ph.D. throughout this country, more have been from this very distinguished—but small—college than from any other institution in the United States. . . . This is a proven environment where the aspirations and abilities of young women can and do flourish. Where else in America can you attend a small, first-rate women's college with its own superb faculty and at the same time draw upon the resources of a major university and the leading international urban center of the world?" To those who contend that the whole idea of a women's college is hopelessly behind the times, she has countered that it is rather the "old, Victorian" definition of a women's

college that is out of date. "The notion of a women's college as anachronistic would be tantamount to saying that women have completely come of age," she told Maeroff. "I think there are very few today who would say that."

As part of her efforts to attract more and better qualified students, Miss Futter, working closely with a faculty committee, introduced in 1983 a new interdisciplinary curriculum designed to meet the "need for a balance between specialized knowledge and broader skills," as she put it. The new curriculum requirements put more emphasis on computer science, mathematics, and statistics and insured that every student sampled the full range of the liberal arts programs. Summarizing her commitment to the development of quantitative skills, she told Edward B. Fiske of the New York Times (February 27, 1983) that such skills were "increasingly necessary to be a successful student in the liberal arts, to be successful in one's professional life, and to be a successful participant in a democratic society." To demonstrate their broad application, she pointed to the new quantitative-reasoning course, which is taught jointly by a mathematician, an economist, and an anthropologist. "All over America, colleges are responding to enrollment problems and financial crises in conservative ways—covering their flanks, rear-guard actions," Charles S. Olton, Barnard's dean of faculty and vice-president for academic affairs, remarked, as quoted in the New York Times Magazine profile of Ellen Futter. "What Ellen has done is taken a new initiative and then reached out and found money to make it work."

Since Columbia College became a coeducational institution in the fall of 1983, 4,740 women have applied for admission to Columbia and 3,864 to Barnard. Of those who approached both schools, the majority eventually chose Columbia, at least partly because of Columbia's generous financial aid packages. But the caliber of the incoming freshman classes at Barnard in 1983 and 1984 remained unusually high. In 1983, for example, the number who ranked in the top 10 percent of their high-school graduating classes was 75.6 percent, up from 62 percent in 1982. Eager to preserve that academic edge, Miss Futter instituted a more aggressive recruitment program. Among other things, she dispatched recruiters to urban centers throughout the country and, for the first time, invited some 400 candidates to spend a few days on campus.

Ellen Futter herself is perhaps Barnard College's best advertisement. As Georgia Dullea observed in the New York Times Magazine, she is, in effect, a "fulfillment of the Barnard prophecy" that "'you can do anything you want to do, be anything you want to be.'" In the words of one admiring undergraduate, as a successful career woman, wife, and mother, Barnard's president was "doing it all." For her part, Miss Futter has been quick to point out to interviewers and to her students that she has benefitted from advantages not shared by all working mothers: a supportive husband, a home on campus near her office, full-time household help, and "the economic wherewithal to help [herself] out to do other things." Speaking to Elisabeth Bumiller of the *Washington Post* (March 16, 1982), she added, "I think it would be a great sadness if women's liberation meant that talented women felt like failures because they couldn't juggle four balls at one time." Nevertheless, she has regularly advised Barnard women to "shoot for it."

At Columbia's commencement exercises in the spring of 1984, Michael Sovern, in awarding Miss Futter an honorary doctor of laws degree, applauded her as "the embodiment of the Barnard ideal: *magna cum laude* alumna, college trustee since your student days, graduate of our law school, successful New York lawyer, active community volunteer, devoted family woman, acclaimed educational leader." In her capacity as president of Barnard College, Miss Futter serves on the executive committee of the Women's College Coalition and as trustee of the New York State Commission on Independent Colleges and Universities, and she is an active member of the New York State Governor's Committee of College and University Presidents. Her other memberships include the National Institute of Social Sciences, the Helsinki Watch Committee, an international human-rights monitoring organization, and several bar associations.

A trim five feet two inches tall, Ellen Futter has short, thick dark brown hair and dark eyes. She regularly puts in a twelve-hour workday, either on campus or on her increasingly frequent travels around the country to raise money or recruit students, but in her rare hours of leisure she enjoys playing tennis, cooking, shelling, which, in her words, "fits in with my balance between work and play," and reading. Her taste in books is eclectic, ranging from light romance to historical biography. On August 25, 1974 Ellen Futter married John A. Shutkin, a lawyer whom she met while both were students at Columbia's law school. They have a daughter, Anne Victoria, who was born on her mother's birthday in 1981. When questioned about her plans for the future, Miss Futter told Georgia Dullea, "I never thought I'd be doing what I'm doing today at thirty-five, which proves you can't predict or project. Early retirement sometimes sounds attractive," she admitted, but she would not rule out returning to law practice or, as some have speculated, embarking on a political career.

*References: Chicago Tribune XII p3 F 14 '82 por; N Y Times B p3 Jl 28 '80 por; N Y Times Mag p44+ D 2 '84 por; Washington Post C p6 Mr 16 '82 por; Who's Who in America, 1984–85*

## Gandhi, Rajiv (Ratna)

(gän´dē rä-jēv)

*Aug. 20, 1944– Prime Minister of India. Address: b. Office of the Prime Minister, New Delhi, India*

With the assassination, on October 31, 1984, of India's Prime Minister Indira Gandhi by Sikh extremists who belonged to her security force, her only surviving son, Rajiv Gandhi, was thrust into the position of leadership of his nation's 750 million people. A former airline pilot with no particular political ambition, Rajiv Gandhi had reluctantly agreed, at his mother's urging, to succeed his politically active younger brother, Sanjay Gandhi, as heir apparent, following Sanjay's death in an air crash in 1980. Elected to his brother's seat in the Lok Sabha—the lower house of India's parliament—in 1981, he became his mother's chief aide and adviser. His accession as his country's sixth and youngest prime minister was confirmed by an unprecedented landslide electoral victory in late December 1984. During his first few months in office, Rajiv Gandhi, a self-styled member of the Beatles Generation, seemed to be fulfilling his pledge to bring his tradition-bound and unwieldily bureaucratic land "into the twenty-first century" and to cope with its perennial and seemingly insurmountable problems, including hunger, disease, overpopulation, corruption, and sectarian violence.

Rajiv Gandhi's designation as his mother's successor was viewed by some observers as an attempt to perpetuate a dynasty. His great-grandfather Motilal Nehru, a close associate of Mohandas K. Gandhi (not a relative), pioneered in the Indian independence movement under British colonial rule, and his grandfather Jawaharlal Nehru served as independent India's first prime minister from 1947 to 1964. Indira Gandhi, who was elected president of the Indian National Congress party in 1959, served as her father's aide and official hostess during his years in office and was prime minister of India from 1966 to 1977 and again from 1980 until her death. During her dynamic and often controversial rule, she continued her father's campaign to establish India as a major influence within the non-aligned bloc of nations and on the world scene, a task that now devolves on Rajiv Gandhi.

Rajiv Ratna Gandhi was born on August 20, 1944—almost three years to the day before India attained independence from Great Britain—in Bombay, to which his mother had traveled from the family home in Allahabad to take advantage of its superior medical facilities. Rajiv's father, Feroze Gandhi, a Parsi lawyer and journalist, became a member of India's parliament in 1950 and died a decade later. His brother, Sanjay, was born in 1946.

Recalling her elder son's birth, Indira Gandhi wrote in her autobiographical *My Truth* (1981), "I think it was one of the most joyful moments in my life, although I must say at the time he seemed quite ugly." She remembers proudly displaying her newborn son for inspection by his grandfather through the bars of the British prison where Jawaharlal Nehru was confined at the time. According to a profile in *Maclean's* (November 12, 1984), "On January 29, 1948, Rajiv visited Mahatma Gandhi with his mother and two relatives and, while the adults bantered, the child decorated Gandhi's big toe with a chain of flowers. A day later, the mahatma was assassinated."

According to Krishna Nehru Hutheesing, a sister of Jawaharlal Nehru, "Indira was a tender mother. . . . Remembering her own loneliness as a child, she wanted [her children] to have a normal childhood. She supervised their meals, played with them, and took them to a film if a suitable one for children was being shown. The boys were secure in their mother's affection." Although Indira Gandhi and her husband were estranged during much of their marriage, Feroze Gandhi remained a devoted parent, who often saw his sons, constructed toys for their amusement, and encouraged their interest in science and technology.

When Indira Gandhi became her father's official hostess in 1947, she moved with Rajiv and Sanjay to the Teen Murti house, the prime minister's residence in New Delhi, where she placed them in the care of Anna Orsholt, a Danish governess who had been in the service of the Nehru family for some years. In 1951 the boys were admitted to the Shiv Niketan (Abode of Serenity) elementary school, where they were instructed in the Hindi language, arts and crafts, and general knowledge.

After completing his secondary education at the exclusive Doon School at Dehra Dun in the Himalayan foothills, Rajiv Gandhi studied for three years at Trinity College of Cambridge University—his grandfather Nehru's alma mater. He then attended the Imperial College of Science and Technology in London. In 1965 he obtained a degree in

mechanical engineering. It was at Cambridge that he met his future wife, Sonia Maino, the daughter of an Italian businessman. Although Indira Gandhi at first opposed her son's marriage to a foreigner, she eventually gave her approval and later grew quite fond of her Italian daughter-in-law.

Rajiv Gandhi's enthusiasm for aviation prompted him to embark on flight training on his return to India. After qualifying for his commercial pilot's license, he obtained employment with Indian Airlines, the government-owned domestic air carrier, flying twin-engine propeller-driven planes between the subcontinent's minor cities, looking forward to the time when he might qualify to pilot the more sophisticated Boeing jet planes, and eventually attaining the status of senior pilot. He introduced himself to his passengers as "Captain Rajiv" instead of as the more impressive-sounding "Captain Gandhi."

The sedate and reflective Rajiv Gandhi and his flamboyant and impetuous brother, Sanjay, lived with their families under one roof in the prime minister's house, but the two brothers had little in common. While Rajiv seemed content with his quiet family life and his work as an airline pilot, Sanjay—after indulging in an ambitious but unsuccessful automobile-manufacturing venture—plunged headlong into politics. He was soon recognized as Mrs. Gandhi's presumptive heir. Even though Sanjay had not yet been elected to public office, as his mother's chief adviser he was largely responsible for the controversial "national regeneration" program, including an excessively zealous birth-control campaign, under the state of emergency, established in mid-1975, that gave Indira Gandhi virtually dictatorial power.

Public discontent with Mrs. Gandhi's emergency rule and with the growing influence of Sanjay Gandhi led to her defeat in the elections of March 1977 and the taking over of the prime ministership by Morarji Desai, the head of the newly organized Janata party. Facing charges of corruption and the misuse of power, Indira Gandhi was aided by Sanjay and his wife, Maneka, in her effort to make a comeback. In 1978 she broke with the old guard of the Congress party and formed her own political party, the Indian National Congress-I ("I" for Indira), which in the elections of January 1980 returned her to power as prime minister and brought Sanjay Gandhi into the Lok Sabha as a member of parliament for Amethi in Uttar Pradesh. Meanwhile, during the 1970s, Rajiv Gandhi had remained aloof from national affairs and rarely expressed himself politically, though he apparently disapproved of his brother's questionable tactics, which reportedly included sending "strong-arm types" into the streets, blocking traffic, disrupting court proceedings, and hijacking aircraft.

On June 23, 1980 Sanjay Gandhi died in an air crash after losing control of the Pitts aerobatic biplane that he was flying in a daredevil stunt over New Delhi. His death, after only six months as a member of parliament and barely ten days as one of the general secretaries of the Congress-I party, left a vacuum that his grieving mother and her supporters hoped Rajiv Gandhi would fill. But it was only with great reluctance that Rajiv consented to enter the political arena. "The way I look at it is that Mummy has to be helped somehow," he said in an interview in *India Today*, soon after his brother's death. "She had a lot of support from Sanjay and now it's not there. . . . I don't know much about politics, so there's no question of my stepping into his shoes."

While he continued to fly domestic runs in northern India, Rajiv Gandhi began to act as his mother's unofficial assistant. He undertook liaison duties, met with politicians and petitioners, and screened visitors, but because he remained behind the scenes, he provoked some criticism in the press on the ground that he was exercising power without responsibility. Nevertheless, he resisted formally entering politics, even after a petition submitted in August 1980 by some 300 members of parliament urged him to do so.

Finally, in early May 1981, Rajiv Gandhi resigned from Indian Airlines, relinquished plans to start training to fly Boeing jets, and joined the Congress-I party, declaring his candidacy for his late brother's parliamentary seat. Opposed by thirteen candidates in a by-election on June 15, 1981, Gandhi won the Amethi constituency with 258,884 of the 307,523 votes cast. His election seems to have been carefully orchestrated by Indira Gandhi. Ten days after his election, Rajiv Gandhi was appointed an executive committee member of the youth wing of the Congress-I party, a position that his late brother had used to build up his national strength.

While representing Amethi in the 542-member Lok Sabha, Rajiv Gandhi continued as his mother's unofficial assistant and was soon recognized as an important political force, despite his disdain for the venality and sycophancy that characterized much of Indian politics. He toured the country extensively with his mother, addressed public meetings, held discussions with officials, met with foreign dignitaries, and organized the Asian Games in New Delhi in 1982. In his own district he helped to obtain a massive federally funded development program that improved the quality of life in that economically depressed region. In February 1983 he was appointed by his mother as one of the Congress-I party's general secretaries and eventually became the most powerful among them.

Deploring what he saw as a flagrant abandonment of the ideals of Mohandas K. Gandhi, Rajiv Gandhi established such a reputation for high standards of morality in politics that he earned the nickname "Mr. Clean." He reorganized the inefficient and faction-ridden Congress-I party machinery, dismissed his late brother's more disreputable associates, and removed those state and local officials whom he regarded as corrupt or incompetent. Gathering around himself a coterie of young and upwardly mobile professionals, businessmen, and technicians, many of them former classmates at the Doon School, Rajiv Gandhi introduced modern management methods, including up-to-date advertising techniques and computerized poll forecasting, into Indian politics. One of his few disputes with his mother was over her insistence on consulting astrologers in making political decisions, to which he was said to have responded, "We aren't living in the Flintstone age."

By early 1984, Rajiv Gandhi, as the second most powerful political figure in India, seemed to be well-versed in the techniques of politics, even though one veteran political commentator described him at the time as "a rosebud in a bed of overripe cabbages." To prepare for national elections scheduled for late 1984 or early 1985, he and his fellow general secretaries were busily screening candidates, a function that, having been taken from the state party organizations, was now concentrated in the hands of officials of the national Congress-I party organization.

For the forthcoming elections, Rajiv Gandhi faced a challenge from his late brother's politically ambitious young widow, Maneka Gandhi, a former model and journalist, whom Indira Gandhi had evicted from the family home in March 1982 for allegedly plotting with opponents to her government. In April 1983, Maneka formed her own party of the opposition, the Rashtriya Sanjay Manch (National Sanjay Organization), and in January 1984 she announced her candidacy for Rajiv Gandhi's seat in Amethi, capitalizing on public sympathy as Sanjay's widow.

Although Rajiv Gandhi presumably did not develop a clearly defined political program of his own during his mother's prime ministership, he indicated in his public statements that his priorities for India were population control, education, social reform, dealing with religious and ethnic strife, and getting "the poor and the weak . . . out of the morass they're stuck in." In foreign policy, he favored continuing close ties with the Soviet Union and at times criticized what he saw as American attempts to weaken Indian neutrality. On the other hand, while giving lip service to socialism, he was said to have persuaded his mother to relax government financial controls and grant greater incentives to private business and foreign investors.

Although serving as his mother's chief adviser, Rajiv Gandhi occasionally acted on his own. In March 1984 he was credited with having persuaded the government to refrain from amending an existing law in such a way as to enable a prominent member of the Congress-I party, A. R. Antulay, to escape prosecution on pending charges of corruption. His efforts did not always succeed, however. It is not clear whether, in response to increasingly militant Sikh demands for autonomy, he had a hand in his mother's decision, in June 1984, to order the army raid on the Golden Temple in Amritsar, the holiest shrine of the Sikh religion, at the cost of more than 600 lives, but observers have suggested that it seems unlikely that she would have taken such a drastic step without consulting him.

In the morning hours of October 31, 1984, while walking in the garden of her official residence in New Delhi, Indira Gandhi was gunned down by two Sikh members of her security guard, apparently in retaliation for the Golden Temple massacre. Rajiv Gandhi, who rushed back from a campaign trip in West Bengal on learning of the assassination, was unanimously elected prime minister that same day in an emergency meeting of the cabinet. As Hindus rioted against Sikhs in retaliatory violence that eventually resulted in some 2,000 deaths, Rajiv Gandhi called for calm. "This is a moment of profound grief," he declared, shortly after being sworn in by President Giani Zail Singh. "We can and must face this tragic ordeal with fortitude, courage, and wisdom." Over the next few days, he managed to stem the worst of the violence and met with Sikh leaders to assure them that their community would not be held responsible for the assassination. Pending new elections, he retained most of his mother's ministers in his temporary cabinet.

Indira Gandhi's funeral was attended by nearly 100 foreign dignitaries, including British Prime Minister Margaret Thatcher, Soviet Premier Nikolai Tikhinov, and President Mohammad Zia ul-Haq of Pakistan—the first Pakistani head of state to attend the funeral of an Indian prime minister. The United States was represented by Secretary of State George P. Shultz, who commented after meeting with the new prime minister, "Gandhi came through with a sort of quiet strength that I find reassuring."

On November 12, 1984, following a twelve-day period of mourning, Rajiv Gandhi was unanimously elected as president of the Congress-I party and gave his first national policy speech, in which he affirmed his adherence to the policies of Mahatma Gandhi, Jawaharlal Nehru, and Indira Gandhi. He called for national unity, world peace, continued adherence to socialism and planning, promotion of science and technology, and adoption of "a new work ethic." On the following day the government announced national elections for December 24 and 27, four weeks earlier than the dates required by the constitution. Starting his "national unity campaign," Rajiv Gandhi toured the country by helicopter amid shouts from cheering crowds of "Long live Rajiv!" and "Indira will live forever!"

In the midst of the election campaign, India was struck by one of the worst manmade disasters in history when on December 3, 1984 poison gas leaks from an American-owned Union Carbide insecticide plant in the city of Bhopal caused the deaths of as many as 2,500 people. Breaking off his election tour to visit the stricken city, Gandhi announced emergency measures to provide relief and to stop the spread of toxic effects of the chemical. He declared that his government would review its policies regarding location of factories producing hazardous substances and demand compensation from Union Carbide for victims and their families.

The elections of December 24 and 27, 1984 brought Rajiv Gandhi what has been described as "the most complete, comprehensive triumph" in India's history. With over fifty percent of the popular vote, more than had been received by any of his predecessors, Gandhi won 401 of the 508 contested seats in the Lok Sabha. (Elections for the remaining seats, in the potentially troublesome states of Punjab and Assam and in disaster-ridden Bhopal, were postponed). In his own Amethi district, Rajiv Gandhi won an easy victory over Maneka Gandhi, with a margin of about 314,000 votes. His overall victory was attributed by political observers to sympathy over his mother's death, disarray among the parties of the opposition, and his lack, as yet, of formidable enemies.

Armed with what he considered to be his mandate to "take India swiftly forward," Rajiv Gandhi was formally inaugurated on December 31, 1984, along with his thirty-nine-member council of ministers, in which he retained the foreign-affairs portfolio. He indicated that he would monitor their performance and dismiss those who proved to be ineffective. Among his first actions in early 1985 were his replacement of some of his mother's top aides and his appointment of a special cabinet group to deal with the separatist political crisis in the Sikh stronghold of Punjab. "The size of [his] victory proves that Rajiv Gandhi is his own man—not just the relative of his relatives," Joseph Kraft wrote in his syndicated column, published in the New York Post (January 3, 1985).

In his first year as prime minister, Rajiv Gandhi managed to hold his own and was in some areas remarkably successful. He took strong measures to weed out corruption; introduced legislation to stiffen penalties for terrorist activities; promoted high technology, private enterprise, and foreign investment; made progress toward resolution of longstanding regional and sectarian disputes in Punjab, Assam, Gujarat, and Kashmir; and persuaded the government of neighboring Sri Lanka and leaders of its insurgent Tamil minority to enter negotiations to resolve their long-standing civil conflict.

On a visit to the USSR in May 1985, Gandhi obtained two new trade agreements that affirmed the special relationship between India and the Soviet Union. The following month he made a five-day state visit to the United States, where he addressed a joint session of Congress. Although he criticized American military aid to Pakistan and expressed "deep reservations about the militarization of outer space," he seemed to establish rapport with President Ronald Reagan.

On July 24, 1985, in what was considered a political triumph for Rajiv Gandhi, the Indian government concluded a far-reaching agreement with Sikh leaders that, among other provisions, gave the Sikhs greater political and economic influence in Punjab, where they constituted 61 percent of the population. Although the assassination, in August, of the moderate Sikh leader Sant Harchand Singh Longowal by Sikh extremists was a major setback, the relatively peaceful elections in Punjab on September 25, 1985 seemed to indicate that the agreement was a success. Meanwhile, in a major reshuffle, Gandhi expanded his cabinet to fifty-one ministers and relinquished the foreign-affairs portfolio while taking on the duties of minister of defense.

Rajiv Gandhi and his Italian-born wife, Sonia, whom he married in 1968 and who is now an Indian citizen, have a son, Rahul, and a daughter, Priyanka. A tall, portly, soft-spoken man, Gandhi has thinning hair, an ingratiating manner, and a boyish appearance. According to Shyam Bhatia, writing in the London Observer (December 23, 1984), he has been characterized as "the most 'English' of India's prime ministers," with "perfect command of the language, dry humor," and a "persistent habit of understatement." His recreational interests include ham-radio operation, photography, and listening to classical music.

References: London Sunday Times p10 O 21 '84 por; Macleans 97:30+ N 12 '84 por; N Y Times A p1+ N 1 '84 pors, p1+ D 30 '84 por; N Y Times Mag p40+ Je 13 '82 por, p39+ D 2 '84 pors; Newsweek 104:42+ N 12 '84 pors; Time 124:42+ N 12 '84 por; Ali, Tariq. An Indian Dynasty: The Story of the Gandhi-Nehru Family (1985); Mehta, Ved. A Family Affair (1982); Sharma, Satinder and Indra. Rajiv Gandhi: An Annotated Bibliography (1983)

## Garcia Pérez, Alan

*May 23, 1949– President of Peru. Address: Palacio del Gobierno, Lima, Peru*

On July 28, 1985 thirty-six-year-old Alan García Pérez succeeded the aging Fernando Belaúnde Terry as president of Peru, marking the first time in four decades that an elected president relinquished power to an elected successor in that perennially crisis-ridden South American nation of some 19.7 million people. A lawyer by profession, García was elected in 1978 to the constituent assembly and in 1980 to the national congress, and in 1982 he became general secretary of the Alianza Popular Revolucionaria Americana (APRA), also known as the Peruvian Aprista party. Founded in 1924 by Victor Raúl Haya de la Torre as a militant leftist movement to challenge the oligarchy that had ruled Peru for over a century, APRA gradually mellowed over the years into a moderate social democratic movement, with strong support from the middle class and organized labor. Although it had not previously elected a president, APRA has played a key role in Peruvian politics in the six decades of its existence.

During his early months in office, García Pérez drastically shook up his country's military and police forces, launched a vigorous campaign against government corruption, declared war on the cocaine trade in the Amazon region, established a commission to seek rapport with extreme leftist guerrilla forces, and instituted an economic program that included a price freeze, concessions to industry and agriculture, restrictions on foreign exchange, and a balanced budget. Although his insistence on bypassing the International Monetary Fund in foreign-debt negotiations and limiting debt payments for the time being to 10 percent of export earnings have brought him criticism from the international banking community and United States government officials, García Pérez is widely regarded as the best hope for the survival of democracy in Peru.

Alan García Pérez was born in Lima, Peru on May 23, 1949. His parents, Carlos García Ronceros and Nyta Pérez de García, were both members of APRA, and during the first five years of Alan García's life, his father, a prominent figure in the Aprista party, was imprisoned for political reasons by the military government of General Manuel A. Odria. To avoid further harassment, the mother moved with her children to the southern part of Peru. At eleven, García joined the youth organization of APRA and during his adolescence became active in the party, eventually becoming a protégé of Haya de la Torre.

After completing his secondary education at the Colegio Nacional José Maria Eguren in the Barranco district of Lima, García Pérez studied literature and law at the Universidad Católica de Lima and in 1973 graduated with a law degree from the Universidad Nacional Mayor de San Marcos in his home city. Feeling restless, García decided to continue his studies in Spain and France. While in Europe, he adopted the bohemian lifestyle of many other young expatriate Latin Americans, occasionally picking up some extra money by singing in bistros.

García obtained his doctor of law degree at the Universidad Complutense de Madrid after completing a dissertation on the juridical concept of society and constitutional law in the achievement of American independence. His supervisor was the noted Spanish professor and political leader Manuel Fraga Iribarne. He then moved to Paris, where he studied sociology at the Sorbonne and at the Institute of Higher Studies on Latin America, and wrote a dissertation on sociological factors influencing elections in the history of the Aprista party, under the guidance of François Bourricaud, a distinguished sociologist and authority on Peru.

Returning to Lima in 1977, García immersed himself in party work. In the following year he was designated by Haya de la Torre as secretary of organization and president of the commission on ideology of APRA. On July 18, 1978, in Peru's first nationwide balloting in a decade and a half, García was elected to the 100-member constituent assembly, which drafted the new constitution that went into effect on July 28, 1980, paving the way for a return to democracy after twelve years of military rule. In the elections of May 18, 1980 Fernando Belaúnde Terry, the leader of the moderately right-of-center Acción Popular, who had served as president from 1963 to 1968, won the presidency with 45.4 percent of the votes cast. Armando Villanueva del Campo, who had succeeded as leader of APRA after Haya de la Torre's death in August 1979, came in second, with about 27 percent of the vote in the fifteen-candidate contest. Heading the list of APRA candidates, García Pérez won a seat in the chamber of deputies, the lower house of the national congress, for the term 1980 to 1985.

In 1982, after winning the support of the younger elements of APRA and successfully negotiating with other factions, García Pérez was elected secretary general of the party, a position that assured him the presidential candidacy for the next elections. Formally nominated in 1984 for the national elections scheduled for April of the following year, García carefully organized his campaign and presented himself as heir to the leadership of APRA by adopting Haya de la Torre's language, gestures, and sober manner of dress. At the same time, in addressing himself "to all Peruvians," he toned down the party's radical image in order to reach out to the middle classes as well as to slum dwellers. "You'll notice that he waves the Peruvian flag and not the APRA flag at meetings," one of his aides observed, as quoted in the New York Times (January 9, 1985), "because there are people who like him but don't trust APRA."

During the years of Belaúnde Terry's presidency, Peru's economy had steadily declined, despite the government's strict austerity measures. By the eve of the 1985 elections, the inflation rate was steadily increasing, unemployment was rampant, and the foreign debt exceeded $14 billion. Floods had caused extensive damage, the nation was beset by strikes, and guerrillas of the extreme left, notably the Sendero Luminoso (Shining Path)—inspired by Mao Zedong—spread terror throughout the country, prompting the military to launch a violent counterinsurgency campaign. Into that grim atmosphere, García Pérez tried to introduce a note of self-assured optimism, seeking to implant in Peruvians some hope for their future and pledging himself to combat hunger, disease, and unemployment. He avoided commitment to a detailed program, arguing that many of Peru's problems required long-term solutions rather than radical panaceas, and he refused to engage in polemics with his opponents of the left or right.

Because of the worsening economic crisis, during his campaign García stressed the need for greater national self-sufficiency. He called for a shift in investment from urban centers to agricultural areas to eliminate the need for food imports, discourage the tide of migration to the cities, improve nutritional standards, and establish new markets for industry. With reference to Peru's staggering national debt, García criticized the "recessive practices" prescribed by the International Monetary Fund (IMF) and proposed selective increases in tariffs to protect local industry and a slowing down of the devaluation of the national currency. "We will pay," he told voters, "but not at the time that they want. First we'll pay off our debt to the people by providing food and jobs. It's not fifty bankers who pick the president of Peru." Although he insisted that he would have to "apply the law" against the excesses of Sendero Luminoso, García maintained that the movement could not be defeated through violence. Instead, he called for an understanding of historical and racial factors in dealing with that largely Andean Indian guerrilla organization.

Although Sendero Luminoso and another guerrilla group known as Movimiento Revolucionario Tupac Amaru threatened to disrupt the voting, the elections proceeded relatively peacefully when some 90 percent of Peru's 8.2 million eligible voters went to the polls on April 14, 1985. In the nine-candidate race, García received a plurality, with 3,457,030 votes, or 45.74 percent of the total. His nearest opponent, with 21.26 percent of the vote, was Lima's independent Marxist mayor, Alfonso Barrantes Lingán, heading a multiparty coalition known as Izquierda Unida (United Left) that included Communists as well as democratic socialists. In third place, with some 12 percent of the vote, was Luis Bedoya Reyes of the right-wing Partido Popular Cristiano (Popular Christian party), while Javier Alva Orlandini of Belaúnde Terry's Acción Popular received only about 5 percent. In the congressional elections on the same day APRA received narrow majorities in both the senate and the chamber of deputies. As Barrantes commented after the election, the right had been virtually "erased from the scene" in Peru. Since the vote received by García fell short of an absolute majority, a runoff contest between the two leading candidates was required under the constitution, but that requirement was waived when Barrantes on April 26 withdrew from the race. On June 1, 1985 the national election board formally declared García Pérez the president-elect of Peru.

Addressing a crowd of some 5,000 Peruvians after the polls had closed on election day, amid shouts of "Alan, Presidente!", García said: "We have been left a fatherland like this, indebted, sacrificed, hungry, and with violence. Now the Peruvian people will change the government, change the economy, change politics, and reaffirm our democracy." In outlining his plans two days later, García affirmed that he would bypass the International Monetary Fund in foreign-debt negotiations and support joint efforts by Latin American debtor countries in seeking more lenient terms. "We need to go back to the concept of a new world economic order," he declared. "Now only the debtors are paying the cost of the world crisis. . . . Latin America has to give a common answer." García praised the Sandinista government of Nicaragua as the "progressive affirmation of democracy in Central America" and criticized what he called the "distorted concepts of Latin America" held by Ronald Reagan. He added that his government would pursue the policies of the "nonaligned" Third World bloc in foreign affairs and would look for regional solutions to its international debt and its relations with the United States.

On July 20, 1985 García appointed his new seventeen-member cabinet, including members of other parties besides APRA. Eight days later, under strict security in the wake of guerrilla violence, he was sworn in for a five-year term as president of Peru and received the red and white presidential sash from his predecessor, Belaúnde Terry. Among the dignitaries attending the inauguration were the presidents of Argentina, Uruguay, Colombia, Bolivia, Panama, and the Dominican Republic. The United States was represented by James Baker 3d, secretary of the treasury.

In his two-hour inaugural address, García announced that over the next twelve months Peru would restrict its foreign-debt payments to 10 percent of the national export income while its debt was being renegotiated. He indicated that his government would deal directly with its creditors and bypass the International Monetary Fund, which he held partly responsible for his country's economic woes. Peru would refuse to accept "imposed economic policies," he declared. García called on Latin American countries to act in concert to obtain more favorable conditions for their debts and urged them to promote trade with developing nations. Among other proposals, he called for establishment of a commission that would seek a peaceful resolution to the government's five-year war with Sendero Luminoso. He promised to put an end to "injustice, exploitation, and misery" and to intensify the campaign against narcotics traffickers, and he pledged to reduce military spending and urged other Latin American countries to do likewise. For the immediate future, García put forth several pieces of legislation to be presented to congress, including measures to combat corruption among government officials and in the police force, to promote agricultural development, and to decentralize public administration and business monopolies.

García's debt plan drew sharp criticism from United States officials. James Baker 3d remarked that it was "counterproductive" and would reduce the willingness of banks to extend credit, a view with which the Federal Reserve Board chairman, Paul A. Volcker, concurred. International bankers voiced some concern that other Latin American debtor nations might follow Peru's example in restricting their debt payments. Taking an opposite point of view, Cuban President Fidel Castro called on Latin American nations to suspend debt payments outright and criticized García's proposed social and economic reforms as inadequate. But some Western observers saw in García's debt program a sound compromise. Tom Wicker, for example, described it in his *New York Times* column (July 30, 1985) as "the most imaginative idea yet offered by a leader of a debt-ridden Latin American nation, . . . one that avoids both extremes—default or years of extreme economic austerity threatening political upheaval."

Two days after García's inauguration, representatives of twenty Latin American nations issued the Declaration of Lima, in which they agreed in principle with the Peruvian president's policy of linking debt payments with export earnings but made no reference to his refusal to deal with the International Monetary Fund or his specific plans for coming to terms with the debt. On the same day, García declared a two-day bank holiday, reportedly to prevent a run on international reserves. When the banks reopened on August 1, García ordered a ninety-day freeze on dollar accounts to stem the flight of capital and announced a series of emergency measures, including adjustments in prices of gasoline and certain basic foods, along with a 50 percent rise in the minimum wage, to be followed by a freeze on wages and prices.

During August, in collaboration with the government of Colombia and the United States Drug Enforcement Agency, García launched an extensive airborne anti-narcotics campaign known as Opertion Condor that resulted in raids on major cocaine-processing laboratories and distribution sites. He also forced the retirement of a number of police generals suspected of being involved in the illegal drug trade and signed into law a congressional authorization to revamp the 65,000-man national police force. Responding to reports of mass killings by government troops of scores of Andean peasants in the army's campaign against guerrillas, García moved in September to assert his authority over the military. Several high-ranking officers, including the chairman of the joint chiefs of staff, were dismissed, and trials were ordered for officers and troops implicated in the killings.

Within a few weeks of taking office, García appeared to have made substantial headway toward resolving many of the seemingly insoluble problems that had long plagued Peru. Inflation had slowed down considerably, and according to a government report in early September, Lima's cost-of-living index had risen less than 1 percent since the emergency measures went into effect, as compared with 11 percent in July. To reduce government expenditures, he placed a ceiling on salaries of high-ranking officials and canceled the major part of an order for fighter planes from France. He announced plans to bring government closer to the people by holding cabinet meetings in the various regions of the country and established the promised "peace commission" to deal with the guerrilla problem. "I have the satisfaction of having contributed to restoring to Peru part of its lost will," Garcia told Michael L. Smith in an interview in the *Washington Post* (September 15, 1985). "Now we have to make up for lost time. We've put an end to the domination of the government by the economy, which existed up to now." An independent opinion poll published a little over a month after he took office gave Garcia an approval rating of 96 percent.

Addressing the United Nations General Assembly in New York City on September 23, 1985, on the occasion of the world organization's fortieth anniversary, Garcia reaffirmed his government's intention to limit debt payments to 10 percent of export earnings and indicated that Peru would withdraw from the International Money Fund unless substantial reforms were made to ease terms for repayment. "We are faced with a dramatic choice," he declared. "It's either debt or democracy. This is the crux of the current Latin American situation."

Alan García Pérez and his wife, the former Pilar Nores, have four daughters. A darkly handsome, sturdily built man, six feet three inches tall, with a thick shock of black hair, Garcia exudes self-confidence and charisma and—despite his youth—a paternalism that some observers view as authoritarianism. In his book *Futuro Diferente* (A Different Future), published in 1983, he updated the ideas of Haya de la Torre and emphasized the importance of the foreign-debt problem for Latin America. Garcia takes his inspiration from the achievements of Peru's ancient Inca empire and from Spain's social democratic prime minister Felipe González, rather than from Marx and Lenin, and some consider him a suitable successor to Fidel Castro as the leading representative of the Latin American left.

References: N Y Times A p12 Ja 9 '85 por, A p1+ S 3 '85; N Y Times Mag p23+ Jl 14 '85 por; Time 125:56+ Ap 29 '85 por; Wall St J p34 S 25 '85 por

Garn, Edwin (Jacob) *See* Garn, Jake

## Garn, Jake

Oct. 12, 1932- United States Senator from Utah. Address: b. 505 Dirksen Office Bldg., Washington, D.C. 20510

In April 1985 Jake Garn, a Republican senator from Utah, became the first well-known civilian to be launched into outer space. As chairman of a Senate subcommittee that oversees spending by the National Aeronautics and Space Adminstration, Garn asked for and finally received permission from NASA officials to join the crew of a space shuttle as a congressional observer. He was criticized in the *New York Times* for allegedly using the shuttle flight to advance his own political ends and had the dubious honor of being lampooned in Gary Trudeau's satirical *Doonesbury* comic strip. But as a former Navy pilot, Garn believed that he was well qualified for the trip, and he underwent considerable pre-flight training. After an adventurous week in space, the shuttle *Discovery* brought Garn and six other astronauts safely back to earth on April 19, 1985.

One of a new breed of conservatives in public office, Garn was first elected to the Senate in 1974, where he wields considerable influence, especially in his post as chairman of the Committee on Banking, Housing and Urban Affairs. Known for his in-depth grasp of such key issues as banking reform and the SALT II arms limitation agreement, Garn is a foe of big government and, at the same time, a hard-line proponent of strong military preparedness.

Edwin Jacob Garn—who prefers to use Jake as his given name—was born in Richfield, Utah on October 12, 1932 to Jacob Edwin Garn and Fern (Christensen) Garn and was reared according to the precepts of his family's Mormon faith. His father, who had been an airman during World War I and had his own airplane, served as an official of the Bureau of Air Commerce and as Utah's first director of aeronautics. In 1937 the family moved to Salt Lake City, where Garn attended East High, graduating in 1951. He then went on to the University of Utah, where he majored in business and finance, and obtained his B.S. degree in 1955.

Garn, who already had learned to fly an airplane as a teenager, trained as a pilot on joining the United States Navy in 1956. During his tour of duty he piloted antisubmarine patrols over the Sea of Japan and Yellow Sea and reconnaissance patrols up and down the east coast of China, and he advanced in rank from ensign to lieutenant senior grade. Although he had planned at first to become a career officer, Garn decided, because of family obligations, to resign from the Navy in 1960. Returning to Salt Lake City, he was a special agent for the John Hancock Mutual Life Insurance Company in 1960-61, then served for five years as assistant manager of the Salt Lake City branch of the Home Life Insurance Company of New York, and worked from 1966 to 1968 for the Mutual Trust Life Insurance Company.

While pursuing his business career, Garn became involved in community affairs, devoting his free time to the American Cancer Society, the Boy Scouts, the Salvation Army, Little League baseball, the Jaycees, and other organizations. He also was active in local politics, serving as Republican voting district chairman from 1960 until 1964, as Republican legislative district chairman from 1962 to 1966, and as a member of the board of directors of the Salt Lake County Young Republicans from 1960 until 1966.

From 1963 to 1979 Garn was a command pilot with the Utah Air National Guard, eventually reaching the rank of colonel. When he tried to negotiate a lease on a local airport, he came up against some frustrating bureaucratic restrictions. According to one story often recounted in the press, Garn decided to seek elective office when he took up the challenge of a Salt Lake City commissioner, who invited him to run for public office if he did not like the way the city was being managed. Another account, by Harry Jones in the *Deseret News* (November 4, 1972), maintained that Garn as a public speaker "had a great bit on the podium about the apathy of people in relation to their government. It stirred a lot of people into action. Some were so stirred, they asked [Garn] to run for a Salt Lake City commission post." Although it meant resigning from his insurance position and taking a lower salary, Garn accepted the offer and was elected. He served on the city commission of Salt Lake City as director of the water and sewer systems from 1968 until 1972, and during that period he was also acting commissioner of the city fire department.

After a relatively short time in public life, Garn decided to run for the mayoralty of Salt Lake City in 1971, when the incumbent, J. Bracken Lee, declined to seek reelection. Running on a pledge to modernize and consolidate city government, Garn defeated parks commissioner Conran B. Harrison in the November election with a landslide majority of 39,690 to 15,008, or 73 percent of the vote. Sworn in on January 3, 1972 as mayor—a nonpartisan position in Salt Lake City—Garn launched a city beautification project. His efforts to widen streets, plant trees, and build fountains were at first criticized but later brought him considerable praise. As mayor, Garn often fired away at what he called the "police state tactics" of the federal government, whose regulations, he felt, were crippling municipal government. In connection with his mayoral duties, Garn served as president of the Utah League of Cities, which conferred on him its Tom McCoy Award as the state's outstanding municipal official. He was also a vice-president of the National League of Cities and was one of three mayors selected to serve on the New Coalition, which was established in 1973 to deal with key issues on the national, state, and local levels.

In 1974 Garn decided to declare his candidacy for the United States Senate seat being vacated by the retirement of Wallace F. Bennett. In the wake of the Watergate scandal and the resulting resignation of President Richard Nixon, Republican candidates from coast to coast faced stiff opposition. Running against the relatively liberal Democratic Congressman Wayne Owens, who was backed by Senator Edward M. Kennedy and actor Robert Redford, among others, and who had a lead in the preelection polls, Garn amassed a solid majority of some 25,000, winning 50 percent of the vote to Owens' 44 percent.

In his freshman term in the Senate, then under Democratic control, Garn exercised his conservative credentials on a variety of issues and showed himself to be a foreign policy "hawk" who favored a strong military and defense policy. He criticized the administration of Gerald R. Ford for its 1975 relaxation of the United States trade embargo with Cuba, and he also opposed ratification of the Panama Canal treaties, which after arduous debate finally won Senate approval in 1978. On domestic issues, Garn successfully led a filibuster effort in 1976 to prevent the passage of "clean-air" legislation that would have restricted industrial growth in Utah and other largely rural states. He was opposed to most social welfare measures, including federally funded abortion and union-backed labor reform. In keeping with his commitment to a free-market ideology, Garn entertained misgivings about federal loan aid to the Chrysler Corporation, and he failed to support the financial bailout package for New York City in the late 1970s.

Garn's most significant effort during his freshman term concerned the debate over the second strategic arms limitation agreement, SALT II, which, after having been signed by President Jimmy Carter and Soviet leader Leonid I. Brezhnev in June 1979, was sent to the Senate for ratification. As a member of the Senate's Select Committee on Intelligence, Garn had devoted considerable attention to the details of the treaty. Convinced that the United States had been shortchanged during the negotiations, Garn recommended that the treaty not be ratified. "It is absolutely the major legislative effort I have," he said in an interview for the *New York Times* (May 28, 1979). "I have put two and one half years of my life into it, trying to learn every single nut and bolt that I can." After much debate, SALT II ratification became a moot issue as a result of the Soviet invasion of Afghanistan in August 1979, which caused President Carter to suspend efforts to gain Senate approval.

By the end of his first term, Garn had become a significant force in the Senate. He had served on the Armed Services Committee and had become the ranking minority member of the Committee on Banking, Housing and Urban Affairs. According to Sanford J. Ungar, writing in the *Atlantic Monthly* (February 1979), Garn already wielded "a surprising amount of raw power." Together with Paul Laxalt of Nevada, Malcolm Wallop of Wyoming, and several other relatively young senators from Western states, Garn was one of a group identified by Ungar as "new conservatives," who constituted "the virtual, if not the official, leaders of the opposition in the Senate." Garn's conservative voice had won him an approval rating of 87 percent from the right-wing committee for the Survival of a Free Congress in 1980, while in the same year he received an approval rating of only 11 percent from the AFL-CIO.

Easily reelected in 1980 over Democratic challenger Dan Berman with 74 percent of the Utah vote, Garn returned to the Senate which, in the gathering conservative tide of Ronald Reagan's presidential victory, had come under Republican control. In the ensuing shift of power, Garn was named chairman of its Committee on Banking, Housing and Urban Affairs. From that position of influence, Garn proposed comprehensive legislation to restructure banking laws—the first such major reform since 1933. Garn's proposals were aimed at permitting commercial banks to compete with the rapidly expanding money-market funds and allowing them to underwrite revenue bonds. Eventually, in 1982, modest revisions in the banking laws were passed, though they were not as strong as Garn had desired. He met with somewhat greater success, in the ninety-seventh Congress, with his proposals for cuts in federally subsidized housing and in aid to mass-transit systems. According to the 1984 edition of *Politics in America*, "Garn's tenure as Banking Committee chairman has not been without difficulties. Sometimes his control of the panel seems shaky, and more than once he has had to postpone committee action on bills because he did not have the votes to determine the outcome. But he has been a chairman with a clear idea of where he wants to go."

As a "pro-lifer," in 1981 Garn cosponsored a version of a proposed constitutional amendment designed to make abortion illegal except where the life of the mother was at stake. His relationship with fellow anti-abortionists was, however, somewhat strained when it was revealed that the National Pro-Life Political Action Board had developed a "hit list" of liberal or quasi-liberal congressmen targeted for defeat in the 1982 elec-

tions. Garn resigned from the advisory panel of the action board when that list was publicized in mid-1981. "Members of a group's advisory board should be asked to advise," Garn said at the time, "and since I was not, I intend to resign."

Another issue that concerned Garn was the much-debated question of extra income that members of Congress earned as honoraria for lectures and writings. Although Garn had voted against efforts to raise senators' salaries, he outspokenly favored allowing them to earn as much outside income as they wished through speaking engagements and writing. Maintaining that outside earnings were necessary for the financial solvency that allowed him to remain in public office, Garn supported the Senate's action to lift the ceiling on such earnings. Without the additional $48,000 that he received in 1981 for his speeches and writings, he maintained, he "would not be able to run again in '86."

In May 1981 Garn made his first request that he be allowed to take part in a space mission as an astronaut. As chairman of the Senate appropriations subcommittee that reviewed spending by the National Aeronautics and Space Administration (NASA), Garn contended that his participation in a space flight would perform a legitimate fact-finding function. At a 1982 hearing he declared his "continuing desire sometime in the future to personally check out the space shuttle so that we can provide continuing appropriations." He repeated his request in 1983, and finally in November 1984 NASA officials invited Garn to become the first public official to fly in one of the space missions.

The announcement of NASA's offer evoked considerable comment in the press. Because Garn had fiscal supervisory responsibilities to NASA, an editorial in the *New York Times* suggested that the invitation resembled a bribe. During the ensuing months, such criticism provided background accompaniment to his preparations for his approaching space flight. Although polls showed Garn had considerable support for his flight in his home state, one letter to the *Salt Lake City Tribune* asked: "Is it really necessary to send Senator Garn into space? And could they do us all a favor and lose him out there?"

Early in 1985, at Johnson Space Center in Houston, Texas and Kennedy Space Center at Orlando, Florida, Garn underwent more than six weeks of special training, including exposure to conditions of weightlessness and simulated transport in an altitude chamber. He did not conceal his excitement as the date for the shuttle's flight approached. In an article by Storer Rowley in the *Chicago Tribune* (February 24, 1985), he was quoted as saying, "I don't know I'm going. It's still unreal. It's like the little kid waiting for Christmas and Christmas never comes." Garn answered critics of his space junket by pointing out that he was credited with over 10,000 hours of flight time during thirty-six years as a pilot, and that his trip would be valuable for his Senate committee's dealings with NASA. During the flight, Garn was to serve as a "payload specialist"—that is, as a human guinea pig to be subjected to a variety of tests measuring the effects of long periods of weightlessness on body fluids and organs. The tests were designed to help scientists understand the motion sickness that is often experienced in space.

Garn had originally been scheduled to fly aboard the space shuttle *Challenger,* but some difficulties led to cancellation of the original voyage on March 1, 1985. He was reassigned to a flight on the shuttle *Discovery,* which finally rocketed into orbit from Cape Canaveral, Florida on April 12, 1985 with a crew of seven. The week-long mission was notable for the successful deployment of a Canadian communications satellite, Anik C-1, and for the intrepid but unsuccessful efforts by the crew to repair a second satellite, the Leasat 3, which malfunctioned after its deployment in space. The spacecraft also encountered a variety of problems in landing. When it finally landed on April 19, Garn was somewhat unsteady on his feet, and he said later that he had been ill during the first two days of the flight. But he concluded, "I have never had a more fantastic experience and I have never been so proud of any people I've ever worked with." While in orbit, Garn cast the first vote in history by space proxy, in support of President Reagan's request for $14 million in nonmilitary aid to contras fighting the Sandinista regime in Nicaragua.

Trim, bald Jake Garn is said to be personable and friendly in individual conversation and is noted for his sense of humor. But he also is known for his "mean stare" and his sharp temper, especially when speaking out on issues that infringe on his long-standing conservative beliefs. On February 2, 1957 he married Hazel Rhae Thompson, and the couple had four children, Jacob Wayne, Susan Rhae, Ellen Marie, and Jeffrey Paul. In 1976, Hazel Garn was killed in an automobile accident, and some nine months later, on April 8, 1977, Jake Garn married Kathleen Brewerton, who has a son from her previous marriage to Garn's administrative assistant, Jeff Bingham. The couple has since had two more children, Matthew Spencer and Jennifer Kathleen. Garn is a high priest in the Church of Jesus Christ of Latter-Day Saints. His military decorations include the Armed Forces Expeditionary Medal, the Vietnam Service Medal, the Combat Readiness Medal, and the National Defense Medal. He is cochairman of the Coalition of Peace Through Strength.

References: *Deseret News* T p1+ N 4 '72 por; *N Y Times* p8 Ap 13 '85; *Almanac of American Politics, 1984; Congressional Directory, 1983–84; Leaders in Profile (1975); Politics in America, 1986; Who's Who in America, 1984–85.*

---

## Getty, Gordon P(eter)

*Dec. 20, 1933– Businessman; philanthropist.*
*Address: b. c/o J. Paul Getty Museum, 17985 Pacific Coast Highway, Malibu, Calif. 90265*

Although Gordon P. Getty was ranked in *Forbes* magazine as the wealthiest man in the United States both in 1983 and 1984, he is more often identified with the arts and sciences than with business. As a result of his maneuvers, his wealth and that of the Getty family trust, which he administered, was vastly expanded, through the sale to Texaco in early 1984 of the Getty Oil Company, founded by his grandfather, the Oklahoma oilman George Franklin Getty, and presided over by his father, J. Paul Getty, until his death in 1976. Gordon P. Getty fell from first place to fifteenth among the nation's wealthiest persons, when, under an agreement he signed with other members of the family in May 1985, the Getty trust was divided into six parts, reducing his share in the $4.1-billion fortune to about $950 million. But in any case, he would rather compose music, sing operatic arias, write poetry, or fulfill his role as a Maecenas of the arts and sciences while keeping a low profile in the business world. "I'm a businessman," he says, as quoted in *Forbes* (October 1, 1984), "because I had to be one."

Gordon Peter Getty, the fourth of the five sons of J. Paul Getty, was born on December 20, 1933. His mother, the former Ann Rork, who later mar-

ried Dr. Rudolph Alvin Light, was the fourth of J. Paul Getty's five wives, and by the time Gordon was born his parents were already planning their divorce. His oldest half-brother, George F. Getty, was apparently his father's favorite and served as executive vice-president and chief operating officer of Getty Oil until his death in 1973. The second of J. Paul Getty's sons, J. Ronald Getty, was briefly involved in the management of Getty enterprises but for reasons that are unclear received only a few thousand dollars a year from the family trust. The third son, J. Paul Getty Jr., who is a year older than Gordon P. Getty and has the same mother, is a recluse living in London. He was in the news in 1973, when his son, J. Paul Getty 3d, had an ear severed by terrorist kidnappers. In 1983 he and Gordon P. Getty were each receiving $28 million a year from the family trust. The youngest of J. Paul Getty's sons, Timothy, died in 1958 at the age of twelve.

After spending his early childhood in the Los Angeles area, Gordon P. Getty lived with his mother in the Pacific Heights section of San Francisco and received his education at private schools and military academies. His father, whom he recalls as "very Victorian" and as "distant but devoted," saw him only about once a year but always remembered him with gifts at Christmas and on his birthday. Although his mother seems to have been well provided for, because, as he recalled, she always had a cook, a maid, and a gardener, Getty's allowance in grade school was only twenty-five cents a week, and even while he was attending St. Ignatius High School, a Jesuit school in San Francisco, it was limited to five dollars a week. He did not realize the extent of his family's wealth while he was in school, and it was not until he was twenty-four that he read in *Fortune* that his father was the wealthiest man in the United States. Getty earned a B.S. degree in English in 1956 from the University of San Francisco, with average grades. In a three-day interview with Henry Brandon in the *Washington Post* (September 16, 1984), he commented on the premium he placed on education. "The best things in life require effort and study rather than money," he asserted. "You can't buy education, and it's worth more than a billion dollars."

In 1957, after serving for six months in the United States Army, where he achieved the rank of second lieutenant, Gordon P. Getty went to work for his father, first as a $500-a-month management trainee with Tidewater, a subsidiary of the Getty Oil Company. His chores included pumping gas in San Rafael, California and working at a San Francisco tire-and-battery plant. During 1958-59 Gordon P. Getty was in the Middle East, in the neutral zone between Kuwait and Saudi Arabia, as a consultant for Getty Oil, where one of his tasks was to try to collect a substantial debt that the local Saudi Arabian governor owed to the company. But before he was able to carry out that assignment, a Getty oil truck crashed into a pipeline, causing some damage. As the company's representative, Getty was held responsible, and after spending ten days under house arrest he decided to leave the area and return home. After that, he was given no more supervisory jobs with the company. In the 1960s and early 1970s his father used him on occasion as a "troubleshooter," but his efforts met with little success.

Until the early 1960s, Gordon P. Getty's income from Getty interests consisted of $15,000 a year that he received from the Sarah C. Getty Trust, which was established in 1934 in the name of his paternal grandmother. That annual income was increased in about 1963 to $50,000. Although in 1966 he was reportedly unsuccessful in a lawsuit against his father to obtain more income from the family trust rather than having his share reinvested, by 1967 he was collecting $500,000 a year. After the death, in 1973, of his oldest half-brother, George, who had become executive vice-president of the Getty Oil Company, Gordon P. Getty seems to have succeeded him as his father's favorite, though at the time he remained aloof from the company's affairs. When J. Paul Getty died in 1976, Gordon P. Getty took his seat on the company's board of directors and became co-trustee of the Sarah C. Getty Trust, which held 40.2 percent of the stock in Getty Oil and included three generations of family members among its beneficiaries. It was not, however, until about six years later that he became directly involved in the company.

The death, in May 1982, of co-trustee C. Lansing Hays Jr., a long-time family adviser who according to one acquaintance considered himself "J. Paul's messenger on earth," made Gordon P. Getty the sole trustee of the Sarah C. Getty Trust and advanced him to the forefront of family business affairs. In the words of Sidney R. Petersen, chairman and chief executive of Getty Oil since 1980, as quoted in the *New York Times* (December 11, 1983): "Following Hays's death, Gordon began a period of evolution in his vision of himself, his relation to the company, and his vision of the company itself."

Determined to play a more active role in Getty Oil—then the fourteenth-largest oil producer in the United States—Gordon P. Getty began to explore means of raising the value of its stock, which stood at $48.50 per share at the beginning of 1983. In an effort to offset a decline in the oil business, Sidney R. Petersen had in recent years diversified the company's activities into such areas as cable television and insurance, but Gordon P. Getty, like his father before him, placed the main emphasis on oil exploration and production and wanted the company to divest itself of non-oil ventures. When he tried to persuade the Getty Oil board to reconsider corporate strategy, he was rebuffed by Petersen. The machinations that ensued were compared by some observers to the corporate intrigues depicted on such television soap operas as *Dynasty* or *Dallas*.

In July 1983 an independent study undertaken at Gordon P. Getty's insistence by the investment-banking firm of Goldman, Sachs & Company proposed among other things a $500-million-a-year stock repurchase program, but it was rejected by the Getty Oil board of directors because it would have eventually given Gordon Getty majority control of the company by decreasing the number of its shares on the open market. Then, in early October, the Getty board under Petersen made initial authorization for the issuance of 9 million new Getty shares under an employee stock-option program, a move that would dilute Gordon P. Getty's influence in the company.

Later that month, the company arrived at a one-year "standstill" agreement with Getty and his ally Harold M. Williams, the chief executive of the J. Paul Getty Museum, which owned 11.8 percent of Getty Oil stock. Under its provisions, Williams was to obtain a seat on the Getty Oil board, and Gordon P. Getty was authorized to name four new board members. The agreement prohibited any signatory from joining with any group to control the company and prevented the issuance of new shares of stock or the repurchase of old ones. But the agreement lasted only one month. It ended when the company board voted to support a lawsuit by J. Paul Getty Jr. in behalf of his teenage son Tara Gabriel Galaxy Gramophone Getty to force Gordon P. Getty to share control over the Sarah C. Getty Trust by having the Bank of America appointed as co-trustee. In response, Gordon P. Getty and Harold M. Williams moved unilaterally in December 1983 to amend the company's bylaws, as they were authorized to do under Delaware corporate law because together they controlled a majority of the company stock. The amendments gave veto power to Gordon P. Getty's allies on the board and required fourteen of the sixteen directors to approve any significant action. Furthermore, the board was forced to withdraw from the lawsuit involving control of the Sarah C. Getty Trust.

In late December 1983, J. Hugh Liedtke, the president of Pennzoil, approached Gordon Getty with a $1.6-billion offer for the purchase, at $100 per share, of up to 20 percent of Getty Oil stock not owned by the family trust or the Getty museum. After several days of negotiations, a $5.4-billion agreement was reached under which the Sarah C. Getty Trust and Pennzoil were to buy up the available stock for $112.50 a share, making the company a private firm owned 57 percent by the family heirs and 43 percent by Pennzoil, with Gordon P. Getty as board chairman and Liedtke as president. But final action was delayed when Claire Getty, a niece of Gordon P. Getty, obtained a restraining order that blocked the sale pending full disclosure of the terms to the beneficiaries of the family trust, thus enabling a new bidder to enter the scene.

Then, on January 4, 1984, the day the Pennzoil deal was approved by the Getty Oil board, John K. McKinley, chairman of the giant Texaco, Inc., which was badly in need of additional oil reserves, came into the picture with an offer to buy the entire Getty Oil Company and its holdings at $125 a share, for a total of about $9.98 billion. Superseding the Pennzoil deal, the Texaco agreement, approved by the Getty Oil board on January 6, 1984, was the biggest merger deal on record, making Texaco the second-largest oil company in the United States, just behind Exxon. The 40.2 percent of Getty Oil stock owned by the Sarah C. Getty Trust, previously valued at $2.3 billion, was sold to Texaco for about $4 billion, thus nearly doubling the wealth controlled by Gordon P. Getty, even though, without playing any role in the company's management, he failed to achieve his goal of gaining control of his father's oil empire. As Thomas C. Hayes observed in the New York Times (January 10, 1984), "The windfall will further help support a private life as both a patron and occasional participant in opera and anthropology, in addition to commercial real-estate investment on the West Coast."

After eighteen months of litigation resulting from lawsuits filed by other members of the Getty family who sought greater influence over the family fortune, an agreement was signed by Gordon P. Getty and his relatives in May 1985. Under its provisions, the Sarah C. Getty Trust was divided into six separate trusts, and Gordon P. Getty was removed as the sole trustee of the $4.1-billion family fortune, while the amount under his personal control was reduced to some $950 million.

Although Gordon P. Getty's musical training was limited to some piano lessons that he took as a child and a year of courses in music theory that he attended at the San Francisco Conservatory, music became his major interest. He began to compose at an early age, and published his first work, an a capella chorus to a poem by Tennyson, in 1959. During the 1960s and 1970s he continued to write music, but he failed to complete any of his compositions because none satisfied him. Then, during a stay in Paris in 1980, he came upon a book of poems by Emily Dickinson and decided to set thirty-two of them to music. The resulting song cycle, "The White Election," was performed in December 1983 by mezzo-soprano Mignon Dunn of the Metropolitan Opera at Alice Tully Hall in New York's Lincoln Center. Although "The White Election" met with some favorable comment, it failed to evoke much enthusiasm from the critics. "Mr. Getty has evidently responded to the laconic style of the poems," Bernard Holland observed in the New York Times (December 4, 1983). "There is . . . great deference to the text but hardly any music at all. What there is, is expressed in popular nineteenth-century American harmonies, colored by occasional Schubertian devices and interrupted with a dissonant chord or two. Many of the songs avoid melody altogether and replace it with chanted text and single line accompaniments."

In March 1985 the San Francisco Symphony Orchestra under Edo de Waart introduced a new work by Gordon P. Getty, Plump Jack, a thirteen-minute cantata about Sir John Falstaff that is based on scenes from Shakespeare's Henry IV Parts I and II and Henry V. Getty has also composed some other choral works and several pieces for solo piano. In September 1985 he was honored for his compositions by the Northwood Institute and the Institute for Advanced Studies in the Theatre Arts, both in New York City.

In addition to spending hours in his study composing music at his Yamaha piano, Getty enjoys indulging his love of opera, which he attributes to the inspiration of his mother and some of his music teachers. He has sung with the Marin Opera Company, based near San Francisco, performing in such baritone roles as that of Cascart in Leoncavallo's *Zaza*. Although he rarely attends his wife's lavish social gatherings, he sometimes acts as host of operatic soirées, joining in song with such honored guests as Plácido Domingo, Luciano Pavarotti, or Leontyne Price. Otherwise, he often spends evenings in his study listening to some of the 10,000 classical recordings in his collection, which dates back as far as 1880 and includes performances by virtually every great singer and musician of the century, as well as the voices of the Victorian poets Robert Browning and Alfred, Lord Tennyson. Getty is a major benefactor of the San Francisco Opera, reportedly spending $250,000 or more a year underwriting new productions, and he also helps to support other opera houses in the United States and abroad.

According to the *New York Times* (January 10, 1984), Getty is listed in anthropological journals as a "specialist in the antiquities, archaeology and culture of the Indians of the American Southwest" and serves as a "working chairman" of the L. S. B. Leakey Foundation of Pasadena, California, which supports research in human evolution. He is also a director of the Institute of Human Origins in Berkeley, California, and he serves as president of the Jane Goodall Institute, named for the British ethologist who pioneered the study of chimpanzees in their natural habitat. Not surprisingly, Getty also helps to support the San Francisco Zoo.

One of Gordon P. Getty's major cultural interests is the J. Paul Getty Museum in Malibu, California, which he serves as one of fifteen trustees. Modeled on an ancient Roman seaside villa, the museum building, opened in 1974, contains an extensive collection of Greek and Roman antiquities, Renaissance and Baroque paintings, and French decorative arts. As a result of the Texaco purchase, the trust that funds the museum was valued in 1984 at $2.2 billion and is required by law to spend 4.2 percent of its worth each year. That vast endowment allowed the museum to purchase, in 1984, nine private photography collections comprising some 18,000 rare historic items and to hire the Metropolitan Museum of Art's former curator of prints and photographs. The purchase, which reportedly cost $20 million, gave the Getty Museum instant prominence as one of the nation's most significant repositories for photography.

Getty and his fellow trustees have drawn up plans for the construction of a new headquarters for the museum trust, combined with the establishment of a center for the history of art and the humanities and a conservation institute on a 742-acre site in Los Angeles. He believes that the museum should devote itself mainly to classical antiquity, but he wants it to be a "grant-maker to other great institutions and, especially, to enrich the culture of Southern California in fields other than visual arts." Cultural institutions to which the Getty museum has contributed substantially also include the Los Angeles County Museum of Art, the Museum of Contemporary Art, the UCLA Museum of Cultural History, and the Plaza de la Raza, a Hispanic arts center in East Los Angeles.

Gordon P. Getty and Ann Gilbert were married on Christmas Day of 1964, after eloping to Las Vegas. The oldest of their four sons, Gordon, is a student at Harvard University; the second son, John, is studying at Exeter, New Hampshire; and the youngest sons, Andrew and William, attend school in California. The Gettys' neoclassical five-story stucco mansion in Pacific Heights, overlooking San Francisco Bay, which was built in 1913 by the San Francisco architect Willis Polk, was featured in the October 1977 issue of *Vogue*. In addition, they maintain a four-bedroom apartment on Fifth Avenue in New York City. Actively involved in her husband's business affairs, Mrs. Getty invited four executives to sit on the board of the Getty Oil Company when it was expanded in 1983, and while her father-in-law was alive, often "mended fences" between him and her husband. In 1985, she and Lord George Weidenfeld became co-owners of Grove Press. Although Getty is a Republican who remains aloof from party concerns, his wife is a committed Democrat who served as cochairman of the host committee for the party's 1984 convention in San Francisco. Getty does not belong to any church and describes himself as "never very religious nor much of a joiner."

Six feet two inches in height, Gordon P. Getty weighs about 180 pounds and has black, curly hair. He has been variously described as a "shy and reserved" man, who is mathematically brilliant, as a "preoccupied, absent-minded professor type," and as "an exceptionally modest and trusting man." According to Henry Brandon of the *Washington Post* (September 16, 1984), Getty "holds views on almost everything, from music and chess to politics, business, and the state of the world." He rates himself as a "terrible" golfer, a "pretty good" chess player, and a "decent" bridge partner. During his sojourn in the Middle East he was ping-pong champion of the Neutral Zone.

Disputing published reports of his net worth, Getty points out that the $4.1 billion that *Forbes* gave as his personal fortune when it placed him at the head of its 1984 list of the 400 richest Americans was actually the amount of the Getty family trust, which he controlled and had the power to invest, but did not own outright. His share of the trust's income was 33 percent. According to his own estimate, his personal wealth was somewhere between $30 million and $50 million. Indifferent to his status as one of the wealthiest persons in the United States, he has no desire to be another J. Paul Getty but would like some day to be remembered for his musical accomplishments.

*References: Bsns W* p29+ D 12 '83 por; *Forbes* 374:70+ O 1 '84 por; *Fortune* 108:6+ D 26 '83 por, 109:106+ F 6 '84 por; *N Y Times* III p1+ D 11 '83 por, D p1+ Ja 10 '84 por, III p4 Ap 22 '84 por; *People* 20:120 O 17 '83 por; *Washington Post* L p1+ S 16 '84 pors

## Goldberg, Whoopi

*1950– Actress. Address: b. c/o Solters, Roskin, Friedman, Inc., 45 W. 34th Street, New York City, N.Y. 10001*

After winning fringe-theatre followings on both coasts, the innovative performance artist Whoopi Goldberg brought her eponymous one-woman show to Broadway, resoundingly, during the 1984–85 theatrical season. Although her antic monologues contain elements of improvisational standup comedy, the pseudonymous Miss Goldberg is essentially a character actress (or actor, as she sometimes insists) whose original routines are really short seriocomic plays, "written" in her head. Frustrated by the dearth of work for black character actors in the straight theatre, she began several years ago to create her own varied repertoire, a gallery of offbeat social types whom she fleshes out into believable individuals by virtuosic shifts in voice, body language, and facial expression, in addition to narration. Six of her characterizations comprised the Broadway production of *Whoopi Goldberg,* of which Mel Gussow wrote in the *New York Times:* "Whoopi Goldberg is a slight, sprite-like comic actress whose mind and body are inhabited by some of the drollest and most touching characters one is ever likely to encounter. . . . She has the face and personality of the wise child—with ingenuous eyes and a puckish smile. As she tells her tales of misfits and outcasts, and even as she offers wry satiric comments, she is consistently disarming."

The actor who calls herself Whoopi Goldberg assiduously keeps secret her real name. She was born in 1950 in New York City, where she and a younger brother were raised by their mother in a housing project in the Chelsea section of Manhat-

tan. Abandoned by her husband, the mother took a succession of jobs, including Head Start teacher. She still lives and works in New York City. Whoopi Goldberg attended St. Columba Church on West 25th Street, and she received her elementary education in the parish school, under nuns of the Congregation of Notre Dame. She gained her first stage experience at the Helena Rubinstein Children's Theatre at the Hudson Guild, on West 26th Street, where she acted in plays from the age of eight to the age of ten. "That's all I ever wanted to do," she told Wayne Robbins of *Newsday* (October 21, 1984).

A born mimic, with a natural, flawless eye and ear for details of character, Miss Goldberg began in childhood her practice of storing up such details in her imagination. Watching situation comedies and old movies on television, she was early on influenced by comedy actresses ranging from Gracie Allen to Carole Lombard (in the romantic film comedy *My Man Godfrey*) and Claudette Colbert (in *It Happened One Night,* her favorite film). "I won't admit to studying with anyone," she told Harry Haun in an interview published in the national theatre magazine *Playbill* (volume three, number two, 1984). "What it is is I'm a real sponge in terms of seeing things and absorbing them. And, with the people I have admired over the years, I've stolen from them and added the things that I know instinctively. It was always the character actors I went for. Dustin Hoffman, for example, is a character actor. John Garfield was essentially a character actor, Robert Duvall, Spencer Tracy, Robin Williams, Carole Lombard, Clark Gable, Diana Sands. And since character is the basis, the very bottom line of theatre, I watched these people to see what they did." Next to romantic comedies of the 1930s, horror movies of the 1950s were her favorite screen fare.

Dropping out of high school, Miss Goldberg, "like everyone" in the 1960s, "was a hippie, on the fine line between the Lower East Side and something spiritual." "I asked myself," she recounted to David Remnick of the *Washington Post* (December 25, 1984), "am I going to keep doing drugs and kill myself or figure out what I'm going to do with my life?" She became involved in "hippie politics," participating in civil-rights marches and the student demonstrations at Columbia University; worked as a counselor at an Ethical Culture summer camp in Peekskill, New York; and found work on Broadway in the choruses of the musicals *Hair, Jesus Christ Superstar,* and *Pippin.* In the early 1970s she was married briefly; from her marriage she has a daughter, Alexandrea Martin.

In 1974 Miss Goldberg flew to Los Angeles with her daughter on an airline ticket sent to her by a friend. "What happens when people give you those tickets is you're so excited you forget you don't have the money to go back," she told Guy Trebay of the *Village Voice* (October 30, 1984). From Los Angeles she drove to San Diego, intending to spend a week there. Instead, she remained for six years, becoming a founding member of the San Diego

Repertory Theatre and joining Spontaneous Combustion, an improvisational troupe. With the repertory company she played the lead in *Mother Courage* and roles in *The Grass Is Greener, Don't Drink the Water,* and *Getting Out.*

It was during her sojourn in San Diego that Whoopi Goldberg invented her stage name. "The name came out of the blue," she explained to David Remnick in the *Washington Post* interview. "It was a joke. First it was Whoopi Cushion. Then it was French, like Whoopi Cushon. My mother said, 'Nobody's gonna respect you with a name like that.' So I put Goldberg on it. Goldberg's a part of my family somewhere and that's all I can say about it."

With her newly invented name, Whoopi Goldberg joined a standup comic named Don Victor in two-character performances in and around San Diego. Victor quit the duo on the eve of a scheduled engagement in San Francisco, and Miss Goldberg flew alone to the Bay Area, where she was met by David Schein, a comedian who was booked to share the bill with Goldberg-Victor. "I got off the plane saying, 'I'm really sorry, but it is just going to be me,'" she recalled in the interview with Harry Haun. "David said okay. He said, 'Just do what you do when you work with Don and make the audience your partner.' Then he said, 'What's the worst that can happen? You do twenty minutes, and, if you're bad, you'll know it and you'll get off the stage.' Well, sure enough, I went on, and I did an hour. At the end of it, I knew that I could do a solo performance."

Deciding not to return to San Diego, Miss Goldberg settled in Berkeley, across the bay from San Francisco. There, she moved in with David Schein and joined the Blake Street Hawkeyes, an experimental theatre collective that Schein had cofounded. With Schein she wrote *The Last Word,* a two-character satire on male-female relationships that the couple performed in Berkeley in 1981. According to some sources, they later performed *The Last Word* in London, England—an undertaking that must have severely strained their financial means. By her own account, Miss Goldberg throughout her fringe-theatrical apprenticeship in California depended for her livelihood on either welfare or extra-theatrical jobs, including bricklayer, bank teller, and licensed cosmetician. After graduating from beauty college, she took a job at a mortuary, dressing the hair of and applying makeup to corpses, because she was "tired of working on living people who *all* wanted to look like Farrah Fawcett." "It was great work," she told Guy Trebay of the *Village Voice,* "much better than working on live people. You could push them around like big dolls. And they never complained about how they looked." Another advantage of the job was that "nobody ever bothered" her, "because people don't like to come in and be around the dead for some reason."

The first of the score of solo characterizations Miss Goldberg developed was the "surfer chick," a hyperkinetic thirteen-year-old Catholic girl telling, in vapid California "Valley girl" lingo, how she became pregnant, was rejected by her family, and gave herself a damaging abortion with a wire coat hanger after unsuccessfully experimenting with a mixture of whisky and scouring powder. That creation, like many of those to follow, was a theatrical structuring of real-life experience reflecting the sensitive conscience of a social activist as well as the bright wit of an entertainer. Across from Miss Goldberg's home in Berkeley was a hospital, in front of which right-to-life advocates were picketing daily. After failing to reach the anti-abortionists through rational argument, and to get the city to stop them, she and David Schein counter-picketed, handing out wire hangers to demonstrate that "this is the alternative" to legalized abortion.

In 1983 Miss Goldberg brought together in a one-hour presentation titled *The Spook Show* four of her characterizations: the self-aborting Valley girl; Fontaine, a jive-talking, comically cynical drug addict and thief of ambiguous gender who has a Ph.D. degree in literature that he "can't do *jack* with . . . but stand in this unemployment line"; a nine-year-old black girl who covers her nappy hair with a yellow skirt and tells her mother she doesn't "want to be black no more" because "you have to be white to be on *Love Boat*"; and a grotesquely crippled young woman who becomes normal in her dreams—a transformation that Miss Goldberg executed, as one witness put it, as gracefully "as a time-lapse bloom of a flower."

Her handicapped character was inspired by wheelchair-bound friends of Miss Goldberg in Berkeley, who didn't want people patronizing them as if they were less than full human beings. Explaining that characterization to Betsy Barns for *Interview* (December 1984), Miss Goldberg said, "After the dream, she goes back to being handicapped, but she is still going to marry this wonderful person. It shows how 'normal' is in the eye of the beholder. . . . This is a woman who understands people's fear of her, and she has to chuckle because it's so ridiculous." The black child feigning long blonde hair emerged from her own childhood and that of her daughter, Alexandrea. Miss Goldberg was angry when she saw Alexandrea putting a skirt on her head until she realized that she herself had not worked through the television images of her own childhood. "The people who we saw on TV, growing up, were the people we all wanted to emulate—and we never could . . . ," she explained to Betsy Barns. "When I started doing this little girl, I found that it wasn't just black women who are like this. White women feel it too. We were taught that to be 'ordinary' is not okay."

After premiering in Berkeley, Miss Goldberg took *The Spook Show* (alternatively titled *A Broad Abroad* and *Whoopi Goldberg Variations*) on the road, across the United States and to Europe. During the 1983-84 Off-Broadway season, David White, the executive director and producer of the Dance Theatre Workshop in Manhattan, asked her to perform the show as part of a workshop series called "Character and Confession; New Experiences in Narrative Theatre." Her workshop engagement was a sellout, and New York critics, while remarking "sentimental gimmicks" and looseness in some of her material, were impressed with "her incredibly accurate perception and portrayal of gesture and personal style of both blacks and whites" and her "uncanny" ability to "transform her face and body, as well as her voice." "Her characters . . . are the disinherited, the ghosts of the earth," Sally Banes wrote in the *Village Voice* (February 21, 1984). "And Goldberg's rendition of them haunts us, as she leads us in with laughter and then suddenly turns the tables, casting us into horror or awe or just quiet dignity."

Among those who caught Miss Goldberg's act at the Dance Theatre Workshop early in 1984 was the prominent director and producer Mike Nichols, himself a veteran actor and comedian, who saw in her "one part Elaine May, one part Groucho, one part Ruth Draper, one part Richard Pryor, and five parts never seen before." Nichols told Harry Haun: "I went backstage to tell Whoopi and to meet her and I burst into tears, made a complete fool of myself. She has a gigantic spirit, and you're sort of slowly exposed to what she's like. Her compassion and her humanity are enormously moving and quite startling in somebody that funny. She has a way of cutting through everything, both personally and professionally. She just gets right to it."

Before deciding to accept Mike Nichols' offer to produce her on Broadway, Miss Goldberg went home to Berkeley, where she did *Moms*, a re-creation of Moms Mabley that she and Ellen Sebastian wrote, using the material of the late black standup comedienne. For that performance, she won a Bay Area Theatre Award. Then, returning to New York City, she expanded the material of *The Spook Show* and, under Mike Nichols' "supervision," took the result uptown at the beginning of the 1984-85 Broadway season. *Whoopi Goldberg*, produced by Nichols in association with Emanuel Azenberg and the Shubert organization, opened at the Lyceum Theatre on October 24, 1984. The show witnessed by the Broadway first-nighters consisted of six characterizations. Added to the four carried over from *The Spook Show* were Ugmo, an old male panhandler recalling his days in black vaudeville, and a tart-tongued Jamaican woman who comes to the United States as the live-in domestic and companion of a lecherous octogenarian millionaire.

Mel Gussow of the *New York Times* (October 28, 1984), an early champion of *The Spook Show*, was just as enthusiastic about *Whoopi Goldberg*, reiterating that "before long, people [will] try to compare future comics to the inimitable Whoopi Goldberg." The *Times*'s principal critic, Frank Rich, was less enthusiastic. "Her jokes, however scatological in language, can be mild and overextended, and her moments of pathos are often too mechanically ironic and maudlin to provoke," Rich wrote in his opening-night review. "[But] Whoopi Goldberg's liberating spirit fills up the theatre, even as her considerable comic promise is left waiting to be fully unlocked."

Other reviews ranged from the adulatory ("a brilliant diseuse" with "the gift of tongues," who "can slide effortlessly out of Fontaine's jive talk into the syntax and accent of every university-educated German who's ever talked to you in English" and "can reproduce the lilt of West Indian English without caricature") to John Simon's scathingly dissenting opinion in *New York* (November 5, 1984) that *Whoopi Goldberg* was "a first draft" turned, perhaps partly through the "magic" of Mike Nichols' name, "into a second coming." Even Simon, however, could not fault Miss Goldberg's "good timing, lively facial expressions, considerable flexibility in her impersonations, and real skill with accents." Brendan Gill of the *New Yorker* (November 5, 1984), while recognizing her as a "highly gifted" performer, "skillful" in mixing "farcical bravado and touching woebegoneness," thought that her act, requiring "intimacy," suffered in its translation from small room to cavernous Broadway theatre. Some critics tempered their admiration for *Whoopi Goldberg* with the demurral that "Whoopi as writer isn't in the same class as Whoopi the performer," that "she is so good that she deserves better." Miss Goldberg found "nothing" in the negative criticism that "can help" her improve her performance. "I am my show," she told a reporter for *Time* (November 16, 1984). "The characters I play on the stage have been on a long voyage of discovery."

Miss Goldberg's stated purpose on the stage is "to make people laugh *and think*." In an interview for the *New York Amsterdam News* (February 25, 1984) she described her craft as "a blend of straight theatre, stand-up comedy, Greek comedy, political satire, and world assessment through characters." "Everywhere I go," she said, "I see incidents, or I meet someone who sticks in my mind. And people tell me stories. Then I develop a character and try it on different audiences until I get what I want right in my head." Even after she gets it right, she demands "the active participation of the audience"—and sometimes tells the audience so, in more colorful language—because you can't "change people if they just sit there," and because acting before a "half-dead" audience "becomes work." Depending on the responsiveness of the audience, her Broadway performance ran from a minimum of ninety minutes to as much as 120 minutes. A performance of *Whoopi Goldberg* taped before the show closed in the spring of 1985 was shown on Home Box Office, the pay-television channel, beginning on July 20, 1985.

"I don't 'write' characters," Miss Goldberg explained to Harry Haun in the *Playbill* interview. "I just do them on the stage. Some lines I know work, so I remember to use them, but I don't write them down. These characters are people, very much living in my head. They are all distinct, different individuals, and it's the job of the actor to keep them that way. Actors are schizophrenics essentially, which is how we can produce these vastly different people. In a sense, I see myself as a medium, something from which these people spring. If I had not lucked out and gotten into theatre, I could be in Bellevue."

Miss Goldberg stressed to Wayne Robbins of *Newsday* (November 4, 1984) the importance of her being called an actor and not a comic. "What they call me has a lot to do with what I'm going to be able to do. . . . If I get stuck being called a comedienne, I'd find myself inundated with work for a black comedienne. This is not what I do." Although her act is "not fast-food comedy," as she told Betsy Barns in the *Interview* conversation, "a gag element shows up periodically," and "some of [her] stuff has no 'serious' value" but is "just weird stuff" that she thinks about. One of the subjects she thinks about "a lot" is death, a preoccupation vented in her character Inez Beaverman, an elderly woman wearing a shabby fox fur and speaking in a thick Jewish accent about her visits to the gynecologist and her worry about the high cost of dying these days.

In the summer of 1985 Miss Goldberg finished shooting the lead in director Steven Spielberg's motion picture *The Color Purple* (Warner Brothers), based on Alice Walker's Sapphic novel about a black teenaged bride in the deep South, and she began filming a Twentieth Century-Fox movie with the working title "Sweet Dreams," in which she stars as a computer operator who becomes the recipient of messages from an American secret agent trapped behind the Iron Curtain. Mike Nichols thinks that Miss Goldberg is "going to be big in the movies, as an actress" because, while playwrights aren't writing many roles for women, especially black women, "movies can be tailored to someone." Robin Williams is looking for a film property to do with her. (Williams and his family have been very close to her and her family and have shown her that "people don't have to go crazy in this business.") "Love stories and adventure stories should involve people who look normal, like you and me," she told Betsy Barns. "There's no reason why I shouldn't be able to do a love story with Robin Williams or William Hurt, except that people say, 'We can't do this. Our distributors in the South won't be able to handle an interracial relationship.' That keeps the stupidity alive."

Whoopi Goldberg, who wears her hair in what she calls "do-do braids," is petite and supple of physique and, normally, sweet, even radiant, of countenance, and warm of manner. With her daughter and her little white dog, Otis, Miss Goldberg recently moved into a new apartment, a floor-through in a brownstone in New York City. The only vice to which she confesses is smoking cigarettes. Regarding her pseudonymity, she told David Remnick of the *Washington Post*: "I'm protecting my family. As it is now, I can go home and live as this other person and even though I look like Whoopi Goldberg on the street, I can whip out my driver's license and say, 'Hey, but I'm not.'"

References: N Y Daily News p3 O 21 '84 pors; N Y Times II p1+ O 21 '84 pors; Newsday II p3+ N 4 '84 por; Newsweek 103:63 Mr 5 '84 pors; People 21:72+ My 28 '84, 22:106 Ag 13 '84; Village Voice p54+ O 30 '84 por; Washington Post C p1+ D 25 '84 pors

## Goode, W(illie) Wilson

Aug. 19, 1938- Mayor of Philadelphia. Address: City Hall, Philadelphia, Pa. 19107

W. Wilson Goode, elected on November 8, 1983 as Philadelphia's 126th mayor—the first black man ever to attain that office—is generally acknowledged as a deft administrator and an articulate spokesman for the concerns of minorities. The swiftness of Goode's emergence as a national political figure after a number of years as a municipal and state civil servant was made clear by the fact that he was for a time seriously considered as a vice-presidential running mate by the 1984 Democratic presidential candidate Walter F. Mondale. Even the storm of controversy surrounding Goode's role in the tragic May 1985 confrontation between Philadelphia police and MOVE, a radical back-to-nature cult, failed to tarnish the reputation of the man who, in the words of Amy Wilentz of *Time* magazine (May 27, 1985), had been "perceived as perhaps the most promising black politician of the late '80s."

Willie Wilson Goode's life has followed the scenario of the classic American success story. The son of a sharecropper, he was born on August 19, 1938 in a wooden shack on Jordan Mill Pond Road just outside Seaboard, North Carolina, a farming community some seventy miles northeast of Raleigh. Indoor plumbing and electricity were luxuries of which the parents, Albert and Rozella

Goode, only dreamed. The family was dirt poor but possessed of a gritty determination to escape the racial segregation and grinding hardship of Southern rural life. It was from his parents that Goode learned the value of an honest day's labor. Years later, he proudly explained to Thad Martin, who interviewed him for *Ebony* (May 1984), how his parents managed to survive through sheer hard work. "They didn't mind telling the owner of the land, 'Look, I'm not going to take any of this abuse from you. We are going to do our job . . . ,'" Goode recalled. "We moved often because my father refused to put his family through that kind of thing."

Goode received his early education in a succession of one-room schools. He was fifteen when his parents joined in the massive postwar migration of blacks to the industrial cities of the northeast. The Goodes and their seven children relocated in a black working-class district of west Philadelphia, and Wilson attended John Bartram High School, where he was an honors student. The first member of his family to attend college, he obtained his B.A. degree in 1961 from Morgan State University in Baltimore. His enrollment in the Reserve Officers Training Corps at the university led to a tour of duty, in 1962-63, in the United States Army, where he commanded military police troops, rising to the rank of captain, and earned a commendation medal for meritorious service.

On his return to civilian life, Goode worked at a succession of jobs, as a probation officer, supervisor at a building maintenance firm, and insurance claims adjuster. He also became involved in community affairs, including activities at the First Baptist Church of Paschal, near his southwest Philadelphia home, and he attended courses at the Wharton School of the University of Pennsylvania, which awarded him the master of public administration degree in 1968. In 1969 Goode became executive director of the Philadelphia Council for Community Advancement, a non-profit organization established to help neighborhood groups and promote housing construction. It was there that Goode first came to public attention and made some of the contacts that later became the source of his grassroots political support. In 1969-70 he was one of the five finalists in the Jaycees Philadelphia community awards, and in 1972 that organization named him outstanding young leader of the year.

But as busy and successful as he had become, Goode was plagued by the nagging suspicion that something seemed to be missing from his life. When he startled his family and friends by announcing that he was seriously thinking of devoting himself to the Baptist ministry, his church pastor advised him not to rush into anything and to take time to pray over his decision. Goode did so and, as he later recalled, he opted instead for "a ministry of a different kind, a ministry of public service."

Goode's administrative abilities were rewarded when in 1978 Governor Milton J. Shapp appointed him head of the three-member Pennsylvania Public Utility Commission (PUC), the influential body that oversees utility rates in the state. In the aftermath of the March 28, 1979 disaster at the Three Mile Island nuclear generating station near Harrisburg, Goode conducted an investigation into the incident and suspended a rate-hike recently granted to the Metropolitan Edison Company, which owned the plant. It was Goode who was largely responsible for ensuring that the public was protected and at the same time provided with an uninterrupted flow of power.

Meanwhile, in Philadelphia, the flamboyant Democratic mayor Frank L. Rizzo was nearing the end of eight years in office. The tough ex-police chief let it be known that he would seek an unprecedented third straight term, if some way could be found to circumvent a restriction in the city charter. Rizzo was popular with ethnic whites, but his dogmatism, his casual attitude toward what some considered institutionalized racism, and his apparent indifference toward alleged police brutality earned him the enmity of Philadelphia's liberal Democrats and of most blacks. For many people, the final straw was Rizzo's handling of an incident in the summer of 1978 involving city police and members of the now infamous MOVE group. MOVE, a militant radical movement founded in 1972 by Vincent Leaphart, an unemployed black handyman with a limited education, was little known outside Philadelphia in 1978. The apparent acronym in MOVE's name actually stood for nothing. Leaphart and his few dozen followers espoused a disjointed back-to-nature philosophy and most of them adopted the surname "Africa." MOVE members ate natural foods, recycled garbage and human wastes in the yards of their communal homes, and rejected modern conveniences.

After fifteen months of fruitless efforts to evict MOVE from a rundown dwelling in west Philadelphia's Powelton Village district, Rizzo ran out of patience, and on August 8, 1978 he gave police permission to oust the group forcibly. Hundreds of police officers surrounded the commune and after a brief, heated gun battle they succeeded, although one officer was killed and two were seriously wounded. In the wake of the attack a MOVE member was brutally beaten by police as reporters and television cameras looked on. A dozen MOVE members were arrested on murder and weapons charges. Nine of them were eventually convicted, and the MOVE house was demolished by city work crews. Rizzo's critics charged that his approach to the MOVE problem had been typically heavy-handed and confrontational, and he only made matters worse when he referred to MOVE members as "idiots" and "pigs" and urged whites to band together for mutual protection.

Rizzo lost his bid for a third-term candidacy in November 1978, when Philadelphia voters, by a two-to-one margin, defeated a proposed charter amendment that would have allowed him to run again. His successor, elected as mayor on the Democratic ticket in November 1979, was former United States congressman William J. Green 3d, whose advent was seen by many as the dawning of a new era at city hall. But despite his announced plans to promote racial harmony and get the city moving again, relations between the new mayor and city council soon deteriorated. The press made much of what appeared to be an underlying racial element in the split and that theme remained constant even after Green in early 1980 hired W. Wilson Goode away from the PUC, appointing him as the city's first black managing director. Skeptics saw Green's move as an attempt to buy off the black community. But although Goode's race may have been partly responsible for his appointment, there was no question about his credentials as Philadelphia's top non-elected official and the man responsible for the city's ten operating divisions. Green was fully aware that Goode was a superb administrator and that he was well-educated and had deep roots in the community. The fact that he was black in a city where color mattered to many people was an added bonus.

As the most visible member of Green's team, Goode worked as much as seven days a week, held neighborhood meetings about city problems in all parts of Philadelphia, and adopted measures to streamline city hall operations. People were amazed to see him riding city garbage trucks as he monitored the performances of sanitation workers or taking part in neighborhood cleanups. As the date of the November 1983 mayoralty elections approached, Goode's name was increasingly mentioned as a successor to Green, who was not seeking a second term.

After some serious soul searching, Goode declared himself as a candidate for mayor. His main opponent for the Democratic nomination was Frank Rizzo, who after a term out of office was eligible to try for a comeback. The stage seemed set for a bitter battle between the two men, but to everyone's surprise the primary campaign was relatively tame, as a result of an April 1983 gentlemen's agreement—in which even the Republicans joined—to disregard the racial question and concentrate on the real issues. Rizzo reportedly spent $1.5 million on the primary campaign, while Goode spent some $1 million, contributed by such diverse backers as business leaders, women's groups, and labor unions.

Early opinion polls showed Goode with a twenty-two-point lead, but Rizzo, buoyed by the advice of consultants hired to help soften his abrasive public image, seemed smugly confident of victory. Ironically, it was Goode who campaigned like a veteran, greeting rush-hour commuters, making appearances on downtown streets and at public functions, and waving to people from what seemed like an endless series of motorcades through black and ethnic neighborhoods. He methodically gathered endorsements from all but two of sixty-nine Democratic ward leaders and from most of the city's major labor unions. With that assured backing, Goode was able to avoid the "black power" appeal some supporters pushed him to make and which his opponents both predicted and feared.

Goode declined the Reverend Jesse Jackson's offer of campaign help but endorsed Walter Mondale's candidacy for the Democratic presidential nomination, insisting that "Philadelphia needs a friend in the White House."

When attempts to link Goode with police corruption failed, the most Rizzo could do was joke about Goode's absentmindedness in forgetting his children's names in an interview and about his sober style. A Goode aide drew a sketch of a happy face on his notes for a television debate to remind him to smile. But on primary day, May 17, 1983, it was Goode who had the last laugh. He swept about 98 percent of the black vote, which makes up 40 percent of the city's 900,000 registered electors, and also drew some 23 percent of white votes, in defeating Rizzo by a margin of 53 to 46 percent, or 59,000 votes. After the primary, Rizzo lent his support to Goode for the November election.

Since Democrats outnumber Republicans five to one in the City of Brotherly Love, the November mayoralty election turned out to be something of an anticlimax. Goode's two white rivals, Republican John J. Egan Jr. and independent Thomas A. Leonard, split the opposition vote. Even so, Goode took nothing for granted, campaigning hard throughout the long, hot summer and running a dignified, business-like campaign in what Time magazine called "textbook style." Preferring policy papers to polemics, he stressed his record as an administrator and appealed to Philadelphians' sense of civic pride in their resilient ability to bounce back from tough times. The race issue was a troubling, yet muted campaign theme that Goode did not sidestep entirely. Speaking to a mostly black audience one evening, he displayed a rare flash of his sometimes biting humor when he remarked: "In spite of all the things they say about us, I can't sing. I can't dance. But I can run this city. Will you help me?" On another occasion, facing a persistent heckler, Goode showed grace under pressure when he declined to take refuge behind the guise of an angry black. "Sir, you have a choice," he said. "I respect your right to vote for who you want to vote for. So if you don't like me, don't vote for me." Goode knew that in order to win he had to reassure whites, who feared a repetition in Philadelphia of what was happening in Chicago. The sizable black community there had rallied to a militant call by black congressman Harold Washington and had supported him en masse as the Democratic candidate. Many whites were clearly uneasy at that turn of events, and when the Reverend Jesse Jackson visited Philadelphia during the mayoral campaign and was reported to have observed, with reference to Washington's victory in Chicago, that "the newest thing is simply to vote black," Goode was quick to distance himself from the comment, which Jackson himself later maintained was a misquote.

On November 8, 1983 Goode received some 55 percent of the votes cast—including 27 percent of the white vote—to Egan's 37 percent and Leonard's 8 percent. His victory was generally seen as part of the decade-long shift in voting patterns that had enabled blacks—with the aid of "crossover" white votes—to gain the mayor's offices in four of the nation's largest cities—Detroit, Chicago, Los Angeles, and now Philadelphia—and in fifteen other towns with populations over 100,000. Goode told interviewers he saw his victory as part of a great change that was bringing into the political process a growing number of "non-traditional" groups, such as blacks, Hispanics, Asians, and women. Furthermore, Goode added, no longer did electors aspire to a house in suburbia, two cars, and a $50,000-a-year job. "The American dream is that if I am willing to work, then give me a job," Goode told Victoria Irwin of the *Christian Science Monitor* (April 29, 1985). "Let me work and earn my keep and take care of my family . . . and maybe live in my row house in Philadelphia, in the Bronx, in Detroit, Chicago. Give me an opportunity to use my skills, to use my brain, to use my muscles."

Goode's top priority on taking office on January 2, 1984 was what he saw as the need for a revival of the idealism of William Penn, who had been the city's founding father some 300 years earlier. More specifically, he spoke of the crying need for jobs, affordable housing, cleaner streets, a more accessible city hall, new contracts for city employees, a more efficient garbage disposal system, and improved relations between the city council and the mayor. Goode was keenly aware too of Philadelphia's need for major reconstructive surgery. Population was down 13 percent in a decade, with Houston displacing Philadelphia as the nation's fourth-largest city; jobs were disappearing from a decaying industrial base at a rate of 10,000 annually; and the middle-class was abandoning the inner city to the elderly, to the poor, and to urban blight.

In an attempt to reverse those trends, Goode appointed a new six-member cabinet that was equally divided among blacks and whites and among men and women. He recruited local business leaders to take part in a business roundtable that he established to find ways of luring industry to the city, and he appealed for volunteers to keep alive programs—such as an adult literacy project—that were in danger of failing for lack of funds. During his first year in office Goode was constantly in the news for his praiseworthy actions. He resolved a long squabble with the city council over cable television franchising authority, abolished an archaic and unpopular mercantile tax, opened a new commuter transit system in record time, and persuaded Philadelphia Eagles owner Leonard Tose to keep his National Football League team in the city. Philadelphians were dazzled by Goode's accomplishments, and some press reports referred to the mayor as "Wilson Too Goode."

Fortunately for Goode, he was riding the crest of a wave of popularity when he had to face his greatest challenge, the May 1985 MOVE debacle. The radical group now occupied a row house in the Cobb's Creek district of west Philadelphia, some two miles from the site of the ill-starred encounter of seven years earlier. As in 1978, there was a pattern of escalating confrontation, with MOVE members threatening and bullying neighbors and police and resisting all efforts to evict them. They refused to speak with authorities until nine of their number who had been jailed in 1978 were freed. At first, Goode contended that there were no legal grounds for action against MOVE, prompting Chuck Stone, a leading black Philadelphia journalist, to comment: "For a mayor who will tap-dance in a minute to cut a ribbon, Goode was notoriously absent . . . as the man in charge." Finally, as a result of neighborhood pressure and the discovery of housing violations in the commune, the mayor decided to act.

On May 12, 1985 police surrounded the heavily fortified MOVE house, and early the next day they tried to arrest four MOVE members. When a furious police assault, first with guns and then with fire department water cannons, failed to dislodge the group the situation was deadlocked. Impatient police asked for and received Mayor Goode's approval of a plan to drop a bag of water-based gel explosive on the roof of the MOVE house to destroy a bunker-like fortification there. That afternoon the bomb was dropped from a helicopter. There was a loud explosion followed by flames that soon spread to adjacent buildings. Firemen at first made no effort to douse the blaze because they feared MOVE gunfire. By the time they moved in, the fire, apparently fueled by explosives stored in the compound, had turned the entire area into a blazing inferno. When the damage was tallied later, sixty-one buildings had been destroyed, 250 persons were homeless, and an estimated $8 million in property damage had been caused. Authorities found the bodies of eleven persons, including four children, in the rubble of the MOVE house at 6221 Osage Avenue.

As the official who had given final approval for the bombing, Goode was at the center of a furious debate. Some critics blamed the entire situation on the mayor alone. When New York City mayor Edward I. Koch termed the Philadelphia police's tactics "stupid," Goode responded angrily, "Let him run his city. I'll run mine." Accepting full responsibility for all that had gone wrong, Goode pledged to do whatever was needed to rebuild the neighborhood as quickly as possible. Surprisingly, that seemed to satisfy most Philadelphians. Local polls showed that as many as 71 percent of the city's residents approved of the mayor's actions, despite the fact that everything went wrong that could have gone wrong.

In the tragedy's aftermath the homeless filed a multimillion-dollar class-action lawsuit against the city, the mayor appointed a commission to look into the bombing, and the FBI launched an investigation to determine whether federal civil rights had been violated. Mayor Goode was outwardly untroubled by the uproar and announced his intention to put the MOVE incident behind him as quickly as possible. "I've had a charmed life as mayor because I've learned the arts of compromise and negotiation," Goode told Amy Wilentz of *Time* (May 27, 1985). "I will run again. There's work here that has to be done and that cannot be finished in this term. We have to rebuild that neighborhood."

On October 8, 1985, the eleven-member Philadelphia Investigating Commission began its inquiry into the MOVE disaster and Goode's role in dealing with it, amid criticism that the investigation by the panel, which had been appointed by the mayor himself, was like "the palace guard investigating the king." Several city officials, testifying before the commission, blamed the MOVE debacle on the long delay by the city administration in taking action against the radical group. In his own testimony, Goode staunchly defended his position, but his charges that his senior subordinates had misled and misinformed him and had disregarded his instructions were disputed by Police Commissioner Gregory J. Sambor and other officials.

Meanwhile, in response to a long-standing federal investigation into alleged police corruption in Philadelphia, Goode announced a program in September 1985 for upgrading the standards of the city's police department. Its provisions included appointment of a special prosecutor, a requirement for all senior police officers seeking promotion to take polygraph tests, a strengthening of the department's internal-affairs unit, and an upgrading of

educational standards for members of the police department.

W. Wilson Goode has been married since 1960 to the former Velma Helen Williams, an administrative aide at the University of Pennsylvania. Their children are Muriel, who works for a law firm; W. Wilson Jr., a student at the University of Pennsylvania; and Natasha, who attends public school. Goode, who is five feet eight inches tall, has been described as a meticulous, sober man who maintains a tight rein on his emotions. He has few hobbies, rarely watches television, and never goes on vacation. Still a deeply religious man, he serves as a church deacon and fervently believes everything he does is with God's guidance. In his speaking style he shows occasional flashes of the oldtime gospel preacher.

References: Christian Sci Mon p3+ Ap 29 '85 pors; Ebony p44+ My 84 pors; Macleans p17 My 30 '83 por; N Y Times D p27 N 10 '83; Time 125:22 My 27 '85 por; Who's Who Among Black Americans, 1980–81; Who's Who in the East, 1985–86

---

## Gorbachev, Mikhail (Sergeyevich)

(gŏr-bä-chof´)

*Mar. 2, 1931- General Secretary of the Communist Party of the Soviet Union. Address: b. Central Committee of the Communist Party, Staraya Ploshchad 4, Moscow, USSR*

Mikhail Gorbachev's election, on March 11, 1985, to succeed the late Konstantin U. Chernenko as general secretary of the Communist party marks a new epoch in the history of the Soviet Union. Articulate, well-educated, and confident, Gorbachev "typifies the style and substance of the upcoming generation in Moscow," according to Serge Schmemann in the *New York Times Magazine* (March 3, 1985). The youngest Soviet leader since Joseph Stalin succeeded Lenin in 1924, Gorbachev served for twenty-two years as a party official in the southern district of Stavropol before his appointment as agriculture secretary on the Central Committee of the Communist party in 1978, and he soon became part of the Kremlin's inner circle. Since his election, he has continued the program of economic and social reform begun by his mentor, Yuri Andropov, and while maintaining a tough stance toward the United States, he has indicated a desire to pursue a course of peaceful coexistence in the spirit of the détente of the 1970s.

As is often the case with Soviet leaders, relatively little is known of Mikhail Sergeyevich Gorbachev's early life. A native of the fertile agricultural area of southern Russia, just north of the Caucasus mountains, he was born on March 2, 1931 into a family of peasants in the village of Privol-

noye, in the Krasnogvardeisky district of Stravropol territory, where he was educated in local schools. Although he was only eleven when the Germans occupied Stavropol during World War II, the experience left a deep impression on him. From 1946 to 1950 he worked summers at a machine and tractor station as an assistant combine harvester operator in the grain fields of the collective farms of his home area.

At Moscow State University, where he entered law school in 1950, apparently under the sponsorship of the Stravropol regional Communist party organization, Gorbachev invested more energy in politics than in his studies. According to a former schoolmate, who was quoted in *Time* (March 25, 1985), he was only an average student who "didn't have a lot of original ideas" but "made an effort to be everybody's buddy." Apparently Gorbachev never intended to practice law, which was not a particularly prestigious field of study in the Soviet Union at that time, but regarded the law primarily as preparation for party work. After joining the Communist party in 1952, he became active in the Young Communist League, or Komsomol.

Accounts differ about Gorbachev's political views in the last difficult years of Stalin's regime. According to some observers, he supported Stalin's "anti-cosmopolitan" line, while others maintain that he criticized the dictator's repressive regime long before Nikita Khrushchev's famous 1956 speech made it safe to do so. Whatever the case, Gorbachev's devotion to politics was obviously paramount, and as soon as he obtained his law degree in 1955, he returned to Stavropol to immerse himself in party work.

At first, Gorbachev worked with the Komsomol, the traditional training ground for Soviet party officials. From 1956 to 1958 he was first secretary of the Stavropol city Komsomol organization, and for the next four years he served the Komsomol committee for the Stavropol territory, first as deputy chief of the propaganda department, then as second secretary, and later as first secretary. In March 1962 he moved to the more demanding job of party organizer for the territorial production board of collective and state farms, and in December of that year he became head of the department of party organizations of the Stavropol territory Communist party committee. In 1963 Gorbachev became chief of the agricultural department for the entire Stavropol region, an important post for one so young. At the same time he took courses in farm economics at the Stavropol Agricultural Institute, from which he obtained a diploma in agronomy in 1967.

Rising steadily in the Communist hierarchy, Gorbachev became in September 1966 first secretary of the party committee for the city of Stavropol. In August 1968 he was chosen second secretary of the Stavropol territory party committee, and in April 1970 he was named its first secretary, becoming at thirty-nine one of the youngest provincial party chiefs in the USSR. Gorbachev helped to reorganize his district's vast and productive grain farms, improving living conditions for the workers, expanding the size of private plots, and allowing the collectives a greater voice in planning.

His innovations apparently were effective, since recognition by the authorities in Moscow soon followed. In 1970 Gorbachev became a deputy to the Soviet of the Union within the bicameral Supreme Soviet—the formal legislative body of the USSR—and he was named to its conservation and youth affairs commissions, becoming chairman of the latter in 1974. Within the national party organization, he became a member of the powerful Central Com-

mittee in 1971. He served as a delegate to a number of party congresses in the USSR and was sent on trips abroad, heading party delegations to Belgium in 1972, to West Germany in 1975, and to France in 1976.

No matter how able, even the most promising Soviet party officials need mentors to get ahead, and Gorbachev was particularly successful in attracting the favor of powerful men. His first important mentor was Mikhail A. Suslov, a former Stavropol party chief who served as Leonid I. Brezhnev's ideology minister. Gorbachev also gained the backing of the Suslov faction in the Kremlin, which included KGB chairman Yuri Andropov, and the agriculture secretary, Fyodor Kulakov. After Kulakov died of a heart attack, Gorbachev was brought to Moscow in November 1978 to replace him on the ten-member secretariat of the party's Central Committee, giving him "a swift leg up in the Soviet succession ladder," as his biographer Thomas G. Butson noted in his book *Gorbachev* (1985).

But Gorbachev's new position was "as dangerous as it was enticing," in the words of the London *Observer* (November 11, 1984), because the limited amount of arable land and uncertain climate, combined with problems involving collective management, had long made agriculture the Achilles' heel of the Soviet economy. Despite their strenuous efforts, many party leaders, among them Nikita S. Khrushchev, had met with failures in that area.

As agriculture secretary, Gorbachev tried to revive Soviet agriculture by supervising Brezhnev's massive program of farm investment as well as promoting innovations of his own, such as transferring control over agricultural production from the ministries in Moscow to regional agro-industrial authorities, and using the "brigade system" under which groups of workers were assigned to farm specific plots of land and rewarded according to the results. But Gorbachev fared little better than his predecessors. In fact, during his tenure in agriculture, harvests were so poor that the government stopped publishing crop statistics and had to spend billions to buy grain abroad. Yet the crop failures had little effect on the "Teflon Commissar," as Gorbachev was dubbed in *Newsweek* (March 25, 1985). Continuing to advance his career under the patronage of Suslov and Andropov, he became a candidate, or nonvoting, member of the Politburo in November 1979, and was advanced to full membership in October 1980, the youngest member of the Central Committee's policy-making organ.

Gorbachev's early years in the Politburo were troubled ones for the Soviet leadership. As the elderly Brezhnev grew increasingly infirm, the government drifted, and corruption became widespread. After Brezhnev died in 1982, the reformers within the Kremlin succeeded in electing Yuri Andropov as general secretary, and he immediately launched a broad-ranging program of reform. As Andropov's right-hand man, Gorbachev helped to carry out his mentor's bold reform initiatives, including a purge of corrupt and incompetent party officials that resulted in the removal of one-fifth of the regional party secretaries, one-third of their staffs, and thousands of local managers and party workers. Gorbachev also supervised Andropov's "five ministries" program, inaugurated in January 1984, which introduced a measure of decentralization and technological innovation in a small number of industries and granted managers greater flexibility in establishing goals.

As Andropov's health worsened, Gorbachev became increasingly conspicuous both inside and outside the walls of the Kremlin, acting as the ailing leader's liaison with the party hierarchy, making major speeches, and attending important diplomatic functions. In May 1983 he led a Soviet delegation on a highly publicized trip to Canada. Many observers believed that Andropov was grooming Gorbachev for the succession. But he died too soon to guarantee a chosen successor, and the mossbacked old guard, apparently convinced that younger leaders were too inexperienced to take over power, elected the elderly Konstantin U. Chernenko, a Brezhnev loyalist, as general secretary in February 1984.

It soon became evident to Kremlinologists that Gorbachev had emerged from the succession struggle in a very strong position. Although he had some opposition within the Kremlin, notably from the party secretary for defense industry administration, Grigory Romanov, who was considered his chief rival, Gorbachev began to act as the unofficial "second secretary" in charge of the key areas of ideology, economics, and party organization. In April 1984 he became chairman of the foreign affairs committee of the Supreme Soviet. Loyally supporting Chernenko, Gorbachev gradually assumed more and more of the ailing chairman's public leadership functions. As one informed observer noted in *Time* (March 25, 1985), "Gorbachev was smart not to push Chernenko out. He just waited for the old man to drop."

When Gorbachev led a Soviet delegation on an exchange visit to the British Houses of Parliament in December 1984, accompanied by his chic wife, he demonstrated a sense of humor, mercurial intelligence, and sophisticated style that made him an instant media sensation. Even Prime Minister Margaret Thatcher, whose anti-Communism is beyond question, was much impressed with him and remarked, "I like Mr. Gorbachev. We can do business together."

Following his nomination by the veteran foreign minister, Andrei A. Gromyko, Gorbachev was elected general secretary in an emergency meeting of the Central Committee, on March 11, 1985, only a few hours after the official announcement of Chernenko's death. The speed of the succession confirmed conjectures that it had been arranged long in advance. In making his acceptance speech on the same day, Gorbachev emphasized the need for rapid economic development as the most important goal and called for "further perfection and development of democracy" and "socialist self-government." With reference to the resump-

tion of Geneva arms limitation talks, scheduled for the following day, Gorbachev pledged to maintain the "defense capacity of the motherland" but asserted that his nation was not striving to "acquire unilateral advantages" over the United States and the NATO powers and promised to follow the "Leninist course" of "peaceful coexistence."

The new general secretary moved confidently and vigorously ahead with Andropov's program of reform. His first order of business was to consolidate his power after years of drift and diffusion. Vacancies on the Politburo allowed him in April 1985 to appoint three Andropov protégés, Yegor K. Ligachev, Nikolai I. Ryzhkov, and Victor M. Chebrikov, thus giving himself a substantial majority on the thirteen-member ruling body. Furthermore, Gorbachev had ample time to prepare for the twenty-seventh party congress, scheduled for late 1985 or early 1986, which under his direction was to adopt a new party program and five-year plan as well as elect new members to the Central Committee. Finally, he could count on old age to remove the last members of the monolithic old guard who had long resisted change in the Soviet system.

At the lower levels of party organization, Gorbachev renewed the drive to remove corrupt and incompetent functionaries. Several officials concerned with production of energy, an area vital to Soviet economic recovery, were "retired" after denunciations in the press, and a number of provincial party chiefs along with dozens of local officials were dismissed in what some observers described as a purge.

Building an effective party organization was essential to Gorbachev's primary concern, economic revitalization. In recent years, the Soviet economy had shown alarming signs of weakness: a drop in oil production, the nation's chief export commodity; a disappointing increase of only 2 percent in gross national product, well below those of China and the United States; and continued poor performance in agriculture. The Soviet leadership was clearly worried that the continued economic crisis threatened national security. "We cannot remain a major power in world affairs unless we put our domestic house in order," Gorbachev had warned in a speech to the Central Committee in December 1984.

Like his patron, Andropov, Gorbachev did not intend to dismantle the system of centralized planning but wanted merely to make it more efficient. His program involved enforcing greater worker discipline, including a campaign against alcoholism, while rewarding better efforts with cash bonuses and consumer goods. At the management level, he wanted to introduce greater independence and use incentive schemes to increase productivity. He was also enthusiastic about modernizing the Soviet economy by introducing new technology. Having spoken favorably of Hungary's more market-oriented socialist economy, he stressed in speeches the need for "intensification," a Soviet code word for introducing market principles into a planned economy.

On foreign policy issues, Western observers predicted that Gorbachev would be less innovative because of the collective nature of Kremlin policy-making and his relative lack of experience in that area. Yet he demonstrated what Hedrick Smith of the New York Times (April 9, 1985) called a "knack for diplomatic theater" by announcing on Easter Sunday that the Soviet Union would observe a six-month moratorium on deployment of its SS-20 medium-range nuclear missiles. Critics pointed out that the Soviet Union had virtually completed the deployment anyway and was already testing a new version of the missile. Nevertheless, Gorbachev's political showmanship reinforced the perception that he would be a formidable diplomatic adversary.

A major point in Gorbachev's foreign policy and defense views was his opposition to the proposed Strategic Defense Initiative, or "Star Wars" plan, of the United States, which he regarded as a dangerous militarization of space. He accused the Americans of violating the guidelines for the Geneva arms talks by refusing to negotiate simultaneously on the space program and on strategic and medium-range nuclear weaponry. In view of the Soviet Union's failure to block deployment of the Pershing II and cruise missiles in Western Europe in 1983, Gorbachev's emphasis on the Star Wars plan has been seen by Western observers as an effort to drive a wedge between the United States and its NATO allies, many of whom are uneasy about the American space initiative.

Although Gorbachev has denounced the United States as "the forward edge of the war menace to mankind," he has also referred to superpower confrontation as "an anomaly," and at Moscow trade talks in May 1985 he told United States Secretary of Commerce Malcolm Baldrige that it was "high time to defrost the potential for Soviet-American cooperation." Many analysts believe that Gorbachev's domestic problems are too pressing for him to take any assertive action that might threaten the current uneasy state of détente.

Gorbachev has announced his resolve to cement ties with other Communist countries, especially China. His statement in his inaugural speech that he intended to "expand cooperation with socialist states" and to "enhance the role and influence of socialism in world affairs" was seen by Western observers as an assertion of continued Soviet dominance within the Communist bloc. In May he signed two economic agreements with visiting Indian Prime Minister Rajiv Gandhi and discussed with him, among other matters, the possible threat to India and the USSR posed by Pakistani aid to Afghan rebels fighting Soviet-backed troops. He has indicated willingness to accept a political settlement with the Afghan rebels, and a possible rapprochement with Israel, with which the Soviet Union had broken relations in 1967.

In June 1985, rejecting a draft economic five-year plan, Gorbachev called for less emphasis on construction of new factories and more on improving the quality of consumer products. He demanded the retooling and renovation of existing industrial plants, elimination of waste and incompetence, and more efficient state supervision of the economy, and he strongly criticized some of the holdover officials from the Brezhnev era for having allowed the economy to stagnate during the 1970s.

In a major shakeup, in July, Gorbachev consolidated his own authority, permitting his chief rival, Grigory V. Romanov, to retire on "health grounds" from the party Secretariat and Politburo. He named the veteran statesman Andrei A. Gromyko, who had been foreign minister for twenty-eight years, to the largely ceremonial but prestigious presidency of the USSR and placed the foreign affairs portfolio into the hands of his close associate Eduard Shevardnadze, who had been Communist party chief in the Soviet Republic of Georgia. He also reorganized the military, replacing the commander of Warsaw Pact forces and other high-ranking officers.

As a prelude to summit talks between Gorbachev and President Ronald Reagan scheduled to be held in November 1985 at Geneva, Gorbachev announced a unilateral five-month moratorium on Soviet nuclear tests effective August 6, 1985 and offered to extend the freeze on testing if the United States were to take similar action. But American officials contended that the Soviet Union had already completed its 1985 testing program and that the move was in effect a Soviet propaganda ploy. The Reagan administration also dismissed Gorbachev's endorsement, in September, of a plan for a Central European zone free of chemical weapons because such a ban could not be easily verified.

In a meeting, in September, with eight United States senators headed by Democrat Robert C. Byrd of West Virginia, Gorbachev offered "radical proposals" to reduce offensive nuclear arms on condition that the Reagan administration would agree to bar development and deployment of the "Star Wars" missile defense project. Then, in early October, he was well received in Paris, where he affirmed a Soviet proposal, made earlier at the Geneva arms talks, for a 50 percent reduction in American and Soviet strategic weapons. He failed however, to win support for his offer to hold separate arms-reduction talks with France and Great Britain.

Drafts for a new Communist party program, the first in twenty-five years, and two new economic development plans, were presented by Gorbachev at a meeting of the Communist Party Central Committee in mid-October 1985. Replacing the excessively ambitious document introduced by Nikita S. Khrushchev in 1961, the political program indicated that the Soviet Union was still in the stage of "developed socialism," which precedes communism, and warned against "going ahead too fast" while emphasizing the need to consider "the level of society's material and spiritual maturity." The economic plans called for increased labor productivity that could nearly double the national income within fifteen years.

Experts on Soviet affairs have warned against confusing Gorbachev's more open style with a more liberal political philosophy. He has been described, like his mentor, Andropov, as an "intellectual authoritarian." Although he has indicated an unusual willingness to consult public opinion and a more relaxed attitude toward censorship, Gorbachev is not expected to be especially tolerant of dissidents. As Andrei Gromyko said of Gorbachev in his nomination speech, "Comrades, this man has a nice smile, but he's got iron teeth."

Nevertheless, analysts also note the absence of evidence in Gorbachev's career of the "killer instinct" often found in Soviet leaders. They point out that he rose through the ranks as a result of his own ability and the help of powerful patrons, rather than by means of military prowess or bloody purges. Too young to experience personally the full impact of Stalinism or of World War II, he came of age in an era of expanding Soviet power. As a result, he has a self-confidence and freedom from paranoia noticeably lacking in the old guard. In any case, many observers agree that after a long period of uncertain leadership, the Soviet Union has a strong, effective, charismatic man at its helm. After a meeting with Gorbachev, Speaker of the House of Representatives Thomas P. ("Tip") O'Neill Jr., heading a United States congressional delegation to Moscow, told Celestine Bohlen of the *Washington Post* (April 11, 1985): "He's a master of words, a master of the art of politics and diplomacy. . . . He's hard, he's tough, he's strong."

Mikhail Gorbachev's wife, Raisa Maksimovna Gorbacheva, whom he met when they were both university students, is an unusual asset for a Soviet leader. The attractive, poised, and stylish Mrs. Gorbachev holds a doctor of philosophy degree and teaches Marxist-Leninist theory at Moscow State University. The Gorbachevs are said to have two children, although only one, their daughter Irina, who is a physician and mother of their granddaughter Oksana, has appeared in public with them. The couple have an apartment near the Kremlin and a lakeside dacha outside Moscow. Gorbachev enjoys hiking and listening to classical music, and he has read widely in world literature. He and his wife regularly attend the ballet and the theatre, and they have taken motoring vacations in Italy and France.

Gorbachev is a somewhat bald, stocky man, five feet ten inches tall, who bears a resemblance to the American actor Rod Steiger. He dresses in well-cut but conservative dark suits. A prominent strawberry-colored birthmark on his pate is usually airbrushed out of official photographs. Observers describe him as a soft-spoken, mild-mannered man who is very direct without being abrasive. Westerners used to the dour demeanor that often characterizes Soviet politicians are particularly struck by his expressive face, sense of humor, and ready smile. He reportedly puts in a six-day-a-week, twelve-hour-a-day work schedule. Among his many decorations are three Orders of Lenin, the Order of the October Revolution, and the Order of the Red Banner of Labor.

References: *London Observer* p9 N 11 '84 por; *London Sunday Times* p10 N 11 '84 por; *N Y Times* A p1+ Je 17 '85 por; *N Y Times Mag* p40+ Mr 3 '85 por; *Newsweek* 105:22+ Mr 25 '85 por; *Soviet Life* p1 My '85; *Time* 125:15+ Mr 25 '85 por; *Washington Post* E p1+ Mr 17 '85; Butson, Thomas G. *Gorbachev* (1985); *International Who's Who, 1985-86*

## Greene, Harold H(erman)

*Feb. 6, 1923– Federal judge. Address: b. United States District Court for the District of Columbia, United States Court House, Third and Constitution Aves., Washington, D.C. 20001*

On August 5, 1983, Judge Harold H. Greene of the United States District Court for the District of Columbia gave final approval to a consent decree breaking up the largest corporation in the world—the American Telephone and Telegraph Company. The settlement, which concluded a 1974 antitrust suit filed by the United States Department of Justice to end the regulated monopoly that AT&T had exercised for decades over the American telephone network, was attributed in large part to Greene's skills as a trial judge and to his gift for synthesizing highly complex issues. In a remarkable display of judicial activism, Greene assumed responsibility for modifying and administering the terms of the settlement in accordance with what he perceived to be the public interest. Earlier in a distinguished judicial career that spans twenty-five years, Greene helped to restructure the criminal court system of Washington, D.C. and played a major role in drafting the groundbreaking civil rights legislation of the 1960s.

Of Jewish parentage, Harold Herman Greene was born Heinz Grünhaus on February 6, 1923 in Frankfurt an der Oder, in what is now the German Democratic Republic. In an interview with Jim Hoagland for the *Washington Post Potomac* magazine (September 25, 1966), Greene could recall no "overt acts" taken by the Nazi government against him or his parents before their flight from the country in 1939. He has nonetheless remained reticent about his childhood in Germany. "I don't think about it too much," he told Hoagland. "Too many people are concerned with what they were in Europe, before they came to the United States."

After passing through Belgium, France, Spain, and Portugal, the Grünhaus family finally settled in the United States in 1943. The following year, Heinz became a naturalized American citizen, Americanized his name to Harold Greene, and enlisted in the United States Army. Assigned to military intelligence, he spent most of his two-year tour of duty in Allied-occupied Germany. On his discharge from the service with the rank of staff sergeant in 1946, Greene joined his parents, Irving and Edith, in Washington, D.C., where they had opened a jewelry shop. Supporting himself by working as a translator for the United States Department of Justice, Greene attended night school at George Washington University. He received his B.S. degree in 1949 and, graduating first in his class, his J.D. degree in 1952. Shortly after that, he was admitted to practice before the bars of the District of Columbia, the State of Maryland, the United States Supreme Court, and the Military Court of Appeals.

Following a year's apprenticeship as a clerk for the United States Court of Appeals in Washington, Greene was hired as an Assistant United States Attorney for the District of Columbia, a post he held until 1957, when he accepted a job in the Justice Department's office of legal counsel. A year later, he was chosen to head the appeals and research section of the Department's civil rights division, which Congress had recently established to enforce existing civil rights measures and to prepare comprehensive legislation that would ban discrimination based on color, race, national origin, religion, or sex. "Harold either wrote, reviewed, argued or somehow participated in every significant civil rights case heard in the most crucial era of civil rights litigation," one Justice Department official told Jim Hoagland. "And he had more to do with the writing of the Civil Rights Act of 1964 and the Voting Rights Act of 1965 than anyone else."

In July 1965, a month before Congress passed the Voting Rights Act, President Lyndon B. Johnson appointed Greene to the post of associate judge of the District of Columbia Court of General Sessions. Greene's decision to trade in his promising Justice Department career for a term on the bench of Washington's problem-plagued "peoples' court" surprised some observers, but he evidently relished the challenge of reforming a court notorious for its lack of decorum and turnstile justice.

During his first year on the General Sessions bench, Judge Greene wrote 235 pages of opinions—more than the court's other fourteen judges combined. His diligence won him the admiration of the *Washington Post,* formerly a sharp and frequent critic of General Sessions. The *Post's* legal correspondent was also impressed by Judge Greene's scrupulous regard for the rights of criminal defendants. In order to insure the best available representation for the poor defendants who crowded his courtroom, Greene sought to extend a stipulation in the Criminal Justice Act of 1964 that provided for fixed payments to court-appointed attorneys who represented indigents charged with felonies in federal courts. Arguing that the federal compensation program attracted better qualified lawyers and thus substantially improved the quality of justice for indigents, Greene eventually persuaded the United States Comptroller General to draw up a similar scheme to cover the serious misdemeanor cases that made up the bulk of the General Sessions trial docket. The new fee system went into effect in December 1966.

Impressed by Greene's accomplishments in his short time on the General Sessions bench, President Johnson named him the court's chief judge in November 1966. Immediately on taking office, Greene implemented sweeping administrative reforms intended to reduce the huge case backlog without jeopardizing defendants' rights. To that end, he set up an assignment court to distribute incoming criminal cases to lawyers and judges and arrange for adjournments. Greene's plan succeeded in preventing defendants' lawyers from deliberately postponing their cases while they "shopped" for a lenient judge or tried to improve plea-bargaining terms, but at the cost of a sharp increase in the demands for jury trials. By adding several new judges to the bench and by lengthening the workday, however, Greene still managed to trim the average delay between arrest and trial for criminal defendants from three months in 1966 to about six weeks in 1970.

In an effort to curb the capital's escalating crime rate, Congress passed, in 1970, an omnibus legislative package that called for, among other things, a reorganization of the District of Columbia's peculiar judicial system of overlapping federal and local jurisdictions. The reorganization, which Greene lobbied hard for, combined the Court of General Sessions and the various other separate courts into the District of Columbia Superior Court, with a general jurisdiction comparable to that of a state circuit court. In recognition of his achievements at General Sessions, Congress confirmed Greene to a five-year term as chief judge of the expanded court, beginning in 1971.

Determined to speed up criminal trials "so that law enforcement can retain its lost deterrent power," as he expressed it, Judge Greene pledged to reduce felony processing lags to sixty to ninety days, but despite some initial progress, that goal eluded him as a tide of criminal cases swamped Superior Court in the mid-1970s. He was more successful in improving conditions for juveniles charged with serious crimes. In one of his first actions as head of the restructured court system, Greene ordered city officials to develop an alternative to detaining juveniles awaiting trial in the dilapidated and overcrowded Receiving Home for Children. When the city failed to meet his two-year deadline, the judge shut the facility down and transferred the 250 children confined there to other prisons and halfway houses or to their own homes under an innovative home-detention program. Praised by the independent judicial tenure commission for his skills as a trial judge and as an administrator, Greene easily won reappointment to a second term as chief judge of Superior Court in 1976.

Two years later, on May 17, 1978, President Jimmy Carter named Harold Greene to the federal bench of the United States District Court for the District of Columbia. Within days of his taking the oath of office, he inherited the case that was to occupy most of his time for the next six years: the Justice Department's antitrust suit, filed in 1974, against the American Telephone and Telegraph Company and its research and manufacturing affiliates, Bell Telephone Laboratories and Western Electric. The lawsuit—by far the largest antitrust case in American history, dwarfing even the 1911 breakup of the Standard Oil trust—turned on Justice's contention that AT&T (known colloquially as "Ma Bell") and its affiliates had combined and conspired to monopolize telecommunications service and equipment in the United States in violation of the Sherman Antitrust Act.

The Communications Act of 1934 had recognized AT&T's exercise of a so-called "natural monopoly" over telephone service as being consistent with the principle of providing every American household with access to a telephone at a low cost, but in 1949 the Justice Department filed an antitrust suit against AT&T, alleging that the company had extended its monopoly from telephone service to equipment manufacturing. That suit was settled in a 1956 consent decree—widely criticized as ineffective—that allowed the parent company to keep Western Electric on the condition that it withdraw from all business not directly connected with communications and that it freely license existing patents. With the technological revolution in the 1970s, however, came a host of new telecommunications companies eager to compete with Ma Bell. Through court decisions and FCC rulings, a number of them won the right to establish private long-distance service and to hook up to existing Bell System facilities. The 1974 suit was filed in response to complaints from those new competitors that Bell had tried to squeeze them out by restricting access to its local telephone networks and by using the profits from its local service monopoly to subsidize its long-distance rates.

Some antitrust specialists thought the AT&T case was too complex for any single court to handle, but Judge Greene quickly stamped the proceedings with his customary mark of no-nonsense efficiency. Just three months after taking the case, he issued a pretrial directive putting lawyers for both sides on a strict schedule intended to get the trial underway by September 1980. Moreover, he insisted on establishing deadlines for filing legal papers and considerably pared down the trial workload by obliging the litigants to identify and stipulate agreement to those facts not in dispute, thus separating "the contested wheat from the uncontested chaff," as he put it.

The non-jury trial finally began on January 14, 1981, only to be almost immediately suspended while the disputants made an unsuccessful, last-gasp effort to reach an out-of-court settlement. Refusing to countenance further delays without a formal agreement in place, Greene restored the case to his docket in March over the protest of both parties. Ten months later, on January 8, 1982, AT&T and the Justice Department announced that they had come to an agreement. Under the terms of the settlement, AT&T agreed to spin off its twenty-two wholly owned local telephone subsidiaries, which were worth an estimated $80 billion, into seven independent regional phone companies. In return, the company was allowed to keep its Western Electric and Bell Laboratories affiliates and to expand into such highly lucrative telecommunications fields as electronic data processing and computer-to-computer transmissions.

On learning of the surprise settlement, Judge Greene, who was on vacation at the time, issued a statement announcing that he would review the terms of the accord to ensure that it met the "public interest" requirement for out-of-court antitrust settlements mandated by the 1974 Tunney Act. Both the Justice Department and AT&T sought without success to avoid judicial review by describing the agreement as a modification of the 1956 consent decree. Denouncing that tactic as "a mere act of labeling" intended to subvert the "clearly expressed will of Congress," Greene convened hearings on the proposed settlement and, over the next few months, reviewed some 8,000 pages of commentary from 600 interested individuals and organizations.

In a 178-page opinion delivered on August 11, 1982, Greene approved the basic framework of the settlement as being "plainly in the public interest," but insisted on important modifications designed to safeguard customers and competitors alike. To forestall anticipated consumer rate increases, he sought to boost the regional companies' earnings power by allowing them to sell telephones and related equipment and by returning to them the lucrative publishing rights to the Yellow Pages directories. To permit competitive conditions to develop in the burgeoning electronic publishing industry, he prohibited AT&T from offering an electronic information service "until the risk of its dominance of that field has abated," or for at least seven years. He also took the unusual step of empowering his court to review and approve each step of AT&T's divestiture in order to monitor compliance with the decree and ensure the financial viability of the new regional companies. Before giving the settlement his final approval, the judge ordered AT&T to relinquish the Bell name and logo for the exclusive use of the regional companies, noting that the shared name confused consumers and gave AT&T an unfair advantage in long-distance service.

The court-ordered modifications were welcomed by Samuel A. Simon, the executive director of the Telecommunications Research and Action Center, a Washington-based consumer advocate group, as "an extraordinary pro-consumer decision," an opinion that was echoed by Congressman Timothy Wirth, the chairman of the House Telecommunications Subcommittee, which had drafted legislation incorporating similar provisions. Some legal experts and industry analysts, however, contended that Judge Greene had exceeded his authority. Arguing that the proposed agreement preempted the power of a state to regulate telephone service within its borders, Maryland and twelve other states went so far as to challenge the settlement in the Supreme Court, but the Court affirmed Greene's decision.

Since the consent decree took effect on January 1, 1984, Greene has continued to spend more than one-third of his time on the case and on related telecommunications issues, amid demands from industry officials that he surrender at least some of his oversight responsibility to a permanent regulatory agency. Responding to consumer complaints about poor service, broken equipment, and a confusing array of choices, Greene defended the breakup of AT&T. "Competition has served the country well in other areas, and I see no reason why competition shouldn't serve the public as well in telecommunications," he told Robert D. Hershey Jr. in an interview for the New York Times (December 30, 1983). "There's no reason whatever why the quality should go down, and there's every reason to believe, based on past experience, that competition will drive the price down for the consumer."

Judge Greene found himself on the front page once again in February 1984, after he criticized Attorney General William French Smith's refusal to appoint a special prosecutor to look into the so-called "Debategate" scandal, which involved the unauthorized transfer of President Carter's debate briefing papers from the White House to Ronald Reagan's 1980 presidential campaign committee. Greene's comments came in response to a civil suit filed in his court to compel Smith to appoint such a prosecutor under the provisions of the 1978 Ethics in Government Act. Calling Smith's handling of the matter "arbitrary and unlawful" and drawing "parallels" to Watergate, Greene took the unprecedented step of ordering the Attorney General to seek an independent counsel to investigate possible criminal behavior by top Reagan aides. Greene's action tested the issue of whether the Attorney General's failure to comply with the Ethics Act was subject to judicial review. Answering unanimously in the negative, the United States

Court of Appeals for the District of Columbia reversed Greene's order in June 1984.

Harold H. Greene has a commanding courtroom presence despite his relatively short stature and slight build. An affable and soft-spoken man, he is known for his sharp sense of humor, which can turn bitingly sarcastic when he is faced with incompetence on the bench or at the bar. He has a keen intellectual interest in the law, and he confessed to one reporter that he felt a twinge of disappointment when the negotiated settlement of the AT&T suit deprived him of writing a major antitrust opinion.

An admitted workaholic, in his rare moments of leisure the judge enjoys reading and playing bridge. Greene and the former Evelyn Schroer, a native of the Saar region on the German-French border, have been married since September 19, 1948. They have two children, Michael David, a physician, and Stephanie Alison, an elementary school teacher. The Greenes make their home in northwest Washington, D.C.

References: N Y Times D p30 D 30 '84 por; Newsweek 99:51+ Ja 25 '82 por; Time 123:53 Ja 2 '84 por; Washington Post B p1+ O 19 '70 por, F p1+ D 2 '84 por; Washington Post Potomac mag p7+ S 25 '66 por; Congressional Directory, 1983–84; Federal Judicial Almanac (1984)

## Gregorian, Vartan

Apr. 7, 1935(?)- Library administrator; educator; historian. Address: b. New York Public Library, 42d St. and Fifth Ave., New York City, N.Y. 10018; h. 40 E. 94th St., New York City, N.Y. 10028

New Yorkers owe the revitalization of their once-declining public library system in large measure to an Armenian-American scholar, Vartan Gregorian, who came to their rescue in 1981 from the University of Pennsylvania, where he had been dean, provost, and professor of history. Combining his credentials as an educator with a flair for management, salesmanship, and showmanship and a crusader's sense of mission, he campaigned successfully to make patronage and use of the New York Public Library seem desirable, necessary, and even fashionable. For Gregorian, the library that he heads as president and chief executive officer is one of "the last refuges of rationalism in the world" and should serve as "a cultural center for New York and for the nation." As Douglas Davis noted in Newsweek (June 25, 1984), "It's the juxtaposition of high scholarship and broad popular appeal—last year 1.5 million people visited the Fifth Avenue library—that distinguishes New York from the great libraries of Europe and the larger Library of Congress in Washington."

*Vartan Gregorian*

An authority on the Armenian community in Iran, among other aspects of Armenian culture and history, Vartan Gregorian was born on April 7, 1935 to middle-class Armenian parents Samuel B. and Shushanik G. (Mirzaian) Gregorian in Tabriz, northern Iran. His grandfather operated a caravansary, or inn for camel caravans, and his father worked in management for a large oil company. When Vartan was seven years old, his mother died. To console him, his relatives said that she had gone to America, a country that he imagined to be paradise and set his heart on seeing. The care of Vartan and his younger sister fell to their maternal grandmother, who passed along to them her store of folk wisdom. "She was everything. She taught me everything is negotiable except your dignity," her grandson has recalled.

During World War II, when his father was away from home in military service, Gregorian saw his grandmother struggling to cope with food shortages and other economic hardships of war. But at the age of ten he got a job as a page at the Armenian Library in Tabriz and there made the discovery that he has said changed his life. Through his contact with books he entered "the only stable world, and the only world that was immutable," as he was quoted as saying in the *New York Times* (March 14, 1982). "Your sense of justice, of human compassion," he went on to explain, "—these were all awakened by books, and in retrospect, I can see that this for me was an outlet, a wonderful outlet for hope, and a way to transcend my culture and see the world."

A few years later Gregorian, then about fourteen, met a French diplomat of Armenian descent who was stationed in Tabriz and recovering from an illness at the home of a mutual friend. The diplomat taught him to play chess and urged him to go to Beirut for study at Collège Armenien. On arrival he learned that all the courses were taught in French. Within a year he had overcome the handicap of his unfamiliarity with that language and began to excel scholastically. After his graduation in 1955, he worked for a year as a reporter for various Beirut newspapers while qualifying for a diploma in Armenian studies from Collège Armenien, which then awarded him a scholarship for study abroad.

Gregorian enrolled in Stanford University in California in 1956. The following year he was elected president of the International Club, an office that he held until 1959, when the Institute of International Relations named him as the student who had contributed most to international understanding. Meanwhile, having majored in history, to which he had switched from English literature, he earned his B.A. degree in history and humanities in 1958. A two-year teaching fellowship in the department of history enabled him to remain at Stanford to begin graduate study.

During the years in which he worked for his Ph.D. degree in history and humanities, awarded in 1964, Gregorian steadily developed the role of an educator in which he continues to find his identity. In a part-time appointment in 1960 he taught a class in Armenian history and culture at the University of California at Berkeley, and back in Beirut during 1961 he was an instructor of Armenian history at Collège Armenien. But for the most part he acquired his early experience in teaching at San Francisco State College, where he was an instructor in history in 1960 and from 1964 to 1966 and an associate professor from 1966 to 1968. For about six months in 1968 he was also visiting associate professor of history at the University of California at Los Angeles.

Meanwhile, as he had done since his arrival in the United States, Gregorian continued to contribute articles on Armenian literature and other subjects to Beirut periodicals, including "The Cult of Stalin and Process of Destalinization in Armenian Literature" (*Aztag*, April 1962) and "Soviet Armenian Literature: A Critical Analysis" (*Bagin*, June-July 1962). (He sometimes wrote under the pseudonym V. Herian.) His paper "Mahud Tarzi and *Saraj-ol-Akhbar*, The Ideology of Modernization and Nationalism in Afghanistan" appeared in the *Middle East Journal* in the summer of 1967, and in 1969 Stanford University Press published his book *The Emergence of Modern Afghanistan, Politics of Reform and Modernization, 1880-1946*.

San Francisco State College's 17,500 or more racially diversified students had a lively share in the social and political ferment that beset urban campuses during the 1960s. "[Gregorian] has had a way of placing himself in the eye of the tornado wherever he has worked," Jennifer Allen observed in *New York* (January 16, 1984). "At San Francisco . . . he seems to have been acquainted with every radical, every faction, on and off campus." Believing that organizations of all types had a right to be heard, he agreed to serve as faculty adviser to the Progressive Labor group so that it would be officially recognized on the campus. When he left the college, all factions called a temporary truce to join in a farewell party for him.

With his move in 1968 from San Francisco to Austin as associate professor of history at the University of Texas, Gregorian combined teaching with a growing number of administrative and other academic assignments outside the classroom. Besides serving on committees for European, American, and Middle East studies, among others, he was director from 1969 to 1971 of the special programs of the College of Arts and Sciences, of the independent studies program, and of the junior fellows program. Meanwhile, in 1970, he had advanced to a full professorship in history.

Administrative responsibilities became increasingly important for Gregorian during nearly a decade at the University of Pennsylvania, where he taught as professor of history and Tarzian Professor of Armenian and Caucasian History from 1972 to 1981. He was faculty assistant to the university's president and provost in 1973-74, first dean of the Faculty of Arts and Sciences from 1974 to 1978, and provost from 1978 to 1980. During his tenure as dean, according to Joseph Deitch's profile of Gregorian in the *Wilson Library Bulletin* (December 1981), "his leadership and magnetism helped raise as much as $32 million for this university unit and form a new alumni society, a new board of overseers, and such new programs as an Italian Studies Center, a Center for Medieval Studies, and the Philadelphia Center for Early American Studies." One of Gregorian's colleagues at Pennsylvania, Deitch went on to report, attributed his success to an asset beyond his ability to utilize the skills of his staff: "the human element, in sensitivity and understanding, was uppermost in everything he did."

When, therefore, Martin Meyerson, president of the University of Pennsylvania, made known his intention to retire in 1980, Gregorian, an eager candidate for the office, was favored on the campus as his likely successor. The search committee nevertheless preferred Sheldon Hackney for the position. Upon hearing the announcement on his automobile radio, Gregorian abruptly resigned as provost, in part, apparently, because he felt that the committee's treatment of him had been somewhat shabby. "I never questioned the decision—I questioned the manner," Jennifer Allen quoted him as saying. Pennsylvania students and faculty members protested his rejection in vain.

Another search committee, however, this one engaged in finding a replacement for Richard W. Couper, president of the New York Public Library, selected Gregorian unanimously. He also had the unstinted support of Andrew Heiskell, former chairman of Time, Inc., who was slated to become chairman of the library. Both men assumed their new posts on June 1, 1981. Although Gregorian had not at first sought the NYPL presidency, from the day his appointment was announced, in April 1981, he showed unbounded zeal for the library and the role he envisaged for himself in its future. At a press conference in April he indicated that his move to the new job was a natural development in his career as a teacher, not a turn to a different profession: "The library is essential for higher education. I will be dealing with students and scholars. In a sense I am only changing my focus, not my interests."

An essential part of the equipment that Gregorian brought to his office on Fifth Avenue was the experience he had acquired as a fund-raiser at the University of Pennsylvania. "The New York Public Library is the trustee of a national treasure," he said at the same press conference. "With that comes not only pride but the question of cost. . . . We will raise funds everywhere and what we will negotiate is the amount, not the question of whether contributions should be made at all." Partly because of the New York City fiscal crisis that necessitated budgetary cuts during the 1970s, the library had been forced to reduce its services, neglect repairs to its physical facilities, and dip into its $80 million endowment. Gregorian accepted the challenge of reversing that downturn, of regenerating the entire library system, and of restoring the magnificence of its main building.

The "national treasure" that Gregorian has described as "a free university, library, and museum rolled into one" comprises some 27 million items, including over 7 million books, 11 million manuscripts, and 20,000 periodical subscriptions—acquisitions that in the United States rank in number below only those of the Library of Congress and the Harvard University libraries. In addition to the famed main reference facility—the Central Research Library at 42d Street and Fifth Avenue—the system includes the Library of the Performing Arts at Lincoln Center, the Schomberg Center for Research in Black Culture in Harlem, and more than eighty branch, or circulating, libraries in Manhattan, the Bronx, and Staten Island.

Unlike the branch libraries, which are maintained by city, state, and federal funds, the research libraries have to draw almost two-thirds of their income from private sources. "We're the only major library that is public but primarily privately supported," Gregorian has pointed out. The NYPL, in fact, began in 1895 as a privately incorporated merger of the libraries of James Lenox and John Jacob Astor. Through bequests from Astor and Samuel J. Tilden, the books became available to the public in a building provided and maintained by the city. Because of the library's dependence on private funds, one of Gregorian's first tasks as its president was to stimulate the flow of contributions by increasing public awareness of what it offered.

As part of his fund-raising campaign, Gregorian launched a series of special cultural events at the Central Research Library, including the presentation there for the first time of the National Book Critics Circle Awards and the Commonwealth Literary Awards, reading performances by well-known actors and authors, literary luncheons sponsored by the Friends of the Library donors, and $1,000-a-plate Literary Lion Dinners. Those and other gatherings were attended by such celebrities as Isaac Bashevis Singer, William F. Buckley Jr., Jacqueline Kennedy Onassis, and the Walter Annenbergs. A recent scheme for raising money was a library raffle offering, as Gregorian described them in one of his promotional letters, "scores of exquisite, exciting, extra-special prizes," topped by a twelve-day, first-class vacation for two in London.

Gregorian's warmth and ebullience won him many allies, captivated, it would seem, by what Heiskell has called "a strange combination of scholarship, energy, drive, salesmanship, enthusiasm and even a certain naiveté." His new friends included New York City's Mayor Edward I. Koch, who had access to the city's purse strings, and Mrs. Brooke Astor, widow of Vincent Astor, grandson of the library's cofounder. An influential civic leader and philanthropist, she redoubled her long-time efforts in behalf of the library's advancement. Three years after Gregorian become president of the NYPL, its number of donors had risen to over 40,000, who during that time had contributed a total of some $34 million. The National Endowment for the Humanities increased its matching grant for 1984 from the $2 million of the two preceding years to $2.2 million, and New York City raised its support for the library's operating budget to $50 million in 1985, considerably up from the $28 million figure of 1981.

Contributions from many diverse sources, including foundations and corporations, enabled Gregorian to undertake the most visible demonstration of his leadership, a massive $45 million restoration of the main library building, at 42d Street and Fifth Avenue. Much of the beauty and grandeur of the beaux arts edifice designed by Thomas Hastings and John M. Carrère in 1911 had been obscured by years of decay, neglect, and mistreatment. Its marble walls, for example, had been concealed by partitions to provide office space, and carved wooden ceilings had been plastered over.

The first of three phases of the "efforts to rebuild this national landmark," as Gregorian put it, included extensive roof repairs, landscaping of the Fifth Avenue plaza, and cleaning of the Fifth Avenue facade and the entrance's two imperious marble lions, which Mayor Fiorello LaGuardia had nicknamed "Patience" and "Fortitude." Among other first-phase accomplishments were improvements in temperature and humidity controls for reading rooms and bookstacks and the restoration of three elegant first-floor interiors—the Periodical Room, the grand entrance hall (Astor Hall), and the exhibition hall (Gottesman Hall). Later phases of the program call for renovation of the public catalogue room and main reading room. In a separate project plans have been drawn up for the rehabilitation of the library's nine-acre Bryant Park, long a stamping ground for derelicts, prostitutes, and drug addicts.

On May 24, 1984 the New York Public Library celebrated the completion of the first phase of its restoration with a preview of "Censorship: 500 Years of Conflict," its first major exhibition in two generations and the first to be held in the newly reopened Gottesman Hall. Some 300 items—books, manuscripts, and prints—mostly drawn from the library's own holdings, documented a five-century struggle for freedom of expression. Concomitant exhibitions, lectures, and forums on censorship were held at other reference libraries and branch libraries throughout the city.

Aside from preserving and enlarging the library's acquisitions, expanding its staff, and increasing its public-service hours, Gregorian has been involved in the enormous job of computerizing the catalogue. Eventually the computer system will supersede the old bound catalogues that now list the majority of entries. Nevertheless, in the true spirit of librarianship Gregorian has affirmed that "the book is here to stay." "What we're doing," he said, as quoted in Time (February 25, 1985), "is symbolic of the peaceful coexistence of the book and the computer." The main library has about fifty terminals for patron use. Also concerned with linking up with information-retrieval centers, he said at his first press conference, "The crucial task is to transform information into knowledge. It is essential that computers serve as tools to knowledge."

Gregorian's achievements in library administration have been made at the expense of his scholarly work-in-progress, including an updating of his book on Soviet-Afghan relations. Many of the scores of committees, boards, and organizations with which he is associated, however, pertain to education and research. Since he became head of the NYPL he has been awarded at least nine honorary doctorates, among other academic tributes.

While a graduate student and teaching fellow at Stanford University, Vartan Gregorian met Clare Russell, also a student, whom he married on March 25, 1960. They have three sons, Vahe, Raffi, and Dareh. Jennifer Allen of New York found that "he protects his private life zealously." He is a stocky, bearded man with bushy graying hair. Walking, attending concerts, going to the movies, listening to Armenian music, reading, traveling, and playing chess are his recreations. He would probably also fully enjoy the rounds of parties that his job imposes on him if there were opportunity for prolonged intellectual discussion. But Gregorian, who can communicate in Armenian, Turkish, Arabic, Persian, Russian, French, and English, laments, "The art of conversation has died."

References: N Y Daily News People p3 Ja 27 '85 por; N Y Times C p9 Ap 14 '81 por, p64 Mr 14 '82 por, C p10 Jl 19 '83; New York 17:34+ Ja 16 '84 pors; Time 124:87 Ag 13 '84 por; Wilson Lib Bul 56:278+ D '81 por, 58:625+ My '84 por; Contemporary American Scholars (1982); Contemporary Authors 1st rev vols 29-32 (1978); Who's Who in America, 1984-85

cation home in the woods, where his two sons and two daughters spent their summers and acquired their lasting love of nature. Consequently, Hagegard still considers himself as being "at heart a country boy," as he assured Dorle J. Soria during an interview for *High Fidelity/Musical America* (March 1983). Growing up in a house where his mother played the piano and sang, and his father played the violin, he developed a precocious interest in lieder and chamber music.

Although he originally studied to be an architect, Hagegard kept up his music studies at the Karlstad Conservatory and at the Royal Academy in Stockholm. When, at nineteen, he definitely decided that his aptitude for music was far greater than his aptitude for architecture, he made up his mind to spend the summer studying with Erik Werba in Salzburg, Austria. Werba's classes were already full, but after auditioning Hagegard, he graciously agreed to make room for one more. Two years later, Hagegard returned to Salzburg for a summer of study with Gerald Moore, the renowned British accompanist for some of the greatest singers in the world, and an authority on lieder. "That's when the lights started to go on," Hagegard recalled during an interview with Mark Steinbrink for the *New York Times* (February 24, 1984). "He was such a wonderful musician, he got me hooked on lieder singing right away." But then the Swedish army claimed Hagegard for two years of compulsory military service, after which he finally settled in Stockholm for full-time study at the Royal Academy of Music.

Hagegard's audition for the role of Papageno at the Swedish Royal Opera came about by accident when its general manager, the late Goeran Gentele, invited him to try out for the part, after failing to sign up his cousin, Erland Börje Hagegard, who had a conflicting commitment in Vienna. Not long before that, Hakan had filled in for his ailing cousin on short notice in a church concert, and Gentele was apparently impressed by the similarity between their voices. That Stockholm debut, in 1968, at the age of only twenty-three, caused a furor in the Swedish press, with one headline the next day asking: "Could this be another Birgit Nilsson?" That, Hagegard has said, was "a rather confusing compliment."

After that first season at the Royal Opera, Goeran Gentele generously agreed to allow Hagegard to return to the Royal Academy of Music to continue his lieder studies and complete his operatic training. He also studied with the great Italian baritone, Tito Gobbi, who was especially noted for his acting in the role of Scarpia in *Tosca*. In paying tribute to Gobbi, Hagegard has said: "He really opened my eyes to opera. In the beginning I was not sure if I should become an opera singer. I didn't believe in it. But he taught me to love acting as well as singing and since it is natural for me to act I began to enjoy it. He also taught me to know when I was ready for a role."

When he finished his studies at the Royal Academy of Music, Hagegard returned as a regular

## Hagegard, Hakan
(hä´ge gärd hä´kän)

*Nov. 25, 1945- Swedish lyric baritone. Address: b. c/o Thea Dispeker, 59 E. 54th St., New York City, N.Y. 10022*

One of the most admired lyric baritones of his generation, Swedish-born Hakan Hagegard first achieved worldwide recognition in 1975 as the irrepressible bird-catcher Papageno in Ingmar Bergman's lapidary-like film version of Mozart's *The Magic Flute*, the role in which he made his debut in 1968 at the Royal Opera in Stockholm. Since that much applauded film performance, Hagegard has turned down offers to reprise that portrayal, in order to avoid being typecast as one of Mozart's most endearing oafs. After a decade spent in establishing an enviable reputation as a lieder and operatic singer of uncommon interpretive ability, Hagegard agreed to sing Papageno in his debut at La Scala, which is scheduled for 1985. Like the other great male lieder singers of our time, Dietrich Fischer-Dieskau and Hermann Prey, he prefers the intimacy and direct communication with the audience afforded by solo recitals to the more impersonal and formalized framework of the operatic stage. As a concert artist, he has appeared with symphony orchestras throughout Europe, and with American symphony orchestras based in Atlanta, Dallas, Baltimore, Cincinnati, Pittsburgh, Seattle, Cleveland, and Chicago.

Hakan Hagegard, who by now is resigned to seeing the diacritical marks over his name omitted in English-language newspapers, magazines, and press releases, was born on November 25, 1945 in Karlstad, a city in southwestern Sweden that is located between Stockholm and Oslo, on the shores of Lake Vänern. His father, a teacher, bought a va-

member of the Royal Opera in Stockholm in a repertory that included Marcello, the painter, in *La Bohème*; Figaro in *The Barber of Seville*; Rodrigo in *Don Carlo*; Harlequin in *Ariadne auf Naxos*, and the title role in *Rigoletto* (after he had studied it for four years). In 1973 he appeared as Crispin in the world premiere of Lars Johan Werle's *Tintomara* in Stockholm, and he sang the male lead in Debussy's *Pelléas et Melisande*, which was the last new production that Goeran Gentele mounted at the Royal Opera House. He sang his first *Don Giovanni* at the little Drottningholm Court Theatre, where he has returned many times because he finds it "a fantastic place to sing," and wears a gold medallion with the baroque initials "D.G." as a souvenir of his first performance there. It was at another comparatively small theatre—that of Glyndebourne in Sussex, England—that Hagegard made his first appearance abroad, in the summer of 1973, when he appeared with his compatriot Elisabeth Söderström in Richard Strauss's one-act conversation piece, *Capriccio*. He was invited back to Glyndebourne for the following season, as Count Almaviva in Mozart's *The Marriage of Figaro*. His most recent appearance there was in Richard Strauss's *Arabella* in the summer of 1984.

Hakan Hagegard's portrayal of Papageno in the 1975 film version of *The Magic Flute*, directed by Ingmar Bergman, made him known to audiences around the world. Although critics felt that his beguiling performance as the bumptious bird-catcher was one of the highlights of the production, Hagegard was somewhat dismayed with the aftermath of that success. "After the film," he told Steinbrink, "the only role that people offered me to sing was Papageno. I could see nothing else in my future. So I turned down the jobs. I wanted to try new things. Gradually people got the idea, and started offering me other roles. Now I feel secure enough to go back to it, and I'll perform it for my La Scala debut next year [1985]."

Meanwhile, Hagegard had been extending his song repertory with works by Mahler, Dallapiccola, Orff, Ligeti, and Swedish composers of the past and present. "Some people think that lieder are like gold and diamonds—just for the very few. I think they are for everybody," he told Dorle J. Soria during his interview with her. And he informed Steinbrink during the *New York Times* interview: "Lieder singing gives you the greatest chance to communicate with an audience. And for me that's the best part of my job. In a recital hall the house lights are higher, you can look into people's eyes."

When Hagegard made his Metropolitan Opera debut on December 7, 1978 as Doctor Malatesta in Donizetti's opera buffa *Don Pasquale*, Harold C. Schonberg hailed him in the *New York Times* (December 9, 1978) as a "young, handsome, absolutely professional actor, and the possessor of a dependable, well-focused baritone voice." "It is not a large instrument, but it projects well and is used with security," Schonberg added. Hagegard's past ten years with the Royal Opera of Stockholm had obviously paid him their dividends. He was invited

back to the Met as Figaro in *The Barber of Seville* and as Wolfram in *Tannhäuser* in February 1984.

Audiences and management alike have been so hospitable to Hagegard at the 92d Street YMHA in New York City that he has come to regard it as a kind of home away from home. When he gave a 1981 song recital there in works by Schubert, Brahms, Ravel, Stenhammar, and Rangstrom, Robert S. Clark of *High Fidelity/Musical America* (August 1981) welcomed him enthusiastically to the diminishing ranks of contemporary practitioners of art song, celebrating his "firmly centered, well-schooled, and characterful voice" and his "full spectrum of colors and dynamic values." Accompanying Hagegard at the piano that evening, as he has done at so many of his recitals since 1972, was Thomas Shuback, a conductor at the Royal Opera of Stockholm.

After attending a joint recital that Hakan Hagegard gave with the Metropolitan Opera soprano Judith Blegen (who also is of Scandinavian descent) at the YMHA in the autumn of the following year, Edward Rothstein of the *New York Times* (October 8, 1982) called the evening "a lesson in the nature of vocal music" because of their perfection in matters of pitch, modulation, and phrasing. That same autumn both singers were invited to Minneapolis to take part as soloists, along with Birgit Nilsson and Martii Talvela, in a concert inaugurating the "Scandinavia Today" Festival that was attended by royalty and other dignitaries. On that gala occasion the Minnesota Orchestra was conducted by Neville Marriner.

Hagegard has also performed at the New York YMHA with the Y Chamber Symphony, the orchestra in residence at the landmark cultural center. When he interpreted four of Mahler's *Rückertlieder* there with the Chamber Symphony, Edward Rothstein wrote in his review for the *New York Times* (February 29, 1984) that he made "the songs' miniature worlds seem more resonant because of his sensitivity to the music's elusive 'aura'." That same month Hagegard traversed the entire song cycle of Schubert's *Die Winterreise* in the YMHA auditorium for a capacity audience. Although Speight Jenkins, the music critic of the *New York Post*, reportedly said when Hagegard first performed the monumental song cycle in New York City in 1981 that he had "the God-given gift to make his art seem an expression of his feelings," Hagegard himself feels that he has yet to master all the nuances of the work. He has admitted: "In a way I wish that I had never recorded *Die Winterreise*, because even after this little time there are so many things that I'd do differently if I could do it again." Hagegard once filmed a production of *Die Winterreise* for Swedish television, using an actor as well as a singer and pianist. Written by him, the script called for the scene to shift occasionally from the castle where the recital was taking place out into the snowy landscape where the rejected lover was wandering.

By working his magic in much larger auditoriums, such as Carnegie Hall, Hagegard has transformed them for the nonce into chamber theatres with his introspective and beautifully sung selections of composers ranging from Mozart to Alban Berg. Noted for his advocacy of avant-garde contemporary composers, he has undertaken not only such difficult works as Berg's *Seven Early Songs*, endowing them with what one critic called "a languid poetry," but has also become known for his performance of world premieres. One notable instance was his premiere of Dominick Argento's song cycle *The Andrée Expedition* at O'Shaughnessy Auditorium in St. Paul, Minnesota in February 1983. His Swedish accent added an authenticity to the text of the forty-five-minute work, which was inspired by the tragic deaths of three Swedish balloonists who were forced down on an island in the Arctic shortly before the turn of the century.

In the United States, Hakan Hagegard has fulfilled engagements with the Santa Fe Opera in the title role of *The Barber of Seville* and as the dashing Danilo in *The Merry Widow* with the San Francisco Opera. His operatic bookings have taken him as far afield as the Sydney Opera House in Australia, the Teatro Colón in Buenos Aires, Argentina, and the Teatro Municipal in Rio de Janeiro, in Brazil. Among the stops on his frenetic schedule have been Salzburg, Austria for its winter festival, Ravinia, Illinois for its summer festival with the Chicago Symphony, and Cleveland, Ohio for the Blossom summer festival with the Cleveland Orchestra. And his recitals have taken him all over the North American continent, including Boston, Massachusetts, the Kennedy Center in Washington, D.C., and Toronto, Canada.

For a relatively young artist, Hagegard's discography is already impressive. When he made his recording debut in his late twenties with the orchestra of the Royal Opera of Stockholm, Harold Rosenthal of *Opera* (July 1976) praised his voice as "beautiful in quality, even throughout its scale" and took special note of his faultless technique on that album of arias for the Caprice label. Now under exclusive contract to RCA Victor, Hagegard first appeared on its Red Seal label with a digital recording of Carl Orff's *Carmina Burana*, with André Previn and the Pittsburgh Symphony. His first solo venture for RCA Victor was Schumann's song cycle *Dichterliebe*, with five Brahms lieder to round out the recording, and he was featured in the 1984 digital recording of the Brahms *Requiem*, with James Levine conducting the Chicago Symphony.

But the most discussed of Hagegard's recordings for RCA Victor by far has been his complete performance of Schubert's *Die Winterreise* on two discs. In reviewing it for the *New York Times* (April 24, 1984), Dale Harris represented a minority opinion among critics when he observed that Hagegard was not yet ready for "the highest peaks of artistic achievement." Although he found Hagegard's interpretation of the somber song cycle pleasing, he felt that Hagegard was wanting "in the kind of insight and the feeling for nuance, both verbal and coloristic, which alone can realize their full profundity."

Tall, personable, and ruggedly built, Hakan Hagegard has a joviality, ready smile, and spontaneous laugh that never fail to make an agreeable impression on interviewers. By his marriage to his former wife, Anna, from whom he is now divorced, he is the father of two young sons. He has moved out of Stockholm to a large house—furnished in traditional eighteenth-century style—where he can indulge to the full his favorite outdoor recreations, including hiking, fishing, and cross-country skiing. Although now fully booked until 1988, Hagegard continues to take his life "one step at a time," as he has always done, without too much concern for the future. Someday he would like to weigh other possibilities, such as a Broadway musical or more films. "Films and lieder are somewhat alike," he has explained. "They both require an intimacy of gesture that is obviously out of place on the opera stage." Meanwhile, he continues to be refreshingly levelheaded about his career. "You see, musical stardom has never been very important to me," he told one interviewer. "I do my job because I enjoy it. If it ceases to be fun, I don't think I'd do it. For me my voice is very close to my soul. When I'm feeling well about myself, I sing well."

References: Hi Fi/Mus Am 33:6+ Mr '83 por; NY Times II p23+ F 26 '84 por; Who's Who in Opera, 1976; Who's Who in the World, 1982-83

## Hale, Clara

*Apr. 1, 1905– Social activist. Address: Hale House, 154 W. 122d St., New York City, N.Y. 10027*

In his State of the Union address in February 1985, President Ronald Reagan cited Clara Hale as "a true American hero." In so doing, the President called to national attention Hale House, the unique Harlem facility where Mother Hale, as everyone who knows her calls her, cares for babies born to mothers addicted to heroin, methadone, cocaine, and other hard drugs. Since 1969 Mother Hale has taken in 500 children born with congenital addictions and nursed them through the pains of withdrawal. With rare exceptions, the children at Hale House are ultimately returned to their mothers, who meanwhile have undergone rehabilitation from drugs.

At least 5,000 drug-addicted infants are born in the United States each year—almost half of them in the metropolitan New York City area—and Hale House is the only facility in the country that cares for and treats those innocent victims of maternal drug abuse. The house is located in central Harlem in New York City, where its residential program is carried out in a five-story brownstone at 154 West 122d Street. The administrative offices, at 68 Edgecombe Avenue, are directed by Mother Hale's daughter, Lorraine R. Hale, who has a Ph.D. de-

*Clara Hale*

didn't want to go home. So what started as day care ended up being fulltime. The parents would see the children on weekends."

In addition to caring for the children of women who went off to work as live-in maids, Clara Hale began to take in foster children, wards of the city, which paid her two dollars a week per child. For twenty-seven years her five-room walk-up apartment on West 146th Street in Harlem was home for seven or eight foster children at a time. "My daughter says she was almost sixteen before she realized all these other kids weren't her real sisters and brothers," Mrs. Hale told Seligson. "Everyone called me 'Mommy.' I took care of forty of them like that. They're now all grown up. They're doctors, lawyers, everything. Almost all of them stay in touch. I have about sixty grandchildren."

In 1968 Clara Hale, feeling it was time for her to "just kinda take it easy," retired. The retirement was brief. One day in 1969 Lorraine Hale encountered a young woman heroin addict nodding off in a Harlem park with a two-month-old baby girl falling from her arms. Rousing the woman, she gave her Clara Hale's address as a place "where you can get help." "My mother has always been committed to the belief that there is a little bit of God in every person," Lorraine told Irene Verag of *Newsday* (January 29, 1985). "She feels it is her responsibility to respect and honor everyone. I knew she wouldn't turn that baby away."

The next day the young woman arrived with her baby at Clara Hale's door. "Before I knew it," Mother Hale recalled for Irene Verag, "every pregnant addict in Harlem knew about the crazy lady who would give her baby a home." Within two months, she was caring for twenty-two addicted babies packed wall-to-wall in cribs in her apartment. Working overtime or at two jobs, her daughter, Lorraine, and her sons, Nathan (a certified public accountant) and Kenneth, provided the sole financial support for the operation for a year and a half. At the behest of Percy Sutton, then the president of the borough of Manhattan, New York City began funding the project in the early 1970s. The present annual funding of $190,000 (70 percent of which is federal, 15 city, and 15 state) is channeled through the New York City Department of Social Services for Children, which monitors Hale House. An additional $30,000 comes from private gifts. The best-known and most generous of the private benefactors coming to Mother Hale's aid was the late rock star John Lennon. He contributed $20,000 in 1978, and the John Lennon Spirit Foundation, directed by Lennon's widow, Yoko Ono, continued to send Mother Hale a $20,000 check annually after Lennon's murder in 1979.

In addition to expediting official funding for Mother Hale's work, Percy Sutton helped to begin the search for a house that would suit her needs. A vacant five-story brownstone at 154 West 122d Street was selected; gutted and rebuilt with a federal grant, it opened as Hale House in 1975. The first floor of the impeccably maintained, cheerfully decorated house comprises a kitchen, a dining

gree in child development. "In an age of cynicism and immunity to human despair," Lorraine Hale has said, "it may sound corny to say that Mother Hale's 'secret ingredient' has been her ability to convey love and concern to each of these infants while helping their afflicted mothers break the cycle of shame, guilt, and drug-dependency which almost destroyed them."

The youngest of four children, Clara Hale was born Clara McBride in Philadelphia, Pennsylvania on April 1, 1905. Her father died during her infancy and her mother supported the family by taking in boarders and by cooking. She credits her mother with giving her "the foundation for all [she has] done," teaching her "to love people," "be proud" of herself, and "always look people in the eyes." After graduating from high school in Philadelphia, she married Thomas Hale and moved with him to New York City, where he opened his own floor-waxing business. "He didn't make enough money," Mother Hale recalled in an interview with Tom Seligson for the syndicated Sunday supplement *Parade* (November 18, 1984), "so I did domestic work at night, cleaning theatres. I was at Loew's about four years."

When Clara Hale was only twenty-seven, her husband died of cancer, leaving her to raise alone her two natural children, Lorraine, then six, and Nathan, then five, and her adopted son, Kenneth, then two. To make ends meet, she doubled her domestic work for several years, cleaning homes by day and theatres by night, but she was unhappy with that arrangement because it meant leaving her children alone. "So I began caring for other people's children during the day," she recounted to Tom Seligson. "The parents paid me. I didn't make a whole lot, but I wasn't starving. And the kids must've liked it because once they got there, they

room, and a room for play and preschool activities. Much of the wall space in the dining room is mirrored, to encourage the children to "walk with their heads up, to have pride in themselves." "I want my kids . . . ," Mother Hale has explained, "when they pass by these mirrors [to] see themselves and say to themselves that they look nice." The second floor of Hale House is a nursery for detoxified babies. New arrivals, usually about ten days old, stay with Mother Hale in her bedroom on the third floor during their period of withdrawal. For weeks, the drug-addicted infants suffer from stiff legs and backs, diarrhea, and vomiting, and they often manifest their need for drugs by inflicting bloody scratches on themselves as well as crying inconsolably.

A study conducted by the New York City Department of Health estimated that 2,290 of the 300,000 children born in the city between 1979 and 1981 were born chemical-dependent, but only two programs were concerned with the multigenerational drug problem. One was the state-funded New York Medical College Pregnant Addicts and Addicted Mothers Program, with its health counseling and supervision services. The other was Hale House. As Mary Ann Giordano pointed out in the New York Daily News (November 14, 1983), "Only Hale House takes these children in after birth, cares for them through the withdrawal process, and raises them until their mothers complete a drug-treatment program—or simply decide they are ready to take their children back."

President Ronald Reagan, who admires Mother Hale's work and shares her philosophy that "what you have to do, you do" without "expecting something that the city or someone owes you," invited her to be present when he gave his State of the Union address before Congress on February 6, 1985. "When the President called, I was sick, but I went anyway," she later said. "I wanted the kids to see it and know it. . . . The doctor said I shouldn't go, I couldn't travel, [I] might have a stroke. . . . But I told him, when the President calls, I go. . . . I'm an American." Mother Hale was sitting near the First Lady, Nancy Reagan, in the visitors' gallery of the House of Representatives when the President cited her as "a true American hero." The citation was greeted with a standing ovation from the spectators, including all of the members of Congress, the Supreme Court, and the cabinet. On February 7, 1985, the day after the State of the Union address, Mother Hale visited President Reagan in the Oval Office of the White House, where the President told her that her work was "an inspiration for our people."

The other person cited by President Reagan in his State of the Union address was Jean Nguyen, the first West Point female cadet of Vietnamese descent. Kathleen Jamieson, a professor of communications at the University of Maryland, saw the President, in his customary "skillful" way, using both women as "rhetorical figures." Miss Jamieson explained, as quoted by Elizabeth Kastor in the Washington Post (February 8, 1985): "What he's done is get the Democrats in Congress to stand in applause. . . . The people he cites tend to be persons who are not generally considered to be part of his natural constituency. When he smiles up and Hale smiles and says 'Thank you' to Reagan, it short-circuits all you ever heard that says Reagan has not helped blacks."

Whatever cynical interpretation others might put on the presidential citation, Clara Hale and her daughter welcomed the national attention it brought to Hale House. Back on 122d Street, Mother Hale told reporters of the surge of phone calls coming in with offers of support from around the country. "I am not begging anybody [for] anything," she said. "But I tell them the circumstances." Specifically, she told the prospective supporters of her regret in having to turn away half of those applying to Hale House and of her need for a larger site. The site she had in mind was a "double house" on 122d Street at Adam Clayton Powell Jr. Boulevard. "Right now the house is the most important thing. Get the house and we will fix it up and everything else will be all right."

The Hales's second priority in seeking more space is to create a residential facility where reunited mothers and children who have successfully undergone treatment may live together under Hale House supervision and care for at least a year before resuming their independent lives. Lorraine Hale is also in the process of developing a research facility containing up-to-date medical, psychological, and social-work data both for Hale House's use and for that of other inner-city agencies across the country. Miss Hale wants Hale House "to become an institution" because she doesn't "want it to die" with her and her mother. "That's why we're bringing in people who can work independently of Mother and me," she has explained. "Of course, our real dream is to expand. We'd like to open Hale Houses all across the country, run by people we could train. There's such a need."

In overseeing the administrative details of Hale House, Lorraine Hale leaves her mother free to care for the children. Mother Hale has trained seven child-care workers and three sleep-in aides to assist and spell her in her job, which is, in her words, "just to love the children." Other staff members include a house parent, a social worker, a teacher, a cook, and a maintenance worker, all of whom interact with the children. A part-time health staff provides medical and dental care in conjunction with a local clinic, and volunteers assist in providing recreational activities. The devoted staff works for an average of $175 a week.

Unless and until plans for expansion go through, the number of children at Hale House at any one time is limited by the city government to fifteen, most of whom are referred by police, clergy, and hospital or social workers and admitted without regard to race, religion, or sex. They range in age from ten days to four years. Mother Hale awakes each morning in time to give six o'clock bottles to the several drug-addicted infants who share her royal-blue bedroom. She cleans up their vomit, changes their diapers, feeds them lunch and dinner, and naps when they do. When they cry in the agony of withdrawal, she walks the floor with them, talks to them, and sings to them, but gives them no medicine, not even aspirin. "I don't want them to get in any habits," she has explained, "so they go cold turkey." She rocks them and waits, knowing that "one day they'll smile" at her.

After several weeks or months, when withdrawal is complete and the infants can sleep peacefully through the night, they are moved from Mother Hale's bedroom to the floor below, where the child-care workers Mother Hale has trained watch over them until their mothers can take them home. Older children share rooms on the fourth floor. While undergoing rehabilitation (usually for eighteen months), the mothers must visit their children regularly at the house, which is "not an orphanage," as Mother Hale often reminds people. The aim is to reunite parents and children, and adoption is a last and only rare resort. Only twelve of the 500 children who have lived at Hale House during its sixteen years of existence have been put up for adoption. "When we can send a child back to his family," Lorraine Hale told a reporter for the *New York Times* (March 12, 1984), "that's a precious moment for me."

Clara Hale is short and slight and looks younger than her years. "Despite her thin white hair," Tom Seligson wrote in *Parade*, "her face is barely lined,

and her eyes are bright. She looks right at you when she talks, her voice warm and confident. Short and straight-backed, she moves slowly and nimbly." When Seligson asked Lorraine Hale if her mother ever relaxes, he was told: "Only when we get her away from here. And I mean totally away. I live up in Scarsdale [about 10 miles from Manhattan], and my mother won't even come visit. She says it's too quiet. I try to send her on trips twice a year. She just came back from Israel."

Mother Hale believes that "everyone comes into this world to do something" and that she has "found what [she] was meant to do." "I love children and I love caring for them," she has said. "That is what the Lord meant me to do." Her generosity is not limited to children, however. According to her daughter, "Anybody can come to my mother for a handout, and she'll give it. She gets paid a salary and she gives it all away. We finally got her to open a checking account at the age of seventy-six. Every month, I write thirty envelopes to different causes she supports." For "her devotion to suffering children and their parents" Clara Hale was awarded an honorary doctorate in humane letters by the John Jay College of Criminal Justice in June 1985.

References: N Y Daily News p21 N 13 '83 por, p29 N 14 '83, p15 N 15 '83 por, p2+ F 10 '85 pors; Newsday p1+ Ja 29 '85 pors; People 21:211+ Mr 5 '84 pors; Read Digest 125:49+ S '84 por; Washington Post C p1+ F 8 '85

## Hamilton, Scott

*Aug. 28, 1958– Skater. Address: b. c/o Ice Capades, 4 Pennsylvania Plaza, New York City, N.Y. 10001*

Throughout the 1970s men's figure skating was dominated by such balletic performers as John Curry and Robin Cousins, the gold medalists at, respectively, the 1976 and 1980 Winter Olympics, whose grace and purity of line rivaled those of a premier danseur. Since 1981, however, the preeminent skater internationally, with eight consecutive national and world titles to his credit, has been Scott Hamilton, a pint-sized powerhouse known for his extraordinary speed and virtuoso stunts, among them a battery of triple jumps. Contending that figure skating is a sport rather than an art form, the deceptively fragile-looking Hamilton has created for himself surprisingly athletic free-skating routines in an energetic, "apple pies and Chevrolets" style, to use his words, that have won over audiences and judges alike. His gold medal in men's figure skating at the 1984 Winter Olympics was the first for an American since David Jenkins took that honor in 1960.

Six weeks after his birth on August 28, 1958, Scott Hamilton was adopted by Ernest and Dorothy Hamilton, professors of, respectively, biology and

family relations at Bowling Green [Ohio] State University. He has an older sister, Susan, and a younger brother, Steven, who is also adopted. When he was about two, Scott contracted a mysterious illness that caused him to stop growing. Tests indicated that the boy was, in effect, suffering from malnutrition because his body was not digesting and absorbing food properly, but his physicians were at a loss as to how to correct the condition. Although bedridden for the better part of the next few years, Scott "never really felt sick," as he recalled to Jane Leavy of the *Washington Post* (January 18, 1984). He "just felt short."

Throughout his childhood, Scott Hamilton was in and out of hospitals as a series of doctors prescribed a variety of treatments and special diets without success. Finally, after his illness was mistakenly diagnosed as cystic fibrosis, and he was given just six months to live, the Hamiltons took their son, then eight years old, to the Boston Children's Hospital in Boston, Massachusetts, where a team of specialists identified his ailment as Schwachmann's syndrome—paralysis, or as in Hamilton's case, partial paralysis of the intestinal tract—complicated by severe respiratory problems. Armed with a vitamin-enriched, high-protein diet plan and a moderate exercise program, Hamilton returned to his home in Bowling Green. Within a few months his condition stabilized, and he felt well enough to accompany his sister on an ice-skating outing. "Scotty went along to watch . . . ," Ernest Hamilton told Bob Ottum in an interview for *Sports Illustrated* (February 6, 1984). "He had a feeding tube in place; it went to his stomach. One end of it came out his nose, and when he wasn't using it, we taped it out of the way behind one ear. This frail little kid with the tube running across his cheek turned and said, 'You know, I think I'd like to try skating.'"

Almost from the beginning, Hamilton skated with confidence and uncommon speed. Reveling in his apparent natural ability and in the cool, humid atmosphere of the ice rink, which seemed to soothe his lungs, he progressed rapidly. At the suggestion of the rink's teaching pros, he signed up for regular lessons and joined the ice hockey team at the local elementary school that he attended. Within six months of his stepping out on the ice for the first time, he was skating in local and regional "sub-juvenile" competitions. More important, within one year his illness disappeared, and he began growing again, although he would always be considerably smaller than his peers. Hamilton's doctors attributed his miraculous recovery to the beneficial effects of intense physical activity in the cold atmosphere of the rink.

When he was thirteen, Hamilton left home to live and train with Pierre Brunet, the former Olympic gold medalist and noted figure skating coach at the Wagon Wheel Figure Skating Club in Rockton, Illinois. His training over the next few years took him to so many parts of the country that his high-school education was sporadic at best, and in his senior year alone, he attended three different schools. Following his graduation in 1976, Hamilton abruptly decided to quit competitive skating and enroll at Bowling Green State University. "My folks had spent all the money they could possibly afford to keep me going," he explained to Bob Ottum. But before he began classes, an anonymous, wealthy couple, who had financially supported other potential Olympic medalists, volunteered to sponsor Hamilton. Elated, the skater immediately resumed training, first with Carlo Fassi, a respected teacher of school figures in Denver, Colorado, then with Don Laws, a specialist in free skating in Philadelphia, Pennsylvania and, later, Denver.

Despite what he has called his "outrageous ambition," Hamilton was at the time rather lackadaisical about his training regimen, and even in competitions, he was more apt to be perfunctory than letter-perfect. "I just felt the off-ice stuff was more important than on-ice things," he explained to Jane Leavy. At the United States national figure skating contest early in 1977, for example, he turned in a slipshod, uninspiring performance and finished a disappointing ninth. His mother's death of cancer shortly after that profoundly affected his outlook on life and his attitude toward skating. "Everything I do is pretty much for my mom," he told Miss Leavy. "She gave and gave and gave and sacrificed and sacrificed and really I gave nothing in return." After her death, he went on, "I realized I have a responsibility to do what I'm doing now in a way that's almost obsessed."

Over the next several years, Hamilton's renewed dedication paid off in steadily improving rankings in the national championships. When one skating judge pointedly told him that he would never be taken seriously in international competition because of his diminutive size, he immediately changed his jumping style in order to "create an illusion" of height on the ice. He also worked on increasing his extension and perfecting his line. By 1980 he was good enough to capture third place in the national competition and thus win a berth on the United States Olympic figure skating squad. In recognition of his perseverance in the face of seemingly insurmountable obstacles, the captains of the American teams elected him to carry the United States flag and lead the entire troupe into the arena in the opening-day ceremonies of the 1980 Winter Games at Lake Placid, New York.

Hamilton's solid fifth-place finishes at the 1980 Olympics and at the world championship a few weeks later put him in a good position for an international title, particularly after the then world leaders, among them Robin Cousins, turned professional. He entered the 1981 world competition fresh from his triumph at the national medal event in San Diego, California, where he had taken the top prize with relative ease. At the "worlds," as the international meet is popularly known, in Hartford, Connecticut in March 1981, the skater got off to a slow start and stood in third place going into the third and final round of the tournament—the five-minute free-skating program, which counts for 50 percent of the overall score.

Opening his program with a perfectly executed triple lutz, Hamilton skated his difficult routine with dazzling flair. Not even a spill while running on the ice marred his performance in the eyes of the nine judges, who awarded him scores of 5.8 and 5.9 (out of a possible 6.0) for technical merit and 5.7 to 5.9 for artistic impression. Coupled with his scores for the compulsory school figures and the short program, the total was more than enough for him to overtake fellow countryman David Santee and Igor Bobrin of the Soviet Union, who finished second and third, respectively, and win the title. He was only the second American to win the men's championship since 1970. Later in the year, Hamilton took an individual gold medal at the first annual Skate America tournament, an international competition organized by the United States Figure Skating Association, at Lake Placid. The back-to-back titles undoubtedly contributed to his being voted Male Athlete of the Year by the United States Olympic Committee.

Determined to protect his national and world championships, for the next three years Hamilton practiced eight hours a day, six days a week under the watchful eye of Don Laws at the Colorado Ice Arena in Denver. His punishing training regimen also included regular workouts at a local gym. He devoted a considerable amount of time to devising original free-skating programs, too. In 1982, for example, he collaborated with Laws and dancer Ricky Harris on a new routine set to a medley of big-band–era tunes that was at the same time technically taxing and engagingly whimsical. "Skating is the only sport in which your individual personality can come out," he explained to Melinda Stivers Leach in an interview for the Christian Science Monitor (December 14, 1982). "It's . . . not just technical perfection. It involves how you display yourself and how you impress an audience."

Impressing the judges as well as his audiences with daring free-skating programs that featured multiple triple jumps, Scott Hamilton held on to his national and world titles in 1982 and 1983. At the 1983 world championship, he simply overwhelmed his opposition with his explosive free skating, tossing off no fewer than six triple jumps, including a triple lutz–triple toe loop combination. His virtually flawless execution of the demanding routine earned him a raft of 5.8s and 5.9s, among them a rare 5.9 from the Soviet judge for artistic impression. His only challengers, Norbert Schramm of the Federal Republic of Germany and Canada's Brian Orser, finished well behind Hamilton in second and third place.

It was at the 1983 world tournament that Hamilton unveiled his unorthodox new costume—a sleek, form-fitting one-piece suit similar to those worn by speed skaters. There were no sequins or beads—none of the "glitz and glitter" that made some of his fellow contestants look like, in his words, "a Las Vegas lounge act." The streamlined costume was just part of his campaign to change the image of the male figure skater. "There's been too much emphasis on ballet," he told Bob Ottum for the Sports Illustrated profile. "Too much artistry by graceful men in jeweled costumes. I don't hate spangles; they just get to be too much. At the end of a performance, people shouldn't swoon.

They should look upon it as a sporting event." To that end, he began consciously to stress the prescribed stunts and technical figures over the artistic elements in his free-skating routines.

In preparation for the 1984 Winter Olympics, Hamilton created a new routine designed to showcase the power of his jumps, the blinding speed of his spins, and the intricacy of his straight-line footwork. After spending hours listening to musical selections, he finally chose the overture to George Duke's futuristic Guardian of Light for the attention-grabbing opening section of triple jumps and fleet-footed patterns; Hiroshima's haunting "Third Generation" for the slower middle section of combinations and spins; and modern jazz for the slam-bang finale of Russian split jumps, double axels and salchows, ending in a blurring scratch spin. "The secret is that the music sort of gets under your seat . . . ," he said, in outlining his program to Bob Ottum. "Open with some technical stuff to show them you're proficient, and then hit them with some drama to get their approval. Then put in an ominous mood. Without realizing it, they're out of their seats. Then they're back in. Then out. And back again. If I do a triple jump, they go 'yea.' But if I follow that up immediately with another triple, they all rise and go 'yea!'" When Hamilton presented his new free-skating program for the first time, at the United States national championship early in 1984, it won him five 5.9s and four perfect 6.0s for artistic impression. No competitor had ever before received so many perfect marks at the national tournament.

As the winner of fifteen straight championships since 1980, Scott Hamilton was heavily favored to take the gold medal in men's figure skating at the 1984 Winter Olympics in Sarajevo, Yugoslavia, and after achieving a first-place finish in the school-figures segment of the competition, which accounts for 30 percent of the final point tally, he seemed to be well on his way to the title. But in the two-minute short program of seven required elements, which by his own admission has never been "[his] event," he was outpointed by Brian Orser. With nothing to lose, Orser, a dynamic free skater, pulled out all the stops in his final routine, hitting all five triple jumps. His caution-to-the-winds performance earned him seven 5.9s and two 5.8s for technical merit.

Following Orser onto the ice, Hamilton began his program well enough, with a spot-on triple lutz. Then, inexplicably, he "started losing the edge," as he put it. Like Orser, he had planned to use the prescribed limit of five triple jumps—a triple lutz, a triple flip, a triple toe loop in combination with a double loop, a triple toe walley, and a triple salchow. He succeeded in only three of the five and didn't even attempt the triple flip. Moreover, knowledgeable observers noticed that he appeared to be off-balance and that his axis on the jumps was tilted rather than upright. His tentative and uncharacteristically subdued performance brought him his lowest marks for technical merit in some years. Although his scores for artistic impression were considerably higher, he ended up in second place in the free-skating segment, with only six 5.9s to Orser's eleven. Still, when computed with his scores from the other two events, it was enough to win the gold medal. Brian Orser was awarded the silver medal and Jozef Sabovtchik of Czechoslovakia, the bronze. After taking the traditional victory lap, Hamilton, holding high a large American flag borrowed from a rink-side spectator, led his fellow medalists on another circuit of Zetra Arena to thunderous applause.

At a post-competition press conference, an admittedly embarrassed Hamilton told reporters, as quoted in the Chicago Tribune (February 17, 1984), "It wasn't pretty, but I did it. All the pressure got to me, I guess. I felt like I was skating with twenty-pound weights on my shoulders. I really wanted this night to be something special. I wanted it to be the most memorable program of my life, and it was." In response to newsmen's questions, he acknowledged that he had been taking antibiotics to cure a persistent ear infection, but he made no excuses for his below-average performance. Feeling that he still had "something to prove," Hamilton took some consolation in his stunning victory at the world championships in Ottawa, Canada a month later. Shortly thereafter, he announced his retirement from amateur skating competition.

Deluged with million-dollar–plus contracts from all the major ice shows and an enticing offer to head his own touring company, Hamilton decided to sign on with the Ice Capades. He has been on the road with the troupe since August 1984, skating twice at each performance. Although he misses the challenge of competition and the "feeling of accomplishment" that comes with a victory, he takes pleasure in performing before the Ice Capades' enthusiastic, sell-out crowds. "It's not the same high-high [as winning a title], but it's a consistent fix, an audience fix," he told Malcolm Moran of the New York Times (January 26, 1985). "It's like a disease. You like being in front of them, and you like showing off and you like the applause. It's a feeling of acceptance."

Lithe and muscular, blue-eyed, blond-haired Scott Hamilton stands five feet three-and-one-half inches tall and weighs 115 pounds. As he explained to Frank Litsky, who spoke to him for a New York Times (March 7, 1983) profile, his size is "perfect" for skating: "I have a lower center of balance. I don't have as much body to adjust when I make a mistake, and not as much body to get tired." The only drawback to his short stature, as he tells it, is having to shop for clothes in the boys' department, where the selection is often limited to blazers that have a "little duckie on the pocket." Hamilton's self-deprecating sense of humor and friendly, easygoing manner have made him the most popular figure skating champion in decades, especially among younger skaters, to whom he is unfailingly generous and helpful. In his spare time, Hamilton enjoys listening to music and attending Denver Broncos football games. Reflecting on his future, he told Bob Ottum, "Physically, you can only do

this stuff so long. It's a great destroyer of bodies. And then, too, you can only hang on publicly as long as the people want to see you in action. You've got to balance these factors carefully. So what I want to do is get the most out of these few years I've got coming." The skater makes his home in Denver.

References: N Y Times C p7 Mr 7 '83 pors; Sports Illus 54:68+ Mr 16 '81 por, 58:58+ Mr 21 '83 por, 60:88+ F 6 '84 pors; Washington Post D p1+ Ja 18 '84 por; Steere, Michael. Scott Hamilton (1985)

## Havel, Václav

(hä´ vel vä´ tsläv)

Oct. 5, 1936– Czechoslovakian playwright; poet; essayist. Address: c/o Robert Lantz, The Lantz Office Inc., 114 E. 55th St., New York City, N. Y. 10022

Probably no Czech playwright since Karel Čapek has had a national and international impact comparable to that of the brave dissident and human-rights champion Václav Havel. Delighting in wordplay, Havel began writing absurdist explorations of the power of language during the short period of relative freedom artists enjoyed in Czechoslovakia in the 1960s. His full-length play The Memorandum, a satire on official gibberish, is generally regarded as his best of that period. The most important of his later, samizdat works are the three one-act grimly ironic plays Interview, A Private View, and Protest, all of which are about the rationalizations of conformists trying to reconcile with conscience their selfish collusion with an oppressive system. A political "agnostic," Havel never "consciously decided to become a dissident." "We just happened to," he has explained. "We don't know how. And we started landing in jails—we also don't know how. We just did some things that seemed the decent things to do."

Václav Havel was born on October 5, 1936 in Prague, Czechoslovakia to Václav M. and Božena (Vavrečková) Havel. His father was a very wealthy man, a prominent restaurateur and the owner of extensive real estate in the commercial center of Prague. An uncle owned the Barandov studios, the dominant motion-picture company in Czechoslovakia. When the Communist government nationalized business and industry in 1948, the father's restaurant and properties were confiscated; he became an office clerk, and his wife went to work as a tour guide.

As an officially despised, downgraded scion of the *haute bourgeoisie* in a "people's republic," Václav Havel was denied easy access to an education beyond elementary school. While doing menial work days in a chemical laboratory, he continued his schooling nights, completing secondary school and then studying successively at a technical college and at the Prague Academy of the Arts. At the age of nineteen he began publishing critical essays, the most important of which was a monograph on the Czech writer and painter Josef Čapek, the older brother of the more famous Karel Čapek, the playwright, novelist, and essayist. At first torn between fiction and theatre, Havel finally decided, "Drama for me is the better genre . . . , not novels or short stories." He did not rule out verse, however, and he went on to write concrete poetry in addition to his plays and occasional essays.

After doing his compulsory military service, in the late 1950s, Havel worked for a year as a stagehand with a theatrical company known as Divadlo ABC before joining Divadlo na Zábradlí, the Theatre on the Balustrade, an avant-garde troupe founded in 1958 by Ivan Vyskočil. Under the direction of Vyskočil's successor, Jan Grossman, the Theatre on the Balustrade became the leading dramatic ensemble in Prague during the political thaw that began modestly in 1962 and reached its peak in 1968. Its repertoire included such Czech works as dramatizations of Jaroslav Hašek's novel *The Good Soldier Schweik* and Franz Kafka's novel *The Trial* in addition to translations from the foreign theatre of the absurd, including Samuel Beckett's *Waiting for Godot* and Eugene Ionesco's *The Lesson* and *The Bald Soprano*.

Havel joined the Theatre on the Balustrade as a stagehand and electrician and went on to become, successively, secretary, manuscript reader, and dramaturge, or literary manager and resident playwright. His first play was *Hitchhiking* (*Autostop*), a satire written in collaboration with Ivan Vyskočil that had its premiere at the Theatre on the Balustrade in 1961. His first solo play was *The Garden Party* (*Zahradní slavnost*). First staged at the Theatre on the Balustrade in 1963, *The Gar-*den *Party* was subsequently translated into all of the major European languages. The English-language version is by Vera Blackwell, the Czech emigré and friend who has translated, impeccably, all of Havel's plays into English.

*The Garden Party* is a four-act play set in the Prague of 1963, when the nascent, and ultimately aborted, transition from totalitarianism to limited liberalism was running into linguistic impasses and, thus, into vicious logical circles. The play's apparent protagonist is Hugo Pludek, an ambitious young man who is a sort of idiot savant, good at two things: playing chess and parroting political buzz words and platitudes; so brilliant is his mimicry of officialese, he rises quickly in a government faced with a political problem based on a linguistic one. The real hero of *The Garden Party*, as Jan Grossman observed, is "cliché": "Man does not use cliché; cliché uses man. Cliché . . . causes, advances, and complicates the plot, determining human action and, deviating further and further from our given reality, creating its own." At the sacrifice of his humanity and individuality, Pludek becomes a linguistic automaton, whose brilliant mouthing of bureaucratic lingo wins him the twin posts of director of the old Office of Liquidation and of the new Office of Inauguration. The latter is intended to dissolve and replace the former, but bureaucrats in the Office of Liquidation insist that their office technically cannot be liquidated except by itself—an impossibility because, once the liquidation were to begin, the office would no longer exist and the job could not be completed. The solution is the creation of a new, bigger bureaucratic monster, the Central Office for Inauguration and Liquidation.

Havel's best-known and most performed play, *The Memorandum* (*Vyrozumění*), is also his most conscientious. Begun in 1960, it was five years in the writing and did not reach production at the Theatre on the Balustrade until 1965. In it, the theme of *The Garden Party* was extended beyond the dehumanizing power of piecemeal words and phrases to a view of language as a total ideological web—in Havel's words, a "kind of dictatorship," made so by "the people who are for this language" for the sake of their own careers.

Although Havel intended *The Memorandum* as a political metaphor "not only about socialism or Communism" but "about all systems that destroy human personality," it is difficult not to read it as a parody of the Stalinization and de-Stalinization processes. The twelve-scene play is set in a vast business enterprise, a bureaucracy that obviously represents politico-social systems that serve, not society, but themselves. It opens with Josef Gross, the managing director of the company, reading aloud the memo of the title, a document he cannot fathom because it is written in Ptydepe, an artificial "scientific" language newly imposed by nefarious forces seizing control of the company, ostensibly for "precision" in inter-office communications, although Ptydepe makes such communication virtually impossible. All employees accept the language without complaint, lest they be judged "reactionary." The catch is that Gross cannot request a translation of the message except in Ptydepe itself. Because of his incompetence, he is reduced in rank to "staff watcher," or internal spy, and he regains his executive position only after Maria, a sympathetic office typist, comes to his aid and translates the memo, which turns out to be a scathing critique of Ptydepe. The group that seized power through the language leads the campaign against it, imposing a new, antithetical gibberish, known as Chorukor. The chastened Gross now goes along, and when Maria, who has been dismissed, comes to him for support he mouths high humanitarian concerns and ethical standards—and turns his back on her for having broken the rules.

Tom Stoppard, the Czech-born English-language playwright, who discovered Havel's work in 1967 and has since become a good friend of his, wrote in his introduction to the Grove Press edition of *The Memorandum* (1980) that he considers that play of Havel's "the one that best shows off the hallmarks of his gift: the fascination with language; the invention of an absurd society raised only a notch or two above the normal world of state bureaucracy . . . , and, not least, the playfulness with which it is done, the almost gentle refusal to indulge a sense of grievance, the utter lack of righteousness or petulance or bile." "Here," Stoppard concluded, "one relishes the joyous freedom of Havel's imagination. In 1965 joy and freedom seemed possible." *The Garden Party* and *The Memorandum* were included in Havel's collection *Protokoly* ("Protocols," 1966), along with two essays on the theatre and some of his poetry.

Havel's sardonic comedy *The Increased Difficulty of Concentration* (*Ztížená možnost soustředění*), first produced at the Theatre on the Balustrade in April 1968, reaches beyond satire about totalitarian bureaucracies to include comment on the universal themes of alienation, loss of communication, and fragmented consciousness. The theme of fragmentation is underscored by the cubistic structure of the plot, which spirals repetitively, playing events back, like a film rewinding, and ending where it began. The protagonist is Edouard Huml, a social scientist who, as the play opens, is dictating an essay on human values. His professorial words are counterpointed by the moral and emotional chaos of his private life, in which he seeks escape from a dehumanized society by indulging in romantic excess. What makes concentration increasingly difficult for him are the demands of his wife, his mistress, and his secretary. A fourth woman, an interrogator, enters the picture with Puzak, a computer that is programmed to analyze Huml as a "random sample." In trying to measure and classify Huml's identity, Puzak is stymied, and comes up, understandably, with a zero. The moral of the play, stated by Huml at the beginning and reiterated by him at the end, is an affirmation of the human heart's uncomputable motivations, especially its need for needs.

The thaw within the Communist party in Czechoslovakia in the 1960s was brought about under the leadership of two members of the Slovakian national minority, Alexander Dubček and Gustav Husák. Dubček, the more staunchly liberal of the two, led the opposition to the regime of Antonin Novotný and in January 1968 forced the resignation of Novotný and replaced him as party first secretary and premier. During his brief term, Dubček introduced many reforms, relaxing censorship, placing liberal Communists in high state positions, beginning the pursuit of an independent foreign policy, and promising a gradual democratization of the system.

During the accelerated reform movement of 1968, Havel, whose passport had previously been confiscated, had it restored to him. In April and May 1968 he visited the United States on the occasion of the first American production of *The Memorandum*, by Joseph Papp's Public Theatre in New York City. That production received the Obie Award for the best Off-Broadway foreign play of 1967-68, and a production of *The Increased Difficulty of Concentration* at the Forum of the Repertory Theatre of Lincoln Center in New York City two seasons later was similarly honored. To Edith Oliver of the *New Yorker*, *The Memorandum* "seemed acute and entertaining" and *The Increased Difficulty of Concentration* "whimsical, redundant, and laden with weighty irony" but "worth putting on." Writing in the *Nation* (December 22, 1969), Harold Clurman described *The Increased Difficulty of Concentration* as "a farce of no great subtlety [that means] something vital to the Czech citizen" and that "for us . . . offers sidelights on contemporary 'history' agreeably mixed with bedroom imbroglio."

Alarmed at the course of events under Dubček, the Soviet Union, along with other Warsaw Pact armies, invaded Czechoslovakia in August 1968. Immediately following the invasion, Havel made a radio broadcast from an underground station, monitored by Radio Free Europe in Munich, in which he addressed to Western intellectuals "in the name of all Czech and Slovak writers . . . an urgent plea for support." He also addressed groups of Czech artists and workers, exhorting them to unite in the cause of human rights, and he attracted around him a dedicated cell of theatre people and others, no more than a dozen in all, committed to working as best they could to protest the repression.

Under Soviet pressure, Dubček agreed to cancel his reforms, but he was replaced anyway with the more pliable (in the Soviet view) Husák, who resolidified Czechoslovakia's ties with the Soviet Union and reimposed strong party control over Czech political and economic life. The production of Havel's plays and the publication of his writings were banned and his passport was permanently confiscated. Because of his resistance to the repression and his human-rights advocacy, he was during the 1970s repeatedly arrested, jailed twice, and forced to earn his livelihood by doing menial work, stacking barrels in a brewery. His lifestyle, once almost dandyish, was downgraded radically.

In his condition of persecution, Havel "had to rethink and reconsider his way of writing plays, and he underwent a crisis of creativity," as Walter Schamschula pointed out in his essay on Havel in *Fiction and Drama in Eastern and Southeastern Europe* (1980), edited by Henrik Birnbaum and Thomas Eckman. The first fruits of Havel's crise of creativity, written in the early 1970s, were two cerebral, didactic satires, *The Conspirators* and *The Mountain Hotel*. In *The Conspirators*, Havel used a cyclical structure to picture the history of the Communist revolution in Czechoslovakia, personified by four power-struggling public officials, as static, returning always where it was at the beginning.

*The Mountain Hotel* is set in an edifice of "windowless cages"—in Walter Schumschula's words, "Thomas Mann's Magic Mountain turned into a madhouse with no escape." The characters are holiday-makers who take turns remembering and forgetting the same sets of words, gestures, occurrences. As Marketa Goetz-Stankiewicz observed in her book *The Silenced Theatre* (1979), "Havel tried to make these occurrences the subject matter of the play, in order to find out 'to what extent they are capable—all on their own—to create meaning.' The themes of the disintegration of human identity and existential schizophrenia, which Havel has repeatedly called his main concerns, are obviously apparent again insofar as they can be expressed solely by these automatized occurrences."

Marketa Goetz-Stankiewicz went on to observe that the closer Havel's writing "reflects a situation he knows personally, the better he writes and the broader his appeal will be." In 1975 Havel returned to realism based on personal experience, writing two semi-autobiographical one-act plays, *Interview,* also known as *Audience,* and *A Private View,* also known as *The Vanishing Day* (*Vernissage*), which he and his group performed clandestinely, in private homes. The protagonist of both plays is a dissident artist named Ferdinand Vaněk, who confronts conformists who contribute to the official tyranny but pretend not to be part of the repression. In *Interview* Vaněk, who is working in a brewery, is approached by his boss with several unethical schemes. The most outrageous of the suggestions, all of which are rejected by Vaněk, is that he become a self-informer. The boss is tired of reporting on Vaněk to the secret police, and his idea is that Vaněk, being a writer, could more easily create acceptable reports on himself.

*A Private View* is an indictment of the hollowness of materialistic values. In that play Vaněk visits a conformist couple who, surrounded by creature comforts in their apartment, tell him he is foolish to continue living in his deprived state of rebellion. "As a comment on contemporary Czechoslovakia," Marketa Goetz-Stankiewicz observed, "it is certainly a fascinating document about a society, the official, constantly reiterated ideals, aims, and evaluations of which bear no re-

lation whatsoever to the value of an individual who thrives under this regime."

Following an amateur production of Havel's adaptation of *The Beggar's Opera* in 1975, even members of the audience became subject to police reprisal. In an open letter to First Secretary Husák during that year, Havel wrote: "Society can be enriched and cultivated only through self-knowledge, and the main instrument of society's self-knowledge is its culture. Where total control over society is sought, the first thing to be suppressed is its culture."

In January 1977 hundreds of Czech intellectuals and artists signed Charter 77, a manifesto protesting the failure of the Czechoslovakian Socialist Republic to abide by the Helsinki Covenant on Civil and Political Rights, to which it was a signatory. The official response was a wave of arrests, accompanied by the statement that "freedom of expression" had to be "consistent with the interests of the working people." As one of the Charter's three principal elected spokesmen, Havel was arrested for the fifth time and jailed for four months, until May 1977. The following October he was brought to trial on a new charge, "subversion of the Republic," for sending banned writings out of the country for publication abroad, and given a fourteen-month suspended sentence. In 1978 some dozen Chartists, including Havel, founded an offshoot of the Charter 77 movement known as the Committee for the Defense of the Unjustly Persecuted. The membership of the committee was arrested piecemeal during 1979. In October 1979 the Prague people's court convicted six of the dissidents, including Havel, on charges of "subversion" and contacts "with a foreign agent." Havel was sentenced to four-and-a-half years at hard labor.

Meanwhile, in the period between his two incarcerations, Havel had written a third one-act play—generally regarded as the best of the three—with the character Vaněk as hero. In *Protest,* Stanek, a successful television writer, a spineless sellout, wants the help of Vaněk and his human-rights group in the matter of a young man, the boyfriend of Stanek's daughter, who has been arrested for allegedly subversive remarks. After telling Vaněk how much he admires his integrity and courage, Stanek brings up the subject of the arrested young man. It so happens that Vaněk has in his briefcase a protest petition, already prepared, relating to the very case. Throughout the remainder of the play Stanek squirms his way out of signing the petition through doubletalk about "true ethicality" requiring that attention be paid to "relentless objective reflection" rather than "subjective inner feeling." His ultimate sophistry is the argument that for him to sign the petition and thus expose his liberalism would be a disservice to Vaněk and his dissident group.

Repeatedly mailed out of Czechoslovakia, complete copies of *Interview, A Private View,* and *Protest* ultimately reached the West. Reviewing a production of *Protest* at the Olivier Theatre in London, Benedict Nightingale of the *New Statesman*

(February 15, 1980) wrote: "*Protest* is a *samizdat* play dealing, like several of Havel's others, with those trying to reconcile their consciences with their privileges in Husák's Czechoslovakia; and, since its author is presently incarcerated for the monstrous crime of refusing to make any such accommodation himself, it's nice to be able to report that it is a particularly successful one. . . . Why doesn't some enterprising producer transform this into part of a Havel double or triple bill?"

One such enterprising producer was Joseph Papp, who brought the three Vaněk one-acters to his Public Theatre in New York City in the 1983–84 Off-Broadway season. Directed by Lee Grant, a woman especially empathic with Havel's plight because of her blacklisting as an actress during the McCarthy witch-hunt of the 1950s, the three plays were presented under the overall title *A Private View*. Edith Oliver of the *New Yorker* (December 5, 1983) found that Miss Grant maintained "the correct tone and the European Absurdist style from beginning to end." Although John Simon detected some "difficulties" with the plays—chiefly the problem of the playwright-protagonist necessarily emerging "as such a saint"—Simon observed in

*New York* (December 5, 1983) that *A Private View* "contains noble and harrowing truths that needed saying" and that the triple bill was "an act of justice as well as satisfaction."

Václav Havel and the former Olga Splíchalová were married in 1965. They have no children. During his last incarceration Havel fell seriously ill with pneumonia complicated by a lung abscess. Following an urgent appeal from the international intellectual community, his sentence was suspended in February 1983, ten months short of its completion. In November 1983 Vera Blackwell, Havel's translator, after speaking to the playwright by telephone from London, reported that he "was physically fit now" but "depressed." A volume of Havel's letters to his wife from prison, published in West Germany in 1984, is scheduled for publication in English translation by Alfred A. Knopf in 1986 under the title *Letters from Olga*.

References: *New Statesman* 105:16 Mr 18 '83 por; *N Y Post* p58 My 15 '68 por; *N Y Times* A p3 O 25 '79 por; *N Y Times Mag* p32+ N 12 '67; *Contemporary Authors* vol 104 (1982); *International Who's Who, 1985–86*; *World Authors 1970–75 (1980)*

---

## Hawkins, Paula (Fickes)

*Jan. 24, 1927– United States Senator from Florida. Address: b. Rm. 313 Hart Senate Office Bldg., Washington, D.C. 20510*

Political observers have been hard-pressed to pigeonhole Paula Hawkins, the outspoken and unpredictable freshman Republican senator from Florida. To some, she is a "rambunctious inspiration," to others, an "intellectual lightweight" less interested in issues than in images. The first woman to be elected to the United States Senate whose career was not based on her relationship to a husband or other male relative, Mrs. Hawkins brought to her post twenty years of experience in state government and Republican political organizations. Generally speaking, the senator, who won her seat in the Reagan landslide of 1980, is a conservative on economic issues and a moderate on some social issues. "[Voters] don't want specifics," she said, as quoted in the *New Republic* (October 25, 1980). "People are looking today for somebody that will shake it up. . . . That's all they want. They want a fighter."

The oldest of the four children of Paul B. and Leone (Staley) Fickes, Paula Hawkins was born Paula Fickes on January 24, 1927 in Salt Lake City, Utah. Her family moved frequently over the next few years, as Paul Fickes, a chief warrant officer in the United States Navy, was transferred from one naval base to another. "We sometimes were not in a community long enough to make friends," Paula Hawkins told Fred Grimm in an interview

for the *Washington Post* (June 2, 1985). Consequently, she was especially close to her two sisters, Carole and Karma, and her brother, Llewellen. After the father retired from the Navy in 1934 to accept a teaching position at the Georgia Institute of Technology, the family settled in Atlanta, and it was there that Paula Fickes spent most of her childhood and adolescence.

When her parents separated in 1944, Paula Fickes moved with her mother and siblings to Logan, Utah, where she completed her secondary education. Upon her graduation from Cache High School in nearby Richmond later in the same year, she turned down a scholarship to the University of Utah in Salt Lake City in favor of enrolling at Utah State University, which was nearer her home. She attended classes there for several years, but she did not complete the program and earn her bachelor's degree. As she explained to Elizabeth Bumiller in an interview for the *Washington Post* (December 2, 1980), "I just didn't settle down to a major. I never liked the rules they had." Meanwhile, at her mother's urging, she took secretarial courses so that she could, in her words, "earn a living." She eventually dropped out of college to take a job as secretary to Utah State's director of athletics.

On September 5, 1947 Paula Fickes married her high-school sweetheart, Walter Eugene Hawkins, and returned to Atlanta, where her husband studied electrical engineering while she worked as a model for local department stores and as a secretary. For the next twenty years, Paula Hawkins' life revolved around her husband, who built a successful career as an electronics engineer, and her three children, Genean, Kevin Brent, and Kelley Ann. A devout Mormon, she is committed to the concept of the nuclear family and that commitment has greatly influenced her political philosophy. "The family is the basic unit of government," she has said, as quoted in *Ms.* magazine (February 1981). "A strong family produces a strong citizen."

The Hawkins family moved to Florida in 1955, settling first in Winter Park, then in the rapidly growing new suburb of Maitland. Mrs. Hawkins quickly became involved in community affairs, serving as an officer of the local chapter of the Parent Teacher Association and of several other civic organizations. An experienced community activist by the late 1950s, she helped to mobilize the so-called "Dirty Dozen"—a group of Maitland residents who lobbied for installation of a sewer system in their expanding community. In press accounts of their unsuccessful effort, Mrs. Hawkins was invariably identified as "the Maitland housewife," a tag she went on to use to great effect in subsequent political campaigns, where she frequently portrayed herself as a representative of the average citizen.

A longtime volunteer for the local Republican party organization, Paula Hawkins was chosen as her precinct's representative to the Orange County Republican Executive Committee in 1964. Over the next decade, she took on positions of increasing responsibility, beginning with her being selected in 1966 to become a member of the Orange County Republican organization's finance committee. Later in the same year, she coordinated Edward J. Gurney's successful run for the United States Congress. Impressed by her political know-how, state Republican party officials named her cochairman of Richard Nixon's presidential campaign activities in Florida in 1968. That year also marked her election as a delegate to the first of four successive Republican National Conventions. Mrs. Hawkins capped her career in the Republican party organization in 1972, when she served as cochairman of the Florida Committee to Reelect the President and chairman of the host committee at the Republican National Convention, held that year in Miami.

In the 1972 general election, Paula Hawkins won a seat on Florida's Public Service Commission. She was reelected to the post in 1976, making her the first Florida Republican to be reelected to a statewide office since Reconstruction days. During her seven years on the commission, the last three as its chairman, she cultivated her image as the battling "Maitland housewife" willing to take on both big business and big government. As a staunch consumer advocate, Mrs. Hawkins consistently opposed telephone and utility rate increases. She also fought to end weekend service cutoffs, to lower the required utility deposit, and to improve the insulation in housing for the poor, where, in her words, the utility bills were often "higher than the payments on the house." Although she generally opposes federal regulation, claiming that "the federal government could mess up a two-car funeral," she argued that because they were "life support services," utilities "must be regulated." Twice during her tenure on the commission Paula Hawkins unsuccessfully sought election to higher office—to the United States Senate, in 1974, and to the lieutenant governorship of Florida, in 1978.

Mrs. Hawkins left the Public Service Commission in 1979 to become vice-president of consumer affairs for Air Florida, but her absence from politics turned out to be only short-lived, for in May 1980 she resigned that post to enter the Republican senatorial primary election. The best-known of the six contenders, she failed to win the necessary majority by just a few percentage points, but in the subsequent runoff she overwhelmed her competitor for the candidacy, former Congressman Lou Frey Jr., by taking 62 percent of the vote to his 38 percent. Her Democratic opponent in the November general election was Bill Gunter, the popular state insurance commissioner. In a campaign that was, by all accounts, unusually short on specific issues, Mrs. Hawkins earned points for her assertive and forceful personality. When the votes were tallied on November 4, 1980, Paula Hawkins emerged victorious by a margin of some 117,000 votes. Many political analysts credited her election to the nationwide landslide for Ronald Reagan, who headed the Republican ticket.

One of fourteen Republican freshman senators who took office in January 1981, Paula Hawkins assessed the meaning of the one-sided election results in a wide-ranging interview with Bill Peterson that was published in the May 31, 1981 edition of the *Washington Post*. "I don't think any of us came here to stay a long time," she said of the incoming senators and congressmen. "I get the feeling we're a product of the times, and that the electorate was looking for someone to come to Washington for a few years and then go home again. You feel a certain impatience with the freshmen you don't get with the seniors. There are a lot of us who are zealous and want response faster." Senator Hawkins defined her own priorities as being "to simplify government and try to make it relate to the man in the street."

By all accounts, including her own, Paula Hawkins' first year in the United States Senate was, in the words of New York Times reporter Phil Gailey, "a public relations disaster." Her outspokenness and apparent eagerness to make a name for herself in the unusually large freshman class earned her the enmity of her fellow Florida legislators and prompted some of her home state newspapers to label her "Betty Boop," referring to a vacuous cartoon character. The low point in her estimation was reached with what has since become known as the "steak and jail" luncheon. After treating reporters, farm lobbyists, and other invited guests to a lavish lunch of sirloin, asparagus, and strawberries in an elegantly appointed private Senate dining room, Senator Hawkins annouced her plan to imprison "truly greedy" food stamp chiselers. "It was the wrong setting to make such an announcement," she admitted later, as quoted in the New York Times (December 15, 1981).

Recognizing that her flamboyant style was receiving more media attention than her legislative initiatives, Senator Hawkins recruited a new press secretary from the staff of the liberal Democratic representative Claude Pepper and determinedly set out to improve her image. Perhaps most important, she began to make real gains on the legislative front. A member of the Senate's Children's Caucus, she has been especially effective in the area of child welfare, her goal being to try "to raise the public's awareness that a child who looks protected may still be vulnerable," as she once put it.

In response to an alarming increase in the number of children reported missing by their families, Paula Hawkins, as chairman of the Senate Labor and Human Resources Committee's subcommittee on investigation and oversight, conducted a year-long probe of the problem. The subcommittee's findings led to the passage of the Missing Children Act of 1982, which established a national clearinghouse for information about missing children. At Mrs. Hawkins' insistence, the measure included a provision giving parents the right to request the FBI to enter a missing child's name and physical description into its computerized National Crime Information Center. In 1983 alone, more than 2,000 children were located in that way. Continuing her crusade, Senator Hawkins initiated and steered through Congress the Missing Children's Assistance Act. Signed into law by President Reagan in 1984, the bill provided federal funding for a permanent National Center for Missing and Exploited Children to assist individuals and organizations in finding missing children and to coordinate local safety and public awareness programs. For her efforts, Mrs. Hawkins earned an award for excellence in legislative achievement from Child Find, Inc., a national nonprofit organization devoted to locating missing children.

Appalled by the shocking reports of sexual abuse in several day-care centers and other child-care facilities, Senator Hawkins cosponsored legislation that encouraged state governments to require tougher screening procedures for child-care and juvenile-welfare workers. She also persuaded her colleagues to approve a resolution recommending that state legislatures enact reforms designed to protect the young victims, such as accepting a child's testimony of sexual assault without corroboration and making the courtroom setting less intimidating. The senator's suggestions carried special weight because, as she confessed in her opening remarks at the Third National Conference on the Sexual Victimization of Children, in Arlington, Virginia in April 1984, she herself had been sexually abused by an elderly neighbor when she was just five years old. Her mother and the parents of other molested children took the man to court, but the judge, finding the youngsters' allegations "impossible" to believe, dismissed the case. "It's bothered me all this time that the 'nice old man' got off and went on abusing children for the rest of his life," Mrs. Hawkins said, as quoted in the Washington Post (April 27, 1984). "The embarrassment and humiliation of being called a liar will stay with me the rest of mine."

Mrs. Hawkins' failure to take a similarly strong stand on women's issues angered many feminists. The senator, who likes to describe herself as "feminine" rather than "feminist," is opposed to the legalization of and federal funding for abortions, which she sees as "tampering with human life," and to what she has called "the oversold, vaguely worded, and ambiguous" Equal Rights Amendment. "As women, we're all for equality—or superiority," she explained to Jo Thomas in an interview for the New York Times (November 7, 1980). "But there are better ways to attack problems which have come to be known as women's issues. Elect more women to the United States Senate. It's women's fault for not running for office."

On other domestic social and economic matters, Senator Hawkins has generally taken the conservative line. In 1984, for example, she voted with the conservative coalition on 77 percent of the roll-call votes. She strongly supports Reaganomics and has approved measures intended to stimulate the economy, tame inflation, and balance the federal budget, but while she has agreed to cutbacks in some social welfare programs, she has repeatedly drawn the line at entitlement and so-called "safety net" programs affecting the elderly and children with special needs.

Among other things, Senator Hawkins has refused to okay a cap on cost-of-living adjustments to the pensions of federal retirees or to freeze the retirement fund benefits of railroad workers. On the Senate floor, she helped to lead the fight for the continuation of a variety of essential services to the elderly mandated by the Older Americans Act, including Meals on Wheels, legal aid, senior community employment, residential repairs, and transportation. Largely because of her efforts, Congress recently amended the Older Americans Act to provide special assistance to the victims of physical and psychological abuse and to those suffering from Alzheimer's disease.

Long concerned about drug abuse and its related social problems, Paula Hawkins, the chairman of the Senate subcommittee on alcoholism and drug abuse, was instrumental in the passage of legislation authorizing federal programs specifically for the treatment and prevention of substance abuse in women. Believing that only sure and harsh punishment will deter drug dealers, she sponsored bills making drug-related murder a federal offense and imposing mandatory life sentences for the possession of large amounts of heroin and cocaine.

In an attempt to cut off the supply of drugs to the United States at its source, Senator Hawkins introduced, in 1983, an amendment to a foreign assistance bill that gives the president the option of blocking economic aid to any country that fails to implement an effective program for reducing the production and export of illegal narcotics. After the bill's passage, she visited heads of state in Pakistan, Turkey, the People's Republic of China, and several South American countries, explaining the harm caused by drugs smuggled from those areas. She believes the fight against international drug trade is "a war that we cannot afford to lose. . . . [But] it will take more commitment of resources to stop it. We need more volunteers in every community, more clamor from the public."

On the whole, Senator Hawkins has supported President Reagan on foreign policy and defense issues. Among other things, she has approved increased appropriations for the production of such sophisticated weapons as the MX missile and the B-1 bomber and for the research and development of Reagan's ambitious Strategic Defense Initiative, or "Star Wars" program, which calls for the installation of a space-based defensive "shield" against incoming nuclear missiles. A staunch advocate of the president's hard line toward Communism, she has been especially supportive of the administration's efforts to counter Communist interference in Central America. Her commitment is so strong that when the Senate, after months of wrangling, voted in June 1984 to delete an amendment authorizing $21 million in additional military aid to the antigovernment Nicaraguan rebels from an emergency domestic spending bill, she cast the sole dissenting vote.

Reflecting the sentiments of her constituency, Mrs. Hawkins has been a steadfast ally of Israel. In 1984, she added an amendment to a foreign aid bill prohibiting the United States from negotiating with the Palestine Liberation Organization until that group rejects the use of terrorism to achieve its political objectives and publicly recognizes Israel's right to exist. Sensitive as well to issues of interest to Florida's large Cuban-American population, Senator Hawkins was a driving force behind the passage of legislation establishing Radio Martí, a Spanish-language radio station under the jurisdiction of the Voice of America that broadcasts news and entertainment to Cuba.

With her large, brown eyes, fine-boned features, and dazzling smile, Paula Hawkins is an unusually photogenic woman who looks considerably younger than her years. Disciplined and well-organized, she is, according to her aides, a "classic 'A' type personality." Although she regularly puts in sixteen-hour days on Capitol Hill, she still finds time for such domestic chores as gardening and cooking. Paula Hawkins and her husband have a large, Spanish-style house in Winter Park, Florida and an apartment in the Watergate complex in Washington, D.C. Senator Hawkins is the recipient of numerous "woman of the year" awards, including the 1981 Republican Woman of the Year and the 1983 Mother of the Year Award for Statesmanship.

References: N Y Times A p29 N 6 '80 por, A p18 N 7 '80 por: People 16:90+ Ap 20 '81 pors; Washington Post B p1+ D 2 '80 pors, A p1+ S 2 '85 por; Working Woman 7:76+ S '82 por; Congressional Directory, 1984; Politics in America, 1986; Who's Who in America, 1984–85; Who's Who in American Politics, 1983–84

## Helmsley, Harry B(rakmann)

*Mar. 4, 1909– Real-estate developer. Address: b. Helmsley-Spear Inc., 60 E. 42d St., New York City, N.Y. 10165; h. 36 Central Park South, New York City, N.Y. 10019*

"The best advice I ever got was from my mother. It was simply, 'Buy real estate.' And like a dutiful son I bought and bought and continue to buy throughout this country," Harry B. Helmsley reported in *Good Housekeeping* (May 1983). Through a combination of thorough knowledge of his markets, sound instincts, bold entrepreneurship, and frugal management, Helmsley, who began his career in 1925 as an office boy in a real-estate firm, built a vast empire that includes luxury hotels, apartment buildings, offices, and other properties. As Manhattan's largest landlord and one of New York's biggest boosters, he can almost literally take inventory from his midtown office window. Known as a wily negotiator with a knack for making money without investing any of his own, the seventy-six-year-old real-estate tycoon shows no sign of slowing down. When asked if he plans to retire soon, he invariably replies, "I'm having too much fun."

Henry Brakmann Helmsley was born on March 4, 1909 in Manhattan to Henry Helmsley, a notions buyer for a wholesale dry-goods business, and his wife. Formerly a Lutheran, Harry Helmsley, as he is usually called, is now a Quaker. He and his younger brother, Walter P. Helmsley, who died in 1974, were raised in the Bronx, where Harry attended Evander Childs High School. On graduating at sixteen, he went to work to help support the family, but whenever he could he took extension courses, particularly in history, from Columbia and New York universities and the YMCA.

Since her own father had been a fairly successful apartment landlord, Helmsley's mother encouraged his real-estate interest. Beginning as a twelve-dollar-a-week office boy for the real-estate firm of Dwight, Voorhis & Perry, he soon got a raise in salary and was collecting rents and managing apartments in the notorious Hell's Kitchen section of New York, among other duties, which allowed him to become thoroughly familiar with the city's buildings. Within seven years he was made an executive, and in 1938 he bought into the firm, which then became known as Dwight, Voorhis & Helmsley. As a partner, he was able to hire his brother, Walter, who continued to work for him until his retirement in 1961. In 1955, his firm, which by then had become Dwight-Helmsley, merged with Leon Spear's management company to become Helmsley-Spear.

His first important real-estate deal took place in 1936, when the owners of a ten-story office building on East 23d Street were about to default on its $100,000 mortgage. "They were willing to let me buy their mortgage for $1,000—my only $1,000—and I took over the building's debt," he told Nicholas Pileggi of *New York* (May 19, 1980). "The mortgage at the time was 3 percent, and it cost me $3,000 a year . . . ," he continued, "but I was confident I could turn the building around." As soon as he had acquired the property, he installed his father, who had lost his job in the depression, as the building's superintendent. "I was supporting him anyhow," he explained to Randall Smith in the *Wall Street Journal* (December 28, 1982). "One of the reasons I wanted to buy the property was so he could get a job."

By paring the building's expenses to the bone ("One extra employee could cost $3,000 . . . [and make] the difference as to whether I could pay the mortgage") and filling vacancies, Helmsley realized a $65,000 profit when he finally sold the building in the late 1940s. Nevertheless, buying and only rarely selling became Helmsley's trademark. "Why sell the corner of 58th and Park?" he commented in *Nation's Business* (October 1980). "They're not making any more of them." Draft-exempt during the Second World War because of his poor eyesight, he continued to manage and acquire properties, many of them commercial buildings that had been foreclosed during the depression.

In 1949 Helmsley formed an alliance that not only would prove extremely profitable over the next several decades but would also transform him from a relatively minor property holder into a major power in New York City real estate. In conjunction with Lawrence A. Wien, a Columbia University–trained real-estate and tax lawyer, he pioneered the syndication of real-estate properties, using a system developed by Wien. First, Helmsley found desirable properties and participated in the negotiations for purchase. "I've never seen anyone who could isolate the one or two key factors in a deal and figure exactly what they're worth as Harry can," Wien claimed in an interview for *New York* (June 21, 1971). "He is the canniest negotiator you'll find anywhere." Wien's responsibility was to find the money needed to close the deals. To do that, he lined up wealthy investors willing to contribute a set amount toward the purchase of the building for a fixed return on their investment and certain tax write-offs. The profits were not subject to the high corporation tax rates because the investors leased the property back to an operating group—one that Helmsley and Wien owned or had a controlling interest in—that collected the rents and issued monthly payments to the investors. Helmsley usually substituted his hefty broker's fee for his share of the purchase price. As a result, he would earn profits from his "investment" and fees for managing the building in addition to his share of the "fair advantage" (a fee paid the principal members of the syndicate for their contributions of time and expertise)—all without actually putting in any of his own money. Wien would be paid legal fees and part of the fair advantage and be retained to represent the syndicate and the operating company. In addition, while the investors' rate of return was fixed, Helmsley and Wien's income would expand as the profits from the operation of the building rose.

Although during the 1950s Wein and Helmsley acquired warehouses and office buildings, many of them just outside Manhattan's prime midtown area in the aging garment district, through nearly 100 public syndications involving about 15,000 investors, their crowning achievement was the syndicated purchase in 1961 of the Empire State Building. The price, variously reported to be from $65 million to $85 million, set a record for the price paid for a single building, and as late as 1982 it was still the largest syndication ever. Over 3,000 investors anted at least $10,000 each to form a syndicate to lease the building; Wien and Helmsley each contributed $500,000 and a $4 million deposit repaid to them when the deal was consummated. The syndicate then obtained a $6 million mortgage from Colonel Henry R. Crown, the previous owner; a $3 million loan from the shipping magnate Daniel Ludwig; and $20 million from the Prudential Life Insurance Company in return for giving it title to the building. Prudential, which already owned the land, then leased the building back to the syndicate until the year 2075. The syndicate, in turn, subleased the property to the Empire State Building Company, an operating company owned principally by Wien and Helmsley, which would manage the property. For their part in the deal, Helmsley received $500,000 in broker's fees and a $90,000-a-year management contract while Wien's law firm was paid $1.1 million in legal fees and given an annual retainer of $190,000.

To increase the Empire State Building's profit yield to about 12 percent, Helmsley cut expenses by automating the elevator service and bookkeeping to reduce the payroll, restricting overtime, installing air-conditioning to justify rent increases, and taking over the cleaning operation—the most expensive single item in maintaining a building—with his own company, Office Maintenance Corporation. In less than a year, the building's net profit was increased by $1.5 million.

During their association of more than twenty years, Wien and Helmsley came to own, control, or manage about $2.5 billion in properties, including the posh St. Moritz and Carlton House hotels in Manhattan, but after 1961 they limited themselves to small, private syndications of fifteen or twenty investors. Continuing to expand, in 1965 Helmsley bought the Charles F. Noyes Company, a real-estate firm specializing in lower Manhattan office buildings, and Brown, Harris Stevens, Inc., which handles cooperative apartments. By 1968 Helmsley-Spear was one of the country's largest real-estate firms and Harry Helmsley, one of America's largest property owners.

Helmsley's brilliance at making huge amounts of money on limited or no personal investment and his solid reputation with financial institutions were demonstrated again in 1968 when he decided to establish a real-estate investment trust of his own. On what Peter Hellman of New York (June 21, 1971) called, "so far as anybody knows, the largest signature loan ever made to an individual," Helmsley, with co-signer Irving Schneider, who was executive vice-president of Helmsley-Spear, borrowed $78 million from Chase Manhattan Bank to buy out the Furman-Wolfson Trust, which owned thirty-three properties in seven states valued at $165 million. Helmsley took some of those properties out for himself, put in some of his own, and renamed the resulting group of twenty properties Investment Properties Associates. He and Schneider then offered to the public partnership participation units of $1,000 each. The loan was paid back immediately with the public subscription proceeds, leaving Helmsley and Schneider with fees for operating the trust and with any profits exceeding those promised to the public investors. In addition, Helmsley-Spear would receive the property management income.

His fascination with getting a good bargain quickly led Helmsley into new areas. Constructing skyscrapers of his own, in the late 1960s he commissioned the Pfizer and Marine Midland buildings, followed in the early seventies by the fifty-seven-story One Penn Plaza and two office towers in the Wall Street area. Nor did he neglect the New York City housing market. In September 1968 he announced his plans to buy from the Metropolitan Life Insurance Company the Parkchester apartment complex, the largest in the nation, comprising 171 buildings with a total of over 12,000 apartments, a shopping center, post office, and other facilities. Attracted by the "glamour of buying a city within a city," Helmley assembled a six-man syndicate that purchased that complex in the Bronx for $90 million, then the record price for a single property. During the early 1970s he further expanded his rental property holdings, buying Horizon House, a high-rise apartment in Fort Lee, New Jersey; Tudor City, another huge apartment complex near the United Nations building in Manhattan; and the 3,493-unit Parkmerced apartment complex in San Francisco.

At that time, Helmsley, among other Manhattan landlords, began converting some of his rental properties into cooperatives, often over the protests of tenants. He offered one of his rental buildings to the tenants on a condominium basis, the first such conversion attempt in the city, and planned eventually to convert Parkchester as well. Tenant groups at the Parkchester complex, suspicious of Helmsley's claim that the units would be offered as condominiums only as they were vacated so that no renter would be forced out of his apartment, pushed through changes in state law that seriously hindered his efforts at condominium conversion. In addition, throughout the decade renters at Tudor City and the Fresh Meadows complex in Queens, which he bought in 1972, protested his reduction of services and plans to build on what had been landscaped parkland, complaints that Helmsley countered in 1981 by offering the disputed sites to the city for public use in exchange for rights to build on other city parkland.

By the fall of 1983, Parkchester residents' fears had been allayed somewhat by a dozen years' experience of conversions and they eased their opposition to converting the rest of the complex. As of 1985, his disputes with the tenants of Tudor City and Queens Meadow remained unresolved. Convinced by the low return on his investment and the stress of tenant-landlord conflicts that "rental housing is [not] a viable economic business today," Helmsley sold off his Tudor City holdings in 1985.

In the early 1970s Helmsley constructed three major office towers, won the right to develop three office buildings in New York's Battery Park City

project, and in 1974 bought the city's largest manufacturing building at a foreclosure sale. By 1973,
however, the boom in New York was over, the demand for office space slowed to a trickle, and increased costs and vacancies led Helmsley to turn
back several office buildings to their mortgage
holders. In addition, projected completion dates
for Helmsley's three Battery Park City buildings
and an uptown office tower were pushed forward
to 1978 or later. To help ease the city's fiscal crisis,
on June 6, 1975 Helmsley and other major property
holders prepaid their real-estate taxes in exchange
for an 8 percent discount on those taxes, which allowed the city to raise $200 million. Nevertheless,
Helmsley explained to Carter Horsley in the *New
York Times* (February 15, 1976) that future construction projects and business expansion hinged
"on the political climate and whether the city can
face its problems and make itself more desirable
for business." Although New York City teetered on
the edge of bankruptcy in the mid-1970s, Helmsley's vast holdings shielded him from serious financial harm, and the holders of mortgages on his
residential properties offered him concessions
rather than take over buildings that were rent-
controlled and therefore difficult to convert into
more profitable condominiums.

As the city's financial state improved later in the
1970s, Helmsley again bought buildings and assembled properties for new projects. "I negotiate
leases every day and I have a feel for the market,"
he explained in *Fortune* (April 10, 1978). "The
whole country is improving." Although he had previously purchased several hotels, in May 1971 he
had opened the elegant Park Lane hotel overlooking Central Park, which was the first hotel he had
built and the first new hotel in the city since 1965,
and, gambling on his optimistic instinct at the end
of the decade, he constructed two more luxury hotels to cater to the moneyed traveler: the Helmsley
Palace, built behind St. Patrick's Cathedral on
property belonging to the Catholic Archdiocese of
New York, and the Harley, located near Grand
Central Station. According to *Business Week* (May
11, 1981), his strategy was to use his hotels "to reduce his dependence on residential properties and
to balance the inflation-impacted long-term leases
of his commercial properties."

A storm of protest arose when Helmsley announced his plans to incorporate into the Helmsley
Palace the Italian Renaissance Villard houses that
had been designated historic landmarks. Architectural interests, community boards, and far-flung
members of the Villard family battled for nearly
four years before the final plans, which preserved
the gold music room Helmsley had originally
planned to scrap, were approved. When his 1,050-
room Palace opened in September 1980, kudos
poured in. Hailed as a "miracle of restoration" in
*Travel/Holiday* (May 1981) and as "a dream re-
freshed in every detail" by *Town and Country's*
Peter Dragadze (October 1980), the hotel earned
the coveted five diamonds rating from the Automobile Association of America. The Harley, its name

a contraction of the first names of Helmsley and his
wife Leona, encountered no such opposition. Complete with Harry's bar and Mindy's (from Leona
Helmsley's middle name) restaurant, the Harley
opened in February 1981 and became the flagship
of a chain of Harley hotels across the country, including the Hospitality Motor Inns, which he acquired in 1979. (The Harley was renamed The
Helmsley in 1985.)

To operate his growing hotel portfolio, Helmsley
formed two new companies: Deco Purchasing,
which buys the supplies and furnishings for the
Helmsley hotels, and Helmsley-Spear Hospitality,
which he broke off from Helmsley-Spear in 1979
to manage and broker his other hotel properties. By
1980 he had incorporated his holdings into Helmsley Enterprises, an umbrella company.

Still wheeling and dealing at an age when most
people have retired, in 1981, without borrowing
funds or spending any of his own money, Helmsley
took control of the valuable land holdings of Investors Funding Corporation, a bankrupt title company, by liquidating its assets, transferring real estate,
and issuing stock in his new, reorganized company,
Realesco Equities Corporation. But such impressive successes notwithstanding, Helmsley's business instincts have occasionally failed him. In 1984
he defaulted on a $16 million mortgage in Miami
and postponed plans to build offices there. At the
same time, rumors circulated that he was trying to
sell the midwestern motels in the Harley chain as
well as the St. Moritz hotel in Manhattan. Nevertheless, Helmsley plans to construct a film studio
on the West Side Manhattan site he bought in 1981
and once again make New York the home of the
world's tallest structure by erecting a skyscraper
taller than Chicago's Sears Tower.

In operating his businesses, Helmsley admits to
watching every penny. He has, however, contributed generously to several charities, including the
National Council to Combat Blindness and the
Federation of Protestant Welfare Agencies, and
donated $2 million to New York University Hospi-
tal's cooperative-care building. Over the years, he
has been appointed to the board of directors of
dozens of organizations, ranging in scope from the
Commerce and Industry Association to the Lincoln
Center for the Performing Arts.

Harry B. Helmsley, who stands six feet three
inches tall and has brown eyes, married Leona
Roberts on April 8, 1972, about a year after he hired
her as a senior vice-president of one of his firms.
A former real-estate broker, she is now president
of the Helmsley hotels. His marriage of more than
thirty years to Eve Helmsley ended in divorce in
1972. Since he has no children, Leona Helmsley
stands to inherit the bulk of his personal assets of
over $900 million and the $5.5 billion more he controls. By all accounts, they have an idyllic marriage,
and her annual March 4th "I'm Just Wild About
Harry" birthday celebration, to which about 200
guests are invited, is already legendary. In 1973
Leona Helmsley nearly lost her life and Helmsley
was seriously wounded in a robbery attempt at

their Palm Beach penthouse, but the couple still enjoys flying to Florida in their private jet to spend time there or getting away to their Greenwich, Connecticut estate. When in New York, he swims daily in the pool in his Park Lane Hotel penthouse, and he and his wife also enjoy ballroom dancing several times a week. Nevertheless, his favorite recreation seems to be negotiating business deals, in each of which he insists on retaining a controlling interest. "When I sit down," he noted in *Forbes* (October 1, 1984), "the board of directors has arrived."

*References: Nations Bsns 68:55+ O '80 por; New York 13:27+ My 19 '80 por, 17:6+ Mar 12 '84; People 14:128+ D 8 '80 por; Wall St J p1+ D 28 '82 por*

## Heseltine, Michael (Ray Dibdin)

*Mar. 21, 1933– British government official. Address: b. House of Commons, Westminster, London SW 1A OAA, England; h. "Thenford House," near Banbury, Devon, England*

Michael Heseltine, the secretary of state for defense in Prime Minister Margaret Thatcher's Conservative government, represents a new breed of Tory politician. A self-made man with an entrepreneurial outlook and a flair for management, he accumulated a fortune in real estate and publishing before rising to national political prominence. First elected to Parliament in 1966, Heseltine held ministerial positions in the transport, trade and industry, and environment departments before assuming, in 1983, the top post at the Department of Defense.

Michael Ray Dibdin Heseltine was born in Swansea, an industrial seaport in South Wales, on March 21, 1933, the son of Rupert D. and Eileen (Ray) Heseltine. Both his maternal and paternal grandfathers were involved in trade, one as a commercial traveller in tea, the other as a shipping and coal magnate. His father, a structural engineer, managed a local steelworks and served as a colonel in the Territorial Army, the British military reserves. Heseltine attended Shrewsbury, an elite public school across the English border, in Shropshire, where he became known not for his prowess as an athlete or his achievements as a scholar, but for his skill as a craftsman. The fourteen-foot canoe that he constructed himself was the envy of his classmates. Heseltine rarely speaks about his years at Shrewsbury, probably because throughout his career there he felt overshadowed by more talented boys, as his longtime friend and former schoolmate Anthony Howard has surmised. As Howard told Tim Heald in an interview for the London *Sunday Telegraph* magazine (May 1, 1983), Heseltine's experience at Shrewsbury left him with "an indomitable determination to show that whatever the record books and the school reports might indicate—he was every bit as good as they were."

As an undergraduate at the University of Oxford Heseltine found an outlet for his ambition in politics. Objecting to the elitism of the university's Conservative Association, whose officers were appointed rather than elected, he founded a splinter group called the Blue Ribbon Club. According to Tim Heald, Heseltine was "widely regarded as a maverick" by his fellow students, but he was nonetheless elected president of the Oxford Union in 1954. He made his mark in that post as an enterprising entrepreneur who turned the Union restaurants into a profitable operation and converted its cellars into a nightclub. Recalling Heseltine's accomplishments, Anthony Howard told Heald, "I often think that he'd have made a superb hotel manager."

His involvement in campus politics left Heseltine little time for his academic studies, but by working hard during his last year at Pembroke College, Oxford, he managed to take a respectable second in politics, philosophy, and economics. After receiving his B.A. degree in 1955, he went to London to learn accountancy at an apprenticeship salary of £7 a week. Realizing that he would need a substantially higher income in order to pursue a political career at the national level, he decided to invest the £1,000 legacy left him by his maternal grandparents in a business venture. With a partner, he began buying, rehabilitating, and reselling houses and small hotels in London, and gradually built up a lucrative real-estate business.

Heseltine's career as a property developer was not without its setbacks. One year, he and his business partner lost a reported £250,000 due to cost overruns in a public housing project in the Stepney section of East London. A planned model estate in Tenterden, Kent turned into an even bigger debacle. Novices at house-building, they erected their model home too far from the main road, only to find themselves marooned by a prolonged rainy spell in a sea of mud. "Sitting there waiting for buyers was the worst nightmare of my life," Heseltine recalled to Tim Heald.

After completing his national service, during which time he was commissioned in the Welsh Guards, Heseltine became, in 1961, director of Bow Publications. Five years later, he was named chairman of the Haymarket Press. As head of the Haymarket publishing group, he oversaw the development of a series of successful specialized periodicals, including the business monthly *Management Today* and such do-it-yourself magazines as *Greenhouse* and *Practical Camper*. "I had a commercial flair. I suppose one must say that," he told Terry Coleman, who interviewed him for a *Guardian* (February 20, 1977) profile. But Heseltine made his share of mistakes, too. Both *Topic,* a weekly news magazine, and *Town,* a glossy, expensive monthly magazine for men, folded after losing a good deal of money. Still, under Heseltine's direction, the Haymarket Press's annual sales revenues rose from £700,000 in 1965 to £25 million in 1980, making it one of the largest independent trade and technical publishing houses in Great Britain.

Meanwhile, Michael Heseltine was also laying the foundations for his political career. After two unsuccessful parliamentary bids, as the Tory candidate for Gower, near Swansea, in 1959 and for Coventry North in 1964, he was finally elected to the House of Commons from Tavistock, in Devon, in 1966. Heseltine was never entirely comfortable with his blue-blooded Tavistock constituency, for as Tim Heald observed in the *Sunday Telegraph* magazine, the voters "tended to think of him as a parvenu and he was reminded of the exclusive, snobbish Tory establishment at Oxford." In 1974 he took advantage of a boundary reorganization and stood for election from Henley-on-Thames, thus exchanging what Heald called "feudal Devon" for "outer commuter-belt stockbrokerdom."

Not long after taking his seat in Parliament in 1966, Heseltine was recruited for front bench duty. He was named vice-chairman of the Conservative Parliamentary Transport Committee in 1968, and the following year, he was chosen to be his party's spokesman on transport. Extensive traveling around the country to organize opposition to the Labour government's proposed transport bill put an admitted strain on his family life and severely limited the time he could devote to constituency matters, but Heseltine's diligence paid off when the Conservatives won the general election in June 1970, and the new prime minister, Edward Heath, appointed him parliamentary secretary, Ministry of Transport. A few months later, he was made undersecretary of state in the Department of the Environment, a post he held until he was promoted to minister for aerospace and shipping in the Department of Trade and Industry in August 1972. During his tenure there, he presided over the government's campaign to promote international sales of the Concorde, the controversial supersonic transport plane developed and manufactured by the British Aircraft Corporation and its French counterpart, Aérospatiale. Despite his efforts, the plane was not a commercial success, largely due to its high operating costs, and Heseltine looks back on the experiment with little enthusiasm.

After a Labour government, under Prime Minister Harold Wilson, was returned to office in March 1974, Heseltine served as the Conservative party's parliamentary spokesman on industry, from March 1974 to November 1976, and on the environment, from November 1976 to May 1979. One of the most vocal members of the Opposition in the House of Commons, he excelled at passionate denunciations of Labour's nationalization policy. Even members of his own party occasionally objected to his histrionic style. For example, in a widely publicized incident during a heated debate on nationalization in the Commons in May 1976, an overwrought Heseltine seized the ceremonial mace and waved it about until he was physically restrained by his colleagues. However unpopular they were on the floor, Heseltine's theatrics gained him national attention and won him a loyal following among the Tory rank-and-file.

When Margaret Thatcher became prime minister following the Conservatives' victory at the polls in May 1979, she named Michael Heseltine to the cabinet-level post of secretary for the environment. He was created a privy counsellor at the same time. As head of the sprawling Department of the Environment, which is responsible for planning and land use, local government, housing, parks and historical buildings and monuments, environmental protection, and sports and recreation, he quickly earned a reputation for being an efficient and somewhat ruthless administrator. To streamline procedures and coordinate programs, he devised a "Management Information System for Ministers," or MINIS, that proved to be popular with civil servants. In keeping with the government's efforts to rein in spending, Heseltine waged war with local authorities over proposed cutbacks in funding, prompting Philip Jordan, writing in the *Guardian* (August 16, 1981), to call him "the Mad Axeman of the spending cuts." Heseltine also took the heat when he introduced in the House of Commons a plan to sell to tenants all six million municipally owned houses and apartments at discounts of up to 50 percent from the market price in an attempt to extend property ownership to the middle and working classes and to reduce government involvement in housing. The government's bill "lays the basis for perhaps as profound a social revolution as any in our history," he said on the floor of the Commons, as quoted in the *New York Times* (February 7, 1980). "Certainly no piece of legislation has enabled the transfer of so much capital wealth from the state to the people."

At the height of the summer of 1981, riots broke out in London and Liverpool and quickly spread to more than thirty cities and towns, especially in the industrial midlands. In his post as temporary minister for the inner cities, Heseltine was dispatched in late July to the racially mixed Toxteth district in Liverpool, where some of the worst rioting occurred, to look into the problems behind the violence and suggest solutions. At the end of his own two-and-a-half-week, on-the-scene investigation, Heseltine unveiled a plan to create new jobs, improve low-income housing, and expand community facilities—all to be financed out of existing government programs. He received high marks from the press and even from his political opponents for ingenuity and sincerity, but most predicted that without additional funds for those urban areas hit hardest by unemployment, Heseltine's ambitious package would accomplish little. Moreover, some Liverpool residents complained that his proposals failed to correct what they considered to be the root cause of the unrest: deteriorating relations between the virtually all-white police force and the racially mixed community. Heseltine's book on urban revitalization, *Reviving the Cities*, was published by the Conservative Political Centre in 1983.

In a cabinet shuffle on January 6, 1983, Prime Minister Thatcher appointed Heseltine to succeed Sir John Nott, who had decided to retire from politics, as secretary of state for defense. Confronted by the greatest political challenge of his career— namely, to carry out Prime Minister Thatcher's defense build-up in the face of determined resistance from the nuclear disarmament movement and from Opposition critics of defense spending— Heseltine threw himself into his new job with his customary determination and energy. In his first White Paper on defense, which he delivered in July 1983, he stressed his firm intention to modernize Britain's nuclear deterrent capability and, at the same time, to make the Department of Defense more efficient and economical.

Heseltine's first major task was to oversee the delivery, installation, and on-site testing of the 160 ground-launched cruise missiles that Britain was to deploy as part of NATO's new intermediate-range nuclear force. The impending arrival of the cruise missiles sparked massive protest demonstrations by the Campaign for Nuclear Disarmament, the Greenham Common Women's Peace Encampment, and other antinuclear groups, and for a time, it looked as though the protesters might actually be able to block the missiles' deployment. But under Heseltine's deft direction, the cruise missiles were delivered safely to Greenham Common, a Royal Air Force base operated by the United States, in mid-November 1983. In a well-executed maneuver that caught the protesters by surprise, the first training exercises were carried out without a hitch in March 1984.

The Thatcher government's decision to modernize Britain's independent deterrent program, by replacing its aging nuclear-armed Polaris submarines with American-made Trident submarine-launched ballistic missiles, also aroused widespread controversy. Opponents of the plan argued that the prime minister and her defense secretary were pushing the Trident program, which is projected to cost upwards of £10 billion over the next decade, to the detriment of more effective and less expensive conventional weaponry. To cover the cost of the Trident program and finance operations at the Falkland Islands garrison, which Britain had established after regaining control of the islands from Argentina in 1982, Heseltine had to cut back on other programs. The minister had repeatedly insisted that new equipment expenses can be included in future budgets, but some political observers, among them Richard Holme, a former president of the Liberal party, have countered that by that time, Britain's conventional forces will be hopelessly outdated.

Still, even Heseltine's critics have expressed admiration for his energetic attempts to streamline the Department of Defense, long "Whitehall's most cumbersome and overmanned department," according to John Connell, writing in the London *Sunday Times* (March 18, 1984). Determined to eliminate duplication and centralize planning, Heseltine announced a major shakeup in the department's organizational hierarchy in March 1984. Among other things, he drastically reduced the personnel of all three branches of the armed services, merged the formerly independent civilian and military central staffs, and set up a separate office of management and budget to oversee the financial planning and control of all defense programs. Heseltine's bold reorganizational blueprint met with considerable resistance from within the Department of Defense itself, but most outsiders tended to regard the plan as a definite improvement. As Richard Holme observed in the *Guardian* (January 20, 1985), "Any one who will take on the generals, admirals, and air-marshals, armed only with a briefcase full of management textbooks, deserves some sort of medal."

At NATO meetings in recent months, Heseltine has increasingly found himself playing the role of mediator between the United States and its European allies. While he agrees with his American counterpart that a state-of-the-art nuclear defense system, including the deployment of American missiles on British soil, is the only effective deterrent to Soviet aggression, he has steadfastly insisted on an equal, independent role for Britain and the other Western European nations. Fearing that American domination of heavy weapons production will diminish his country's strength both economically and politically, he has pushed for joint production of some matériel and shared knowledge of advanced weapons technology. "There has to be a genuine two-way street across the spectrum of defense equipment," he explained, as quoted in the *New York Times* (April 29, 1984), "or the Europeans will have no choice but to rationalize among themselves and buy from each other." As if to reassert Britain's standing as a leader in advanced weapons technology, Heseltine negotiated the sale of 132 British-made combat aircraft to Saudi Arabia in September 1985. The largest single export order in British history, the multibillion-pound purchase was expected to save from 25,000 to 30,000 jobs in the British aerospace industry.

To decrease international tensions, Heseltine has argued in favor of adopting a less confrontational stance toward the Soviet Union. "A rhetoric solely of confrontation cannot be helpful in overcoming the genuine—as opposed to the manufactured and propagandist—security concerns among all the peoples of Eastern Europe," he explained, as quoted in the *New York Times* (April 29, 1984). Part of the problem, he went on, stems from American misperceptions of its European allies as being "soft" on Communism, loath to make additional contributions to NATO, especially in the area of conventional forces, and not grateful enough for the shelter of the American nuclear umbrella. On the floor of the Commons, Heseltine has repeatedly warned against Britain's making any unilateral reductions in nuclear weapons, contending that the Soviet Union would almost certainly take advantage of the weak link in NATO's defense chain.

Of his political orientation in general, Heseltine told Tim Heald, "I'm not what you'd call a doctrinal politician, nor one who's hitched his wagon to the art of the possible." Distrustful of centralized authority, he maintains that the proper function of government is to check power rather than exercise it. He also believes in the free enterprise system, despite the inevitable distinctions in wealth and status that it produces. "To have a free society," he said in the *Guardian* interview with Terry Coleman, "you must accept and welcome the ability of people to create fortunes for themselves." Within the Tory establishment, Heseltine, who has served as president of the Association of Conservative Clubs since 1982, is considered to be a moderate, and the prime minister is known to be somewhat wary of him. As R. W. Apple Jr. remarked in the *New York Times* (January 7, 1983), "He has never been a full-blooded Thatcherite, standing somewhere between the left and right wings of his party. And, with his shock of golden hair and well-tailored good looks, he is a potential rival much beloved by the Tory rank-and-file."

Heseltine has been described as a strong, energetic personality with few intimate friends. He works long hours, priding himself on his efficiency and self-discipline. "Read fast, decide fast" is his motto, he once said, as quoted in the London *Sunday Times* magazine (April 27, 1980), adding, "The pace of ministerial life is such that the flow of adrenalin helps you through." In his leisure hours, he watches old movies, especially comedies and Westerns, on television, and he attends performances of the Royal Shakespeare Company in Stratford-upon-Avon, which is just a few miles from his Palladian country estate, Thenford House. An enthusiastic gardener and ornithologist, he takes great pride in the aviary he built on the grounds there. Although he has claimed to dislike the social side of politics, Heseltine and his wife, the former Anne Edna Harding Williams, a partner in a London art gallery whom he married in 1962, entertain frequently and lavishly. The couple has

one son and two daughters. In addition to Thenford House, the Heseltines own a Georgian house in Belgravia, London and a six-bedroom thatched cottage at Exford on Exmoor.

References: Guardian Weekly 116:19 F 20 '77 por; London Sunday Telegraph mag p36+ My 1 '83 pors; London Sunday Times mag p68+ Ap 27 '80 pors; International Who's Who, 1984-85; International Yearbook and Statesmen's Who's Who, 1985; Who's Who, 1985-86

## Himmelfarb, Gertrude

*Aug. 8, 1922– Historian; university professor.*
*Address: b. Graduate School, City University of New York, 33 W. 43d St., New York City, N.Y. 10036*

With the kind of "high seriousness" of which Matthew Arnold himself might have approved, the American historian of ideas Gertrude Himmelfarb has been writing for four decades about the political and cultural values of Victorian England. Dr. Himmelfarb's academic training in New York City and at the University of Chicago during the intellectual ferment of the 1940s gave her an abiding appreciation of the conservative worldview of the Victorians, with their commitment to moral values and their awe of civil power. In her prodigious output of essays, reviews, books, and in her editing of reprints from the period, she has explored the meaning behind the debates and personalities of that age of "economic, political, social, and cultural revolution," as she has called it. As her latest book, *The Idea of Poverty* clearly indicates, her concerns about power, legitimacy, and social cohesion are highly relevant to the urgent issues of the present time. Since 1978, Dr. Himmelfarb has been a distinguished professor of history at the Graduate School of the City University of New York.

Gertrude Himmelfarb was born in Brooklyn, New York on August 8, 1922, the second child of Max Himmelfarb, a manufacturer, and Bertha (Lerner) Himmelfarb. Her brother, Milton, is a noted political observer in his own right and a contributing editor of the neoconservative magazine *Commentary*. After graduating in 1939 from New Utrecht High School in Brooklyn, she went on to Brooklyn College, where her studies in history and philosophy were supplemented by classes at the Jewish Theological Seminary in Manhattan. There she studied religious history, some scriptures, and Judaic literature. She received the bachelor's degree from Brooklyn College in 1942.

In the late 1930s and 1940s the University of Chicago was a magnet for European thinkers, some of them German Jews, who, partly influenced by Max Weber, addressed the "modernism" of the "age of anxiety" as a political problem. Concerned with the nature of political freedom, and aroused by the terrors of power gone awry in fascism, Nazism, and Stalinism, they reexamined political values, often in the light of earlier modern or classical thought. (Among those associated with the university, for example, were Leo Strauss, Hannah Arendt, and Friedrich Hayek.) Certain tendencies of the Chicago School were conservative, so that by the late 1940s "conservative liberalism" was recognized as a distinctive political approach. In 1942, the same year in which she married Irving Kristol, a recent graduate of the City College of New York, Gertrude Himmelfarb arrived at the University of Chicago. She has said that she found its atmosphere highly stimulating.

There she studied under Louis Gottschalk, the distinguished specialist in the French and American revolutions. Other important influences on the development of her thinking, along with Max Weber, were the British economist R. H. Tawney and the Viennese psychoanalyst Sigmund Freud. In 1944 she received her master's degree after submitting a thesis on Maximilien Robespierre, the complex figure who led the Reign of Terror after the French Revolution of 1789. Gertrude Himmelfarb then began her doctoral studies on John Emerich Edward Dalberg-Acton—Lord Acton, the Roman Catholic parliamentarian, political philosopher, and historian, who lived from 1834 to 1902. A history department fellowship in 1946–47 took her to Girton College, at Cambridge University in England, to read Acton's manuscripts. Miss Himmelfarb edited a collection of his *Essays on Freedom and Power* (The Free Press, 1948) and in 1952 produced *Lord Acton: A Study in Conscience and Politics* (Univ. of Chicago Press), based on the doctoral thesis she had completed in 1950.

That "biography of a mind" rather than of a life, as Dr. Himmelfarb described it in her preface, presented as "one of our great contemporaries" the

statesman best-known for his dictum that power tends to corrupt and absolute power corrupts absolutely. A friend of William Gladstone, Lord Acton was a man who, though of a liberal and scientific disposition, also believed in God and traditional institutions. Because human sinfulness was the basic social evil, according to Acton, fatuous optimism in scientific and social progress, aggrandizing both the state and the majority will, could not supplant the rule of law and absolute moral principles. That rule would encourage "a practical, temporizing, expediential politics, . . . that would find freedom in a judicious mix of authority, tradition, and experience." Such a view, Dr. Himmelfarb explained, recognized that individual moral character was neglected or stunted—at a high political cost—by so-called "enlightened" advancement, and it spoke directly to twentieth-century readers made all too familiar with the catastrophes of two world wars and totalitarianism. Widely hailed as "an extremely well-written" "triumph of American historical scholarship" that "evoke[d] anew enthusiasm for a majestic figure," *Lord Acton: A Study* established Dr. Himmelfarb's reputation as an historian of ideas and as a political critic.

Her Lord Acton studies had been the focus but not the limit of Gertrude Himmelfarb's interest in the relevance of political thinkers of the past for contemporary readers. During the postwar years she published several essays on the subject, among them "Edmund Burke: The Hero as Politician" (*Modern Review*, Summer 1949), "The Carlyles at Home" (*American Mercury*, August 1952), and "Henry Adams: A Skeptic's Faith in Democracy" (*Commentary*, December 1952). "Prophets of the New Conservatism" (*Commentary*, January 1950), an article reviewing recent books by Peter Viereck, Bertrand de Jouvenel, James Burnham, and Leo Strauss, was punctuated throughout with her opinions on the conservative point of view. There she argued that conservatives, as distinct from liberals, championed the validity of an intellectual or political "aristocracy" and of the institutions that grant legitimacy to that elite. Twentieth-century conservatism's "strongest talking point," in her opinion, was its suspicion of the "absolute state," a political structure that liberals inadvertently supported "in their zeal for democratic equality and economic security." Dr. Himmelfarb worked as an independent scholar during the 1950s, receiving funding from American Association of University Women and American Philosophical Society fellowships (1951–52) and Guggenheim fellowships (1955–56, 1957–58). In 1954 Brooklyn College honored her with a distinguished alumni award.

In 1959 Doubleday published Gertrude Himmelfarb's semibiographical volume *Darwin and the Darwinian Revolution*, an analysis of the impact of the theory of natural selection on nineteenth-century political and religious thought. Even where crude "social Darwinism" was rejected, evolution as a "law of nature" entered politics in a more subtle way: such intangibles as equality, justice, and natural rights paled before the brute fact of the struggle assumed to be taking place in organic development. In place of the earlier "humanistic order," a scientific rationale for power was now sought, as an analogue to the "Darwinian dream in which man had only to probe nature to elicit its metaphysical truths." Although it was criticized as an "unconvincing case against the quality of Darwin's mind," Dr. Himmelfarb's challenge of Charles Darwin's scientific rigor was less a technical than a philosophical one. In 1968 W. W. Norton published a revised edition of the text.

Although she disputes reductionist models of social class relations, that subject has been an underlying theme of much of Gertrude Himmelfarb's writing. As one facet of her interest, her studies of the "proto-Victorian" Thomas Robert Malthus, as she termed him, whose *Essay on the Principle of Population* (1798) had a sweeping effect on attitudes and policies toward the poor, extend at least as far back as her article entitled "Malthus," which appeared in *Encounter* in August 1955. Replying to the utopians William Godwin and the Marquis de Condorcet, who dreamed of an egalitarian happiness born of the supposed perfectibility of the human mind, Malthus offered his gloomy "scientific" prognosis on the natural obstacles to such progress: the ever-conflicting, primitive pressures of population growth and food supply. As the class most constrained by those factors, the poor would be cruelly trapped by schemes to secure Godwin's illusory ideal. Although she faulted his demographic studies, Dr. Himmelfarb viewed Malthus as a moralist. His opposition to the Poor Law then in effect in England, which granted poor relief in the form of a living allowance or "dole," derived from his concern that indolence and misery would be perpetuated if the poor were supported as dependent paupers.

The solution Malthus eventually arrived at was a "prophecy," as Dr. Himmelfarb called it in her introduction to the Modern Library edition (1960) of his tract, *On Population*, which reprinted both his original *Essay* and the salient parts of his revised argument, first published in 1803. Neglected by most scholars, the "revision," as she pointed out, actually overturned his earlier stark predictions by introducing the possibility of "moral restraint." Malthus now foresaw the poor improving their condition by attaining the sober, industrious virtues of the middle classes—through entering political life and receiving schooling and other cultural benefits. His modern editor cited that ultimate vision with approval: "For the *embourgeoisement* of the lower classes, more than the inexorable pressure of population, has been the saving both of the lower classes and of society."

Having devoted herself to scholarly pursuits, without formal academic affiliation, since 1950, in 1965 Gertrude Himmelfarb became a professor of history at Brooklyn College, then incorporated with the City University of New York, and at the City University's Graduate School. In 1968 Alfred A. Knopf published *Victorian Minds*, a collection of

Gertrude Himmelfarb's essays, some of which were new, while others had been previously published. In one of its key chapters, "The Victorian Ethos," she discussed the "conservative revolution" in which not only the lower and working classes but also a portion of the aristocracy came to share the prudential ethic of the middle class during the sixty-four years of the Victorian era. In keeping with her recognition that religious perspectives have profound political implications, she saw as the impetus for that revolution the evangelical spirit of John Wesley's religious reform in the eighteenth century, which though conservative and superficially opposed to democracy, diffused the same moral code throughout most social strata and bridged the "two nations" of the rich and the poor. The zeal of evangelicalism helped to spur England to extend the voting franchise in the nineteenth century. As she suggested in "The Politics of Democracy: The English Reform Act of 1867" (*Journal of British Studies*, November 1966), Liberals feared that development more than did Conservatives, who trusted the masses to identify themselves with "established traditions and authorities."

That reading of Liberals' motives has led Gertrude Himmelfarb to challenge the beneficent promises found in the Victorian philosophy of Utilitarianism. According to her view, its cold material calculus of "the good" as the greatest happiness (or pleasure) for the greatest number pandered to the crass ideology of majority opinion, in competition with the humanistic ethics of the conservatives. Although the Utilitarians James Mill and Jeremy Bentham contended that they advocated liberal egalitarianism, she pointed out in another essay in *Victorian Minds*, "The Haunted House of Jeremy Bentham," which first appeared as a contribution to the festschrift *Ideas in History: Essays in Honor of Louis Gottschalk* (Duke Univ. Press, 1965), that Bentham actually placed scant value on the natural rights of individuals.

But in her editions of writings by James Mill's son, John Stuart Mill's *Essays on Politics and Culture* (Doubleday, 1962) and *On Liberty* (Penguin, 1974), and in her study of John Stuart Mill's life and work, *On Liberty and Liberalism* (Knopf, 1974), Gertrude Himmelfarb tried to set the record straight on that much vaunted proponent of liberalism and toleration. Postulating "two Mills" at variance with each other in the thought of John Stuart Mill, she found in his discourses an appreciation for "natural authority" and a recognition that "what is right is not the will of the people but the good of the people." Although some reviewers of *On Liberty and Liberalism* questioned her contention that Mill's liberal credo *On Liberty* (1859) was written under the spell of Mrs. Harriet Taylor, his longtime companion who later became his wife, many acknowledged as authoritative her argument that "absolutized liberty destroys particular liberties."

Her frequent reflections on methodology testify to the attention that Gertrude Himmelfarb—who suggests that modernist distortions in scholarship may subvert clear thinking about past and present—pays to contemporary intellectual culture. Taking to task in "The 'New History'" (*Commentary*, January 1975) the modish disciplines of psycho-history and quanto-history, which arrogate to themselves the authority of science, she pointed out that without a humanist perspective, knowledge is lost. And in "Political Thinking: Ancients vs. Moderns" (*Commentary*, July 1951) she exposed that type of empiricism in the social sciences that accepts only motives of wealth, power, and prestige as politically "real," thus impoverishing the philosopher's quest for "the good," "the true," and "the just." As she had written earlier: "Eliminating from the universe of political reality anything that smacks of morals, of non-material and non-individual interests, [depletes] reality of much that gives it texture and depth."

One of the greatest challenges to historians lies in maintaining both the integrity of the past—its real, independent existence—and that of the historian's own selective reconstruction of it. In her essay "Supposing History Is A Woman—What Then?" (*American Scholar*, Autumn 1984), Gertrude Himmelfarb reached the provocative conclusion that Friedrich Nietzsche, who thought the study of history important in the promotion of life and action, "pays Clio [the muse of history] the compliment of thinking her capable of telling, not the truth—there is no truth in history any more than in philosophy—but something important about the past and therefore about the present." "Finally what is wanted," she declared in "The Writing of Social History" (*Journal of British Studies*, November 1971), "is not social history, or political history, or any other kind of history, but good history," the kind that will not only analyze but also speak out against the corruptness of politics.

In the *Idea of Poverty: England in the Early Industrial Age* (Knopf, 1984) Gertrude Himmelfarb incorporated in a much larger study a subject that she had touched upon in many previous works. Comparing her approach, with certain exceptions, to that of the French *annaliste* historians, she used economic, political, sociological, and literary sources to illuminate the Victorians' evolving interpretations of poverty as a social problem. The pressimism of the early Malthus and Robert Mayhew's study called *London Labor and the London Poor* "gripped the imagination of contemporaries," who came to see poverty "as primarily, fundamentally, a moral problem . . . for the poor as responsible moral agents, and for society as a legitimate moral order." The resulting New Poor Law of 1834 at first stigmatized all the poor as paupers, but it broke the cycle of dependency and contributed to an improved condition for the lower classes. Written on a grant from the Woodrow Wilson International Center and a humanities fellowship from the Rockefeller Foundation, *The Idea of Poverty* was widely praised by reviewers. She has planned a second volume, covering the later nineteenth and early twentieth centuries.

While taking part in a symposium entitled "What is a Liberal—Who is a Conservative?" in *Commentary* (September 1976), Gertrude Himmelfarb vented some spleen in her contention that the recent term "neoconservative" was concocted "to permit us to speak about the unspeakable." She wrote that the conservative disposition "looks to other areas [than social activism] for the satisfaction of some of man's most basic needs—to the family, religion, job, neighborhood, to a host of private associations and personal commitments." She elaborated that view in a less compelling light in the *Commentary* symposium "Is Liberalism Good for the Jews?" (January 1980), in which she suggested that strong military defense, strong economy, and strong family ties set the boundaries for a minimally healthy society. Perhaps her abiding mission as a political commentator was defined by her in an addendum to the early "Prophets of the New Conservatism" article, in which she called for the restoration of "a sense of complexity to a problem that will not respond to the simplemindedness of any school."

Among other awards, Gertrude Himmelfarb has received a National Endowment for the Humanities senior fellowship (1968–69), a Phi Beta Kappa visiting scholarship (1972–73), and an American Council of Learned Societies fellowship (1972–73). No stranger to public service, she has served on the Presidential Advisory Commission on the Economic Role of Women; as an overseer to the Hoover Institution on War, Revolution, and Peace; on the boards of the National Endowment for the Humanities and the National Academy of Arts and Sciences; and as a fellow of the Woodrow Wilson International Center in Washington, D.C. She continues to contribute essays and reviews to intellectual journals on a regular basis. Dr. Gertrude Himmelfarb and her husband, Irving Kristol, who is a professor of urban studies at New York University and a noted spokesman for neoconservative views, make their home in Manhattan. The couple have two grown children, William and Elizabeth.

References: N Y Times Bk R p4+ Ja 1'84; *Contemporary Authors* vols 49–52 (1975); *Who's Who in America*, 1984–85

# Hines, Gregory

Feb. 14, 1946– Dancer; actor. Address: b. c/o Orion Pictures Corp., 1875 Century Park East, Los Angeles, Calif. 90067

After being relegated for more than two decades to show-business limbo, tap dancing began to stage a revival in the 1970s, and its comeback was clinched with the jazz-tapping of Gregory and Maurice Hines in the musical revue *Eubie!* (1978). The Hines brothers, who had been known internationally when they were younger as two-thirds of an

*Gregory Hines*

act called Hines, Hines and Dad, went on to spell the song-and-dance lead in the Broadway smash *Sophisticated Ladies* (1981-83), and they danced together in Francis Ford Coppola's *The Cotton Club* (1984), a multi-plotted jazz-era film in which Gregory had one of the more important acting roles. Gregory, a more improvisational dancer than his brother, is a consummate, versatile showman, bringing an engaging brio even to his singing (in which he is untrained) and a wry sense of humor, when needed, to his acting. On stage, he played the lead in the musical comedy *Comin' Uptown* (1979-80), and his motion-picture acting credits in addition to *The Cotton Club* include major roles in *Wolfen* (1981) and *Deal of the Century* (1983).

Gregory Oliver Hines was born on February 14, 1946 in New York City, where his father, Maurice Hines Sr., worked as a soda salesman and a night-club bouncer. The father was also a semipro ball-player, and in recent years he has been employed as a restaurant captain in Las Vegas. Like his father, Gregory was athletically inclined, and he might have become a professional football player had he had the heft of his brother, Maurice, who is two years his senior. The Hines brothers' paternal grandmother was Ora Hines, who had been a showgirl at the Cotton Club, the famous Prohibition-era Harlem nightclub were blacks entertained a well-heeled white clientele.

Growing up in Harlem and Brooklyn, Maurice and Gregory were steered toward a tap-dancing career by their mother, Alma Iola (Lawless) Hines, who, in Gregory's words, wanted them "to have an outlet . . . out of the ghetto" and envisioned them emulating the Nicholas Brothers, prime exemplars of what is now known as the "old technique" of tap. Gregory was barely walking when Maurice, already attending dancing classes, began teaching him the steps he had just learned himself. In addition to enrolling both boys in dancing school, Mrs. Hines regularly took them to the Apollo Theatre, Harlem's vaudeville mecca, and introduced them to as many song-and-dance professionals as she could. At the Apollo, Gregory became a special fan of such masters of improvisational tap as "Sandman" Sims and Teddy Hale.

The Hines brothers began performing together locally when Gregory was five, and they were held over (for a total of two weeks) at the Apollo when he was six. By the time he was seven, they were enrolled in professional children's schools and were touring during summer vacations. In 1954 Maurice and Gregory were cast, respectively, as the newspaper boy and the shoeshine boy in the shortlived Broadway musical comedy *The Girl in Pink Tights*, starring the French ballerina Jeanmaire.

Under the guidance of the Broadway tap coach Henry LeTang and the chaperonage of their mother, the Hines Kids, as they first called themselves, became an international attraction. When Maurice reached his teens, they changed their name to the Hines Brothers, and they were known as Hines, Hines and Brown during a brief period when the singer and pantomimist Johnny Brown joined the act. Finally, in order to be with his family during tours, Maurice Hines Sr. learned to play the drums and, in 1963, joined the act, which accordingly underwent another name change, to Hines, Hines and Dad. With Gregory functioning as comedian, Maurice as straight man, and the elder Hines as percussionist, the trio guested on the *Ed Sullivan Show* and other television programs, including Johnny Carson's *Tonight Show*, where they made more than a dozen appearances. Their European itinerary included such prestigious houses as London's Palladium and Paris' Olympia Theatre. Recalling the act's final years, Gregory told David Hinkley of the New York *Daily News* (December 23, 1984): "Tap had died, and we were doing lounge routines. So I didn't dance for seven years. Didn't even own a pair of tap shoes."

Eventually Gregory, who had been influenced by the 1960s counterculture and wanted to write songs and perform rock-style music, had a falling out with Maurice, who was interested in legitimate theatre and felt that his brother had "gone showbiz." "I was going through a lot of changes," Gregory Hines recounted to Leah Y. Latimer in an interview for the *Washington Post* (January 25, 1981). "Marriage. We'd just had a child. Divorce. I was finding myself." In 1973 the Hines act disbanded and Gregory moved to the beachfront town of Venice, California, where he became, in his words, "a long-haired hippie." In Venice he organized a jazz-rock group, Severance, for which he wrote songs, sang, and played guitar. In addition, he worked as a waiter, busboy, and karate instructor (he is a black belt), joined a men's consciousness-raising group, and met his present wife, Pamela Koslow.

Although he found life in Venice spiritually and emotionally therapeutic, Gregory Hines returned

East in January 1978, partly because he missed being near his daughter, Daria, then seven years old, who was living in New York with her mother, Hines's first wife, Patricia Panella, a dance therapist. On the day he arrived back in New York City, Maurice, with whom he had become reconciled, told him about an audition for a Broadway-bound revue, *The Last Minstrel Show*. Gregory landed a tap-dancing part in that production, which opened and closed in Philadelphia.

Critics generally agreed that Gregory and Maurice Hines were "the brightest stars" in the all-black galaxy of the Broadway musical revue *Eubie!* (1978-79), a homage to the then ninety-five-year-old composer Eubie Blake that was tap-choreographed by their mentor, Henry LeTang. In that string of Blake compositions, Gregory sang a soul-wrenching "Low Down Blues" and his machine-gun tapping of "Hot Feet" was repeatedly interrupted by applause. Gregory and Maurice teamed their flashing feet in the duet "Dixie Moon" and joined others in the tango "There's a Million Little Cupids in the Sky." Writing after a New York newspaper strike had been settled, Richard Eder of the *New York Times* (January 5, 1979) called Gregory's dancing "a kind of inspired graffiti." Eder, like several other reviewers, noted that Gregory gave the show most of its humor: "When he is not tap dancing, or singing, Mr. Hines is clowning, which he does very well, and with a fraudulent innocence." For his performance in *Eubie!*, Hines won several awards, including one from the Outer Critics' Circle, and he was nominated for a Tony Award as outstanding featured actor in a musical.

Gregory Hines did his first genuine acting (in addition to singing and dancing) as Scrooge in *Comin' Uptown* (1979-80), a Broadway musical-comedy version of *A Christmas Carol* that was set in present-day Harlem. The show flopped at the box office, and many critics regarded it as a flat and witless confection, unworthy of its talented cast and especially of Hines, "the only substantial reason for bothering to see *Comin' Uptown*." Some reviewers noted but none quibbled over the fact that in bringing his own *joie de vivre* to the role, Hines turned Scrooge from the beginning into an endearing character and thereby rendered his climactic conversion redundant. Hines came across as a "marvelous," "inhumanly agile" performer, graceful in his acting, soulful in his singing, and, above all, "elegant" but "almost shattering" in his tapping. "Every time he began to move he carried the audience along with him, and they shouted out encouragement . . . ," Sally R. Sommer reported in the *Village Voice* (December 31, 1979). "He plays around with the tempo, hitting a fast, loose flurry with gusto and precision after he has set it up by teasing us with a long, slow stride." For his performance as Scrooge, Hines received his second straight Tony nomination, for outstanding actor in a musical.

Hines choreographed *Blues in the Night*, an electric revue based on classic blues songs that ran for six weeks Off-Broadway early in 1980. With Charles (Honi) Coles, John Bubbles, Nell Carter, and others, he participated in *Black Broadway*, impresario George Wein's salute to black Broadway musicals of the past, presented at Town Hall in New York City in May 1980. Later in the same year a pair of Hines's tap shoes was placed on the "Wall of Fame," alongside shoes of Fred Astaire, Ruby Keeler, and other dance greats, at Roseland, the venerable Manhattan dancehall.

Hines headed the cast of *Sophisticated Ladies*, a selective, handsomely mounted showcase of Duke Ellington's music conceived by director-choreographer Donald McKayle (who called the musical revue a "choreomusical") and tap-choreographed by Henry LeTang. The production had a history as volatile as some of its numbers, beginning in December 1980, when reviewers of its Philadelphia tryout complained that it was too long and encumbered with wooden narration and dialogue and with ambitious Ellington suites and religious music that minimized the song-and-dance talents of Hines and Judith Jamison. When the show moved to Washington, D.C. in January 1981 Hines voiced his own complaints in what he later described as "not too nice a way" and was dismissed. After the other cast members rallied behind him, he was rehired and Michael Smuin replaced McKayle as director.

Smuin eliminated all vestiges of a book from *Sophisticated Ladies* and revamped the entire show, so that the production that reached Broadway in March 1981 was no longer a sprawling tour of Ellington's musical life and times but, rather, a sleek, sumptuous, and sassy Saturday night party at the old Cotton Club. With Mercer Ellington, Duke's son, conducting the on-stage orchestra, Hines presided over the revels with a combination of insouciance and manic energy, singing the title song as well as "Don't Get Around Much Anymore" and "Something to Live For," exchanging antiphons with Miss Jamison in the duet "I Let a Song Go Out of My Heart," joining with others in such numbers as "Take the A Train" and "It Don't Mean a Thing (If It Ain't Got That Swing)," bringing down the house with a phenomenal, almost unchoreographable Bill Robinson-style solo tap dance up and down (backwards) a staircase, and even rolling off a rousing, Buddy Rich-caliber drum solo. While some critics of the Broadway production felt that *Sophisticated Ladies* did not do justice to Duke Ellington's music, most agreed that the elegant production was a "seductive" machine, a "gilded, speeding" juggernaut of "fun" to which the audience could only capitulate. The critic for *Variety* (March 4, 1981) registered a dissent, viewing *Sophisticated Ladies* as "another elaborate cabaret show" in which "Gregory Hines can only occasionally suggest his remarkable variety of hoofing, singing, and slyly casual comedy." Others described Hines as singing "with engaging feeling," wielding "the fastest pair of spats in the East," and "constantly tickling us with his droll sense of humor."

For his part in *Sophisticated Ladies*, Hines received his third straight Tony nomination, for best actor in a musical. The show itself was a solid hit, running on Broadway for two years, until January 1983. Midway through the run, in January 1982, Hines turned his Broadway role over to his brother in order to head up the West Coast production of *Sophisticated Ladies*, a move that fit in with his increasing involvement in motion pictures. Hines first appeared on the screen as a Roman-era slave in Mel Brooks's grossly farcical epic *History of the World—Part I* (Twentieth Century-Fox, 1981). Many critics thought that one of the best things in the humans-versus-wolves horror flick *Wolfen* (Orion, 1981) was his portrayal of a hip medical examiner investigating a series of mysterious deaths who himself ends up as a lupine *pièce de resistance*. In *Deal of the Century* (Warner Brothers, 1983), an unfocused, heavily panned satire on the state of ethics in the military-industrial complex, Hines was cast as a born-again test pilot enlisted by a shady armaments dealer (Chevy Chase) in a scheme to peddle a line of rejected unmanned aircraft in Latin America.

While he was in Los Angeles with the West Coast company of *Sophisticated Ladies*, Gregory Hines heard about plans for *The Cotton Club* (Orion, 1984), a movie recreating the heyday of the legendary Harlem nightspot, when the members of white high society flocking there were joined by the capos of the white underworld, including rival mobsters forcibly vying to take over the black-founded numbers racket. Hines also heard that Robert Evans, the producer of the film, was interested in casting him, but the interest seems at first to have been ambivalent at best, for Hines had to importune Evans daily for approximately two weeks before Evans would agree to give him the role that he wanted, that of "Sandman" Williams, an upwardly mobile Cotton Club tap dancer. That role was as yet embryonic, like the whole screenplay, which Francis Ford Coppola, the scenarist as well as the director of the movie, would, with the help of William Kennedy, rewrite forty or fifty times before he was satisfied with it. The cost of the film came to approximately $1 million a rewrite, or $47 million in all.

In rewriting *The Cotton Club*, Coppola relied heavily on his cast's real-life experiences. After hearing Hines describe the breakup of Hines, Hines and Dad, he made "Sandman" Williams one half of a feuding brother act, with Maurice Hines playing the other half. The overly ambitious "Sandman" meets his match when he falls in love with Lila Rose Oliver (Lonette McKee), a light-skinned chanteuse who plans to "pass" her way to Broadway glory and considers "Sandman's" darker skin a threat to her career. Coppola alternated or interwove "Sandman's" story with several other plots, the chief of which concerned Dixie Dwyer (Richard Gere), a white cornetist who jams with the black musicians at the club and becomes involved with Vera Cicero (Diane Lane), the young mistress of gangster Dutch Schultz, the bootleg-beer baron.

In impressionistic, video style, Coppola crosscut the sight and sound of dancing feet and musical instruments with that of machine guns, leaving many critics unhappy. "Coppola, with his staccato imagery fragmenting the songs and dances, knocks the life out of the performers," Pauline Kael wrote in the *New Yorker* (January 7, 1985). "[He] doesn't seem to know that it's criminal not to let these artists do their thing." Miss Kael, like many other reviewers of *The Cotton Club*, felt that what Coppola intended to be "an epic view of the Jazz Age" was actually "a composite of old Warners musicals and gangsters pictures."

Following the completion of *The Cotton Club*, Hines went to Europe for the filming of "White Nights" under the direction of Taylor Hackford. That motion picture is the story of the prolonged encounter of a Soviet emigré ballet dancer (Mikhail Baryshnikov) and an embittered American Vietnam veteran (Hines) who defects to the Soviet Union and marries there before becoming disillusioned with the Soviet system. In keeping with Hackford's intention to make "a film in which dance functioned integrally to advance both story and character," the two men are thrown into a mutually catalytic situation in which they "dance for their lives," taking turns demonstrating their respective tap and ballet styles and then joining in a series of duets synthesizing elements of both.

Hines looks forward to more motion-picture opportunities in the future, and he has expressed special interest in the possibility of starring in a film biography of Bill "Bojangles" Robinson, the legend of dance and musical comedy. Hines returned to nightclubs in March 1985 with a seventy-minute solo act combining dancing, singing, and guitar playing. Among the more recent of his numerous television credits was a performance on the star-studded two-hour NBC network show *Motown Returns to the Apollo* (May 19, 1985), a condensed version of a six-hour taping that took place at the official reopening of the historic Harlem theatre on May 4, 1985.

Gregory Hines stands a willowy five feet ten inches tall and has angular features, large, heavy-lidded eyes, a rakish smile, and, usually, an earring hanging from his left ear. Interviewers, who invariably find him "friendly" and "charming," correctly surmise that he is more relaxed and spontaneous than his brother Maurice. "Gregory loves . . . improvisation," Maurice has acknowledged. "I hate it. . . . He picks up steps quickly, much more quickly than I do, but I retain them longer and teach them back to him long after he's forgotten them. And Gregory is more Californian than I am . . . laid-back, mellow."

Hines met his second wife, Pamela Koslow, during his stay in California in the mid-1970s. She was a high-school guidance counselor at that time but has since changed to a career in theatrical producing. They were married in 1981 and now live in Manhattan with their son, Zachary. They share custody with their respective previous spouses of Pamela's daughter from her previous marriage,

Jessica, and Hines's daughter from his first marriage, Daria. Long interested in the problems of divorced fathers, Hines organized a single-parents' group for theatre people in 1979. In his leisure hours, the entertainer is a good cook, and he likes to play softball.

References: *Christian Sci Mon* p12 Mr 24 '81 por; *New York* 12:27+ Mr 30 '81 pors; *N Y Daily News* mag p12+ D 23 '84 pors; *N Y Times* C p10 N 24 '78 por; *People* 16:105+ Ag 17 '81 pors; *Time* 117:59 Ap 27 '81 por; *Washington Post* H p1+ Ja 25 '81 pors, H p1+ F 24 '85 pors; *Who's Who in America*, 1984–85

## Hogwood, Christopher

Sept. 10, 1941– British conductor; harpsichordist; musicologist. Address: b. c/o Jasper Parrott, 12 Penzance Pl., London W11 4PA, England; h. 2 Claremont Hills Rd., Cambridge CB2 1PA, England

"Every piece of music should be looked at as a painting that dissolved off the wall when you closed the gallery door," Christopher Hogwood, the early music specialist and founder and conductor of the Academy of Ancient Music, told Stuart Isacoff during an interview for *Keyboard Classics* (March/April 1985). "If all the colors dripped down into a huge pot and you took this pot, along with a recipe of how to reassemble the colors back into Van Gogh's 'Sunflowers,' you would be very careful to get all the reds and the yellows in the right places, and not to paint it bigger or smaller than it was. I think music carries with it this responsibility."

Along with his older contemporary, the Austrian Nikolaus Harnoncourt, with whom he is often compared, Hogwood is internationally recognized as one of the leaders in the movement to restore historically correct (he frowns on the word "authentic") performances of seventeenth- and eighteenth-century music to modern practice. Together with the Academy of Ancient Music, which he founded in 1974, Hogwood has made over sixty recordings of music of the baroque and classical periods, using the instrumentation and performing techniques known to have been in use at the time of their composition. Most notable among them is their seven-volume set of the complete symphonic works of Mozart, in which each symphony is performed by an orchestra exactly like the one for which it was originally composed. As a conductor, solo harpsichordist, and editor, Hogwood has also been responsible for helping to restore such long-neglected works as Handel's oratorio *La Resurrezione*, William Byrd's *My Ladye Nevells Booke,* and the keyboard works of the baroque English organist William Croft. But Hogwood's recognition extends far beyond the ranks of purist baroque scholars. In its 1982 list of the ten most popular classical artists, *Billboard* ranked Hogwood in ninth place, ahead of Sir Georg Solti, and Hogwood and his Academy of Ancient Music had four of the thirty best-selling classical albums on *Billboard*'s chart of March 2, 1985.

Christopher Jarvis Haley Hogwood was born on September 10, 1941 to Haley Evelyn Hogwood and the former Marion Constance Higgott in Nottingham, England. "My parents were active in quite different professions," he told Gerhard Persché for an interview in *Opernwelt* (1984). "But there was music-making at home." His own interest in music failed to flower during childhood, perhaps because of a series of piano lessons that he took at the age of eight with a teacher whom he has characterized as "a very stern old lady, not very encouraging." As for his discovery of the harpsichord, Hogwood told Persché, "I don't know how it came about—perhaps I heard a record of Wanda Landowska—suddenly I became . . . enormously interested in the harpsichord, if only still as a hobby."

When Hogwood entered Pembroke College at Cambridge University in 1960, it was with the intention of studying Greek and Latin, but he was quickly "seduced by music," as he put it. It was Raymond Leppard, the conductor and musicologist whose editions of Monteverdi's operas helped return them to the modern repertory, who encouraged him to switch to music study. The teachers with whom Hogwood studied also included Thurston Dart, the harpsichordist and conductor whose research into authentic scores and their sources, especially Bach's *Brandenburg Concertos*, served as something of a model for Hogwood's later work, and Rafael Puyana, the harpsichord virtuoso, with whom Hogwood later recorded François Couperin's *Pièces de clavecin* for the Philips label. The first of his major musical projects as an undergraduate, however, was his organizing of an orchestra of his fellow students who were devoted to modern music. "At Cambridge," he recalled for Allan Kozinn during an interview for *Symphony Magazine* (December 1984), "I spent more time playing contemporary music than early music. I ran my own orchestra there and I commissioned new pieces for it. We spent a great deal of time playing through avant-garde compositions."

Hogwood's interest in the harpsichord and in baroque music also flourished at Cambridge. When he began studying early keyboard instruments, at first it was as much out of a personal interest in their historical development as it was in their musical characteristics. The harpsichord and its repertory were also a way of his surmounting a natural physical limitation, since his hand was too small for the stretches demanded by the Romantic piano literature. More important, however, was Hogwood's friendship with David Munrow, an English scholar and wind player one year his junior who had a consuming interest in baroque and pre-baroque music.

Hogwood and Munrow began playing baroque music together on modern instruments at Cambridge. Following his graduation in 1964, Hogwood left for a year of study at Charles University in Prague, Czechoslovakia, where he devoted much of his time to research in its centuries-old archives. "When I came back from there my interest in baroque music had lessened," he told Persché. "I had somehow come up against the barrier of what one can do in this area on modern instruments. At the same time, David Munrow had gone the same way, and so we plunged into what was then for us the so exotic, if still hypothetical, sound world of mediaeval music." In 1967 Hogwood and Munrow founded the Early Music Consort of London, an ensemble devoted to the restoration of mediaeval music to the concert hall and recording studio. The original quartet of Munrow and Hogwood with counter-tenor James Bowman and Oliver Brooks on viol made its debut in Louvain, Belgium in 1967, a year before they were first heard in London. Within five years, the Early Music Consort was one of the most acclaimed groups of young musicians in Europe and America, with recordings on both the Decca and EMI labels, first performances of Peter Dickinson's *Translations* (1971) and Elizabeth Luytens' *Tears Of Night* (1972) to their credit, and a Peter Maxwell Davies score (*Taverner*, 1972) composed specifically for them. Hogwood's work with the Early Music Consort continued until Munrow's tragic suicide in 1976, although in the meantime other musical relationships were changing his thinking about the Early Music Consort's work. In 1966 he had also joined Neville Marriner's chamber orchestra, the Academy of St. Martin-in-the-Fields, as continuo player both in their live appearances and on recordings, and he began performing as a solo harpsichordist. That same year he became a lecturer at the Cambridgeshire College of Art and Technology, a post that he held until 1969.

Hogwood's studies and his duties with the academy of St. Martin-in-the-Fields, which included the preparation and editing of baroque scores, gradually began to conflict with his work in Munrow's Early Music Consort. Of his years with that mediaeval group, he recalled for Persché: "It was at that time a wholly new world for all of us, and good for the public too, since it became acquainted with a new repertoire. There was a lot of showbiz attached to it. Finally my interest in this kind of music became exhausted, because we did not know whether or not what we were doing was authentic." The result of what at best could only be viewed as assumptions, and of what Hogwood himself saw as the inevitable "guesswork" inherent in the Early Music Consort's work, was that though their recordings became increasingly popular, Hogwood grew ever more uncomfortable with it. "I turned to an area, to a period, which offered me reliable sources. That was the music of the seventeenth and eighteenth centuries," he has explained. He also began to appreciate the limitations of the St. Martin Academy's work with that music, confined as it was to the use of modern instruments, including the harpsichord. His own research into the capabilities of original period harpsichords, coupled with his work in editing scores, first as assistant to the musicologist Howard Ferguson and later on projects of his own for the Folio Society, transformed the way he heard music. "I tried increasingly to give my solo recitals on historical instruments," he told Persché, "because the harpsichords built in modern times had a sound that one could only place in the realm of the imagination or, better, of toys." As the 1970s began, Hogwood met many members of smaller chamber groups who were also interested in creating historically aware performances.

The Academy of Ancient Music came about partly as a result of the chance meeting, in 1973, between Hogwood and Peter Wadland, a producer for Decca Records, at a concert at Nash Terrace in London. Wadland was interested in recording a group of Britain-based baroque music specialists working on original instruments, modeled roughly along the lines of Nikolaus Harnoncourt's Concentus Musicus, but there was no such group at the time, though Hogwood knew musicians interested in exploring that repertory. The first project on which the two collaborated was a recording of Thomas Arne's eight harpsichord sonatas on the Decca Group's newly acquired L'Oiseau-Lyre label. "We got on particularly well on these sessions," Wadland recalled in 1983, "maybe because we were both rather inexperienced at our respective jobs! And I decided that Christopher Hogwood would be the perfect director and founder of the baroque orchestra I envisaged." Wadland then followed up on those initial sessions by offering Hogwood the opportunity to record with a baroque studio ensemble performing the orchestral music of Thomas Arne, the British composer who lived from 1710 to 1778.

In what was in effect the debut of the Academy of Ancient Music, Hogwood and the twenty-five musicians who took part in that 1974 session got to know each other for the first time in the recording studio, but they soon found their style because most of them came from the same background and approached the material in the same way. Critical and commercial success greeted their first recordings of Arne and Purcell and encouraged both the Academy and the management of L'Oiseau-Lyre to become more ambitious in planning new records, which included Vivaldi, Bach and his sons, Stamitz, and Haydn. Their most important project, however, materialized when Decca's executives began contemplating a new recording of all of Mozart's symphonies. The result was the Academy's recording of the composer's symphonic works in performances prepared under the guidance of Hogwood, concertmaster Jaap Schroder, and musicologist Neal Zaslaw that recreated the exact musical forces of Mozart's day. Recorded between 1979 and 1982 and released over a three-year span, the complete cycle constituted a landmark for listener and performer alike, and helped to establish Hogwood internationally as "perhaps the most persuasive present-day translator of musicological scholarship into actual performance," to quote a reviewer writing for the New York Times (August 12, 1982). Despite some reservations about tempos and a lack of emotional inflection that he detected in certain of the symphonies, the musicologist Stanley Sadie, the editor of the New Grove Dictionary of Music and Musicians, called the cycle a "remarkable achievement."

The Academy's massive commitment of time and effort to its Mozart cycle and L'Oiseau-Lyre's allocation of its resources for the project did not preclude other monumental projects from their consideration. Under Hogwood, with soprano Emma Kirkby, bass David Thomas, tenor Ian Partridge, contralto Carolyn Watkinson, and soprano Patrizia Kwella, the Academy of Ancient Music gave the first performance of Handel's oratorio La Resurrezione in London at Easter time in 1981 and recorded it for record release in May of the following year. As Stanley Sadie described it in Gramophone (June 1982): "Not often have I heard authentic instruments serve the music so well. Lucid textures, distinct articulation, well-defined lines add to the freshness of effect already residing in the music itself. . . . Christopher Hogwood, as always, is intent on keeping the performance moving along at a good pace, and the work can stand it." The Academy of Ancient Music also numbers on its discography works by Handel, Vivaldi, Geminiani, Purcell, Stamitz, Haydn, and Bach and his sons, among other composers, including critically praised performances of Handel's Messiah, the complete Water Music, and the complete Royal Fireworks Music. Attesting to Hogwood's considerable contribution to contemporary understanding of music of the baroque period are the nine articles on the subject that he wrote for the New Grove Dictionary of Music and Musicians (1980).

As a result of its Mozart cycle, the Academy seems to be linked to that composer's work during the 1980s as firmly as Nikolaus Harnoncourt's Concentus Musicus, through its Bach cantata series, was associated with Bach in the 1970s. Hogwood's latest brisk-selling triumph with the Academy is the 1984 recording of Mozart's unfinished Requiem based on an edition by Richard Maunder in which the work is stripped of all the posthumous additions to the score made by Mozart's contemporary Franz Xavier Sussmayr. In their place Maunder substituted passages based on material left behind by Mozart, thus giving the Requiem a new overall shape suggested by the composer himself. Reviewing the recording for Newsweek (December 17, 1984), Alan Rich wrote, " . . . What makes it memorable is the tremendous intensity of Hogwood's vision of the piece, and the astounding clarity with which his superb ensemble performs it." Hogwood's Mozart's Requiem was listed as the fourth-best-selling classical album in America in Billboard's issue of March 2, 1985.

"I'm for democracy to the point of anarchy," Hogwood told an interviewer for the London Sunday Times (April 22, 1984), in describing his approach to conducting. "Your oboe d'amore player is fully aware of the art regarding his instrument, its technology and history. You accept what he feels is best in the circumstances. Other players will make their own suggestions. You are the umpire. No one wants to get back to the maestro situation of a bunch of mice playing baroque instruments and a great conductor telling them to do it his way." Because the Academy, which supports itself entirely on proceeds from its recordings, did not tour with Hogwood in the United States until 1985, he often found himself dealing with American orchestras that were unaccustomed to such permissiveness from conductors. During his 1983 appearance with the Boston Symphony, Hogwood placed the orchestra's second violins on the opposite side of the podium from the first violins, rather than behind them as is usual with modern orchestras, for a performance of Haydn's Symphony No. 104 in D Major ("London"). More important than simply emulating the configuration of the orchestra of the classical period, that arrangement emphasized the antiphonal relationship between the two sections in Haydn's writing. "I spoke briefly with the leader of the seconds, Marylou Speaker Churchill," he told Patrick J. Smith in an interview for Ovation (December 1983), "who said she was happy to be liberated from her usual position behind the firsts."

Hogwood has also reintroduced into practice at his concerts Mozart's own custom of dividing the first three and final movements of his symphonies between the beginning and end of the programs, and in recognition of the festive occasions for which most eighteenth-century concert music was written, he encourages his audiences to applaud between movements and carries on an interchange of dialogue with them when the circumstances are intimate enough to allow it. In addition to the Boston Symphony, he has conducted the Chicago Symphony, the Los Angeles Philharmonic, and the San Francisco, St. Louis, and Detroit symphonies on recent tours, and he brought the Academy over for its American debut in 1985. During the summer of 1983, a year after he made his own Mostly Mozart debut in New York, Hogwood inaugurated the first Mostly Mozart Festival in London, which proved so successful that it was repeated the following year.

In recent years, as his commitments with the Academy have multiplied along with his conducting engagements on four continents, Hogwood has had to curtail his concertizing as a solo harpsichordist. Going to some lengths to avoid being pigeonholed as an early music specialist, during his 1983 Australian tour he conducted works by Mendelssohn, Shostakovich, and Verdi, and he has expressed an interest in someday performing the work of several modern English composers. During 1983 he began talking about splitting the Academy into two groups, explaining to the *Ovation* interviewer: "Some of my players want to stay with Bach and Handel and not play later music; they will be in an orchestra for baroque music. The others will play Haydn, more Mozart and even some nineteenth-century works—the first five Schubert symphonies, and perhaps music of neglected composers like Hummel." The Academy has already recorded the first two Beethoven symphonies with

period scoring, instruments, and technique, undoing a century and a half of Romantic practice, and plans to release a complete set of the nine symphonies performed in the same fashion. And for all of his planned activity with early nineteenth-century music, he has continued his interest in Handel, as witnessed by the publication by Thames & Hudson in 1985 of his *Handel*, a critically acclaimed biographical study of the composer based on historical sources arranged in documentary fashion. Hogwood hopes someday to foster a revival of interest in the clavichord, which, in his opinion, is "such a perfect instrument."

Christopher Hogwood lives in a university-owned house at Jesus College of Cambridge University, where he has served on the music faculty since 1975, surrounded by an enviable collection of original harpsichords, virginals, and clavichords. His musical commitments oblige him to keep an apartment in London as well, but he still considers Cambridge to be his home. Hogwood's diversions, apart from his collection of period instruments, include the viewing of paintings, especially those dealing with musical subjects.

References: London Observer S 2 '84; Opernwelt 25:58+ n2 '84; Ovation 11:17+ D '83; Symphony p24+ D '84; New Grove Dictionary of Music and Musicians (1980); International Who's Who In Music and Musicians Directory (1980); Who's Who, 1985–86

## Horne, Lena

June 30, 1917– Singer; actress. Address: b. Sherman Sneed-Ralph Harris, 765 River Rock Rd., Santa Barbara, Calif. 93108

NOTE: This biography supersedes the article that appeared in *Current Biography* in 1944.

One of the high points of the 1980–81 Broadway theatrical season was *Lena Horne: The Lady and Her Music*, essentially a one-woman tour de force, although it included three backup singer-dancers. The show reviewed the highlights of the legendary singer's career, including her mid-1930s stint at Harlem's Cotton Club; her appearances in such Hollywood movies as *Cabin in the Sky* and *Stormy Weather*; her years as one of the top nightclub entertainers in the United States; and her starring role on Broadway in 1957-58 as Savannah in *Jamaica*. During much of her career, Lena Horne was noted for her work with civil-rights organizations. In the words of John Simon, writing in *New York* (May 25,1981), Lena Horne "is ageless. More young than old, perhaps, but tempered like steel, baked like clay, annealed like glass; life has chiseled, burnished, refined her."

Lena Calhoun Horne was born on June 30, 1917 in Brooklyn, New York into one of that borough's

"first black families." Her grandmother, Cora Calhoun Horne, was a prominent member of the NAACP and the National Urban League; her maternal grandfather was the first black member of the Brooklyn Board of Education; and an uncle, Dr. Frank Smith Horne, was a scholar, educator, and government administrator who served occasionally as unofficial adviser on race relations to President Franklin D. Roosevelt. Lena Horne's ancestors included natives of the former French West African colony of Sénégal, as well as Blackfoot Indians and white slaveowners. Her father, Edwin F. ("Teddy") Horne, a civil servant who was also a numbers runner and gambler, left home when she was three. Her mother, the former Edna Scottron, became a touring actress with the Lafayette Players, then the leading black stock company on the east coast. For several years, Lena was left at a succession of homes in various parts of the South, including that of her Uncle Frank in Fort Valley, Georgia.

"I never let myself love anybody," Lena Horne explained, as quoted in People (January 4, 1982), "because I knew I couldn't stay around." When she was twelve, she returned to Brooklyn to live first with her grandmother and then with her mother, who had remarried after her divorce. Over the years, she attended several different schools, including the Brooklyn Ethical Culture school, Public School 35, Girls High School in her home borough, and the Rosenwald Endowed Public Grade School in Fort Valley.

At sixteen, Lena Horne left school to help support her ailing mother. Through family connections, she landed a job as a chorus girl at Harlem's most famous nightspot, the Cotton Club, which was run by white racketeers. Over the next two years, she appeared in shows there with such personalities as Cab Calloway and Avon Long, eventually graduating to featured spots. In addition, for a brief period in October 1934 she played the small part of a quadroon girl in the Broadway play Dance With Your Gods, which ran for only nine performances. In 1935 she left the Cotton Club to become a singer with Noble Sissle's orchestra, with which she toured the East and Midwest for about a year, doing well enough to become the band's temporary leader, under the name Helena Horne, after Sissle was injured in an accident.

Largely because, as she explained to Audreen Buffalo in an interview for Essence (May 1985), she felt that she "had to get away from show business," Lena Horne was married in January 1937 to Louis J. Jones, a friend of her father who was active in Democratic party politics in Pittsburgh. Their two children, Gail and Edwin ("Teddy"), were born in 1937 and 1940, respectively. As it turned out, Miss Horne was forced to continue working, since her husband had difficulty obtaining employment during the Depression. In addition to singing at private parties in the Pittsburgh area, she made her screen debut in the low-budget, independently produced all-black film The Duke Is Tops (Millon Dollar Productions, 1938) and was a principal in Lew Leslie's short-lived Broadway revue Blackbirds of 1939.

Partly because Louis J. Jones felt resentment over his wife's career, the couple separated in 1940 and were divorced in 1944. Returning to New York in the autumn of 1940, Miss Horne was hired as a vocalist for Charlie Barnet's orchestra, becoming one of the first black performers to sing with a major white band. One of her recordings with Barnet, "Good for Nothing Joe," was a hit, and another, "Haunted Town," later became a collectors' item. After she left the band, John Hammond, the noted impresario and record producer, recommended her to Barney Josephson, the manager of the Cafe Society Downtown club in Greenwich Village, where she began a seven-month stint as a solo singer in March 1941, billed as Helena Horne. At the time, Miss Horne told Audreen Buffalo in the Essence interview, she was "only a fairish jazz singer" and "loved the blues but couldn't sing them," but that opinion was shared by few.

As soon as Lena Horne opened at Cafe Society Downtown, business increased dramatically, and three weeks later Josephson sponsored a concert for her at Carnegie Hall. While still at the club, Lena Horne made recordings with Teddy Wilson, who led the Cafe Society house band, and with Artie Shaw and Henry Levine's Dixieland Jazz Group. Later that year she made her first four solo records for RCA Victor, including "I Gotta Right to Sing the Blues" and "Moanin' Low." About that time, she also appeared regularly as a featured vocalist on radio shows.

Lena Horne has described her Cafe Society engagement as one of the happiest periods of her life, since she was educated about politics by Josephson and about singing by such artists as Teddy Wilson and Billie Holiday—who was then appearing at a nearby club. Nevertheless, in February 1942 she left for Los Angeles to star, along with Katherine Dunham's dancers and other black performers, in a show at the Little Troc nightclub in Hollywood. A New York Times correspondent wrote of the opening performance: "People who never went to night clubs pushed their way into the place four or five nights a week." And songwriter-producer Buddy de Sylva called Lena Horne "the best female singer of songs" he had ever heard.

After seeing her act, Roger Edens, a staff composer and arranger at Metro-Goldwyn-Mayer, arranged an audition for Miss Horne at that studio, where her singing so impressed mogul Louis B. Mayer and other executives that she was offered a contract. Despite personal reservations about whether she really wanted a film career, Lena Horne signed the long-term contract on the urging of friends, including the NAACP executive secretary Walter White and the bandleader Count Basie, who felt she might pave the way for other black artists.

After making her MGM debut with a small part in Cole Porter's Panama Hattie (1942), Lena Horne had her first major assignment, that of Georgia Brown, the devil's temptress, in the all-black musical Cabin in the Sky (MGM, 1943). In their 1984 biography, Lena; A Personal and Professional Biography of Lena Horne, James Haskins and Kathleen Benson asserted that "as played by Lena,

Georgia was not evil, but naughty, more impish than destructive. . . . [She] caused critics to appreciate the underlying humor in the story." Another all-black musical, *Stormy Weather* (Twentieth Century-Fox, 1943), based loosely on the life of Bill ("Bojangles") Robinson, featured such megastars as Robinson himself, Cab Calloway, and Fats Waller, but it was Lena Horne who had top billing. She was singled out for praise by Thomas M. Pryor of the *New York Times* (July 22, 1943), who called the film "a joy to the ear, especially when Miss Horne digs deep into the depths of romantic despair to put across the classic blues number, after which the picture is titled, in a manner that is distinctive and refreshing." Miss Horne had already sung the song "Stormy Weather," in her club act and recorded it, and over the years it became the song most closely associated with her.

Cabin in the Sky and Stormy Weather established Lena Horne as a star, but afterwards an impasse developed between the actress, who refused to portray maids or prostitutes, and her studio, which would not cast her in nonstereotyped roles. Furthermore, her light complexion did not fit the conventional image of what a black person should look like. As a result, her later film appearances were limited to musical numbers, separate from the main plot, which could be cut when the pictures played in the South. They included "Jericho" in the Red Skelton vehicle *I Dood It* (1943); "Honeysuckle Rose" in *Thousands Cheer* (1943); "You're So Indifferent" in *Swing Fever* (1943); "Somebody Loves Me" in *Broadway Rhythm* (1944); "Paper Doll" in *Two Girls and A Sailor* (1944); and "Love" in *Ziegfeld Follies* (1946). Often she sang while leaning against a pillar, a pose that became her trademark. In the *Show Boat* sequence of MGM's *Till the Clouds Roll By* (1946), a musical biography of composer Jerome Kern, Lena Horne played the mulatto Julie. She was considered for the same role when MGM remade *Show Boat* itself five years later, but lost out to Ava Gardner, who ironically wore the "Light Egyptian" makeup that Max Factor had devised especially for Miss Horne's skin. Lena Horne's last two films under her MGM contract were *Words and Music* (1948) and *Duchess of Idaho* (1950).

During World War II, Lena Horne was the favorite pinup girl of black soldiers. She personally contributed to the war effort, appearing as a regular at the Hollywood Canteen and making frequent tours of army bases around the country. Often her audiences were segregated, but the "last straw" for Miss Horne came when, at Fort Riley, Kansas, she found German prisoners of war seated in the front rows and American black soldiers behind them. Accounts of what happened next differ. Some maintain that she walked out, while according to others she simply complained to the NAACP and the tour's sponsors.

Between films and war-related activities, Lena Horne continued to work in nightclubs. The first black performer ever to play such spots as the Savoy-Plaza Hotel and the Copacabana in New York, she set box-office records at both places. By 1948 *Life* magazine could call her "the season's top nightclub attraction," and by 1952 the singer, who was by then a fixture in such cities as St. Louis and Las Vegas, was earning as much as $12,500 a week for her nightclub performances. During that period, Miss Horne deliberately cultivated a cold and aloof performing style. As she explained to Joan Barthel of the *New York Times* (July 28, 1968), "The image I chose to give is of a woman the audience can't reach and therefore can't hurt. They were not getting me, just a singer." In 1947 she traveled for the first time to London and Paris, where she also became a favorite. On the day after her Paris opening, *France Soir* put a three-column picture of her on its front page, with the caption "Un Triomphe." Her later trips abroad also took her to Scandinavia and Israel, and on a return visit to England she was presented to members of the royal family. In December 1947, in Paris, Lena Horne married Lennie Hayton, who had been a musical director at MGM and later served as her conductor and arranger. Their interracial marriage was a happy one until his death, in 1971.

Over the years, Lena Horne had been involved in social and political organizations such as the NAACP—in which she was enrolled by her grandmother when she was two. She was also active in the Hollywood Independent Citizens' Committee of the Arts, Sciences and Professions, the Hollywood Victory Committee, and Franklin D. Roosevelt's election campaigns. During the McCarthy witch-hunts of the early 1950s some organizations to which she had belonged became suspect, and that, along with her friendship with Paul Robeson, resulted in her being listed in the anti-Communist publications *Red Channels* and *Counterattack*. For a time she was unable to find work in films, radio, television, and some nightclubs, but she eventually overcame the blacklist. In 1956 she made a guest appearance in the MGM movie *Meet Me in Las Vegas* and signed a new recording contract with RCA Victor. One of her first LP records under that contract, *Lena Horne at the Waldorf-Astoria*, became the largest-selling album by a female performer in RCA's history. At about that time, also, she started to appear as a frequent guest with such television hosts as Ed Sullivan, Steve Allen, and Perry Como.

When Lena Horne starred for the first time in a Broadway musical, Harold Arlen and E. Y. Harburg's *Jamaica*, produced by David Merrick, critics expressed reservations about the show as a whole but lauded her performance. The observations of Richard Watts Jr. in the *New York Post* (November 1, 1957) were typical: "With her grace, her lithe dignity, her quiet humor, her curious combination of sullenness and sweetness, and her enormous and stirring skill at projecting a song for everything that is in it, she is one of the incomparable performers of our time." Thanks largely to its star, *Jamaica* ran for 555 performances at the Imperial Theatre in 1957–58. Lena Horne's next venture into the legitimate theatre, *Nine O'Clock Revue*, closed after its Toronto and New Haven engagements in 1961.

Lena Horne was strongly affected by events of the 1960s civil-rights movement, beginning with the first student sit-in at a Greensboro, North Carolina lunch counter. Once, in 1960, she threw ashtrays, plates, and a lamp at a patron of the Luau Restaurant in Beverly Hills in response to a racial slur. For the rest of the decade, she was one of the most visible black celebrities involved with the civil-rights movement, traveling South to sing and speak at rallies; taking part in a 1963 meeting between black leaders and Attorney General Robert F. Kennedy; and adding songs with civil-rights messages to her repertoire. In 1966 she took part in a series of round-table discussions sponsored by the National Council of Negro Women and its collegiate affiliate, the sorority Lambda Kappa Mu. Meanwhile, in 1965, Doubleday had published her autobiography, Lena, which she wrote with Richard Schickel.

Aside from appearing at civil-rights rallies and benefits, Lena Horne, who had never been especially fond of nightclubs, cut down considerably on her live performances during the 1960s. She could be seen, however, in her own television specials, including Lena in Concert, shown on NBC-TV in 1969, and Harry and Lena, a 1979 ABC-TV special, in which she was teamed with Harry Belafonte, as well as several that were made in Great Britain. In the Western Death of a Gunfighter (Universal, 1969), her first film in over a decade and the first in which she was cast in a straight dramatic role, she played the madam of the town brothel and the mistress of the hero, who was portrayed by Richard Widmark.

During a period of about a year, in 1970 and 1971, Lena Horne had to endure the deaths of her father, with whom she had become reconciled some years earlier, her son, who had been suffering from a kidney ailment, and her second husband, Lennie Hayton. At first, she did not want to go back to work, but then, as she told John Gruen during an interview, "I suddenly felt very strong—I felt tremendously alive." She resumed her tours of theatres and clubs throughout the United States, appearing with such co-stars as Alan King, Tony Bennett, or Count Basie. Her joint show with Bennett, called Tony and Lena, came to the Minskoff Theatre on Broadway for a three-week stand in 1974. In his review, John S. Wilson of the New York Times (November 1, 1974) noted: "Because of [Miss Horne's] more obvious attributes, the fact that she also has a remarkably good, flexible voice has often been overlooked. It is a voice with range and color and control that are rare in top singers." Also in 1974, Lena Horne portrayed Glinda the Good Witch in The Wiz (Universal), the all-black film version of The Wizard of Oz.

In the words of Newsweek's culture critic, Jack Kroll, the premiere of Lena Horne: The Lady and Her Music at the Nederlander Theater on May 12, 1981 "had the sort of effect that only the greatest theatrical events have." The show included many of the songs with which she had been identified during her career, including "Surrey With the Fringe on Top," "Can't Help Lovin' Dat Man," "Love Me or Leave Me, "Bewitched, Bothered and Bewildered," and, as the closing number, "Believe in Yourself" from The Wiz. She sang "Stormy Weather" twice, first imitating the way she had done it in Hollywood. Then, toward the end of the evening, she repeated the song to demonstrate how she had matured as a singer, prompting Frank Rich to comment in the New York Times (May 13, 1981): "Not only have we heard a great singer top what we thought to be her best work, but we've also witnessed an honest-to-God coup de théâtre." Originally scheduled for six weeks, the show was continually extended, running for a total of 333 performances, nearly all of them sold out. Although it opened too late to be eligible for the Tony awards, the public clamor was so great that it was given a special award, and it also won a Drama Desk Award, a special citation from the New York Drama Critics Circle, and two Grammys for the original cast album. In addition, Miss Horne received New York City's highest cultural award, the Handel Medallion, as well as the Emergence Award from the Dance Theatre of Harlem, and she had a scholarship established in her name at the Duke Ellington School of the Arts in Washington, D.C. More recently, she has won the Governor's Arts Award from New York State Governor Mario Cuomo and the Paul Robeson Award from Actors' Equity.

After Lena Horne: The Lady and Her Music finally closed in New York, on its star's sixty-fifth birthday, she took it on a tour of the United States and then, in the summer of 1984, to London, where the response was tumultuous. A televised version was shown on PBS's "Great Performances" series in December 1984, shortly after its star was feted, along with four other artists, at the annual Kennedy Center Honors ceremony in Washington, D.C. In early 1985 Miss Horne entered into discussions with Bill Cosby about the possibility of his producing a regular television series in which she would star.

Lena Horne is five feet five inches tall, weighs about 125 pounds, and has black hair and brown eyes. Although her performing trademarks of perfection, style, and taste remain as strong as ever, she now presents to audiences a mellowed persona compared to the aloofness of her early career. The fact that her popularity has been the result of her beauty and sex appeal as well as her talent has not always been gratifying to her. Under a Virgil Partch cartoon of a nightclub patron shouting, "Hey, Lena, sing something dirty," she once wrote, "The story of my life." Praised for keeping her looks over the years, she once attributed that fact, on the Mike Douglas Show, to "good strong stock and voodoo." She keeps her weight down by maintaining a careful diet and may frequently do without food she likes. Her surviving child, Gail, was divorced from film director Sidney Lumet in 1978. Miss Horne has five grandchildren. She makes her home in a converted olive mill in Montecito, near Santa Barbara, California. Her hobbies include landscape gardening, reading anything from murder mysteries to *The Autobiography of Malcolm X*, and listening to classical music and the latest popular hits. The singer and actress, who once had the ambition to become a schoolteacher, was awarded an honorary L.H.D. degree by Howard University in 1979.

References: Ebony 23:125+ Jl '68 pors, p39+ My '80 pors; Esquire 88:67+ Ag '77 pors; N Y Times II p13 Jl 28 '68 por, II p1 My 3 '81 pors; New York 14:16+ My 4 '81 pors; Show 3:62+ S '63 pors; Katz, E. Film Encyclopedia (1982); Notable Names in the American Theatre (1976); Who's Who in America, 1984-85

## Jarrett, Keith

*May 8, 1945– Musician; composer. Address: b. c/o Vincent Ryan, 135 W. 16th St., New York City, N.Y. 10011*

The gifted improvisational virtuoso Keith Jarrett is a unique phenomenon in contemporary music, and he may well turn out to be a profound force. Jarrett, whose primary instrument is the acoustic piano, is a lyrical visionary who "spontaneously" composes what he has called "a universal folk music." In his rapt, sustained musical explorations, he brings elements of pre-Schoenberg classicism together with a variety of other modes, especially jazz, in freeform collages, which he executes seamlessly and, often, spellbindingly. Trained in classical music, Jarrett apprenticed in the jazz quartets of Charles Lloyd and Miles Davis. The first of his recordings (which now number in the scores of discs, and

which routinely contain full-side cuts) were with his own jazz ensemble, but he solidified his reputation and amassed a surprisingly large (by alternative music standards) and predominantly young and fanatic following with the solo concert albums he began taping under the producer Manfred Eicher in Germany in 1972. Several years ago Jarrett, ever-changing in obedience to his personal muse, turned to orchestral settings, and since 1983 he has concentrated on classical recitals, chiefly of Baroque music.

Keith Jarrett is not partly Afro-American, as many have assumed, but wholly of European descent—Hungarian and Scottish-Irish to be precise. He was born on May 8, 1945 in Allentown, Pennsylvania, the first of five children, all sons, of Daniel Jarrett, a real-estate salesman, and Irma Jarrett. Eleven years later the parents separated, and from then on Mrs. Jarrett raised the children by herself, with the help of her mother. None of the boys scored less than 140 on I.Q. tests, according to Mrs. Jarrett; all became musicians. Mrs. Jarrett, long interested in metaphysical ideas, has in recent years been writing on mysticism.

"Keith learned to talk at six months," Irma Jarrett recalled in an interview with James Lincoln Collier for the *New York Times Magazine* (January 7, 1979). "We had a cheap record player, and when he was around two, I'd play symphonic music to him and ask him, 'What does this sound like?' Then he started to do the same thing on the piano—you know, make the sound of birds or thunder. He had perfect pitch. When he was three, I got him a teacher." Jarrett entered elementary school at the third-grade level, and he always, in his words, "consorted with older kids." Although a prodigy, he led a "normal" childhood. "If I awoke a half-hour early," he recalled in an interview with Jim Jerome of *People* (August 22, 1977), "it was to sneak past my grandmother and shoot baskets outside."

Jarrett began giving piano recitals in Allentown when he was seven, and it was not long before he was introducing compositions and improvisations of his own into the performances. Under a succession of teachers during childhood and adolescence, Jarrett was trained in a classical repertoire ranging from Bach to Debussy, Bártok, and Ravel. He studied composition for a year, when he was fifteen, worked a season on the road with Fred Waring's Pennsylvanians, and then turned his attention to jazz, in which he was strongly influenced by the impressionistic piano reveries of Bill Evans. After studying for a year on a scholarship at the Berklee School of Music in Boston, Jarrett, then nineteen, moved to New York City, where he and his wife lived impecuniously, in roach-infested cold-water flats in Spanish Harlem and on the Lower East Side, while he sought his fortune as a jazz musician.

At that time some of the biggest names in jazz in the New York area would congregate on Monday evenings at the Village Vanguard, the Greenwich Village club, for jam sessions organized by Rahsaan Roland Kirk, the late experimental saxophonist and composer. Being gigless most of the time, Jarrett attended the sessions, hoping for a chance to sit in. Finally, one night he was asked up to help finish the last five minutes of a set and, with the aplomb of a seasoned pro, proceeded to play not only the regular rhythmic backup expected of him but also a line to fill in for a missing bass. That "audition" was his passport to steady employment. After playing briefly with Rahsaan Roland Kirk, Art Blakey's Jazz Messengers, and Tony Scott, he began his first major apprenticeship, with the Charles Lloyd quartet. Lloyd indulged his bright young pianist in extended solos, one of which created a stir at the 1966 Newport Jazz Festival. Between 1966 and 1969 Jarrett toured Europe six times with Lloyd, becoming better known there than he was in the United States at the time. During the group's visit to Moscow in 1966, a performance of Jarrett's composition "Days And Nights Waiting" opened what was the first appearance by an American jazz ensemble at a Soviet music festival. A year later, Jarrett's "Sorcery" was performed at the Prague International Jazz Festival by the Moscow Radio-Television Orchestra.

In the United States the Charles Lloyd quartet was in the vanguard of "fusion" jazz. When the hippie "flower children" flocked to San Francisco in the late 1960s, the Lloyd group joined the pilgrimage, assuming "psychedelic" airs and giving breakthrough performances at the Fillmore Auditorium, the acid rock palace. Jarrett's theatrics—including, on occasion, climbing into the piano and plucking the strings directly with his hands—were eminently compatible with the countercultural spirit of the time. In 1970, after the Lloyd group broke up, Jarrett joined Miles Davis' fusion ensemble, which came to be known as the Davis Fillmore band. His tenure with that innovative Davis group was spasmodic, and it lasted only a year, but it was as congenial as could be expected, given the group's electrified instrumentation. Although he realizes that there was "no other way of playing what Miles was coming up with," he has always felt that "just being in the same room" with electric music "is harmful, like smoking cigarettes."

Meanwhile, between gigs with Lloyd and Davis, Jarrett was finding relief from electric music in acoustic sessions with bassist Charlie Haden and drummer Paul Motian. His first recording was the trio album *Life Between The Exit Signs* (Vortex, 1968), made with Haden and Motian. Later in the same year Jarrett, with an unidentified string quartet as backup, cut *Restoration Ruin* (Vortex), a three-ring showcase for his songwriting, his singing, and his playing of a variety of instruments, including soprano saxophone, harmonica, African percussion, and recorder. The album consisted of ten folk-rock-style vocals, some whimsical, some ironic or sardonic, and some romantic. On all of the tracks, Jarrett accompanied himself on guitar, usually overdubbing himself on several other instruments behind his singing. Reviewers of the album heard in it the strong influence of Bob Dylan, especially in the song "Fortunate." For some, the song

best suited to Jarrett's "thin" voice was the wispy "Sue New."

In 1971, after Jarrett left Miles Davis' band, the Jarrett-Haden-Motian trio became a quartet with the addition of saxophonist Dewey Redman. In the quartet's sessions, Jarrett often played soprano saxophone duets with Redman, and he pushed small-group conventions to new experimental limits. The quartet made its recording debut in June 1971 with *Birth* (Atlantic), and two months later Columbia Records released *Expectations*, on which the quartet was backed by other musicians. In a variety of musical settings—solo, in trio and sextet, and with string orchestra and brass section—Jarrett let loose on *Expectations* an unbridled, sustained pianistic flourish probably unprecedented in the history of jazz.

The American response to *Expectations* was mixed, and Columbia, following suit to Atlantic, dropped the Jarrett quartet. In France, however, the album was awarded the Grand Prix du Disque for best jazz album of the year, and the recording's reception was even more favorable in the Federal Republic of Germany. Early in 1972 the pianist Chick Corea suggested to the German record producer Manfred Eicher that he and Jarrett, along with two bass players, do an album for Eicher's ECM (Editions of Contemporary Music) label. Jarrett vetoed that proposal, but said that he would be willing to do a solo album. Eicher accepted the offer, and Jarrett left for Europe.

With ECM, Jarrett began a second, stronger career, thanks in part perhaps to the stimulus of the Northern European ambiance, and thanks certainly to Manfred Eicher, who granted Jarrett total freedom of artistic choice and whose meticulous production work gave Jarrett's recordings a shining finish. His work for ECM quickly took on a commercial and critical life separate from his work with his American quartet (which moved from Columbia to ABC-Impulse). Each of his solo albums for ECM was a new adventure, conceived and cast differently from the one before it. Together, those albums would represent Jarrett's definitive work for most of his fans during the 1970s.

Jarrett's first piano solo recording and his first disc for ECM, *Facing You* (1972), stunned European discophiles with its variety of styles, from the pianistic stridency of "In Front" to the measured passion of "My Lady; My Child." Writing of *Facing You* in *High Fidelity* just after the album's American release by Polydor three years later, Robert Hurwitz said: "One would be hard-pressed to find a more brilliant recent example of the delicate art of spontaneous composition. . . . One is struck by the pianist's enormous musical (as opposed to merely jazz) knowledge—his feeling for harmony and counterpoint, the wealth of melodic invention, his impeccable sense of time, perhaps most importantly his ability never to be locked into a rut or to have to draw on clichés. His music is always changing. Technically, there is little he cannot do." Hurwitz remarked that Jarrett is "a two-handed pianist," that unlike most jazz pianists, "who use their left hand as a harmonic anchor and their right as a singing line," Jarrett often uses both hands as "separate and equal voices," and he never does so "for mere pyrotechnic display."

The next Jarrett album released by ECM was *In the Light* (1973), consisting mostly of difficult music for chamber ensembles, including a brass quintet piece that Jarrett himself admitted was "nearly unplayable." From that recording, regarded as "flawed" by some critics, Jarrett moved to his "sublime" second solo album for ECM, the three-disc *Bremen/Lausanne* (1974), also titled *Solo Concerts*, consisting of live recordings of two concerts in those European cities. In his liner notes for that album, Jarrett described himself as "one artist creating spontaneously something which is governed by the atmosphere, the audience, the place (both the room and the geographical location), the instrument; all these being channeled . . . through the artist so that everyone's efforts are equally rewarded." In *Solo Concerts* and the subsequent live double album *Köln Concert* (ECM, 1975), recorded in Cologne, Jarrett "freely mixed," as Mikal Gilmore observed in *Rolling Stone*, "gospel, impressionist, and atonal flights into a consonant whole."

In Germany, Jarrett "evoked an extraordinary response," as the German writer Norbert Ely reported in an American edition of *Scala*. "His night concerts in Cologne and at the Hamburg State House and his improvisation on the organ at the Ottobeuren Benedictine Abbey are among the most important attempts to integrate a wide variety of cultural traditions in a common vision. Like Philip Glass, Jarrett is friendly with Stuttgart's general music director, Dennis Russell Davies, who . . . is attempting to implement his vision of a comprehensive new culture."

With the German connection came Jarrett's international apotheosis, especially in Japan. In the United States in the years following the release of *Facing You*, although the ECM recordings were slow in reaching American release through Polydor, he found and cultivated a widening audience that appreciated his lyrical, melodic music and his spontaneous, idiosyncratic playing and respected the demands he made upon it, the audience. His increasingly popular performances remained intimate affairs in which all applause between movements and compositions was forbidden and any distractions from the audience, including coughing, could bring a halt to his playing. Jarrett on stage was a study in Lisztian histrionics, twisting and gyrating his body over trills and ostinati, humming ecstatically, and commanding audience absorption in his own inner concentration and effort.

Jarrett was named jazz artist of the year in a 1973 *Rolling Stone* poll. The international jazz critics polled by *Down Beat* voted *Solo Concerts* the best jazz recording of 1974, and *Time* cited the same album as the best "pop" recording of the year. ("I'm pleased that they did that," Jarrett said. "They said, to hell with categories, we're going to put that album first.") *Köln Concert* sold 500,000 copies in four years, making it one of the largest-selling solo-piano recordings in history.

Meanwhile, Jarrett had not abandoned his ensemble work. In Europe he recorded several quartet albums, beginning with *Belonging* (ECM, 1974), with the Scandinavian musicians Jan Gabarek, Jon Christensen, and Palle Danielsson. With his American colleagues Redman, Haden, and Motian, he recorded three quartet albums for ABC/Impulse between 1973 and 1975: *Fort Yawuh* (recorded live at the Village Vanguard), *Treasure Island*, and *Death and the Flower*. When Jarrett performed with Gabarek, Christensen, and Danielsson at the Village Vanguard for five nights in 1979, the house was sold out each night and a thousand reservations were turned away. Jarrett's solos during that Vanguard gig were full of allusions to Bach, Monk, Copland, Beethoven, Debussy, and Gershwin, among others.

At the Newport Jazz Festival in 1976 Jarrett castigated members of the audience for returning to their seats too slowly, and on other occasions he scolded audiences not only for being noisy but also for being too quiet ("because you know they're being silent because they're not sure whether they should relax"). At a concert in Montreal he had just begun his program when a member of the audience coughed, followed by another, and another. Jumping up from the piano bench, Jarrett told the audience: "O.K., everybody cough!" "I've been considered—what's the word?—a typically touchy artist," Jarrett once explained to a reporter. "But people don't understand that I'm almost playing on the audience, instead of the piano. I mean, the audience is in the room and it's vibrating."

*Staircase* (ECM, 1977) consisted of studio improvisations by Jarrett. Five concerts he gave in Japan in 1976 were recorded live for the ten-disc ECM album *Sun Bear Concerts*. Released in December 1978, that album sold fairly well despite its list price of seventy-five dollars. The sales were abetted by a two-month tour of Australia, Japan, and the United States undertaken by Jarrett on the occasion of the album's release. While in Japan he rehearsed his symphonic orchestral composition, "The Celestial Hawk," which he planned to perform with conductor Seiji Ozawa and the Boston Symphony Orchestra in 1980. That plan fell through, and he performed the work instead with the Syracuse Symphony, in March 1980 at Carnegie Hall. As soloist, Jarrett did not use a full score but instead improvised his part from a lead sheet. John Rockwell of the *New York Times* described "The Celestial Hawk" as "popsy, trivial kitsch, prolix and pretentious, with passing moments of coloristic charm."

The following year, another *Times* reviewer, Stephen Holden, in reviewing the ECM studio album *Invocations* (to which digital recording brought an aural clarity unprecedented in Jarrett's discography) found the pianist to be, "after an uneven period in his career . . . at the peak of his powers." "Clarity of tone and dynamic control have always been two of Mr. Jarrett's greatest assets as a pianist," Rockwell wrote. "And the new album reveals just how important hearing, as opposed to harmony and compositional structure, is to Mr. Jarrett's spiritually-attuned aesthetic."

In the early 1980s Jarrett appeared with numerous orchestras in the United States and abroad in performances of Bartók's Second and Third Piano Concertos, the Samuel Barber Piano Concerto, the Stravinsky Concerto for Piano and Woodwinds, concertos by Mozart, and works composed especially for him by Lou Harrison, Colin McPhee, and Peggy Glanville-Hicks. In 1983 he announced that he was indefinitely suspending solo performances of his own work in order to concentrate on interpreting the compositions of others. Don Heckman, reviewing the album *Standards, Vol. 1* (ECM, 1983), found Jarrett's interpretations of old pop favorites such as "It Never Entered My Mind" and "The Masquerade is Over" to be "an absolute delight." Heckman especially liked the cut "All the Things You Are," where Jarrett's "intense melodicism pays off."

Since 1984 Jarrett has been confining his public performances to classical recitals, chiefly of Baroque works by Bach, Scarlatti, Beethoven, and Shostakovich, "ecstatic" composers for whom he feels a special affinity. Reviewing a sold-out recital by Jarrett at Avery Fisher Hall in 1985, John Rockwell observed in the *New York Times*: "Mr. Jarrett may not be Glenn Gould, but then again, Mr. Gould never had minions selling Gould T-shirts at his concerts either. That cross-over appeal drew an alert, sympathetic audience on Friday. More crucially, Mr. Jarrett plays well, and with further experience in this repertory he may play much better. He has a venturesome musical mind, eager to embrace new music and new ways of playing familiar music."

Jarrett has studied the works of G. I. Gurdjieff and Kahlil Gibran, and he is familiar, apparently, with the Tao and, certainly, with the Sufi theory of octaves ("a certain thing meets another thing until it isn't really notes anymore"), but he professes not to "know what the words 'philosophical' and 'spiritual' mean," especially as they apply to the "mysterious" process that goes on when he is spontaneously playing. Before his fingers touch the keys of the piano, he empties himself of thought, so that he is "a receptacle instead of machine." (That is why "what the audience does matters an awful lot.") "I don't believe that I can create, but that I can be a channel for the Creative," he explained in his notes for the album *Solo-Concerts.* "I do believe in the Creator, and so in reality this is His album through me to you." Because the piano and its condition are important in the process, he insists that concert promoters supply him with a concert grand and that they have it tuned both before and midway through each performance.

Keith Jarrett is of medium height and slight, wiry build. His complexion is swarthy and his hair, which he once wore Afro style, is curly. Intense, soft-spoken, and not given to small talk, he gives an initial impression of shyness and a more lasting

one of moodiness. Mikal Gilmore, who had difficulty buttonholing him for *Rolling Stone,* described his temperament as "haughty." Jarrett lives with his wife, Margot (whom he met in high school), and his two sons in a renovated Dutch Colonial farmhouse near the town of Oxford, New Jersey. Summers, he swims in the pool in his yard or plays tennis on a community court; winters, he skis on a nearby slope. Unless he changed vehicles in recent years, he drives an Alfa Romeo, a Jaguar, and a Jeep.

*References: Hi Fi 25:63+ My '75 por; N Y Times XII p1+ S 28 '75 por; N Y Times Mag p17+ Ja 7 '79 por; New Yorker 55:94+ My 28 '79; Newsday II p3 D 6 '81 por; People 8:60+ Ag 22 '77 pors; Rolling Stone p13+ Ja 25 '79 pors; Washington Post G p1+ D 7 '75; Rockwell, John. All American Music (1983); Who's Who in America, 1984-85*

## Jarvik, Robert K(offler)

*May 11, 1946– Physician; inventor; businessman. Address: b. 825 N. 300 W. St., Salt Lake City, Utah 84103*

In December 1982 "Jarvik-7," the first artificial heart to be permanently implanted in a human being, replaced the natural heart of Barney Clark, a terminally ill cardiac patient, who survived for 112 days with the plastic and aluminum device. Its designer is the physician and inventor Dr. Robert Jarvik, a protégé of Dr. Willem Kolff, the pioneer of biomedical engineering. The Jarvik-7 heart has since been successfully placed in the chests of several other seriously ill coronary patients. Jarvik is an assistant research professor of surgery at the University of Utah, as well as president of Symbion, Inc., a company that manufactures the prosthetic heart and other artificial organs.

Robert Koffler Jarvik, the son of Norman Eugene Jarvik, a physician, and Edythe (Koffler) Jarvik, was born on May 11, 1946 in Midland, Michigan and grew up in Stamford, Connecticut. Mechanically-minded and skillful with his hands, he assisted his father during operations, and while still in his teens designed surgical tools and invented an automatic surgical stapler.

In 1964 Jarvik entered Syracuse University in New York State, where his artistic inclinations prompted him at first to study architecture and mechanical drawing, but after his father had to undergo heart surgery for an aortic aneurysm in the following year, he decided to change to a premedical curriculum. In 1968 he obtained his B.A. degree in zoology. Jarvik has attributed his mediocre college grades to the fact that he was "not a conventional thinker" and did not put his major effort into his studies. As a result, he was repeatedly rejected when he applied to medical schools in the United States. For two years in the late 1960s Jarvik studied in Italy at the University of Bologna school of medicine, and after leaving that institution without graduating he entered New York University, from which he obtained an M.A. degree in occupational biomechanics in 1971.

Still determined to qualify as a physician, Jarvik considered applying to the University of Utah, with the hope that he might be accepted if he were a state resident. Meanwhile, the surgical supply house for which he was then working, Ethicon, Inc., offered to pay his salary if he could obtain a position with the Institute for Biomedical Engineering and Division of Artificial Organs in Salt Lake City, an affiliate of the University of Utah directed by Dr. Willem Kolff, the noted pioneer of "spare parts medicine."

In an article in the Wall Street Journal (July 24, 1984), Jarvik recalled that at first Kolff did not want to hire him even as a lowly lab assistant. "Then he asked what kind of car I drove. I said I had a Volvo, his car. And he changed his mind." According to Kolff, who was interviewed by Allen B. Weisse for Conversations in Medicine (1984), Jarvik was recommended to him by a colleague associated with Ethicon who described him as "a very ingenious fellow." A trailblazer in the field of artificial-organs research, Kolff had invented, during World War II, the first kidney dialysis machine, and began in the 1950s to work toward developing a total artificial heart. It was on that project that Jarvik concentrated his effort after he joined Kolff's institute.

Although envisioned since the early part of the nineteenth century, the idea of a man-made heart replacement had only in recent years been viewed as a feasible goal in modern medicine and was still encountering, when Jarvik entered the field, considerable technical obstacles. Consisting of a blood-pumping mechanism with a power supply system, the first devices, built by Kolff and others in the late 1950s, proved too cumbersome and heavy to fit within the chest cavity. Although that problem was alleviated by later models that replaced only the ventricles, or pumping chambers, of the natural heart, and used an external drive mechanism powered by compressed air, a variety of problems remained to be solved. In general, the successful artificial heart would need to be small in size, durable and dependable, and yet gentle in its action upon the circulatory system. The experimental mechanisms were implanted in dogs and calves, but early success had been limited, and the animals lived for only a short time.

In 1971 an artificial heart designed by Clifford S. Kwann-Gett, a member of Kolff's artificial-organs team, used a flexible rubber diaphragm as the pumping element which, activated by compressed air, actually forced blood in and out of the artificial heart. That innovation eliminated problems involving mechanical dysfunction, and survival periods for the experimental animals increased from one to two weeks in 1972. But a significant problem with that heart, and similar models, was a tendency for blood clots to form upon the diaphragm surface, a phenomenon that could eventually result in bleeding and death.

Jarvik's first important contribution helped to allay the problems inherent in the Kwann-Gett heart and similar devices. First designed in 1972, the Jarvik-3, as it was called, was better suited to fit the anatomy of experimental animals, and in later designs it had extremely flexible diaphragms made of multiple layers of smooth polyurethane instead of rubber. Biomer, as the material utilized by Jarvik is called, is an elastic material similar to the Lycra used in girdles. Animals receiving the Jarvik-3 were able to live for four months or longer in experiments carried out during the 1970s.

Meanwhile, with the help of Dr. Kolff, Jarvik had entered the University of Utah college of medicine in 1972 and received his M.D. degree in 1976. But instead of serving the customary internship and residency, Jarvik decided to devote his complete attention to the artificial heart, and to work full-time for Dr. Kolff in the artificial-organs division at the University of Utah Medical Center. In 1979 he became research assistant professor of surgery and bioengineering at the University of Utah School of Medicine.

In addition, in 1976 Jarvik became a prime associate in an artificial-organs research firm, a business venture that had been started by Dr. Kolff. Concerned that the research money made available for the artificial-organs program by the National Institutes of Health might someday be cut off, Kolff believed that a private company could best raise the necessary funds to continue work on the artificial heart. Originally known as Kolff Associates, and later named Kolff Medical, Inc., the company was started with limited capital and an uncertain source of revenue, and it was several years before its financial situation improved. In an article in Money magazine (April 1983), Jarvik told journalist Malcolm N. Carter, "We were a start-up company with a very long start-up phase . . . very long." At first Jarvik was the company's vice-president for research and development.

With a view toward imminent human implantation, Jarvik developed a model of the artificial heart that was smaller than earlier devices and designed to fit inside the chest of an average human patient. The Jarvik-7, as it was known, was being tested in calves and sheep by the late 1970s. Like previous models, it consisted of two artificial ventricles that would be attached to the natural atria of the human heart, and it was powered by compressed air from an electrical unit, located outside the patient's body and connected by tubes.

Early in 1981 Dr. Kolff made a formal request to the Food and Drug Administration, asking permission to implant the Jarvik-7 in a human patient. Although the FDA granted the request in September of that year, it took more than a year before a suitable subject was found, in accordance with the stringent guidelines set down by the FDA and the University of Utah. Finally, Barney Clark, a retired dentist suffering from cardiomyopathy, a degenerative and irreversible disease, was judged acceptable, and on December 2, 1982 he received the first artificial heart. Dr. William DeVries performed the surgery, and Jarvik assisted in the operation, which lasted seven-and-a-half hours.

The operation on Barney Clark brought worldwide attention to focus upon the artificial heart and those principally responsible for its development and implantation. Closely observed by the media, Clark lived for 112 days after surgery, in the face of a variety of complications. Except for a broken valve, which was replaced, the Jarvik-7 functioned perfectly throughout, and was still beating when Clark suffered multiple organ failure, and death, on March 23, 1983. Regarding the operation as a success, since it proved that artificial hearts could sustain life for a long time, Jarvik, DeVries, and others on the Utah team looked toward future implantations.

Concurrently with events leading to the operation on Clark, Jarvik played a major role in business dealings relating to the artificial heart. According to the article by Malcolm N. Carter, Jarvik had emerged as an aggressive corporate officer of the company established by Kolff, now known as Symbion, Inc. In 1981 he had prevailed upon Kolff to name him president of the company, and to allow him to exercise the powers of chief executive officer. Together with businessman W. Edward Massey, he also sought venture capital from investors, and succeeded in gaining the backing of the investment firm of E. M. Warburg Pincus & Company. In the subsequent deal, arranged with Jarvik's approval, Kolff was deliberately left out of the management affairs of the company, although he remained chairman of the board. That caused a rift between the two men, and though they were said to have been reconciled, Jarvik told David Zinman, as quoted in Newsday (April 9, 1985), that

Kolff remained "very unhappy" with him. With reference to some of Kolff's proposed innovations, he added: "If the company were to succeed, it could not spend a lot of money playing around with a lot of impractical ideas. The company is there to succeed financially. It has to." According to Kolff, he and Jarvik had at first developed a very good relationship. "It would be described as a father-son sort of thing," he remarked, "but sometimes the son revolts against the father."

When approval for another artificial-heart operation was slow in coming, as a result of stringent requirements laid down by the University of Utah, William DeVries—the only physician whom the FDA had authorized to carry out the implantation—moved his practice to Humana Hospital Audubon in Louisville, Kentucky in October 1984. A private hospital corporation, which had also been a backer of Symbion, Inc., Humana committed itself to an aggressive policy to continue experimentation with the artificial heart.

The second recipient of the Jarvik-7 artificial heart was fifty-two-year-old William J. Schroeder, who received a device with an improved valve and smaller external drive mechanism, in a six-and-a-half-hour operation, on November 25, 1984. In an article in the Wall Street Journal (November 20, 1984), Jarvik expressed his belief that even though Schroeder could conceivably die during surgery or soon after, he might also hope to live a year following the implant. Jarvik forecast four possible complications: formation of blood clots, calcium buildup, mechanical failure, or infection stemming from the drive lines that connected the heart to the power source.

Although Schroeder survived the initial heart operation, eighteen days after the implant he suffered a stroke that caused impairment of his memory and speech. Nevertheless, his postoperative physical condition improved enough so that he was able to leave Humana in early April 1985 and move to a specially equipped "transition apartment" across the street from the hospital. Jarvik told David Zinman of Newsday (April 9, 1985) that for him, Schroeder's stroke "was probably one of the biggest disappointments . . . of anything that has ever happened."

The implantation of the Jarvik-7 in other terminally ill patients lent a sagalike character to the story of the artificial heart, and each new operation was widely reported in the press. The third recipient of the Jarvik-7 at Humana Hospital was Murray P. Haydon, a fifty-eight-year-old retired auto worker, whose three-and-a-half-hour operation on February 17, 1985 was described by Dr. DeVries as "perfect." On April 9, 1985 Dr. Bjarne K. H. Semb at the Karolinska Thoracic Clinic in Stockholm, Sweden implanted the Jarvik-7 in an anonymous patient who was later identified as Leif Stenberg. Jarvik, who as in the previous implant operations was present in the operating room to lend assistance and advice, revealed afterward that Symbion donated the $15,500 Jarvik-7 heart to the Karolinska clinic because it was felt that much could be learned from working with Dr. Semb and his team.

Jack. C. Burcham, a sixty-two-year-old retired railroad engineer, became the fifth recipient of the Jarvik-7 artificial heart in a six-hour operation by Dr. DeVries at Humana on April 14, 1985 but died ten days later, following complications. In late August 1985, at the University Medical Center in Tucson, Arizona, a Jarvik-7 pump was implanted by Dr. Jack G. Copeland into twenty-five-year-old Michael Drummond of Phoenix, as a stopgap measure, pending availability of a human heart. A few days later, in early September, Dr. Copeland successfully replaced the Jarvik-7 in Drummond with the living heart of a recent motorcycle accident victim.

Jarvik is currently refining a fully portable Jarvik-8 heart that will be battery-powered and as easy to carry as a briefcase. Although the main emphasis at Symbion in Salt Lake City has been on the artificial heart, under Jarvik the company has branched out to the development of other synthetic organs, including an artificial ear. Research on the artificial heart has also recently begun in such locations as Cleveland, Phoenix, and Hershey, Pennsylvania, as well as Austria, France, West Germany, Czechoslovakia, and Japan. In May 1985 a panel of experts convened by the National Heart, Lung and Blood Institute endorsed the artificial-heart program and recommended increased federal support for development of a fully implantable synthetic heart, free of outside support systems.

Robert K. Jarvik and his ex-wife, the former Elaine Levin, a journalist, whom he married on October 5, 1968, have two children, Tyler and Kate. Jarvik was described by David Zinman of Newsday (April 9, 1985) as slight of build and dark-haired, with "the face of a Russian ballet dancer." His avocations include skiing and weightlifting; he also reads poetry and retains an interest in theoretical physics; and he once sculpted a bust of his mentor, Dr. Kolff. According to his former wife, during their engagement Jarvik drove to Alaska to pan for gold, from which he fashioned a wedding ring for her. And on being informed of the birth of his son, he immediately put a Handel trumpet suite on the record player, so that the child could arrive with the proper fanfare.

Jarvik is the author of more than sixty scientific publications since 1972 and holds five United States patents. In February 1983 he was named inventor of the year by the National Inventors Hall of Fame. At the time he declared that he was "not really the inventor of the artificial heart" and held no patents on it, but he acknowledged that he helped to develop the Jarvik-7 and accepted the award in behalf of a series of artificial-heart developers, going back more than twenty years. The Utah chapter of the National Conference of Christians and Jews honored Jarvik with a Brotherhood Citation in 1983. That same year, Jarvik won the John W. Hyatt Award of the Society of Plastics Engineers, the Golden Plate of the American Academy of Achievement, and the Gold Heart Award of the Utah Heart Association. He holds an honorary doctor of science degree from Syracuse University.

In 1984 he received a creative leadership award from the New York University Alumni Association and was chosen by Esquire magazine as one of the outstanding Americans under forty. In 1985 the governor of Connecticut designated February 14 as "Dr. Robert Jarvik Day." He is a member of the American Society for Artificial Organs and a fellow of the United States Public Health Service.

Sometimes described as a visionary, and often noted for his tendency to court publicity and attention, Jarvik set forth the goal of his invention rather simply in his article "The Total Artificial Heart," in the January 1981 issue of Scientific American: "If the artificial heart is ever to achieve its objective, it must be more than a pump. It must also be more than functional, reliable and dependable. It must be forgettable."

References: Money 12:131+ Ap '83 por; Newsday Discovery p3 Ap 9 '85 por; N Y Times A p24 D 3 '82 por; Who's Who in America, 1984-85

## Johnson, Sonia

Feb. 27, 1936– Social activist; educator. Address: h. 3318 Second St. South, Arlington, Va. 22204

Since 1977, when she began her active support of the Equal Rights Amendment to the United States Constitution, thus setting off a train of events that led to her excommunication in 1979 from the Church of Jesus Christ of Latter-Day Saints, or Mormon church, Sonia Johnson has adopted a public life that is focused on a radical feminist message of social transformation. Before that time, as she has recounted in her autobiography From

*Housewife to Heretic* (1981), her perspective was that of a traditional, church-loving Mormon, a wife and mother, and a former teacher and missionary with a Ph.D. degree who struggled to adapt to a structure that she now believes was meant to control and oppress women.

With a reputation as a rousing speaker and controversial tactician, Sonia Johnson has become a familiar figure in the American political left, whose feminism is a comprehensive philosophy of living and governing: "All the ways that have been called 'womanly,' and therefore weak and dumb, are the nonviolent, cooperative ways we need now to prevent atomic destruction," she has declared. Her campaign as presidential candidate for the Citizens Party in 1984 enhanced her prominence in left-of-center politics and extended her interests into international work in behalf of women and of peace.

A fifth-generation Mormon, Sonia Johnson was born Sonia Harris in Malad, Idaho on February 27, 1936. The family also included an older brother and sister, Paul and Joyce, and two younger brothers, Michael and Mark. Around the time of Sonia's birth, her religiously devout parents were teachers at a Shoshone Indian reservation across the state border in Utah. For most of the time until she was twelve, the Harris family lived in Preston, Utah, where her father taught at a Mormon seminary. They then settled in Logan, Utah.

In her autobiography *From Housewife to Heretic* (Doubleday, 1981; Anchor, 1983) Sonia Johnson recalls the tightly knit Mormon culture in which she was raised as "a warm, secure world . . . where heaven and its powerful inhabitants were intimately involved in human affairs and perpetually on call." Family prayer gatherings each morning and evening, long Sunday services, and neighborhood "family home evenings," as well as the traditions of tall-tale telling and accounts of miracles, made the church the center of life and a powerful formative influence. "I realized that my religious training at home far surpassed that of most Mormons," Sonia Johnson has recalled, "partly because discussion of religion was going on in one way or another most of the time, and partly because I had a philosophical bent and searched it out myself with interest and enthusiasm." From the time she entered her early teens she played the organ for Sunday services.

But her protective cocoon of religious doctrine and practice was not without its contradictions. A "longing and often lonely child," Sonia became progressively more puzzled about herself, a sense of unease she now ascribes both to the adult conspiracy of silence about the quakings of pubescent sexuality and to endemic sexism. "I felt," she wrote in her autobiography, "as if something were deeply awry and, as females are taught to do, assumed something must be deeply awry within *me*." Just as her mother sacrificed all her energy to the family, Sonia and her sister were expected to cater to their brothers and father in household chores. That pattern she now sees as an iron lesson that all her

"human talent and complexity were to be focused into the narrow goal of finding a man." Her rare acts of rebellion, such as her outspoken repudiation of a church lecture on the irreparable defilement that sexually active girls—but not boys—supposedly brought upon themselves, ran up against a stone wall of resistance. The blame and confusion she felt as an adolescent began to gnaw at her self-confidence.

After she graduated from Logan High School, Sonia Harris attended Utah State University, where she received a bachelor's degree in English in 1957. She took her graduate work at the University of Minnesota and also at Utah State in Logan, where, in the summer of 1958, she met Rick Johnson, a graduate student in educational psychology and a Baptist. Impressed by the consideration and intellectual respect he showed her, she came to love him and began to hope for marriage. Although Rick Johnson's qualities were genuine, she now looks back at her "desperation" for a wedding ring somewhat ruefully: "I was a perfectly conditioned patriarchal woman. . . . As a woman, I had to have a man front for me in society, a man to lean on, to depend on for my definition of myself." Rick Johnson converted to the Mormon faith, and they were married at her parents' home on August 21, 1959.

After working for several months as a bookkeeper to support her husband's completion of his studies for a master's degree, Sonia Johnson traveled with him and her brother Mark in early 1960 to western Samoa, where they were teaching missionaries for about a year. The couple next moved to Minneapolis, where both attended graduate school at the University of Minnesota, but Sonia Johnson discontinued her studies after a few semesters when their first child was born. She resumed her academic pursuits, however, at Rutgers University in New Jersey, where Rick Johnson secured a teaching position after receiving his doctoral degree. By switching her earlier English credits into the university's education program, Sonia Johnson was able to complete an education degree in the teaching of English, finishing her doctoral dissertation a few days before the birth of their second child in about 1965.

There followed a long period of global travel for the family, first in Palo Alto, California in 1967, where Sonia Johnson taught a night school course while Rick Johnson taught at Stanford University. They then went to Korea, Malawi, and Malaysia, where they again combined teaching with missionary work and enjoyed several "good years, full years" of an active and devout life. When Mormon church directives were issued in 1968 restricting women's prayer leadership at sacrament meetings and placing women's auxiliary groups, according to Sonia Johnson, under men's administrative control, she felt only a vague uneasiness. Yet an occasional awareness of "something lacking" in herself caused her guilt and depression. Her sporadic but satisfying teaching career, which conflicted with the role of a "sanctified housewife," might, she feared, incur God's displeasure—and that of the powerful men who claimed to speak for God. A serious bout of fatigue she suffered during that period, culminating in an attack of rheumatoid arthritis, was apparently cured after she attended a healing prayer session with the Mormon bishop of the Palo Alto area and her husband, but in her autobiography she reflected, "I may very well have given myself arthritis to punish myself for not being happy doing God's will. . . . I'd turned my body into a battlefield for my emotions."

During 1975 the Johnsons traveled across country in a mobile home, evaluating Title I teaching projects for the United States Office of Education. They finally bought a regular home and settled with their four children in Sterling Park, Virginia in mid-1976, where Sonia Johnson worked part-time at an editing job and, later, taught composition classes at George Mason University in Fairfax, Virginia. Meanwhile she gave lessons in doctrine at a local Relief Society church group for women and played the organ at Mormon services. At the suggestion of a Mormon friend, she and her husband began to read books on feminism, and her interest in that subject grew. Meanwhile, the proposed Equal Rights Amendment (ERA), which would constitutionally prohibit discrimination on the basis of sex, was attracting public attention—and formal Mormon disapproval.

Her "epiphany" came one night in the spring of 1977, when she attended an address by the regional parish (or "stake") president on the Mormon church's opposition to the ERA. To her dismay, she found his remarks to be condescending and ineptly prepared, and his argument that the ERA was unnecessary because Mormon women were exalted rather than stifled seemed to her ludicrous. In a flash of radicalization, she "saw through their rhetoric to the pervasive and profound sexism of the leaders of [her] church. . . . " "I knew instantly what the women's movement was all about; I knew it in my very bones. . . . I knew where women were in this society and where they had been for thousands of years," she has recounted. From that date she consciously began "a painful, beautiful birth" as a "full human being" who understood that patriarchal, or male-dominated, culture oppressed women's lives.

During the next two-and-a-half years, Sonia Johnson's radical new approach to the social status of women increased in articulateness and fervor. She helped to found Mormons for ERA, a lobbying and public-education group that gained a small but loyal nationwide following of about 500 members. Under that banner she joined some 100,000 marchers in Washington, D.C., in July 1978 who supported an extended ratification time for the ERA, which was still unapproved after seven years of state-by-state deliberation. At the invitation of the staff of Senator Birch Bayh, chairman of the Senate Subcommittee on Constitutional Rights, she testified in the Senate hearings on the extension measure, coming during questioning into direct confrontation with Senator Orrin G. Hatch of Utah,

a Mormon and an opponent of the ERA. In the fall of that year the Congress agreed to a three-year extension.

Although Sonia Johnson continued her church activities and was assured by some Mormons that support for the ERA was not doctrinally heretical, her bluntly feminist stance inevitably brought her into friction with her basically conservative church. She admits that, like "guerrilla warriors," Mormons for ERA pressured the church structure with conspicuous publicity displays and continual but unsuccessful requests for meetings with the church president. A revival by feminist Mormons of a minor church tradition about the eternal "Mother" in heaven who cared for her children with as much authority as the eternal "Father" also aroused some ire within church circles. During that turbulent time, Sonia Johnson had the full support of her husband in her work for the ERA.

As her own political involvement and public speeches gained media attention, church leaders came to see Sonia Johnson as directly undermining the church's authority. The tension came to a head when she claimed publicly that the church was operating a well-funded anti-ERA lobby in several states under the cover of its missionary work. Thanks to her efforts, the Virginia LDS Citizens' Group, a Mormon group that had been organizing opposition to the measure, was required to register as a political lobby in March 1979. Then, in the fall of 1979 Sonia Johnson was informed by regional church leaders that an excommunication action was being considered against her. The charges—influencing members and non-members to oppose church programs; advocating diminished support for church leaders; and presenting false doctrine on the nature of God—avoided any direct mention of her political activities. Despite her growing impatience with the local Mormon leaders, Sonia Johnson still called herself a loyal adherent to the faith and tried to rally a defense that would demonstrate that she had never challenged the Church's doctrinal authority.

The excommunication trial of December 1, 1979 was held in a closed session at an Oakton, Virginia church center while reporters and hundreds of supporters waited outdoors. According to Sonia Johnson's account, her presentation was hobbled by a prohibition against direct testimony about the ERA and by the announcement of several new, unfamiliar charges, factors that prevented her from fully defending her actions. Several days later, the verdict finding her guilty of "seditious actions" and "serious defection from the church and its doctrines," and therefore excommunicated, was announced. Stunned and tearful, she told the press, as reported by Ellen Goodman in the *Washington Post* (December 8, 1979), that she still loved the church and did not believe that God was "bound by men's mortal errors." "I'm not afraid of God doing something that 'old boyish,'" she told Ellen Goodman. Sonia Johnson suffered another blow at that time, when her husband informed her that he wanted a divorce, for reasons having nothing to do with the political issues they had faced together.

Cut off from her two most important relationships, Sonia Johnson nevertheless reaffirmed her commitment to women's rights and, in fact, expanded her view of the drastic changes needed in society if women—and men—were to achieve liberation. For the next two years she brought that message to the lecture circuit, speaking before such groups as the American Association of University Women, the Women's Bar Association, the League of Women Voters, the American Humanist Society, and college students. In the summer of 1980 she addressed the Democratic National Convention in New York City and attended the World Conference on Women in Copenhagen, Denmark. More controversial were the several civil disobedience protests in front of the White House that she helped to initiate in opposition to Reagan administration policies that she considered sexist or militaristic. When *From Housewife to Heretic* was published in 1981, reviewers generally applauded her impassioned and revealing account of her life story and of her change in social consciousness.

As the extended deadline for ratification of the Equal Rights Amendment drew near in mid-1982, supporters focused their lobbying attention upon the undecided states of Florida, Oklahoma, North Carolina, and Illinois—three of which would have to approve the amendment to meet the constitutional requirement of passage by three-fourths of the state legislatures. Sonia Johnson joined seven other pro-ERA women in a thirty-seven-day "Women's Fast for Justice," staged, beginning on May 18 of that year, at the rotunda of the Illinois State Capitol building in Springfield. The fast was described by its participants, among them a Roman Catholic nun and a California businesswoman, as a "life-giving process" and "religious witness." The group drank only bottled water during that period, taking no solid food. A support team from the National Organization for Women (NOW) attended them as they grew progressively weaker in their daily trek (via a van funded by *Ms*. magazine editor Gloria Steinem) from a nearby motel to the rotunda for each day's three-hour vigil, often conducted from wheelchairs. Sonia Johnson was hospitalized three times for physical complications caused by her fast.

Reaction to the hunger fast was decidedly mixed, even within the feminist community. Gloria Steinem, for example, was quoted in *Newsday* (June 8, 1982) as questioning whether "a piece of paper is worth losing one life." And there was also outright hostility, such as that demonstrated by an opposition group who pointedly consumed a full-course meal alongside the fasters one afternoon. Some legislative supporters of the ERA tempered their enthusiasm out of reluctance to be identified with the potentially fatal protest, but Sonia Johnson defended the cause of women's rights as worth dying for. As she later explained to a reporter for the Madison, Wisconsin journal *Feminist Connection* (December 1982): "When Patrick Henry said, 'Give me liberty or give me death,' nobody said, 'Oh, come on! What an extreme statement!'" Although the Illinois lawmakers defeated the ratification proposal at the end of June, thus sealing the ERA's demise, Sonia Johnson declared the fast a success in a homecoming speech at National Airport in Washington, D.C., because, she said, "it show[ed] that ordinary women can do extraordinary things. We're much greater than we dreamed. The women's movement has just begun." On the same occasion she announced her candidacy to become president of NOW. That election, held in October 1982, was won by Judy Goldsmith, with Sonia Johnson taking 40 percent of the vote. (A second bid for the NOW presidency, which she attempted in July 1985, yielded Sonia Johnson only a small percentage of votes, as Judy Goldsmith's main challenger, Eleanor Smeal, won the post for a second time.)

Early in 1983 the Citizens Party, a national left-wing political party dedicated to economic democracy, environmental protection, and nuclear disarmament, among other issues, approached Sonia Johnson as their potential candidate in the 1984 presidential election. (Barry Commoner, the economist, ran as the Citizens Party's presidential choice in 1980.) At first she rebuffed the suggestion, but after six months of encouragement from party members and a warm reception at the party's national convention in San Francisco in September 1983, she agreed, convinced that her feminist analysis of problems confronting the United States and the world dovetailed with the organization's overall criticism of systemic injustice. Soon after becoming the party's virtually unopposed nominee for president, she was joined by Richard Walton, a foreign-policy analyst and party activist from Rhode Island, as her vice-presidential running mate. As Sonia Johnson made clear in an early campaign letter, she hoped her candidacy would prove that "war, pollution, poverty, inequality, and powerlessness of individuals are *not* inevitable. . . . I am running to say that there cannot be peace in the world without justice, without compassion, without mercy at home." In addition, the backing of a coordinated political network amplified her message that the injustices women face are a key to global problems.

Throughout 1984 Sonia Johnson stumped in almost every state in the nation, outlining policy proposals that departed emphatically from the views expressed by President Ronald Reagan and Walter F. Mondale, the presidential contenders for the two major parties. She advocated a foreign policy committed primarily to human rights, which would entail, in her view, the withdrawal of United States military personnel from Lebanon and Central America, the halving of the United States' military budget, and the removal of Pershing II and Cruise nuclear missiles from Western Europe. With the savings realized from a decreased military budget she would reduce the national deficit and restore social programs. In other areas of domestic policy, Sonia Johnson called for the scrapping of nuclear power projects, pointing to safety and financial concerns; supported a policy of equal pay for comparable work by both sexes; favored legislation requiring industrial plants to give their workers a two-year advance notice before plant relocation; and advocated homosexual-rights measures. Those basic left-wing platform planks were complemented by her more "creative" proposals to declare a "national emergency plan" to eradicate the militarized "conquistador" mentality from the culture and to bring global arms decisions under the control of an international group of "non-patriarchal" women. Sonia Johnson's unorthodox status as a presidential candidate was underscored when she announced, in April 1984, that she would refuse to pay federal income taxes that year in protest of military expenditures and, in May, that she was joining the Center for Constitutional Rights in a plan to make a citizen's arrest of President Reagan for violation of the War Powers Act and of international law in his foreign policies.

By raising more than $180,000 from private contributions for her campaign fund, Sonia Johnson became the first third-party presidential candidate to qualify for federal primary matching funds. Her campaign was not successful, however, in its case requesting the Federal Communications Commission to order Sonia Johnson's inclusion in the televised presidential debates, which are sponsored by the League of Women Voters. The campaign committee filed suit in October 1984 with the U.S. Court of Appeals in Arlington, Virginia, charging a violation of First Amendment rights on the basis that the debates had become a virtual public institution and participation in them was a prerequisite for winning an election. No decision was announced in time to affect the 1984 election.

In the hard-fought presidential election of November 1984, all third-party candidates combined received only about 1 percent of the vote nationally, as voters of different liberal stripes, loath to expend their ballots on lesser known contenders, rallied behind Walter Mondale, the Democrat, in an unsuccessful effort to defeat the Republican incumbent, Ronald Reagan. Sonia Johnson appeared on the ballot in eighteen states, including California, Pennsylvania, Illinois, New Jersey, Utah, and Michigan, and she was an official write-in choice in sixteen other states. Despite the disappointing, if unsurprising, result, Sonia Johnson believed that her effort may have achieved "other victories." "The idea is to change people's values . . . ," she remarked. "To help raise the consciousness about women, to help empower women, to begin to get into people's minds new ideas about women. I would consider that winning."

Sonia Johnson is an attractive, dark-haired woman whose well-groomed personal appearance gives the lie to images of radical activists as blue-jeaned, hirsute ragamuffins. Since her divorce from Richard Johnson she has been the sole support of herself and their four children: Eric, Kari, Marc, and Noel. While she was a presidential candidate she broadened her political efforts into the international arena, notably as a member of a women's delegation that traveled to Nicaragua, Honduras, and El Salvador and as a founder, after a visit to Europe in early 1984, of Women's International Disarmament Alliance, a network for coordinating women's peace movements throughout the world. She has said that she sees herself as a "pioneer" who plans to continue her public work for women and for the survival of the human species.

References: Chicago Tribune XII p1+ D 7 '80 por; Ms 8:39+ Mr '80 pors; N Y Times A p18 D 3 '79; People 14:67+ D 29 '80 pors, 17:93+ Je 28 '82 pors; Washington Post D p1+ Je 11 '82 por, A p5 O 29 '84 por

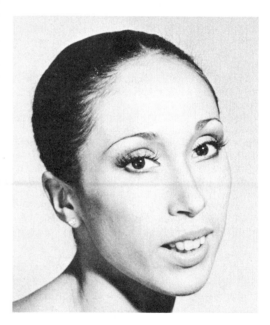

## Johnson, Virginia

Jan. 25, 1950– Dancer. Address: b. c/o The Dance Theatre of Harlem, Inc., 466 W. 152d St., New York City, N.Y. 10031

Unquestionably the reigning prima ballerina in the unranked Dance Theatre of Harlem, Virginia Johnson has a technical and emotional range that is ideally suited to the company's eclectic repertory. Although she is essentially a lyrical dancer known for her purity of line, superb extension, and exquisite musical phrasing, she has over the years extended her command of the dance vocabulary, becoming versatile enough to move with ease from such flamboyant, technically taxing classical showcases as the Don Quixote pas de deux to the muscularly modern style of Voluntaries. A member of the Dance Theatre since its founding in 1969, Miss

Johnson came into her own in the 1980s as an affecting dance-actress in a series of dramatic ballets, including *A Streetcar Named Desire* and *Fall River Legend*, and perhaps most spectacularly, in the so-called "Creole" *Giselle*, Arthur Mitchell's inspired reinterpretation of the Romantic classic.

Virginia Alma Fairfax Johnson was born in Washington, D.C. on January 25, 1950 to James Lee Johnson, a naval architect, and his wife, Madeline (Murray) Johnson, a physical education instructor at Howard University. She has an older sister, Suzanne, who works in merchandising for the fashion designer Calvin Klein, and a younger brother, Kurt, a bank manager. Reared in a home filled with music, Virginia Johnson exhibited at an early age the superior dancer's innate musicality. Recognizing their daughter's natural ability, the Johnsons enrolled the little girl in the Washington School of Ballet when she was just three years old, where her instructor was Mary Day, the renowned teacher and choreographer and the school's cofounder. Although her initial training was classically oriented, Virginia Johnson eventually expanded her study to include modern dance.

Following her graduation from the Washington, D.C. public school system, Virginia Johnson, who had been named a University Scholar, enrolled in the dance program at New York University's School of the Arts. Because there were so few opportunities for black performers in classical ballet companies, her instructors encouraged her to concentrate on modern or jazz dance, but having resigned herself to becoming a ballet teacher, she resisted. "The trouble was classes were mostly in modern dance . . . ," she explained to Frances Herridge in an interview for the *New York Post* (January 2, 1981). "I kept wanting to do the traditional ballet technique. Then I heard that Arthur Mitchell was teaching just that up in Harlem. So I started spending my Saturdays there."

Under the tutelage of Mitchell, a former principal dancer with the New York City Ballet, and Karel Shook, the former ballet master of the Dutch National Ballet, who joined together in 1969 to found the Dance Theatre of Harlem, Miss Johnson, a charter member of the new troupe, progressed rapidly. At the time, there were only a handful of dancers in the company, and it had "no repertory, no costumes, and no building—nothing," as she recalled to Burt Supree in an interview for the *Village Voice* (September 25, 1984). "It was just a dream. But a belief in Dance Theatre made it a special place to work from the start. We knew we were a serious company." She made her first professional appearance in the company's official debut performance, at the Solomon R. Guggenheim Museum in New York City on January 8, 1971, dancing leading roles in the world premieres of three works by Arthur Mitchell: *Rhythmetron*, a formal "court ball" dance with jazzy accents, the neoclassic *Fête Noire*, and *Tones*, in which she and partner Walter Raines shone in the brisk, Balanchinian central pas de deux.

Over the next few years, in Dance Theatre of Harlem performances in New York City, at other venues in the Northeast, and in Europe, most notably, at the Spoleto (Italy) Festival in 1971, Virginia Johnson appeared in virtually every work in the company's growing repertory. She was perhaps most effective in John Taras' romantic pas de deux *Design For Strings*, as the earth goddess in Walter Raines's episodic oriental allegory *Haiku*, in the fluttery love duet in Louis Johnson's *Wings*, and in the sassy "Shout" solo in his *Forces of Rhythm*, which traces the development of black dance. Her special affinity for the choreography of Arthur Mitchell was never more evident than in *Holberg Suite*, a well-crafted, plotless exercise enlivened by her crisp, picture-perfect pirouettes and quicksilver *batterie*.

Despite a classical technique that was arguably the strongest in the entire company, Virginia Johnson, who is by nature somewhat reserved and serious, spent her first few years with the Dance Theatre of Harlem in the shadow of Lydia Abarca, a lyrical dancer with instinctive audience rapport. In his assessment of the troupe for *Ballet Review* (no. 6, 1974), Robert Greskovic chided Miss Johnson for dancing "under her towering potential" and suggested that she take on "even more challenging" parts. "She's undoubtedly 'ballerina' material," he concluded, "and an extra inch of effort could make her even more outstanding." Aware of her shortcomings, she threw herself into her work with renewed vigor and dedication. "The dream wasn't enough," she explained to Anita Finkel in an interview for a *Ballet News* (January 1983) profile. "I would have to change tremendously before I could even fully dream of being a dancer. Otherwise, all of it would be only a fantasy, a silly thing, like dreaming of being a princess."

Consciously pushing herself to the limits by extending her range, Virginia Johnson, in the late 1970s, accepted guest engagements with the Washington Ballet, the Capitol Ballet, and the Stars of the World Ballet. She tried her hand at choreography, too, creating and dancing a solo in Alan Miller's television film of George Crumb's "Ancient Voices of Children" and devising the dances for her first one-woman concert, at Marymount College in New York City in 1978. With her home company, she added to her personal repertory roles in a variety of ballets that tested her versatility as well as her virtuosity, including the fearful wife of a jealous preacher in *The Beloved*, Lester Horton's spare, macabre dance drama; the Ballerina in Karel Shook's new version of the pyrotechnical *Don Quixote* pas de deux; the Swan Queen in Frederic Franklin's staging of the second act of *Swan Lake*; and Glauce, Jason's second wife, in *After Corinth*, Walter Raines's skewed retelling of the legend of Medea's revenge. Other congenial works were Mitchell's sentimental duet *The Greatest Love of All*; *Invasion*, Royston Maldoom's athletic ensemble piece; Geoffrey Holder's exotic *Dougla*; and *Mirage (The Games People Play)*, Billy Wilson's spoof of a smart cocktail party, in which she touchingly portrayed an elegant but lonely woman.

With her long arms and legs and elegant line, Virginia Johnson is the quintessential Balanchine ballerina. In the mid- and late 1970s, she mastered leading roles in most of the Balanchine classics that make up such an important part of the Dance Theatre of Harlem's repertory, including *Concerto Barocco*, a pure exploration of musical structure, the sparkling *Tchaikovsky Pas de Deux*, the "Sanguinic" variation of *The Four Temperaments*, and the lyrical *Serenade*. An exceptional allegro dancer, she excelled in the solo variations of Balanchine's *Allegro Brillante*, tossing off its series of whipping turns with dazzling flair. The rhythmic intricacies of the second movement of *Agon* were equally to her taste. Indeed, Virginia Johnson was confident enough to spice the master's work with her own inflections. As Nancy Goldner, for one, noticed in her review for the *Christian Science Monitor* (May 1, 1975), the dancer added "a few wiggles to the faintly Spanish solo"—a little frill that Miss Goldner thought looked "delightful on her and in *Agon*."

One of the qualities that most endeared Virginia Johnson to audiences and critics alike was her attention to dramatic nuance—her ability to find and convey meaning even in such seemingly plotless contemporary ballets as Glen Tetley's *Greening*. Described somewhat cryptically in a program note by its choreographer as "a work about waiting for something else," *Greening* is nonetheless nonnarrative in structure and employs angular movements and acrobatic double work rather than traditional dramatic gestures. But in her interpretation of the central female role, particularly in a contemplative solo of small, swirling steps, Virginia Johnson is more than a cipher in a kinetic design; she is a real woman torn by "intense conflicts in her soul," a woman "divided against herself," as Fernau Hall observed in his review for the London *Daily Telegraph* (July 30, 1981). In explaining her total commitment to her roles, the ballerina told Tobi Tobias, as quoted in *Dance* magazine (January 1982), "I want to be a dancer with every part of myself. I don't just want to have a dancer's feet or a dancer's back. I want to be dancing completely, down to the ends of my hair."

Realizing that only in dramatic roles could she achieve her goal, Virginia Johnson responded with enthusiasm when the Dance Theatre of Harlem began to include more dance dramas in its programs in the early 1980s. One of her first assignments was the part of the faded Southern belle Blanche Dubois in Valerie Bettis' dance treatment of Tennessee Williams' *A Streetcar Named Desire*. Overcoming the limitations of Miss Bettis' "swoop-and-flutter" choreography, as one critic termed it, she etched an affecting and consistently convincing portrayal of an emotionally unstable woman trying to hang on to her self-respect, even as she is being led away to a mental hospital, a faint smile hovering on her face. "It is a haunting final picture," Patricia Barnes wrote in her review of the ballet for the British periodical *Dance and Dancers* (May 1982). "As the self-immersed, fastidious

Blanche, Virginia Johnson is wonderful. She manages to be touching in spite of her airs, for underneath them we can sense that, despite the shabby circumstances of her life, she is attempting against all odds to retain her dignity and her sanity. It is this layer that Johnson eloquently reveals."

Virginia Johnson's next dramatic role—the Accused in *Fall River Legend*, Agnes de Mille's melodramatic account of the celebrated case of Lizzie Borden, the spinster accused of hacking her father and stepmother to death in 1892—presented an even more daunting challenge. To perform the part, the dancer explained to Janice Berman of *Newsday* (January 2, 1983), "you have to step back in time, to think what it was like to be an unmarried woman in the 1890s, to feel those extreme constraints in your lifestyle, and to see your life stretching before you in a similar manner for the next fifty years. Her [Lizzie's] life was so spiritually and emotionally bleak."

Coached by Agnes de Mille and by Sallie Wilson, a former principal dancer with the American Ballet Theatre and one of the role's foremost interpreters, Virginia Johnson concentrated on communicating to the audience the Accused's extreme states of mind, ranging from euphoria, in her joyful dance with the kindly minister, to murderous rage after her stepmother thwarts her budding romance, to inconsolable anguish as she stands at the foot of the scaffold. That she succeeded is borne out in the overwhelmingly favorable notices that greeted her debut in *Fall River Legend*, in February 1983. Even those critics, among them Clive Barnes, who has always disliked the piece, were won over by her towering performance. Leading the applause was Anna Kisselgoff of the *New York Times*, who in her encomium of February 5, 1983 pronounced the production "a sheer utter triumph" for Agnes de Mille, for the Dance Theatre of Harlem, and especially for Virginia Johnson: "From the start, she's frail rather than strong, stricken in the heart when her hopes for happiness are killed. It is not only Miss Johnson's excellent acting that one should praise but the quality of her dancing, its broken quality of despair, its desperate intensity."

Critical bouquets also greeted Virginia Johnson's interpretations of Zobeide, the imperious concubine in Frederic Franklin's faithful restaging of Michel Fokine's sensual Oriental fantasy *Schéhérazade*, Desdemona in John Butler's *Othello*, and the mysterious, sexually ambiguous Garçonne in *Les Biches*, Bronislava Nijinska's sophisticated comedy of manners about a fashionable house party in the 1920s. Although Miss Johnson appeared to be focusing her attention on dramatic ballets in the early 1980s, she did not neglect pure dance works, annexing to her repertory Glen Tetley's elegiac display piece *Voluntaries*, *Bélé*, Geoffrey Holder's Creole spectacle, and three classical showpieces: *Paquita*, the pas de dix from *Raymonda*, and the *Sylvia* pas de deux. Perhaps the most delightful addition, however, was Holder's *Songs of the Auvergne*, a rapturous extended solo originally created for Carmen de Lavallade.

Realizing a long-held dream, in 1984 Arthur Mitchell mounted for the Dance Theatre of Harlem, as its first full-length offering, a sumptuous production of *Giselle*. Working in collaboration with Frederic Franklin, the director, and Carl Michel, the designer, he boldly transplanted the Romantic classic from a mythical village on the Rhine to a plantation on the Louisiana bayous, where a free black society had flourished just before the Civil War. Virginia Johnson, who has always deplored the prevailing tendency to regard the great nineteenth-century ballets as "little holy shrines," enthusiastically endorsed her mentor's effort to bring *Giselle* "back to life," as she put it.

To prepare for her role as the frail young woman driven mad by a broken heart (identified, in Mitchell's version, as Giselle Lanaux, the sheltered, half-caste daughter of a recently freed slave), Miss Johnson studied films and photographs of earlier productions of the work and read histories of antebellum Creole society. She found the key to her characterization in the Romantic style itself. "Approaching it from a Romantic point of view gave me a kind of freedom . . . ," she told Burt Supree in the *Village Voice* interview. "To capture the essence of a Romantic ballet the emotion is the important thing." In rehearsals with Frederic Franklin, the ballerina gradually perfected the distinctive Romantic technique, with its feathery footwork, light, airy jumps, and soft, relaxed upper body.

When the Dance Theatre of Harlem's *Giselle* opened in July 1984 at the Coliseum in London, England, where the company has enjoyed considerable success over the years, British dance critics lavished praise on Virginia Johnson and her partner, Eddie J. Shellman, who took the part of Albrecht (called Albert Monet-Cloutier in Mitchell's version). While they applauded her strong, sure dancing, the reviewers were especially taken by her remarkable suggestion of "ghostly insubstantiality" as a Wili in the ethereal second act and by her quality of "luminous innocence," which made "every thought and feeling transparent." Their American counterparts were no less effusive following the production's American premiere in New York two months later. Veteran reviewer Deborah Jowitt spoke for her colleagues in her assessment for the *Village Voice* (October 9, 1984): "Virginia Johnson's Giselle is a triumph of intelligence, sensitivity, and good taste. . . . Her expressive ability shapes and dominates even steps she's weak in. Her Giselle is delicate, childish, and she plays a touching mad scene—a wan Ophelia gradually becoming as stiff and fragile as the flower she holds."

At five feet eight inches in height, Virginia Johnson is tall for a ballerina. Her long, oval face, with its aquiline features, finely arched eyebrows, and "large, lambent eyes" reminded Olga Maynard of the portraits of fifteenth-century noblewomen. A quiet, thoughtful woman with a self-effacing modesty, she rarely grants interviews, preferring to let her work speak for her. Like most dancers, she spends virtually all of her waking hours in classes, rehearsals, and performances. "It's a cliché, but you do sacrifice a lot to dance," she told Valerie Brooks, who interviewed her for a *New York Sunday News* (June 16, 1985) profile. "I don't think I would encourage a daughter to become a ballerina. But I love it, and I'm greedy now—I'm giving all my time to dancing, and it is giving me back more and more." Despite her demanding schedule, Miss Johnson manages to conduct master classes for young dancers and to give frequent public lecture-demonstrations. Her willingness to share her time and her art earned her the 1985 Young Achiever Award from the National Council of Women of the United States. Miss Johnson guards her body against illness and injury, which can be especially debilitating for an older dancer, by following a nutrition-rich diet. In her spare time, she enjoys cooking, reading, especially history, writing short stories, and visiting art galleries and museums. The ballerina shares her Manhattan apartment with several cats.

References: Ballet N 4:10+ Ja '83 pors; Dance N 65:1+ Ja '80 pors; N Y Daily News People p4 Je 16 '85 pors; N Y Post Ja 2 '81 por; Newsday II p5 Ja 21 '83 pors; Who's Who in America, 1984-85

## Kane, Joseph Nathan

Jan. 23, 1899- Historian; journalist. Address: b. c/o H. W. Wilson Co., 950 University Ave., Bronx, N.Y. 10452

For more than half a century the research historian Joseph Nathan Kane has been tracking down elusive and obscure items in American history and presenting his findings in books, magazines, newspapers, over the airwaves, and on the lecture circuit. The most popular of his forty-six books is *Famous First Facts*, a monumental compilation of more than 9,000 miscellaneous first American happenings, discoveries, and inventions that has become a staple in reference collections everywhere. First published in 1933, that work is now in its fourth edition, and the octogenarian author continues to investigate new data for authenticity and possible inclusion in an expanded fifth edition. His next most widely consulted compendium is *Facts About the Presidents* (1959; fourth edition, 1981), offering a trove of information about the presidents of the United States and their terms in office and much about the office itself. During his long career Kane has served as a consultant to the radio, television, and motion-picture media and to corporations wanting certifiable information about "firsts" relating to their products or services. In the 1940s and 1950s he was the foremost authority for the questions asked on radio and television quiz shows, supplying all the questions for the long-lived *Break the Bank* and syndicating to many other programs.

The oldest of three children, Joseph Nathan Kane was born at 12:15 P.M. on January 23, 1899 at 201 West 117th Street on Manhattan's Upper West Side to Albert Norman Kane, an importer of furs, and Hulda (Ascheim) Kane. His maternal grandfather was a wholesaler of woolens and passementeries, and his paternal grandfather was a composer whose works were played by such bands as those of John Philip Sousa and Patrick Gilmore. Kane's brother, Albert, a former legal adviser in the Bureau of Indian Affairs, lives in Washington, D.C., and his sister, Ann, lives in West Palm Beach, Florida.

Inheriting the paternal talent for music, Kane played the mandolin, violin, and banjo for his own amusement as a youth. He also collected stamps and foreign currency, and in school he was especially interested in world geography. He attended Public School 10, directly across the street from his parents' home on West 117th Street. That school, which no longer exists, numbered among its other illustrious graduates Bennett Cerf, the late publisher, Henry Dreyfus, the late industrial designer, Richard Rodgers, the late composer, and many jurists, including several high-court justices. Kane is secretary of P.S. 10's still active, although dwindling, alumni association.

At Townsend Harris High School, then one of the elite New York City public secondary schools, now defunct, Kane constantly stymied his teachers with his demand for proof of their assertions. "At school I would ask, 'How do you know?'" he recalled in an interview for *Current Biography*. "And that was usually the end of the discussion." As editor of the *Academic Herald* at Townsend Harris, he interviewed John Wanamaker, the department-store mogul, among others, and later, for the Jewish press, he interviewed Vicente Blasco-Ibáñez, the Spanish novelist and politician,

Lord Balfour, the British statesman, H. G. Wells, the English novelist, and other prominent figures in politics, the arts, the sciences, music, and the theatre. Even then, he told the interviewer for *Current Biography*, he was trying to "shed light on facts generally unknown."

At Columbia University from 1917 to 1920, Kane followed his own bent, taking classes in theatre and journalism but studying for the most part off the course and improving his knowledge of foreign languages. "I did not like to play follow-the-leader in education," he recalls. "If everyone was forced to read *The Merchant of Venice*, I would read *Twelfth Night*." Anticipating military service in World War I, he earned a certificate in electrical engineering from the Columbia School of Engineering in order to qualify as a radio and Morse-code operator. He enlisted in the army but never saw service, because he contracted influenza (from which he nearly died) during the great epidemic of 1918.

After the war, Kane, responding to a classified newspaper advertisement, applied for a clerical position with D. Auerbach & Sons, New York City confectionery manufacturers. Because of his knowledge of world geography and currency and his ability to speak French, German, and Spanish as well as English, he was made manager of the company's export department. Following a year with D. Auerbach & Sons, he worked for two years as export manager of the Universal Export Corporation.

While with D. Auerbach & Sons, Kane began writing monthly articles on export matters, including international finance, for the *Confectioners Journal* and *Export Trade*, and soon he was syndicating his articles to other trade journals, making revisions to suit the specific commodity interests of each. Over the following two decades he syndicated hundreds of articles to more than twenty publications, including *Exporters' Digest and International Trade Review* (of which he was an editor for several years), *American Hatter*, *Underwear and Hosiery Review*, *Fur Age*, *Cracker Baker*, *National Costumer*, and *Playthings*. He also contributed articles to such magazines and newspapers as *American Hebrew*, *American Magazine*, *Advertising Age*, *Printers' Ink*, *Nation's Business* and the *New York Times*, *Sun*, and *World*. As a State Department–accredited correspondent for his own Kane Feature News Syndicate, he covered, among other events, the 1921 Conference on the Limitation of Armaments in Washington, D.C.

As a free-lance, self-syndicated journalist, Kane between 1922 and 1932 spent eleven months of each year traveling around the United States. He visited every state in the union and most of the cities in each, traveling by rail, bus, his own car, and sometimes even by air. An aviation aficionado, he became acquainted with many pilots, including stunt pilots, and he wrote the column "The Back Seat Driver" for *Aeronautical Industry* and *Air Transportation*.

Kane's career as a seeker of "firsts" dates back to his period of journalistic traveling in the 1920s. It began with an abortive commission from Simon & Schuster Inc. to write a popular history of inventions, the usual story of Morse and the telegraph, Edison and the electric light, Bell and the telephone, the Wright brothers and the airplane, and so forth. Planning the book on inventors in the generally accepted manner, Kane encountered many problems traditionally ignored by popular historians. One was a difficulty in terminology: an airplane is an aircraft, for example, but so is a balloon; similarly, automobiles used to be called motorcycles, and motorcycles used to be called automobiles. Among other problems were the simultaneity of several variations of the same invention; the difference between the actual invention and its refinement or development, manufacture, and promotion, leading to conflicts in claims; the inaccuracy or dishonesty of some claims; and the inadequacy of many of the records accepted as documentation for the claims.

Kane came away from his initial research realizing that often "a lot of people" appeared responsible for the same invention and that "nobody knew who did it first." "The credit always seemed to go to the inventor with the best publicity agent," he recounted in an article he wrote for *Liberty* magazine (December 1938), "and the little man, too engrossed in his beloved work to advertise his exploits, was simply lost in the shuffle."

Deciding to write a book on the achievers of "firsts" whom history had overlooked or forgotten, not only in invention but in general, Kane was told by librarians and other experts at the Library of Congress, the Smithsonian Institution, the New York Historical Society, and elsewhere that such a definitive work could not be done, given the difficulty of establishing "firsts" with certainty. Their doubts only fired Kane's determination the more, while making him aware of the enormity of the task before him. He realized that every item in the book would have to be specific and exact as to full name, date, place, and description, backed by unassailable documentation and corroboration. Partly because he was "chauvinistic" and partly because available worldwide records were not commensurate with such a rigorous standard, he limited his scope to the United States, where he could find proof to substantiate his claims and not be bothered with "mostly unsubstantiated" counterclaims made by foreign countries for their nationals.

Seeking out leads to and verification of interesting "first" facts, Kane in his travels gathered information from local people everywhere, including "achievers" or their descendants; frequented museums, used-book stores, historical societies, and libraries ranging from special collections and one-room rural libraries to the Library of Congress; pored over public documents and records, including patents, sales records, and newspaper files; and obtained data from government departments and private organizations and associations. Much of the information came to him by serendipity. Often

consulting numerous sources and engaging in lengthy correspondence to establish a single fact from mounds of conflicting data, he bit by bit completed his book.

Rejected by eleven other publishers, Kane finally approached the late Halsey W. Wilson, the founder and then president of the H. W. Wilson Company, with his manuscript. Wilson was hesitant, unsure that there would be a market for such a work. By mail or in person, Kane showed the manuscript, or photostated portions thereof, to reference librarians across the United States. Letters requesting the book poured into the H. W. Wilson Company, and on the strength of that demand *Famous First Facts: A Record of First Happenings, Discoveries, and Inventions in the United States* was published by Wilson in 1933.

In his introduction to the first edition of *Famous First Facts* Kane pointed out that he was not attempting "to remold public conceptions, but merely to present impartial facts" and thus "to replace romantic history with commonplace truth." "Whenever rival claims have been put forth," he explained, "the one best substantiated has been given credence. Only those 'firsts' for which there are definite records are included; it is possible that further research into hitherto unpublished records may disclose additional data."

The 757-page book cataloged some 3,000 facts (one third the number in the current edition), arranged alphabetically according to subject and indexed chronologically and geographically. Among the entries were such diverse items as the first distinctly American disease (tularemia, 1906); the first imported sheep (1609), cows (1624), and camels (1856); the first Afro-American army major (Martin Robinson Delaney, 1865); the first subway (the Beach Pneumatic Underground Railway, New York City, 1870); the first steamboat to carry a person (built by John Fitch in 1787, twenty years before Fulton introduced regular steamboat service); and the first lock-stitch sewing machine (made by Walter Hunt between 1832 and 1834, a dozen years before Elias Howe obtained his patent).

Reviewers of the first edition of *Famous First Facts* hailed it as "something new under the sun," "a book more fascinating . . . than the dictionary," and "a very valuable tool for the reference library," and they marveled at the "patient plugging away at dry statistics" that must have gone into its creation. "It was surely a happy inspiration that set Joseph Nathan Kane at the task of producing so intriguing a volume," the reviewer for the *New York Times* (May 14, 1933) wrote, "and a dogged resolution of almost superhuman force that kept him at work so incessantly grilling until it was finished."

Its supplement, *More First Facts,* was published by the H. W. Wilson Company in 1935. Only slightly slimmer than *Famous First Facts,* it presented an additional, entirely different collection of "firsts." The scope and general arrangement was the same as in the original volume, but a new feature was added, an index showing the various "firsts" occurring on each day of the year, including the material covered in the first volume. The second edition of *Famous First Facts*, published by Wilson fifteen years later, included, in revised form, the material in both the original volume and *More First Facts* as well as new entries.

From August 1938 to July 1939 Kane hosted the weekly half-hour radio program *Famous First Facts*, broadcast coast to coast by the Mutual Broadcasting System. The program opened with a dramatization of a "first," followed by an interview with an achiever or an achiever's descendant. Among those interviewed by Kane were a nine-year-old descendant of John Hanson, who headed the first Continental Congress; Henry A. Walden, who built and flew the first monoplane in 1909; and the son of Charles E. Duryea, the builder of the first practical American gasoline automobile.

In the heyday of radio and television quiz shows, Kane supplied some of the questions for *The $64,000 Question* and *Double or Nothing*, among other answer-for-money programs, and he wrote all of the questions for *Break the Bank* from the inception of that half-hour weekly show on the ABC radio network in 1945. In 1948-49 *Break the Bank* was simulcast on ABC television, and the following season it moved to the NBC television network, where it remained for five years, with the exception of one year on CBS. It returned to ABC for two-and-a-half years beginning in January 1954. During *Break the Bank's* first eight years the contestants, drawn from the studio audience, competed for sums in the magnitude of $10,000. Renamed *Break the $250,000 Bank* and featuring guest "experts" rather than studio contestants, the program ran on NBC from October 1956 to January 1957.

In 1958 Kane wrote for the short-lived prime-time television quiz show *Dotto*. As recounted by Tim Brooks and Earle Marsh in their *Complete Directory to Prime Time Network TV Shows* (1979) and by Alex McNeil in his *Total Television* (1980), the scandals that ended the popularity of the quiz shows had their origin in a daytime version of *Dotto* predating the nighttime program. They were precipitated by charges of rigging brought by a disgruntled would-be daytime contestant, one Edward Hilgemeier Jr. Kane, who supplied the questions and served as the authority for the correct answers but never participated in the production of any of the shows or met the contestants, later told a reporter that the rigging of quiz shows, where it existed, probably consisted of matching questions to contestants. "I know that *Break the Bank* . . . was principally on the up and up," he said. The quiz show scandals not only affected the television industry but ruined the salability of Kane's excellent little book *How to Win on Quiz Shows* (Bartholomew House, 1956).

The H. W. Wilson Company published the first edition of Kane's *Facts About the Presidents* in 1959. "This torrent of factual matter is arranged systematically and is accompanied by a valuable index," Robert C. Woodward observed in his review in the *Library Journal* (January 1, 1960). "No more useful volume than this will come the way of reference workers during the forthcoming election year." The fourth and latest edition of *Facts About the Presidents* (Wilson, 1981) presents data concerning the lives, the backgrounds, and the terms in office of the thirty-nine men who have held the office of president of the United States, from George Washington to Ronald Reagan. Between editions, supplements are issued, bringing the reader up-to-date about the administration of the incumbent president. A supplement on the Reagan administration, for example, was published early in 1985.

The most recent edition of *Famous First Facts* (Wilson, 1981) is a 1,350-page volume presenting more than 9,000 first discoveries, inventions, and happenings in American history, from the birth of the first child of European (Norse) parents on American soil in 1007 to the graduation of the first woman from West Point in 1980. In addition to the geographical and chronological indexes, there is a personal names index. Soft-cover editions of both *Famous First Facts* and *Facts About the Presidents* have been published by Pocket Books and Ace Books. Pocket Books also published Kane's *Perma Quiz Book* (1956) and *The Second Perma Quiz Book* (1958). Kane has adapted his fact research to journalism in several magazine and newspaper series, including "Accidentally Ours," in *Coronet*, "Who Was First," an illustrated daily feature syndicated to hundreds of newspapers by the NEA service, and "It Happened Here First," which ran in *New York* magazine beginning in 1977.

Kane has also written *1,000 Facts Worth Knowing* (Whitman, 1938); *What Dog Is That?* (Greenberg, 1944), containing descriptions of the 122 pure breeds recognized by the American Kennel Club, illustrated by Walter Edward Blythe; and *The Centennial History of King Solomon Lodge No. 279, Free and Accepted Masons 1852-1952* (published by the lodge, to which Kane belongs, in 1952). The Scarecrow Press has published four editions of Kane's *The American Counties*, the latest in 1981. The same press issued *Nicknames and Sobriquets of U.S. Cities and States* (1970; revised, 1979), written by Kane in collaboration with Gerald L. Alexander. Kane has been a consultant to the American Foreign Credit Underwriters Corporation, and his expertise has often been tapped by television news departments, by Congress, by the White House, and by other governmental agencies, especially the Department of the Interior.

Joseph Nathan Kane is five feet eight inches tall, white-haired, still somewhat wiry of physique, and brisk in his movements. His only noticeable physical failing is a hearing loss in his right ear. Because that defect diminishes his enjoyment of stage productions, he seldom goes to the theatre anymore, preferring motion pictures. (He does not watch television.) Kane has a constant sense of humor and likes to tell jokes and droll stories, which he delivers with a poker face. A seasoned world traveler, he has a smattering of many languages, and he retains his ability to speak Spanish, French, and

German quite well. Periodically, he vacations at an isolated spa in Mexico where there is no television, radio, telephone, or even telegraph and where only fruits, nuts, and vegetables are served. (Normally he is not a vegetarian.) Most of his time is spent in his apartment or in libraries or other places of research because he is, as he says, "a workaholic." When he speaks before conventions of librarians or other groups he delivers not lectures but what he calls "rambles," during which the audience is invited to interrupt him at any time with questions.

A childless widower, Kane maintains bachelor quarters in a penthouse apartment overlooking the Hudson River on Manhattan's Upper West Side, a few blocks southwest of his birthplace. The apartment is cluttered, in a workmanlike way, with books, index files, and cartons of newspaper clippings, photostats of documents and other source material, and recordings of the radio show he hosted in the late 1930s, two of which he played for the Current Biography interviewer on a vintage phonograph. He told the interviewer of two collections he keeps in his bank safe deposit box. One is his stamp collection. The other is a collection of curious old inventions, with patent tags. Among the inventions are the first safety pin, the first fountain pen, a paper collar, and a shoe with a revolving heel (to compensate for wear), all invented by Kane's hero, Walter Hunt.

Although Kane calls himself a Reform Jew, he does not attend synagogue except to please his brother when he is in Washington. A skeptic who describes himself as a "factualist," a "fatalist," and a "universalist," he belongs to no political party and believes that "the world would be a better place" without parties, nationalities, churches, and color lines. On one wall of his apartment is a placard reading, "The person with a new idea is a crackpot—until it succeeds." Another favorite motto of his is Seneca's "Veritas simplex oratio est": Simple truth is the most eloquent oratory.

References: Cleveland Plain Dealer E p4 Jl 31 '85 por; Liberty p42+ D '38 pors; N Y Daily News p7 Ag 26 '76 por; Palm Beach Daily News p5 Je 16 '85 por, C p2 Ja 21 '83 por; Who's Who in America Monthly Supplement No. 9, 1943

## Kean, Thomas H(oward)

(kān)

*Apr. 21, 1935– Governor of New Jersey.*
*Address: b. State House, Trenton, N.J. 08625; h. 123 Shrewsbury Dr., Livingston, N.J. 07039*

The forty-eighth governor of New Jersey, Republican Thomas H. Kean, who succeeded Brendan Byrne in January 1982 and was reelected by a landslide in 1985, came from a family with a long history of privilege and power, but he earned his own political fortune through investments of ingenuity and energy that turned foes into friends and wrung robust good health from New Jersey's sickly economy. Combining political sophistication with a determined optimism, Kean believes that most people in government have some idealism, but that one has to search for it. "Sometimes it takes a little longer with some people than with others," he says, "but it's usually there."

Thomas Howard Kean was born on April 21, 1935 in New York City, the fifth of the six children of Robert Winthrop Kean and Elizabeth (Stuyvesant) Kean. His father, a distant cousin of Theodore Roosevelt, served two decades as a member of the United States House of Representatives from New Jersey, earning the nickname "Mr. Social Security" because of his sponsorship of legislation to benefit the aged, and he was one of the first Republicans to speak out against the excesses of Senator Joseph R. McCarthy. Thomas Kean's paternal grandfather, Hamilton Fish Kean, and his great-uncle John Kean, were United States senators from New Jersey. His ancestors also included five Colonial governors, as well as John Kean, a Continental

congressman from South Carolina, who married Susan Livingston, for whom the town of Livingston is named. The town of Keansburg and Kean College in Union bear the family name. The Keans' high profile derived also from the family's financial prominence, a result of investment in real estate, public utilities, and banks.

Thomas Kean's first elected office was as a member of the student council at St. Mark's School, a prestigious preparatory school in Southboro, Massachusetts, where he enrolled at thirteen.

His ability to please the public was noted by a fellow student who wrote in his yearbook: "A politician is a walrus who can sit on a fence and yet keep both ears to the ground." In 1957 Kean obtained his B.A. degree in history at Princeton University after submitting a senior thesis on the Polish patriot Count Julian Ursyn Niemcewicz (1758–1841), a distant relative, by marriage, of the Kean family. After completing a tour of active duty with the Army National Guard, he campaigned for his father in his unsuccessful 1958 bid against Harrison A. Williams for a seat in the United States Senate and then returned to St. Mark's to teach government and history. Enrolled at Columbia University while working for an investment company, Kean earned his M.A. degree in 1963 and completed his course work for a Ph.D. degree in history and education.

Postponing his dissertation for what he intended as a brief detour on his route to an academic career, Kean was persuaded to serve as national youth coordinator in the 1964 presidential primary campaign of former Pennsylvania governor William W. Scranton, a family friend. Once sidetracked into politics, Kean never found his way back to academe. After Scranton lost, Kean worked for Senator Barry Goldwater's unsuccessful presidential campaign and then became director of the northern New Jersey chapter of the Committee of Sixty-Eight, a community service organization sponsored by the GOP to establish goodwill with black voters. By then he had become executive vice-president of the Realty Transfer Company, his family's land development and real-estate investment firm, in Elizabeth.

In 1967 Kean took over the presidency of the Realty Transfer Company, and won, against great odds, a seat in the New Jersey state assembly. During his ten years in the assembly, he established a reputation as a moderate and honed his leadership skills, serving in 1970–71 as assistant majority leader, in 1971–72 as majority leader, and from 1972 to 1974 as speaker—the youngest in New Jersey history. During 1973 he also served temporarily as acting governor, replacing Governor William Cahill. After the Democrats, under Governor Brendan Byrne, won control of the administration, Kean served from 1974 to 1977 as assembly minority leader.

As a state legislator, Kean tried to improve his state's image as well as its economic standing in the region. He acted as co-chairman of the New Jersey Coalition for Fair Broadcasting, a public-interest group that crusaded to force the Federal Communications Commission to eliminate what Kean called a "television news blackout" of New Jersey. He persuaded President Gerald R. Ford to campaign in New Jersey, which Ford did with some success, despite his defeat by Jimmy Carter in 1976. Among other legislation, Kean sponsored the bills that created New Jersey's Department of Environmental Protection and its Division of Consumer Protection. He introduced New Jersey's first rent-control bill and promoted measures to extend state control over ecologically sensitive regions, to restrict industrial development on the Atlantic and Delaware River shorelines, to provide aid for urban areas, to ease the burden of tuition for college students, and to ban the easily accessible handguns popularly known as "Saturday night specials."

In the spring of 1974 Kean ran in the Republican primary for a seat in the United States House of Representatives for New Jersey's fifth congressional district, only to be defeated by Millicent Fenwick, an old friend, by a slim margin of eighty-three votes out of some 25,000 cast. A 1977 Republican gubernatorial primary also ended in defeat for Kean. The key issue at the time was the passage, during Governor Brendan Byrne's administration, of the state's first income tax. Although Kean and his primary rival, Raymond H. Bateman, the minority leader in the state senate, had supported a broad-based income tax, both had opposed the legislation that became law and was scheduled to expire in June 1978. Bateman campaigned with a pledge to reject reinstatement of the tax, while Kean—whose slogan was "Byrned up? Let's raise Kean"—promised to consult the public on that issue. Both advocated stricter economies to compensate for reduced revenues. Bateman handily won the primary, with 193,654 votes to Kean's 129,463, but lost the November election to the incumbent Byrne.

On January 28, 1981 Kean once more announced his candidacy for the Republican gubernatorial nomination. Because outgoing Governor Byrne was constitutionally ineligible to succeed himself, and because any candidate able to raise $50,000 could receive matching funds from the state election law enforcement commission, a record total of twenty-one candidates—thirteen Democrats and eight Republicans—filed for the June gubernatorial contest. To counter efforts to depict him as something of an elitist snob, Kean tried to modify his patrician image. At the same time, he sharpened his political definition, moving somewhat to the right while refraining from alienating his moderate support. Abandoning his earlier opposition to the death penalty, he proposed a vigorous anti-crime program. His four-year plan for the budget, he said, was to allow the size of the state payroll to drop 10 percent by attrition and cut the sales tax 20 percent, while slashing the corporate tax in half to lure business into the state, a program that would work "hand in glove" with national supply-side economics.

Supported by former President Gerald R. Ford and by New York Congressman Jack Kemp, Kean won the gubernatorial nomination with a plurality of 31 percent. James Florio, the United States Representative from the Camden area of southern New Jersey, was the Democratic choice. Although radically different in background, style, and politics, the two rivals were well matched in age and telegenic appeal. Florio was the son of a second-generation Italian-American shipyard worker, in a state where a substantial minority of voters were of Italian descent, and a Navy veteran who earned a law degree at Rutgers, the state university, on a scholarship. He had served three terms in the state assembly and four in the United States Congress. Though lacking Florio's national legislative experience, Kean was strongly backed by President Ronald Reagan and Vice-President George Bush, who viewed the New Jersey race, one of only two gubernatorial elections in 1981 (the other was Virginia's), as a referendum on Reaganomics. Florio repudiated Reagan's fiscal policies, particularly as applied to New Jersey, but suggested few alternative tactics.

While Florio warned that Kean would "superimpose the meanness of spirit coming out of Washington" upon New Jersey, Kean tried to divest himself of the image of being a mere rubber stamp of the Reagan administration. "It's great to have the support of the President, but it's distracting to people," Kean complained, as quoted in the *New York Times* (October 26, 1981). "I spent most of the day the other day talking about toxic waste, and the headlines of the stories I saw were jobs and taxes. I spent a day talking about urban enterprise zones in the cities; a lot of the stories that day were jobs and taxes. I put out a crime package of fifteen points . . . and the top of the stories that day were jobs and taxes." At the same time, he tried to make known his opposition to cuts in transportation aid and Social Security and his support of the Equal Rights Amendment and of the Supreme Court decision granting women freedom of choice with regard to abortions. Florio, for his part, was placed on the defensive regarding certain Democratic policies, in particular, Governor Byrne's unpopular tax increases, which Kean charged had turned New Jersey from a "boom state" in the 1960s into a "basket case" in the 1970s.

A week before the election, the *New York Times* endorsed Kean. The outcome of the November 3, 1981 election, determined by a mere 1,677-vote margin out of some 2.3 million votes cast, required a recount and was not officially certified as a victory for Kean until four weeks later. The mandate was further obscured by the revelation that on election day the Republican National Committee had organized a so-called ballot security program in which some 200 armed off-duty policemen wearing official-looking armbands, and lawyers carrying written challenges to voter eligibility, patrolled the polls in certain predominantly Democratic districts with large black and Hispanic populations. A state superior court judge ruled the activities illegal, and the "National Ballot Security Task Force" was disbanded, on the same day, but not before resentment was aroused. While denying any personal involvement, Kean said, "It was designed to prevent people from voting illegally—it should not have had a chilling effect on a legal voter." Donald Sanchez, a vice-president of the New Jersey AFL-CIO, retorted: "The inference seems to be that these people are more inclined to dishonesty, and that's a slur." Despite charges that the illegal tactic had discouraged some eligible voters from casting ballots, Florio conceded the race to Kean on November 30, 1981.

"Let New Jersey show the nation that the Northeast can grow and prosper . . . not by what it takes from Washington, but by what it makes on its own," Kean declared in his inaugural address as he took office as governor on January 19, 1982. He said that with both houses of the state legislature controlled by Democrats he expected "clashes of ideas and ideology" but also bipartisan cooperation. Despite his inaugural optimism and his friendship with the administration in Washington, the new governor was dismayed when informed that as a result of Reagan's "new federalism" New Jersey would be receiving some $700 million less in federal aid in the coming fiscal year than in the current one. The Democrats in turn complained when Kean announced that he intended to cut business taxes but extend the sales tax to gasoline and cigarettes, raise mass-transit fares 25 percent, and increase tuition at state colleges 10 percent to eliminate a deficit in the budget for fiscal 1983. Calling the governor a "Robin Hood in reverse," assembly Speaker Alan J. Karcher asserted that "he taxes the poor to give to the rich."

In a budget battle that lasted through December 1982, Kean was narrowly defeated in his effort to obtain a 5 percent surtax on gasoline. Forced to renege on campaign pledges, he signed legislation to increase the state sales tax from 5 to 6 percent and to boost income taxes for those earning over $50,000 a year. "It's not what I wanted or what anybody else wanted," he commented. "It's basically a compromise." Although frustrated in his financial plans, Kean succeeded in other areas. He signed bills clamping down on juvenile offenders and reinstating the death penalty in New Jersey. His proposal for a bond issue to build new prisons won legislative approval. But his handling of the budget tended to rub off the bloom from those successes. Assembly minority leader Dean A. Gallo tried to analyze the difficulty, saying: "I think he is very reluctant to use gubernatorial tactics that are sometimes needed to get bills through. He would rather appeal to legislators to follow their consciences and do the right thing, but as we all know that doesn't always work."

The year 1983 got off to a better start, partly as a result of the improved economic outlook. Kean's proposal for a $6.8 billion austerity budget met with easy acceptance. Even his most vociferous critic, Alan J. Karcher, who habitually referred to the governor as "a clone of Ronald Reagan," responded with only mild criticism. The governor's budget contained no new taxes, but it provided for increases in state college tuition and in train and bus fares. "This budget imposes a system whereby government will be managed from the top down, not controlled by demands coming up from the bottom," the governor said with new firmness. Other legislation that he signed included bills to raise the legal age for gambling and drinking from eighteen to twenty-one, an appropriation of $80 million to alleviate prison crowding, and a bill requiring manufacturers to inform not only their employees but also the public of any toxic substances used in their products. With sixty-five sites on the federal Environmental Protection Agency's list for high-priority clean-up, New Jersey, which also led the nation in population density and cancer rate, was in dire need of those strict environmental guidelines. In September 1983 the governor introduced several proposals to upgrade public education, including raising teachers' salaries, certifying qualified professionals to teach without requiring education courses, and imposing tougher graduation standards on students

Two fiascos in public relations marred Kean's second year in office. Cries of poor taste, ignorance, and waste of public funds were heard when he complained about the American Empire furniture selected for the restoration of Drumthwacket, the nineteenth-century official governor's residence in Princeton, and requested replacements. To calm the furor, he announced that he had decided to continue to live at his home in Livingston and pay his own expenses, thereby saving the state $60,000 a year. Shortly thereafter, he raised the hackles of Democrats by sending invitations to 12,000 businessmen and professionals, asking them to make gifts of $1,000 a year to join the newly formed Governor's Club. Private meetings with the governor and his cabinet were listed as membership privileges. The state Commission on Ethical Standards began a review, which was dropped when a subsequent letter to the club's 150 members redefined the members' benefits, omitting references to the private meetings.

Although the state legislature remained Democratic following the November 1983 elections, the governor was better able to assert his will in the second half of his term. In his January 1984 State of the State address, he announced among other things his intention to exercise greater control over the Port Authority of New York and New Jersey. He obtained New York Governor Mario Cuomo's consent to a plan for the Port Authority to invest $150 million in redeveloping the Hoboken waterfront, to increase its payment for lease of Newark Airport, and to build new office space in downtown Newark. His $7.6 billion budget plan included substantial increases in expenditures for mental health, education, and transportation, but no new taxes or fare increases. It relied on improvement in the economy to generate most of the new revenues needed. In addition, the governor asked the legislature to pledge to appropriate $88 million a year for ten years to finance $3.3 billion in revenue bonds, which along with increased truck registration fees and toll-road surpluses were to be used to gain the maximum in federal matching funds to make badly needed repairs on New Jersey's 10,000 miles of highway and 6,000 bridges. Expected to create 120,000 construction jobs, the program attracted the support of labor, and in June 1984 the budget was passed virtually intact.

Governor Kean built on his popularity when, in response to delayed public-school openings because of the detection of airborne asbestos in classrooms, he proposed legislation to make New Jersey's standards for asbestos the strictest in the United States. In addition, he signed legislation to eliminate pay discrimination against minority and female state employees, and supported a bill to allow the New Jersey Sports and Exposition Authority to bring a major-league baseball team into the state. A principal sponsor of the baseball bill was Kean's former adversary, assembly Speaker Karcher, who after the governor's January 1985 State of the State message, which emphasized environmental clean-up, was heard to comment, "If I didn't know he was a Republican, I would have sworn he had changed parties."

The $8.8 billion budget proposed by Kean in January 1985 for the fiscal year beginning in July included $794 million in tax-relief programs, as well as funding for education, anti-crime, and environmental programs, and it was designed to please all constituencies. The budget plan prompted Karcher to comment: "Tom Kean has proven to be as liberal a Republican as there is in the country. . . . He's doing exactly what the Democrats have asked him to do." The Republican minority leader, Charles Hardwick, also praised the governor's fiscal package, calling it "a budget he can run on."

On May 16, 1985 Governor Kean declared a drought emergency throughout New Jersey. Noting that reservoirs in some areas were filled only to 55 percent of capacity, he imposed special restrictions, including mandatory water rationing, on ninety-three communities in six northeastern counties that were especially hard hit as a result of inadequate precipitation. In addition, outdoor water restrictions were imposed in 120 communities in the Delaware River basin, and voluntary water conservation measures were encouraged in the rest of the state.

Kean announced his candidacy for reelection to the governorship on April 2, 1985 and remained unopposed for the Republican nomination. Meanwhile, his 1981 Democratic opponent, James J. Florio, had withdrawn his candidacy, a move that Republican spokesmen interpreted as a tacit acknowledgement of Kean's strength. Nevertheless, five major Democratic candidates entered the contest for the gubernatorial nomination: Newark mayor Kenneth R. Gibson, state senate majority leader John F. Russo, Essex County executive Peter Shapiro, former state senator Stephen B. Wiley, and former United States attorney Robert J. Del Tufo. In the primary election, on June 4, 1985, Peter Shapiro won the nomination with a plurality of about 31 percent.

In the summer and fall of 1985, Kean signed, among other measures, legislation to withdraw $2 billion in state investments from companies doing business in South Africa, to establish minimum salary levels for public-school teachers, and to regulate smoking in the work place and in public areas, and he released $1 million in state funds to help victims of a disastrous Labor Day fire in Passaic. In late July he became chairman of the Education Commission of the States, a coalition of state education officials and governors.

The election campaign between Kean and Shapiro was relatively low key, with both candidates agreeing on such issues as the need to reduce automobile insurance rates and to improve the quality of public education. Much of the debate centered on the issue of toxic-waste cleanup. Shapiro maintained that the Kean administration had taken "by and large minimal remedial action," while Kean asserted that no other state had done as much as New Jersey in cleaning up toxic waste sites. In september, Kean became the first New Jersey Republican gubernatorial candidate to win endorsement from the state's AFL-CIO. A month before the election, President Ronald Reagan gave his endorsement to Kean, calling New Jersey "a bellwether for the national recovery," and he urged voters to place Republicans in control of the state assembly for the first time in a dozen years. By mid-October, Kean had a lead of some 40 to 50 percentage points in opinion polls. Those predictions were confirmed on election day, November 5, 1985, when Kean, with 1,352,459 votes to Shapiro's 574,980, scored a landslide victory that also swept the Republicans into power in the New Jersey Assembly.

Governor Kean is a former chairman of the Coalition of Northeastern Governors and has headed the human resources committee of the National Governors Association. He has served as a commentator and reporter on public television news programs, and he has appeared with actress Brooke Shields in television advertisements promoting tourism in New Jersey. He is a member of the New Jersey Historical Society and the Audubon Society. In 1985 he was named "person of the year" by the New Jersey conference of the NAACP for his efforts in behalf of affirmative action.

By his marriage, in 1967, to Deborah Elizabeth Bye, a debutante from Wilmington, Delaware, Kean has twin sons, Thomas Jr. and Reed, and a daughter, Alexandra. Kean has been described as a paradigm of paradox: an opera lover who is also a boxing fan, a millionaire who tells anecdotes about his own frugality, a fiscal conservative who demonstrates generosity. But in most respects predictability and convention seem to prevail. Kean is described by friends as consistently diligent and genuinely affable, despite a shyness that sometimes causes him to appear aloof or pompous. He is an Episcopalian.

References: N Y Times B p11+ O 26 '81 por, B p8 Ja 20 '82 por; N Y Times Mag p60+ N 1 '81 por; Who's Who in America, 1984-85; Who's Who in American Politics, 1983-84

---

## Keillor, Garrison

(kē´ lər)

*Aug. 7, 1942- Writer; broadcaster. Address: b. Minnesota Public Radio, 45 E. Eighth St., Saint Paul, Minn. 55101*

The droll and low-keyed Midwestern storyteller Garrison Keillor describes himself as "a champion of small pleasures." Keillor began regaling readers of the *New Yorker* as well as listeners of Minnesota Public Radio with his affectionate yarns about and parodies of small-town life more than a decade ago, and his national audience has swelled in the five years since his live Saturday night MPR show, *A Prairie Home Companion,* began satellite transmission. Beamed to stations affiliated with American Public Radio, Keillor's elegantly homespun two-hour variety program reaches an estimated two million–plus listeners coast to coast and in Hawaii and Alaska. Only the news-oriented program *All Things Considered* has more listeners on public radio.

Set in rustic Lake Wobegon ("where all the women are strong, all the men are good-looking, and all the children are above average"), a Minnesota hamlet born of Keillor's imagination, as well as his experience, *A Prairie Home Companion* evokes the fun and flavor of radio's golden age, when families gathered around the parlor console to hear *Fibber McGee and Molly* and *Grand Ole Opry.* Among the regulars on the show are Miss

Stevie Beck, who plays the autoharp, harmonizes with Keillor in songs written by him and others, and takes part in dramatic sketches; the bluegrass band Stoney Lonesome; and Butch Thompson and his trio, who play music ranging from New Orleans jazz and ragtime to blues and seasonal favorites and who back up guests ranging from American and Scandinavian folksingers to an occasional classical violinist. As host, Keillor banters with the musicians, does amusing commercials for such "sponsors" as Ralph's Pretty Good Grocery ("Remember, if you can't find it at Ralph's, you can probably get along without it") and Powdermilk Biscuits ("Heaven's, they're good . . . and expeditious"), and delivers the centerpiece of the program, his rambling monologue, a whimsical "news" report that begins, "It's been a quiet week in Lake Wobegon. . . ." Keillor expanded on and refined his radio narratives in his humorous fictionalized memoir *Lake Wobegon Days* (1985), in which, as Veronica Geng observed in the *New York Times Book Review* (August 25, 1985), Lake Wobegon "joins Thurber's Columbus as an absurd definition of a very real Midwest." The book shot to the top of the bestseller lists in the fall of 1985.

Garrison Edward Keillor's first name was originally Gary. As he explained to Diane Roback in an interview for *Publishers Weekly* (September 13, 1985), he began using Garrison when, as an eighth-grader submitting poetry to the school paper "at a time when boys didn't write poetry," he wanted "to hide behind a name that meant strength." Keillor was born on August 7, 1942 in Anoka, Minnesota, a Minneapolis suburb where his grandfather had settled as a farmer after migrating from Canada in 1880. He is the third of six children of John P. Keillor, a railway mail clerk and carpenter, and Grace R. (Denham) Keillor, who raised her children lovingly but strictly in the religion of her Scottish forebears, the Plymouth Brethren, disputatious, fundamentalist dissenters from the Church of England's formalities of prescribed ritual and ministerial ordination and from its comparatively liberal moral code. Growing up in the Plymouth Brethren's Anoka "meeting," Keillor remembers chafing under proscriptions against "dancing, drinking, card playing, liberal education, and too-friendly association with nonbelievers" but enjoying the parables that highlighted the Sunday church gatherings and the tales his older relatives and other adults told. "The people were wonderful storytellers," he recounted to James Traub for *Esquire* (May 1982), "and the purpose of their stories was to imbue us with compassion." His chief early model for storytelling was, he has said, his great-uncle Lou Powell, "a real traveling carnival" in "a family of taciturn people."

As a humorist, L. S. Klepp observed in the *Village Voice* (September 10, 1985), "Keillor owes a great deal to the narrow, repressive religious training that he had to throw off to become a humorist. . . . In this he resembles . . . Peter De Vries. Both express considerable ambivalence toward the spartan virtues of the provincial Midwest, taking refuge from them in urbane sophistication, and taking refuge from urbane sophistication in them." In her article in the *New York Times Book Review*, Veronica Geng pointed out that the Brethren (fictionalized by Keillor as the Sanctified Brethren), being "stricter than the strict Lutheran and Catholic majority, . . . guard the Wobegonian ideal at its narrowest point, where going east in any way, shape, or form means going to hell."

A socially withdrawn child, Keillor was slow in learning to read but when he "finally got the knack of it" he "couldn't get enough." "When I was fourteen, I was happy to read all day every day and into the night," he recounts in the introduction to his collection of humorous prose pieces *Happy To Be Here* (Atheneum, 1981; Penguin Books, 1983). "I hid in closets and in the basement, locked myself in the bathroom, reading right up to the final moment when Mother pried the book from my fingers and shoved me outdoors into the land of living persons." He fell in love with words and the weaving of words, spoken and, especially, written. "I have been writing since I was a little boy and always knew that was what I wanted to do," he told Mervyn Rothstein in an interview for the *New York Times* (August 20, 1985), explaining that his detour into radio came about because when he "got out of college [it was] a more possible way to make a living."

After reading and writing, his favorite childhood pastime was listening to the radio, at a time when that medium had not yet quite lost its imaginative creativity, especially in the upper Midwest. No radio personality influenced him more than Cedric Adams, an announcer and commentator at station WCCO in Minneapolis who played the laid-back sage, ruminating about life in the American heartland in a neighborly way and boosting the bread sales of his sponsor, the Purity Baking Company, with the credibility of his warm, soft-sell pitches—the distant foil for Keillor's Powdermilk Biscuits parodies on *A Prairie Home Companion*. Another radio program from Keillor's youth that would influence him in the creation of *A Prairie Home Companion* was *Grand Ole Opry*, a five-hour "barn dance" featuring "hillbilly" singers and fiddlers like Roy Acuff and bumpkin comedians and comediennes like Cousin Minnie Pearl, broadcast live on Saturday nights from "the Mother Church of country music," Ryman Auditorium in Nashville, Tennessee. (Minnie Pearl is today among the devoted fans of *A Prairie Home Companion*.)

Keillor's parents subscribed to *Reader's Digest, Popular Mechanics, National Geographic, Boy's Life,* and *American Home,* but none of those magazines appealed to him as did the *New Yorker,* which he discovered in the Anoka public library in 1956. "My people weren't much for literature, and they were dead set against conspicuous wealth, so a magazine in which classy paragraphs marched down the aisle between columns of diamond necklaces and French cognacs was not a magazine they welcomed into their home," he recalled in the introduction to *Happy To Be Here.* "I was more easily dazzled, and to me the *New Yorker* was a fabulous sight, an immense, glittering ocean liner off the coast of Minnesota, and I loved to read it. I bought copies and smuggled them home, though with a clear conscience, for what I most admired was not the decor or the tone of the thing but rather the work of some writers, particularly the *New Yorker's* great infield of Thurber, Liebling, Perelman, and White. They were my heroes . . . and in my mind they took the field against the big mazumbos of American Literature, and I cheered for them. I cheer for them now . . . and still think that it is more worthy in the eyes of God and better for us as a people if a writer makes three pages sharp and funny about the lives of geese than to make 300 flat and flabby about God or the American people."

According to his teachers, the brilliant academic reputation of Keillor's older brother, Philip, sapped his own interest in most subjects. Deloyd Hockstetter remembers Keillor as a student in his junior and senior high-school English classes in Anoka. "He was a tall, thin kid sitting in the back . . . ," Hockstetter recalled when interviewed for *Saturday Review* (May/June 1983) by John Bordsen. "Most of the kids knew who he was but didn't know him. . . . He never contributed to class discussions, but one time he gave a laid-back satire about what's in the records in the principal's office. He had them rolling in the aisles, but everything was written out—that's how shy he was. The only subject that interested him was writing. One year his class was to put out the student newspaper. . . . In the baskets in the back of the room I'd find articles written by a student who used the name 'Garrison Edwards.' It turned out they were by Gary." Hockstetter took a strong personal interest in Keillor, encouraging him in his writing, reading the manuscripts he was trying to sell to the *New Yorker*, and spending hours at a time talking over coffee with him in Minneapolis restaurants.

In 1960 Keillor enrolled at the University of Minnesota in Minneapolis. During his protracted, interrupted pursuit of a B.A. degree, he spent much of his time editing and writing for the student literary magazine, the *Ivory Tower*; married a fellow student, Mary Guntzel (1965); and earned money for his living and college expenses by parking cars (1960–62) and by staff-announcing on KUOM, the campus radio station (1963–66). As soon as he took his degree, in 1966, he traveled east by bus in an unsuccessful search for employment with a major magazine. He has recalled his debacle when interviewed at the *Atlantic Monthly* in Boston: "I think that during the interview they could tell that I was somebody who had just changed in a public rest room. I had a kind of hangdog look about me. I looked a little too stiff, too, because I had to keep my hand on my leg where I had spilled some Orange Julius two days before."

Returning to the University of Minnesota, Keillor resumed broadcasting for the campus radio station while studying, abortively, for an M.A. degree in English and putting in long hours at the typewriter, working on a novel (which he ultimately threw out with "the other trash") and humorous pieces intended for the *New Yorker*. "When you write . . . fiction for the *New Yorker*," he told John Bordsen, "and you feel as I did then about the *New Yorker*, you tend to be an extremely careful writer. I went through a great many drafts, and I studied every sentence, and it was work that I enjoyed doing, but it was also very difficult." His diligence at the typewriter contributed to the breakup of his marriage (which ended in divorce in 1974), but it also won him acceptance at the *New Yorker*, which began publishing his stories in 1969.

Keillor began his tenure with Minnesota Public Radio in 1968, hosting a three-hour morning "drive-time" classical music show. With brief departures, he worked that program four days a week for fourteen years, first from KSJR-FM in Collegeville (the original and, for a time, the solitary MPR outlet) and later from KSJN-FM in Saint Paul, which has been his base ever since. Early on, he began using mythical Lake Wobegon as the location for some of the make-believe sponsors of the program. "Lake Wobegon sounded sort of vague, and had an Indian sound to it, as so many towns in Minnesota do," he explained to John Bordsen. "And so, it sat around for a time simply as that—a fictitious name—before I ever started putting people in it."

Thus some of the elements of *A Prairie Home Companion* were already in place when the *New Yorker* assigned Keillor to do an article on the Grand Ole Opry's move in March 1974 from its historic home in Ryman Auditorium to a new home in Opryland U.S.A., an entertainment park on the outskirts of Nashville that also holds two country-music museums. His visit to Nashville stirred memories of the *Grand Ole Opry* broadcasts he had heard as a boy, jelling in his mind the concept of a Lake Wobegon radio show in which a cast of rustic regulars would offer a leisurely blend of listenable music, clean fun, and old-fashioned story-telling.

On his return from Nashville, Keillor presented his idea to Bill King, the president of Minnesota Public Radio. Approved by King, *A Prairie Home Companion* made its debut two months later on a network of thirty upper-Midwest public radio stations anchored by KSJN-FM. The first broadcast took place before a small audience at Macalester College in Saint Paul. As its popularity grew, the show moved to larger sites, and in 1978 it found a permanent home in the 800-seat World Theatre in downtown Saint Paul. Since January 1984 it has been broadcasting temporarily from another downtown St. Paul theatre, the 1,700-seat Orpheum, pending completion of repairs at the World. Cargill, Inc. has provided major financial support for the program since 1974, and the National Endowment for the Arts began funding *A Prairie Home Companion* with grants in 1977.

*A Prairie Home Companion* was first heard nationally as part of a public radio special called *Folk Festival USA* in February 1979. The favorable listener response to that trial run persuaded Keillor and the producers of Minnesota Public Radio to go national on a regular basis, and they began beaming *A Prairie Home Companion* to a few stations across the country by satellite in 1980. (The program received a Peabody Award in 1981.) In January 1982 Minnesota Public Radio and four major public radio stations elsewhere (WNYC in New York City, KUSC in Los Angeles, KQED in San Francisco, and WGUC in Cincinnati) created

American Public Radio, a national distributor and marketer of public radio programming. Under the aegis of APR, *A Prairie Home Companion*'s station carriage expanded to 219 outlets. As its listenership grew, the show extended its periodic tour engagements; in the early days its tour itinerary was restricted to the five-state area including North Dakota, South Dakota, Iowa, and Wisconsin; in October 1981 *A Prairie Home Companion* traveled to Boston, Massachusetts, Washington, D.C., and Swarthmore, Pennsylvania; in June 1982 it toured the West Coast; and in May 1983 it made its first visit to New York City, where it was broadcast live from Town Hall.

Keillor begins his program singing his diffidently romantic trademark song "Hello Love." In his monologues he populates Lake Wobegon with such characters as Senator Knute Thorvaldson, an unelected citizen named "Senator" by his mother because she "thought it had sort of a ring to it"; Pastor Ingqvist of the Lake Wobegon Lutheran Church; Mayor Clint Bunsen; Father Emil, the archtraditionalist pastor of Our Lady of Perpetual Responsibility Church, whose voice can be heard wafting from the confessional on Saturdays ("Oh, you *didn't!*"); Dr. Newt and his wife, Marva; and Margaret Haskins Derber, the town's unmetrical poet laureate. The townsfolk save at Bob's Bank, "at the sign of the sock"; buy tiny waterbeds for their cats at Bertha's Kitty Boutique in the Dales; "really do find things that cost only a nickel" at Skoglund's Five & Dime; lunch at the Chatterbox Cafe, "where the coffeepot is always on, which is why it tastes that way"; have their cars fixed at Jack's Auto Repair, "where the bright flashing lights lead to complete satisfaction"; go to the movies at Nights in the Garden of Spain Theatre, "formerly the Bijou, formerly the Roxie, where hearts beat in black and white"; have their "phobia needs" served at the Fearmonger's Shoppe in the Dales ("When it comes to safety, don't expect to save money"); and unwind at the Sidetrack Tap, the "dim little tavern on Main Street" whose motto is, "Don't sleep at our bar; we don't drink in your bed."

All of the imaginary local establishments get promoted on *A Prairie Home Companion*, but the chief beneficiary of Keillor's mock advertising is Powdermilk Biscuits, "made from whole wheat raised by Norwegian bachelor farmers in the rich bottomlands of the Wobegon valley, so you know they're not only good, they're also pure mostly, the biscuit with that whole-wheat goodness that gives shy persons the strength to get up and do what needs to be done; biscuit mix in the big blue box or biscuits already baked in the big brown bag with the dark stains that indicate freshness."

In addition to Stevie Beck, the Butch Thompson Trio, and Stoney Lonesome, Keillor's cohorts on *A Prairie Home Companion* include the fiddler and mandolinist Peter Ostrovshko, the folksinger and lyricist Greg Brown, and Howard Mohr, a rural Minnesota poet and essayist whose collection *How to Tell a Tornado*, published by Minnesota Public Radio, is typified by the prose piece "Waving, Its

Ins and Outs," an analysis of the country custom of greeting one's neighbors manually. The Butch Thompson Trio has recorded *A Prairie Home Companion* on the label of the same name, and on that label Keillor has cut *The Family Radio*, an album offering a sampling of his monologues and songs. Among other *A Prairie Home Companion* products are such items as T-shirts and women's flowered bonnets. The production solicits contributions for folk song lyrics as well as birthday, anniversary, and other such messages, which Keillor reads, selectively, on the air.

In his best-selling collection *Happy To Be Here* Keillor gently lampoons science fiction, little magazines, *Life* magazine, Richard Brautigan, corporate reports, transit-system publicity pamphlets, and war comic books as well as small-town mores. Reviewing the collection in *National Review* (December 11, 1981), D. Keith Mano proclaimed Keillor "damned brilliant," especially in his "burlesque masterpiece," the essay "Shy Rights." "His kind derision operates the way a voice stress analyzer might: it is a knowing of some special, audible sort . . . ," Mano wrote. "His wit is so reactive that it turns even claptrap into a goddam genre." In his review of the book in *Time* (February 1, 1982), John Skow wrote of Keillor: "He is in love with the upper Midwest, with the region and the people that Sinclair Lewis derided. He is rooted, fond of hickishness, fascinated by the utter, daft strangeness of the ordinary."

Keillor rejects the notion that his creation of Lake Wobegon is naively nostalgic. "The simple and pure rural life . . . never was," he pointed out to Edward Fiske of the *New York Times* (October 31, 1982). Don Druker, the radio coordinator for the National Endowment for the Arts, told Fiske: "What Garrison is saying is that nothing has been lost. Writers like Sherwood Anderson . . . were saying that if you want corruption . . . you don't have to go to the big city to find it. Garrison stands that on its head. If you are looking for transcendence and affirmation and eternal values, you don't have to go to a university or big city to find them. You can find them in your own hometown."

Keillor's book *Lake Wobegon Days: Recollections of a Small American Town* (Viking, 1985), a gently comic work of fiction combining aspects of the personal memoir, the anecdotal novel, and the local history, is in varying ways comparable to (although warmer than) the fiction of his fellow Midwestern humorists George Ade, Mark Twain, Ring Lardner, James Thurber, Jean Shepherd, and Peter De Vries. "The book was my project to get myself back to being a writer, a writer as I dreamed I might be when I was a child," he told Mervyn Rothstein in the *New York Times* interview. "Even when I began publishing with the *New Yorker* in 1970 I was still torn between radio, which is improvisational and colloquial and more intimate and sentimental to me, and my other writing, which tended to be a little drier, a piece of craft. And in the conflict between radio and writing . . . I arrived at doing this monologue on Saturday nights . . . the favorite thing I had done on radio. It was based on writing, but in the end it was radio . . . [where] there's the sound of the human voice to sort of carry [the narrative] over the imperfections. But in writing on the page, you have to create that voice artificially, and it's a very delicate job."

Gary Edward Keillor, the narrator of *Lake Wobegon Days*, describes the manners and mores that oppressed him as a child and that Garrison Keillor the adult can appreciate for their humor and integrity. Contributing to the Wobegonian way of life is an obstinate belief that virtue and happiness lie in less, not more. "Left to our own devices," the narrator says, "we Wobegonians go straight for the small potatoes. Majestic doesn't appeal to us; we like the Grand Canyon better with Clarence and Arlene parked in front of it, smiling." Joined to that contentment with small pleasures is a nagging doubt about the direction one should be taking, symbolized in Lake Wobegon's landmark, the Statue of the Unknown Norwegian, who symbolizes "confidence in the New World" and at the same time seems to be saying, "Wait here. I think I forgot something." In her *New York Times Book Review* article, Veronica Geng pointed out that Keillor's insight into "the way a community's core ideas and experiences get attenuated into funny-looking motifs" shapes "not just this local history but a lineage in American comedy [that] you could call Qualm Humor. . . . *Lake Wobegon Days* is about the way our beliefs, desires, and fears tail off into abstractions—and get renewed from time to time. . . . This book, unfolding Mr. Keillor's full design, is a genuine work of American history." In the *Village Voice*, L. S. Kleep credited Keillor with giving us "a gallery of shrewdly observed American characters, set in a comic light but with compelling sympathy and truth," so that "his collected Lake Wobegon small potatoes add up and in the end outweigh a lot of celebrated contemporary novels."

In his small office at Minnesota Public Radio, Keillor works at a word processor, turning out his magazine pieces (some of which now go to *Atlantic Monthly*) and other prose from Monday to Wednesday and preparing his radio show on Thursday and Friday. On Friday afternoon he rehearses with Butch Thompson and several other key members of his troupe, but he does not memorize his material and he finds it "amazing" when he delivers his monologue without script verbatim on Saturday night. The performance is a victory over shyness. "When he gets up in front of a microphone," his friend Russell Ringsack told Linda Witt of *People*, "he really bares himself. He'd never be able to talk so openly in public." Keillor explained to Bryan Wooley in an interview for *Dial* (May 1984): "As terrifying as getting up in front of an audience was—and still is today—nobody can resist laughter. The chance to make people laugh has a powerful attraction."

Garrison Keillor, who is six feet four inches tall, has a warm, beguiling baritone voice that often becomes mournful or whispery in his monologues. A former cigarette addict, who would belie the relaxed tone of the broadcasts by his nervous chain-smoking of Camels, he now smokes an occasional cigar. Keillor lives in a stately Victorian house in suburban Saint Paul with Margaret Moos, his program coordinator, Jason, his son from his marriage to Mary Guntzel, and two cats named Ralph and Tuna. The Lake Wobegon humorist is a Democrat politically, and in religion he still considers himself a Christian.

References: N Y Times II p23 O 31 '82 por, C p3 My 13 '83 por, p14 Jl 8 '84 por, C p18 Ag 20 '85; Newsday mag p12+ O 13 '85; People 21:42+ F 6 '84 pors; Sat R 9:12+ My/Je '83 pors

## Kennedy, William

Jan. 16, 1928- Author; educator. Address: b. State University of New York, 1400 Washington Ave., Albany, N.Y. 12222; c/o Viking Penguin, 40 W. 23d St., New York City, N.Y. 10010

With the publication of his Pulitzer Prize-winning *Ironweed* (1983), the third novel in his "Albany trilogy," William Kennedy vaulted from long-term obscurity, sparked an unwonted demand for his previous novels, put his unlikely native city on the literary map, and helped restore the good name of regionalism to American literature. In his richly textured stories, dark tales relieved by a comic sense sometimes raucous and sometimes quietly ironic and by a zest for life and language, Kennedy takes his readers into the streets, saloons, and gambling dens of Albany in its "sin city" days of the

Prohibition and Depression eras and introduces them to scoundrels who are more innocent than they look and wretched losers who are more spiritually resilient. He is interested not only in evoking a time and place, but also in revealing "the human being concealed within a bum or gangster." "When you take a character into his most extreme condition," he has explained, "you begin to discover what lurks in the far corner of the soul." A former newspaper reporter and rewrite man, Kennedy was a part-time lecturer at the State University, Albany, from 1974 to 1982, and he is now a tenured professor of English there.

William Joseph Kennedy was born in Albany on January 16, 1928 to William Joseph Kennedy Sr. and Mary Elizabeth (McDonald) Kennedy, working-class parents whose Irish ancestors settled in the city more than five generations ago. The initial impetus for Kennedy's fiction was his obsession with the fact that he was "an only child—the only child in practically the whole family." "It was that phenomenon," he told Curt Suplee of the *Washington Post* (December 28, 1983), "that made me want to write my first novel—what happened to this family, why are there no kids?"

Kennedy's mother worked all of her life as an accountant, and his father was a barber, foundry worker, pie salesman, and, finally, deputy sheriff. William Sr. was also a gambler and a ward heeler in the Albany political machine of Daniel P. O'Connell, and he often took his son on his rounds of political clubs and gaming rooms. Margaret Croyden, an old friend of Kennedy's, when interviewing the novelist for an article in the *New York Times Magazine* (August 26, 1984), asked him if he was "nostalgic for that vanished world." "Up to a point," he replied, "but I'm aware of all the negative elements, the power that some had to destroy lives, the vote-buying and the election-stealing."

Sartorial metaphors abound in Kennedy's novels, and his main characters, however low-life, tend, like their creator, to be fastidious about their clothing. In all probability, he inherited "that feeling," he says, from his father, who was "a fanatic about clothes" and could not abide "a wrinkle in his collar." He keeps discovering elements of his father in himself, he told Curt Suplee: "I keep hearing phrases, representing values that were his, which he never really tried to impose on me but did in the same way that the church and the Democratic party and the North End of Albany did—that matrix."

Growing up in Albany's North End, an Irish-American Catholic Democratic enclave, Kennedy hung out in pool halls and bowling alleys and idolized the baseball players and hustlers whom he sees as "the living embodiment" of that age. At the same time, he was an altar boy, and he attended the Christian Brothers Academy in Albany. As he has pointed out, "there is no doctrinaire element of religion" in his work, but his current editor at Viking Press, Gerald Howard, a fellow Irish-American Catholic, "recognized the Irish link immediately" in Kennedy's fiction. "If you grow up

Irish, the sense of sin, death and suffering is in your bones," Howard explained to Margaret Croyden. "If you grow up Irish, you have a gloomy view of the possibilities of people. His Irishness is a real key to who he is and what he is thinking."

Kennedy enrolled at Siena College, a Franciscan school in Loudonville, New York, with the intention of preparing for a career in chemical engineering, but after he flunked solid geometry he changed his major to English and turned his attention to journalism. He became editor of the campus newspaper, and after taking his bachelor's degree in 1949 he went to work as a sportswriter for the *Glens Falls* (New York) *Post-Star*. Following his term of service in the United States Army he joined the staff of the *Albany Times-Union* as a general assignment reporter.

After three-and-a-half years with the *Times-Union*, Kennedy had had enough not only of court trials, city hall, and the police blotter but also of Albany itself, which at that time seemed to him to have become "an old man's town—moribund, no action." With alacrity, he accepted an offer to go to San Juan in 1956 as assistant managing editor and columnist for a new English-language newspaper, the *Puerto Rico World Journal*. Within months, that paper folded and, after a short stint spent in reporting for the *Miami Herald* in Florida, Kennedy earned his living for two years as a Puerto Rico correspondent for the Knight newspapers and Time-Life publications. In 1959 he helped found the *San Juan Star*, of which he became managing editor.

While in Puerto Rico, Kennedy began trying his hand at fiction. In that effort he was encouraged by Saul Bellow, the novelist, under whom he took a creative writing course at the University of Puerto Rico. At first, the setting of his tentative stories was Puerto Rico, but soon he found himself writing about Albany. That writing seemed "to come more easily, with a richness that was absent" in his attempts to be "exotic." "It proved to me," he has recounted, "that I really didn't have . . . to go anywhere else. It really was a young writer's education in discovering his own turf."

In 1961 Kennedy returned temporarily to Albany to take care of his gravely ill father, who was by then a widower and alone. "He was really a stubborn Irishman, wouldn't pay attention to anybody," Kennedy recounted to Curt Suplee of the *Washington Post*. "Well, we got him straight and then I decided I'd have to come back to keep him straight for a while. I didn't think I'd stay long but I was interested in my family's history, my neighborhood's history. And by inchworm accumulation of imaginative progress it became interesting to me . . . an inexhaustible context . . . as abundant in mythical qualities as it was in political ambition, remarkably consequential greed, and genuine fear of the Lord."

Refusing to take a full-time job lest he "never write fiction again," Kennedy offered himself to the *Albany Times-Union* as a part-time feature writer, and his offer was accepted. From 1963 to

1970 he wrote for the newpaper local-color stories about Albany, its history, its neighborhoods, and its people, especially the politicians, ethnic working people, bookies, barkeeps, and derelicts—the grist of his fiction. He was nominated for a Pulitzer Prize for a series he wrote on the city's slums in 1965.

A strike at the *Times-Union* inspired a short story that Kennedy expanded into his first published novel, *The Ink Truck,* a rollicking, sardonic, and often surreal narrative that was edited at Dial Press by D. L. Doctorow and published by Dial in 1969. The protagonist of the novel is Bailey, a lusty, foolhardy former newspaper columnist who leads a bizarre, futile rearguard action against his former employers in a newspaper strike. At the time of the novel's publication, reviewers described *The Ink Truck* as "inventive, circular, multilayered," its protagonist as "a loser of heroic dimensions," and its author as a man with "a keen sense of the absurd and a profound understanding of the ludicrous side" of humanity. Fifteen years later, Joel Conarroe, writing with hindsight in the *New York Times* (September 30, 1984), described *The Ink Truck* as revealing "an energetic but as yet undisciplined artist working his way somewhat clumsily to the flexible style that would become his trademark, a style indebted to Joyce, Fitzgerald, and Beckett, yet very much his own."

Several years of obsessive research and rewriting (eight drafts) went into the writing of *Legs* (Coward, 1975) Kennedy's fictionalized account of the last year-and-a-half in the life of Jack ("Legs") Diamond, the fast-living Prohibition-era "celebrity" gangster who made his last stand for mob power in Albany, where his criminal rivals finally gunned him to death in his underwear in a rooming house in 1931. "It's the last time I ever intend to research a novel . . . ," Kennedy told an interviewer. "Too much research can overburden the imagination."

Kennedy was drawn to Diamond as a fictional subject not so much because the gangster was "an impious presence in the city" as because he was a fascinating personification of the moral ambiguity of the American ideal of "success," glamorized by a press that superficially reviled him, raised to "a mythic dimension" in the popular romantic imagination, and viewed by Kennedy himself as "a venal man of integrity." "He [was] not merely the dude of all gangsters, the most active brain in the New York underworld," the narrator of the novel, Diamond's lawyer, friend, and admirer Marcus Gorman, says, "but . . . one of the truly new Irishmen of his day: Horatio Alger out of Finn McCool and Jesse James . . . a pioneer, the founder of the first truly modern gang, the dauphin of the town for years."

One critic questioned the value of such devoted chronicling of the last days of "a Babbitt with weapons, a gangster . . . parched for glory, famished for public love." More typical were those who appreciated *Legs's* "rolling prose and informed anecdote" and described the novel as "a peculiarly seductive portrait" and "a very skillful story, full of bounce and wit." Critics who faulted Kennedy for giving no evidence that he questioned his narrator's "mindless life-force worship" were answered, in effect, by the reviewer for the *New Republic* (May 24, 1975), who pointed out that the author's sociological and psychological interests were subordinate to his pursuit of "indefinite and suggestive truth germane to fiction, hostile to statistics, and finally dependent on the lode of language mined in the privacy of imagination."

The basis for Kennedy's densely textured and fast-paced third novel, *Billy Phelan's Greatest Game* (Viking, 1978), was the bungled kidnapping in 1933 of John O'Connell Jr., the nephew of Boss O'Connell and the heir apparent to the Albany Democratic machine. In the novel, the O'Connells become the McCalls, John Jr. becomes Charlie Boy McCall, and the year is moved forward to 1938. The story is narrated by its one savory character, Martin Daugherty, a journalist tapped by the McCall brothers to help keep the facts about the kidnapping of Charlie Boy from the public. The protagonist is Billy Phelan, a young whoring, gambling pool shark and barfly, a petty dependent of the McCall machine, who finds himself caught up in the corruption and pitted against his political patrons in the reluctant role of an informer.

Like Kennedy's two previous novels, *Billy Phelan's Greatest Game* was ignored by the *New York Times.* Compensating for that omission were reviews elsewhere that remarked Kennedy's "energetic, argot-filled style" and his "true comic spirit, conveyed by a tumult of fierce and wonderful language." In the *Saturday Review* (May 2, 1978) Doris Grumbach wrote: "He [Kennedy] knows more about his special Hibernian turf than anyone else. [His] pitch is perfect. . . . The cast of *Billy Phelan* is, quite simply, a wonder—a magical bunch of thugs, lovers, and game players. No one writing in America today . . . has Kennedy's rich and fertile gift of gab; his pure verbal energy; his love of people, and their kith and kin."

Francis Phelan, Billy's reprobate father, the protagonist of *Ironweed,* was the next central character created by Kennedy. After a series of tragedies for which he was responsible—including the killing of a scab in a trolleyworkers strike and the accidental death of Billy's thirteen-day-old younger brother Gerald—Francis flees Albany and does not see his family again for twenty-two years, a period during which shame and guilt drive him to dereliction and drink as well as into a caring relationship with an equally desperate woman. Returning to Albany in 1938—the time of the story—to make money by voting (twenty-one times, at five dollars a vote), he ends up working in the cemetery, where the shades of his past, including his dead father, mother, and infant son, haunt him. In the end (which is anti-sentimental) he finds within himself a surprising inner strength, when he realizes that "the trick" is to reject self-victimization and "to live . . . to survive the mob."

Because the sales of Kennedy's previous books were deemed insufficient, Viking Press at first rejected *Ironweed*, and the book made the rounds of other major publishing companies, encountering rejection a total of thirteen times. After Saul Bellow wrote Viking a scolding letter ("That the author of *Billy Phelan* should have a manuscript kicking around looking for a publisher is disgraceful") and Corlies M. ("Cork") Smith returned to Viking as an editor, the publishing house not only decided to publish *Ironweed* but to reissue the two previous novels in the "Albany cycle." In January 1983 *Ironweed* was published in hardcover and *Legs* and *Billy Phelan's Greatest Game* were reissued as Penguin paperbacks.

Reviewing *Ironweed* in *Newsweek* (January 31, 1983), Peter S. Prescott noticed the novel's "refusal of sentimentality" and its "freshness of language," and he judged Kennedy worthy of a place "among the best of our current American novelists." George Stade, who admitted to residual "prejudices" against Kennedy's fiction, found *Ironweed*, "for all the rich variety of prose and event, from hallucination to bedrock realism to slapstick and blessed quotidian peace," to be "more austere than its predecessors." "In spite of my prejudices," Stade wrote, "Kennedy's defiant humanism has left me chastened but feeling good." Curt Suplee in his *Washington Post* article described *Ironweed*'s dialogue as being "so keen you can smell the rye on the speakers' breath" and its style "taut and springy, cadenced like good bar talk but rich with impromptu fluorescence of metaphor"—all that despite "themes that dare the heart's enigmas."

*Ironweed* sold more than 100,000 copies in two years. In addition to the Pulitzer Prize for fiction, the novel won the National Book Critics Circle Award for fiction. In December 1983 the MacArthur Foundation named Kennedy a winner of one of its no-strings, tax-free fellowships for "exceptionally talented individuals," worth $264,-000, paid out over five years. Early in 1984 the novelist received the New York State Governor's Award, and the following September the State University of New York and various citizens groups in Albany sponsored a four-day "William Kennedy's Albany" celebration that included a "Sunday in the Park" party, walking tours, a talk by Kennedy, and a photographic exhibit. Kennedy used a lagniappe award from the MacArthur Foundation ($15,000 annually for five years) to set up the Writers Institute at Albany, where aspiring writers can attend lectures and workshops given by established authors.

A collection of affectionate and engaging essays by Kennedy on Albany, its history, and its folklore, along with personal memoirs, was published in 1984 by Viking in association with Washington Park Press under the title *O Albany!* and the subtitle *Improbable City of Political Wizards, Fearless Ethnics, Spectacular Aristocrats, Splendid Nobodies, and Underrated Scoundrels.* In 1984 Kennedy resumed work on "Quinn's Book," a long-fallow novel about two adolescents, ancestors of Billy Phelan, growing up in Albany during the Civil War. In addition, he was working on a screenplay of *Legs* for producer Gene Kirkwood, who also bought the film rights to *Billy Phelan's Greatest Game.* Earlier, Kennedy had collaborated with filmmaker Francis Ford Coppola on the script for Coppola's *Cotton Club* (1984).

Despite some thinning of his brown hair, Kennedy looks younger than his years. His "earthy manliness," according to Margaret Croyden, is combined with a "boyish naiveté" and his face is "full of vitality and vigor." In her *New York Times Magazine* article Miss Croyden described Kennedy "drink in hand, rock[ing] back and forth in an old office chair, smiling, his eyes mischievous but intense." To some interviewers the novelist seemed "mild," "pleasant," and "friendly but reserved," but his friends know him to be a convivial party thrower who has on occasion entertained them until dawn with his banjo and ukelele playing and singing of popular songs.

William Kennedy and Ana Daisy Dana Segara, a former dancer, singer, and actress who is a native of Puerto Rico, were married on January 31, 1957. They have three children, Dana, Katherine, and Brendan, and one grandchild, from Dana's marriage. Katherine serves as Kennedy's secretary, neatly transcribing to word processor the many, heavily rewritten drafts of his manuscripts, which he typewrites and then copiously emends in handwriting. The Kennedys live in a nineteenth-century farmhouse in the Albany suburb of Averill Park, where the novelist's study is adorned with photographs of William Faulkner, Samuel Beckett, Robert Penn Warren, Saul Bellow, Louis Armstrong, Mae West, and Frank Sinatra. Kennedy also has an office in the two-story former boarding house on Dove Street in downtown Albany in which Legs Diamond was murdered. That building, now an official landmark, is owned jointly by the Kennedys and Gene Kirkwood, the film producer.

References: *Guardian* p11 Ja 26 '84 por; *N Y Times* p23+ S 17 '83 pors, C p15 S 6 '84 por; *N Y Times Bk R* p35 N 13 '83 por; *N Y Times Mag* p33+ Ag 26 '84 por; *Newsweek* 103:78+ F 6 '84 por; *Time* 124:77+ O 1 '84 por; *Pub W* 224:52+ D 19 '83; *Contemporary Authors* vols 85–88 (1980)

## Kim Dae Jung

(dĭ zhun)

Jan. 6, 1924– South Korean opposition leader. *Address:* c/o Korean Institute for Human Rights, P.O. Box 11618, Alexandria, Va. 22312

The politically courageous and devoutly religious Kim Dae Jung has challenged South Korea's unstable and often repressive government system for three decades. He continues to champion democ-

*Kim Dae Jung*

When Communist North Korean forces invaded South Korea in 1950, setting off the Korean war, Kim was arrested in Mokpo by the occupying forces as a "reactionary capitalist" and barely escaped execution by a firing squad. After the resolution, in 1953, of that conflict, which divided North and South Korea as allies of the Soviet Union and of the United States, respectively, Kim embarked on his political career, running unsuccessfully three times, beginning in 1954, as a representative in the party opposing President Syngman Rhee. In the brief and unstable period of democracy that followed Rhee's forced resignation in 1960, he served as official spokesman for Prime Minister Chang Myon and went on to win an assembly seat in a by-election that year. But Kim's tenure had barely begun when a military coup led by Major General Park Chung Hee overthrew the government and dissolved the legislature in May 1961. Along with many other political figures, he was arrested and briefly imprisoned by the junta. The electoral process was restored in 1963, and Kim, determined to "agitate for democracy," won a landslide victory as assembly representative from the Mokpo district. He won reelection in 1967, a mandate that, in his opinion, indicated a general discontent with Park's autocratic policies.

Exploiting his advantageous position, which was further strengthened by two more successful reelections, Kim roundly opposed Park's rightist political agenda for South Korea. The surprise choice over older opposition figures, he then emerged as the favored candidate for the New Democratic party in the campaign for the presidential election slated for 1971. Addressing huge crowds throughout the country, he advocated liberal reforms that, unlike Park's views, acknowledged the thaw in the Cold War: a softened diplomacy with North Korea and the USSR; gradual disbandment of the South's two-million-member home militia; and a "hands-off" agreement by the United States, Soviet Union, China, and Japan with regard to Korea. On the domestic front, Kim called for economic policies that would benefit all Koreans, not just an elite. He accused Park's government of excessive corruption and charged Park himself with blatantly seeking to crush democratic institutions in order to "prolong his regime in the name of anticommunism and national security." Although Kim lost to Park in the April 1971 election, amid charges of government fraud, the 46 percent of the vote he drew testified to his popularity and marked him as a formidable challenge to the establishment.

After his defeat Kim continued to press for more democratic processes in South Korea, though his voice was muffled by the ban against mentioning his name that had been imposed upon the newspapers. That year he was injured in an automobile accident that was later acknowledged to be an assassination attempt staged by the South Korean Central Intelligence Agency (KCIA). Despite the harassment and surveillance that he endured during that trying period, Kim managed to cultivate ties with the international Korean community. In

racy for his people, despite at least one assassination attempt, a kidnapping, and repeated imprisonment, prompting political observers to compare him to Lech Walesa, the Polish Solidarity leader, and to Benigno Aquino Jr., the martyred Filipino opposition leader. Ever since Kim made a strong bid for the presidency in South Korea's last open election, in 1971, he has spearheaded a sometimes illegal popular struggle to restore human rights and economic justice to his homeland, which he boldly hopes will be one day reunited with North Korea. After the death sentence that had been pronounced on him in 1980 was commuted, Kim came to the United States, where he spent two years. His less than cordial reception when he returned to Seoul in early 1985 refocused international attention on his country's political difficulties, but some cautious observers believe that South Korea may be inching toward the democratic foundation that Kim, a convert to Roman Catholicism since the late 1950s, has long demanded and is helping to build.

Kim Dae Jung was born on January 6, 1924 on the island of Hayi-do off South Korea's southwestern Cholla province, the second of seven children born to a middle-class farmer and his wife. In 1943 Kim graduated from a commercial high school in the port city of Mokpo in Cholla, and he later studied economics at Kyung Hee University in Seoul. When he entered the freight-shipping business, Kim demonstrated such acumen that he headed his own company within a few years, as the relatively wealthy owner of nine small freighters; at the same time, he published a daily provincial newspaper. Although Kim joined a hybrid Korean nationalist organization in 1946, he soon repudiated its Communist elements by quitting the group.

San Francisco, for example, he established a chapter of the National Congress for the Restoration of Democracy and Promotion of the Unification of Korea, known as the Han Min Tong, with the stated aim of opposing Park's "dictatorial regime." In October 1972, while Kim was away on a trip to Japan, his worst fears were realized by Park's imposition of martial law, suspension of the constitution, and roundup of opposition critics under what was called the Yushin, or "revitalization," system.

Refusing to return to Korea lest he be silenced there, Kim mounted a vigorous protest against the repressive developments in his native land, and he sought American diplomatic intervention for the restoration of parliamentary democracy. But in August 1973 his activity was cut short. While attending a conference in Tokyo to do spadework for establishing a Han Min Tong chapter there, Kim was abducted from his hotel by suspected operatives of the KCIA. Gagged and tied with weights, he was taken back to Korea by boat and delivered in a dazed condition, after five days, to his home in Seoul, where he was placed under arrest. It was widely believed that only the international outcry that followed his disappearance had spared his life, and relations between South Korea and Japan, which argued that its sovereignty had been violated, were strained for a considerable time afterward.

A Japanese diplomatic initiative brought about Kim's release from house arrest after two months. Because, as he put it, South Korea offered "no freedom of the press, no freedom of assembly, no freedom of political activity," he hoped to continue his organizational work abroad, possibly in the United States. Although the government promised no discriminatory delay in acting on his passport application, some eight months later Kim was still languishing in Seoul under sporadic surveillance. There he was charged with minor election-law violations dating back to 1967 and 1971, along with a miscellany of other indictments for criticizing the administration. The verdict in that case, given in December 1975, sentenced him to a year's confinement and fined him $100.

By South Korean standards of the time, Kim had received only a mild rebuke. If anything, President Park's grip on the country, which he vowed not to relax any time soon, had intensified in the mid-1970s. Although his restrictions on basic freedoms had somewhat eased following a visit from President Gerald R. Ford in late 1974, a new "emergency" decree in 1975 proscribed all political actions that could remotely be construed as being antigovernment in nature. Denouncing that measure as "a method to suppress the people's will," Kim decried the official pretext that national security required the curtailment of political and religious expression, and he called for "moral support and sympathy" for his stance from the United States, which still had some 40,000 troops based on South Korean territory.

In early 1976 Kim joined a dozen distinguished Koreans, among them religious leaders, university professors, and a former president, in signing a statement urging Park's resignation, restoration of the parliamentary system, and an independent judiciary. Arrests swiftly followed the letter's public reading, on the March 1 anniversary of the Koreans' uprising against their Japanese overlords in 1919, at Myongdong Roman Catholic Cathedral in Seoul. The subsequent trial provoked clashes between police and the dissidents' supporters, some of whom placed tape over their mouths in the form of a cross to signify the "crucifixion" of democracy. Incarcerated while the case dragged on, with no opportunity for bail, the ailing Kim was hit that August with an eight-year prison term for advocating the overthrow of the government. He served about thirty-three months of that time, during which he was allowed one ten-minute visit each week from his wife.

In the same month that Kim was released from prison, in December 1978, under a suspended sentence because of ill health, the New Democratic party (NDP), tamed but still existing under the Park regime, outpolled the ruling Democratic Republican party in the general election. That victory, though in name only, emboldened Kim Young Sam, the NDP leader, to mount more vocal criticisms of Park than he had attempted for some years, and in so doing, he inspired a popular reawakening as well. Although Kim Dae Jung no longer held an official NDP position, he gave behind-the-scenes support, despite his restricted status under house arrest, to Kim Young Sam's "determination to fight . . . to restore democracy." He welcomed President Jimmy Carter's visit to South Korea in 1979, calling him "a man of faith" who had spelled out a clear human-rights policy, but warned in an interview for Sojourners magazine (October 1979) that Carter's praise of South Korea's "economic miracle" "implied that economic development should come first, sacrificing everything else, including human freedoms and workers' rights." "You cannot break a person's body, mind, and spirit and then tell him he's free to exercise his rights," he continued. " . . . The spirit, the determination, the moral fabric of the nation is steadily declining under the present system. People are saying, 'What's the use?'"

On October 26, 1979 President Park was assassinated by the chief of the KCIA, Kim Jae Kyu, and Choi Kyu Hah, a career diplomat, was installed as acting president by the martial law commanders, who seemed ready to end Park's authoritarian system. Taking advantage of the hiatus as an opportunity for reform, Kim Dae Jung lifted his moratorium on political activity by releasing a statement, a week after the assassination, that called for direct election of the president and the national assembly "according to the will of the people." "If this can take place," the text continued, "the government can stabilize the political situation with the broad support of the people and the defense posture can be firmly and securely strengthened." He also asked the United States to "assure the neutrality of the [South Korean] military" during the transition. When he was released from confinement the following month, under a general amnesty that freed some seventy other dissidents at the same time, Kim voiced his fears of political and social chaos if the restoration of democracy were delayed. At the same time he made clear that he hoped to run for president. To bring the political life of South Korea back to normal, he advocated the early lifting of martial law, amendment of the constitution, and appointment of a cabinet representing the diverse political parties, dissidents, journalists, and scholars who had previously been silenced.

When his civil rights were restored in March 1980 along with those of several hundred other activists, Kim began to criticize the NDP and the passivity, vacillation, and personal ambition of its leader, Kim Young Sam. He apparently took preliminary steps to form his own opposition party, and his stance, which was later termed "political suicide" by one observer, led army leaders to accuse him of having a Communist background and of holding radical views. But he refuted the charges, which originated from the cadre surrounding Lieutenant General Chun Doo Hwan, the strongest figure in the new junta, by declaring: "I am a moderate, a pragmatist. I am a Christian and have made Christianity the standard for all my actions. Above all, I believe in nonviolence. At the same time, I never compromised. . . . I am not a socialist."

Impatient for the vaguely promised reforms, thousands of student demonstrators took to the streets of Seoul and other cities in early May. On May 16 Kim was arrested, following the release of a military report charging him with sedition in the form of "mass agitation," sympathies with North Korea, Marxist connections, and incitement of student leaders. The next day rebels successfully overran Kwangju, capital city of the Cholla province, in a fierce uprising that was quelled, with some 1,000 Koreans reportedly killed, over the next few weeks. When Kim was hauled into military court in July to be tried for sedition by four generals, responsibility for that revolt was added to his indictments, along with accusations of Communism that largely stemmed from his involvement with the Han Min Tong, which in 1978 had been declared "antistate" on claims that it was funded by North Korean sources. An official campaign to discredit him inundated the Korean press. "Kim has the erroneous image of a patriot, a democrat, an anti-Communist, a hero and a martyr," one writer fumed. "Kim's positive image abroad is a mask behind which hides a dedicated, ruthless, methodical, and lifelong revolutionary idealist."

Kim later reported that he underwent sixty days of continuous questioning under threats of torture before his trial, which was joined to that of twenty-three of his supporters, including one of his sons and a younger brother. Faced with a prosecution that failed to call witnesses, and saddled with "gagged" and court-appointed lawyers, he denied every major charge, arguing that he "sought to gain power through elections" and had "never advocated the use of violence for political purposes." (No independent source has ever confirmed claims of the Han Min Tong's Communist backing.) Many demands for leniency, along with assertions that the charges were "farfetched," came from the United States, including a personal letter from President Jimmy Carter to Lieutenant General Chun, while Japanese diplomats also applied pressure for a fair and rational handling of the case. But in September 1980 Kim was sentenced to death by hanging for sedition, despite his conciliatory summing up in which he admitted that he had not reported American and Japanese currency that he held, conceded that he had held meetings without permission, and accepted "some moral responsibility for the demonstrations."

Chun Doo Hwan, who became president following Choi Kyu Hah's resignation, commuted Kim's sentence to twenty years' imprisonment in early 1981, just before leaving for Washington, D.C. as the first head of state received by President Ronald Reagan. Then, in December 1982, Kim was released from prison, for official reasons of "humanitarianism and the desire to promote national unity"—and with the proviso that he leave South Korea. Ostensibly to receive medical treatment for arthritis, Kim arrived in Washington, D.C. with his wife and two of his sons that month. Although grateful for his American reception, he lamented what he considered to be official United States support for "dictatorial regimes in the name of anti-Communism, security, and economic rehabilitation." During his American exile, Kim helped to create the Korean Institute for Human Rights in Arlington, Virginia and accepted a fellowship at the Center for International Affairs at Harvard University. He tried to visit President Reagan during his stay, but without any success.

Dissatisfied with his efforts to sway events in South Korea from a point as remote from Seoul as Washington, D.C., in the fall of 1984 Kim announced his plan to return there, even though the Chun regime made clear its view that "political and social instability" would ensue. After consulting Seoul authorities, members of the State Department tried to persuade him to delay his trip until after the national assembly elections, slated for February 1985, offering Chun's guarantee not to rearrest him if he did so. But, encouraged by the eager anticipation of his arrival among opposition groups, who had formed the New Korea Democratic Party (NKDP) in early 1985, Kim rejected the compromise proposal.

With memories still fresh in their minds of Benigno Aquino Jr.'s fatal shooting when he returned from exile to the Philippines in 1983, some twenty American human-rights activists concerned about official reaction to Kim joined his flight on February 8, 1985, along with a number of reporters. When they disembarked at Seoul airport, which had been made off-limits to thousands of Kim's supporters, security guards apparently forced Kim and his wife out of the grip of their companions—

among them Robert E. White, the former ambassador to El Salvador, and Patricia Derian, an assistant secretary of state for human rights in the Carter administration—who said they had been kicked and punched and Kim had been knocked down in the scuffle. Making headlines around the world, the incident was either downplayed as mere "manhandling" or inflated into a "beating," and Richard L. Wilbur, the United States ambassador to South Korea, registered an official complaint requesting an inquiry. Kim was then confined to his home in Seoul.

By capturing an electoral majority in South Korea's largest cities and winning nearly 30 percent of the vote nationwide, the NKDP emerged as a strong, legitimate contender in the national assembly elections that were held four days after Kim's return. The party had openly campaigned for constitutional reforms, including direct presidential elections for 1988, when Chun is scheduled to step down, and Kim's presence in South Korea was widely credited with inspiring the voters' trust in that platform. Perhaps most surprising was the official response to the NKDP groundswell: a spokesman for Chun's ruling Democratic Justice Party, which retained the assembly majority, acknowledged the balloting as "a demand for change in our attitude . . . [and for] gradual democracy and more liberalization."

Even Kim expressed much optimism, which was borne out the following month when he and Kim Young Sam were among the last names removed from a political blacklist in recognition of the "new political climate . . . born of a harmonizing blend of freedom and order." Because he was still barred from joining or organizing a political party, Kim restricted his activity to co-chairing, with Kim Young Sam, the Council for the Promotion of Democracy, which worked as a support group for the NKDP. In April several opposition parties, reportedly shepherded by Kim, merged under the NKDP banner, arousing hopes that a genuine democratic dialogue was finally underway in South Korea.

Yet those prospects appeared less certain by the fall of 1985. Kim, informed that he must "repent" in order to regain his full rights and threatened with reinstatement of his suspended twenty-year sentence, had to bear surveillance and periodic confinement, and a new series of campus arrests and dismissals of activists was started. " . . . I am much afraid of the possibility of polarization, with the military dictatorship on one side and radical elements on the other," Kim explained, as quoted in the New York Times (October 1, 1985). "In that case, we moderate democrats will lose our base."

Kim Dae Jung, who stands five feet six inches tall, walks with a slight limp and sometimes uses a cane. Abstemious by nature, he drinks very little and only occasionally smokes a pipe. He has two sons by his marriage to his first wife, who died in 1959, and one son by Lee Hee Ho, a former YWCA administrator in South Korea, whom he married in 1962. She has often joined Kim in his antigovernment activities, sharing his harassments or detainments. Kim, who has acquired a mastery of calligraphic writing, sells his scrolls as part of his fundraising, and he enjoys indoor gardening.

References: Christian Sci Mon p2 Jl 9 '79; N Y Times p2 Mr 29 '71 por, A p1+ S 17 '80, A p1+ F 9 '85 por; N Y Times Mag p20+ D 23 '84 pors; Sojourners 8:11+ O '79 por; Washington Post A p16 Ag 25 '73, C p3 Ag 26 '73 por; International Who's Who, 1985-86

## King, Larry

Nov. 19, 1933– Broadcaster; newspaper columnist. Address: b. 1755 S. Jefferson Davis Highway, Arlington, Va. 22202

From midnight to dawn for more than seven years, Larry King has presided over a national radio show that serves as a forum for Americans to air their often controversial views and gives its host the opportunity to chat with celebrities, experts in various fields, and lesser-known but undeniably interesting personalities. When The Larry King Show had its premiere on the Mutual Broadcasting System in January 1978, only twenty-eight small stations carried it, but by the early 1980s, about 250 stations in all fifty states as well as the Armed Forces Radio Network were broadcasting it to an estimated weekly audience of three million. In a competitive market glutted with talk shows, the unique format of The Larry King Show, the first national late-night talk program, and its host's inimitable style have made it overwhelmingly successful.

Tom Shales, the radio and television critic of the Washington Post, observed in his column of August

18, 1984: "If a person holds the opinion that the world needs no more talk shows, a very valid opinion to hold, it still might be worth making an exemption for King. He's smart and he asks good questions, and that puts him a couple of steps ahead of the pack." During his twenty-eight-year career, King has also been a newspaper columnist, a television-show host, and an autobiographer, having written, in collaboration with Emily Yoffe, *Larry King by Larry King* (Simon and Schuster, 1982). More recently, he played cameo roles in the films *Ghostbusters* and *Lost in America*.

Born Lawrence Harvey Zeiger on November 19, 1933 in Brooklyn, New York, Larry King was the second child of Jennie and Eddie Zeiger, both Russian-Jewish immigrants. Their first child, a boy six years older than King, died of appendicitis shortly before King's birth. His only other sibling, Martin, is now a vice-president and corporate counsel for the Revco drugstore chain. Although his parents' bar-and-grill in the Brownsville section of Brooklyn was fairly successful, Eddie Zieger sold the business when World War II broke out in order to contribute to the war effort by working at a defense plant in Kearny, New Jersey. On June 10, 1944 he died of a heart attack while working at the plant, forcing Jennie Zeiger to take relief payments before she found work in Manhattan's garment district a year later.

His idolized father's sudden death traumatized the ten-year-old Larry King. Although he had done so well in school that he skipped from the second to the fourth grade, he now neglected his studies and gained the reputation of a troublemaker at Brooklyn's Junior High School 128. His record did not improve at Lafayette High School: he graduated in 1951 with a grade average of sixty-six, one point above the minimum for passing.

Reflecting on his father's death and his problems at school in an interview for *Current Biography*, King explained that, at first not understanding what had happened, he simply thought that his father had left him. "And if he left me, who would leave me next? And so nothing else was worth it but the things I liked—and the things I liked were broadcasting and sports." When his mother moved her family from Brownsville to an attic apartment in Bensonhurst, he spent most of his time watching the Brooklyn Dodgers, talking about sports, or listening to Arthur Godfrey, whom he worshiped, Walter Winchell, and the team of Bob Elliott and Ray Goulding and to such popular radio series as *Armstrong Theater of Today*, *The Lone Ranger*, *Vox Pop*, *Grand Central Station*, and *Town Meeting of the Air*. He often went to Manhattan to see his favorite shows being broadcast.

Although he was certain that he wanted a career in broadcasting, King did not know how to break into the field, so he marked time in Brooklyn for four years after high school, working as a delivery boy and mail clerk, among other odd jobs. Finally, in 1957, at the age of twenty-three, he took a bus to Miami where, he heard, a neophyte could start a

radio career. He only got a job sweeping floors at the 250-watt AM station WAHR (now WMBM), but when the disc jockey for the station's 9 A.M.-to-noon show suddenly quit, King was asked to replace him. On May 1, 1957, having changed his name moments before he went on the air from Zeiger to King at the station manager's suggestion, he found himself in front of a microphone for the first time.

"I was petrified," King admitted to John Pekkanen of *People* (March 10, 1980). "The theme music was supposed to fade, and I was supposed to do a voice-over. But every time the music faded, I'd turn it back up again. Finally the station manager stuck his head into the studio and said, 'Remember, this is a communicating business.' I let the music go down and told the audience what had just happened. Those were my first words on radio."

Never again suffering from "mike fright," King was soon attracting the attention of larger Miami radio stations. Promised better pay and the enviable morning "drive-time" slot, he joined WKAT late in 1958. Reaching for a wider audience, the station encouraged its DJs to be imaginative. King took advantage of that latitude "to break away from being a standard disc jockey," by creating such offbeat characters as Captain Wainwright of the Miami State Police, whose unorthodox suggestions included placing horse-racing wagers with police officers to save a trip to the track. The popularity of the character led to King's being hired by Pumpernik's Restaurant to serve as host for a four-hour, on-location radio show designed to boost its flagging breakfast-time business.

Culling his guests from the restaurant's clientele, King interviewed whoever happened to be there at the time rather than relying on prearranged bookings. As a result, during the show's first week, he interviewed the restaurant's waitresses, some plumbers in town for a convention, and the then still relatively unknown comedians Don Rickles and Lenny Bruce. On the fourth day, the pop singer and movie actor Bobby Darin, his curiosity piqued by the unusual format of the show, dropped in and was interviewed. Soon other celebrities made a point of stopping by Pumpernik's whenever they were in Miami.

As he recounted in his autobiography, *Larry King by Larry King*, the Pumpernik assignment proved to be a turning point in his career. "I found I could do more than shtick. I found I had an ability to draw people out in an interview. The key to my success as an interviewer is in the fact that I am truly interested in a person's craft, in his or her work. And when you sincerely want to find out why people do what they do, and how they do it, you are going to learn a lot." Never knowing who his guests would be and so unable to prepare in advance, King perfected his interviewing technique by listening carefully to what his guests said and then gestating questions as the interview progressed. King continues to rely on that ad-lib method of interviewing. "The less I know in advance," he explained to Gary Deeb in an interview for the Times of London syndicate, "the more curious I am on the air."

In 1962 King moved to WIOD in Miami while continuing his interview show from Pumpernik's. But the next year, at the urging of the WIOD management, he moved the show from the restaurant to a houseboat that was used as the setting for the ABC television series *Surfside 6* and began broadcasting at night. He also dabbled in television work at the local station WLBW, hosting on Sundays a late-night talk show with no time limits, but in 1964 he left that station for a weekend show on WTVJ-TV. A year later King incorporated newspaper work into his repertoire, writing a regular column first for the *Miami Beach Sun-Reporter* and later for the Miami *Herald* and the Miami *News*. With his radio, television, and newspaper jobs, King was earning approximately $70,000 a year by 1966.

Ironically, as King became increasingly successful, his financial problems worsened: gambling on horse races, buying expensive clothes, and renting Cadillacs left him deeply in debt in spite of his impressive income. "At my most egotistical moments, of which there were many, I felt as if I owned Miami—and I lived as if I did, too . . . ," he admitted in his autobiography. "I felt that whatever Larry King wanted, Larry King should have." But it was his friendship with the wealthy financier Louis Wolfson, whom he met in 1966 at the Hialeah race track, that eventually shattered his career. In 1968 Wolfson gave King $5,000 to relay to the New Orleans district attorney Jim Garrison to help in his investigation into the assassination of President John F. Kennedy. Instead, King used the money to pay his taxes. That alleged misappropriation of funds, King's inability to pay his large debt to Wolfson, and his subsequent failure to use his influence with important government officials in behalf of Wolfson, who had been sentenced to prison for stock violations, infuriated the financier. After his release, Wolfson, unappeased by King's offer of a $5,000 cashier's check, pressed grand larceny charges against King, who was arrested in December 1971. The matter was finally resolved when the charges against King were dropped because the statute of limitations had expired.

In the meantime, however, King's career was ruined by the scandal. He not only lost his positions as disc jockey and color commentator for the Miami Dolphins' games for WIOD, as talk-show host for WTVJ, and as columnist for the *Miami Beach Sun-Reporter*, but also found himself deeply in debt. Suddenly, at the age of thirty-eight, he faced the challenge of starting over. Recalling that bleak period for the *Current Biography* interview, King explained, "The thing within my makeup that makes me so very good and also makes me so harmful to myself is an incredible impetuosity, which I bring to the air and also to my personal life. . . . Impetuous is the right word—someone who acts on the moment. Instinct. I go to my instinct."

Scrambling to make a living, King worked from 1972 to 1975 as a freelance writer and broadcaster. In 1974 he landed a job in public relations for a horse-racing track in Shreveport, Louisiana, and

during that fall he was once again behind a microphone, serving as a radio color commentator for the Shreveport Steamers of the short-lived World Football League. However, early in 1975 the racing track was sold and new personnel brought in. Out of work again, King traveled to San Francisco to look for a broadcasting position. After about a month, he accepted the post of announcer for University of California football games. Since the job did not begin until September, King returned to Miami to visit his mother. When he arrived, he learned that WIOD had a new general manager, who had heard King's old tapes and wanted to rehire him for an evening interview show.

Despite his misgivings about returning to the station that had so unceremoniously dismissed him, King accepted the offer and notified the University of California that he would not be announcing its football games. On returning to WIOD, King used the same format as before, interviewing a guest and then taking calls from listeners. Soon he was also rehired as a TV interviewer, as a columnist for the Miami *News*, and as the radio color commentator for the Miami Dolphins football team. But even though he now had a steady income and had quit gambling on horse races, King, unable to repay his debts of $352,000, declared bankruptcy in 1978. Since then, his finances have been handled by others, who give him a weekly allowance for his personal expenses.

Shortly before he declared bankruptcy, the Mutual Broadcasting Network approached King about leaving WIOD to do a national, late-night talk show. Because Mutual's two previous attempts at such a program had failed, King had reservations about the network's ability to attract celebrities at such an unlikely hour, let alone a sizable audience, but he nevertheless took the assignment. "For my part, I decided I would give the show my best try, and if it didn't work, I could always go back to Miami or to another city," he recalled in his autobiography. "I just didn't have that much to lose."

On January 30, 1978 *The Larry King Show* made its debut in twenty-eight cities over the Mutual Broadcasting System. It was originally broadcast from WIOD in Miami, where King continued to host the show for nine weeks, but since April 1978 it has emanated from Mutual's studios in Arlington, Virginia, which overlook the Capitol in Washington, D.C. Although fond of Miami, King prefers hosting the show from the Washington area because of the city's "mystique" and because it gives him ready access to top government officials, who often appear as his guests.

The show originally ran for five-and-a-half hours, from midnight to 5:30 A.M. (EST), but its last half hour was later cut. In spite of the program's unfashionably late time slot, both the calibre of King's guests, who have ranged from porno film star Marilyn Chambers to Frank Sinatra and from the New York governor, Mario Cuomo, to the Reverend Jerry Falwell, and King's unique and often controversial style quickly attracted a large, faithful following. By the early 1980s, *The Larry King*

*Show* was being carried by about 250 Mutual Broadcasting affiliates and could claim a weekly audience of between three and five million people. In 1982 the University of Georgia honored the show with a George Foster Peabody award, which King considers the highlight of his career.

Hewing to a tripartite formula, King first conducts an hour-long interview with his guest, who usually stays on for two more hours to answer the listeners' questions. During the last segment, called "Open Phone America," King has to cope with a barrage of comments and questions from callers on virtually every subject, including the economy, nuclear war, social issues, sports, and current events. Thanks to its live transmission, *The Larry King Show* has been able to break important news stories, such as the failed rescue attempt of the American hostages in Iran in 1980 and the end of the major-league baseball strike in 1982. The show often goes on the road, traveling to Hawaii in February 1985 and visiting San Francisco and Dallas for the Democratic and Republican conventions in 1984. But not all of the proceedings are serious. King often cavorts in comedy sketches featuring his fictional alien, Gork of the planet Fringus, and several regular callers, among them the Portland Laugher and the Brooklyn Scandal Scooper, also provide antic relief.

King takes great pride in the quality of his audience and gives it most of the credit for the show's success. Surveys indicate that the listenership is 52 percent male and heavily weighted with graduate students and professionals, with a mean age of twenty-nine. Although only about 1 percent of his audience phone in, more than once his listeners, who call at their own expense, have jammed the entire 703 area code.

Even though King has the right to veto or suggest guests, he rarely disagrees with his producer's bookings. "The best guest is anyone passionately involved in what he does, anyone with a deep, emotional caring about what he does," King has said. "That means Jerry Falwell is a terrific guest, and so are Mario Cuomo, Studs Terkel, Phyllis Schlafly, and Muhammad Ali." Of the more than twenty thousand people he has interviewed during his career, he considers architects to be the most outspoken professionals, politicians the least, and criminal defense lawyers the most interesting because "they hold a person's future in their hands."

In May 1985 King signed a new five-year, $1.85 million, no-options contract with Mutual. He also agreed to do a similar call-in interview show—*Larry King Live*—for the Cable News Network for $250,000 a year and to provide the color commentary for about thirty-five Baltimore Colts and Washington Capital games for Home Team Sports, a pay-TV channel. "I'm on a roll," he told Jacqueline Trescott of the *Washington Post* (May 1, 1985), "but even though the schedule is tough, the shows aren't tough." In addition to *The Larry King Show*, he conducts a two-and-a-half-minute interview during each day for Mutual and a longer one each month for Voice of America's *Talk to America* program. He writes columns once a week for *USA Today* and the *Sporting News* and hosts the weekly *Larry King: Let's Talk* program on WJLA-TV in Washington, D.C. In spite of his demonstrable successes in radio, in television, and in the print media, King has yet to realize all his goals: he wants to publish two more books.

According to Marc Lee of the *Washington Times* (January 7, 1985), Larry King, who has dark hair and wears thick glasses, is "handsome in a peculiar way." After a teenage marriage that was annulled before being consummated, he wed Alene Akins (1961-63, 1967-71), a former Playboy bunny; Mickey Sutphin (1964-66); and Sharon Lepore (1976-82), a former math teacher. Each of those marriages ended in divorce. He and Alene Akins have a daughter, Chaia, who was born in 1967. King, who has said unequivocally that he will never marry again, lives with Chaia in an Arlington, Virginia apartment. When his busy schedule permits, he enjoys reading and traveling.

References: *People* 13:49+ Mr 10 '80 pors; *Quest/81* p24+ Mr '81 pors; *Contemporary Authors vol 111* (1984); King, Larry. *Larry King by Larry King* (1982)

## Korda, Michael (Vincent)

*Oct. 8, 1933– Publishing executive; author.*
*Address: b. Simon & Schuster, 1230 Ave. of the Americas, New York City, N.Y. 10020*

Few people have enjoyed more success in merging two careers than Michael Korda. The flamboyant and controversial editor in chief of Simon &

Schuster, Korda has guided the fortunes of that publishing house, which numbers among its stable of authors such luminaries as Graham Greene, Joan Didion, and Carlos Castenada. Moreover, he is himself an unusually prolific and eclectic writer, with credits ranging from scores of magazine articles of the self-help genre to the captivating memoir *Charmed Lives* to the randy *roman à clef* called *Queenie*. He is not the only publisher who writes, but as he has pointed out, he is "the only publisher who writes *successfully*."

Michael Vincent Korda was born in London, England on October 8, 1933, the son of Vincent Korda, the Hungarian-born motion picture art director, and his wife, Gertrude Musgrove, an English actress. His father was one of three brothers, all of whom became prominent figures in the British film industry. The middle brother, Zoltán, was a director who specialized in exotic adventure epics like *The Four Feathers* and *The Macomber Affair*; the oldest, Alexander, who directed or produced some of the biggest box-office hits of the 1930s and 1940s, including *The Private Life of Henry VIII*, *The Scarlet Pimpernel*, and *That Hamilton Woman*, eventually won a knighthood for building the British cinema into a temporary rival of Hollywood. An exceptionally gifted scenic designer, Vincent Korda created the lavish sets for most of his brothers' motion pictures and for dozens of other large-scale productions.

Reared in what one writer called an atmosphere of "richly indulged and cultivated glamour and wackiness," Michael Korda was a shy and lonely child, and for years he tried, by his own admission, to repress his "glitzy" background. As he told Tony Schwartz in an interview for the *New York Times Book Review* (June 27, 1982), he has since changed his mind: "I think I'm so much invested in the Korda myth that a lot of the world seems strangely unimportant by comparison. . . . I come from a family that was very strong, very successful, very bizarre, and terrifically exciting. Being a Korda is something I regard as special—not wonderful, or worthy of a national monument, but special."

During most of his boyhood, Michael was something of an "extra" in the ongoing saga of the eccentric Kordas. He spent most of his time in a series of boarding schools and military academies in England and the United States. After his parents separated in 1941, he lived for a time with his mother in New York City; then, in about 1946, he rejoined his father in London. A few months later, Korda enrolled at Le Rosey, the exclusive Swiss boarding school favored by European royalty. It was there that he consciously began to cultivate the flamboyant image, modeled after his idolized Uncle Alexander, that has stayed with him. "He was fat and quite foppish, an American-English dandy, very elegant and slightly strange," his classmate Warner LeRoy told Julie Baumgold in an interview for *New York* magazine (April 1, 1985). "In that school where we had kings and the Shah and the Aga Khan, everyone was a little strange, but he was very different. I have a vision of lace, just a vision, an impression of a lace handkerchief."

Following his graduation from Le Rosey, Korda fulfilled his British military obligation by serving in the Royal Air Force from 1952 to 1954. On his discharge, he took a low-level job with the *Financial Times* in London for a few months, then entered Magdalen College, Oxford University. He interrupted his studies in 1956 to join the insurgents in the short-lived anti-Communist revolution in Hungary. As he explained in his book *Charmed Lives; A Family Romance* (Random House, 1979), his decision to take part in the revolt stemmed from a desire to emulate his Uncle Alexander, who had died earlier in the same year: "His successes and his aura—financial, sexual, professional—all seemed to crush and reduce me, and I felt suffocated, haunted by the possibility of being a failure all my life, of having to compete with Alex long after his death."

After the Soviet Union crushed the rebellion early in 1957, Korda returned to Oxford to complete his studies, taking his B.A. degree in modern languages in 1958. Shortly thereafter, he decided to move to New York City, where he hoped to become a journalist "in the Evelyn Waugh tradition." Unsuccessful in his attempts to find employment with a news magazine, he eventually settled for a job reading scripts for the much praised CBS-TV dramatic anthology series *Playhouse 90*. When the network liquidated its story-reading department a few months later, Korda signed on at Simon & Schuster as an assistant editor. He has cheerfully admitted that he got the position as a result of his family connections. "When I came into publishing, Alex was still a very much remembered figure and my father and Zoli were still very active," Korda told Stephen E. Rubin of the *Los Angeles Times* (October 21, 1979). "I benefited enormously from it because people are snobs. I got hired like *that* and I was made an editor's assistant like *that*."

First assigned to reading the "sludge pile" of unsolicited manuscripts, Korda, an admitted workaholic, threw himself into his disagreeable task with characteristic determination and singlemindedness. "Nobody in book publishing succeeds except by longevity, fifteen years in the office doing donkeywork," he told Julie Baumgold. "For the first eight or nine years, all I did was work behind the scenes, and six people knew." Over those years, his obvious professionalism, supercharged energy, and clairvoyant ability to anticipate the changing tastes of the American reading public paid off in increasingly responsible positions. Among his early editorial successes were Irving Wallace's best-selling novel *The Chapman Report* and *The Forest People*, the social anthropologist Colin Turnbull's eminently readable study of the Pygmies of the Ituri Forest in Zaire.

By the mid-1960s, Korda had risen to the post of executive editor at Simon & Schuster, with an impressive string of best sellers to his credit. Nonetheless, as he told Karen De Witt of the *Washington Post* (October 27, 1977), he gradually came to feel that his work was unappreciated and that he himself was "very underpaid." Then, in 1968, Robert A.

Gottlieb, the editor in chief of Simon & Schuster, resigned. Immediately named acting editor in chief, Korda eventually managed to parlay that temporary appointment into a permanent assignment. Working closely with Richard E. Snyder, Simon & Schuster's publisher and, since 1979, chief executive officer, he has since continued the blockbuster tradition of the publishing house, making it, in Stephen Rubin's words, "glitzy, high-pressured, popular, and successful."

Korda outlined his views on the publishing industry and discussed his approach to his job as Simon & Schuster's editor in chief in an interview that appeared in the November 28, 1979 edition of the Chicago Tribune. "Publishing is a business and a literary activity . . . ," he told Mary Patton. "The ideal book is one that wins the Pulitzer Prize, gets made into a movie, and sells a lot of copies—in other words quality and profit." In Korda's opinion, too many publishers ignore the marketing aspect of book publishing. "It's a retail business, at a certain level," he went on, "and you've got to have the instincts of a good merchandiser if you want to sell copies."

In selecting books for Simon & Schuster's list, Korda generally bypasses first novels and what he calls "flaky idea books." Contending that his role is to recruit and sign those "solid name authors" whose titles will "keep our list going," he has published books by such perennial best-selling writers as Harold Robbins, Anthony Burgess, Carlos Castaneda, Susan Howatch, Richard Adams, and Jacqueline Susann, among others. Korda himself edits the work of Graham Greene, Joan Didion, Larry McMurtry, Jackie Collins, and Shirley Conran—all of whose novels have the backbone of narrative he favors. His specialty is the "overnight read"—digesting, criticizing, and reorganizing sprawling, 1,000-page novels in a matter of hours. One of the most meticulous text editors in the business, he is especially adept at detecting and correcting structural flaws and inconsistencies in characterization. On occasion, he has even rewritten weak endings, imitating the writer's style so well that the carpentry is invisible.

Korda's talent for mimicry has served him well at Simon & Schuster's semiannual sales conferences. "He never prepares," Korda's longtime colleague Joni Evans told Tony Schwartz, "but he'll stand up before 150 people, with twenty-five books to present, and summarize the essence of every single one, remembering every last character, dramatizing the whole thing, and probably writing half the books himself while he's talking. He's also the only editor who consistently gets applause when he's done."

During his tenure as editor in chief, Korda has generally managed to avoid controversy, but in 1984 he became personally involved in the imbroglio surrounding Simon & Schuster's publication of Vengeance; the True Story of an Israeli Counter-Terrorist Team. Written by George Jonas, Vengeance purports to tell the story of five young Israelis who were selected to seek out and kill the terrorists responsible for the deaths of eleven Israeli athletes at the Summer Olympic Games in Munich, Germany, in 1972. The book's accuracy was publicly questioned by both the New York Times and the London Times after Korda and Jonas admitted that they could not confirm the identity of the group's leader or independently verify his statements. "We don't have a staff of hundreds of reporters to check every book we publish . . . ," Korda said, as quoted in the New York Times (May 2, 1984). "If it isn't libelous, the weight of responsibility is to let the author tell his story."

In the early 1970s Korda reached a point in his life where being the editor in chief of a major publishing house simply seemed not enough. Having grown up in a famous family, he hungered for public recognition. "It's a part of my character," he admitted to Julie Baumgold for the New York magazine profile. "I don't drink or chase women, I'm not particularly greedy, but I don't like being anonymous." At least partly to satisfy his need for celebrity, Korda began writing magazine articles, mainly on cultural trends, in 1972. Since then, he has contributed scores of pieces to such varied publications as Glamour, Newsweek, Playboy, Vogue, and Family Weekly. He also writes columns regularly for Penthouse, Success, and Self.

One of those magazine articles formed the basis for Korda's first book, Male Chauvinism! How It Works (Random House, 1973), a glib, anecdotal discussion of sexual politics in the office. Male Chauvinism! sold only moderately well, but Korda's second book, Power! How To Get It, How To Use It (Random House, 1975), a guidebook for the upwardly mobile that one critic described as reading "much like a collaboration between C. Northcote Parkinson and Niccolò Machiavelli," landed on the best-seller list despite mostly negative reviews. Although Korda insisted at first that he had intended Power! to be a spoof of corporate oneupmanship, when it became evident that readers were apparently taking his manipulative advice to heart, he decided to play along. "I did get caught up in it all . . . ," he told Tony Schwartz. "I was buoyed by the attention. Touring, talking, and lecturing was a high, and I enjoyed it enormously."

Success! (Random House, 1977), which was directed at ambitious middle-managers, enlarged upon the self-promotion techniques that Korda had introduced in Power!. Like its predecessor, Success! survived a barrage of critical disparagement to become one of the year's top sellers. Growing "tired of being the Norman Vincent Peale of upward mobility," as he put it, Korda scrapped plans for yet another self-help book in favor of writing a long-delayed biography of his illustrious family. A highly personal account, spiced with gossip, of his fairy-tale childhood among the rich and famous, Charmed Lives brought Korda a measure of the critical esteem that had so far eluded him. According to Peter Bogdanovich, the motion picture director, who reviewed the book for the Washington Post, Charmed Lives was good enough to join "that very small handful of books about movie people that are worth reading: literate without being pretentious, candid without being exploitative, worldly without being jaded, sensitive without being mawkish." Despite such accolades, the book sold fewer copies—about 30,000 in hardcover—than anticipated. It proved to be more popular in Great Britain, where it was read over the radio in nightly installments.

As more than one reviewer pointed out, Korda continued to explore the themes of ambition, power, and wealth that had long fascinated him in his first novel, *Worldly Goods* (Random House, 1982), a tightly constructed, fast-paced potboiler about the power struggle between two multimillionaire financiers—one of them the son of an ex-Nazi the sordid past of whom comes back to haunt him—and the woman who was mistress to them both. Reviews were mixed, and Korda himself has since dismissed the book as "an apprenticeship." "I wanted to prove to myself that I could write a novel . . . ," he explained to Tony Schwartz. "You don't try to make a magnificent piece of period furniture as your first effort. You start with a simple table. Unless you're a genius, you have to accept imperfections to be productive."

Korda regained his status as a best-selling author with the 1985 release of his second novel, *Queenie* (Linden Press/Simon & Schuster). Based on the life of the late Merle Oberon, the actress who was Alexander Korda's second wife, the book "was written to have all the elements," as Julie Baumgold observed in her profile for *New York*, including India under the Raj, murder, incest-rape, homosexuality, ambition, lost love, an "unabashed delight in money and textures," and a "shockingly beautiful, eventually powerful heroine with a criminal heart and secrets." Within days of its publication, *Queenie* had earned a place on *Publishers Weekly*'s hardcover best-seller list, and it was recently sold to ABC-TV for a projected miniseries.

A slight, wiry man, Michael Korda stands five feet two inches tall and weighs about 130 pounds. He has a rather impish face, blue eyes, and long hair that becomes "ever blonder with age," according to Julie Baumgold. An early riser, he writes for three hours every morning before setting off, usually by subway, for his office, where he regularly puts in a nine- or ten-hour day. In his spare time, he jogs, goes horseback riding, or reads. His taste in literature is eclectic, but he is especially fond of the novels of Joseph Conrad. He is an avid gun collector. Korda has been married to the former Margaret Mogford, an English model whom he met while horseback riding in Central Park, since 1978. An earlier marriage to Carolyn Keese, by whom he has one son, Christopher Vincent, ended in divorce. The Kordas divide their time between an apartment overlooking Central Park on Manhattan's Upper West Side and a 150-acre farm near Poughkeepsie, New York.

References: Los Angeles Times p6+ O 21 '79 por; N Y Times Bk R p13+ Je 27 '82 por; New York 118:38+ Ap 1 '85 pors; Newsday II p3 Ja 2 '80 por; People 12:139+ D 17 '79 pors; Washington Post B p1+ O 27 '77; Contemporary Authors vol 107 (1983); Who's Who in America, 1984–85

## Kremer, Gidon

(krā´ mer ge´ dōn)

*Feb. 27, 1947– Violinist. Address: b. c/o ICM Artists, Ltd., 40 W. 57th St., New York City, N.Y. 10019*

Gidon Kremer, the Soviet-born violinist who is considered by many music critics to be one of the most accomplished musicians of his generation, first came to international attention in 1970, when he won the gold medal in Moscow's prestigious Tchaikovsky Competition. A pupil of the late David Oistrakh, whose grand, heroic style made a lasting impact on him, Kremer is most celebrated for the passionate originality he brings to his performances of both classical and contemporary music—an originality underscored by his highly expressive stage persona. Traditionalists have criticized his unconventional stage manners, which include taking deep kneebends and occasionally turning his back to the audience, his audacious addition of a note or two to Beethoven's scores, and his frequent performances of little-known—and some would say superficial—contemporary works. But no one questions his remarkable technical command or his dedication to his art. "When I am onstage I want the people not just to like what I am doing, but to need what I am doing," he once remarked.

Gidon Kremer was born in Riga, Latvia on February 27, 1947, the descendant of noted musicians on both sides of his family. His mother, Marianne Brückner, and his father, Markus Kremer, were violinists in the highly regarded Riga Symphony Orchestra, and his maternal grandfather, Karl Brückner, was an internationally acclaimed violinist and an instructor at the Riga School of Music. In commenting on his musical background, Kremer told a reporter for *People* (May 3, 1982), "There was no question that I would become a musician. It was only a question of how good." When he was just four years old, he began taking regular violin lessons, with his father and grandfather taking turns as his teacher. A conscientious pupil, the child practiced by the hour in the kitchen of his family's two-and-one-half-room apartment. By the time he was seven, he was proficient enough to play the first movement of Vivaldi's Violin Concerto in G.

Recognizing their son's talent, the Kremers enrolled him in the Riga School of Music, where he continued his studies with Professor V. Sturestep. Although Kremer has insisted in interviews that he "wasn't a genius, not even a child prodigy," he made such rapid progress that he was only sixteen when he captured the top prize in a national violin competition. In 1965 Kremer was accepted as a student at the renowned P. I. Tchaikovsky State Conservatory in Moscow. He spent the next eight years there, primarily under the tutelage of the famed violinist David Oistrakh. "I felt I had been born anew," he said years later of that experience. Confident of his grandson's future success as a violinist, grandfather Brückner gave the young man the violin he had himself played on countless tours—a treasured eighteenth-century instrument by the master Giovanni Battista Guadagnini. Kremer performed on it exclusively until the late 1970s, when, during an American concert tour, he purchased a Stradivarius.

Although he himself disagrees with the belief that one musician can be judged to be better than another, Kremer realized that competition prizes could serve as a springboard to a concert career. From an early age, he distinguished himself in the competitive arena, winning a bronze medal in the 1967 Queen Elizabeth Competition in Brussels, a silver medal in the 1968 Montreal Music Competition, and a gold medal in the 1968 Paganini Competition in Genoa. After he took the coveted gold medal at the Fourth International Tchaikovsky competition in Moscow in 1970, the young violinist was deluged with invitations to perform abroad. Normally, Soviet artists are granted permission to tour abroad for about ninety days each year, but from the beginning, the authorities were unusually strict with Kremer. In 1970, for example, he was permitted to play only short engagements with orchestras in Budapest and Vienna, and from 1971 through 1973 he was not allowed to leave the Soviet Union at all. Finally, in 1974, the ban on his travel was lifted, and he began touring regularly in Western Europe, performing with orchestras in Vi-

enna, West Berlin, Munich, Salzburg, and the Bavarian city of Ansbach. Over the years, Kremer's circle of admirers grew, especially in Germany, where in 1976 critics voted him "Musician of the Year." In the same year, Herbert von Karajan, who had invited him to perform in the opening concert of the 1976 Salzburg Mozart Festival, introduced Kremer from the podium as "in my opinion, the greatest violinist in the world." Grateful as he was for the maestro's unqualified support, Kremer told Eleanor Blau, who interviewed him for a *New York Times* (August 27, 1980) profile, that he felt "terrible" as he walked onstage. "I am not interested in being best or first," he explained. "I really am interested only to do my job—to give all my experience and all my feeling in music."

During his first United States tour, under the auspices of the impresario Sol Hurok, Gidon Kremer made his New York debut in a recital at Avery Fisher Hall in the Lincoln Center for the Performing Arts on January 14, 1977. He opened his concert with Stravinsky's "Elegie for Unaccompanied Violin" followed by Bach's Partita no. 1 in B minor; then, accompanied by the pianist Xenia Knorre, he played Beethoven's Sonata no. 10 in G opus 96 and Charles Ives's Sonata no. 4 ("Children's Day at the Camp Meeting"). He also introduced his New York audience to an unusual piece by Alfred Schnittke, the contemporary Russian composer whose works he has championed throughout his career. The Schnittke work he selected on this occasion was "Preludio in Memoriam Dmitri Shostakovich," which concludes with a duet for taped and live violin.

Audiences and critics alike responded to Kremer's New York debut with enthusiasm and admiration. In his highly favorable appraisal of the performance for the *New York Times* (January 16, 1977), Peter G. Davis noted approvingly that Kremer, "unlike so many violinists that the Russians send us these days," was "far from a flashy, glamorous personality, either in appearance or in style of playing." To the contrary, Davis went on, Kremer's "tone tends to be on the dry side, he phrases with an elegant sense of understatement and although his technique is second to none, it is never used for surface effect." Davis was especially taken with Kremer's "unconventional yet convincing" interpretation of the Bach Partita: "Precisely articulated and flawlessly intoned, this was letter-perfect Bach playing, yet cunningly accented to suggest the inherent contrapuntal nature of the music and its extraordinary surface tension."

Peter Goodman, the music critic for *Newsday*, echoed his colleague's assessment of Kremer's special affinity for Bach. "He played as if caressing each note," Goodman wrote in his review of January 17, 1977. "Every nuance received loving consideration like individual gems in a delicately crafted setting. His trills were like butterflies on the strings. . . . His concentration was such that he could spring from the most featherlight sound to powerful fortes in a single bow." For Goodman, the "joy of the concert" was in the sensitive interpretations Kremer accorded each piece, and "they were spellbinding."

Late in 1977, at the conclusion of a tour of West Germany and Austria with the Vilna Chamber Orchestra, Kremer and his wife, the pianist Elena Bashkirova, who is his regular accompanist, formally applied to the Soviet Ministry of Culture for permission to reside in the West for two years. In making the application, Kremer was careful to point out that their motives were not political, but artistic. As he explained to Paul Moor in an interview for the March 1978 issue of *High Fidelity/Musical America*, "It is really very important for every artist, not only for me, to see and experience a lot, not only in his own country but in the whole world." After lengthy discussions with ministry officials, permission was granted.

In the meantime, Kremer's father, a Latvian Jew, and his mother, who was German-born, applied for and received visas to immigrate to Israel. En route, however, they stopped in Heidelberg and decided to settle there instead. When Gidon Kremer's two years abroad expired at the end of 1979, he and his wife applied for permission to remain with Gidon's aged and ailing parents. For several months, Kremer heard nothing. Then, in February 1980, a concert he had been scheduled to give in Moscow with the Moscow Philharmonic was abruptly canceled, allegedly because his application to remain in West Germany was still pending. Kremer was admittedly puzzled by the Soviet government's reaction, for as he told Eleanor Blau, "We would have the legal right to stay with my parents; in the Soviet Union children may join their parents. But this might be the first example of a known artist doing that." (Contrary to some published reports, the Kremers never requested political asylum.)

Eventually, the Kremers were allowed to remain in the West, while retaining their Soviet citizenship. But although he can visit his homeland, Gidon Kremer cannot perform there, his government having taken the position that his resident status abroad precludes his giving concerts in the Soviet Union. At the same time, since he remains a Russian citizen, he cannot tour the country as a foreign artist. "It is, let's say, a very complex situation which I hope will be solved someday," he said in a recent interview with Allan Kozinn for the *New York Times* (December 30, 1984).

The longer Gidon Kremer has stayed in the West, the greater his stature in the music world has grown—along with his reputation for being something of an eccentric with a decidedly "different" musical taste and an idiosyncratic performing style. After hearing him play Stravinsky's "Duo Concertante," Prokofiev's Sonata in D opus 115, six melodies from *Zodiac* by Karlheinz Stockhausen, Tchaikovsky's "Sérénade mélancolique" and "Valse-Scherzo," and Schubert's *Phantasie*, for violin and piano, in C major at Carnegie Hall in New York City in March 1979, Donal Henahan, the *New York Times*'s music critic, asked his readers, "When did you last hear a violin played quite so

beautifully?" Kremer's tone, "while not far or richly vibrant, carried through the yawning hall with unfailing ease," Henahan went on, in his encomium of March 27, 1979. "No matter how brusquely he appeared to be attacking the strings, the sound that emerged was all butter and honey. Even in flying staccato passages and slashed double stops, there was no rasp. That astonishing bow stayed glued to the strings, no matter what the provocation, and this program offered more than the usual quota."

Henahan was even more taken by Kremer's debut performance as a soloist with the New York Philharmonic in November 1980. In his view, the violinist's interpretation of the Sibelius Violin Concerto was, quite simply, "flabbergasting." "For once, the grandiose gestures of this score, which in other hands can seem no more than pseudo-Romantic posturing, came into focus as genuinely emotional outpourings," Henahan maintained in the *Times* of November 8, 1980. "One could easily have been sidetracked into admiring Mr. Kremer's fleet, unerring fingers, his purely produced harmonics at dashing tempos, or his success in attacking the strings brusquely without giving out any hint of rough sound. But on this occasion we heard something beyond all that: a consistently thrilling singing voice that just happened to be funneled through a violin."

While some critics, among them Jonathan Dove, a reviewer for the British music publication *Strad*, have openly admired "the extraordinary affection" with which Kremer "cherishes each note," to use Dove's words, others have argued that the violinist's vaunted "affection" for the individual notes sometimes obscures the music. As a case in point, Peter G. Davis, writing in the *New York Times* (October 20, 1980), cited Kremer's "extremely wispy" performance of Brahms's Sonata no. 1 at a Carnegie Hall recital. Although "full of sensitive detail," his interpretation was "so attenuated and tonally disembodied that the musical personality of the piece barely registered at all," in Davis' opinion. Still others have objected to Kremer's penchant for including in virtually every one of his concerts an unknown or controversial contemporary work. "In music-making, we must explore different areas of emotional and spiritual life," the violinist explained to Jane Rubinsky in an interview for *Keynote* magazine (May 1984). "It would be too dangerous to ignore the classics. But young musicians should do at least something that would show they are living in a certain time. Otherwise the profession of the performer becomes a little bit like a museum profession."

Among the contemporary composers whose works are frequently featured in Kremer's programs are Hans Werner Henze, Karlheinz Stockhausen, and George Rochberg, and the lesser-known Soviet avant-gardists Arvo Pärt, Sofia Gubaidulina, and Alfred Schnittke. It is perhaps Kremer's fondness for introducing Schnittke's cadenzas into Beethoven's Violin Concerto that has most offended the less "musically permissive" reviewers. One of them is Henry Roth, who in an appraisal for the Strad (January 1984) dismissed the Schnittke cadenzas as "a scarcely cohesive collection of insignificant pizzicato pluckings, rambling double-stops and chordal salvos . . . which may or may not be related to the concerto's basic themes." In his own defense, Kremer told Allan Kozinn, "I think a cadenza has a right to be heard on its own. It is a space where the performer has the right to say something about the relationship to the piece. . . . For me, the Schnittke cadenza was a statement I could believe in. It was my way of confronting the concerto."

Although he is best-known as a soloist, Kremer is an ardent devotee of chamber music. Besides giving frequent recitals with chamber groups, most notably, the English Chamber Orchestra, he has established an annual chamber-music festival in the remote Austrian village of Lockenhaus. Begun on a shoestring in July 1981 as a noncommercial alternative to what Kremer has called "the supermarket of music," the Lockenhaus "anti-festival" quickly acquired an international reputation. Kremer described the great satisfaction he found in playing "in different combinations" with such friends as Heinz Holliger, Andrós Schiff, and Misha Maisky at Lockenhaus in his conversation with Jane Rubinsky. "I felt as if in a kindergarten," he said. "It was all fun, all pleasure, all excitement—and not just the usual excitement after playing a concert, but that of people meeting each other, people understanding each other, people having time to communicate, to make music, to listen to music."

Kremer's already extensive discography includes some fifty record albums, among them recordings of Schnittke's Concerto Grosso for Two Violins, Strings, Cembalo, and Prepared Piano, backed by Sibelius' Violin Concerto in D minor, both with the London Symphony Orchestra under the baton of Gennady Rozhdestvensky (Vanguard); Brahms's Violin Concerto in D major, under Herbert von Karajan (Angel); Stravinsky's "Duo Concertante" for violin and piano paired with Prokofiev's unaccompanied Violin Sonata in D (Philips); the complete sonatas and partitas for solo violin by J. S. Bach (Philips); Milhaud's "Le Boeuf sur le toit" and "Printemps," both on the Philips label; and a Vivaldi violin concerto paired with a performance of his The Four Seasons with the London Symphony Orchestra (Deutsche Grammophon). Kremer also presided over the live recording of a series of chamber music concerts at the Lockenhaus Festival in 1982. His LPs have earned him the Grand Prix du Disque and the Deutsche Schallplattenpreis.

A lean and angular man, Gidon Kremer stands five feet nine inches tall and weighs a spare 125 pounds. When he first appeared in the West, he sported shoulder-length hair and a beard, leading a reporter for Time magazine to describe him as looking like "an intellectual rock-'n'-roll star badly in need of a square meal." He recently shaved his beard and cut his thinning, sandy-colored hair short, yet according to several interviewers, he still exudes an intensity and energy that hints of radicalism—an impression confirmed by his vigorous attacks on musical conformity. "For me, a performance is only successful if it is a dialogue between those who produce it—the composer and the player—and those who listen," he told Allan Kozinn. "If that dialogue takes place, then it's worth the work it takes to go on stage. But if the point is to show off, to be conventional, and to satisfy people by giving them what they expect in return for a lot of loud applause, then there's no point. If it had to be that way, I would not continue in my profession."

Kremer, who has performed recently with the Cincinnati Orchestra, the Montreal Symphony, the Philadelphia Orchestra, the Rochester Philharmonic, and the San Francisco Orchestra, among others, spends most of the year on tour. To prepare for his hectic performing and recording schedule, he practices two or three hours daily, often on a new instrument handcrafted for him by the American violin maker Bellini in order to "hear the new wood." For recreation, he visits museums and art galleries and attends plays and concerts. He likes jazz and what he calls "good rock" as well as classical music and is especially fond of the rock groups Genesis, Pink Floyd, and King Crimson. Recently divorced from Elena Bashkirova, Kremer maintains bachelor apartments in New York City, Paris, and Lucerne. An earlier marriage, to the violinist Tatiana Grindenko, also ended in divorce. According to a report in the New York Times of November 2, 1980, he has one daughter, who lives in Moscow.

References: Hi Fi/Mus Am 28:MA-35 Mr '78 por; Keynote 7:31 My '84 por; N Y Times C p20 Ag 27 '80 por, C p3 Ja 29 '82 por, II p17+ D 30 '84 por; New York 18:48+ O 21 '85; People 17:74+ My 3 '82 por; Time 109:77 Ja 24 '77 por

## Lamm, Richard D(ouglas)

Aug. 3, 1935- Governor of Colorado. Address: b. 136 State Capitol, Denver, Col. 80203; h. Colorado State Executive Residence, 400 8th Ave. E., Denver, Col. 80203

To political observers, Colorado's chief executive, Richard D. Lamm, is "Governor Gloom," since he foresees a bleak future for the United States, unless the nation regains control of its domestic and military budgets, limits its population growth, conserves its resources, and protects its environment. Much of his reputation comes from the way he states his case rather than from the arguments that he advances. Speaking to the Colorado Health Lawyers Association at Denver's St. Joseph's Hospital on March 27, 1984, for example, Lamm warned against using technology to keep the hopelessly ill alive and in prolonged agony, but many

*Richard D. Lamm*

Americans focused their attention on his much criticized offhand remark that, at some point, people have "a duty to die and get out of the way." The three-term Democratic governor remains very popular in Colorado, however, and many expect him to run for the United States Senate in 1986, if Gary Hart should abandon his seat in order to prepare for the 1988 presidential campaign. Lamm's career to date has demonstrated the acumen of the editors of *Time* magazine when they selected him, in 1974, as one of "200 Young Leaders of America."

Richard Douglas Lamm was born on August 3, 1935 in Madison, Wisconsin to Arnold E. Lamm and Mary (Townsend) Lamm. Lamm's father was a high-level executive with a coal company that operated major mines in several western states, including Colorado. Although his family later moved to Lancaster, Ohio, Lamm returned to his birthplace to attend the University of Wisconsin in Madison. While an undergraduate, he majored in accounting and was active in the Society for the Advancement of Management and in the Chi Psi fraternity. He graduated in 1957 with the degree of Bachelor of Business Administration. During the summers he worked as a runner on the New York Stock Exchange, as a lumberjack in Oregon, as a deckhand on a Great Lakes oreboat, and as a workhand at a Canadian resort.

After completing an active-duty obligation as a lieutenant in the United States Army, Lamm enrolled in law school at the University of California at Berkeley in 1958. During the summers of 1959 and 1960, respectively, he worked in San Francisco as a tax clerk at the California Franchise Tax Board and as a law clerk at the firm of Michael, Best and Friedrich. He completed work on his LL.B. degree in 1961 and set off for Colorado, a state that he had found inviting during his tour of military service.

Settling in Denver, Lamm began to build a career as a certified public accountant and as a lawyer. He worked for a year as an accountant with Ernst and Ernst and then became an attorney for the Colorado Anti-Discrimination Commission. In 1963 he joined the law firm of Jones, Meiklejohn, Kilroy, Kehl and Lyons, where he remained until he entered private practice in 1965. Four years later, he added to his existing responsibilities those of an associate professor of law at the University of Denver.

Not long after his arrival in Denver, Lamm became active in Democratic politics by serving as president of Denver's Young Democrats in 1963 and as vice-president of Colorado's Young Democrats in 1964. Two years later he made a successful bid for a seat representing Denver in the Colorado House of Representatives, where he served for four two-year terms. In 1967, as a freshman legislator, Lamm sponsored a bill that made Colorado the first state to legalize therapeutic abortions, later backed the state's no-fault automobile-insurance plan, and so strongly advocated legislation against child abuse that his supporters dubbed him the "champion of the battered child." Perhaps most important, he emerged as a defender of the environment and as a vigorous proponent of restrictions on water and air pollution by devising a rigorous land-use ordinance that twice won approval in the Republican-controlled House and that failed by only one vote in the Republican-dominated Senate.

Selected by his fellow Democrats in 1971 as assistant minority leader, or "whip," Lamm won his most important environmental victory of the decade outside the halls of the legislature. In the middle of 1970 he and a group called Citizens for Colorado's Future began what seemed like a quixotic crusade to convince the citizens of their state to withdraw Denver's offer to host the Winter Olympics in 1976. Repeating concerns of the Environmental Protection Agency, Lamm and his associates argued that construction for the Olympic games and the accompanying sudden influx of people to the state would endanger Colorado's water and air resources and would impose a severe strain on its waste disposal and public transportation systems. Moreover, they contended that the experiences of cities like Sapporo, Japan showed that members of the Denver organizing committee were badly underestimating the likely financial costs of the Winter Games. When a measure to cut off state funding for the Olympics failed by just one vote in the Colorado House, Lamm took the issue to the people in the form of a referendum. On November 7, 1972 the voters of Colorado, by a margin of 537,440 to 358,906, rejected a bond issue that would have raised state funds for the Games, and one day later, Denver withdrew its bid to be the site of the international competition.

Following that triumph, Lamm began preparing for the 1974 gubernatorial election. During his fourteen months of campaigning he generated a lot of publicity by walking almost 900 miles throughout the state, and in the Democratic primary he defeated Thomas Farley, a state representative who had a strong base in the steel-making city of Pueblo and who commanded much support in Denver's party organization. The general election promised to be even more of a challenge because, although registered Democrats outnumbered Republicans 398,000 to 320,000, the Republicans had enjoyed twelve years of uninterrupted control in Colorado and could usually count on swaying to their side most of the state's 415,000 unaffiliated voters.

The gubernatorial contest pitted Lamm against John D. Vanderhoof, a popular Republican incumbent who had taken over as chief executive when Governor John Love resigned in 1973 to join the Nixon administration in Washington. Although Vanderhoof had a commendable record as a conservationist, he had supported the movement to make Denver a site for the Winter Olympics, and had encouraged the rapid economic growth then occurring in the state. Moreover, he was willing to tolerate the expansion of strip mining, especially in parts of the state remote from tourist centers. Inevitably, Lamm stressed his own environmental record, but he also emphasized inflation and honesty in government, and in the wake of Watergate, he even issued a hefty report on his personal finances. His strategy worked, and in November he emerged with a 61,846 vote victory out of 820,442 ballots cast.

In his first years in office Lamm found himself caught between the high expectations of environmentalists, who wanted him to address all their issues as directly as he had handled the Olympics, and the hostility of the business community, which considered him an archenemy of economic growth. As inflation and the fears of unemployment put pressure on the broad base of Colorado's electorate, the governor compromised and tried to promote himself not as an opponent of immigration and economic development but as a foe of congestion and industrial pollution. "When people said I was no-growth, I think that came pretty close to the truth," he later commented. "I have not really backed out, but have come to the painful conclusion that my only realistic alternative is to accommodate growth the best I can."

Although he confronted a legislature controlled by the opposition, Lamm accomplished much in his first term. He recruited professional administrators from outside the state; improved conditions in the prison system; sought to correct abuses in nursing homes; and managed to maintain a budget surplus while providing tax relief, especially for the poor, by means of new revenues from higher corporate taxes and from a mild severance tax imposed on the extraction of Colorado's mineral wealth. And he convinced President Jimmy Carter to locate in Golden, Colorado a federally sponsored Solar Energy Research Institute that Vice-President Walter F. Mondale and Senator Hubert H. Humphrey had coveted for Minnesota.

Despite his successes, Lamm faced a tough battle for reelection in 1978 against Ted L. Strickland, a conservative state senator. He blamed at least some of his problems on President Carter, who had eliminated from the 1978 federal budget eight major Western water projects, including five directly affecting Colorado. The president, he commented, is "as popular in Colorado as Sherman in Georgia," pointing out that in the arid West the storage of water through damming is a critical component of conservation and not a wasteful alternative to it. Fortunately for the governor, Strickland fell into a pattern of making allegations that he later had to withdraw or modify, and as a result, Lamm defeated his opponent by a margin of 483,885 votes to 317,232. It was a remarkable feat in light of the conservative tide that enabled the Republicans to recapture from the Democrats one of the Colorado seats in the United States Senate. Four years later, Lamm earned a third term by taking an even more impressive 66 percent of the vote in his race against John Fuhr, the Republican contender.

During his tenure as governor, Richard D. Lamm has emerged as one of the leading spokesmen for the mountain and desert states of Montana, Idaho, Wyoming, Colorado, Utah, Arizona, and New Mexico. He has often written on his region's problems in the "Op-Ed" page of the New York Times and in other publications, and he collaborated with Michael McCarthy, a journalist from Denver, on a book entitled The Angry West: A Vulnerable Land and Its Future (Houghton Mifflin, 1982). Lamm's consistent theme has been that the American West, fundamentally an arid and fragile environment capable of sustaining only limited growth, has been exploited for more than a century by Eastern investors and industries, and has been substantially controlled by the federal government, which owns half of the land in the area.

The nation's interest in achieving independence from foreign energy suppliers through the rapid development of the coal, oil, and oil shale in Colorado and adjacent states prompts Lamm's most pressing concern for the West, for he fears a repetition of the boom-and-bust cycle characteristic of the economic history of the region. He has referred to the communities that mushroom overnight around mines and drilling sites, only to disappear as deposits are exhausted and technology changes, as "tomorrow's ghost towns." Recoiling from the prospect of despoiled landscapes and other forms of pollution associated with vast strip-mining operations, Lamm worries that the great volume of water required for the long-distance transportation of coal slurry through pipelines and especially for the processing of oil shale may undermine agriculture. "I'm not going to trade a good food-producing industry," he has said, "for a disruptive mining industry that hasn't even been proved economically feasible."

Although Lamm understands the hostility that many Westerners feel toward the remote bureaucracy in Washington that sometimes seems to control their fates, he has been sharply critical of the political "Sagebrush Rebellion" in which James Watt, Ronald Reagan's controversial former Secretary of the Interior, played such a prominent role. In The Angry West Lamm and McCarthy described the protest against federal control of the region's vast public lands as "part hypocrisy, part demagoguery, partly the honest anger of honest people" and called the movement one "of confusion and hysteria and terrifyingly destructive potential." Lamm argues that the Sagebrush Rebellion's demand for the transfer of public land to state control lacks constitutional justification and that, in any case, the supposed beneficiaries would go bankrupt trying to maintain and manage their acquisitions. In the end, the cycle of despoliation would resume as the states voluntarily or involuntarily sold off the public lands to "the Exxons, the Mobils, and the Gulfs."

According to Lamm, the West ought to abandon even the appearance of radicalism and avoid the risk of trading control by big government for control by big business. The solution to the West's problems, as he sees it, lies not in "protective sectionalism" but in a "positive regionalism" that will re-assert the importance of a federal system in which the needs of the states are balanced against those of the central government, which is dominated by the non-Western majority of the nation's population. "We're all happy to be Americans, but we're not going to let you rip us off," the governor has warned in behalf of his fellow Westerners. "We're simply asking the rest of the country to recognize that you can't leave us the way you left West Virginia, Tennessee, and Kentucky. What we're really demanding is that growth pay its way."

In recent years Lamm has extended his message from the specific concerns of Colorado to the broader ones of American society. He has noted that during his ten years as governor the United States has seen an annual trade surplus of $9 billion deteriorate into a deficit of $69 billion and that between 1970 and 1980 the nation's share of the world's gross product declined from 40 percent to 30 percent. In Lamm's opinion, Democrats have failed to recognize the imperative of limiting domestic spending, Republicans have allowed the military budget to get out of control, and public demands for benefits have turned elections into bidding contests.

To underscore what he views as the gravity of the present situation, Lamm has speculated in public about the future. In an article for *Playboy* (August 1984) he offered predictions for 1994, and in some of his speeches he has dramatically cast himself in the roles of the American secretaries of the interior and of the treasury as they assess the late twentieth century from the perspective of the year 2005. His grim forecasts warn of a depression brought about by fiscal insanity, of bitter battles for a shrinking number of jobs, of grave unrest among deprived minorities, of catastrophic environmental and economic problems caused by the abuse of resources and by overpopulation, and of the curtailment of personal liberties by a government finally forced to deal with overwhelming realities. Implicit in Lamm's predictions is the assumption that the future can be different, however, if Americans make some hard choices today. The governor, who

supported his fellow Coloradan, Senator Gary Hart, in the 1984 Democratic presidential primaries, holds out hope that the American people may become receptive to unpleasant but necessary ideas. "My platform," he says, "would be to raise your taxes and cut your services."

Much of Lamm's thinking on fiscal reform had focused on the control of America's health-care costs, which amounted to an average of $45 million for every hour of 1983 and which are rising at two-and-a-half times the rate of inflation. In the governor's view the nation must do more to make those who are able, including the children of nursing-home patients, relieve the financial drain on Medicare, and it must consider reallocating resources now spent on measures to prolong the lives of the terminally ill. For a society facing limited resources, the decision to spend $100,000 treating a person's last months amounts, in his opinion, to a decision not to inoculate 4,000 children against polio. Lamm would take the money saved by reforming the health-care system and put it into "restarting America's industrial engine and in the education system," both of which, he believes, are deteriorating.

Some critics have denounced Lamm's predictions and prescriptions. In an article in the *Wall Street Journal* (December 12, 1984) Dan Griswold of the *Colorado Springs Gazette Telegraph* noted a predilection for bureaucratic coercion in Lamm's proposals and pointed out that several of his forecasts, including the existence of gasoline rationing by 1985, have not materialized. An Hispanic state senator accused Lamm of trying to "make political points with racial bigots and nativists" when the governor, who believes that "population is the ultimate environmental issue" and that a high volume of immigration to the United States condemns many Americans to unemployment, suggested that illegal immigrants be denied public-health care benefits at a Denver city hospital. Likewise, Lamm's doubts about the wisdom of spending large sums to educate hopelessly retarded children "to roll over," or to put "a lift on every bus in America for the few handicapped people who will use them" has led many to view him as hardhearted. To State Senator Ralph Cole of Littleton, Lamm has proved himself to be "a rich man's son who has never had to make a living" and a person who lacks "the milk of human kindness."

His defenders note that Lamm tends to speak in aphorisms, so that his rhetoric tends to be both memorable and open to misinterpretation. Far from advocating euthanasia, for example, he meant by his remark about "a duty to die" to identify the imposition of fruitless treatments on the terminally ill as an illogical use of medical resources. He points out, moreover, that he has made a "living will" that prohibits the use of heroic measures to extend his own life. But Lamm does not apologize for his role as a gadfly. "If politicians can't discuss sensitive issues," he says, "we're all lost."

Slated for publication in October 1985, both of Lamm's new books—one a first novel on which he collaborated with Arnold Grossman, his media consultant and jogging partner, and the other a work of nonfiction, share one thing in common: a sense of impending doom. The novel, which bears the Orwellian title of *1988* (St. Martin's), is a convoluted tale of terrorism and perfidy in national politics; *Megatraumas: America at the Year 2000* (Houghton, Mifflin) charts the inevitable decline of "a democracy addicted to excess," unless Americans rouse themselves in time.

Richard D. Lamm runs five miles every morning, likes to backpack and ski, and by the time he took office as governor, had climbed Pike's Peak and thirty-six other Colorado mountains that exceed 14,000 feet in elevation. On May 11, 1963 he married Dorothy ("Dottie") Vennard, who was trained as a psychiatric social worker and now writes a popular newspaper column in Colorado. The Lamms have a son, Scott Hunter, and a daughter, Heather Susan.

*References: Chicago Tribune II p1+ My 5 '85 pors; Economist 264:55 S 17 '77 por; N Y Times Mag p34+ O 27 '74 pors; Newsday II p3 Ap 4 '84 por; Newsweek 100:26+ Jl 19 '82 por; Time 104:12 N 18 '74 por; Wall Street J p28 D 12 '84; Who's Who in America, 1984-85*

## Lange, David (Russell)
(lon´ gē)

*Aug. 4, 1942– Prime Minister of New Zealand. Address: b. Office of the Prime Minister, Executive Suite, Parliament Bldg., Wellington, New Zealand; h. 282 Massey Rd., Mangere, Auckland, New Zealand*

A former crusading lawyer and member of Parliament, David Lange, who was elected on July 14, 1984 to succeed Sir Robert Muldoon as prime minister of New Zealand, is the second-youngest and the best-educated leader in the history of that small, tranquil, and remote South Pacific nation of some 3.3 million people. A moderate socialist with a marked social conscience, Lange became head of New Zealand's Labour party in 1983, and in the months following his inauguration as prime minister he instituted measures aimed at resolving New Zealand's economic problems. On the international scene, his insistence on excluding from New Zealand waters nuclear-powered and nuclear-armed ships brought him into direct confrontation with the administration of President Ronald Reagan, but, like the majority of New Zealanders, he supports the ANZUS pact, linking New Zealand with the United States and Australia in a defensive alliance.

A native of Otahuhu, a working-class suburb of Auckland, David Russell Lange was born on August 4, 1942, the son of Eric Roy Lange and Phoebe (Fysh) Lange. Some of his ancestors had come from England to New Zealand's North Island during the 1870s gold rush in the Coromandel fields. His father, a brilliant physician of German descent, had given up the rewards of a lucrative medical practice to serve the poor. David Lange was raised in a liberal Methodist tradition and taught the values of compassion and duty.

Educated at the Fairburn Road primary school in Otahuhu, the Otara Intermediate school, and Otahuhu College, Lange was a bright but indifferent student who took an interest in politics and debate but was easily bored by classroom routine. After obtaining his LL.B. degree at Otahuhu College of Auckland University in 1966, he was admitted as a barrister and solicitor of the New Zealand supreme court. Lange's life might then have followed the fast track into high-paying legal work, had he not gone to London in 1967. There he obtained a job with a reinsurance company and devoted his free time to the West London Mission of the renowned Methodist preacher Lord Soper, whose oratory and efforts in behalf of the city's poor greatly impressed him. It was there that he met his future wife, Naomi Joy Crampton, a volunteer at the mission.

Returning to New Zealand in 1968, Lange practiced law privately at Kaikohe, in the northern part of New Zealand's North Island, working with the poor among the Maori people as well as with "pakehas," or persons of European origin. He then went back to Auckland University, where he did some tutoring while completing work on his LL.M. degree. He graduated in 1970 with first-class honors in criminal law, criminal behavior, and medico-legal problems. From 1970 to 1977 Lange practiced law in Auckland and earned a reputation as a crusading lawyer and a diligent worker, handling as many as a dozen court pleas a day. Because of his strong opposition to military involvement in Vietnam on the part of the United States and New Zealand, Lange was for a time denied an American visa.

Dissatisfied with merely defending the downtrodden in the law courts, Lange decided to enter politics. "You meet all the powerless, all the moneyless, and the hopeless," he has said, as quoted by David Barber in the *Christian Science Monitor* (July 17, 1984). "And you think about it and you get mad about it. That's why I am in politics." Lange's first foray into national politics was his unsuccessful candidacy for the parliamentary seat of the northern district of Hobson in the 1975 general election. In March 1977 he ran in a by-election in the Auckland region for the Mangere seat in New Zealand's unicameral Parliament, the House of Representatives. His resounding victory helped to reverse the Labour party's smashing defeat by the National party under Sir Robert Muldoon in November 1975.

Within the House of Representatives, Lange became shadow minister of justice and opposition spokesman on social welfare in 1978, and that year he was a member of official delegations visiting Singapore, Thailand, India, and Japan. In 1979 he visited the European Parliament, and attended an Inter-Parliamentary Union conference in Prague and a Commonwealth Parliamentary Association seminar in England. In 1981 he visited Western Samoa and Great Britain.

Virtually unrivaled as a debater and orator, Lange impressed his colleagues in Parliament as a member of the selected committees on statutes revision, foreign affairs, social services, Maori affairs, and privileges. In 1980 he was shadow minister of overseas trade, regional development, foreign affairs, and Pacific islands affairs, and in 1982, as foreign affairs shadow minister, he went to the United States under a visitor program.

Meanwhile, persuaded by party colleagues, Lange, who had been elected deputy leader of the opposition in November 1979, decided in 1980 to challenge Sir Wallace Rowling as Labour party leader. But that effort failed, and it was blamed for the discord within Labour ranks that led to Prime Minister Muldoon's reelection by a narrow margin in November 1981. Rowling's third consecutive failure to gain the prime ministership convinced the Labour party caucus that he must be replaced, and following his retirement on February 3, 1983 Lange was elected to succeed him as leader of the Labour opposition. In his role as opposition leader, Lange visited the United States, Western Europe, and Asia in 1984.

As the Labour party's candidate challenging Muldoon in the 1984 elections, Lange focused much of his attention on economic issues. Under Muldoon a modified corporate socialism had emerged, with big business and agriculture receiv-

ing large government subsidies. But while inflation had dropped from 16 percent in 1982 to 4.7 percent on the eve of the election, the economy lay stagnant. Unemployment had reached 7 percent, high for New Zealand, and the government deficit amounted to $2 billion in United States currency. The foreign debt stood at about 45 percent of gross domestic product.

Muldoon's open support of nuclear capability in a country where opposition to all forms of nuclear power was increasingly part of the respectable mainstream worked to his disadvantage, as did the voters' growing dislike of what they considered his abrasive and "bullying" personality. Despite Muldoon's attempts to paint Lange as a "bumbling incompetent" and to depict him derisively as a "brilliant entertainer," as well as repeated references to his inexperience and to his personal weight problem, the latter stood firmly by Labour's campaign pledges to resolve New Zealand's economic crisis and to keep the country free from nuclear facilities. On July 14, 1984, 91 percent of New Zealand's registered voters went to the polls. Labour outpolled the ruling National party by two to one, taking fifty-five seats in the ninety-five–seat Parliament, leaving the Nationals with thirty-eight, while the Social Credit party received only two seats.

Lange did not have to wait long to fulfill his campaign pledges. A bank run resulted in the flow of hundreds of millions of dollars from the country in the first few days. In an effort to stop the financial hemorrhaging, New Zealand's Reserve Bank suspended all transaction in foreign exchange on the day following the elections. Ignoring Labour's call, outgoing Prime Minister Muldoon refused to act as the incoming government's agent and devalue the Kiwi dollar but finally gave in at the urging of his party colleagues, to avert a constitutional crisis.

On July 18, Lange announced his economic recovery package, which included an immediate 20 percent devaluation of the New Zealand dollar; a three-month price freeze; wage restraints; the lifting of restrictions on interest rates to attract capital; a review of farm and export subsidies; and a freeze on professional fees and service charges. That same day the Reserve Bank reopened exchange markets with the new rate of exchange.

Formally sworn in as prime minister on July 26, 1984, along with his twenty-member cabinet, including two women and two Maoris, Lange decided to retain the foreign-affairs portfolio for himself and to appoint two ministers to assist the minister of finance, to underscore the significance that his government placed on those areas. In the week following his inauguration, Lange attended a regional meeting of Commonwealth heads of government at Port Moresby, New Guinea.

Admittedly less interested in economics than in such issues as racial equality, the interests of the consumer, the quality of life, and a return to idealism among New Zealanders, the new prime minister advanced economic principles that are surprisingly conservative. His advocacy of more free enterprise and a lesser role for government in the marketplace earned him the support of businessmen and international financiers.

In September 1984 Lange assembled some ninety leaders from industry, labor, and government in an economic summit conference aimed at achieving a new social consensus. His first budget, issued in November, reduced total government spending, allowed only minor increases in defense, and made more money available for social expenditures. His actions brought him praise from the Anglican archbishop of New Zealand, who generally remained aloof from national issues.

Lange's insistence on an "independent international affairs policy, made in Wellington, not in Washington or London," brought him into confrontation with New Zealand's most powerful ally and ANZUS partner, the United States. Signed by Australia, New Zealand, and the United States in September 1951, the ANZUS treaty is less formal than NATO. Dependent on the military cooperation of its members to protect South Pacific seas lanes, it is no longer directed against Japan or China, but against a perceived Soviet threat. While New Zealand's military force consists of only 12,700 troops and a navy of four frigates, six patrol boats, and seven helicopters, access to its ports is considered essential to ANZUS. According to the terms of the treaty, however, the United States must request New Zealand's permission for the harboring of nuclear-powered or -armed vessels, a condition that it also concedes to other allies, including Japan and NATO powers. But since those countries generally do not press the United States, which refuses to divulge which of its vessels are so equipped, the question had remained largely academic.

At a meeting in Wellington in July 1984, United States Secretary of State George P. Shultz and Prime Minister-elect Lange had reached an agreement to the effect that the United States would defer any test of New Zealand's commitments to ANZUS and to its antinuclear policy until early in the following year. Shultz reportedly assured Lange that there would be no American trade sanction against New Zealand because of its nuclear policy. Lange told a interviewer for the Canadian Broadcasting Corporation at the time that he hoped to reestablish the cooperation maintained between the two nations during the last Labour party government, from 1972 to 1975, when the United States respected New Zealand's ban on port calls by American nuclear warships.

Over the next few months Lange walked a tightrope, opposing demands by grass-roots members at the Labour party conference in September for a withdrawal from ANZUS, while at the same time informing the United States that New Zealand's antinuclear stance was not negotiable. On September 21, 1984 he visited the UN, where he stressed that his antinuclear efforts were not aimed solely at the United States. Shortly thereafter, the New Zealand cabinet established a policy under which admissibility of each American ship to New Zealand waters was to be judged on an individual basis.

On January 21, 1985 the United States government requested permission for a harbor visit to New Zealand by the U.S.S. *Buchanan*, a conventionally powered destroyer, as part of the March 1985 ANZUS Sea Eagle maneuvers. Before the scheduled visit Lange worked behind the scenes to gain assurances that the *Buchanan* carried no nuclear weapons, but his requests were rebuffed, and he therefore refused permission. In response, spokesmen for the United States State Department called the refusal "a matter of grave concern which goes to the core of our mutual obligation as allies" and asserted that New Zealand was no longer viewed as a "loyal and faithful ally," while Secretary Shultz charged that Lange's position had in effect "changed the operational character of ANZUS."

American pressure on Lange continued to mount. Members of both houses of Congress threatened economic sanctions aimed at New Zealand's trade with the United States, which at the time amounted to about 14 percent of New Zealand's total. A planned visit of a New Zealand parliamentary delegation to United States Pacific headquarters in Hawaii was canceled, as were the Sea Eagle maneuvers and other joint military exercises scheduled for the coming weeks. In late February 1985 the United States announced plans to phase out attendance by New Zealand officers at American military academies and to curtail intelligence sharing with New Zealand, the first time it would be taking such action against an ally. In early March the United States pressured Australia to postpone indefinitely any further ANZUS meetings.

The strong American reaction was not aimed only at New Zealand but was intended to prevent the spread of what came to be termed "Kiwi disease" among United States allies in the South Pacific, in Japan, and in NATO countries, which all have substantial nuclear disarmament movements. As State Department spokesman Bernard Kalb put it: "We would hope that our response to New Zealand would signal that the course these movements advocate would not be cost-free in terms of security relationships with the United States."

Regional reaction was less negative. Australian Prime Minister Bob Hawke asserted that New Zealand's decision was that of a sovereign nation and in no way impaired relations between the two South Pacific countries. Prompted by domestic opposition, he then reversed an earlier decision to offer Australian tracking facilities for American MX missile tests in the South Pacific. After further pressure was exerted from Washington, however, Hawke termed the ANZUS alliance "inoperative" until Lange lifted the nuclear ban. On the other hand, Lange's antinuclear stand received support from several of the nations in the thirteen-member South Pacific Forum, of whom eight, including New Zealand, signed a treaty in August 1985, declaring the South Pacific a nuclear-free zone.

Lange's policies of banning nuclear ships while at the same time stressing New Zealand's loyalty to the ANZUS alliance drew strong support among New Zealand voters. In early February 1985 an estimated 15,000 New Zealanders marched in downtown Auckland to support the prime minister, while 95 percent of Lange's mail supported the ban. Opinion polls showed a measured, but firm, consensus in his favor. The increasing bitterness with which New Zealanders viewed the American reaction reflected not only a nationalist pride but also a true consensus on the question of nuclear weapons. As Lange had observed in September 1984, the ban was "not the concern of a minor or weird minority cult or political sect—it's mainstream, and that has to be conveyed."

In Lange's words, it was "unacceptable that another country should by threat or coercion try to change a policy which has been embraced by the New Zealand people." While insisting that New Zealand wanted neither American nuclear weapons nor nuclear protection, Lange affirmed his commitment to "those values of justice, equality, and individual liberty which New Zealand shares with the Unites States." He observed that the ANZUS alliance was the "result of the relationship, not the cause of it" and noted that the present conflict was really over "whether nuclear weapons have become the whole character of the ANZUS alliance."

Taking New Zealand's case aggressively around the world, Lange warned in February 1985 that American policy would force his country to curtail its surveillance of Pacific sea lanes. In Great Britain, Lange differed with Prime Minister Margaret Thatcher on nuclear policy, but received her assurances that British trade with New Zealand would continue, and he also indicated his rejection of Soviet efforts to intervene in the controversy. On March 1, 1985 Lange met with the American Fundamentalist leader Jerry Falwell in an Oxford Union debate that was later televised. Taking the affirmative view on the proposition that "nuclear weapons are morally indefensible," Lange won the debate by a vote of 298 to 250 among those present.

Press reaction to Lange's challenge to the United States was mixed. William F. Buckley Jr., in his syndicated column published in the *Washington Post* (February 19, 1985), saw a "good argument for simply waiting until the leftist distemper in New Zealand wheezes away." One British analyst at the Brookings Institution noted that the United States needed ANZUS far more than the reverse and warned that American coercion of a democratic ally might be construed as "bullying." And the *Manchester Guardian Weekly* (February 17, 1985) editorialized, "If Mr. Lange's stand helps to prevent the spread of the nuclear cancer to a remote, beautiful, and strategically little important part of the world, congratulations seem to be in order." In February 1985 the Swedish Peace and Arbitration Society nominated David Lange for the Nobel Peace Prize.

Lange has also begun to fulfill his election promises in support of the peoples of the Third World. A staunch critic of apartheid, he won wide support for his opposition to the policies of South Africa, which closed its consulate in Wellington in August 1984. Citing the violent reaction to the South African rugby team's 1981 tour, which some 275,000 New Zealanders had protested, he banned their scheduled return in 1985. Although the New Zealand Rugby Union defied Lange's plea not to send an all-black rugby team to South Africa, the tour was ultimately canceled, following judicial proceedings.

In April 1985 Prime Minister Lange visited the Seychelles, Kenya, Tanzania, Zambia, Botswana, and Zimbabwe and announced his intention to establish New Zealand's first diplomatic mission on the African continent. At Harare, Zimbabwe, he promised increased aid to South African refugees but warned that his government would not "fund or identify with the violent overthrow" of the South African government.

New Zealand became the center of worldwide attention when on July 10, 1985 the *Rainbow Warrior*, a 160-foot trawler that served as a flagship for the antinuclear organization Greenpeace, was sunk in Auckland harbor as a result of two explosions, and a photographer for the group was killed. The ship had been scheduled to sail for Mururoa atoll as part of a campaign to protest French nuclear testing in the South Pacific. Although two French citizens, later identified as secret service agents, were arrested by New Zealand authorities and charged with the bombing, the French government at first denied responsibility. But in September 1985, following months of investigations and reports and the resignation of Defense Minister Charles Hernu, French Prime Minister Laurent Fabius confirmed that the bombing had been carried out by French agents acting on official orders. Referring to the bombing as "international terrorism," Lange demanded "very substantial" compensation as well as a formal apology from France but also indicated a willingness to fly to Paris and consult with President François Mitterrand on the matter. In October 1985 Lange addressed the United Nations General Assembly in New York on the theme, "The UN's role: protector of the weak."

David Lange, who stands six feet tall, once weighed as much 380 pounds, but a crash diet and a stomach bypass operation brought his weight down to about 225 pounds by early 1985. Lange, who is described as an unassuming man, enjoys reading, working crossword puzzles, and swimming. He is a Methodist lay preacher. Lange and his wife, the former Naomi Joy Crampton, were married in 1968. They have two sons, Roy and Byron, and a daughter, Emily.

*References: Christian Sci Mon p9+ Jl 17 '84 por; London Observer p9 F 24 '85 por; London Sunday Times p20 Jl 15 '84; N Y Times p7 F 17 '85; New Statesm 105:20+ Ja 7 '83 por; International Who's Who, 1985–86; International Year Book and Statesmen's Who's Who, 1985; Who's Who in the World, 1984–85*

## Larkin, Philip (Arthur)

*Aug. 8, 1922– British writer; librarian. Address: b. c/o Faber and Faber Ltd., 3 Queen Sq., London, WC1N 3AU England*

From the speculation over succession that followed the death of England's poet laureate, Sir John Betjeman, in May 1984, the laconic librarian of the University of Hull, Philip Larkin, emerged as the favorite candidate. When the poet laureateship was offered to Larkin, he turned it down, however, on the ground that he had published no poetry since the appearance of *High Windows* in 1974, and the post went to Ted Hughes instead. Clive James once compared Larkin to Italy's Nobel Prize winner Eugenio Montale in meagerness and fastidiousness of output, noting in *Encounter,* "Neither writes an unconsidered line." Two early novels, set in wartime England, and a warmly welcomed collection of critical essays on literature and jazz, *Required Writing* (1983), make up his best-known work in prose. It is as a writer of verse that he is beloved—of witty and elegiac poetry, condensed, commonsensical, and formally flawless. In four slender books that contain 117 mainly brief poems, he established himself as "both the unofficial laureate of postwar Britain," John Press recorded in *Southern Review,* "and the poet who voices most articulately and poignantly the spiritual desolation of a world in which men have shed the last rags of religious faith that once lent meaning and hope to human lives."

Philip Arthur Larkin was born on August 8, 1922 in Coventry, Warwickshire, England, the second child and only son of Sydney and Eva Emily (Day) Larkin. His father served as that city's treasurer. "We lived in quite respectable houses and had a succession of maids and that sort of thing, as one

did before the war," Larkin said of his middle-class home life when interviewed by Miriam Gross for the London *Observer* (December 16, 1979). In his poem "Coming" he describes his boyhood as "a forgotten boredom." Shy and withdrawn because of a stammer, he grew to dislike other children, perhaps experiencing in his relationship with them the brutishness that he depicted in another form in "Take One Home for the Kiddies." A brief poem about "living toys," it ends, "Fetch the shoebox, fetch the shovel—/'Mam, we're playing funerals now.'"

Larkin's undiagnosed nearsightedness, along with a reluctance to speak up in class, made him what he has called "an unsuccessful schoolboy." But his discomfort lessened during his final terms at King Henry VIII School in Coventry, a day school that he attended from 1930 to 1940. Playing cricket and football and listening to jazz helped to brighten his high school years. His father's large collection of books, including all the novels of Thomas Hardy, had given him an appetite for reading, and in his teens he began writing verse and prose pieces. He continued writing at Oxford, where he enrolled in St. John's College in 1940, seeing his poetry in print for the first time when, that year, the *Listener* published "Ultimatum." Later poems appeared in the *Cherwell* and other undergraduate magazines.

At an Oxford overcast by World War II, Larkin studied English language and literature, became an admirer of the poetry of W. H. Auden and William Butler Yeats, and enjoyed the friendship of, among others, Kingsley Amis, to whom he transmitted his enthusiasm for jazz. Presumably because of poor eyesight, he failed his medical examination for military service and thus was able to remain at the university and take a First Class B.A. degree in 1943. He received an M.A. degree in 1947.

Because of his stammer, which persisted until about the age of thirty, Larkin ruled out the possibility of a teaching career. After he had been rejected in two attempts to enter the Civil Service, he secured an appointment in 1943 as librarian of the Wellington urban district council in Shropshire. Having then earned professional accreditation in librarianship through correspondence courses, he moved along to the post of assistant librarian at the University College of Leicester in 1946 and to that of sublibrarian at Queen's University in Belfast, Northern Ireland four years later. In 1955 he became librarian of Brynmor Jones Library of the University of Hull in Yorkshire.

"Work encroaches like a weed over the whole of my life. . . . It's all the time absorbing creative energy that might have gone into poetry," Larkin complained in an interview for the *Guardian* (May 20, 1965), also grumbling, "I equate librarianship with stoking boilers." But years later, in his talk with Miriam Gross for the London *Observer,* he admitted, "Librarianship suits me—I love the feel of libraries—and it has just the right blend of academic interest and administration that seems to match my particular talents. . . . I've always thought that a regular job was no bad thing for a poet." Two semi-humorous poems, "Toads" and "Toads Revisited," written some years apart, offer parallel testimony in verse to his change of attitude. In the former he protests, "Why should I let the toad *work*/Squat on my life?/Can't I use my wit as a pitchfork/And drive the brute off?" But after watching the idleness of retired old men in "Toads Revisited," he decides, "No, give me my in-tray,/My loaf-haired secretary,/My shall-I-keep-the-call-in-Sir?/. . . . Give me your arm, old toad;/Help me down Cemetery Road."

While at the public library in Shropshire, Larkin wrote two novels, *Jill* (Fortune Press, 1945; Faber; St. Martin's, 1964; Overlook, 1976 and 1984) and *A Girl in Winter* (Faber, 1947; St. Martin's, 1957; Overlook, 1984). "In essence an unambitious short story," according to Larkin himself, *Jill* portrays a Huddlesford scholarship student in wartime Oxford, John Kemp, whose attempts to imitate and impress his obnoxious upper-class roommate include the invention of a girl named Jill. Although the American critic James Gindin credited Larkin with having produced the earliest example of "that characteristic landmark of the British postwar novel, the displaced working-class hero," Larkin's feckless protagonist lacks the defiance and bitterness of Britain's "angry young man," as he reaches a gloomy and inconclusive rite of passage.

Cheerless also is the struggle of Katherine Lind, the heroine of *A Girl in Winter*, to come to terms with life's limitations as a public-library employee and a foreigner in a provincial English town during World War II. A lonely and introspective young woman, she strives, by lowering her expectations, to protect herself against disillusionment in her relationships with others. Both novels have been admired for their sensitively drawn landscapes and townscapes, among other qualities, and the critical reception of *A Girl in Winter* was so encouraging that for several years Larkin's publisher, Faber and Faber, pressed him for a third novel. Despite repeated efforts, he failed to revert the flow of his creative imagination from poetry to fiction.

Before the appearance of his novels Larkin had published a collection of thirty-two short lyrics, *The North Ship* (Fortune Press, 1945). When the book was reissued by Faber and Faber in 1966, its author, who had come to regard his early poems as "complete rubbish, for the most part," acknowledged in his introduction to the new edition that he had been excessively influenced by Auden, Dylan Thomas, and, especially, Yeats, whose melodiousness had infatuated him. Reading the poetry of Hardy at the end of World War II, however, had liberated Larkin from the romantic elements that in his own work had been artificial. Hardy taught him to write from life, not from literary concepts, to write about whatever aroused his feelings and to trust his feelings.

The Hardian tonic may account in considerable measure for some changes in style and the greater maturity of Larkin's verse in *The Less Deceived* (Marvell Press, 1955; St. Martin's, 1960), which included several of the poems that he had earlier assembled in the privately printed pamphlet *XX Poems* (1951). With the publication of *The Less Deceived*, his poetry caught public attention, a recognition reinforced by the inclusion of his work in Robert Conquest's *New Lines* (1956). The young poets, including Elizabeth Jennings and D. J. Enright, who were represented in that anthology came to be labeled "The Movement," although they did not form an organized group. Like the others, Larkin favored an emphasis on communication and directness, a return to more traditional prosody, and a rejection of esoteric symbolism, of themes remote from reality, and of emotion unrestrained by rationality. "As a guiding principle," he explained in a note about his verse in another anthology of the 1950s, "I believe that every poem must be its own sole freshly-created universe, and therefore have no belief in . . . a common myth-kitty or casual allusions in poems to other poems or poets."

Almost a decade passed before Larkin published his next book, *The Whitsun Weddings* (Faber; Random, 1964), containing thirty-two poems, some of which had appeared in the *Atlantic Monthly*, the *New York Review of Books*, the *Partisan Review*, and other periodicals. Another slim volume, *High Windows* (Faber; Farrar, 1974), followed ten years later. Critics differ in their views as to whether Larkin's talents have improved or declined from one collection to another and as to what degree his attention has moved from private to public concerns. He himself has maintained that a poet is not required to develop, and for the most part he has continued to explore the same themes of desolation, loneliness, disappointment in love, the passing of time, the purposelessness of life, and the inevitability of death. Introducing new perspectives and expending his remarkable technical resources, he clarifies, sharpens, and deepens his feelings about the way things are in England in his time.

"Deprivation is for me what daffodils were for Wordsworth," Larkin admitted in the London *Observer* interview. The rapist in "The Less Deceived" is seen "stumbling up the breathless stair/To burst into fulfilment's desolate attic." In "I Remember, I Remember" Larkin regrets an "unspent childhood": "And here we have that splendid family/I never ran to when I got depressed/. . . . And, in those offices, my doggerel/was not set up in blunt ten-point, nor read/By a distinguished cousin of the mayor." Referring in "Annus Mirabilis" to the permissiveness that followed the advent of the birth-control pill, he laments, "Sexual intercourse began/In nineteen sixty-three/ (Which was rather late for me)."

The most pervasive form of deprivation in Larkin's poetry is death. An awareness of his own mortality shadows him. "Dockery and Son," in which he describes himself as "death-suited," ends with the lines: "Life is first boredom, then fear./ Whether or not we use it, it goes,/And leaves what something hidden from us chose./And age, and then the only end of age." Senility in "The Old Fools" and a hospital setting in "The Building," two of the finest poems of *High Windows*, give distressing tangibility to Larkin's contemplation of death.

Occasionally, expressions of joy, as in "The Coming," which hails the approach of spring, and of contentment, as in "At Grass," a poem about retired racehorses, relieve Larkin's overall desperation. Sometimes love may stir a guarded and qualified departure from negativism. In "An Arundel Tomb," for instance, he observes the linked hands of the earl and countess in effigy and reflects that the endurance of that gesture in stone has come "to prove/Our almost-instinct almost true:/What will survive of us is love."

A traditionalist in many respects, Larkin once said that he writes poetry to preserve experience. His regard for continuity and for ritual observance is especially evident in his much-anthologized "Church Going." That poem, one of his longest, unfolds his own agnosticism but acknowledges the historical significance of the church, its ceremonial function in connection with marriage, birth, and death, and its role in filling a human spiritual need: " . . . someone will forever be surprising/A hunger in himself to be more serious,/And gravitating with it to this ground."

Long-cherished customs are part of the everyday English life from which Larkin derives his poetry. Nuptial celebrations, wedding couples and their relatives, and a panoramic landscape combine to make "The Whitsun Weddings" one of his most popular poems. Ordinary objects such as a department store's "Cheap suits, red kitchen-ware, sharp shoes, iced lollies,/Electric mixers, toasters, washers, driers—" along with "grain-scattered streets, barge-crowded water," and other commonplaces of an urbanscape sum up Hull in "Here."

Like the young Wordsworth of *Lyrical Ballads*, Larkin not only finds the content of his poetry in familiar scenes and situations, but writes in "language really used by man." The conversational tone of "Toads Revisited" is typical: "What else can I answer,/When the lights come on at four/At the end of another year?" If there is a literary purpose, such as the need to characterize the narrator of a poem, he does not hesitate to use four-letter words and other vulgarisms. But he moves easily from slang and colloquialisms to language that seems fresh and sharp because the words may retain their original meaning. A master of traditional verse forms, he has achieved an impressive metrical and stanzaic variety. His unassertive style accommodates meters that follow the offhand rhythms of ordinary speech. Because of his somewhat sparing use of metaphor, his poems often have a deceptive simplicity and literalness. As Elizabeth Brownjohn, however, noted in the *New Statesman* (July 26, 1974), Larkin "needs to be read with concentration, and repeatedly, to find the meaning behind the surface words." A fairly obvious example is "Sunny Prestatyn," in which he uses an all-too-common present-day sight, the obscene deface-

ment of a billboard, to suggest, among other themes, the elusiveness of the ideal and the corruption of innocence.

Larkin's detractors have charged him with excesses of pessimism, nostalgia, and insistent self-diminishment and with "bellyaching," narrowness of emotional range, and provincialism. But few critics dispute the elegance and beauty of much of his verse. His wit, moreover, in such an observation as "Nothing, like something, happens anywhere," of "I Remember, I Remember," lightens the gloom. "If Larkin is not merely admired but loved," Calvin Bedient argued in *Eight Contemporary Poets* (1974), "it is partly because finding poetry and humour even in sterility, he makes it bearable; he shows that it can be borne with grace and gentleness."

Many of the merits of Larkin's poetry belong also to his prose. They include "clarity, a sense of rhythm and asymmetry . . . and a deflating, all but despairing defiance of cant," Robert Pinsky pointed out in his comments in the *New York Times Book Review* (August 12, 1984) on *Required Writing: Miscellaneous Pieces 1955-1982* (Faber, 1983; Farrar, 1984). As the title suggests, the book is largely a collection of commissioned reviews and essays that he wrote as a jazz critic and literary journalist, together with memoirs and interviews. Openly opinionated, he is forthright in his enthusiasm for Hardy, John Betjeman, Stevie Smith, Barbara Pym, and Anthony Powell, in his reservations about Emily Dickinson, among others, and in his disappointment with the work that Auden produced after he left England for the United States.

A partiality for England over "abroad," in fact, sways much of Larkin's taste. His love of American jazz is an exception, as the critical pieces he wrote for the London *Daily Telegraph* from 1961 to 1971 testify. Ninety-three of his reviews were reprinted in *All What Jazz; A Record Diary 1961-1968* (Faber; St. Martin's, 1970), a book that, according to Robert Craft in the *New York Review of Books* (June 28, 1984), "contains some of the best-written music criticism of its time." An updated edition, entitled *All What Jazz, A Record Diary 1961-1971*, was published by Farrar, Straus & Giroux in the autumn of 1985. Larkin's likes and dislikes in jazz, which make up a major section of *Required Writing*, help to clarify his views on other arts. Saluting Louis Armstrong, Pee Wee Russell, and Bix Beiderbecke as among the jazz greats, he compared what he considered to be Charlie Parker's detrimental postwar influence on jazz to Ezra Pound's modernization of poetry and Pablo Picasso's modernization of painting.

The antimodern bias in Larkin's critical writings is also reflected in his choice of poems for *The Oxford Book of Twentieth Century English Verse* (Clarendon, 1973), which he edited. He worked for several years on that anthology, including the year 1970-71, which he spent at All Souls College, Oxford as a visiting fellow. Although regarded as not so eccentric in its selection as Yeats's *Oxford Book of Modern Verse* (1936), Larkin's compilation of

584 poems by 207 poets shows that "he has little time for anything that is obscure, oblique, or experimental," A. Alvarez found in his review for the London *Observer* (April 1, 1973).

Faber and Faber observed Larkin's sixtieth birthday with the publication in 1982 of *Larkin at Sixty*, a collection of tributes from Anthony Thwaite, who edited the book, the Faber editor Charles Monteith, Clive James, Kingsley Amis, and other friends and colleagues. Larkin's honors also include several doctorates (from the universities of Belfast, Leicester, and Warwick, among others) and appointments to the National Manuscript Collection of the Contemporary Writers Committee, the literature panel of the Arts Council of Great Britain, the board of management of the Poetry Books Society, and the panel of judges of the Booker Prize. His literary awards include the Queen's Gold Medal for Poetry in 1965 for *The Whitsun Weddings*, the Loines Award for Poetry in 1974 for *High Windows*, and the W. H. Smith Annual Literary Award in 1984 for *Required Writing*. In June 1985 Larkin was made a Companion of Honour in the Queen's Birthday Honours list.

As much a conservative in politics as he is in aesthetics, Philip Larkin adheres to right-wing preferences that make him a wholehearted supporter of British Prime Minister Margaret Thatcher. His religious affiliation is with the Church of England. He is a tall (six feet one inch), scholarly looking bachelor with a slight hearing defect. Once when asked about having made not getting married a theme of his poetry, he replied, "I see life more as an affair of solitude diversified by company than as an affair of company diversified by solitude," as Miriam Gross quoted him in the London *Observer*. In his conversation with her he explained also that living in Hull satisfied him because he felt "the need to be on the periphery of things." What he told John Horder of the *Guardian* (May 20, 1965) two decades ago is likely to be true today: "I lead a very simple life. I'm not the type of person who has always to be collecting theatre programmes or cooking Turkish dishes." Larkin does not read his poetry in public, but Listen Records issued long-playing records of his readings of *The Less Deceived* in 1955 and of *The Whitsun Weddings* in 1964, and on a Faber cassette of 1984 Larkin and Douglas Dunn both read a selection of their verse.

*References:* Encounter 42:65+ Je '74; Guardian p12 Mr 31 '73 por; Harper's 267:57+ N '83 por; Southern R 13:131+ Winter '77; Bedient, Calvin. *Eight Contemporary Poets* (1974); *Contemporary Poets* (1980); *International Who's Who, 1984–85*; Larkin, Philip. *Required Writing* (1983); Martin, Bruce K. *Philip Larkin* (1978); Schmidt, Michael. *A Reader's Guide to Fifty Modern British Poets* (1979); Thwaite, Anthony, ed. *Larkin at Sixty* (1982); *World Authors 1950–1970* (1975)

## Lasch, Christopher

June 1, 1932– Historian; social critic; educator.
Address: b. University of Rochester, Department of History, Rochester, N.Y. 14627

Christopher Lasch, a professor of history at the University of Rochester, is a well-known, if imperfectly understood, theorist of contemporary culture who speaks from a position on the intellectual left. His specialization in history is late nineteenth-century America and the progressive reformist spirit that arose when urbanization and centralized government became part of the national scene. According to Lasch in his book *The New Radicalism (1889–1963)*, that age of industrial and technological progress, capitalist enterprise, and great monopolies gave birth to our own, and he believes that the responses to the social problems of that time have helped to generate twentieth-century confusion and despair, while political power has remained entrenched in elite economic sectors. Although he sympathizes with the efforts of leftists, since the 1960s, to change that state of affairs, Lasch nevertheless mistrusts their murky rhetoric and superficial analyses, as he has explained in his *The Agony of the American Left* (1969).

A thoughtful socialist and occasional apologist for Marxism, Lasch gained national attention with his sixth book, the best-selling *The Culture of*

*Narcissism* (1979), a study of modern personality that draws heavily on the literature of psychoanalysis. Because it serves as a sort of Rorschach test for the political persuasions of its readers, that jeremiad fueled a debate between those who viewed it as a neoconservative cry against contemporary permissiveness and those who saw in it a deeper, more radical argument: that contemporary "liberation" plays into the hands of the powers-that-be very much as the old strictures did. With *The Minimal Self* (1984) Lasch spelled out the political directions that may hold out hope for a more democratic and less psychologically repressed future. Considered as a whole, Lasch's work resonates with his guiding conviction that the cultural historian should seek "not merely to understand [society] but to transform it."

Christopher Lasch was born on June 1, 1932 in Omaha, Nebraska to Robert Lasch, a journalist and editorial writer for the *Omaha World Herald*, and Zora (Schaupp) Lasch, a social worker who later became a philosophy professor. Not much information is available about Lasch's childhood and youth until his enrollment at Harvard University, in 1950. There he roomed for a time with John Updike, the novelist and essayist. Lasch graduated *summa cum laude* with a B.A. degree in history in 1954, receiving Harvard's Bowdoin Prize the same year.

Going on to Columbia University in New York City for his postgraduate work, Lasch earned his master's degree in 1955 and took his first teaching post the following year, at Williams College in Williamstown, Massachusetts. He held an Erb Fellowship (1955–56) and Gilder Fellowship (1956–57) from Columbia while serving as a history instructor until 1959. In the meantime he continued his doctoral studies, and while teaching at Roosevelt University in Chicago (1960–61) he obtained his Ph.D. degree from Columbia, in 1961.

While only a student and junior instructor, Christopher Lasch began his prodigious writing career by publishing essays on historical trends that revealed, in his view, the deeper currents of American cultural and political life. In one of his early articles, "The Anti-Imperialists, the Philippines, and the Inequality of Man" (*Journal of Southern History*, August 1958), he presented evidence that Americans who opposed the annexation of the Philippines after the Spanish-American War (1898) held attitudes fully as racist as did those who favored the move. That study was an early adumbration of a theme that runs through much of Lasch's later work: that many supposedly "alternative" viewpoints in American culture partake of the very errors they claim to challenge. Another early piece, "'Realism' as a Critique of American Diplomacy" (*Nation*, November 24, 1962), analysed the concept of national interest in light of the strategies of George F. Kennan, who was appointed United States ambassador to the Soviet Union in 1952.

During his assistant professorship at the University of Iowa (1961–63), Lasch's first book-length study, *The American Liberals and the Russian Revolution* (1962), was published by Columbia University Press. It dealt in part with the domestic political consequences for American liberals who looked favorably on communist theories, and received some approval from reviewers. Lasch be-

came an associate professor at the University of Iowa in 1964 and a full professor there in 1965.

With his second book, *The New Radicalism in America (1889–1963); the Intellectual As a Social Type* (Knopf, 1965), Lasch examined in a series of biographical sketches the new, self-conscious intelligentsia that became a force for reform in the United States in the pre–World War I era. Scorning the repressive hypocrisy of provincial bourgeois society and identifying with the social outcasts and urban masses for whom "respectable" America found no place, Randolph Bourne, Jane Addams, Mabel Dodge Luhan, Lincoln Steffens, and other radicals combined their skepticism of tradition with a hardheaded approach to political realities. They pinned their faith on the "scientific progressivism" of such measures as city planning, prison reform, "clean politics," and public education as the means for achieving mature personal freedom and a less constricting social milieu. Lasch follows the development of that perspective in the thought of mid-century intellectuals, among them Walter Lippmann, Reinhold Niebuhr, Arthur Schlesinger Jr., Dwight Macdonald, and Norman Mailer, only to conclude that the legacy of the zealous reformers ironically has been a "responsible conservatism" and "philosophy of adjustment" that helped create a managerial culture of social engineering.

Critics on the whole greeted the book as did the reviewer for *Newsweek* (May 17, 1965), who called it an "ingenious, imaginative composite of social history, depth psychology, and textual analysis." Even Benjamin DeMott, who, in writing a review for the *Washington Post's Book World* (June 27, 1965), termed Lasch's style "inelegant and muddled," conceded that *The New Radicalism* pointed a way "toward an adequate radical politics in which 'social awareness' nourishes the sense of intellectual responsibility instead of canceling it."

The problems of intellectual responsibility and effective radicalism concerned Lasch not only in their historical setting but also as crucial issues for the generation emerging into political consciousness in the 1960s—including Lasch himself, who had just turned thirty in 1962. Several articles a year appeared with his byline in periodicals during that decade—among them a discussion of the imperatives facing "The Moral Man" in the *Nation* (November 28, 1966), book reviews in *Commentary* and the *New York Review of Books*, and discussions such as "The Cold War, Revisited and Re-visioned" in the *New York Times Magazine* (January 14, 1966). In his "New Curriculum for Teach-Ins" (*Nation*, October 18, 1965) Lasch attributed the American left's failure to extricate foreign policy from the moral and military quagmire of Vietnam to its acceptance of "anti-communism as the *sine qua non* of political respectability," making it "the prisoner of its own immediate success." He called for two means of using power in order to turn the political tide: mass civil disobedience and the building of a coherent political force that resisted the ideology of the Cold

War and unified the diverse factions calling for change.

Student and racial protest had begun in earnest by 1966, the year that Lasch became a professor of history at Northwestern University in Evanston, Illinois. In 1969, under the somber title *The Agony of the American Left*, Knopf published a collection of five of his essays on populism, socialism, black power, the Students for a Democratic Society (SDS), and related topics. Lasch described a fractured and inchoate radical movement that since World War I had ceased to influence American politics in any significant way. Combining his own commitment to radical change with a respect for the traditions of populist democracy, he scored the left's emphasis on sexual liberation, personal expression, and degradation of authority as evidence of inner fears that denied the possibility of rational discourse in a rational society. In Lasch's opinion, those Americans who were excluded from the centers of entrenched power needed an effective political party, not a chorus of naive, hate-filled "revolutionaries." Among the mixed reviews, the judgment of Malcolm Muggeridge on the lament was perhaps the most telling: "Professor Lasch's cry from the heart . . . lacks one essential ingredient—comedy," he observed in the *Chicago Tribune's Book World* (March 16, 1969). "The theme deserves a Cervantes; it usually gets, as in this case, a stricken academic."

In 1970 Christopher Lasch accepted an appointment as professor of history at the University of Rochester, a post he has held to the present time. His next volume, *The World of Nations* (Knopf, 1973), consisting of eighteen essays and book reviews published since 1958, was divided into three sections: "The Limits of Liberal Reform," "Alternatives to Liberalism," and "The So-Called Post-Industrial Society." The collection takes its title from the Italian historian Giovanni Battista Vico's exhortation to "philosophers" to undertake "the study of the 'world of nations' or civil world, which, since men [have] made it, men could hope to know," and Lasch applied that dictum to such diverse but culturally related topics as the origin of the "insane asylum," rising divorce rates, the thought of Jacques Ellul, a French critic of modernist ideologies, the role of the foreign-policy elite in the Vietnam war, and the feasibility of revolution in the late capitalist era. Critics differed in their appraisals of *The World of Nations*, with one reviewer seeing it as "a valuable dialogue across disciplinary lines" and another as "a wavering between a fitful socialism and a plea for culture."

Aided by grants from the Ford Foundation (1974-75) and the Guggenheim Foundation (1975), Christopher Lasch next completed his study *Haven in a Heartless World; The Family Besieged* (Basic Books, 1977, 1979). The book appeared at a time of public debate about the fate of the nuclear family, which appeared to be in crisis because of changing sexual mores, "women's liberation," high divorce rates, and other symptomatic trends. Lasch disavowed the books then flooding the publishing market in response to that phenomenon as "vague speculations . . . and trendy cultural criticism, much of which, ostensibly radical in its condemnation of existing arrangements, is churned out merely to satisfy the demand for cultural novelties." Instead he offered a "study, not of the family, but of the study of the family," discovering that its "crisis," as a subject of social concern, extended at least as far back as the late nineteenth century. Using both neo-Marxist and Freudian paradigms, Lasch argued that the industrial revolution, which first appropriated work from the jurisdiction of the family, later produced ideological justifications that also robbed the family of its private relations. Social scientists, health professionals (both medical and mental), and "expert" advisers of all persuasions—heirs to those reformers he had discussed in *The New Radicalism*—eroded parental confidence and authority, so that children received neither the discipline nor the love needed for healthy maturity. The result, Lasch maintained, has been a new generation of narcissistic adults with broken ideals and a fear of emotional intensity, who live in a state of "chronic mild depression [as] the dominant mood" of a culture they can neither understand nor change.

The diverse responses to *Haven in a Heartless World* testified to its originality. Reviewers on the conservative end of the spectrum, such as George Gilder in the *National Review* (February 17, 1978), applauded Lasch's "shrewd and brilliant critique of the pretensions of modern social science" in his "marvellously reactionary book" that seemed to Gilder to uphold traditional family values. Some writers on the left, similarly, mistook Lasch's analysis as a "nostalgic" tract glorifying "the old bourgeois family." But more perceptive readers, like D. B. Davis in the *New York Review of Books* (February 23, 1978), hailed *Haven in a Heartless World* as a "brilliant exposure of the collective self-deception of a 'therapeutic' society in quest of psychic security"—a security shaped "in the interests of marketing new services and products." Replying to his critics in his preface to the book's paperback edition, Lasch pointed out that he was really indicting the capitalist organization of work and the consumerist manipulation of human affections.

Having examined the repressive aspects of modern society from several angles, Lasch next turned to an in-depth view of the modern individual. *The Culture of Narcissism* (W. W. Norton, 1978) scrutinizes in detail the syndrome of contemporary narcissism, a personality structure that, Lasch suggests, reached epidemic levels in the United States after World War II. Characterized by their inability to experience directly any reality beyond the self and by a harsh internal superego, narcissists are fascinated by celebrity and "performance"; unable to embrace any cause wholeheartedly, they are nevertheless susceptible to external control because they fear their own impulses. From that clinical description Lasch moves on to analyze historical and cultural patterns, finding that narcissism is a pathological but valid response to the overwhelming grimness of our times, marked as they are by the Holocaust, fears of nuclear annihilation and environmental waste, and the futility of personal dreams in a society regulated at all levels of behavior by capitalist norms.

Even art offers no alternatives: for example, the literature of Norman Mailer, Philip Roth, Donald Barthelme, Kurt Vonnegut, Erica Jong, and others is based on self-parodies and garrulous monologues on the voyage into the interior void. Lasch's book includes scathing chapters on the awareness movement, sports, education, "the sex war," fears of death and old age, and bureaucracy as the new paternal figure. That cultural milieu and the narcissistic personality it sustains are geared toward a consumer ethic of manufactured gratification to substitute for real satisfaction or achievement. Short on answers, The Culture of Narcissism concludes with only a few lines of hope that holders of "traditions of localism, self-help, and community action" might find "the vision of a new society, a decent society, to give them new vigor."

"We need discipline; we need punishment; the man who would recall us to it is called Professor Lasch, and he wields a mean whip," retorted Norman Snider in his review of The Culture of Narcissism in the Toronto Globe & Mail (February 17, 1979). Labeling him as "an authoritarian" (but unable to determine "whether he is an authoritarian of the right or left"), Snider dismissed Lasch as an exponent of the "crotchety, irritable spleen demonstrated by writers of letters-to-the-editor." The book's anecdotal, sometimes rambling style irked some critics, and several of them, perhaps unaware of Lasch's impressive historian's credentials, accused him of "narcissism-of-the-moment" in his "inclination to think that [his] culture is, somehow, magnificently worse off spiritually than any other culture hitherto."

Other readers, such as Michael Rogin, a political scientist at the University of California, believed that Lasch had gone "to the heart of our culture," and Robert Coles, the social psychologist, agreed in his assessment for the New Yorker (August 27, 1979) that Lasch had aptly described a society caught in a serious bind. The Culture of Narcissism was enshrined on the New York Times best-seller list for seven weeks and was widely translated, and its popularity reportedly led to an invitation for Lasch to advise President Jimmy Carter on a national address about the country's "crisis of confidence," which was delivered in July 1979. But when it was named for an American Book Award in 1980, Lasch declined the nomination, on the ground that the awards process gave priority to commercial success and so sanctioned "the worst tendencies in publishing today."

Christopher Lasch received an honorary doctorate in humane letters from Bard College in 1977. Since 1979 he has been Don Alonzo Watson Professor of History at the University of Rochester. Taking a leave from the university in the winter of 1980–81, he delivered the Freud Lectures at University College in London, England, in which his main target was the faulty and "irrelevant" interpretations that thinkers of the new left have imposed on Freud's thought. Back in New York, Lasch received in 1983 an American Council of Learned Societies–Ford Foundation fellowship for research in the progressive movement in American politics and social thought.

In The Minimal Self; Psychic Survival in Troubled Times (W. W. Norton, 1984), a sequel to The Culture of Narcissism, Lasch seeks to clarify contentious points made in the earlier book. Its first section analyzes the stark ethic of "survivalism" found both in mainstream culture and in leftist doomsayers, but the final chapters discuss an alternative approach that owes something to radical feminism. Feminists who criticize destructive control of nature—in the arms race, pollution, or technological ubiquity, for example—accurately understand the dangerous course of modern society. That awareness should lead not to a dream of narcissistic union with nature but to a commitment to political action, which remains, Lasch wrote in his preface, "the only effective defense against disaster." At the same time, he says, we must learn how to "mourn" internally for what we have lost as a society in the drive for power; only then can we reclaim what is ours. Like its predecessor, The Minimal Self inspired both praise for its incisive radical stance and complaints in some quarters about its unrelieved negativism.

Throughout the 1970s and into the 1980s Lasch was a consulting editor to the Partisan Review, and from 1979 to 1983 he served on the editorial board of Democracy, a journal of left-liberal political theory. He keeps abreast of contemporary currents of American thought by reading such journals of opinion "for intellectuals as opposed to scholars" as Dissent, Commentary, and The Public Interest. Telos and Salmagundi are among the "good, small left-wing magazines" he scans, and for psychological perspectives he turns to the American Journal of Psychoanalysis or Psychology Today.

On June 30, 1956 Christopher Lasch married Nell Commager, the daughter of Henry Steele Commager, the American historian. Mrs. Lasch is a professional potter. The couple make their home in Avon, New York with their four children, Robert, Elisabeth, Catherine, and Christopher. Commenting on his own ability to face a culturally impoverished era, Lasch told Barbara Rowes during an interview for People (July 9, 1979): "The only things worth living for are love and work. I have a family I like to live with and work I enjoy. Every day I make compromises, but I don't know how else to live." He has described himself as an amateur musician with a classical interest whose taste is "anti-Wagnerian."

References: Atlantic 254:141+ N '84; N Y Times Bk Review p6+ Je 13 '65, p6+ Ja 15 '78; New Yorker 55:98+ Ag 27 '79; Contemporary Authors vols 73-76 (1978); Who's Who in America, 1984-85

## Lauper, Cyndi

(lawp´ ər)

*June 20, 1953– Singer; songwriter. Address: b. c/o Premier Talent, 3 E. 54th St., New York City, N.Y. 10022; c/o CBS Records Division, 51 W. 52d St., New York City, N.Y. 10019*

A new figure on the national pop-music scene who is changing the contours of rock 'n' roll with her songs and her personality, Cyndi Lauper emerged with her first solo album, *She's So Unusual* (1983), as a powerhouse vocalist, imaginative composer, and witty comedienne. Her first starring video, "Girls Just Want to Have Fun," based on the hit single from that album, was a rousing departure from the macabre themes of some video artists, and her bright and wacky persona, abetted by a new-wave fashion style that merges Betty Boop with the Queen of Outer Space, has won her a huge following that runs the gamut from youngsters who emulate her street toughness to feminists who admire her fierce independence. But the emotional depths she plumbs when she sings, her four-octave vocal range, and the creative variety of her music prove that Cyndi Lauper is no fleeting media darling. With three hit singles and a clutch of music awards already to her credit, she has staked out a claim to stardom that should yield gold or platinum for years to come.

Cyndi Lauper was born on June 20, 1953 in Queens in New York City. She has an older sister and a younger brother. The family lived in the Williamsburg section of Brooklyn until Cyndi was five, when her father and her Italian-American mother, Catrine, were divorced. The mother then moved with her three children to the Ozone Park district of Queens, where she worked as a waitress. "I'd see her come home dead tired . . . so that she could feed us," Cyndi Lauper explained in an interview with David Frankel for *New York* (December 26, 1983). "I saw her suffer an enormous amount, and I was angry." She remembers that the women in her extended Catholic family were often relegated to the kitchen. Early on, she has said, she came to believe that family, church, and state "are the three biggest oppressors of women that will ever come along."

During her childhood of anger and confusion, singing provided an outlet for Cyndi Lauper. As she told David Frankel, "I always sang. I sang before I talked. When I was sad I would sing, and I'd feel better." She began to learn vocal techniques by accompanying her mother's recordings of performers like the dramatic soprano Eileen Farrell, Louis Armstrong, and the tenor Mario Lanza, and she studied the phrasing styles of Billie Holiday and Lester Young. In 1964, at eleven, she joined an informal music group that sang Beatles tunes in a basement, and she was precociously interested in painting and drawing.

But Cyndi Lauper, by her own admission, felt herself to be a "no good" misfit. By the age of twelve she had begun to dye her hair in bright shades and to dress in extravagant outfits, becoming the target of insults and an occasional hurled rock from her more conformist peers. An inferior student whose teachers, according to her mother, were blind to her other talents, including her artwork, singing ability, and verse writing, she became a self-styled "delinquent" and "street kid," who when she reached high school felt "out of step" with the others. "Everything became unreal for me," she told an interviewer for *People* (September 17, 1984). "I felt there just wasn't any room for me in this world." She flunked out of four schools, including a Catholic boarding school and the High School of Fashion Industries in New York City, and her wild behavior left her the survivor of several automobile crashes. She recalls "incredible fights" during that period with her mother, who had taken to praying to the saints in her behalf. Meanwhile she somehow managed to continue her amateur singing career, playing the guitar and performing folk songs in parks and at local clubs.

When she was seventeen, Cyndi Lauper dropped out of school (though she later received a graduate equivalency degree) and left home. She tried working as an office girl, then as a horse-walker at the Belmont Park racetrack on Long Island, before finally deciding to leave New York City. A trip to Canada landed her eventually in Vermont, where she studied art for a year. Later she waited on tables, cleaned dog kennels, and modeled for art classes. "I was one of those people that was always running away," she said of those years of self-rejection. Finally, after having tried everything else, she committed herself to a career in music, convinced in spite of the dissenting opinions of her friends that her voice was her strongest talent.

In 1974 Cyndi Lauper returned to New York and began touring the Long Island music-club circuit as a lead singer with various bands, including Doc West's disco band and a rock group called Flyer that she formed herself. She usually performed her own versions of hits by Rod Stewart, Grace Slick, Janis Joplin, and others. Although she fit easily into the music scene, where her associates were as "weird" as she was, so that she no longer felt like an outcast, she had to take "a lot of abuse" in that predominantly male environment and had little money to show for her efforts. "And singing other people's songs didn't sit well with my creative process," she later commented to David Frankel.

A problem with cracked vocal cords in 1977 sent her to Katie Agresta, a rock 'n' roll vocal coach in New York with whom she has studied ever since. That same year she met John Turi, a saxophonist, keyboardist, and composer, and shortly afterwards they organized Blue Angel, a group specializing in 1950s-style rockabilly numbers, many of which they wrote themselves. Over the next few years, the band received considerable attention from critics but found only a local audience. Catching them at the Ritz club in New York City, Robert Palmer of the *New York Times* (October 26, 1980) wrote, "The focus of the group is Cyndi Lauper, who has a marvelous, piercing voice. . . . Miss Lauper is a natural, and, at her best, a riveting rock-and-roll performer." The band's album on the Polydor label, entitled *Blue Angel,* won similar praise after its 1980 release, most of it bestowed on what Kurt Loder, writing for *Rolling Stone* (May 24, 1984), called Cyndi Lauper's "spectacular octave-vaulting vocals on such doo-wopish tunes as 'Maybe He'll Know,'" "Cut Out," and "Anna Blue." In Miss Lauper's words, however, the unsuccessful LP "went lead" commercially. Although they had toured Germany with the British singer Joe Jackson and were featured in a German television music program, by 1982 the group's musical and financial resources had run out. As Miss Lauper put it, "We were starving. . . . After a while we just couldn't fight it." The resulting acrimonious breakup led to Miss Lauper's filing for bankruptcy.

While charting her bearings in the months after Blue Angel disintegrated, Cyndi Lauper obtained some engagements as the opening act at New York clubs like the Palladium and as a "geisha" singer at a Japanese restaurant. After some eight years of professional cultivation, the astonishing power and texture of her voice were now fully developed, with a stylistic range from soulful cries and broken shouts and whoops to an "electronic sound . . . with character" that she especially worked to achieve. A repertory of new-wave numbers, hard-rock originals, torch songs, and her own compositions showcased those abilities, so that she reminded some listeners of a "wired" Brenda Lee or the "girl groups" of the 1950s. The dizzying energy of her stage act, coupled with her distinctive thrift-shop costumes and glowing pink or orange mane, marked Cyndi Lauper as an original personality and as a potential star.

With the help of David Wolff, her new manager, she signed a recording contract in 1983 with Por-trait Records, a label owned by CBS. Produced by Rick Chertoff, her first solo album, *She's So Unusual,* was released in the fall of that year. Its cuts, several of which she co-wrote, included "He's So Unusual," a souped-up version of a hit from 1929; the pounding rocker "She Bop"; "Money Changes Everything," a snarling cult classic first performed by the Brains; the haunting ballad "Time After Time"; and "Girls Just Want to Have Fun," an upbeat chant Cyndi Lauper had reworked with help from its original composer, Robert Hazard. It was originally written from a male point of view, but by the time that song became Cyndi Lauper's own "the title was different, the melody lines were different, the feel was different, and it meant something else," as she put it. An irresistible tribute to the unencumbered freedom and vitality of young women, it was the first single release from the album.

At first *She's So Unusual* went unnoticed on the music charts. The turning point came in December 1983, with the premiere of Miss Lauper's video movie of "Girls Just Want to Have Fun" on MTV, the rock-music cable network. Directed by Edd Griles, one of whose videos for Blue Angel had won a New York Film Festival award, and with Cyndi Lauper as artistic consultant, that video won instant acclaim as "one of the most high-spirited rock videos ever released." In it, Cyndi Lauper sang her anthem as she led a crowd of exuberant young people in motley garb dancing through the streets of Manhattan, winding up with a free-for-all party at the home of her distraught parents, who were played by her actual mother and Lou Albano, a friend from earlier days. The video's popularity and its ubiquity on MTV propelled "Girls Just Want to Have Fun" to the number-two spot on the popular-music charts and spurred sales of *She's So Unusual.*

That success also brought Cyndi Lauper renewed attention from music critics, many of whom believed, as suggested by Joe Brown in the *Washington Post* (April 29, 1984), that she had "the strongest persona of rock's new women." John Rockwell, writing for the *New York Times* (June 17, 1984), called *She's So Unusual* "an album both nutsily endearing and potentially enduring— moving in a way that suggests Miss Lauper may well have things to tell us for years to come. . . . She has a distinctive and affecting soprano, strong, multicolored and equally adept in rhythmic dance songs and ballads." In acknowledging those accolades, Cyndi Lauper has said: "I like to take real life and make it into art. . . . I sang my best and tried to do something that was real. That kind of sincerity goes across to the people. They aren't stupid; they know when it's real."

Shortly after opening for the rock group the Kinks at the Roseland Ballroom in New York City in December 1983, Cyndi Lauper embarked on a successful tour of Japan, Australia, Hawaii, and England. When she returned, her schedule expanded to include not only concerts but also television appearances, where her good-natured mugging—a "new wave Gracie Allen," one observer termed her—enlivened a skit with Rodney Dangerfield on the Grammy Awards program in February 1984. She charmed Johnny Carson and David Letterman on their late-night talk shows with her running comic routines, delivered in a squeaky Brooklynesque dialect, and the television producer Lorne Michaels praised her well-timed zaniness when she taped a segment for his short-lived program The New Show. That spring Cyndi Lauper's video for "Time After Time" appeared on MTV, and soon that evocative ode, co-written by her, held the number-one singles spot. At the American Video Awards ceremony in April, she was named best female performer.

During her concert tour of the United States and Canada in mid-1984 Cyndi Lauper galvanized a loyal following that encompassed everyone from prepubescent girls, who decked themselves out in her devil-may-care image, to their staid grandparents. Performing at her best in smaller halls, where she could project more intimately to her audiences, she dominated the stage as she whirled, boogied, and clambered up on the loudspeakers while belting out piercing numbers like Jackie Wilson's "Baby Workout," Gene Pitney's "I'm Gonna Be Strong," Prince's "When You Were Mine," and other cuts from her "She's So Unusual" album. She was backed by a four-man rhythm section, Sandy Gennaro on drums, John K. on bass, Keni Hairston, and John McCurry, to whom she gave credit without any reservations: "I love my band. I come from a band, so if you take [it] away from me, then you take my tools away from me and I can't work." Although one reviewer thought her song lineup "too versatile," suggesting "a new talent struggling to find the right sound," and others considered her neon clown's outfit a distraction more than an invitation, pop-music mavens acknowledged that her "voice of uncommon resonance" elevated her "stylistic mannerisms into something timeless and emotionally involving," "so that her songs can touch heart, mind, or soul."

When the first annual MTV Video Music Awards were held in New York City in September 1984, Cyndi Lauper was nominated in five categories and collected the prize for best female video for "Girls Just Want to Have Fun." Edd Griles won as best director for the "Time After Time" video. Other honors she received included a Grammy in February 1985 as best new artist of 1984; two American Music Awards, in the female vocalist and female video artist categories; and six American Video Awards that April for "Time After Time" and the new "She Bop" video. In addition, in January 1985 Ms. magazine named Cyndi Lauper as one of its twelve "women of the year" for 1984, praising her for holding "fast and strong to two principles, solidarity with women and a fierce belief in individual expression." That estimation was seconded in June 1985 by the Los Angeles–based organization Women in Film, which honored her enlightened video work. "I'm glad to have a girl-following," she was quoted as saying in

Newsweek (March 4, 1985). "Because I want to encourage them. I try to beget strength and courage and purpose. I want to show a new woman." "If you can live by what you believe in . . . ," she told Sid Smith for the Chicago Tribune (April 15, 1984), "as long as you love it and mean it, that's the most you can hope for. Then, if you have success, it's success on your own terms. And nothing beats that. Nothing at all."

Worldwide sales of She's So Unusual reached the six-million mark in early 1985, and the auto-erotic "She Bop" reached the top three on the singles parade, the first time a woman had earned three hit singles from a debut album. "Money Changes Everything" and "All Through the Night" became hit singles soon afterward. At the request of film producer Steven Spielberg, Cyndi Lauper cowrote and sang the title song, "The Goonies 'r' Good Enough," for the 1985 movie The Goonies (Warner Brothers), and she coproduced its soundtrack album, The Goonies (Epic). With Richard Donner, the film's director, she made a two-part "cliff-hanger" video, in which Spielberg appears, based on her song—her sixth Top Ten success. The New World film Girls Just Want to Have Fun (1985), a teenage dance story, used the original version of Robert Hazard's song as its theme, and Cyndi Lauper had no part in its production.

Cyndi Lauper's scrappy comedic flair has been carefully nurtured by her manager, David Wolff, who suggests routines to her and may have orchestrated a much ballyhooed "feud" between Miss Lauper and "Captain" Lou Albano, a sometime sports manager. Purportedly in response to Albano's incorrigible sexism, but also because she is "very serious about wrestling," as she claims, she became the manager of a champion woman wrestler, Wendi Richter, who defeated Albano's candidate in a wrestling match televised live on MTV in the summer of 1984 with the two offended parties conspicuously at ringside. A reconciliation was staged during a New York concert that fall. On television talk shows she has announced her plan to write a cookbook with manic recipes like "squirrel spaghetti sauce," and she will satirically espouse the "P.E.G." philosophy of politeness, etiquette, and grooming while undercutting its tenets with her own freewheeling style. "I try to be free and not have any inhibitions . . . ," she commented in the People article. "I'm an entertainer, trying to express the fact that you can liberate yourself, and say, hell, yes, I can do it. Life is not a prison sentence."

Believing that "the human voice is a great healer," Cyndi Lauper strives to portray in her music "real life . . . that kind of beauty . . . full of emotion." She has described her creative method: "I take from what's around me and what I see. Maybe it's because I'm from New York. I'm used to seeing people with a lot of character in their faces, a lot of color." She attributes her "folksy" touch and musical success to her love of people. "That's where real rock 'n' roll comes from—real people," she remarked to David Hinckley, who interviewed her for the New York *Daily News* magazine (August 26, 1984). "That's why my songs work." Obviously agreeing on the authenticity of her material, Miles Davis, the jazz trumpeter and composer, is planning to record an instrumental version of "Time After Time." In the spring of 1985 Cyndi Lauper joined a host of rock-music luminaries to record Lionel Richie's composition "We Are the World." Proceeds from sales of the resulting song and video—which received attention worthy of a major public event—were earmarked to aid victims of Ethiopia's ravaging famine.

Cyndi Lauper is five feet three inches tall and weighs 108 pounds. She insists that she would "probably become a crazy person" if ever induced to forgo her wild hairdo ("a bird's nest gone berserk"), her "tiger-striped eyes" and "pea-soup green lips," her trinkets and *faux* jewels (she needs "a chain cutter just to get undressed"), and her tatterdemalion-chic clothing. "I'm not *trying* to be different," the singer assured Cathleen McGuigan

of *Newsweek* (March 26, 1984). "I'm just saying it's OK to be yourself, and if you have a few quirky things, that's OK, too." At least one New York boutique has introduced a line of clothing and accessories in Cyndi Lauper's style.

Cyndi Lauper would like to make "a real rock 'n' roll movie" of her own, possibly with the production team responsible for her videos. While her busy work schedule leaves her little time for hobbies, she enjoys shopping, watching old movies and reruns on television (particularly the Jackie Gleason series *The Honeymooners*), listening to the radio, and playing miniature golf. She shares an apartment on Manhattan's Upper East Side with David Wolff.

*References: Chicago Tribune* XIII p9+ Ap 15 '84 por; *Ms.* 13:72+ O '84 por; *New York* 17:112+ D 26 '83–Ja 2 '84 por; *N Y Post* p31 F 26 '85 pors; *N Y Daily News* mag p4+ Ag 26 '84 por; *Newsweek* 105:48+ Mr 4 '85 pors; *People* 22:83+ S 17 '84 pors; *Rolling Stone* p13+ My 24 '84 pors; *Washington Post* B p1+ S 7 '84 pors

---

**Leakey, Mary (Douglas)**

Feb. 6, 1913– Archaeologist; paleoanthropologist. Address: b. c/o National Museum, P.O. Box 30239, Nairobi, Kenya

The name Leakey is synonymous in most people's minds with the successive dramatic discoveries of fossilized hominid bones and stone artifacts that have, over the years, pushed the origins of true man further and further back in prehistory. Less flamboyant and publicity-conscious than her hus-

band, Louis S. B. Leakey, or her son Richard Leakey, Mary Leakey was the "unsung hero," to use Stephen Jay Gould's term, of the clan for years, even though she was, in fact, responsible for many of the spectacular Leakey finds, including the nearly complete skull of *Zinjanthropus*, which was at first thought to be the missing human evolutionary link. Mrs. Leakey finally received a measure of long-overdue public recognition with her discovery, in 1978, of 3.5-million-year-old fossilized hominid footprints at Laetoli in Tanzania, proving beyond a doubt that the australopithecines had walked upright, and with the publications of her books *Olduvai Gorge: My Search for Early Man* (Collins, 1979) and *Disclosing the Past* (Doubleday, 1984).

Mary Leakey was born Mary Douglas Nicol on February 6, 1913 in London, England, the only child of Erskine Edward and Cecilia Marion (Frere) Nicol. Her father was a prolific and fairly successful landscape painter, as was his father before him, and Mary apparently inherited from the two artists the natural talent for drawing that was to prove so important in the development of her career. She may owe her archaeological curiosity to a maternal ancestor, the British prehistorian John Frere, the father of the more celebrated John Hookham Frere, who in 1797 had first recognized Stone Age flint implements as primitive tools and weapons. Unwilling to "stretch [her] faith in genetic inheritance," as she put it in her autobiography *Disclosing the Past*, the scientist herself ascribes her early interest in archaeology to her father's passion for the study of antiquities, particularly Egyptology, and to her childhood adventures in the prehistoric caves of southwestern France, where her father went regularly to paint. One winter, while the Nicols were staying in Les Eyzies-de-Tayak, Elie Peyrony, the noted French prehistorian, was excavating at nearby Laugerie Haute, a treasure-trove of finely shaped flint tools from the Upper Paleolithic age. With Peyrony's permission, Mary Nicol eagerly combed through his "spoil heaps," getting her first taste of the joy of sorting and collecting prehistoric objects. A few years later, at Cabrerets, she explored Pêch Merle Cave with the Abbé Lemozi, the amateur archaeologist who had discovered the remarkable prehistoric rock paintings there. "The abbé kindled my interest in prehistory and also gave me a very sound groundwork in excavating," she told Melvin M. Payne in an interview for the National Geographic (February, 1965). "After that, I don't think I ever really wanted to do anything else."

Mary Nicol was very close to her father and, consequently, she felt his death, when she was only thirteen years old, keenly. Because of her family's frequent travels, she had thus far had "no proper settled schooling," as she put it, although her father had taught her to read. Deciding that it was time for her daughter to begin her formal education, Mrs. Nicol enrolled the girl in convent schools, first in Kensington, then in Wimbledon, where she had bought a small house. Neither school was able to tame the independent, high-spirited teen-ager. After Mary's second expulsion, Mrs. Nicol abandoned her attempt to make of her child an obedient and well-mannered Catholic young lady.

Far more important to Mary Nicol than her sporadic formal education was her chance encounter with Alexander Keiller and Dorothy Liddell, who were excavating a Neolithic site near Avebury, during a summer vacation in the late 1920s. Recalling that meeting in her autobiography, she wrote: "Perhaps when I met Miss Liddell this first time I absorbed there and then the notion that a career in archaeology was certainly open to a woman." From 1930 through 1934, she served as one of Miss Liddell's two chief assistants at a dig at Hembury, in Devon, one of the earliest major Neolithic sites of southern Britain. Between summer seasons in the field, she made drawings of some of the finds, including stone tools, for publication, and she attended lectures in geology and archaeology at London University and at the London Museum. Mary Nicol's illustrations attracted the attention of the archaeologist Dr. Gertrude Caton-Thompson, who subsequently asked her to draw the stone tools from her Egyptian excavations for her book The Desert Fayoum (1934).

It was Gertrude Caton-Thompson who introduced Mary Nicol to Louis Leakey, at a dinner party that followed his lecture at the Royal Anthropological Institute in London in 1933. In the course of their conversation, Leakey asked her to help him with the drawings for his forthcoming book Adam's Ancestors (1934), and she readily agreed. When the two met again a few months later, at the annual meeting of the British Association for the Advancement of Science, they became in-

separable companions, despite the fact that he was ten years older than she and already married. The following year they worked together at a Lower Paleolithic site in Swanscombe, and Leakey frequently visited Miss Nicol at nearby Jaywick, where she was supervising her first dig.

Before Leakey returned to Africa in October 1934, he and Mary Nicol decided to marry as soon as he could obtain a divorce. In the meantime, they made arrangements so that she could join him in the field in Tanzania in a few months. The following April, she was looking "spellbound" for the first time at Olduvai Gorge—"a view that has since come to mean more to [her] than any other in the world," she wrote in Disclosing the Past. Her first experience in Africa was rich in discovery, adventure, and excitement. Immediately in harmony with the wild and beautiful landscape, she delighted in observing the behavior of vast herds of migrating animals and in excavating the fossil-rich strata at Olduvai and at other nearby sites. She was especially entranced by the naturalistic Stone Age rock paintings at Kisese and vowed to return one day to make a thorough study of the hundreds of human and animal figures. By the time she went back to England in September 1935, she knew she was not the same woman who had left. As she once put it, "Africa had cast its spell" on her.

For the next year, Mary Nicol and Louis Leakey, still unmarried but "blissfully happy," in her words, lived together in a cottage in rural Hertfordshire. Shortly after his divorce became final, the two were wed, on December 24, 1936. A few weeks later, they set out for Africa. While Louis Leakey worked on a major study of the customs of the Kikuyu tribe for the Rhodes Trust, Mary Leakey began excavations at Hyrax Hill, in the Great Rift Valley north of Nairobi in Kenya. There she found not only Late Stone Age obsidian implements and Iron Age pottery, but also the remains of a Neolithic settlement, including a cemetery with nineteen burial mounds. In 1937 and 1938, the Leakeys, working in tandem, excavated the Njoro River Cave, which turned out to be a Late Stone Age cremation ground. As a result of the cremation process, many fragile objects, such as bead necklaces and wooden drinking vessels, had been carbonized and thus preserved.

During World War II Louis Leakey called a temporary halt to his field research in order to work for British intelligence in East Africa. Mary Leakey, however, continued some of their projects alone, taking time out only for the births of her sons Jonathan, in 1940, and Richard, in 1944. (Her second child, Deborah, died in infancy.) As she explained in her autobiography, "I quite liked having a baby—I think I won't put it more strongly than that—but I had no intention of allowing motherhood to disrupt my work as an archaeologist." At Olorgesailie, in the Kenya Rift Valley, she came across a phenomenal deposit of thousands of hand axes and cleavers from the Late Paleolithic period. (The impressive concentration of implements was left in place and is today a major tourist attraction.)

Occasionally accompanied by her husband, Mrs. Leakey also explored Rusinga Lake Island in Lake Victoria, with its rich deposits of Miocene fossils, and wrote a detailed descriptive study of dimple-based Iron Age pottery from Kavirondo in western Kenya.

After the end of the war the Leakeys paid a brief visit to England, but in 1946 they returned to Kenya, where Louis assumed his new post of curator of the Coryndon Museum in Nairobi. Both Louis and Mary Leakey devoted much of their time to organizing the First Pan-African Congress of Prehistory and Paleontology, which was convened in Nairobi on January 14, 1947. The success of the congress brought to the fore the groundbreaking work the Leakeys had been carrying out over the past decade, but it was Mary Leakey's discovery the following year of the ape-like skull of the Miocene human forerunner *Proconsul africanus* that focused world attention on the Leakeys and on East Africa as the possible cradle of mankind. After painstakingly fitting the thirty-odd separate pieces of the skull together, she carried it by hand to England for analysis by Wilfred Le Gros Clark, then the leading authority in primate evolution. The find of *Proconsul* had personal as well as professional ramifications for the Leakeys, for they decided that "quite the best celebration would be to have another baby." Their son Philip was born nine months later.

The 1950s were years of political turmoil in Kenya. Both the Leakeys strongly supported Kenyan independence, but Mary Leakey more and more sought "blessed relief" from the interracial violence at Olduvai and at other remote excavation sites. She has rated as "one of the highlights" of her career her recording, in 1951, of some 1,600 of the thousands of Late Stone Age paintings in the Kondoa-Irangi region of Tanzania. After carefully tracing the scenes onto sheets of clear cellophane, she transferred them, reduced to half-scale, onto gray or buff drawing paper. The meticulous work gave her "a great sense of happiness and well-being," she wrote in *Disclosing the Past,* not only because of the sheer beauty of the paintings and the "fascination and excitement of disentangling the figures," which were often superimposed, but also because the drawings afforded a glimpse of the lives of the hunter-gatherers who painted them. "There were details like clothing, hair styles and the fragile objects that hardly ever survive for the archaeologist—musical instruments, bows and arrows, and body ornaments depicted as they were worn. . . . No amounts of stone and bone could yield the kinds of information that the paintings gave so freely." Mary Leakey's long-delayed book about the Tanzanian rock paintings, *Africa's Vanishing Art,* was finally published in 1983 by Hamish Hamilton/Rainbird in Great Britain and by Doubleday in the United States.

On July 17, 1959 Mary Leakey made her second major discovery. The Leakeys had been excavating a site at Olduvai Gorge for several weeks, but on that particular day, Louis Leakey was confined to camp with a fever. Accompanied only by her two Dalmatians, Mary Leakey set off to investigate the oldest layer at the site. As she surveyed the exposure with her practiced eye, a scrap of bone protruding from the ground caught her attention. Gently brushing aside some of the deposit, she saw two large hominid teeth in place in an upper jaw. As Ruth Moore recounted the story in her book *Man, Time, and Fossils* (1961), Mrs. Leakey raced back to camp to rouse her husband from his sick bed, shouting, "I've got him! I've got him!" Using camel's-hair brushes and dental picks, the Leakeys gingerly uncovered a full palate and set of teeth; by sifting through tons of eroded scree, they eventually found about 400 bone fragments, which when pieced together formed an almost complete hominid skull, later dated at 1.75 million years, of the genus *Zinjanthropus*. Over the next few months, Mary Leakey found on the "Zinj" floor other hominid bones and 164 stone tools of twelve different types, including choppers, scrapers, anvils, and hammerstones.

As luck would have it, a camera crew for the British television series *On Safari* arrived on the scene the day after Mary Leakey's momentous find, and thus it was that "Zinj" came to international public attention. For the Leakeys, it meant not only worldwide recognition, but also the beginning of substantial funding from the National Geographic Society. Fame brought controversy, too, and it was not long before Louis Leakey's bold assertion that "Zinj" was the so-called "missing link" between the primitive ape-men and *Homo sapiens* was proved to be incorrect. Subsequent discoveries by the Leakeys and by other archaeologists suggested that "Zinj" was in fact a new species of the manlike australopithecines, a hominid line that developed parallel to the genus *Homo*. In the course of large-scale excavations at Olduvai over the next few years, the Leakeys dug out of the same sedimentary layer as "Zinj" a hominid skull that was clearly more similar to that of modern man. They named the creature *Homo habilis*, or "able man," for his apparent technological skills, and the crude stone tools originally attributed to *Zinjanthropus* now had to be considered the handiwork of his bigger-brained contemporary. As Mary Leakey observed in her autobiography, "Until then the idea that two hominids could occupy the same area at the same time had been unacceptable to most scientists." (Conclusive fossil proof that bands of *Homo habilis* coexisted with *Austrolopithecus* was unearthed by Richard Leakey at Lake Rudolf in 1972.)

By the mid-1960s, the Leakeys had established a permanent camp at Olduvai Gorge, and it was there that Mary Leakey lived for most of the year, while her husband stayed in Nairobi to direct activities at the Coryndon Museum, visiting the site only on weekends and holidays. Louis Leakey was by this time making twice-yearly visits to the United States, too, to lecture and raise funds for field research. As he became more and more caught up in the celebrity whirl of foreign lecture tours, Mary

Leakey became more and more independent—professionally as well as emotionally. She could no longer support some of her husband's archaeological positions, particularly his "unscientific," to use her word, contention that Calico Hills, in the Mojave Desert in southern California, was the site of a sizable human settlement some 80,000 years ago. For his part, Louis Leakey, who was in poor health, undoubtedly felt that his wife had, as she put it, "become cold and uncaring," that she had "abandoned" him in a time of trouble. The Leakeys' marriage—which, as Mary Leakey underlined in her autobiography, "in its best years had been an idyllic partnership"—was, for all intents and purposes, over in 1968, and though they never officially separated, the pair lived apart until Louis Leakey's fatal heart attack in 1972.

After her husband's death, Mary Leakey had of necessity to take a more public role. Although she once was hesitant about speaking more than a few words before an audience, she soon blossomed into a spellbinding lecturer and a persuasive fund raiser. In those capacities, she traveled widely in Europe and in the United States, while continuing to spend as much time as possible in the East African bush. In 1978, at Laetoli, on the Serengeti Plain some thirty miles south of Olduvai Gorge, she stumbled upon what she has since described as "the most significant" of her finds: a twenty-three-meter-long trail of hominid footprints, "so sharp that they could have been left this morning," preserved in volcanic ash that had been dated at 3.6 million years.

Mary Leakey theorized that the tracks were made by three individuals—two adults, whom she was tempted to see as a man and a woman, and a youngster. The smaller of the two adults had deliberately stepped into the prints left by her larger companion, apparently in play. As she wrote in an article for the *National Geographic* (April 1979), Mrs. Leakey experienced "a kind of poignant wrench" as she followed the path of the "female" figure: "At one point, and you need not be an expert tracker to discern this, she stops, pauses, turns to the left to glance at some possible threat or irregularity, and then continues to the north. This motion, so intensely human, transcends time." Despite large-scale excavations, the surrounding beds, while rich in hominid remains and in unusual animal fossils, yielded not a single tool, suggesting that bipedalism preceded formalized toolmaking. Mary Leakey commented on the crucial importance of bipedalism to man's evolutionary development in her piece for the *National Geographic*: "This unique ability [to walk upright] freed the hands for myriad possibilities—carrying, toolmaking, intricate manipulation. From this single development, in fact, stems all modern technology. Somewhat oversimplified, the formula holds that this new freedom of forelimbs posed a challenge. The brain expanded to meet it. And mankind was formed."

A slight and soft-spoken woman with blue eyes and the weathered skin of one who has virtually lived outdoors, Mary Leakey was described by Nan Robertson, who interviewed her for the *New York Times* (February 8, 1980), as "schoolmarmish in mien and manner"—a description belied by Mrs. Leakey's fondness for a good cigar and a stiff glass of bourbon. Although she prefers working and living "among the animals" in the bush, she has had to curtail her field research somewhat since she lost the vision in her left eye due to a thrombosis in 1982, and she recently turned over the Olduvai Gorge camp to the Tanzanian Department of Antiquities. Mrs. Leakey shares her home at Langata in Nairobi with several Dalmatians and a menagerie of other small animals. Among her frequent visitors are her sons Jonathan, a herpetologist; Richard, the director of the Kenya National Museum and the founder of the Louis Leakey Memorial Institute for African Prehistory in Nairobi; and Philip, the only white member of the Kenyan parliament and the assistant minister in foreign affairs; and her grandchildren.

In the preface to her autobiography Mary Leakey disclaimed somewhat wryly any great interest in philosophical profundities. "You find poets and philosophers telling us of Man's unceasing search for his own identity and for self-knowledge," she wrote. "I'm not sure I believe them, though it sounds very impressive." When asked by Nan Robertson to explain the impetus behind her life's work, she replied simply, "Curiosity. What made man, man?" Elaborating on that theme in the concluding chapter of *Disclosing the Past*, she explained that, unlike her husband, she had "never believed that knowledge of the past would help us to understand and possibly control the future. . . . Nature . . . will take its course, and man's activities will follow an irreversible pattern." Moreover, the "small pieces" of the past that have been preserved and uncovered "may give us a biased view of the picture as a whole." Nonetheless, Mrs. Leakey has derived her greatest satisfaction from studying man's early tools for "any insights we can get into the lifestyles and activities in succeeding stages of human evolution." Mary Leakey has received many awards, most notably the National Geographic Society's Hubbard Medal, which she shared with her husband in 1962, the Gold Medal of the Society of Women Geographers, and the 1980 Bradford Washburn Award, which is given annually by the Boston Museum of Science to honor outstanding contributions to the public's understanding of the natural sciences. She holds honorary doctorates from Oxford University, Yale University, the University of Chicago, and the University of Witwatersrand.

References: *Christian Sci Mon* B p13+ Mr 18 '84 pors; *N Y Times* A p18 F 8 '80 por, C p1+ O 30 '84 por; *N Y Times Mag* p13+ Mr 3 '74 pors; *Nat Geog Mag* 127:2+ F '65 pors; *Washington Post* B p1+ F 5 '80 pors; Cole, Sonia. *Leakey's Luck* (1975); *Contemporary Authors* vols 97–100 (1981); *International Who's Who, 1985–86; Who's Who, 1985–86*

**Lehman, John F(rancis), Jr.**

*Sept. 14, 1942– United States Secretary of the Navy. Address: b. Navy Department, The Pentagon, Room 4E686, Washington, D.C. 20350*

In 1981 John F. Lehman Jr. became the youngest secretary of the navy in this century when, at the age of thirty-eight, he was appointed to that office by President Ronald Reagan. Through deft political maneuvering and well-publicized efforts to run the navy more economically, he has destroyed in just four years the image of that office as a sinecure to become, according to *Newsweek* magazine, "the most effective Navy secretary in recent memory." Modeling himself on Admiral Alfred Thayer Mahan, the late-nineteenth-century strategist who insisted that the United States had to have a navy capable of operating on a worldwide scale, Lehman has successfully fought for an expansion of the nation's sea force to a fleet of 600 vessels, including new nuclear-powered submarines and aircraft carriers. Nevertheless, the outspoken and sometimes abrasive young secretary of the navy differs on one vital point with Mahan. The admiral "believed that democracies were unwilling to pay the price of continued naval power . . . ," Lehman once pointed out. "This particular view is one which we must all work together to disprove in our own case."

John Francis Lehman Jr. was born on September 14, 1942 in Philadelphia, Pennsylvania. A member of one of that city's most prominent families, he is the oldest of the three sons of John F. Lehman, a plant manager for Continental Can Company, and Constance (Cruice) Lehman. The late Princess Grace of Monaco was his cousin. After graduating from La Salle College High School, a Christian Brothers day school in Philadelphia, Lehman ma-

triculated at St. Joseph's College, a Jesuit institution also in Philadelphia, and while an undergraduate there won the double sculls national championship. On taking his B.S. degree in international relations in 1964, he continued his studies in that field on an Earhart Fellowship at Gonville and Caius College, Cambridge University, from which he received, in 1967, a B.A. degree with second-class honors in law and an M.A. degree in international law and diplomacy. Off and on over the course of the next several years he pursued his advanced studies further, as a visiting fellow at Johns Hopkins University's School of Advanced International Studies, as a Chubb Fellow at Yale University, and as a graduate student at the University of Pennsylvania, where he earned M.A. and Ph.D. degrees. His doctoral dissertation, *The Executive, Congress, and Foreign Relations: Studies of the Nixon Administration*, was published by Praeger in 1976.

Throughout his education Lehman maintained a clear academic focus on issues involving nuclear arms and the balance of power. As an undergraduate he was a principal organizer of the March 1964 Philadelphia Collegiate Disarmament Conference. With James E. Dougherty, a professor at St. Joseph's College, he edited *The Prospects for Arms Control* (Macfadden-Bartell, 1965), a collection of papers from that conference, and *Arms Control for the Late Sixties* (Van Nostrand, 1967), which brought together papers presented at the Bendix Corporation–University of Pennsylvania Third International Arms Control Symposium, held in Philadelphia in April 1966, of which Lehman had been the executive director. Both volumes reflect Lehman's generally conservative approach to disarmament.

In January 1969, after a year and a half on the staff of the Foreign Policy Research Institute at the University of Pennsylvania, Lehman joined the administration of the newly elected president, Richard Nixon, for whom he had worked during the 1968 campaign, as a staff member of the National Security Council (NSC). At first an aide to Richard Allen, in September 1971 he was promoted to the position of special counsel and senior staff member, in which post he worked directly for Secretary of State Henry A. Kissinger (who headed the NSC) as a liaison between the NSC and Congress. At that time, large personnel cuts were made in various departments and agencies of the executive branch, including the Arms Control and Disarmament Agency (ACDA). Lehman, Senator Henry Jackson, and Richard Perle, now an assistant secretary of defense, were implicated in the administration's so-called "purge" from the ACDA of Democrats and critics of Nixon's arms-control policies, but Lehman maintains that his only role in the shakeup was submitting personnel recommendations for vacancies throughout the executive branch to H. R. Haldeman at Haldeman's request. Lehman himself worked directly with the ACDA beginning in July 1974 as a member of the United States delegation to the Mutual and Balanced Force Reduction

(MBFR) talks with the Soviet Union held in Vienna, Austria, where he served as the disarmament adviser to Stanley Resor, another American delegate, and as the representative of Fred Ikle, the ACDA's director. Six months later, President Gerald R. Ford nominated Lehman for the post of deputy director of the ACDA.

Facing a hostile Senate Foreign Relations Committee during his confirmation hearings in February and March 1975, Lehman fielded a barrage of sharp questions from the committee's Democratic members on the ACDA "purge" and his alleged criticisms of the committee and its former chairman, J. William Fulbright. The nominee came under attack from other sources as well, but after Henry Kissinger sent a cable from Europe expressing his support for Lehman, a coalition of the Republican minority and of some Democrats was able to muster nine favorable votes against six Democratic nays. The full Senate approved the nomination by a voice vote.

The agency's director, Fred Ilke, paid little attention to administration and left the new deputy director more or less in charge of day-to-day operations. Critics of Lehman, whom a former ACDA employee described as "a real super-conservative hawk," claim that he used his position to hire strategic-arms hardliners and to undermine Henry Kissinger's's efforts to get SALT (Strategic Arms Limitations Treaty) II ratified. Lehman admitted in an interview for the book *Reagan's Ruling Class* (1982) that he "had many problems with many of the drafts that Henry at various times carried around with him." The provisions that he opposed vigorously within the administration included the proposed ban on shipboard Tomahawk cruise missiles, which he considers among "the most effective conventional weapons for war at sea."

Leaving office when Democrat Jimmy Carter took office in January 1977, Lehman remained a vocal adversary of the SALT II treaty, joining the Committee on the Present Danger, which opposed that treaty and what it saw as the escalating military power of the Soviet Union, and writing frequently on the permanent advantage that he believed SALT II would afford the Soviet Union. Lehman eventually combined his essays and others by Seymour Weiss in *Beyond the SALT II Failure* (Praeger, 1981). As one of the leading Republican critics of the Carter administration's defense policies, he also lambasted the budget cuts that, in his view, left the navy and other armed services inadequately prepared and pushed for an expansion of the nation's nuclear-powered fleet. In *Aircraft Carriers: The Real Choices* (Sage Publications, 1978), for example, he articulated many of the arguments in favor of those giant vessels that he would later advocate as secretary of the navy. In addition, he established the Abington Corporation, a defense consulting firm, and was president of Intruder, Inc., an aircraft operator. He also served as the director of both the Foreign Policy Research Institute in Philadelphia and Transco Energy, Inc., in Washington, D.C.

From 1977 to 1980 Lehman chaired the Republican National Committee's defense advisory committee, which shaped the hardline section on defense in the party's platform. After Ronald Reagan's election, Lehman admittedly not only "lobbied all of the President's staff" in his effort to win the position of secretary of the navy but also refused to consider any other position in the administration. "I felt so strongly about the Navy—that it was undervalued as an asset and was being dismantled by the Carter administration," he explained, as quoted in *Reagan's Ruling Class.* "Under strong pressure from congressional defense experts to include some defense specialists in the Pentagon hierarchy," according to the 1981 *Congressional Quarterly Almanac,* President Reagan nominated Lehman as secretary of the navy on January 24, 1981, and, after a cordial one-day confirmation hearing before the Senate Committee on Armed Services, his appointment was confirmed by the full Senate on January 29, 1981. As secretary of the navy, Lehman is the highest ranking civilian in the Department of the Navy and is responsible for the 553,000 active-duty navy personnel, the 192,000 servicemen in the Marine Corps, and an annual budget of about $70 billion.

On taking office, Lehman supported in congressional hearings the president's position that an American navy adequate to meet its responsibilities would require 600 ships, a 33 percent increase. "We are attempting to cover three oceans with a one-and-a-half ocean Navy," he complained. "It's like pulling a too-small sheet from one side of the bed to the other." In Secretary Lehman's opinion the growth of the Soviet navy, and especially its development of a Pacific fleet, had eroded the margin of maritime superiority once held by the United States. "Our national security," Lehman told the Senate Committee on Armed Services at his confirmation hearing in 1981, "demands maritime superiority and nothing less; no euphemism, no fancy academic hedgewords." In addition to enhancing the navy's ability to protect the nation's vital commercial sea lanes, an expanded American fleet, he argued, would enable the United States to prevent the Soviets from both closing the Persian Gulf and supporting their allies in the Pacific. Perhaps most important, the larger navy could stop the Russians from quickly defeating Norway and using that nation as a submarine base 1,500 miles closer to the North Atlantic than their own station at the Kola Peninsula in the Barents Sea. To achieve those goals, Lehman wanted two more Nimitz-class nuclear-powered aircraft carriers and three additional carrier battle groups for a total increase of 150 ships.

The buildup enjoyed wide support within the administration and on Capitol Hill, but a vocal minority quickly criticized the secretary's call for a "visibly offensive" navy capable of operating simultaneously in several regions, including the Norwegian Sea close to the Soviet homeland, as destabilizing. Lehman retorted that a strong navy would deter an enemy from initiating a conflict and, if deterrence failed, the United States would be able to choose theatres of operation favorable to itself and not simply have to respond to attacks at points, such as central Europe, advantageous to the Soviets.

Other opponents of Lehman's program questioned his reliance on expensive nuclear-powered vessels, especially aircraft-carrier groups. Senator William Proxmire, for example, charged that each of the three proposed carrier groups would cost $30 billion rather than the $15 billion that the navy projected. "And what will we get?" the Wisconsin Democrat asked. "A large floating target for advanced Soviet missiles—like hitting a bull in the butt with a bass fiddle." Such fears were exacerbated by the Falkland Islands war in 1982, during which Argentina sank the British destroyer *Sheffield* with a relatively inexpensive French Exocet missile.

Conceding nothing to foes of the expensive nuclear navy, the secretary maintained that if a conventional conflict broke out, rather than being easy targets, the ninety-one-ton nuclear aircraft carriers, which have triple-armored decks, and their escort vessels would use their high-performance interceptors, advanced radar, and anti-missile missiles to prevent attacking forces from coming close enough to inflict the kind of damage seen in the South Atlantic; and in case of a nuclear war surface ships would be much less vulnerable than land-based facilities.

Also facing some opposition from within the Pentagon, Lehman proved to be a skillful bureaucratic infighter. For example, Admiral Hyman G. Rickover, who was the director of the navy's nuclear-propulsion program and the "father of the nuclear navy," maintained that the proposed buildup was unnecessary and that the United States had as many nuclear submarines as it could possibly need. But by the end of his first year in office, the secretary had persuaded President Reagan to retire the eighty-two-year-old critic of the arms race on the ground that the navy needed "a younger man who can be available, perhaps, for the next decade in that job to give the stability that is so necessary." Lehman also survived a struggle with Deputy Secretary of Defense Paul Thayer, who questioned the expense of the navy's building programs and sought to transfer $10 billion of the navy's appropriation to the army. "I don't think it's any secret that the toughest part of the track was when Secretary Thayer was aboard," Lehman stated in the *New York Times* (September 13, 1984). "He fundamentally disagreed with the president's and Cap's [Secretary of Defense Caspar Weinberger's] and my approach to the Navy. . . . There was a lot of heated discussion." When Lehman publicly complained in October 1983 of the "guerrilla warfare" waged on Capitol Hill by "senior defense officials," implying Thayer, he was rebuked by Weinberger, but the navy nevertheless emerged the winner when Thayer was forced to resign early in 1984 under allegations that he had passed inside information to friends playing the stock market.

By the end of Reagan's first term, appropriations were secured for the 600-ship navy, which centered around fifteen carrier groups and included four recommissioned battleships that had been refitted at relatively low cost, but Secretary Lehman's most celebrated victory has been controlling the soaring costs of building the expanded fleet. In 1982, for example, Lehman threatened to terminate the $40 billion F-18 fighter program unless the McDonnell Douglas and Northrup corporations agreed to reduce their prices. His longest battle has been an ongoing struggle with the General Dynamics Corporation, whose Electric Boat division in Groton, Connecticut builds the Trident submarine.

In 1981 Lehman barred Electric Boat from bidding on three attack submarines and threatened to suspend the costly and much-delayed Trident program unless General Dynamics dropped a $100 million claim—the cost of correcting errors made by its own workers—instituted against the navy. Then, in May 1985, after the oversight subcommittee of the House Energy and Commerce Committee forced General Dynamics' chairman, David S. Lewis, to admit that the corporation had improperly billed the government for such overhead expenses as personal travel and entertainment, Lehman disciplined the organization again. The secretary canceled $22.5 million in existing contracts and blocked General Dynamics from obtaining contracts for Electric Boat and for its Pomona, California division until the corporation paid back $75 million in overcharges and established a "rigorous code of ethics for its officers."

In addition, Lehman fined General Dynamics $676,283 for giving $67,628.30 in illegal gratuities to Admiral Rickover during the period between 1961 and 1977, and, taking the strongest action possible given the statute of limitations, he sent a letter of censure to Rickover for having "encouraged or even demanded" the gifts. In August 1985, after General Dynamics paid its fine, instituted the required ethics code, and backed away from $111 million in claims against the government, the navy declared its business with the corporation "back to normal" and began lifting the suspensions on $1 billion worth of contracts for Electric Boat and Pomona.

To contain expenses further, Lehman ended cost-plus contracts, which committed the government to pay for all cost overruns in shipbuilding, and introduced competitive bidding into the allocation of contracts. As a result of those and other measures, by 1984 the navy had had twenty-one ships built at $500 million under budget and had saved enough money to allow it to refit the battleship *Missouri* without any further appropriations from Congress. To ensure that the navy continues to be run economically, Lehman has reserved almost half of the 253 slots for admirals for those officers who were trained at Wharton, Harvard, and other prestigious business schools specifically to handle naval procurement.

Nevertheless, Secretary Lehman's relationship with defense contractors has not escaped criticism.

Early in 1985, P. Takis Veliotis, a former General Dynamics executive vice-president now living in Athens to avoid prosecution for taking kickbacks, turned over to United States investigators the tape of a telephone conversation he had with David Lewis in which Lewis alleged that, at General Dynamics' insistence, White House counselor Edwin Meese had pressured Lehman to settle the dispute and that the secretary of the navy had granted Electric Boat a higher margin of profit on future contracts in return for its dropping of existing cost-overrun claims. Lehman and Meese denied that any such deal was made.

The outspoken secretary's tenure has been marked by other controversies, the most publicized of which occurred in 1982, when Congress questioned Lehman's apparent noncompliance with a promise made at his confirmation hearings to sell the Abington Corporation. The secretary denied that any conflict of interest existed and explained that he had sold the overseas rights to the company but had kept Abington alive in the United States as a personal holding company in case he wanted to use that name in some future consulting venture.

His most recent crisis involved the revelation in May 1985 that a spy ring of retired and active navy personnel had over the course of two decades engaged in espionage in behalf of the Soviet Union. Lehman joined Secretary of Defense Weinberger in calling for the death penalty for peacetime espionage. He also asked Congress to authorize the expanded use of random polygraph tests specifically aimed at espionage activities and strongly suggested that the number of Soviet personnel allowed into the United States be reduced. Commenting that it was "very clear that our security system has left a lot to be desired," Lehman instituted random inspections of people entering or leaving ships and navy installations, ordered often-ignored security regulations to be enforced, stepped up counterintelligence investigations, and cut the number of security clearances by 10 percent immediately, with the goal of an eventual 50 percent reduction.

However, in October 1985 both the navy and the United States intelligence services won unanimous plaudits for the interception of an Egyptian plane carrying four PLO terrorists. The aircraft carrier *Saratoga*, operating in the Mediterranean Sea, served as a base for the E2-C early-warning aircraft that tracked the Egyptian plane and for the F-14s that forced it to land at an Italian-American naval air facility in Sicily where the terrorists were apprehended. The operation was launched in response to the murder of Leon Klinghoffer, an American tourist aboard the *Achille Lauro*, by the terrorists who had seized that Italian ocean liner. "What this demonstrates," Secretary Lehman was quick to point out, "is despite the cheap-shot artists that try to portray the military as not being able to tie their shoelaces, we have the highest quality we've ever had."

John Lehman, who is a Catholic, has been married since 1975 to Barbara Thornton Wieland. The couple have three children: Alexandra, John F. 3d,

and Grace Virginia. Lehman, a former Air Force reservist and now a commander in the Naval Reserve, has flown as the bombardier-navigator in the navy's two-man A-6 Intruder attack-bomber and is a qualified helicopter pilot. Even during his tenure as secretary of the navy, he has made a point of serving his annual two weeks on active duty, without pay, as a member of Medium Attack Wing One at the Oceana Naval Air Station near Virginia Beach, Virginia because, as he explained in the *New York Times* (August 12, 1982), "the operational people have a very much better feel than we do up here for what works and what doesn't work and where we ought to be putting our bucks."

References: Barrons 64:16+ Je 11 '84 pors; Bsns W p171+ Jl 20 '81 por; N Y Times B p18 S 13 '84 por; Brownstein, Ronald, and Easton, Nina. Reagan's Ruling Class (1983); Who's Who in America, 1984–85; Who's Who in American Politics, 1983–84

## Leonard, Elmore

Oct. 11, 1925– Author. Address: b. c/o H. N. Swanson, 8523 Sunset Blvd., Los Angeles, Calif. 90069

For three decades, Elmore Leonard was a prolific but relatively obscure "genre" entertainer, appreciated for the most part by aficionados of western and crime fiction. Leonard gained wider recognition with *City Primeval* (1980) and *LaBrava* (1983), gritty contemporary action thrillers set in the cops-and-robbers netherworlds of Detroit and Miami, respectively, and he hit the best-seller jackpot with

*Glitz* (1985), another naturalistic and hard-edged crime suspense novel, set in the sleazier strata of Miami, San Juan, and Atlantic City. In addition to his twenty-three novels, Leonard has written more than thirty short stories (dating back to his pulp western days), and some dozen screenplays. Central to most of the plots in his offbeat, menace-laden stories are the motivations of greed or revenge.

"I've always taken exception to being placed in the mystery genre," Leonard told Bill Dunn in an interview for *Publishers Weekly* (February 25, 1983). "I'm certainly not in the middle of the genre. I'm more on the edge, where a lot of everyday things are happening." His characters are generally low-lifers, including some of the most insane and despicable villains in the history of fiction, and even his protagonists, including some of the street-smart cops, are, in his words, "the almost good guys," trying "to make a score one way or another." With seeming artlessness, Leonard lets his characters "perform." They set the intricate plots in motion, and their hip and often obscene dialogue tells the story, lean and terse, with minimal descriptive intrusion and frequent deadpan humor. Behind the scenes, of course, is Leonard, with his uncanny ear for the colorful argot and edgy rhythms of contemporary American urban speech and his eye for the authentic local color of what W. H. Auden, writing of Raymond Chandler, once called "the criminal milieu, the Great Wrong Place."

Elmore John Leonard Jr. was born in New Orleans, Louisiana on October 11, 1925 to Elmore John Leonard Sr. and Flora Amelia (Rive) Leonard. He was raised in the Roman Catholicism of his parents. His father's occupation, locating new auto dealerships for the General Motors Corporation, kept the family moving around the country until 1935, when the Leonards settled in Detroit. Referring to the fact that "guns are vital" in his stories (even though he doesn't glamorize violence), Leonard told Beaufort Cranford in an interview for the *Detroit News* (October 9, 1983) that he "used to play with [toy] guns when [he] was little."

The boyhood writing Leonard remembers doing was confined to a World War I combat drama, which he and his classmates performed in their fifth-grade classroom, and a short story, which he wrote in high school. He learned "to write in scenes" from watching motion pictures, as he recalled in an interview with Diane K. Shah of *Rolling Stone* (February 28, 1985): "In grade school, I used to 'tell' movies. I'd get with friends and tell *Captain Blood* and anything Errol Flynn was in." It was as a baseball pitcher in high school that he acquired the nickname "Dutch," after Dutch Leonard, the knuckleballer who won twenty games for the Washington Senators in 1939. Elmore ("Dutch") Leonard's tenure on the mound was short, but the nickname has survived to this day.

During the last two years of World War II, Leonard served with the Navy Seabees in the South Pacific. Following the war he majored in English at the University of Detroit on the GI Bill and married his first wife, Beverly Claire Cline. After he took his Ph.B. degree in 1950, he was determined to become a professional writer of fiction, but he had a growing family to support. To assure himself of a regular income, he took a job with Campbell-Ewald, a Detroit advertising agency, and began his efforts at fiction in his spare time.

Unable to "afford to be a literary writer," Leonard set about learning how to do "commercial" writing. "It seemed best to pick a genre," he told Beaufort Cranford in the *Detroit News* interview, "and I chose westerns, probably because I like western movies. I subscribed to *Arizona Highways* and started reading about Apaches and the cavalry." He told Bill Dunn of *Publishers Weekly* that he "learned to write from *For Whom the Bell Tolls*," but that his "attitude is different" than Hemingway's, that he sees "humor everywhere." John O'Hara was another early influence, and in the course of Leonard's development as a writer he was impressed with the way Mark Harris, Richard E. Bissell, and Kurt Vonnegut Jr. "see absurdities." George V. Higgins was a later influence. Leonard was "not influenced . . . at all" by "the Chandler-Hammett-MacDonald school."

Getting up at five, Leonard would spend two hours writing a daily quota of two pages of pulp western fiction each morning before going to Campbell-Ewald to spend the day turning out ad copy for the agency's Chevrolet account. His distaste for the advertising style ("cute, alliterative, full of similes and metaphors") reinforced the clean economy of style in the westerns he was writing at home. He sold his first story to *Argosy* in 1951 and was soon selling regularly to *Dime Western*, *Zane Grey's Western*, and other pulp magazines. Two of the stories became motion pictures. One was *3:10 to Yuma* (Columbia, 1957), written by Halsted Welles, directed by Delmer Daves, and starring Van Heflin as a poor farmer who brings in a notorious desperado (Glenn Ford) for the reward money, braving a barrage of gunfire from the outlaw's accomplices in order to do so. The other was *The Tall T* (Columbia, 1957), written by Burt Kennedy, directed by Budd Boetticher, and starring Randolph Scott as an Arizona rancher who outwits three stagecoach bandits holding a hostage.

Leonard's first published novel was *The Bounty Hunters*, issued in hardcover by Houghton Mifflin in 1953 and in paperback by Ballantine Books the following year. Over the next seven years Leonard published two additional hardcover novels, *The Law at Randado* (Houghton, 1955) and *Escape from 5 Shadows* (Houghton, 1956), and two paperbacks, *Last Stand at Saber River* (Dell, 1957) and *Hombre* (Ballantine, 1961). *Hombre* has been voted one of the twenty-five best western novels of all time by the Western Writers of America.

When Campbell-Ewald's profit-sharing plan came due in 1961, Leonard took his money and quit the agency. His hope was to write fiction full time, but, with four children to feed and the western market drying up, he ended up writing no fiction at all for four years. Instead, he free-lanced advertising copy, wrote a recruiting film for the Franciscans, and scripted some dozen educational films for Encyclopaedia Britannica Films. Leonard felt that he could afford to return to the writing of novels only after Twentieth Century-Fox bought the screen rights to *Hombre* for $10,000.

Written by Irving Ravetch and Harriet Frank, directed by Martin Ritt, and starring Paul Newman as a white man raised by Indians, *Hombre* was released in 1967 to appreciative notices. Leonard himself especially liked the faithful rendering of the opening scene, which he had written in response to the unrealistic "white flag" situation he had seen a hundred times in television westerns, in which the good guy approaches the holed-up bad guy with a white flag, makes a deal, and walks away, all problems solved. In *Hombre*, it is the bad guy (Richard Boone) who does the white-flagging, only to be asked by the good guy (Newman), "How you gonna get down the hill?" The Boone character says, "Now, *wait* a minute," runs, and is shot dead in his tracks. "That's what it's all about: realism," Leonard pointed out to Bill Kelly in an interview for *American Film* (December 1984). "Boone, incidentally, is the only actor who has delivered my lines exactly as I wrote them, accent and all, and he did it twice—in *Hombre* and *The Tall T.*

Changing genres, Leonard wrote his first contemporary novel, *The Big Bounce*, a melodrama about the sexual and criminal misadventures of a drifter working at a California motel. When Leonard's New York agent, Marguerite Harper, fell ill, the legendary Hollywood agent H. N. Swanson, who had been handling movie sales for Leonard, became his literary agent as well. After numerous rejections, Swanson sold the publishing and movie rights to *The Big Bounce* simultaneously, to Fawcett Books and Warner Brothers, respectively. Fawcett published the book as an original Gold Medal paperback in 1969, and in the same year Warner Brothers released the motion picture *The Big Bounce*, scripted by Robert Dozier and starring Ryan O'Neal and Leigh Taylor-Young. Leonard regards the film as "maybe the worst movie ever made."

In his Prohibition-era novel *The Moonshine War* (Doubleday, 1969), Leonard told the sometimes comic story of a revenue agent who, to his regret, enlists the help of a sadistic gangster in his hunt for illegal whiskey in the hills of Kentucky. He also wrote the screen adaptation of *The Moonshine War* (MGM, 1970). Leonard reverted to the western genre (of which he was growing tired) temporarily with the paperback originals *Valdez Is Coming* (Gold Medal, 1970) and *Forty Lashes Less One* (Bantam, 1972) and the screenplay *Joe Kidd* (Universal, 1972), a Clint Eastwood vehicle. (Roland Kibbee and David Rayfiel wrote the screen adaptation of *Valdez Is Coming*, released by United Artists in 1970.) Leonard also wrote the film *Mr. Majestyk* (United Artists, 1974) for Eastwood, but Charles Bronson replaced Eastwood in the title role, that of a Colorado melon grower at war with the local Mafia. The motion picture was highly re-

garded by critics, but Leonard considers the Dell paperback *Mr. Majestyk*, which he wrote after the screenplay, superior, because he "worked up the characters more."

Transferring his action to the urban scene, Leonard wrote the paperback *Fifty-Two Pickup* (Dell, 1974), the story of a Detroit auto-parts manufacturer who, with his forgiving wife, fights back against hoodlums who have kidnapped and murdered his porn-model mistress and are trying to blackmail him, and *Swag* (Delacorte, 1976; also published under the title *Ryan's Rules*), in which a Detroit auto thief, Ernest J. ("Stick") Stickley Jr., and an ex-car salesman named Ryan become partners in armed robbery. "The dough starts rolling in," Ken Tucher wrote of *Swag* in a retrospective review in the *Village Voice* (February 23, 1982), "and Leonard takes off on an assiduously detailed account of two mugs with new money that is matched in modern fiction only by Bruce J. Friedman's underrated *About Harry Townes*. Both Leonard and Friedman have a knack for describing the tastes of no-class bachelors—the cheap swank of new apartments that look like motel rooms; the rubbery sheen of leisure suits; the clunk of gold chains against hairy breast bones—without being condescending; with tender interest, in fact."

The protagonist of the hardcover novel *Unknown Man No. 89* (Delacorte, 1977) is a caddish process server who discovers the full humanity within himself under pressure, after he breaks his number-one rule ("Never get personally involved") and, at great risk, goes to the rescue of a damsel being duped by a dangerous confidence man. Bantam Books published Leonard's *Switch* and *Gunsight* as paperback originals in 1978 and 1979, respectively. In *Switch*, two ex-convicts kidnap the wife of a rich builder, only to learn that her philandering husband is glad to be rid of her and won't pay a ransom. The ironic plot thickens when the bitter, vengeful wife joins forces with her captors to give her mate his comeuppance. Chiefly because he needed the money offered for the job ($50,000), Leonard wrote the television oater *High Noon, Part II: The Return of Will Kane*, a sequel to the 1952 big-screen classic. He was less than satisfied with that 1980 CBS production, in which Lee Majors played the gun-dueling hero originally created by Gary Cooper.

Leonard's literary fortunes took a sharp upward turn when he became associated with Arbor House, the hardcover publishing company founded by Donald I. Fine, who had bought several of Leonard's paperbacks when he was editor-in-chief at Dell Books. Aggressively promoted by Fine, *City Primeval: High Noon in Detroit* (Arbor House, 1980), perhaps the toughest of Leonard's novels, became the first to be treated by critics as "literature," "strong stuff but compelling." *City Primeval* is the classic frontier shootout tale transposed to the blighted inner city, where Raymond Cruz, a committed Detroit cop, bravely faces down a vicious murderer in behalf of a complacent citizenry.

*Split Images* (Arbor House, 1982), *Cat Chaser* (Arbor House, 1982), and *Stick* (Arbor House, 1983) brought renewed raves from literary critics. *Split Images* is a chilling story, set in Detroit and Palm Beach, about a demented, homicidal multimillionaire, his ex-policeman chauffeur, and the imperfect but basically good cop who trails them. The sprawling novel *Cat Chaser* is about a motel owner in Pompano Beach, Florida (where Leonard's mother owns a motel, bought for her by him) whose life is placid until he meets the American wife of a rich, corrupt Dominican political exile, along with an assortment of disreputable confidence men. Reviewing *Cat Chaser* in the *New York Times* (June 11, 1982), John Leonard credited the author with writing dialogue better than any active novelist except Philip Roth and putting "the fun back into adultery."

Ernest J. Stickley Jr., the protagonist of *Swag*, surfaces again in *Stick* (Arbor House, 1983) in a guise clearly inspired by Jack Henry Abbott—that of an ex-con struggling to readjust to life outside prison walls. Fresh from a seven-year prison term in Michigan, Stick drifts to Miami's South Beach where he tries to go straight but is caught up in the fast-buck world of high-rolling drug dealers and petty stock manipulators, whom he learns to beat at their own games. George Stade, who reviewed *Stick* for the *New York Times Book Review* (March 6, 1983), complained that the novel's scenes were "slack" and its bull sessions "long." "For the rest," Stade wrote, "when Mr. Leonard is . . . thickening the air with menace [and] exposing the black holes behind the parts people play . . . he gives us more serious fun per word than anyone around." Although he collaborated on the screenplay, Leonard was disappointed in the film adaptation of *Stick* (Universal, 1985), directed by and starring Burt Reynolds. "You see," he explained when Pete Hamill interviewed him for the New York *Daily News* (April 21, 1985), "my thing is really pretty deadpan. If everybody starts acting, it won't work." The money he received for the movie rights to *Stick*, $350,000, was by far the largest sum he received for his work to that point.

*Stick* was a Book-of-the-Month Club alternate selection, and *LaBrava* (Arbor House, 1983) won the Edgar Allan Poe Award of the Mystery Writers of America. In *LaBrava*, the setting is again Miami's sleazy South Beach area. The title character is a retired Secret Service agent turned photographer who becomes embroiled in thwarting a deceptively simple-minded extortion scheme that threatens a former film actress, one of the matinee idols of his childhood. To Peter S. Prescott of *Newsweek* (November 14, 1983), *LaBrava* suggested that Leonard is "the legitimate heir of James M. Cain." "Leonard is particularly adept at depicting both human frailty . . . and the temptation to prey on that frailty . . . ," Prescott wrote. "Like Cain, Leonard takes great care with dialogue, employing the utmost artifice to create an illusion of inarticulate speech. It's hard to read *LaBrava* without imagining the movie that will surely be made from

it." Such a movie is being planned by producer Walter Mirisch, and Leonard is rewriting the script, for the third or fourth time. Roy Scheider, who is slated for the title role, discussed the problems of translating Leonard's novels into films with Pete Hamill: "The stuff that makes Elmore Leonard unique—all that texture, the runs of dialogue, the riffs between characters—a lot of it has to go by the boards in a movie."

The swell of critical praise for Leonard peaked with *Glitz* (Arbor House, 1985), which was a Book-of-the-Month Club selection, reached third place on the *Publishers Weekly* best-seller list, remained on the *New York Times* list for eighteen weeks, and attained an estimated readership of three million. The protagonist of *Glitz* is Vincent Mora, an off-duty Miami police lieutenant who falls in love with Iris Ruíz, a prostitute, in Puerto Rico and later goes to Atlantic City, the New Jersey gambling mecca, to free-lance investigate her murder there. The murder, it turns out, has been committed by his old nemesis, the vengeful psychopathic rapist Teddy Magyk, as bait for him. The few critics who were disappointed with *Glitz* included Jefferson Morley, a Leonard admirer who detected in the book an unwonted "self-consciousness," compounded by "recycled devices." Writing in the *New Republic* (March 25, 1985), Morley pointed out that Leonard's books "are a revelation because he is such a self-effacing writer, because he makes his point by never making any points." Fearful that the author was "getting lost in, well, the glitz" of critical adulation, Morley advised, "Keep your eye on the ball, Elmore."

The original advance for *Glitz*, $40,000, was upped to $200,000 on the eve of its publication. Warner Books paid $450,000 plus bonuses for the paperback rights, and the screen rights have been purchased for another $450,000. (Leonard is writing the screenplay.) Five other Leonard novels are being groomed for the movies, and Bantam Books is reissuing seven of his western novels and two of his crime novels in paperback. MGM-TV has contracted with Leonard for a television crime series, and the author is at work on his twenty-fourth novel, about ex-cons who get together for one more big heist. The novel is set chiefly in New Orleans, but it will also apparently involve Nicaragua, on which Leonard says he has been doing "a lot of clipping." Under the umbrella title *Elmore Leonard's Dutch Treat*, Arbor House in November 1985 reissued *Mr. Majestyk* and *Swag*, along with *The Hunted*, about an American pursued in Israel by hitmen from Detroit.

Leonard researches his novels by reading books, the popular press, and such publications as crime commission reports and prison newsletters; by spending time with a private detective he knows in Florida and with homicide detectives and prosecutors in Detroit and elsewhere; by visiting and conversing with prisoners; and by being a good listener generally. His wife lends her ear to the task of eavesdropping, reporting to him the colorful conversations she overhears. Leonard also employs a part-time researcher, Gregg Sutter, who does much of his legwork and provides him with albums of pertinent photographs.

Five-foot-nine and wiry of physique, Elmore Leonard sports a trim beard, wears horned-rim glasses, and dresses rather casually, usually in jeans or slacks, a tweed jacket, and a Kangol cap. He is quiet and soft-spoken, with a subtle sense of humor and an air of serenity that he attributes to his experience in Alcoholics Anonymous, which he joined in 1974, three years before he took his last alcoholic drink. Having learned to "live one day at a time," he now has "complete trust in God" and feels that he is "in His hands." Leonard writes from nine-thirty in the morning to six in the evening five or six days a week. He does his first drafts in longhand, polishes them at the typewriter, and turns the pages over to a professional for final typing. In breaks from his work, he sometimes plays tennis with his son Peter.

From his first marriage, which ended in divorce in 1977, Leonard has five grown children and three grandchildren. With his second wife, the former Joan Shepard, whom he married in 1979, he lives in a comfortable brick house, with swimming pool, in Birmingham, Michigan. The two live quietly, spending most of their evenings at home, watching movies on their video recorder and television or reading. Among Leonard's favorite authors currently are the novelists Raymond Carver and Bobbie Anne Mason. "My heroes are bumbling along, trying to make it," "Dutch" Leonard has said. "My guys don't play roles. I suppose they're me."

References: N Y Times Mag p20+ D 30 '84 por; Newsday mag p19+ Ap 21 '85 pors; Newsweek 105:62+ Ap 22 '85 pors; People 23:73+ Mr 4 '85 pors; Time 123:84+ My 28 '84 por; Washington Post C p1+ F 6 '85 por; Contemporary Authors new rev vol 12 (1984); Tuska, Jon and Pietarski, Vicki. Encyclopedia of Frontier and Western Fiction (1983); Who's Who in America, 1976–77

## Lortel, Lucille

(lôr tel ´)

1902(?)– Theatrical producer. Address: b. White Barn Theatre Foundation, Inc., Westport, Conn. 06880

Affectionately known as the "Queen of Off Broadway," Lucille Lortel, the producer and theatre proprietor, has provided pioneering, quality theatre to the New York area for almost forty years. First conferred by Washington Post drama critic Richard Coe in 1962, the title is proclaimed on a plaque in the Lucille Lortel wing, opened in 1981, of the theatre gallery in the Museum of the City of New York. Always ahead of her time, the former actress founded the still thriving White Barn Theatre in Westport, Connecticut in 1947 as a sanctuary from the pressures of the commercial theatre, where playwrights could test new plays and actors could stretch their talents in a variety of challenging roles. Shortly after taking ownership of the Theatre de Lys in New York City's Greenwich Village in 1955, Miss Lortel launched the now legendary Matinee Series as "a laboratory for innovation" in the theatre. "If you love the theatre, you must be innovative," she explained, as quoted in Fifty Plus magazine (June 1980). "You must try new ideas and new faces. That's the only way the theatre can develop. You can't do it on Broadway because it costs too much. The costs are lower Off Broadway, so you can afford to take a chance, and you must take a chance."

The daughter of Harry Lortel, a garment-industry executive, and his wife, Anna (Mayo) Lortel, Lucille Lortel was born in New York City in about 1902. Some sources give her year of birth as 1906 or 1910. After briefly attending Adelphi College, now Adelphi University, in Garden City, New York, Miss Lortel enrolled at the American Academy of Dramatic Arts in 1920. The following year, she traveled to Berlin, Germany to study acting with Arnold Korf, the expatriate American actor and teacher, and with the theatrical director and producer Max Reinhardt. On her return to the United States, Miss Lortel made her stage debut in 1924, with a stock company in Albany, New York. A year later, she appeared on Broadway in a minor role in the short-lived Two by Two; as a Handmaiden and, in the final week of the run, as Iras in the Theatre Guild production of Shaw's Caesar and Cleopatra, with Helen Hayes and Lionel At-will in the title roles; and as Inez in David Belasco's production of Willard Mack's melodrama *The Dove*, starring Judith Anderson.

Lucille Lortel's stage credits for the 1920s also include the roles of the virginal Clara Rathboone in *One Man's Woman*, a comedy drama by Michael Kallesser, Elsa in William Francis Dugan's comedy *The Virgin Man*, and the nymphomaniac Poppy in the national touring company of *The Shanghai Gesture*. During the 1928-29 New York season and, subsequently, on the Orpheum circuit, she appeared in vaudeville as a Spanish dancer in the play *The Man Who Laughed Last*, with Sessue Hayakawa. A screen version of *The Man Who Laughed Last* was released by Vitaphone in 1929. The actress also made a series of short films for Warner Brothers. Her budding career was cut short by her marriage, on March 23, 1931, to Louis Schweitzer, a chemical engineer and cigarette-paper manufacturer. Because her husband strongly disapproved of her continuing to perform, Miss Lortel retired from the stage, returning only to play the French Maid in the ephemeral drama *The Man Who Reclaimed His Head*, with Claude Rains, at the Broadhurst Theatre in 1932.

Except for making occasional appearances on such radio programs as *Advice to the Lovelorn* and *Great Women of History*, Lucille Lortel acceded to her millionaire husband's wish for the next fifteen years. But as she admitted to Haskel Frankel in an interview for the *New York Times* (August 5, 1979), she became increasingly "restless." "Just going from party to party watching people outdo each other didn't mean much to me," she explained to Frankel. "It can't compare to the thrill of seeing a play or performance come to life." Almost by chance, that "thrill" became a reality for her in the summer of 1947. While her husband was in Europe on a business trip, she was approached by her long-time friends Canada Lee, the noted black actor, and Philip Huston, the playwright, who wanted to try out Huston and Elizabeth Goodyear's new play *The Painted Wagon* before a discriminating audience. She immediately offered them the use of the empty stable on her eighteen-acre Westport, Connecticut estate. Moreover, she equipped the stable with a raised platform and folding chairs, decorated it with Japanese lanterns and lithographed advertisements for nineteenth-century melodramas, and invited some of the most influential people in New York theatre to attend a staged reading of the new piece. After the performance, on July 27, 1947, the actors—among them Lee and Huston—joined the audience for coffee and sandwiches and a discussion of the play. By the time Louis Schweitzer returned home, the White Barn Theatre was "a fact," Miss Lortel told Frankel. "I told my husband that I needed this, and he backed me up."

Inundated with scripts following the success of *The Painted Wagon*, Lucille Lortel presented over the first two seasons of weekend dramatic reading of the White Barn Theatre such varied fare as the musical revue *No Casting Today*; *Ivory Tower*, with Eva Marie Saint in one of her first major roles;

Zero Mostel in William Saroyan's *Jim Dandy*; the North American premiere of Sean O'Casey's *Red Roses for Me*, starring Kim Hunter; and *Alive and Kicking*, a new musical revue by Hoagy Carmichael. After her return from a survey of contemporary theatre in Europe in 1949, she remodeled the White Barn along the lines of the Club Theatre of England. To accommodate the more elaborately staged productions, complete with sets and costumes, that she envisioned, she had a permanent stage constructed. The first play in this phase of the White Barn Theatre's development was a translation of Federico Garcia Lorca's *Amor de Don Perlimplin con Belisa en su jardin*, directed by a then unknown Sidney Lumet.

Under Lucille Lortel's direction, the White Barn Theatre soon earned a reputation as a showcase for diverse theatrical troupes, ranging from the Lemonade Opera Company, which presented the American premiere of Felix Mendelssohn's opera *The Stranger*, to the Oxford University Players, who appeared in Jonson's *The Alchemist*, to Geoffrey Holder and his Trinidad Dance Troupe. The unquestioned highlight of the White Barn's 1951 season was the initial American appearance of the Dublin Players Company, which numbered among its actors the future Tony Award nominee Milo O'Shea, in the American premieres of *The Rising of the Moon*, a short comedy about peasant life by Lady Augusta Gregory, and Yeats's *The Words Upon the Window Pane*, followed by Sean O'Casey's melodrama *The Shadow of a Gunman* and John Millington Synge's *The Shadow of the Glen*. "When the White Barn began, it was to summer theatre what Off Broadway is to the commercial theatre," the actress Eva Le Gallienne said recently, as quoted in *Avenue* (June-July-August, 1981). "An avowed pioneer, it proved that summer productions could be stimulating, avant-garde, and enthusiastically received."

In 1951 the White Barn Theatre was chartered as a non-profit foundation by the State of Connecticut. Its officially stated purpose was "to create an opportunity for new playwrights, composers, directors, actors, and designers to showcase their talents and develop in their craft; and for more established artists to work free of the stereotypes to which so many are confined after they have arrived." To that end, Lucille Lortel, newly appointed president of the White Barn's board of directors, expanded the theatre's physical plant and launched a comprehensive theatre-crafts training program. Scenic designer Ralph Alswang extensively remodeled the 155-seat auditorium, enlarged the stage, installed state-of-the-art lighting and sound equipment, and supervised the setting up of a closed-circuit television system to accommodate overflow audiences on the terrace. Lucille Lortel herself was the driving force behind the establishment of the White Barn Theatre Apprentice School, the introduction of regular summer seminars in Shakespeare, Ibsen, and Chekhov for advanced students and professional actors, and the creation of an actors' residence hall, Derwent House, named for the actor and playwright Clarence Derwent, then the president of the Actors' Equity Association of America and the vice-president of the White Barn's board of directors. According to Mildred Dunnock, who was among the actors interviewed for the *Avenue* magazine profile of Lucille Lortel, by the mid-1950s the White Barn Theatre "was a wonderful opportunity, a place to try out new things, with great freedom to live and work. And yet," she went on, "as progressive as it was, no actor who ever worked there ever felt he was taking a chance with his career because he knew no production would be shoddy."

Besides Mildred Dunnock, the list of established actors who appeared at the White Barn Theatre over the years comprises Zero Mostel, Eva Le Gallienne, James Coco, Kim Hunter, and Peggy Wood. Numbered among those performers who got their first big breaks there are Peter Falk, Vincent Gardenia, Sada Thompson, George Peppard, and Lois Nettleton. The smorgasbord of plays given their initial performances at the White Barn, which opened its thirty-sixth season in July 1984 with *Sprechen Sie Brecht*, includes such contemporary American classics as Murray Schisgal's *The Typists*, Paul Zindel's Pulitzer Prize–winning *The Effect of Gamma Rays on Man-in-the-Moon Marigolds*, and Terrence McNally's *Next*.

With the White Barn Theatre entrenched as a stimulating showcase for experimentalism in theatre, Lucille Lortel broadened her scope in 1955 with the acquisition of the Theatre de Lys, a twenty-fourth anniversary gift from her husband. She had intended to use the 299-seat theatre in Greenwich Village as a proving ground for White Barn productions that seemed to merit a New York run, but her first production there, in September 1955, was a revival of Marc Blitzstein's adaptation of Bertolt Brecht and Kurt Weill's abrasive musical *The Threepenny Opera*. "I chose *Threepenny* because I thought it should have another chance," she has explained simply. The production chalked up 2,611 performances before closing on December 17, 1961.

*The Threepenny Opera*'s seven-year run—the longest for a musical in the annals of the American theatre up to that date—launched the Off-Broadway boom. As Stuart W. Little observed in his book *Off-Broadway: The Prophetic Theater* (1972), "For thousands of theatergoers, a visit to the de Lys was the authentic off-Broadway experience. Off-Broadway meant the discovery of new talent and fresh theatrical experiences in unfamiliar parts of the city. . . . The de Lys at the far end of Christopher Street, near the Hudson River docks, was situated in a borderline neighborhood between the known residential part of the city and the open seaport. The unknown world beyond, in imagination, merged with the pulsing underworld life of *The Threepenny Opera* and became sinister, exotic, and menacing."

Because she craved the freedom to experiment, Lucille Lortel was somewhat frustrated by the runaway success of *The Threepenny Opera*. Determined to stage works of an unusual or experimental nature, she sought and received the support of the Greater New York chapter of the American National Theater and Academy (ANTA) for her proposed Matinee Series, which was modeled on the White Barn showcase concept. Miss Lortel's choice of Felicia Komai's verse adaptation of Alan Paton's novel *Cry, the Beloved Country* as the Series' inaugural venture, on May 15, 1956, typified her dedication to giving new playwrights a hearing. So, too, did her selection of Paul Shyre's adaptation of John Dos Passos' best seller *U.S.A.*, which became the first of many Matinee Series productions to go on to successful Off-Broadway runs. She also encouraged the presentation of adventurous new forms, such as Anna Sokolow's Kafkaesque dance drama *Metamorphosis* and May O'Donnell's modern-dance interpretation of Maeterlinck's *Pelleas and Melisande*. Accepting Miss Lortel's open invitation to actors to appear in works of their own choosing, Siobhan McKenna took the title role in an unusual staging of *Hamlet*, in which she was supported entirely by offstage voices, Helen Hayes performed in the Shakespearean anthology *Lovers, Villains, and Fools*, and Dame Sybil Thorndike and Sir Lewis Casson gave a joint dramatic reading. Seen only once, those first-season programs ably demonstrated the aims of the Matinee Series, outlined in the program for the Series' twentieth anniversary gala—namely, "to serve the actor, to serve the director, and to serve the playwright."

The first of the many honors netted by the Matinee Series was an Obie Award for the dramatization of Frank O'Connor's *Guests of the Nation* as the best one-act play of 1958. Accompanying the award was a special citation from the *Village Voice* applauding Lucille Lortel "for fostering and furthering the spirit of theatrical experiment." In its 1959-60 season, the Series distinguished itself by recreating a ground-breaking White Barn production—*Shakespeare in Harlem*, a dramatization by an all-black cast, including Godfrey Cambridge and Isabelle Sanford, of Langston Hughes's poems. Adaptations of poetic works by Robert Frost, Archibald MacLeish, W. H. Auden and Conrad Aiken followed. During the same season, the Series established its prestigious connection with the Library of Congress with the performances of two rarely seen Irish plays, O'Casey's *Time to Go* and Paul Vincent Carroll's *The Coggerers*.

To open the 1961-62 season of the Matinee Series, Lucille Lortel selected the illuminating compendium *Brecht on Brecht: His Life and Art*, a "living anthology" of the German playwright's work compiled by the actor George Tabori. So positive was the public response to *Brecht on Brecht* that she finally shuttered the long-running *Threepenny Opera* in order to give her second Brecht production a wider audience as a regular attraction at the Theatre de Lys, where it played to packed houses for more than a year. Brecht was just one of the many contemporary European dramatists championed by Lucille Lortel long before they were widely accepted in the United States. Ever on the lookout for new and offbeat material, she met with O'Casey, Eugène Ionesco, and Jean Genet, among other playwrights, on her trips abroad. Following those encounters, she mounted productions of several previously unknown plays by O'Casey, Ionesco's *The Shepherd's Chameleon* and *Victims of Duty*, and perhaps most notably, Genet's *The Balcony*, which she coproduced at the Circle-in-the-Square in 1960. She also oversaw the first American productions of plays by the Italian writer Mario Fratti and by Athol Fugard, the South African playwright whose *The Blood Knot*, starring J. D. Cannon and James Earl Jones, was a critical and commercial success at the Off-Broadway Cricket Theatre in 1964.

Lucille Lortel also provided a stage for the early noncommercial work of such major American playwrights as Tennessee Williams, Edward Albee, and William Inge. Over the years, she has staged at the White Barn or the Theatre de Lys productions of Inge's *Glory in the Flower*, Albee's *Fam and Yam*, and Williams' *The Purification, I Rise in Flames Cried the Phoenix, Three Players of a Summer Game,* and *Talk To Me Like the Rain.* Among those new writers whose works were entries in the Matinee Series schedules were Adrienne Kennedy, Terrence McNally, Norman Rosten, and Anna Marie Barlow.

Largely because of increased competition from burgeoning Off-Off-Broadway showcase theatres, Lucille Lortel ended the Matinee Series at the Theatre de Lys in 1975 with a twentieth-anniversary gala at which the original actors reenacted thirty-five scenes from the Series' most distinguished productions, documenting its historical and artistic impact. The Theatre de Lys, however, continued to house stagings of notable modern plays, including the long-running musical spoof *Dames at Sea*, Tom Cole's *Medal of Honor Rag*, David Mamet's *A Life in the Theatre*, Sam Shepard's Pulitzer Prize-winning *Buried Child*, and *Getting Out*, an early work by the Pulitzer Prize winner Marsha Norman. In 1981 the landmark playhouse was rechristened the Lucille Lortel Theatre, a name change the owner had long been modestly resisting. At the time, the theatre was housing the British playwright Caryl Churchill's arresting *Cloud Nine*, which Lucille Lortel, to her later regret, had originally rejected. Among its more recent occupants were the Obie-honored *Woza Albert!* and the Playwrights Horizons' production of Wendy Wasserstein's *Isn't It Romantic*, which settled in for a long run in June 1984.

At the Harold Clurman Theatre on the ever-expanding "Theatre Row" on West 42nd Street in New York City, Lucille Lortel coproduced the world premiere, on June 15, 1983, of Samuel Beckett's trilogy of one-act plays, *Ohio Impromptu, Catastrophe,* and *What Where.* The following year, she acted as coproducer of another Beckett trio—*Enough, Footfalls,* and *Rockaby*—at the newly opened Samuel Beckett Theatre. Outside her usual Off-Broadway bailiwick, she has spon-

sored the production of O'Casey's *I Knock at the Door*, at the Belasco Theatre in 1957, and a revival of Williams' *A Streetcar Named Desire*, at the St. James Theatre in 1973, among other plays. A long-time member of the boards of directors of the national and New York chapters of ANTA and of the Lincoln Center for the Performing Arts, Miss Lortel was a cofounder of the American Shakespeare Festival Theatre and Academy in Stratford, Connecticut, which was established in 1955.

Her long list of honors includes the State of Connecticut's Distinguished Award in the Arts, the Double Image Theatre Award, and the Theatre Hall of Fame Arnold Weissberger Award. She was, in addition, the first recipient of the Margo Jones Award for her dedication to the production of new plays, in 1962, and of the Lee Strasberg Lifetime Achievement Award, in 1984. In recognition of her "outstanding contribution to the furthering of theatre in America," the University of Bridgeport (Connecticut) awarded Lucille Lortel an honorary doctorate in May 1984.

A trim, petite woman who appears to be years younger than her chronological age, Lucille Lortel has large, heavy-lidded brown eyes and classic features. She usually wears her dark hair smoothed back from her forehead into a chignon. For recreation, she attends plays and concerts, some of which she has supported financially. In 1980, for example, she rescued the debt-ridden New York Senior Concert Orchestra, which performs yearly at Carnegie Hall, with a large donation. "That's what money is for," she explained in an interview for *Fifty Plus* (June 1980). Miss Lortel lives alone in an elegant apartment filled with theatrical memorabilia, atop a midtown Manhattan hotel. A widow since 1971, she has no family. "My theatres are my children," she once said, as quoted in the *New York Times* (April 8, 1981).

References: After Dark 14:80 Ag–S '81 por; Christian Sci Mon p31+ Je 18 '85 por; Fifty Plus 20:23 Je '80 por; N Y Times III p7 S 30 '80 por, II p8 Ap 8 '81 por, XXIII p17 Jl 10 '83 por, III p3 Ag 5 '83 por; Stages 1:1+ Ap '84 pors; Washington Post A p26 Ap 3 '62; Biographical Encyclopedia and Who's Who of the American Theatre (1966); Notable Names in the American Theatre (1976); Who's Who in the Theatre (1981)

---

## Mackerras, Sir Charles

Nov. 17, 1925– Conductor; composer; musicologist. Address: b. c/o ICM Artists, Ltd., 40 W. 57th St., New York City, N.Y. 10019; h. 10 Hamilton Terrace, London NW8 9UG, England

"Australia has had a cultural inferiority complex for a long, long time," Sir Charles Mackerras once observed in an interview with John Rockwell in *Opera News* (July 1973). "It's rather similar to

*Sir Charles Mackerras*

America in that respect, apart from New York. If you are a bright young person, you really have to go away to establish your reputation with the people back home." An Australian national who was born in the United States, Mackerras has impressed his countrymen by conducting symphony and opera company orchestras on three continents. Although he has been acclaimed as a Wagner and Mozart conductor of the first rank, Mackerras has often ranged far afield from the German repertory, as with his ballet score *Pineapple Poll*, adapted from the music of Sir Arthur Sullivan, his highly praised recording of Handel's *Messiah*, and his authoritative recordings of the operas of Leoš Janáček that have made Mackerras something of a cultural hero in the composer's native Czechoslovakia.

The third son of Alan Patrick and Catherine Mackerras, Sir Charles Mackerras was born Alan Charles MacLaurin Mackerras on November 17, 1925 in Schenectady, New York, where his father, an Australian scientist, was working on a scholarship from General Electric. Two years later, the family resettled in Sydney when the father returned to Australia to begin work on the electrification of New South Wales. At both the Sydney Grammar School and the prestigious King's School, Charles Mackerras soon showed signs of being the most gifted musician among the five Mackerras sons (his brothers' interests gravitated towards law, teaching, Chinese studies, and statistics), and the first such talent to appear in his family since the heyday of his maternal great-great-great-grandfather, Isaac Nathan (1792–1864), a singer, composer, writer on music, and intimate friend of Lord Byron. Nathan, who emigrated from England in 1841, is remembered as the "Father of Australian Music," an epithet he earned by founding two choral societies, publishing a music periodical, and pioneering in producing operas down under.

While still in his teens Mackerras entered Australia's leading music school, the New South Wales State Conservatorium of Music, as a student of oboe, piano, and composition. The standards he set for himself, however, came straight from England. As he later informed Alan Blyth in *Gramophone* (March 1975), "Because I came from what was then the backwoods in Australia, the only way you could get to know what standards abroad were like was by listening to records. We used to buy every record that came out, and anyone who went to England brought back everything he could get hold of. I learned a great deal of my music that way, and certainly gained my first love of opera through them. I was an oboe player and the real yardstick I had was the sound of Leon Goossens in the LPO (London Philharmonic Orchestra) of that time. I could also hear that his method was vastly different from that of the players in the Vienna Philharmonic. I tried to emulate the Goossens sound by listening to the records over and over again."

At the age of eighteen, following his graduation from the Conservatorium, Mackerras became the principal oboist of the Sydney Symphony Orchestra, a position he held from 1943 until 1946. His earliest professional contact with the orchestra transformed his conception of himself as a musician, not because of the few occasions on which he was given the chance to conduct but, rather, because of the opportunity to play under great conductors from time to time. He recalled for Blyth a visit by Eugene Ormandy, the music director of the Philadelphia Orchestra: "[Ormandy] did some amazing things with the Sydney Symphony just after the war. The young players then in that orchestra had no experience; he was the first really competent conductor they had played under. It shook them to find someone who knew so much."

It also jolted Mackerras into questioning his own choice of instrument as a means of eventually reaching the podium. He told an interviewer for the *New York Post* (November 21, 1972), "I realized that Toscanini and Barbirolli had been string players first and I thought hell, I'll never be a great conductor unless I learn to play a string instrument." The immediate result was his decision to leave Australia in 1947 for a job as second oboist with the Sadler's Wells Opera Company in London and for study under its conductor, Michael Mudie. It was at Sadler's Wells that Mackerras met his future wife, a young clarinetist named Helena Judith Wilkins, who spent her childhood in India as the daughter of a government official. He also applied for and won a British Council Scholarship for a year's study at the Academy of Fine Arts in Prague under Vaclav Talich, the most distinguished and influential Czech conductor of his generation. Mackerras now jokes about the two "honeymoons" he spent in Prague in 1948: one with the former Helena Judith Wilkins and the other with the music of Leoš Janáček under Talich.

It was, for Mackerras, perhaps the best possible time to discover Prague, Talich, and Janáček. With Czechoslovakia newly liberated from the Nazis and with its capital city largely intact, a renaissance in Czech culture was taking place. Talich, a conductor of international stature since 1903, when he led the Berlin Philharmonic, had been a passionate exponent of Czech music for forty years, and Czech nationalism had reasserted itself in Prague. During his stay, Mackerras attended a performance of Janáček's opera *Káťa Kabanová* and, in an article in *Gramophone* (October 1977), described his response: "I was vastly impressed by the dramatic impact and originality of the music, but I did not realize that the orchestration had been changed and 'normalized' by the conductor, Vaclav Talich. Nor did I know that it was common practice in Prague to retouch Janáček's orchestration, because it was apparently so unconventional, clumsy almost." He began a close and exacting study of the music of Janáček that would bring him back to Czechoslovakia many times after his work with Vaclav Talich had formally ended.

On Mackerras' return to London from Prague in 1948, he was appointed assistant conductor at Sadler's Wells and made his debut at the podium on October 28, 1948 in a performance of *Die Fledermaus*. Three years later, in 1951, he was given the honor of conducting the British premiere of *Káťa Kabanová* at Sadler's Wells, his first experience of working with a Janáček opera outside of Czechoslovakia. Mackerras found his preparations for the performance to be a revelatory experience. "When I first started to work on *Káťa* at Sadler's Wells," he recalled in *Gramophone* (October 1977), "I couldn't understand why it all sounded so different from the beautiful velvety quality of the performance I had heard under Talich four years before. Also, I was quite bewildered by the huge amount of corrections I had to make to the parts, not only in phrasing, rhythm, and tempo but even in the notes themselves." The questions that arose resulted in his making many trips back to Czechoslovakia to Janáček's publisher, Universal Editions, in order to compare the composer's original work with the copies used for publication.

What he and many enthusiasts of Czech music began to realize was the drastic extent to which Janáček's scores had been altered by copyists and earlier editors, who were bent on "correcting" compositional innovations that they regarded as examples of clumsiness and error. Consequently, Mackerras began a thirty-year process of reconciling and rethinking disparate editions of the operas and their original scores. By the late 1970s, Mackerras was not only the leading Janáček interpreter outside of Czechoslovakia but also the editor of several authoritative scores for publication as well as performance. He conducted the first British performances of *The Makropoulos Affair* (1964) and *From The House Of The Dead* (1965), the premiere of his own edition of *Káťa Kabanová* (1973), and *Jenufa* (1974) at Covent Garden. Sir Charles Mackerras has also conducted the operas in Brno, and was honored by Czechoslovakia in 1978 with the Janáček Medal.

Mackerras' recording career, which began in 1952 with a set of shellac discs of his own ballet score *Pineapple Poll* (EMI-Columbia), now includes the Janáček operas, in their first recordings outside of Czechoslavakia, on Decca/London. His *Káťa Kabanová* received the 1978 International Record Critics Award, and *From The House Of The Dead* won the 1981 Grammy Award as the Best Opera Recording. In Great Britain, beginning with the granting in 1978 of its first Record of the Year Award to *Káťa Kabanová*, *Gramophone* magazine has honored and acclaimed the entire operatic series.

After he left Sadler's Wells in 1953, Sir Charles Mackerras was associated for a time with Benjamin Britten's English Opera Group. He also traveled around the world as a freelance conductor in London, Europe, South Africa, Australia, and the United States, gaining a reputation for his attention to the finest points of interpretive detail. Before he made his Covent Garden debut in 1963 in a performance of Dmitri Shostakovich's *Katerina Izmailova*, he visited the Soviet Union to discuss the work with its composer. His subsequent engagements at Covent Garden included the conducting of operas by Mozart, Puccini, and Verdi. His performance of Benjamin Britten's *Peter Grimes* with the Sadler's Wells company on their 1965 appearance in Hamburg led to a series of trial engagements with the Hamburg State Opera in *Fidelio*, *Il Trovatore*, and *Così Fan Tutte* and his appointment as its conductor from 1966 through 1970.

In 1967 Sir Charles Mackerras led the English Chamber Orchestra, the Ambrosian Singers, and world-class soloists including contralto Dame Janet Baker in a recording of Handel's *Messiah* (Angel Records), based on Basil Lam's reconstructed authoritative edition of the work, which set a new standard for re-creation of Baroque performing techniques. Its authentic bowing and phrasing and judicious use of Baroque embellishment revolutionized the manner in which conductors, musicians, and listeners conceived of *Messiah* and set Mackerras apart from not only the "big band" Handelians of the past but also from some contemporary Baroque scholar-musicians. "I take a stand halfway between two opposite poles of interpretation," he told Raymond Ericson of the *New York Times* (October 7, 1979), "the old-fashioned tradition with the big symphonic style, and the performances on old instruments with the strings using no vibrato, natural horns, etc. I find the latter too bland in sound, too lacking in color. I like to do something in between, adopting the practices of Baroque and Classical times but not using old instruments. I know many people don't agree with me, and I feel this way principally about familiar music. For the less familiar, I do like old instruments." His interest in authenticity and variant editions has manifested itself in a recording of Mozart's edition of the Handel work, *Der Messias* (Deutsche Grammophon-Archiv), in German with the Austrian Radio Orchestra and Chorus and soloists including Peter Schreier and Edith Mathis. It is one of his as yet unrealized goals to record the Mozart operas using Baroque period performance technique on modern instruments, an idea to which the record companies have not yet responded favorably.

Sir Charles Mackerras' convictions about the authenticity and validity of certain scores and approaches to music-making have occasionally surprised even his supporters. In the *Opera* interview entitled "Is the Conductor the Boss?" (October 1967), he cited to Arthur Jacobs the example of a production of *Carmen* he once conducted for which he elected to use Ernest Guiraud's 1875 grand-opera adaptation, with large cuts and recitatives in place of the authentic comic-opera original. He attributed that decision to his realistic appraisal of the forces available to him: "The fact that some of the singers were French would only show up the others—in speech. Whereas in singing, the fact that some of the performers do not pronounce the French really correctly hardly detracts from their performances."

During the late 1960s and throughout the 1970s Mackerras perfected his sense of dramatic pacing in opera houses around the world. In addition to becoming one of London's leading Wagnerian specialists, building on the scaffolding of the pioneering work of Reginald Goodall at the English National Opera (formerly Sadler's Wells), he became a guest conductor at all of the world's major opera houses. His debut at the Metropolitan Opera House on October 31, 1972 in a performance of Gluck's *Orfeo ed Euridice* was singled out for praise by Harold C. Schonberg in the *New York Times* (November 2, 1972), except for the indistinct presence of the harpsichord in the orchestral sector. His other American engagements took Mackerras to Boston, Chicago, Dallas, Los Angeles, St. Louis, the San Francisco Opera, and the New York Philharmonic.

In Great Britain during the 1970s, Mackerras became a major force in the musical life of London, holding the posts of music director (1970–77) and chief guest conductor (1978–80) of the English National Opera and of chief guest conductor of the BBC Symphony Orchestra (1976–79). In recognition of his service, he was honored by the crown with the rank of Commander of the British Empire in 1974 and with a knighthood in 1978. A longtime guest conductor with the Sydney Symphony Orchestra, he returned to his hometown in 1973 to conduct one of the early opera performances at the newly inaugurated Sydney Opera House. And bringing his career full circle, in 1981 Mackerras became the first Australian to be appointed chief conductor of the Sydney Symphony Orchestra. Since 1982 he has also served on the Australian Broadcasting Commission.

In recent years, Sir Charles Mackerras has managed to work on several extended projects with the English Chamber Orchestra, with which he has enjoyed a thirty-year relationship. The most notable of these was their 1983 tour of the United States

and their recording, in the summer of 1984, of the soundtrack for a film about the life of George Frideric Handel.

A large, outgoing, gregarious man with an easy laugh and cheerful disposition, Sir Charles Mackerras seems the antithesis of the olympian, mystical conductor or the cerebral musicologist. With his reddish-blond hair and ruddy, freckled complexion, and the trace of Australian accent that lingers in his speech, he appears even less to be the dignified holder of a knighthood. He and Lady Mackerras reside in a four-story Regency house in St. John's Wood in London. Although his work takes him all over the world each season, he prefers certain cities as much for the cuisine they have to offer as for their orchestras and opera companies, most notably Paris and Aix-en-Provence. He also admits to a weakness for Manhattan's restaurants and to a passion for fine vintage wines. Lady Mackerras cited one example for Dorle J. Soria in *High Fidelity/Musical America* (January 1980): "Some years ago at a Rothschild wine sale I bought some Chateau Lafitte but was told it was not to be drunk before 1980. I did have the hardest time to keep him from drinking it."

Now that their two daughters are grown, Sir Charles and Lady Mackerras have time to pursue other major interests: sailing, and visits to Australia and their second home on the Isle of Elba. Sir Charles retains strong personal as well as professional ties to Sydney, where much of his family still lives, and to which, apart from his musical obligations, he returns as often as he can. He conceded to John Rockwell in an *Opera News* interview (July 1973) however, that even twenty-six years after his move to England, and the development of international jet travel, the journey home is still physically trying. "It takes twelve hours from Europe to Australia," he said, "and I need about a week to adjust to it."

References: *High Fi 30:7+ Jan '80; Gramophone 52:1626 Mar '75, 55:596 O '77; Guardian D 3 '71; NY Post p33 N 21 '72 por; Baker's Biographical Dictionary of Musicians (1978); Conductors on Record (1982); International Who's Who in Music and Musicians Directory, 1980; New Grove Dictionary Of Music and Musicians (1978); Who's Who, 1985–86*

## Madden, John

Apr. 10, 1936– Sports commentator; former football coach. Address: b. c/o Random House, 201 E. 50th St., New York City, N.Y. 10022; c/o CBS Sports, 51 W. 52d St., New York City, N.Y. 10019

Bluff and boisterous John Madden, formerly a football coach and currently a television pitchman and commentator, as well as author of a best-

*John Madden*

selling, entertaining autobiography, has become heralded nationwide as perhaps the best football "color caster" on the airwaves. Thirty seconds of exposure on his first Miller Lite Beer television commercial brought him more popular recognition than his decade, from 1969 to 1978, as head coach of the mighty Oakland Raiders. The youngest football coach at the time of his appointment, at thirty-three, John Madden guided his troops to seven division championships, an American Football Conference championship, and a world championship in Super Bowl XI, in 1977. With a career record of 103 games won, thirty-two lost, and seven tied, and a .763 percentage, Madden was the second coach in forty years with 100 or more victories in ten seasons—an achievement equaled only by the Miami Dolphins' Don Shula.

As Sarah Pileggi wrote of John Madden in *Sports Illustrated* (September 1, 1983): "His big, doughy, unmade bed of a face and his hulking figure are known and loved by total strangers from Meridian, Mississippi to Missoula, Montana. He is both the good-natured but slightly dangerous—to himself as well as others—goof who breaks through the paper walls in all those Miller Lite commercials and the CBS football pundit with the common touch who leads us all through television's swamps of verbal hogwash onto the high ground of enlightenment."

John Madden was born in Austin, Minnesota, on April 10, 1936, the son of Earl and Mary (O'Flaherty) Madden. He has two younger sisters, Dolores and Judy. His family moved to Daly City, California, south of San Francisco, when he was six. He played his first football and baseball games in the small vacant lot behind his family's house. Working as a batboy for the Sarto Athletic Club at nearby Marchbank Park, he recycled the discard-ed baseballs and splintered bats for his own use. John Madden's best friend, whom he considered almost like a brother, was John Robinson, who later became coach of the University of Southern California Trojans football team and then head coach of the Los Angeles Rams. They met in the fifth grade while at Our Lady of Perpetual Help School. "We had fun with no money," Madden reminisced in an interview in the *Los Angeles Times* (December 25, 1983). "We started as kids sneaking into things"—the movies, Seals Stadium for the baseball games, Kezar Stadium for the San Francisco Forty-niners football games, and the Cow Palace. Until Madden's father gave him an old 1940 Cadillac, the pair caught freight trains and hitched rides on the backs of trolley cars to get to San Francisco. "No kid ever had a better time growing up than I did," Madden recalled in his book. "My dad was an auto mechanic, . . . but he hated his job. That's probably why he never pushed me to get a job when I was a teenager."

At Jefferson Union High School, John Madden played basketball, football, and baseball. In the *Los Angeles Times* article (December 25, 1983), John Robinson is quoted as relating how Madden, as the school team's catcher, became "the only man in baseball who ever threw a home run" when he made a wild throw that enabled the opposing team to score on an error. In his senior year, Madden was courted by the New York Yankees and the Boston Red Sox to sign to play in the minor leagues. But while caddying for pocket-money at the San Francisco Golf and Country Club, Madden realized that "the one thing all those very successful guys had in common was that they'd gone to college." In 1954 he and John Robinson enrolled at the University of Oregon on football scholarships. Temporarily disabled by a knee operation during his first year, Madden returned to California to attend the College of San Mateo near his home and also spent a semester at Grays Harbor College in Aberdeen, Washington. When California Polytechnic State University at San Luis Obispo recruited him, he switched from his earlier pre-law major to education. In 1957 and 1958 he was all-conference tackle, as well as a baseball catcher. After receiving his B.S. degree in education in 1959, Madden joined the Philadelphia Eagles, who had drafted him in the twenty-first round, as a guard.

But rookie John Madden was never to play in a National Football League game, for in one of his first scrimmages at the Eagles' training camp, a ball-carrier tripped over his left leg, injuring ligaments and cartilage in Madden's knee. While undergoing treatment all that season in Philadelphia, Madden started to think in earnest about coaching as a career. He watched game films of other teams alongside the star quarterback Norman Van Brocklin, listening carefully to the comments of the future Hall of Famer and learning from him "the basic philosophy of being a coach." He returned to Cal Poly to pursue an M.A. degree in education, which he obtained in 1961, and he continued to take courses in physical education until he was within a year of a doctorate. While practice teaching at San Luis Obispo High School, Madden coached the entire football team in spring practice for a three-week stint that led to his first official position, from 1960 to 1962, as line coach at Allan Hancock Junior College in Santa Maria, California. After serving as head coach at Hancock from 1962 to 1964, Madden moved to California State University at San Diego, where he was defensive coordinator under Don Coryell from 1964 through 1966. During his three years there, the Aztecs, with a record of 8-2, 8-2, and 11-0, were the top-ranked small-college team in the United States. In addition to fulfilling his coaching duties, Madden taught health, recreation, and physical education at both the junior college and the university, and that teaching experience helped to prepare him for his chosen career. "Coaching football is basically the same thing," Madden has observed. "You teach in meetings. You discuss on the practice field. You test in the game." To enhance his competence in his chosen field, Madden attended many coaches' clinics, including an eight-hour lecture on a single play, "The Green Bay Sweep," by the famed Vince Lombardi.

In 1967 John Madden was mustered into professional football by the American Football League's Oakland Raiders, as linebacker coach under head coach John Rauch. That year the Raiders compiled a 13-1 record, the best in AFL history, and won the league's championship, but in 1968 they were overpowered in Super Bowl II by the Green Bay Packers, 33 to 14. When Rauch departed suddenly to join the Buffalo Bills because of clashes with the Raiders' managing general partner, Al Davis, John Madden was elevated to the position of head coach on February 4, 1969. "He relates well to people," Davis declared succinctly of Madden's qualifications. Football prognosticators believed that Madden was tapped because he had a firm grounding in fundamental football and, in contrast to the self-proclaimed organizational "genius," Al Davis, his personality was, in the words of Wells Twombly in *Sport* (November 1976), "comfortably low-key and suitably obscure."

As Madden later wrote, he regarded himself not as head coach *per se*, but as "*learning* how to be the head coach—learning as I went along, learning from other people's advice, learning from what I remembered." Soon after he took over, Madden innovated the now common practice of conducting minicamps for rookies before regular training camp, partly for the opportunity to practice for his own benefit. In 1969 the Raiders posted the best season mark in pro football, 12-1-1, winning their third consecutive AFL Western division title, and John Madden was named the league's coach of the year.

During his ten years at Oakland the untrumpeted Madden developed into an outstanding coach, winning games when his team was beset with problems and never suffering a losing season. With the merger realignment in 1970, the Raiders joined the Western Division of the American Football Conference in the National Football League. That year the Raiders had to restructure their defense, but Madden managed to bring the team into the playoffs and he nearly did so again the following year. Finishing 10-3-1 in his fourth season, Madden's team forfeited a trip to the Super Bowl to the Pittsburgh Steelers by a fluke. On December 23, 1972 a disputable pass deflection on the fourth down in the final twenty-two seconds scratched Oakland's 7-6 lead. A fuming Madden later tried to prove that the Steelers and the officials had stolen the game, but the blurred game films proved inconclusive. The Steelers' victory, as Art Rosenbaum noted in the *San Francisco Chronicle* (July 15, 1979), remained a persistent controversy. In 1973 the Raiders were back in the AFC championship game with a 33-14 playoff win over Pittsburgh but then lost 27 to 10 to the Miami Dolphins.

"Nobody helped me maintain the Raiders at a high level more than Al did," Madden has recalled, contradicting those who viewed the coach as a mere puppet of Al Davis, the team's managing general partner. Davis, who had coached the team from 1963 to 1966, when he became the AFL commissioner who masterminded the merger with the NFL, admitted that he was still trying to coach during Rauch's incumbency but was now intent on functioning "strictly in the capacity of an advisory assistant coach." At first, Madden would often ask Davis for advice, but as he became more knowledgeable about pro football, he became more independent. He bucked Davis for the first time in 1973 when he placed Horace Jones at defensive end instead of Davis' choice, Bubba Smith. A long-running difference of opinion that Madden mentioned in his book involved Davis' contention that a team should be built with cornerbacks and his own view, favoring offensive linemen. In 1974, Madden's Raiders, with twelve wins and two losses, garnered the best record in the NFL and defeated the world-champion Miami Dolphins in the AFC playoffs, 28 to 26. On January 4, 1976 the Raiders were outperformed by the Pittsburgh Steelers, 16 to 10, in the AFC championship game. Proud of his squad, Madden asserted, as quoted in *Sport* (November 1976): "I just don't consider the Raiders to be losers because we aren't in the Super Bowl. . . . The Oakland Raiders were winners, too. We had a fantastic year in seventy-five. Only a fool would call us losers." But Madden was miffed when a newsman addressed him as "Al." "My name's John. That's a helluva thing at this point," he sputtered, as quoted by Dave Anderson in the *New York Times* (January 6, 1979).

Despite four other job offers over the years, including one from the New York Jets, John Madden did not want to leave the Raiders, and especially Al Davis, whom he described as "my friend, about the best I've ever had." In the interview in *Sport* (November 1976), he reminded Wells Twombly: "Most head coaches have to make their reports to people who aren't football men, guys who don't understand. Would you rather talk to Al Davis or to a guy who owns an oil company?" Aware that coaching "isn't a popularity contest," Madden said, "I'm not out to make a name for myself. . . . This is a cooperative effort and I'm a happy man." As Twombly pointed out, John Madden was "the most successful unknown coach in the world," the only helmsman who ever won seventy games in his first seven years, coached six division championships in that span, and commanded more winning streaks of five games or better than any other active coach.

The Super Bowl XI coup was finally in Madden's grasp on January 9, 1977, when the Raiders walloped the Minnesota Vikings, 32 to 14, at the Rose Bowl in Pasadena. The 1976 season had been especially burdensome for Madden because of an onslaught of charges of "dirty play" on the part of the Raiders. With a patched-up team weakened by injuries in training camp, he switched to a three linemen–four linebackers defense from a four-three formation. In addition, he aimed for an entirely unpredictable offense. As described by William N. Wallace in the New York Times (January 11, 1977), Madden used psychological approaches to build confidence in his players. Significantly, Bud Grant's Vikings had reached the Super Bowl three times in the preceding four years, while the Raiders had not attained that goal in nine years. Oakland dominated the game, particularly the first half, running forty-eight plays and controlling the ball for twenty-one-and-a-half minutes of a possible thirty. "We didn't throw much in the second half," Madden said, "because our two interceptions led to touchdowns." Al Davis commented at the time: "I am especially happy for John Madden today. This will establish him as one of the truly great coaches in the game from an organization standpoint. And it's just a matter of time before he is recognized as the greatest coach." On January 29, 1977 Madden was named the Washington Touchdown Club's coach of the year, and in 1979 he was the first coach to be honored with the Vince Lombardi Dedication Award.

After the excitement of Super Bowl XI, Madden began to contemplate giving up coaching. His ambition of winning 100 games in his first ten years was realized on November 5, 1978, when he became the thirteenth coach in NFL history—and the second in forty years—to rack up 100 victories. His final tally was 103 games won. Madden's distinction was that he had accomplished that record with the same team. And his winning percentage of .790 at the beginning of the 1978 season was the best all-time record for NFL coaches with fifty or more wins. Madden was, however, beginning to burn out, and at summer minicamp in 1978 he developed a stomach ulcer. That year for the first time since 1971, the Raiders, with nine wins and seven losses, missed the playoffs. A major factor in Madden's decision was the plight of Darryl Stingley, the wide receiver for the New England Patriots who collided with the Raiders' free safety, Jack Tatum, in an exhibition game on August 12, 1978 and was paralyzed with a broken neck. Madden quietly made daily visits to Stingley, but he felt that "not

enough people seemed to care." Another factor, Madden indicated, was a conversation with his wife that corrected his assumption, brought on by his confused state of mind, that his older son was at that time about twelve when he was actually sixteen. At a press conference on January 4, 1979 Madden emotionally announced: "I'm not resigning, quitting for doing anything else. I'm retiring. I'll never coach another game of football. I gave it everything I had for ten years, and I don't have any more." Al Davis then put Madden on the Raiders' administrative staff in charge of "special projects."

"Madden: A Frank and 'Human' Leader" was the title of a profile in the New York Times (January 9, 1977), which noted that "not many football coaches are so free of ego display as Madden, so outspoken in common-sense terms, so down to earth in player relations." Working successfully with varied eccentrics—problem players from other teams who were astutely scouted by Al Davis—Madden brought a sense of stability to them through his communication skills and genuine concern. When they got into scrapes, "John would be there night and day, fighting to help them," as Raider guard Gene Upshaw remarked. With regard to his perception of his men, Madden explained in a profile in Sports Illustrated (September 1, 1983): "I don't know that I ever had a great player that was normal. To get outstanding performance you get some people that are a little left of plumb. I believed in letting them alone, personality-wise, giving them freedom, not thwarting them. In football," he continued, "you're doing things that aren't normal—running at high speed, hitting and being hit, and getting tired and sore and hurt. . . . Yet some coaches want that same person to take off his gear and go be normal."

Madden had only a few rules of his own. In his book he wrote: "To me, discipline in football occurs on the field, not off it. Discipline is knowing what you're supposed to do and doing it as best you can. On the field, the Raiders were, and are, a disciplined team. On third down and short yardage, the Raiders don't jump offside. That's discipline—not a coat and tie, not a clean shave. I had only three rules on the Raiders—be on time, pay attention, and play like hell when I tell you to." Pep talks did not figure in Madden's mode of operation. And he considered game plans "overrated" because they do not take into account the unplanned human factor. "Is the guy hurt? Is he tired? Have we beaten on him awhile?" Madden asks.

Discovering that members of his family had become accustomed to going their own ways during his absences, John Madden felt restless in retirement. He soon embarked on several new occupations in 1979—teaching, acting in commercials, and broadcasting commentaries on television and radio. At the University of California at Berkeley, he held two-day seminars on "Man to Man Football." He also wrote a weekly newspaper column and presented motivational speeches for corporation executives. Hired by Miller Lite, to his surprise he encountered instant fame with his first beer commercial.

As a media "coach," John Madden continued to enjoy the football "season" he craved since boyhood. Joining CBS-TV as an "extra analyst" in 1979, Madden took over three years later as the network's number-one analyst and color commentator alongside veteran play-by-play announcer Pat Summerall, with his first Super Bowl assignment in 1982. Using the Telestrator Chalkboard in the broadcast booth, Madden diagrams plays as he did on the field. One of his assets is his uncommon ability to see and recall each man in an entire play. CBS producer John Silman credits Madden with having "added a new dimension to broadcasting" by bridging "the gap betwen the too-technical and the too-entertaining." As Steve Gelman wrote in TV Guide (January 8, 1983), "Madden has an eye for our idiosyncrasies, an ear for our quirks, and a mind that delivers them back with an original tilt." And John Leonard wrote wryly in New York (January 9, 1984) of Madden's imminent coverage of Super Bowl XVIII: "We need him because we are otherwise in danger of confusing fun and games with serious news." In 1981 and 1982, John Madden was presented with television Emmy awards in the sports personality analyst category, and in 1982 he was the first color commentator to receive the Golden Mike award from the Touchdown Club of America.

"I'll tell ya something," Madden often says in opening his commentary, which is exuberantly punctuated with the same gestures he uses in his conversations with people in trains and hotel lobbies. As classified by Ray Kennedy in his article "Clear the Tracks for Big John" in Sports Illustrated (November 17, 1980), Madden's characteristic gestures include "the point, a wagging, accusatory jab; the touchdown, a rapid pumping of both hands overhead; the explosion, a smashing of right fist into left palm; the boogie, a series of uppercuts with fingers wiggling and hips swaying; and the double sweep, a backward swing with both arms that has been known to fell potted palms and an occasional passerby." In his broadcasts, Madden tries to avoid presenting his personal opinions and experiences or repeating clichés. He briefs himself thoroughly by studying media guides and newspaper clippings about opposing teams, attending football practice, watching game films and videotapes, and chatting with players and coaches off the record. Dispensing with notes in the broadcast booth, he depends on his "instantaneous reaction to the monitor." In one interview, Madden asserted, "The key to the whole thing is to be natural. . . . I talk and act like I would if I were talking things over with my quarterback or my wife."

Toiling with less intensity in broadcasting than he did in coaching but with similar dedication, John Madden does much of his homework in a leisurely manner on his cross-country trips between California and New York. He admits to claustrophobia and a fear of flying that dates back to 1960, when a plane carrying the Cal Poly San Luis Obispo football team crashed and some of his friends perished. Traveling by train allows Madden time for recreational reading, mainly biographies of celebrities ranging from George Steinbrenner to Luciano Pavarotti, and to indulge his hobbies of people-watching and conversation. A confirmed advocate of AMTRAK, Madden says, "The train is the closest I've come to fulfilling my fantasy of seeing America as John Steinbeck did in his book, Travels with Charley, with his dog."

Madden's list of activities continues to increase. With Dave Anderson, he wrote the genial little volume Hey, Wait a Minute, I Wrote a Book!, published by Random House in 1984, in which he relates his own life and anecdotes about the Raiders. In addition to his industrial film credits and the Miller commercials, Madden has made commercials for Krylon spray paint and MIC Insurance. He has appeared as guest host on Saturday Night Live on NBC-TV but rejected a regular role on the hit NBC Thursday-night sitcom Cheers because it would have conflicted with his other commitments.

John Madden is married to the former Virginia Fields, whom he met while they were both working on M.A. degrees in education. Their son Michael is a student at Harvard University, and the other son, Joseph, attends the Choate School in Wallingford, Connecticut. The Maddens, who have two English bulldogs, divide their time between their ranch-style tract home in Pleasanton, a suburb southeast of Oakland, and a duplex apartment at the Dakota on Manhattan's Central Park West.

As a broadcaster, Madden projects the same image as he did as coach of the Oakland Raiders—"corpulence, wrapped in sartorial indifference," in the words of Peter J. Boyer in the Los Angeles Times (January 23, 1982). Six feet four inches tall and weighing 270 pounds, Madden has blue eyes and reddish-blond hair that looks "as if combed with his ax," according to one waggish observer. Usually in shirt sleeves, he has been described as looking "like a lumpy laundry bag." Madden doffs his mandatory CBS blazer whenever he can and takes every opportunity to keep his shoelaces untied. Glen Dickey, writing in the San Francisco Chronicle (October 9, 1978), has commented on Madden: "There is depth to the man. He is no saint, to be sure. He has his share of human weaknesses; he can be rude and overbearing and bullying. . . . But he has a genuine concern for other people, and not just those who can do him some good."

References: Los Angeles Times II p1+ Ja 23 '82 por, III p3+ D 19 '82 por, III p1+ D 25 '83 por; N Y Times p35 Ja 6 '77, V p3 Ja 9 '77, p14 Ja 6 '79 por; Newsweek 103:66+ Ja 9 '84 pors; People 17:99+ Ja 25 '82 pors: Sport 63:45+ N '76 pors, 74:59 Ag '83 por; Sporting News 187:31 Ja 20 '79 por; Sports Illus 53:77+ N 17 '80, 59:38+ S 1 '83 pors; TV Guide 31:20+ Ja 8 '83 pors; Washington Post C p3+ Ja 8 '84 pors; Madden, John and Anderson, Dave. Hey, Wait a Minute, I Wrote a Book! (1984); Who's Who in America, 1984-85

## Marton, Eva

(mär-tôn´)

*June 18, 1943– Opera singer. Address: b. Eric Semon Associates, 111 W. 57th St., New York City, N.Y. 10019; Metropolitan Opera, Lincoln Center, New York City, N.Y. 10023*

Since 1968, when she made her debut at the Budapest State Opera house, the Hungarian dramatic soprano Eva Marton has forged her way into the front rank of world-class operatic singers. Her technically brilliant, vocally secure, and psychologically convincing interpretations of some of the most demanding roles in opera, including that of Leonore in Beethoven's *Fidelio* and that of the title role in Puccini's *Turandot,* have been favorably compared to the performances of the legendary soprano Birgit Nilsson, now retired, and have made her one of the most sought-after singers at the world's leading opera houses. Although she now commands a repertoire of more than forty roles in four languages, Eva Marton is continually looking for such new challenges as the role of Brünnhilde in Wagner's *Ring,* which she sang with great success at the San Francisco Opera in 1985, and she plans to portray all of Wagner's heroines eventually. "This was a path I picked out for myself," she explained to Michael Walsh of *Time* (December 19, 1983). "I want to do these roles while I am still young. My voice is probably the most profound expression of myself, of my deepest thoughts that I cannot and do not speak. The time I have been waiting for has come."

Eva Marton was born Eva Heinrich on June 18, 1943 in Budapest, Hungary, about a year and a half before the city was almost destroyed at the hands of battling German and Soviet troops. "It was very hard for [my parents], after the war," she told Peter

Goodman of *Newsday* (January 8, 1984), "because they had to start all over again." Even though her father was a famous chef at the Hotel Bristol in Budapest and a lecturer at the High School for Culinary Science, her family was in such straitened circumstances that she did not get her first pair of shoes until she was six years old.

Nevertheless, Eva Marton remembers her childhood as a pleasant time, partly because of her early discovery of music. When she was five, she heard someone singing on the radio and, enthralled, began singing herself. "I don't know why," she told Peter Goodman. "When I sang, I was very glad, I was very happy." Her first instrument, however, was the piano, which she studied for three years. "My teacher was a pupil of Bartók, a wonderful woman," Marton recalled for Thomas P. Lanier in *Opera News* (February 12, 1983). "But I didn't have the patience, the nerves or the talent to make it my career. On the other side, she told me I had a marvelous voice, so I changed my studies to singing when I was fourteen." She could not afford an opera ticket until she was fifteen, but a year later she attended a performance of Wagner's *Lohengrin,* which made an indelible impression on her.

As a teenager, Eva Marton sang folksongs, appeared in operas staged for schoolchildren, and sang for two years in the Budapest Radio Chorus before entering the Ferenc Liszt Academy of Music in Budapest, where her teachers included the famous tenor Endre Roessler. In Hungary, or any Eastern bloc nation, she explained in an interview with Gary Lipton in the *New York Times* (November 28, 1982), "music was an ideal profession. The state subsidized all my studies at the Liszt Academy . . . and I followed a rigorous curriculum." While working on her voice and technique and studying Italian, she played on the Hungarian National Volleyball team. "When I started adding two or three pounds a year," she told Lipton, "it was time to hang up the uniform." However, she credits the breathing and stamina she developed as an athlete with helping her to perfect the physical side of her musicianship. After her stunning interpretation of the soprano role in the last act of Puccini's *Manon Lescaut,* which she performed as her final examination at the Liszt Academy, Eva Marton graduated with honors, receiving diplomas in both opera singing and singing instruction.

While a student she had met Zoltán Marton, a medical intern only a few years older than herself. "She came in complaining of a stomach ache," he recalled for Lanier in *Opera News* (February 12, 1983). "It was two in the morning, and I was half asleep, but one look and I instantly woke up. Later that morning . . . I went to her house. Her father reluctantly let me in. Here was this barefoot girl, a mass of red hair covering her pillow, dressed in a flimsy nightgown. I told her she had an intestinal virus, not appendicitis. Then I asked for a date." The two were married while Eva was still at the Liszt Academy, and despite opposition from her mother, she chose to take her husband's name and pursue her career as Eva Marton. The early years of their marriage, however, proved very difficult. "My husband's father, also a physician, gave up his practice so we could live in his examining room," she told Annalyn Swan of *Newsweek* (December 19, 1983). "One corner was for the baby, one for our bed, one for the piano and the fourth for an armoire. But something inside me kept saying, 'Out, out, out: your voice is your passport out of this misery.'"

Joining the Budapest Opera in 1968, she made her debut there in the coloratura role of the Queen in Rimsky-Korsakov's *Le Coq d'Or*, though she considers the speaking part of the Queen in Szokolay's *Hamlet* to have been her actual debut. During a little more than three years with that company, she added more than eight roles to her repertoire, including the Puccini heroines Manon Lescaut and Tosca and the Countess Almaviva in Mozart's *The Marriage of Figaro*, but she first gained wider attention as Freia in its Hungarian-language version of Wagner's *Das Rheingold*. After the internationally acclaimed conductor Christoph von Dohnányi, then the director of the Frankfurt Opera, heard her sing that part, he offered her a series of guest appearances in 1971 as Alice Fell in the Frankfurt Opera production of Verdi's *Falstaff*. Before undertaking that role, she went on tour with the Budapest State Opera, during which she sang Virtù in Monteverdi's *L'Incoronazione di Poppea* and Manon Lescaut at the Bolshoi Theater in Moscow. Later in 1971, she portrayed the avenging Odabella in Verdi's *Attila* and made her Italian debut in the thirty-fifth Maggio Musicale Fiorentino festival as Mathilde in Rossini's *William Tell*, conducted by Riccardo Muti.

During her five seasons with the Frankfurt Opera, she appeared at a number of other opera houses throughout Europe, including the Vienna State Opera, where she sang Tatyana in a new production of Tchaikovsky's *Eugene Onegin*. In addition, she gave her first performance in the United States—in the February 23, 1975 world premiere of Alan Hovhaness' *The Way of Jesus* at St. Patrick's Cathedral in New York—and on November 3, 1976 made her American operatic debut as Eva in Wagner's *Die Meistersinger von Nürnberg* at the Metropolitan Opera in New York. "Those were difficult but rewarding years," Marton recalled for Lanier, "because I was able to build my entire repertory. In one insane year, for example, I learned eight operas, including *Aïda*, *Un Ballo in Maschera*, *La Forza del Destino*, *Die Meistersinger*, all in the original language. I wanted to move on from Frankfurt, however, and was lucky that Dohnányi became Intendant in Hamburg and brought me there on a per-evening contract which, *Gott sei Dank*, left me free for guest appearances."

One such guest appearance—as Tosca in a 1977 production at Marseilles—provided her with her first great triumph and proved to be a "key that opened many doors." Since she performed Tosca at the Vienna State Opera in 1973 (her first appear-

ance there and the first time she sang the role in Italian), she had won praise for her interpretation of the part, but "after the [Marseilles] performance," she recalled in the *Opera News* interview, "there were so many people crowding around that I couldn't leave until the police came. I worked hard and honestly for many years to earn such acclaim." Marton has since sung Tosca at more than twenty opera houses. For her exceptional portrayal of the role at La Scala in 1980, in a performance that featured Luciano Pavarotti and Ingvar Wixell and had Seiji Ozawa on the podium, she was awarded the Silver Rose and named Italy's Singer of the Year. Her debut as Elisabeth and Venus in *Tannhäuser* on August 1, 1977 at the Bayreuth Festival, a role she reprised there the following year, was also well received. "How refreshing it was to hear a new Venus/Elisabeth," James Helme Sutcliffe wrote in *Opera News* (October 1977), "both encompassed by an appealing bright soprano voice with a not unattractive 'beat' that receded to perfect control in the pianissimos of the prayer."

Continuing her string of taxing soprano roles, on June 17, 1978 Eva Marton made her debut at La Scala in Milan as Leonora in Verdi's *Il Trovatore*, under the baton of Zubin Mehta. Later that year she appeared there as Amalia in a revival of Pier Luigi Pizzi's production of Verdi's *I Masnadieri* and also essayed the role of Judith, the fourth of Bluebeard's ill-fated wives, in Béla Bartók's *Duke Bluebeard's Castle*. She was particularly pleased to take part in the latter production, since it was the first Hungarian opera to be performed at La Scala in the original language. During the 1978–79 season, Marton also returned to the Metropolitan Opera to give a favorably received performance as Chrysothemis, the gentler younger sister in Strauss's *Elektra*, her first appearance in that role on a major stage. Next, she earned encomiums when, expanding her Wagnerian repertoire, she portrayed Elsa in *Lohengrin* at the Teatro Colón in Buenos Aires on September 18, 1979. Assessing that performance for *Opera* (March 1, 1980), Eduardo Arnosi unequivocally termed it "undoubtedly the best Elsa heard here since the unforgettable Rose Bampton in 1942."

Eva Marton credits Gerard Mortier, the director of the Brussels Opera, with encouraging her to undertake her most challenging roles. "He persuaded me to attempt the 'impossible' parts," she told Gary Lipton of the *New York Times* (November 28, 1982), "like the Empress in *Die Frau Ohne Schatten*. Every time I threw down the Strauss score and cried, 'No, never, I can't do it!,' Mortier gave me the courage to pick it up and start again." She not only mastered that exacting role—after working on it every day for six months—but made it a hallmark of her repertoire. After giving acclaimed performances of the Empress in Hamburg with Dohnányi and in Geneva, she enjoyed, by her own account, one of "the greatest successes of [her] career" when she sang that role in a Teatro Colón production that featured Birgit Nilsson as the

Dyer's Wife. For that performance, her debut at that house, and for her appearance there as Elsa in *Lohengrin*, the Argentine Republic named her the best *débutante* of all time. Moreover, it was her first performance in *Die Frau* at New York's Metropolitan Opera on October 12, 1981 that finally established her among American aficionados of opera as a soprano of world-class stature.

The production's drawing card had been Birgit Nilsson in her first Met performance as the Dyer's Wife, but it was Eva Marton who captivated press and public alike with the searing brightness of her opulent instrument and with her confident, seemingly effortless delivery of the role's demanding high C's and D's. In a glowing review in *New York* magazine (October 26, 1981), critic Peter G. Davis summed up the shared reaction: "At the end, Nilsson received the respect due an old favorite, but Marton was greeted with the tumultuous approval of an audience that had unexpectedly discovered a star."

Recalling that Met appearance during the *Opera News* interview, Eva Marton said, "How can I fully explain what that evening meant? I knew exactly who had sung this role before. I knew exactly that my time had come. I knew exactly that I had to grab this chance. I knew exactly what I know and what I can do. What I didn't know was how the public would accept me. . . . This evening was important because it was a measure of how far I had come, how strong I am." Other Metropolitan triumphs followed: her Venus/Elisabeth in *Tannhäuser* (November 29, 1982); Leonore in *Fidelio* (December 14, 1983), in a production that marked the Met debut of the conductor Klaus Tennstedt; and Ortrud in *Lohengrin* (September 24, 1984).

Her work in the Met's *Die Frau Ohne Schatten* led directly to Eva Marton's next substantial success in the United States. As she recalled in *Opera News* (February 12, 1983), during their last performance of that opera, Birgit Nilsson offered her some advice. "'You know,'" she quoted Miss Nilsson as saying, "'I've been thinking over what would be a good part for you. . . . Turandot—I made my career with that one.'" On November 27, 1983 Eva Marton made her American debut as Puccini's imperious Chinese princess in the Opera Company of Boston's lavish 1983 production that also starred the tenor James McCracken as Calaf and Sarah Reese in the soprano role of Liù. Michael Walsh rhapsodized in *Time* (December 19, 1983) that Eva Marton's dazzling interpretation of the glacial Turandot "could serve as an object lesson in how the role should be sung," and in an equally rapturous review in *Newsweek* (December 19, 1983), Annalyn Swan declared that "even more than her fire-and-ice performance as the Empress in the Met's 'Die Frau,' . . . Turandot establishes Marton as the crown princess of the dramatic-soprano repertory." Her beautifully sung and skillfully acted Brünnhilde in the acclaimed San Francisco Opera production of Wagner's *Ring* in 1985 fully justified such high praise.

Although she studies the correspondence of the composer and librettist, their other works, and critical analyses, Eva Marton's approach to a new role is subjective as well as technical, as much a matter of resonating to a dramatic setting as mastering a musical score. Furthermore, she is always careful that "[her] every sound and gesture [is] rooted in the dramatic situation," and she credits the director Götz Friedrich, with whom she worked at Bayreuth, Munich, and Hamburg, with helping her learn how to move in a theatrically effective manner.

Her preparation for her debut in Amilcare Ponchielli's *La Gioconda*, which she described to Thomas P. Lanier in *Opera News*, is typical. "It is no news what [the librettist Arrigo] Boito himself thought of this miserable text, so what should I say about it? Right from the beginning I saw the big difficulty would be how to make this part believable. If I can't believe it, how can I present it to the audience? So I tried to find something relevant, and what I came up with is the anguish of loving a man more than he loves you." But she was still not content. "I spent many sleepless nights searching for [Gioconda's] moment of decision," she further explained in the *New York Times* interview with Gary Lipton. "Finally, I heard it in the orchestra, that stabbing C-sharp chord that precedes the aria. These little things make all the difference in the best performances."

Her meticulous preparation was generously rewarded. Like most critics, Peter G. Davis became ecstatic over that September 1984 Metropolitan Opera production of *La Gioconda*, which also marked the first appearance there of Placido Domingo as Enzo. "Here at last," Davis wrote in *New York* magazine (October 11, 1984), "was an honest-to-God dramatic soprano who met the vocal challenges of the role without compromising." "The flamboyant temperament that made her Gioconda such a vivid character, passionately involved during every moment of this supercharged melodrama," Davis concluded, rendered hers "a performance of thrilling intensity."

Despite her grueling schedule of appearances around the world, Eva Marton has found time for making recordings. Her discography includes several albums for Hungarian labels, among them Verdi's *La Forza del Destino* and Mendelssohn's *Midsummer Night's Dream*, as well as three for CBS: Erich Korngold's *Violanta* with the Munich Radio Orchestra; *Turandot*, performed with the cast from the Vienna State Opera production and conducted by Lorin Maazel; Beethoven's *Ah! Perfido*, with the English Chamber Orchestra; *Die Walküre*, under the baton of Zubin Mehta; and an all-Strauss recording with the Toronto Symphony Orchestra. Her first solo album was a recording of Wagner's arias and operatic scenes for the Sefel label, with the Philharmonia Orchestra under the direction of Arpad Joo.

Eva Marton is a striking redhead with a speaking voice that, according to Thomas P. Lanier in *Opera News* (February 12, 1983), is "a plummy mix of Hildegard Knef and Eva Gabor." Throughout her career, she has tried to strike a balance between the demands of her art and her life with her husband, Zoltán, and their two children: Zoltán Jr. and Diana. She relishes the little time she can spend at home in Hamburg, where she and her family have lived since her engagement with the Hamburg Opera in 1977, and she occasionally takes her children with her when she has to travel. Her husband, who maintains a surgical practice in Hamburg, also travels with her as her business manager. Eva Marton confesses to being too busy to feel homesick for Budapest, but as a cook—when she finds time to cook—she likes to create variations on native Hungarian goulash, and as a musician, she continues to take an interest in the music of her homeland. For example, she is eager to record Franz Liszt's oratorio St. Elisabeth, because if she, a Hungarian, does not do it, "who," she asks, "will?"

Although Eva Marton continually adds challenging roles to her repertoire, to protect her voice she is careful not to accept a part for which she is not yet ready. In Opera News (February 12, 1983), she explained her rationale with one of her favorite jokes: "There were two bulls standing in the hills looking down on a valley where there were many cows grazing. The young one said, 'Oh, I have to go down there right now. I need one of those beautiful cows.' The old bull gave him advice: 'Go slow and have them all.' This is my philosophy when it comes to my repertory, my career and my life."

References: Newsday II p19 Ja 8 '84 pors; N Y Times II p1+ N 28 '82 por; Opera News 47:9+ F 12 '83 pors; Who's Who in America, 1984-85; Who's Who in American Music: Classical (1982); Who's Who in Opera (1976); Wilkens, Carol. Eva Marton (1982)

## McEwen, Terence A(lexander)

Apr. 13, 1929- Opera director. Address: b. San Francisco Opera Association, War Memorial Opera House, 301 Van Ness Ave., San Francisco, Calif. 94102

One of the world's leading connoisseurs of the singing voice, Terence ("Terry") McEwen realized a lifelong dream when on January 1, 1982 he took over the direction of the San Francisco Opera. A fanatical opera lover since childhood, McEwen is only the third man to manage America's second-ranking opera house, succeeding Kurt Herbert Ad-

ler who became its director on the death of the company's founder, Gaetano Merola. McEwen, who had never before managed an opera company, was formerly the executive vice-president in charge of the classical music division of London Records. The judicious choice of an opera aficionado and astute business executive combined in one person seems to have paid off, for at the end of its 1984 season the San Francisco Opera found itself not only critically acclaimed but solvent once more.

Terence Alexander McEwen was born in Thunder Bay, Ontario on April 13, 1929, the son of a steamship executive, but grew up in Montreal, where he attended Strathcona Academy and took pre-law courses at Sir George Williams College. He used to listen to the Metropolitan Opera's Saturday afternoon radio broadcasts while doing his homework and according to Robert Jacobson of Opera News (October 1982), maintains that he has been "a maniac opera-lover since the age of twelve." At that time, McEwen and a precocious friend were already dreaming up ideal opera casts, and he was collecting opera recordings to play on the gramophone that his mother had given him as a Christmas present. When the Metropolitan Opera came on one of its annual spring tours to Montreal with the Brazilian soprano Bidù Sayão as Manon, the fourteen-year-old McEwen fell hopelessly in love.

In those days Montreal had two local opera companies in residence and was regularly visited by the companies of the Met and San Carlo. Looking back on his adolescent infatuation with the lyric stage, McEwen told Deborah Karpf of Opera Canada (July 1983): "I would also creep in after the first act without buying a ticket, when I didn't have any money, which was hard on the nerves. But when you're fourteen, fifteen, or sixteen, you don't care about nerves. Anyway, for a long time I never saw the first acts of any of my favorite operas." Later, as a college student, he helped to subsidize his passion by taking on jobs as a waiter, record-store clerk, and junior music critic for a Montreal newspaper. He traveled to New York to hear the Met during a Christmas vacation and attended opera performances in Toronto and other cities. A term paper he wrote at the time entitled "Opera As the Sublime Experience" clearly indicated where his interests lay.

Despite his father's wish that he become a lawyer, McEwen decided to travel to Europe in 1950 to study singing, and began his trip with a visit to London. Finding himself without funds and discovering that he would be unable to get a work permit while studying voice in Italy, he managed to get a job at fifteen dollars a week in the warehouse of Decca Records. Even at that minuscule wage, he spent his spare cash on recordings and opera tickets and had the good fortune to hear some of the world's greatest singers at Covent Garden.

McEwen advanced quickly at Decca Records, and when its executives discovered that he spoke fluent French, he was sent to its Paris office, where he stayed for five years before returning to London. His Paris sojourn gave him the opportunity to hear opera all over Europe and to become familiar with singers like Kirsten Flagstad, Beniamo Gigli, and others who were nearing the end of their great careers in that post–World War II era. Although McEwen's responsibilities lay ostensibly in the business rather than the artistic end of the company, his interests were much broader than marketing and sales. "I was always interfering with Decca's operatic operations, although I had no right to," he admitted during his interview with Deborah Karpf.

In 1959 McEwen was transferred to New York City to become the manager of the classical music division of London Records, Decca's American branch, which accounted for one-half of Decca's total world sales. Again he played a key role in casting and in selection of repertory, not just because he had the power to control release of recordings, but also because he had such an encyclopedic knowledge of singers and conductors.

Many budding vocal careers were promoted by McEwen, though some of his critics viewed him as merely a publicist or salesman. The veteran New York Times music critic Harold C. Schonberg emphasized his clout, however, by quoting Richard Rollefson of London Records in an article for the New York Times Magazine (November 6, 1983). In Rollefson's opinion, McEwen was "very influential in his suggestions to Decca. He also had an 'in' with singers. They would listen to his ideas, and it was Terry who was one of the strongest forces in the development of the Decca operatic catalogue." Using his lavish expense account to good advantage, he entertained artists and persuaded even some temperamental singers who did not very much care for each other to take part in the same recording project. Because he overflowed with creative ideas and

enjoyed the confidence of Decca's head, Sir Edward Lewis, McEwen was able, according to Robert Jacobson, to bring London Records "to the forefront of the business . . . especially in building certain stars." Such milestones as Joan Sutherland's early album The Art of the Prima Donna were products of McEwen's fecund mind, and he had a hand in the recording of such superstars as Luciano Pavarotti, Plácido Domingo, and Renata Tebaldi.

Above all, McEwen was a fan. When an article criticizing one of his favorites appeared in the New York Times, he was among those who rallied to her defense by writing a letter to the publication (May 20, 1973): "I am upset, hurt and outraged by the article on Renata Tebaldi because I am one of the thousands who will be eternally grateful for the unique kind of radiance this great artist has shed on me consistently since I first heard her 23 years ago." From the time he arrived in New York, McEwen's colorful personality was on display to the public. He was a mainstay of the Texaco Opera Quiz aired during the intermissions of the Saturday Met broadcasts, wrote with gusto, as in an article on the ill-fated nineteenth-century French tenor, Adolphe Nourrit (Opera News, March 9, 1963), and set to work on a biography of Rossini. Lecturing engagements and television appearances also crowded his schedule.

When Sir Georg Solti became music director of the Covent Garden opera in 1961, he approached McEwen about becoming its artistic administrator, offering him a chance to fulfill a lifelong fantasy. But there was still much for the hyperactive McEwen to achieve at London Records where, as he told Deborah Karpf, he "continued to climb the ladder" until he "ran the company." By the late 1970s he felt he had accomplished what he had set out to do and he feared the possibility of burnout. He decided to retire from London Records in 1980 and move to Hawaii, where he could produce a syndicated radio program and write books, for two of which he already had signed contracts.

At that point, in 1979, Kurt Herbert Adler offered Terry McEwen the chance to become his successor at the San Francisco Opera, thus substituting his long-held dream of running an opera company for his fantasy of a retreat to Hawaii. The dream soon became reality when, on June 7, 1979, the appointment was officially announced, with the agreement that McEwen would leave London Records in June 1980 and join the San Francisco Opera in September with a five-year contract. He and Adler were to work together until the septuagenarian Adler finally retired from the directorship and McEwen took over in January 1982.

The projected arrangement had an auspicious beginning. Allan Ulrich of the Los Angeles Times (June 9, 1979) quoted Adler's tribute to McEwen: "The San Francisco Opera must progress or it will regress. The structure is good here, and Terry has the ability to build on it. He has done a phenomenal job as an administrator, and he is a close friend to the world's greatest artists, and that includes conductors. Many of them can be expected to appear here." McEwen countered with a pledge to "continue the policy of adventurous repertory and casting offered by Maestro Adler."

While McEwen made himself acquainted with the staging and technical aspects of the San Francisco Opera, Adler directed a major expansion of its program. A new orchestra had to be developed to replace the San Francisco Symphony, which was finally getting a house and season of its own, and an ambitious spring-summer season was undertaken. Meanwhile, Adler's company continued to be, as John Rockwell put it (New York Times, July 5, 1981), "totally dominated by his authoritarian personality." McEwen remained in the background, avoiding interviews, but also making his own plans without much consultation with Adler.

Although Adler and McEwen had been warm friends for many years, so much so that Adler, trading on his long-standing credibility, had virtually forced the San Francisco Opera's board to accept his choice of a successor, the relationship soon began to turn sour. As the time neared for him to relinquish the helm, Alder began to hedge about his actual retirement date and he was outraged by a reorganization that McEwen had planned. Above all, McEwen was not using Adler's services as a conductor nearly as much as the older man had expected. Retirement for an autocrat accustomed to complete control was galling.

Over the years Adler had introduced a number of innovative adjunct companies to the San Francisco Opera's main fall season, enhancing its excellent reputation: Spring Opera, to experiment in repertory and production methods; Western Opera Theater, which took younger artists and smaller productions on tour in western towns; the educational Brown Bag Opera; Affiliate Artists, now called the Adler Fellowship Program, designed to give young artists practical experience; the American Opera Project; and the Merola Opera Program for young singers. McEwen combined all of those enterprises under one umbrella organization called the San Francisco Opera Center in order to impose a logical sequence on the training programs, and he dropped, at least for the time being, the Spring Opera, which had been Adler's special pride. Founded in 1960 with an emphasis on new and unusual operas, Spring Opera had been losing money over three recent seasons and, with an underpublicized first summer season in 1981, had left McEwen with a substantial deficit to face at the beginning of his tenure. It may also be that his avowed enthusiasm for great voices, in contrast to Adler's interest in repertory, influenced his decision.

When, in 1982, McEwen became the general director of the San Francisco Opera, the first fruits of his management soon became apparent. In March the new Center inaugurated a showcase series of performances, featuring singers who had been selected through nationwide auditions. The Summer Festival, McEwen's first international season, opened its five-opera, one-month run with Handel's Julius Caesar. Robert Jacobson of Opera News (September 1982) was happy to report that it "received miraculous handling on every level, restoring the work to its proper balance." The critic for the British publication Opera (September 1982) found the production "without doubt, more beautiful than the celebrated New York City Opera production of the '60s, but also less immediate," and pronounced the Turandot that followed it "quite exceptional." That view was not shared by Jacobson, who thought it "offered precious little to illuminate or make dramatic sense of Puccini's fairy tale." The Summer Festival concluded on July 4 with Stravinsky's The Rake's Progress.

Writing in the Summer Festival edition of San Francisco Opera (1982), McEwen discussed his preoccupation with the financial future of the company and the planning of the future seasons, and asserted that "the combination of traditional and adventurous seems appropriate for an artistic endeavor in our great city." As part of the traditional, he emphasized the need to strengthen the standard repertory. "Kurt [Adler] left me mostly icing and very little cake," he candidly told Robert Jacobson in the Opera News article. "I'm not saying my predecessor didn't have a company of great musical integrity, but some of my aims are perhaps more earthbound than his, more realistic. Kurt was a great adventurer. So am I, in a way, but my background is as a businessman and that gives me a realistic look at things." Part of that realism consists in making ends meet in a country that is much more niggardly with government subsidies for opera than is Europe. With a top fee of $8,000, McEwen can afford in any one season only a few of the superstars who are treated with greater generosity in the heavily underwritten opera houses abroad. While still at London Records, he argued that artists must be prepared to give the public what it wants in return for their high fees. In San Francisco, McEwen's seasons will balance musical rewards with financial outlay, but will always try to feature the beautiful voices he treasures most.

McEwen's first full season opened on September 10, 1982 with a benefit performance of Verdi's Un Ballo in Maschera with his predecessor, Adler, conducting and Pavarotti singing. For Bellini's Norma McEwen engaged Joan Sutherland and Marilyn Horne; Leontyne Price and Régine Crespin sang in Poulenc's Dialogues of the Carmelites. Lohengrin, Tosca, and the other productions of the season fully documented McEwen's penchant for hiring magnificent voices. As Paul Moor commented in Musical America (April 1983): "Put it all together and it adds up almost to an embarrassment of vocal riches. Even supporting roles sometimes received really memorable performances." He regretted, however, McEwen's retreat from the venturesome programming of Kurt Herbert Adler.

For the Summer Festival of 1983, McEwen launched the first two of his projected new productions of Wagner's "Ring" cycle, explaining that "if we're to have a summer festival, it is very logical in my mind to lead towards some kind of artistic unity. And Wagner was the only person who wrote a series of operas to be performed in a festival." Unable, primarily because of costs, to do all four operas in 1983, he decided to start out with *Das Rheingold* and *Die Walküre* for the Wagner centenary in 1983, add *Siegfried* in the summer of 1984, and feature the complete cycle including a new production of *Götterdämmerung* in the 1985 Summer Festival.

"Our 'Ring' has been planned as a return to romanticism, color and the kind of majestic beauty that most of the music suggests," McEwen informed representatives of the press. No devotee of contemporary stage directors, who take their ego trips at the expense of the composer's intentions, McEwen himself exercised some control over the whole production, not only the casting. Although he is not a shouter and screamer like his predecessor, he is nevertheless very firm in seeing his ideas carried out. He listens attentively and engages in consultations, but he has no interest in sharing control over artistic policy. Harold C. Schonberg in the *New York Times* (November 6, 1983) quoted him as saying: "I intend to run the place by myself."

Not surprisingly, it is in the casting of his "Ring" that McEwen has shown his true mettle. The veteran Viennese bass-baritone Walter Berry was persuaded to sing the role of Alberich for the first time, only because of his faith in McEwen's instincts about singers' voices. Similarly, McEwen convinced the American bass James Morris to be his Wotan in 1985 after many others had tried unsuccessfully to lure him into a Wagnerian role. Like many others, Morris believed that Wagnerian roles harm the voice but he went along with McEwen, who assured him that it was the Wagnerian singers whose voices lasted longest.

Critical reception of the 1983 "Ring" performances was mixed. Andrew Porter of the *New Yorker* (June 13, 1983) quarreled with the conducting, the staging, and even some points of the singing, but conceded in the end of his lengthy review that "this San Francisco half cycle is a high, serious, and beautiful achievement. . . . One looks forward eagerly to 'Siegfried' and 'Götterdämmerung.'" In the *New York Times* (June 2, 1983) Schonberg also objected to the staging but conceded, "At least McEwen is living up to his reputation as a connoisseur of voices. The cast was international, and as good as any that can be brought together today."

Since opera singers in the jet age must be signed up years in advance, the San Francisco season beginning in September 1983 with Verdi's *Otello* was really the first that was totally McEwen's. Here again, his knowledge of and personal friendships with opera stars worked to the advantage of his audience. When Sherrill Milnes had to cancel his promised Iago because of vocal problems, Silvano Carroll filled in, and when Carlo Cossutta, whom McEwen considers one of the three leading tenors for the title role, developed inflamed vocal cords on the morning of opening night, McEwen's pleading brought Plácido Domingo flying in by private jet for a late but triumphant one-night appearance to open San Francisco's season, one of those cliffhangers that seem to occur in opera more often than in any other of the performing arts.

Tight money and last-minute cancellations have plagued Terry McEwen's early years with the San Francisco Opera, but he appears to take those headaches in stride. The *Siegfried* of his 1984 Summer Festival was met with wild enthusiasm, as was the singing, if not the staging, of *Aida* and *Don Pasquale.* The innovation of having English-language subtitles projected below the proscenium arch was so widely admired that McEwen now contemplates more Russian operas. For the fall season he scheduled the little-known Mussorgsky work, *Khovanshchina,* in a production that Alan Rich, writing in *Newsweek* (December 3, 1984), declared "revealed a masterpiece worthy to stand beside the far-better-known 'Boris'." Rich quoted a gratified McEwen: "I've had a passion for Russian opera since I first saw the Bolshoi in Montreal during Expo 67, but it wasn't until we began projecting English 'supertitles' that I decided to go ahead. There's a sound quality in sung Russian that you just can't translate."

Terence McEwen concedes that the critics who worry that he is more concerned with the box-office than with artistic innovation are partly correct, but he had, with his somewhat more conservative repertory, brought the San Francisco Opera back to solvency by the end of 1984. And works such as Tippett's *The Midsummer Marriage* and Janacek's rarely heard *Katya Kabanova* of the 1983 season, not to mention the 1984 production of *Khovanshchina* and his brave new "Ring" cycle, attest to his artistic commitment.

Those critics who, along with Andrew Porter, had looked forward to a complete San Francisco "Ring" were far from disappointed when it was unveiled to standing ovations at the sold-out War Memorial Opera House in the summer of 1985. To Alan Rich of *Newsweek* the production, which was directed by Nikolaus Lehnhoff, designed by John Conklin, and conducted by Edo de Waart, was a "Ring" that was "more for the eye than for the ear," perhaps because its handsome sets, inspired by the German Romantic landscape painter Caspar David Friedrich and the German architect Friedrich Schinkel, were deliberately intended to distance the action in the nineteenth century.

Writing in the *New York Review of Books,* Joseph Kerman summed up the McEwen "Ring" as "carefully thought out, well rehearsed, and skillfully executed." John von Rhein of the *Chicago Tribune,* who considered the production "as much the 'Ring' of the '80s as Patrice Chereau's was the 'Ring' of the '70s," asserted that "there can be little doubt that this is one of the most visually appealing, musically and dramatically cogent productions in modern 'Ring' history. It deserves long life and wide exposure."

Whether presiding at the oval desk of his ample office on the fourth floor of the San Francisco War

Memorial Opera House or in his large bachelor apartment, larger-than-life Terry McEwen is surrounded by the recordings and pictures of the great musical stars he has treasured all his life. The ebullient impresario is a portly and bald six-footer, who smokes incessantly. As he often says, his idea of a wonderful evening may be to stay home and listen to his historical recordings, but he is also known as a highly gregarious person and a talented raconteur.

References: N Y Times II p15 Jl 5 '81 por; N Y Times Mag p130+ N 6 '83 por; Opera Canada p18+ Jl 9–30 '83 por; Opera News p8+ O '82 por, p30+ N '82 por

Irving Penn, courtesy Vogue, © 1983 Condé Nast

## Meier, Richard (Alan)

Oct. 12, 1934-Architect. Address: b. Richard Meier & Partners, Architects, 136 E. 57th St., New York City, N.Y. 10022

The jury that selected Richard Meier as the 1984 laureate of the Pritzker Prize, the highest accolade in architecture, cited him for his "single-minded pursuit of new directions in contemporary architecture," for his "search for clarity and his experiments in balancing light, forms, and space," and for "works which are personal, vigorous, original." Rejecting the geometric inventions and applied, historically eclectic ornamentation of post-modernism, Meier is an unrepentant modernist in the functional tradition of Le Corbusier, who defined architecture as "the masterly, correct, and magnificent play of mass brought together in light." Within that tradition, however, Meier has devel-

oped a personal, elegant style that makes him not only current but avant-garde. His gleaming white and silver buildings, clean-lined and often austerely high-tech in appearance, are actually elaborate, picturesque sculptings of space and light, in dialogue with their settings. "Fundamentally," Meier said in an address at a symposium on "The Pursuit of Excellence" sponsored by the LTV Corporation in 1981, "my meditations are on space, form, light, and how to make them. My goal is presence, not illusion." Among Meier's works are the High Museum of Art in Atlanta, Georgia, the Hartford (Connecticut) Seminary, the Atheneum in New Harmony, Indiana, several medical facilities and housing projects, and many private homes.

Richard Alan Meier was born in Newark, New Jersey on October 12, 1934 to Jerome and Carolyn (Kaltenbacher) Meier. In the questionnaire he returned to Current Biography, Meier lists two brothers, James and Thomas. Meier graduated from high school in 1952 and took his bachelor of architecture degree at Cornell University five years later. Following his graduation from college, he vacationed in Europe, where he met Le Corbusier, the Swiss architect who, in antithesis with Frank Lloyd Wright, gave modern architecture much of its aesthetics and philosophy. Whereas Wright was concerned with the horizontal extension of space and the organic blending of a building with the natural environment, Le Corbusier was an exponent of efficient urbanized architecture designed for the vertical penetration of space and based on geometric rather than organic principles. The intellectualism of Corbusier's approach was modified and warmed by his insistence on "sun, space, and silence."

Meier apprenticed in New Jersey with the architectural firm of Frank Grad & Sons (1957) and in New York with the firms of Davis, Brody & Wisniewski (1958–59), Skidmore, Owings & Merrill (1959–60), and Marcel Breuer & Associates (1960–63). While working for the Breuer firm he designed a Fire Island beach house that gave little indication of the distinctive style for which he would soon become known. During his years of apprenticeship, Meier spent many of his after-office hours working in the studio of his artist friend Frank Stella, painting large abstract-expressionist canvases and making collages. From 1960 to 1962 he was visiting architectural critic at Pratt Institute in Brooklyn, and he taught architectural design as an adjunct professor at the Cooper Union for the Advancement of Science and Art in Manhattan for eleven years beginning in 1962.

Working out of his New York City apartment, Meier in 1963 launched his private practice (first known as Richard Meier & Associates) with a commission for his parents, a residence in Essex Fells, New Jersey done under the acknowledged influence of Frank Lloyd Wright's "Falling Water" house. Also in 1963, Meier visited the opening of an exhibition of models and drawings by Le Corbusier at the Museum of Modern Art in Manhattan. He remembers that exhibition as "a turning point" in his life, a reinforcement of his "vertical interest, more so than the horizontal, at least in the Wrightian sense." In an interview for *Newsday* (April 24, 1984), Meier told Doris Herzig: "I think he [Wright] was wrong. Unlike nature, architecture doesn't grow and doesn't change. It is inert. What is important to me is the dialogue between what is natural and what is inert." He believes, he said, that a building should contrast with its surroundings, rather than blend with them, to "heighten one's awareness of nature."

"At the beginning, the design of a number of private houses provided me with an excellent opportunity to develop my ideas about architecture," Meier recalled in an address at the seminar on "The Pursuit of Excellence." "With them, I found and tested my vocabulary and set of values." In addition to the residence for his parents, he designed a studio and apartment for Frank Stella in New York City (completed 1965), the Dotson house in Ithaca, New York (1965), and the Hoffman house in East Hampton, New York (1967), among other early residential commissions.

The project that first brought Meier national attention was his innovative Smith house in Darien, Connecticut (1967), widely admired for its clarity, openness, direct articulation of private and public spaces, and relation to land and water. Looking back on that work fifteen years later, Paul Goldberger wrote in *Vogue* (June 1983): "It was already clear that something else beside the standard modernist impulse was at work—a kind of picturesque, compositional design sense, as sure and fine an intuitive design ability as had been seen in years. The Smith House was lighter than most modernist houses of the 1960s, more a kind of frame; it was very beautiful as an object, and nothing about it said, 'This is an awkward form, but you will like it when you get used to it.' One became used to it instantly, and this alone set it apart from all sorts of buildings that were going up at the same time." Single-family dwellings subsequently designed by Meier included the Saltzman house in East Hampton, the Douglas house in Harbor Springs, Michigan, and the Maidman house in Sands Point, New York. Among the more ambitious of the private homes he created was an eleven-bedroom house in Old Westbury, New York described in *Newsweek* (December 24, 1973) as "a joy to see and romp in."

Meier's first large commission was Westbeth Artists' Housing, a pioneering example of what is now known as "adaptive re-use." That commission, funded by grants from the National Council on the Arts and the J. M. Kaplan Fund, involved the creative restoration of the old Bell Telephone Laboratories buildings, thirteen-story steel-and-concrete structures occupying the full square block bounded by West, Bethune, Washington, and Bank streets across from the Hudson River piers on the western edge of Manhattan's Greenwich Village. Beginning in 1968, Meier transformed the former commercial buildings into 383 loft-type studio-residences constituting the largest housing facility for artists in the world and the first of its kind in the

United States. The complex, financed as middle-income housing by the Federal Housing Administration, opened in May 1970.

The New York State Urban Development Corporation commissioned Meier's second major project, Twin Parks Northeast Housing in the Bronx, completed in 1972. The architectural historian Kenneth Frampton described that project as "an exemplary piece of housing" and observed, "Few are the projects, in America or elsewhere, in which the modulation of form and surface has such rhythmic authority, or in which acknowledgement of the existing context has in no way inhibited the creation of a new situation."

Following a proposal by Meier, the Villa Strozzi in Florence, Italy was modified in 1973 to serve as the enclosure for a new museum. During the 1970s Meier designed several facilities for the New York State Department of Mental Hygiene, the largest of which was the Bronx Developmental Center, commissioned in 1971 as an addition to Bronx State Hospital and planned as a total-care facility (home and school as well as hospital) for almost 400 mentally handicapped people ranging in age from seven to seventy. Creating "a sense of place that would respond to the special feelings and needs of these people" was a challenge for Meier, given the traffic-island site he had to work with, a twelve-acre triangular hill surrounded by an amorphous hospital campus, a parkway, and a network of railroad tracks. Always sensitive to context, Meier decided in this instance to ignore the context and allow the new structure to "open inward" and, like a monastery, "create its own context," a "microcosm world, a sanctuary with a strong sense of community."

Adopting that strategy, Meier created a sleek, silvery multi-structure comprising three elements joined by such connective tissue as glass-enclosed passageways. The outer element, or "public realm," housing administrative offices, lecture hall, and other support services, was designed as a filter, a vast aluminum-and-glass wall controlling access to the second and third elements, "the inner realms." The first of the inner realms, as conceived by Meier, was the residential, consisting of smaller, domestically scaled, staggered L-shaped living units; the second was recreational courtyard space. As Meier explained in the LTV Corporation symposium, "progression from public to private" was "established through a nuance of surface detail," especially "the location of the glass plane in relation to the surface; in the public areas it is set back from the face, in the private it is set flush."

Completed in 1977, the Bronx Developmental Center was criticized by some lay people concerned as "unhomelike" and "art for art's sake," but architects from around the world considered it a landmark achievement. "In smart and important ways," Mark Stevens observed in *Newsweek* (May 30, 1977), "this building enriches the way people live by shaping the way they see." Writing in the *New York Times* (May 3, 1977), Ada Louise Huxtable commended Meier for bringing "a rigorous intellect and sensitive esthetic" to "nearly insoluble problems" and putting together "form and purpose . . . style and function . . . structure and skin, circulation and use . . . like a fine, expensive watch." "The whole structure is marked by an extremely disciplined interlocking of logic and art . . . ," Mrs. Huxtable wrote. "In spite of its fashionably 'minimalist' components, this building has a richness of composition and a finesse and originality of form that mark an important new phase of architectural design."

The plans for Frank Lloyd Wright's Solomon R. Guggenheim Museum in Manhattan designated a bulge of space at the southwest corner of the building for use as an "architectural archive," but the space served merely as a utility room for nineteen years, until 1978, when Meier converted it into the Ave Simon Reading Room, housing a collection of international art periodicals for the use of museum members and visiting scholars. The furnishings Meier designed for the room led to other such designs, including a collection of furniture for Knoll International, completed in 1982. The aesthetic of his furniture is much the same as that of his buildings of recent years, as Paul Goldberger observed in Vogue (June 1984): "His work has become more concerned with curves, with the playing off of soft lines against the hard ones, with the using of hard edges to enclose and shelter soft interiors."

In 1979 Meier completed the Atheneum, a visitors' center in the restored historic town of New Harmony, Indiana, famous for the planned communities that George Rapp and Robert Owen founded there in the early nineteenth century and as the site of the country's first free public school and free public library. The Atheneum stands in a field on the banks of the Wabash River, so that when the field floods in the spring the building, in Meier's words, "built on a podium of earth, floats above the water—an object from another context and time, a porcelain-paneled 'boat of knowledge' docking on New Harmony's shores."

Meier conceived the Atheneum "in terms of the linked ideas of architectural promenade and historical path." Inside the building, the visitor is channeled to a series of historical exhibits and presentations by an upwardly winding ramp. "By the time he has made his way from the ground floor to the rooftop terrace for the view of the river and the town," Ada Louise Huxtable wrote in the New York Times (September 30, 1979), "he has become familiar with the story and spirit of New Harmony. He has also been exposed to an extraordinary series of architectural impressions in which the sense of the past is heightened, both physically and poetically, by the experience of the present." Mrs. Huxtable judged "this gleaming white structure" to be "as radical an addition to the rural American landscape as Le Corbusier's Villa Savoie was to the French countryside at Poissy half a century ago."

In designing the Hartford (Connecticut) Seminary, completed in 1981, Meier evoked "the character of the building as a center of educational and spiritual enlightenment . . . not by preconceived and superimposed symbols, but wholly by the way in which light and space are configurated."

Meier submitted a proposal for the design of the administrative headquarters of the Renault automobile plant in Boulogne-Billancourt, France in 1981, and the following year he completed the Bartholomew Consolidated School in Columbus, Indiana. In 1983 he completed the Giovanetti house in Pittsburgh, Pennsylvania and a tableware collection for Swid Powell Designs and began designing an office building for Siemens AG in Munich, Germany.

Meier's High Museum of Art in Atlanta, Georgia, completed in 1983, is a complex structure of white porcelain panels, glass, some granite, and pipe rails. Like the Guggenheim Museum, it has a ramp ascending a central atrium, but the gallery plan and intent are almost an inversion of the Guggenheim. The art is exhibited not within the curved central atrium but off of it. "The movement through the museum is designed so that we move back and forth from gallery to atrium to gallery again, changing levels on a system of ramps that offers views of the city outside as well as views that turn back inside," Paul Goldberger wrote in the New York Times (October 5, 1983). "So . . . there is none of the hermetic sense of some museums. At the High Museum we move back and forth from the experience of art to the experience of architecture—and each enriches the other." In Goldberger's opinion, the High Museum "is not only Atlanta's most important piece of recent architecture, it is among the best museum structures any city has built in at least a generation."

In 1984 Meier had two major commissions under construction: the Des Moines (Iowa) Art Center, an addition to a complex already comprising structures designed by Eliel Saarinen and I. M. Pei; and the Museum für Kunsthhandwerk in Frankfurt, West Germany. The latter, like other recent museum work by Meier, is in the Enlightenment tradition of joining educational to collection and display functions. In Frankfurt, the architecture is calculated to lead the visitor "through a prescribed didactic and evocative sequence" and at the same time to allow him to see a work close up, then from a distance, and finally perhaps in different contexts or from different perspectives. While the architect's design serves to frame the art, it is itself art. "The role of the architect is seen as that of encouraging people to use the museum to experience the art of architecture as well as the art displayed in it," Meier said in the LTV symposium. "As the institution is committed to . . . cultural illumination, its architecture should be both literally and symbolically radiant. It should both contain and reflect light."

The Hyatt Foundation established the Pritzker Architecture Prize in 1979 as a way of honoring achievement in a field of creative endeavor overlooked by the Nobel prizes. On April 17, 1984 Meier was named the sixth recipient of the prize, which consists of a tax-free $100,000 cash award and a small sculpture by Henry Moore. In his speech at the cash-award ceremony on April 17, Meier softpedaled his differences with the post-modernists. "In architecture, history is making a triumphant comeback," he said. "Architectural history can be seen as a repertoire for new design. My own sources include many from the history of architecture, but my quotes and allusions are never literal. Fundamentally, my meditations are on space, form, light, and how to make them." He elaborated in a interview with Benjamin Forgey for the *Washington Post* (May 16, 1984): "There is today an aspect of architecture in which buildings refer to things outside themselves, historical references which are outside the context. . . . My concern is with the quality of the product, without the overlay of other elements." On the same subject, he was quoted by Wolf Von Eckardt in *Time* (November 12, 1984): "Sure, I think he [Le Corbusier] was the greatest architect of the century. But then I am also a disciple of Borromini, and I'm affected no less by Bramante and Bernini, whose work I studied in Rome."

On October 26, 1984 the J. Paul Getty Trust, which administers the most lucrative visual-arts endowment in the world, selected Meier to design a gigantic, $100-million–plus arts complex on a 700-acre site in Los Angeles, a commission dwarfing all of the architect's previous work. Meier told Wolf Von Eckardt that the Getty complex will not be a porcelain-clad structure like his previous museums. "It would be out of place on that site," he explained. "Besides, I felt ready to shift direction . . . even before this commission came along.".

An impressive-looking six-footer, Richard Alan Meier weighs 170 pounds, has bespectacled blue eyes, wears his gray hair in a longish mane, prefers conservative, dark suits (offset by colorful silk ties), and is as poised personally as he is assured in his designing. Meier and Katherine Gormley, also an architect, were married on January 21, 1978. They have two children, Joseph Max and Ana Moss. The Meiers live in a Manhattan apartment that has been totally redesigned and reconstructed by Meier, even to the lowering of the floor. The furniture was also designed by him, except for pieces designed by Le Corbusier and Marcel Breuer, and Stella paintings adorn the walls. He still makes collages, which he considers his "workout" for architecture. His many awards include the Arnold Brunner Memorial Prize from the American Academy of Arts and Letters (1977), the R. S. Reynolds Memorial Award (1977), and awards of excellence from the publications *Architectural Record* and *Progressive Architecture*.

References: N Y Times C p20 Ap 18 '84 por; Newsday (At Home) p2 Ap 24 '84; Newsweek 89:59 My 30 '77; Time 124:111 N 12 '84 por; Vogue 173:196+ Je '84 por; Washington Post B p1+ My 16 '84 por; Meier, Richard and Rykwert, Joseph. Richard Meier, Architect (1984); Who's Who in America, 1984–85

---

## Merrifield, R(obert) Bruce

July 15, 1921– Biochemist. Address: b. Rockefeller University, 1230 York Ave., New York City, N.Y. 10021

The 1984 Nobel Prize in Chemistry was awarded to R. Bruce Merrifield, the John D. Rockefeller Jr. Professor at Rockefeller University, for developing a revolutionary new method of manufacturing proteins in the laboratory. Since its inception in the early 1960s, "solid phase peptide synthesis," as the process is called, has opened vast new horizons for basic biochemical research and laid the groundwork for new advances in medicine, pharmacology, and related fields. With a ready supply of enzymes, hormones, and other proteins, scientists have eagerly explored their chemical structures in order to understand their functions better, with a view toward treating or even preventing a number of diseases and genetic disorders. Merrifield's technique has also been adapted to produce nucleic acids, which has greatly stimulated progress in genetic engineering.

Robert Bruce Merrifield, the son of Lorene (Lucas) and George E. Merrifield, a furniture salesman, was born on July 15, 1921 in Fort Worth, Texas but spent most of his childhood in California. During the Great Depression, the Merrifields

moved repeatedly up and down the California coast to take advantage of what opportunities there were for work; R. Bruce Merrifield later estimated that as a result he had attended forty different schools in his youth. But for five years during his adolescence, his family remained in Montebello, California, where he attended the local high school. His desire to become a chemist crystallized there while he was writing a required essay on his career plans.

After graduating in the late 1930s, he pursued that interest first at Pasadena Junior College, which was nearby and inexpensive, and then at the University of California at Los Angeles (UCLA), from which he received his B.A. degree in 1943. While an undergraduate there, he paid his expenses by synthesizing dehydroxyphenylalanine (DOPA), an amino acid that in certain forms is used in the treatment of Parkinson's disease, in the amino-acid manufacturing laboratory run by Max Dunn, a professor of biochemistry at UCLA.

On graduating, Merrifield was hired as a chemist by the Philip R. Park Research Foundation, but after a year he decided to return to UCLA for graduate work. He originally planned only to complete a master's degree, but a fellowship from Anheuser Busch, the beer manufacturer, enabled him to work for a Ph.D. During his four-and-a-half years of graduate work, he served first as a teaching assistant in chemistry and in 1948-1949 as a research assistant at UCLA's medical school. In connection with his fellowship, Merrifield analyzed purines and pyrimidines in yeast samples and developed an innovative bioassay—a test for determining the strength of a substance—for them based on how essential they were for the growth of certain bacteria. His technique, however, was soon eclipsed by a simpler one, devised by Dr. Erwin Chargaff, that used chromatography.

Having received his Ph.D. degree on June 19, 1949, Merrifield moved to the East Coast to begin work as an assistant biochemist in the laboratory of Dr. Dilworth Wayne Woolley at Rockefeller University (then known as the Rockefeller Institute for Medical Research) in Manhattan. Early on, he conducted further experiments in nucleic-acid chemistry, but by the time he was promoted to research associate in 1953 Merrifield was immersed in the study of protein chemistry, which was one of the main interests of Woolley's laboratory and one of the primary focal points of biochemical research at the time. "The proteins are key components of all living organisms," Merrifield once explained. "All of the enzymes that catalyze biological reactions and many of the hormones that regulate them are proteins. If we are to understand, and eventually control, the events that occur in the body, we must first understand the composition, structure, and function of the individual proteins."

Progress toward that goal had been slow and difficult because of the complexity of the gigantic protein molecules. Nineteenth-century scientists discovered that proteins consist of amino acids, and several of the amino acids were isolated. In 1901 Emil Fischer, a German organic chemist, devised a method for bonding amino acids to form a peptide—a tiny fragment of a protein, containing the same elements (but fewer in number) as a pro-

tein and arranged in the same sequence. As a result, the synthesis of biologically active peptides and even of true proteins became theoretically possible, but fifty more years elapsed before the necessary first step—establishing the exact sequence of amino acids in a peptide or a protein molecule—was completed. In 1953 the American scientist Vincent du Vigneaud determined the composition of and used the method pioneered by Fischer to synthesize the small pituitary hormones oxytocin and vasopressin, which are used in obstetrics and the treatment of diabetes, respectively. However, the process for synthesizing even a relatively simple peptide like oxytocin, which consists of only nine amino acids, was lengthy and complicated; furthermore, the final yield was usually low and the product often impure. Labs, therefore, could not adequately meet the demand for those hormones and other synthetic peptides to be used in research and for therapeutic purposes.

The principal dilemma in peptide synthesis is the formation of the peptide bonds that link the amino acids. An amino acid is a chemical compound consisting of several reactive groups—that is, several possible sites where it might bond with another molecule: one amino group, one carboxyl group, and often another group on a side chain. The two classical methods of joining amino acids to form peptides are "fragmentation," in which the amino acids are bonded in short, separate chains that would then be linked together to form the desired peptide; and the "stepwise" technique, in which the peptide is formed in a single chain by adding one amino acid at a time in the correct sequence. To control the peptide synthesis with either method, all but a single reactive group of each amino acid must be chemically protected, or blocked, so that when two are added together they can combine in only one way. In addition, the correct bonding site on each amino acid must be activated in order to form the desired peptide. If a third amino acid is to be added, a certain one of the previously protected reactive groups must be chemically deprotected and then activated before the next bond can be formed. To further complicate the procedure, the byproducts of each bonding reaction and the reagents (the chemicals used to protect, deprotect, or activate reactive sites) have to be removed from the reaction vessel and the remaining material purified, often over the course of several days and by more than one method, before the next amino acid may be introduced. At each step, some of the growing peptide chain is unavoidably lost. For example, it was estimated in *Chemical & Engineering News* (October 22, 1984) that the final yield in synthesizing a peptide chain of 100 amino acids using the stepwise method would be only about .003 percent.

Working in Woolley's lab, Merrifield, who had been promoted to associate professor in 1958, had successfully used those classic methods to make structural analogs of some peptides as well as controlled variants of them in order to compare their biological activity. He had also bonded chains of twenty to forty amino acids of random sequence to form polypeptides that seemed to act like certain catalytic enzymes. But his studies were seriously hindered by the inefficiency of the available methods of synthesis. As Merrifield noted in a May 26, 1959 entry in his research journal, "There is a need for a rapid, quantitative, automatic method for synthesis of long chain peptides." He further speculated in his journal that if the first amino acid were anchored to a solid support, the researcher would not have to remove the growing peptide chain from the reaction vessel in order to purify it after each step but could simply filter out the byproducts of the bonding reaction and the reagents: the support would prevent the chain from being washed out also. Much less of the peptide would be lost with this process, and so the final yield would be dramatically increased. Once the chain was completed, the support would be chemically removed and the product purified by conventional methods.

Soon afterwards he discussed his theory with Dr. Woolley, who encouraged him to try it out. Although Merrifield hoped that he could show in a few months that his method was practicable, the initial work took three years. "You can't get away with a dry spell like that at just any old place," he told John F. Henahan in Chemical & Engineering News (August 2, 1971). "If I had been at Harvard or Berkeley, I think people would have begun to look at me a little funny."

After much research and several false starts, Merrifield found an insoluble, solid support that worked: minute beads of polystyrene that had been rendered reactive to amino acids by chloromethyl ether. Although the tiny plastic beads could barely be seen by the human eye, in theory each could support a trillion peptide chains. But other problems remained to be solved. He had to find the correct reagents and solvents to use at each juncture in the procedure to ensure a yield of 100 percent for every bonding reaction. As Merrifield explained in an article for Scientific American (March 1968), if only 90 percent of the second amino acid bonded correctly to the first, when a third amino acid was introduced it would bond as expected with the dipeptide but also with the remaining 10 percent of the second amino acid, forming an unwanted second chain. Such incorrect bondings might occur several times, especially during the synthesis of a long peptide chain. Since with his procedure the product is not purified after each step, separating the desired peptide from the final product would be very difficult. Consequently, careful testing and planning were essential.

Trying out his procedure, Merrifield linked the amino acid alanine to the pretreated plastic beads, and with the necessary steps for filtering, adding reagents, and refiltering, he introduced the amino acid leucine. Chemically detaching the polystyrene bead, he obtained a dipeptide. Repeating that process with four amino acids (leucine, alanine, glycine, and valine, in that order), he synthesized a tetrapeptide in a fraction of the time it would normally take, and with a yield of almost 100 percent

after each coupling step. In 1962 Merrifield reported the results of his "solid phase peptide synthesis," as he called the process, to a meeting of the Federation of American Societies for Experimental Biology. A year later he published in the Journal of the American Chemical Society the results of his solid-phase synthesis of the hormone bradykinin, an important nonapeptide. Using his procedure, biochemists could produce large yields of bradykinin in a short time, thus facilitating the then-intensive study of the hormone as a pain transmitter.

Since automation of the process—which was basically a step-by-step procedure—promised to speed up peptide synthesis further and to make possible the synthesis of the more complicated proteins, Merrifield next set out to devise a synthesizing machine. "Originally, the idea was sort of helter-skelter," Merrifield told John F. Henahan in the Chemical & Engineering News interview, "until John Stewart [a colleague at Rockefeller University], who was also a ham radio man, cooperated on the electrical end of things. I functioned as plumber, and between the two of us we put something together in the basement at home." The basic tasks of the machine were twofold: to add, at the appropriate junctures, the amino acids and the various reagents and solvents to a specially designed reaction vessel that contained the growing peptide chain, and then to allow the unwanted byproducts to be filtered out. Merrifield and Stewart linked a series of containers for these agents and chemicals to a rotary valve system, whose twelve valves were each activated by precisely positioned nylon pins that were hammered into a timer-controlled rotating drum—on the order, for instance, of a player piano. The first working model of the machine could add six amino acids to a peptide chain every day—each acid requiring about ninety steps on the drum. It was completed in 1965, with the additional help of Nils Jernberg, who worked in the Rockefeller Institute's instrument shop.

Merrifield and his colleagues were soon using his machine to synthesize bradykinin, peptide hormones such as oxytocin, and finally a protein—insulin, which consists of fifty-one amino acids and is the smallest true protein. (The average protein has 120 amino acids.) With the aid of the machine, Merrifield and Dr. Arnold Marglin completed the synthesis of that protein, a process that had previously taken months, in only twenty days.

An even more impressive achievement was the automatic solid synthesis of the enzyme ribonuclease by Merrifield and Dr. Bernd Gutte in 1969—the first synthesis of an enzyme by any means. (Almost simultaneously, a team of scientists at the Merck Sharp & Dohme Research Laboratories in Rahway, New Jersey synthesized it by means of the traditional fragmentation method.) Ribonuclease had long been associated with Rockefeller University, where it was first isolated by René Dubos in 1938, crystallized by Moses Kunitz in 1940, and the sequence of its 124 amino acids determined by C. R. W. Hirs, William Stein, and Stanford Moore in

1960. It was appropriate, then, that Merrifield chose it for his first enzyme synthesis.

A complex process, it required 369 chemical reactions and 11,931 separate steps by the machine, performed during several weeks of continuous operation. Nevertheless, the solid phase synthesis of ribonuclease was considerably quicker than conventional techniques and boded well for rapid advances in research on and treatment of many diseases and genetic disorders, such as the form of mental retardation known as phenylketonuria, that had been linked to the lack or dysfunction of an enzyme.

Prompted by the ribonuclease synthesis, scientists used automatic solid phase peptide synthesis to produce peptides and proteins for a broad spectrum of medical and experimental purposes. For example, researchers have manufactured a wide variety of analogs, that is, the man-made equivalents of substances produced by the human body, such as calcitronin, a hormone produced by the thyroid gland that affects calcium metabolism, and the pituitary-gland hormone adrenocorticotrophin (ACTH). Others are currently trying to make various vaccines that would use the simulated protein "coats" of viruses rather than the dead viruses themselves, thus stimulating the production of antibodies while avoiding the danger of viral infection associated with vaccination. Furthermore, through solid phase synthesis, neurochemists are studying a variety of hormones produced in the brain that affect such psychophysiological activities as emotions and memory. Adapting his technique, genetic engineers and biochemists have devised a "gene machine," which couples nucleotides to form nucleic acids. Beckman Instruments and Vega Biotechnologies, among other companies, now commercially produce sophisticated versions of Merrifield's synthesizer.

In recognition of his "simple and ingenious" method, which has revolutionized protein and peptide chemistry and stimulated important research in other fields, the Royal Swedish Academy of Sciences awarded R. Bruce Merrifield the 1984 Nobel Prize in chemistry, which carried with it a premium of $190,000. His many other honors include the prestigious Lasker Award (1969), the Gairdner Award (1970), an award from the American Chemical Society (1972), the Nichols medal (1973), and numerous honorary degrees from leading universities. In addition to his duties at Rockefeller University, he served in 1968 as the Nobel guest professor at Uppsala University in Sweden and since 1969 as the associate editor of The International Journal of Peptide and Protein Research. He was elected to membership in the National Academy of Sciences in 1972, and he also belongs to other professional organizations. A full professor at Rockefeller University since 1966, he was named the John D. Rockefeller Jr. Professor in 1983.

On June 20, 1949 R. Bruce Merrifield married Elizabeth Furlong, who for the past several years has been working in the Merrifield laboratory, specifically on synthesizing a molecule of interferon—the promising anti-tumor agent. The couple has six children: Nancy, James, Betsy, Cathy, Laurie, and Sally. Described as soft-spoken and unassuming, Merrifield has continued in recent years to refine his method and to search for expanded applications of automatic peptide synthesis. His interest in and study of the relation of structure to function in synthetic, biologically active peptides and proteins has also continued unabated. He lives in Cresskill, New Jersey.

*References: Chemical & Engineering News p22+ Ag 2 '71 pors; New Scientist 104:11+ O 25 '84; N Y Times A p1+ O 18 '84 por; Science 226:1151+ D 7 '84; American Men and Women of Science, 15th ed (1982); Who's Who in America, 1984–85*

## Mikulski, Barbara A(nn)

*July 20, 1936– U.S. Representative from Maryland. Address: b. 2404 Rayburn Bldg., Washington, D.C. 20515*

Earthy, flamboyant, feisty, and outspoken, Barbara Mikulski, who has represented Maryland's 3d Congressional District in the House of Representatives since 1977, has never been a typical member of the United States Congress. A former social worker turned social activist, Miss Mikulski first came to national political notice in the early 1970s as the self-styled "Queen of the Ethnics" and a favored daughter of the women's movement. After easily winning the House seat vacated by Democrat Paul S. Sarbanes in 1976, Miss Mikulski headed for Congress promising, with her customary lack of reserve, "to raise hell," but the plainspoken liberal and feminist has played the congressional political game with considerable finesse. The national cochairman of the unsuccessful Mondale-Ferraro 1984 presidential campaign and a candidate for one of Maryland's Senate seats in 1986, Barbara Mikulski is becoming a powerful force on Capitol Hill.

Born on July 20, 1936 in Baltimore, Maryland, Barbara Ann Mikulski grew up in Highlandtown, one of that city's ethnic, working-class neighborhoods, where she attended the Sacred Heart of Jesus elementary school and from 1950 to 1954 the Institute of Notre Dame High School. Her parents, William and Christine Eleanor (Kutz) Mikulski, ran a small grocery store in Highlandtown called "Willy's Market." "We were a family of entrepreneurs and the women always worked side by side with the men," she told Judith Michaelson of the New York Post (January 27, 1973); her own efforts on behalf of the women's movement are a natural byproduct of that tradition.

Although she briefly considered becoming a nun and later entered Mount Saint Agnes College, a small women's school that is now part of Loyola University, to study medical technology, she finally decided to pursue a career in social work and received a B.A. degree in sociology from Mount Saint Agnes College in 1958. After graduation, she was a caseworker for a number of social work agencies in Baltimore: the Associated Catholic Charities (1958–61), the Department of Social Services (1961–63, 1966–70), and the York Family Agency (1964). At the same time she took evening courses toward a master's degree in social work. On receiving that degree from the University of Maryland in 1965, she taught at the VISTA training center in Baltimore for five years. She also worked for REASON (Responding to the Elderly's Ability and Sickness Otherwise Neglected), Narcotics Anonymous, and other community projects.

Social work slowly began to raise her political consciousness. As she explained in the New York Times (September 22, 1973): "The more I worked with people on a one-to-one basis, the more I saw that institutions were really the problem." While working in the Kennedy and Johnson campaigns, she became increasingly involved with the civil-rights movement and the battle over residential desegregation in Baltimore. Her personal independence also increased; at the age of twenty-seven she shocked her parents, who believed children should remain at home until they married, by moving into her own apartment and later left the old neighborhood entirely to live in an integrated area across town for four years. But when Barbara Mikulski and other civil-rights activists returned home for visits, their families argued with them about their work. "Not that they objected to us helping the Negroes," she told Thomas H. Clancy in America (December 26, 1970), "but they pointed out the needs of our own people in our old neighborhoods." "People in ethnic communities felt that black people were getting everything," she

explained. "Yet I know that black programs were token efforts. . . . The result was that the two groups were turned against each other instead of the system."

Those rising tensions not only convinced Barbara Mikulski of the wisdom of blacks and ethnics working together toward a common goal—coalition politics—but also forced her to come to terms with her own heritage. Her grandparents, who emigrated from Poland around the turn of the century, were living embodiments of Old World culture. In contrast, her parents were eager to make their three daughters, of whom Barbara was the oldest, "real Americans," which often meant downplaying their ethnic heritage. As a result, like many third-generation ethnics, Miss Mikulski felt torn between her Polish and American identities. She finally resolved, as she explained in America (December 26, 1970), "to be [herself] . . . a woman, a Polish-American, and a Catholic." She also became deeply involved in the "back-to-your-roots" ethnic revival, or "White Ethnic Movement," of the late 1960s and 1970s, so much so that she was recognized as one of its principal spokesmen and its "first lady." In addition to writing articles about the movement in Redbook, the New York Times, and other periodicals, she became an associate of the National Center for Urban Ethnic Affairs and an active member of the Polish Women's Alliance.

The final stage in her transformation from social worker to social activist came in 1968. The assassinations of Robert F. Kennedy and Martin Luther King Jr. not only left her angry and bewildered but inspired her to "completely change [her] life." At first she looked for answers in more study and in teaching, at Mount Saint Agnes College in 1969 and then in the field of urban affairs at Baltimore Community College in 1970–71, in addition to her social work. But she finally determined that political activism was the solution. After all, as she explained in the New York Post (January 27, 1973), "Politics is social work with power. I always wanted to help people." Moving back to her old neighborhood, she helped to found the Southeast Baltimore Organization, a coalition of Polish, Italian, black, and Lumbee Indian groups, and led it in a successful campaign to stop the construction of a proposed freeway that would have necessitated tearing down 400 homes of retired and elderly persons in the neighborhood. In addition, the coalition started a neighborhood restoration project and persuaded the city to build a park in its community.

"The community action revealed other problems . . . related to inadequate schools, libraries, and health services," Barbara Mikulski explained to Essie E. Lee for the book Women in Congress (1979). "I decided that rather than knock on the doors of city hall, I'd be more effective inside helping people get their fair share of governmental services." Making the case for the "misunderstood Ethnic American," the needs of the elderly, and the potential for coalition politics, Miss Mikulski built upon her already enthusiastic following in Baltimore to form a political power base. In 1971 she was ready to challenge two old-line political organizations for a seat on the Baltimore City Council. Aided by her family, who distributed circulars with the weekly grocery specials saying, "Please vote for our daughter," by her image as a liberal reformer, and by a tenacious, door-to-door campaign, she confounded political experts by winning the election. During her tenure on the council, she successfully introduced legislation to create the Commission on Aging and Retirement Education (CARE), to reduce bus fares for the elderly, and to establish a commission to study the impact of rape on its victims. In *Women in Congress* (1979), Miss Mikulski said that the results of the latter study were used to improve treatment of and services to rape victims and "to bring about changes in state laws related to the use of evidence and criminal procedures in rape cases."

Meanwhile, Barbara Mikulski's political style and message quickly gained national attention. Originally backing Edmund S. Muskie in his short-lived 1972 presidential campaign, she then worked for George S. McGovern as a special adviser to his vice-presidential candidate, R. Sargent Shriver. After the election, Jean Westwood, the Democratic national chairman, appointed her as cochairman of the important Commission on Delegate Selection and Party Structure. Succeeding Leonard Woodcock, the president of the United Auto Workers, as chairman of that panel in January 1973, Miss Mikulski had to mediate between reformers and conservatives, both of whom saw the delegate selection process as critical in their bid to control the Democratic party's future. The guidelines that had been used at the 1972 Democratic convention, she explained in the *New York Post* (January 27, 1973), had been "enforced as quotas in certain states. Delegates were elected openly and then at the convention the judgment of the electorate was superseded" to ensure a set ratio of women and minorities in each delegation. Under her guidance, the commission voted unanimously in October 1973 to replace that strict quota system with a more flexible "affirmative action" rule to ensure the equitable representation of all Democrats but "with particular concern for minority groups, native Americans, women and youth in the delegate selection process." As a result, state delegations need only give evidence that the selection process had been open and fair. A new Compliance Review Commission was set up to enforce the rules and monitor affirmative-action efforts. The commission also instituted other changes, including abolition of the "winner-take-all" primaries in favor of apportioning delegates according to the popular vote for each candidate. Reflecting in 1976 on the Democrats' presidential victory, Barbara Mikulski claimed some of the credit, saying in an interview with *U.S. News and World Report* (November 15, 1976) that her commission had "laid the groundwork for a harmonious convention and also a unified Democratic party."

During her term as councilwoman, she had stressed repeatedly in her speeches two themes: re-

vitalizing the Democratic party and getting women to run for high office. Taking her own advice, in 1974 Barbara Mikulski decided to run for the United States Senate against the popular Republican incumbent, Charles McC. Mathias Jr. With no established politicians willing "to be the sacrificial lamb in a hopeless campaign," as she phrased it in *Ms.* magazine (July 1975), she easily beat a field of ten men in the Democratic primary. But since both she and Mathias were liberals and supporters of the Equal Rights Amendment (ERA), Miss Mikulski faced the problem of having few different ideas to offer the electorate, and, as Ben A. Franklin pointed out in the *New York Times* (October 23, 1974), the "debates" between the candidates were little more than a "dialogue of sameness." Shifting her attack to the economic and anti-inflation policies of the Ford administration, she fared no better, for Mathias, too, was often dissatisfied with its programs.

Undaunted by those problems and her limited finances, Barbara Mikulski, who described herself as a "progressive populist" and "a cross between Eleanor Roosevelt and Harry Truman," ran a feisty campaign on a shoestring. Unable to afford expensive hotel rooms on the campaign circuit, she toured the state in a camper, and logging over 10,000 campaign miles, she tirelessly shook hands at factory gates, addressed senior citizens' groups, and danced at Greek festivals. The nation's leading feminists, including Gloria Steinem and Bella Abzug, took to the stump for her. Barbara Mikulski lost to Mathias but won a respectable 43 percent of the statewide vote and carried Baltimore and suburban Baltimore County.

As Ben A. Franklin of the *New York Times* predicted before the election, her gutsy campaign left her "a valuable legacy of high visibility across the state and good marks from admiring Democratic party officials" in Baltimore. So when Democrat Paul S. Sarbanes resigned in 1976 as the representative of Maryland's 3d Congressional District in order to run for the Senate, Barbara Mikulski, who had won reelection in 1975 to the Baltimore City Council, entered the race for Sarbanes' seat. After a victory in the primary—which, in that Maryland district, is tantamount to election—against a field of ten Democratic contenders, she changed her "roly-poly" image by shedding fifty pounds, conducted a hard-hitting, issue-oriented campaign, and went on to take 75 percent of the vote against Republican Samuel A. Culotta in the general election.

Although heralded in advance as "a likely successor to Bella Abzug as the chamber's most strident feminist voice," according to *Politics in America* (1986), the freshman representative from Maryland soon showed critics that she would not be so easily stereotyped. Her first move was to endorse Jim Wright of Texas for majority leader rather than one of the two more liberal candidates; when Wright won, she gained not only a reputation for shrewdness but also an appointment to serve as the first woman on the powerful Interstate and

Foreign Commerce Committee and a seat on the Merchant Marine and Fisheries Committee, whose rulings are important to the Baltimore port. (She is currently chairman of the Marine Committee's oceanography subcommittee.) She gave further proof in her first term of her political know-how while serving as the only woman appointee on the Ad Hoc Energy Committee, which had been set up to handle President Jimmy Carter's energy package. After Carter ignored her proposed amendment that would have allotted $65 million to help cities install energy conservation in municipal buildings, she let it be known that she might not be around to give the president a critical vote he needed against gas deregulation. Carter suddenly decided that he liked her amendment, and Congresswoman Mikulski cast her vote against deregulation.

Reelected to the House four times in succession, Barbara Mikulski has earned a reputation as a liberal, pro-labor Democratic party loyalist: she has received average approval ratings of 90 percent from both the liberal Americans for Democratic Action and the AFL-CIO and has voted with her party about 88 percent of the time. On the Interstate and Foreign Commerce Committee, for example, Barbara Mikulski has consistently sided with the Democratic pro-consumer faction that favors strict regulation of the energy industry, including price controls. She also favored a tough "superfund" bill that would force chemical companies to pay for the cleanup of toxic wastes, the establishment of minimum "domestic content" requirements for motor vehicles sold or distributed in the United States, and dairy price supports. As a member of the Commerce Committee's transportation and health subcommittee, she fought less successfully for a child health insurance program, national health insurance, and hospital cost regulation. However, she did help to pass legislation that tied reductions in federal Medicaid funding to "good-guy" bonuses (states that were making progress in containing hospital costs would suffer less severe cutbacks), which saved Maryland about $9 million in 1981, and successfully opposed freezing physicians' fees under Medicare.

True to her social-work background, Miss Mikulski has been a passionate opponent of President Ronald Reagan's cutbacks in social spending. Detailing the impact of budget cuts on her constituents, she concluded in *Working Woman* (January 1983), "If the government truly wants to nourish the family, it must give the family what it needs"—decent jobs, education, and health care. In keeping with that belief, the Congressional Women's Caucus, of which Barbara Mikulski is a founding member, joined in 1979 with other women's groups, social-service organizations, and civil-rights advocates in supporting a bill that would have allocated $65 million over three years to preventing domestic violence and to setting up services and shelters for battered spouses and children. Although the bill passed by a wide margin in the House, it died in the Senate.

One of the prime movers behind the 1984 Child Abuse Act, Congresswoman Mikulski has also backed the passage of the ERA and has opposed prohibiting the use of health benefit funds to pay for abortions. However, she has not neglected issues of more local concern. In the 98th Congress, for example, she fought for funding to dredge Baltimore's port and clean up Chesapeake Bay and tried to prevent staff cuts in the Social Security Administration, whose headquarters is located within her district.

Under the Reagan administration, the congresswoman became more involved in foreign-policy issues. Close ties to the Maryknoll order heightened her concern with conditions in El Salvador, where a group of American women, including two Maryknoll nuns, was brutally murdered in 1980. Her fact-finding trip to the troubled Central American nation early in 1981 convinced her to oppose further military aid to El Salvador. "It is morally wrong and wrongheaded," she maintained. "A generation of villagers is growing up who will hate the sight of a U.S. symbol, because it means to them that someone is coming to shoot." She has also voted against aid to the contras in Nicaragua and, as a proponent of a nuclear freeze, opposes the MX missile program.

Miss Mikulski's memberships include the National Women's Political Caucus and the Democratic National Strategy Council, and she also serves on the national board of directors of both Valley House and the Urban Coalition. She holds several honorary degrees and has been named Maryland's Outstanding Young Woman of the Year (1968), Woman of the Year (1973) by the Business and Professional Woman's Club Association of Baltimore, National Citizen of the Year (1973) by the Buffalo (New York) American-Political Eagle, and Outstanding Alumnus by both the University of Maryland's School of Social Work (1973) and Loyola College (1974).

Barbara Mikulski stands four feet eleven inches tall, has brown eyes and brown hair, and wears glasses. She has never married. Her demanding political schedule leaves little time for her favorite recreations of sailing, reading, and talking to old friends. Determined to keep in touch with her constituents, she commutes to Washington from her home, a 180-year-old brick Federal house in east Baltimore, in a car equipped with a cellular telephone. Miss Mikulski's constituency may soon widen since late in 1985 she announced her candidacy for the United States Senate seat that will be vacated by the retirement in 1986 of Senator Mathias.

References: N Y Post p21 Ja 27 '73 por; N Y Times p15 S 22 '73 por; Almanac of American Politics (1986); Lee, Essie E. Women in Congress (1979); Politics in America (1986); Stineman, Esther. American Political Women (1980); Who's Who in American Politics, 1985–86

## Monk, Meredith

*Nov. 20, 1942- Composer; performance artist; choreographer. Address: b. c/o The House Foundation for the Arts, Inc., 325 Spring St., New York City, N.Y. 10013*

Recently described by the *New York Times*'s music critic John Rockwell as "the archetypal multimedia artist, having managed to work—one art at a time or in combination—in dance, theatre, film, and video," Meredith Monk has been a leading innovator in the so-called "Next Wave" since the mid-1960s, when she was a choreographer and performer with the now legendary Judson Dance Theater. Over the years, her dances gradually evolved into imagistic, nonverbal theatre pieces in which she layered and juxtaposed movement, filmed sequences, elaborate special effects, and, perhaps most important, haunting, primitivist music of her own composition. Among Miss Monk's best-known works are the evening-length "opera epics" *Vessel* and *Quarry*, which earned her Obie awards for outstanding contribution to the Off-Broadway theatre in, respectively, the 1971–72 and 1975–76 New York seasons. In 1985 she celebrated her twentieth year as a performing artist with three special events: a revival of her multimedia opera *Quarry* at the La Mama Theatre, a retrospective of her films and videotapes at the Whitney Museum of American Art, and her debut performance at Carnegie Hall, where she introduced *Book of Days*, an ambitious new work in progress.

The daughter of Theodore Glenn and Audrey Lois (Zellman) Monk, Meredith Jane Monk was born on November 20, 1942 in Lima, Peru, where her mother, a professional singer, was giving a series of concerts. She spent her early childhood in New York City in a home filled with music. "I sang before I talked and read music before I read words—at three," Miss Monk has said, as quoted in the *New York Times* (March 28, 1976). While still a toddler, Miss Monk began her formal training in music and movement with classes in eurhythmics, a method of analyzing music by translating rhythm into bodily movements developed by the Swiss composer Émile Jaques-Dalcroze. After moving to Connecticut with her parents in about 1950, she expanded her music-related studies to include lessons in piano, ballet, modern dance, and mime.

At the George School, a Quaker coeducational preparatory school in Bucks County, Pennsylvania that she attended in the late 1950s, Miss Monk choreographed several student musical-comedy productions. She further explored her choreographic interests as a performing-arts major at Sarah Lawrence College, where her instructors included Bessie Schonberg and Judith Dunn. "Sarah Lawrence was a revelation," Miss Monk told Lelia K. Telberg in an interview for a *Music Journal* (September/October 1979) profile. "I was encouraged to work with a feeling, an idea . . . and let the medium and the form find itself. It seemed that finally I was able to combine movement with music and words, all coming from a single source . . . a total experience."

Shortly after receiving her B.A. degree from Sarah Lawrence in 1964, Meredith Monk joined the fledgling Judson Dance Theater, an experimental troupe based at the Judson Memorial Church in New York's Greenwich Village and dedicated to expanding the dance vocabulary to embrace natural "non-dance" movements. In addition to dancers and choreographers, the group included composers, poets, painters, and sculptors. During her years with the Judson Dance Theater, Meredith Monk performed in works by other choreographers and created a number of pieces—beginning with *Cartoon*, a humorous solo with deliberately exaggerated movements, in 1964—in which she turned away from what she has called "'dancey' dances" toward increasingly theatrical investigations of space, scale, and movement itself. *Portable* (1966), for example, consisted of Miss Monk's wheeling a portable "house" around the stage and marking its progress with tape, and *Duet for Cat's Scream and Locomotive* (1966) featured barely perceptible movements and gestures to a partly inaudible score. Perhaps the most discussed of her journeyman compositions was *16mm Earrings* (1966), a mixed-media theatre piece that employed projections and films to suggest the deceptiveness of outward appearances. For many critics, *16mm Earrings* was the highlight of Miss Monk's contribution to the controversial avant-garde dance festival at the Billy Rose Theatre in New York City in February 1969.

Most of Meredith Monk's early creations were solos or duets, but in the late 1960s she began working on ensemble pieces requiring large numbers of performers. Most of them were composed in collaboration with members of The House, the semi-communal performing-arts troupe that she founded in 1968. Committed to an interdisciplinary approach to performance, The House immeasurably influenced the direction of her career, for as Robb Baker pointed out in his retrospective analysis of Miss Monk's work for *Dance* magazine, (April 1976), many of the ideas and images that later surfaced in such major works as *Vessel* were improvised on the spot during the company's 1969 national tour of colleges and art centers. The company's repertory for the tour included *Barbershop*, in which Meredith Monk explored the personal relationship between a spectator and a work of art by encouraging the audience to roam around Chicago's Museum of Contemporary Art, where various members of The House were performing simultaneously in separate galleries, and *Dedicated to Dinosaurs*, an "offstage experience for dancers and audience," to use Miss Monk's words, designed to make viewers aware of a particular space—on that occasion the rotunda and the adjoining whale and dinosaur halls of the Smithsonian Institution's Museum of Natural History in Washington, D.C.

Meredith Monk continued her experiments with space and scale in her panoramic "live movie" *Needle-Brain Lloyd and the Systems Kid* (1970), which she staged outdoors on the Connecticut College campus as part of the annual American Dance Festival, and in *Juice* (1969), the three-part "theatre cantata" that she has described as an investigation of "the idea of compression." Presented in three evening-length installments at three different locations, ranging from the vast, spiraling central gallery of the Solomon R. Guggenheim Museum to the intimate confines of The House's SoHo loft, and separated by "intermissions" of a week or more in length, *Juice* zeroed in on a quartet. First glimpsed as four red-dyed figures marching through ranks of white-clad performers at the Guggenheim Museum, the four characters gradually came into focus over the course of the performance until, in the final segment, they appeared in close-up on videotape. "Seen as a whole, *Juice* was a true abstract drama . . . ," Anna Kisselgoff wrote in her review of the piece for the *New York Times* (December 9, 1969). "It was nonlinear in content, but its characterization of the protagonists unfolded steadily and progressively. . . . In their public confessions, voiced as a parallel to the discarded costumes from other sections, the four protagonists were now stripped bare to essentials about themselves. In this sense *Juice* was as specifically about the human situation as it appeared to be abstract."

In *Vessel* (1971), her mixed-media "opera epic" loosely based on incidents in the life of Joan of Arc, Meredith Monk reversed the "zoom lens" effect she had used in *Juice*, moving from her loft, where she presented scenes of everyday domestic life in the Middle Ages, to a "hand-made mountain" of muslin draped on an existing set in a nearby "environmental" theatre, to a vacant parking lot. There, amid bonfires, she staged her heroine's immolation in the light of a welder's blowtorch. Critics at the New York premiere of *Vessel* and at

subsequent revivals in Liverpool, England in 1972 and Chicago, Illinois in 1973 invariably singled out for special praise Miss Monk's arresting sound score. As Merete Bates wrote in her review for the *Guardian* (June 19, 1972), "The imagery compels. But it is the rhythm and quality of sound and movement that force you . . . to endure a level and depth of being normally submerged, ignored. The rhythm is insistent, repetitive, remorseless, inevitable. The variation within is of sounds as nervily harsh, explosive, as they are familiar."

Sound and rhythm have always played an important part in Meredith Monk's choreographic constructions, but it is her own extraordinary voice, with a range of several octaves, that characterizes or even determines her unique style. Resolved to "stretch the voice" in as many ways as she could, she devoted several years in the late 1960s to developing a vocal vocabulary that would be as varied and flexible as her dance vocabulary. "I was interested in using the voice as an instrument, as a source of energy and impulse, to get different registers and kinds of texture," she explained to David Sterritt of the *Christian Science Monitor* (January 18, 1982). Drawing on the sounds of the natural world, ancient forms of liturgical chant, and the vocal traditions of folk cultures, among other sources, Miss Monk gradually extended the parameters of vocal expression to become, in the words of Alan M. Kriegsman, a "one-person vocal synthesizer, reinventing the technique and art of singing with each new composition."

In her early compositions, Meredith Monk vocalized wordlessly over repeated, minimal piano phrases. Some of those simple, haunting mood pieces, which Deborah Jowitt, the dance critic, once described as a "textured backdrop for daydreams," were collected in the LP *Key* (Increase Records, 1971). Her discography also includes *Our Lady of Late* (Minona Records, 1974), a series of songs sung to the accompaniment of the eerie drone created by rubbing the rim of a thin-stemmed water glass which she composed for William Dunas' dance of the same name, *Songs from the Hill/Tablet* (Virgo, 1979), *Dolmen Music* (ECM/Warner, 1981), which German music critics voted the best recording of the year, and *Turtle Dreams* (ECM/Warner, 1983). As she gained skill and confidence in her craft, Meredith Monk added other voices and instruments to her increasingly elaborate musical constructions, but because she believes the voice itself is a "strong, rich language" she has continued to dispense with lyrics. "People can respond directly, without having to go through language," she told David Sterritt. "I'm trying to approach a vocal music that's both primordial and futuristic. Maybe there won't be language differentiation in the future."

Meredith Monk's hypnotic, ritualistic music was perfectly suited to her award-winning visionary theatre pieces *Education of the Girlchild* (1973), which took first prize at the 1975 Venice Biennale, and *Quarry* (1976). An allegorical "biography of womenkind," to use Deborah Jowitt's term,

Education of the Girlchild concluded with a forty-five-minute tour-de-force solo in which Miss Monk, in the central role of the Girlchild, passed through all the stages of a woman's life in reverse. In her skillful transformation from withered crone into a strong and agile young girl, Miss Monk "tells us what it is to grow up by growing down," as Anna Kisselgoff observed in her New York Times (February 10, 1979) review of a revival of the piece.

Like Girlchild, Quarry depended for its impact at least partly on shared experience and collective memory. Indeed the title refers to what Miss Monk has called "a digging up of memory, or racial unconsciousness." Set during World War II, Quarry presents jumbled images of the world as perceived by a feverish child. She turned in such a brilliant performance as the fitfully sleeping youngster that most reviewers were willing to overlook the highly personal and in some instances incomprehensible symbolism that threatened to overwhelm the piece.

While preparing for the premieres or revivals of her major opera epics, Meredith Monk created several chamber theatre works that can be linked by imagery into broad categories. They are the "travelogue" series (Paris, Chacon, and Venice/Milan), which she made in collaboration with Ping Chong, and the so-called "archaeology" pieces (Small Scroll, Anthology, The Plateau Series, and Recent Ruins). In Paris (1973) and Chacon (1974), she played with inverse ratios, devising an episodic, largely nonverbal duet, which she performed with Ping Chong, to represent a stroll through the streets of the French capital and an ensemble work for twenty-eight dancers and musicians to illustrate life in the tiny New Mexican hamlet of Chacon. A more complex work than either of its predecessors, Venice/Milan (1976) presented the collaborators' impressions of those cities in a series of Felliniesque tableaux vivants.

In the extended solo Anthology (1975), the fragmented group piece Small Scroll (1975), and the reduced-scale work The Plateau Series (1978), Meredith Monk treated such mundane daily activities as running, petting a dog, sewing, washing clothes, and chopping wood as ritualistic "task-dances." Props—the artifacts of civilization—took on an added significance in each of those pieces, particularly in Small Scroll, which reminded Deborah Jowitt, who reviewed a performance of the piece at St. Mark's-in-the-Bouwerie for the Village Voice (June 16, 1975), of "the mysterious scenes in Babylonian cylinder seals," where "everything is clear, but nothing is clear." The most ambitious of the archaeology pieces was Recent Ruins (1979), in which Meredith Monk used mechanical props, elaborate period costumes, special effects, and an extended film sequence set on New York City's own "recent ruin," Ellis Island, to show how generations of archaeologists contributed to the destruction of ancient cultures by deliberately distancing themselves emotionally from them.

The film Ellis Island won major prizes at the Atlanta and San Francisco film festivals. In making Ellis Island, which she has described as "a poetic, atmospheric look at a place and a time," she used visuals, natural sounds, and her own evocative music to re-create the ambience of Ellis Island at the turn of the century, when it served as the chief immigration station of the United States. Ellis Island has since been telecast nationwide by the Public Broadcasting Service, and it has also been shown on West German television. Miss Monk's video version of Paris brought station KTCA-TV in Minneapolis, Minnesota the Corporation for Public Broadcasting's first prize for performance programming, and her video Turtle Dreams (Waltz), a segment from her multimedia cabaret Turtle Dreams (1983), took the grand prize at the first Video Culture Canada festival in 1983.

In the late 1970s, Meredith Monk began to concentrate on musical composition and performance, primarily because she had grown to "distrust the theatre a little bit," as she explained to John Rockwell in the New York Times interview. "All that hiding behind 'the fourth wall,'" she went on. "I began to think of music concerts as more honest." Since then, she has given a number of solo and group concerts throughout the United States and in Europe. At one such recital, billed as a "music concert with film," at the City Center Space in New York City in May 1981, she offered an eclectic program of solos for voice and piano, most notably a condensed version of her second-act solo from Education of the Girlchild, vocal ensembles, instrumentals, and excerpts from her films Ellis Island and Quarry. According to Wayne Robins, in his review of the concert for Newsday (May 21, 1981), Meredith Monk explored a "breathtaking" range of vocal possibilities in her solos, sounding at times "like a cross between Joni Mitchell and the Velvet Underground's Nico" or "like a barking dog who can mimic the sounds of an alto saxophone." Writing in the Christian Science Monitor (May 2, 1981), David Sterritt agreed that the effect of Miss Monk's "utterly unique" sound, "with its enormous leaps from cozy coloratura to keening wails, hollers, and sighs," was "dizzying," but he was even more enchanted by what he called the "enormously emotional implications" of her group compositions. For him, "Dolmen Music," a piece for six singers, cello, and percussion, "summed up what Monk's chameleonlike art is all about: a cry from the heart refined by a busy intellect and expressed with shivering immediacy."

Two major new multimedia theatre pieces joined the Monk canon in the early 1980s—Specimen Days in 1981 and The Games in 1983. Specimen Days, which derives its title from Walt Whitman's book about his experiences as a male nurse during the Civil War along with other autobiographical material, including reminiscences of childhood and travel sketches, examines the devastating effects of war on the lives of individuals through a series of poignant domestic vignettes (a family gathering around a dinner table or posing for a group photograph) and stunning visual effects (a huge cannonball flattening hundreds of miniature white tents). Although grounded in the Civil War era, *Specimen Days* is concerned about the future. Its final image is a turtle lumbering along a deserted city street—the sole survivor of "the last of all civil wars," as David Sterritt put it.

Meredith Monk pursued her apocalyptic vision of the future in *The Games*, a parable that she created with Ping Chong about a post-nuclear society struggling to preserve the vestiges of civilization in the mechanical repetition of half-remembered rituals. "It's about loss, about loving what we have now and fighting for what we have now," Miss Monk has explained, as quoted in the *Village Voice* (October 9, 1984). "Not that it won't change, but that we won't let it be destroyed." Commissioned by Peter Stein's Schaubühne repertory theatre in West Berlin in 1983, *The Games* received its American premiere the following year at the Brooklyn (New York) Academy of Music's Next Wave Festival. Miss Monk came in for special praise from the New York critics for her chilling portrayal of the Orwellian Gamesmaster who referees the competitions and for her unusually rich score, in which she combined vocal chants and wails with otherworldly instrumental passages for such exotic instruments as the Chinese shawm and the alto rauschpfeife.

A slender, lithe woman who stands five feet two inches tall, Meredith Monk has a long, pale face with large, expressive eyes and brown hair, which she often wears in braids. Although her family history is integral to her semi-autobiographical works, she carefully guards her privacy and rarely grants interviews. On one of those rare occasions, she looked back on her career for Jon Pareles of the *New York Times* (May 17, 1985): "I never wanted to make the kind of piece where you walk in at 8:30, sit down in front of a proscenium stage knowing what to expect, and forget about it the next morning. . . . What I love about the theatre is that it gives you the chance to walk into a different world." In addition to the honors mentioned above, Miss Monk has won six ASCAP awards for her musical compositions and a Creative Arts award from Brandeis University, and she has received grants and fellowships from the National Endowment for the Arts, the Creative Artists Public Service, the New York State Council for the Arts, and the Guggenheim Foundation. She has served on the performing arts faculties of New York University, Goddard College, Sarah Lawrence College, and the Naropa Institute. She makes her home in a loft in the SoHo section of Manhattan.

References: *Christian Sci Mon* p14 Ja 18 '82 por; *Dance* 50:56+ Ap '76 pors; *Music J* p6+ S/O '79 pors; *N Y Times* II p8 Mr 28 '76 por, Cp3 My 17 '85 por; *Newsweek* 104:124+ O 29 '84 pors; *Performing Arts J* p3+ Spring/Summer '78; *Women & Performance J* 1:19+ Spring/Summer '83; *Encyclopedia of Dance and Ballet* (1977); *Who's Who of American Women, 1983–84*

## Moreno, Rita

(mô-rä´nō)

Dec. 11, 1931– Actress; singer; dancer. Address: b. c/o William Morris Agency, 1350 Avenue of the Americas, New York City, N.Y. 10019

The only performer ever to win all four of the entertainment world's most important awards—a feat that landed her in the *Guinness Book of World Records*—Rita Moreno has finally emerged from the "fiery Latin" image that dogged her during her early years as a Hollywood starlet. She won the 1962 Oscar as best supporting actress for her performance in the classic movie musical *West Side Story*; a 1975 Tony for her hilarious impersonation of Googie Gomez in Terrence McNally's Broadway comedy *The Ritz*; the recording industry's Grammy, in 1972, for her participation in the soundtrack album of her popular children's television series *The Electric Company*; and two Emmy awards, for guest appearances on television's *The Muppet Show* in 1977 and *The Rockford Files* in 1978.

Rita Moreno was born Rosa Dolores Alverio on December 11, 1931 in Humacao, a small town near the rain forest of Puerto Rico. Her parents, Paco Alverio and the former Rosa Maria Marcano, were so soon divorced that she can only vaguely remember her father. Her mother then went to the United States, leaving her in the care of relatives until she could earn enough money as a seamstress to come back for her five-year-old daughter. After making the twelve-day sea voyage to New York in stormy weather, the future actress settled with her mother and several other relatives in a tenement in the Washington Heights section of Manhattan.

Soon after arriving in New York, Rita Moreno began taking dance lessons from Paco Cansino, an uncle of Rita Hayworth, and before long she was performing professionally to supplement the meager family income. At the same time she attended Public School 132 in New York—the extent of her education, except for some extension courses taken years later at the University of California at Los Angeles and a year of acting lessons with Jeff Corey. She appeared in the children's theatre in the toy department at Macy's and at weddings and bar mitzvahs, sometimes with bananas on her head in imitation of the Latin idol of the day, Carmen Miranda. At thirteen, billed as "Rosita Cosio," she had a part in a Broadway play, that of Angelina in Harry Kleiner's war drama, *Skydrift*, which ran for only seven performances in November 1945. In her teens she sang and danced in tacky nightclubs in such cities as Las Vegas, Boston, Montreal, and New York.

In the mid-1940s Rita Moreno did the dubbing for such child stars as Elizabeth Taylor, Margaret O'Brien, and Peggy Ann Garner in Hollywood films destined for Spanish-speaking countries. She made her own film debut as a delinquent in the reform-school melodrama *So Young, So Bad* (United Artists, 1950), and she was signed that year to a contract by MGM, after a talent scout arranged a meeting for her with studio head Louis B. Mayer. By that time she was calling herself "Rosita Moreno," having adopted the surname of her stepfather, Edward Moreno. Then, at the request of MGM officials, she shortened her first name to Rita. For MGM she appeared in small parts in the Mario Lanza vehicle *The Toast of New Orleans* and the Esther Williams aquatic extravaganza *Pagan Love Song*, both in 1950. "Then I was dropped from MGM, to my *great* shock," she recalled for Allan Wallach of *Newsday* (May 4, 1975), "because I really thought I was going to be the biggest, hottest star that ever happened."

Reluctant to admit defeat, Rita Moreno kept herself busy for a time by freelancing in Hollywood. Although she managed to obtain a small role, as Zelda Zanders, in MGM's *Singin' in the Rain* (1952), she was usually stereotyped as a sultry Latin temptress, in such grade-B films as *The Fabulous Senorita* (Republic, 1952), *The Ring*, (United Artists, 1952), *Cattle Town* (Warner, 1952), *Latin Lovers* (MGM, 1953), and *Jivaro* (Paramount, 1954). On the then prevailing Hollywood theory that one type of exotic foreigner was interchangeable with another, she was also cast as an Arab, in Columbia's 1953 war drama *El Alamein*, and occasionally, as in *Fort Vengeance* (Allied Artists, 1953) and *The Yellow Tomahawk* (United Artists, 1954), in American Indian roles. An early attempt to escape from what she once described, in an interview with Jack Hicks of *TV Guide* (January 15, 1983), as "the Yonkee Peeg school of acting" by going on stage failed when she was dropped from the cast of the play *Camino Real* after one week of rehearsals, because the playwright, Tennessee Williams, did not like her voice.

The "Rita the Cheetah" image created by her film roles was reinforced by Miss Moreno's turbulent private life, especially her relationship with Marlon Brando, then at the peak of his stardom.

They dated, off and on, for about eight years and, as she explained to Jack Hicks, "if we had an argument, the press knew about it before my best friends did." Another boyfriend, Geordie Hormel of the meat-packing family, was falsely arrested in 1954 on charges of marijuana possession, and Miss Moreno added to her notoriety at the time when she got into a fight with policemen who found her asleep in Hormel's living room and wanted to search her belongings. Underneath the vibrant facade, however, she suffered from deep feelings of inferiority, in large part a residue of her Hispanic childhood. To combat her depression, she underwent psychoanalysis for six-and-a-half years.

A 1954 appearance on the cover of *Life* magazine helped Rita Moreno to obtain a contract with Twentieth Century-Fox, where, after being assigned a small role as a singer in *Garden of Evil* (1954), she appeared in parts that were somewhat more substantial but generally followed the same pattern as before. Reviewing the adventure film *Untamed* (1955), set in South Africa, Archer Winsten of the New York *Post* (March 13, 1955) noted that she was "again billed as a fiery love machine" and queried: "Will the powers in Twentieth Century-Fox wait patiently until Miss Moreno loses half of her youth, vitality and beauty before they get around to giving her a romantic break?" Winsten's plea went unheeded by the makers of the semi-historical Western *Seven Cities of Gold* (1955), in which she asked soldier Richard Egan, "Why joo no luv Oola no more?" and, on hearing his disheartening reply, jumped off a cliff.

After appearing in the Tom Ewell comedy *The Lieutenant Wore Skirts* (1955), in which she did a takeoff on Marilyn Monroe, Rita Moreno obtained what she considered her best movie role of the 1950s, that of the Burmese slave girl Tuptim in the adaptation of Rodgers and Hammerstein's Broadway musical hit *The King and I* (1956). With her romantic partner, Carlos Rivas, she sang "We Kiss in a Shadow" and "I Have Dreamed," and she narrated the film's ballet, "The Small House of Uncle Thomas," choreographed by Jerome Robbins. A year later, Robbins suggested that she try out for the ingenue lead part of Maria in Leonard Bernstein's new Broadway musical *West Side Story*, but she did not do so because of film commitments.

After appearing as the tavern wench Huguette in the Paramount production of the operetta *The Vagabond King* (1956) and finishing her Twentieth Century-Fox contract with *The Deerslayer* (1957), Rita Moreno did not make another movie until *This Rebel Breed* (Warner, 1960). Turning again to the stage, she played Catherine in Arthur Miller's *A View from the Bridge* at theatres in La Jolla, California and in Seattle, launching a successful career in summer stock and regional theatre that over the years included such roles as Sally Bowles in *I Am a Camera*, Annie Sullivan in *The Miracle Worker*, Lola in *Damn Yankees*, and Adelaide in *Guys and Dolls*. Her personal problems, meanwhile, had come to a head when, despondent over career frustrations and emotional problems, she tried to kill herself by taking an overdose of sleeping pills. On finding herself in a hospital, however, she decided she wanted to live. Her therapist told her, as she recalled for Arthur Bell of the *Village Voice* (August 23, 1976), that "it was the most therapeutic attempt he had ever seen. It was as if I had exorcised all my demons and had turned a real corner."

Rita Moreno's fortunes took a turn for the better when director-choreographer Jerome Robbins cast her in the film version of *West Side Story* (United Artists, 1961), not as Maria, but in the more ebullient, supporting role of Anita. As in *The King and I*, Miss Moreno did all her own singing, and she spent hours with Robbins rehearsing her dance numbers, especially "America," a sardonic song comparing life in the United States with that in Puerto Rico. *West Side Story* was acclaimed as a landmark in film-musical history, ultimately winning a total of ten Academy Awards, including best supporting actress honors for Rita Moreno. Summing up the reactions of preview audiences, Joe Hyams wrote in the *New York Herald Tribune* (September 26, 1961): "Miss Moreno emerges as a first-rate dramatic talent in one of the best pictures of the year. Some people claim she steals the picture."

Although Rita Moreno had hoped that her Oscar would lead to better assignments, her performance as Anita only confirmed the "Latin spitfire" image in the minds of Hollywood executives. After portraying Rosa Zacharias in the screen adaptation of Tennessee Williams' *Summer and Smoke* (Paramount, 1961) and appearing as a camp follower in the World War II film *Cry of Battle* (Allied Artists, 1963) she left what she felt was "the dead-end environment" of Hollywood and moved to London. There she replaced Dawn Porter, who was indisposed, in the role of Ilona Ritter in Hal Prince's 1964 West End production of the American musical *She Loves Me*. But although she received excellent notices, her hopes of remaining in London were dashed by the strict British Equity regulations regarding importation of performers. Returning to Broadway, she played Iris Parodus Brustein, in her words, "the only Greco-Irish-Indian hillbilly in existence," in Lorraine Hansberry's play *The Sign in Sidney Brustein's Window*. The drama of Greenwich Village life acquired a cult following and managed to eke out a 101-performance run.

With the help of Marlon Brando, Rita Moreno returned to films in the role of a drug addict in *The Night of the Following Day* (Universal, 1969). The kidnapping thriller failed to evoke enthusiasm from critics, but it brought Miss Moreno some favorable reviews, including one from Pauline Kael of the *New Yorker* (March 8, 1969), who wrote that she did the "only acting in the picture" and gave "an expert stylized performance." It proved to be a steppingstone to more films, including *Marlowe* (MGM, 1969), with James Garner as Raymond Chandler's famous detective, and *Popi* (United Artists, 1969), a comedy set in East Harlem, in which she played Alan Arkin's girlfriend. Her part

in Mike Nichols' production of Jules Feiffer's successful comedy *Carnal Knowledge* (Avco-Embassy, 1971), as the prostitute whom Jack Nicholson visits to cure his impotence, was even smaller, but also brought her favorable notices.

On stage, Rita Moreno's 1968 impersonation of Serafina in Tennessee Williams' *The Rose Tattoo* at the Ivanhoe Theatre in Chicago brought her repeated standing ovations and the Joseph Jefferson Award from that city's critics. In 1970 she portrayed the evangelist Sharon Falconer in the short-lived Broadway musical *Gantry*, based on the Sinclair Lewis novel, and then replaced Linda Lavin in Neil Simon's long-running hit comedy *Last of the Red Hot Lovers*. A 1973 revival of Sidney Kingsley's *Detective Story*, in which she played the shoplifter, closed in Philadelphia without making it to Broadway.

Meanwhile, in 1971, the Children's Television Workshop, producers of the widely acclaimed program *Sesame Street*, offered Rita Moreno the chance to appear in its new Public Broadcasting System series, *The Electric Company*, designed to teach seven- to ten-year-old children to improve their reading skills. As she told Neil Hickey in a *TV Guide* interview (December 2, 1972), she jumped at the opportunity because of the show's educational value and because it gave her the chance to do "low comedy—zany, bizarre, eccentric stuff." Her continuing characters on the show included Otto, an autocratic and constantly frustrated movie director, and Pandore, "a bratty WASP girl with blonde curls." A soundtrack recording of *The Electric Company* brought Rita Moreno, along with Bill Cosby and others, a 1972 Grammy award for the best recording for children.

At a party for James Coco, Rita Moreno was asked to perform a routine that she had originated during breaks in the filming of *West Side Story*, in which she sang "Everything's Coming Up Roses" with an exaggerated Spanish accent. One of the guests was playwright Terrence McNally, who doubled over with laughter. Early in 1974 Miss Moreno, who was then appearing in Peter Nichols' *The National Health* in New Haven, was invited to a performance at the Yale Repertory Theater of McNally's new play, *The Tubs*, a farce set in a homosexual bathhouse. Flabbergasted to find that one of the characters, an untalented but ambitious Puerto Rican chanteuse named Googie Gomez, "was doing *my* number," she agreed to McNally's request that she play Googie when the play, retitled *The Ritz*, came to Broadway, after fulfilling her commitment to appear in *The National Health* at the Circle in the Square in New York City.

After *The Ritz* opened at Broadway's Longacre Theater on January 20, 1975 for a 400-performance run, Bernard Drew of the *White Plains Reporter Dispatch*, representing a consensus of critical opinion, wrote of Rita Moreno's performance: "In fractured English, she creates a portrait of tattered glory. . . . Hot, cold, tempestuous, wiggling, seething, cursing, . . . so that she tears the house down every time she opens her mouth or does a bump and grind, she is showing a new generation of the-atergoers what stars are all about." Miss Moreno, who felt that by playing Googie she was thumbing her nose at the screenwriters who had created her earlier stereotyped parts, was happy to win the Tony Award, but somewhat disappointed that it came only in the "supporting actress" category.

Rita Moreno repeated her Googie characteriza-tion in the film version of The Ritz (Warner, 1976), which was less successful than the play, with critics divided as to whether her natural affinity for the role had been impaired by what some felt was Richard Lester's inept direction. Since then, she has appeared as a Jewish mother in The Boss's Son (American Cinema Ltd., 1978); as an Italian-American mistress in Happy Birthday, Gemini (United Artists, 1980), based on the Broadway play Gemini; and as the wife of dentist Jack Weston in The Four Seasons (Universal, 1981), actor-director Alan Alda's comedy-drama about three married couples who take vacations together. Commenting on the latter, which proved to be one of the year's box-office sleepers, David Ansen noted in Newsweek (May 25, 1981) that Miss Moreno was "a delight, though underused."

Since 1978 much of Rita Moreno's time has been taken up with the nightclub act which she pres-ented that year in Chicago and at the Grand Finale II in New York City. When she opened for Bill Cos-by at Harrah's in Lake Tahoe later that year, Variety's critic (November 8, 1978) acclaimed Rita Moreno as "one of the most exciting things to come this state's way in a long time." Since then, she has taken her act to such places as Toronto and Atlantic City, as well as to the Queen Elizabeth II and other cruise ships.

Two pilots for projected television series made by Rita Moreno during the 1970s were unsuccess-ful, but beginning in 1982 she played Violet, the head of a large company's secretarial pool in the ABC-TV situation comedy Nine to Five, spun off from Jane Fonda's 1980 feminist movie. One of her purposes in delineating the character, she told Jack Hicks, was to "show the women out there that you don't shrivel up like a raisin when you hit forty." The show finished in sixteenth place among all prime-time network series for the 1982-83 season, but after its time slot was changed and the original executive producers were replaced, the ratings slipped, and Nine to Five was "put on hiatus."

In addition to her film, television, and nightclub work, Rita Moreno found time to co-star with James Coco and Sally Struthers in Wally's Cafe, a Broadway comedy by Sam Bobrick and Ron Clark that ran for only twelve performances in June 1981. A revival of Neil Simon's hit comedy The Odd Couple, which the playwright rewrote so that its two main characters could be played by women, opened at Broadway's Longacre Theater on June 11, 1985, following a national tour, with Rita More-no as the slovenly Olive Madison and Sally Struth-ers in the role of the compulsively tidy Florence Unger. Although most critics liked both the play and its stars, with Rita Moreno, in the words of the

Christian Science Monitor critic John Beaufort (June 12, 1985), playing the "designated slob of the duo with her state-of-the-art finesse," some felt that its principals were miscast and that The Odd Couple did not easily lend itself to a "sex-change operation."

Rita Moreno is five feet two inches tall, weighs about 110 pounds, and has dark hair and brown eyes. In June 1965 she married Dr. Leonard Gor-don, an internist and cardiologist at New York's Mount Sinai Hospital. Dr. Gordon, who is Jewish, did not realize that she was "that Rita Moreno" un-til their sixth date. Their daughter, Fernanda Lu, briefly performed in her mother's act at the Sands Hotel in Atlantic City in 1984 before beginning her freshman year at Tufts University. Rita Moreno and her husband, who retired following a heart at-tack and is now her personal manager, have a house in Pacific Palisades, California and an apart-ment in upper Manhattan. In an interview with Helen Dorsey of the Chicago Tribune (October 13, 1982), she referred to her family as "the best thing that ever happened to me . . . my answer to sanity." Her favorite recreations are cooking, nee-dlework, and growing vegetables. She has served on the boards of directors of Third World Cinema and the Alvin Ailey Dance Company, and on the theatre panel of the National Foundation of the Arts. In August 1985, in Chicago, she received the Sarah Siddons Award.

References: Chicago Tribune I p14+ O 13 '82 pors; N Y Daily News III p1 F 2 '75 pors; N Y Sunday News mag p10+ Ag 22 '76 pors; N Y Times II p1+ Mr 30 '75 pors; TV Guide 31:26+ Ja 15 '83 por; Village Voice p156 Ag 23 '76 por; Notable Names in the American Theatre (1976); Who's Who in America, 1984-85; Who's Who in the Theatre (1981)

## Murray, Bill

Sept. 21, 1950- Actor; comedian. Address: b. c/o Columbia Pictures, Columbia Plaza, Burbank, Calif. 91505

With his scruffy appearance, deadpan face, laid-back manner, and cheeky delivery of sardonic wisecracks, Bill Murray the comedian is a walking inside joke, a caricatured embodiment of the sensi-bility of the young mass audience that flocked to his zany motion pictures Meatballs (1980) and Stripes (1981) and made his occult horror spoof Ghostbusters (1984) one of the top-grossing film farces of all time. An alumnus of the Chicago im-provisational company Second City, Murray honed his brash and breezy persona on The Na-tional Lampoon Radio Hour and in the cabaret re-vue The National Lampoon Show. He began his ascent to stardom as a member of the Not Ready for Prime Time Players on the NBC television show Saturday Night Live.

*Bill Murray*

When Pauline Kael first watched Bill Murray on *Saturday Night Live*, in 1976, he struck her as the kind of person who "would think up fraternity-initiation rites." "He seemed like something out of a swamp—cold-blooded yet sweaty . . . ," Miss Kael wrote in the *New Yorker* (July 13, 1981). "Was his obnoxiousness a wimp's revenge? He seemed the shiftiest of comics, . . . smug, dislikable. . . . Yet the more I saw of him the funnier he became. He's a master of show-business insincerity. . . . There's a wild strain loose inside the doughy hand-someness which saves him from predictabili-ty. . . . Murray seems enormously likable now—the more so, maybe, because he has been wearing his suave put-on expressions so long that he has no way to be straight without appearing even phonier."

Bill Murray was born in the Chicago suburb of Wilmette, Illinois on September 21, 1950, the fifth child and the self-described "black sheep" among the nine children of Lucille Murray and the late Ed Murray, a lumber-company salesman. According to Bill Murray, humor was a family affair, in which each of the children was a "cutup," vying for their father's risibility. "He [the father] was real funny, and he was . . . very tough to make laugh," Mur-ray told Timothy Crouse in an interview for *Rolling Stone* (August 16, 1984). "He was very dry. [But] my father's father was the real nut . . . the kind of guy who had the light-up bow tie. But you'd really have to beat up on him to get that bow tie out there. He would do it only at the most tastefully tasteless occasions."

Murray received his primary education under Franciscan nuns at coeducational St. Joseph's pa-rochial school in Wilmette and his secondary edu-cation under Jesuit priests at the Loyola Academy for boys in the same city. As a Catholic schoolboy

he was, in his words, "an under-achiever and a screw-off." "I just didn't care for school much," he explained to Timothy Crouse. "Studying was bor-ing. I was lazy. I'm still lazy. And I had no interest in getting good grades." He was good at sports, however, especially baseball and basketball, and he acted in high-school theatre, playing Keefer in *The Caine Mutiny* and dancing in the chorus of *The Music Man*. His original motivation for partic-ipating in dramatics was ulterior: "You got to get out of class for a few hours . . . and there were girls."

By the time their father died, in 1969, the older Murray children were either on their own or pay-ing their way through Catholic school by golf-caddying and baby-sitting. How his mother "managed to get all the rest of the family raised" is still "amazing" to Bill Murray. Before training his sights on show-business, Murray aspired to careers in medicine and baseball. (Several years into his acting career, he was still debating between it and minor-league baseball.) In the meantime, in addi-tion to caddying, he worked in a pizza parlor.

Murray's brief stint as a pre-med major at Jesuit-run Regis College in Denver, Colorado marked the beginning of what he refers to as his "bad phase." According to David Felton in *Rolling Stone* (April 20, 1978) he devoted more energy to soft drugs than to his studies. Felton reported that Murray was ar-rested twice on marijuana charges; on the first oc-casion, in Sterling, Colorado, charges were dropped for lack of material evidence; on the sec-ond, he was apprehended carrying a suitcase full of the weed at O'Hare International Airport in Chi-cago, found guilty, and put on probation.

Meanwhile, Bill Murray's older brother Brian Doyle-Murray (who added the Doyle to his name to avoid confusion with the British actor Brian Murray) had joined Second City, the Chicago com-edy company known for its fresh satirical revues and intense improvisational training program. While hanging out at Brian's apartment in Chica-go's Old Town neighborhood on the Near North Side, Bill met the Second City troupers John Belushi, Harold Ramis, and Joe Flaherty, the direc-tor Del Close, and Bernie Sahlins, who ran Second City. After what he has described as "a lot of watching experience" at the Second City theatre, he began taking workshops there on a scholarship.

During the 1972–73 Off-Broadway season John Belushi moved to New York City to join Chevy Chase and others in the cast of *National Lam-poon's Lemmings*, a rock musical revue conceived by Sean Kelly, the senior editor of the adult satiri-cal magazine *National Lampoon*. In 1974, when John Belushi was helping to produce the *National Lampoon Radio Hour*, he recruited Joe Flaherty, Harold Ramis, and the two Murray brothers for that project, which was taped in New York and syndicated nationally. Gilda Radner, an alumnus of the Toronto offshoot of Second City, and Chevy Chase were also in the cast of the radio show.

From the *National Lampoon Radio Hour* the Murrays, Belushi, Ramis, and Miss Radner moved into the topical cabaret revue *The National Lampoon Show*. The broadly satirical words and lyrics of that show were written by the cast members ("overlooked by Sean Kelly") and set to music by Paul Jacobs. Bill Murray's contributions included a city dweller ridiculously ecstatic over such urban wonders as the neighborhood delicatessen and a prurient priest satisfying his voyeurism in the confessional. Produced by Toronto-based Ivan Reitman and directed by Martin Charmin, *The National Lampoon Show* toured Philadelphia, Ontario, Toronto, and Long Island before opening at the New Palladium, a Manhattan bar-restaurant, on March 2, 1975. New York critics hailed the "no-holds-barred assault on icons and institutions," and it ran at the New Palladium for 180 performances.

Among the many show-business people in the *The National Lampoon Show*'s audience were the Canadian-born television producer Lorne Michaels, who was preparing to launch *Saturday Night Live* on the NBC network, and the sportscaster Howard Cosell, who would soon become the host of the short-lived variety show *Saturday Night Live with Howard Cosell* on ABC. Cosell recruited Bill Murray and Brian Doyle-Murray for his show, which premiered on September 20, 1975. Michaels signed Belushi and Gilda Radner for his, which began telecasting three weeks later, on October 11, 1975. Because of the duplication in name, the title of Michaels' show was temporarily changed, first to *Saturday Night* and then to *NBC's Saturday Night Live*. Among the original Not Ready for Prime Time Players were Chevy Chase and Dan Ackroyd, another Second City alumnus.

ABC canceled *Saturday Night Live with Howard Cosell* after just half a season, in January 1976, and Bill Murray spent most of the rest of 1976 in California, contributing comic relief to television documentaries directed by Mike Shamberg. After Chevy Chase left the Not Ready for Prime Time Players, Lorne Michaels tapped Murray as Chase's replacement, in January 1977. Beginning as a second banana, Murray slowly worked his way to prominence in the ensemble. Among the comic personae he developed were an oily lounge singer; a name-dropping, ostentatiously hip movie critic; a gossip columnist who takes personal umbrage at the misbehavior of celebrities ("I'm sorry, but that's the way I feel. Now get out of here."), and other personifications of sleaziness and boorishness. A favorite with the television audience was his characterization of Todd Loopner, an uncouth adolescent "nerd" whose idea of fun is giving people "noogies" (knuckle raps on the skull). When he puts his arms in a hammerlock around his wretched, nasally congested girlfriend, Lisa (Gilda Radner), it is to utter, not terms of endearment, but, "How about a couple noogies?"

"Perhaps no one is better than Murray at lampooning the kind of show-biz fatuousness that saturates much of the prime time on NBC and the other two networks as well . . . ," Tom Shales wrote in the *Washington Post* (May 31, 1978). "That the

*Saturday Night Live* people are around to mess up executive hair [an allusion to an off-air incident in which Murray hammerlocked and repeatedly "noogied" Herbert S. Schlossler, then the president of NBC, who kept trying to pat his hair back down] is one of the best protections NBC has against creative atrophy. There is nothing on television at any hour to compare with the breakneck spontaneity and derring-do of *Saturday Night Live*."

A year later Frank Rich observed in *Time* (July 16, 1979) that "one of the happier developments" on *Saturday Night Live* during the 1978-79 season was "the unleashing" of Bill Murray. "When he finally seized centerstage, he stopped being a straight man and became a live—or maybe frazzled—wire. Murray is a master of comic insincerity. He speaks in italics and tries to raise the put-down into an art form. His routine resembles Steve Martin's, with a crucial difference. Where Martin is slick and cold, Murray is disheveled and vulnerable. One feels that Murray's manic behavior is a cover for some rather touching neuroses."

In his first motion-picture appearance, Murray was an extra leaning against a barroom wall in Paul Mazursky's *Next Stop Greenwich Village* (Twentieth Century-Fox, 1975). His opportunity to star in a film came three years later, through Ivan Reitman. Fresh from his huge success in coproducing *National Lampoon's Animal House* (Universal, 1978), a college-fraternity burlesque starring John Belushi, Reitman wanted to try his hand at directing a similar broad spoof—but one with heart—of life in a boys' summer camp, with Murray in the role of a head counselor who, despite his bluff talk, becomes an effective father figure to a troubled camper. Approached by Reitman early in 1978, Murray rejected the idea. Undaunted, Reitman wrote the rough script for *Meatballs* and pursued Murray to Oregon, where his prospective star was hoping to spend the summer playing for a Triple A baseball team. "There was no second choice," Reitman told Dave Hirshey of the New York *Daily News* (July 15, 1979). "I felt he had the perfect image that the part required, an ability to play a semi-loon and at the same time relate to a confused, lonely kid."

Murray finally relented, after working on Reitman's script, fleshing out the characters with the help of Harold Ramis and other writers. Much of *Meatballs* was improvised during the shooting, at Camp White Pine, near Haliburton, Ontario, Canada. Produced on a shoe-string budget of $1.5 million and released by Paramount Pictures with limited optimism, the film turned out to be the surprise hit of the summer of 1979, attracting a vast juvenile audience as well as older, hard-core Murray aficionados and grossing $64 million. Reviewers of the movie during its first run thought that Murray, in the role of Tripper, the wisecracking but warmhearted head counselor at crisis-ridden Camp North Star, held the ramshackle slapstick together and turned the film *Meatballs* into "a joyous entertainment," "a lovely, airy cartoon." In her 1981 *New Yorker* piece, Pauline Kael looked back on the film as "eminently forgettable" but credited Murray with playing "big brother to a gooey-eyed kid with a crush on him [without] embarrassing himself (and us) by somehow contriving to look above the kid's head, off-screen—anywhere but at that moist, adoring face."

In *The Jerk* (Universal, 1979), a comic vehicle for his friend Steve Martin, Murray had a cameo role as a homosexual Jewish interior decorator, and he was featured in part of the motion picture *Mr. Mike's Mondo Video* (independently released, 1979), a mock documentary written and produced by Michael O'Donoghue, comprising television sketches that had been rejected by the NBC censors as violations of good taste. As the deranged grounds keeper, he was one of the numerous professional flakes, headed by Chevy Chase, in the somewhat less offensive golf-course comedy *Caddyshack* (Warner Brothers, 1980), and he had an uncredited and largely improvised supporting role as the roommate of Dustin Hoffman's transvestite character in *Tootsie* (Columbia, 1982).

Murray starred in the commercially unsuccessful *Where the Buffalo Roam* (Universal, 1980), subtitled "A Movie Based on the Twisted Legend of Dr. Hunter S. Thompson." In the view of most critics, that film, produced and directed by Art Linson, turned the inspired lunacy of countercultural journalist Thompson into a farrago of set-piece gags and madcap adventures without conveying the excellence of Thompson's creative reportage and the pain and moral outrage beneath his facetiousness. "Murray is as engaging as he was in *Meatballs*," Jack Kroll wrote in *Newsweek* (May 12, 1980), "but he plays Thompson as a collage of mechanical attributes and accouterments." Kroll blamed producer-director Art Linson for failing "to give his movie any real shape and energy."

Applying his low-comedy formula and still relatively frugal pocketbook ($10 million) to the "new Army," Ivan Reitman, this time as both producer and director, again scored big at the box office with *Stripes* (Columbia, 1981), a frenetic farce about a hip misfit who, with his buddy (Harold Ramis, who co-wrote the screenplay), turns the basic-training manual upside down and relentlessly mocks the military establishment. Most initial critical assessments were more negative than positive: "a cheerfully moronic farce for the male sodality," "two hours of jiveass schtick," "a needlessly infantile movie that blunts the excellent on-camera work of Murray and Ramis." "It's just a flimsy, thrown-together service comedy . . . ," Pauline Kael wrote in the *New Yorker*. "But you can't take your eyes off Murray. . . . He's so anxiously aware of everything going on around him that you almost feel he's watching you. . . . Bill Murray is like a bomb ticking, and he keeps erupting with smartass remarks. At the same time, he's the supreme practitioner of going with the flow; he's never surprised. It's a rare comic who acts superior to the people around him and is still funny. Maybe Murray's know-it-all hipness isn't offensive because it seems compulsive and just gets him into trouble. And because he's in

direct contact with the audience. Or should be." Regarding the nihilism in *Stripes*, Miss Kael observed that the makers of the movie were "still operating in the post-counterculture comedy terms of the late seventies." "The recruits here don't believe in anything at the beginning of the film or at the end either," she wrote. "This may be a silly, dated view—a remnant of stoned alienation—but it's a useful premise for a comedy. And could Bill Murray believe in anything? I wouldn't want to be within fifty yards of anything he believed in."

Dan Ackroyd and Harold Ramis wrote *Ghostbusters* (Columbia, 1984) as a departure from the spook-movie formula that requires even take-offs of the genre to maintain a reverential fear of the supernatural. "We are taking a mundane attitude toward the supernatural," Ramis wrote in the production notes. "We're simply janitors cleaning up someone else's mess with a little bit of high technology." The technology to which Ramis referred was the state-of-the-art special-effects work of Richard Edlund. The "janitors" were three university researchers of the paranormal (Murray, Ackroyd, and Ramis) who, discredited as quacks in academe, turn for a living to serving the "supernatural elimination needs" of New York City, setting up shop as spook-exterminators just in time to confront an apocalyptical uprising of the forces of darkness—the first omen of which is a nasty ectoplasmic entity devouring the junk food in the refrigerator of their initial client, a pretty Central Park West penthouse dweller named Dana Barrett (Sigourney Weaver). As Dr. Peter Venkman, the coolest and most earthly of the team of commercial exorcists, Murray takes more interest in Miss Barrett than in the blob in her frig, and throughout the film he comments on the cataclysmic happenings with unimpressed, denigrating wit.

Produced and directed by Ivan Reitman at a cost of more than $30 million, *Ghostbusters* was released in June 1984 and by October it had grossed $202 million. Strong notices recommended it, and Murray especially, as "a hoot," "deflating pomposity." Reviewers described *Ghostbusters* as a showcase for Murray, whose "irrepressible common man" slinks through the movie, "thoroughly enjoying himself" and humanizing the awesome, Armageddon-like terrain of special effects with his one-liners.

Murray made *Ghostbusters* as half of a package deal with Columbia Pictures. The other part of the package was the reluctant concession from Columbia that he be allowed to play his first dramatic role, that of Larry Darrell in *The Razor's Edge* (Columbia, 1984), a remake of the 1946 film classic (which starred Tyrone Power) based on Somerset Maugham's 1944 novel about a young American who, traumatized by his battlefield experience as a medic in World War I, drops out of bourgeois society and repudiates Western materialistic values for Eastern mysticism. The film was directed by John Byrum, who had introduced Murray to the novel and who wrote the screenplay in collaboration with him. The shooting was done for the most part on location in France, England, and India. John Belushi's recent death from an overdose of drugs gave working on it "a greater dimension" for Murray.

Only a very small minority of reviewers responded favorably to *The Razor's Edge*. Some critics viewed its "vaporous" spiritual message as "dated," especially in an age inundated with gurus from the East, meditation cults, and second thoughts about the hippie mysticism of the 1960s, and others considered the film remake either unnecessary or misbegotten. "The problem with Bill Murray's performance in *The Razor's Edge* stems from a confusion . . . of comedy and drama," Michael McWilliams wrote in the New York *Daily News* (October 28, 1984). "In the movie, huge chunks of hackneyed drama are interspersed with Murray doing Murray." David Ansen of *Newsweek* (October 22, 1984) observed that Murray's portrayal of Larry Darrell as "a holy fool" removes "the taint of sanctimony" from the role but "it can wreak havoc with the movie's tone."

Bill Murray, whose weight fluctuates between slightly and very much over the average, has thinning, usually unkempt hair and a wardrobe of Hawaiian shirts and other rumpled, tacky, and seedy items consonant with his casual image. According to Gene Siskel of the *Chicago Tribune* (June 10, 1984), he usually "looks like he's been out all night . . . both off-screen and on." In the course of his series of interviews with Timothy Crouse of *Rolling Stone* Murray occasionally lapsed into "brooding silences," surprising Crouse with "this somber side of his personality." Crouse reported that "boorishness is not" part of his private life style, that his manners are often "elegant," that he is "attentive" to others, especially family, and that he is "interested in spiritual disciplines, and they seem to have had a salutary effect on him." Among Murray's favorite foods are yogurt with bananas and sandwiches made of peanut butter, mayonnaise, and lettuce on pumpernickel.

Murray's wife, the former Mickey Kelley, was a talent coordinator for the *Tonight* and *Dick Cavett* television shows before she settled down to homemaking, but Murray did not meet her in show business but back home, when he was in high school. The two were married in a civil ceremony on January 21, 1981 and in a religious ceremony arranged by a sister of Murray's who is a nun on March 25, 1981. They have a son, Homer Banks Murray, born in 1982 and named in part after Chicago Cubs baseball player Ernie Banks. The Murrays live in a large rented house at Sneden's Landing on the Hudson River a short distance north of New York City, and they maintain a sparsely furnished pied-à-terre in Manhattan.

References: *Chicago Tribune* VI p8, Je 21, '81 por, XIII p5 Je 10 '84 pors; *N Y Daily News* L p5+ Jl 15 '79 pors; *N Y Post* p21 O 1 '84 pors; *Rolling Stone* p21+ Ag 16 '84 por; *Toronto Globe and Mail* p36 Je 30 '79 por; *Who's Who in America*, 1984–85

## Nakian, Reuben

*Aug. 10, 1897– Sculptor. Address: 810 Bedford St., Stamford, Conn. 06901*

According to Reuben Nakian, the "grand old man of American sculpture," as he has been called, "sculpture should have a powerful human content" and "should be poetry." Practicing what he preaches, he vigorously affirms the spirit of humanism in his own quasi-abstract art. Now in his late eighties, Nakian conceives of himself as an inheritor of the ancient Mediterranean tradition, and he has always taken as his subject matter Greek and Roman mythology, especially those stories that deal with the erotic conquests of the gods. Far from free and romantic, his approach to his material is carefully worked out and self-critical. For any one of his surviving sculptures he has made copious drawings as the concept developed, and he painstakingly modeled his smaller studies. Nakian has deliberately destroyed many of his "finished" larger works because they failed, in his opinion, to convey the degree of feeling and spontaneity that he demands of art. "If it isn't 100 percent right, zing, I'll smash it," he has said.

Although by the 1930s Nakian was renowned for his portrait sculpture and by the 1960s enjoyed an international reputation, he is now somewhat out of the public eye. Between 1966, when the Museum of Modern Art held a retrospective of his sculpture and drawings, and 1982, when the Marlborough Gallery in New York mounted an exhibition of his recent work, nothing much by Nakian had been shown. No longer part of the New York art scene by reason of geography (he lives in Connecticut) and because of age, he has gone his own way, an anachronism in the era of pop and minimal art. For those contemporary trends—the art of "an age of zombies" he terms them—he evinces unconcern if not frank disdain.

The youngest of the five children of the Armenian immigrants George and Mary (Malakian) Nakian, Reuben Nakian was born on August 10, 1897 in College Point, Long Island, New York. When he was nine the Nakians moved to New York City and from there to suburban New Jersey. With the encouragement of his parents, he began to take drawing lessons at the age of thirteen with a teacher in Jersey City, and he also started to model in clay.

In 1912, after graduating from elementary school, Nakian studied for a month at the Art Students League in New York City; his subsequent formal art school training was equally desultory, so that he learned his craft primarily through the age-old method of apprenticeship. From 1913 to 1915 he did lettering for an advertising agency, for mail-order houses, and for Century magazine. After taking evening classes in life drawing at the Independent Art School and in clay sculpture at the Beaux Arts Academy, Nakian set out in 1916 to be taken on as an apprentice to a sculptor. Accepted by Paul Manship, he worked with that influential figurative artist and his chief assistant, Gaston Lachaise, until 1920. When Manship left for Europe, Nakian and Lachaise shared a studio for three years. Much later, in decrying Manship's and Lachaise's influence on his style, Nakian was to proclaim that Cézanne and Brancusi were his first real inspirations.

Nakian's early sculptures (in marble, wood, and bronze) and drawings were of animals, stylized in form, and with smooth, flowing arabesque contours. One of his first works, a bank in the shape of a cow, which was designed in 1917 for the "Free Milk for France" campaign, was replicated widely. Praise was also lavished on his works that were shown in the "Salons of America" exhibition at the Anderson Galleries in New York in 1922, at the Whitney Studio Club in 1923, and at the American Art Association Galleries, also in 1923. In the meantime, with the aid of a stipend from the Whitney Studio Club, Nakian had taken his own studio in Weehawken Heights, New Jersey. In 1925 he moved back to New York, to Greenwich Village, and for many years maintained studios in various locations there. He held his first one-man show in 1926, at the Whitney Studio Club.

With the aid of a Guggenheim Fellowship that was bestowed on him in 1931, Nakian was able to spend eight months in France and Italy. He returned to the United States in 1932 to embark on what may be considered the second phase of his career: a series of plaster busts of celebrities. In 1933 a one-man show of portraits of nine of his fellow artists was shown at the Downtown Gallery, followed by a commission to do a portrait of General Hugh Johnson, then the head of the National Recovery Administration. Armed with further commissions, he "invaded" the offices of members of President Franklin D. Roosevelt's cabinet and managed to capture life-size likenesses of such dignitaries as Cordell Hull and Harry Hopkins as they worked. The result, including a portrait of the president done from photographs, was an exhibition called "Portrait-Heads of Officials of the Present Administration," which was shown at the Corcoran Gallery of Art in Washington, D.C., and then in New York City at the Downtown Gallery in 1935. Also in that social-realist mode was an eight-foot-high plaster statue of Babe Ruth in characteristic batting stance. The widely publicized homage to America's baseball idol was shown at the First Municipal Art Exhibition, in Rockfeller Center, in 1934. The heroically proportioned "ton of plaster," as one sportswriter of the day referred to it, was never cast in bronze as Nakian had hoped it would be, and it has since disappeared.

Besides striking up friendships with fellow sculptors such as Constantin Brancusi and William Zorach, Nakian established in 1935 a close personal and working relationship with another Armenian-American artist, the painter Arshile Gorky, that proved important to his career. Through their conversations about Cézanne, Picasso, Ingres, and the contemporary surrealist movement, Nakian's approach to his art was drastically modified, and it was also Gorky who introduced him to Willem de Kooning. For the rest of the 1930s and for most of the 1940s Nakian virtually relinquished sculpture, confining himself to ink drawings in which he worked out new ideas of style and subject matter. And in 1936, in his home on Staten Island, Nakian began to work on assignments for the Federal Art Project of the Works Progress Administration.

The tentative beginning of a third phase in Nakian's development can be recognized in an abstract Europa and the Bull, begun in 1938, completed in 1942, and later, as with so many of his works, destroyed. His new abstractionist impulse is also evident in the famous Head of Marcel Duchamp, which he modeled in plaster in 1943 and later cast in bronze. A radical departure from the realistic, smoothly modeled heads of other artists of the early 1930s, that rough-textured, vigorous work forecasts the "dramatized surfaces" of Nakian's later style.

In 1944 Nakian and his family moved from Staten Island to Stamford, Connecticut, though he continued to maintain a studio on Washington Square South until 1948, when he moved it to Stamford. From 1946 to 1951 he taught at the Newark School of Fine and Industrial Arts, in Newark, New Jersey, and from 1952 to 1954 he was an instructor at Pratt Institute in Brooklyn, New York.

In about 1947, in Newark, Reuben Nakian began work on a series of small terra-cotta plaques and groupings on which, in the wet clay, he incised frankly erotic drawings of mythological scenes involving gods and satyrs at their amorous pursuits. As the critic Alfred Frankenstein described them in the San Francisco Sunday Examiner and Chronicle (July 10, 1966), the "swiftness, humor and liveliness of the linear performance reminds one of Picasso; the bulge and taper of the figures is indebted to Gaston Lachaise . . . the effect is altogether unique and totally Nakian's own." In the firing of larger terra-cotta variations of those pieces, he was helped by one of his students, Larry McCabe, who became his first permanent assistant. Some of those "stone drawings" (so called because of their hardness after the clay had been fired) were patinated in earth colors; others were done in pastel tones, "à la Fragonard," as Nakian styled them. The stark contrast between the fast, fluid drawing and the permanence both of the material and of the age-old stories incised on it is intriguing. As with all of Nakian's mature work, the momentary and the permanent exist side by side.

From then on, Reuben Nakian's art became "soaked in history," as the art critic Thomas B. Hess once phrased it. Enlarged variations of the themes of the plaques were worked in clay or plaster—sometimes cast in bronze—or steel. Abstraction now began to absorb the more figurative quality of the first smaller pieces; heads and features were replaced by generalized allusions to drapery-clad figures, often achieved by a technique of dipping burlap in wet plaster, which then encased and preserved the folds and draping of the cloth.

Notable among Nakian's earlier large abstract pieces are the terra-cotta *Voyage to Crete* series (1949-1952), which represent a nude woman courted by Jupiter in the shape of a bull; the plaster *Chambre à coucher de l'empereur* (cast in bronze in 1958); and his largest piece, the twelve-foot-high *Rape of Lucrece* (1955-1958), one of Nakian's first steel sculptures. In the *Rape of Lucrece*, as with the *Duchess of Alba* (1959) or *Mars and Venus* (1959-1960), the image is formed of shaped sheets of steel painted black, supported on rods that function as armature but that are also integral to the imagery. Apart from aesthetic considerations, Nakian turned to steel because often he could not afford the cost of bronze casting.

Reuben Nakian has been termed an abstract expressionist in three dimensions, and his work, beginning with the 1960s, certainly has affinities with the paintings of his friend de Kooning, or the other action painters. It is evident that the concern of those artists, in their respective media, is with surface and texture, so that forceful gesture either of brush or hand has resulted in manipulated, gouged, rough-hewn textures and forms. Like Nakian's "spread-legged altar of bronze," *Goddess with the Golden Thighs* (1964-1966), which was the "centerpiece" of his 1966 Museum of Modern Art retrospective, those works are meant to be seen frontally, since they are, characteristically, wider than deep.

A new series of terra cottas devoted to the priapic play of nymphs and satyrs and of Leda and her swan began to occupy Nakian in 1962, and the next year he embarked on plaster studies for his highly regarded *Judgment of Paris* (1963-1966), a group of free-standing, monumental abstract representations of Paris, Venus, Juno, and Minerva. Again, in 1979, Nakian returned to the nymph-satyr and Leda themes—this time cast in bronze. Along with his plaster and bronze versions of *Garden of the*

*Gods* I and II, they formed a major part of his 1982 Marlborough Gallery show. But among the work shown there, a new style emerged—a trend toward long, thin tubular forms, an almost architectural representation of coupling bodies and entwined limbs.

Public honors bestowed on Reuben Nakian include, in addition to the Guggenheim Fellowship, a $10,000 Ford Foundation grant in 1958 and, in 1978, membership in the American Institute of Arts and Letters. In 1960 he was invited by New York University to compete with five other well-known American sculptors for the commission to ornament the north facade of the Loeb Student Center, the former site of his Washington Square studio. Installed in 1961, his winning design consists of fifteen curved rectangles of aluminum sheeting in three groupings, supported on thin steel rods. Sometimes called *Birds in Flight*, the abstract design suggests birds, or leaves. Fixed in place, seemingly gravity-defying, the metal forms are so played on by light that they seem to float across the wall. Also in 1961 a selection of fifty-eight of Nakian's works represented the United States at the São Paulo Bienal in Brazil.

Exhibitions of his art span the entire course of Nakian's long career, with some gaps in the 1940s and 1950s, reflecting the ten years or so he "took off" to redefine his directions. Nevertheless, he has been generously represented in group shows of contemporary sculpture in both the United States and abroad. In 1965, for example, five of his works were shown in "Etats Unis: Sculptures du XXe siècle," organized by the Museum of Modern Art and shown first at the Musée Rodin in Paris and then in Germany, through 1966. In 1968 he was one of the entrants representing the United States in the 34th Venice Biennale. Recognized for their important role in his total oeuvre, Nakian's ink and wash drawings are shown in conjunction with his sculptures, and in 1964 a group of them was given separate treatment at the Solomon R. Guggenheim Museum's "American Drawings" show. Nakian is well represented in the collections of the major American museums.

Besides the Loeb Student Center facade, two other large sculptures by Nakian embellish New York City structures. His bronze *Voyage to Crete* (1960-1962) stands in the foyer of the New York State Theatre at Lincoln Center, and his ten-foot-high *Descent from the Cross*, modeled in heavy pieces of plaster over iron and wire-mesh in 1972 and cast in bronze in 1977, looms in a corner of the plaza outside St. Vartan Armenian Cathedral on Second Avenue. (Originally, the Metropolitan Museum of Art had planned to purchase it if it could obtain funds for casting.) Begun as a protest against the corruptions of contemporary society, it turned out to be Nakian's sole religious work. The self-styled pagan, acknowledging the influence of Rubens' *Descent from the Cross* in the Antwerp Cathedral, produced what the critic Hilton Kramer called in the *New York Times* (November 5, 1976) "an expressionist outburst of feeling elevated by an austere formality." Another rare departure for Reuben Nakian from Mediterranean mythology was *Hiroshima* (1965-1966), a nine-foot-high bronze, one cast of which is now displayed in the outdoor setting of the Storm King Art Center, Mountainville, New York. The first cast is owned by the Museum of Modern Art.

Reuben Nakian is a stocky man, with large, strong hands that are well suited to his media. It is said that when he was young he looked like an American Indian, an impression reinforced by his supple grace of movement. With his bold features and long, straight hair, now completely white, he remains an arresting figure, so much so that one recent interviewer described him as looking like "a weather-beaten sailor" with "a vocabulary to match." Still living in Stamford, Connecticut with his wife, the former Rose St. John, whom he married in 1934, and one of their four children, Nakian retains the vigor and drive of a much younger person. Despite two heart attacks and recurrent eye trouble, he insists that if he has enough energy, he can work "like lightning." In 1981 he started to do some red-chalk drawings, in a return to a medium he had not used since the 1920s, and in 1981-82, under the auspices of the National Endowment for the Arts, he worked on a bronze Juno for a park in Norwalk, Connecticut. Beginning to explore print-

making, he made etchings of his mythological images. "The thing to do when you get stale," the indefatigable Nakian maintains, "is to quit and try something new."

The abiding, passionate interest that Nakian retains in art is attested to by visitors who report his eagerness to talk about it with animation and volubility, one thought leading him on to a new one. Like many of the artists of his generation who are still active today, such as Louise Nevelson and Willem de Kooning, Nakian is grateful that he was born at a time when an artist could mature slowly, remaining unrecognized and poor for many years, to be sure, but not caught up in the market-place pressures of today's art world. As Nakian views it, that maturing process involves seeing oneself as constituting part of the whole tradition of art. "Art comes out of art," he says, emphasizing not a regression to the past, but the evolution of artistic approaches. And so, while Reuben Nakian may dismiss most of the younger sculptors, he looks confidently ahead to his next challenge. As he once said of himself, "I'm not a storage warehouse. . . . My ideas are changing all the time."

References: Marks, Claude. World Artists (1984); O'Hara, Frank. Nakian (1966); Who's Who in American Art (1984)

---

## Newman, Paul

Jan. 26, 1925– Actor; motion-picture director and producer. Address: b. c/o Rogers & Cowan Inc., 9665 Wilshire Blvd., Beverly Hills, Calif. 90210; 2048 Century Park E., Suite 2500, Los Angeles, Calif. 90067

NOTE: This biography supersedes the article that appeared in Current Biography in 1959.

In forty-six motion pictures, among them the American classics *The Hustler, Hud, Cool Hand Luke, Butch Cassidy and the Sundance Kid,* and *The Sting,* over some thirty years, Paul Newman has, in his various screen personae, singularly mirrored the changing tenor of his times. As Susan Toepfer observed in her recent profile of the actor for the New York Sunday News magazine, he symbolized for millions of viewers the "indifference" of the 1950s, the "danger" of the 1960s, the "mellowing" of the 1970s, and the "individualism" of the 1980s. A self-described "cerebral" actor who learned his craft on the stage and on television during the 1950s, Newman refined his technique with each succeeding role and with occasional ventures into directing, most notably, *Rachel, Rachel,* in 1968. Many critics felt that he scaled the summit of his acting career with his portrayal of the down-and-out lawyer in the 1982 release *The Verdict,* in which he "goes right down to the butt ends of his

soul and then renews himself," as David Denby put it. "When you've seen this movie, you have not only experienced Newman in a new way, you have experienced yourself in a new way. And perhaps only an actor who is also a great star can do that to us." A six-time Oscar nominee, Paul Newman was the recipient of the 1984 Cecil B. De Mille Award for his "outstanding contribution to the entertainment field."

Of German and Hungarian descent, Paul Leonard Newman was born on January 26, 1925 in Cleveland, Ohio, the second of the two children of Arthur S. Newman, a partner in a thriving sporting-goods store, and his wife, Theresa (Fetzer) Newman. His older brother, Arthur S. Newman Jr., is a film production manager. Raised in the affluent upper-middle-class suburb of Shaker Heights, where he attended the local public schools, Paul Newman was encouraged to pursue his early interest in the arts, especially literature, by his uncle, Joseph F. Newman, a well-known Ohio journalist and poet, and by his mother, who described to him in detail the plays she regularly attended at the Hanna Theater in downtown Cleveland. Although he felt, by his own admission, "uncomfortable" onstage, Newman appeared in several elementary and high-school productions, and he played the leading role in the Cleveland Play House's staging of the children's play St. George and the Dragon.

Following his graduation from Shaker Heights Senior High School, in January 1943, Newman enlisted in the United States Navy. While waiting to be called for naval flight training, he attended Ohio University in Athens, Ohio. During his four months there, he auditioned for and won the part of boxer Speed McFarland in a campus production of The Milky Way, the comedy by Lynn Root and Harry Clork. Disqualified from the Navy's pilot-training program because of color blindness, Newman finally began his World War II tour of duty in the summer of 1943 as a radioman, third class, on torpedo bombers in the Pacific. After his discharge from the service three years later, he enrolled at Kenyon College in Gambier, Ohio, on the G.I. bill. An indifferent student, he devoted as much time to his extracurricular activities as to his academic pursuits. When, in his junior year, he was kicked off the football team after a barroom fracas landed him in jail overnight, he turned to acting to fill his newly acquired spare time. Over the next two years, he played leading roles in ten undergraduate productions, ranging from the contemporary staples The Front Page and Charley's Aunt to the classical comedies The Taming of the Shrew and The Alchemist. "I was probably one of the worst college actors in history . . . ," he said years later, as quoted in the book The Player; a Profile of an Art (1962). "I had no idea what I was doing. I learned my lines by rote and simply said them, without spontaneity, without any idea of dealing with the forces around me onstage, without knowing what it meant to act and react."

Despite his misgivings about his talent as an actor, Newman set off within hours of receiving his B.A. degree in English, in June 1949, for Williams Bay, Wisconsin to appear in summer-stock productions of John Loves Mary, a comedy by Norman Krasna, and Tennessee Williams' The Glass Menagerie, in which he portrayed the Gentleman Caller. He then signed on with the Woodstock Players, a repertory company in Woodstock, Illinois, near Chicago, for the 1949–50 season of some sixteen plays. His credits for the company include the role of Christian de Neuvillette in Rostand's Cyrano de Bergerac. On his father's death, in May 1950, Newman reluctantly shelved his developing acting career to take over the family sporting-goods store in Cleveland. Freed of his obligation when the business was sold the following year, he immediately entered Yale University's School of Drama in New Haven, Connecticut. "I wasn't driven to acting by any inner compulsion," Newman has explained, as quoted in Time (December 6, 1982). "I was running away from the sporting-goods business." After a year at Yale, with the encouragement of his instructors he decided to try his luck in New York, where he found employment in television almost immediately.

In the early 1950s Newman appeared in episodes of The Mask, ABC's short-lived crime drama, the CBS dramatic anthology series The Web, and the popular NBC sitcom The Aldrich Family. For CBS's You Are There, a public-affairs series that re-created historical events, he portrayed Socrates, Aristotle, Julius Caesar, and Nathan Hale. Newman made his Broadway debut on February 19, 1953, in the Theatre Guild's production of Picnic, William Inge's Pulitzer Prize-winning play about a group of sex-starved women in a small Kansas town. Under the direction of Joshua Logan, he earned excellent notices for his sensitive interpretation of the role of Alan Seymour, an ineffectual college lad. His performance also netted him a mention in Theatre World annual's list of "promising personalities" of the 1952–53 New York season. Throughout that period, Newman, who considered himself to be "an untuned piano," as he phrased it, studied at the Actors Studio, where his teachers included Lee Strasberg, Elia Kazan, and Martin Ritt.

Newman left the cast of Picnic in the spring of 1954, having signed a long-term contract with Warner Brothers. Embarrassed by his inauspicious screen debut, as a Greek sculptor in The Silver Chalice (1954), an overblown religious costume drama based on Thomas B. Costain's best-selling novel of the same name, Newman fled back to Broadway, where he redeemed himself with an arresting portrayal of a psychotic killer in Joseph Hayes's literate thriller The Desperate Hours, which opened at the Ethel Barrymore Theatre in February 1955 to critical salvos. While in New York, then the center of television production, he appeared in two episodes of the CBS series Appointment with Adventure, starred in The Death of Billy the Kid, a presentation of NBC's Philco Television Playhouse, and joined Eva Marie Saint and Frank Sinatra in a musical version of Thornton Wilder's Our Town for NBC's Producers' Showcase. In an effort to extend his range, he also accepted the part of a fifty-five-year-old punch-drunk fighter in The Battler, the television adaptation of Ernest Hemingway's classic short story, which was broadcast on NBC's dramatic anthology series Playwrights '56.

Newman's assured performance as the washed-up pugilist no doubt contributed to the decision of MGM executives to cast him in the central role in *Somebody Up There Likes Me*, the life story of the boxer Rocky Graziano. In his customary thorough-going manner, Newman prepared for the role by spending two weeks with Graziano, but he took pains to avoid aping the fighter on screen. "I tried to play *a* Graziano, not *the* Graziano," he explained, as quoted in *Player*. That Newman succeeded in his characterization of the juvenile delinquent turned world heavyweight champion was borne out by the glowing reviews accorded the film on its release in 1956. The actor also scored in *The Rack* (MGM, 1956), in which he played an American army officer on trial for collaboration with the enemy during the Korean war. Bosley Crowther, writing in the *New York Times* (November 6, 1956), rated Newman's "brilliantly detailed performance" of a man in moral torment as "a remarkable tour de force." Newman followed up, in quick succession, with leading roles in the motion pictures *The Helen Morgan Story* (Warner Brothers, 1957), *Until They Sail* (MGM, 1957), a wartime romance, and *The Left-Handed Gun* (Warner Brothers, 1958), Arthur Penn's offbeat psychological western, and in several acclaimed television dramatic specials, including *The 80-Yard Run*, *Bang the Drum Slowly*, and *The Rag Jungle*. His film work earned him a Golden Globe Award from the Hollywood Foreign Press Association as one of the most promising newcomers of 1957.

Fulfilling his promise, Newman netted the "outstanding actor of the year" award at the 1958 Cannes Film Festival for his performance as the unprincipled Ben Quick in *The Long Hot Summer* (Twentieth Century-Fox), an adaptation of several William Faulkner works in which he costarred for the first time with his wife, Joanne Woodward, and an Academy Award nomination for his subtly shaded interpretation of the embittered alcoholic Brick Pollitt in Richard Brooks's screen adaptation of Tennessee Williams' Pulitzer Prize-winning play *Cat on a Hot Tin Roof*. The last-named film, which also starred Elizabeth Taylor and Burl Ives, was MGM's top money-maker in 1958 and Paul Newman's first box-office hit. The actor was, by his own admission, "weak" in *Rally Round the Flag, Boys!* (Twentieth Century-Fox, 1958), a send-up of suburban life, and he fared only slightly better in the slick soap operas *The Young Philadelphians* (Warner Brothers, 1959) and *From the Terrace* (Twentieth Century-Fox, 1960). After the completion of *From the Terrace*, he bought his freedom from Warner Brothers for a reported $500,000.

In 1959 Newman took time out from films to star in Elia Kazan's Broadway production of Tennessee Williams' *Sweet Bird of Youth*, another variation on the author's favorite theme of the corruption of innocence. As Chance Wayne, the parasitic young gigolo, he drew the best notices of his career to that date by managing to arouse in the audience feelings of compassion as well as contempt. To quote Walter Kerr, who reviewed the play for the *New York Herald Tribune* (March 22, 1959), he kept his ambiguous character—"half vulgar greed, half yearning idealism—recklessly balanced on the slopes of Hell." Newman remained with the stage production for nearly a year. He and costar Geraldine Page subsequently re-created their roles for "a tamer and tidied" film version released by MGM in 1962. Newman made only one more stage appearance. In 1964 he and Joanne Woodward, working for scale, teamed up to star in the Actors Studio Theatre production of James Costigan's comedy *Baby Want a Kiss*.

Following his understated performance as Ari Ben Canaan, the isolationist leader of the Palestinian underground in *Exodus* (United Artists, 1960), Newman turned in what many film critics and historians regard as his best work, in his series of so-called "lucky 'H'" pictures: *The Hustler, Hud, Harper,* and *Hombre*. His incarnation of the cocky, small-time pool shark Fast Eddie Felson in *The Hustler* (Twentieth Century-Fox, 1961), Robert Rossen's downbeat melodrama, brought him his second Oscar nomination for best actor. Newman confirmed his place in the front rank of motion-picture actors and earned his third Academy Award nomination with his performance as the amoral Hud Bannon in Martin Ritt's landmark contemporary western *Hud* (Twentieth Century-Fox, 1963). The stylish *Harper* (Warner Brothers, 1966), an adaptation of Ross Macdonald's murder mystery *The Moving Target*, further attested to Newman's versatility, as he took on the identity of a cynical private eye in the Humphrey Bogart trenchcoat style. In *Hombre* (Twentieth Century-Fox, 1967), which was a suspenseful, *Stagecoach*-like western directed by Martin Ritt, the actor gave life to a stoic outcast—a white orphan raised by Apaches. Some critics saw traces of each of those characters in Newman's portrayal of the rebellious, "Cool Hand" Luke, the quintessential "triumphant anti-hero," to use Judith Crist's term, who repeatedly defies the system—in this case, a vicious Southern penal system—and is eventually defeated by it. One of the biggest hits of 1967, *Cool Hand Luke* (Warner Brothers) garnered Newman his fourth Oscar nomination.

Interspersed among Newman's triumphs in the 1960s were appearances in a handful of disappointing films. Reviewers generally agreed that he was unsuited to his roles as an expatriated jazz musician in *Paris Blues* (United Artists, 1961), an alcoholic writer in both *A New Kind of Love* (Paramount, 1963) and *The Prize* (MGM, 1964), an anarchist in turn-of-the-century Paris in Peter Ustinov's rambling *Lady L* (MGM, 1966), and a double agent in Alfred Hitchcock's labored thriller *Torn Curtain* (Universal, 1966), among others. It was at least partly because of a dearth of suitable roles that Newman temporarily turned his attention from acting to producing and directing, with the release, in 1968, of the solidly acclaimed *Rachel, Rachel* (Warner Brothers), about a lonely spinster's awakening to life. In a conscious effort to "keep the direction invisible," Newman employed a rather unorthodox technique that he has described as "a sort of eavesdropping." Admiring critics, including Renata Adler, Judith Crist, Penelope Gilliatt, and Richard Schickel, applauded Newman's "sensitive and discreet" direction, "immaculate" casting, and "beautiful choices of which character to watch at what moment." *Rachel, Rachel* received four Academy Award nominations, including best picture and best actress, for Joanne Woodward in the title role, and earned Newman the best director of the year award from the New York Film Critics. Newman later directed his wife in the filmed versions of the Pulitzer Prize-winning plays *The Effect of Gamma Rays on Man-in-the-Moon Marigolds* (Universal, 1972) and *The Shadow Box*, which was broadcast on ABC-TV in 1980.

Perhaps in an effort to gain more control over his film projects, Newman joined forces, in 1968, with John Foreman to form the Newman-Foreman Company. Over the next few years, the company produced several motion pictures starring the actor, among them *Winning* (Universal, 1969), about the personal problems of a professional automobile racer; *WUSA* (Paramount, 1970), a political parable set in a right-wing Southern radio station; *Sometimes a Great Notion* (Universal, 1971), the film version of Ken Kesey's sprawling chronicle of a family of self-reliant lumberjacks that Newman also directed; and *The Mackintosh Man* (Warner Brothers, 1973), John Huston's convoluted spy thriller. The pair's most successful venture by far was George Roy Hill's picaresque western *Butch Cassidy and the Sundance Kid* (1969), which Foreman produced for release by Twentieth Century-Fox. The highest-grossing western in motion-picture history, *Butch Cassidy* teamed Newman, as the affable, gun-shy Butch, with Robert Redford, in the role of his sharpshooting sidekick, as outlaws who had outlived their day. The two actors were reunited in Hill's *The Sting* (Columbia, 1973), a Depression-era comedy about two con men who set up an elaborate scam to revenge themselves on a gangster. The duo's superlative comic timing undoubtedly contributed to *The Sting's* enormous popularity at the box office and to its seven Academy Awards.

With the exception of the part of Henry Gondorff in *The Sting*, Newman found few rewarding roles in the early 1970s. "What's an actor to do?" he asked David Sterritt of the *Christian Science Monitor* (December 3, 1981). " . . . You have to keep the instrument tuned. So you take the best there is and hope for the best." Among the parts that Newman selected during those years were a bumbling, good-natured cattle-buyer in the modest contemporary western *Pocket Money* (National General, 1972), the title character in *The Life and Times of Judge Roy Bean* (National General, 1972), a shaky amalgam of fact and legend about a famous outlaw judge of the old West; an architect in the disaster spectacle *The Towering Inferno* (Twentieth Century-Fox/Warner Brothers, 1974), and the detective Lew Harper in *The Drowning Pool* (War-

ner Brothers, 1975), a lackluster sequel to *Harper. Pocket Money* and *Judge Roy Bean* were financed and distributed by First Artists Productions, which Newman had founded in partnership with fellow actors Barbra Streisand, Sidney Poitier, and Steve McQueen.

At least partly because of his disenchantment with undemanding roles, Newman, who was admittedly "getting very bored with acting," plunged actively into auto racing, a sport he had learned for his film *Winning*, in 1972. "Racing is the best way I know to get away from all the 'rubbish' of Hollywood," he explained, as quoted in *People* (June 25, 1979). Within four years, he was good enough to pilot a Triumph TR-6 to his first national amateur championship. Later in the same year, he was awarded the President's Cup, the highest amateur trophy given by the Sports Car Club of America. Turning professional in 1977, he and two teammates, driving in shifts, took fifth place in the grueling twenty-four-hour endurance race at Daytona, Florida. After Newman and his team came in second in the prestigious Le Mans contest in 1979, veteran driver Sam Posey proclaimed the actor "one of the top endurance racers in the world."

Newman, who was then entering as many as twenty-five events in the annual April-to-October racing season, always returned to his acting career reinvigorated. As he explained to Charles Champlin in an interview published in *Newsday* (November 21, 1982), "What seems possible as I look back is that my passion for racing has bled back into the acting." Whatever the reason, film reviewers began to notice a renewed commitment in his work with the release, in 1976, of Robert Altman's *Buffalo Bill and the Indians, or Sitting Bull's History Lesson* (United Artists), an eccentric version of Arthur Kopit's play *Indians* that was remarkable only for Newman's characterization of Buffalo Bill as a boozy, egomaniacal "showbiz cowboy."

Since then, with the minor exceptions of Altman's murky surrealistic allegory *Quintet* (Twentieth Century-Fox, 1979) and Irwin Allen's cliché-ridden disaster epic *When Time Ran Out* (Warner Brothers, 1980), Newman has turned in a series of winning portrayals in what were for him unorthodox roles. His gutsy interpretation of a foul-mouthed, over-the-hill minor league ice hockey coach in *Slap Shot* (Universal, 1977), George Roy Hill's comedy, offended some of his fans, but Pauline Kael rated his performance "casual American star-acting at its peak." Newman shattered the superstar mold with his characterization of a compassionate cop in Daniel Petrie's *Fort Apache, the Bronx* (Twentieth Century-Fox, 1981), an unflinching look at life in the crucible of a high-crime precinct in the blighted South Bronx.

During the on-location shooting of *Fort Apache*, Newman and the film's producers became involved in a running battle, fueled by inaccurate news reports, with some of the neighborhood's black and Hispanic residents, who felt that the picture portrayed them in a negative light. Irked by the careless reporting of a local tabloid, Newman chose as his next project *Absence of Malice* (Columbia, 1982), a lacerating examination of media abuse in which he played an honest businessman victimized by an irresponsible journalist. For his compact, low-key characterization that was "realer than his role" as written, in Stanley Kauffmann's assessment, Newman earned his fifth Academy Award nomination as best actor.

Newman put his image on the line when he accepted the assignment of Frank Galvin, a washed-up, alcoholic attorney redeemed by his heroic pursuit of justice in the courtroom drama *The Verdict* (Twentieth Century-Fox, 1982). "It's so comforting not to have to be a movie star . . . ," he explained. "It's a relief to have an unprotected character to play. This guy's an open wound." In bringing Galvin to life, as he takes on two powerful establishments—the medical profession and the Catholic church—in a malpractice suit, Newman was for the first time photographed in a manner that attested to his age. David Denby observed in *New York* magazine (December 20, 1982), "The icon has become mortal. He's also become a great actor." Previously never an admirer of Newman's work, Stanley Kauffmann noted in the *New Republic* (December 20, 1982) that Newman's performance was "affectingly colored by—that lovely paradox of acting—his own feelings about the character and his own personality. This is realistic American film acting at its veristic/imaginative best." *The Verdict* brought Newman his sixth best-actor Oscar nomination.

Recently described as having a face that "doesn't age" but "purifies," Paul Newman has piercing, cobalt-blue eyes, thinning, silvery hair, and stands about five feet eleven inches tall. He follows a program of daily exercise that includes jogging, riding a stationary exercise bicycle, and working out on a Nautilus machine. Treasuring his privacy, he rarely grants interviews, and he refuses to sign autographs because, according to a longtime friend, "the majesty of the act is so offensive to him." Nevertheless, the appreciation fans often express to him touches him deeply. Close friends know Newman as a man who shuns pretension and has a genuine desire for simplicity and "sanity" in his way of life. According to a profile in *People* (March 19, 1984), he believes the key to being a good actor is knowing how "to be a child." He claims never to read reviews of his movies—"If they're good you get a fat head and if they're bad you're depressed for three weeks." Among his recreations are fishing, going to the theatre, and listening to classical music, especially Bach and Beethoven.

Since the early 1960s, Newman and Joanne Woodward, whom he married on January 29, 1958, have made an eighteenth-century farmhouse in Westport, Connecticut their home base. The couple also maintains a house in Malibu, California and an apartment overlooking Central Park in New York City. The Newmans are the parents of Elinor (Nell), Melissa, and Clea. In addition, the actor has two daughters, Susan and Stephanie, from an earlier marriage to Jackie Witte that ended in divorce. His oldest child and only son, Scott, died of an accidental overdose of alcohol and Valium in 1978. Traumatized by the tragedy, Newman set up the Scott Newman Foundation, which finances the production of anti-drug films for children.

A sizable portion of the Scott Newman Foundation's funding comes from the profits of the sales of "Newman's Own" salad dressing, spaghetti sauce, and natural popcorn. In 1982 the actor and his Westport neighbor A. E. Hotchner, the writer, set up a corporation to manufacture and market Newman's original oil-and-vinegar dressing. Within two years, what had started "as a joke" was parlayed into a multimillion-dollar business. *Newman's Own Cookbook*, a collection of the actor's favorite all-natural recipes, was published by Contemporary Books in the fall of 1985. All the company's profits—some $4 million as of January 1985—are donated to charities and social welfare organizations. Newman's dedication to public service was first manifested in the early 1950s, when he stuffed envelopes for Democratic presidential candidate Adlai E. Stevenson. He has since served as an official delegate from Connecticut to the Democratic National Convention in 1968 and as a citizen delegate to the United Nations Conference on Disarmament in 1978. An outspoken liberal, he has lobbied for civil rights, environmental protection, and a nuclear freeze. Although he has for years maintained that he would never run for public office because he'd "get elected for all the wrong reasons," in June 1984 Newman informed *USA Today* that he was giving the idea serious consideration.

Aside from random thoughts of running for political office or becoming a gentleman farmer or marine biologist, Paul Newman remains intensely interested in writing, producing, and directing films. His most recent directorial effort, *Harry and Son* (Orion, 1984), a domestic drama about an ailing construction worker at odds with his artistically inclined teenage son, was not a commercial success. "The kind of pictures I want to do and enjoy doing aren't fashionable today," Newman told Clarke Taylor in an interview for the *Los Angeles Times* (February 1, 1981). "People don't want to see the heavy stuff. They want to be entertained. . . . If there's anything I'm interested in in this anesthetized society, it's emotion. I really want to get to audiences and wake them up."

References: *Ladies Home J* 100:94+ Ag '83 por, 102:102+ Mr '85 por; *Life* 7:17+ F '84 pors; *Los Angeles Times* III p1+ S 19 '78 pors, III p6+ O 7 '83 por, VI p1+ Mr 6 '84 por; *N Y Sunday News mag* p15+ D 5 '83 pors; *N Y Times C* p15 F 9 '81 por; *Rolling Stone* p14+ Ja 20 '83 pors; *Time* 120:68+ D 6 '82 pors; *Contemporary Theatre, Film, and Television* (1984); Godfrey, Lionel. *Paul Newman: Superstar* (1978); Landry, J. C. *Paul Newman* (1983); Quirk, Lawrence J. *The Films of Paul Newman* (1971); *Who's Who in America, 1984–85*

## Novak, Michael

*Sept. 9, 1933– Social critic; philosopher. Address: b. c/o Donald Cutler, Sterling North Agency, 660 Madison Ave., New York City, N.Y. 10021*

The provocative social critic Michael Novak, who is now the resident scholar at the American Enterprise Institute for Public Policy Research, the conservative think tank in Washington, D.C., began his career as a liberal Catholic intellectual, a democratic socialist who joined the drive for "the open church," the phrase that became the title of his 1964 book on Vatican Council II. In the course of moving from left to right in his politics—which he now describes as "neoliberal"—Novak wrote a score of books, including *The Rise of the Unmeltable Ethnics* (1972), with which he became a leading champion of ethnicity; *The Spirit of Democratic Capitalism* (1982), a Judaeo-Christian apologia for a free political economy; and *Moral Clarity in a Nuclear Age* (1983), in which he challenged the theology of the American Catholic hierarchy's condemnation of nuclear weapons.

Michael Novak's roots are in the working class of which he wrote in *The Rise of the Unmeltable Ethnics*. The grandson of Slovak immigrants, he was born in Johnstown, Pennsylvania on September 9, 1933 to Michael John and Irene Louise (Sakmar) Novak. He became a junior seminarian in the Congregation of Holy Cross in 1947, when he was fourteen years old. A younger brother who followed him into the religious community went on to the priesthood and became a missionary in Pakistan, where he was killed in the riots near Dacca in 1964.

The Congregation of Holy Cross runs several colleges and universities, including Stonehill College in North Easton, Massachusetts and the Uni-

versity of Notre Dame in South Bend, Indiana. Michael Novak received his B.A. degree in philosophy *summa cum laude* at Stonehill in 1956 and his bachelor's in theology *cum laude* at the Gregorian University in Rome, Italy in 1958. His most influential teacher in Rome was the theologian Bernard Lonergan. Obtaining a dispensation from his religious vows of poverty, chastity, and obedience, he left the Congregation of Holy Cross before ordination, early in 1960. He spent the next several years in graduate study at Harvard University, which awarded him a master's degree in 1966.

While a seminarian in Rome, Novak began writing for the liberal Catholic journal of opinion *Commonweal* and the Jesuit weekly *America*, and he later became a contributor as well to such secular journals as the *New Republic* and such Protestant publications as *Christian Century*. His first book was the novel *The Tiber Was Silver* (Doubleday, 1961), apparently inspired by his experience in Rome. His second was *A New Generation: American and Catholic* (Herder & Herder, 1964), a patchwork of his journalistic essays concerned with the changing church in the United States and the place in it of "realistic" young Catholics. Several of his articles in *Commonweal* were addressed to "the gap between theology and marital reality," especially in the area of birth control, and he edited *The Experience of Marriage* (Macmillan, 1964), in which thirteen anonymous Catholic married couples candidly described the physical aspects of their marriages and the moral dilemmas encountered therein.

A recurrent theme in Novak's early essays was the "renewal and reform" of the church that were set in motion by Vatican Council II (1962–65). He reported on the council in the American Catholic press from Rome, and he chronicled the proceedings of the second session of the council in *The Open Church* (Macmillan, 1964), the liberal perspective of which he later repudiated. During a personal crisis of faith following the Vatican Council, Novak wrote *Belief and Unbelief* (Macmillan, 1965), in which he tried to restate the case for Christian theism in a "post-religious" age through a rigorously argued philosophy of self-knowledge.

As assistant professor of humanities at Stanford University from 1965 to 1968, when sentiment against the war in Vietnam was peaking, Novak became intimate with the spirit and sentiments of the antiwar activists and other student radicals, and he proposed an incarnational theology for the "new left" in the essays eventually brought together in the book *A Theology for Radical Politics* (Herder & Herder, 1969). The morality of the Vietnam war was among the diverse subjects covered in *A Time To Build* (Macmillan, 1967), a collection of lectures, essays, and articles that had originally appeared in periodicals ranging from *Concilium* to the *Saturday Evening Post*. In the Democratic presidential primaries of 1968 Novak helped Eugene McCarthy to enter the race and later campaigned for the late Robert F. Kennedy, whom he still regards as his "chief political hero."

From Stanford, Novak moved to the faculty of the State University of New York at Old Westbury, where he was associate professor of philosophy and religious studies from 1968 to 1973. During those years he completed the novel *Naked I Leave* (Macmillan, 1970) and wrote *Ascent of the Mountain, Flight of the Dove: An Introduction to Religious Studies* (Harper, 1971). The novel, which was greeted with middling notices, is the spiritual odyssey of Jon Svoboda, a virginal ex-seminarian of untroubled faith from a Pennsylvania steel town who discovers the world, the flesh, and spiritual turbulence on his route from Greenwich Village, through a nudist island on the Riviera, to journalistic duty at Vatican Council II.

Novak aimed *Ascent of the Mountain, Flight of the Dove* primarily at the college audience, translating the theme of *Belief and Unbelief*—religion as a search for personal identity—into a summons to adventure. Four lectures he delivered at Lake Forest College in 1969 were published under the title *The Experience of Nothingness* (Harper, 1970). Speaking for and to an American counterculture disillusioned with establishment myths and the values those myths buttressed, Novak proposed a Christian existentialist ethics of alienation reminiscent of atheistic existentialism's handling of the problem of meaningful choice in an "absurd" world. Echoing Jean-Paul Sartre as much as St. John of the Cross, he argued that the subjective "experience of nothingness," like St. John's "dark night of the soul," is a primal experience that need not lead to despair if, out of prior commitments to honesty, courage, freedom, and community hidden in the emptiness, one forges his or her own tentative mythology and acts on it. Novak wrote and his wife, Karen Laub-Novak, illustrated (with pen-and-ink drawings) *A Book of Elements; Reflections on Middle-Class Days* (Herder & Herder, 1972), consisting of prose hymns to everyday experience, both exhilarating and depressing, from conjugal love and seasonal celebration to problems between parents and children and encounters with cultural kitsch.

Turning his sights away from theology, Novak entered the mainstream of social criticism resoundingly with *The Rise of the Unmeltable Ethnics* (Macmillan, 1972). That book, like *Belief and Unbelief*, had its origin in an identity crisis of sorts. As a professor at the State University of New York in Old Westbury, Novak realized that he was by birth and breeding alien not only to the life style of colleagues who were Jewish but also to that of those who were Anglo-Saxon Protestant. For the first time, he looked seriously into his own roots and began to see that ethnic diversity is a reality denied in the myth of homogeneity in which he, like Americans generally, was schooled. That myth, imposed by the dominant WASP culture, demanded "the reconstruction of the self" in accordance with the white Protestant Anglo-Saxon model.

In *The Rise of the Unmeltable Ethnics* Novak asserted that the United States is not a melting pot, at least at the top; that ethnic groups immigrating to America from southern and eastern Europe brought with them complex value systems as worthy of appreciation as the dominant Nordic style; and that it was time for "a new cultural pluralism" and a politics based on that pluralism. Central to the new politics would be a coalition of blue-collar whites and blacks. Novak blamed "elite Protestant politics" for pitting blacks and Catholic minority whites against each other in a struggle for economic survival. While resenting the greater concern of liberals about anti-black prejudice than anti-ethnic prejudice, he pointed out that blacks and Catholic working-class whites are natural allies, with a common enemy. "The enemy is educated, wealthy, powerful—and sometimes wears liberal, sometimes radical, sometimes conservative disguise. The enemy is concentrated power."

Garry Wills, another prominent Catholic pundit, was dismayed to see Novak, "a very moral man" and "a naturally pleasant person," contributing his "bright aphorisms and seductive phrases" to the "rapidly growing literature on the social uses of hatred." Reviewing *The Rise of the Unmeltable Ethnics* in the *New York Times Book Review* (April 23, 1972), Wills described Novak as straining to "prove his own ethnicity, merrily inventing angers as he goes, . . . working his gentle soul into Zorba-the-Greek exhibitionism." In other reviews Novak was complimented for having "brilliantly explored ethnic angst" and for "dispelling the myth that ethnic politics is fundamentally racist."

To shape the new white ethnic consciousness into a "progressive force," Novak founded the Ethnic Millions Political Action Committee (EMPAC). At first trying to unite ethnic factions behind Democratic political candidates, he wrote speeches for R. Sargent Shriver and Senator Edward Muskie and was a member of Senator George McGovern's campaign staff in the 1972 presidential race, in which McGovern identified himself with the "new politics" generated by the antiwar movement.

After President Richard Nixon trounced McGovern at the polls, Novak and others, from old-line Democrats and labor leaders to deradicalized intellectuals, reassessed the new politics and rejected it, separating themselves from McGovern-style activists and forming the Coalition for a Democratic Majority. Novak faulted McGovern for having used rhetoric that ignored the cultural realities in which Americans actually live, for failing to understand, for example, why a black audience in the Los Angeles ghetto of Watts "went blank" when he spoke of the need to return to the America of the Founding Fathers.

Novak's exegesis of the 1972 presidential election went into his *Choosing Our King* (Macmillan, 1974), an insightful, imaginative analysis of the importance of symbolism in American politics, which he described as a civil religion, and especially in the president—a "priest, prophet, and king." He diagnosed the national malaise as that of a society looking for the refreshment of new public symbols; and, finally, proposed that we elect two presidents, one to manage the nation and the other to exercise symbolic authority.

The religious analogy in *Choosing Our King* was given a different application in *The Joy Sports: End Zones, Bases, Baskets, Balls, and the Consecration of the American Spirit* (Basic Books, 1976), a highly readable explanation of the spiritual excitement in sports, even for reviewers who took issue with his "theologizing" of the mundane. In Novak's view, the athletic events for which Americans have a passion are "far deeper in significance" than mere "entertainment." For him, "play, not work, is the end of life," and sports are "creations of the human spirit," cathartic secular ceremonies analogous to the drama of religious liturgy. A football game is "a public liturgy," and those involved in it who are "believers" know that it is not "just a game" but "a bout with death in advance," a contest in which one team or the city or school it represents "is blessed [and] the other rejected . . . by a power—Fate, Fortune—neither one controls." Novak is fond of quoting the French Catholic writer Georges Bernanos' dictum, "Grace is everywhere."

Following a stint as director of humanities at the Rockefeller Foundation (1973-74), Novak concentrated on researching and writing *The Guns of Lattimer* (Basic Books, 1978), a resurrection of the almost forgotten "legacy of simple, weary men, blown back by a sudden explosion on a hot September day" in 1897. The men were striking Slavic miners in the anthracite town of Lattimer, Pennsylvania. Fired upon by a sheriff's posse, nineteen of them were killed and thirty-one were seriously wounded; all members of the posse were acquitted by a jury of their peers. Novak reconstructed the massacre by embellishing historical fact with fictional vignettes. Even reviewers who found the blend lumpy leaned to the consensus view of the book as a "useful" contribution to "the literature of injustice"—"a paean to the millions of Slavic immigrants who lived and endured in America" and "a welcome reminder of a profound national bias."

From 1977 to 1979 Novak was Watson-Ledden professor of religious studies at Syracuse University. He became resident scholar at the American Enterprise Institute for Public Policy Research while still on the Syracuse faculty, in 1978. The institute and the university's department of religion in 1979 jointly sponsored a seminar on the problems posed for the world religions by rival economic systems. Ten lectures given at the seminar, together with highlights from the discussions, were edited by Novak and published by the institute under the title *Capitalism and Socialism; A Theological Inquiry* (1979).

Novak, who had opposed the California gubernatorial candidacy of Ronald Reagan while at Stanford University in the 1960s, supported Reagan's successful presidential candidacy in 1980. In an article in *Commonweal* (October 24, 1980) titled "Switch to Reagan: For a Stronger America," he characterized Reagan as "a builder, not a knocker" and a man of "implacable affability." Before en-

dorsing Reagan, he had hoped that the Democrats would nominate Daniel Patrick Moynihan or Edward M. Kennedy rather than President Jimmy Carter. He opposed Carter chiefly on foreign-policy grounds.

With the proverbial fervor of the convert, Novak wrote *The Spirit of Democratic Capitalism* (Simon & Schuster, 1982), a defense of the "much despised system" that is "perhaps our last, best hope" for "alleviating poverty and for removing oppressive tyranny." Rejecting the assumption that capitalism is inherently unjust and that Christians ought to espouse some form of socialism, at least ideally, he argued that democratic capitalism is the most propitious setting for the flourishing of Western religious and cultural values. Within democratic capitalism, he pictured "democratic polity, an economy based on markets and incentives, and a moral-cultural system which is pluralistic and, in the largest sense, liberal" functioning harmoniously, "as one." "Democratic capitalism is neither the Kingdom of God nor without sin," he wrote. "Yet all other known systems of political economy are worse. . . . Judaism and Christianity do not *require* democratic capitalism. It is only that without it they would be poorer and less free." Reviewers on the left tended to relegate *The Spirit of Democratic Capitalism* to *The Gospel of Wealth* tradition of the late nineteenth century. Others, on the right and in the center, regarded it as "perhaps the first serious attempt to construct a theology of capitalism" and an inspiration to "those just now beginning to lay siege to the heretofore sacrosanct citadel of liberation theology and the claim that 'Christianity is the religion of which socialism is the practice.'"

Partly in emulation of G. K. Chesterton's *Orthodoxy*, Novak rendered a public account of his beliefs in *Confession of a Catholic* (Harper & Row, 1983), a sometimes idiosyncratic *confessio* structured as a gloss on the Nicene Creed, followed by a generally baleful description of the state of the post–Vatican II church. His reflections ranged from eloquent statements of Catholic spirituality and apologetics (including passages on the Resurrection of Jesus and the remission of sins), through lament for the old Latin mass and deprecation of the aesthetics of the new liturgy, to sociopolitical criticism of radical feminism, gay liberation, utopian socialism, and geopolitical neutralism. Chiefly concerned with the church's "compromises" with Marxism and the "gnosticism" of the age, he offered a *mea culpa* for his own earlier complicity in the liberalization of Catholicism and excoriated the liberal and liberation theologians who continue to "subvert" Catholic doctrine. In Novak's view, Vatican Council II "set in motion both positive forces and forces that squandered the inheritance of the church." Relating the changes in the church to "the many individual lives" he has seen "ravaged by novel interpretations in faith and morals," he judged "the new libertinism" to be "less the result of human frailty than of the ideology of 'openness' and 'liberation.'" Traditionalists in the church gave a warm reception to *Confession of a Catholic,* which for them contained probably only one major point of contention: Novak's demurrer on the current Catholic teaching on contraception, an issue on which he has never changed position.

The American Catholic bishops began drafting their pastoral letter on war and peace in 1981. That controversial document, challenging some of the most fundamental aspects of United States nuclear-arms policy and strategy, was two arduous years in the making. Novak contributed significantly to the arduousness, writing his own open letter defending nuclear deterrence as a peace-keeping strategy. Successive drafts of his letter, rebutting the early episcopal drafts, were sent to the bishops and probably contributed to whatever "just war" weight balanced the dovelike pronouncements in the completed document, "The Challenge of Peace: God's Promise and Our Response," issued in 1983. Novak's open letter, first published in the periodicals *Catholicism in Crisis* and the *National Review,* was issued in revised book form as *Moral Clarity in the Nuclear Age* (Thomas Nelson, 1983).

Novak again confronted the American bishops in November 1984, when they issued the first draft of their pastoral letter on "Catholic Social Teaching and the U.S. Economy." Taking a dim view of "privileged concentrations of power, wealth, and income" in a nation where 15 percent of the population "lives below the official poverty level," the bishops called for aggressive, government-led action to remove the "social and moral scandal" and to raise economic rights to the same "privileged position" that political rights "hold in the cultural and legal traditions of our nation." In answer to the hierarchy, Novak and William Simon, the former Secretary of the Treasury, headed up a prestigious group of lay Catholics calling itself the Lay Commission on Catholic Social Teaching and the U.S. Economy. In its own open letter, the group faulted the bishops for failing to acknowledge the capacity of United States capitalism to create jobs and help lower the poverty level, and it asserted, "Poverty is . . . a personal and community problem which each of us and all our appropriate associations, not only the state, ought to address." Reiterating many of the ideas he had earlier formulated in *The Spirit of Democratic Capitalism,* Novak provided his own "neoliberal" perspective on Catholic social thought as it relates to economics, especially in Latin America and the Third World, in *Freedom with Justice* (Harper & Row, 1984). When the bishops issued the second draft of their economics letter, in the autumn of 1985, Novak was happy to see the "good-faith changes" they had made and the "less condemnatory" tone of their words, because "it really isn't much fun criticizing the works of one's own bishops."

Michael Novak and the artist Karen Laub were married on June 29, 1963. With their three children, Richard, Tanya, and Jana, the Novaks live in the Chevy Chase section of the District of Columbia. Novak's office at the American Enterprise Institute

for Public Policy Research is decorated with large lithographs of the Four Horsemen of the Apocalypse by his wife and a photograph of Novak with Pope John Paul II. Novak is a columnist for the *National Review,* and a column he wrote for the now defunct *Washington Star* was nominated for a Pulitzer Prize for commentary in 1979. For the Reagan administration, he has served as head of the United States delegation to the United Nations Human Rights Commission and as a member of the board responsible for Radio Free Europe and Radio Liberty, among other positions. He has approximately thirty engagements on the lecture circuit each year.

Novak is a round-faced man with thinning, graying hair and a voice, normally low, that sometimes pipes in the heat of argument. Colman McCarthy of the *Washington Post* (May 11, 1983) reported that "one Novak trait that came across in three interviews [was] a love of attention." According to McCarthy, Novak "sees intellectual development, not inconsistency," in his philosophical and political changes over the years. "The world has changed a great deal," Novak told McCarthy. "I've always argued that you should question your positions. When I've seen things not work the way I thought they would work, I've adjusted accordingly."

*References: Washington Post B p1+ My 11 '83 pors; Contemporary Authors new rev vol 1 (1981); Who's Who in America, 1984–85*

---

# O'Neill, William A(tchison)

*Aug. 11, 1930– Governor of Connecticut. Address: b. Office of the Governor, Rm. 202, State Capitol, Hartford, Conn. 06115; h. Governor's Residence, 990 Prospect Ave., Hartford, Conn. 06115; Meeks Point, East Hampton, Conn. 06424*

On December 31, 1980 the popular governor of Connecticut Ella T. Grasso, terminally ill with cancer, stepped down in the middle of her second term, relinquishing the office to her lieutenant governor, William A. O'Neill, a humble man of working-class background. "I am in a position I never in my wildest imagination thought I would attain," O'Neill has said." "But because of happenstance, luck, and tragedy, I stand before you as the eighty-fourth governor of the great state of Connecticut." A manager rather than an innovator, O'Neill has demonstrated his greatest strength as a broker of compromise while pursuing the moderate Democratic policies of his predecessor.

William Atchison O'Neill was born in Hartford, Connecticut on August 11, 1930, the only child of Joseph O'Neill, a private chauffeur, and Frances (Quinn) O'Neill. The family moved from the state capital, when William was seven, to East Hampton,

*William A. O'Neill*

a small town on the shore of Lake Pocotopaug, about twenty miles southeast of Hartford. There the parents opened O'Neill's Restaurant, a neighborhood gathering place that William O'Neill later took over.

Although O'Neill earned only average grades in the local public schools that he attended, he impressed his teachers and classmates with his leadership qualities. In high school he was a singer and played basketball and soccer. "He was not the type to throw in the towel," one of his school teammates has recalled. "He was never a quitter."

As a teenager, O'Neill demonstrated his interest in politics by engaging in such civic activities as driving voters to the polls on election day. After high-school graduation he was for a time uncertain as to his career plans. He studied for a year at New Britain Teachers College, then took a job at Pratt & Whitney Aircraft Corporation, but quit in 1950 to enlist in the United States Air Force. He flew fourteen combat missions as a B-29 tail gunner during the Korean war, attaining the rank of staff sergeant by the time of his discharge in 1953. Back in civilian life, he returned to Pratt & Whitney, at the same time taking night classes in engineering at the University of Hartford, and then he accepted a job as a salesman with the Prudential Insurance Company.

O'Neill took his first step into formal politics in 1954, when he won election to a seat on the East Hampton Democratic town committee that he retained for twenty-five years. His low-keyed style of leadership and his quiet, persevering competence in financial management won him the admiration and friendship of local politicians. But as a Democrat in a strongly Republican district he failed in his first two attempts to win a seat in the house of representatives, the lower house of the state gener-

al assembly, losing by 100 votes in 1960 and by fifty votes in 1962. Wrangling over legislative reapportionment resulted in cancellation of the 1964 election.

In 1966 the young East Hampton aspirant won the Democratic nomination for the house seat of the newly defined 52d assembly district, over the candidate for Middletown, the district's political center, and then went on to win the seat by a margin of sixty-seven votes. Reelected in 1968, 1970, 1972, 1974, and 1976, he served a total of twelve years in the general assembly. His colleagues chose him as assistant majority leader for the 1971-72 term, assistant minority leader for the 1973-74 term, and majority leader for the terms spanning 1975 through 1978. He also served on the Connecticut governor's finance advisory committee for six years, beginning in 1968, and he was chairman of the house committee on executive nominations.

O'Neill's reliability came to the attention of two veteran Connecticut politicians, Ella T. Grasso and John M. Bailey. A former Connecticut state legislator and secretary of state, Mrs. Grasso went on to serve two terms in the United States House of Representatives. When she decided to run for the Connecticut governorship in 1974, she invited O'Neill to head her campaign committee, and he accepted. In a landslide victory in November, Mrs. Grasso became the first woman in the United States to be elected governor in her own right, rather than as the widow of an incumbent.

Immediately on taking office in early 1975, Governor Grasso was beset with serious problems, including a $70-million debt and a 10-percent unemployment rate that she inherited from her Republican predecessor, Governor Thomas J. Meskill. Soon afterward she suffered a major loss with the death, in April, of her closest political adviser and mentor, John M. Bailey, who as chairman of the Democratic state central committee had steered the Connecticut party machine for nearly three decades. Mrs. Grasso named O'Neill as her personal choice for the vacated committee chairmanship, and the seventy-two–member committee unanimously elected him on April 28, 1975. It was an important career boost that surprised some observers. His hometown newspaper, the *Middletown Press*, was quoted as describing him at the time as "a respected figure, but not one destined for instant stardom." But as Lawrence Fellows pointed out in the *New York Times* (April 29, 1975), O'Neill had "made few enemies, if any, on either side of the political aisle." In the same article O'Neill was quoted as saying: "I think the term 'boss' is a word out of the past. I wouldn't try to be one." In a departure from the style of his predecessor, O'Neill promised to consult on a regular basis with local party leaders.

Mrs. Grasso's first year as governor was fraught with fiscal misfortune. She failed to fulfill her promises of financial aid to cities, sliced the welfare budget, and, just before Christmas, laid off a number of state workers. Frustrated, she blamed O'Neill for her inability to move legislation intact through the assembly. By July 1976 it was apparent that Governor Grasso no longer supported the man whom she had previously endorsed. She announced that, contrary to custom, she would not suggest a candidate for the July 19 election for the Democratic state central committee chairmanship. Meanwhile, her aides were reported to be rounding up support for Peter G. Kelly, the Hartford Democratic party chairman. Mrs. Grasso gave as her reason for failing to support O'Neill that she wanted the election process to be more truly democratic, and she suggested that by holding both the party chairmanship and the house majority leadership O'Neill tended to divide his loyalty between the executive and legislative branches. Reporters speculated that she was bitter because, despite Democratic majorities in both houses, the assembly had rewritten her budgets and balked at her proposals for a wage freeze and an increase in the work week for state employees.

Feeling ran high against Mrs. Grasso for what some observers perceived as a lapse of loyalty. Ironically, the challenge solidified support for O'Neill, who was reelected to the chairmanship in a secret ballot, winning forty votes to Kelly's twenty-eight. O'Neill's surprise victory was ascribed to the support of many small constituencies. And the rift was soon healed, thanks in part to O'Neill's remarkable equanimity. "I hold no grudges," he said, as quoted in the New York Times (July 21, 1976). In November 1976 Democratic party support for O'Neill was again demonstrated when he was unanimously reelected as house majority leader.

In 1978, in a move that was unprecedented for Connecticut, Governor Grasso decided to allow the Democratic state convention to choose her running mate in her bid for reelection. Her lieutenant governor, Robert K. Killian, was challenging her in the primary, but the convention in July endorsed Mrs. Grasso and designated O'Neill as her running mate in a campaign that opened with nine candidates for lieutenant governor. Ella Grasso defeated Killian by a vote of two to one in the September Democratic primary. On election day, November 7, after a campaign in which she stressed her opposition to a state income tax, Mrs. Grasso trounced the Republican challenger, United States Representative Ronald A. Sarasin, and O'Neill was elected as her second-in-command.

As lieutenant governor, O'Neill presided over the state senate, continued to carve out behind-the-scenes compromises to support the frugal policies of the governor, and acted as stand-in for her at fund-raising events and civic functions. While Governor Grasso was popular with the public, O'Neill was quietly effective as her backup. As described in a profile in the New York Times (December 5, 1980), he became known as a politician who handled issues "with a lot of caution and preparation, and very little public flair."

Little more than a year into her second term as governor, Mrs. Grasso was beset by a series of illnesses, including cancer, that led to her resignation from office on December 31, 1980 and her death on

February 5, 1981. Informed of her intention to resign, O'Neill made a statement to the press that typified his humility and honesty: "I'm not sure that anyone is ever ready to be the chief executive," he said, as quoted in the New York Times (December 5, 1980). "But you somehow find yourself when called upon to fulfill duties that you yourself and perhaps many others do not feel you capable of. I therefore feel as though I will do this job to the best of my ability."

On the day she handed over the governorship, Ella Grasso wrote a letter to O'Neill that read in part, "This afternoon, your time of challenge and promise begins." Sworn in on December 31, 1980 as Connecticut's eighty-fourth governor, O'Neill pledged to continue Mrs. Grasso's policies. "To do anything less would be a travesty of justice," he said. The vacated post of lieutenant governor was filled, as dictated by the Connecticut constitution, by the president pro tempore of the state senate, Joseph J. Fauliso, a Hartford Democrat. Among O'Neill's first actions as governor was a shakeup in the command of the state police in response to stepped-up activity by the Ku Klux Klan in Connecticut in early 1981.

The new governor found himself facing fiscal difficulties, compounded by his tenuous authority, which Richard L. Madden of the New York Times (January 2, 1981) likened to that of a lame-duck governor. With only four weeks to propose a budget of some $3 billion for the fiscal year beginning July 1 and to bridge a gap between anticipated revenues and projected spending estimated at $200 million, O'Neill was hampered by having no direct mandate from the voters. His initial recommendation stunned both parties. On January 7, 1981, in his first state of the state address, he called, among other things, for cancellation of Connecticut's urban problems block grants, a revenue-sharing program scheduled to distribute $23.8 million that March to municipalities. That recommendation displeased legislators from urban districts, and the general assembly voted to cancel only half of the program. In February he surprised legislators by proposing a 10-percent tax on unincorporated businesses in hopes of balancing the budget, but the assembly, after a long and heated struggle, granted only part of his demand. Nevertheless, the governor had at last taken a stand and, in the process, made some enemies. Some criticized his new, more aloof style as well as his politics. "He should have been a lot softer about sitting down with his people," complained George L. Gunther, Republican leader of the Connecticut senate, as quoted in the New York Times (May 5, 1981). "When the king doesn't sit down with the princes, you have all sorts of problems out there." An interim budget, signed in June, did not take into account expected cuts in federal aid.

When the general assembly reconvened in mid-November 1981 for an emergency budget-balancing session, the budget was running a deficit estimated at about $83 million, partly as a result of the reduction in federal funds. As stress mounted, the governor's health failed, and he suffered a mild heart attack. In early December he underwent double coronary bypass surgery at Hartford's Saint Francis Hospital. Lieutenant Governor Fauliso took on the budget battle during O'Neill's recuperation. The budget passed by the general assembly in late January 1982 featured a deficit estimated at $30 million but also included tax hikes and budget cuts that would add approximately $100 million in revenue to the state in the next fiscal year. Governor O'Neill in his first public appearance after his release from the hospital announced his intention to run in the 1982 gubernatorial race.

Although O'Neill's illness had won him sympathy, it had also caused him to yield center stage to House Speaker Ernest N. Abate, who announced his own candidacy. But despite the respect in which Abate was held by his legislative colleagues, the liberal Democratic lawyer from Stamford was unable to raise the requisite 20 percent of the vote at the Democratic state convention in July 1982 to force a primary runoff. Consequently, Governor O'Neill and Fauliso, the unchallenged candidate for lieutenant governor, won the Democratic nomination. Shortly afterward, the Republican state convention endorsed Lewis B. Rome, a former mayor of Bloomfield, who had been the running mate of gubernatorial candidate Ronald A. Sarasin in the 1978 election.

In a campaign that offered few opportunities for divergence of opinion, Rome accused O'Neill of poor management, pointing as an example to a well-publicized case in which a commissioner of transportation, appointed by former Governor Grasso and retained by O'Neill, was arrested on charges of accepting gifts from companies doing business with the state. He complained that O'Neill, with his practice of campaigning as litte as possible, was conducting a "Rose Garden strategy," and he ridiculed O'Neill's campaign slogan, "Quiet Courage and Yankee Determination," by asserting, "It's not quiet courage, it's silence."

For his part, O'Neill stressed his record of tight budgeting and a low unemployment rate—less than 7 percent, in contrast to a national rate of more than 10 percent—that he attributed to his party's job-creation programs. On other issues, the candidates were in basic agreement. Both vowed to veto a state income tax—Connecticut was one of only seven states with no tax on earned personal income—and both expected the anticipated budget gap to be resolved by national economic recovery that would result in greater revenues from Connecticut's sales tax, which at 7.5 percent was the state's greatest source of income.

O'Neill also identified himself with such relatively noncontroversial measures as a law that would raise Connecticut's drinking age from eighteen to nineteen, legislation that would require companies in the state to provide information about toxic substances used by their plants, and a bill that would discourage use of a victim's sexual history in a rape trial. He prided himself on having created "enterprise zones" in designated areas of six cities, where the state would provide incentives to lure industry into depressed neighborhoods. Following a catastrophic rainstorm in June 1982, O'Neill applied for federal aid for Connecticut and succeeded in obtaining status for the state as a major disaster area. At the same time he was strongly critical of the administration of President Ronald Reagan for its cutbacks in federal aid to the states.

On election day, November 2, 1982, O'Neill won 54 percent of the vote to Rome's 46 percent. The election also resulted in strong Democratic majorities in both houses of the state general assembly. Granted an electoral mandate, Governor O'Neill abandoned his caretaker stance, and his confidence appeared to soar. His basic moderation, however, did not alter. One of his first moves as governor-elect was to request the resignations of 134 politically appointed top executive-branch officials, but in the end he replaced only seven.

Budget troubles continued to dominate Connecticut politics. Shortly after the election, new estimates predicted a budget gap for the fiscal year beginning July 1983 at nearly $300 million. Amid demands for a total overhaul of Connecticut's tax structure, he called instead for the state sales tax to be cut from 7.5 to 7 percent but extended to items not previously taxed, such as medical services and children's clothing. Described as "just another patchwork" in a *New York Times* editorial (February 12, 1983), the proposal drew fire from all sides. "Bill O'Neill is levying heavy taxes on the very people he claims to support—the poor, the handicapped, and the needy," the senate minority leader, Philip S. Robertson, a Republican, said, as quoted in the *New York Times* (February 13, 1983). The recommendation was rejected, and a compromise was finally arrived at that included new taxes on interest income and real-estate sales.

In response to public concern, O'Neill endorsed the raising of the state's minimum drinking age once more, from nineteen to twenty, and signed a bill to phase out tolls along the Connecticut Turnpike, beginning in late 1985. He also signed legislation, the first of its kind in the United States, placing limits on the cost to customers of a nuclear power plant, Millstone 3, that was being built in Waterford.

In 1984 O'Neill was among the early backers of Democratic presidential candidate Walter Mondale. The upbeat economy enabled the governor to propose a $4-billion budget with tax increases in only one area, that of transportation. The legislature approved his tax package nearly intact, including a ten-year program to upgrade Connecticut's roads and bridges that would be financed in part by increased gasoline taxes and motor-vehicle fees. The fiscal year ending June 30, 1984 yielded an unexpected $144-million surplus for the state.

Governor O'Neill's newfound confidence prompted senate majority leader Richard F. Schneller to comment, as quoted in the *New York Times* (May 19, 1984): "Rather than events taking their own course, he is now shaping events." And

Speaker of the House Irving J. Stolberg called the 1984 legislation "the apex of cooperation" between the governor and the assembly. But although O'Neill indicated that he intended to seek another term as governor in 1986, the nationwide GOP landslide victory in November 1984—which brought the Republicans substantial majorities in both houses of the Connecticut state general assembly—left little doubt that he would face a major challenge over the next two years.

Nevertheless, O'Neill reached substantial agreement with the Republican-controlled legislature. During the first five months of 1985 he signed over 200 bills sent to him by the general assembly and vetoed only two relatively minor measures. In May he signed a bipartisan compromise $3.95 billion state budget that included provisions for tax cuts amounting to $155 million, although he failed to win assembly approval for his proposal to send a substantial amount of the state's surplus funds to cities and towns for local property tax relief. In September he proposed a minimum starting salary of some $19,000 a year for Connecticut teachers, and an increase from 40 to 50 percent of the state's share of local education costs, beginning with the 1986-87 school year.

In December 1962 William A. O'Neill married Natalie ("Nikki") Scott Damon, a schoolteacher from Massachusetts, whom he had met at a party six months earlier. The O'Neills, who have no children, make their home in a five-room house on Lake Pocotopaug. Although his gubernatorial responsibilities have left him little time for recreational activities, he enjoys taking his motorboat out for a spin on the lake, playing golf, dining informally with friends, and reading historical novels and books on science and United States history. The American political personality he most admires is President Harry S. Truman, whose common touch he has tried to emulate. Sometimes given to malapropism, O'Neill has been known to quote such "old Chinese *adverbs*" as "The longest march in the world begins with a very short step," or to promise to govern "in the *mannerism*" that the people have come to expect. Among the honors that O'Neill has received is a distinguished humanitarian award from the National Jewish Hospital and Research Center and the 1981 man of the year award of the Elks.

References: N Y Times B p8 D 5 '80, B p2 My 11 '84; International Who's Who, 1985-86; Who's Who in America, 1984-85; Who's Who in American Politics, 1983-84

## Özal, Turgut

(û´ zäl tōor´ get)

1927- Prime Minister of the Republic of Turkey.
Address: Halaskargazi Cad. No. 336/1 D. 6, Şişli, Istanbul, Turkey

After his conservative Motherland party won a clear majority of parliamentary seats in the November 1983 general election, Turgut Özal, a pragmatic technocrat with twenty-two years' experience in the civil service, automatically became prime minister of Turkey. A self-described "monetarist and supply-sider," he was the chief architect of the free-market economic recovery program that reversed Turkey's economic decline and virtually saved the country from bankruptcy in the late 1970s. As prime minister, Özal has devised a bold strategy of industrial growth and trade expansion designed to make Turkey, in his words, "the Japan of the Middle East." But like Kemal Atatürk, the founder of the Turkish Republic who, in modernizing the country, transformed it from an Islamic-theocratic state to a Westernized, secular one, Özal is mindful of the nation's Islamic heritage. "Technologically, managerially and economically we should follow the liberal Western system," the prime minister, a devout Moslem, said shortly before taking office, as quoted in the *Wall Street Journal* (December 3, 1983), "but we also have to keep the important Islamic social background and moral values. These make a nation."

The oldest son of Mehmet and Hafize Özal, Turgut Özal was born in 1927 in Malatya, Turkey, 465 miles east of the capital city of Ankara, in the Anatolian highlands. The fortunes of his parents reflected the sweeping social and political changes then transforming Turkey. "My mother was a teacher," Özal told Alison MacLeod in an interview for *Euromoney* (March 1981), "my father was an *imam*. He was a religious teacher, a preacher in the mosque. But when the Republic came in he became an ordinary teacher. Then my father became a banker. . . . " From his mother, he learned the dutifulness to the Islamic faith that has guided his life; from his father, whom he often accompanied on his travels around the country for the Turkish Agricultural Bank, he acquired an astute business sense. The Özal family itself moved often during Turgut's boyhood, first to Ankara, then to the central highland towns of Konya and Kayseri, to Mardin, near the Syrian border, and finally to Mersin, on the Mediterranean Sea.

After graduating in 1950 from Istanbul Technical University with an M.S. degree in electrical engineering, Özal went to work for Turkey's Electrical Power Resources Survey Administration, where he oversaw the country's electrification program and helped plan the construction of several hydroelectric projects. In 1952 he was sent to the United States to study the American electric-power industry. By the time he returned home, in 1953, he was an expert statistician and cost-benefit analyst. For the next several years, he divided his time between the Power Resources Survey Administration and the State Planning Organization. He even fulfilled his compulsory military obligations on assignment to the State Planning Organization, although he also served on the Scientific Advisory Council of the Ministry of Defense.

When Süleyman Demirel, Özal's former boss at the Power Resources Survey Administration, became prime minister of Turkey in 1965, he named his longtime friend and colleague special technical advisor to the prime minister's office. Özal remained in that post until his appointment, in 1967, as undersecretary of the State Planning Organization. Out of a job after Demirel was ousted in a military coup in 1971, Özal accepted an appointment as a special projects advisor and senior economist at the World Bank in Washington, D.C. In his two years there, he focused on industrial and mining projects in developing countries. On his return to his homeland in 1973, he entered the private sector, working first as a managing director of the Sabanki Combine and then for the Asil Celik Steel Works. His business associates from that period sing his praises: "I worked with him," Ali Koçman, the president of Tusiad, a businessmen's organization, said, as quoted in *Euromoney* (March 1981). "He is the most strict, the most honest, the most fair man I have ever met in business life in Turkey."

Back in office in 1975, Prime Minister Demirel named Özal governor of the central bank, but the nomination was blocked. It was not until Demirel's next term began, in 1979, that Özal rejoined the government, as undersecretary of the State Planning Organization. At the time, Turkey was reeling under the effects of the 1974 Arab oil embargo. Huge balance-of-payments deficits, resulting in an enormous foreign debt, and the drying up of Turkey's credit had provoked financial and political chaos. Parliament, shackled by the stalemated coalitions of Prime Minister Demirel and his chief rival, former liberal Prime Minister Bülent Ecevit, failed to find solutions to the problems of runaway inflation, labor unrest, 40 percent unemployment, and increasing social disorder. As parliament's authority crumbled, political extremism, fed by the influx of the uprooted and easily radicalized rural poor into the already overcrowded cities, flourished. From 1978 through 1980, as many as 13,000 Turks were slain or wounded in street violence.

In January 1980 Demirel managed to force through his cabinet a five-year plan of economic reforms and austerity measures that has come to be known as Turgut Özal's "Turkish miracle." Demirel's faith in his deputy was strong, his message to the cabinet simple: "Sign, or return to parliament." Such firmness eventually proved the undoing of Demirel's minority government. The political opposition stepped up its attacks, and on September 12, 1980 the armed forces, under command of General Kenan Evren, overthrew the Demirel government. Acting swiftly to restore political and economic stability, the ruling five-man junta placed in custody hundreds of political leaders, including Demirel and Ecevit, abolished all political parties, banned labor-union activity, and imposed martial law. Ranking civil servants were ordered to return to the management of their ministries. Turgut Özal, whose austerity measures were beginning to show measurable results, was asked to stay on as deputy prime minister to see his economic plan through.

Özal devised an economic package that, over the next three years, brought inflation down from 120 percent a year to 30 percent, doubled Turkey's exports, opened up its domestic markets to foreign competition, ended shortages at the bazaars and gas pumps, and rekindled modest growth in the gross national product. He accomplished this remarkable reversal in classic monetarist fashion by keeping strict control over the money supply, freeing bank interest rates to rise higher than the inflation rate, which encouraged increased savings and investments, reforming the tax system, devaluing the Turkish lira, and beginning the restoration of Atatürk's state economic enterprises to private ownership and control. Perhaps most important, he brought immediate relief to Turkey's ailing economy by arranging, in January 1981, a rescheduling of the country's $3.2 billion foreign debt, thus reopening the country's credit lines. Despite his obvious successes, criticism of and opposition to his austere economic recovery program continued to mount. In July 1982, following the forced departure of his finance minister, Kaya Erdem, Özal himself submitted his resignation. Almost immediately, he began preparing for the upcoming general election, scheduled for November 1983.

Although as a technocrat he was protected from the shifting political winds throughout most of his career, Turgut Özal was no newcomer to electoral politics. In the mid-1970s he had made an unsuccessful bid for parliament as a candidate of the Islamic fundamentalist National Salvation party in Izmir. He had decided to run, he has since explained, as a "sentimental" gesture to his younger brother, Korkut, a deputy leader of that party who had served as agriculture minister in the administrations of both Ecevit and Demirel. On May 20, 1983, just a few weeks after officials lifted the twenty-two-month ban on political activity, Özal founded the Motherland party in accordance with the government's strict rules. Because the old "pre-coup" parties, including Ecevit's Republican People's party, Demirel's Justice party, and the National Salvation party, had been permanently outlawed, Özal's new party held the center position, between the Nationalist Democracy party, led by retired General Turgut Sünalp, and the officially sanctioned left-wing opposition party, the Populists, headed by Necdet Calp, a civil servant.

Özal's Motherland party draws its strength from what Özal has called the "middle pillar,"—the "workers and government employees, farmers, artisans and craftsmen and small businessmen," who had recently begun to reassert themselves after years of being subjugated under the influence of the Westernized urban elite, the traditional ally of the army since the days of Atatürk. Yet the party also represents Turkey's young technocrat and business class, who see Özal as one of their own. Having once favored the military's authoritarian rule as the best way to insure stability and economic growth, those voters were now eager for the establishment of a free-market economy. As Özal told Sam Cohen in an interview for the *Christian Science Monitor* (November 30, 1983), "We are conservative on moral issues, liberal on the economy, and progressive on social justice. . . . This is quite different from the conservative parties in the West. It shows that we are a different society."

Özal presented his particular blend of religion and economics to the Turkish voters in a hard-fought, American-style campaign complete with campaign buttons, mass-media advertising, and public-relations consultants. At home before the cameras, he came across as open and confident in the nationally televised debate with his opponents, and he mesmerized Turks in a series of twenty-minute televised chats in which he outlined the country's economic problems and his solutions to those problems in straightforward terms. Worried by Özal's increasing popularity, the government at first pressured him to merge his Motherland party with its tacitly supported Nationalist Democracy party, then attempted to stem the tide in his favor by stopping the publication of an eleventh-hour public opinion poll that showed him to be the clear frontrunner. Finally, on the eve of the election, President Evren tipped the junta's hand by publicly warning voters against Özal's "false statements and sweet promises."

When the ballots were counted in the general election on November 6, the Motherland party emerged victorious, taking 45 percent of the popular vote and 212 of the 400 seats in the unicameral parliament. It was the first time a party had won an absolute majority since the early 1970s. Calp's Populist party came in second, with 30 percent of the vote and 117 seats, while the army-backed Nationalist Democracy party received only 23 percent of the vote and seventy-one seats. Quelling some fears that the military might challenge the results, on November 24 parliament met for its first session. Two weeks later, the junta stepped down, and on December 7, President Evren formally asked Turgut Özal to form a new government.

Despite his clear-cut victory at the polls, Özal had still to tread a narrow path between implementing his ambitious program of economic growth and democratization and propitiating the military, which retained considerable power. Under the terms of Turkey's 1982 constitution, which had been ratified by 90 percent of the registered voters, Kenan Evren, who will remain president until 1989, has the final say in matters of defense, foreign policy, and internal security. "Confident that democracy will be safeguarded," as he expressed it, Evren approved, with only minor changes, Özal's cabinet choices, most of them young technocrats, and on December 13, 1983, he turned over the reins of government to the new prime minister. As if to endorse Özal's administration, Turkish voters overwhelmingly favored the Motherland party's candidates in the nationwide municipal elections on March 25, 1984, virtually guaranteeing Özal's position for the next five years.

Prime Minister Özal had conceded that the economic recovery, on which he believes Turkish democracy rests, will not be easy. "We are not blessed with oil, and it will take a tough recipe of blood, sweat and sacrifice to earn our way," he explained, as quoted in *Institutional Investor* (January 1984). In a subsequent interview for the *New Yorker* (October 15, 1984), he predicted that "the next five years" would be "the hardest in the history of Turkey." Recent economic statistics seem to support his statements. By October 1984, the devaluation of the lira from its artificially high level of twenty-five to the dollar, in 1980, to 400 to the dollar had increased exports by 32 percent over the previous year, and exports to the Middle East had grown from a meager $400,000 in 1980 to over $3.2 billion by late 1984, accounting for 42 percent of Turkey's foreign market. At the same time, despite the elimination of many restrictions, imports went up by only 8 percent. More important, the trade deficit declined by 27 percent and the gross national product rose by 5.7 percent in real terms—a growth rate rivaled by few countries.

But Özal's economic policies were not without their social costs. His supply-side, free-market experiment failed to slow inflation, which reached an annual rate of 52.4 percent by October 1984, at least partly because the end of state subsidies doubled the price of many basic commodities. The elimination of import controls hurt domestic industry, too, provoking an increase in the number of bankruptcies and pushing the unemployment rate up to slightly over 20 percent. Moreover, the devaluation of the lira made imported goods all the more expensive for the average consumer. Having made the restoration of "peace and calm" a top priority, at first Özal took a hard line on human rights. Indeed, a writer for the *Economist* (November 19, 1983) described his approach as "not so different from the generals'." According to Amnesty International and Helsinki Watch, the human-rights watchdog organizations, as recently as late 1984 Turkish jails held upwards of 20,000 political prisoners, including labor leaders, civil-rights activists, and intellectuals as well as terrorists. Some Western analysts, however, saw signs of hope in Özal's gradual lifting of martial law. By April 1985 he had restored civilian rule in forty-four of Turkey's sixty-seven provinces.

In the area of foreign affairs, Prime Minister Özal has pledged to improve economic and political relations with Greece, which have deteriorated considerably since Turkish Cypriots issued a unilateral declaration of independence in November 1983. Reaffirming Turkey's allegiance to NATO, he vowed that, under his administration, the country would live up to its commitments as the alliance's second-largest military force. In meetings with President Ronald Reagan and other government and business leaders in Washington, D.C. in April 1985, Özal sought to forge closer links to the United States through expanded trade agreements and increased private American investment in Turkey. At the same time, however, he has been cautious about negotiating for membership in the EEC, and some of his countrymen see him as less pro-Western than he seems, from all outward appearances, to be. As one Turk told the British journalist Edward Mortimer, like Sheik Ahmed Zaki Yamani, the Saudi Arabian oil minister, Özal is fully conversant with Western economic and political ways but fundamentally committed to Islam. Özal has sought new commercial and economic ties with the Soviet Union and its Eastern Bloc allies, too, and he has revived political and trade arrangements with Pakistan, strengthened bonds with Libya, Turkey's chief source of oil, and increased trade with Iran, which has recently become the country's most important trading partner. In several interviews over the past few months, Özal has repeatedly stressed his desire to make Turkey the new "bridge" between East and West. But some veteran political analysts contend that his methods may instead undercut Atatürk's Westernizing legacy and turn Turkey into an inward-looking, Eastern-oriented regional power.

Turgut Özal, a portly, round-faced man with thick black hair and a bristly moustache, stands five feet, five inches tall. Fond of food, from Turkish seafood grill to American hamburgers, he has battled obesity for years. By following a strict diet, he recently managed to get his weight down to 170 pounds, although he has, in the past, tipped the scales at 240 pounds. A practicing Moslem, he neither smokes nor drinks, and he carries his worry beads at all times. "I don't say I'm 100 percent Islamic," he said, as quoted in *Euromoney* (October 1981). "I try to pray five times a day. But sometimes that gets delayed. Above all I believe in religious freedom." Married since 1954 to the for-

mer Semra Yeginmen, he has two grown children—a son, Ahmet, and a daughter, Zeynep Gonenc, who is married to an engineer—and a younger son, Efe, with whom he shares a love of computer games and electronic toys. Whenever possible, he enjoys vacationing with his family at a Turkish seaside resort.

References: N Y Times A p11 N 9 '83 por; New Yorker 60:134+ O 15 '84; U S News 98:42+ Ap 1 '85 por; International Who's Who, 1985–86; Who's Who in the World, 1982–83

## Payton, Walter

*1954– Football player. Address: b. Chicago Bears, Halas Hall, 250 N. Washington Rd., Lake Forest, Ill. 60045*

The Chicago Bears' durable and overworked running back Walter Payton, widely rated the best all-purpose yardage gainer in National Football League history, was for many years denied the celebrity he deserved by the mediocrity of his team, which has had only three winning seasons since he joined it in 1975. Payton's superstar status did not become generally known until 1984, when he set a new NFL career record in rushing, finishing the season with a career total of 13,309 yards in 3,047 attempts, and in combined yardage (receiving as well as running), with 17,304 yards. Not the most graceful of runners, Payton compensates for finesse with his consistency, intensity, never-say-die attitude, and the aggressiveness with which he vaults over or, more often, gallops into would-be tacklers. A versatile team player, he is as fearsome at blocking as he is at running and receiving, and on the occasions he is called on to pass he can be expected to complete one-third of his throws for touchdowns. Payton has started in 140 of 146 games in his professional career, and he enters his eleventh pro season with 124 consecutive starts.

Walter Jerry Payton was born in Columbia, Mississippi in 1954 to Alyne Payton and the late Peter Payton, a factory worker. His older brother, Eddie, is a former professional football player, a kick-return specialist and utility running back with the Minnesota Vikings, among other teams. A hyperactive, strong-willed, and prankish child, Payton was often corporally disciplined by his father. His parents instilled in him an ideal of excellence, "to be the best," that, he says, has stuck with him throughout his life. Strict Baptists, they also imbued him with their religious faith. In childhood, he was more interested in music than in sports, always playing the drums, tapping or beating on anything within reach, or dancing.

At Columbia High School, Payton was a drummer in the school band, and after school he played and sang in jazz-rock combos. While he set local schoolboy records in the long jump in track, he avoided football so long as his brother was starring at halfback for the school team. Although his mother did not forbid him to play football, he sensed that she worried over Eddie coming home from games with bruises and that she hoped that he, Walter, would not do the same. In addition, according to his mother, he seemed to be intimidated by his more demonstrative brother. "Eddie was always running outside to practice things he'd seen in televised football games," Mrs. Payton recalled in an interview with Paul Bellow for *Sport* (December 1977), "but Walter never did that. He'd just sit and watch and that was all."

When Eddie Payton graduated from Columbia High School, Walter, at the urging of the football coach, tried out for the team, in his junior year. From the first day of practice, his physical prowess set him apart, and in his first high-school carry he ran more than sixty yards for a touchdown. Partly because he did not want to upset his mother with torn uniforms, Payton eschewed the stutter step as a runner and developed his characteristic straight-arm technique during his high-school career.

Courted widely by college recruiters on his graduation from high school, Payton considered Kansas State but finally followed his brother to nearby Jackson State University. He quickly outshone Eddie as a punter, touchdown passer, and rusher, eventually registering the most points in National Collegiate Athletic Association history, with 464. Academically, he earned his B.A. degree in special education in three-and-a-half years.

In the 1975 professional draft of college players Payton was the first-round choice of the Chicago Bears. Insisting on a signing bonus surpassing Archie Manning's record for a National Football League player from Mississippi, he was conceded a $126,000 bonus by the Bears. As a pro rookie Payton, suffering an ankle injury, was kept out of one

game (a mar on his otherwise perfect "attendance" record that he resented for years afterward), and in the other games he was used only sporadically. Although limited in his rushing opportunities, he averaged 3.5 yards per rush, and as a kickoff returner he led the league, with 444 yards in fourteen returns. The Bears, who had not had a winning year since 1967, finished the 1975 season with four wins and ten losses, just as they had in 1974.

With Payton rushing for 1,390 yards in 311 attempts, Chicago broke even, 7-7, in 1976, for the first time since 1968. Only a last-game injury deprived Payton of a chance at the NFL rushing title. When he scored his first touchdown in 1976, he began his tradition of handing the ball to one of the linemen who block for him to share in the glory by spiking it. Following the 1976 season, Payton returned to Mississippi to work for his master's degree at Jackson State and spend time at home, where he engaged in dialogues with his mother that helped relieve him of some of the pressure he was feeling as a pro neophyte and made him realize that "all he could expect was to do [his] best." "I told him how I believe everybody's life is pre-planned by God," Mrs. Payton told Paul Bellow. "There's no need worrying about it. Whatever's gonna happen is gonna happen." Bellow noted, however, that as the 1977 season approached Payton "appeared as fully wired as ever . . . edgy, nervous, and irritable" and that "he stopped talking to newsmen."

In 1977 Payton, along with his fellow running back and friend Ron Harper, paced the Bears to their first winning season (9-5) in ten years and their first playoffs in fourteen. Payton led the National Football League in yards rushing with 1,852, and he did so in 339 attempts, for an average of 5.5, his career best. He set a new NFL single-game record for most yards in a game against Minnesota on November 20, 1977, with 275, two more than O. J. Simpson's previous mark. Of the twenty-seven passes he caught (for 269 yards), one was the longest of his career—a seventy-five-foot heave from Bob Avellini at Detroit on November 24.

Explaining the problem Payton posed for the defense, Los Angeles defensive end Jack Youngblood was quoted by Paul Bellow in his December 1977 *Sport* article: "You can't flow with the play because he'll cut back, and you can't tackle him below the waist because his legs are going all over the place. The best place to zero in is right at his belly button. But you don't try to punish him, because you'll miss him. You've got to grab him and get a firm hold." After the Bears overwhelmed the Dallas Cowboys in the 1977 playoffs, Dallas coach Tom Landry told a reporter: "You really don't appreciate a Walter Payton until you are on the sidelines against him. We were hitting him with two and three men."

Payton was voted the Most Valuable Player in the 1977 Pro Bowl, and he was the league's consensus MVP, the youngest player ever to achieve that distinction. Among his numerous other honors in 1977 were the UPI Athlete-of-the-Year designation, won over baseball's Steve Carlton, and several similar player-of-the-year awards. Negotiating for a higher salary on the strength of his proven worth, Payton finally signed three one-year contracts for an estimated $400,000 in 1978, $425,000 in 1979, and $450,000 in 1980. The contracts contained clauses for additional incentive payments as high as $97,000 a year.

Under Neill Armstrong, who replaced Jack Pardee as head coach of the Bears in 1978, Payton and Harper became the best running combination in the NFL, together surpassing Tony Dorsett and Robert Newhouse of Dallas by almost 500 yards and accounting for 72 percent of the Chicago offense. Individually, Payton made the longest run of his career, for seventy-six yards against Denver on October 16, and the most yards receiving in a game, 119 yards against Detroit thirteen days later. Reflecting NFL rule changes favoring passing that were then being introduced, Payton doubled his receptions in 1978, bringing them to fifty, for 480 yards. A Pro Bowl starter, he was an all-Pro pick in several polls and the leading vote-getter for the UPI's 1978 all-National Football Conference team. The Bears finished the season in the red, 7-9.

With the change in coaching staff, Payton changed his running style. "Instead of free-lancing," he told Clifford Terry in an interview for the Chicago Tribune (September 2, 1979), "I stuck more to the planned patterns." He explained that under Coach Pardee the offensive line had blocked all over the field, making it easier for him to pick his holes. "The new staff wants to confine everything to one area. Whatever, I'd rather run up the middle than around the end. It's more power running, and you're less susceptible to injuries to the knees. When you're running outside, you get strung out, with the defenders coming in on you. In the middle, everything is compact."

"Walter's a trickster . . . like a young kid . . . chasing cats, throwing rocks . . . ," the Chicago offensive guard Ted Albrecht told Clifford Terry. "We all have some of the little kid in us, but he has more than normal—which I think is absolutely beautiful." Terry quoted the Bears' former backfield coach Fred O'Connor regarding Payton's physique: "The first time I saw Walter Payton in the locker room I thought God must have taken a chisel and said, 'I'm gonna make me a halfback.'" He also quoted O. J. Simpson's describing Payton as an "insane" runner and explaining: "There is no rhyme or reason to what he does, but it all works out." Payton agreed: "I guess my running comes by instinct. I don't try to define it or explain it . . . only to improve it." He added that he would "actually rather block than run."

Coach Armstrong enjoyed his first and only winning season in Chicago in 1979, when the Bears went 10-6. In addition to forcing a change in Payton's running style, Armstrong gave him a chance to pass occasionally, in keeping with the team's new, more varied offense. During the 1979 season Payton threw once, for fifty-four yards and a touchdown. On the ground he gained 1,610 yards in 369 attempts and scored thirteen TDs. He was again a Pro Bowl starter, and he was voted to the all-NFC team in the Associated Press poll. In a wildcat divisional playoff loss (17-27) to the Philadelphia Eagles, he rushed sixteen times for sixty-seven yards and caught three passes for fifty-two yards and two TDs. He performed all those season and postseason exploits despite a painful shoulder-nerve injury.

"The guy's amazing . . . ," Chicago free safety Doug Plank said of Payton in an interview with Kevin Lamb for the Sporting News (September 27, 1980). "Week after week I see him put his head down and hit guys in the chest and they get carried off. His ability to come up with a big play each week is amazing. . . . He's doing things nobody else could have done." The former Chicago running back Rick Casares observed to Lamb that Payton is "one of the guys from the old school who . . . makes a better [game film] clip than talk show appearance, and he sticks his nose in there." Bobby Bryant, the Minnesota cornerback, compared efforts to tackle Payton to "trying to rope a calf." According to Lamb, statements that "Walter Payton is the Bears" rankle Payton, who wants "to leave the game with people saying, 'Now that Walter Payton, he was a team player.'"

In 1980 Payton won an unprecedented fifth consecutive National Football Conference rushing title with 1,460 yards, sixty-nine of them gained in one touchdown run, and he went to the Pro Bowl with more votes than any other member of the NFC team. The following season the Bears, with a 6-10 record, finished in last place in the NFC Central. A demoralized Payton, playing with cracked ribs in addition to a recurrence of the pain in his shoulder and with a broken-down offensive line, ran for only 1,222 yards, the fewest since his rookie season, and he failed to win the NFC rushing title for the first time in five years. In 1981 he signed a three-year contract worth almost $2 million.

In 1982, when Mike Ditka replaced Neill Armstrong as head coach, the Bears went a dismal 3-6. During that strike-shortened season Payton gained 596 yards in 148 rushes and thirty-nine in one completed pass. In addition, he was on the receiving end of thirty-two passes worth 311 yards. After the season ended, Phil Elderkin wrote of Payton in the Christian Science Monitor (January 7, 1983): "After watching his short, choppy steps, most people would probably not agree with any description of his running that includes the word cruise. But I maintain that he is smoother than he looks; that there is no one in the NFL right now who runs better laterally; that his secret is a low center of gravity that makes him tough to knock off his feet and eyes that seem to pick up on everything going on around him." Elderkin quoted Hank Kuhlmann, the Chicago backfield coach, as pointing out that other running backs "can't touch" Payton's all-around skills, including catching passes out of the outfield and pass-blocking for the quarterback. Kuhlmann added that he had never "seen Walter loaf on a play."

Rushing for 1,421 yards, catching for 607 (the most receptions of any Bear, for the fourth time in six years), and passing for ninety-five, Payton in 1983 had a combined total of more than 2,000 yards for the second time in his professional career. That yardage accounted for more than 36 percent of the total yardage of the Bears, who won six and lost six games. Payton was a Pro Bowl backup and a consensus second-stringer on the 1983 all-NFC team. At the Super Bowl, he worked as a color commentator for WLS-TV, the Chicago affiliate of the American Broadcasting Company.

Following the 1983 season, Payton signed the most lucrative contract in NFL history, guaranteeing him $240,000 a year for life. In the spring of 1984 he underwent arthroscopic surgery on both his knees. Commenting on his ability to prepare for every season regardless of the quality of the team or his own condition, the Chicago defensive lineman Dan Hampton observed in an interview in the summer of 1984 that Payton plays with the enthusiasm of a tenth grader, unlike "a lot of players who are jaded on the job." Coach Ditka, who was trying to take some of the pressure off Payton by having quarterback Jim McMahon share the load, pointed out to Steve Fiffer in an interview for *Inside Sports* (October 1984) that "Walter is still our best weapon," only "now we get production out of him running, catching, throwing, and as a decoy." Up to Ditka's arrival in Chicago, Payton had averaged twenty-one carries per game, a tally matched only by that of Houston's Earl Campbell.

On October 7, 1984 Payton surpassed Jim Brown's career rushing record of 12,312 (which had stood for nineteen years), and his running and blocking made the Bears the best team on the ground in the 1984 season. In addition to running for 1,684 yards in 381 carries, he passed for forty-seven yards in the three (out of six) passes he completed, and he caught for 368, leading the team in receptions and breaking the club record for career receptions. A consensus All-Pro, he made his seventh appearance in the Pro Bowl. Finishing the season 10-6, Chicago defeated the Washington Redskins in a divisional playoff game in which Payton ran for 104 yards, threw a nineteen-yard touchdown pass, and blocked with such ferocity that he broke the collarbone of Washington safety Curtis Jordan. In the National Football Conference championship game in January 6, 1985, the San Francisco 49ers swamped Chicago 23-0. After waiting ten years for a chance at the championship, Payton found the rout "the hardest thing [he has] ever had to deal with."

Coach Ditka, who had come to Chicago "committed to the pass," explained to Steve Jacobson of *Newsday* (January 6, 1985) why he was changing his mind and letting Payton carry the ball after all: "I wanted to show people we could open up the offense. Now I'm committed to winning. I think the best way of winning is doing things the players believe in. Our players believe in running. . . . Our line responds to it; it makes sense."

The muscular, solidly built Payton is five feet ten-and-a-half inches tall, weighs 205 pounds, and has a firm abdomen, a thick neck, and massive thighs and buttocks—the center of his balance. As a runner, he stands out not so much for his speed as for his extraordinary acceleration. He runs out or in, but he prefers the middle and the off-tackle dive play, and he surprises defenders with his frequent, sudden cutbacks. He runs on his toes, and one of the secrets of his durability, rare in a running back, is his short, stiff-legged stride, a series of consistent kicks or bursts that saves wear and tear on his knees. Compact, he darts quickly this way and that, punishing would-be tacklers with his helmeted head or his strong forearm, and dragging opposing linemen with him as he spins out of clogs. In the off-season he follows an almost fanatical training schedule, which includes gymnastics, weight lifting, and running barefoot in sandbanks.

With the help of a secretary, an accountant, and a lawyer, Payton runs Walter Payton Enterpises, which encompasses a number of investments and businesses, including Mississippi and Tennessee timberland, real estate, and restaurants in Chicago and Jackson, Mississippi. He has done commercial endorsements for cars, shoes, and the Hilton hotel chain, but he has turned down most commercial offers, partly because they would not have projected him as he wished and partly because they would have been too time-consuming for a man who treasures his privacy and his family life. Most of his television spots have been public service ads for such causes as the Peace Corps and United Way. He is involved in many charities, especially benefits for deaf and retarded children. His graduate work at Jackson State was in education for the deaf.

According to a teammate, Payton is "a classic moody guy" who "can be just as up as down." He is known to be "unpredictable" off field and "very, very shy," but virtually all his acquaintances agree that he is likeable, gracious, and humble. Payton sometimes expresses his "up" moods by spontaneous outbursts of dancing.

Walter Payton, whose nickname is "Sweetness," lives with his wife, Connie, whom he met in college, and his son, Jarret, in a home he recently had built in a Chicago suburb. The house is situated on five wooded acres, along with a shooting range and a pond stocked with fish. Payton's favorite recreations are fishing, hunting, golf, baseball, archery, dancing, and playing the drums. He speaks in a soft, high-pitched voice, and, obsessive achiever that he is, he seems to be in perpetual motion, like a man driven, especially when reporters are trying to buttonhole him. Just as he deceives defenders on the field, he enjoys "juking" the press and playing pranks on his teammates. Although he does not "get to fellowship as much as [he would] like," he often prays and reads the Bible (which he packs in his suitcase) the year round.

References: N Y Times A p21+ Ja 4 '85 por; Newsday S p1+ Ja 6 '85 pors; Newsweek 90:63 D 5 '77 por; Sport 65:57+ D '77 pors; Sporting News p2+ O 1 '84 pors; Sports Ill 57:18+ Ag 16 '82 pors; Payton, Walter and Jenkins, Jerry B. Sweetness (1978)

## Penzias, Arno A(llan)

*Apr. 26, 1933– Astrophysicist. Address: b. Bell Labs, Murray Hill, N.J. 07974*

"I guess it's kind of corny to say," the German-born astrophysicist Arno A. Penzias once admitted during an interview, "but I've realized the American dream." Forty years after fleeing to the United States from Nazi Germany, Penzias was awarded the 1978 Nobel Prize in Physics, which he shared with his colleague Robert W. Wilson for their detection of microwave background radiation, a discovery that finally proved that the universe had been created by the "big bang" that took place ten to twenty billion years ago. Continuing their profitable collaboration at AT&T Bell Laboratories, the two scientists soon detected an abundance of the fossil element deuterium in space. Its presence substantiated the theory that the universe is "open"—continually expanding until it loses momentum, becoming still and lifeless—rather than "closed"—eternally oscillating between expansion and a sudden collapse that fuels another big bang. Today, Penzias is vice-president for research at Bell Labs, where he continues both his theoretical work, with an emphasis on the origin of the elements, and his studies of practical applications for theoretical breakthroughs in the rapidly growing telecommunications industry.

Arno Penzias was born on April 26, 1933 in Munich, Germany, the son of Karl Penzias, a Polish-Jewish national and owner of a small leather business, and Justine (Inge Eisenreich) Penzias, who had converted to Judaism at the time of her marriage. Arno Penzias, who attended Jewish schools in Germany, recalls his earliest years as unmarred by any overt anti-Semitism, but in the fall of 1938 the German government began deporting residents who did not have German passports. Although the Penzias family missed by one hour the deadline for Polish Jews to return to Poland, that may have saved their lives, for on their return to Munich Karl Penzias, who had been ordered to leave the country within six months, began making immediate arrangements to immigrate to the United States.

Under those circumstances it is not surprising that "affidavit" was the first English word Arno Penzias ever learned, for an affidavit from a sponsor in America provided the magic key to an exit permit from Germany. In the late spring of 1939, when children were still allowed to leave freely, six-year-old Arno was put in charge of his younger brother, Gunter, on their unescorted train trip to England. A few days later their father was also able to leave, and within a few months Justine Penzias joined her husband and sons in England. In December 1939 they boarded a ship for the United States, arriving in New York City in the first week of January 1940. Having settled in the Bronx, Karl Penzias supported his family as an apartment-building superintendent while Justine Penzias worked as a cleaning woman in various homes. (To this day, Arno Penzias remembers the opened cans of Hershey syrup she would bring home as tips.) Within a few years, his father was employed in the carpentry shop of the Metropolitan Museum of Art and his mother went to work in the garment district. Arno Penzias became a naturalized citizen in 1946, at which time he added "Allan," the name he had been known by since his arrival in the United States, as his middle name. He has since reverted to using his given name but retains the middle initial "A." in his signature as "a vestige of [his] attempt to Americanize [himself]."

At first, Penzias' foreign accent and lack of skills at children's games made him something of a social misfit, a problem perhaps exacerbated by his frequent transfers as an elementary school student: he attended about six different New York public grade schools and a junior high school in the Bronx. But when he entered Brooklyn Technical High School in 1947, he finally began to find his niche and to make friends. At that "fairly elite" school, as he once described it, he pursued an interest in chemistry, which his father encouraged, in order to prepare himself for a career in engineering, both because it offered good job prospects and because he found the scientific and technical fields less culturally biased and so more open to immigrants. In 1951 Penzias enrolled as a chemical engineering major at the tuition-free City College of New York, but after one semester he found that he was "sick of chemistry" and decided to study physics. "Physics was unglamorous then. This was before Sputnik . . . ," he told Jeremy Bernstein in an interview for the *New Yorker* (August 20, 1984). "The top kids seemed to be attracted to it for aesthetic reasons. I didn't get into it, at first, for those reasons, but I found that, as I studied it, it was something I liked. The competition was extraordinarily tough. I had a feeling at that time of not being terribly good—of being a barely adequate physicist."

In 1954 Penzias graduated from City College in the top 10 percent of his class. While still in college, he had joined the Reserve Officers' Training Corps, and following graduation he served as a radar officer in the Army Signal Corps at Fort Devens, Massachusetts, for a stint that he later termed "a clear waste of two years of [his] life." On his discharge in 1956, Penzias decided to continue his studies, but his first application, to the Massachusetts Institute of Technology, was turned down. Spurred by that rejection and his determination to return to New York City, he applied to Columbia University, which granted him a research assistantship at its radiation laboratory.

The physics department at Columbia in the mid-1950s was a center of high-powered research. Its staff included the Nobel Prize–winning scientists Polykarp Kusch and I. I. Rabi as well as Tsung-Dao Lee and Charles H. Townes, both of whom would later be honored with that award. A few years previously, Townes and two of his students had built the first operating maser receiver, a device for the amplification of high-frequency radio waves. For his thesis, which Townes directed, Penzias built a second maser receiver to detect radiation with a wavelength of twenty-one centimeters. Since hydrogen atoms emit radiation of that wavelength, Penzias thought it would be fairly simple to use his maser and a sensitive antenna to detect hydrogen in outer space by positioning his antenna according to previously published calculations of where hydrogen should occur. When he discovered that those calculations were wrong, he redesigned his experiment to set upper limits for hydrogen in certain clusters of galaxies, but with disappointing results. He has since dismissed his thesis, entitled "A tunable maser radiometer and the measurement of 21 cm line emission from free hydrogen in the Pegasus I cluster of galaxies," as "dreadful." "I felt that I had just barely got through it," he admitted in the New Yorker (August 20, 1984). "It was something I felt I had to live down or, at least, do over, better." "There were two things that I was good at," he continued. "One was that I had an ability to organize things in mechanical terms—to build things—and the other was that I had, and have, a great ability to endure pain. These were the two things that got me through Columbia." In spite of the difficulties he had there, he received his M.A. degree in physics in 1958 and his Ph.D. degree in physics four years later.

When in the spring of 1960 Townes took some students to see the Bell Labs Radio Research Laboratory at Crawford Hill, New Jersey, Penzias was attracted by the facilities available there for reworking his thesis. Later that year, he asked the director of the lab, Rudolf Kompfner, if he could have a temporary appointment in order to work on his project, but Kompfner instead offered him a permanent position, which he accepted in 1961. "I had always thought that Bell Labs would be a great place to work," Penzias told Jeremy Bernstein. "I liked the connection between the work and useful things. I have always wanted to do something practical."

Although at first Penzias worked in the field of satellite communications at Bell Labs, he soon returned to radio astronomy. In 1963, Robert W. Wilson joined Bell Labs as a second radio astronomer, and the two split the duties of the one radio astronomy position while working half-time in other areas. They were given wide freedom as to the type of project they wished to pursue since radio astronomy in general was close enough to satellite communications to have a relationship to the work of the other scientists at Bell Labs and since Bell Labs funded many experiments in pure science as part of an ongoing exchange with the scientific community at large. For the most part, Wilson handled the electronics and calculations involved in each experiment while Penzias was in charge of the mechanics and article writing.

In 1960 a horn reflector antenna had been built at Crawford Hill to receive signals from the Echo balloon that the National Aeronautics and Space Administration had launched. By the time that Wilson arrived, that antenna was still in place but no longer needed, and so he and Penzias were permitted to dismantle the communications receiver and make a radio telescope. Their intention was to measure the radio signals from Cassiopeia A, a supernova remnant, and from the halo of the Milky Way. Precise measurement required that the horn reflector antenna introduce no radio noise of its own. To test the antenna, Penzias constructed a liquid-helium-cooled device—a "cold load"—that emitted a known amount of radiation or radio "noise" (expressed as a temperature on the Kelvin scale) to use as a reference. As he recounted in the New Yorker, for his part Wilson "made a good switch to connect the receiver alternately to the antenna and this reference source." By then aiming the antenna, which was attuned to seven-centimeter radio waves, at a precise point in the sky from which no radiation was expected, the scientists should have detected only the constant and already measured noise emitted from the earth's atmosphere and terrestrial sources. If that proved to be the case, they could then proceed with their experiments, certain that their properly working equipment would not distort their findings.

However, the horn reflector antenna immediately began picking up unexpected noise. For a year Penzias and Wilson tried to account for the problem: they took the antenna apart, machined its moving parts, and reassembled it; they sealed the antenna joints (put together with aluminum rivets) with aluminum tape and an electrically conductive glue; they turned the antenna in the direction of New York City to test if the static was coming from there; they even banished a pair of pigeons that had made their home in the antenna throat and painstakingly cleaned away the pigeon droppings. Nothing eliminated the puzzling noise, measured as 3.5° Kelvin.

Throughout a whole year, that 3.5° K noise level remained constant, no matter what the time of day or season, that is, no matter what the position of the earth might be. It was, Penzias remarked much later, "like cigar smoke in a room with no cigar." The Bell engineers who had initially worked with that same antenna for the Echo satellite project had been aware that it was picking up more noise than expected, but since it did not affect their task, they could afford to ignore the anomaly; but Penzias and Wilson, still baffled after exhausting all possible solutions to the problem and unable to conduct their experiments until the static had been accounted for, faced a dead end. But through a conversation he had in January 1965 with Bernard Burke, a radio astronomer at M.I.T., Penzias happened to learn that a group of physicists at Princeton University—P. J. E. Peebles, Robert H. Dicke, P. G. Roll, and D. T. Wilkinson—might have an explanation for the mysterious noise. According to their theory, there ought to be detectable microwave background radiation, or fossil radio noise, left over from the formation of the universe.

In the 1960s the controversy over the origins of the universe still raged in the scientific community. "Steady state" theorists maintained that the universe has always existed in its current form and that as it expands, new matter is spontaneously created in space to fill the void. On the other hand, exponents of the "big bang" theory, including the Princeton scientists, argued that the universe originated ten to twenty billion years ago in a fiery explosion of such awesome proportions that it is still fueling the expansion of the universe. The remnant energy of so tremendous an explosion, they reasoned, should still be detectable. With the expansion of the universe, however, the original light waves would have been stretched to radio waves, which Peebles at first predicted would have a temperature of 10° K.

The 3.5° K that Penzias and Wilson had found was close enough to what the Princeton scientists were expecting, and they excitedly came to visit Bell Labs for a discussion with the two radio astronomers there. Both Penzias and Wilson expressed interest in the Princeton theory but were not yet certain that it was the definitive explanation of the phenomenon they had detected, partly because theorists held that when the spectral distribution of the microwave background radiation was plotted on a graph it would form the so-called Planck black-body curve. With a measurement of the radiation at only one wavelength, Penzias and Wilson could not yet show that their 3.5° K noise would fit that model. Nevertheless, when they published their findings in the July 1965 issue of the Astrophysical Journal, they cautiously noted that "a possible explanation for the observed excess noise is the one given by Dicke, Peebles, Roll, and Wilkinson in a companion letter in this issue."

According to science writer Malcolm W. Browne of the New York Times (March 12, 1978), the Penzias-Wilson observations set in motion a "surge of cosmological discovery" that fleshed out the picture of the microwave background radiation. Measurements of the radiation at fifteen different wavelengths by 1972 showed that it clearly fit the Planck black-body curve, a finding that dealt a deathblow to the steady-state theory. For their remarkable achievement, Penzias and Wilson were honored by the Royal Swedish Academy of Sciences with the 1978 Nobel Prize in Physics. They shared the award with the eminent Russian scientist Pyotr Leonevich Kapitsa, who was recognized for his work in low-temperature physics. Penzias planned to donate a part of his $40,000 premium to charities serving either Jewish immigrants or youths.

As a physicist who had made an astounding discovery in a field in which he had, in his opinion, too few credentials, Penzias felt compelled to delve more deeply into astronomy, so beginning in the mid-1960s he turned to study of the unexplored millimeter-wavelength segment of the radiation spectrum produced by interstellar molecules. Led by Penzias and Wilson, the group Penzias organized detected many of the interstellar molecules that are now widely known. "When we opened up this field, it was a tremendous step forward," Wilson explained in the New Yorker (August 20, 1984), "and it was very profitable both professionally and scientifically."

Continuing their research collaboration at Bell Labs, Penzias and Wilson made yet another startling discovery: they detected an abundance of the fossil element deuterium in the Milky Way galaxy. That find ended yet another cosmological controversy. Some scientists had believed that the universe was "closed," that is, that it continually oscillates between expansion following a big bang and a sudden collapse back to its center that fuels yet another big bang and the recreation of the universe. As Ronald Kotulak explained in the Chicago Tribune (May 1, 1979), "if there were sufficient matter to eventually cause [the] gravitational collapse [of the universe], deuterium nuclei . . . all would have formed helium at the moment of the big bang." Its abundance in our galaxy supports the theory of the "open," ever expanding universe, a concept that Penzias finds philosophically appealing. "A closed universe, one that explodes, expands, falls back on itself and explodes again, repeating the process over and over eternally: that would be a pointless universe . . . ," he explained in the New York Times (March 12, 1978). "But it seems to me that the data we have in hand right now clearly show that there is not nearly enough matter . . . for the universe to be able to fall back on itself ever again." "The best data we have," he added, "are exactly what I would have predicted, had I had nothing to go on but the five books of Moses, the Psalms, the Bible as a whole."

A steady series of promotions during his years at Bell Labs culminated in 1981 with Penzias' appointment as vice-president of research. No sooner did he take on his new position than an out-of-court settlement broke up AT&T, impelling the research group at Bell Labs to direct less of its resources to pure science and more to finding applications for its research in the field of information systems and telecommunications. In addition to his scientific and administrative responsibilities

at Bell Labs, Penzias has served as a visiting professor at Princeton University since 1972, as a guest
lecturer at several universities across the country,
and as vice-chairman of the Committee of Concerned Scientists, an organization that works for
the political freedom of scientists worldwide. In
keeping with that commitment, immediately after
receiving his Nobel Prize, he went straight from
Stockholm to Moscow, where he delivered his Nobel lecture in the apartment of Viktor Brailovsky,
a Russian dissident scientist, as a gesture of support. Penzias also chairs the editorial committee of
AT&T's *Bell System Technical Journal* and is a
member of the National Academy of Sciences, the
American Academy of Arts and Sciences, and the
American Astronomical Society, among other pro-

fessional groups. He is also the only American ever
to receive an honorary degree from the Paris Observatory.

A hard-working man who is as demanding of
others as he is of himself, Penzias nevertheless
finds time to jog two or three miles every other day.
He and the former Anne Pearl Barras, whom he
married on November 25, 1954, have three children—David Simon, Mindy Gail, and Laurie
Ruth—and make their home in Highland Park,
New Jersey.

References: *New Yorker* 60:42+ Ag 20 '84;
*Physics Today* 34:261 N '81; *Today* C p11 O 19
'78 por; *Who's Who in America,* 1984-85; *Who's
Who in the World,* 1984-85

---

## Pickens, T(homas) Boone (Jr.)

*May 22, 1928- Corporation executive. Address:
b. Mesa Petroleum Company, Box 2009, One
Mesa Sq., Amarillo, Tex. 79189*

Probably the most feared of the so-called
"corporate raiders" is T. Boone Pickens, the president and chairman of the board of the Mesa Petroleum Company, the streamlined independent oil
and gas producer that he founded in 1964. The
flamboyant, fiercely competitive Pickens came to
national attention in 1982, when he made the first
in a series of unsuccessful attempts to gain control
of such industry giants as Gulf and Unocal. Although Pickens has been accused by his critics of
practicing "greenmail"—the strategy of buying
huge blocks of a corporation's stock with the sole

intention of selling them back at a premium so that
the company can avert a takeover—his tactics have
generated estimated pre-tax profits of nearly $1
billion for Mesa Petroleum and its shareholders.
Speaking in his own defense, Pickens, who is fond
of describing himself as "the champion of the small
stockholder," has said simply, as quoted in *Time*
(January 14, 1985), "My job is to do the best I can
with the capital I have to work with."

Distantly related to the legendary American
frontiersman Daniel Boone, Thomas Boone Pickens Jr., the only child of Thomas Boone Pickens
and Grace Marclen (Molonson) Pickens, was born
on May 22, 1928 in Holdenville, Oklahoma, a cattle
town virtually surrounded by oil wells. His father,
an attorney for the Phillips Petroleum Company's
land acquisition department, was something of a
gambler who often risked the family's capital on
oil-lease speculations; his mother, on the other
hand, was so practical that she was chosen to manage Holdenville's gasoline-rationing program during World War II. "I was very fortunate in my gene
mix," Pickens told an interviewer for a *Time*
(March 4, 1985) magazine cover story. "The gambling instincts I inherited from my father were
matched by my mother's gift for analysis."

In the mid-1940s the Pickens family moved to
Amarillo, Texas, where T. Boone, as he prefers to
be known, made a name for himself as the star
guard on the Amarillo High School basketball
team. His prowess on the basketball court won him
an athletic scholarship to Texas A & M University,
but his stay there was short-lived. When a broken
elbow cost him his scholarship, he transferred for
his sophomore year to Oklahoma State University.
After receiving a B.S. degree in geology from Oklahoma State in 1951, Pickens took a job as a well-site
geologist with Phillips Petroleum. Frustrated by the
company's entrenched conservatism, he resigned
in 1955 and struck out on his own. The following
year, with only $2,500 in cash, a $100,000 line of
credit, and what *New York Times* reporter Lydia
Chavez called "an uncanny ability to find oil and
gas," Pickens launched the Petroleum Exploration
Company.

Based in Amarillo, Petroleum Exploration thrived, spurring Pickens to incorporate in 1964 as the Mesa Petroleum Company. The course Pickens charted for his new enterprise was, in the jargon of the oil business, "upstream"—that is, he confined Mesa's activities to drilling, exploration, and production and resisted the temptation to expand into such other areas as service stations, refineries, tankers, and pipelines, as the so-called "integrated" companies, among them Gulf and Exxon, had done. Unencumbered by money-losing sidelines, Mesa realized an impressive profit almost from the beginning. By 1969 Mesa was prosperous enough for Pickens to acquire Hugoton Production Company and its vast gas field north of Amarillo. Four years later, he added Pubco Petroleum to Mesa's holdings. Pickens was unsuccessful, however, in his bid for Southland Royalty in 1970, and in 1976 Southland took over Aztec, a natural gas producer that he had once coveted. Pickens was also stung when his only attempt to diversify Mesa backfired in 1974 and he was forced to sell the company's cattle business at a $19 million loss.

Believing that the oil industry was "gradually winding down," Pickens sought in the late 1970s an appropriate new direction for Mesa Petroleum. Because the skyrocketing costs of exploration in Alaska were beyond Mesa's means and the oil fields abroad were, in his words, "at the mercy of radical and unreliable foreigners," Pickens decided to spin off some of Mesa's production properties into the newly created Mesa Royalty Trust. Thus, on November 1, 1979, every Mesa shareholder received a unit of the royalty trust for each Mesa share he owned, with Mesa retaining 10 percent of the trust units. Within three months, the price of Mesa's stock, which had been forty dollars a share in July 1979, rose to nearly sixty dollars a share, and a unit of the oil trust sold at thirty-five dollars. Those healthy figures, coupled with the OPEC-led bull market in oil, resulted in high profits for Mesa's shareholders and for Pickens himself. As L. J. Davis observed in an analysis for *Harper's* (January 1985), "Pickens had divested himself of a full half of his company and, at the same time, he had kept it."

A shrewd businessman with an uncanny knack for making the right decisions at exactly the right time, Pickens, in 1979, surprised energy analysts by selling Mesa's Canadian assets for slightly more than $500 million. Several months later, the Canadian government instituted new energy regulations that put American companies at a decided disadvantage, and the oil and gas prospects in Canada turned sour. Displaying similar foresight, Pickens realized a $65 million profit by divesting Mesa of its operations in the North Sea shortly before the British government levied a heavy tax on North Sea oil production.

On May 31, 1982 Pickens made his first big takeover bid when Mesa tried to buy out Cities Service Company, a middle-sized Oklahoma-based oil company. At the time of the bid, Mesa already owned 5 percent of Cities' outstanding shares. Pickens offered to pay fifty dollars a share for enough additional stock to raise Mesa's stake in Cities Service to a controlling 51 percent. Charles J. Waidelich, the chairman of Cities Service's board of directors, countered by purchasing Mesa Petroleum stock, and, on June 9, 1982, the *Wall Street Journal* reported that Cities Service had made a $1.4 billion offer to purchase Mesa. The bidding war continued until August 1982, when Occidental Petroleum emerged as a corporate "white knight" and bought Cities Service for fifty-five dollars per share. According to *Time* (March 4, 1985), the merger brought Pickens and his Mesa group a $31.5 million profit.

A few months later, in December 1982, Pickens announced a $520 million cash tender offer for a majority of the shares in the General American Oil Company, an enticing takeover prospect because of its rich domestic oil reserves. "Looking for oil and gas isn't going to do you any good now, with prices stabilized or dropped back to some degree . . . ," Pickens explained to Robert J. Cole of the *New York Times* (December 21, 1982). "Consequently, you've got to do something different. We're not going to commit big dollars to exploration. We're going to commit big dollars to acquisition."

Stymied by a series of tactical maneuvers begun by General American to block the takeover, Pickens filed suit in federal court charging that General American's "kamikaze defensive tactics" prevented Mesa "from having a fair opportunity to bid" for the larger company. He withdrew the suit in January 1983 after Phillips Petroleum negotiated an agreement to purchase General American for $1.2 billion. Pickens had "lost" another prospect, but the Mesa group nonetheless came away ahead by a reported $43.6 million. Moreover, in return for Pickens' pledge to abandon his quest for General American, Phillips paid Mesa $15 million to cover the costs of its "unfriendly" bid. The Mesa group of investors also realized a tidy profit—reportedly, $31.6 million—when Pickens sold the 2 percent interest in Superior Oil that he had foresightedly acquired shortly before that company was taken over by the giant Mobil Oil Corporation.

In the late summer of 1983, Pickens began accumulating stock in Gulf Oil Corporation, which was then trading at a fraction over thirty-eight dollars a share. The mammoth Gulf, the fifth-largest American oil company, with some 40,000 employees, seemed to be an unlikely choice for a buyout by Mesa Petroleum, which ranked ninety-second among American oil producers and had only 700 employees. Pickens' takeover attempt, however, came in the wake of several costly errors in judgment by Gulf's management that had cut deeply into the company's financial reserves. As a result, Gulf had been written off by Wall Street analysts, but Pickens felt that the company's stock, which was then trading at less than forty dollars a share, was worth far more.

In late January 1984, Pickens and his investment group, who by then held 13.2 percent of Gulf's stock, offered the company's stockholders fifty-five dollars per share for all outstanding Gulf stock. A few days later, Pickens' proposal was bettered by Robert O. Anderson, the chairman of the Atlantic Richfield Company, who submitted a bid of seventy dollars per share. Unable to match Anderson's figure, Pickens decided to tender for 13.5 million shares of Gulf at sixty-five dollars a share. The additional stock would give Pickens' investment group 21.3 percent of the oil firm—"enough," as L. J. Davis observed, "for the investors group to take over the company." Calling Pickens' offer "unfair and inadequate," Gulf's board of directors sought alternatives to the bid from several prospective buyers. Gulf ultimately reached an agreement with Standard Oil Company of California for Standard to purchase Gulf for eighty dollars a share. (The new oil company was renamed Chevron, after Socal's trademark.) The transaction netted Pickens and his partners a $760 million profit. Smaller investors benefited as well, for over the course of the protracted takeover battle, the value of a share of Gulf stock more than doubled, as Pickens has been quick to point out.

Setting his sights next on Phillips Petroleum, on December 4, 1984 Pickens proposed a tender offer for 9.7 percent of the company's outstanding shares at sixty dollars a share. The next day Phillips executives obtained a temporary restraining order that prevented the Pickens-led group, which had previously acquired a 5.7 percent interest in the Oklahoma-based corporation, from obtaining the additional shares necessary for control of the board of directors. Rather than submit to Pickens, Phillips eventually opted to take a "poison pill" in the form of a recapitalization plan that doubled the company's long-term debt, thus making the cost of the takeover prohibitively expensive for Pickens. The Mesa partners nonetheless realized an $89 million profit when Phillips bought back the stock purchased by the group before the tender offer at fifty-three dollars per share. In his New York Times (March 5, 1985) analysis of the fight for control of Phillips Petroleum, Fred R. Bleakley reported that there was "unqualified admiration" on Wall Street for Pickens' "ability to come out ahead—and improve the lot of all Phillips shareholders in the process."

While embroiled in the struggle for Phillips, Pickens was quietly accumulating huge blocks of shares in Unocal Corporation, formerly known as Union Oil of California. Like his earlier targets, Unocal was considered by energy analysts to be worth considerably more than the trading value of its stock, which was then selling at less than forty dollars a share. Openly acknowledging Unocal's solid twelfth-place position in the industry, Pickens told an interviewer for the New York Times (February 25, 1985), "Union is obviously strong, but its executives haven't done very much for the stockholders."

The battle for Unocal, which pitted Pickens against Unocal's feisty chairman, Fred L. Hartley, began in earnest on March 12, 1985, when Unocal sued its principal lender, Security Pacific National Bank, for "breaches of contract" because the bank had lent money to Pickens to finance his purchase of Unocal stock. Undeterred, Pickens secured alternative financing, and less than three weeks later he purchased an additional 6.7 million shares of Unocal to increase his holdings to 13.5 percent of the company. In an attempt to gain a controlling 50.1 percent interest, on April 8 Pickens offered to buy 64 million shares of Unocal at fifty-four dollars each. Rejecting Pickens' proposal as "grossly inadequate," Hartley countered with a "fair value" bid to buy back its outstanding stock at seventy-two dollars a share, a figure well above the market price. The offer was open to all shareholders—except Pickens' Mesa Partners II group. Pickens immediately brought suit, but the Delaware Supreme Court, in a surprising reversal of a lower-court decision, upheld Unocal's unorthodox plan. To cut his losses, which Time (June 3, 1985) estimated could be as high as $300 million, Pickens struck a deal with Hartley. Under the terms of the settlement, Unocal agreed to pay Pickens the seventy-two-dollar-a-share price, but only for about one-third of his group's 23.7 million shares. Perhaps more important, Hartley extracted from Pickens a pledge to sell off his remaining shares at a slow pace and to refrain from further takeover attempts for twenty-five years. Although most financial analysts predicted that the arrangement would cost the Mesa chairman and his investors group between $80 and $130 million, Pickens claimed an after-tax gain of about $83 million. Moreover, he said that his takeover bid had created some $2 billion in additional value for Unocal's shareholders.

According to Business Week (May 6, 1985), in 1984 Pickens was the highest paid corporation executive in the United States, earning more than $20 million in salary, cash bonuses, and deferred compensation. While it is true that the value of Mesa Petroleum's stock has dropped slightly since Pickens "got serious about takeovers," as Jack Willoughby observed in an article for Forbes (April 22, 1985), Mesa's stock continues to sell at over 90 percent of its appraised value—double the ratio of many major oil stocks. Believing that top managers ought to have a real stake in their companies' operations by owning stock, Pickens holds some 1.5 million shares of Mesa, and he has options for nearly five million more. Taken together, his stocks and options were estimated to be worth, in March 1985, about $100 million. "Chief executives, who themselves own few shares of their companies, have no more feeling for the average stockholder than they do for baboons in Africa . . . ," Pickens once explained, as quoted in Time (March 4, 1985). "It infuriates me to see them invest their own money in Treasury bills rather than work to improve the value of their companies' stock."

A member of the boards of directors of two Texas banks, the Hughes Tool Company, and the National Petroleum Council, T. Boone Pickens also devotes a considerable amount of time to public service organizations. He is, among other things, the chairman of the board of the M. D. Anderson Medical Center in Houston, the head of the executive committee of the Texas Research League, and the chairman of the board of regents of West Texas State University. In 1981 and 1982 he received the Wall Street Transcript's gold award, given annually to the top chief executive in the oil-producing industry. He received the Transcript's bronze award in 1983 and its silver award in 1984. Largely because of Pickens' unique managerial ability, Nelsons Survey of Wall Street Research chose Mesa as the best managed among eighty-nine companies in the oil-and-gas production category for 1982. Long active in politics, in 1984 Pickens spearheaded a fund-raising drive for the reelection of President Ronald Reagan and later served as a delegate to the Republican National Convention. In recent years, he has become a familiar figure on the lecture circuit, giving an average of two speeches a week, usually on the subject of stockholders' rights.

A wiry five feet eight inches tall, the blue-eyed, sandy-haired Pickens, who has been described as "a classic country boy," looks years younger than his chronological age. He keeps in fighting trim by playing tennis, racquetball, and golf and by working out daily in the physical fitness center he had built for the employees at Mesa's corporate headquarters. An expert marksman, he enjoys hunting quail. Over the years Pickens has ridiculed the "toys" and "perks" beloved by some corporation executives and has earned a reputation as a demanding, no-nonsense employer who regularly puts in a twelve-hour workday and expects no less from his associates. "What people don't understand is that there really are more than twenty-four hours in a day," he told an interviewer for *Time*. "I'm well organized, and I keep up with what's going on." Pickens occasionally spends his rare days off at his vacation retreat in Palm Springs, California, in the company of his second wife, the former Beatrice Louise Carr, whom he married on April 27, 1972. An earlier marriage to Lynn O'Brien, by whom he has several children, ended in divorce in 1971. The Pickenses also own a palatial home in Amarillo and two cattle ranches, one in north Texas, the other in Oklahoma.

References: *Financial World* 152:8+ D 31 '83 pors; *Fortune* 108:54+ D 26 '83 pors; *Harper's* 270:53+ Ja '85 por; *N Y Times* D p1+ Je 7 '82 por; *Time* 125:51 Ja 14 '85 por, 125:52+ Mr 4 '85 pors; *Who's Who in America*, 1984–85

---

## Reed, John S(hepard)

*Feb. 7, 1939– Chief executive officer and chairman of Citicorp. Address: b. 399 Park Ave., New York City, N.Y. 10022*

Citicorp, the world's largest private banking institution and parent of Citibank, ended years of speculation in June 1984 when it tapped John S. Reed as its new chief executive officer to replace retiring chairman Walter B. Wriston. The forty-five-year-old Reed skyrocketed to prominence in the late 1970s when he guided Citicorp's thrust into consumer banking and helped to shape Citicorp into the first truly national retail consumer bank. Like Wriston, he is an imaginative businessman and an enterpreneurial genius in a traditionally conservative field. "In selecting Mr. Reed," Ronald I. Mandle of Paine Weber, Inc., asserted in the *New York Times* (June 24, 1984), "Citicorp is sending a signal that this is a changing world and Citicorp intends to lead that change."

John Shepard Reed was born in Chicago, Illinois on February 7, 1939. His father was a plant manager for an Armour Company subsidiary in South America. As a result, John Reed spent most of his formative years in Argentina and Brazil and is fluent in both Spanish and Portuguese. After graduating from high school, Reed enrolled in a five-year, dual-degree program. During its first three years he studied American literature at Washington and Jefferson College in Pennsylvania and received his

B.A. degree in 1959. He was a member of Lambda Chi Alpha fraternity and graduated seventh in his class of 130. Reed then studied physical metallurgy at the Massachusetts Institute of Technology, which granted him a B.S. degree in 1961.

After working briefly for the Goodyear Tire and Rubber Company in Akron, Ohio, as a systems analyst, Reed served from 1962 to 1964 in the Army Corps of Engineers in Korea. On his discharge from the Army, he enrolled at MIT's Sloan School of Management and obtained his M.S. degree, the equivalent of an M.B.A., in 1965. At MIT, he was spotted by James Q. Griffin, the personnel director for the international division of First National City Bank. (In 1976 its name was officially changed to Citibank.) Reed was one of the thirty-four people, out of 350 Griffin interviewed at colleges across the country, to be hired for that division in 1965. "He was considered one of the bright lights [at MIT]," Griffin told Fred R. Bleakley of the *New York Times* (June 21, 1984), "and he impressed me as a man who made a point of absorbing as much of the world as he could. His interests ranged from Brazilian music, to farming, to what was going on in research at MIT."

Because of his overseas upbringing and foreign-language fluency, Reed, although still in his twenties, was made an officer's assistant, rather than a trainee, in the international division's planning department. Reporting directly to Walter B. Wriston, who was then an executive vice-president in charge of that department, Reed helped to chart the bank's worldwide business strategy. A tireless worker, he was promoted several times during the next few years. Shifting to the New York headquarters staff in 1967 as an assistant cashier, Reed designed a management information system for the comptrollers area, and in 1968—the year in which First National City Corporation (Citicorp) was formed and took over the bank's ownership—he traveled widely as assistant vice-president and as an aide to the head of the overseas department. Promoted to vice-president and transferred to the bank's Operations Group later in 1968, Reed impressed William I. Spencer, the group's head, with the drive, vision, and technological expertise he displayed in preparing his study of the tangled check-processing, or so-called back-room, operations. Named senior vice-president in 1969, the youngest person to hold that title in the bank's history, Reed was placed in charge of the back room by Spencer and given the massive and intimidating job of reorganizing it, a project described by John A. Byrne in *Forbes* (July 16, 1984) as "a risky venture—and potentially a ticket to oblivion" because it was a thankless job far removed from the center ring—the overseas department—of Citicorp.

At the time, the back-room operation was in disarray. Expenses were rising at 15 percent annually—more quickly than bank earnings—and if that trend continued for five years, Reed admitted to Michael C. Jensen in a *New York Times* interview (November 29, 1970), "it would be impossible to make any money." To make matters worse, employee turnover in the division was 50 percent, and the backlog of uncorrected errors exceeded 25,000. "It was an administrative mess," Reed told Jensen. "We found that there was no record of what resources were being consumed to produce what. The departments were organized in a helter-skelter manner. There were no clean flows of

activity." In a series of bold strokes, Reed dismantled the ponderous bureaucratic machinery that characterized the clogged back office, computerized it, and introduced mechanisms like those used in General Motors and other major companies to "inject productivity changes," which would "absorb the very legitimate and necessary labor cost increases." He then recruited what John A. Byrne described in *Forbes* (July 16, 1984) as "several tough-minded, demanding technocrats" from Ford Motor Corporation and Grumman Aerospace. Citicorp managers who could not adjust to the new, highly automated system were placed in dead-end jobs, forcing a number of them to resign. "That caused John more problems than anything else in his career," a former colleague recalled in the *Forbes* article. Labeled "cold and abrasive," Reed responded to plunging employee morale by calling in Jay Lorsch, a behavioral specialist from Harvard, which led to a case study now taught at Harvard, Columbia, and other business schools.

Partly as a result of Reed's success in making the back room more efficient, in 1970 Spencer was named president of Citicorp, and Reed succeeded him as executive vice-president in charge of the Operations Group, which had 8,000 employees and a budget of $100 million. In that position, he continued his reorganization of back-room operations and also represented Citibank in studying the feasibility of "paperless transaction processing systems," which he hoped would eventually eliminate most of the two million checks and other documents his group handled daily.

Reed remained involved in back-room operations until 1974 when he sought the assignment of investigating First National City's retail consumer business in order to find possibilities for expansion. According to Daniel Hertzberg and Michael R. Sesit of the *Wall Street Journal* (June 21, 1984), the bank's executives had concluded that the company derived a "dangerously increasing share" of its income from foreign operations and that the bank relied too much on large money-market deposits for funding. They viewed a push into consumer banking as a means of developing a more stable funding base. In his new position as head of the Consumer Service Group, John Reed compiled profit-and-loss data for the first time for the bank's retail consumer division and discovered that it was showing small losses. But instead of advocating caution, Reed argued for new strategies to expand retail consumer banking.

Convinced that computerization was the key to cost-efficient consumer services, Reed pioneered the development of automated teller machines, which were programmed to handle routine banking transactions. In the mid-1970s, those devices were placed in most of the company's 247 New York City branches while many other banks were still considering the idea. However, a stipulation that customers with less than $5,000 on deposit could bank only by machine elicited so great a backlash that Reed was forced to rescind the measure. Another ill-considered consumer-banking strategy involved "password" traveler's checks, which enabled individuals to order by telephone traveler's checks with their names imprinted on them. Not only did Citibank overestimate the demand for traveler's checks, but other banks objected to Citibank's dealing with their clients, and the postal service was unable to deliver the checks within twenty-four hours as the bank had promised. The cost of the "password" traveler's-checks gamble was estimated at $8- to $10 million.

Even more costly was Reed's move to expand Citicorp's credit-card operations. In 1977 twenty-six million Visa applications were mailed to Americans, making Citicorp the largest issuer of bank credit cards in the nation. So vast—and so indiscriminate—was that recruitment effort that a substantial percentage of card holders turned out to be poor credit risks. Ultimately, Citicorp wrote off nearly $80 million in bad consumer debts. No less damaging to Reed's reputation was his decision to issue long-term mortgage loans—at fixed interest rates because of usury ceilings in many states—and to fund short-term in the money markets. Those strategies backfired when interest rates began spiraling upward in the early 1980s. "We failed to appreciate the reality of the potential disaster," Reed later admitted in an article for *International Investor*. "In retrospect I sort of say, 'John, how dumb can you be?'" In spite of that costly error, in 1979 Reed was appointed senior executive vice-president, a newly created title, and put in charge of Citicorp's worldwide consumer banking.

By the end of 1981, it was estimated that Reed's tactics had cost Citicorp almost $300 million. Long an unpopular figure with Citicorp's rank and file—his youth and reputation as a brusque, insensitive technocrat had earned him the nickname "the brat"—Reed also became a target of the bank's hierarchy. When the red ink from Reed's consumer segment drained profits from Citicorp's successful undertakings, resulting in a loss of bonuses for a number of high-level Citicorp officials, rumors surfaced that Reed would be eased out of his position.

But Reed, firmly supported by Wriston, persevered in his aggressive game plan even after Moody's Investor Service lowered Citicorp's bond rating from AAA to AA. Despite the Visa fiasco, Reed engineered the acquisition of the Carte Blanche and Diners' Club travel and entertainment cards. Holders of those cards are generally affluent and subject to careful credit checks, making default unlikely, and the yearly maintenance fee paid by those who use the bank's various charge cards provides a reliable source of income for the consumer division. In addition, Reed's canny transfer in 1981 of Citicorp's credit-card operations from New York State to Sioux Falls, South Dakota, where legislators had responded to the promise of increased jobs by lifting the state's usury ceiling, allowed the bank to raise the finance charges on its credit cards by almost eight points to 19.8 percent. With great success, Citibank introduced its own "Choice Card" in Washington, D.C., in February 1980 and has since offered it to its cus-

tomers in Denver, Colorado. Another major innovation pioneered by Citibank to reach the consumer market is HomeBase, a computer system that allows individuals to do almost all of their banking at home for a small monthly fee. After four years of research and testing, HomeBase was officially introduced in July 1984.

To reach an even wider consumer market, Citicorp and, to a lesser degree, other banks circumvented federal laws that prohibited interstate banks by opening "non-bank banks," or "consumer banks." Since the Bank Holding Company Act of 1956 defined a bank as an institution that accepted demand deposits and made commercial loans, if an institution served only one of those functions the interstate banking restrictions would not apply. As a result, Citicorp was able to establish a network of more than 800 consumer-banking and finance offices in forty-four states, in part through purchases of several failed savings and loan associations: in 1982 it acquired Fidelity Savings and Loan in San Francisco, and in 1984 it bought New Biscayne Federal Savings and Loan in Miami, Florida and First Federal Savings and Loan in Chicago. With the acquisition of the San Francisco savings and loan, which had assets of $2.9 billion, Citicorp surpassed BankAmerica Corporation as the largest bank holding company in the United States. According to Robert A. Bennett, writing in the *New York Times* (June 20, 1984), it was Reed who engineered those important acquisitions.

Going even further, Citicorp led an intensive lobbying effort to convince federal authorities to deregulate the banking industry. "You might say that Citicorp both forced the issue of deregulation and created it to meet its own ends," a former Citibank executive claimed in *Datamation* (August 1, 1984). "At any event, by settling for nothing less than a free and unrestricted financial services market, Wriston and Reed probably saved the banking industry." But as of June 1985, the efforts of Citicorp and other major banks to establish nationwide chains of non-bank banks had been blocked in court and Congress was considering outlawing such limited-service offices.

By the first quarter of 1982, Reed's division was solidly in the black, and in June of that year he was elected a director of Citicorp and vice-chairman in charge of the Individual Bank, the consumer-banking division. The Individual Bank's net earnings increased in 1983 by 206.1 percent, from $66 million to $202 million. Perhaps more important, by 1984 Citicorp could boast that it did business with one out of every seven American households, and financial analysts credited Reed with the successful establishment of the Individual Bank as the United States' only truly "national" retail consumer bank.

Even before Walter Wriston announced his intention to resign, speculation regarding his successor focused on three people: John S. Reed; Thomas C. Theobald, who directs Citicorp's business with corporations, governments, and other financial institutions; and Hans H. Angermueller, who has led the corporation's lobbying and legal efforts. Like Reed, Theobald and Angermueller had been promoted to the post of senior executive vice-president on January 1, 1980, and two years later each of the three men had been given the title of vice-chairman and director and the responsibility for one of Citicorp's three main divisions. Although Wriston never explicitly said that one of those three men would be the next head of Citicorp, the apparent horserace among Reed, Theobald, and Angermueller made them the focus of industry gossip.

The decision to name Reed chairman and chief executive officer of Citicorp was announced by the corporation's board of directors on June 20, 1984. Although many of Citicorp's competitors had expected the job to go to Theobald, who has the experience that Reed lacks in the traditional banking areas of lending to big business and governments, most industry analysts agreed that Reed was the logical successor to Wriston, since both are known for their irreverence, intellectual curiosity, and restless creativity. Indeed, a year before Reed was given Citicorp's top post, Robert Bennett wrote in the New York Times Magazine (May 29, 1983) that Reed was the candidate most likely to maintain a "permanent revolution within Citicorp."

As chairman and chief executive officer of Citicorp, a position he formally assumed on September 1, 1984, Reed is expected to develop even further Citicorp's multifaceted individual-banking enterprises. He is also likely to work toward the realization of Wriston's vision of Citicorp as a worldwide force in investment banking, insurance, and information processing. In keeping with that aim, in September 1985 Reed announced that Citicorp and McGraw-Hill had formed a joint-venture company, Gemco, to provide, through an electronic system, information and markets for buyers and sellers of crude oil. Of more immediate concern, however, are Citicorp's diminished profits in the corporate lending arena. Many financial analysts believe that the ascendancy of Citicorp's consumer division has taken place at the expense of traditional corporate-banking operations, resulting in a schism between executives in those two camps. "One of John Reed's jobs will be to integrate the corporate and the retail side, . . . " Anthony M. Santomero, a professor of finance at the Wharton Business School, told Leslie Wayne in the New York Times (June 24, 1984). "[He] will have to make evident his commitment to the entire bank."

Another key issue is the huge debt owed to Citicorp by third-world nations. In Latin America—most notably in Brazil, Mexico, Venezuela, and Argentina—Citicorp has issued over $10 billion in loans. Because payments on those loans account for about one-third of Citicorp's earnings, a series of missed payments, a debt moratorium, or the imposition of lower fees and interest rates would seriously reduce Citicorp's profits. Accordingly, in mid-September 1984 Citicorp purchased loan insurance of $900 million from the Philadelphia-based Cigna Corporation to cover a portion of the

monies owed to the bank by the four Latin American republics and the Philippines. To ease the drain on profits, Reed has already implemented a cost-cutting program that, according to several insiders, is reminiscent of his drive to modernize Citicorp's back-room operations in the early 1970s.

Still youthful looking, John Reed has brown eyes, brown hair, a straightforward manner, and a disarming smile. Solidly built, he stands five-feet, nine-inches tall. A registered Democrat who takes liberal stands on many issues, Reed is a board member of the Russell Sage Foundation, the Sloan-Kettering Institute for Cancer Research, Philip Morris, and United Technologies. Once a workaholic who spent little time at home, Reed, according to a colleague, reassessed his priorities in the wake of a "normal life crisis" in the mid-1970s. "John may have been a robot before," an associate recalled in the New York Times (June 21, 1984), "but suddenly he became people-oriented and sensitive." The metamorphosis strengthened Reed's position in Citicorp and may have been partly responsible for his ascension to the organization's top post.

Reed and his wife, the former Sally Foreman, whom he married in 1964, have four children: Traci, a student at Denison University, Timothy, Tefford, and Tenley. According to Traci, Reed relaxes on the weekends at their home in the affluent suburb of Greenwich, Connecticut by preparing breakfast for the family or by taking care of various fix-it jobs. An excellent golfer with a seven handicap, he takes to the links of the local Stanwich Club during the warm weather or to skis on the slopes near his vacation home in Stratton, Vermont.

References: Business Week p104+ Je 18 '84 pors; Forbes 134:150+ Jl 16 '84 por; N Y Times III p5 N 29 '70 por, D p1+ Je 21 '84 pors, III p1+ Je 24 '84 por

---

## Reid, Kate

Nov. 4, 1930– Canadian actress. Address: b. Reid Willis, 14 Binscarth Rd., Toronto, Ontario M4W 1Y1, Canada

"Kate Reid may not be a household name to the general public," wrote a New York Times reporter, Carol Lawson, in 1984, "but she is to the theatre industry, which knows her as an actress who works constantly." A self-described "chameleon" who finds something of herself in every role she plays, Miss Reid learned her craft as a member of Canada's distinguished Stratford Festival Company, where her roles have included Lady Macbeth, Katharina, Juliet's Nurse, and Madame Ranevskaya. Her sensitive portrait of Linda Loman in the 1984 Broadway revival of Death of a Salesman was preceded by critically acclaimed performances in Who's Afraid of Virginia Woolf?, Dylan, and The

*Kate Reid*

Chekhov's *The Seagull*. On the strength of her performances at Hart House, Miss Reid was invited to join the Straw Hat Players in 1948. Over the next few years, she sharpened her theatrical skills in a number of summer-stock productions across Canada and at the Herbert Berghof Studio in New York, where she studied with the actress and teacher Uta Hagen. By the mid-1950s, she was proficient enough in her craft to take the leading part of Lizzie Curry, the spinster who loses her heart to a con man, in the Canadian premiere of N. Richard Nash's romantic drama *The Rainmaker*, at the Crest Theatre in Toronto.

Miss Reid reprised the role of Lizzie on tour in England in 1956. Two years later, she made her West End debut, as Catherine Ashland in *The Stepmother*, Warren Chetham-Strode's short-lived drama about family relationships. Although she had little more to do than "stand around in marvelous Worth dresses," as she put it, Miss Reid made quite an impression on R. B. Marriott, who reviewed the production for the British trade newspaper *The Stage* (November 13, 1958): "Kate Reid, on the first night starting somewhat uneasily, gradually developed her performance with skill and intelligence, making one think that she might be outstanding dealing with a character that made worthwhile demands on her."

Eager to tackle the classical repertory, Miss Reid returned to Canada in the spring of 1959 and signed on with the Stratford (Ontario) Festival Company, Canada's premier classical repertory troupe. Before beginning rehearsals for the Festival's summer season, she studied privately with a voice coach for several months in order to master the technique of Shakespearean verse speaking. Cast as Celia in *As You Like It*, and Emilia in *Othello*, Miss Reid turned in a pair of well-rounded and seemingly effortless characterizations. She was, by all accounts, especially effective as Emilia, Iago's sharp-tongued wife, giving the role a "womanly warmth," to use Judith Crist's words, that was often missing from other interpretations.

Spurning enticing offers from Broadway, Miss Reid rejoined the Stratford Festival Company in 1960 to play Juliet's garrulous Nurse in *Romeo and Juliet* and the lovelorn Helena in *A Midsummer Night's Dream*. She stayed on at Stratford for three more seasons, taking the parts of Queen Katharine in George McCowan's acclaimed production of *Henry VIII*, Jaquenetta in *Love's Labour's Lost*, and Elly Cassady in Donald Lamont Jack's satirical contemporary play *The Canvas Barricade* in summer of 1961; Katharina in *The Taming of the Shrew* and Lady Macbeth in *Macbeth* in 1962; and Cassandra in *Troilus and Cressida*, Adriana in *The Comedy of Errors*, and Lise and Sister Marthe in Edmond Rostand's *Cyrano de Bergerac* in 1963. She was perhaps most successful as Lady Macbeth. Peter Coe's unorthodox and turbulent production of Shakespeare's tragedy left many viewers cold, but most drama critics were dazzled by Miss Reid's ability to illuminate Lady Macbeth's relentless de-

*Price*. Although her screen credits are limited, she has appeared in more than 200 television shows in Canada, England, and the United States. "Acting is not something you do because you're good at it, but because you have to," she once remarked. "It's not a job. You've got to do it."

Daphne Kate Reid, the daughter of Walter Clarke and Helen Isabel (Moore) Reid, was born in London, England on November 4, 1930. Shortly after that, her father, a colonel in the 32d Bengal Lancers, retired from the military and moved with his family to Canada, settling in Oakdale, Ontario, near Toronto. He died three years later. "My mother . . . raised me single-handed on dad's pension in a three-room cottage," Kate Reid told Ronald Evans in an interview for the Toronto *Telegram* (March 13, 1965). "We were so hard up, I once suggested she take in laundry." Nevertheless, Mrs. Reid managed to send her daughter to Havergal College, an elite girls' boarding school in Toronto, for several years. Little else is known about Kate Reid's life before she began studying acting with Ernest Sterndale Bennett at the Toronto Conservatory of Music at the age of fifteen. "There *was* nothing before that," she once explained, as quoted in the Toronto *Globe and Mail* (January 14, 1978). "I don't think I ever thought about acting before I fell into it. . . . Looking back, I don't think I had much of a choice. It turned out to be something I liked doing."

While Miss Reid was a student, Bennett arranged for her to play the part of Daphne Randall in a production of *The Damask Cheek*, a comedy by John Van Druten and Lloyd Morris, at the University of Toronto's Hart House Theatre. The young actress' assured portrayal caught the eye of Robert Gill, the new director of Hart House, who subsequently cast her in the plum role of Nina in

termination and her gradual disintegration into madness.

Among the admirers of Miss Reid's virtuoso performances at Stratford in 1962 was Alan Schneider, the renowned stage director. Schneider, who was then preparing for the upcoming Broadway opening of Edward Albee's searing domestic drama *Who's Afraid of Virginia Woolf?*, hired the actress to substitute for Uta Hagen in the taxing role of Martha at the matinee performances. One of the most talked-about plays of the 1962–63 Broadway season, *Who's Afraid of Virginia Woolf?* focuses on two couples who, during the course of a long and liquor-laced night, engage in a series of savage verbal duels. Even those critics familiar with Miss Reid's mastery of the classical repertory were astounded by the depth and range she displayed as Martha, the sluttish, vitriolic wife of an ineffectual history professor. "She makes the play her own, as she does the part . . . ," Herbert Whittaker wrote in his review for the Toronto *Globe and Mail* (February 2, 1963). "She comes on looking unkempt, over-plump, bleary. By the end, she is [a] lovely, and hurting child. This is an old trick of Miss Reid's. It is a flagrant example of stage magic."

To the surprise of none of her friends, one of whom once accused her of "fighting success," Miss Reid turned down an offer to lead the evening company of *Virginia Woolf* in order to return to Stratford for the 1963 summer season. By the next year, however, she was back on Broadway, portraying Caitlin Thomas in *Dylan*, Sidney Michaels' drama about the chaotic last years of the Welsh poet Dylan Thomas. The play, which opened to generally enthusiastic reviews in January 1964, was an excellent showcase for its two stars: Sir Alec Guinness, who played the title role, and Miss Reid, who received a Tony Award nomination for her portrayal of Dylan's bitter, loving wife. "Playing opposite an actor of the Guinness stature could be a perilous assignment without a matching talent," Richard Watts Jr. observed in his *New York Post* (January 20, 1964) review of *Dylan*, "and Miss Reid's moving and honest characterization meets this challenge beautifully."

After appearing as Martha in a Manitoba Theatre Centre production of *Who's Afraid of Virginia Woolf?* and as Madame Ranevskaya in Chekhov's *The Cherry Orchard* and as Portia in *Julius Caesar* at Stratford in the summer of 1965, Miss Reid returned to Broadway once again to costar with Margaret Leighton and Zoe Caldwell in *Slapstick Tragedy*, a double bill comprising Tennessee Williams' one-act plays *The Mutilated* and *The Gnädiges Fräulein*. Skewered by the critics, *Slapstick Tragedy* closed after only seven performances, but Miss Reid, who portrayed a raucous, aging whore in the raunchy *The Mutilated* and essayed the role of a slovenly landlady in its companion piece, escaped unscathed, garnering her second Tony Award nomination, as best actress in a play.

Continuing to divide her time between stage appearances in New York and Canada, Kate Reid starred in the Canadian premiere of *The Subject Was Roses*, Frank Gilroy's Pulitzer Prize–winning domestic drama about the devastating effect a soldier's homecoming has on his family, at the Toronto Playhouse in December 1966. Her sensitive reading of the penultimate scene, in which the mother expresses her own unhappiness, was the high spot of the otherwise lackluster production for many reviewers. She was equally effective in *The Price*, Arthur Miller's penetrating study of guilt, responsibility, and family relationships, which opened at the Morosco Theatre on Broadway on February 7, 1968. As Esther Franz, the despairing wife of the less successful of two brothers who meet after a sixteen-year estrangement in order to dispose of their deceased father's meager estate, Miss Reid offered a carefully drawn study of a practical woman hamstrung by her husband's stubborn pride. Miss Reid remained with the production when it transferred to London's West End in March 1969.

Having established herself as a stage actress, Kate Reid decided, in the late 1960s, to take on the challenge of acting before the motion-picture camera. She made her Hollywood film debut in *This Property Is Condemned* (Paramount, 1966), a rather free adaptation of Tennessee Williams' Depression-era one-act play. Overcoming the limitations of the script, Miss Reid made the most of the role of the slatternly landlady who uses her beautiful daughter (played by Natalie Wood) to lure customers to her decaying boarding house. The actress was given little opportunity to display her talent in *The Andromeda Strain* (Universal, 1971), a sci-fi thriller based on Michael Crichton's best-selling novel of the same name. Cast as a grumpy microbiologist, she found herself playing a supporting role to the technological wizardry that was the centerpiece of the film. She fared better in *The Rainbow Boys* (Mutual, 1973), a comic romp that reviewer John Hofsess called "a strong contender for best Canadian film of the year." As he pointed out in his review for *Maclean's* (April 1973), Hofsess was especially taken by the "keen" rapport between Miss Reid and her costar, Donald Pleasence. Miss Reid's screen credits also include the part of Claire, the alcoholic sister in Tony Richardson's stagey film version of *A Delicate Balance* (American Film Theatre, 1973), Edward Albee's Pulitzer Prize–winning play about a contentious New England family, in which she shared top billing with Paul Scofield and Katharine Hepburn, and supporting roles in *Equus* (United Artists, 1977), the film version of Peter Shaffer's psychological drama, and the Canadian horror film *Death Ship* (Astral Bellevue Pathé/Bloodstar, 1980).

After an absence of several years, Miss Reid returned to the stage in 1973 to portray the indomitable Juno in the Philadelphia Drama Guild's production of *Juno and the Paycock*, Sean O'Casey's realistic tragedy set in 1922, at the height of the Irish "troubles." Ireland was also the setting of Miss Reid's next Broadway venture—the Irish playwright Brian Friel's *The Freedom of the City*.

Although some critics ranked Friel's contemporary political drama with O'Casey's classic *The Plough and the Stars,* the play closed on February 23, 1974, after only nine performances. Miss Reid, however, scored yet another personal triumph as the good-natured, middle-aged mother of eleven who is mistaken for a terrorist and killed by British soldiers. She was no less effective in another Broadway flop—John Guare's ambitious *Bosoms and Neglect,* in which a neurotic young computer analyst tries to come to terms with his mother, who is dying of cancer. Despite the actress' touching and "resourceful"—to use Douglas Watt's word—characterization of the dying woman, the play survived for just four performances toward the end of the 1978–1979 Broadway season.

Several months later, Miss Reid agreed to try her luck in another piece by John Guare: the film *Atlantic City* (Paramount, 1981). Directed by Louis Malle, the Canadian-French motion-picture production won the acclaim that had eluded *Bosoms and Neglect. Atlantic City* is the bittersweet story of three of life's losers—Lou Pasco (Burt Lancaster), an aging, lonely small-time numbers runner for the mob, Grace (Kate Reid), the reclusive, hypochondriac widow who is Lou's occasional lover; and Sally (Susan Sarandon), an opportunistic young waitress—whose lives are transformed when Lou comes into possession of a fortune in cocaine. When *Atlantic City* had its premiere in the United States in April 1981 to salvos of praise from the critics, Miss Reid came in for a generous share of the credit for a thoughtful supporting performance that was at once comical and profoundly sad.

Late in 1980 Miss Reid replaced Nancy Marchand in the successful Broadway revival of *Morning's at Seven,* Paul Osborn's 1939 comedy about four quarrelsome sisters living in adjoining houses in a small Midwestern town. Assuming the role of Ida, a dimwit who has to contend with an eccentric husband and a foolish son, she blended smoothly into a cast that had been roundly praised for its ensemble qualities. She subsequently played the role in the national tour of the production.

Kate Reid was the only actress considered for the part of Linda Loman when *Death of a Salesman* was resurrected in 1984 as a Broadway vehicle for Dustin Hoffman. Considered by many theatre critics and historians to be the supreme American tragedy, Arthur Miller's Pulitzer Prize-winning drama had first come to Broadway in 1949, with Lee J. Cobb as the self-deluded, middle-aged traveling salesman Willy Loman and Mildred Dunnock as his devoted, put-upon wife. Playing Linda as a woman who, in Miss Reid's words, "is totally motivated by her husband," the actress was an excellent match for Hoffman, whose unorthodox interpretation of Willy as a feisty, overaged adolescent was widely praised. Summing up the critical consensus, Richard Schickel, writing in *Time* (April 9, 1984), contended that Miss Reid's performance in the problematic role of Linda was "in its way as awesome as

Hoffman's." A film of the Broadway production was telecast by CBS-TV in September 1985.

Over the years, Miss Reid has regularly taken time out from her work in the more lucrative commercial theatre to appear in such noncommercial venues as Hart House, where she starred in the fiftieth anniversary production of Eugene O'Neill's *Mourning Becomes Electra,* and the Shaw Festival in Niagara-on-the-Lake, Ontario, where she played leading roles in Somerset Maugham's *The Circle* and in Bernard Shaw's *Arms and the Man, The Apple Cart, Major Barbara,* and *Mrs. Warren's Profession.* She has also undertaken for the Stratford (Ontario) Festival Company the parts of Mrs. Bat in Slawomir Mrozek's *Vatzlav*; Esther, the terminally ill revolutionary in Arnold Wesker's dreary *The Friends*; and Fonsia Dorsey in *The Gin Game,* D. L. Coburn's two-character dark comedy, among other roles. Her classical repertory credits for the American Shakespeare Festival Theatre in Stratford, Connecticut include Queen Gertrude in *Hamlet* and Masha in Chekhov's *The Three Sisters.* The American Shakespeare Festival Theatre's summer 1974 revival of Tennessee Williams' *Cat on a Hot Tin Roof,* starring Elizabeth Ashley as Maggie, Keir Dullea as Brick, Fred Gwynne as Big Daddy, and Kate Reid as Big Mama, eventually moved to Broadway, where it was enthusiastically received, although in the view of most critics Miss Reid's broad interpretation of Big Mama fell considerably short of the mark. Most recently, she appeared in John Wood's production of Robert Lowell's colloquial adaptation of the *Oresteia,* at the National Arts Centre in Toronto.

A seasoned television performer whose credits extend back to the early days of the medium, Miss Reid was nominated for Emmy Awards for her performances in two *Hallmark Hall of Fame* productions: *The Invincible Mr. Disraeli* (1963), in which she played Queen Victoria, and *Abe Lincoln in Illinois* (1964), in which she was cast as Mary Todd Lincoln. Her long list of television appearances also includes a great number of productions for the Canadian Broadcasting Corporation, among them *Candida, Little Women, Mother Courage, A Month in the Country, Hamlet,* and *The Three Sisters.* More recently, she had an ongoing role in the short-lived action-adventure series *Gavilan,* an NBC entry in the 1982–83 television season, and she played Aunt Lil in several episodes of CBS's long-running prime-time soap opera *Dallas.*

A full-figured woman of medium height, Kate Reid has large, expressive brown eyes, ginger-colored hair, and a mellifluous speaking voice that has been described as "cello-toned." After a youthful marriage to Michael Sadlier ended in divorce, Miss Reid wed the actor Austin Willis on July 13, 1953. The couple, who divorced in 1962, have two children, a son, Reid, and a daughter, Robin. It was primarily because of her reluctance to be separated from her children that the actress turned down several choice parts—such as the title role in the touring-company production of *The Killing of Sister George*—during the 1960s and 1970s.

Her own most severe critic, Miss Reid has admitted to having exorcised some personal demons, including a reported drinking problem. "Anybody who survives in this business learns from the school of hard knocks," she told John Fraser of the Toronto *Globe and Mail* (June 26, 1976), "and I seem to have taken a long time to grow up as a human being. . . . I had to learn you don't have to be defiant twenty-four hours a day." Miss Reid, who is an Officer of Canada, is the recipient of an honorary doctorate from York University, and in 1976 she was awarded a senior arts grant by the Canada Council. The grants are given to professional artists who have made a significant contribution to their fields over a number of years. The actress makes her home in Toronto.

References: *Macleans* 77:22+ Ap 18 '64 pors; *Toronto Globe and Mail* p11 Jl 15 '67 por, p8 Je 4 '73 por, p31 Je 26 '76 por, p33 Ja 14 '78 por; *Canadian Who's Who, 1982; Notable Names in the American Theatre (1976); Who's Who in America, 1984–85; Who's Who in the Theatre (1981)*

## Rochberg, George
(rok´bûrg)

*July 5, 1918– Composer. Address: 285 Aronimink Dr., Newtown Square, Penn. 19073*

George Rochberg, a former serialist and one of the most celebrated of contemporary American composers, enjoys the paradoxical distinction of having become controversial in recent years for his passionate advocacy and adherence to musical tradition and for his love of beautiful sound. Although devotees of more structured, experimental forms of composition may scorn him as reactionary, his unabashed lyricism has earned him the increasing admiration of audiences, musicians, and large segments of the public and has brought him prestigious awards, fellowships, and commissions. From 1960 to 1983 Rochberg was associated with the music faculty of the University of Pennsylvania.

George Rochberg was born on July 15, 1918 in Paterson, New Jersey and raised in nearby Passaic.

His parents, Morris Rochberg, an upholsterer, and Anna (Hoffman) Rochberg, had immigrated to the United States from the Ukraine around 1912 or 1913. The middle of three children, Rochberg began playing piano at the age of ten and started composing music almost immediately after that.

At Passaic High School, Rochberg played piano for school dances and composed popular tunes with lyrics by his friend Bob Russell, which the two tried unsuccessfully to peddle to publishers. (Russell later became a lyricist for Duke Ellington.) After graduating from high school in 1935, Rochberg worked his way through Montclair State Teachers College by teaching piano and playing in jazz bands, majoring in history because the curriculum made no provision for majors in music. Concurrently with his senior year in college, Rochberg won a scholarship to study composition at the Mannes School of Music in New York City under Hans Weisse and George Szell. He continued those studies for two more years, interrupting them to serve in the United States Army in Europe from 1942 to 1945, where he earned a Purple Heart with oak-leaf cluster as a lieutenant in the infantry.

In 1945, after his discharge from the army, Rochberg won a second scholarship, this time to the Curtis Institute of Music in Philadelphia, where he studied theory and composition under Rosario Scalero and Gian-Carlo Menotti. He obtained an M.A. degree from the University of Pennsylvania in 1949 and received a Fulbright fellowship and a Prix de Rome in 1950. From 1949 until 1954 Rochberg served as a faculty member at the Curtis Institute, and from 1951 to 1960 he also worked as director of publications for the Theodore Presser Company, a well-known music publisher based in Bryn Mawr, Pennsylvania.

The first piece by Rochberg to attract the attention of the music establishment was an orchestral score in the impressionistic mode entitled *Night Music* (1948). Originally intended as one of two slow movements in his five-movement Symphony No. 1, Rochberg removed it in order to shorten the symphony and eventually won a $1,000 George Gershwin Memorial Award and a performance of the excerpt by the New York Philharmonic. Reviewing the April 1953 concert at Carnegie Hall, the *New York Times* critic Howard Taubman commented, "Every page of this ten-minute score makes its effect, and a dark, almost grim, mood is sustained." Taubman was equally impressed by Rochberg's First Symphony when the Philadelphia Orchestra performed it at Carnegie Hall in April 1958. "Mr. Rochberg's Symphony No. 1 proclaims him a real composer," he wrote in his column for the April 2, 1958 edition. "It has a highly promising vitality and exuberance. It bespeaks a young talent full of ginger and ideas."

Throughout most of the 1950s and the early 1960s, Rochberg considered himself a disciple of Arnold Schoenberg and a serialist composer. As he wrote in the liner notes that accompanied a recording of his Third String Quartet by the Concord Quartet for the Nonesuch label: "I was convinced of the inevitability of the 12-tone language—I felt I was living at the very edge of the musical frontier, of history itself." His Symphony No. 2 (1955–56) exemplified Rochberg's commitment to serialism and his ability to use any form to achieve the power and intensity he desired. Although he based the piece on a single twelve-tone row, he exploited the lyric possibilities of the form by breaking the row into halves called "hexachords" that became the melodic motifs of the symphony.

After the Cleveland Orchestra performed Rochberg's Symphony No. 2 at Carnegie Hall on February 15, 1960, Ross Parmenter commented in the New York Times of the following day: "By the time he is done, one has the impression of having heard a work of considerable lyricism. Yet it is also dark and intense, and its inherent gravity is what gave it its strength and its power to move the audience." In 1961 the work won Rochberg the Naumburg Recording Award, entitling him to have that symphony recorded by Columbia Records and performed by the New York Philharmonic at a special Naumburg Foundation concert in October 1961.

Rochberg's String Quartet No. 2 (1959–61), another venture into rigorous atonality, paid an obvious debt to Schoenberg by incorporating a soprano solo in the final portion, as Schoenberg had done in his String Quartet No. 2. After it had its New York City premiere at the Museum of Modern Art in May of 1962, the New York Times critic Harold Schonberg, a longstanding enemy of serialism, reviewed it in his column of May 11, 1962 as "a work of some strength but without charm or variety." In contrast, Donal Henahan, who heard the work ten years later in a performance by the Concord String Quartet at Carnegie Recital Hall on May 7, 1973, found, as he made clear in his review of two days later, that it "became completely individual and urgent in the final episode," while "never slipping into the facelessness that makes much academic serial music of the 1950s and 1960s a trial to endure nowadays."

In 1964 the death of Rochberg's twenty-year-old son, Paul, a promising writer of fiction and poetry, plunged him into a crisis of creative identity. While composing Contra Mortem et Tempus, his first work after that personal tragedy, Rochberg discovered that atonality was far too desiccated and arid

a medium to express his sorrow and bereavement. After more than ten years of working with it, serial music was for him "finished, empty, meaningless," as he told Tim Page when interviewed for an article in the New York Times Magazine (May 29, 1983). He began to try out different modes of composition and even incorporated the work of other composers, past and present, into his own pieces.

Rochberg first employed that "collagist" or "assemblage" technique in Music for the Magic Theatre (1965), an orchestral work in three movements that took its title from a passage in Hermann Hesse's Steppenwolf, in which the artistic imagination is described as a kind of magic theatre, and Mozart appears as a guide to the protagonist. The composition quoted not only from Mozart's Divertimento K. 287 but also from Beethoven and Mahler in a manner that Donal Henahan, in reviewing a performance of the work at Aspen, Colorado for the New York Times (July 19, 1972), found too literal and lengthy. Yet he also noted that Rochberg was a composer who was "unafraid to invite the listener into his personal universe, and technically fully able to do so."

Described by its composer as a "passion according to the twentieth century," Rochberg's Symphony No. 3 (1966–69) was scored for solo voices, chamber chorus, double chorus, and large orchestra, with a text of four lines from sacred writings set to music by Schütz, Bach, Mahler, and Ives. The result, according to Allen Hughes, who reviewed the work for the New York Times (November 26, 1970) after its premiere at the Juilliard Theater in New York City, was the "musical equivalent of a Joycean prose technique," which could be heard as "a kind of journey through a musical dream" or as an autobiographical stream of consciousness. Given its New York premiere by the National Orchestra of New York at Carnegie Hall on April 17, 1985, Rochberg's "skillful and palatable" Symphony No. 4 sounded to Donal Henahan's ears as if "haunted by Mahler's ghost," with occasional hints of Ravel, Prokofiev, and even Sir Edward Elgar.

In 1960 Rochberg had left the Theodore Presser Company to become chairman of the music department at the University of Pennsylvania, a position he held until 1968, when he became a professor of composition and composer-in-residence. In 1979 he was appointed Annenberg Professor of Humanities, but despite his administrative and teaching responsibilities Rochberg continued to compose prolifically, producing a new symphony, string quartet, or concerto every two or three years, along with many smaller-scale works.

Among Rochberg's best-known briefer works are Zodiac, a twelve-tone composition consisting of twelve bagatelles he wrote for piano in 1952 and richly rescored for full orchestra in 1964; La bocca della verità (1958), which has been described as "post-serialist" because it uses superimposed tempi to relieve the constraints of the twelve-tone row; several pieces set to words by his late son, Paul, including Tableaux—Sound Pictures (1968) and Eleven Songs (1969); and Nach Bach (1966), a jocular commentary on Bach's Partita in E minor.

Throughout the early and mid-1970s, Rochberg kept edging closer to complete tonality in his compositions, while continuing to use the collage technique. His String Quartet No. 3 (1972), written for the Concord String Quartet, had its premiere at a concert presented by the Naumburg Foundation at Alice Tully Hall in May 1972. In his *New York Times* review (May 17, 1972) Donald Henahan reported that the quartet "began with a series of atonal chords, reiterated as though the composer were trying to get them out of his system." It continued with borrowings from and allusions to Ives, Stravinsky, Beethoven's final quartets, Bartók's dances, and Mahler's waltzes, returning briefly to its opening atonalism before its finale. Henahan concluded: "The appeal of this work . . . lies not in any literary stance but its unfailing formal rigor and old-fashioned musicality. Mr. Rochberg's quartet is—how did we used to put it?—beautiful. It is one of the rare new works that go past collage and quotation into another, fairer land." Two years later, when the Concord String Quartet brought Rochberg's String Quartet back to Alice Tully Hall along with his new, totally tonal composition called *Ricordanza—Soliloquy for Cello and Piano,* Henahan observed in the *New York Times* (April 26, 1974) that *Ricordanza,* as performed by Rochberg at the piano and with Norman Fischer on cello, could not be "dismissed as nostalgia or even as a nosethumb at those sectors of the Academy where serialism is still believed to be the music of the future." "In what seemed to be Mr. Rochberg's deepest plunge yet into the tonal world most composers feel is dead," Henahan added, "he forces us to remember past pleasures and to re-examine prejudices and superstitions."

Rochberg achieved his most resounding critical and popular success with his five-movement, thirty-seven-minute work *Concerto for Violin and Orchestra,* which was commissioned by the Pittsburgh Symphony in memory of the music critic Donald Steinfirst and funded by a Bicentennial grant from the National Endowment for the Arts. Isaac Stern introduced the concerto, a work in the grand tradition of Brahms and Sibelius, with the Pittsburgh Symphony in April 1975 and later performed it with the major orchestras of Chicago, San Francisco, Detroit, and Boston. Its acrobatic and virtuosic writing for the violin gave Stern free rein to dazzle the audience, while its rich tonalities, ranging in mood from joyous to elegiac, added to its popular appeal. During an interview with John Guinn for the *Detroit Free Press* (March 19, 1976) Isaac Stern remarked: "Everywhere I've seen it performed up to now, I've noticed that audiences seem to take to it almost instantly. That's because it's largely tonal, and it also has tunes one can whistle."

Continuing his close association with the Concord String Quartet throughout the 1970s, Rochberg composed no fewer than four more works for the group during the relatively brief period from 1977 to 1979. Three of them, his String Quartets Number Four, Five, and Six, collectively known as *The*

*Concord Quartets,* had their premiere in Philadelphia in January 1979 as part of a belated celebration of his sixtieth birthday. Intended, in the composer's words, "to ensure the maximum variety of gesture and the broadest possible spectrum," the fourteen movements of the *Concord Quartets,* performable as one long suite as well as three separate quartets, ranged from fugue to fantasy, from tonality to atonality, and from snatches of Beethoven to bits of Schoenberg. The critical consensus was that Rochberg, by traversing a wide range of styles and emotions with extraordinary skill, had composed "perhaps the most enjoyable" work of chamber music in recent years. Similar superlatives greeted the first hearing of Rochberg's String Quartet No. 7, in a performance by the Concord String Quartet, to whom the piece was again dedicated, and by the baritone Leslie Guinn, who sang a text by Paul Rochberg.

Critics in general worked up less enthusiasm over the premiere performance, in Santa Fe, New Mexico in August 1982, of Rochberg's first venture into opera, *The Confidence Man,* which he based on Herman Melville's bleakly pessimistic novel about a protean swindler who fleeces his victims aboard a Mississippi river boat. The blackness and cynicism of Melville's mood in the mid-1850s, when he wrote the novel, at an emotional nadir, is mirrored in its series of vignettes. For a libretto fashioned by his wife, Gene—centering on a naive candlemaker named China Aster who borrows $1,000, invests it unwisely, and dies—Rochberg composed a primarily tonal score. More than one reviewer attributed the limitations of *The Confidence Man* to its unpromising and intractable source material: the density, complexity, and amorphous structure of Melville's novel itself.

After teaching for twenty-three years on the faculty of the University of Pennsylvania, Rochberg retired in 1983, as Emeritus Annenberg Professor of Humanities, to devote himself exclusively to composing. He was honored on that occasion by a concert by the pianist Jerome Lowenthal, who dedicated the entire evening to performing Rochberg works from every phase of his career. Since his retirement, the composer has continued to live with his wife, the former Gene Rosenfeld, to whom he has been married since 1941, in a split-level brick-and-stone house in Newtown Square, in Delaware County, Pennsylvania. The couple have a grown daughter, Francesca Rochberg-Halton. Rochberg is a tall, gray-haired gentleman, who manages to reconcile his courtly manner with a lively sense of humor. Although his commitment to the musical idiom of an earlier period continues to exercise his confreres, Rochberg feels rewarded by the abundance of his creative energy. "I used to feel hemmed in," he told a *Newsweek* reporter who interviewed him in 1979. "Now I feel free. I used to feel uncertain and dissatisfied; today I have incredible energy. For the first time in my life I'm saying what I feel."

In 1985 the University of Michigan Press published Rochberg's *The Aesthetics of Survival: A*

Composer's View of Twentieth-Century Music, a collection of essays written between 1955 and 1982, in which he propounds his conviction that the value of music depends on its intelligibility to the ear. According to Rochberg, that requirement can only be met when music relates to "historical tonality."

References: Chicago Tribune Ja 20 '80 por; N Y Times II p20 Jl 15 '73 por; N Y Times Mag p24+ My 29 '83 por; New Yorker 54:109+ F 12 '79; Newsweek 93:70 F 19 '79 por; Opera N 47:14+ Jl '82 pors; Time 105:57 My 5 '75 por; Washington Post B p1 Ap 7 '75

## Rothenberg, Susan

Jan. 20, 1945– Painter. Address: b. c/o Willard Gallery, 29 E. 72d St., New York City, N.Y. 10021

"I am an image maker who is also an image breaker—trying for a little more," says Susan Rothenberg, who, in a series of paintings using the horse as the major motif, emerged in the mid-1970s as one of the new wave of figurative artists reacting against the somber and austere visual purities of minimalist abstraction. In the 1980s Miss Rothenberg's sensuously painted canvases have been populated by the human figure and by subjects taken from the natural landscape—hauntingly poetic and mysterious images that are built up out of brushstrokes rather than from the drawn line, and are laid down on a brushily abstract monochrome ground redolent of both minimal reductiveness and the action-painting wing of abstract expressionism. And with the rise in the early 1980s of the neoexpressionist movement, which eclipsed the dominant styles of the 1960s and 1970s and signaled a dramatic change in artistic taste, Susan Rothenberg has been acclaimed as a transitional figure linking the "cool" abstraction of the previous generation to the turbulent figure painting of the contemporary scene. In the estimation of the art critic Peter Schjeldahl, "[Susan Rothenberg] is, quite simply, one of the most thoroughly convincing artists in the world, one of a handful who have laid hold of a medium and muscled it into perfect accord with their temperaments."

Self-described as having been "a middle-class, urban kid," Susan Rothenberg was born on January 20, 1945 and reared in Buffalo, New York, the daughter of Leonard and Adele (Cohen) Rothenberg. Her parents' financial circumstances were comfortable, and for a time her father was co-owner of a chain of supermarkets. "I think you often become what you are praised for when you are pretty small," Rothenberg told Lisbet Nilson of Artnews (February 1984), adding that her childhood efforts at drawing and painting were "about [all] I was praised for. I was not a real well-behaved child."

The encouragement emanating from her parents and gradeschool teachers was augmented by the enthusiasm shown her work by Dr. Joseph Rosenberg, the family's physician and neighbor, who transmitted his own excitement about art to Susan Rothenberg and let her paint in his studio on Sundays. She visited Buffalo's prestigious Albright-Knox Art Gallery and in high school received strict academic instruction in art from a Hungarian immigrant named Laszlo Szabo who, as Susan Rothenberg recalled in her interview with Lisbet Nilson, "made you draw from a plaster eye and a plaster nose for a year; after three years you got to use the colors red, yellow, and blue. He thought everything from Picasso on was pure garbage."

Enrolled in the fine-arts department of Cornell University in 1963, Miss Rothenberg elected to study sculpture because, as she has explained, "painting had always come easy to me and I wanted something I couldn't do." She produced mixed-media works—"dangerous little objects," according to her—which were influenced by the artist Lucas Samaras' menacingly surreal assemblages of items from everyday use. And when, after two years, her experiments culminated in a cement block bristling with small spikes, the head of the department bluntly informed Susan Rothenberg that she had no talent. Her rambunctious response was a hedonistic, five-month visit to the Greek island of Hydra, where she seems to have dabbled with alcohol and drugs and experimented with the lifestyle of the 1960s counterculture. After returning to Cornell, she took courses in painting, and completed requirements for her bachelor's degree in 1966.

The late 1960s are now remembered by Susan Rothenberg as "that awful post-college time between 21 and 25," as she remarked to the art critic Grace Glueck in an interview for the New York

Times Magazine (July 22, 1984). The confusion and restlessness of her life from 1967 to 1969 calls to mind the sense of spiritual drift discernible in the writer Ann Beattie's chronicles of the generation that stumbled from exultant youth to uncertain adulthood in the late 1960s and early 1970s. In 1967 Miss Rothenberg enrolled in the master's degree program of the Corcoran School of Art in Washington, D.C., but dropped out after only two weeks. Staying on in Washington, she did some painting—"weird little satirical suburban paintings," she told Lisbet Nilson, "spray-painted sheep in front of a tract house, that sort of thing"—but mostly she "stayed in a room and . . . spent a lot of time in a jazz bar," as she informed Grace Glueck. "The whole year of 1968 is lost to me," she said. "I don't remember where I was, nor do I my parent or friends." By about mid-1969 Susan Rothenberg had returned to Buffalo, and that autumn she set out for Nova Scotia, intending, she told Grace Glueck, "to get lost in the woods and teach English in some backwater town."

In Montreal, however, Miss Rothenberg changed the train ticket from Halifax to New York City, where, with help from college friends and money from home, she was soon ensconced in a downtown loft. Her impulsive move to West Broadway in lower Manhattan was to prove serendipitous, for in the early 1970s that area, known as SoHo, teemed with experimental artists who, though they worked in different media, cross-pollinated each other. Dancers collaborated with painters and sculptors, who worked with vanguard classical composers influenced by rock musicians, and those rock musicians in turn collaborated with poets who helped to stage dances. All those performers and artists made up a cohesive community that consolidated the cultural gains won by two earlier generations of the New York School avant-garde. Indeed, Susan Rothenberg met the sculptor George Trakas, whom she was to marry in 1971, when they were both performing in a dance piece by Joan Jonas.

"He taught me what work was," Susan Rothenberg said of Trakas in the interview with Grace Glueck. "He was completely dedicated to being a sculptor, and I took on his work ethic. He made me see how demanding and committed an artist's life had to be." Influenced by process art at the time she met Trakas, Miss Rothenberg, according to Lisbet Nilson, "punched holes in paper and plastic, worked with torn polyethylene and carved-up aluminum mesh, with graphite and gunpowder," while her geometric pattern paintings were in the then prevailing minimalist style. "I was working through all the influences around me," the artist told Lisbet Nilson. "And finally I realized that I was boring myself in the studio—which is really a basis for change."

A marked transformation in Susan Rothenberg's art took place in 1973, one year after the birth of her daughter, Maggie, when she began painting to hold on to her identity within her new status, concerned lest she become merely a wife and mother. In her pattern paintings she had been dividing her canvases into open book-like halves with a line drawn down their middle, and when doodling one day she "drew a line down the middle" and suddenly there was "half a horse on either side. The horse held the space," she has explained, "and the line kept the picture flat."

Although the image of the horse would dominate her canvases for the next six years, at first Susan Rothenberg was certain that the horse paintings would put her "right out of the ballpark" in the New York art world. Developing out of the formalist theories of the critic Clement Greenberg and Frank Stella's austerely reductive stripe painting of the late 1950s, minimal doctrine was rigidly anti-illusionist—to respect the "integrity" of the picture plane, painting must use geometric strategies to keep things absolutely flat—and it proscribed painterly gesture and pictorial subject matter. Consequently, even abstract representations of the horse were verboten. Executed with what Lisbet Nilson has called a "brushy, insistent stroke" that made her canvases painterly and sensual, Susan Rothenberg's work seemed provocative to the taste of the mid-1970s.

Nevertheless, Miss Rothenberg's horses—depicted either in profile or frontally, sometimes standing, sometimes in motion, and all painted in acrylic on canvas or paper—were executed with a formalist rigor that kept the work, to quote Lisbet Nilson, "as cool and intelligent, as spare and formal," as minimal aesthetics demanded. At first, Rothenberg managed, as she put it, "to stick to the philosophy of the day—of keeping the painting flat and anti-illusionist"—by geometricizing the image, laying the horse down against a monochrome ground on a canvas divided by vertical or diagonal lines or bars. The use of a single line down the center of the canvas proved specially effective in this respect, because separating the canvas into halves that resembled an opened book forced the viewer to read the painting from left to right, or vice versa, rather than in depth. Eventually, Miss Rothenberg dismembered the animal, abandoning verticals and diagonals and introducing large bones, whose sharp lines competed with the soft contours of the horse shape to create tension-filled areas of canvas. "One of the big elements that the geometry gave the painting was tension," Rothenberg has said, as quoted in Artnews. "And . . . I found that a bone could create that same feeling, so the bones took over the tension factor. . . ." And because bones were more integral to the subject matter, "the work got more psychologically intense, since bones have so many connotations," to quote the artist.

The horse is an image that, as Grace Glueck noted, is "steeped in mythology and history, a domesticated creature, yet one evoking a wild one," but Susan Rothenberg insists that the animal is not for her psychologically compelling. Despite having taken riding lessons, she was, as a child, more interested in dogs. Instead, she speculates that because she was uncomfortable working in an abstract idiom, the horse "was a way of not doing people, yet it was a symbol of people, a self-portrait, really." But however unfashionable representational painting was at that time, Rothenberg's series of horses, publicly unveiled at solo shows in SoHo in 1975 and at the uptown Willard Gallery the following year, seemed "to touch a cultural nerve," as Lisbet Nilson has put it. Reviewing an early Rothenberg show at the Willard Gallery, the influential *New York Times* critic Hilton Kramer wrote: "It is the quality of the painting that is so impressive, the authority with which a highly simplified image is transformed into a pictorial experience of great sensitivity and even grandeur. It is the kind of painting that invests every area of the canvas with feeling without ever spilling over into Expressionist abandon." At about that time, what critics dubbed "New Image Painting" emerged in reaction to minimalism, and Rothenberg's spare yet evocative imagery on monotype fields of paint strokes epitomized the new style's combination of iconic content and structural rigor.

The end of the 1970s seems to have been a stressful period for the artist. In 1979 she and George Trakas were divorced, and the following year she did her last horse painting. Unwilling at that point to paint the human figure, and having exhausted the theme of the horse, Rothenberg had reached an artistic cul-de-sac, until one day, while doodling with her daughter's crayons, the image of a human head and hand appeared. Rothenberg found private, autobiographical significance in that image—because, as she wrote in an *Art in America* article (December 1982), she usually works with a head and a hand. In 1980, working from what she called a "mesmerizing" series of nine-inch studies, she did five paintings of a superimposed head and hand, which, she has said, became "very confrontational" when produced on the large scale of a ten-foot-square canvas.

Images began to proliferate in Susan Rothenberg's work in 1981, while she was spending a summer vacation with her daughter on Long Island. There she taught herself to paint in oil, a medium whose possibilities she has continued to explore. Her subject matter—nonrealistic depictions of boats, trees, and swans, traditional subjects of oil painting—came from what she saw outside the barn she used as a studio, which was situated on a creek in a rustic area. "What I think the work was starting to talk about," she commented in *Art in America*, "[was] growing, taking journeys. The boat became a symbol to me—about the freedom I was feeling."

According to Miss Rothenberg, her series of sailboats led her "down a different avenue of painting," inasmuch as she was forced to deal in painterly terms with the seeming fragility of boats, their dependency on wind, and the "qualities of light and atmospheric conditions" that they suggest. As a result, she began to represent shadow, movement, and even the action of forces of nature, such as streaming sunlight or gusting winds, and her canvases, unremittingly flat in the previous de-

cade, began to admit some shallow spatial depth. Since about 1982, when Rothenberg began to jettison all rules for what she does and does not paint, she has been depicting the human image. Those works include representations of figures in realistic situations—as in *Grandmother* (1983-84), in which an adult is lovingly intertwined with a small child, and *One-Armed Float* (1982), a partly submerged swimmer—and even of scenes from her family history, such as *Maggie's Cartwheel* (1981-82), the happy domesticity of which is counterbalanced by the somber black and gray strokes that comprise the two figures.

In late 1982 Susan Rothenberg was the only woman included in "Zeitgeist," a mammoth and influential show in Berlin, mounted just yards across the western side of the line separating East and West. Most of the artists in "Zeitgeist" were young neoexpressionists from Germany, Italy, and the United States, who had broken decisively with the calculated geometric and intellectual purities of 1970s abstraction to revive interest in the painterly gesture, depiction of the human figure, and often convulsive psychological narrative. Critics, however, have been careful to point out that Susan Rothenberg's images, unlike those of, say, Julian Schnabel and Jörg Immendorff, are not icons of contemporary *angst* and that, as Robert Storr declared in *Art in America* (May 1983), her work "is interesting not only for its poetry but for the ways it challenges Expressionism by linking the heady intuitions of private symbolism to the discipline of radical abstraction." And the *Time* magazine art critic, Robert Hughes, noted that "Rothenberg is trying to salvage a way of presenting the human figure that owes nothing to mass media, that comes out of painting alone, abstract painting included." "A painting needs something else," she has said, "something from another state of reality." The human figures appearing in her recent work seem to have come from that realm: so evocative are the mysterious forms that she has called them "the unnameable."

What Robert Hughes called the "difficulty of depiction" is a central issue in Susan Rothenberg's painting. Her figures are as spare as Alberto Giacometti's etiolated sculptures, but despite the simplicity of her often spectral shapes, they have a hard-won quality, as if they had been wrenched from murky depths to the surface of her agitated, monochrome grounds. According to Storr, the "most consistent device" she has used to establish the "materiality" of her painterly surfaces is the fiercely animated gesture of her brushstroke, "which functions not so much to simulate feeling as to activate the canvas. . . . Rothenberg's simplifications and corrections [of the figure] are, like Giacometti's, part of a search for the essential characteristics of form. . . . Thus her gesture is more a matter of anticipation and release than of desperation."

As quoted by Lisbet Nilson, Susan Rothenberg herself has described her painting as being "about . . . essences, or the feelings you get from the objects you see." For example, when she paints from nature, she is "*truly* not interested in repeating how beautiful a tree is, but [is] very interested in interpreting 'treeness.'" Nor is she interested in the beauty of the human image. "It's more thoughts about people than the figure I'm talking about," she explains. "I'm painting human beings. And that bespeaks a generalized common form for them, which is not specific—and, actually, probably not even of a specific sex. . . . It's trying to get at something very basic—you could call it primitive desire."

In the fall of 1985 Miss Rothenberg was accorded the honor of a two-month exhibition at the prestigious Phillips Collection in Washington, D.C. The fourteen large oils and two drawings displayed were all new works that demonstrated a more complex, naturalistic style and a wider range of imagery and emotion—as indicated, for example, by their balancing of stark monochrome shades with new, colorful elements. Piet Mondrian, the late modernist painter, appeared in four paintings in the highly regarded show, bathed in a halo of light in *The Golden Moment* (1985) and standing in a field in *ING-Spray* (1984–85). Although Miss Rothenberg was at first surprised when the figure of that abstractionist master emerged on her canvas—"I said, 'Oh my God. Mondrian has come to visit'"—art critics lavishly praised the harmony of "narrative illusionism and pure painterliness" she was able to achieve in the series.

Susan Rothenberg is a tiny, compact woman who seemed "pixieish" to Lisbet Nilson. Although her manner is cheerful and relaxed, that interviewer perceived in her "a streak of self-deprecating, rather deliberate naiveté—she calls it her Little Orphan Annie act—[that] clearly masks a disciplined private seriousness." The artist lives with her daughter in the rapidly gentrifying lower Manhattan district known as TriBeCa, in a spacious loft that serves her both as home and studio.

Susan Rothenberg works by means of a painstaking process of trial and error, because, as Grace Glueck pointed out, "inspiration doesn't always arrive so quickly" for the artist, despite her "electric energy." Sometimes her imagery develops out of an earlier work, but "the genesis of her paintings is [usually] complex," the *New York Times* critic commented, "triggered by interior or outside events." "The magic part," Miss Rothenberg told her, "usually frames itself in my head like a question, a phrase, like, 'What should it be? What picture should be? Here.' And I don't know if I mean here in my studio, or here in this world. . . . 'What should be?' is a kind of prior thought to letting an image come up. It will happen any time; it happens sometimes just thinking, 'I know what I want to do,' and then starting. I mean, I mess up the canvas as soon as I can with some sort of paint." After "messing up" a canvas with paint, she relaxes, contemplating her work-in-progress from a rocking chair made by her ex-husband, with whom she has remained friends.

Although Susan Rothenberg told Grace Glueck that she regards herself as "probably on the down

side of prolific," she nevertheless produces about fifteen canvases a year, whereas she used to turn out eight or ten. The artist attributes her increased productivity in part to her "new sobriety," having recently given up the drinking that had consumed so many of her evenings since college. She now believes that drinking kept her more inside of herself, less aware of the exterior. "I used not to realize that I had hangovers. . . . I don't think I really saw," she has said. "My work is changing because I'm a lot clearer about things."

Susan Rothenberg is still represented by the Willard Gallery, and her larger canvases can be purchased for about $55,000. Although her work is frequently included in exhibitions featuring such young American contemporaries as Julian Schnabel and David Salle, Rothenberg now refuses to participate in group shows in which she is the only woman artist. She explained to Grace Glueck: "I got sick of people saying, 'How does it feel to be the only woman in the show?' And I would reply, 'It feels lousy, it's not fair. . . .' Not to be singled out as a woman painter is taking a small step in the right direction." Her paintings are in the collections of such prestigious institutions as the Museum of Modern Art, the Whitney Museum of American Art, the Walker Art Center in Minneapolis, and the Stedelijk Museum in Amsterdam, which mounted a solo Rothenberg show in 1982. After touring nearly a dozen American cities earlier in 1984, an exhibition of her recent work, organized by the Los Angeles County Museum of Art, was shown in November of that year at London's Tate Gallery.

References: N Y Times D 8 '78, Ap 13 '79, S 23 '79, S 20 '81; Saturday Review 8:12+ F '81 por; Vanity Fair 46:82+ Ag '83; Village Voice Je 9 '80, Ap 29 '81; Contemporary Artists 2d ed (1983); Who's Who in America, 1984–85

---

## Rubbia, Carlo

*Mar. 31, 1934– Italian physicist. Address: b. Department of Physics, Harvard University, Cambridge, Mass. 02138; European Organization for Nuclear Research, Geneva 23, Switzerland*

Described in *New Scientist* (October 25, 1984) as "an ebullient yet irascible Italian, whom fellow physicists love to hate," Carlo Rubbia is known both for his brilliant high-energy experiments with subatomic particles, which resulted in the electrifying discovery of the hitherto hypothetical $W^-$, $W^+$, and Z particles, and for his controversial personality. In his relentless drive for knowledge, Rubbia, who is professor of physics at Harvard University and senior scientist at the European Organization for Nuclear Research in Geneva, sometimes rushes into a new project before the previous one is finished and spends so much time flying between international commitments that friends dubbed him

*Carlo Rubbia*

the "Alitalia scientist." "I am so pushed in my profession, my curiosity is so great, that I cannot resist trying to respond to these natural questions all the time," he admits. "It is hopeless. My desire for getting somewhere is so large, so strong, that my mind keeps running all the time." But even his critics concede that "he's done great physics," a fact confirmed by two prestigious prizes: the title of *Discover* magazine's 1983 "scientist of the year" and the 1984 Nobel Prize for Physics, which he shared with the Dutch accelerator architect Simon van der Meer.

Born on March 31, 1934 in the small town of Gorizia in northern Italy, Carlo Rubbia is the oldest son of an electrical engineer. He loved science from an early age; indeed, he has called that passion "a birth defect, so to speak." When he was ten years old, the ravaging armies of World War II destroyed his home, but in their wake they abandoned communications equipment that the young Rubbia collected and experimented with, developing in the process the deep understanding of electronics that has remained one of his strengths as a physicist. When he was eleven, his father having been transferred, the family moved to Pisa, where Carlo Rubbia studied physics at the Scuola Normale Superiore and later at the University of Pisa, from which he received a degree in physics in 1958. Before graduating, he was also a physics instructor there.

As a research fellow in 1958–59 at Columbia University, then the pivotal American center of high-energy physics research, Rubbia worked with such luminaries as Steven Weinberg, who later contributed to the theory predicting the existence of the W and Z particles; Leon Lederman, now the director of the Fermi National Accelerator Laboratory (Fermilab) in Batavia, Illinois; and Nicholas

Samios, now the director of the Brookhaven National Laboratory. Rubbia thrived in that intellectually stimulating atmosphere, though by his own admission he had first to overcome an inferiority complex resulting "from jumping from the countryside into the middle of the action." In 1960 he returned to Italy to join the faculty at the University of Rome.

In 1961 Rubbia accepted a position as a physicist at the European Organization for Nuclear Research (CERN), a Geneva-based intergovernmental institution sponsored by thirteen European nations that had been established in the years immediately following World War II. One of CERN's initial projects was the building of a particle accelerator, a fundamental tool in high-energy particle physics research, which was completed in 1959. For years, scientists had studied subatomic particles with particle accelerators, which increase tremendously the velocity of certain elementary particles and then hurl them against fixed targets. The energy generated by the impact occasionally converted itself into certain subatomic particles whose existence had up to then been hypothetical. Since the energy needed to create a particle increases in proportion to the particle's mass, CERN's so-called "proton synchrotron," the most powerful accelerator in the world at that time, boded well for the creation of theoretical particles that previously had been too "heavy" to be produced experimentally. "For fifty years," Rubbia told Gary Taubes in an interview for *Discover* (January 1984), "if you really wanted to become famous in our field, you had to get yourself the biggest and the largest and the most powerful accelerator." As a result, intrigued by both the research possibilities and the concept of international cooperation, the ambitious young physicist was particularly excited about joining the CERN staff.

One year before Rubbia began working at CERN, a little-heralded hypothesis had been advanced that was to have a major impact on his career. According to physics theory, atoms and subatomic particles are held together by and interact through the four fundamental forces of nature: gravity, which holds the universe together; electromagnetism, which binds all atoms and molecules and governs such physical and biochemical reactions as fire and human metabolism; the "weak interaction," or "weak force," which is responsible for radioactive decay and is the key to nuclear fusion; and the "strong interaction," or "strong force," which holds protons, neutrons, and other subatomic particles together within the nucleus. According to quantum field theory, each force is transmitted between two elementary particles by the exchange of a specific third particle, a bundle of energy called a "quantum"; in fact, photons, which carry the electromagnetic force, are readily observable as light.

A constant goal of physics has been a "unified field theory," which would establish that the four forces are actually four different manifestations of one basic force and thus subject to a single set of laws. In the nineteenth century the Scottish physicist James Clerk Maxwell showed that electricity and magnetism, long thought to be distinct, were the same force—electromagnetism—and the scientific genius Albert Einstein devoted the latter part of his life to trying to demonstrate mathematically the underlying unity of electromagnetism and gravity, but in vain.

In 1960 the American physicist Sheldon Glashow, then a postdoctoral student at the University of Copenhagen, wrote a paper postulating the unity of electromagnetism and the weak force and predicting the existence of three weak force quanta, now known as the W$^-$, W$^+$, and Z particles, or as "intermediate vector bosons." (The Z particle has no charge.) Glashow's preliminary prediction about the intermediate vector bosons was incomplete in that it was unable to make specific, testable propositions about the properties of the bosons, including their mass. In 1967 the physicists Steven Weinberg of Harvard University and the Pakistani Abdus Salam of the International Center for Theoretical Physics at Trieste, working independently of each other, completed that step.

According to the resulting "electroweak" theory, both electromagnetism and the weak force stem from a more fundamental property of nature, and at extremely high energies, like those generated by the "big bang" that created the universe, electromagnetic events would be the same as "weak" ones. Consequently, the weak force quanta would have to be related to the photon, the known quantum of electromagnetism. In fact, the electroweak theory maintains that immediately after the "big bang" those four quanta were identical, but as the universe cooled they became outwardly distinct. Although no longer apparent, their underlying "symmetry" is nonetheless real. However, since the mass of a quantum is inversely proportional to the range of the force it transmits (electromagnetism, for example, has an infinite range and so the photon is massless), the weak force, whose range is limited to the atomic nucleus, must be carried by "heavy photons" or "heavy light." That is, the W and Z particles must have considerable mass. According to Weinberg and Salam's careful calculations, the W particles, for instance, would have a mass eighty to ninety times that of the proton—ten times that of the heaviest known subatomic particle. For their important contributions, Weinberg, Glashow, and Salam were jointly awarded the 1979 Nobel Prize in physics.

Rubbia was instrumental in the first phase of the experimental confirmation of the electroweak theory, though in the process he tarnished his professional reputation for several years. In 1969 he agreed to join Alfred Mann of the University of Pennsylvania and David Cline in searching for the massive W particles with a new accelerator at the Fermi National Accelerator Laboratory (Fermilab) outside of Chicago, which by the time of its completion in 1973 was the most powerful in the world. However, in 1971 physicists began to accept that, as postulated by the electroweak theory, there existed "neutral weak currents." All previously known weak force interactions had entailed a change in the electrical charge of the particles involved, but the electroweak theory contended that in some weak interactions the particles retain their charge, just as they do in electromagnetic interactions. Only the existence of the hypothetical Z particle could account for that phenomenon. Laboratory verification of neutral weak currents not only would considerably strengthen the electroweak theory but would also be a coup for the physicists who conducted the successful experiment. Consequently, Rubbia's team redirected its search from the elusive Ws to the currents and thus placed itself in direct competition with physicists at CERN, who were using a huge bubble detection chamber called Gargamelle. No one doubted that the two teams were racing to see which one would discover the current first.

In January 1973 members of the CERN team discovered virtually conclusive proof of neutral currents, and they published their results in July. The physicists on the Fermilab team were also seeing evidence of neutral currents and, pressured by CERN's "lead," publicly reported their own, still inconclusive, findings. Just then, as fate would have it, Rubbia's visa expired and he had to leave the United States. In his absence, his colleagues overhastily repeated the experiment—and found no neutral currents. They prepared a report on those findings, distressing the physicists at CERN who had already committed themselves publicly to the existence of the neutral currents.

Then, in another reversal, researchers on Rubbia's team discovered that their second experiment had been flawed; continued work did indeed reveal the existence of neutral currents. In December 1974 the Fermilab group members published a definitive paper on the existence of neutral currents, but their earlier flawed experiment had left a bad taste in many people's mouths. A joke spread through the physics community that Rubbia's team had discovered "alternating neutral currents." Discussing that fiasco in Discover (January 1984), Rubbia admitted that "in a way, we blew it"; but, he added philosophically, "the definition of an expert that I like best is one who has already made all the mistakes."

With the existence of neutral weak currents confirmed, attention shifted again to the search for means of creating and detecting both the Z and the W$^-$ and W$^+$ particles. However, no existing accelerator could reach the energy levels required to produce such massive particles, and while new giant accelerators were being constructed in the United States, they would not be operational until the mid-1980s. At that point, in 1976, Rubbia conceived a brilliant, but seemingly farfetched, method for creating the weak force quanta by modifying an existing accelerator and immediately applied all his energies to convincing others of its feasibility. Rubbia, David Cline, and Peter M. McIntyre reasoned that if, instead of hurling a proton beam against a fixed target, beams of protons and antiprotons (the antimatter twins of protons), speeding in opposite directions, were trained against each other, the colliding particles would completely destroy each other and be converted into pure energy. As a result, virtually all the released energy—about twenty times that produced in a conventional accelerator—would be free for the creation of new particles. Rubbia and his colleagues were sure that at such tremendous energy levels even the massive W⁻, W⁺, and Z particles would be generated. That idea at first met with scornful scepticism from the scientific community. The director of Fermilab told Rubbia (whom he called "that jet-flying clown") to go elsewhere, and when Rubbia, Cline, and McIntyre submitted a paper on the proposal to the prestigious *Physical Review Letters*, the editors rejected it for publication. Fortunately, Rubbia found a more receptive audience among CERN's directors, who agreed to finance the $100 million project to convert its existing proton synchrotron into a particle collider.

To implement his theory, Rubbia and his team of over 100 physicists had to solve several problems. First, antiprotons, which do not occur naturally on earth, had to be generated in sufficient quantities for the experiment by a conventional particle accelerator and then stored for roughly twenty-four hours until enough—about one hundred billion—had accumulated. Here, Rubbia found a critical ally in the Dutch accelerator physicist Simon van der Meer. He designed a storage ring that not only held the antiprotons but also forced them into a single beam of particles of uniform speed—a necessity if they were to be used successfully in the particle beam collider—by "stochastic cooling," a technique van der Meer devised that uses computer signals and electromagnets to discipline the erratic antiprotons. A magnet then kicks the prepared antiproton beam into the beam collider, a tubular ring four miles in diameter that is in an underground installation on the French-Swiss border. There the proton and antiproton particle beams, moving in opposite directions, make 50,000 revolutions each second. To record the resulting collisions—the most violent on earth—and the matter they produce, a 2,000-ton cylindrical chamber that contains intricate webs of wiring encases the ring, and that cylinder, in turn, is encircled by a calorimeter. Newly created particles pass first into the detector ring, thereby generating electrical signals that are detected and analyzed by computers, and then into the calorimeter, which measures their energy. As a result, clear identification of each particle is possible. "We actually sacrifice each one of the particles and go through an autopsy," Rubbia explained in *Discover* (April 1983). "Each particle tells its own story, and an event [a single proton-antiproton collision] is a collection of stories."

The first moments of the experiment were tense for Rubbia and van der Meer. Many scientists had predicted that the two beams would destroy each other totally at the initial impact, negating any possibility of an ongoing experiment. Rubbia himself was "scared stiff the beam wouldn't work." In *Discover* (January 1984), he described that crucial first run: "We were there, and the beams were injected and we looked at the damn thing and the beams were still there, and we looked again and they were still there, and it came around and they still didn't kill each other as they were supposed to. That was the most exciting moment in my whole experience."

Within the first month, five Ws were detected. To each, Rubbia and his team drank a champagne toast, but, still mindful of the "alternating neutral currents" debacle, he did not announce the results immediately. Instead, he took the longest vacation he has ever had, spending ten days sailing the Nile with his family, while he waited for evidence to accumulate. Finally, in January 1983 he announced the discovery of the W⁻ and W⁺, and a few months later he also confirmed the existence of the Z. The verification of the weak force quanta was hailed globally as one of the most important achievements of the century in physics and as a significant step toward the confirmation of the unified field theory. In 1984 the Royal Swedish Academy of Sciences honored Rubbia for his discovery and van der Meer for the technology that made it possible by awarding them jointly the 1984 Nobel Prize in physics.

In July 1984 Rubbia's team announced another dazzling discovery: they had detected the sixth "quark." Quarks are the basic, indivisible constituents of matter, and the sixth quark, also called the "top" or "truth" quark, was the last to be found. Like the intermediate vector bosons, it is so heavy that it is produced only at extremely high energies, such as those that occurred during the "big bang" or that are generated in the proton-antiproton collider.

Rubbia's design for his proton-antiproton collider has become the model for future particle accelerators and has propelled Europe into the vanguard of high-energy physics, a field that had been dominated by the United States since before World War II. His current undertakings include making the CERN accelerator more powerful in order to learn even more about the properties of the intermediate vector bosons and other particles that may appear at high energies as yet unachieved. Already the detectors at the CERN project have picked up what may be unpredicted anomalies at energies higher than those that created the W and Z particles, but Rubbia is not content. With the United States gearing up to build the "superconducting super collider" (SSC), which would be by far the most powerful accelerator in the world, Rubbia is lobbying for the construction at CERN of the "large hadron collider," which would piggyback the "large electron-positron" (LEP) collider that is already being built. It would be only half as powerful as the SSC, but since it would be built on top of the LEP instead of in a separate tunnel, construction time and costs would be greatly reduced.

Rubbia is also one of the leaders of a collaborative project, based deep in an abandoned silver mine in Utah, that is designed to detect any sign of proton decay, which would disprove the long-standing belief that matter is stable. In addition, beneath an abandoned iron smelter in Wisconsin he is looking for the hypothetical magnetic monopole, which has one pole (electrical charge) instead of the usual two. Looking up to the heavens, he intends to search for antimatter throughout the universe and hopes to use the space shuttle to detect cosmic rays.

Since 1970 Rubbia has divided his time between Harvard University, where he teaches physics during one semester each year, and CERN, where, as senior scientist, he oversees experiments and, as of February 1985, headed a committee to plan the future of the laboratory. He and his wife, Marisa, a high-school physics teacher whom he met while they were students at the University of Pisa, have two children: Laura, a medical student at the University of Geneva, and André, an electronics whiz. He and his family live in Geneva but Carlo Rubbia maintains his Italian citizenship. The full-faced and stocky Rubbia, who speaks Italian, French, German, and English fluently, does find time to enjoy his private yacht and to indulge his love for his native cuisine, but physics remains his all-consuming passion. "Make no mistake about it," he insisted in *Discover* (January 1984). "Physics is fun. Forget about everything else. Physics is fun."

*References: Christian Sci Mon p1+ D 10 '84 por; Discover 4:18+ Ap '83 por, 5:34+ Ja '84 pors; N Y Times B p13 O 18 '84 por; International Who's Who, 1985–86*

---

## Sabato, Ernesto

*June 24, 1911– Argentine writer. Address: Severo Langueri 3135, Santos Lugáres, Buenos Aires, Argentina*

With the awarding in 1985 of the Miguel de Cervantes Prize—considered the equivalent of the Nobel in Hispanic letters—the Spanish government paid homage to the Argentine writer Ernesto Sabato's four decades of literary endeavor. His three novels and many volumes of essays, which have been translated into twenty-eight languages, have moved readers the world over with their unsparing examination of the human condition and their concern for the survival of moral values in the modern world. Sabato's fame as a writer is enhanced by his role as a champion of social justice, which has recently received international attention because of his work as president of the commission investigating the cases of those persons who disappeared during Argentina's military dictatorships.

Ernesto Sabato was born on June 24, 1911 in Rojas, a small town in Buenos Aires province, 160 miles west of Argentina's capital. He was the tenth of eleven sons of Francisco Sabato and Juana Maria Ferrari de Sabato, Italian immigrants who settled in Argentina at the end of the nineteenth century and established the town's flour mill. Eight of their sons survived into adulthood. Ernesto Sabato's childhood was indelibly colored by the death, just four days before his own birth, of his immediately older brother, who had also been named Ernesto. Fearing that he too might die, his mother smothered him with her solicitude, and as a result, Sabato remembers, he became "pathologically attached" to her. The birth of his younger brother Arturo so maddened him with murderous jealousy that throughout his childhood he suffered from nightmares, hallucinations, and bouts of sleep-walking. Because his mother kept him and Arturo indoors, out of harm's way, isolation drove Ernesto to cultivate the inner world of his imagination, and he showed early signs of artistic aptitude. "As far back as I remember, my vocation was artistic: painting and fiction," he told Maria Angélica Correa in an interview for her book *Genio y figura de Ernesto Sabato* (1971).

In 1924 Sabato was sent away to secondary school because Rojas did not have one. He attended the Colegio Nacional in La Plata, capital of the province of Buenos Aires, where the forced separation from his mother plunged him into emotional crisis. His private agony led him to seek relief in the study of mathematics, which he says offered him "all the order, all the purity, all the rigor that was lacking in my adolescent's world." He completed his high-school education in 1928 and, determined to dedicate himself to science rather than to art, enrolled the following year in the Instituto de Fisica at La Plata's Universidad Nacional. But swept up by the political currents of the day, he was distracted from his studies for several years by his involvement in anarchist and Communist movements. Although an important figure in Argentina's Communist Youth organization, having been appointed to the post of secretary general in 1933, he suffered a crisis of faith in Communism while attending a party congress in Brussels and fled to Paris rather than go to the Soviet Union for an indoctrination course. In Paris, as he later recalled for María Angélica Correa, he filched a volume of mathematical analysis from a bookstore and once again found "inner peace" in the order and logic of scientific thought. He returned home to Argentina and his university studies, and completed work on his doctorate in 1937.

In 1938 Sabato received a fellowship from the Asociación Argentina para el Progreso de las Ciencias to study atomic radiation at the prestigious Joliot-Curie Laboratory in Paris. Once in France, he was irresistibly drawn to the world of art and became involved with the surrealist group living there, particularly with André Breton. He began writing a never-finished novel, La fuente muda (The Silent Fountain), and at the same time continued his scientific research. In 1939 he moved to the United States because his grant was transferred to the Massachusetts Institute of Technology (MIT) in Cambridge, where he studied radiation with Professor Manuel Sandoval Vallarta. After returning to Argentina, Sabato accepted professorships in quantum theory and the theory of relativity at the Universidad Nacional in La Plata and in physics at the Instituto del Profesorado in Buenos Aires. He held those appointments from 1940 to 1945, when he was dismissed from them because of his opposition to Juan Domingo Perón's government.

While teaching, Sabato continued to write. In 1941 he became a regular contributor to Sur (South), Argentina's leading literary magazine, and a frequenter of the social gatherings held by its circle of writers. He later told María Angélica Correa that the group, which included Jorge Luis Borges, Argentina's most famous poet, gave him his literary education. "Sur was my university," Sabato said.

Deciding to abandon the world of science after he took a year's leave of absence from teaching in 1943, Sabato retreated to the hills of Córdoba province to write. On his return to Buenos Aires, he weeded out all the math and physics books from his personal library and gave them away to friends. In 1945 he published the book he had worked on during his sabbatical, Uno y el universo (One and the Universe, Sudamericana), which presented Sabato's condemnation of the moral neutrality of scientific thought, as well as his scrutiny of a variety of philosophical and literary issues. The critic Harley Dean Oberhelman has called its essays "units of thought . . . on the road to self-discovery." The book was well received in Buenos Aires, where it won both the Municipal Prose Prize and the Sociedad Argentina de Escritores' Sash of Honor.

Because he still did not have enough money to live on, despite that literary recognition, in 1947 Sabato accepted an appointment with the United Nations Educational, Scientific, and Cultural Organization (UNESCO) in Paris, but finding himself unable to cope with the bureaucratic nature of the work, he left after only two months. On his way back to Buenos Aires he began writing his novel El túnel (The Tunnel). After several publishing houses in Buenos Aires rejected the finished manuscript, Sabato's friends at Sur had it printed in 1948. An immediate bestseller, El túnel gained international recognition. Admiring its "dryness" and "intensity," the existentialist writer Albert Camus selected the novel for Gallimard's collection of Spanish-language works translated into French, and it was praised by such luminaries as Thomas Mann and Graham Greene. It was published in English translation, as The Outsider (Knopf, 1950), and eventually in a number of other languages as well.

In El túnel the painter Juan Pablo Castel tells how his tormented love for Maria Iribarne compels him to murder her, though she is the only person equipped to understand him and his work. Sabato chose to use the device of first-person narration for the novel because, as he later explained, "it was the best way to achieve the identification of the reader with the protagonist." Thanks to that technique, the reader enters into Castel's mind, lost on the frontiers between romantic idealism and mental illness, and penetrates his obsessive, pseudo-logical thought processes. Castel's narrative has a neat circular structure that suggests his enclosure within prison walls and his own hellish isolation. Because the novel so forcefully evokes the painter's solitude, María Angélica Correa has called El túnel "a devastating allegory of the human condition."

During the 1950s Sabato produced several books of essays, working at the same time on El hombre de los pájaros (The Bird Man), a novel that he never finished. Hombres y engranajes (Men and Machinery, Emecé, 1951) and Heterodoxia (Heterodoxy, Emecé, 1953) deal with philosophical problems generated by life in the modern world. Other books reflected his ongoing concern with Argentine political problems, among them El caso Sabato (The Sabato Affair), privately printed in 1956, which explains his resignation from the editorship of Mundo Argentino (given him the year before), as a protest against the injustices of the interim military government that had replaced the dictatorship of Juan Perón. Although Sabato had opposed Perón's policies, in El otro rostro del peronismo (The Other Face of Peronism, Imprenta Lopez, 1956) he urged Argentina to take a lesson from the fallen dictator whom the masses loved because he gave them their first representation in politics. He also called for such reforms as an end to politically motivated vengeance and persecution.

Impressed by the ideas set forth in El otro rostro, Arturo Frondizi, the democratically elected president who took office in 1958, appointed Sabato to the post of director general of cultural relations. He held that position only until 1959, when he resigned because he disagreed with administration policies. As the writer Carlos Tarsitano has noted, from the 1950s on, Sabato has been known for his "posture in favor of 'a social democracy' that does not sacrifice liberty to social justice or the reverse."

In 1961 Ernesto Sabato published *Sobre héroes y tumbas* (On Heroes and Tombs, Fabril Editorial), the novel that is widely acknowledged to be his masterpiece. It was not made available in English until 1981, when David Godine issued it in a masterly translation by Helen Lane, though it had long been available in French, Italian, and German. Its themes of love, death, rebirth, incest, solitude, and madness are woven through the fabric of a tale about the fascination that Fernando and Alejandra, a sinister but brilliant father and daughter couple, exert on Martín and Bruno, a pair of innocents. The story is told by a variety of voices speaking in different time frames, a narrative technique that creates what one critic has called "a veritable gallery of mirrors in which each fact is seen, commented on, and lived from different angles." The time scheme of *On Heroes and Tombs* encompasses the entire range of Argentine history, giving the work a comprehensiveness that makes it "the most representative national novel of Argentina written in the twentieth century," according to Harley Dean Oberhelman.

The centerpiece of *On Heroes and Tombs* is the "Report on the Blind," supposedly written by Fernando and found only after Alejandra has murdered him and committed suicide by self-immolation. Although Fernando's treatise on the nature of evil uses the investigative tools and single-minded focus of science, it is based on the insane premise that blind people belong to a secret sect that rules the world through terror. Critics have written extensively about the "Report on the Blind," interpreting it as a "dream journey" or as an "encounter with the origins and secrets of existence," or explaining it with the aid of Freudian analysis or the scholarly investigation of ancient myths.

In 1963 Sabato published *El escritor y sus fantasmas* (The Writer's Ghosts, Aguilar), whose essays, he notes, are variations on a single theme that has obsessed him since he began writing: "Why, how, and for what purpose is fiction written?" He explains that novelists write fiction because "they feel the obscure but obsessive necessity to offer testimony of their drama, their unhappiness, their solitude." By showing their readers "the essential mystery of existence," the novelists change their lives. Similarly, in his preface to *On Heroes and Tombs*, Sabato wrote: "There exists a certain type of fictional narrative whereby the author endeavors to free himself of an obsession that is not clear even to himself. For good or ill, this is the only sort of fiction that I am able to write." For Sabato, the writing of novels is the exploration of "that dark labyrinth that leads to the central secret of our life."

Other collections of essays by Sabato include *Tango* (Losada, 1963); *Tres aproximaciónes a la literatura de nuestro tiempo: Robbe-Grillet, Borges, Sartre* (Three Approaches to the Literature of Our Time, Editorial Universitaria, 1968); *La convulsión política y social de nuestro tiempo* (The Political and Social Convulsion of Our Time, Edicom, 1969); *La cultura en la encrucijada nacional* (Culture at the National Crossroads, Ediciónes de Crisis, 1973); *Apologías y rechazos* (Apologies and Rejections, Seix Barral, 1979); and *Robotización del hombre* (The Robotization of Man, Centro Editorial del América Latina, 1981). He also took part in a series of conversations about life, death, dreams, and literature with Jorges Luis Borges that were duly recorded by the Argentine writer Orlando Barone and published as *Diálogos* (Emecé, 1976). Sabato's anthologies of work otherwise unpublished in book form include *Itinerario* (Sur, 1969) and *Páginas de Ernesto Sabato* (Pages from Ernesto Sabato, Editorial Celtia, 1983).

Published by Sudamericana in 1974 and not yet translated into English, Sabato's third novel, *Abaddón el Exterminador*, is noteworthy for its technical innovation. In order to confront his perennial themes and the characters who act them out, Sabato enters into his third novel as another character and lives among them. The purpose of adopting that fictive strategy was, as he has explained, "to make a novel of the novel, something like a novel raised to the second power . . . to write something that was at once a fiction and a questioning of fiction, a form of inquiry into the very essence of the genre . . . the secret of its origins in the greatest depth of the human soul." In 1976 *Abaddón el Exterminador* won one of France's most prestigious literary awards—the Prix au Meilleur Livre Etranger.

During the military regimes with which Argentina was saddled from 1976 to 1983, Sabato was a bold and outspoken critic of repression and violations of human rights, despite the repeated threats that were made against his life. Those threats continued after Raúl Alfonsin, the democratically elected president, named him in 1983 to head the twelve-member National Commission on the Disappearance of Persons, which spent nine months in investigating the kidnapping and torture of alleged opponents of the military governments. Presented to the government in September 1984, the completed report, known as "El Informe Sabato," is a damning 50,000-page collection of evidence documenting the disappearance of 8,961 people at the hands of the armed forces. That revelation of "the greatest and most savage tragedy" in the history of Argentina was later condensed into a 500-page book entitled *Nunca Más*. As a consequence of the work of the commission, nine former heads of military governments went on public trial the following April to establish their responsibility for the disappearances.

Since 1934 Ernesto Sabato has been married to Matilde Kuminsky-Richter, whom he met when she attended a course he taught on Marxist theory.

Herself a writer, Matilde reads and discusses all of Sabato's manuscripts with him. In dedicating *On Heroes and Tombs* to her, Sabato wrote: "I dedicate this novel to the woman who has persistently encouraged me at moments when I lacked faith, which is most of the time. Without her, I should never have had the fortitude to finish it." The couple has two sons: Jorge Federico, born in 1938, and Mario, born in 1945. Sabato and his wife live in Santos Lugáres, a working-class suburb an hour away from downtown Buenos Aires, in a house they first occupied some forty years ago. When at home, Sabato devotes much of his time to painting, a hobby that he took up in the late 1970s, when lesions of the retina forced him to cut back on reading and writing. Although Sabato can be difficult to get along with at times because of his abrupt mood swings, his biographer, Maria Angélica Correa, points out that he has countless friends and admirers, thanks to "his dazzling intelligence, his sense of humor, his humanity."

In addition to the Miguel de Cervantes Prize, which he has called "the highest honor" of his life, Sabato has won many other awards. In 1964 he received the French title of Chevalier des Arts et des Lettres, and in 1974 he earned both the Grand Prize of Honor from the Sociedad Argentina de Escritores and Argentina's Premio Consagración Nacional. In 1979 the French government named him Chevalier de la Légion d'Honneur, and the Spanish government awarded him the Gran Cruz al Mérito Civil. In 1984 the Colombian government decorated him with the Cruz de Boyaca, and the Organization of American States bestowed on him its newly created Gabriela Mistral Prize. One honor that Sabato has refused to accept is membership in Argentina's Academy of Letters, because of what he terms his philosophical rejection of "all attempts to crystallize the Spanish language."

*References: Contemporary Authors vols 97–100 (1981); Contemporary Literary Crtiticism vol 10 (1979) and vol 23 (1983); Correa, Maria Angélica. Genio y figura de Ernesto Sabato (1971); Oberhelman, Harley Dean. Ernesto Sabato (1970); Sabato, Ernesto, with prefatory essay by Carlos Catania. Páginas de Ernesto Sabato (1983)*

## Sacks, Oliver (Wolf)

*July 9, 1933– Physician; writer. Address: b. Albert Einstein College of Medicine, Bronx, N.Y. 10461; h. 119 Horton St., Bronx, N.Y. 10464*

The neurologist Oliver Sacks is a physician, writer, and humanist whose career has evolved as a search to overcome the rigid categorizations and thinking of contemporary medical science. His three major books and his essays for laymen in such journals as the *New York Review of Books* have focused on some of the most challenging and complex problems facing modern neurology, in a quest for a holistic, humanistic view and practice transcending the confines of standard scientific empiricism. In short, Sacks is leveling boundaries in medical thinking, and in all probability, his work has just begun.

Oliver Wolf Sacks was born on July 9, 1933 in London, England to Dr. Samuel Sacks and Dr. Muriel Elsie (Landau) Sacks. Both of his parents were physicians, trained in neurology, and his father had worked under the famed neurologist Sir Henry Head, whose work was later to influence Oliver Sacks's thinking. Samuel and Muriel Sacks were so successful in instilling a love of medicine in all their children that not only Oliver but also his three older brothers Marcus, David, and Michael went on to pursue medical careers. In the Sacks household medicine meant a conjunction of science with personal relationships, and it was precisely that conception that was to guide Oliver Sacks's professional development.

Oliver Sacks attended St. Paul's School in London and on graduating in 1951 was granted a schol-

arship to the Queen's College, Oxford, where he majored in physiology. He obtained his B.A. degree from the college in 1954, and his M.A., B.M., and B.Ch. in 1958, as well as his M.D. from Middlesex Hospital, where he studied from 1955 to 1960. As a diversion from his studies, Sacks engaged in such sports as swimming, competitive weightlifting, and motorcycling.

In 1960 Sacks came to the United States, where he has made his home ever since, though he retains strong ties with relatives in England. He engaged in further study at the University of California in Los Angeles, from 1960 to 1965. Then, in 1965, he accepted a position as instructor in neurology at Albert Einstein College of Medicine in the Bronx, New York City, as well as the post of consultant neurologist to Bronx State Hospital. At that point in his development he considered himself "fairly orthodox" as a neurologist, and he later pointed out that his first book, *Migraine: The Evolution of a Common Disorder* (Univ. of California Press, 1970), was "well within the established medical 'canon.'"

Perhaps in comparison with Sacks's later work, *Migraine* may appear "orthodox." Nonetheless, it was neither a standard medical text for physician and student, nor a standard scientific work written for the lay reader, though it aimed to reach both of those audiences. He spelled out his concept of medicine in his frontispiece epigraph, which he took from Robert Burton's seventeenth-century treatise *The Anatomy of Melancholy*: "Socrates, in Plato, would prescribe no Physick for Charmides' *headache* till first he had eased his troublesome mind; body and soul must be cured together, as head and eyes. . . . " Sacks himself wrote in the preface that though he had at first considered migraine as no more than a peculiar type of headache, he came to see, in the course of treating a thousand migraine patients, that "many migraine attacks were drenched in emotional significance, and could not be usefully considered, let alone treated, unless their emotional antecedents and effects were exposed in detail."

Oliver Sacks was beginning to challenge the dominant school of contemporary medicine in the West that divorces mind from body, emotion from sickness, and attempts to cure disease through technique and mechanics rather than through a concentration on the whole person. Rejecting both the exclusively chemical or neurological answer of the somatically oriented physician, and the exclusively psychological answer of the psychiatrist, Sacks delved into the complex, multidimensional phenomenon of migraine to seek the interaction between physiological, biological, and psychological factors. Above all, his focus remained the patient, the individual, the human being. Whatever form of treatment the physician chooses, Sacks wrote, "one must always *listen* to the patient. For if migraine patients have a common and legitimate complaint besides their migraines, it is that they have not been listened to by physicians. Looked at, investigated, drugged, charged; but not listened to." In recommending *Migraine* to the readers of the *New York Review of Books* (June 3, 1971), W. H. Auden wrote: "I am sure . . . that any layman who is at all interested in the relation between body and mind, even if he does not understand all of it, will find the book as fascinating as I have." An expanded and updated edition of *Migraine* was published by the same press in 1985.

In fact, Oliver Sacks himself had experienced debilitating attacks of migraine since childhood, but *Migraine: The Evolution of a Common Disorder* as yet remained orthodox enough to preclude the detailing of his own personal experiences. Much later, in his book *A Leg to Stand On*, Sacks described his own migraines, including the phenomenon of *hemianopia*, or half-vision, in which he would completely lose his visual field to the left. He recalls his acute sensitivity as a child to being considered either a story-teller or "crazy," if he confided to others his bizarre changes of perception.

It was while he was completing work on *Migraine* that Oliver Sacks went to work in a New York charity hospital, where he encountered an extraordinary group of patients who were to have a pivotal influence on his life's work. They were the surviving victims of a global pandemic of *encephalitis lethargica* ("sleeping sickness") that had appeared in Europe in the winter of 1916–17 and, spreading all over the world, affected some five million people over the next decade. The symptoms of disease were many and contradictory, and fully one-third of those affected died in the acute stages of the disease's ravages, "in states of coma so deep as to preclude arousal," Sacks was to write, "or in states of sleeplessness so intense as to preclude sedation."

Some patients who contracted the disease staged a complete recovery, or so it only seemed, since many years later the majority developed "post-encephalitic syndromes," variants of neurological or psychiatric disorders that showed symptoms similar to acute cases of Parkinson's disease, including catatonia, melancholia, trance, and immobility. Some almost became "living statues," remaining motionless for months or even years on end, speechless and cocooned.

When Oliver Sacks arrived in 1966 at the hospital he has called "Mount Carmel," there were eighty post-encephalitic patients there, constituting the largest such group remaining in the United States, and one of the few remaining such groups in the world. Those patients were scattered in isolated wards throughout the hospital, and Sacks immediately set about bringing them together and attempting to instill some sense of belonging and community. About one-half of the group were in a state of deep, pathological "sleep"; the rest were able to maintain some minimal form of social interaction. At that point, Sacks had no sanguine expectations of any treatment or "cure." It was simply his conviction that a human, personal atmosphere was more healthful than an impersonal, institutionalized, repressive one.

In 1967 research and experimentation with a new drug, laevodihydroxyphenylalanine, commonly known as L-DOPA, showed it to have remarkable success in the treatment of Parkinsonism. Sacks began to consider using it with his post-encephalitic patients, but hesitated for two years, both because of the prohibitive cost of the drug in its first years on the market and because of his own uncertainties. As he wrote later in the *British Medical Journal* (December 24, 1984): "These were not 'ordinary' patients with Parkinson's disease: they had far more complex patho-physiological syndromes . . . they had been 'institutionalized,' and 'out of the world,' for decades. . . . I was faced by scientific and human complexities."

Nevertheless, early in 1969 Sacks decided to embark on a limited scientific study with the drug, a ninety-day double-blind trial. The spectacular, decisive effects of the drug on the patients compelled him to discontinue the experimental use of the placebo and to extend the treatment beyond the original ninety days. "Suddenly . . . ," he wrote in his book about the experience, *Awakenings*, "in the lugubrious and vaulted silence . . . there burst forth the wonder, the laughter, the resurrection of awakenings. Patients motionless and frozen, in some cases for almost five decades, were suddenly able, once again, to walk and talk, to feel and think, with perfect freedom."

Tragically, the miraculous effects of the drug brought in their wake unforeseen consequences. After the initial "awakening" period, most, though not all, of the patients, each in his or her own individual way, began to relapse, to deteriorate, and no dosage level of the drug was effective in returning them to their briefly found vitality. "That L-DOPA," Sacks quotes one patient as saying, painfully depressed at regressing from such tremendous heights, "that stuff should be given its proper name—*Hell*-DOPA!"

In August 1969 Oliver Sacks began to write up his observations and experiences in the form of biographical case histories of the patients, convinced that no standard "scientific" presentation could capture the depth and complexities of what those patients experienced with L-DOPA, and he later wrote letters to the *British Medical Journal* and the *Lancet*, attempting to convey the density of the human drama involved. Yet when he submitted papers to the medical journals, though he dutifully wrote them up in conventional scientific format, they were rejected, often out of hand.

Saddened by what he saw as the narrow scope of interest of the medical community, Sacks probed deeper into the "why" of the apparent success and then the abject "failure" of L-DOPA. He began to realize that a purely medical format could not contain his observations, which touched on the philosophical and existential as well as on the clinical. Although he had so much to say, he found no forum in which to say it. When an article he wrote for the *Journal of the American Medical Association* was roundly attacked by his colleagues, he felt, by his own admission, bewildered and frustrated, angry and sometimes despairing.

In September 1972 the editor of the British Broadcasting Corporation publication, *The Listener*, invited Oliver Sacks to write an article on his experiences wih L-DOPA. He wrote "The Great Awakening," as he called his article, at a single sitting, and when it was published in the October 26, 1972 issue of the magazine, it met with an enthusiastic reception. The resulting fervor prompted Sacks to return to the case histories he had written three years earlier. Adding eleven more, within two weeks he completed *Awakenings*, which was published by Duckworth in London in 1973 and by Doubleday in New York in 1974.

The heart of *Awakenings* is its case histories, but they are prefaced and followed by Sacks's musings on the relationship of science and metaphysics, body and mind, physiology, biology, consciousness, and environment. He also discusses the nature of hospitals as "total institutions" that promote disease rather than aid in the healing process and presents a bill of indictment against "assembly-line medicine" in which "everything human, everything living, [is] pounded, ground, pulverized, atomized, quantized, and otherwise 'processed' out of existence."

Sacks concludes that the answer as to the "why" of the effects of L-DOPA on post-encephalitic patients lies not in the nature of the chemical but in the totality of the life-experiences, consciousness, and relationships of the patients. What did life mean to a woman whose suddenly vital consciousness found itself in a body 40 years older than she expected, and 40 years later in historic time? "The limitations of L-DOPA are as clear as its benefits," Sacks wrote, "and if we hope to reduce the one and increase the other we must go *beyond* L-DOPA, beyond all purely chemical considerations, and deal with the *person* and his being-in-the-world."

Such a conclusion was hardly standard neurology, and the publication of *Awakenings* met, for the most part, with a stony silence from the medical profession. One exception was the *British Clinical Journal*, whose editor named *Awakenings* as his "editor's choice" for 1973 and felt impelled to comment on "the strange mutism" of the medical community towards the book. In the opinion of the great neuropsychologist A. R. Luria, the book revived the important tradition of clinical case studies "common to the great neurologists and psychiatrists of the nineteenth century," and poets, novelists, and humanistically oriented social scientists showered it with praise. W. H. Auden called it "a masterpiece," and Doris Lessing wrote, "It makes you aware of what a knife-edge we live on." Writing in the *Journal of the American Institute of Planners* (April 1978), Martin H. Krieger recommended *Awakenings* to social planners, those who think of themselves as "problem solvers, managers, and visionaries."

The generally cool reception to *Awakenings* on the part of his colleagues disquieted Sacks, who was, after all, aiming to expand the horizons of neurology, not to disavow the field altogether. In 1976 he had a personal experience which once fully integrated with his professional knowledge—a process that took several long years—finally enabled him to define to his own satisfaction where he stood in relationship to the neurological tradition.

It happened while Sacks was on a mountaineering vacation in Norway. He set out one morning to climb the six-thousand-foot mountain above the

SANTMYER

Hardanger fjord, but on his way up found himself confronted by a threatening bull, and running wildly down the mountain in panic, slipped and fell, tearing the quadriceps tendon of his left thigh. In *A Leg to Stand On* (Summit Books, 1984) Sacks details the harrowing afternoon of making his way down the mountain with only one good leg, the thoughts that passed through his mind on his life and the possibility of his death, and his rescue, just as darkness came, by reindeer hunters. Yet, as Sacks was only to realize later, his odyssey had only begun. It was not the accident in itself but the following weeks he spent as a doctor who had become a patient, the slow process of his recovery, the intertwining of physical injury and consciousness of self, that impelled Sacks to write a book based not on his observations of others, but on his own observations of himself.

Sacks, who had never before been a patient, now experienced from the inside that sense of stigma and impotence attached to what he calls "the social caste of patients . . . out-cast, outcasts, set apart by society." Furthermore, his severe but uncomplicated wound had unforeseen effects on him that the medical "experts" quickly dismissed with the abrupt reassurance, "You'll be fine." But far from feeling fine, Sacks was experiencing the paralysis of his leg not merely as a physical paralysis but as a profound alienation from the very concept of his left leg. He could not restore to his consciousness the image of his left leg as part of himself; he could not reconnect his will to his leg even at the point when, physically, he "should" have been able to move it.

In the process of reconnecting his mind to his leg, Sacks drew on both his profound knowledge of neurology and the consolations of poets and philosophers. In fact it was *music* that helped him break through to a rediscovery of his whole body-self—music, and the spontaneous action elicited by a healer who listened fully and attentively to Sacks's subjective reality, and proceeded on that basis.

Several years passed before Oliver Sacks set down in writing his experiences in *A Leg to Stand On*. He had corresponded with A. R. Luria on his ordeal, and Luria had replied that "such symptoms are perhaps common, but very uncommonly described. . . . Please publish your observations." And when Sacks read for himself the masterful works of the early-twentieth-century British neurologist Sir Henry Head, the previously irreconcilable pieces finally came together for him, both the debt he owed to tradition, and the new trails he was seeking to blaze. Consequently, *A Leg to Stand On* concludes with Sacks's vision and perspective of a "new" neurology or neuropsychology, one that goes beyond the bounds of empirical science "to assert and affirm the living subject, to escape from a purely objective, or 'robotic,' science, to find and establish what was missing—a living 'I'."

In fact, it is more than a "new" neurology or a new "human medicine" that Sacks envisions. In the last chapter of *A Leg to Stand On*, called "The

Long Road," he invokes images of "a new and wholly delightful sphere of life and mind . . . a wonderful continent, an infinite open country, a new realm, to which the neurology and medicine of the future might aspire." In appraising *A Leg to Stand On* for the *New York Review of Books* (September 27, 1984), Jerome Bruner came to the conclusion that it is "a story about the nature of selfhood—a narrative comparable to Conrad's *The Secret Sharer*."

Oliver Sacks continues to write for the lay press as well as for his medical colleagues. His article "The Lost Mariner" (*New York Review of Books*, February 16, 1984), about a man with severe memory loss, presents Sacks's further musings on the integrity of the human spirit—especially in contemplation of nature or art or God—despite handicaps that empirical science calls "hopeless." The *New York Review of Books* received a fervent and almost unprecedented outpouring of reader comment on that essay. And *Awakenings*, in a dramatic adaptation by the playwright Harold Pinter, was shown on British television in late 1984. Although Sacks maintains his active teaching post as professor of neurology at Albert Einstein College of Medicine, he told *Current Biography* that his "*essential* work (and habitat) is in chronic hospitals, charity hospitals, asylums, homes, etc."

Oliver Sacks, who is six feet tall and weighs about 220 pounds, rises early most mornings for an hour-long bicycle ride, and following his day's work he takes a long swim. He lives in the Bronx in a small red house with a white picket fence. An omnivorous reader, he often quotes the philosophers and poets in his books and articles, and he delights in browsing through the volumes of the *Oxford English Dictionary* in bed. Behind his gold-rimmed glasses there is a gentle gaze that befits a man who once said: "I think [Martin] Buber's comment, 'We must humanize technology, before it dehumanizes us,' applies *desperately* to medicine."

References: British Medical Journal D 24 '83; Newsday mag p18 D 9 '84 pors; Newsweek 104:70+ Ag 20 '84 por; Contemporary Authors vols 53–56 (1975); Sacks, Oliver. A Leg to Stand On (1984)

## Santmyer, Helen Hooven

Nov. 25, 1895– Writer. Address: b. Harper & Row, 10 E. 53rd St., New York City, N. Y. 10022; h. Hospitality Home East, N. Monroe Dr., Xenia, Ohio 45385

After writing in relative obscurity for more than sixty years, Helen Hooven Santmyer skyrocketed to national attention at the age of eighty-eight with the republication of her fourth book, " . . . And Ladies of the Club." Originally issued in a limited

*Helen Hooven Santmyer*

printing by the Ohio State University Press, Miss Santmyer's saga of life in a small midwestern town gathered dust on library shelves until it was "discovered" by the mother of a Hollywood writer-director and became a publishing event. Within months, " . . . *And Ladies of the Club*" was republished by G. P. Putnam's Sons; chosen as a Book-of-the-Month Club main selection; proposed as a television miniseries; and propelled to the top of the *New York Times* best-seller list. Ironically, Helen Hooven Santmyer has become a literary celebrity and a darling of the media at an age when she feels she is too old to write another book.

Born in Cincinnati, Ohio on November 25, 1895, Helen Hooven Santmyer was the first of the three children of Bertha (Hooven) Santmyer and Joseph Wright Santmyer, a drug salesman. When she was five, the Santmyers moved to the home that her great-grandfather, a carriage maker, had owned in Xenia, Ohio, a small town steeped in the Republican and Protestant values cherished by her family. Helen Hooven Santmyer was to spend most of her life in Xenia.

Admittedly a tomboy, Miss Santmyer enjoyed a carefree childhood, but she also admired intellectual achievement, and, inspired by the books of Louisa May Alcott, decided at an early age to become a writer. She was also influenced by the Women's Club of Xenia, which met once a month for "the mutual benefit which may be obtained by its members in intellectual culture," according to its bylaws. "We always stopped whatever noisy game we were playing when we saw the ladies beginning to assemble," she told Jane Howard in an interview for *Life* (June 1984). "We had great respect for them; they had a reputation for being very well educated, very full of ideas. They were an example to me."

Convinced that a college education—though unusual for women in that era—was essential if she were to become a writer, Helen Hooven Santmyer attended Wellesley College in Massachusetts, where she wrote poetry, belonged to a literary club called the Scribblers, and was one of ten graduating seniors in the class of 1918 elected to the yearbook's Hall of Fame. Staying on in Boston after receiving her B.A. degree, Miss Santmyer worked for a year for a radical suffragist group but found it not to her liking. "They considered a day lost when they hadn't succeeded in getting into jail," she explained to Jane Howard. "That's not my approach. My own approach is to *avoid* getting into jail."

Moving to New York in 1919, Helen Hooven Santmyer worked as a secretary to the editor of *Scribner's Magazine*, where she met such literary luminaries as Ernest Hemingway and F. Scott Fitzgerald. Her New York apartment, which she shared with a friend from Wellesley and their black housemaid from Xenia, was close enough to the Metropolitan Museum of Art to allow her to "dash in, whenever [she] had a spare fifteen minutes, to look at the Egyptian collection or whatever else [she] felt like seeing." But in spite of the attractions of the metropolis, she returned to Xenia at her father's bidding and taught English at the local high school in 1921-22. "My father told me that if I would come home for a year, he would pay my way for three years at Oxford University in England," she recalled in an interview with Paul Galloway for the *Chicago Tribune* (June 10, 1984). "I agreed. I would have never saved enough money otherwise." That promised trip was delayed two more years while Miss Santmyer taught as an assistant professor of literature at Wellesley, but in 1924 she began her studies at Oxford University.

After Oxford granted her a B.Litt. degree in 1927, she once again returned to Ohio. The following year she was elected to membership in the Women's Club of Xenia, on whose roster she has remained ever since. Like the other ladies of the club, she was required to deliver papers from time to time on such wide-ranging topics as "Religion South of the Sahara," "Lucretia Mott," "J. M. Synge and Lady Gregory," "Glimpses of Early Japan," and "Ohio Journalism."

In 1925, while she was studying at Oxford, Houghton-Mifflin published her first novel. *Herbs and Apples* tells the story of Derrick Thornton, a young midwestern girl with an ambition for independent achievement. Like Miss Santmyer herself, Derrick attends an Eastern college, is celebrated there for her writing talent, and then moves to New York where she is a moderately successful contributor to literary magazines. Although she claims to "loathe the idea of marriage," Derrick falls in love with and is betrothed to Jack Devlin, but he is killed in Europe while fighting in World War I. Finally—in a plot twist that foreshadowed Miss Santmyer's own future—she returns to her Ohio town, giving up her ambition for laurel leaves in exchange for the midwest's "herbs and apples."

*Herbs and Apples* was hospitably received. Voicing the critical consensus, a *New Republic* reviewer noted that "Miss Santmyer is lacking in the ability to sift her material so as to make it sustain her theme, and the narrative drags accordingly. Yet scattered through this oddly compounded book are passages of a breathtaking delicacy and poignancy of insight and power beyond cavil."

*The Fierce Dispute* (Houghton-Mifflin, 1929), her second novel, chronicles an intense battle of wills, waged between a child's mother and grandmother over her future. After her divorce from an unfaithful Italian musician named Paolo, Hilary Baird returns with their daughter, Lucy Anne, to her mother's fine old home in the midwest. Still in love with Paolo in spite of his infidelity, Hilary determines that Lucy Anne will follow in his footsteps by becoming a musician, but grandmother Baird so detests her former son-in-law that she is equally adamant that the child will not study music. Although the dispute ends only with the grandmother's death, in her last will and testament she acknowledges her capitulation. The book was greeted with only lukewarm praise from reviewers, who found the plot improbable and the relationships between characters artificial, but most critics were impressed by the delineation of young Lucy Anne. Helen Hooven Santmyer herself has characterized her two first novels as "youthful" and has confessed to Edwin McDowell in a *New York Times* interview (January 12, 1984) that she "would just as soon forget them."

In the early 1930s, Helen Hooven Santmyer moved with her parents to Orange County, California, where her father managed the R. A. Kelly rope factory, but the family returned to Xenia five years later when he retired. In 1936 she accepted a position as dean of women at Cedarville College, a small Presbyterian school only eight miles from Xenia. She stayed at Cedarville for seventeen years, eventually becoming head of its English department. When the college was taken over by fundamentalist Baptists, she left Cedarville to become a reference librarian at the Dayton (Ohio) and Montgomery County Public Library, where she remained until she retired in 1960.

During her career as an educator and librarian, Helen Hooven Santmyer had continued to write in her spare time, but only after her retirement could she indulge the luxury of devoting her full time to literary pursuits. She had long been interested in the history of Xenia and its landmarks, and one of her articles on the town, "Cemetery: A Reminiscence," had been published in the *Antioch Review* (Spring 1956) before her retirement. A second, "There Were Fences," appeared in the *Antioch Review's* Spring 1961 issue. Continuing to mine that lode, she wrote eleven more historical essays, and in 1962 the Ohio State University Press, in Columbus, published all thirteen as *Ohio Town: A Portrait of Xenia.*

With thoroughly researched and lovingly recalled detail, she evoked such historic landmarks as the courthouse square, the Opera House where traveling troupes once performed, and the imposing Presbyterian church she attended as a child. Using those sites as opportunities for retailing autobiographical anecdotes and stories about some of Xenia's citizenry, both living and dead, she effectively conveyed the quintessence of small-town life. Although the book received little national attention, *Ohio Town* was extravagantly praised in her home state and won the 1963 Ohioana Book Award.

Turning once again to fiction, in the mid-1960s Helen Hooven Santmyer began what many consider to be her *magnum opus*: a quasi-historical narrative about a small-town women's club, modeled after the Women's Club of Xenia, and its members. Finally completing it in 1975, she shipped the longhand manuscript in eleven boxes to Weldon A. Kefauver, the director of the Ohio State University Press, to whom she "felt under obligation" because of her satisfaction with his handling of *Ohio Town.* Although university presses rarely publish fiction, Kefauver persuaded the editorial board to accept the massive work for publication; however, when after six years the editing process was finally completed and 1,631 copies of the 1,344-page volume were issued in 1982, only about 300 copies were sold, primarily to libraries.

The enthusiasm of one reader, however, revived the flagging fortunes of *" . . . And Ladies of the Club."* Extolling its merits, Grace Sindell, a resident of the affluent Cleveland suburb of Shaker Heights, Ohio, persuaded her son Gerald, a director, writer, and producer in Hollywood, to read it. Convinced that the book would provide grist for a television miniseries, early in 1984 he flew to Ohio with the Los Angeles producer and former book publisher Stanley Corwin to negotiate with the Ohio State University Press for the world publication, television, and motion-picture rights to the novel, which they finally acquired in January 1985. G. P. Putnam's Sons then paid them $50,000 for the right to publish the book in a trade edition, and Berkley Books, in turn, purchased from Putnam's the paperback rights for $396,000. When the Book-of-the-Month Club paid $110,000 for the privilege of offering the novel as one of its main selections for the summer of 1984, the sale was reported on the front page of the January 12, 1984 edition of the *New York Times.* Even before its official republication by Putnam's on June 25, 1984, *" . . . And Ladies of the Club"* was ranked number two on the *New York Times* best-seller list, instantly making its octogenarian author a celebrity.

Structured by the device of the fortnightly meetings of the local women's club, the monumental, minutely detailed novel chronicles the day-to-day occurrences that shape the lives of several families in the fictional town of Waynesboro, Ohio (a thinly veiled version of Xenia) from the founding of the club in 1868 to the election of Franklin Delano Roosevelt as president in 1932. (When one interviewer asked Miss Santmyer why she ended her novel with the beginning of the Roosevelt administration, she snapped, "What I thought of the New

Deal wasn't fit to print.") Its two central characters, both charter members of the women's club, are Anne Gordon, the wife of the town's physician, John Gordon, whose efforts to endure her husband's infidelities and recover from the tragedies that befall their two children turn her into a kind of stoical heroine by the end of the book; and Sally Rausch, whose energetic German husband, Ludwig, becomes the proprietor of a rope factory, a leading industrialist, and a power broker in the Republican party. Interwoven with their life stories and those of their neighbors and kin are such important events in American history as the assassinations of Presidents Garfield and McKinley (both Ohio Republicans), the introduction of electricity, the telephone, and the automobile, the Crédit Mobilier affair, the Spanish-American War, and World War I.

" . . . And Ladies of the Club" was widely billed as a retort to Sinclair Lewis' derogatory portrait of Middle America in Main Street. It was also commonly reported to have been in work since the 1920s, when Main Street was first published. Miss Santmyer denies both rumors, though she admittedly regards Lewis' book as "prejudiced and unfair" and even has a character in her novel who "seethed" when she thought about the defamation of small-town life in Main Street. "Lewis wrote his version and I wrote mine," she said in an interview for Newsweek (June 18, 1984). She also made it clear that while she had been planning such a novel for most of her life, she did not actually begin to write " . . . And Ladies of the Club" until she was seventy.

In spite of all its prepublication fanfare and impressive advance sales, the book failed to impress most critics. While applauding her scrupulous attention to detail in describing period costumes and architecture, her grasp of history, and her discretion in dealing with the characters' intimate lives, many critics complained that the prose was labored, the narrative dull. Other reviewers, equating the viewpoint developed in the novel with that of the author, objected to Helen Hooven Santmyer's infatuation with her upper-middle-class, white, Republican, and Protestant characters, and found her heroes small-minded, self-absorbed, even bigoted.

Writing in the conservative National Review (October 5, 1984), Francis X. Marnell joined a minority of critics in praising the novel as an admirable "domestic history" and as an interesting sociological study, but in a more representative review, Susan Brownmiller asserted in the Chicago Tribune's Bookworld (June 10, 1984) that " . . . And Ladies of the Club" is "the sometimes inspired, sometimes embarrassing, uneven work of a writer with flashes of talent who labored in a vacuum and lost her perspective, most likely because she cared too much about Waynesboro's lost world to grasp the destructiveness of its dreadful limitations."

Nevertheless, its chilly critical reaction did not dim the popularity of " . . . And Ladies of the Club": by the third week after publication, it had climbed to the number-one spot on the New York Times best-seller list, and over 200,000 copies were in print by mid-July. Having bought the rights to Ohio Town from the Ohio State University Press for $25,000, Harper and Row capitalized on the success of " . . . And Ladies of the Club" by reissuing Ohio Town in August 1984 and Herbs and Apples in October 1985. A new edition of The Fierce Dispute, a serialization of " . . . And Ladies of the Club" in Family Circle magazine, and a TV miniseries of that novel were also in the works. For her accomplishments, she received in 1985 an honorary doctorate in the humanities from Wright University and the Governor's Award for Literature.

Helen Hooven Santmyer lives today in a nursing home, confined to a wheelchair because of arthritis. Although she suffers from emphysema, she is a chainsmoker of Chesterfields. She is blind in one eye and has a cataract in the other. Her closest friend, Mildred Sandoe, who for many years shared her home in Xenia and traveled with her to Canada and Mexico, now lives in the opposite wing of the nursing home. Despite her poor health, strained by the stress of instant celebrity, and her pride in her accomplishments, Miss Santmyer retains a firm hold on her perspective and common sense. "Ninety percent of the hoopla," she sniffed to Jane Briggs-Bunting in an interview for People (July 16, 1984), "is because I'm such an old lady."

References: Chicago Tribune II p1+ Je 10 '84 por; Life 7:31+ Je '84 pors; N Y Times A p1+ Ja 12 '84 por; Newsweek 103:93 Je 18 '84 por; People 22:75+ Jl 16 '84 pors; Contemporary Authors 1st rev vol 4 (1967)

## Sawyer, Diane

Dec. 22, 1945- Broadcast journalist. Address: b. CBS News, 524 W. 57th St., New York City, N.Y. 10019

In 1984, just six years after joining the Washington bureau of CBS News in the relatively lowly position of general assignment reporter, Diane Sawyer was named coeditor of the slickly produced, multi-Emmy-winning 60 Minutes, the prime-time news magazine that has consistently ranked among the top five television programs in the country for more than a decade. Miss Sawyer, 60 Minutes' first woman correspondent, brought to her new job journalistic skills acquired during an early stint at an understaffed local television station and, later, as coanchor of CBS's national morning news broadcast, an unsurpassed knowledge of politics learned during her eight years as a staff assistant to former President Richard Nixon, and what a writer for Newsweek magazine called a "special blend of the cerebral and the glamorous." With her low-key, businesslike delivery and warm, gracious manner, she manages to be at once authoritative

*Diane Sawyer*

Miss Sawyer capped her high-school career by winning, in her senior year, first place in the annual national Junior Miss contest, largely on the strength of her poise in the final interview and her thoughtful essay comparing the music of the North and the South during the Civil War. Winning the Junior Miss title was, in her words, "a frightening experience," but as she told Jamie Loughridge for *Harper's Bazaar* (November 1984), "there was education in the terror," for as she travelled around the country making public appearances she learned to think on her feet and to speak extemporaneously "without panicking."

Upon her high-school graduation in 1963, Miss Sawyer enrolled at Wellesley College in Wellesley, Massachusetts on a scholarship. An excellent student, she maintained a high grade-point average despite a heavy extracurricular schedule that included singing with the Wellesley Blue Notes, acting in campus theatrical productions, and serving as vice-president of the student body. After receiving her B.A. degree in English in 1967, Miss Sawyer returned to Louisville and talked her way into a job as a "weather girl" and part-time reporter for WLKY-TV, the local ABC affiliate. Thinking that her lack of meteorological expertise made her weather reports "extraordinarily boring," she attempted to enliven them by quoting from appropriate poems.

Miss Sawyer's initiative and her composed on-the-air performance soon earned her a promotion to full-time correspondent. Often serving as her own one-woman field crew at the small non-union station, she covered a variety of stories. To obtain a long sought-after interview with Supreme Court Justice William O. Douglas, she once shouldered a television camera and sound equipment and accompanied him on a five-mile hike along a perilous stretch of Kentucky's Red River Gorge. As an "antidote" to her work, in her off-hours she took courses at the University of Louisville's law school.

Feeling at the time "sort of nonspecifically undernourished," as she put it, Miss Sawyer left Louisville in 1970 and moved to Washington, D.C. in search of "an intellectual vitamin." Unable to find work as a broadcast journalist, she made the rounds of the government offices and eventually landed a job as an assistant to Jerry Warren, the White House deputy press secretary. First assigned to write press releases, she quickly graduated to more demanding tasks, including drafting some of President Richard Nixon's public statements. After a few months, she was promoted to administrative assistant to White House press secretary Ron Ziegler and, eventually, to staff assistant to the president. Her choice of a White House job "was not ideological," as she insisted to Tony Schwartz of the *New York Times* (September 30, 1981). "I was catholic in my politics. I had also interviewed on Capitol Hill, and if someone like George McGovern had offered me a job, I'd almost certainly have taken it." But as the weeks passed, she developed an intense loyalty to the Nixon administration, particularly to the president himself. "You

and appealing. Although Miss Sawyer has turned out over the years a number of penetrating, issue-oriented investigative pieces, it is as an interviewer that she has made her mark. Eschewing the confrontational interviewing techniques favored by many of her professional colleagues, she believes in being "smart" rather than "tough." "I think you really have to use your instincts," she said recently. "Interviewing is about using good instincts, about listening and curiosity."

The younger of the two children of E. P. and Jean W. (Dunagan) Sawyer, Diane Sawyer was born in Glasgow, Kentucky on December 22, 1945. Her father was a county judge and an amateur composer of country music; her mother taught elementary school. Not long after their second daughter's birth, the Sawyers moved to nearby Louisville, where Diane attended the public schools. "Madly extracurricular," she took "every imaginable lesson on earth," ranging from ballet, tap, piano, and voice to horseback riding and fencing.

At Seneca High School, Diane Sawyer served as an editor in chief of the campus newspaper, the *Arrow,* and participated in many artistic activities. Growing up in the shadow of her talented older sister, Linda, she was insecure, doubt-riddled, and "boringly serious." "Part of me longed to be like the other girls, to wisecrack, flirt, and ride in open cars, screaming with pleasure," she recalled to Patricia Bosworth, who interviewed her for the *Ladies' Home Journal* (February 1985). "But part of me wanted nothing to do with it, and I was something of a loner instead. I was just happy going off by myself or with my group of friends. We called ourselves 'reincarnated transcendentalists' and spent our time reading Emerson and Thoreau down by what I'm sure was a terribly polluted creek."

can't work in that kind of crucible and not become attached to the people," she explained to Schwartz. "You see the goals, the good goals people are working toward. There were a lot of people there I liked and [policy] initiatives I admired."

As the Watergate scandal unravelled from mid-1972 to mid-1974, an increasingly "tormented," to use her word, Diane Sawyer put in sixteen-hour days in the White House press office monitoring media coverage of the affair. According to some veteran Washington reporters, she occasionally attempted to dissuade them from publishing or broadcasting potentially damaging information. "She was a total nonsource, close to the cuff," Dan Rather, then CBS News's chief White House correspondent, told Tony Schwartz. "But she was very competent about her job, and if you needed a statistic or a spelling at the last minute, she was always the one you went to."

When President Nixon resigned on August 9, 1974, Diane Sawyer was among those staff members asked to accompany him to his political exile at the former "California White House" in San Clemente. She accepted without hesitation, "out of a sense of what was honorable," as she put it. "It was a human consideration," she said several years later, as quoted in *Broadcasting* (November 22, 1982) magazine. "Here was a man whose dreams were shattered. If I didn't come through for him at a time when he needed me, I couldn't have lived with myself." Having intended to stay only long enough to organize her voluminous Watergate files, Miss Sawyer remained instead for four years, first as a member of the team assigned to facilitate the transition from Nixon's administration to that of the new president, Gerald R. Ford, then as a research assistant to the former chief executive, who was writing his memoirs. As she told Tony Schwartz, during the three years she spent working closely with Nixon on his autobiography *RN*, she "learned a great deal about self-discipline and self-renewal" and "came to appreciate the way in which experience hones perception."

Upon her return to the nation's capital in mid-1978, Diane Sawyer signed on with the Washington bureau of CBS News as a general assignment reporter. Impressed by her articulateness and intelligence, William Small, then a senior vice-president in the news division at CBS, hired the relatively inexperienced broadcast journalist over the strong objections of some of CBS's most respected senior correspondents, including Dan Rather and Robert Pierpoint, who contended that she had "no credibility," to use Rather's words, as a reporter because of her years on the White House staff. Aware of her colleagues' apprehension, Miss Sawyer gradually won them over with her cheerful willingness to work weekends and holidays, her uncomplaining acceptance of "drudgery" assignments, such as prolonged stakeouts, and most important, her clear, concise, objective reporting.

Miss Sawyer's on-the-scene coverage of the accident at the Three Mile Island nuclear-power facility in eastern Pennsylvania in 1979 earned her a promotion to correspondent in February 1980. Six months later, she joined Robert Pierpoint on the State Department beat, where, up against such old hands as NBC's Marvin Kalb and ABC's Barrie Dunsmore, she found her familiarity with governmental bureaucracy invaluable in developing a network of reliable sources. Among the stories she covered at the State Department were the efforts to free the American hostages being held by Islamic extremists at the United States Embassy in Teheran, Iran, the controversial role assumed by Secretary of State Alexander M. Haig immediately following the attempted assassination of President Ronald Reagan, the Soviet military buildup along the Polish border late in 1981, and President Reagan's decision to make El Salvador a test case of his tough new foreign policy in Latin America. In addition to supplying regular reports to the network's morning and evening newscasts, Miss Sawyer frequently appeared on *CBS News Sunday Morning*, the network's ninety-minute magazine, and occasionally anchored its mid-evening *Newsbreak*.

During the Iranian hostage crisis, Miss Sawyer was a fixture on the weekday broadcasts of *Morning With Charles Kuralt*, and after giving her reports, she often discussed them extemporaneously with Kuralt. Their off-the-cuff conversations, liberally laced with historical references and literary allusions, were considered by many television critics to be a welcome contrast to the superficiality and arch badinage that had become characteristic of broadcast journalism. When CBS decided early in 1981 to expand its morning news show from sixty to ninety minutes, Kuralt and Robert Northshield, his senior executive producer, lobbied network news executives, who were searching for someone to coanchor the broadcast, in Diane Sawyer's behalf. They argued that her sensibility, personal warmth, and considerable journalistic talent perfectly suited the tone of the program, which had always relied on the reporting and writing skills of its correspondents rather than on homey sets and electronic wizardry. The top brass apparently agreed, for on May 13, 1981, William Leonard, then the president of CBS News, announced that Miss Sawyer had been chosen to coanchor the program, which was rechristened *Morning With Charles Kuralt and Diane Sawyer*.

Within weeks of her debut in the coanchor spot, on September 28, 1981, Miss Sawyer had put her own stamp on the broadcast. Refusing to be restricted to the soft features traditionally associated with women correspondents, she contributed on-the-scene coverage of fastbreaking stories, developed special pieces on a variety of subjects, ranging from domestic politics to profiles of such disparate individuals as the writer Eudora Welty and the international soccer star Pele, and conducted hard-hitting interviews with such policy makers as James A. Baker, then the White House chief of staff, Dean Hinton, the United States ambassador to El Salvador, and perhaps most notably, former President Nixon, on the tenth anniversary of the Watergate break-in. "To me, the reading of the news is the thing that least defines what I consider my mission to be in the morning," she told Morgan Strong of *USA Today* (May 4, 1985). "My mission is to try to take that kinetic, uncontrollable, unpredictable encounter that is the live interview and make it both probing and persevering and penetrating and engaging for the person who is doing it, for myself, and, therefore, for the person who is watching."

Perennially last in the early-morning ratings sweepstakes, behind ABC's chirpy *Good Morning, America* and NBC's durable *Today* show, CBS's entry finally began to gain some ground on its competitors. From March 1982, when Bill Kurtis succeeded Kuralt as Miss Sawyer's coanchorman, to March 1983, the show's ratings jumped some 30 percent, an increase most broadcast analysts attributed to Miss Sawyer's presence. But the gains were short-lived, and in mid-1984 CBS announced a major overhaul of the morning newscast and the reassignment of Diane Sawyer to the staff of *60 Minutes*. According to one *CBS Morning News* veteran, as quoted in *TV Guide* (October 20, 1984), Miss Sawyer lacked the "calm reassurance" and "nonthreatening quality" deemed necessary for the early-morning viewing hours. She was "just too radiant, too brilliant," he said, "and she didn't work for the show's good—no matter how hard she tried." She was, however, ideal for *60 Minutes*, whose executive producer, Don Hewitt, had long been looking for "a strong woman reporter."

Miss Sawyer officially joined the *60 Minutes* team, comprised of Mike Wallace, Harry Reasoner, Morley Safer, and Ed Bradley, in August 1984. She was to have been moved into rotation with those "tough old tigers," as she affectionately calls them, gradually, but because Wallace was involved in the lengthy trial of a libel suit brought against CBS News by General William Westmoreland she began contributing pieces to the show almost immediately. Her initial offering, broadcast in October 1984, was a profile of convicted murderer Velma Barfield, who would become the first woman to be executed in the United States in twenty-two years. At least partly because they took less time to prepare than in-depth investigative reports, she followed up by submitting interviews with, among others, Andreas Papandreou, the prime minister of Greece; the novelists William Kennedy and Saul Bellow; the stepchildren of Claus von Bulow, a socialite on trial for attempting to murder his heiress wife; and retired Admiral Hyman G. Rickover, the former head of the United States Navy's nuclear submarine program, who had not agreed to an interview for more than a quarter of a century.

In sharp contrast to her colleague Mike Wallace's abrasive and inquisitorial interviewing technique, Miss Sawyer, who sees interviews as "explorations of character," probes gently. "Within a single interview you and the subject may go through a whole range of reactions to each other," she told Lawrence Eisenberg for a *Good Housekeeping* (September 1985) profile, "but I re-ally don't go in with a strategy that says I'm going to beat up a little here and then smooth it over a little there." By her own account, her only "strategy" in interviewing is "to overcompensate." Convinced that preparation is "the soul of wit and brevity," she invariably reads "the extra book" and makes "the extra phone call." With her amiable and disarming manner, Miss Sawyer often catches her subjects off guard and elicits from them unusually revealing remarks. Before she was temporarily sidelined by hepatitis in the spring of 1985, she had filed nearly a dozen pieces for *60 Minutes*, including an exclusive interview with British Prime Minister Margaret Thatcher and—at the urging of Don Hewitt, who thought it was time for her to do what he called a "dirty-face Diane" story to counteract her elegant image—an on-location report on hunger in western Africa.

Over the course of her career with CBS News, Miss Sawyer has covered, in addition to her regular assignments, the nationl conventions of both the Republican and Democratic parties and the subsequent election campaigns in 1980 and 1984. In the closing weeks of the 1984 election campaign, the League of Women Voters sponsored a series of nationally televised debates between Ronald Reagan, the Republican incumbent, and Walter F. Mondale, the Democratic challenger. Miss Sawyer was one of only three journalists, out of the eighty-three suggested by the League as possible questioners, to be acceptable to both candidates. She has also occasionally contributed pieces to *Walter Cronkite's Universe*, the network's irregularly scheduled science magazine, and to *American Parade*. Recognizing the unique quality of her work, the New York chapter of Women in Communications named her one of the six winners of its 1984 Matrix Award.

Diane Sawyer, who stands slightly more than five feet nine inches tall, has shoulder-length, honey blonde hair and large, laughing eyes that have been described as being "sapphire" in color. Despite her unquestionable attractiveness, she has admitted to having "a fundamental belief in the inadequacy" of her looks. "It probably goes back to my sister, who was always so lean and elegant and lovely," she explained to an interviewer for *Newsweek* (March 14, 1983). "I always saw things that bulged, like baby-fat cheeks and a pug nose." To maintain her trim figure and keep her energy level high, she exercises on the rowing machine she keeps in her apartment on Manhattan's Upper East Side, swims and jogs at a neighborhood health club, and plays tennis on weekends.

Admittedly "addicted" to her job, Miss Sawyer seems to thrive on her hectic schedule, although she occasionally worries that it will "take over" her life. To unwind, she goes to the movies (she has been known to see as many as three in a day) or reads. A self-described "dreary believer in self-improvement," she devours books on a wide variety of subjects. Her taste in literature is similarly eclectic, but she has a special fondness for late nineteenth-century fiction, especially the novels of

Henry James, whom she admires for his depiction of women who "are never careless about their lives." At any given time, she has, by her own count, "two or three books going," but only rarely is that number likely to include the latest best seller. "They seem like an indulgence when you haven't done justice to George Eliot," she once explained.

References: Broadcasting 103:37+ N 22 '81 por; Harpers Bazaar 118:232+ N '84 por; Ladies Home J 102:28+ F '85 por; N Y Daily News p77 N 25 '81 por; N Y Daily News Leisure p1+ F 2 '83 pors; N Y Times C p23 S 30 '81 por, C p20 O 22 '84 por; Newsweek 101:74+ Mr 14 '83 pors; TV Guide 29:17+ F 28 '81 por; Who's Who in America, 1984-85

## Scargill, Arthur

Jan. 11, 1938– British labor union leader.
Address: b. National Union of Mineworkers, 2 Huddersfield Rd., Barnsley, Yorkshire, England

One of the most controversial personalities in Great Britain is Arthur Scargill, the fiery Marxist president of the 185,000-member National Union of Mineworkers (NUM), a post he took over from the moderate Joseph Gormley in 1982. Under his leadership, the NUM was embroiled for a year beginning March 1984 in the longest and most violent strike in British post-World War II history. The son and grandson of Yorkshire coal miners, Scargill spent seventeen years in the pits before becoming a full-time union official. He first came to national prominence in the coal strike of 1972 and played

a key role in the 1974 strike, which resulted in the downfall of Conservative Prime Minister Edward Heath. In the recent strike, Scargill was pitted against the Conservative government of Margaret Thatcher, and observers agreed that the stakes were high in what seemed to be a battle to the death between "King Arthur" and the "Iron Lady."

Arthur Scargill was born in Barnsley, Yorkshire on January 11, 1938, into a household in which mining and radicalism were family traditions. Except for World War II service in the Royal Air Force, his father, Harold Scargill, worked most of his life in the coal pits. A member of the Communist party, he taught his son that "your life depends on your power to master words" and introduced him to the Daily Worker and to such radical works of fiction as Jack London's The Iron Heel and Robert Tressell's The Ragged Trousered Philanthropists.

Although Scargill's family was poor, as were most miners in those days, he had a moderately comfortable childhood. When he was three, the Scargills moved from their basic two-room miners' cottage to a simple but modern crescent home. Scargill's mother, Alice, who died when he was seventeen, openly spoiled her only child, who grew up to be a self-assured, even "cocky" schoolboy with a loyal following at the Worsborough Dale School. But after failing his eleven-plus exams, he had to face the inevitable fate of the working-class boy and get a job. So, against his mother's wishes, Arthur Scargill became a miner at the age of fifteen.

"I thought I'd been put into hell," Scargill recalled of his first day of work at the Woolley Colliery, with its noise and dust and its "Captain Bligh" of an overseer. "It left an indelible mark on me," he told Bernard D. Nossiter of the Washington Post (February 1, 1974). But young Arthur Scargill was not long intimidated; he soon began to agitate in behalf of his fellow apprentices for better working conditions. At eighteen he led his first strike against his own union to compel the local branch to have its meetings on weekends, when he and other apprentices could attend. Coal-board officials soon recognized Scargill as a troublemaker and put him on the night shift for two-and-a-half years to keep him "away from the lads," he told Michael Parkin, as quoted in the Manchester Guardian Weekly (December 18, 1977).

Scargill's militancy found other avenues of expression as well. Having written to the Labour party about becoming a member and receiving no reply, he wrote to the Communists, who sent around a comrade named David Larder. Tremendously impressed by Larder, the seventeen-year-old Scargill joined the Young Communist League because, in his words, he "wanted to put the world right—which wasn't a bad idea."

Scargill flourished in that militant and highly disciplined organization, soon winning a place on its national executive committee. In 1957 the party sent him to Moscow as a delegate to the World Youth Festival, where he met Nikita S. Khrushchev and other Soviet leaders. But Scargill left the Communist party in 1961, because he felt that its discipline conflicted with his union duties. Explaining the break to the *Guardian* interviewer, Scargill said, "I have always argued—and I think my record proves it—that my first consideration was my trade union, to the exclusion of all else." In 1963 he became a member of the Cooperative party, and eventually he followed his father into the Labour party. He also became active in the Campaign for Nuclear Disarmament.

While still a member of the Communist party, Scargill made one brief foray into electoral politics, standing at the age of twenty-two as its candidate in a local council election. But he received only 12.8 percent of the vote, against the Labour candidate's 87.2 percent. After that, he confined his efforts to union politics, where his growing reputation as a shrewd, articulate union man brought better results. Realizing that he needed more education to play an effective leadership role, Scargill began, at twenty-three, a three-year course in history, economics, and industrial relations at nearby Leeds University, financed by the union and the National Coal Board. At twenty-six he became his local branch's representative to the area meetings of the NUM, a position that thrust him into the thick of Yorkshire mining politics.

National prominence came to Scargill in the coal strikes of 1972 and 1974. To combat inflation, Conservative Prime Minister Edward Heath tried to enforce a strict limit on wage increases, but his plans were thwarted by a growing militancy among the young miners, who after a decade of relative acquiescence were determined to fight for better pay. During the strike of January and February of 1972, Scargill, who served as regional spokesman of the strike committee, gained fame as the organizer of the "flying pickets," squads of hundreds of miners who would mass unexpectedly to close down mines and coal-storage depots. During the 1972 strike there occurred what Scargill described in a *Washington Post* interview (February 1, 1974) as "the most glamorous moment in the history of the trade union movement"—the closing of the Saltley coke depot in Birmingham by some 20,000 union men with Arthur Scargill at their head. Virtually overnight, the young Yorkshire miner became a folk hero to the nation's miners.

Scargill's role in the 1972 strike brought him rapid advancement within the Yorkshire union organization. In the same year he obtained his first full-time post above ground, that of compensation agent, with responsibility for advancing benefit claims in behalf of the mine workers. Then, in 1973, following the death of the president of the Yorkshire area union organization, Scargill was elected to replace him, obtaining some 30,000 votes against about 6,000 received by each of his two conservative opponents. At thirty-five he became the youngest man ever to lead a regional union in Great Britain, assuming the lifetime presidency of the elite of British coal miners, who themselves were widely considered to be the "aristocracy" of the nation's working class.

As head of the powerful Yorkshire miners' union, Scargill refurbished the antiquated union offices and addressed himself to such matters as the investigation of the Lofthouse colliery incident that resulted in seven deaths in 1973. In the miners' strike of early 1974, which helped to bring down the government of Edward Heath, Scargill played an important role. Faced with the miners' demands for wage increases, the Prime Minister called for an election on the issue and lost. During the last weeks of Heath's government, Scargill met with him to point out that as a result of an anomaly dating from the nationalization of the coal industry in 1947, the miners' wages had been calculated in a way that made them appear to be better paid in comparison to other industrial workers than they actually were. Heath refused to accept the argument, although the government pay board later did so. With customary flamboyance, Scargill told Terry Coleman, as quoted in the *Manchester Guardian Weekly* (December 20, 1981), "The irony of the whole thing is that Heath could still have been Prime Minister had he only accepted that argument."

With the victory over Heath behind them, the miners experienced relatively good times in the mid-1970s under Labour Prime Minister Harold Wilson, partly as a result of a sharp rise in oil prices that made coal a more attractive fuel. But a recession in the late 1970s put an end to the coal boom and brought serious financial problems to the industry. Elected in May 1979 on a platform opposing union demands and stressing a free-market economy, Conservative Prime Minister Margaret Thatcher was determined to make the British coal industry more efficient, with or without the cooperation of the NUM. To meet the challenge of Mrs. Thatcher's policies, the miners needed strong leadership. When Joseph Gormley, the moderate president of the NUM, stepped down in December 1981, they elected Arthur Scargill to take his place, with a solid 70 percent majority, over three moderate candidates.

Taking office as president of the NUM in early 1982, Scargill moved its headquarters from London to Sheffield, Yorkshire, his power base. He suffered a setback when in January some 55 percent of the voting NUM members chose to accept a 9.3 percent pay-increase offer rather than hold out for 24 percent, as Scargill wished to do. The recommendation of outgoing president Gormley that the miners accept the offer was described by Scargill as "an unparalleled act of betrayal," but a motion to censure Gormley was defeated at a union executive meeting by one vote. In November 1982 and again in March 1983, Scargill failed to obtain the 55 percent of the union vote necessary for his demand for a national coal strike in response to the Thatcher government's policies.

Then, in the fall of 1983, Mrs. Thatcher appointed Ian MacGregor, a Scottish-born American businessman, to head the National Coal Board. Having just finished rehabilitating the British Steel Corporation, at the cost of some 95,000 jobs, MacGregor was determineed to close the unprofitable coal pits whose upkeep was making British coal so expensive. In early March 1984, MacGregor announced plans to close twenty pits and lay off some 20,000 miners. One of the mines to be closed was Cortonwood, in Yorkshire, where a group of miners had been resettled from a previously closed pit with the promise they would never be transferred again.

With the threatened Cortonwood closing, MacGregor had finally given Scargill the spark he needed to ignite a miners' strike. This time, the union leader bypassed the rulebook and did not call for a national strike vote, but instead called the men out district by district. Beginning on March 12, 1984, mines across Britain began to close. Ultimately over two-thirds shut down, and some 80 percent of the NUM's 185,000 members went on strike.

From the beginning, the strike was unusually bitter and violent. Many miners, especially those in the profitable pits where wages were comparatively high, simply did not strike. An estimated 40,000 to 50,000 men, primarily in Nottinghamshire, remained at work. Elsewhere, miners were prevented from working by "flying pickets" and even intimidated in their own homes. Night after night throughout the summer of 1984, the news media kept the public informed of violent clashes between police and strikers, with barricades of burning cars in the background. As of mid-August, almost 5,500 men had been arrested, 591 people had been injured, and two miners had been killed. Scargill himself was briefly placed under arrest near Sheffield in May, on charges of obstructing a highway.

During the course of the strike, Scargill became in the eyes of many a national "bogeyman," accused of trying to destroy British political traditions of democracy and fair play. Some observers feared that as a result of the violence, Great Britain was turning into a police state. "Thanks to Mr. Scargill's class war," an editorial in the *Economist* (March 24, 1984) observed, "the right to go where one pleases may have been damaged in the process." Prime Minister Thatcher characterized his tactics as an "attempt to substitute the rule of the mob for the rule of the law." For his part, Scargill has responded with equal vehemence. Speaking before the British Trade Union Congress at Brighton in September 1984, he referred to MacGregor as the "butcher of British industry" who was "out to destroy our pits, our jobs, our way of life, our future" and who "talks of quotas, and good management, and cost efficiency," but never "about human beings."

At the annual Labour party conference at Blackpool in October 1984 Scargill so dominated the proceedings that he was accused of virtually "hijacking" the party, and he seemed to provoke much popular opposition, even among members of the left. Anxious to steer his party on a less radical course, Labour party leader Neil Kinnock, though he supported the coal strike, condemned its violence and tried to keep his distance from Scargill. A national public-opinion poll taken at the time of

the Blackpool conference gave Labour an approval rating of only 35 percent as compared to 43 percent received by the Conservatives and 19 percent by the Liberal–Social Democratic coalition, a result attributed largely to the miners' strike. The trade union movement in general was lukewarm in its support of the NUM. Although there were brief slowdowns and strikes among printers, railwaymen, and dock workers, other key groups, such as the steelworkers, refused to support the miners in any tangible way.

Meanwhile, in October, as negotiations between the NUM and the National Coal Board appeared to be deadlocked, a British High Court judge declared the strike illegal in the absence of a national strike vote, and when Scargill ignored a subpoena to answer the charges, he and the NUM were fined for contempt of court. By late 1984 there seemed little hope for a resumption of negotiations, and material hardship forced thousands to return to the mines, but Scargill continued to command an impassioned following among the miners of a kind rarely seen in British politics. As Godfrey Hodgson pointed out in the *New York Times Magazine* (September 30, 1984), the strike had to be viewed against the background of "more than 100 years of radicalism and solidarity" in the pits. As 1984 drew to a close, Scargill's popularity appeared to be on the wane, and there were increasing defections from the NUM. A Gallup poll in November showed public opinion favoring the National Coal Board over the union by 53 to 26 percent.

Finally, on March 3, 1985, with over 52 percent of the miners already back on the job, the NUM, by a vote of ninety-eight to ninety-one of its delegates, ended the strike—the costliest in British history, with losses estimated at $3.2 billion. Some 85 percent of the miners returned to the pits, but those in Scotland and Kent remained out, pending amnesty for some 700 miners dismissed for various offenses, a demand rejected by the coal board. Although the NUM was totally defeated in its key demand—an end to government policy to close unprofitable mines—Scargill claimed that his union had won "the greatest battle of all" by "struggling against this government's policies." While castigating most of the trade union movement for its lack of solidarity with the miners, he declared that the "struggle would continue."

The badly divided NUM suffered a further setback in July 1985, when the miners of Nottinghamshire broke away to form a separate union. But Scargill won a personal victory at the NUM conference in Sheffield that month, when union rules were changed to enable him to remain president for life. His position was further enhanced when delegates at the Labour party conference at Blackpool in September approved his motion to require a future Labour government to reimburse the NUM for losses incurred during the strike, to reinstate dismissed miners, and to close down only those mines that were totally exhausted.

Once characterized by Michael Parkin in the *Manchester Guardian Weekly* (December 18,

1977) as engaging in a "terrier-like pursuit of what he sees as objective truth," Scargill finds Marxism to be a compelling political philosophy but opposes the repression practiced in some Communist countries. Although he admires Fidel Castro's Cuba, he finds much to dislike about the Soviet Union. "They can't tolerate criticism and how they can equate that with Marxism is beyond me," he once commented. He does, however, agree with the Soviet opposition to the Polish Solidarity movement, which he has described as "an anti-socialist organization aimed at toppling a socialist government," as quoted in the *Manchester Guardian Weekly* (October 23, 1983). In the fall of 1984 he and other NUM leaders came under fire for establishing a liaison with the Libyan dictator, Colonel Muammar el-Qaddafi, and with the Soviet government, with the hope of obtaining financial aid.

Although he is sometimes accused of using undemocratic means to achieve his goals, Scargill professes to believe in change by the ballot box. "You have to win power with accepted democratic standards," he told Bernard D. Nossiter of the *Washington Post*. Nevertheless, Scargill has repeatedly turned down opportunities to stand as a Labour candidate for Parliament. As John Mortimer observed in the *Sunday Times* (January 10, 1985), it would be difficult for a man such as Scargill to forsake the "reality of union rule for the pallid pretensions of Westminster." Aware of his unpopularity among many of his fellow citizens, Scargill told Mortimer, "When Christ was about to be crucified he couldn't even find a seconder, let alone anyone to vote for him."

Described to John Mortimer by associates as "funny, charming, ruthlessly ambitious and 'as English as Yorkshire pudding,'" Scargill is known as a powerful orator who packs the house wherever he speaks. A compulsive worker, he has been forced to take time off because of exhaustion, and he occasionally suffers from a nervous tic. Stocky and of medium build, he dresses fashionably and blow-dries his thinning red hair to disguise "a poorly accepted baldness." Described in the *Guardian Weekly* (October 23, 1983) as looking like "Pinocchio caught telling a whopper," Scargill has been much caricatured in the British press.

Arthur Scargill lives in a bungalow in Barnsley, the Yorkshire village where he was born, with his wife, Anne, their daughter Margaret, who is a student, and his father. The daughter of a union leader, Anne Scargill is his strongest supporter, and he once quipped that she would leave him if he ever changed his politics. Apart from his union activities, Scargill enjoys a quiet home life, exercising his Airedale terriers and watching football. A non-observant Christian who believes that Jesus was a socialist, he loves old churches and the hymns of Moody and Sankey. His musical favorites also include Basin Street blues and Tchaikovsky's "1812 Overture" played simultaneously by three brass bands.

References: *Guardian Weekly* 117:4 D 18 '77 por, 125:19 D 20 '81 por; *London Sunday Times* p17 Ja 10 '82 por, p8 Jl 15 '84 por; *N Y Times* A p2 F 6 '84 por; *Washington Post* A p19 F 1 '74 por; *International Who's Who*, 1985–86

## Scavullo, Francesco

Jan. 16, 1929– Photographer. Address: b. 212 E. 63rd St., New York City, N.Y. 10021

Since he shot his first cover for *Seventeen* magazine in 1948, the photographer Francesco Scavullo has devoted himself to recording high fashion, beauty, and celebrity for such diverse magazines as *Harper's Bazaar*, *Vogue*, *Town and Country*, *Cosmopolitan*, *Time*, *Newsweek*, *People*, *Good Housekeeping*, *Interview*, and *Playboy*. Called "the court painter of our time" by the *Washington Post*, Scavullo, a master of light, is perhaps best known for his idealized personal portraits.

Scavullo expressed his credo in an interview in the *Los Angeles Times* (November 28, 1976): "Somebody's got to come out for a view of life that is beautiful. I know there are times of unrest. But I also know there is beauty. There are sunsets. And there is love. And no one wants to look bad. I don't care if they are into looking dirty and protesting the Establishment. When a camera clicks, they want to look good. That's essentially what I do."

One of the five children of Angelo and Margaret (Pavis) Scavullo, Francesco Scavullo was born on January 16, 1929 in Staten Island, New York. In about 1937, Angelo Scavullo, who was in the catering and cooking-utensil business, moved with his family to an elegant townhouse in Manhattan, near the Central Park Casino, the swank supper club that he had recently purchased. An imaginative child, Francesco Scavullo was enthralled by his mother's anecdotes about the celebrities who dined there, and he enjoyed strolling along Fifth Avenue with her, admiring the gowns and jewels on the mannequins in the windows of the city's most exclusive shops. From his earliest days he had been entranced by the advertisements and photographs in his mother's fashion magazines. His innate visual sense was also fed by his frequent trips to the neighborhood movie theatres. As he recalled in his introduction to *Scavullo* (Harper & Row, 1984), he was "spellbound" by the luminous Greta Garbo in *Queen Christina*, the first motion picture he ever saw. "The camera almost choked me with this close-up of a woman called Garbo," he told Stephanie Mansfield in an interview for a *Washington Post* (January 8, 1985) profile. "Magic, it was for me. Images. Fantasy. . . . It was total escape into a world of imagination."

Eager to "capture something equally beautiful," as he expressed it, Scavullo borrowed his father's camera to take snapshots of his sisters playing on the beach, but the developed photographs invariably lacked "the magic" he was after. "I had no idea how to create the transformations I wanted to create," he explained in *Scavullo*. "I only knew that someday I'd learn how." When he was nine years old, he finally persuaded his mother to buy him a small Univex motion picture camera. Recruiting his friends to serve as actors and production assistants, he remade "bits and pieces" of his favorite films, including *Gone with the Wind*. "I lit the scenes with bridge lamps and flood lights, and we burned Atlanta by burning in the fireplace the little cardboard houses my mother used for Christmas decoration," he wrote in *Scavullo*. "We wrapped little Gigi [his nextdoor neighbor] up in draperies and I put birds of paradise I had found in my mother's drawer in her hair. I made her up with my mother's lipstick and eyeshadow, and I directed and shot scenes from every movie I had seen."

Applying the techniques he had used in his fledgling filmmaking efforts to his still photography, Scavullo soon began to pose, dress, and make up his two older sisters, often in the images of the movie actresses Dorothy Lamour and Vivien Leigh, for what he called "serious" pictures. He learned how to retouch prints in the darkroom, too. "I'd begun to do what I'd always wanted to do—transform faces into their most beautiful possibilities," he said years later. As the photographer recalled in his first book, *Scavullo on Beauty* (Random House, 1976): "It wasn't long before all my sisters' girlfriends lined up in front of my house, prom dresses over their arms, begging me to 'make them over.'" In the interview for the *Washington Post* profile, he admitted to Miss Mansfield that his skill with a camera had a beneficial effect on his personality: "When I was a kid, I was very self-conscious. I thought I was a very ugly little boy, and I only admired attractive people. . . . I didn't think I was bright. I didn't think I had a personality. I was very

quiet. I didn't speak. . . . The camera made me very bold."

By the time he was in high school, Scavullo had decided to become a fashion photographer, much to the disappointment of his father, who had hoped that his son would enter the restaurant management business. During one summer vacation, he took a part-time job as a general assistant in a small photographic studio in order to get professional experience. The studio specialized in taking snapshots of travelers about to board cruise ships. Scavullo found the assignment "boring," but it did give him the chance to snap his first celebrity, the Latin American singer and actress Carmen Miranda. Following his high-school graduation in 1945, Scavullo bypassed college to accept a position as an assistant at Becker's Studio, which put together fashion catalogs. A hard worker and "quick study," he picked up the tricks of the trade quickly, and after a few months began scouting around for a more interesting and responsible job. Tipped off about an opening at *Vogue* magazine by a co-worker, he arranged for an interview, and to his surprise and delight, was hired on the spot. During his three years on the staff of *Vogue*, he worked with such famous high-fashion photographers as Cecil Beaton and John Rawlings, but, most often, with Horst. As luck would have it, Horst's assistant abruptly resigned one day, and Scavullo was chosen as his replacement. He spent the next three years as Horst's apprentice, performing such tasks as adjusting the lights for a sitting and focusing the camera.

Eventually craving more independence, Scavullo agreed to help Jerry Plucer, an artist whose fashion sketches appeared regularly in *Harper's Bazaar*, to set up shop as a photographer. As he reported in *Scavullo*, he called on his jack-of-all-trades experience with Horst to redesign his friend's studio: "I had a big screen made, of unbleached muslin; I got spotlights and big drum floods. I did Plucer's sittings—lit them, put the film in, took the exposure, squeezed the rubber ball, and often stayed up all night developing and printing. . . . Everything was a new experience." Among those new experiences was the unforgettable day when Diana Vreeland, the fashion magazine editor, brought in a new model named Betty Bacall to shoot a blouse layout for *Harper's Bazaar*, and Scavullo took the very first picture of what became known as the "Look."

While working with Plucer, Scavullo met Eleanore Hillebrand, the fashion editor of *Seventeen*, a new magazine targeted for the adolescent market. In an interview arranged by Eleanore Hillebrand with the magazine's editorial staff, the photographer talked his way into shooting the cover for the next issue. To illustrate its theme, "Boy Meets Girl," Scavullo photographed two teenaged models dressed in yellow slickers and huddled under an umbrella through a sheet of glass that he had sprayed with water. "It looked as if they were walking to the movies on a rainy day," he said later. The cover was an immediate hit, and within a month the nineteen-year-old photographer was under contract. From 1948 through 1950, Scavullo traveled extensively for *Seventeen*, shooting fashion layouts in such exotic locations as Machu Picchu in Peru and the Australian outback. During those years, he usually did his models' makeup and hairstyles himself, and he often selected their clothes. In his view, he "sparked up the teenage look away from those terrible Vicki Vaughn dresses and those awful Toni permanents," but his preference for natural-looking hair and makeup nearly cost the magazine much-needed advertising revenue when some manufacturers of cosmetics and hair-care products threatened to cancel their lucrative accounts.

Within weeks of his signing the contract with *Seventeen* magazine, in 1948, the photographer opened Scavullo Studio in a converted carriage house on Manhattan's Upper East Side, where he continues to live and work. In addition to his regular assignments for *Seventeen*, from 1948 to 1950 Scavullo contributed covers and fashion spreads to the *Ladies' Home Journal, Good Housekeeping, Woman's Home Companion, Today's Woman,* and *Town and Country.* For the last-named magazine, he also photographed socialites and debutantes. He numbers two of the covers he took for *Town and Country*—Gloria Vanderbilt in a Pierrot collar and Countess Anna Camerana Bozza, "wearing nothing but jewelry," in his words—as among the best of his career. He finally broke into the pages of *Harper's Bazaar* in August 1955, with a dramatic layout of sophisticated designer gowns photographed in the trainyard of the New Haven Railroad.

During the 1950s, Scavullo developed and perfected the innovative lighting techniques for which his work is celebrated. To achieve a soft, natural daylight effect, he shaded his models from the direct glare of the spotlights with white umbrellas. He achieved the same effect on location by diffusing the light through muslin sheets sewn together and strung on bamboo poles like a canopy. If he wanted the light to pinpoint a model's face directly, he surrounded her, top and sides, with large pieces of cardboard known as "barn doors." On bright days, he used strips of black curtains at the studio windows to control the amount of light, sometimes highlighting a sitter's face with a single sunbeam.

By the mid-1960s, Scavullo felt that he knew how to work his "personal style," as he phrased it, into any assignment. In 1965, at the request of Helen Gurley Brown, the editor in chief of *Cosmopolitan,* he came up with an entirely new look for the magazine's cover—the seductive "Cosmo girl" covers—which were, as Scavullo pointed out, far "sexier" than those of other women's magazines. He has been designing them ever since. Sean M. Byrnes, the editor who began assisting Scavullo in 1972, explained the unusual arrangement in an interview for *Camera 35* magazine (October 1979). "Francesco and I have complete control. We pick the girls. We tell them what to wear. Everything is what we decide. Helen trusts our taste implicitly." Sensing Farrah Faw-

cett's potential when he photographed her for a Wella Balsam shampoo ad, Scavullo promptly chose her for his next *Cosmopolitan* cover. According to the photographer, that issue sold more copies than any other, and soon afterward the blonde actress was tapped to star in the television series *Charlie's Angels.* Scavullo was also responsible for posing and photographing *Cosmopolitan's* controversial nude male centerfolds. His shot of Burt Reynolds, the first of the centerfolds, in 1971, reportedly helped to revive the actor's stalled career.

It was at about that time that Scavullo began to offer his services as an image-maker to performers and other celebrities as well as to professional models. "It's like gathering moss," he remarked in an interview for the *Washington Post* (December 1, 1977). "The models liked what I did for them, and now I do personalities." After he glamorized recording star Helen Reddy, his office was flooded with requests for portraits. Among those who benefited from Scavullo's magic touch were broadcast journalist Barbara Walters, actress Elizabeth Taylor, Martha Mitchell, the wife of former United States Attorney General John Mitchell, whose astonishingly transformed face adorned the Christmas 1974 cover of *New York* magazine, and Barbra Streisand and Kris Kristofferson, in a romantic portrait that was used to advertise the pair's 1976 remake of the motion picture *A Star Is Born.* His "favorite sitting" of the hundreds of celebrities he has photographed over the years is Janis Joplin, the late whisky-voiced rock singer. "All the other photogs did was the regular shots of her running and jumping and straddling walls," Scavullo told Alan Cartnal of the *Los Angeles Times* (November 28, 1976). "She told me [Richard] Avedon made her feel like a pole-vaulter. Then I got her to sing. I got her to tell me her life. And she was beautiful."

Originally hired as a consultant to glamorize Margaux Hemingway for the motion picture *Lipstick* (Paramount, 1976), Scavullo wound up playing, in his words, a bit part "with a phony voice two octaves lower than usual and saying phony stuff like: 'Great, baby—give me that smile for the camera, baby.'" Scavullo's own technique for eliminating tension in the studio is a nonstop patter calculated to animate his subjects. "I don't want my pictures to look like Clairol ads . . . [or] Ultima II atrocities," he told Alan Cartnal. "These are people. And when you engage them—find out about them—tell them they're beautiful—suddenly you see the life in them." Scavullo reportedly turns down any prospective client he "can't relate to."

Scavullo begins a photographic session by taking a series of preliminary Polaroid shots. Then, after trying to make his sitter as relaxed and comfortable as possible, he takes several dozen exposures "by eye," as he once put it. "Something reminds me," he told one interviewer. "Maybe there's a computer in me. . . . Pictures remain in my mind from museums, from everything." Because of the time that has to be allotted to makeup and hairstyling, he often devotes an entire afternoon to shooting a portrait of a woman. In contrast, a man's sitting usually lasts about forty minutes. "There's no illusion" with men, Scavullo has explained, as quoted in the *Los Angeles Times* (December 4, 1977). "You're going to get what's there." On the average, he photographs ten subjects each week. His fee is reportedly $10,000 per sitting.

The "Scavullo-ization" process, as it has been called, is spelled out in detail in the photographer's books *Scavullo Women* (Harper & Row, 1982), a guide to makeovers, with "before" and "after" photographs, that he wrote with Sean M. Byrnes, and the best-selling *Scavullo on Beauty*. *Scavullo on Beauty* contains, in addition to striking black-and-white photographs of fifty-nine of Scavullo's "favorite women," frank dialogues between the photographer and his subjects, who in the course of the conversations reveal their psyches and life-styles as well as their beauty routines. Although most of the women, among them Mary Tyler Moore, Barbra Streisand, Lauren Hutton, and Bette Midler, are internationally famous, Scavullo maintains that his purpose in writing the book was "to show you [the average woman] how you can start to bring out the best in yourself." In his opinion, "every woman is glamorous and desirable—if she would only believe it," for "beauty includes your outlook, your optimism about life, your enthusiasm, your intelligence, and so on, every bit as much as what you do with your physical features."

After leafing through *Scavullo on Beauty*, Blair Sabol, a writer for the *Village Voice* who had herself undergone the "Scavullo treatment" in preparation for a portrait sitting, wrote, as quoted in *Newsweek* (November 22, 1976), "You get the feeling that everyone lives on diets of tea with honey and a single bean sprout per day, baths of scented Evian water, inherited good skin and teeth, summer homes in Montauk . . . and a great admiration for Diana Vreeland or Liz Taylor." As for her own Scavullo makeover, Miss Sabol reported, "Not only did it have nothing to do with the normal me. It had nothing to do with my own fantasy of me."

For the companion volume, *Scavullo on Men* (Random House, 1977), which he wrote in collaboration with Bob Colacello, the photographer focused his Nikon 35-mm camera lens on fifty "men of achievement," including Milos Forman, the Academy Award–winning motion picture director, actor Alan Bates, the novelist and political commentator William F. Buckley Jr., Arthur Ashe, the former world-class tennis player, playwright Arthur Miller, architect Philip Johnson, cancer researcher Dr. William Cahan, and Harry Reasoner, the veteran broadcast journalist, who agreed to be photographed only after his colleague Barbara Walters assured him that Scavullo didn't have "a cruel lens." In addition to the photographs and candid discussions of grooming, diet, and attitudes toward sex and death, the book offers biographical sketches of Scavullo's subjects and descriptions of their careers. A selection of Scavullo's portraits of men is housed in the permanent photography collection of the Metropolitan Museum of Art in New York City.

At the request of Mikhail Baryshnikov, the artistic director of the American Ballet Theatre, Scavullo took portraits and suspended-in-motion photographs of the company's principal dancers for its 1981 souvenir program. An exhibition of those photographs, funded by Hasselblad, the camera manufacturer, ran for several weeks at the Andrew Crispo Gallery in New York City and later traveled around the United States. A few of the photographs are also included in *Scavullo* (Harper & Row, 1984), a retrospective compilation of more than 200 of the photographer's favorite pictures, many of them previously unpublished. Scavullo has described that coffee-table book as "kind of like a social document" of the years 1948 through 1984. Perhaps to underscore the country's changing attitudes toward morality, he chose to open the book with a picture, taken in 1948, of a demure little girl in a frilly party dress and to close it with the seductive portrait of a five-year-old model, made up to look like a sexy, older woman, which he had taken for a lavish *Harper's Bazaar* layout featuring several expensive perfumes. At the time of its publication in December 1983, the spread's headline—"Tiny Treasures: Fabulous Christmas Fantasies"—raised the hackles of some media critics. But as Scavullo insisted in a conversation with Jeanine Stein for the *Los Angeles Herald Examiner* (October 22, 1984), he was not exploiting the child's sexuality: "There *is* a sexuality about her. And why not? She's been looking at the tube since she could see. I'm only trying to show what *we* are doing to the children, not what *I* am doing to them."

To coincide with the publication of his most recent book, Scavullo funded major exhibits of his work at the Light Gallery in New York and at the G. Ray Hawkins Gallery in Los Angeles. The photographer's celebrities often looked "unpleasantly exhibitionistic" to the *New York Times*'s Gene Thornton. "Scavullo seems to have created out of public figures a flamboyant world of his own imagination," Thornton concluded in his review of November 4, 1984. Robert L. Pincus, who commented on the show for the *Los Angeles Times* (October 26, 1984), was similarly unimpressed. "Each portrait feels like an homage to his subject, intended to heighten their star mystique rather than reveal character . . . ," he wrote. "Only the people who fill celebrity magazines exist for Scavullo; humanity is simply the anonymous masses who adore them. His viewpoint makes for utterly ephemeral photography." Speaking in his own defense, Scavullo described his distinctive touch in a *Washington Post* interview (January 8, 1985): "I think I do what no one else does. My pictures are alive. They are never dead. They're never *negative* of people."

A member of the Directors Guild of America, the American Federation of Television and Radio Artists, and the Screen Actors Guild, Scavullo recently branched out into film and television directing. His credits to date include Ella Fitzgerald's commercials for Memorex recording tape ("Is it live or is it Memorex?") and the *Crystal Gayle Special*, which was broadcast by CBS-TV in December 1979. The last-named show was judged to be "a well-balanced, musically diverse hour of entertainment with an unmistakable touch of class" by the *Los Angeles Times*'s television critic, James Brown. In 1984 Scavullo and Dennis Powers set up a production company to film television commercials.

A small, compact man, Francesco Scavullo stands five feet seven inches tall and weighs 125 pounds and has close-cropped dark hair, brown eyes, and, according to one reporter, "a kindly self-effacing manner." He habitually dresses in black, from head to toe. "I hardly ever have time to shop," he said in a recent interview. "I wear this same outfit every single day. A black silk shirt over a white cotton voile shirt, with black pants." Preoccupied with environmental purity, he eats only organically grown foods, breathes filtered air, and eschews tap water not only for drinking and bathing, but for developing his negatives. A longtime sufferer from arthritis, he keeps the condition under control with a daily exercise routine. Scavullo used to frequent Studio 54 and other night spots favored by the Beautiful People, but he has recently confined his social life to serving as host of small dinner parties, at his Manhattan townhouse or at his summer retreat in Southhampton, New York. He has decorated both homes with large blowups of his favorite photographs and with the brightly colored abstract compositions that he paints in his spare time. Scavullo's marriage to the former Carol McCallson, a model, ended in 1956.

References: *Biog N* 2:429 Mr '75; *Los Angeles Times* V p1+ N 28 '76 por, V p8 D 4 '77 por, V p1+ N 19 '82 por; *Newsweek* 83:54 F 4 '74 por, 88:73+ N 22 '76 por; *Washington Post* C p1+ D 1 '77 por, C p1+ Ja 8 '85 pors; *Contemporary Authors* vol 102 (1981); *Macmillan Biographical Encyclopedia of Photographic Artists and Innovators* (1983); *Who's Who in America*, 1984–85

## Schaller, George B(eals)

*May 26, 1933– Zoologist; author. Address: b. Animal Research and Conservation Center, New York Zoological Society, Bronx Park, N.Y. 10460*

Although George B. Schaller is currently the director of the Animal Research and Conservation Center at New York City's Bronx Zoo, his lifelong contact with animals has ranged far beyond the confines of that or any other zoo. His studies of animals in the wild have extended from the gorillas in the rain forests of Zaire to the tigers in central India to the giant pandas in the mountains of southwestern China. Schaller's goal has been to make the human race aware of its animal relatives, many species of which are fast disappearing, and his painstaking documentation of animal behavior in the wild has destroyed long-held myths and misconceptions that were based on the fanciful accounts of hunters and trophy seekers. Among his many books that have won wide acclaim is *The Serengeti Lion* (Univ. of Chicago Press, 1972), which was honored with the National Book Award in 1973. For his conservation efforts Schaller has received several national and international awards, including the 1980 Gold Medal of the World Wildlife Fund.

George Beals Schaller was born on May 26, 1933 in Berlin, Germany, the son of Georg Ludwig Schaller, a businessman, and Bettina Byrd (Beals) Schaller. When he was a teenager, his mother brought him to the United States, to an uncle's home in Missouri. (His parents were later divorced.) It was in the woods of Missouri that Schaller began to discover wildlife. "I turned over rocks and caught lizards," Schaller told Dawn Clayton of *People* (September 15, 1980). "Later on I found I could make a living doing almost the same thing." Because of his interest in wildlife and wilderness areas, Schaller chose to attend the University of Alaska at Fairbanks and obtained both a B.S. degree in zoology and a B.A. degree in anthropology in 1955.

Schaller's fieldwork in Alaska included a survey of the birds of Colville River and stints with the United States Fish and Wildlife Service and the National Park Service. In 1956 he served as an assistant to the naturalist and conservationist Olaus Murie on an expedition to the Brooks Range in northeastern Alaska, which is now the Arctic Wild-life Range. Schaller, who still considers Murie one of his role models, cited his "undimmed capacity for wonder" and "tremendous generosity of spirit" in an interview for *Omni* (December 1983). Another inspiration was the famed conservationist Aldo Leopold, whose *A Sand County Almanac* has become a classic of the ecological movement, though he died too early for Schaller to have known him personally.

Schaller decided to continue his graduate studies at the University of Wisconsin, where he specialized in the behavior of birds. One day in January 1957 he entered the office of his professor, Dr. John T. Emlen, who confronted him with the half-joking question: "Would you like to study gorillas?" Emlen explained that Harold Coolidge, of the National Academy of Sciences, was contemplating an expedition to study the behavior of gorillas in the wild. That evening Schaller sent Coolidge a letter of application. It took two years for the expedition to materialize—and in the interim Schaller had married the former Kay Suzanne Morgan, a trained anthropologist, on August 26, 1957—but on February 1, 1959 Schaller and Emlen, together with their wives, set out from New York City for Africa. Schaller remembers his exhilaration at leaving the concrete and steel of the metropolis behind, exchanging the asphalt jungle for a green one.

For six months Emlen and Schaller studied the habitat and distribution of the mountain gorilla, looking for the best site at which to study its behavior. They finally settled on the high mountain forest of the Virunga Volcanoes region of Albert National Park (now Kivu National Park) in what was then the Belgian Congo. The Emlens then departed, leaving George Schaller and his wife to discover the nature of gorilla behavior.

Both the popular and "scientific" literature on gorillas abounded in accounts of gorilla character and behavior that were based not on careful study but on the chance encounters of hunters or students. Small wonder, then, that gorillas were considered ferocious, bloodthirsty animals that were highly aggressive and terrifying. Discounting those impressions as exaggerated, Schaller was determined not to take a rifle or revolver with him into the field. In all of his field expeditions, starting with his earliest study of gorillas and extending to his later work with lions and tigers, Schaller has held to the principle that an animal will only attack a human being when provoked and will become instinctively wary and hostile in the presence of a man carrying a gun. For his daily encounters with the gorillas, Schaller wanted to adopt the role of another friendly primate.

It was precisely that pattern of daily, patient, quiet, and unobtrusive observation that rewarded Schaller with a wealth of results. He would set out early each morning to track a band of gorillas and, when he found them, would sit quietly, watch, and take notes for up to seven hours. Occasionally he would take along his sleeping bag and sleep at the edge of a gorilla troop in order to record their sleeping habits.

What Schaller discovered was that gorillas in the wild are virtually the absolute opposite of their belligerent image. They are amiable, peaceful, and cooperative animals living in bands of from five to twenty-seven members headed by a mature male who is generally affectionate and well-liked. They show a relaxed interdependence and lack both sexual jealousy and territorial instinct. Quarrels are rare. Moreover, Schaller was struck by the similarities of some gorilla mannerisms to human behavior: they stamp their feet and throw things when they are annoyed; when tense, they put something in their mouths; they stretch their arms and yawn in the morning and like to lie in the sun. In his book *The Year of the Gorilla* (Univ. of Chicago Press, 1964), a work for the layman that followed the publication by the same university press in 1963 of his scientific monograph *The Mountain Gorilla: Ecology and Behavior,* Schaller noted both the similarities and differences between gorillas and humans and wrote that for him the most important reason for studying animals is "that man learns to understand himself."

In 1957 Schaller received his M.S. degree from the University of Wisconsin, and he obtained his Ph.D. degree from that institution in 1962. During the academic year of 1962–63 he served as a fellow at the Center for Advanced Study in the Behavioral Sciences in Stanford, California. He then received an appointment as a research associate at Johns Hopkins University in Baltimore, Maryland, where he had advanced to the rank of assistant professor by the time he left in 1966.

An association with Johns Hopkins University was nothing new to Schaller, for it was under its auspices that Schaller had set off in 1963 on his second major expedition into the wild, with the assignment of studying big game in Kanha National Park in the state of Madhya Pradesh in central India. Inevitably his focus of interest became the tiger, much feared and little studied "except along the sights of a rifle," as Schaller once put it in an article in *Life* (June 25, 1965). As he had earlier done with the gorilla, Schaller set himself the task of studying the tiger in its natural habitat. For more than a year he roamed the forests alone and unarmed, quietly observing the tiger eating, sleeping, caring for its young, and hunting for food.

The tiger, Schaller noted, is shy by nature and generally moves and hunts alone, though several may gather together at night and share their kills. An animal of contrasts, both gentle and fierce, it moves with a self-assured power and grace. Schaller discovered that he had little reason to fear it. He once surprised a tiger from its nap and was chased up a tree. "I clapped my hands and said, 'Go away, tiger, go away,'" Schaller told John Stein, who interviewed him for *Omni* (December 1983), "and the tiger got up like a big Saint Bernard and walked off." Schaller recorded his experiences and observations on that expedition in both *The Deer and the Tiger: A Study of Wildlife in India* (Univ. of

Chicago Press, 1967) and, in collaboration with Millicent E. Selsam, in a children's book, *The Tiger: Its Life in the Wild* (Harper, 1969).

In 1966 Schaller began his long association with the New York Zoological Society, when he became one of its research associates. In June of that year its Institute for Research in Animal Behavior, together with Rockefeller University, sponsored Schaller's expedition to Serengeti National Park in Tanzania, to which he had been invited to study lions by John Owen, director of the Tanzania National Parks. Schaller was eager to undertake the challenge, both because of his excitement over the aura of beauty and power that surrounds the lion and because of his strong conviction that detailed information about lion behavior was urgently needed in order to act quickly to ensure its preservation in the wild.

In *Golden Shadows, Flying Hooves* (Alfred A. Knopf, 1973), one of several books Schaller has written about his experiences in the Serengeti, he stressed the fact that the preservation of a species within the confines of a national park demands detailed knowledge about its eating habits, patterns of travel, rate of reproduction, and other matters. "Answers to these problems are particularly important with respect to predators," he writes, "for their habit of killing prey has engendered much revulsion and false sentiment on the part of man." In their ignorance of the balance of nature, men have killed off predators in national parks, from the mountain lions and wolves of Yellowstone National Park to the lions and cheetahs of South Africa's Kruger National Park. In Schaller's opinion, only through knowledge can we successfully argue for the rights of predators to exist freely; yet, ultimately, we should not have to place a value on free animal life. "Indeed," he concluded in his introduction to *Golden Shadows, Flying Hooves*, "to watch animals satisfies an urge to explore past the limits of knowledge and to contemplate life in all its diversity; it teaches sympathy and humility; and it strengthens man's feeling of belonging to the natural world."

From June 1966 to September 1969, Schaller lived in the Serengeti with his wife, Kay, and their two small sons, Eric and Mark. He would rise every day at dawn to spend the morning watching lions, a chore, as he has emphasized in interviews, that can be often mundane and boring, since the Serengeti lion sleeps an average of twenty-one hours a day. After years of patient research he was able to draw a detailed portrait of the lion's character and habits, including its generally amiable and cooperative nature that changes to a short-tempered aggression only when its food supply is threatened.

As had previously happened with his field studies of gorillas and tigers, Schaller eventually came to recognize individual animals by their distinctive markings and to feel that they were his friends. Those feelings left their imprint on his National Book Award–winning *The Serengeti Lion: A Study of Predator–Prey Relations*, of which the

noted Harvard biologist E. O. Wilson wrote in *Science* (February 2, 1973): "If you have only enough time to read one book about field biology, this is the one I recommend. . . . Schaller has the master's ability to enliven his scientific report with brief personal anecdotes and expressions of personal emotion that do not lose objectivity or even noticeably digress from the data."

Not all of Schaller's research has concerned animals that used to be considered hostile to human beings. Starting in 1969, he embarked on an ambitious project of studying the wild sheep and goats of the Himalayas. He made several trips through the mountains of Pakistan and Nepal in 1970 and 1972, then moved with his entire family to Pakistan in mid-1972, where they remained for two years, and in late 1974 and early 1975 he returned for two more trips to Pakistan. Schaller documented his scientific findings in *Mountain Monarchs: Wild Sheep and Goats of the Himalaya* (Univ. of Chicago Press, 1977), in which he recorded his detailed observations of the behavior and ecology of several Himalayan animals, both the sheep and goats and their predators such as the snow leopard, and made an impassioned plea for the conservation of rare species.

Parts of Schaller's *Stones of Silence: Journeys in the Himalaya* (Viking, 1980) were written while he was engaged in his next field project, which involved the observation of jaguars in the forests and swamps of Mato Grosso in southwestern Brazil. In that book, Schaller orchestrated the data he had presented in *Mountain Monarchs* into a lyrical chronicle of his Himalayan odysseys, a kind of meditation on the beauties of solitude and nature. In reviewing it for the *Christian Science Monitor* (March 10, 1980), Spencer Punnett observed: "In this book, science is never separate from imagination and emotion. . . . In one sense, this is not an adventure story; it does not involve much suspense or a dramatic plot. Nevertheless, as the ruminations of a literate man with an exotic career, 'Stones of Silence' offers a kind of quiet delight."

In 1979 George Schaller was appointed director of the Animal Research and Conservation Center of the New York Zoological Society, a post that enables him to concentrate his full energies where his most abiding interest lies: a determined effort to educate the American public on the urgent necessity of conserving endangered animal species. During the interview for *Omni* magazine, Schaller ruefully noted that virtually all government funding for the Center's projects had dried up, deploring the billions of government dollars spent on military muscle power while the natural environment and its living species were dying off. He commended privately funded groups such as the Sierra Club and the Audubon Society for their conservation efforts in America, and the National Geographic Society and the World Wildlife Fund for their support of conservation work globally.

"Preventing the extermination of species is one of the most basic, and probably the most urgent, issue facing us today," Schaller told John Stein of

*Omni.* Rejecting the demurrer that animal conservationists are "choosing animals over people," Schaller underscored the interdependence of all living species and noted that not only does our food come from plants and animals, but about forty percent of all the drugs we use are based on animal or plant products. Beyond this, Schaller argued, our commitment to wildlife preservation and ecological balance represents a commitment to our future and the future of our planet.

It so happens that it is exactly that type of commitment to the future that underlies the ongoing effort of the Chinese government to save from extinction the giant panda of the bamboo forest of Sichuan province. In 1980 the Chinese invited the World Wildlife Fund to study panda behavior, especially their food habits, in response to the death by starvation of about a quarter of the panda population when their sole source of food, bamboo, died off. Invited to head the American delegation, Schaller set up a Chinese-American cooperative program of panda research. The first Westerner in half a century to be allowed to view the pandas in their native habitat, he stayed for almost two years in the snowy mountains of the Wolong Nature Preserve. The aim of the research was to gain knowledge that would help both the breeding of pandas in captivity and the conservation programs in the wild. *The Giant Pandas of Wolong* (Univ. of Chicago Press, 1985), which Schaller wrote with three of his Chinese colleagues, Hu Jinchu, Pan Wenshi, and Zhu Jing, recounts the team's observations and conclusions about panda behavior.

In spite of discouraging trends, Schaller maintains an optimism on the possibility of animal conservation. In interviewing him for *Omni,* John Stein noted that "his quiet confidence coolly masks whatever pressure he feels." In many ways a solitary, self-contained man, he prefers to work alone in the field and counts among his most exhilarating experiences those times when he felt completely accepted by another animal. Yet, when asked to recount the best thing that has ever happened to him in his career, he unhesitatingly names his marriage, pointing out that his wife, Kay, has provided a much needed stability in his unconventional life by traveling with him to distant lands when possible and by staying home to raise their children when needed. Their sons, Eric and Mark, are now in their twenties, and the Schallers share a home in rural Connecticut. John Stein noted that in coming to interview Schaller he "was prepared for a robust trekker, replete in khaki safari suit," but found that his subject is modestly built and trim. "But his eyes hold the power to snare you," Stein observed.

References: Omni p85+ D '83 por; People 14:113+ S 15 '80 por; Contemporary Authors new rev vol 9 (1983); Schaller, George. Golden Shadows, Flying Hooves (1973), Stones of Silence (1980), The Year of the Gorilla (1964)

## Scholder, Fritz

*Oct. 6, 1937– Painter; printmaker. Address: b. Galisteo, N.M. 87540; 118 Cattletrack Rd., Scottsdale, Ariz. 85251; 260 W. Broadway, New York City, N.Y. 10013*

Acknowledged by many of his peers to be the leader of what has been called "the new American Indian art," Fritz Scholder is also denounced by others as the man who singlehandedly "messed up" Indian art and demeaned the Indian. The conflict between those appraisals echoes the larger paradox implicit in the status of the Native American in contemporary society, and that paradox, in fact, has been the central, enduring theme in Scholder's art since 1967. "The New American Indian Art is not a stylistic movement—it really encompasses many styles," Scholder has declared. As painter, printmaker, and sculptor, he has freely mixed abstract expressionist, surrealist, and pop approaches with a basically traditional figurative emphasis to create his own combination of literal truth and low-keyed irony. "In today's world," Scholder has said, "love, art, and magic are greatly needed."

Fritz Scholder, who is one-quarter Indian (his paternal grandmother was a member of the Luiseño tribe of the Southern California Mission

Indians), is the son of Fritz William Scholder 4th and Ella Mae (Haney) Scholder. His father, a school administrator employed by the United States Bureau of Indian Affairs, was stationed at

the Wahpeton Indian School in Wahpeton, North Dakota. The artist was born on October 6, 1937 in Breckenridge, Minnesota. His youth was a peripatetic one, since his father was transferred to other parts of the Midwest and Far West, but he himself went to school off the reservations. Indeed, he never thought of himself as an Indian, for his family was completely assimilated and he grew up in homes devoid of a single Indian artifact. In Pierre, South Dakota he did take a high-school art course with Oscar Howe, a noted Sioux painter, but Howe had spent some time after World War II in Paris and was intent on introducing his talented young student to contemporary Western painting. Under his tutelage, Scholder decided that he was going to become a serious artist.

In 1957, when the Scholders moved on to Sacramento, California, he transferred to Sacramento City College and there took courses with Wayne Thiebaud. Whatever elements of pop art can be traced in Scholder's style are largely owing to Thiebaud's influence. Another stylistic trait also stems from those California years. The strong design sense and verticality of many of his compositions are, according to the critics, due to Richard Diebenkorn, an artist Scholder admired, who was then working as an abstract expressionist.

It was Thiebaud who arranged for Scholder's first one-man exhibition, which was held in 1958 at the Sacramento City College Art Gallery. After obtaining his B.A. degree from Sacramento State College in 1960, Scholder taught in the Sacramento public-school system until, in 1961, he was awarded a scholarship (for which he was eligible because his father had entered his name at birth on the Indian rolls), that enabled him to take part in the Southwest Indian art project at the University of Arizona, under the auspices of the Rockefeller Foundation.

It proved to be the turning point in Scholder's career, for during those summers of 1961 and 1962 in Tucson, first as a participant and then as a teacher, he made his first conscious self-identification as an Indian and began to search for ways to combine traditional Indian art with contemporary non-Indian styles and techniques. Scholder continued his quest at the newly established Institute of American Indian Arts in Santa Fe, New Mexico, where between 1964 and 1969 he taught advanced painting and art history. In the meantime, in 1964 he earned his Master of Fine Arts degree at the University of Arizona.

On arriving in Santa Fe, Scholder had vowed he would not paint Indians, noting with some chagrin that "the non-Indian had painted the subject as a noble savage and the Indian painter had been caught in a tourist-pleasing cliché." Instead, he devoted himself to abstract landscapes inspired by the mesa and mountain scenery of New Mexico, but, increasingly fascinated by Indian artifacts and the still very much alive traditional life of the pueblos, he retracted his vow and on one winter evening early in 1967 decided to paint an Indian. From that point on, the theme dominated his art,

with *Indian No. 1* being only the first of over 300 paintings, boldly brushed in vivid expressionist colors, that he devoted to the subject.

Far from romanticized stereotypes, Scholder's paintings, and the graphics that came later, are his attempt to forge a new idiom in Indian art. They are concerned with modern Indians living in a technological society, who are perceived as individuals and who are dealt with realistically, honestly, often with quizzical humor, always with affection and compassionate respect. *Super Indian No. 2* (1971), one of his most famous oils, shows a hulking seated figure of a man in a buffalo-horn headdress, wearing beads and a loincloth, engaged in eating a double-dip strawberry ice cream cone. The incident depicted was one Scholder had actually seen. Just after taking part in a ritual buffalo dance, now debased into a tourist carnival, the Indian had stepped up to a concession booth and ordered the cone. Although it may contain an element of a pop art, the painting, far from being cool and hip, makes a serious social observation in its own offhand way. Similarly, *Bicentennial Indian* (1974), a color lithograph of an Indian draped in the American flag, is neither cliché-deflating pop art nor overt political satire. Scholder supplies a footnote explaining that in the late nineteenth century the U.S. Bureau of Indian Affairs, for reasons unknown, sent surplus flags to the reservations, and the Indians used them for decorative costumes. *Indians with Umbrellas* (1971), one of the *Indians Forever* lithographs suite, is forthright in its humor: a row of Indians are riding on horseback, silhouetted against the far horizon, and four of them are carrying big, sunny-colored umbrellas.

On the other hand, such paintings as *Indian in Gallup* (1970), which depicts a figure with skull-like face, dressed in white man's clothes, standing outside the blinding white walls of a bar, or *Indian with Beer Can* (1969), which displays a seated man, his face hidden by dark glasses and a sombrero, are outspoken comments on such major social problems endemic on the reservations as alcoholism and acculturation. "I have painted the Indian real, not red," Scholder has declared.

Fritz Scholder resigned from the Institute of American Indian Arts in 1969, so that he could devote himself full-time to painting. During that year he made his first trip abroad, a three-month journey to North Africa and Europe, and while in London, at the Tate Gallery, he encountered the bizarre and savage work of the figurative painter Francis Bacon. "I just sat down there and had to absorb him!" he has recalled. Bacon's vibrant colors and his manner of applying them undoubtedly influenced the American painter's style, so that now, characteristically working with a long-handled brush, he applied his often strident colors with vigor. According to Scholder, no color stands alone; it is what it is next to that creates excitement. Bacon's mordant approach, too, may have contributed to the sharpening of Scholder's treatment of his theme, which deals with the torment of people caught between two rapidly evolving cultures. In any event, paintings like *Screaming Indian No. 2* (1970), depicting a figure standing on the desert sands under a harsh blue sky, seem to reflect Bacon directly.

In recognition of his role as mentor and leader, Fritz Scholder was asked in 1970 to deliver a paper on "New Indian Art" at the First Convocation of American Indian Scholars, held at Princeton University in New Jersey. Toward the end of that year he made an important decision: to take up a new medium, though his earlier attempts at lithography, made during his college days, had been a failure. As one of the first artists invited by the prestigious Tamarind Institute to work in their new facilities in Albuquerque, New Mexico, Scholder undertook a major project: a suite of large (22 x 30-inch) lithographs, in black and white and in color, entitled *Indians Forever*. In the course of his first morning in the workshop he completed his first drawing, made his first attempt at color lithography on the third day of work, and by the end of March 1971 had completed the project. Small wonder that he was exhilarated by the successful outcome, for he had found a new and enlarged audience and had mastered a new medium. Soon, with his so-called Woman series, Scholder undertook to portray what he considers to be "the most misunderstood minority in the country." "The real, the raw woman" appears in highly sensuous nude poses in five lithographs from 1971, only to drop almost wholly from his repertoire, except for some representations in different media of an image called *Crucified Woman*.

Characteristically, Fritz Scholder explores his subjects in sequences of paintings or prints, but each depiction of the same image is unique in terms of its color harmonies, and therefore of its mood and texture. Explaining his fascination with the procedure, Scholder has admitted, "I never know when a series will begin or end. I love that surprise." Finished with the Woman series, he went on to images conveying his interest in the occult, and his belief in magic has engendered and sustained much of his subsequent art. In 1972 a small series of paintings called Vampir led the way. The impetus came from a trip to Transylvania that Scholder made in the course of another European journey, in 1972, while accompanying the touring exhibition "Two American Painters." The show, featuring his work and that of one of his Indian pupils, T. C. Cannon, had opened in Washington, D.C., at the National Collection of Fine Arts.

Scholder's fascination with otherworldly forces was nourished by another trip, this time to Egypt, in 1974, which resulted in his paintings of the pyramids and the Great Sphinx. A decade later he turned to the Shaman theme in a series of monotypes and oils representing the single figure of an Indian shaman seen against various brightly colored backgrounds. Its pivoting shape suggests the shaman's flight to the spirit world: the arms terminate in bird's feathers, and the supple robed form with its obscured face alludes to the shaman's an-

drogynous nature. *Shaman and Dog*, a large oil, dissolves the bound between a conjuror and his animal familiar. In the Conjuring Shaman monotypes a transparent ghost figure looms up behind the shaman's torso. Those works from 1984 were exhibited at the ACA Galleries in New York City in 1984-1985.

As an artist-in-residence at Dartmouth College in Hanover, New Hampshire in the fall of 1973, Fritz Scholder worked on what came to be known as his Dartmouth Portraits. Some of them are based on old photographs of Indians, and are painted in non-naturalistic colors laid on with bold strokes. Fantasies rather than individual likenesses, they are assertions of the proud and indomitable Indian spirit.

Over the years, Fritz Scholder has added to his technical repertoire aquatint, etching, and monotype, painting in acrylics, and sculpture in bronze and mixed media. First produced in 1977, his work in monotype was inspired by his visit to the studio of the noted American printmaker Nathan Oliveira. The haunting, magic-laden presence of his sculptured pieces, which have been described as his personal fetishes, transcends their small size. Examples are a circular face in bronze called *Screaming Indian* (1969); figures of mummified animals and crucified women; and *Eagle Fetish No. 1* and *Eagle Fetish No. 2* (1975), both in mixed media. Scholder has also done some photographs, examples of which were first shown in the 1978 exhibition of "Indian Kitsch" at the Heard Museum in Phoenix, Arizona.

After 1979, though the image of the Indian still recurred throughout his work, many other subjects also claimed Scholder's attention. A Flower series, painted in 1979, with its vivid closeups of blooms, undoubtedly shows the influence of another Southwest painter, for as Scholder has himself remarked, "the shadows of Georgia O'Keeffe are long." The Dream series, dating from 1981, centers on two embracing figures silhouetted against backgrounds of different hues that convey a range of moods from the tender and melting to the darkly mysterious. When, in 1982, Scholder purchased a New York City loft in lower Manhattan, views of the Empire State Building to the north inspired a series of brightly colored paintings in 1984 that make of its soaring shaft an urban totem. But the Western landscape has returned in the Arizona series, which he began in 1983.

As successful as he is prolific, Fritz Scholder has had exhibitions every year since his first one-man showing in 1958, at galleries and museums across the United States and in Europe and Japan. He was accorded his first solo show in New York City in 1968, and a major exhibition of 109 works, entitled "Fritz Scholder/The Retrospective: 1960-1981," was mounted at the Tucson (Arizona) Museum of Art in 1981. His paintings and prints, which now command superstar prices, can be seen in the major public and university museums, and he has been avidly collected by private owners. His long list of honors includes the painting award of the

American Academy and Institute of Arts and Letters in 1977 and governor's awards in the arts, in North Dakota and New Mexico, in 1981 and 1983. He has received an honorary doctorate in fine arts from Ripon College in Wisconsin and an honorary doctorate in fine arts from the University of Arizona in Tucson. A book by the American Indian writer Jamake Highwater entitled *Anpao: An American Indian Odyssey,* which was published by Lippincott in 1977 with illustrations by Fritz Scholder, was named a Newbery honor book by the American Library Association in 1978. Several film documentaries have been produced about the man and his art, the most recent example of which is *Fritz Scholder: American Portrait,* which was telecast nationwide in the United States by PBS-TV in 1983.

From time to time Fritz Scholder has insisted that he is not an Indian artist but "a non-Indian Indian." He has even gone so far as to declare: "I have never been an Indian. I am proud of that one-quarter of my heritage, but a person cannot be something he is only one-quarter of." Such statements seem to refer to the problem of identity that lies at the heart of the modern American Indian experience, and to Scholder's conviction that the Indian must come to terms with the outside "Anglo" world. Throughout his career he has revealed his own conflicting moods and personae in confrontational self-portraits that show him as laughing or scowling, or with his face contorted in a scream (a la Edvard Munch) or stoically impassive. Sometimes he stares defiantly at the viewer with his hands thrust into a belt buckled with a large Indian turquoise.

Indeed, Fritz Scholder often wears Indian jewelry and his long and flowing hair is swept back from his face in Indian style. In person, belying some of his self-portraits, he is gentle, soft-spoken, and quick to smile; although somewhat reserved, he is warm and open in his eminently quotable conversation. Commonsensical in his approach to his work and realistic about showings and sales, he sees no reason why art and business should not mix. He loves "goodies" (as he calls them) and lives comfortably, surrounded by furnishings in the latest style and by his collections of Native American, Pre-Columbian, and African art. Since 1972 he has maintained two adobe-style homes, with ample studio space. Although he spends his winters in Scottsdale, Arizona and his summers in Galisteo, outside Santa Fe, Scholder is equally at home in the New York art world and in the places he visits on his frequent travels abroad. By his marriage in 1958 to his first wife, the former Peggy Stephenson, Fritz Scholder has a son, Fritz Scholder 6th. Divorced in 1965, he married the former Romona Attenberger in 1966.

References: *Art N* 73:90+ O '74, 80:166+ D '81; *Toronto Globe & Mail* pE5 My 11 '85 por; Adams, Clinton. *Fritz Scholder: Lithographs* (1975); Taylor, Joshua C., ed. *Fritz Scholder* (1982); Turk, Rudy H. *Scholder/Indians* (1972);

*Who's Who in America, 1984-85; Who's Who in the World, 1982-83*

## Schwartz, Tony

*Aug. 19, 1923- Communications specialist. Address: b. 455 W. 56th St., New York City, N.Y. 10019*

"I'm always puzzled when people ask me to tell them what I do," says Tony Schwartz, a telecommunications expert and audio specialist whose credits include radio and television commercials for more than 300 corporations, some twenty phonograph records, and sound design for more than a dozen Broadway shows and several films. Perhaps best known for the controversial media campaigns he created for such political candidates as Lyndon B. Johnson, George S. McGovern, and Jimmy Carter as well as for many organizations and social causes, Schwartz is also in the forefront of advances in audio technology. He invented the "mnemonic" technique that allows portions of a word to be edited out without rendering it unintelligible: the brain automatically fills in the missing phonemes. As a result, the same amount of information can be conveyed in a radically shortened, and thus less expensive, commercial. He also actively supports a more effective use of media as an educational tool. Although he believes that its potential is sadly underexploited, Schwartz maintains that "television is perhaps the best reading-readiness tool ever invented." Schwartz has charted his development as a communications specialist and explained the theories behind his work in two books: *The Responsive Chord* (1973) and *Media: The Second God* (1982).

Anthony ("Tony") Schwartz was born in Manhattan on August 19, 1923 to Samuel Schwartz, a Romanian-born civil engineer, and Esther (Levy) Schwartz, a writer. He has one brother, Larry Schwartz. When Tony was four, his family moved up the Hudson River to Peekskill, New York, where he received his elementary and high-school education. Schwartz credits Norman A. Kropf, his high-school art teacher, with influencing him in his choice of communications as a career, but, as he explained in the introduction to his first book, The Responsive Chord (Doubleday, 1973), even as a child he was fascinated by sound: "Radio and I grew up together, and my ear developed a sensitivity to audio communication, which carried over to other areas of my life. I couldn't read, work, or do homework without the radio on. My mother often complained that people could not read and listen at the same time. She was half right. . . . Although I was not simultaneously perceiving two sensory inputs, the oscillation process was so quick that I could readily absorb distinct auditory and visual information occurring simultaneously. This discovery encouraged me to look deeper into the new communication environment."

Nevertheless, Schwartz's interest in audio remained avocational for some time, and on graduating from Peekskill High School in 1941 he studied advertising design at the Pratt Institute in Brooklyn, New York, from which he received a certificate three years later. He then joined the civil service as a graphic artist for the United States Navy at its training aids development center. After World War II ended, Schwartz resumed his career in commercial advertising design, working as the art director of the Graphics Institute for five years and then as a designer at the Wexton Company, an advertising agency he founded with Howard Wechsler in 1950.

By that time, Schwartz's interest in sound was steadily coming to the fore. In 1945 he bought one of the first available Webster wire recorders, the precursors of the tape recorder. Intrigued since youth by the folk songs and stories of various cultures, he had learned to use a short-wave radio in order to converse with people from distant countries. However, as he recalled in the New Yorker (November 21, 1964), that experiment had proved disappointing: "I found that most short-wave radio fans were interested in how they were being received in Australia, say, rather than what was going on in Australia. My interest was in people, not in technique." His wire recorder solved that problem. Although at first he limited his recordings to jazz and folk songs that could only be heard on the radio, he was soon preserving the work of then unknown folksingers, such as Moondog, Pete Seeger, and Harry Belafonte, who were too poor to afford their own "sound mirrors," as recorders were then called. Beginning in 1946, he also exchanged recordings of folk material with people from around the world, eventually cataloging 20,000 songs and stories from fifty-two different countries.

Schwartz made use of those recordings on his weekly morning radio program, which aired on WNYC in New York from 1946 to 1972 and won the Prix Italia at the prestigious World Radio Festival in Rimini, Italy, in 1956. Having listened enthusiastically to some of his work, Robert Rosenwald, the heir to the Sears, Roebuck fortune, offered in 1952 to finance a sound study on a subject of Schwartz's choosing, provided that the final product was not censored in any way. Readily agreeing to that generous proposal, Schwartz immediately quit his job to make an in-depth audio profile of his postal zone, New York 19, on Manhattan's West Side, and in 1952 he handed over the Wexton Company to his brother and a cousin to devote himself to sound studies. Although there were no portable recorders at that time, Schwartz developed his own fourteen-pound, battery-operated tape recorder so that he could record the sounds of the neighborhood in their natural environment. During the next eighteen months, he captured on tape the area's "noncommercial music—the songs of its many national groups, its children's games and songs, its street musicians, its church services and festivals, its parades, and just the beautiful music in people's talk."

When Moe Asch of Folkways Records heard of his "sound documentary," he asked Schwartz to produce some records of everyday sounds for his company. Schwartz complied, creating about a dozen records for the Folkways label. Among the best known are New York 19; Nueva York, a selection spanning eight years of recording that Nat Hentoff described in the Reporter magazine (October 1, 1959) as "a painfully evocative self-portrait of the [Puerto Rican] emigrants" in New York; 1, 2, 3, and a Zing, Zing, Zing, which captures the songs that accompany children's games; and You're Stepping on My Shadow, the title vignette of which features a child who admonishes Schwartz that he is stepping on her shadow and later has him move aside to make room in an elevator for her imaginary pet donkey. For that album, he also caught museumgoers' unguarded comments on a portrait of Abraham Lincoln and on the Metropolitan Museum of Art's controversial $2.3 million acquisition: Rembrandt's Aristotle Contemplating the Bust of Homer. As Herbert Kupferberg noted in his review of that album for the Herald Tribune (May 20, 1962), "Tony Schwartz didn't exactly invent the tape recorder, but he has put it to some original and fascinating uses."

Perhaps Schwartz's most original contribution in his recordings was the use of "live" sounds captured as they occurred in their natural environment rather than created in a studio. When several advertising agencies approached him in the mid-1950s about creating sounds for their commercials, Schwartz again relied on natural ones to produce the desired effect. In preparing his commercials for Johnson & Johnson baby products, for example, he spent days recording a woman and baby playing together at their home and then edited the hours of tape to create an appealing humming-cooing duet between the mother and infant—the first time an actual child's voice, rather than a woman imitating a child, was used in a commercial.

Those commercials, among others, earned him the title of a "great specialist in children's sound," but Schwartz considers such epithets "deadly compliments": he is a specialist in the effects of sound on people, not in sound effects themselves. His well-known ad for Coca-Cola is a case in point. Almost poetic in its simplicity, the commercial was devoid of narration: the camera merely focused on two temptingly dewy bottles of Coke as random sounds of people at play are heard in the background.

His imaginative advertisement for Coca-Cola won the top prize for commercials at the Cannes Film Festival, and by the early 1960s Schwartz had won a number of other awards for his audio work, including a special prize at the Venice Film Festival for his sound track on the documentary film *My Own Backyard to Play In*. In addition to his work on radio, he began presenting his recordings in public, first at Columbia University's McMillan Hall as part of a music education program, and later at Hunter College, New York University, Town Hall, and the Museum of Modern Art. He also designed the sound for some films and Broadway productions, wrote regular columns on sound for the magazines *Art Direction* and *Popular Photography*, and gave regular Saturday night "concerts" at the Baq Room, a Manhattan nightclub, for six years.

His discovery in the early 1960s of the writings of Marshall McLuhan, the renowned Canadian communications theorist, helped Schwartz to formulate the theory behind his work in audio, which he presented in two generally well-received books: *The Responsive Chord* (Doubleday, 1973) and *Media: The Second God* (Random House, 1982). According to his "resonance principle" of electronic communications, advertisers can most effectively evoke the desired response (that is, buying a certain product) by focusing on the audience's prior experiences. His commercial for Bosco chocolate syrup, for instance, consisted almost entirely of the sound of a child eagerly gulping down a glass of chocolate milk and then contentedly gasping for breath. Aware from past experience that a child only relishes drinks that are delicious, the listener naturally concludes that children love chocolate milk made with Bosco syrup. Such an ad—one that strikes the "responsive chord"—is more likely to persuade the listener to buy Bosco than one that bombards him with claims, however true, about the product's merits. "Credibility in electronic media," Schwartz wrote in *Media: The Second God*, "comes mainly from how the commercial makes you *feel*."

Applying that same principle to political advertisements, Schwartz created for Lyndon B. Johnson's 1964 presidential campaign a commercial that is still generating controversy. Johnson's campaign advisers were aware that many Americans were concerned that his opponent, the conservative Republican Barry Goldwater, would too readily employ nuclear weapons. The spot that Schwartz designed featured a little girl counting as she plucked the petals from a daisy while the countdown for an atomic rocket is heard in the background. Suddenly, the screen erupted in a radioactive mushroom cloud. In a voice-over at the end of the ad, Johnson intoned, "Either we must learn to love each other or we must die." Vigorous protests from Goldwater's supporters, who claimed the ad accused their candidate of being trigger-happy, forced its withdrawal after one showing. However, as Schwartz points out in *The Responsive Chord*, Goldwater's name was never mentioned in the ad; instead, the effectiveness of the ad depended on a listener's first recalling that Goldwater had endorsed the use of tactical nuclear weapons and then worrying that he might actually use them. "This mistrust was not in the *Daisy* spot," Schwartz maintained. "It was in the people who viewed the commercial. The stimuli of the film and sound evoked those feelings and allowed people to express what they inherently believed." Lyndon B. Johnson later gave that ad a good deal of the credit for his victory in the November election.

Although that commercial served its purpose, even some of Johnson's backers had qualms about Schwartz's methods. Bill Moyers, who was then Johnson's press secretary, told Tom Shales of the *Washington Post* (February 17, 1983) that the *Daisy* spot "was good advertising, but bad politics." An anonymous "Democratic political image maker" acknowledged Schwartz's expertise in communications, but voiced similar reservations about Schwartz's political ads in the *Washington Star* (July 29, 1979): "His stuff is just too heavy-handed, too negative and negative in a way that is often unfair."

Unperturbed by such criticisms, both Schwartz and his clients have since 1964 developed several thousand radio and television commercials for political campaigns, mostly for Democrats. Schwartz often works with Joseph Napolitan, a campaign consultant, public-affairs analyst, and "brilliant researcher," whose advice and analyses help him to determine how best to strike a specific audience's "responsive chord." When Hubert H. Humphrey of Minnesota ran against the Nixon-Agnew ticket in 1968, Schwartz evoked the public's concern about Spiro T. Agnew's effectiveness in a one-minute ad that consisted almost entirely of a man laughing uncontrollably and then gasping, "Agnew for vice-president." The camera then faded to a card reading, "This would be funny if it weren't so serious." In spite of Schwartz's valiant efforts, Humphrey lost the election, and in 1972 Nixon and Agnew again defeated one of his clients, George S. McGovern, by a landslide.

Nevertheless, Schwartz's carefully planned media campaigns have usually succeeded. In 1976 alone his work helped to engineer the victories of Jimmy Carter in his run against President Gerald R. Ford; of Daniel Patrick Moynihan in his bid for the United States Senate seat held by Conservative-Republican James L. Buckley of New York; of Senator Edward M. Kennedy of Massachusetts in his run for reelection; and of John D. Rockefeller 4th in his gubernatorial campaign in West Virginia.

In an interview with Tom Shales of the *Washington Post* (February 17, 1983), Schwartz maintained that the success or failure of a campaign is no criterion of the effectiveness of his commercials. To substantiate his contention he cited the interest generated by his work in Massachusetts for the ill-fated 1982 gubernatorial campaign of Edward J. King: "He lost, but I won. Everyone comments on the media up there." Furthermore, Schwartz asserts that he is more concerned with a politician's integrity and positions on important issues than in his viability as a candidate. In 1980 he shocked Washington insiders by crossing party lines to help Warren Rudman, a New Hampshire Republican, defeat Democratic Senator John Durkin, who had also asked Schwartz to work for him. He explained that Durkin's refusal to withdraw false charges that he had leveled against his opponent convinced him to work for Rudman. "I don't mind fighting hard, but I never want to fight dirty," he later said, "because both my reputation and the reputation of my client are on the line." Appealing to the public's "sense of shame," Schwartz designed a television commercial that featured a drawing of Pinocchio's head. As the announcer scolded Durkin for spreading lies, the character's nose grew and grew.

Schwartz also played on that sense of shame in ads he designed to promote certain social causes or to change negative behavior patterns. As he pointed out in *Media: The Second God*, shame has always been an effective deterrent: in primitive cultures, some wrongdoers were literally ridiculed to death, and Puritans relied on the humiliation of the public stocks to punish lawbreakers. Electronic media can be used to the same purpose: a person's misconduct can become public knowledge almost as soon as it occurs, and one can only escape the embarrassment of further public scrutiny by modifying his behavior. Often those advertisements are aimed at only a few people—a technique that Schwartz calls "narrowcasting." One successful effort targeted by name the members of a board that had ordered the closing of the John Jay College of Criminal Justice in New York, a school that offers advanced training to law officers and firefighters. The ads not only pressured the board into keeping the college open but so heightened public awareness of the school that its enrollment increased markedly the next year.

In other media campaigns, Schwartz succeeded in helping to block the passage in the New York State legislature of blue laws prohibiting Sunday shopping; to prevent a strike by New York City police by involving Mayor Ed Koch in the negotiations; and to force a revision in the Massachusetts state budget by running a commercial questioning allocations for "herdsmen, poultrymen, dairymen, swineherdsmen, and even an assistant herdsman" for state institutions that had no animals. He also designed a series of commercials for the American Cancer Society, helped persuade Alaska's voters to endorse a 1982 pro-abortion referendum, and went to bat for a nuclear-freeze referendum that was re-

jected by Maine's electorate in 1982. In 1984 Schwartz, at the behest of Roman Catholic bishops in the United States, put together a sixty-second plea for arms control that featured a message from Pope John Paul II. Many of Schwartz's ads were made at his own expense, and he has estimated that he designs about a half-million dollars' worth of free public-service commercials each year.

Tony Schwartz, who stands six feet tall, weighs about two hundred pounds, and wears glasses, has greying brown hair and unusual eyes: one is blue and the other hazel. On September 27, 1959, he married Reenah Lurie. The couple has two children, Michaela and Anton. Although Schwartz is an agoraphobic who leaves his home only for his daily swim at a nearby gym or for occasional vacations, with the help of one assistant and a secretary he is able to run his several companies—New Sounds, Environmental Media Consultants, and Planned Reactions—out of the office and studio adjoining the brownstone on Manhattan's West Side where he lives with his family. He relies heavily on the telephone, using it to tape commercials, transmit scripts, and lecture throughout the United States, and his clients, including many high-ranking government officials, come to him. Schwartz is more than content with that arrangement. "I have zero interest in seeing places," he insists, "and great interest in meeting people."

References: Herald Tribune III p7 Jl 12 '64 por; New Yorker 40:49+ N 21 '64; Popular Photography 53:58+ S '63 pors; The Reporter 21:40+ O 1 '59; Washington Post C p1+ F 17 '83 por; Washington Star F p1+ Jl 29 '79 por

---

## Serra, Richard (Antony)

*Nov. 2, 1939– Sculptor; experimental filmmaker. Address: b. c/o Leo Castelli Gallery, 420 West Broadway, New York, N.Y. 10012; h. Post Office Box 645, Canal Street Station, New York, N.Y. 10013*

For almost two decades Richard Serra has been celebrated by the mandarins of the New York art world as one of the most innovative of the minimalist sculptors who gained prominence in the late 1960s. Because at that time Serra, a committed abstractionist, was conducting sculptural experiments that called attention to the activity of making art, those works prompted influential critics to label him a "process artist." In the following decade, Serra came to the attention of the general public through his controversial large-scale urban sculptures, more than a dozen of which have been erected in Western Europe and North America. Made of Cor-Ten steel, a raw and rusty-looking industrial material, those uningratiating structures are called "site-specific," meaning that Serra has,

*Richard Serra*

er, described by Serra as "more than a Sunday painter," took him to museums and provided him with "a host of art books to look at," Serra said, "so that I could identity paintings as well as most kids could identify cars." His father, a blue-collar worker in a candy plant, was descended from artisans of Spanish origin, and Richard's paternal grandfather had been a woodcarver. Indeed, Richard's parents reviewed his artistic output on a daily basis, and when he was angry, he "punished" them by refusing to draw. Another source of encouragement for Serra came from the di Suvero family, who also lived on the Avenues and were the Serras' close friends. Their son Mark, who had begun creating art at an early age, later became a prominent New York School sculptor in the 1960s.

Richard Serra enrolled at the Berkeley campus of the University of California in 1957, but soon transferred to the University of California at Santa Barbara. Although he majored in English literature, he also elected many courses in art, an activity he now found "totally interesting and totally private," as he told Harriet Senie. At that time Santa Barbara was, as Serra remembers, "a hotbed of intellectual activity," with a student body of only 2,400 and a faculty that included such luminaries as Aldous Huxley, Reinhold Niebuhr, and Hugh Kenner, among others.

To help finance his undergraduate studies, Serra worked periodically in steel mills, because, as he told an interviewer for *Art in America* (May/June 1976), it was "sweat work" that was "fun to do" and served as "the quickest way [to make] a great deal of money." In the mid-1960s, after he had begun to exhibit in New York City galleries, Serra resumed working in steel mills on an on-again, off-again basis, a practice he has continued because it has deepened his understanding of the intrinsic structural potential of steel and has given him superior skills in manipulating it.

After leaving the Santa Barbara campus in 1961, Serra, acting on a whim, sent a portfolio of twelve drawings to the Yale School of Art and Architecture. At the bottom of that institution's acceptance letter was a note saying that its faculty members were interested in Serra because they thought they could teach him something. When he arrived, the school was in a state of transition. Josef Albers, the influential head of the department of design, had retired, and the abstract-expressionist painter Jack Tworkov had recently joined the faculty. Unlike Albers, a former Bauhaus teacher whose advocacy of geometrical abstraction verged on the dogmatic, Tworkov emphasized "spiritual" autobiographical content and painterly gesture in his canvases. Tworkov also invited leading critics and New York School painters to the New Haven campus, and in Serra's last year there he studied with Robert Rauschenberg, Frank Stella, and Philip Guston. "When such diverse artists came to criticize your work, all with a dogmatic opinion of what was right and what was wrong," Serra recalled in the *Artnews* interview, "within the same week two people might tell you things that were totally con-

to quote Calvin Tomkins, "taken into consideration the character, the topography, and the surroundings of the site when designing the piece. . . ." Nevertheless, the public has, on more than one occasion, greeted Serra's work with what one writer has described as "distrust and hostility."

The public's misunderstanding of Serra's aesthetic intentions stems partly from the artist's visual language, a vocabulary of spare, often stark, minimalist forms, and partly from the rigorous theoretical underpinnings of his work. His sculpture is addressed to such conceptual issues as repetition, space, and process or to investigations of the basic principles of building—weight, tension, balance, and counterbalance. As a result, even sophisticated gallery-goers have sometimes been baffled by Serra's experimental work, either because they are uninterested in his answers to conceptual questions or because his nonexpressive minimalist forms give cold comfort to viewers whose aesthetic values are tied to traditional concepts of beauty. Moreover, many viewers have been troubled by the sense of menace emanating from his aggressively stacked pieces, which are made of several tons of precariously balanced steel or lead plates.

Richard Antony Serra was born in San Francisco on November 2, 1939 in a working-class Russian and Italian neighborhood known as "the Excelsior." In about 1943 his mother and father moved their family of three boys to "the Avenues," an eight-mile-square area of sand dunes near the beach. "It was bordered," Serra recalled in an interview with Harriet Senie for *Artnews* (March 1984), "by the zoo and by the concessions, comparable to Coney Island, which we called 'playland' or the 'Golden Gate Park.'"

Strongly encouraged by his parents, Serra began to draw and paint in early adolescence. His moth-

tradictory. . . . It destroyed the myth of the genius artist and threw you back on your own work, which was a very healthy thing. It made the transition from being a student to being a working artist much easier."

In 1964, when he left Yale with a Master of Fine Arts degree and a B.A. degree, Serra won a traveling fellowship that took him to Paris, where he painted and became close friends with the experimental composer Philip Glass. The following year he received a Fulbright grant that enabled him to live in Italy, where he absorbed the avant-garde composer John Cage's ideas about the role of chance in art, and so produced a series of works in which paint was used as a "found object." Unhappy with that experiment's outcome, Serra decided to forget about chance and began incorporating, in arte povera fashion, sticks, stones, and branches into his work. In 1966 he had a solo show at Rome's Galleria La Salita, exhibiting found objects, including dead animals, in boxlike houses of his own construction.

By 1966 Serra had returned to New York, where minimalism was on the rise in the art world. Influenced by the formalist theories of critic Clement Greenberg and by the austere paintings of Frank Stella, young minimalist sculptors like Don Judd, Carl Andre, and Robert Morris were producing "specific objects"—reductive, geometrical forms with smooth, impersonal surfaces. Although the impact of their work was beginning to be felt, Serra told art historian Barbara Rose: "One day I woke up and saw that no one was playing the sculpture game and I decided to play it for myself."

Serra's first sculptures were strips of metal, or slashed rubber, or neon tubing, or metal rods which, unlike traditional sculpture, were not vertical and had no formal base or "pedestal"; instead, they were simply hung from a wall or arranged on a floor in seemingly random patterns. In those exploratory works, Serra shifted the aesthetic focus from an exclusive, "fetishistic" concern with the end-product, the finished art object, to the physical procedures of making art. And because he shared with minimalists like Judd and Andre a commitment to an abstract art that was nonillusionist, nonmetaphorical, and nonhumanistic, Serra's work was discussed within the context of minimalist doctrine.

In 1967 Leo Castelli, a powerbroker in the art world, took Serra into his prestigious gallery, providing the unknown young sculptor with a regular monthly stipend even though he had no expectation of selling any of Serra's experimental works for at least three years. Later in 1967 Serra spelled out his approach to sculpture in his "Verb List," a kind of process-art manifesto that comprised eighty-four transitive verbs and twenty-four phrases. The verbs—"to roll, to crease, to fold, to store, to bend, to shorten, to twist, . . . to tear"—identify the various physical activities that the sculptor can perform. The phrases—"of tension, of gravity, of entropy, of nature, . . . of location, of context, of time"—describe the external forces that may, as Harriet Senie wrote, "determine or control the form of the work."

In the late 1960s Serra investigated the issue of process in works that also demonstrated the value of his "Verb List" as a practical manual. For example, in his "Tearing Lead" series (1968-69) he methodically ripped away, by hand, successive edges of lead squares, letting those crumpled "tears" simply fall to the floor. In his "Splashed Lead" series, he spattered molten lead against the juncture of a floor and a wall, allowed the "tossings" to cool and harden, then pried them from the corner and laid them one after another in sequence. In both series, viewers were forced to reconstruct visually the physical procedures that had brought those pieces to a completed state. That was Serra's way of elevating process to the same plane of aesthetic importance as the finished artwork. To explain his aesthetic intentions, Serra quoted the philosopher of science Alfred North Whitehead, who said, "Process and existence presuppose each other."

From 1968 to the early 1970s Serra explored weight, balance and counterbalance, tension, and gravity in a series of propped or stacked pieces. The propped pieces generally took the form of a broad, thick, rectangular sheet of metal held flush against a wall by a rolled cylinder of lead, the bottom end of which rested on the floor. Having already rejected the use of a formal base, Serra eschewed the use of welded joints to steady his propped pieces. Using the floor as a base, the heavy forms were supported entirely by their weight and the pull of gravity. Serra's disavowal of welding, which he dismissed as mere "stitching," was a departure from the whole tradition of welded sculpture in modern art, which had been developed by Picasso and Julio González in the 1930s and which was continued after World War II by such abstract-expressionist sculptors as David Smith and Anthony Caro.

What Harriet Senie called a "threat of imminent imbalance" was most dramatically felt in Serra's "Skullcracker Series" of 1969, which consisted of gravity-defying piles of metal plates or slabs that were much larger than the propped pieces. Stacked Steel Slabs was a twenty-foot-high stack of eight-foot-by-ten-foot steel slabs that tilted dangerously toward the ground, as if they were on the verge of toppling over. One-Ton Prop (House of Cards) consisted of four rectangular plates of lead antinomy that leaned together to form a large, menacing house of metal cards—one that might collapse with a 2,000-pound crash at any moment.

The "Skullcracker Series" took its name from its construction site, the Skullcracker Yard of the Kaiser Steel Corporation's plant in Pomona, California. While working there for ten weeks in conjunction with the 1969 "Art and Technology" exhibition at the Los Angeles County Museum, Serra had access to an overhead magnetic crane, a large open steelyard, and enough scrap metal to build a battleship. As a result, he "recognized the possibilities of working on [the] large scale" that would culminate in his public sculptures, as he told

Douglas Crimp during an interview for *Arts Magazine* (November 1980).

Two of Serra's first site-specific public sculptures were erected in landscape settings. His *Untitled* piece of 1971 consists of six cast-concrete walls set outside of Toronto in a field that slopes down two small hills and ends in a valley. Positioned at irregular angles, they articulate the site's gradual slope, "mimicking the field's curves, reflecting its rise and fall," as one critic noted. Similarly, Serra's *Spin-Out* (1973) is the embedment of three rectangular steel plates in an isolated grove in the sculpture garden of the Rijksmuseum Kröller-Müller in Otterloo, The Netherlands. Discussing *Spin-Out* in *Art and Artists* (March 1974), John Anthony Thwaites praised the artist for positioning the slender plates so unobtrusively that, instead of dominating the landscape, they point up its verdant beauty.

Encouraged by the success of his outdoor pieces, and of such indoor sculptures as *Circuit* (1972), which redefined the space of a room and exerted so forceful a presence that viewers experienced them viscerally as well as optically, Serra began work on his urban public sculptures in the late 1970s. One of the first was *Terminal* (1977), an enormous forty-one-foot-high sculpture made of four heavy plates of Cor-Ten steel that inhabits a traffic island in the West German city of Bochum. *Terminal* was followed in 1980 by *T.W.U.*, a thirty-six-foot-high temporary construction of three Cor-Ten steel plates set on a traffic island in the SoHo section of downtown Manhattan, and *St. John's Rotary Arc*, a 200-foot-long, twelve-foot-high curved wall of Cor-Ten steel that bisects a traffic island near the exit from the Holland Tunnel in lower Manhattan.

Now widely considered a successful practitioner of site-specific public sculpture, Serra in 1981 installed *Tilted Arc* on the rather drab plaza of the Jacob Javits Federal Building in lower Manhattan. Commissioned two years earlier by the General Services Administration, (GSA), *Tilted Arc* is a twelve-foot-high, seventy-three ton, 120-foot-long curved wall of Cor-Ten steel that tilts one foot off its vertical axis. Although Serra thought that his piece "transformed the context . . . of the plaza from one of decoration to one of sculpture," about 1,300 office workers signed petitions requesting its removal, complaining that it was an eyesore, a "graffiti-catcher," and disruptive of pedestrian traffic. The controversy grew more heated when Peter Schjeldahl, a critic usually sympathetic to experimental art, denounced *Tilted Arc* in the *Village Voice* (October 14, 1981), calling it "so mistaken, so wrong, so bad" that it epitomized the failure of recent public art. Serra responded to those criticisms in the *Soho News* (November 17, 1981), asserting that his sculpture—which remains in place—describes "a truly lyrical line," one that, with its slight tilt, has no analogue either in nature or in earlier artistic forms. He also argued that abstract sculpture must be free from ideas of what constitutes a popular or eye-pleasing form; other-

wise it is impossible for an artist to dissolve the sculptural object in the sculptural field, which is Serra's aesthetic objective.

*Tilted Arc* became an international art-world cause célèbre in early 1985, when the New York office of the GSA scheduled public hearings to determine the fate of Serra's work as a public sculpture. Fifty-six people, all of whom were either workers in the Javits Building or residents of lower Manhattan, called for the "relocation" of Serra's lyrical yet intimidating wall. One hundred eighteen speakers—including Mrs. Jacob S. Javits, Senator Howard Metzenbaum, William Rubin of the Museum of Modern Art, and the artists Frank Stella and Phillip Glass—opposed any tampering with *Tilted Arc*. Nevertheless, on May 31 Dwight Ink, the acting head of the GSA, announced that the controversial sculpture would be moved to an alternate, not-yet-determined site. Because *Tilted Arc* was of site-specific design, Serra angrily insisted that relocation amounted to destruction, and threatened to expatriate himself to West Germany. "I can't stay in a country that commissions my work and then wantonly and willfully detroys it," he declared, as quoted in *People* magazine (April 1, 1985).

The furor over *Tilted Arc* was not Serra's first experience of public controversy. His *Terminal* piece had been censured as an ugly waste of money by the local branch of the conservative Christian Democratic Party in Bochum, and in 1978 Serra had angrily resigned "from what would have been the most important public commission of his or any other contemporary artist's career," to quote Calvin Tomkins, who profiled him in the *New Yorker* (April 5, 1982). Serra had been chosen by the Pennsylvania Avenue Development Corporation of Washington, D.C., to participate in the construction of a huge plaza near the White House and the Treasury Building. Asked to collaborate with the architect Robert Venturi, Serra designed a vertical sculpture for the site, but Venturi's concept called for two pylons that would "frame" the Treasury Building, a device that Serra dismissed as "reactionary and rhetorical." When he failed to convince Venturi and the corporation's advisory board that the pylon installation was "Hitlerian," he abandoned the project, saying, "It's not the nature of my work to reassert ideological values of the government." Serra believes that his public sculptures are sometimes misunderstood because "they do not relate to the history of monuments. They do not memorialize anything. They have none of the symbolic values communicated by monuments. They relate to sculpture and nothing else. . . . A steel curve is not a monument."

Two of Serra's recently installed public sculptures that have been acclaimed are *Twain* (1982), in Saint Louis, and *Clara-Clara* (1983), which frames the entrance to the Tuileries in Paris. *Twain* is an irregular polygon made of eight forty-to-fifty-foot-long plates of Cor-Ten steel. Each of the ten-foot-high plates is separated by a three-foot-wide gap, and the opening at the piece's apex lines up with the architect Eero Saarinen's Jefferson Memorial Arch, which, just ten blocks away, soars over the city.

Clara-Clara was originally designed for placement at the Centre Pompidou at Beaubourg, where Serra had been given a retrospective exhibition. But the piece—two curved steel arcs, each 118 feet long and eleven feet high—failed to fit the Beaubourg site, and museum officials had Clara-Clara placed at the Tuileries, a historic seventeenth-century sanctuary where Serra's side-by-side curved walls lined up with the famous obelisk on the Place de la Concorde and the Arc de Triomphe in the distance. The French press praised Clara-Clara extravagantly.

Since 1970 Serra has had prime exhibition space in New York City's two major art districts, in SoHo at the Leo Castelli Gallery and in midtown at the Blum-Helman Gallery. In addition to his sculpture, Serra regularly exhibits drawings and models of sculptural projects, as well as experimental films. Early films, like Hand Catching Lead and Hands

Scraping, both from 1969, addressed the aesthetic issues of repetition and process, but more recent works have been overtly political, leveling coruscating criticisms of aspects of American mass culture that are only implicity indicted in his sculpture. A retrospective exhibition of Serra's works in all media was scheduled to open at the Museum of Modern Art in New York City in 1986.

Richard Serra is a sturdily built man with blue eyes and curly graying hair, which he wore long and flowing in the 1960s but is now close-cropped. His characteristic dress is workman's clothes, which he wears to express his identification with the working class. Serra's wife is the German-born Clara Weyergraf, with whom he collaborated on the 1979 film Steelmill/Stahlwerk.

References: Art in America My/Je '71, Summer '81, S '85; Artforum F '70, My '72; New Yorker My 20 '85; N Y Times My 19 '85; Studio International O '73; Contemporary Artists 2d ed (1983); Pincus-Witten, Robert. Postminimalism (1977)

## Shevchenko, Arkady N(ikolayevich)

Oct. 11, 1930– Foreign-policy consultant; former Soviet diplomat; former United Nations official. Address: b. c/o Alfred A. Knopf, Inc., 201 E. 50th St., New York City, N.Y. 10022

The West's knowledge of the inner workings of the Kremlin and of the thinking and attitudes of the men who make policy there has been enhanced by the transplanted expertise of the former senior Soviet diplomat Arkady N. Shevchenko. A specialist

in disarmament policy, Shevchenko was a close adviser in the 1960s and early 1970s to Andrei A. Gromyko, now the chairman of the presidium of the Supreme Soviet, and to the Soviet delegates to the Strategic Arms Limitations Treaty talks. He was an undersecretary general of the United Nations from 1973 to 1978, when he shocked the international diplomatic community by defecting to the United States. In his best-selling memoir Breaking with Moscow (1985), which some critics regarded as "self-serving," Shevchenko issued another shocker, revealing that he had secretly cooperated with American intelligence agencies for two-and-a-half years before his defection.

"It is not my purpose . . . ," Shevchenko explains in Breaking with Moscow, "to instill feelings of hostility in Americans toward the Soviet people, or to complicate in any way efforts to promote peace. The world has enough madmen trying to do that. . . . What I want is to share . . . my experience under the Soviet system; to tell the truth about it as I lived it; to inform the public of Soviet designs, and to warn of the dangers they present to the world. In so doing I hope also, in however small a way, to help the Soviet people eventually find their way to liberty." While dialogue and accommodation with the USSR are "imperative, if we are to avoid cataclysm," he points out, the United States must be firm in its policy toward the Soviet Union if it is to force Moscow "to restrain itself."

The son of a physician, Arkady Nikolayevich Shevchenko was born on October 11, 1930 in Gorlovka, a coal-mining town in the Ukraine. In 1936 the Shevchenkos moved to Yevpatoriya, a resort town on the Crimea's Black Sea coast, where the father became the administrator of a children's tuberculosis sanitarium. When the Germans invaded the Crimea during World War II, Shevchenko was temporarily evacuated, with his mother, to Torgai in Siberia. His older brother, Gennady, his only sibling, a pilot, was killed in the war, and Arkady became, in his words, "a pampered only child."

Early in his childhood Shevchenko was imbued by his mother with a love of reading, and he later became a regular theatregoer and a movie buff. In school, he showed little interest in mathematics or science but scored top grades in literature, history, and world geography, and he took pride in his activities as a member of the Young Pioneers, the Soviet equivalent of the Boy Scouts, and the Komsomol, the Communist youth organization. As a teenager, he played basketball and chess, collected stamps, and learned to drive a car.

His first aspiration was to become a film director, but Shevchenko's interest in politics, foreign affairs, and international peace prevailed. In 1949 he gained admission to the Moscow State Institute of International Relations, the exclusive school for political and diplomatic cadres, generally known by its Russian acronym, MGIMO. "MGIMO had become popular," he explains in *Breaking with Moscow* (Knopf, 1985), "attracting the 'golden youth,' the children of the highest party and government officials, because it opened the door to travel abroad, an alluring prospect to many for no better reason than that it facilitated the acquisition of foreign goods."

Shevchenko completed his undergraduate work at the Moscow State Institute of International Relations in 1954. As a graduate student from 1954 to 1956, he chose as his field of expertise the problem of atomic weapons in relation to international law and peaceful coexistence. In addition to his dissertation on Soviet disarmament policy (which finally brought him his doctorate in international law in 1963), he began publishing articles on arms control and world peace. One of the articles was cowritten with a fellow student, Anatoly Gromyko, a collaboration that served as the occasion for Shevchenko's meeting Anatoly's father, Andrei A. Gromyko, then the first deputy foreign minister in the Soviet government.

In 1956 Shevchenko joined the Soviet ministry of foreign affairs as an attaché in the department concerned with the United Nations and disarmament. He was promoted to third secretary the following year, and in 1958 he became a member of the Communist party, a prerequisite for further promotions and for assignments abroad. "I was promoted very fast because I was a very hard worker," he told Leo Seligsohn in an interview for *Newsday* (July 4, 1982). "And I was lucky. My superiors were intelligent people. What it took fifteen years to do, I did in three years. I'm a workaholic. In fact, in 1961 I had to spend three months in the hospital in Moscow for exhaustion. I had been working twenty hours a day."

Shevchenko's "dream since childhood" was to visit the United States. He realized that dream in 1958, when he spent three months in New York as an adviser with the Soviet delegation to a special

UN session on disarmament. He returned to the United Nations as a disarmament expert with the Soviet delegation to the 1960 session of the General Assembly, which was personally led by Premier Nikita Khrushchev, and he spent most of 1962 with the Soviet delegation to the Committee on Disarmament in Geneva, Switzerland. He was a counselor (finally senior counselor) with the permanent Soviet mission to the United Nations from 1963 to 1970, and for three years beginning in 1970 he was stationed in Moscow as the personal political adviser to Andrei A. Gromyko, then foreign minister. With the title of ambassador extraordinary and plenipotentiary (which he retained) he made a diplomatic tour of Third World and Soviet bloc countries in Gromyko's behalf in 1971. While in Moscow, he was a part-time senior research fellow in the Institute of United States and Canada Studies at the USSR Academy of Sciences, and he finished the work for his doctorate at the Moscow State Institute of International Relations. In keeping with his high diplomatic status, he became accustomed to the life of the Soviet *nomenklatura* hierarchy, enjoying superior housing in Moscow and a dacha, or country house, in one of the best areas outside the city.

According to Edward Jay Epstein in the *New Republic* (June 15 and 22, 1985), Shevchenko's "principal job" both at the UN and the foreign ministry was "putting the best face possible on Soviet arms control proposals and disparaging American policy." He was the coauthor of the three-volume compendium *The Struggle of the Soviet Union for Disarmament* and, covertly, he prepared propaganda for what he has called "the Soviet disinformation apparatus." That propaganda, disseminated internationally, promoted the Soviet Union as the champion of disarmament. By 1973 he had contributed approximately 200 articles to *Kommunist*, *Pravda*, *New Times*, *International Life*, and other publications, many of them under the pseudonym "N. Arkadyev."

Nominated by Gromyko, Shevchenko in April 1973 became undersecretary general for political and Security Council affairs in the Secretariat of the United Nations, a position traditionally held by a Soviet. In that post he controlled twenty subsections, with a total staff of ninety-one, dealing with disarmament and outer-space issues, and some African problems. On those matters of international concern, he and his staff coordinated information for the Security Council and prepared political analyses for Secretary General Kurt Waldheim.

As the highest-ranking Soviet in the UN Secretariat, Shevchenko graduated to a life-style far beyond the reach of the average Soviet citizen, earning $87,000 a year, living in a maid-attended luxury Manhattan apartment, and riding in a chauffeured limousine. Unlike his wife, Lina, who had difficulty adapting to American ways (except for shopping sprees), he relished "the openness of American society" and resented the strict surveillance of agents of the KGB, the Soviet state security police, who, according to him, "maintained a large presence in New York, particularly in the UN Secretariat." In his book he recalls having to "use and manipulate" the UN Secretariat in violation of his UN oath to behave "as an international civil servant . . . and not to seek or accept instructions . . . from any government or authority external to the organization." "The USSR and the Soviet bloc are not unique in their disregard of (the UN's) international purpose," he explained in *Breaking with Moscow*. "But in the UN the Soviet Union is alone in one respect among the other nations on earth: its mendacity and cynicism are fully institutionalized."

Shevchenko's experience as undersecretary brought to a boil a disillusionment with the Soviet system that had long been simmering within him. Even as a young man rising in the diplomatic service, he recounted in *Breaking with Moscow*, he was aware that he was "part of the stratum that tried to portray itself as fighting what it coveted . . . the bourgeois way of life," but he "smiled and played the hypocrite, not only in public . . . but even in [his] own family." As he "approached the pinnacle of influence," he "found it a desert," and he saw "how easily" members of the Politburo "called vice virtue, . . . how hypocrisy and corruption had penetrated the smallest aspects of their lives, how isolated they were from the population they ruled." After years spent among the Soviet elite, he "finally got [his] fill of its venality and coarseness," its "personal betrayals," its "suspicion and intrigues" and decided that "by continuing to serve the Soviet Union [he] would be helping to support and promote what [he] hated."

Shevchenko considered resigning from his position and joining "the open dissidents to fight the regime" in the Soviet Union, but he realized that if he did so he would spend the rest of his life "in jail or in a mental institution" because he "knew too much for the government to let [him] remain at large at home or exile [him] to the West." Through an American diplomat friend at the UN, he was put in contact with the Central Intelligence Agency, which agreed to help and to protect him in defecting but asked in return that he stay on at the United Nations "a little while" to "provide us with information."

For two-and-a-half years Shevchenko was a self-described "reluctant spy," a role made easy by his reputation as a dedicated Soviet hardliner at the UN. "I have never regarded myself as a spy in the true sense of the word, nor have I felt I betrayed my people or my country," he writes in *Breaking with Moscow*. "I have always loved Russia and always will. For a relatively short time in my life I worked with the U.S. government to help it better comprehend the objectives and actions of the Soviet regime—a regime I knew well and had grown to hate. That regime, and the system that props it up, is what I 'betrayed.'" In his criticism of *Breaking with Moscow* in the *New Republic*, Edward Jay Epstein pointed out that the manuscript for the book was a pedestrian tome, rejected by publishers, until, with the help of ghostwriters,

Shevchenko turned paraphrased material into dramatic verbatim "conversations" with such figures as Nikita Khrushchev and added "all the elements of a spy thriller." Epstein suggested that "much of the material about Shevchenko's espionage career" was either "spun out of formulaic spy fiction or invented out of whole cloth," partly to give the CIA, "at a time of concern about KGB espionage successes, . . . its own success story—the penetration of the walled city of the Kremlin." Ashbel Green, the editor in chief at Alfred A. Knopf, described Epstein's charges as "bizarre fulminations," and the essential reliability of Shevchenko's memoir was corroborated by, among others, Senator Daniel Patrick Moynihan, the former deputy chairman of the Senate Intelligence Committee, Stansfield Turner, the former director of the CIA, and even Judy Taylor Chavez, Shevchenko's alienated former paid companion. Shevchenko observed that if his book is a fraud "then two presidents of the United States are frauds, both Carter and Reagan, who knew about my story, and the several National Security advisers also are frauds."

After receiving a cable summoning him to Moscow for "consultations," Shevchenko became convinced, at the beginning of April 1978, that his secret cooperation with the United States government had been discovered, and on April 6, 1978 he fled to a CIA "safe house" in the Pocono Mountains in Pennsylvania. Once under American protection, he called the UN to have his office sealed and then phoned his wife. To his shock, a man, probably a KGB agent, answered. Lina had disappeared. In anger, he wrote to Leonid Brezhnev, the Soviet Communist party's general secretary, announcing his break with Moscow and offering to resign from the UN discreetly in exchange for a guarantee of his family's immunity from "repressive measures of any sort."

Kurt Waldheim, the UN secretary general, accepted Shevchenko's resignation from his UN post on April 25, 1978, and sixteen days later Shevchenko learned that his wife, flown back to the Soviet Union, had died there of an overdose of sleeping pills. Soviet authorities described Lina's death as a suicide, but Shevchenko, having heard of "medical assassinations," wondered if they could "have murdered her to protect themselves, and perhaps at the same time punish [him]?" He worried about his children—not so much about his son, Gennady, a novice career diplomat from whom he had wisely remained politically aloof, as about his daughter, Anna, living in the Shevchenko apartment with her grandmother. Attempts to contact Anna through government and personal channels failed and Shevchenko came to feel that "the surest, cruelest way the Soviets can punish me is to keep us separated."

During months of debriefing by the CIA and FBI in a succession of locations and under several aliases, Shevchenko recounts in *Breaking with Moscow*, he became starved for "an emotional support they [his male protectors] could not provide." At the suggestion of FBI agents, he finally called an "escort" service, through which he met in May 1978 Judy Taylor Chavez, a Washington call girl on whom he lavished tens of thousands of dollars over a period of five months. The prolonged assignation turned out to be a major embarrassment to both him and the CIA. In October 1978 Miss Chavez lured the former diplomat to a rendezvous at a Washington restaurant where he was taken by surprise by television cameramen from NBC News, and she wrote the paperback exposé *Defector's Mistress* (Dell, 1979), in which she portrayed Shevchenko unkindlily and charged that the CIA was the source of the money he gave her. Shevchenko insisted that the money came from his UN severance pay, although he did acknowledge that the CIA provided him with a generous annuity.

In December 1978 Shevchenko married Elaine Bissell Jackson, whom he had met through his attorney and friend William Geimer. The new Mrs. Shevchenko, a court reporter from North Carolina, quit her job in order to concentrate on helping her husband with his writing. The Shevchenkos live in a house they bought in suburban Washington, D.C., one room of which contains Shevchenko's large personal library. "I don't advertise who I am, and if they [the neighbors] know it, they don't seem to care," Shevchenko told Leo Seligsohn in the *Newsday* interview. "We live quietly."

A poker-faced and somewhat stiff-mannered but amiable man, Arkady N. Shevchenko is round-shouldered and of medium height, with a slight physique. Leo Seligsohn of *Newsday* described him as having a "hyper" personality and speaking English "fast and nonstop." In addition to Russian and English, Shevchenko speaks French and German. His ample, bespectacled visage has become familiar to viewers of American television news programs, which regularly enlist him for commentaries on Soviet affairs. His full work schedule also includes regular lectures at the Foreign Service Institute of the United States Department of State, consultations with various other government departments and agencies, testimony at congressional hearings, and tours of the university and business lecture circuits (at $7,000 a talk). Spending much of his time writing, he contributes to various journals and newspapers and is working on a new book. The motion-picture rights to *Breaking with Moscow* have been purchased by Lester Persky Productions.

For a high-ranking defector who has been sentenced to death in absentia in the USSR, the former diplomat now lives a relatively open life, without bodyguards and other protections offered by the CIA and FBI. He does so for two reasons. One is that he does not see the sense of leaving "one prison for another." The other is that he believes that his best defense against retaliation from the KGB is "to remain publicly active." "What is my life worth, compared to the scandal that would occur if they did something to me now?" he pointed out to Robert Cross in an interview for the *Chicago Tribune* (April 7, 1985). "My face is so well-known in this country."

References: Chicago Tribune III p1+ Ap 7 '85 pors; N Y Times p12 Ap 11 '78 por; Newsday mag p12+ Jl 4 '82 por; Washington Post C p1+ F 18 '85 por; Chavez, Judy Foster. Defector's Mistress (1979); International Who's Who, 1985–86; Shevchenko, Arkady N. Breaking with Moscow (1985); Who's Who in the United Nations and Related Agencies (1975)

## Siles Zuazo, Hernán
(sē´lāz swä´sõ)

Mar. 19, 1914– Former president of Bolivia. Address: Oficina Principal, Moviemento Nacionalista Revolucionario Izquierdo, La Paz, Bolivia

Note: This biography supersedes the article that appeared in *Current Biography* in 1958.

The moderate populist Hernán Siles Zuazo has been in the eye of the Bolivian political storm for over four decades. A founder of the Nationalist Revolutionary Movement (MNR), in 1941, Siles led his party to power in Bolivia's national revolution of 1952 and served as president of his small, landlocked Andean country from 1956 to 1960. He spent most of the following two decades in exile, as one military regime succeeded another and Siles led the left-of-center schism in the MNR that became today's Leftist Nationalist Revolutionary Movement (MNRI). Deprived of the presidency by electoral fraud in 1978 and by a combination of congressional stalemate and military power in 1979 and 1980, Siles was finally inaugurated for a second term as president in 1982, when runaway inflation, chronic popular unrest, and internal division drove the armed forces back to the barracks. More pragmatic than leftist, President Siles reluctantly imposed on his already impoverished nation an austere "war economy." That policy hurt him politically more than it affected the economic imbroglio he had inherited. He called for new presidential elections in July 1985 and was succeeded by Victor Paz Estenssoro the following month.

Hernán Siles Zuazo was born in La Paz on March 19, 1914, the illegitimate son of Hernando Siles Reyes, the last Republican president of Bolivia (1926–30), and Isabel Zuazo Cusicanqui. Raised by his mother, he was never close to his father, although the relationship between father and son was cordial. Siles Zuazo's half-brother, Luis Adolfo Siles Salinas, also served as president of Bolivia, for five months in 1969.

Although he was raised a Roman Catholic, Siles Zuazo received his secondary education at the American Institute, a Methodist school in La Paz. After fighting in the Chaco war (1932–35), a territorial conflict in which the superior Bolivian forces were routed by a frugally armed and trained Paraguayan army, he earned a law degree at the University of San Andrés in La Paz and, in 1939, set up a law practice in the capital city. As a law student and young lawyer, he helped to found the Bolivian National Statistics Bureau and directed the Congressional Library.

The Chaco war, with its high cost in lives, territory, and national pride, was a watershed in Bolivian politics, leaving many of the more literate young veterans of the debacle not only bitter but radicalized. Blaming the ill-advised confrontation with Paraguay on the international oil companies and wealthy tin-mine owners and their political allies, they set out to challenge the traditional political system, in which, in their view, a white upper-class minority protected its narrow vested interests without a comprehensive sense of patriotism and with aristocratic disregard for the general welfare of a population that is predominantly Indian.

Most of the political parties formed in the wake of the Chaco war, whether on the left or the right, called themselves "revolutionary." The first challenge to the old-style politics was that mounted by a group of young army officers who seized power in 1936 and tried to impose a military socialism on the country. Over a period of three years they achieved three of their major goals: a new constitution, a national labor code, and the confiscation of the holdings of the Standard Oil Company in Bolivia.

Meanwhile, civilian dissidents were forming various opposition alignments, from Communist to right-wing falangist. Among the four most powerful groupings to emerge was the National Revolutionary Movement (Movimiento Nacionalista Revolucionario or MNR), which Siles Zuazo helped Victor Paz Estenssoro to found in 1941. In its original state, the MNR was an amorphous blend of Marxist and fascist ideologies. Advocating

land reform, universal suffrage, nationalization of the mining industry, and unionization of the miners, it won the support of the Indians and the mestizos and began building a coalition in the Congress, where Siles was a member of the chamber of deputies. The party would find its identity as a grand coalition only when, after several years, it repudiated its fascist wing. In the meantime, under the influence of that wing, the MNR was allied with a clandestine military movement, Razón de Patria, which in a coup in 1943 installed Major Gualberto Villaroel, a national socialist, in the presidency. Villaroel's reformist but repressive regime was brought to an end by a popular uprising in 1946, when he was lynched by a mob in front of the presidential palace.

Following Villaroel's overthrow, Siles lived in exile in Argentina and Chile, earning a living as a translator for American news agencies. While in exile, the MNR leaders revamped their party, purging it of its extreme right wing and joining forces with the Trotskyite mine-union leader Juan Lechín Oquendo (who is now, along with Paz, an opponent of Siles). At the same time, they made the party's reformist agenda general enough to be acceptable to a broad spectrum of other groups.

From exile, Paz ran for president and Siles for vice-president in 1951. They won a plurality of the vote, but not a decisive majority, and a military junta intervened before Congress could decide the election. Juan Lechín Oquendo's tin miners spearheaded a popular armed uprising against the junta, and Siles returned from exile to help direct the successful historic national revolution of 1952, which installed Paz and Siles in office. Under Paz's four-year presidency, with Siles heading a national commission on agrarian reform, the first MNR government fulfilled the party's most revolutionary promises, nationalizing the three largest tin-mining companies and abolishing the feudal system that had held the Indian population in peonage. It implemented the most sweeping land reform program in the history of the Americas, and, promulgating suffrage for all, struck down the literacy requirement for voting. Supplied with arms as well as with land and the franchise, the Indians were from that time on a force, however passive, to be reckoned with in Bolivian politics. In contrast, the armed forces were stripped of men and matériel, and their officers' ranks, previously a predominantly aristocratic preserve, were opened to the middle and lower classes. Enfeebled as well as democratized, the military would remain politically impotent for a dozen years.

With the revolutionary reforms, unfortunately, came inflation. Elected president in 1956, Siles concentrated on protecting the economic stability of the country, and he succeeded in doing so with the help of loans from the International Monetary Fund and aid from the United States but at the expense of revolutionary programs. He cut back on some of the recently introduced social services, froze wages, quashed incipient strikes (on one occasion by countering with a personal hunger strike, a tactic he would repeat several times during his presidencies), ended worker co-administration of the nationalized mines, and invited American oil companies back into Bolivia. When several Marxist members of his cabinet resigned in protest against what they considered the surrender of Bolivian sovereignty to American interests, the MNR leadership rallied behind Siles, authorizing the purging of dissident left-wingers from the government and the party.

Paz Estenssoro returned to the presidency in 1960 with General René Barrientos Ortuña as his vice-president. During that MNR administration, Siles served as ambassador to Paraguay (1960-63) and to Spain (1963-64). This time around, Paz did not resume the political and social reform he had begun in the early 1950s but, rather, continued the retrenchment initiated by Siles. In addition, with the help of the United States, he rebuilt the Bolivian army and air force, paving the way for a new era of military juntas.

Deposed by military coup in 1964, Paz fled into exile along with the other MNR leaders, including Siles Zuazo, and Bolivia settled into eighteen years of shifting military rule. Midway through those years, there was a period in which more enlightened and socially conscious army and air force officers came to the fore, in regimes that gained the support of the left with their openness to accommodation with organized labor and the radical student movement. That period ended with the ascent to power in 1971 of Colonel Hugo Banzer Suárez, a right-wing nationalist, supported by the urban bourgeoisie, who ruled Bolivia for seven years. The dominant party during the Banzer regime was the Socialist Falange, modeled on the Spanish fascist party of the same name.

In exile, the two MNR leaders moved in opposite directions, Paz to the right of center and Siles to the left. After Paz threw the support of the party behind the Banzer regime (for two years, beginning in 1971), Siles broke away and formed the schismatic Leftist Nationalist Revolutionary Movement (Movimiento Nacionalista Revolucionario Izquierdo, hence MNRI). The MNRI was the principal element in the Democratic and Popular Unity (Unidad Democratica Popular, hence UDP) coalition, the peasant-labor alliance under the auspices of which Siles ran for president in 1978. Paz Estenssoro ran as the candidate of the Historical Nationalist Revolutionary Movement (Movimiento Nacionalista Revolucionario Histórico, hence MNRH), an electoral alliance that solidified into the orthodox successor to the MNR party. General Juan Pereda Asbún was the military candidate.

In the 1978 election Siles outpolled Paz Estenssoro, but the voting was rigged in favor of General Pereda, apparently by right-wing elements in collusion with army and air force factions afraid of losing their prerogatives. Balloting described by the head of an international panel of observers to be "as crooked as a piece of barbed wire" left the results in dispute, and General Pereda was installed in the presidency by military mandate. Four

months later Pereda was ousted by General David Padilla Arancibia, who promised a return to civilian rule in 1979.

In July 1979 Siles won a narrow plurality of votes over Paz, but not a decisive majority. Congress named Walter Guevera Arze, the president of the Senate, to serve as interim chief executive pending a new election in 1980, but Colonel Alberto Natusch Busch seized power on November 1, 1979. Two weeks later, following widespread civil disorder and the suspension of $200 million in aid from the United States, Colonel Natusch Busch was forced to resign, and Congress elected the president of the chamber of deputies, Lidia Gueiler Tejada, provisional chief executive.

Again in June 1980, Siles received the largest number of votes but not an absolute majority. Before Congress could ratify his election, as was expected, officers claiming to head off a "Communist assault" led a bloody military uprising, in which many leftist leaders were arrested, tortured, and killed. Disguised as a peasant, Siles escaped by boat across Lake Titicaca to Peru. The junta that governed Bolivia under three successive chief executives during the following two years found the task increasingly onerous. During the long procession of military regimes preceding theirs, the bureaucrats who had continued to function could do little more than assuage the symptoms of Bolivia's grievous social and economic ills. Although Bolivia had the largest standing army, per capita, of any Andean nation, it had the lowest per-capita income ($550 annually) in the hemisphere after Haiti, and that income was decreasing in real value at an accelerating pace. The national treasury, with a deficit three times greater than the budget, was covering the balance by printing pesos, contributing to a worsening inflation.

By the summer of 1982 Bolivia was technically in default on its foreign debt, and its international reputation was not helped by the presence of an unconstitutional junta at the helm of government. Domestically, the military regime was under pressure from striking miners, demonstrations against the involvement of generals in the cocaine trade, and dissent and division in the armed forces themselves. In September 1982 General Guido Vildoso Calderón, the head of the junta, announced that leadership would be turned over to civilians the following month. Siles wanted a general election, but General Vildoso instead reconvened the 1980 Congress, which elected Siles president.

Returning from exile, Siles was inaugurated on October 10, 1982 as the head of a coalition government made up of members of his own party, the Soviet-line Communist party, and another Marxist group, the Leftist Revolutionary Movement. He began his administration with brave words, declaring in his inaugural address that the time of "those who do not believe in democracy" had "come to an end" and that "we are going to dismantle corruption and . . . start a new road in the national revolution." However, the nearly bankrupt national treasury, the declining productivity, the runaway inflation, the food shortages, and the rest of the economic problems he had inherited from his military predecessors were to prove more than he could handle.

Central to Siles' plan for national recovery was an austerity program calculated in large measure to persuade the International Monetary Fund to refinance on favorable terms Bolivia's foreign debt (which is now $6 billion, and rising), on which the country would have difficulty even paying the interest. Unfortunately, his program damaged him politically without affecting the inflation rate, which soared from 200 to more than 3,000 percent in three years. Over those years, the configuration of his cabinet changed repeatedly (seventy-four ministers came and went in six cabinets) in disagreements over the way to handle the foreign debt and inflation. The chief disagreement on the left came from Juan Lechín Oquendo, the head of Central Obrera Boliviana (COB), the workers' confederation, who wanted the government to halt negotiations with the IMF, repudiate the foreign debt until refinancing could be handled without undue sacrifice from the Bolivian people, and sell its gold reserves to make up for the lack of foreign credit. A "national liberation" program drawn up by the COB called for state control of private banks, worker control of private enterprises, peasant confederation control of the emergency agricultural program, and majority worker representation in all state decision-making bodies.

In May 1984 President Siles temporarily suspended foreign debt payments, pending renegotiation of refinancing. If the suspension pleased the left, it riled many on the right, who called for Siles' resignation, and in June a group of right-wing police and army officers kidnapped the president for ten hours in an abortive coup attempt. Siles was cooperative with other governments in such matters as the capture and extradition of international terrorists and the Nazi war criminal Klaus Barbie, and he tried to cooperate with the United States in fighting the traffic in cocaine and wanted to set up independent courts to hear drug cases, but that was a more difficult matter, for several reasons. The most obvious was the fact that, at a time when Bolivia's traditional chief exports, tin and natural gas, were going begging on the world market, the cocaine industry was earning an estimated $2 billion a year. Another reason was the necessity of defending the state-monopolized cultivation of the coca plant, which, as Siles explained on one occasion, "from time immemorial has been chewed by our people to relieve pain." A third reason was the threat from anonymous powers in the military that they would not tolerate eradication of the cocaine business. When it became known that Siles had authorized a meeting between the head of his anti-drug agency and Robert Suárez Gomez, the so-called "Cocaine King" of Bolivia, who reportedly offered the government assistance in meeting its foreign debt payments, the Congress voted to censure him, on October 24, 1984. He responded to the censure with a five-day fast, his fifth in public life,

to help "restore a climate of peace and reflection by Bolivians."

Pressured by strikes and demonstrations, Siles made some concessions to the COB, including a dominant union role in the management of Comibol, the state mining company, granted in 1983, and a 57 percent wage increase, granted in 1984. He stubbornly refused, however, to abandon outright his austerity program, which included price increases of 400 percent in gasoline and 300 percent in food in 1984. A walkout by tin miners in March 1985 sparked a general strike, in which the union leaders demanded an inflation-adjusted minimum wage increase of at least 400 percent. On March 20, 1985 Siles deployed army troops and riot police against rampaging mobs of strikers disrupting transport and commerce in La Paz. It was his government's first such use of military force.

Even those sectors of Bolivian society not antagonized by Siles' decisions had become impatient with what they viewed as his general indecisiveness. In the summer of 1985 Siles decided to step down, a year before the end of his term. Following elections in which no candidate received a plurality of the vote, the Bolivian congress named Victor Paz Estenssoro to succeed Siles.

Hernán Siles Zuazo is five feet four inches tall and not as chunky as the contours of his face suggest in photographs. He wears thick glasses, and several of the fingers of his left hand are paralyzed, the result of a wound received in the Chaco war. Political friends and enemies alike regard him as honest and skillful, but stubborn. "He's a peaceful, introverted man of good will," Fernando Baptista, the vice-president of the Bolivian Senate, told Edward Schumacher, a special correspondent for the New York Times, in 1982. Siles and his wife, the former Maria Teresa Ormachea del Carpio, have three grown daughters, Marcela, Ana María, and Isabel.

References: Macleans 98:28 Mr 18 '85; N Y Times A p8 O 8 '82 por, p3 O 9 '82, IV p4 O 10 '82 por; Newsweek 100:87 O 25 '82 por; International Who's Who 1985–86; Mitchell, Christopher. The Legacy of Populism in Bolivia (1977)

---

## Slade, Roy

July 14, 1933– Art school president; museum director; artist. Address: b. P.O. Box 801, Bloomfield Hills, Mich. 48013; h. 500 Lone Pine Rd., Bloomfield Hills, Mich. 48013

Energy, enthusiasm, and an unusual combination of talents have helped to shape Roy Slade's career. An innovative teacher of painting and an adept educational executive, Slade has been president of the Cranbrook Academy of Art in Bloomfield Hills, Michigan since 1977. During his tenure he has re-

*Roy Slade*

stored the school to its position—once in jeopardy—as one of the most prestigious academies of art and design in the United States. In addition to shouldering his manifold administrative responsibilities, including lecturing and teaching, he has managed to find time to continue with his own painting, which he has exhibited in group and one-man shows.

Roy Slade was born in Cardiff, Wales on July 14, 1933, the son of David Trevor and Millicent (Roberts) Slade, who encouraged his precocity to such a degree that he exhibited his first painting at the age of five in a children's art show in Cardiff. He obtained his National Diploma of Design (equivalent to an American B.F.A.) from the Cardiff College of Art in 1953, where he won the Silver Medal for being "the student who contributes most to the life of the college and who also produces the best work in the open competition." He received an art teachers diploma from the University of Wales the following year.

After serving in the British Army, and teaching in the Far Eastern School of Language and Method in Singapore and Malaya during the mid-1950s, Slade returned to Wales to head the Arts and Crafts Department of Heolgam School. There, in 1957, he married his first wife, a student-teacher at the school. In 1960 he took the first of a series of teaching posts in England, as a lecturer at Clarendon College in Nottingham, and in 1964 he went on to teach painting at Leeds College of Art, one of the most influential of all European art schools. From 1965 to 1967 he served as its director of post-diploma studies.

At Leeds a new team approach to the teaching of art had been adopted: students, instead of emulating the style of a particular mentor—the so-called atelier system—came under the tutelage of several instructors who encouraged them to experiment and develop their own styles. Slade's contribution to that innovation was recognized with the award of a Fulbright-Hays scholarship for the year 1967–68, under the terms of which he came to the United States to teach painting at the Corcoran School of Art in Washington, D.C. In the course of that year he traveled and lectured extensively, observing the still ultraconservative, formal way in which art was taught in American schools.

On his return to England, Roy Slade spent the academic year of 1968–69 as senior lecturer at Leeds College, until a call came from the Corcoran School. Slade went back as its associate dean, charged with the responsibility of planning a new four-year program incorporating his team-teaching ideas and philosophy of "education is exposure," and, coincidentally, with helping to mend a rift between faculty and administration. Because of his success as a mediator who could also strengthen the school's reputation and financial position, Slade's career took off, and in 1970 he was appointed dean of the Corcoran School. Two years later he was once again chosen to step in to fill a breach, when he was asked to serve as the temporary director of the Corcoran Gallery of Art. The museum's codirectors had resigned their posts after a much-publicized, eyebrow-raising brawl during a formal opening that culminated several years of mounting financial and administrative tensions.

Although Slade was at first reluctant to accept the directorship, he proved to be the correct choice. In the words of the *Washington Post* art critic Paul Richard, he "brought with him one invaluable credential. . . . Slade knows Washington, its artists and its audiences, its dealers and collectors. He gets along with people of all sorts." That included the museum's board of trustees. For six months, while still serving as dean of the art school, Slade held things together, guided by his recognition of the Corcoran Gallery's unique place among Washington museums and by his determination that he would "restore dignity and credibility to the institution [and] get things done with maximum efficiency and minimum expense."

That he proceeded to do by exhibiting more of the Corcoran's somewhat neglected core holdings of eighteenth and nineteenth-century American art, with an eye to the forthcoming 1976 Bicentennial, while continuing to show the work of contemporary local artists. Slade said at the time: "We're one block from the White House. We have a national role to play. We must continue to hang local and regional exhibitions [and] important international shows." During that six-month interim period he managed both to reduce the deficit by paring staff and, at the same time, to put on as many as twenty-seven exhibitions. Despite what was perceived by some observers to be his lack of a national reputation and museum experience, he was named permanent director of the Corcoran Gallery, continuing as dean of its art school, on June 27, 1973.

With his program of "direction, decision, delegation," Slade succeeded in turning what the press habitually labeled "the chronically troubled Corcoran" into what he called a "very much alive" gallery. In late 1973, in conjunction with the publication of the second volume of the catalogue of the museum's American paintings, that core collection was reinstalled. Two years later, all signs pointed to the Corcoran's breaking even financially, thanks not only to his rigorous economies but also to his success in attracting donations. Membership had increased, funds were available for purchases of art for the first time in several years, and the appointment of a chief curator and additional staff provided him with much needed help. Those achievements were crowned by the popular success of the Corcoran's Thirty-fourth Biennial Exhibition of Contemporary American Painting, a show put together by Slade in February 1975. Displaying the mostly monumental works of fifty artists, it was a festive "celebration of the spectacle and spectrum of contemporary art," as Slade described it. Formal recognition of his achievements came with his receipt of the Welsh Society of Philadelphia Award in 1974 and his election to membership in the National Society of Literature and Arts in 1975.

In March 1977 Slade announced his resignation from the Corcoran to become president of the Cranbrook Academy of Art in Bloomfield Hills, Michigan and director of its museum. He assumed his new posts on August 1 of that year. "Cranbrook made me an offer I couldn't refuse," he explained to the dismayed Washington art community. The position not only promised him "money, security, and an academic schedule," but also—and that was the main consideration—"a chance to return to the studio to paint." Perhaps Slade left, as one observer speculated, because he "just wasn't having that much fun anymore."

The Cranbrook Academy was founded in 1923, and formally opened in 1932, by George G. Booth and Ellen Scripps Booth, Detroit newspaper publishers and philanthropists who envisioned the establishment of a community of artists and craftsmen. On a handsomely landscaped estate of 300 acres about twenty-five miles north of Detroit, it includes, besides studios and living quarters, three preparatory schools for boys and girls, a science institute, a museum and library, and a church. Most of the buildings and their furnishings were designed by the great Finnish architect Eliel Saarinen and his family, and Saarinen himself served as president of Cranbrook until 1947. The school became renowned as an American Bauhaus among whose distinguished graduates were the designers Charles Eames and Florence Knoll and the sculptor Harry Bertoia, but after Saarinen's death in 1950 its lustrous reputation began to fade. It was Slade's mandate, as it had been at the Corcoran, to address the problems of a troubled institution. By 1982, on the occasion of Cranbrook's fiftieth anniversary, the design critic Wolf von Eckardt could pronounce the academy to be "in vigorous health, due mainly to an infusion of crackling energy."

Slade's grasp of Eliel Saarinen's philosophy of the unity of arts, craft, and design is reflected in his own statement that an interest in crafts bespeaks "an inherent desire for a return to basic values and human survival." In that spirit, one of his first tasks was the refurbishing of Saarinen's own home and studio. Working from photographs, he restored many of the original furnishings and was able to track down others that had been dispersed. Slade finally reconstructed the Saarinen House as the most important residence created in the art deco and *moderne* styles in the United States.

A kinship also exists between Slade's theories of teaching by exposure and Eliel Saarinen's guiding idea that Cranbrook was to be a supportive environment for creative artists rather than a school with a formal program of courses and credits. Its highly talented graduate students, about 150 in number, work for about two years with a staff of twelve artists-in-residence and visiting lecturers. "We don't teach at Cranbrook. We learn," Slade has declared. As an educator he has always believed that the creative artist's problem is one of self-motivation. "This is what we work on," he has said. "The talent is already there."

Since coming to Cranbrook, Slade has lectured throughout the United States about the academy, has tapped alumni, corporate donors, and collectors for support, and has solicited the return of objects from the Cranbrook collections. Exhibitions of those works, as well as of current productions of the workshops, have been mounted in the Cranbrook Art Museum every year since 1977, and an exhibition of 240 objects, in celebration of Cranbrook's golden jubilee, served to focus public attention on its revived spirit. "Design in America: The Cranbrook Vision 1925–1950" opened in Detroit, Michigan in December 1983. Originated by Slade and organized by the Detroit Institute of Arts and the Metropolitan Museum of Art, it went on to New York City and from there to Helsinki, Paris, and London in the course of a twenty-month tour.

Slade's stewardship of the Cranbrook vision has affected his own art. After finding one of the leaded panes that Eliel Saarinen had designed for his studio windows, he began to use the dominant triangle motif in a series of paintings and drawings. "It was the detail that summed up the whole of Cranbrook for me," he has explained. And in the folder for his 1981 exhibition of those works at the Robert L. Kidd Associates Galleries in Birmingham, Michigan, the artist acknowledged that "the interplay of structure and gesture, of hard and loose forms, of shape and surface, of geometry and line . . . expands the concerns of my earlier work."

That earlier work to which Slade referred began with realistic cityscapes and landscapes and evolved into abstract monochrome studies of forms inspired by trips to the Welsh and English seashores. Later, elements of collage, including shiny paper, strips of mirror, and photographs of seaweed, found their way onto such canvases. Slade's first one-man exhibition was held in a gallery in

Cardiff, Wales; in the years that followed he has had other solo shows, including several at the Jefferson Place Gallery in Washington, and has been represented in group shows in galleries in Great Britain, the United States, and Canada. Examples of his work are owned by, among others, the Arts Council of Great Britain, the British Overseas Airways Corporation, the British Embassy in Washington, and several private collectors.

The list of Slade's activities in behalf of art education and the survival of the independent art school is long and impressive, starting with his 1963-1969 tenure as chief examiner in art for the City and Guilds of London Institute. He has served, in the United States, on the board of directors of the National Association of Schools of Art (1973-74), which, as Slade describes it, "represents schools . . . of the highest traditions and aims in the education of artists" and is a potential "national forum for art education." He had been a member of numerous accreditation committees sponsored by the association and in 1983 was appointed to a four-year term as Commissioner for the Commission on Institutions of Higher Education, North Central Association of Colleges and Schools. Often called upon as an art consultant to institutions or urban centers, Slade has also judged art exhibitions throughout the country. He was the United States Department of State representative to the São Paulo Bienal in 1977, a member of the board of directors of the National Council of Art Administrators (1978-1981), and from 1978 to the present has chaired the Design Michigan Advisory Council, a program sponsored by the Cranbrook Academy to promote design awareness in the state. His career testifies to his belief that "an artist has a responsibility to the world around him to do what he can."

Energy and drive seem consonant with Slade's sheer physical size; he stands six feet one inch. With his blue eyes and abundant wavy gray hair and beard, he is a commanding, almost patriarchal figure. Affable, well-liked by students and colleagues, he steers a diplomatic course through the sometimes murky channels of the academic and museum worlds. Slade has been enthusiastic about all things American since he was a child in wartime Cardiff, and when he arrived in the United States, as he recalls, "Everything grabbed me." He became an American citizen in October 1975.

Slade has readily adapted to the disparate milieus of Washington and Cranbrook. In the nation's capital he and his first wife lived in a rented home filled with their own collection of trendy art that simply had "amused" him and pieces of furniture that he had made himself—"all held together with white paint." He is no longer married to his second wife, whom he wed in 1975. As doyen of the Saarinen House, he keeps it as a living museum, ever conscious of the "stimulus and challenge" presented to him by the unique Cranbrook environment.

References: Washington Post F p1 Jl 8 '73; Who's Who in America, 1982-83; Who's Who in America, 1984-85

### Söderström, Elisabeth
(sû´dər-strûm´´)

May 7, 1927- Swedish soprano. Address: b. c/o Royal Opera House, Stockholm, Sweden; c/o Jonathan Groves, Ingpen & Williams Ltd., 14 Kensington Ct., London W8 5DN, England; c/o Joyce L. Arbib, Columbia Artists Management Inc., 165 W. 57th St., New York City, N.Y. 10019; h. 19 Hersbyvagen, Lidingö 1, Sweden

Elisabeth Söderström, who is often referred to in headlines by Jenny Lind's nickname, "the Swedish Nightingale," is, indeed, not only one of Sweden's greatest singers but also one of the finest and most versatile operatic actresses in the world. An authority on the works of Leos Janacek and Richard Strauss, she is known internationally for her finely molded characterizations in works that range from classical to modern and from comic to tragic. Her repertoire boasts more than fifty operatic roles in ten languages and some 300 songs, which she has performed on stages from Australia to the Soviet Union and on radio, television, and recordings. A member of the Swedish Royal Academy of Music since 1965, she had been selected in 1959 to be a singer of the royal court, becoming at the age of thirty-two the youngest of the dozen holders of Sweden's highest singing honor. Her other honors include the Stelle della Solidarietà d'Italia, the Royal Swedish Academy's prize for best acting, and the Literis et Artibus Award, Sweden's highest decoration for accomplishment in the arts. "An artist should be an instrument and fit in with the great orchestra which consists of both musicians and artists," Miss Söderström believes. "But . . . an artist should also have his or her own personality and be able to produce his or her own personal interpretation of a role."

Elisabeth Anna Söderström, the first of three daughters, was born in Stockholm on May 7, 1927. Her mother was a White Russian concert pianist who had fled the 1917 revolution, and her father was a Swedish businessman who sang tenor as a pastime. Endowed with a good singing voice, Elisabeth was introduced to music by her nurse, a Salvation Army volunteer, who taught her temperance hymns that the three-year-old child sang for the amusement of her parents' dinner guests. Although afflicted with asthma and with allergies to practically anything from nuts and apples to dogs, cats, horses, and feathers, which persisted into adulthood, she was otherwise robust. At Stockholm's Nya Elementary School for Girls, she acted in the dramas the school staged to entertain war refugees. Her father did not encourage her to become a professional singer, but he was eager to see her develop her talents fully, and when she was fourteen she began to take voice training. Her teacher, the Russian coloratura Andreyeva von Skilondz (or de Skilondz), with whom she continued to study for many years, instilled in her a love for Rachmaninoff, Tchaikovsky, and Mussorgsky. It was from her that she learned a technique for focusing her voice without straining it, a skill that she found crucial in surviving performances while suffering from asthma.

Miss Söderström showed herself to be musically adaptable, indeed adventurous, with a talent for languages and particular fluency in English, but her main enthusiasm remained for acting. While studying languages and literary history at Stockholm University, she continued to try her talents in student stage productions. Only after she was turned down by the Stockholm School of Dramatic Arts (out of hundreds of applicants she was ranked ninth, but only eight were admitted) did she turn seriously to singing, with her father's approval. At the prestigious Stockholm Opera School she continued to study languages and also undertook ensemble singing, ballet, acting, fencing, piano, counterpoint, harmony, and solfège. As a student, she was routinely assigned walk-on roles at the Dröttningholm Court Theatre, where she made her debut in 1947 as the shepherdess Bastienne, in Mozart's one-act opera Bastien und Bastienne.

While still in school, Miss Söderström appeared in several minor roles with the Swedish Royal Opera, of which she became a member in 1950. There she worked with, among others, conductor Sixten Ehrling and director Goeran Gentele, a product of Stockholm's Royal Theatre, whose ensemble theatrical experience and attention to subtleties of lighting and blocking helped to revolutionize the Royal Opera. Miss Söderström was delighted by those theatrical infusions of life and nuance into the broadly stylized and static characterizations traditionally associated with opera and saw no inconsistency in the pairing of naturalistic acting techniques with the artificial conventions of opera. In her 1978 autobiography, I Min Tonart (published in English by David & Charles in 1979 as In My Own Key), she wrote, "All my life I have striven to show that it is not in the slightest unnatural to express yourself in song . . . to find a balance between music, words and gestures [to achieve] the work of art I consider an opera performance should be." In the book, she offered a glimpse of her own method of preparing for a role: "When I think myself into a personality, I often start by imagining how that person walks. It sometimes helps to wear the shoes you are going to wear with your costume. . . . "

The year she joined the Swedish Royal Opera, Miss Söderström married Sverker Olow, an officer in the Royal Swedish Navy. That enduring union yielded three sons, Malcolm, Peter, and Jens. Her desire to be with her family was to play a formative role in her career, for by the time her first son was born her versatile voice and powerfully appealing stage presence had earned her an international reputation and invitations to perform worldwide. Her 1955 debut at the Salzburg Festival as Ighino in Hans Pfitzner's Palestrina was followed by her debut at the Glyndebourne Festival in 1957 as the Composer of the opera-within-an-opera in Richard Strauss's Ariadne auf Naxos. Over the years, she became a favorite at Glyndebourne, performing, among other roles, that of Tatiana in Eugene Onegin, in 1968; the countess in Capriccio, in 1973; and Christine in the British premiere of Strauss's Intermezzo, in 1974. Other leading festivals in which she appeared included that in Edinburgh, where she sang the title role in a Royal Opera of Stockholm production of Janacek's Jenufa and appeared as Marie in Alban Berg's Wozzek.

The year 1959 was especially productive for the Swedish singer, who seemed to thrive on diversity and challenge. That summer she was named Hovsangerska, or royal court singer, by King Gustav VI, and in the fall she made her debut with the Metropolitan Opera in New York, beginning a mutually enhancing four-year relationship. Howard Taubman, writing in the New York Times (October 31, 1959), called her opening-night performance as Susanna in Marriage of Figaro "captivating" and praised the "color, size, sweetness and brilliance" of her voice, while Paul Henry Lang wrote in the Herald Tribune that she was "simply a darling, with a bright, delectable, and accurate soprano that carried the treble like a crystal flute."

Elisabeth Söderström's performances at the Metropolitan Opera during 1959 included demanding roles that she sang fluently in three languages—Italian, French, and German. In her portrayal of Marguerite in Gounod's Faust at the Met, she "was fetching of manner and leaden of voice," according to Jay S. Harrison, writing in the Herald Tribune (December 9, 1959). But John

Briggs, in the *New York Times* (December 9, 1959), found the same performance "brilliant" and elaborated: "Miss Söderström has a dark-textured voice of marked individuality, with wide compass and good carrying power. Marguerite's music lies comfortably within her range." A few weeks later, for the Met production of Richard Strauss's *Der Rosenkavalier*, she became "a delightful Sophie" despite some imperfect top notes, according to Francis D. Perkins' review in the *Herald Tribune* (December 27, 1959). In the course of 1959 she sang, in addition to her Met performance as Sophie, the other two soprano roles in *Der Rosenkavalier*: Octavian, at Glyndebourne, and the Marschallin, in Stockholm.

In her next Met season, Miss Söderström reprised Susanna and added the roles of Adina, in Donizetti's *L'Elisir d'Amore*, and Musetta, in Puccini's *La Bohème*, to her repertoire. Although her acting brought only praise, "vocally she did not sound too comfortable" as the village maiden Adina, according to Harold C. Schonberg of the *New York Times* (November 26, 1960). Commenting on her performance as Musetta, the critic for the *Herald Tribune* (January 10, 1961) wrote that she "threw herself into the role with splendid good spirits" but that "it cannot be said that her voice quite matched the animated quality of her characterization." Nevertheless, her dramatic interpretations had brought a fresh earthiness to the familiar roles.

Miss Söderström won hearts and headlines for resourcefulness in her 1962 New York season, when she filled in at perilously short notice for the indisposed Irmgard Seefried as soloist for the Clarion Concerts series at Town Hall. In three days, she learned the two Clärchen songs from Beethoven's *Egmont* as well as an extremely difficult Telemann cantata, *Ino*, which she "flung forth with superb style, as though [she] had been using the cantata as a warm-up piece for the last ten years," according to Alan Rich in the *New York Times* (November 8, 1962).

Engaged in her own right for the Clarion Concerts program in 1963, Miss Söderström sang works by Handel and by David Epstein under the baton of Newell Jenkins. That season, which was to be her last at the Met for nearly two decades, she repeated her Musetta to good notices and sang the Composer in *Ariadne auf Naxos*, a portrayal that brought mixed reviews. While Ross Parmenter of the *New York Times* (February 21, 1964) had only compliments for her "beautiful clarity of line," Louis Snyder, writing in the *Herald Tribune* on the same date, found her voice "wiry rather than substantial."

When Miss Söderström did not reappear in the United States in the seasons that followed, American opera fans assumed that she had retired. In fact, she had given her career a typically idiosyncratic twist, one that enabled her to carry on her family life simultaneously. Previously she had brought her three children with her to New York for her Metropolitan Opera sojourns, but when they reached school age, and her husband was frequently called away from home to sea duty, she found it imperative to remain in Sweden, where she became a member of the Royal Academy of Music in 1965.

Miss Söderström used her reduced radius of movement to broaden rather than narrow her range of activities. Although the Swedish Royal Opera's schedule encompassed ten months out of the year, she was not content merely to fulfill a rigorous commitment there, highlighted by occasional command performances for the King and guest appearances in northern Europe. As she confided to Stephen Godfrey of the Toronto *Globe and Mail* (January 31, 1980): "In my own country I try to spread opera wherever I can—in factories, prisons, hospitals, mental institutions. I'm preaching; I admit it. I'm always on the barricades."

In addition to in-person lecture-demonstrations throughout Sweden, Miss Söderström took on duties as a member of the board of the Swedish Broadcasting Corporation. She wrote and served as hostess of a "music salon" broadcast and she coproduced and costarred in the television show *The Prima Prima Donnas*, aimed at demystifying classical music for a mass audience. As she described the show to Stephen Godfrey, "We mix classical and pop. For example, in a scene from *The Marriage of Figaro*, where Cherubino jumps out of the window, we cut to him landing in a bathtub, and the next song is 'I'm Gonna Wash That Man Right Out of My Hair.'" Altogether, she made about 250 opera, concert, and television appearances a year. In her view, remaining close to home in no way diminished her influence. "When you sing in these vast countries [like the United States] you can't see the results immediately," she told Godfrey. "That's what I like about Sweden: there are only eight million people, and when I go on TV, I know I can reach everyone."

From her base in Sweden in the 1960s and 1970s Miss Söderström on occasion performed on stages in other countries. In 1966 she toured the Soviet Union. At Glyndebourne, her Tatiana in Tchaikovsky's *Eugene Onegin* "radiantly shone and nobly matured," in the words of J. W. Lambert in the *Christian Science Monitor* (July 12, 1968), and at Covent Garden her Fiordiligi in Mozart's *Così fan tutte* was "full of subtleties," according to the same reviewer (April 9, 1971), who found in her aria "Per pietà" "a positive renewal of faith."

Most of Miss Söderström's non-Swedish fans, however, had to rely on recordings to hear her voice. In 1967 London Records released her *Jenny Lind Songs*, and in 1973 Angel Records issued *Le Nozze di Figaro*, conducted by Otto Klemperer, in which Elisabeth Söderström, according to Harvey E. Phillips of the *New York Times* (July 1, 1973), "makes a gorgeous countess, properly aristocratic in her attitudes but able to profit by her voice's attractive, shimmering vibrato to suggest a tremulous vulnerability." By 1979 Angel had issued her fourth volume of *Rachmaninoff Songs*.

In 1977 London Records began a long-term project to record Miss Söderström in the operas of the Czech composer Leos Janacek, including *Katya Kabanova* and *Jenufa*, with her in the title roles, and the *The Makropulos Affair*, in which she sang the part of Emilia Marty. "How fortunate," Peter G. Davis wrote in *New York* magazine (November 28, 1983), "that Elisabeth Söderström's celebrated Janacek impersonations have been captured just in time to convey all the inner radiance and theatrical vibrancy she brings to these wonderful characters." By 1984 she could also be heard on *Elisabeth Söderström Sings Richard Strauss* and on the first recording of Benjamin Britten's *Our Hunting Fathers*, both issued under the EMI/Angel label.

After a thirteen-year absence, in 1977 Miss Söderström was again heard in person in the United States, singing the title role in the San Francisco Opera production of *Katya Kabanova*. Her voice, never perfectly reliable, had lost some of its upper range. Although that voice no longer "could blossom and soar at the music's climaxes," as John Rockwell observed in the *New York Times* (September 29, 1977), she had "evolved . . . into a consummate operatic actress." Later that fall Peter G. Davis, writing in the *New York Times* (October 10, 1977), had an opportunity to analyze the soprano's matured voice, when she gave a recital of songs of Wolf, Sjogren, Kilpinen, Canteloube, Grieg, and Rachmaninoff at New York's 92d Street YM-YWHA. "Judged purely on technical considerations, Miss Söderström does not have a completely unflawed instrument," he observed. "Occasionally a tone will lose support, a difficult phrase may sound a trifle labored perhaps or intonation become a bit suspect. These fleeting moments seem quite insignificant in view of what she does achieve with her voice—beautifully tapered diminuendos, a variety of fascinating colors, gorgeous tonal quality at any dynamic level, controlled pliancy of phrasing and above all the essential sentiment of a song, effects governed by a deep musical intelligence and emotional honesty."

When in 1979 New York's Friends of French Opera was revived after more than a decade of inactivity, Robert Lawrence, its artistic director, chose Miss Söderström to sing the title role of *Sapho* in a much publicized semistaged concert performance of Massenet's love story about a young artist and a middle-aged model. "It's a great personality opera, provided you're lucky enough to have a real singing actress in the title role," Lawrence remarked, as quoted in the *New Yorker* (February 5, 1979). "I've always thought of Elisabeth as a very fine lyric soprano, but now her voice has taken on a darker quality, which enables her to do these dramatically oriented roles. . . . She's like an earthquake." Unfortunately, the preliminary fanfare outshone the performance, in the view of critics.

In the spring of 1980, Clarion Concerts presented Miss Söderström as Dido in *Aeneas in Carthage*, a Swedish opera written in the 1780s by Joseph Martin Kraus. According to Donal Henahan of the *New York Times* (March 28, 1980), Miss Söderström "turned out to be the best reason for attending the performance." The following year, the concert room at New York's Frick Collection was the site of an afternoon recital by Elisabeth Söderström of works by Mendelssohn, Schumann, Schubert, Wilhelm Peterson-Berger, Wilhelm Stenhammar, Sverre Jordan, Carl Nielsen, Sibelius, and other composers. Although the tiny concert room held only 200 people, the recital reached many more with its radio broadcast over WNYC-FM. Miss Söderström kept the atmosphere intimate and informal, chatting with her charmed audience.

In early 1982, Miss Söderström sang Katya Kabanova at the Houston Grand Opera. After a tour that included Toronto, Milwaukee, and Washington, D.C. she was back in New York, singing selections from Rachmaninoff, Grieg, Sibelius, and Tchaikovsky at Alice Tully Hall. "No one alive now can remember Jenny Lind, but the title Swedish Nightingale wouldn't do Miss Söderström justice," Edward Rothstein wrote in the *New York Times* (January 25, 1982). Next on her itinerary was Australia, for a well-received recital tour that included an appearance at the Adelaide Festival as Emilia Marty in the State Opera of South Australia's production of *The Makropulos Affair*. By 1983 Miss Söderström's international career was fully revived, with an active United States schedule that included her performance as the Marschallin in *Der Rosenkavalier* at the Kennedy Center in Washington, D.C. and a recital at the Spoleto Festival U.S.A. in Charleston, South Carolina.

That fall, almost twenty years after she had last sung the Composer in *Ariadne* at the old Met, Miss Söderström made her debut at New York's new Metropolitan Opera House as Ellen Orford in Benjamin Britten's *Peter Grimes*. Just as they had two decades earlier, critics found flaws in her voice while praising her sympathetic and vivid characterization. She made her Santa Fe Opera debut the following winter as the composer's temperamental wife, Christine, in Richard Strauss's semiautobiographical *Intermezzo*. In May 1985 she and mezzo-soprano Frederica von Stade performed works of Brahms, Handel, Tchaikovsky, and Grieg in a recital for the Chamber Music Society of Lincoln Center.

Will Crutchfield, describing in the *New York Times* (January 14, 1985) an Alice Tully Hall recital that included songs by Britten and Tchaikovsky, summed up the singer's ability to communicate despite a flawed voice: "The truth is that Miss Söderström never had an ideal voice for song-singing, only an ideal spirit for it. Neither in dynamics, vocal color nor variety of attack and articulation is it particularly flexible. . . . So she does not do the thousand spontaneous things that Callas or Fischer-Dieskau could do to make character rivetingly manifest in the moment. But everything she *does* do is in character, and not the slightest thing is against it: Thus the spirit emerges, both the song's and the singer's."

This whole-hearted willingness to enter into a role is a reflection of Miss Söderström's absolute commitment to enjoying herself fully. Offstage as well as on, she displays a gusto and vigor that is bolstered by her unwavering refusal to undertake anything she finds onerous and by her consequent sureness and manifest love of what she is doing. Offered the late Goeran Gentele's post as director of the Stockholm Royal Opera in the early 1970s, she declined, declaring that she was "not prepared to stop singing."

When not performing, Elisabeth Söderström makes her home with her husband in a large wooden house on the island of Lidingö, near Stockholm, where she relaxes and indulges in good food and an occasional cocktail. Brown-haired and slim, she is five feet five inches tall and keeps fit by walking, sailing, skiing, and sledding. Her other recreations include reading, writing, embroidery, and solving crossword puzzles and cryptograms. In her autobiography, an assemblage of loosely connected humorous anecdotes, she anticipates with typical fearlessness and good cheer how she will face her last challenge: "I am convinced that just before I draw my last breath, recognising the situation, I will think: 'Ah, yes, this is what I did in *Bohème*, isn't it? . . . '"

References: Hi Fi/Mus Am 21:MA-4+ O '71 por; N Y Times II p9 N 8 '59, II p15 Ja 21 '79 por, C p8 Ja 22 '82 por; Söderström, Elisabeth. In My Own Key (1979); International Cyclopedia of Music and Musicians (1975); International Who's Who, 1985-86; International Who's Who in Music and Musicians' Directory, 1980; New Grove Dictionary of Music and Musicians (1985); Who's Who in Opera (1976)

## Speakes, Larry (Melvin)

*Sept. 13, 1939- Assistant to the president of the United States; principal deputy press secretary. Address: b. The White House, 1600 Pennsylvania Ave. N.W., Washington, D.C. 20500*

When White House press secretary James S. Brady was severely wounded in an assassination attempt against President Ronald Reagan in March 1981, deputy press secretary Larry Speakes was suddenly called upon to perform Brady's duties. Having survived a baptism of fire at his first press briefing, Speakes gradually gained confidence in his own ability and, over the next two years, consolidated his control of the White House press office. In spite of his own occasional gaffes and the frequently strained relations with the press corps, he eventually won the respect of journalists and administration officials alike.

In an interview with Elisabeth Bumiller in the *Washington Post* (March 7, 1982), Speakes noted that the words of the president's press representative "can start a war, or drive the stock market haywire," but the tensions inherent in his position notwithstanding, he relishes the excitement of working at the nation's power base and of having realized his longtime ambition of becoming the chief White House spokesman. "In a way, it's frightening," he admitted. "Every wish has come true."

Born in the Delta town of Cleveland, Mississippi on September 13, 1939 to Harry Earl Speakes, a banker, and Ethlyn Frances (Fincher) Speakes, Larry Melvin Speakes grew up in a comfortably upper-middle-class home in Merigold, a town with a population of less than 600. In 1957 he enrolled at the University of Mississippi in Oxford, where he studied journalism for four years. While an undergraduate, he worked on the *Daily Mississippian*, the college newspaper, and in 1958 he was named its reporter of the year.

Remaining in Mississippi, Speakes made rapid advances in his chosen field. He began his career in 1961 as news editor of the Oxford *Eagle*, the local weekday evening paper, but left that position after a year to become news editor and, in 1965, managing editor of the weekday evening *Bolivar Commercial* in Cleveland, for which he covered such controversial events as the racial integration of the University of Mississippi in 1962. Moving on yet again, he served from 1966 to 1968 as general manager of Progress Publishers of Leland and as editor of its four weekly newspapers: the Leland

*Progress,* the *Hollandale Herald,* the *Bolivar County Democrat,* and the *Sunflower County News.* For six consecutive years, his newspapers won top awards from the Mississippi Press Association, and in 1968 the association honored Speakes with an award for general excellence.

Although he remained in the field of journalism, Speakes's career took a political turn in 1968 when with the help of a friend he landed the job of press secretary to James O. Eastland, the Democratic senator from Mississippi and chairman of the Senate Judiciary Committee. During his six years in that post, Speakes directed press relations for that committee's major hearings, including the confirmation of four Supreme Court justices; served as spokesman for the committee; and coordinated Eastland's successful reelection campaign in 1972.

In spite of the glamour of working on Capitol Hill, Speakes's ambition from the time he arrived in Washington was to hold a post in the White House because, as he explained to Tony Kornheiser in an interview for the *Washington Post* (January 5, 1984), "the town revolved around it, the country revolved around it." His dream was finally realized in the last months of the Nixon administration when he was hired as a staff assistant in the executive office of the president. In May 1974, after only three months in that post, he was assigned to the Boston lawyer James D. St. Clair, the special presidential counsel for the Watergate hearings, as his press secretary, a job he has described as a "tightrope." He survived the change of administrations after President Nixon's resignation on August 8, 1974, however, and remained at the White House, first as assistant press secretary to President Gerald R. Ford and later as press secretary to Ford's vice-presidential running mate, Senator Robert Dole, during the 1976 presidential campaign.

After the Republican Ford-Dole ticket lost to the Democratic standard bearers Jimmy Carter and Walter Mondale, Speakes stayed on as Gerald Ford's press secretary until June 1977, when he joined the Washington office of the international public-relations firm of Hill and Knowlton, Incorporated, as a vice-president. Although he remained with that firm until 1981, he grew increasingly restless. In January 1978, Speakes recalled in the *Washington Post* interview, "I sat down with a friend and said, 'I didn't get enough of it; I want to get back to the White House; I want to be press secretary to the president of the United States, and I'm going to see if I can get in the right campaign to get there.'" Over the next few years, he approached several potential Republican presidential candidates, but his inquiries brought him no closer to his goal. Eventually, however, his persistence paid off. By the time of the 1980 Republican National Convention in Detroit, Michigan, Speakes was once again serving as press secretary to Gerald Ford and helping to promote the ultimately unsuccessful idea of a Reagan-Ford "dream ticket," which might have proved to be Speakes's own ticket back to the White House. He then joined the communications staff of the Reagan-Bush campaign as a liaison to Ford. After Ronald Reagan's landslide victory over Jimmy Carter in November 1980, Speakes contacted James S. Brady, the president-elect's press secretary, who immediately hired him as his deputy spokesman.

On March 30, 1981, just two months into the Reagan administration, Speakes was unexpectedly thrust into the office he had sought for so long. In an attempt to assassinate the president, John W. Hinckley Jr. shot Reagan, two security men, and James Brady, who was severely wounded in the head. As Brady's deputy, Speakes held a press briefing shortly after the incident. When one reporter asked whether the armed forces had been placed on special alert because of the assassination attempt, Speakes answered, "Not that I'm aware of," unintentionally implying that that might actually be the case. In an effort to reassure the press and the public that matters were under control, Secretary of State Alexander M. Haig Jr. quickly took over the briefing, and as Elisabeth Bumiller recounted in the *Washington Post* (March 7, 1982), Speakes, "who had careened from question to shouted question, was relegated to the sidelines. Many say it was Speakes' lowest moment."

In spite of that shaky debut, Speakes remained acting press secretary under the supervision of David R. Gergen, the staff director, and later communications director, of the White House. (Although his doctors were uncertain when—or if—he would be able to resume his duties, James Brady retained the title of press secretary.) Promoted on June 17, 1981 to deputy assistant to the president and principal deputy press secretary, Speakes shared with Gergen the responsibility for the weekday briefings of the White House press corps, with Speakes conducting them three days a week and Gergen, the other two. Both at first claimed to be comfortable with that unprecedented arrangement, but rumors of conflict between the two men were soon circulating freely. Although in March 1982 Gergen delegated all the briefings to Speakes, speculation about press-office infighting continued. Steve Neal reported in the *Chicago Tribune* (October 3, 1982) that certain presidential aides were seeking to replace Speakes after the November 1982 midterm elections with someone who would provide a tougher approach; but voicing the opposition's view, a top White House official quoted in that article praised Speakes as "a first-rate briefer." "He's effective at defending the president," the official continued, "and, more importantly, he doesn't make mistakes. When Gergen was out there, the press could con him into saying about anything they wanted. Speakes doesn't go for the bait."

Speakes materially improved his standing in 1983, partly as a result of a study of press-office operations by John S. Herrington, the White House personnel director, which recommended that Speakes be given a greater role in the White House and a larger staff. On August 5 he was named chief White House spokesman and assistant to the president, and when David Gergen resigned the following December he was left in firm control of the press office. In the months leading up to the promotion, White House officials had gradually allowed him to attend more top-level policy meetings and had given him greater, although still limited, access to sensitive information. Furthermore, while at Reagan's ranch in California in September, he received clearance for the first time to read all the Mideast cables forwarded to the president from Washington.

Acknowledging that Speakes had "grown" (a word used repeatedly by the press and administration officials) in his job, James A. Baker 3d, the White House chief of staff, told Steven R. Weisman in the New York Times (October 3, 1983) that the spokesman "is getting a lot more information, and he's getting it out more quickly. We think he's doing a very, very good job." Somewhat disturbed by the implication of such remarks that he had previously been less capable, Speakes maintained that any improvement in his job performance was due less to an increase in his skills than to the freer flow of information to the press office. However, he conceded to Weisman that he had become more attuned to the president's positions. "If I had been with Ronald Reagan ten years before this job," he explained, "maybe I could have stepped in and reflected his views right away. But it takes time to develop a relationship. I think now there's a recognition that if I'm given the information, I can handle it in a reliable way."

In spite of his increased access to policy meetings, Speakes still remained outside the inner circle of the administration, a fact rendered painfully obvious in the autumn of 1983. When asked on October 24 whether the United States planned an invasion of Grenada, Speakes, acting on the advice of National Security Council officials, labeled such rumors "preposterous," but less than twenty-four hours later a multinational force, largely made up of United States Marines and Rangers, stormed the tiny Caribbean island. Speakes had not been informed of the operation until it had already begun. That blunder not only embarrassed him but also undermined his credibility to a certain degree.

Speakes's sense of humor and sometimes flippant manner have also occasionally led to damaging gaffes. A case in point was Speakes's reaction to a question in November 1983 about the public criticism by Martin Feldstein, the chairman of the Council of Economic Advisors, of certain aspects of the administration's economic program. Prepared for such a query, Speakes responded with a line he and his staff had previously agreed upon as a mild rebuke to Feldstein: "Everybody knows what the president's policy is on deficits, taxes and defense spending—with the possible exception of the chairman of the Council of Economic Advisors." However, during the remainder of the briefing, Speakes, as well as some reporters, repeatedly mispronounced Feldstein's name and made several quips about him. Although Speakes denied the charge that he intentionally mispronounced Feldstein's name to ridicule the CEA chairman, Rea-

gan, who, according to the Washington Post (December 4, 1984), was angered by the occurrence, made it clear that that was "not the way [he wanted] to operate" and reprimanded Speakes.

An incident earlier in the year had proved equally embarrassing for Speakes. When Barbara Honegger, a special assistant in the civil-rights division of the Justice Department, resigned from the administration on August 22, 1983 and denounced as a "sham" the president's efforts to eliminate sex discrimination in federal laws and rules, the Justice Department's spokesman, Tom DeCair, dismissed her complaint as insignificant and belittled Miss Honegger as a "low-level munchkin." On August 24, Speakes joined in the public derision by saying that her "important role" in the administration had consisted of dressing up as the Easter Bunny to entertain the children at the annual White House Easter egg roll. A senior advisor in the administration termed his remark, which irritated women's groups at a time when the president was striving to improve his image among women, "colossally stupid."

Such comments reinforced the opinion of some members of the press corps that Speakes is biased against women, especially female reporters. Ann Devroy of the Gannett News Service, for one, told Tony Kornheiser in an interview for the Washington Post (January 5, 1984) that Speakes "picks on women." "I think he's old-fashioned in the sense that he sees men as more serious and more important," she explained. "He demeans the women's questions by giving flippant answers, or not answering at all." Sam Donaldson, ABC's chief White House correspondent, agreed, telling Kornheiser that "these Southern boys have a cultural view of women. . . . They are to be cared for with great, elaborate courtesy. But they are not to do a man's work." Denying those charges in the same article, Speakes said, "I have no more of a problem with an aggressive woman who flaunts decorum in this White House than I do with a man who flaunts decorum. I'll come down on either of them."

A certain degree of antagonism between the press corps and an administration's spokesman is unavoidable, but the issue of "controlled access" to the president, especially during the 1984 presidential campaign, exacerbated tensions. Reporters protested that presidential press conferences and informal opportunities for discussions with the chief executive were far fewer than in previous administrations and that Speakes himself did not provide the press corps with sufficient information. Some newsmen attributed the meagre offerings at press briefings to an intellectual laziness on Speakes's part, a failure to probe for more details; those more sympathetic blamed administration officials' unwillingness to keep the White House spokesman up-to-date on policy developments; and still others charged that he was simply stonewalling. But Speakes offered no apologies for his tactics, firmly maintaining that his primary duty is to serve President Reagan. "If that means drawing the line here and saying no more, that's what I'm going to do," he told Tony Kornheiser. "A lot of time the press attributes that to a lack of information on my part when it may simply be I just don't want to say any more. I may know everything, but it's not in the president's interest to talk about it. . . . There's 10,000 ways of saying, 'No comment,'" he wryly added. "And I know all of them." His "memo-bait" ploy further alienated some reporters, who, to their chagrin, used some false information Speakes had planted on a secretary's desk, an area understood to be off-limits to newsmen.

Nevertheless, Speakes's adroit handling of such potentially explosive issues as the downing of a Korean commercial airliner by the USSR on September 1, 1983 and his skillful fielding of even commonplace questions have generally earned high marks from administration officials and the somewhat grudging respect of members of the press corps. "There are times when he's faking it," Chris Wallace, an NBC White House correspondent, told Tony Kornheiser, as quoted in the *Washington Post* (January 5, 1984). "And I say this in frustration and admiration: he's pretty good at it. He'll mumble an answer or deflect a question with humor." Speakes's performance as chief White House spokesman has also won him freer access to the president. At least four times a week, he briefly reviews a list of issues with Reagan and then decides how best to communicate to the press the president's sometimes blunt comments. Speakes also helped to develop the concept of the "line of the day," in which every facet of the administration's publicity operation emphasizes a certain point each day, a technique used to great effect during the 1984 presidential campaign. Regulating the flow of information to the press is an integral part of Speakes's duties, and in response to the media's criticism of that control, he has a sign on his desk that reads, "You don't tell us how to stage the news, and we won't tell you how to cover it." Moreover, he explained to Tony Kornheiser, "If any reporter wants more than what is said in the briefing, my office is open. Ten or twelve exercise it [that prerogative] regularly."

During his career, Speakes has received several honors, including the Distinguished Journalism Alumni Award from the University of Mississippi in 1981; the Kappa Sigma Fraternity National Man of the Year Award in 1982; an honorary doctor of letters degree from Indiana Central University in 1982; and the Special Achievement Award for 1983 from the National Association of Government Communicators.

Larry Speakes shares his Annandale, Virginia home with his second wife, Laura Christine Crawford, an executive assistant for *Army Times*, whom he married on November 3, 1968, and their son, Jeremy Stephen. By an earlier marriage to his high-school sweetheart, which ended in divorce, he has two children: Sondra LaNell and Barry Scott. Although he puts in a fourteen-hour day at his White House office, Speakes usually finds some time for recreation: he enjoys jogging several times a week

and listening to the music of country singer Merle Haggard. He is a Methodist.

*References: Chi Tribune I p3 O 3 '82 por; Newsweek 102:50+ D 19 '83 por; N Y Times B p10 O 3 '83 por; Washington Post H p1+ Mr 7 '82 pors, B p1+ Ja 5 '84 por; Who's Who in America, 1984–85; Who's Who in American Politics, 1985–86*

## Stavropoulos, George (Peter)
(sta vrop´ ō ləs)

*Jan. 22, 1920– Fashion designer. Address: b. 16 W. 57th St., New York City, N.Y. 10019*

Among those designers best known for their luxurious evening wear, few can match the longevity of George Stavropoulos, the Greek-born couturier whose magic touch with his favorite fabric—filmy chiffon—has enchanted women for more than three decades. Having established a flourishing salon in Athens in the 1950s, Stavropoulos moved to the United States in 1961, where, starting over from scratch, he gradually built up a multimillion-dollar business. The foundation of his fashion empire— and his perennial bestseller—is a full-length, multilayered chiffon gown with free-floating panels. Inspired by classical Greek sculpture, Stavropoulos' fluid, gracefully draped creations achieve the designer's twin goals of simplicity of form and timeless elegance. "The dress is the frame, not the picture," Stavropoulos explained in a recent interview. "You should see the woman first, not the dress."

George Peter Stavropoulos was born on January 22, 1920 in Tripolis, Greece, the son of Peter Dmitri Stavropoulos, who owned a small tobacco-processing plant, and his wife, the former Dmitra Paraskeveopoulos. He was the seventh—"always the lucky one, too"—of ten brothers and sisters. Interested in painting and sketching from his childhood, Stavropoulos discovered his aptitude for fashion design almost by accident when, as a young teen-ager, he created a ball gown for one of his sisters from an old dress of their grandmother's. "I pinned it with safety pins," he recalled to Charlotte Curtis in an interview for the New York Times (November 8, 1961). "The pins were on the inside so you couldn't see them." Such custom fitting on a model was to become his basic method of designing. Having decided that "sculpting cloth for the body," to quote a writer for Connoisseur magazine, was an intriguing alternative to painting, Stavropoulos learned his craft "only from books and studying classic costumes in the museums," as he explained years later in a guest "Inside Fashion" column for the New York Herald Tribune (August 31, 1965). Appropriately enough, he made his professional debut as a costume designer for theatrical productions of classical plays. He also created the costumes for a production of the ballet Giselle.

In 1949 Stavropoulos opened Nikis 13, a small salon and workshop in Athens. He hired the best seamstresses he could find and plied them with questions. "I stayed with them day and night," he told the interviewer for Connoisseur. "'Explain why you do it this way and not that way,' I would tell them." Within three months, he was deluged with orders for custom designs. "I got famous for coats and suits with my special cut," he wrote in his Herald Tribune column. "I developed artisans to weave woolens for me. . . . I had to learn to sew, to do everything. You must always know everything better than your workers." By 1952 Stavropoulos' reputation was such that Christian Dior invited the young designer to join his high-fashion house in Paris. The fiercely independent Stavropoulos rejected the invitation, preferring to devote his talent and energy to his own salon, which he has described as "a very personal business." "If I didn't like a customer, I never created for her," he admitted in his "Inside Fashion" column. "I would throw her out." And despite the demand for them, he refused to make couture copies of the latest Parisian styles. Nevertheless, over the years Stavropoulos' timeless designs inspired by ancient Greek silhouettes attracted increasing numbers of affluent Athenian women and the wives of visiting foreign diplomats, among them the wife of the United States ambassador.

Although he was at the time the leading couturier in Athens, George Stavropoulos nonetheless shuttered his establishment in mid-1961 and moved to New York City. He took that drastic step at the insistence of his homesick wife, the former Nancy Angelakos, an employee at the United States Embassy whom he had married on October 31, 1960. Unable to find employment with one of the major American fashion designers, the transplanted Greek, who did not yet speak English, took the advice of the couturier James Galanos and went into business for himself. With characteristic determination, he rented a tiny work space on West 57th Street, hired two seamstresses, and set to work on his debut American collection. The day he completed sewing the last dress, the entire group of twenty-five day and evening designs was stolen. Undaunted, Stavropoulos painstakingly re-created every costume and, in November 1961, mounted his first fashion show.

Stavropoulos' first American collection of hand-finished ready-to-wear was comprised mainly of simple, short silk dresses topped by kimono-sleeved jackets sashed with wide crushed-leather belts and of sophisticated evening gowns in such luxurious fabrics as crepe, brocade, silk organza, and French lace. Each garment was lined in thin silk and "so beautifully made," according to Charlotte Curtis, "that it is difficult to believe they can be done by machine." "His designs are simple for the most part," Miss Curtis wrote in her review of the collection for the New York Times (November 8, 1961), "and tend toward Grecian drapery, extravagantly handsome fabrics, and a kind of understated elegance. . . . The clothes are American, too, in that he has analyzed the American figure and found it straighter, taller, and leaner than the Greek figure and has adapted these designs to those new proportions." In her enthusiastic appraisal for the New York Post (November 28, 1961), Ruth Preston also noted with approval the skillful blend of classic design and modern cut and the way the dressmaker details, such as the placement of straps and the curve of the décolletage, were calculated to flatter less-than-perfect figures.

Despite the excitement Stavropoulos' collection generated in fashion circles, it was judged to be a failure by the deparment-store buyers, who felt that it looked, in the designer's words, "too custom" and "not for the American market." For the next two years, Stavropoulos concentrated on designing clothes for private customers, including such prominent socialites as Mrs. Robert Love, the wife of a children's-wear manufacturer, and Mrs. Howard Oxenberg, the former Princess Elizabeth of Yugoslavia, who were often photographed in his creations at chic parties and Broadway opening nights. In 1963 he tried his luck with another ready-to-wear collection. This time, he was rewarded for his effort with a sizable wholesale order from Stanley Korshak, the owner of a posh specialty store in Chicago, Illinois. Geraldine Stutz, the president of Henri Bendel in New York City, and Mildred Custin, who was then the president of Bonwit Teller, followed suit. With wealthy and fashionable women by then clamoring for his designs, Stavropoulos moved in mid-1965 to a larger factory and salon at 16 West 57th Street, his present location. He discussed the happy reversal of his fortunes in a conversation with Marylin Bender, a fashion writer for the New York Times (July 10, 1965): "I haven't changed, but the American market has. Everybody wants a custom touch today and, thank God, I have it."

Stavropoulos' fall 1965 collection was large and varied, but it was his flowing chiffon evening gowns that attracted the most attention. One popular design was a long, black chiffon column with a multilayered skirt floating from a velvet band on the strapless bodice. The top layer could be thrown back over the shoulders like a stole. As graceful and fluid as the chiffons were his bias-cut day dresses in tweed and silk and his versatile suits and coat-and-dress ensembles in mohair, lamb's wool jersey, or cashmere. Giving his collection the ultimate seal of approval, both Bonwit Teller and Henri Bendel showcased his chiffon evening gowns in their Fifth Avenue window displays.

By his own account, the turning point in Stavropoulos' career came when First Lady Claudia Alta ("Lady Bird") Johnson became one of his regular clients. "I already was successful, but a call from the White House helped," Stavropoulos told Timothy Hawkins in an interview for a Los Angeles Times (March 23, 1984) profile. "In 1966, she wore a chiffon gown of mine to the opening of the new Metropolitan Opera House at New York's Lincoln Center and a week later attended the opening of the San Francisco Opera in another of my dresses. I created Mrs. Johnson's look." The First Lady also chose a Stavropoulos dress for her official White House portrait. Among his other influential early clients were Jacqueline Kennedy Onassis, Elizabeth Taylor, Barbra Streisand, Maria Callas, Diahann Carroll, Cicely Tyson, and Shirley MacLaine.

Eager to cash in on the widespread appeal of Stavropoulos' sensuous "Greek goddess" evening wear, fashion wholesalers rushed copies of his designs to department stores across the country. Stavropoulos, annoyed by the realization that others were making a profit at his expense, fought back by devising new ways for handling chiffon. For his spring 1966 collection, he combined it with lace and other fabrics, crystal-pleated it for a three-dimensional effect, and splashed it with shimmering floral designs. By the designer's own estimation, the "masterpiece" of the collection was a simple black chiffon gown topped by a chasuble of black Spanish lace traced with silver embroidery. For his fall 1966 line, Stavropoulos drifted chiffon panels over floor-length lamé slips that flashed and sparkled in the light or superimposed one color of chiffon over another, such as blue over yellow, turquoise over emerald, or red over coral, to create an irridescent effect. The following year, he introduced chiffons in contemporary abstract and geometric prints and in subtly shaded, light-to-dark color gradations.

Most notable among Stavropoulos' other fashion innovations in the late 1960s was the one-sleeved "Calyptra wrap"—a snug-fitting jacket on one side, a side-swept cape on the other. In navy or beige wool for daytime and pink satin for evening, the wrap completely covered its wearer when its detachable stole was wrapped around the head. Although he has never been one to follow fashion trends, Stavropoulos lifted the hemlines of some of his designs fully six inches above the knees in 1967. But as he explained to interviewers, his miniskirts, which were based on the traditional tunics worn by the Evzone guards of the Greek army, were meant to be worn only "for playtime or staying home at night." He added trousers to his line in 1968, after contriving a new method of cutting them so that they required no seams. In lace, satin, crepe, or feather-trimmed chiffon, these "goddess pants," as he called them, were the hit of his spring 1969 collection. Seven years later, Stavropoulos included in his group of clothes for fall and winter wear several pairs of bloomers in a variety of colors and fabrics, such as black wool crepe, brown silk, and green chiffon.

None of Stavropoulos' design innovations, however, was as popular and enduring as his classic, flowing chiffon evening gowns. Over the years, he modified the styles a bit from season to season, but the signature close-to-the-body shape remained unchanged. By the couturier's count, 400 guests at the balls celebrating President Ronald Reagan's inauguration in January 1981 wore his elegant chiffons. The favorite designer of countless women in the public eye, he created a stunning pink satin wedding gown with chiffon bodice and sleeves for Evangeline Gouletas, who married Hugh L. Carey, then the governor of New York, in April 1981. Her Stavropoulos trousseau included a sumptuous ball gown of white-silver satin encrusted with rock crystal that one reporter described as "a dress fit for an empress." Another faithful customer, Eydie Gorme, commissioned Stavropoulos to design the costumes for her 1981 Carnegie Hall engagement. "They're such wonderful entrance clothes," the singer said, as quoted in the New York Times (July 2, 1981). "When you come out on stage, you don't have to open your mouth. The audience is always stunned. The colors are so beautiful. Nobody blends chiffon the way he does."

While he continued to rely on chiffon for his most impressive creations, in 1981 Stavropoulos found a new medium for his artistry—suede, which became in his hands almost as supple a fabric as chiffon. He also began to experiment more with velvet, satin, and silk taffeta because he wanted to make dresses in "stronger shapes" and therefore needed fabrics "stronger than chiffon." The most varied collection in several years, Stavropoulos' spring and summer line for 1983 included, among other items, cotton and linen suits in black and sea green with contrasting buttons; Paris-inspired tight-torso silk dresses; billowing net and taffeta ball gowns with ruffled, off-the-shoulder necklines; culottes that, from behind, looked like a coat; and lavishly embroidered chiffon evening gowns with matching scarves to tie around the waistline or around the neck. At the request of his customers, Stavropoulos added to his 1983 fall line short, wasp-waisted dinner dresses in taffeta, lace, and chiffon; slinky, floor-length cut velvet columns sparkling with exotic metallic birds; and a large group of white evening gowns in a range of fabrics, from chiffon to net to embroidered organdy. His own personal favorite was a white cut velvet dress, with an overlay of chiffon slanting across the body from shoulder to hip.

Explaining that he competed with himself each season to "make the clothes look different," Stavropoulos combined chiffon with organdy, satin, taffeta, and velvet to striking effect for his fall 1984 collection. The standouts from that unusually sophisticated group were sexy, long, skin-baring slip dresses in black or white silk chiffon accented with beading and topped by oversized jackets in box-pleated silk and the so-called "pizza dress"—a black bib-top silk crepe jumper mated with a white chiffon blouse. Stavropoulus, who claims that his designs are prompted by moods rather than trends, has said that the inspiration for the pizza dress was a girl in overalls whom he spotted at a neighborhood pizzeria.

In creating his designs, Stavropoulos follows a few simple "truths," to use his word. "My clothes are for the woman who is a woman," he explained to Joyce Pendola, who interviewed him for *Connoisseur* magazine (June 1983). "She is not a child. She is not a boy. Women *want* to look frail and fragile. If they are not, my clothes will create the illusion that they are." One of the few contemporary couturiers who make their own originals, Stavropoulos has, as he once put it, "complete control" of his designs from beginning to end. Working from his rather free-form and—to the uninitiated—indecipherable sketches, he personally cuts and drapes every costume on a dressmaker's mannequin. (He eschews stitching a preliminary version in muslin, a process he scorns as "too rigid.") With the exception of specially ordered gowns for private customers, he usually makes three to fifty copies of a particular design. His clothes are sold at such prestigious stores as Martha's, Bergdorf-Goodman, Elizabeth Arden, and Neiman-Marcus, among others.

A compactly built man, George Stavropoulos has thick, graying black hair, "bottomless" black eyes, and a mischievous smile. After twenty-three years away from his homeland, he still speaks English with a heavy Greek accent. By all reports, he is so involved in his work, regularly putting in twelve-hour days, that he has given up such former pleasures as swimming and, except for business, traveling. He relaxes by attending the opera and making neckties from fabric scraps, but what pleases him most is "seeing [his] designs put together well on a woman." "It's like a painter seeing his painting well-displayed in a room," he told Timothy Hawkins in the *Los Angeles Times* interview. Stavropoulos and his wife, Nancy, make their home in an apartment on Manhattan's Upper East Side that they have decorated with Near Eastern art objects. He is especially fond of Byzantine icons. The Stavropouloses have one son, Peter George.

References: Connoisseur 213:14+ Je '83 por; Los Angeles Times V p22+ Mr 18 '83, V p23 O 5 '84; N Y Post p33 Ag 14 '71 por; N Y Times p39 N 8 '61 por, p49 N 18 '66, p24 Jl 6 '84; Fairchild's Dictionary of Fashion (1975); Who's Who in America, 1982–83; Who's Who in Fashion, 1980; World of Fashion (1976)

## Sting

Oct. 2, 1951– Singer; musician; actor. Address: b. c/o A&M Records, 595 Madison Ave., New York City, N.Y. 10022

In 1978 a driving, reggae-inflected love song, "Roxanne," broke into the Top Forty popular music charts in the United States, ushering into international celebrity the British rock trio the Police, formed in the previous year. That Police hit, like those to follow, was written and sung by Sting, the band's glacially iconic, much photographed star and the principal creative force behind its unique blend of New Wave rock, Jamaican and other international rhythms, and mainstream melodic pop. Over the following six years the Police sold approximately forty million records, including the hits "Message in a Bottle" and "Walking on the Moon," from their album *Regatta de Blanc* (1979); "Don't Stand So Close to Me," from *Zenyatta Mondatta* (1980); "Every Little Thing She Does Is Magic," from *The Ghost in the Machine* (1981); and "Every Breath You Take," from *Synchronicity* (1983). Many of Sting's sensitive songs, whether personal or cosmic in subject matter, were hymns of alienation, and their melancholy was accented by his reedy, wailing voice.

Although a reunion is possible, the members of the Police have not performed together since their tour to promote *Synchronicity*. Believing that "music is dead because it is largely sectarian" and that "when polarities meet . . . you get that spark" that "makes music lively and meaningful," Sting recently formed a quintet whose other members are American jazz virtuosos, musicians who, in his words, "grew up hearing funk and rock and yet decided to play jazz." Apart from music, Sting has for several years been successfully pursuing a career in motion pictures, where his usual role is what Stewart Copeland of the Police once described as "the dark prince." Among the films in which he portrays a prepossessing but devious villain are *Brimstone and Treacle* (1982) and *Dune* (1984). He exhibited his more tender, vulnerable side in *Plenty* (1985), his best film to date.

Sting was born Gordon Matthew Sumner on October 2, 1951 in Wallsend, Northumberland, England, the oldest of four children of a Catholic dairyman and a hairdresser. Growing up in Newcastle on Tyne—whose industrial ambiance oppressed him—he was educated by Jesuits in parochial schools, which he later blamed, with perhaps a bit of tongue in cheek, for his "venomous nature" while acknowledging a creative debt to Catholicism for the symbolist imagery in his songwriting. In an interview for *Rolling Stone* (September 1, 1983), he told Kristine McKenna that while he is "not a devout Catholic, . . . all that was inculcated into [his] brain as a small child—that there is a heaven and hell, mortal sins and venial sins—is inside [his] psyche and will never come out."

Sting told Miss McKenna that his "very painful" childhood had the salutary effect of giving him "a fighting spirit" and the desire "to escape." "I didn't have an unusually bad childhood. . . . There was just an ache all the time. Heartache. It wasn't my parents' fault, it's just the way my brain was working." Inwardly driven to excel, he was a superior runner and gained local fame as the Northern Counties 100-metres champion, but he quit track after coming in third in the national championships. "I realized when I came in third that there were two people in my age group who were better than I was . . . ," he later explained. "I didn't want to be part of the pyramid. I wanted to be on the top."

A self-taught musician, Sting started off on the guitar, and he took up bass when he was seventeen or eighteen. As a teenager, in the 1960s, he listened to the Beatles, but he "never really had much interest in rock music," and he "loathed" the Led Zeppelin type of hard rock that emerged in the 1970s, a "heavy-handed and sludgy" music, pretentiously "grandiose," that had lost touch with the pop-music tradition and lacked the "very simple tonal code . . . that taps the collective unconscious." His heroes were not rock stars but writers, especially James Joyce and D. H. Lawrence.

After taking a degree in education at Warwick College in Newcastle in 1973, Sting was a soccer coach and music instructor for two years at St.

Mary's, a convent school where most of the other teachers were nuns. Meanwhile he was several years into his musical career, playing double bass nights and weekends with various jazz bands. Early on in that career he acquired his stage name. "I wore outrageous striped yellow-and-black pullovers," he has explained, "and one guy [a trombone player] thought I looked like a bee." His aggressive personality reinforced the aptness of the name. He was, by his own description, a "showoff and egocentric," and an acquaintance of those days told Marcelle Clements in an interview for *Esquire* (November 1983): "He was incredibly nice to me, but many people disliked him because he was arrogant. He loved success even then. He had such a strong personality that he leaped forward, suddenly became really popular, suddenly a [local] name."

The first group Sting played with was a Dixieland band. Later he played backup in cabarets and did gigs with modern and mainstream jazz combos and with dance bands. He was playing with a Newcastle jazz band called Last Exit when Stewart Copeland spotted him in 1976. Copeland, a venturesome American-born drummer, had recently quit the British art-rock group Curved Air, after realizing that the progressive band had, through prodigality, trapped itself in a hopelessly "bogus" situation. "The advances were so high that everything we did had to be commercial," Copeland explained to Kristine McKenna. "We couldn't take any chances musically, so I got bored."

At the time that Copeland was becoming disenchanted with "sterilized music, made from the wallet, not the heart," punk rock bands, led by the short-lived Sex Pistols, were changing all the rules, creating a demand for themselves in clubs and thereby developing a following not primarily dependent on record labels and air play. Copeland decided to form a group of his own, a spartan trio, low in budget but high in energy, playing a music that would be "anti-Eagles, anti–Pink Floyd, anti–Rolling Stones." In the changed musical scene, "if you were a new group it worked for you," Copeland later explained to David Sheff of *People* (January 21, 1980).

Copeland's first recruit was the guitar player Henry Padovani. With Sting rounding out the trio on bass and lead vocals, the Police began performing in January 1977, backing better-known punk headliners in London rock clubs. Copeland's brother Miles, an established rock impresario, became the manager of the group, and his brother Ian, the booking agent. Stewart Copeland was the Police's dominant creative force in the beginning, writing the group's songs to a stripped-down, punk-derived backup, with reggae inflections.

The trio cut its first single, the punk screamer "Fall Out," in February 1977 with £150 in borrowed money. Issued on Stewart Copeland's own label, Illegal Records, it gathered mixed reviews but sold out its initial pressing of 2,000 copies and later pressings totaling 10,000. While touring Europe that spring as part of a British rock show called Strontium 90, the band gained another guitarist, Andy Summers. Not long afterward, Padovani left the group, and in August 1977 the definitive Police lineup made its debut, performing music to which Andy Summers' creative guitar fills lent an often ethereal quality. Stewart Copeland remained in that lineup, but he relinquished most of the songwriting to Sting, the group's frontman, a "shaman" (his word) who, in a trancelike state on stage, moved and danced as he sang and played, provoking primal responses from audiences.

On their way to fame and fortune, the Police made some television commercials, including one for Wrigley's chewing gum, in which they appeared as a punk band (although they did not regard themselves as such). For the Wrigley's ad, the members of the trio bleached their hair, and their blondness became a permanent part of their image. Their prospects brightened dramatically when, in the spring of 1978, A&M Records signed them on the strength of a tape of "Roxanne." The Police's contract with A&M was an unusual one, in which the group, forsaking advances, was guaranteed a higher royalty rate than customary—a gamble on their future success that would pay off more than handsomely.

When A&M released "Roxanne," the Police were in Germany, touring with the electronic composer Eberhard Schoener, and therefore unable to promote the single at home. In addition, the record had radio censorship problems because of its theme (a swain's plea that his beloved renounce her life of prostitution). Although "Roxanne" failed to make the charts, it and the group's second single "Can't Stand Losing You," earned a modest profit. The proceeds from the record sales and the German tour, frugally husbanded, were sufficient to pay for the cutting of the first Police album, completed in August 1978 but not immediately released, and for an initial tour of the United States.

American A&M executives opposed the Police's transatlantic venture in autumn of 1978 because they felt the trio had as yet "no product to support," although "Roxanne" was included in No Wave, a New Wave sampler released by A&M in the United States. The group went ahead anyway, taking a Laker flight across the Atlantic, with their instruments as luggage. Traveling from rock club to rock club along the East Coast in a single van and with a single roadie (Kim Turner), on a budget of twenty dollars a day apiece, they cumulated word of mouth and actually ended with a profit, an unprecedented occurrence for an initial U.S. expedition by a British rock group. Region by region, "Roxanne" made its way into radio playlists and up the charts. The single's American success prompted its rerelease in the U.K., this time to raves.

Immediately after the first American tour, in January 1979, A&M released the Police's first album, Outlandos d'Amour, a hard-rocking blend of new wave and reggae. The LP quickly soared to the Top Forty in the U.S. charts—the first British new wave-style album to do so—and did equally brisk business in Britain. In support of the album, the group made smashing tours of Britain and, again, the United States.

The Police's big commercial breakthrough came with their second album, Regatta de Blanc. That LP sold more than a million copies in the United States; the cuts "The Bed's Too Big Without You," "Message in a Bottle," and "Walking on the Moon" became FM radio favorites; and the two last-mentioned successively hit number one on the U.K. singles charts. A minority of critics found the album "too frenetic for mainstream rock and too clean for hardcore new wave" or dismissed the Police as commercializers of the new wave style, "poseurs" exploiting a punk stance and a reggae beat in the service of "emotionally chilly" or even "banal" music. A majority had a more positive assessment of the group's fresh adaptation of Jamaican folk rhythms to electrified rock and of Sting's spare, raspy wails of "demi-isolation" surmounting his own blunt bass, Summers' more colorful, liquid guitar phrasing, and Copeland's splashy, explosive percussion.

While the Police were becoming perhaps the most highly regarded trio in rock since Cream, Sting was emerging as a teen idol and sex symbol. A "fortunate building block," as he called it, in the structuring of his public image was his cameo appearance as Ace Face, the coolest looking "mod" character in the Who's rock-opera film Quadrophenia (1979). He had a similarly small role in Chris Petit's low-budget motion picture Radio On (1979), an avant-garde mystery set in a rock tour.

In a world tour undertaken early in 1980 the Police performed in India, South America, and other areas where live rock music had seldom been heard. Their success strengthened Sting's "belief in rock 'n' roll as a universal language," and it proved his and the Police's ability to communicate in that language. International eclecticism marked the music of the next Police album, Zenyatta Mondatta (1980), which was produced hurriedly, under industry pressure to feed a demand primed by the success of Regatta de Blanc. Sting was satisfied with only three songs on the LP: "Don't Stand So Close to Me," "Driven to Tears," and "When the World is Running Down, Make the Best of What's Still Around." Nevertheless, Zenyatta Mondatta was an enormous commercial success, spawning two hit singles, "Don't Stand So Close to Me" and "De Do, Do Do, De Da Da Da Da," and going platinum (more than two million copies sold) in the United States, England, Canada, the Netherlands, Austria, Japan, and New Zealand and gold in several other countries.

Sting named the Police's fourth album The Ghost in the Machine (1981) after the book of the same name by Arthur Koestler, which he had been reading. Vocally, that LP offered a full measure of the harmonizing that had been introduced tentatively in Zenyatta Mondatta. Instrumentally, the bare strings and drums of the early albums were beefed up with the densely tailored sounds of synthesizer and multiple guitar, keyboard, and saxophone parts. All the saxophone parts were played, through overdubbing, by Sting, who had recently taught himself to play the instrument. In Sting's lyrics there was a change of emphasis from personal concerns to such social issues as technological change, in the song "Spirits in the Material World," and the Northern Ireland conflict, in "Invisible Sun." The blockbuster single spun off from the album was the love song "Every Little Thing She Does Is Magic," on which the keyboard backup was provided by a guest musician, Jean Roussel.

Sting turned down many offers of stardom in musical films because he had "no desire to become John Travolta." One of the offers he accepted was the role of the bisexual god Helith in David Rudkin's three-hour television fantasy film *Artemis '81*. On the big screen, director Richard Loncraine, who was looking for someone with a "strange" quality ("watchability, I call it"), chose Sting for the key role of Martin Taylor, a charming young London con man who seduces an upper-middle-class *ménage* in Loncraine's wry gothic psychological thriller *Brimstone and Treacle* (United Artists, 1982), written by Dennis Potter. The feral, quasi-diabolical Taylor ingratiates his way into the distressed household of Thomas Bates (Denholm Elliott), a guilt-ridden bourgeois religious hypocrite, brightens the life of Mrs. Bates (Joan Plowright), and takes sexual advantage of their helpless, brain-damaged daughter (Suzanna Hamilton) while convincing the mother that he is the heaven-sent instrument of a miraculous cure.

The reviews of *Brimstone and Treacle* were mixed, but even critics who were disturbed by Potter and Loncraine's perverse sense of humor and their message of moral ambiguity or who saw the film as a victory of style (*Grand Guignol* style) over content generally admitted that it was fascinating to the end and that Loncraine had drawn remarkable performances from his cast, especially Sting. "Where the film comes alive," Sally Hibbin wrote in *Films and Filming* (September 1982), "is in the presence of Sting. The charisma of the rock star undermines the suspect side of Martin, creating an ambiguous personality who is, in equal parts, abhorrent and likable." Sting composed the soundtrack music for *Brimstone and Treacle*, and the Police performed it, along with the Go-Gos.

In 1983 frenzied sales (ultimately eleven million) of their fifth album, *Synchronicity* (viewed by Sting as his "best creative work so far"), and a mid-year sellout tour of the United States gave the Police title to rock's hottest act. On the album they pared down the textured overdubs used in *Ghost in the Machine* and returned to a leaner trio sound while modifying their distinctive reggae rhythms. Sting drew the LP's title from the Jungian concepts of the convergence of acausally related events, and of opposing antinomian forces. Those concepts inspired much of the symbolism in his somber song lyrics on topics ranging from personal angst ("King of Pain") to the chilling possibility of a nuclear holocaust ("Walking in Your Footsteps"). Another influence was the emotional impact of the breakup

of his marriage on Sting, who thinks that "crisis is essential to creativity" and that pop music at its best is cathartic as well as subversive, articulating personal anxieties while challenging social and political indifference and complacency. The cut "Every Breath You Take," which became the top-charting single in the history of A&M Records, is, in Sting's words, the song of "a man abandoned," a maniacally possessive, jealous ex-lover who threatens continued, unrelenting surveillance of his ex-love. It was considered "a fairly nasty song" by its composer, and he was surprised, but not displeased, that "a lot of people thought it was a very sweet love song." "Songs can work on as many levels as possible—and should," he later explained. "That's the magic of music." In *Rolling Stone's* 1983 poll of its readers, the Police, Sting, *Synchronicity*, and "Every Breath You Take" were voted, respectively, the band, songwriter, album, and single of the year.

Following the *Synchronicity* tour, Sting and the other bandmembers went their separate ways. The movie director David Lynch cast Sting as the sadistic but seductive archvillain in *Dune* (Universal, 1984), a screen adaptation of Frank Herbert's science-fiction classic set on the desert planet Arrakis, where a young warrior duke (Kyle MacLachlan) leads a people's army in a rebellion against an evil galactic emperor (Sting). With a $400 million budget, one of the largest in film history, Lynch and his colleagues shot a plethora of extravagant special-effects footage, including scenes of warrior tribesmen riding on gigantic earthworms. In editing the film down to a reasonable length, they left much of the continuity on the cutting-room floor. The end product, in the eyes of many, unrolled pell-mell, with some of the special effects seeming gratuitous. Frank Herbert thought the film did justice to his story, however, and Sting received generally good notices.

The director Franc Roddam, who had given Sting the cameo role in *Quadrophenia* and was impressed with his subsequent development as an actor, cast him as a hip Dr. Charles Von Frankenstein in *The Bride* (Universal), his non-fright retelling of Mary Shelley's classic. From the making of *The Bride*, Sting in early 1985 went immediately into the shooting of *Plenty*, in which he plays a British black marketeer in post–World War II England rejected in love by the female lead (Meryl Streep). *The Bride* was panned by many critics, but *Plenty* was critically acclaimed and Sting's performance in it brought him the best notices of his acting career. Sting has written for himself the screenplay "Gormenghast," an adaptation of Mervyn Peake's trilogy of bizarre gothic fantasy novels set in a vast castle where an eccentric population lives in accordance with arcane rituals. The protagonist is the disingenuous upstart Steerpike, a scullery boy with winning ways who attempts to become ruler of the castle but is foiled by his own hubris. Sting's tentative future plans include motion-picture directing.

In preparation for his first solo album, Sting early in 1985 formed a recording bank of "jazz musicians who have the ability to cross over into larger areas." The musicians he recruited were four young American blacks: Branford Marsalis, saxophone, Kenny Kirkland, keyboard, Omar Hakim, drums, and Daryl Jones, electric bass. Giving the public a taste of what the album would sound like, Sting and the combo performed three sold-out and well-received shows at the Ritz in New York City in February 1985. On those occasions the quintet performed Police hits, the song "I Burn for You" from the *Brimstone and Treacle* soundtrack, and new compositions by Sting, including a blues and a soul song, on which Sting played lead guitar. In November 1985 the Samuel Goldwyn Company released the film *Bring on the Night*, a documentary intended by Sting to show "how this group came together musically."

Beginning in May 1985, Sting and his new band made a highly successful five-month world tour. The group's debut album, *The Dream of the Blue Turtles*, was in second place on the charts in September 1985 and had already gone platinum, with sales of more than 1 million copies. The songs on the LP, written by Sting, included some Police staples and such new compositions as "Children's Crusade" (in which the current peddling of heroin to young people is paralleled with the exploitation of children in the Christian "holy" war against the Muslims in the early thirteenth century), "Russians" (in which Sting imagines saving his son from nuclear warfare), "Fortress Around Your Heart" (in which the site of love has become a mine-strewn no-man's-land) and "We Work the Back Seam" (a rousing anthem about the plight of the British miners and about the nuclear danger). The jazz-pop music of the songs contained borrowings from reggae, the waltz, Prokofiev, and Kurt Weill, among other influences.

The musician and actor lives in the Hampstead section of London with Trudie Styler, the actress and model, and their two children. Nearby live his ex-wife, the actress Frances Tomelty, and two children from his eight-year marriage to her, which ended in divorce in 1984. Those who know Sting well refer to "the polished ambivalence of his charm" and explain his theatrical aplomb not as the usual pop-star bravado but "the confidence of someone who has made himself." He has been variously described as a natural, manic "exhibitionist" who is "guarded" even when acting flamboyant and basically "shy," even melancholy. A keeper of his own counsel, he is in his private life "perspicacious," "very intellectual," "quiet," and often "subdued," with mood shifts from "relaxed, open, and accessible" to "aloof" and "almost reclusive." Armed with a piquant sense of humor, he can be sharp-tongued in the face of ignorance or bad faith, but Jennifer Beals, his costar in *The Bride*, found him to be "fun, sweet, supportive." Published reports have estimated Sting's net worth at $18 million.

Sting, who has described himself as "an actor in the sense that all the world's a stage," feels "blessed" to have "a very mobile face," which changes from "really handsome" to "really ugly" or vice-versa as mood or will dictate. Never having succumbed to the excesses of the rock lifestyle, he is a nonsmoker, a moderate drinker, and a vegetarian who exercises daily, runs often, eats balanced meals, and gets enough sleep. He prefers work to leisure, and fills most of his spare moments with reading. His taste in music extends from Mozart to Miles Davis and Cannonball Adderly, and he "cannot operate without a guitar or piano around." In his political views he is left-leaning but nonideological. "I'm against politics with a capital 'P'," he told Kristine McKenna, "but I think we have to come to terms with the reality of nuclear power. We are in great danger and it's easy to get diverted from that awareness by everyday life. And every time we spend a million dollars on defense, that danger increases." He also said that he does not think "happiness is necessarily the reason we're here." "I think we're here to learn and evolve, and the pursuit of knowledge is what alleviates the pain of being human." Pointing out that he "never unpacks," Sting has said that he is "essentially a traveler," an "itinerant" on the earth.

References: Esquire 100:70+ N '83 por; Films and Filming 336:8+ S '82 pors; Hi Fi 34:90+ Ja '84 por; N Y Daily News p20+ F 21 '82: N Y Post p6 My 6 '85 por; N Y Times C p31 Ja 25 '82; Newsday p3 N 21 '82 pors, II p13 S 15 '85 por; Newsweek 106:66+ S 30 '85 pors; People 17:90 Ja 14 '85 pors; Rolling Stone p14+ S 1 '83 por, p13+ F 7 '80 por; Vanity Fair 48:68+ My '85

## Taylor, Elizabeth

Feb. 27, 1932– Actress. Address: c/o Chen Sam & Associates, Inc., 315 E. 72d St., New York City, N.Y. 10021

NOTE: This biography supersedes the article that appeared in *Current Biography* in 1952.

In 1944, the American moviegoing public fell in love with twelve-year-old Elizabeth Taylor, who had her first starring role in the film *National Velvet*. During the decades that followed, she became, as Stephen Harvey put it in the *New York Times* (June 16, 1985), "the ultimate celebrity." Like many who have written about the actress, Harvey complained that the attention paid to her personal life, particularly her seven marriages, overshadowed her "exceptionally intriguing career on screen." Among the most frequently mentioned examples of the adult Elizabeth Taylor's art are her performances in *A Place in the Sun* (1951), *Raintree County* (1957), *Cat on a Hot Tin Roof* (1958), *Suddenly Last Summer* (1959), and her Oscar-winning tours de force in *Butterfield 8* (1960) and *Who's Afraid of Virginia Woolf?* (1966).

Elizabeth Rosemond Taylor was born on February 27, 1932 in London, England to American par-

*Elizabeth Taylor*

ents from Arkansas City, Kansas. Her father, Francis Taylor, had gone to Europe as a buyer for his uncle, Howard Young, a prosperous St. Louis art dealer, and later established his own art gallery on London's Old Bond Street. Her mother, the former Sara Warmbrodt, acted on stage before her marriage under the professional name of Sara Sothern. Miss Taylor has a brother, Howard Taylor, who is two years older. During her first seven years, the Taylors made their home in the London borough of Hampstead, where she attended Byron House, a coeducational private school. As a small child, she took dancing lessons at a school run by Madame Vacani, and when she was only three she danced in a recital before members of the British royal family at London's Hippodrome. Later, her equestrian skills were nurtured by her adopted godfather, Victor Cazalet, who presented her with a pony and encouraged her to practice riding on his Kent estate.

Just before the outbreak of World War II, the Taylors returned to the United States, settling in Pasadena, California and later in Beverly Hills. Elizabeth's natural beauty and charm soon brought her to the attention of film executives. Sara Taylor strongly supported the idea of a movie career for her daughter, while her husband was somewhat more reluctant, but it was largely Elizabeth's own enthusiasm that led to her obtaining a contract, in 1941, with Universal Pictures. During her year with Universal she played a small part in one film, *There's One Born Every Minute* (1942). Soon afterwards, MGM producer Sam Marx, who at the time served as an air-raid warden alongside Francis Taylor, was seeking a girl to play the granddaughter of an English lord in *Lassie Come Home* (1943), and he arranged a screen test for Elizabeth. As Sam Marx recalled for Brenda Maddox's biog-

raphy *Who's Afraid of Elizabeth Taylor?* (1977), she clearly outshone all the other auditioners and was immediately given an MGM contract. After *Lassie Come Home* she was loaned to Twentieth Century-Fox to play Helen Burns in *Jane Eyre* (1944), and then she appeared in another minor role, in *The White Cliffs of Dover* (MGM, 1944). Meanwhile, in 1942, she transferred from the Hawthorne School in Beverly Hills to the Metro-Goldwyn-Mayer School, and in 1950 she obtained her diploma from the University High School in Hollywood.

Elizabeth Taylor's background and her accomplishments as an equestrienne made her a logical choice for the role of Velvet Brown in *National Velvet*, MGM's film adaptation of Enid Bagnold's novel about a girl who wins a horse in a lottery and rides it to victory in England's Grand National Steeplechase. Because she was at the time too small for the role, producer Pandro S. Berman delayed the shooting of the film until she was tall enough. Eager to play Velvet, she managed, through a rigorous four-month routine of diet and exercise, to add three inches to her height. The result was generally considered to be one of the all-time great performances by a child actress. The usually tough critic James Agee of the *Nation* (December 23, 1944) confessed: "Ever since I first saw the child . . . I have been choked with the peculiar sort of adoration I might have felt if we were in the same grade of primary school." He concluded: "I think that she and the picture are wonderful, and I hardly know or care whether she can act or not." Bosley Crowther of the *New York Times* (December 15, 1944) concurred: "Her face is alive with youthful spirit, her voice has the softness of sweet song and her whole manner in this picture is one of refreshing grace." The animal-loving actress, who in 1946 published a book, *Nibbles and Me* (Duell, Sloan and Pearce), about her pet chipmunk, received top billing for the first time in *Courage of Lassie* (MGM, 1946).

Unlike many child stars, Elizabeth Taylor made a smooth transition to more "grownup" parts. As an invalid in *Cynthia* (MGM, 1947), she received a much-publicized "first screen kiss" from Jimmy Lydon, with whom she was again teamed in *Life With Father* (Warner, 1947), based on the long-running Broadway stage play by Howard Lindsay and Russel Crouse. After playing a "spoiled beauty" in the musical *A Date With Judy* (MGM, 1948), Greer Garson's daughter in *Julia Misbehaves* (MGM, 1948), and Amy in MGM's 1949 remake of *Little Women*, Miss Taylor had her first full-fledged adult role, that of the wife of a Soviet spy, played by Robert Taylor, in *Conspirator* (MGM, 1950) and then appeared as an amateur psychiatrist in *The Big Hangover* (MGM, 1950). In Vincente Minnelli's popular comedy *Father of the Bride* (MGM, 1950), the focus was mainly on the father, played by Spencer Tracy, while she was still "at the promising young actress stage of her career," according to Alton Cook of the *New York World-Telegram* (May 19, 1950). She and Tracy repeated their characterizations in the sequel, *Father's Little Dividend* (MGM, 1951).

Elizabeth Taylor told Richard Meryman of *Life* (December 18, 1964) that the first film in which she was "asked to do any *acting*" was *A Place in the Sun*, director George Stevens' adaptation of Theodore Dreiser's novel *An American Tragedy*, which was filmed in 1949 and released by Paramount in 1951. Critics generally agreed that she brought a new dimension to her delineation of Angela Vickers, the rich girl whose love for George Eastman, played by Montgomery Clift, has tragic consequences. Shelley Winters, who costarred in the film as the ill-fated Alice Tripp, later recalled, as quoted by Stephen Harvey in the *New York Times* (June 16, 1985), that Miss Taylor had "a depth and simpleness which were really remarkable."

After fulfilling her obligations under her initial MGM contract with her performances as a dancing teacher in *Love Is Better Than Ever* (1952) and her portrayal of Rebecca in Pandro S. Berman's film adaptation of Sir Walter Scott's *Ivanhoe* (1952), Miss Taylor starred in *The Girl Who Had Everything* (1953) and *Rhapsody* (1954) under a new seven-year, $5,000-a-week contract with the studio. When Vivien Leigh, the original star of *Elephant Walk* (1954), withdrew from the film because of a nervous breakdown, Elizabeth Taylor took her place, allowing Paramount to salvage some of the original footage. Miss Taylor returned to her home studio for the historical romance *Beau Brummel* (MGM, 1954) and then starred in *The Last Time I Saw Paris* (MGM, 1954), based on F. Scott Fitzgerald's story "Babylon Revisited."

In the course of *Giant* (Warner, 1956), based on Edna Ferber's epic novel, Elizabeth Taylor, in the role of Leslie Benedict, the wife of a Texas rancher, ages some thirty years, but her performance was to a large extent overshadowed by that of James Dean, who had died in an automobile accident just after finishing his scenes in the film, which earned an Oscar for director George Stevens. Her next film, the Civil War epic *Raintree County* (MGM, 1957), was almost unanimously panned by critics, but some praised Miss Taylor's portrayal of a mentally disturbed Southerner who tricks Montgomery Clift into marriage, and William K. Zinsser, reviewing the film in the *New York Herald Tribune* (December 21, 1957), found her to be "the best of the actors."

In the words of director Richard Brooks, Elizabeth Taylor emerged as "the quintessential Tennessee Williams heroine" with her portrayal of Maggie the Cat in MGM's adaptation of Williams's family drama *Cat on a Hot Tin Roof* (1958), costarring Paul Newman. In her *Life* interview with Richard Meryman, Miss Taylor described the film as "a big high point" in her career, and it earned her the number-two spot on Quigley Publications' annual list of top money-making stars for 1958. She remained among the top ten every year except two until 1968, attaining the number-one position in 1961. Her next venture into the world of Tennessee Williams was in the role of Catherine in the gro-

tesque melodrama *Suddenly Last Summer* (Columbia, 1959), directed by Joseph L. Mankiewicz. Although the film was widely panned, critics found Miss Taylor's lengthy monologue, which brought it to its dramatic climax, to be one of its redeeming features.

Meanwhile, Elizabeth Taylor had suffered a major tragedy with the death, in a plane crash in 1958, of her third husband, producer Michael Todd, who, in the words of Brenda Maddox, had changed her "from a dull movie beauty into an international celebrity . . . and into the archetypal star goddess." Her performances in *Raintree County, Cat on a Hot Tin Roof*, and *Suddenly Last Summer* all earned her Academy Award nominations, and she won the award itself for director Daniel Mann's *Butterfield 8* (1960), based on John O'Hara's novel about a New York call girl. Miss Taylor had made the film at the insistence of MGM officials despite her own misgivings, and even after she won the Oscar she believed that the award was largely the result of a sympathy vote, since she had come close to dying of pneumonia just before the awards ceremonies.

Miss Taylor's illness was only one of the troubles that plagued Twentieth Century-Fox on her next movie, the widely publicized *Cleopatra* (1963), under the direction of Mankiewicz. A variety of factors, including Miss Taylor's $1 million fee—the highest paid to any star up to that time—contributed to its record production cost, estimated at $40 million. Critical reaction to *Cleopatra* was sharply divided. Among its ardent defenders, Bosley Crowther of the *New York Times* (June 23, 1963) wrote: "For me, her handsome bearing, her strongly imperious air, her power to convey a conviction of a woman in various states of love offset the distraction of her plumpness and the somewhat grating quality of her voice."

During the filming of *Cleopatra*, Elizabeth Taylor, who was then married to the singer Eddie Fisher, fell in love with Richard Burton, who costarred in the role of Mark Antony. By the time they were married, their second film together, *The VIPs* (MGM, 1963)—which William Peper of the *New York World-Telegram and Sun* (September 20, 1963) described as "old-fashioned entertainment done to a glossy fare-thee-well"—had already been released. It was a financial success, as was the next Burton-Taylor costarring vehicle, *The Sandpiper* (MGM, 1965), despite poor reviews.

Elizabeth Taylor and Richard Burton departed from their glamorous image to play Martha and George, the constantly bickering faculty couple in the film of Edward Albee's play *Who's Afraid of Virginia Woolf?* (Warner, 1966), directed by Mike Nichols. To look properly unattractive as the "fat, foul-mouthed" Martha, Miss Taylor gained about twenty-five pounds. As the critic for *Variety* (June 22, 1966) saw it, her characterization was "at once sensual, spiteful, cynical, pitiable, loathsome, lustful and tender." It earned Miss Taylor her second Academy Award for best actress, as well as the National Board of Review Award, the Foreign Press

Association Award, Italy's Silver Mask, a prize from the British Film Academy, and, in a tie with Lynn Redgrave, the New York Film Critics Circle award.

*The Taming of the Shrew* (Columbia, 1967), directed by Franco Zeffirelli, was the first of the Burtons' own productions and Miss Taylor's first foray into Shakespeare. Bosley Crowther, writing in the *New York Times* (March 9, 1967), called it "forthrightly campy entertainment" and commented on the "sheer theatrical gusto and rollicking sport of the film." Although some critics felt that Miss Taylor, in the role of Katherine, did not have an adequate command of the Shakespearean language, the film further extended her streak of box-office hits.

The subsequent Taylor-Burton pictures, *Doctor Faustus* (Columbia, 1967), *The Comedians* (MGM, 1967), *Boom!* (Universal, 1968), *Under Milk Wood* (Altura, 1971), and Peter Ustinov's *Hammersmith Is Out* (Cinerama, 1972), did not match the success of their first five movies. Furthermore, the grosses of her films without Burton, including John Huston's *Reflections in a Golden Eye* (Warner, 1967), Joseph Losey's *Secret Ceremony* (Universal, 1968), George Stevens' *The Only Game in Town* (Twentieth Century-Fox, 1970), *Night Watch* (Avco Embassy, 1973), and *Ash Wednesday* (Paramount, 1973), hardly seemed to justify her fees, which reached a peak of $1.25 million in 1970. Nevertheless, some critics felt that she grew further as an actress during that period, especially in view of her continued willingness to play unglamorous parts. Commenting on her virtuoso performance in the love triangle drama *X, Y, and Zee* (Columbia, 1972), Pauline Kael wrote in the *New Yorker* (February 12, 1972): "She responds to the zest in Edna O'Brien's material; you can feel her willingness to go all the way with it, and her delight at letting it all spill out. . . . For the first time that I can recall, she appears to be having a roaring good time on camera."

In 1974, Elizabeth Taylor served as one of eleven on-screen narrators for MGM's retrospective of musicals, *That's Entertainment!*, and starred in the Italian-made *The Driver's Seat* (Avco Embassy). She played four characters—the Mother, Maternal Love, the Witch, and Light—in the fantasy *The Blue Bird* (Twentieth Century-Fox, 1976), the first Soviet-American coproduction. After starring as Desiree in director Hal Prince's *A Little Night Music* (New World, 1977), based on Stephen Sondheim's hit musical, Miss Taylor took a sabbatical from filmmaking. During that time she conducted seminars in drama at several Virginia colleges and assisted in the campaign of her husband, John W. Warner, who was elected a United States Republican senator from that state in 1978. She returned to the screen for a cameo role in *Winter Kills* (Avco Embassy, 1979) and then appeared as Marina Rudd, an aging actress, in *The Mirror Crack'd* (EMI, 1980), based on an Agatha Christie novel. The latter was her last appearance in a theatrical film to date, except for her co-narration of *Genocide* (1982), a documentary prepared by the Simon Wiesenthal Center for Holocaust Studies.

Miss Taylor made her Broadway stage debut in 1981, in a revival of *The Little Foxes*, Lillian Hellman's melodrama about machinations among members of a greedy Southern family. The reviews were mixed, but many critics agreed with Frank Rich of the *New York Times* (May 8, 1981) that she had "found just the right vehicle." As Rich viewed it, her role as the evil Regina Giddens "does require the tidal force of pure personality. . . . No doubt it's superfluous to point out that Miss Taylor has charm, grandeur and sex appeal. The news here is that she has the killer instinct, too—and the skill to project it from a stage. . . . Miss Taylor makes us hate her guts—God bless her." The star, who was nominated for a Tony award, received, according to producer Zev Bufman, "the biggest salary ever paid on Broadway" for the 126-performance run at the Martin Beck Theater, which had been sold out almost completely. It was followed by engagements in New Orleans and Los Angeles and, in 1982, a London production.

For her next Broadway venture, a 1983 revival of Noel Coward's comedy *Private Lives*, Miss Taylor was reunited with Richard Burton. Coproduced by Miss Taylor and Zev Bufman through the newly established Elizabeth Theatre Group, it ran for sixty-three performances at the Lunt Fontanne Theater. The production was less successful than *The Little Foxes*, and some critics complained that the two stars were capitalizing on the publicity about their offstage relationship. According to the reviewer for *Newsweek* (May 16, 1983), "Taylor is still magnificent, but it's the bounteous magnificence of an earth mother, not the cool grace of Coward's curvilinear hedonist."

In recent years, Elizabeth Taylor has devoted some of her time and effort to television. With Richard Burton she appeared in the made-for-TV movie *Divorce His: Divorce Hers* (Harlech TV-ABC, 1973). Her other television films include *Victory at Entebbe* (ABC, 1976) and *Return Engagement* (NBC, 1978). Stephen Harvey, in his *New York Times* article, described her as "displaying a flair for caustic comedy" in *Between Friends*, which had its premiere on the pay-cable service Home Box Office in 1983. In the 1985 CBS-TV film *Malice in Wonderland*, she impersonated gossip columnist Louella Parsons. Miss Taylor has also been a guest star on the regular ABC-TV series *General Hospital* and *Hotel* and on that network's miniseries *North and South*.

Elizabeth Taylor's first two marriages, to Conrad Nicholas ("Nicky") Hilton Jr., on May 6, 1950, and to British actor Michael Wilding, on February 21, 1952, ended in divorce, in 1951 and 1957, respectively. Her third marriage, to Michael Todd, on February 2, 1957, ended when he died in a plane crash in March 1958. When she was married, on May 12, 1959, to Todd's close friend Eddie Fisher, she was branded a "homewrecker" by some segments of the press, but both Fisher and Miss Taylor have always maintained that his earlier marriage to the actress Debbie Reynolds had deteriorated before their romance began.

Similar attacks preceded Miss Taylor's 1964 divorce from Fisher and her subsequent union with Richard Burton, whom she married on March 15, 1964, divorced in June 1974, remarried on October 10, 1975, and again divorced in 1976. Elizabeth Taylor and John W. Warner, who were married on December 4, 1976, were divorced in 1982. In her *Life* interview with Richard Meryman, she explained, "I think I ended up being the scarlet woman partly because of my rather puritanical upbringing and beliefs. . . . I always chose to think I was in love and that love was synonymous with marriage. I couldn't just have a romance; it had to be marriage." She is the mother of four children: Michael Wilding Jr., born in 1953; Christopher Wilding, born in 1955; Liza Todd, born in 1957; and Maria Burton Carson, a handicapped German girl whom she adopted in 1961. Miss Taylor first became a grandmother at thirty-nine and has several grandchildren.

"A survivor" is a phrase that acquaintances have often used to describe Elizabeth Taylor. Over the years, she has suffered from ulcers, amoebic dysentery, bursitis, acute bronchitis, and back problems, in addition to her near-fatal 1961 bout with pneumonia. She has undergone over thirty operations and once nearly choked on a chicken bone. Early in 1983, the actress was injured in an automobile accident in Israel, and later that year she entered the Betty Ford Center in California to cure herself of addictions to alcohol, sleeping pills, and painkillers. Several charities, including the American Cancer Society, and the campaign against AIDS, have been recipients of Miss Taylor's generosity, which has taken the form of gifts and participation in benefit events. In 1959, following Mike Todd's death, the actress, whose family background was Christian Scientist, converted to Judaism. Her support of various Jewish and Israeli causes resulted in the banning of her films in some Arab countries. In September 1985, French Culture Minister Jack Lang conferred on Elizabeth Taylor the title Commander of Arts and Letters, France's highest artistic award.

Elizabeth Taylor, who is about five feet four inches tall and has silver-black hair, has often been called one of the world's most beautiful women. Her face, described by Brenda Maddox in her biography as characterized by "the high childishly curved forehead, the black circumflex eyebrows, the perfect nose over the MGM mouth, and the eyes blazing blue, abnormally wide and even," has become legendary, as has her voluptuous figure. She has homes in the Bel Air section of Los Angeles and in Gstaad, Switzerland. Still a lover of animals, Miss Taylor has several pets. Her fine art collection includes paintings by Renoir, Monet, and Modigliani. Among her other hobbies are dress designing, collecting jewelry, cooking, reading, attending rock concerts, and watching old movies, including her own, on television.

References: Life 57:73+ D 18 '64 pors; N Y Times II p19+ Je 16 '85 pors; David, Lester and Robbins, Jhan. Richard and Elizabeth (1977); Katz, E. Film Encyclopedia (1982); Kelley, Kitty. Elizabeth Taylor, The Last Star (1981); Maddox, Brenda. Who's Afraid of Elizabeth Taylor? (1977); Sheppard, Dick. Elizabeth: The Life and Career of Elizabeth Taylor (1975); Thomson, David. A Biographical Dictionary of Film (1976); Who's Who in America, 1984–85

## Tcherkassky, Marianna

Oct. 28, 1952– Dancer. Address: b. c/o American Ballet Theatre, 890 Broadway, New York City, N.Y. 10003

After seeing Marianna Tcherkassky dance her first *Giselle*, in 1976, Clive Barnes, the veteran dance and theatre critic who had been following the ballerina's career with interest since she joined the American Ballet Theatre in 1970, observed that the lyrical Romantic style of her portrayal brought to mind Yvette Chauviré and Galina Ulanova, two of the foremost interpreters of the role. Miss Tcherkassky is perhaps best known for the purity of style that enables her to slip effortlessly from the elegant classicism of *La Bayadère* to the articulated precision footwork of Bournonville's *Napoli Variations* to the Tharpian shrugs and slouches of *Push Comes to Shove*. Recently, however, she has developed into an affecting dance-actress, finding the hidden emotional nuances of even essentially abstract ballets. A favorite of balletomanes long before she was elevated, in 1976, to the rank of principal dancer, Marianna Tcherkassky has rewarded her audiences with sparkling technique, intuitive musical phrasing, and carefully wrought characterizations that breathe new life into well-known works.

Of Russian and Japanese descent, Marianna Alexsavena Tcherkassky was born in Glen Cove, New York on October 28, 1952. Her father, Alexis Tcherkassky, was an opera and concert singer; her mother, the former Lillian Oka, was a leading dancer with the Markova-Dolin Ballet and the Grand Ballet du Marquis de Cuevas. "Born into" the performing arts, as she put it, Miss Tcherkassky received her early ballet training, beginning at the age of eight, from her mother. "There was never any question that I too would be a dancer," she told John Gruen, who interviewed her for a *Dance* magazine (September 1981) profile. An extremely shy child, Marianna Tcherkassky found in dance an emotional as well as a physical outlet. She performed her daily barre exercises assiduously and, after locking herself in her bedroom, practiced the mad scene from *Giselle*. Her diligence quickly paid off, for in the early 1960s she appeared with the New York City Ballet in its production of *A Midsummer Night's Dream* and with the visiting Bolshoi Ballet in a performance of *Ballet School.*

Shortly after she moved with her family to Kensington, Maryland in 1965, Marianna Tcherkassky enrolled in classes at the nearby Washington (D.C.) School of Ballet, where her teachers included Edward Caton and Mary Day, the school's cofounder. Under their tutelage, she progressed so rapidly that Mary Day urged her to enter the prestigious international ballet competition in Varna, Bulgaria, but as Miss Day told an interviewer for *Ballet News* (November 1981), the young dancer "cried and screamed and begged not to go, so we didn't. It's a shame, too, because I know she would have won." Marianna Tcherkassky spent the summer of 1967 in Saratoga, New York, the summer home of the New York City Ballet, as a special student of the renowned instructor Oleg Briansky. Recognizing her uncommon gifts, Briansky arranged for the girl to take daily company class with the City Ballet dancers. One day, George Balanchine, the company's artistic director, spotted her among the ranks and awarded her a Ford Foundation scholarship to study full time at the School of American Ballet, the company's official school.

In the fall of 1967 Marianna Tcherkassy moved to New York City to begin her training at the School of American Ballet. "I was completely miserable . . . ," she confessed to John Gruen. "I had grown so dependent on my family that it was an unbearable wrench to be parted from them. . . . I remember crying myself to sleep for the first three months of that year, and being afraid to tell my parents because I knew that studying at SAB was what they wanted. At any rate, I suffered through it and, little by little, adjusted to the routine." That routine included, in addition to several hours of daily ballet instruction, a regular course of study at the Professional Children's School, from which Miss Tcherkassky received her high-school diploma in 1970.

Among Marianna Tcherkassky's teachers at the School of American Ballet was André Eglevsky, and it was with his small regional company, which is based on Long Island, that she made her professional debut, in 1968. The young dancer dreamed of joining the New York City Ballet on completion of her training, but on the advice of Diana Adams, a perceptive instructor who recognized that she was, by nature, a Romantic ballerina and would be happier dancing the great classical roles, Miss Tcherkassky auditioned for the American Ballet Theatre in 1970 and was accepted into its corps de ballet.

During her years as a corps member, in addition to dancing the standard corps parts in such classics as *Swan Lake, Coppélia,* and *Giselle,* she was entrusted with important solo variations in the world premiere of Dennis Nahat's abstract *Mendelssohn Symphony* and in Rudolf Nureyev's restaging of Marius Petipa's *Paquita.* When the American Ballet Theatre decided to showcase some of its most promising young dancers in a special program celebrating the opening of Mercer Community College in Trenton, New Jersey, she was among those selected. Partnered by Fernando Bujones, she charmed the New York critics with her technically assured performance of August Bournonville's sprightly *Flower Festival Pas De Deux* and the grand pas de deux from *The Nutcracker.*

Elevated to the rank of soloist in October 1972, Marianna Tcherkassky quickly added to her personal repertory such important roles as Prayer in *Coppélia,* the Sweetheart and Mother in *Billy the Kid,* Eugene Loring's folkloric narrative of the Old West, Prelude in *Les Sylphides,* and the Ballerina in *Petrouchka.* She also appeared in the dazzling fouetté competition in David Lichine's rollicking *Graduation Ball;* in the lyrical pas de deux that is the centerpiece of the second movement of Eliot Feld's haunting *At Midnight;* in the "Giggling Rapids" section of Alvin Ailey's jazz suite *The River;* in the Peasant Pas de Deux in *Giselle;* and in the company premieres of Rudi van Dantzig's chilling *Monument for a Dead Boy* and John Neumeier's version of *Le Baiser de la Fée,* in which she danced the role of the innocent and playful Bride with unusual dramatic power.

With her buoyant jumps and feathery beats, Marianna Tcherkassky is particularly suited to the exhilarating and technically demanding works of August Bournonville. In their reviews of performances of Bournonville's *Napoli Variations,* dance critics invariably threw the soloist a special bouquet. "Of the five women, only Marianna Tcherkassky was in enough control to organize the steps into recognizable phrases," Nancy Goldner wrote in the *Christian Science Monitor* (January 11, 1974), "and only she fully conveyed the sheer happiness of the choreography." At the same time, her fluid musicality and elegance made her an ideal choice for Petipa's ballerina roles. Her Princess Florine, for example, in the celebrated Blue Bird Pas de Deux in *The Sleeping Beauty* was "expansive, stylish, and gracious," according to

Jennifer Dunning of the *New York Times* (July 31, 1974). "A balance held just that delicately breathless moment past all expectation . . . was one of those unforgettable treasures of dance-going."

Continuing to annex ballets to her repertory at a prodigious rate throughout the mid-1970s, Marianna Tcherkassky took leading roles in a wide variety of works, among them Sir Frederick Ashton's merry *Les Patineurs*; *Concerto*, Sir Kenneth MacMillan's choreographic translation of Shostakovich's Piano Concerto No. 2; Antony Tudor's lyrical *The Leaves Are Fading*; Jerome Robbins' nonballetic reworking of *Les Noces*; Anton Dolin's version of Jules Perrot's divertissement *Pas de Quatre*; and Michel Fokine's dance poem *Le Spectre de la Rose*.

To prepare for the part of the dreaming young girl in *Le Spectre de la Rose*, Marianna Tcherkassky studied photographs of the original production, featuring Vaslav Nijinsky and Tamara Karsavina, and read extensively about Fokine's life and work. "I wanted to get a feeling for the period, not so much to reproduce . . . but to capture some of the mood of the dances," she explained to Jennifer Dunning a few years later in an interview for a *New York Times* (June 13, 1980) profile. Perhaps most important, she asked André Eglevsky, who had worked with Fokine, to coach her in the mime sequences and in the choreographer's soft, round style. Because of her care, the role of the girl was not overwhelmed, as it so often is in contemporary productions, by the virtuosic choreography for the Spectre.

In her review of the American Ballet Theatre's 1975 New York season for *Dance* magazine (October 1975), Tobi Tobias singled out Marianna Tcherkassky for "the steady, individually distinctive quality" of her work. "With the muted radiance of her stage presence and her serene, beautifully measured dancing in which each phrase is fulfilled," the critic concluded, she performed small parts "like a ballerina in exile." Marianna Tcherkassky came into her own in the 1976 New York summer season with spectacular back-to-back debuts, on just a few days' notice, in two of the most demanding roles in ballet: the Hindu temple dancer Nikiya in the "Kingdom of the Shades" scene from Petipa's classical jewel *La Bayadère* and the title role in *Giselle*, the most celebrated of the Romantic ballets. Her Nikiya was remarkable for the seamless lyricism of her impeccable classical style; her Giselle, for the gossamer delicacy of her dancing and the poignancy of her mad scene, in which she reenacted the ardor of Giselle's love for the double-dealing Albrecht.

Completely won over by her first attempt as Giselle, on August 4, 1976, the New York audience tendered Miss Tcherkassky and her partner, Ivan Nagy, an ovation and showered them with daisies. Although the critics pronounced her debut "a veritable triumph," in Tobi Tobias' words, the ballerina herself was dissatisfied with her interpretation. "It was like a picture without a frame," she told John Gruen. Always in command of the technical

requirements of the role, Miss Tcherkassky gradually mastered its dramatic nuances until she made her Giselle one of the most memorable in recent ballet history. Dance critics have been especially impressed by her transformation from the lighthearted, infatuated peasant girl to the spectral Wili whose unconditional love and generosity of spirit transcended death.

Promoted to principal dancer in August 1976 largely on the strength of her performances in *Giselle* and *La Bayadère*, Marianna Tcherkassky assumed over the next few years leading roles in other classical ballets, including *The Nutcracker*, *La Sylphide*, *Coppélia*, *Don Quixote*, and *Cinderella*. Recognizing her innate musicality and interpretive intelligence, Mikhail Baryshnikov chose her to dance the central role of Clara in his psychological reinterpretation of *The Nutcracker*, which received its world premiere in Washington, D.C. on December 21, 1976. Although many critics carped about Baryshnikov's unorthodox conception, the majority found Miss Tcherkassky's filigreed delicacy and dewy-eyed radiance to be just right for Clara's rapturous "coming-of-age" variations.

Marianna Tcherkassky's mastery of the Bournonville technique made her a natural for the role of the sylph in *La Sylphide*, but her flair for comedy, as the mischievous Swanilda in *Coppélia* and the flirtatious Kitri in Baryshnikov's staging of *Don Quixote*, took critics by surprise. As the heroine in the otherwise disappointing new version of *Cinderella* choreographed jointly by Baryshnikov and Peter Anastos, she managed to overcome the unimaginative choreography to offer "a genuine sweetness and prettiness in her perfect dancing," as Anna Kisselgoff wrote in her review for the *New York Times* (April 27, 1984).

Eager to diversify her repertory, Marianna Tcherkassky accepted the parts of the witty sophisticate in Twyla Tharp's whimsical *Push Comes to Shove*, the alluring gypsy waif in Tudor's *The Tiller in the Fields*, an Arabian dancer in *The Meeting*, a sensuous solo created by the ethnic dancer La Meri, and the grieving woman in Tudor's *Dark Elegies*. She also danced major roles in, among other things, Glen Tetley's angular *Voluntaries*, Harald Lander's technical tour-de-force *Etudes*, Ashton's delightful comedy of manners, *Les Rendezvous*, Lynne Taylor-Corbett's modern dance–flavored *Great Galloping Gottschalk*, and the party piece pas de deux from Petipa's *La Fille Mal Gardée*, restaged for the American Ballet Theatre by Diane Joffe.

The ballerina was especially effective in the title role in *The Firebird*, imbuing her intelligently conceived interpretation with a Slavic passion that reminded Jennifer Dunning of the intensity Maria Tallchief once brought to the role, and as Nikiya in Natalia Markarova's sumptuous production of the full-length *La Bayadère*. Commenting on her performance in the latter work for the *New York Times* (May 22, 1983), Anna Kisselgoff observed, "Miss Tcherkassky was the epitome of the classical dancer imbued with a Romantic spirit. Her duets and solos in the 'Shades' scene could not have been more dreamlike, and yet were also diamond-sharp in outline. Her body placement was perfect: every detail of phrasing caught the climaxes of the music or contributed its own subtleties."

Marianna Tcherkassky's mastery of the various styles of dance and her intuitive appreciation of the different methods of interpretation have made her a favorite of contemporary choreographers. Among those works created especially for her are John Meehan's idyllic duet *Le Retour*, Fernando Bujones' virtuoso divertissement *Grand Pas Romantique*, *In a Country Garden*, Michael Vernon's reworking of his crowd-pleasing *Elssler Pas de Deux*, John McFall's *Interludes*, and Choo San Goh's plotless neo-Romantic *Configurations*.

The music is Miss Tcherkassky's primary source of inspiration, and her first step in preparing a new role is to listen again and again to the score, searching for "those things [that] give what you are dancing a quality beyond the steps," as she explained to Jennifer Dunning for the *New York Times* profile. She also relies heavily on her partners for inspiration and emotional support. Her partners over the years have included such *premiers danseurs* as Mikhail Baryshnikov, Ivan Nagy, Anthony Dowell, John Meehan, Patrick Dupond, and Jean-Charles Gil. In roles of technical virtuosity, she has been best matched with Danilo Radojevic; in Romantic or dramatic ballets, she has been, by most accounts, happiest with Kevin McKenzie or Fernando Bujones.

It was Bujones who partnered Marianna Tcherkassky when she undertook what was perhaps her greatest challenge since *Giselle*—the role of Juliet in Sir Kenneth MacMillan's grandly theatrical staging of *Romeo and Juliet*, which was the showpiece of the American Ballet Theatre's 1984–85 season. In rehearsals, she and Bujones developed for their characters a carefully thought-out relationship based upon the moral change experienced by them both at their initial meeting. Of all the company's Juliets, hers was the "most Shakespearean," according to Anna Kisselgoff, and thanks to the telling details with which she embellished her portrayal, ultimately the most moving. "Miss Tcherkassky's Juliet was above all pure," the dance critic wrote in her review for the *New York Times* (April 26, 1985), "charming and giggly as a child in the initial scenes, modest but eventually maturing away from doll-like fragility." As for her dancing, it "had the beauty of a silken skein, designed to touch the heart—and it did."

Petite and well-proportioned, with raven-black hair, large dark eyes, and delicate features, Marianna Tcherkassky, when seen onstage, bears at times an uncanny resemblance to Dame Margot Fonteyn. Like most dancers, she spends virtually her entire day practicing and refining her technique, rehearsing new roles, or performing. Her sole passion, aside from ballet, is baseball. A rabid fan of the New York Yankees, she attends home games whenever possible, invariably arriving early in order to watch the warmups, and she regularly listens to Yankee games on a transistor radio in her dressing room, particularly when her favorite player, Ron Guidry, is pitching.

As Miss Tcherkassky explained to Sheryl Flatow, who interviewed her for the *New York Daily News* (April 24, 1983), dancers look at sports in a special way. "You're very aware of the physical aspects, of the way athletes move, their coordination and reflexes, their flexibility and agility." She admired Guidry, she said, not only for his strength, speed, and effortless grace, but also for his "dedication" to the Yankee club. "The team is more important to him than being a superstar," she told Miss Flatow, "and I think that kind of commitment is necessary in both our professions." Marianna Tcherkassky lives in New York City with her husband, Terrence S. Orr, an American Ballet Theatre ballet master whom she married in 1980.

*References: Ballet N 5:6 S '83 por; Dance 55:58+ S '81 pors; N Y Times C p3 Jl 23 '76 por, C p12 Ja 13 '80 por; Biographical Dictionary of Dance (1982); Concise Oxford Dictionary of Ballet (1982); Who's Who in America, 1984–85*

# Trottier, Bryan

(trot′yā)

*July 17, 1956– Hockey player. Address: b. New York Islanders, Nassau Veterans Memorial Coliseum, Hempstead Turnpike, Uniondale, N.Y. 11553*

While the flashy and freewheeling Wayne Gretzky of the Edmonton Oilers excels him in brute scoring, the left-shooting Bryan Trottier of the New York Islanders is the most complete center in recent hockey history, a two-way threat as clever as he is hardworking and hard-hitting. A smart, deft puck handler and passer more concerned with feeding his wings than registering goals himself, Trottier leads the Islanders in career points, with 1,018, and assists, with 638. In addition to controlling the team's offense, especially in power plays, he is on defense a rampant and dogged forward, ferociously body-checking (without resorting to Neanderthal use of the stick), going into corners, covering the net when the defenseman is drawn away, and anticipating opportunities to intercept. Exceptionally strong for his size (five feet eleven, 200 pounds) and intensely proud and determined, he seems invulnerable to pain as well as fatigue, often remaining in action, sometimes rashly, when injured. He skates deceptively, with back straight and head up, so as not to alert opponents to the direction in which he plans to move, and his ability to maintain both his balance and his imperturbability under violent contact is uncanny.

As Trottier goes, so go the Islanders, at least in the perception of the New York management, players, and fans. That is especially true in the Stanley Cup playoffs, in which the Isles have created a legend with their comebacks and overtime rallies. Defenseman Denis Potvin and others contributed to the four consecutive Cup championships won by the Islanders between 1980 and 1983, but Trottier increasingly became the key element, the "transmission" to Potvin's petrol, as one close observer analogized. Through 1984, Trottier had ninety-eight career playoff assists, second only to Potvin's ninety-nine in the NHL record books, and 148 points, second to Potvin's team-leading 149.

The oldest of four children in a cattle-ranching family, Bryan John Trottier was born in Val Marie, a high-prairie whistlestop in Canada's western plains province of Saskatchewan, on July 17, 1956. On his mother's side of the family, Trottier's ancestry is wholly Irish; on his father's side, his grandfather was of mixed French and Cree Indian blood and his grandmother was a full Chippewa. His father, Eldon ("Buzz") Trottier, has been a jack of many trades, including cowpunching, rodeo riding, and road construction. As a construction worker, he traveled with his growing family to sites in western Canada and the western United States until 1962, when he took over the Trottier ranch and its herd of some sixty-odd cattle, not including calf crops.

Bryan Trottier began skating when he was six, on the river near his home, which was frozen from October through February. He did not start concentrating on hockey, however, until he was nine (an advanced age by Canadian hockey standards) because of the urgency of the ranch work in which he shared, including cutting, baling, and stacking hay, feeding and watering the horses, and milking the cows. When he was old enough, he also rode herd, checked and repaired fences, and became expert in roping. He continued to help out on the farm off-season well into his hockey career.

According to Trottier, the hockey coach who taught him "the most" was his father, who knows the game "inside out" and was his first mentor. Bryan's brother Monty recalls that Buzz Trottier deemphasized the offensive game, putting more value on body checks than on goals scored. "My father always told him [Bryan] to back-check," Monty told Gerald Eskenazi of the New York Times (April 22, 1979). "It wasn't important to score goals, but to play hockey all over the ice." (Monty is now playing in the Isles' farm system, and the third Trottier brother, Rocky, is in the New Jersey Devils' system.) The father, also an accomplished guitarist, taught Bryan to play that instrument, and in the early 1970s Buzz, Bryan, and Bryan's sister began doing weekend country-and-western and country-rock gigs in honky-tonks in and around Val Marie.

After progressing through the children's leagues, Trottier in 1972 joined a junior hockey club, the Swift Current (Saskatchewan) Broncos of the Western Canada Hockey League, a franchise that moved two years later to Lethbridge, Saskatchewan. After a slow start (forty-five points in 1972-73), he tallied 112 in his second season with the Broncos and 144 in his third, when he was the team captain and the league's most valuable player. Although he was underage, the New York Islanders picked Trottier in the second round of the 1974 amateur draft, and they called him up to New York the following year.

The Islanders had finished eighth in their division, then known as the East Division, in their first two seasons as an NHL franchise, 1972-73 and 1973-74. Defenseman Denis Potvin, in combination with goaltenders Billy Smith and Chico Resch, provided the team with a viable defense for the first time in 1974-75. With the addition of Trottier in 1975-76, the Isles became an offensive threat as well, jumping to league leadership in power plays. Trottier was always on the move, anticipating and intercepting enemy passes, coming up with and controlling the puck in the corners and behind the net, and forcing the other team into mistakes. His forte was setting up his wingers, Billy Harris and Clark Gillies. As opposing players ganged up on him, his linemates were left open, and he would feed them the puck for what, more often than not, would become a goal. Trottier set new NHL rookie records for assists (sixty-three) and points (ninety-five) that season, and he won the Calder Trophy, for rookie of the year. The Isles finished second in the Patrick Division of the NHL's Prince of Wales Conference and seventh overall and they were eliminated in the playoff semi-finals.

"Trottier makes things happen," William A. Torrey, the Isles' general manager, told Sheryl Flatow in an interview for Sport (April 1976). "By that, I don't necessarily mean just when he has the puck. He's cool about everything. His timing is good. He's in the right place at the right time. He has tremendous hockey instinct. There are things that no amount of training can give a boy; he either has them or he doesn't." Aside from the quality of his play, Trottier set a moral example for his teammates, one of athletic devotion and hard work, obeying Coach Al Arbour's commands to the letter and personifying the disciplined position-playing Arbour demanded. In the long, grueling practice sessions imposed by Arbour, Trottier improved the one aspect of his playing in which he was only middling, developing into one of the best faceoff players in the game. He set a similar example off the rink, resisting the big-time life style and residing with a Long Island couple who acted as surrogate parents until his marriage. "He doesn't drink, smoke, carouse, or anything," Clark Gillies said of him. "I've never seen a guy like that—he doesn't do anything. But that's the way he is and it's fine with me."

Hobbled by a twisted knee, Trottier had a slow start in 1976-77, and his total points for the season were twenty-three less than the previous year. The Isles finished second in the Patrick Division and fourth overall in the NHL, and they were again eliminated in the playoff semi-finals. In 1977 the team drafted the Quebec Junior Hockey League goal-scoring ace Mike Bossy, with whom Trottier immediately clicked both on and off the rink. Bossy, who shared Trottier's taste for milk shakes and the quiet life, became a boarder in the home of Trottier and his wife, Trottier's roommate on the road, and his constant companion.

With right wing Bossy complementing left wing Gillies, the Trottier-centered line became the most formidable scoring machine in hockey in 1977-78. Bossy set an NHL rookie record for goals, with fifty-three, and Trottier became the first Islander to pass the 100-points-in-a-season mark, with 123 points (forty-six goals and seventy-seven assists). In mid-season, Trottier made the first-team All-Stars, and in the post-season playoffs he remained in action despite a broken jaw but scored no goals. The Isles, who had finished first in the Patrick Division and third overall, were eliminated in the playoff quarter-finals by the underdog Toronto Maple Leafs.

In 1978-79 Trottier led the Isles to the best record that season in the NHL, 51-15-14. He led the league in scoring, with 134 points, the sixth highest total in NHL history. His assist tally (eighty-seven) was the second highest ever recorded by a forward, and his career points-per-game average (1.37) was second in history only to that of Bobby Orr. Trottier's most memorable performance of the season was against the New York Rangers on December 23, 1978, when he struck for five goals and set up three more in a 9-4 romp. He was awarded the Hart Memorial Trophy as the league's most valuable player, was named player of the year in the Sporting News poll of NHL players, and again made the first string All-Star team. In the playoff semi-finals following the regular season, the Isles again suffered an upset, at the hands of the New York Rangers. Trottier scored only two goals in ten playoff games, bringing his career playoff total to a mere five goals in forty-two games—a performance he would soon spectacularly upgrade. In October 1979 Trottier signed a new contract worth

in excess of $2 million, including bonuses, over five years, plus an option year.

As time went on, Trottier made an effort to be more outgoing and communicative with his teammates, despite his antipathy to partying, and he became noticeably more verbal after he was named assistant team captain in 1979. He fell to sixth place in NHL scoring (forty-two goals and sixty-two assists) in the 1979-80 season, and the Isles' winning percentage was only .500 through the first half of the season. To shake the team out of its lethargy and take some of the pressure off Trottier, the Isles' management made a trade with the Los Angeles Kings and brought in another seasoned center, Butch Goring, on March 12, 1980. During the remainder of the season Coach Al Arbour alternated two offensive lines, one centered by Goring and including Gillies and the other centered by Trottier and winged by Bob Bourne on the left and Bossy or Bob Nystrom on the right. The Isles finished second in the Patrick Division and fifth overall, and they went on to win their first Stanley Cup. Trottier, a dominant force in the playoffs, especially against the Philadelphia Flyers in the final round, won the Conn Smythe Trophy as most valuable player in the cup events.

In 1980-81 Trottier's assists made it possible for Bossy to match Maurice Richard's record of fifty goals in the first fifty games of a season. An injury kept Trottier out of seven games as well as the All-Star game, and he finished the season with thirty-one goals and seventy-two assists, far behind the record 164 points, including 109 record assists, scored by Wayne Gretzky of the Edmonton Oilers, hockey's new wunderkind. But the Isles finished first in the NHL and went on to successfully defend the Stanley Cup. Despite a separated shoulder and an injured foot, he duplicated his twenty-nine-point tally of the year before, and he recorded points in all eighteen playoff games. The eighteen games, joined to the last seven of the 1980 playoffs, gave him twenty-five consecutive scoring games over a two-year period, yet another record.

Interviewed by Gerald Eskenazi of the New York Times following the 1980-81 season, Al Arbour pointed out that Trottier is less impressive in practice than in games. "In practice, the competition isn't there," he explained. "But he's got the knack of getting through at the right time. Take when he's behind the net. It's like everyone knows what he's going to do . . . but you can't stop him. He's a Mack truck." The following autumn Butch Goring told Pat Calabria of Newsday (October 4, 1981): "When I played for Los Angeles . . . the feeling was that if you could stop Trottier or slow him down, you had a chance. But just slowing him down was pretty near an impossible task."

Trottier's 1981-82 season was a lustrous one, in which he scored fifty goals and seventy-nine assists for a total of 129 points. Six of the goals were game winners contributing to a second fifteen-game victory streak by the Isles, and Trottier had a streak of his own, recording points in twenty-five consecutive games. In his most remarkable performance,

Trottier on February 13, 1982 scored five times on five shots against the Flyers, tying NHL records for most goals in a period (four) and most power-play goals in a game (four). In the All-Star selections, he was the second-string center, behind Wayne Gretzky. In the playoffs, the Isles held on to the Stanley Cup, defeating in turn the Pittsburgh Penguins, the New York Rangers, the Quebec Nordiques, and the Vancouver Canucks. Trottier led the scoring in the playoffs, again with twenty-nine points, and he set a new playoff mark with twenty-three assists.

Although Trottier played in all eighty games in the 1982-83 season, back and knee problems contributed to the lowering of his offensive output to thirty-four goals and fifty-five assists. The Isles also slumped, finishing second in their division and sixth overall. Both he and the team responded to the challenge of the 1983 playoffs, however. After sitting out several of the Cup games with an injured right knee, Trottier accumulated eight goals and twelve assists and paced the Isles to their third straight championship. The final playoff series was an historic one against the heavily favored Edmonton Oilers, a match pictured by sports writers as a confrontation between a cocky, devil-may-care aggregation, preeminently typified by Wayne Gretzky, and a conservative team best represented by the disciplined Trottier. The personal duel never materialized, because goalie Billy Smith and the New York defense smothered the Edmonton star and held him goalless, while Trottier played outstanding defense, dominated opposing centers in faceoffs, and contributed a goal and three assists to a 4-0 upset that left the Oilers limp and the Islanders exhausted but jubilant. The sweetness of the victory was such that not even the habitually stone-faced Trottier could maintain his stoic facade. After the game he remained on the rink, a broad smile on his face, skate-dancing with the Stanley Cup held above his head, saluting and hugging fans at all corners of the Nassau Coliseum, and not removing his skates for an hour.

Afterward, Trottier tried to explain his unwonted display of emotion to a reporter in the locker room: "I'm finding as I get older I'm appreciating different things. Knowledge is carrying me. Maybe I'm understanding the Cup differently and what we've been able to accomplish." He also wanted to join with the fans in celebrating because "if you can't share [the elation] with someone, it isn't the same." "I guess I was saying, We're the best, they're the best. They backed us. We're them, or at least a reflection of them."

The 1983-84 season was one of Trottier's finest, and it might have been his best were it not for recurring problems with his right knee. Following injuries to the knee on January 12 and January 21, 1984, he underwent arthroscopic surgery and missed ten regular season games and the All-Star game, in which he was to have been the second-team center. When he went on the inactive list he was fourth in the league in scoring, with seventy-nine points, and his season totals were forty goals

and seventy-one assists. The Isles finished first in their division and second overall, and they reached the final round of the Stanley Cup playoffs, where they again faced Edmonton. In a virtual repeat of the 1983 championship series, the Isles shut out Wayne Gretzky in the first two games, but Gretzky ended up with four goals and three assists and the Oilers took the Stanley Cup away from the New Yorkers, four games to one. Trottier scored two goals and two assists in the championship series and six goals and four assists in the rounds leading up to it.

During the summer of 1984 Trottier stirred a minor controversy by deciding to play for Team USA instead of Team Canada in the Canada Cup international hockey tournament. As a North American Indian, he was entitled to opt for United States citizenship, and he did, to the consternation of many Canadian fans. With citizenship papers in hand, he donned the Team USA jersey for an August 16 exhibition game against Team Canada in Bloomington, Minnesota. When game sites shifted to Canadian soil, fans booed him whenever he touched the puck. When he helped Team USA to trounce Sweden, however, he received a standing ovation and he was named the game's MVP.

In 1984-85 Trottier hit his nadir and the Isles had their worst season (forty wins, thirty-four losses, and six ties) since 1974, when they failed even to make the playoffs. Trottier's still ailing right knee and a strained thigh muscle kept him out of action twelve of the season's first fifteen games, and the flare-up of a chronic lower-back problem contributed to his low point productivity (fifty-nine). On the bright side, Trottier's career point total of 1,018 made him the nineteenth player in NHL history to pass the 1,000 mark. After losing the first two games in the division playoffs against the Washington Capitals in April 1985, the Islanders performed a minor miracle, winning all three of the remaining games in the best-of-five series. Trottier scored the winning goal in one of the games. With the Caps out of the way, the Islanders confronted the Philadelphia Flyers for the division title.

Bryan Trottier has a smooth, boyish face, dark hair, twinkling eyes, and a broad-shouldered, muscular, and chunky build that gives his body checks a devastating cannonball impact. On the rink, he maintains an impassive visage and a quietly confident manner in the most violent of physical collisions, rarely losing his temper and seldom raising his voice to a gladiatorial pitch. Off the ice, he is soft-spoken and modest almost to the point of shyness, cautious in his choice of words in interviews, and reluctant to accept credit apart from his teammates. His sense of humor is reported to be as innocently bumpkin as it was in his Saskatchewan days. According to his former teammate Glenn Resch, Trottier has "a stubborn streak in whatever he does . . . even in video games." Resch told Pat Calabria of *Newsday:* "He just won't give up, and he uses his stubbornness in a positive way. He puts his mind to something, and . . . he's unstoppable."

Trottier and his wife, Nickie, who met at the Islanders' training camp in September 1975 and began dating in January 1976, live with their children, Bryan Jr. and Lindsay Ann, in Manhasset, Long Island, where the Trottiers attend the local Catholic church and Trottier is active in local charities. Nationally, he is president of the Hockey Players Association. He does most of the handy work around his house himself, and he and his wife spend most of their leisure time at home, where Trottier likes to entertain family and friends with his guitar playing and singing. He doesn't need "the attention and all that," he once said, and he will be happy to be remembered years from now, especially by his children, simply as someone who "never got tired, who gave his all . . . that guy [who] always played hard."

References: N Y Post p8 F 16 '79 pors; N Y Times p39+ O 31 '75, V p1+ Ap 22 '79 por, C p7 Ap 8 '85 por; Newsday mag p1+ O 4 '81 pors; Sport 62:92 Ap '76, 73:72+ N '82 por; Sporting News p45 My 2 '81 por; Aaseng, Nathan. Hockey's Super Scorers (1984); Moriarity, Tim and Bereswill, Joe. The Dynamic Islanders (1980)

## Tutu, Desmond (Mpilo)

Oct. 7, 1931– Anglican prelate; social activist. Address: 6981 Orlando West, Johannesburg, South Africa

For his "role as a unifying leader . . . in the campaign to resolve the problem of apartheid in South Africa," and "to direct attention to the nonviolent struggle for liberation" of which he is the chief spokesman, the Norwegian Nobel Committee awarded the 1984 Nobel Peace Prize to the Right Reverend Desmond Tutu, now the Anglican bishop of Johannesburg, the first black to hold that post. Throughout his episcopal career, and especially during his term as general secretary of the South African Council of Churches (1978–84), Bishop Tutu has brought outspoken and tireless Christian witness to the plight of the powerless black majority in a country ruled by a white minority with an official system of racial separatism that is, as he describes it, "as evil as Nazism." Under that system, 4.5 million whites have full dominion over 23 million blacks, who are disenfranchised and deprived of freedom of movement. The Afrikaner government views Tutu as a troublemaker, if not a subversive, but concerned observers in the international community generally see him as he sees himself: a peacemaker in a dangerously polarizing society, preaching racial reconciliation, warning against a "blood bath," and hoping that he is heard before time runs out.

Desmond Mpilo Tutu was born in the gold-mining town of Klerksdorp, Witwatersrand, Transvaal, South Africa, on October 7, 1931. His middle name, meaning "life" in Sotho, a Bantu language, was given him by his grandmother because he was a sickly baby, not expected to survive. "That," he half-jestingly told an interviewer for the London Observer (May 8, 1983), "was my first commitment to faith." His father was Zachariah Tutu, a schoolteacher from the Bantu tribe known as the Xhosas, and his mother was Aletta Tutu, a domestic servant whose tribal ancestry was Tswana.

Tutu was baptized a Methodist, because at the time of his birth his father was teaching in a Methodist school. Later, when an older sister enrolled in an Anglican school, the entire family switched denominations. When Tutu was twelve the family moved to Johannesburg, where the mother found work as a cook at a missionary school for the blind. At that school Tutu was indelibly edified by examples of compassion for and dedication to serving the deprived. It was there that he first came in contact with his chief mentor and role model, the Anglican cleric Father Trevor Huddleston, now Bishop Huddleston, the leading anti-apartheid voice in Great Britain. Then a parish priest in the black Johannesburg slum of Sophiatown, the magnetic Huddleston was on his way to becoming internationally known as the most outspoken and controversial clergyman in South Africa. In the Observer interview, Tutu recalled: "I was standing with my mother one day, when this white man in a cassock [Huddleston] walked past and doffed his big hat to her. I couldn't believe it—a white man raising his hat to a simple black labouring woman." When Tutu was hospitalized for twenty months in his late teens with tuberculosis, Father Huddleston visited him almost daily.

As a teenager, Tutu earned pocket money by selling peanuts at suburban railroad stations and caddying at the Killarney golf course in Johannesburg. When he graduated from Western High School in Johannesburg, he wanted to study medicine, but his family could not afford the medical-school tuition and he turned to teaching instead. After taking a diploma at the Bantu Normal College in Pretoria and a B.A. degree at the University of Johannesburg, he taught at Madibane High School in Johannesburg (1954–55) and Munsieville High School in Krugersdorp (1955–57). When the government introduced a calculatedly second-class state-run system of "Bantu education" in 1957, Tutu, along with many other teachers, resigned in protest.

Once out of the classroom, Tutu saw the church as "a likely means of service," and in retrospect he views his transition from teaching to religious ministry as his being "grabbed by God by the scruff of the neck in order to spread His word, whether it is convenient or not." When he began his theological studies under priests of the Community of the Resurrection, the high-church or Catholic-bent Anglican religious order to which Father Huddleston belonged, he was "not moved by very high ideals," he has admitted, but his spiritual motivation deepened during his religious training, and the community's practices of daily Communion and regular prayer and meditative retreat became essential components of his life.

After taking his licentiate in theology at St. Peter's Theological College in Johannesburg in 1960, Tutu received the Anglican diaconate, in 1960, and was ordained an Anglican priest, in 1961. His first ministerial assignments in South Africa were as curate of St. Alban's Church in Benoni (1960–61) and St. Philip's Church in Alberton (1961–62). While earning his bachelor's degree in divinity and master's in theology at King's College in London, England, he was assigned to St. Alban's parish in London (1962–65) and St. Mary's in Bletchingley, Surrey (1965–66).

From 1967 to 1969 Tutu lectured at the Federal Theological Seminary in the town of Alice in the tribal homeland of Ciskei, and during the following two years he was a lecturer at the National University of Lesotho, then known as the University of Botswana, Lesotho, and Swaziland. A former British protectorate, once known as Basutoland, Lesotho is an independent tribal enclave within South Africa. In 1972 Tutu returned to England as associate director of the Theological Education Fund, a position in which he administered World Council of Churches scholarships for three years. From his base in Bromley, Kent, he traveled widely, especially in Asia and black Africa.

Tutu returned to South Africa as the Anglican dean of Johannesburg in 1975, and the following year he was consecrated bishop of Lesotho. When he saw violence brewing among angry youths in the sprawling black township of Soweto on the outskirts of Johannesburg in the spring of 1976, he worked with the activist Nhato Motlana in trying

to channel it into peaceful demonstrations, and on May 6, 1976 he wrote to Balthazar J. Vorster, then the prime minister of South Africa, warning him of the situation. Vorster dismissed his letter, according to Tutu, "as a political ploy engineered, perhaps, by the political opposition," and "we all know that all hell broke loose on June 16 that year." Six hundred blacks were shot dead in the Soweto riots.

In 1978 Tutu became the first black secretary general of the interdenominational South African Council of Churches, the nation's contact group with the World Council of Churches. The South African Council of Churches represents 13 million Christians, more than 80 percent of them black. Conspicuously absent from membership are the members of the Dutch Reformed Church, the church of the ruling Afrikaners, the descendants of Dutch, German, and French Huguenots who colonized the country from the eighteenth century onward. (Three-fifths of the South African whites are Afrikaners.) Much of the budget of the council is spent in legal and other services for imprisoned blacks and those detained without trial, and for their families.

With the main African nationalist parties banned, the South African Council of Churches under Tutu became an important vehicle of black protest. In 1979 Tutu offended the South African government grievously on two occasions. The first occasion was the enactment of the Group Areas Act, a statute authorizing the government to remove blacks from urban areas to barren tribal lands. After witnessing the pathetic condition in the black squatters' camps, Tutu outraged the government by describing that condition as the government's "final solution" to the black-majority problem. He later retracted his phrasing but continued to insist, "People are starving not because there isn't food but because of deliberate policy, and that in a country that boasts about its maize exports to Zambia!"

More serious in the eyes of the government was Tutu's advocacy of the withdrawal of foreign investments from South Africa. In a television interview in Denmark in the fall of 1979, Tutu called on the Danish government to stop buying coal from South Africa. On his return to South Africa, his passport was confiscated—an action generally interpreted as a warning that he was close to joining the ranks of the 150-odd "subversives" banned from social (beyond family contacts) and political activity in South Africa. Undaunted, Tutu proceeded to exhort parents of mixed ethnic background to support a nationwide school boycott condemned as Communist-inspired by the government; to warn that the arrest and detention of protesters would lead to a resurgence of rioting; and to predict that Nelson R. Mandela, the jailed (since 1964) leader of the outlawed African National Congress (now based in Zambia), or a similar black figure would be prime minister of South Africa within ten years.

After his passport was restored, in January 1981, Tutu toured Europe and the United States, delivering to the international community one constant message: "If you want to see fundamental change in South Africa by peaceful means, you must give assistance by applying pressure on the South African government, political, diplomatic, but above all, economic." When he returned to South Africa in April 1981 his passport was again seized, and since that time his trips abroad have been with "travel documents" on which his nationality is described as "undetermined."

When Columbia University conferred an honorary doctorate of sacred theology on Tutu in August 1982, he was denied permission to go to New York to receive the degree. Because Columbia does not grant degrees in absentia, Michael I. Sovern, president of the university, traveled to Johannesburg for the ceremony. In his citation, Sovern hailed Bishop Tutu as "a stalwart and fearless advocate of justice, peace, and reconciliation among the peoples of [his] troubled land" and as "the voice of [his] oppressed people, a beacon leading them to peaceful opposition to the injustices of apartheid and a symbol of hope for a unified Africa."

Meanwhile, the South African Council of Churches was being investigated by a government-appointed judicial commission, known as the Eloff Commission, after its head, Mr. Justice Eloff. In his submission to the commission, Tutu pointed out that "oppression dehumanizes the oppressor as much as, if not more than, the oppressed" and that "whites need to hear and know that their value as persons is intrinsic to who they are by virtue of having been created in God's image." He also declared against "false or cheap reconciliation," the crying of "peace, peace when there is no peace."

In its report, published in February 1984, the Eloff Commission stopped short of banning the South African Council of Churches, declaring that the council is not a tool of foreign manipulators and that, although "the amount of money spent" in the direction of helping "the needy and deserving" is "meagre when compared with that used mainly for political purposes, innocent people will suffer if the S.A.C.C. were to be rendered largely ineffective." On the negative side, the commission criticized the council's financial administration, pointing out the fraud conviction of a former general secretary; recommended that the government pass a law making the advocacy of international disinvestment in South Africa criminally punishable as "economic sabotage"; and denounced Tutu for making public statements attacking military conscription and lending respectability to the African National Congress. Tutu's response was to express his wholehearted support of the African National Congress' struggle for a "truly democratic," non-racial South Africa.

In September 1984 Tutu began a three-month sabbatical at General Theological Seminary in New York City. It was in the midst of his sojourn in Manhattan, on October 16, 1984, that he, along with the world, received the news that the Norwegian Nobel Committee had named him the 1984 Nobel peace laureate. In announcing the award,

Egil Aarvik, the chairman of the Nobel committee, noted that the peace prize had been awarded to a South African once before, to Albert John Luthuli, the former president of the African National Congress, in 1960. "This year's award should be seen as a renewed recognition of the courage and heroism shown by black South Africans in their use of peaceful methods in the struggle against apartheid . . . ," the Nobel citation read. "It is the committee's wish that the Peace Prize now awarded to Desmond Tutu should be regarded not only as a gesture of support to him and to the South African Council of Churches of which he is leader, but also to all individuals and groups in South Africa who, with their concern for human dignity, fraternity and democracy, incite the admiration of the world."

"Hey, we are winning! Justice is going to win," was Tutu's first reaction to the news of the award. "[It] means we musn't give up." He told reporters that he planned to put much of the $193,000 Nobel cash award into a trust fund for scholarships for indigent South African blacks. In a more negative vein, he expressed scorn for the South African government's recent attempts—including the enfranchisement of Asians and mixed-blood "coloreds" while still excluding blacks—to portray an improvement in social relations. "If things are changing, they are changing for the worse," he said. "So now we have multi-racial sports in order to compete on an international level. But they say nothing about realignment of political power and they still control 87 percent of the land when they only have 20 percent of the population." He warned that "this is our very last chance for change, because if that doesn't happen . . . it seems the bloodbath will be inevitable."

On October 18, 1984 Tutu returned to South Africa to celebrate his award with his people. The joyous welcome he received counterpointed violent confrontations between rioting South African blacks and white security forces, 7,000 of whom raided black townships. In the violence, which had been escalating for two months, eighty blacks were killed; strikes had closed mines and factories; and approximately 200,000 students were boycotting classes. Much of the rioting was precipitated by resentment of rent increases and new utility rates in the townships, along with political frustration. (It was in September 1984 that the new constitution giving separate parliamentary representation to all non-whites excepting blacks took effect.) The worst violence took place in the township of Sharpville, where a black deputy mayor was hacked to death on his porch by blacks. The presidents, mayors, and other tribal leaders in the "homelands" were accused by many blacks of legitimizing forcible resettlement.

At the very time that the Norwegian Nobel Committee decided to give Tutu the peace prize, the white and black Anglican diocesan electors in Johannesburg, the South African Anglican church's largest diocese, a predominantly black see, were deadlocked (reportedly along racial lines) over the choice of Tutu as the diocese's new bishop. The national Anglican hierarchy intervened, and on November 3, 1984 a synod of eleven white and twelve black bishops, meeting in the Orange Free State, elected Tutu the first Anglican bishop of Johannesburg. Tutu was quoted in the press as welcoming the new position with the words, "The time is just right for me to leave the South African Council of Churches. . . . I am fundamentally a pastor. That is what God ordained me to do."

Sermons, speeches, and other statements by Tutu have been collected in two volumes: *Crying in the Wilderness* (Eerdmans, 1982) and *Hope and Suffering* (Eerdmans, 1984). One of the speeches in *Hope and Suffering* addressed the policy of "constructive engagement" pursued by the United States under the presidency of Ronald Reagan, which leans to impartiality regarding South Africa's internal affairs, for strategic reasons. "To be impartial . . . is indeed to have taken sides already . . . with the status quo," Tutu pointed out. "How are you to remain impartial when the South African authorities evict helpless mothers and children and let them shiver in the winter rain . . . ? At least under [President] Carter our morale was upheld by their encouraging rhetoric of disapproval. They did not talk about the overriding strategic importance of South Africa, with her wealth in key strategic resources . . . more important than human freedom. . . . When we are free, South Africa will still be of strategic importance . . . and we will remember who helped us to get free." Following a meeting with President Reagan in the White House on December 7, 1984, the bishop told reporters, "We are no nearer each other than before." For his part, the president cited South Africa's release of eleven imprisoned labor agitators as an example of the effectiveness of his "quiet diplomacy." Spokesmen for South Africa denied that the pressure of demonstrations at South African government offices in American cities had any influence in the decision to release the labor militants.

International political and economic pressure on South Africa mounted sharply in 1985, and even President Reagan began gesturing in the direction of sanctions, ordering a ban on imports of Krugerrands into the United States. Domestically, world disinvestment in South Africa's economy created a financial crisis at the same time that rioting by blacks escalated, resulting in hundreds of deaths (mostly of alleged black quislings) and mass arrests under a state of virtual martial law declared by President Pieter W. Botha. Among those arrested was Trevor Tutu, the bishop's son, for protesting a police roundup of boycotting schoolchildren. Defying a government ban on "political" funerals, Bishop Tutu on August 6 intervened in a confrontation between a procession of black mourners and government security forces and negotiated with police to provide buses to transport the mourners to the burial site. On another occasion he risked his own life to rescue an alleged police informer from a black mob that was beating and trying to burn the man to death.

As self-confident in bearing as he is diminutive in stature, Desmond Tutu is gregarious and ebullient, emanating a spirit of joy despite his intense sense of mission. His conversation is punctuated with high-pitched chuckles, and his wit invades even his political parables. "We had the land, and they had the Bible," one of the parables goes. "Then they said, 'let us pray,' and we closed our eyes. When we opened them again, *they* had the land and we had the Bible. Maybe we got the better end of the deal." When conducting the Eucharistic service in the Sotho language in his old parish in Johannesburg's black township of Soweto, he often breaks into yelps and giggles, and sometimes he dances down the aisle, whooping and laughing with the congregation. As Bishop of Johannesburg, he intends to make his residence in Soweto, because he is "not going to be an honorary white."

Bishop Tutu and his wife, Leah Nomalizo Shenxane, who were married in 1955, have one son and three daughters. The bishop lists his recreations as music, reading, and jogging. He still sees himself as "a simple pastor, passionately concerned for justice, peace, and reconciliation," and, as he constantly points out, the number of preachers of reconciliation in South Africa is fast diminishing. "Most of us are not prisoners of the Gospel," Buti Thiagale, a young black Roman Catholic priest and a member of the Black Consciousness movement, has said. "We want to use it for a certain purpose. He [Tutu] will say, 'Love your enemy.' At his age, he should hate a little bit more. [But] he believes in the Gospel literally."

References: *Chicago Tribune* p1+ Jl 7 '80; *Christian Sci Mon* p15 Ap 26 '79 por, p9+ Mr 28 '84 por; *London Observer* p6 Ag 8 '82 por, p7 My 8 '83 por; *Manchester Guardian Weekly* p9 O 28 '84 por; *N Y Times* p1+ O 17 '84 por; *N Y Times Mag* p23+ Mr 14 '82 pors; *Newsday* II p3 O 17 '84 por; *Newsweek* 104:89 O 29 '84 por; *Washington Post* A p1+ O 17 '84 pors, A p1+ O 19 '84 por; *Who's Who*, 1985–86

---

## Ueberroth, Peter V(ictor)

(ū´ bər roth)

Sept. 2, 1937- Baseball commissioner. Address: b. Baseball, Office of the Commissioner, 350 Park Ave., New York City, N.Y. 10022

Although he was a brilliant entrepreneur, the multimillionaire Peter V. Ueberroth was relatively unknown before he became president of the Los Angeles Olympic Organizing Committee in 1979. His skillful management of the summer games— the first ever to be financed exclusively from private funds—netted a remarkable surplus of over $200 million for the Los Angeles Olympic Organizing Committee and earned him the title of Man of the Year from both *Time* magazine and the

*Peter V. Ueberroth*

*Sporting News.* Taking on another challenge after the Olympics, Ueberroth succeeded Bowie Kuhn as commissioner of baseball. His forceful style and business acumen have led many observers to predict that he will be baseball's most impressive commissioner since Judge Kenesaw Mountain Landis, who originated the position in 1920.

Peter Victor Ueberroth was born in Evanston, Illinois on September 2, 1937, the son of Victor Ueberroth, an aluminum-siding salesman, and Laura (Larson) Ueberroth. His mother died when he was four, and after about a year his father remarried. He and his second wife, Nancy, an accountant, had a son six years later. During Peter's childhood, the Ueberroths lived in Madison, Wisconsin, Upper Darby, Pennsylvania, and Davenport, Iowa, but they finally settled in Burlingame in northern California. He became involved in baseball at an early age as a third baseman, catcher, and pitcher on American Legion and sandlot teams, but he insists that he was merely a mediocre player. Ueberroth continued his interest in sports at Fremont High School in Los Angeles, where he earned letters in baseball, football, and swimming, though sports were not his only extracurricular activity. By the time he entered high school, he was self-supporting, and in his sophomore year he moved out of his parents' home to live and work at Twelveacres, an orphanage for children from broken homes, where he earned $125 a month as its recreation director.

On graduating from high school in 1955, Ueberroth enrolled in the business administration program at San Jose State College. As a result of his high-school coach's recommendation, which was based on his ability as a swimmer, he received a modest athletic scholarship to play water polo, though he had never even seen a match. Neverthe-

less, he became captain of the freshman team, won a letter, and led his conference in scoring during both his junior and senior years. When he tried out for the 1956 United States Olympic team, he was named an alternate. To make ends meet, Ueberroth worked, often for forty hours a week, at odd jobs, and during the summer after his junior year he loaded baggage and performed other chores for a nonscheduled airline in Hawaii.

After obtaining his bachelor's degree in business in 1959, Ueberroth moved to Hawaii, where he landed a job with an association of nonscheduled airlines, but he soon left for a better opportunity with Trans International, a new nonscheduled airline flying between Hawaii and California. It was run by Kirk Kerkorian, who later became well-known as a financier and major shareholder in MGM/United Artists, among other properties. In less than a year as operations manager, Ueberroth expanded its clientele by making flights to the continental United States attractive to residents of the smaller Hawaiian islands, a group ignored by most big airlines. Recognizing his administrative potential, Kerkorian offered him a vice-presidency, the responsibility for running the entire airline, and a salary of $1,000 a month, but he only accepted when he was also given a 3 percent share of the company.

Striking out on his own soon afterwards, Ueberroth established an air shuttle service between Los Angeles and the 1962 Spokane (Washington) World's Fair, but when hotel rates skyrocketed and demand for the charter flights dropped, his company collapsed, leaving him in debt for $100,000. In 1963, shaken but undaunted, with one employee and $5,000, he formed another company, Transportation Consultants International, a centralized reservation service for airlines, hotels, and passenger ships too small to have their own representatives in several cities. There was so great a demand for the service that he opened a dozen more offices and by 1967 was able to make a public stock offering. Over the next decade he built his fortune and reputation by taking over several financially unsound travel agencies—most notably the established firm of Ask Mr. Foster, in which he purchased the majority interest in 1972—and by founding Colony Hotels, which managed resort properties. By 1980, First Travel Corporation, a holding company Ueberroth had formed for his various properties, was the second largest travel company in the United States, with 200 offices worldwide, 1,500 employees, and an annual revenue of $300 million.

Peter Ueberroth's business acumen and sports background led the executive-search firm of Korn/Ferry International to recommend him in 1979 to head the Los Angeles Olympic Organizing Committee (LAOOC), the private organization set up to plan for and manage the 1984 summer games. Ueberroth topped the firm's list of 200 candidates because, according to its report, he "matched the executive profile so well . . . a successful, financially-oriented businessman with proven management and leadership abilities." The LAOOC would need an administrator of Ueberroth's caliber to successfully stage its "Spartan Olympics," so called because of the severe budget restrictions imposed by Los Angeles' refusal to help finance the games and by an amendment to its city charter that prevented federal subsidies. For the first time in Olympic history, the games would depend entirely on private funding.

At first Ueberroth was reluctant to accept the position of president and managing director of the LAOOC. In addition to the drawback of having to take a 70 percent cut in his annual salary of $400,-000, he did not want to become involved in a money-losing project, as most of the recent Olympics had been. And the Los Angeles Olympic Organizing Committee seemed to be following that all too familiar pattern: it was already $300,000 in debt (the cost of securing Los Angeles' bid to serve as host for the Olympics), and to make matters more difficult, lotteries—a traditional and lucrative source of Olympic revenue—were illegal in California. Nevertheless, the enormous challenge of making the 1984 summer games economically viable, perhaps even profitable, appealed to Ueberroth's competitive instinct and he accepted the post. Ueberroth took office on April Fool's Day, 1979, beginning his five-year effort to stage the games with no employees and no bank account (until he opened one with $100 of his own money). For the first week he was locked out of his office because the LAOOC had failed to pay the rent, but he temporarily borrowed office space from a business that was vacating its lease and set to work.

Convinced that the Olympics could only become profitable if run in a businesslike manner, Ueberroth immediately applied himself to cutting unnecessary expenses, such as the $17 million earmarked by the Olympic Committee to finance large groups from various sports federations. He saved millions more by authorizing the construction of only a few new facilities: existing structures, such as the Memorial Coliseum (built for the 1932 Los Angeles Olympics) were used whenever possible, along with college dormitories, which took the place of the usual "Olympic Village" athletes' housing. The LAOOC recruited 50,000 volunteer workers. Ueberroth himself waived his $140,000 annual salary, and nine months after becoming president of the LAOOC he sold First Travel for $10 million (his share was $4 million) to devote his full attention to the Olympics.

Ueberroth next turned his attention to raising the capital to meet the projected budget of $515 million (approximately one-eighteenth of the cost of the 1980 games in Moscow). Taking a calculated risk, he decided to auction through blind bids the right to televise the Olympics. Although his staff predicted that no network would offer more than $150 million, Ueberroth, with the help of the television producer David L. Wolper and attorney John Argue, attracted from ABC an unprecedented bid of $225 million, and the sale of the foreign broadcast rights brought the total to almost $300 million.

Corporate sponsorships accounted for $120 million more. As a result of the LAOOC's aggressive campaign, thirty companies paid between $4 million and $13 million for the title of Olympic sponsor while others underwrote the construction of a fifty-meter swimming pool, the velodrome, eight training tracks, and other facilities. Still others agreed that in exchange for permission to use the Olympic logo on their products and in their advertising they would give up to 10 percent of their profits from the sale of those products or donate merchandise the LAOOC needed.

But Ueberroth did not limit his innovations to financial matters. His primary goal, he said repeatedly, was that the games be remembered "as a great sporting event . . . a return to what the Olympics were meant to be." With that in mind, he appointed envoys from a wide variety of professions to deal with each nation participating in the Olympics and "commissioners"—former competitors or avid fans—for each sport. In a controversial move, he also set up an eighty-two-day relay of the Olympic torch across the United States, with each participant or his sponsor paying $3,000 for the privilege of carrying the torch for five-eighths of a mile, with the proceeds to be donated to nonprofit youth organizations in the United States. Critics contended that the relay commercialized the games, but Ueberroth felt vindicated by its unqualified success, not just in raising money but in fueling enthusiasm for the Olympics and in rekindling patriotism. He has estimated that forty million people turned out to watch the torch pass by.

The date of May 8, 1984 was memorable for not only the start of the torch relay but also for the announcement by the USSR that it would not send its athletes to Los Angeles, on the grounds that security was inadequate and that the games were overly commercial. Several Soviet allies soon followed suit, and the boycott threatened to undermine Ueberroth's years of meticulous planning. Furthermore, if the absence of those teams, especially the excellent Soviet and East German squads, adversely affected television ratings, the LAOOC stood to lose up to $70 million, since a clause in its contract with ABC stipulated that part of the network's payment for broadcasting rights would be waived should television ratings fall below projected levels.

The LAOOC had taken extraordinary precautions to ensure the safety of every athlete at the Olympics, and the United States Defense Department spent over $35 million on sophisticated equipment and a security force of about 16,000 (including an antiterrorist squad)—approximately one security person for each athlete. Armed with those facts and statistics, Ueberroth flew to Lausanne, Switzerland on May 18 to allay the Soviets' fears at an emergency meeting of the International Olympic Committee. In a press conference, Ueberroth expressed his frustration with the result of the parley: "We came here to answer [the Russians'] complaints. There were no complaints." The experience confirmed his belief that the Soviets' only reason for pulling out was to retaliate for the American boycott of the 1980 games in Moscow. The Soviet Union expected sixty or seventy countries to join the boycott, but Ueberroth sent envoys to those countries most likely to withdraw and he himself went to Cuba to negotiate with Fidel Castro. Largely because of the LAOOC's concerted efforts, only seventeen other nations boycotted the Los Angeles Olympics and several Communist nations—Rumania, China, and Yugoslavia—sent teams in spite of the Soviets' absence. Ueberroth managed to deal not only with the boycott, but also with such lesser problems as Los Angeles' traffic and smog and the collapse of the basketball floor. Having been anxious to avoid any tragic incidents such as the massacre of Israeli athletes at the 1972 Munich Olympics, he was pleased by the lack of major disruptions, and when the games ended he was praised by IOC officials. Financially, the summer games were an unqualified success, accruing for the LAOOC a surplus of more than $215 million, which was divided among the United States Olympic Committee and other amateur sports organizations.

Nevertheless, Ueberroth's administrative style irritated a number of his co-workers and others involved in the summer games. During his tenure as LAOOC president some critics equated him with Joseph Stalin, the Ayatollah Khomeini, and Adolf Hitler. Ueberroth admitted that he often came on strong but also pointed out that he is decisive and has a natural aptitude for solving problems. Summing up the majority reaction in a New York Times article (March 11, 1984), Robert Lindsey wrote that "friends and co-workers describe Ueberroth as tough when he wants to be, a smart negotiator and a good organizer, a good man with figures, and a diplomat who is skilled at keeping peace among rival fiefdoms while being unafraid to challenge powerful people when he thinks he is right."

In November 1985 William Morrow published Made in America: His Own Story, Ueberroth's account of his Olympic success, the management techniques he used to achieve it, and the problems he faced along the way. "The organization of the 1984 Games was both painful and rewarding," Ueberroth noted. "From a myriad of standpoints [it] is a story that deserves to be told." The book had a first-print run of 200,000 copies and was given a $150,000 advertising and promotion campaign.

His management skills as well as his often criticized strong-mindedness led a committee of baseball-team owners to hire him as the sixth commissioner of baseball on March 3, 1984, with his term scheduled to begin shortly after the close of the Los Angeles Olympics. At the time that Ueberroth accepted the position, baseball was plagued with problems. The owners' collective annual losses were estimated at between $50 million and $100 million, and the tenuous financial state of the game was exacerbated by a number of other difficulties: disputes with the players' union, squabbles among the owners, declining attendance

made worse by wide-ranging "superstation" broadcasting of games, and the extended lame-duck term of Commissioner Bowie Kuhn. As a result, most owners were delighted that a man of Ueberroth's proved administrative ability was to be in control.

But from the time that Ueberroth and the owners' committee began discussing his becoming commissioner, he made it clear that he would be more than simply the owners' representative and mouthpiece, and he agreed to accept the job only under certain conditions. Since, as Bob Verdi pointed out in the Chicago Tribune (March 6, 1984), Ueberroth, for whom the commissioner's $300,000 salary was not a necessity, held the upper hand in the negotiations, the owners acceded to his demands and, ironically, expanded the powers of the office according to the specifications largely recommended by Kuhn, the commissioner they had fired.

Under the new agreement, the commissioner was given the added title of baseball's chief executive officer, with all departments and the presidents of the two leagues reporting to him on matters relating to the game as a whole; he was empowered to penalize clubs by fining them up to $250,000 (the previous limit had been $5,000) or by taking away their choices in the minor-league and amateur drafts; and he would be reimbursed for any legal expenses resulting from suits the owners might bring against him. Moreover, the commissioner's term of office was reduced from seven to five years, and the reelection procedure was also changed. Previously, the commissioner needed votes of approval from three-fourths of the owners in both leagues—the twelve in the National League and the fourteen in the American League—to stay in office. As a result, Bowie Kuhn was ousted through the opposition of only five National League owners. Ueberroth and his successors, however, will need only a simple majority of the twenty-six owners, with a minimum of five votes from each league.

On taking office on October 1, 1984, Ueberroth asserted that "[he] will not be commissioner for the owners . . . [he] will be commissioner for baseball." With that in mind, Ueberroth announced plans to use sophisticated polling techniques to measure fan opinion on such controversial issues as the designated-hitter rule, and he also vowed not to take part on the owners' side in negotiations with the Players' Association but to "try to encourage [both sides] to meet on some common grounds." Players' union officials were skeptical, but Ueberroth actually did side against the owners in his first major decision as commissioner, the settlement of an umpires' strike during the 1984 playoffs, in which he agreed to the umpires' demand for a post-season fund out of which all of them, not just those who actually work the playoffs and World Series, would be paid. Baseball players and fans were displeased when in February 1985 he upheld Kuhn's decision to prohibit clubs from employing anyone—including Hall of Fame members Willie Mays and Mickey

Mantle—who was also drawing a salary from a gambling casino. But the following month he modified that judgment, respectfully explaining that Kuhn's more stringent ruling had been "made under different circumstances." From now on, baseball personnel may not advertise for casinos but may do public-relations or charity work for them.

But elected in large part because the owners believed that he could help them make more money, the new commissioner has made the game's financial stability a top priority. "Superstations" that beam baseball games nationwide, often infringing on the territories of individual clubs, were one of the major problems. Concerned that superstations would oversaturate the market with baseball games, adversely affecting future contracts with networks for TV rights and hurting attendance for minor-league teams and less popular major-league clubs, by the spring of 1985 he had convinced several superstation-team owners, including Ted Turner of the Atlanta Braves, George Steinbrenner of the New York Yankees, and Nelson Doubleday of the New York Mets, to limit telecasts and to pay up to $7 million into a fund to be shared by the other baseball franchises. He was also credited with helping to avert a lengthy strike during the 1985 season. After a two-day walkout by the players in August, their union and the owners' negotiator reached agreement on a five-year contract that raised to three years the term a new player would have to be with a club before he was eligible for salary arbitration; banned salary caps; raised the starting salary to $60,000 with annual cost-of-living adjustments; and increased the owners' contribution to the players' pension fund to an annual average of $32.6 billion over the life of the contract, with an additional share of television revenues to be used to help financially troubled clubs.

In other actions, the commissioner, alarmed by the growing scandal of drug abuse in baseball, ordered mandatory drug testing of all baseball employees and began negotiations with the players and their union for voluntary testing of players at random, unannounced times during each year. If a player's test results were positive, he would be counseled, not penalized. Ueberroth was concerned not only about the effect of drug abuse on the players' health, on their families, and on their performance but also the possible impact on advertising revenue, on young people's perceptions of the players, and on the reputation of the game. "At whatever level, illegal drug use inevitably involves contact with criminals," Ueberroth explained at a press conference in May 1984. "In the sports world, this connection will just as inevitably involve gambling." In 1985 he also set up a committee of owners to establish criteria for selecting cities for expansion teams.

Peter Ueberroth has dark hair, blue eyes, and a slightly off-center nose, the result of its having been broken five times during water polo games. In September 1959 he married Virginia Nicolaus, his college sweetheart, and they have four children: Vicky, Heidi, Keri, and Joe. Since his family

life is important to him, he is careful to make time for it in his crowded schedule. Still an avid sportsman, he enjoys golf, skin diving, body surfing, tennis, and spearfishing. The Ueberroths maintain homes in Laguna Beach, California, and in New York City, where the headquarters of major-league baseball is located.

References: N Y Times V p1+ Mr 11 '84 por, IV p9 Jl 22 '84 por, V p1+ S 30 '84 por; Newsday Sports p7 Mr 7 '84; Sporting News 199:40 Je 25 '84 por; Time 125:20+ Ja 7 '85 pors; Washington Post D p1+ Ag 11 '84 pors

## Walker, Herschel

Mar. 3, 1962– Football player. Address: b. New Jersey Generals, 3 Empire Blvd., South Hackensack, N.J. 07606

"My mind's like a general and my body's like an army. I keep the body in shape and it does what I tell it to do," the running back Herschel Walker told a sportswriter in 1982, the year he won the Heisman Trophy as the outstanding college football player in the United States. With his awesome combination of speed and power, Walker rushed 5,596 yards—for an average of 5.2 yards per attempt and 155.4 per game—in three consensus All-America seasons with the University of Georgia, breaking ten National College Athletic Association records and fifteen Southeastern Conference records. Sacrificing his final year of collegiate eligibility, Walker turned professional in 1983, joining the New Jersey Generals of the new United States Football League under the most lucrative contract in pro football. He led the league in rushing in 1983, was third in 1984, and set a new pro single-season record for yards gained rushing in 1985, with 2,411. His total professional statistics are 5,562 yards and fifty-four touchdowns in 1,143 attempts rushing and 1,482 yards and seven TDs receiving. His favorite sport, surprisingly, is not football, but track; a world-class sprinter, he forsook a long-held dream of competing in the 1984 Olympics when he lost his amateur standing.

The fifth of seven children, Herschel Junior Walker was born on March 3, 1962 in Augusta, Georgia to Willis Walker and Christine (Taylor) Walker, who instilled in their offspring ideals of honesty, hard work, and drive. He was named Herschel in memory of his paternal grandfather, who in turn had been named after Herschel V. Johnson, a governor of Georgia in the 1850s. When the grandfather was killed in a shooting incident, Willis Walker, twelve at the time, dropped out of school to go to work and help raise his younger sisters. Herschel's older siblings are Willis Junior, Renneth, Sharon, and Veronica; Lorenza and Carol are younger. The Walker children grew up on the rural outskirts of the town of Wrightsville, Georgia, where their parents, who had met picking cotton, were tenant farmers and, later, factory workers. The father eventually became foreman in a clay-processing plant and the mother, supervisor in a clothing factory. When Herschel was eight the family moved from a tenant-farm shanty to a modest wood frame house on a hill up the dirt road from the farm. Two years ago Herschel built a new home for his family, a comfortable four-bedroom brick house, on the slope of the hill.

A religious family, the Walkers attended a local Baptist church, where Herschel sang in the young people's choir. Like their parents, the Walker children were athletic, but Herschel in the beginning was the least so. "I never liked sports when I was young . . . ," he has said, as quoted by Jeff Prugh in Herschel Walker (1983). "I never watched it on TV." (He still has little interest in watching football on television, but he likes to watch boxing matches and karate exhibitions.) In his early years he was short and chubby, the family "runt," according to his mother, and the smallest boy in his class in elementary school. Withdrawn, and suffering a temporary speech impediment, he took refuge in books and versifying. "He was always different, quiet," his mother has recalled, as quoted by John Husar in the Chicago Tribune (October 26, 1980). "He used to fall asleep with a book on his chest. He was a dreamer, and it took me a while to realize that the only way I could know what was in his mind was to go into his briefcase and read the poems that he wrote. That was the only place that he'd say what was on his mind."

Under pressure from his peers, Walker began to play football during recess at school when he was in the fifth grade, and soon he was entertaining thoughts of emulating his brothers Willis and Renneth, who were by that time star high-school varsity football players. The greatest goad to his athletic

development, perhaps, was his embarrassment at being, for many years, a slower runner than his sister Veronica, eighteen months his senior. "One of the things I used to pray for every night was for God to let me beat Veronica," Walker recalled when interviewed for Sports Illustrated (October 4, 1982) by Terry Todd. "I promised that I'd train hard and live a Christian life if only He'd let me get faster."

"Herschel was twelve when he came to me wanting to know how to get big and strong," the local track-and-field coach, Tom Jordan, told Terry Todd, "and I told him what I told the other kids who asked me. 'Do push-ups, sit-ups, and run sprints,' I said." Following the coach's advice in an intense daily regimen, Walker over the course of the following year did 100,000 sit-ups and 100,000 push-ups and sprinted nearly half-a-million miles. Coach Jordan was "amazed at how he'd muscled up" and "was getting faster." Milt Moorman, Walker's closest boyhood friend, has described his progress as a sprinter thus: "By seventh grade he was even with us. By eighth he was pulling away. By ninth there was no hope for us. He was running 9.9 [in the 100-yard dash]." His sister Veronica, as quoted by Gary Smith in Inside Sports (September 30, 1981), remembers how "when he lost all his fat, muscle just came." "One night my mother started feeling him," she told Smith. "She said, 'Something's wrong. We better take you to a doctor. You swolled up.'" On a diet that included between-meal candy bars, hamburgers, and Gatorade, Walker had by the ninth grade grown to five feet ten inches and a solid 185 pounds.

After a freshman season on the B football team of Johnson County High School in Wrightsville, Walker advanced to the starting lineup of the varsity Trojans as fullback. In 1977, as a sophomore fullback, by then about six feet tall and nearing 200 pounds, he mainly blocked for tailback Wannie Cason; on the occasions when he did take the ball, he rushed for a total of 987 yards. In 1978, Gary Phillips, the new Trojan head coach, switched him to tailback. In that position, Walker, burlier and more powerful than most of his adversaries, ran over linemen and outraced those still upright on the field, acquiring the nickname "Hurt" in the process. Phillips described him as a "floater," elaborating: "He floats and glides. He floats, floats, and reads the blocks. Then he finds the alley, and then—boom!—he's gone!" For the first time in twenty years the Johnson County team reached the regional 3-A playoffs, and Walker became a local hero, the first black in Wrightsville to win the admiration and patronage of the local white establishment, including car dealer Bob Newsome, for whom he worked part time.

Meanwhile, track remained his favorite sport. The Johnson County High School track team won the 1979 state Class A track-and-field championship meet largely on the strength of Walker's performance; in addition to the shot put, he won the 100-yard dash, in 9.8 seconds, and the 200, in 21.8; the latter matched the state record. In the summer of the same year Walker was Georgia's representative at the Hertz Number 1 Award Ceremonies, which honor the best high-school track-and-field athletes from every state. He also played basketball (which he prefers to football as a spectator sport); as the starting varsity foward he was an extraordinary rebounder, dubbed "Skywalker" by teammates and fans because of his ability to jump forty-and-a-half inches vertically.

By the beginning of his senior year at Johnson County High School, Walker was just short of present height (which is six feet one-and-a-half inches) and was fast approaching his present weight (222 pounds). As a senior, he rushed 3,167 yards, or 211.1 per game, and scored forty-five touchdowns. The Trojans won the state class-A championship, and Walker was named a consensus All-American and *Parade* magazine's national high-school back of the year. His high-school totals in yards gained rushing and in touchdowns were, respectively, 6,137 and eighty-six. Having maintained an A average academically, he was valedictorian of his class and president of the Beta Club, a scholastic honor society.

The glorious finale to Walker's high-school career was soured by racial tension in Wrightsville, which in the spring of 1980 led to riots, protest marches, and a school boycott. Black activists resented Walker's refusal to join the boycott and contribute his prestige to their cause, and some of his peers anathematized him as a "honky lover." "I was too young," he later explained, as quoted by Henry Leiferman in the *New York Times Magazine* (November 1, 1981). "I was always in and out of town for track meets, and I didn't want to get involved in something I didn't know too much about. I was sent to school to get a good education and learn as much in life as I can. I didn't think that was part of school." "He went into total isolation," Tom Jordan, his track coach, recalled in his interview with Gary Smith for *Inside Sports* (September 30, 1981). "He told me . . . there were blacks threatening to kill him because he wouldn't march and whites threatening to kill him because he was black [and dating a white girl]. Meanwhile, there was all this recruiting pressure."

Probably the most pursued college football prospect in the country, Walker considered over 100 scholarship offers, along with the possibility of joining the United States Marines as an officer candidate. Deciding, at least temporarily, against the Marines, he narrowed the college choices down to the University of Georgia (where his parents wanted him to go, because it was in Athens, only ninety-eight miles from home, and because his sister Veronica was already a member of the track team there), Clemson University, and the University of Southern California. Two flips of a coin decided him on the University of Georgia.

Walker began his freshman season at the University of Georgia a third-stringer, but before the end of the first game, against the University of Tennessee, he had "bulled" his way up to starting tailback. Sent in late in the second quarter of that game, when Tennessee led 15-0, he almost single-handedly turned the tide. "He didn't know *where* he was supposed to go," Vince Dooley, Georgia's head coach, later observed, "or *when* to make his move. He was just taking off *running*—as if for the sheer joy of it. He got only two yards on his first carry, but the speed, the power, the competitiveness . . . were obvious." The two yards were to be multiplied by forty-two as the game progressed. In the third quarter, with the score 15-2 in Tennessee's favor, Walker took a handoff at the Tennessee sixteen-yard line, barreled through the line of scrimmage, knocked over the safety at the seven-yard line, split apart two more defensive backs, and burst into the end zone. A few minutes later he scored again, on a pitchout and a nine-yard run, and the point-after-touchdown gave Georgia the game, 16-15.

As the regular starting tailback during the rest of the season, Walker set a new freshman National Collegiate Athletic Association rushing record with a total of 1,616 yards, forty more than Tony Dorsett's 1973 mark. In his best game, against Vanderbilt, he rushed for 283 yards, demolishing the single-game record set by Georgia's Charley Trippi in 1945. On January 1, 1981 the Georgia Bulldogs capped their perfect 11-0 regular season with a 17-10 Sugar Bowl victory over Notre Dame to bring home Georgia's first national championship ever. Playing with a left arm rendered virtually useless by a dislocated shoulder, Walker contributed 150 yards and two touchdowns to the Sugar Bowl victory, and he was voted the bowl event's most valuable player.

Following the 1980 season, Walker was third in the annual Heisman Trophy voting for the nation's outstanding college football player, a poll in which no freshman had ever before made the top ten. Assessing Walker's impact on the Bulldogs, center Joe Happe said: "I guess what Herschel gave us was a sense of image for ourselves. He hardly talked on the field, but his own discipline seemed to diffuse our rambunctiousness. He set a standard of excellence—to try hard all the time, and damn if anybody was going to let up." Coach Dooley remarked: "He has the rare ability to always say the right thing, to be relaxed, to laugh and be happy a lot. He hustles. He is a team man."

Other observers of Walker's first season at Georgia commented on his combination of speed and strength and his ability to accelerate at will into a supernormal gear. As tailback in the I-formation, he raced quickly to the hole, sometimes through converging linemen, and did not stutter-step when it closed. "I kind of pick my way through the secondary before I start to take advantage of my speed," he told a reporter. "It's not anything anyone ever told me to do." Pointing out that he relied very little on game films, he added, "I think a good runner gets to where he's going by instinct or else he doesn't get there at all." Regarding his habit, when about to be tackled, of lowering his head and charging through for another yard or so, he said: "The defender is going to punish you, so you try to punish him and get yardage."

In 1981 Walker rushed 1,891 yards as he sparked the Bulldogs to a number-two finish nationally in the regular season and to their second Sugar Bowl, where they lost to Pittsburgh. In the Heisman balloting, Walker finished second to Marcus Allen of the University of Southern California. To the relief of Vince Dooley and National Football League Commissioner Pete Rozelle, in 1982 Walker decided not to go ahead with his threat to test the legality of the NFL rule barring the drafting of underclassmen—which he considered to be "basically unconstitutional"—and to return to the University of Georgia for his junior year. As a junior, he rushed 1,752 yards—the second best figure in the nation that year—and scored seventeen touchdowns. With a second 11-0 regular season, the only perfect record among major college teams that year, the Bulldogs ranked first in the nation, just ahead of Penn State, to whom they lost in the Sugar Bowl. Walker was for the third time a consensus All-American, and he won the Heisman Trophy by a landslide vote of the 1,050 sports writers and sportscasters polled, eclipsing Stanford quarterback John Elway and Southern Methodist running back Erick Dickerson.

In three years of college play, Walker set ten NCAA records, including most carries (994) and most yards gained rushing (5,259) over a three-year period. He ranked third on the all-time rushing list, behind the four-year totals of Tony Dorsett and Charles White. In track, which he still enjoyed more than he did football, he was in the top five nationally in the sixty-yard dash, but his best events were the 100-yard (a personal best of 9.1) and the 100-meter (10.10). In those races, as he has recalled, he was toward the end "running with some of the fastest guys in the world and beating just about all of them except Carl Lewis." Among those he outran in the 100-meter was the 1980 Olympian Melvin Lattany. Scholastically, as a pre-law student specializing in criminal justice, he had a B average. His aim outside of sports was to work, like two of his cousins, with the Federal Bureau of Investigation, a goal he still apparently considers a possibility.

By negotiating with the nascent New Jersey Generals of the then aborning United States Football League in February 1983, Walker made himself ineligible for his senior season with Georgia. Apparently he was ambivalent about turning pro at that time, because, after signing a tentative contract with the Generals, he took advantage of an escape clause and backed out of the agreement almost immediately, and at first he denied ever even having looked at a contract. After national headlines, beginning with a story in the Boston Globe, contradicted his denial, he still insisted that, in his view, he had done nothing to compromise his college-football eligibility. To the NCAA, however, the question was not whether he had signed, but whether he had negotiated, and even talking about a possible contract constituted negotiation.

On February 23, 1983, one week after his lawyer, Jack Manton, had started the negotiations, Walker held a press conference to announce his agreement to play for the New Jersey Generals for three years under a contract estimated at $5.5 million. "In denying I signed a contract, I made a mistake," he said. "No one realizes more than I that I am a human being. I apologize [and ] ask for your forgiveness and ask God for His forgiveness." The American Football Coaches Association, representing college coaches across the country, was irate at the USFL and praised the NFL for refusing to waive its hands-off policy toward players with remaining college eligibility. Some NFL coaches, however, thought the policy might have to be changed. "They [the USFL teams] are getting to people before we have a chance," Rankin Smith, the president of the Atlanta Falcons, said. "We couldn't touch Herschel." Most seasoned observers, however, saw the signing of Walker not as the beginning of a trend but as an isolated case, and New Jersey officials later pointed out that their breach of the tradition against campus raiding was born of a rare combination of two factors—Walker's extraordinary talent and the infant team's extraordinary desperation—a combination that is not likely to recur.

In order not to compete with the fall schedule of the NFL, the USFL chose a spring season, beginning in late February or early March and ending in late June. In their inaugural season, in the spring of 1983, both Walker and the Generals had a slow start, not hitting their stride until the fifth game. The team finished the season ingloriously, with a record of six wins and twelve losses, but Walker led the league in rushing, with 1,812 yards. His best game was a victory over the Washington Federals on May 29, when he rushed 194 yards, including eighty-three in one touchdown run, the longest of his eighteen scoring runs that season.

Resuming his studies at the University of Georgia in the first half of the 1983–84 school year, Walker completed all but thirty of the credits necessary for his degree in criminal justice. In March 1984, after Steve Young signed with the Los Angeles Express for a sum surpassing Walker's 1983 deal with the Generals, Donald Trump, the new owner of the New Jersey team, signed Walker to a new contract purportedly more lucrative than Young's. That contract, negotiated by Walker's new agents, the International Management Group, will pay Walker at least $2 million a year through the year 1989, and it is the only existing USFL contract with a clause guaranteeing full payment should the USFL dissolve and Walker go to the NFL. Other contracts promise only to make up the difference should the NFL salary be lower. Trump explained to reporters that he decided to give Walker a new, heftier contract two years before renewal time because he felt certain that the NFL would vie for Walker, and he wanted to raise the ante. "I didn't want to lose Herschel . . . ," he said. "That would have been a devastating blow for the Generals and the USFL."

The newly acquired quarterback Brian Sipe was expected to take some of the pressure off Walker in 1984, but early on Sipe was sidelined with an injury. Walker also suffered an injury, to his right shoulder, requiring caution in movement. Often serving as a decoy for quarterback Glenn Carano, he did not begin picking up yardage until late in March. He finished the season ranking third in the league in rushing, with 1,339 yards on 293 attempts. The longest of his sixteen touchdown runs was for sixty-nine yards. The Generals, with a 14-4 record, finished second in the Atlantic division of the USFL's Eastern conference.

In 1985 Walker rushed for 2,411 yards in 438 attempts, breaking Eric Dickerson's single-season record of 2,105. Twenty-one of his carries were for touchdowns. Receiving, he accounted for twenty-five yards and one TD. The Professional Football Writers Association voted him the USFL's Most Valuable Player. The Generals went 11-7 that season and lost to the Jacksonville Bulls in the first round of the playoffs. Amid speculation that there might never be another USFL season, the league announced that in 1986 it would move its schedule to the fall and early winter, the traditional football time. Gambling on the folding of the USFL, the NFL's Dallas Cowboys picked Walker in the fifth round of the 1985 draft. Walker meanwhile had signed a four-year personal-service contract worth $6 million with the Generals. He also has long-term deals with the Adidas sportswear company and Franklin Sports Industries worth more than $1 million each. In 1985 Doubleday published *Herschel Walker's Basic Training*, written by Walker with Terry Todd.

Herschel Walker has a nineteen-inch neck, a thirty-one-inch waist, and twenty-three-inch thighs. "They . . . ask me how I got so big without lifting [weights] . . . ," Walker told Terry Todd when Todd interviewed him for *Sports Illustrated*. "Up to now my body's gotten stronger and faster every year on my old program, and what I reckon I'll do is try and see how long I can keep improving without the weights. One thing's sure. Soon as I don't make gains, I'm going on a good weight program." In the meantime, to the regular push-ups in his basic exercise program he has added handstand press-ups and push-ups done with someone—often his wife—sitting on his back. He also does sprint swimming, in addition to karate, and he occasionally plays golf and tennis. Needing relatively little sleep, he gets by on about four hours a night. Dancing is one of his favorite recreations. Even-tempered, he is unfailingly patient with importunate autograph seekers and courteous with interviewers.

On March 31, 1983 Herschel married Cynthia De Angelis, better known as Cindy, who is of Italian and Argentinian descent. The two met at the University of Georgia, where they were on the track team together. They maintain homes in both Athens, Georgia and Verona, New Jersey. No sports fanatic, Walker would rather watch a Richard Pryor movie than a football game; he has little patience for sports scholarship and statistics; and he claims not to read "any of the stuff" that's writ-

ten about him, because he knows himself "better than anyone." "I know that my life is based on being a good football player and a good individual," he has said, as quoted by David DuPree in the *Washington Post* (March 23, 1984). "I want to be perfect. I know I can't be, but I at least want to try. I don't consider myself great. I'm just a person who works hard." With rare exceptions—the most notable being a recent gift of $100,000 to the University of Georgia for a new athletic building—the thrifty running back puts most of his money into savings and two businesses, a food franchise and a construction company.

*References: Chicago Tribune* IV p8 Mr 27 '83 pors; *Inside Sports* 3:26+ S 30 '81 pors; *NY Times Mag* p28+ N 1 '81 pors; *Sport* 75:15+ Mr '84 pors; *Sports Ill* 57:95+ 0 4 '82 pors, 58:18+ Mr 14 '83 pors; Burchard, Sue. *Herschel Walker* (1984); Cromartie, Bill. *There Goes Herschel* (1983); Gelfand, Howard. *Herschel Walker* (1983); Prugh, Jeff. *Herschel Walker* (1983)

## Waterston, Sam

*Nov. 15, 1940– Actor. Address: b. c/o Agency for the Performing Arts, Inc., Suite 315, 9000 Sunset Blvd., Los Angeles, Calif. 90069*

With his Academy Award nomination as best actor of 1984 for his performance in *The Killing Fields*, the versatile and accomplished Sam Waterston, after a twenty-year career in motion pictures, television, and theatre, finally emerged as a bona fide star. Preferring to practice his craft on the stage, in roles ranging from Shakespearean tragedy to light comedy, he had been more or less regularly employed in the theatre since 1963, but it was not until 1972, when he portrayed Benedick in the New York Shakespeare Festival's stage and television productions of a "ragtime" *Much Ado About Nothing*, that he attracted widespread attention. His many other memorable roles include Hamlet, Prospero, and Torvald Helmer, on the stage; Tom Wingfield in *The Glass Menagerie* and the title role in *Oppenheimer*, on television; and Nick Carraway in the film version of *The Great Gatsby*. Committed to doing "good work across a broad spectrum," as he has put it, Waterston is more interested in the part, in the project, than in celebrity. Acting, for him, is "a gigantic social service in itself." "If my work has any social value," he told one interviewer, "it will be because I have devoted my life to something that is humane."

One of the four children of George Chychele and Aliça Tucker (Atkinson) Waterston, Samuel Atkinson Waterston was born in Cambridge, Massachusetts on November 15, 1940 with, in his words, "a rusty silver spoon in my mouth." His father, who had emigrated from England to the United States during the Depression, was a semanticist and a teacher of languages at the Brooks School in nearby North Andover; his mother, whose ancestors were among New England's first settlers, was a landscape painter. Since both his parents were interested in the arts, young Sam grew up in what he has described as "an atmosphere that said 'These things are possible.'" Perhaps because of his father's lifelong love affair with the theatre, he was especially drawn to acting. He was only seven when he made his first stage appearance, as Creon's page in the Brooks School's production of Jean Anouilh's *Antigone*, directed by his father. He appeared in other schoolboy productions at the Brooks School and, later, at the Groton School, the prestigious college preparatory academy in Groton, Massachusetts.

Following his graduation from Groton, Sam Waterston enrolled at Yale University on a scholarship to study French and history, but he soon spent almost as much time on theatrical productions as on his studies. Shortly after he arrived on campus, he joined the Yale Dramat, the university's dramatic society, and over the course of his college career, he performed in many Dramat productions, ranging from the classical Greek tragedy *Oedipus Rex* to Samuel Beckett's surrealistic tragicomedy *Waiting for Godot*. It was while he was playing the part of Lucky, the slave in *Godot*, that he had the "Great Experience," as he later termed it, that eventually led to his decision to become a professional actor. In the middle of the final performance of the play, he told Martin Torgoff of *Interview* magazine (April 1981), "I had this sudden, wonderful understanding about the character just the instant before I was supposed to speak. I had a palpable sensation of control from my fingers out to the audience, that what I did affected them, and I thought: 'My God, this is wonderful!'"

Aware of the precariousness of an acting career, Waterston judged it "sensible" to investigate alternatives to the theatre, including architecture. During his junior year, which he spent at the University of Paris, he even tried to give up acting altogether, but within weeks his resolve broke down, and he began taking classes at the American Actors Workshop, organized by John Berry, the expatriate American director. Among other things, Waterston credits Berry with teaching him how to approach a role, how "to find a door into the heart and mind of a character," as he explained to Joanmarie Kalter in an interview for her book *Actors on Acting* (1979). He tested Berry's theories, based on the techniques of Konstantin Stanislavsky and Michael Chekhov, in detailed scene analyses, mining the text for clues to his character. "You can't figure out little, tricky revelations that you do with behavior, that don't have a textual base, and try to slide an interpretation of the part past the lines . . . ," he told Miss Kalter. "You've got to get into the character, try to understand him, figure out what he means by everything he says, and try to make it all matter a lot."

Waterston returned to the United States determined to become an actor at all costs. After taking his B.A. degree from Yale in 1962, he spent several months in summer stock at the Clinton (Connecticut) Playhouse, where his roles included the tragic clown Estragon in *Waiting for Godot*, then opted to try his luck in New York City. Supporting himself by working for Macy's Theatre Club, a now defunct ticket agency, he continued his professional training in classes with Herbert Berghof and Frank Corsaro, and as an occasional observer at the Actors Studio. Waterston made his New York debut at the Phoenix Theater late in 1962, when he took over the role of Jonathan Rosepettle, the sheltered adolescent son in Arthur Kopit's zany black comedy *Oh Dad, Poor Dad, Mama's Hung You in the Closet and I'm Feelin' So Sad*. He then played the part on a national tour and, beginning in August 1963, on Broadway. His touching portrayal of the stammering, overprotected youth generated sympathy as well as laughter, and, perhaps more important, brought him to the attention of Broadway and Off-Broadway producers and directors.

Over the next ten years, Waterston accumulated an impressive list of stage credits in a wide variety of plays. Off Broadway, his roles included Wessy in the short-lived period piece *Thistle in My Bed*, Colin in the long-running comedy *The Knack*, Woodfin in Maxime Furland's one-act play *Fitz*, Kent in the world premiere of Sam Shepard's baffling *La Turista*, and Aburbio in *Posterity for Sale*, an experimental work by Niccolo Tucci. His "natural sense of both whimsical comedy and quiet drama," to quote Richard F. Shepard of the *New York Times* (April 29, 1968), served him well in a twin bill of the one-act plays *Red Cross*, by Sam Shepard, and *Muzeeka*, by John Guare, at the Provincetown Playhouse in New York's Greenwich Village in 1968. He was also effective as the bewildered "mother" in an Americanized version of *Spitting Image*, Colin Spencer's comic fantasy about a male homosexual couple who have a baby, and as the Greek inventor Phanocles in the American premiere of William Golding's elusive parable *The Brass Butterfly*.

Waterston's Broadway credits were equally varied, ranging from the hippie son of a crotchety English general in *Halfway Up the Tree*, Peter Ustinov's antic satire on the generation gap, to the Indian spokesman John Grass in Arthur Kopit's *Indians*, a kaleidoscopic spectacle about the genocide of the American Indian, to the ill-mannered son in a stillborn revival of Noel Coward's 1925 high comedy *Hay Fever*. He was perhaps most affecting as Thomas Lewis, the conscience-stricken art teacher in the chilling courtroom drama *The Trial of the Catonsville Nine*, which transferred to the Lyceum Theatre in June 1971 after several sold-out months Off Broadway. An edited transcript of the trial of the activist priests Daniel and Philip Berrigan and seven others for burning draft records to protest the Vietnam war, the play was essentially an ensemble effort, but several critics singled out Waterston, one of four survivors from the original production, for special commendation. During his first decade as a professional actor, Waterson also occasionally lent his talents to regional theatres, most notably the Mark Taper Forum in Los Angeles, where he took the leading roles of the rascally Mosca in the world premiere of a musical retelling of Jonson's *Volpone*, and Oliver, a novitiate in an Indian monastery in Christopher Isherwood's *A Meeting by the River*.

In mid-1972, on Waterston's return to New York City after fulfilling an engagement at the Mark Taper Forum, Joseph Papp, the producer and artistic director of the New York Shakespeare Festival, offered him the roles of Laertes in *Hamlet* and Benedick in *Much Ado About Nothing*. A veteran of "Shakespeare in the Park" presentations, Waterston had already played the lovesick shepherd Silvius in *As You Like It*, in 1963, Prince Hal in a wildly uneven production of *Henry IV*, in 1968, and the loutish Cloten in A. J. Antoon's nightmarish reworking of *Cymbeline*, in 1971. Most critics found his interpretation of Laertes in Gerald Freedman's star-studded staging of *Hamlet*, which opened the Shakespeare Festival's 1972 season, to be "overwrought," but the *New York Times*'s Clive Barnes was enough impressed by the actor's "heroically tortured" portrayal to venture the forecast that he "would make a good Hamlet one day."

That day came in the summer of 1975, when Waterston took up the challenge of playing the notoriously difficult role for the New York Shakespeare Festival, under the direction of Michael Rudman. Waterston's Hamlet was, in the view of the majority of critics, more the petulant schoolboy than the traditional "melancholy Dane" and clearly no match for Claudius. But there was nonetheless an appealing catch in his voice that signaled the "autumnal despair," as one reviewer put it, "of a young man defeated," and some of his readings offered new insights into the play. By the time the

production moved indoors to the stage of the Vivian Beaumont Theatre in Lincoln Center in December 1975, Waterston had refined and strengthened his characterization to such an extent that one critic—Martin Gottfried of the *New York Post*—went so far as to call it "one of the most memorable Hamlets" of a lifetime of theatregoing. "This is an actor's Hamlet rather than a performer's," he concluded in his review of December 18, 1975, "a touching, vulnerable Hamlet, believably an individual human being."

It was Waterston's talent for investing Shakespeare's characters with a broad humanity that made him such a valuable addition to the Festival's roster in the early 1970s. By portraying Prospero as a vigorous, middle-aged scholar rather than as a wizened magician, he added a poignant dimension to the outpouring of forgiveness and reconciliation that climaxes *The Tempest* and added weight and authority to Edward Berkeley's unorthodox studio production. His interpretation of the complex role of the duke Vincentio in *Measure for Measure*, however, was marred by some physical and vocal mannerisms that occasionally threatened to overwhelm the production. Waterston himself has since admitted that he "could never get [the part] right."

By all accounts, Waterston's most successful Shakespearean creation was Benedick in A. J. Antoon's sunlit production of *Much Ado About Nothing*, the final attraction of the Festival's 1972 summer season at the Delacorte Theatre in Central Park. Transposed from sixteenth-century Messina to turn-of-the-century small-town America, *Much Ado* took on a relevance often missing in more traditional stagings. As Benedick, the misogynistic soldier turned languishing suitor, Waterston easily held his own in repartee with the rapier-tongued Beatrice of Kathleen Widdoes, but he never lost sight of the character's essentially romantic nature, and when he eventually discovered his love—"half-knowingly, but with astonishment nonetheless," as Laurence I. Barrett observed in his review for *Time* (August 28, 1972)—he was "like a child finding the tooth fairy's silver dollar." One of the biggest hits in the history of the New York Shakespeare Festival, *Much Ado About Nothing* was transplanted to the Winter Garden Theatre on Broadway in November 1972. A television version was broadcast by CBS-TV the following February. For his contribution, Sam Waterston, who was, in Laurence Barrett's words, "Benedick to the last corpuscle," took home a Drama Desk Award, a New York Drama Critics Circle Award, and an Obie.

Waterston's superlative performance in the televised version of *Much Ado* won him the role of Tom Wingfield in David Susskind's television production of Tennessee Williams' *The Glass Menagerie*, starring Katharine Hepburn. The actor found the key to his character in Williams' own enactment of the minor part of Doc in the 1972 Off-Broadway staging of his play *Small Craft Warnings*. Among the six Emmy award nominations garnered by the cast of *The Glass Menagerie*, which was telecast by ABC-TV in December 1973, was one for Sam Waterston as best supporting actor. No newcomer to the small screen, Waterston had appeared in some of the most successful prime-time television series of the 1960s, including *Dr. Kildare*, *N.Y.P.D.*, and *Hawk*, and he had played featured roles in such distinguished PBS dramatic specials as *The Good Lieutenant* and *My Mother's House*. His more recent television credits include the made-for-TV motion pictures *Reflections of Murder*, *Games Mother Never Taught You*, *Love Lives On*, *Finnegan, Begin Again*, and the Emmy award–winning *Friendly Fire*, in which he portrayed C. D. B. Bryan, the author of a heart-wrenching best seller that investigated the accidental death of an American soldier in Vietnam.

Perhaps Waterston's most challenging television assignment to date was the title role in the seven-part BBC series *Oppenheimer*. Attracted by what he called the "immensity" of the man and by the in-depth format, the actor jumped at the chance to portray the enigmatic and controversial J. Robert Oppenheimer, the so-called "father of the atom bomb." Waterston's incisive impersonation, "alternately charming and calculating," of the "stoop-shouldered and sad-eyed" Oppenheimer won him a best-actor nomination from the British Academy of Film and Television in 1981. By coincidence, when *Oppenheimer* was broadcast in the United States on PBS's *American Playhouse* anthology in the spring of 1982, it followed hard on the heels of CBS's diverting six-part adventure series *Q.E.D.*, a British import starring Waterston as Quentin E. Deverill, an eccentric American professor turned amateur sleuth in Edwardian London.

Until he was tapped to play Nick Carraway, the narrator of *The Great Gatsby*, in 1973, Waterston's list of motion picture credits, which extends back to the mid-1960s, consisted largely of supporting roles in such low-budget films as *Three* (United Artists, 1969), *Cover Me, Babe* (Twentieth Century-Fox, 1970), and *Who Killed Mary Whats'ername?* (Cannon Group, 1971). The one exception was James Ivory's *Savages* (Angelika Films, 1972), a witty parable of the one-day rise and fall of civilization that enjoyed considerable critical and commercial success in Europe. When Jack Clayton's elaborately mounted and excessively hyped remake of F. Scott Fitzgerald's *The Great Gatsby* was released by Paramount in 1974, Sam Waterston was virtually the sole performer to escape a critical flaying. In the opinion of most of the reviewers, he alone had "the presence and weight as an actor," as Vincent Canby observed in the *New York Times* (March 31, 1974), to give the otherwise disappointing film "a kind of moral heft."

Over the next ten years Waterston displayed his uncommon versatility in a wide range of films. He played, among other parts, a wise-cracking, laid-back halfbreed in Frank Perry's offbeat contemporary western *Rancho Deluxe* (United Artists, 1975), a liberal public defender in the romantic comedy

*Dandy, the All-American Girl* (United Artists, 1976), and a rebellious husband in *Interiors* (United Artists, 1978), Woody Allen's domestic drama. Other congenial roles were a womanizing playwright in *Sweet William* (World Northal, 1982), an astronaut in the ingenious space-flight thriller *Capricorn One* (Warner Brothers, 1978), a ruthless cattle baron in *Heaven's Gate* (United Artists, 1980), Michael Cimino's universally panned epic western, and an undercover agent in the comic cloak-and-dagger adventure *Hopscotch* (Avco Embassy, 1980).

As Waterston explained to one interviewer, his increasing experience as a film actor made it possible for him to play the great classical stage roles "more realistically, more idiomatically." In a 1975 revival of Ibsen's *A Doll's House* at the Vivian Beaumont Theatre, for instance, he avoided the common practice of portraying Torvald Helmer as the stereotypical strait-laced husband. Playing opposite Liv Ullmann's radiant Nora, Waterston made Torvald "as much a victim of his environment as Nora," according to Walter Kerr, who evaluated the production for the *New York Times* (April 6, 1975). "The fatuousness is inbred, scarcely of his own making, and it is much relieved by a sensuality rarely seen in the man." He gave the same thoughtful attention to his interpretation of the self-dramatizing Vershinin in the Manhattan Theatre Club's staging of Chekhov's *The Three Sisters* in 1982. As Frank Rich, for one, remarked in the *New York Times* (December 22, 1982), Waterston's complex characterization, "at once weak and sympathetic," well suited the playwright's intentions. As much at home in contemporary plays as he is in the classics, Waterston has recently tackled the roles of an uptight marriage counselor in Jean Kerr's breezy comedy *Lunch Hour*, which began a respectable Broadway run in November 1980; a cuckolded husband who murders his wife's lover in *Gardenia*, the first play, chronologically, in John Guare's projected epic tetralogy about the death of the American dream; and the disillusioned surgeon in Marsha Norman's bleak *Traveler in the Dark*, which was first performed by the American Repertory Theatre in February 1984.

Waterston found the largest audience of his career in the enormously successful film *The Killing Fields* (Warner Brothers, 1984), Roland Joffe's reenactment of an American journalist's rescue of his Cambodian colleague from war-ravaged Kampuchea. To prepare for his role as Sydney H. Schanberg, the Pulitzer Prize-winning former war correspondent for the *New York Times* whose article "The Death and Life of Dith Pran" served as the basis for the movie's screenplay, Waterston, in his usual thoroughgoing manner, "camped out" in Schanberg's New York office and "read everything he wrote on Cambodia." His diligence paid off in a self-effacing and honest impersonation of the journalist that coupled "a keen intelligence with surprising vulnerability," as David Sterritt noted in the *Christian Science Monitor* (August 8, 1984).

One of the top-grossing motion pictures of the year, *The Killing Fields* netted seven Academy Award nominations, among them one for Waterston as best actor, and actually won three Oscars.

A lean and rangy six feet two inches tall, Sam Waterston has been described as "darkly handsome in an understated, classically small-town USA kind of way." He has dark brown hair, brown eyes, angular features, and a perpetually bemused expression. Because he has spent most of his adult life either "rehearsing or looking for work," as he once put it, he has few hobbies, although he enjoys cooking and gardening, and he occasionally goes skiing. The actor makes his home in a farmhouse in rural Connecticut with his wife, the former Lynn

Louisa Woodruff, a model whom he married on January 26, 1976, and his three children, Elizabeth, Katherine, and James. James, who played his son in *Oppenheimer*, is the child of Waterston's first marriage, to the photographer and writer Barbara Rutledge Johns, which ended in divorce.

*References: After Dark 10:20+ D '68 pors; Interview 11:42 Ap '81 por; L A Times IV p36 D 25 '73 por, VI p8 My 13 '82; L A Times Calendar p88 Je 8 '75 por, p23 N 18 '84 por; New Times 2:58+ Mr 8 '74 por; N Y Times II p3 D 3 '72, III p5 F 27 '81; Notable Names in the American Theatre (1976); Who's Who in America, 1984-85; Who's Who in the Theatre (1981)*

## Wattenberg, Ben J.

*Aug. 26, 1933- Demographer; political writer.
Address: b. American Enterprise Institute for Public Policy Research, 1150 17th St. N.W., Washington, D.C. 20036*

For more than two decades, the demographer and political analyst Ben J. Wattenberg has mined federal census data and public-opinion polls in an effort to illuminate the American experience. In such books as *The Real Majority* (1970), *The Real America* (1974), and *The Good News Is the Bad News Is Wrong* (1984), he has confounded cynics and negativists with carefully documented claims that the quality of life actually is improving for virtually all segments of American society. Warning that the public is in danger of being "catch-phrased and crisis-mongered to death" by those who over-

state rates of poverty, illiteracy, unemployment, and overpopulation, Wattenberg has remained true to his belief that "in American history . . . it is the optimist who has been the realist."

The son of Judah Wattenberg, a lawyer, and Rachel (Gutman) Wattenberg, Ben J. Wattenberg was born in New York City on August 26, 1933. He has a sister, Rebecca Schull. After receiving his B.A. degree from Hobart College in Geneva, New York in 1955 and then spending two years in the Air Force, Ben Wattenberg began a career in journalism. A prolific writer with a talent for fashioning readable prose, Wattenberg at first contributed articles to such popular magazines as *Ladies Home Journal* and *The Reporter* before trying his hand at longer works, including two nonfiction books for young people—*The Story of Harbors* (Sterling, 1961) and *Busy Waterways* (John Day, 1964)—and a geographic, demographic, and historical study, written with Ralph Lee Smith, entitled *The New Nations of Africa* (Hart, 1963).

With the publication of *This U.S.A.* (Doubleday, 1965), his fourth book, Wattenberg first attained national prominence. Written in collaboration with Richard M. Scammon, director of the United States Bureau of the Census from 1961 to 1965, *This U.S.A.* (subtitled "An Unexpected Family Portrait of 194,067,296 Americans Drawn from the Census") was based on the 1960 census. The authors, who spent three years transmuting the 141,000-page census into a multidimensional study of the American people, painted a rosy-hued picture of the state of the Union that contrasted sharply with the darker views of many social critics and political commentators. In spite of the many problems regularly spotlighted by the media—the escalating war in Vietnam, race riots, environmental pollution, and an accelerating nuclear arms race—the authors maintained that the census "shows clearly that the United States is entering a Golden Age, that we have achieved a better America." To illustrate that thesis, they presented evidence that poverty figures are misleading because they include students, military personnel, and certain farm families who live well on little money; that the five-million unemployment figure often cited includes only about 600,000 "hard-core" unemployed male family heads, with those unemployed less than thirteen weeks and housewives and students looking for part-time work accounting for the larger figure; that the birth rate is declining; and that only six-tenths of one percent of the nation's youth are illiterate.

*This U.S.A.* was widely admired for its superb detail, cogent analysis, and deft condensation of the unwieldy census, but, like some other reviewers, Lincoln H. Day cautioned readers in the *New York Times Book Review* (January 2, 1966) that the authors' "aggressive boosterism" detracted from their "otherwise perceptive and informative discussion."

The success of that controversial study catapulted Wattenberg into the political arena, where he served from 1966 to 1968 as a research assistant and speech writer for President Lyndon B. Johnson and "moonlighted" as an advisor to Hubert H. Humphrey, former vice-president under Johnson, during his unsuccessful presidential campaign in 1968. Wattenberg was no more fortunate in his own campaigns: before 1970, he made two unsuccessful attempts to attain public office in Stamford, Connecticut, where he was then living. Nevertheless, his political experiences served as grist for his next book, *The Real Majority: An Extraordinary Examination of the American Electorate* (Cowan-McCann), on which he again collaborated with Richard Scammon.

Published shortly before the 1970 elections, *The Real Majority* is an authoritative psephological analysis that reveals who the American voters are, why they vote the way they do, and how a candidate can reach them. For their study, Wattenberg and Scammon scrutinized polls, surveys, and the 1969 mayoral election results and reached some surprising conclusions. Contravening conventional political wisdom, they contended that the young, the liberal, and the black voters did not hold the key to electoral success: most voters, according to their study, were "middle-aged, middle-class, and middle-minded." Furthermore, among that "unyoung, unpoor, unblack" electorate the pocketbook, traditionally the decisive factor in an election, had taken a backseat to the "social issue." As a result, suddenly a candidate's stand on the rising crime rate, drug abuse, campus unrest, and declining moral standards was more likely to determine the success or failure of his campaign than his economic program.

Translating their findings into political strategy, Wattenberg and Scammon proffered some suggestions to the major parties and some fringe groups. They maintained that the Democratic party's best hope of appealing to the political center—and thus its best hope of recapturing the White House in 1972 or 1976—was to take a firm, "law-and-order" stance on the social issue and to avoid measures that exacerbate racial tensions (such as mandatory busing) while heeding traditional economic concerns. "We recommend to would-be leaders of the people," they concluded, "that they trust the people and listen to the people before leading the people." *The Real Majority*, which was a best-seller in 1970, had a substantial impact on the elections of 1970 and 1972 as conservative Republicans and liberal Democrats alike tailored their campaigns to accord in some degree with the book's precepts and made "law and order" a dominant theme on the campaign trail.

Wattenberg himself put his theories to the test as a strategist for Humphrey in his successful bid to represent once again Minnesota in the Senate and for Senator Henry M. Jackson in his abortive campaigns for the Democratic presidential nomination in 1972 and 1976. When George S. McGovern, who was more liberal than most of his fellow Democrats, defeated Jackson for the party's nomination in 1972 and then led the Democrats to an overwhelming defeat at the polls, Wattenberg responded in December 1972 by cofounding and chairing the Coalition for a Democratic Majority. That organization, which first drew support from such "mainstream liberals" as Humphrey, Jackson, and various labor union leaders, "rejects strongly the politics of the New Left," which McGovern represented, and intends to draw the party back towards the political center by serving as a base through which moderates could influence the party's structure and policies.

In addition to carrying out his duties as chairman of that coalition, Wattenberg continued his demographic studies, which he published in the early 1970s in several monographs, among them *The Demography of the 1970's: The Birth Dearth and What It Means* (1971), which was commissioned by *Family Circle* magazine. In that project he debunked the theory advanced by "ecological crisis-mongers" that a population explosion threatened the United States. Marshaling census data as evidence, he not only showed that the birth rate for the first half of 1971 was the lowest in American history but also pointed out that it might indicate a trend toward smaller families, which, as the author explained, could have a revolutionary impact on "the lifestyle of an entire generation—changing housing patterns, changing income levels, changing roles for women and changing spending patterns, to just begin the list."

Igniting controversy again in 1973, he and Richard Scammon released a study asserting that civil-rights leaders and white, New Left, liberals had, to their own detriment, thrown a "blanket of silence" over data indicating that blacks had made "enormous" economic gains during the Kennedy-Johnson years. In their article "Black Progress and Liberal Rhetoric," which was published in the April and August 1973 issues of *Commentary* magazine, they cited evidence that 52 percent of black families were earning over $8,000 ($6,000 in the South) per year, thus qualifying them for middle-class status. Wattenberg and Scammon argued that by refusing to acknowledge gains, though still insufficent ones, blacks and liberals were giving the Nixon administration justification for its dismantling of the Great Society programs that they supported and that were responsible for those advances. "Liberals," the authors pointed out, "seem to be adopting the strange battle cry: 'We have failed—let us continue.'"

Their report quickly drew fire from blacks and civil-rights leaders, among others. Responding with its own study, the National Urban League disputed Wattenberg and Scammon's definition of middle class, contending that the $11,446 income level set as the "intermediate family budget" by the Bureau of Labor Statistics was a more realistic measure of middle-class status. Using that figure, the League estimated that only one out of four black families would qualify as middle class. Furthermore, according to its study, from 1969 to 1972 the income of black families had decreased in comparison to that of white families, and the black unemployment rate had risen by almost 4 percent. Robert Hill, the director of the National Urban League, added that "while Wattenberg and Scammon prefer to concentrate on the gains of the '60s, black leaders are concerned with the retrenchment of the '70s."

In spite of the criticisms leveled against it, "Black Progress and Liberal Rhetoric" formed a key chapter in Wattenberg's next book, *The Real America* (Doubleday, 1974). Buttressing his argument with Census Bureau statistics and scores of attitudinal surveys by private pollsters, Wattenberg maintained that although environmentalists, feminists, journalists, and antiwar activists, among other members of the "Failure and Guilt Complex," were decrying the quality of life in America, there had actually been "healthy change . . . on almost every measurable front."

Peppering his material with italics, exclamation points, and common sense observations, Wattenberg consequently advised liberals yet again that, given the progress achieved by almost all Americans, their wisest political strategy would be to publicize the fact that the country has particularly "given a better deal to the poor and the black—just what [liberal] legislation said it would do." Most critics found *The Real America* to be eminently readable in spite of Wattenberg's heavy reliance on statistics, and in his review for the *New York Times* (September 29, 1974) Steven R. Weisman termed it "a major contribution to the country's political dialogue."

In 1977 Wattenberg brought his Panglossian message to television as host of the critically praised *In Search of the Real America*, a monthly, six-part PBS series patterned after his similarly styled 1974 study. Subtitled "A Challenge to the Chorus of Failure and Guilt," the series opened with an assault on the negative clichés about big business. In the following installments, Wattenberg and his guests, who included former attorney general Ramsey Clark, economist Milton Friedman, and Senator Daniel Patrick Moynihan, discussed such wide-ranging topics as population growth, the Central Intelligence Agency, Third World nations, Vietnam, and disaffected intellec-

tuals. Returning to public television in 1980, Wattenberg hosted a series of ten half-hour, magazine-format programs aptly titled *Ben Wattenberg's 1980*, in which he used a "walk-about" style to inspect points of interest and interview key figures. Although representatives of opposing viewpoints were usually called upon, Wattenberg freely injected his own opinions and readily admitted that the programs were "advocacy television," prompting the television reviewer Richard F. Shepard to praise the series in the *New York Times* (May 23, 1980) for not immersing the viewer in "a morass of self-canceling views that pass for cautious neutrality." Peter Osnos of the *Washington Post* (May 17, 1980) was less favorably impressed, labeling the program "a paid political announcement, more propaganda than journalism." More recently, in 1981, Wattenberg hosted the PBS documentary series *Ben Wattenberg at Large*.

Toward the end of 1977 Wattenberg made a foray into political fiction with *Against All Enemies* (Doubleday). Written in collaboration with the political consultant Ervin S. Duggan, *Against All Enemies* is about a national crisis precipitated by an American vice-president's open opposition to the president's commitment of troops to Bolivia as a defense against Chilean aggression, and the subsequent duel between the two men for their party's presidential nomination.

*Against All Enemies* was highly regarded by critics for its well-drawn characters, brisk pace, and fidelity to the minutiae of White House life, but Wattenberg's next publication, *The Wealth Weapon* (Transaction Books, 1981), written with Richard J. Whalen, generated less enthusiasm. Its authors argued that the recent reduction of American political influence abroad made it imperative that the government exploit its economic leverage to achieve its foreign-policy objectives. However, F. R. Root, baffled by their presentation of that as a new idea, pointed out in the *Annals of the American Academy of Political and Social Science* (May 1981) that economic sanctions had long been employed by political strategists in Washington, and a reviewer for *Choice* berated the study as "nonscholarly, normative, and polemical, quickly dated material."

With his best-seller *The Good News Is the Bad News Is Wrong* (Simon & Schuster, 1984), Wattenberg found himself back on more familiar terrain. Once again assailing "panic mongering" by both the right and the left, he presented an impressive amount of data, culled from the latest census, other government sources, and opinion polls and surveys, to substantiate his unwavering opinion that Americans live in "a nation that in most respects . . . never had it so good." Nevertheless, he tempered his optimism with his concern about the "bad news bias" in the media, especially television. He cautioned that television's disproportionate number of "gloom and doom" features not only skewed the facts but threatened to undermine Americans' confidence in themselves and their government. The resulting negativism could adversely affect domestic matters—dampening the economic recovery by discouraging investors, for example—and erode the nation's status and influence abroad, thus subverting its ability to achieve its foreign policy goals.

Wattenberg's many honors include appointments by President Carter to serve on the president's board for Ambassadorial Appointments (1977) and in the American delegation to the Madrid Conference on Human Rights (1980). President Ronald Reagan appointed him in 1981 to the Board of International Broadcasting, which oversees the operations of Radio Free Europe and Radio Liberty. Currently, he is vice-chairman of that board and of a bipartisan group studying means of promoting democracy all over the globe.

A slender man whose gray hair is receding, Wattenberg has grown a pointed, salt-and-pepper beard to complement the mustache he has sported for several decades. He and his wife, Diane Abelman, whom he married on July 10, 1983, have one daughter, Rachel, who was born in the spring of 1984. Wattenberg also has three older children—Ruth Elena, Daniel Eli, and Sarah Anita—from his twenty-five-year marriage to Marna Hade, from whom he was divorced in 1981. Since 1977 Wattenberg had been a senior fellow at the American Enterprise Institute for Public Policy Research, a right-of-center think tank in Washington, D.C., and co-editor of *Public Opinion*, its bimonthly magazine. A nationally syndicated newspaper columnist for United Features, Wattenberg is also a commentator for *Spectrum*, a weekly show on the CBS Radio Network. Although he has styled himself an "old liberal" or a centrist, Wattenberg is comfortable with the label of "neoconservative" often assigned to him. "A neoconservative," he wryly explains, "is just a liberal who has been mugged by reality."

References: *Christian Sci Mon* p31 N 5 '84 por; *Contemporary Authors* vols 57-60 (1976); *Who's Who in America*, 1984-85

---

## Wein, George (Theodore)

(wēn)

Oct. 3, 1925– Concert promoter; pianist. Address: b. Festival Productions, Inc., 311 W. 74th St., New York City, N.Y. 10023

Norman Granz and others must be credited with having moved jazz out of the isolation of funky clubs and onto the concert stage, but the impresario who is almost solely responsible for turning concert jazz into staple summer entertainment on a grand scale for a wide audience is George Wein. In 1954

Wein founded the Newport (Rhode Island) Jazz Festival, a marathon fete that became, in the words of the critic Nat Hentoff, "the World Series of this feisty art" and spawned an empire of similar musical galas extending to Tokyo and Nice. Wein's company, Festival Productions, Inc., is the world's largest employer of jazz talent, with an annual payroll of more than $5 million and sales of approximately 750,000 tickets, worth an estimated $9 million. The most spectacular and prestigious of the thirty or more festivals the company produces is the Kool Jazz Festival in New York City, which attracts 100,000 ticket-holding aficionados for more than a week each July. That event, along with nineteen others across the United States, is sponsored by the Brown & Williamson Tobacco Company, makers of Kool mentholated cigarettes. Wein began his career as a pianist, and he still regularly plays (and sometimes sings) with his own sextet.

George Theodore Wein was born on October 3, 1925 in Boston, Massachusetts to Dr. Barnet M. Wein, a plastic surgeon, and Ruth Wein, who played piano. With his older brother, Wein grew up in the Boston suburb of Newton. "I loved to sing," he has said of his childhood, "and a couple of times I got thrown out of movie houses for singing along with Bing Crosby or Nelson Eddy." "I started classical piano lessons at eight," he told Whitney Balliett of the *New Yorker* (June 24, 1972), "and then switched to popular piano, party piano. I had always been intrigued by improvisation, by anyone who could play by ear, so I switched again and took jazz lessons from a teacher named Sam Saxe, and by the time I was fifteen I was playing jazz." Through Saxe, a devotee of Earl ("Fatha") Hines, he picked up some of Hines's style. Teddy Wilson was another important role model for him when he was developing his jazz technique.

Wein organized his own band in junior high school, and he later led a fifteen-piece high-school orchestra. "I knew the limits of my musical talents, [which were] far from the best," he recounted in an interview with Richard Harrington for the Washington Post (May 23, 1982). "But I found that I had a tremendous mind for organizing; that was the natural thing for me to do."

During World War II Wein saw combat in Europe as an army engineer. After the war he took the premedical course at Boston University, out of deference to his father's wishes and with "no real enthusiasm about being a doctor." When he took his B.A. degree, he was, to his relief, not offered a job in the paper company owned by his mother's family. "I would have been miserable, and I guess they sensed it," he told Normand Poirier of the New York Post (July 3, 1962).

Aside from a stint as pianist in a Chinese restaurant, Wein's first professional gigs were with Boston Dixieland bands, including a Dixieland/swing combo he formed with Edmond Hall, the clarinetist, in the late 1940s. The Wein/Hall band was the centerpiece of a concert Wein produced at Jordan Hall in Boston, the success of which encouraged his entrepreneurial bent. Following a job booking groups at the Savoy, the Boston club named after the famous Harlem ballroom, he decided to open his own jazz club.

Subsidized by his mother, Wein opened a jazz club in the Copley Square Hotel and called it Storyville, after the New Orleans red-light district where jazz emerged in the late nineteenth century. Storyville soon became the center of jazz activity in Boston, and it remained so for a decade, until Wein closed it in 1960. For a time he concurrently operated another Boston Club, Mahogany Hall, devoted to traditional jazz, as well as summer clubs in Gloucester and on Cape Cod. During that period, Wein wrote a jazz column for the Simmons (College) News, and he taught a jazz class at Boston University. He was also instrumental in bringing to radio the commentaries of Father Norman O'Connor, the "jazz priest."

Donald Born, a professor at Boston University, introduced Wein to the young socialite couple Louis and Elaine Lorillard, of the tobacco Lorillards, in 1953. The Lorillards, inspired by the Boston Symphony's summer concerts at Tanglewood, Massachusetts, had brought the New York Philharmonic to Newport, Rhode Island, high society's summer colony, in 1952. That venture was a financial fiasco, but, undaunted, they hired Wein to produce two Tanglewood-style evenings of jazz at the Newport Casino in July 1954. For those evenings, Wein lined up, among others, Eddie Condon, Ella Fitzgerald, Billie Holiday, Gerry Mulligan, Lennie Tristano, Stan Kenton, Lester Young, and the Modern Jazz Quartet.

Encouraged by the enthusiastic audience of 13,000 drawn to the Newport Casino in 1954, Wein and the Lorillards, with the support of other Newport residents and the approval of the city fathers, decided to make the Newport Jazz Festival an annual event. They moved it outdoors, to a baseball field, and increased the number of concerts to seven, presented over four days. The festival became the premier event on the American jazz calendar during the last half of the 1950s, attracting growing audiences to witness a parade of performers, from Eubie Blake to Mahalia Jackson, that constituted a live Who's Who in Jazz. In addition, Wein was soon promoting similar festivals in Toronto, Boston, Detroit, Buffalo, and French Lick, Indiana, and he, with others, added to the schedule in Newport a folk festival that became the most important event of its type in the United States.

When 10,000 boozy young people, frustrated at their exclusion from the sold-out field, rioted at the Newport Jazz Festival in 1960, the city government revoked Wein's entertainment license, and, as he later recounted, "word got around that we were bad news." The French Lick Sheraton Hotel, sponsor of the French Lick, Indiana festival, canceled that event, and all but one of Wein's other festivals lost money. By the end of the year he had, by his own account, "nothing left." Biding his time, he earned money doing piano gigs and began taking American jazz artists on tours of Europe.

Staged by other promoters, the 1961 Newport Jazz Festival was a major financial failure. Borrowing $25,000, Wein offered to present the festival at his own risk, and the Newport city government allowed him to return in 1962 under certain conditions, including a curfew, and with the advantage of a new larger festival field, able to accommodate 25,000. Also in 1962, Wein started the Ohio Valley Jazz Festival in Cincinnati (later expanded to include Columbus), and in the years following he began producing festivals in Chicago (in conjunction with Down Beat magazine), Pittsburgh (with the Catholic Youth Organization), Detroit, Atlanta, New Orleans, and Hampton, Virginia. In addition, he took such festival musicians as Thelonius Monk, Duke Ellington, and the Modern Jazz Quartet on concert tours of Japan, Australia, New Zealand, most of the countries of western Europe, and some African nations. Beginning in 1966, he brought singers from the Metropolitan Opera to Newport for an opera festival, as part of an exchange whereby jazz and folk artists performed at the Met's summer concerts in Lewisohn Stadium in New York City.

Looking back on the early years of the Newport Jazz Festival, Gary Giddins of the Village Voice (July 17, 1984) wrote: "The Wein festival . . . once represented a kind of World Series for jazz, in which the enduring heroes and the best rookies were invited to strut their stuff, sometimes in the same game. By spending three days in Rhode Island, you could get a good idea of what the music had to offer that year. When Miles Davis or Cecil Taylor or Ray Charles or Archie Schepp first attracted national attention, they were invited to play Newport; Europeans showed up; youth bands suggested a healthy continuum; elder statesmen were feted." Giddins remembered with special pleasure Louis Armstrong's seventieth birthday celebration, "a concert so compelling that thousands sat rapt in a fierce downpour until Louis sent everyone home," as well as "several small moments, such as a trumpet workshop with Kenny Dorham, Bobby Hackett, and Ray Nance." Giddins also mentioned the "legendary performances," documented on recordings, by Duke Ellington and Joe Williams, an encounter between Thelonius Monk and Pee Wee Russell, and a reunion of Count Basie and Lester Young.

In the late 1960s Wein made increasing concessions to pop music, including rock 'n' roll, booking into the Newport Jazz Festival acts calculated to appeal to the youthful "Woodstock generation." And appeal they did, to a devastating degree. In 1969, 40,000 people showed up at the festival field, 15,000 more than could be accommodated. Instead of going home, the excess crowd remained in Newport for four days, building up what Wein described as "unbelievable pressure" and creating a "mob scene" at the field on July 15, 1969. A worse disturbance occurred in 1971, when rioters broke through the fence and took over the stage, smashing chairs, instruments, and light fixtures. With Wein's acquiescence, the Newport city government stopped the concert and called a halt to the festival, which still had two days remaining.

In 1972 Wein moved the Newport Jazz Festival to New York City, expanding it into a nine-day gala offering forty-five concerts in five major locations: Carnegie and Philharmonic halls, Radio City Music Hall, Yankee Stadium, and the Staten Island Ferry. The joyous reception given the festival by New Yorkers, from city officials on down, along with a paid attendance of 100,000, made Wein feel as though he had "been reborn." The only negative note was struck by a "counter–jazz festival" protesting alleged exploitation of black musical talent without due reward and recognition, especially for the younger and more experimental artists, including local musicians. Wein responded even to that protest positively, pointing out that the counter-festival was itself a contribution to jazz and promising to incorporate it into the festival as a whole the following year (which he did). During 1972 Wein's Festival Productions also staged smaller festivals in Houston and Oakland in addition to those in Hampton, Atlanta, Cincinnati, and New Orleans, and the company was responsible for a twenty-city tour of Europe by a troupe including Jimmy Smith, Dave Brubeck, Sonny Rollins, and Charles Mingus. In 1974 Wein organized his first Grande Parade du Jazz, an annual festival sponsored by the city government of Nice, France.

In his euphoria over the reception given the first New York City concerts, Wein staged his most ambitious Newport Jazz Festival ever in New York in the summer of 1973, scheduling fifty-six events spread out over thirteen locations. (After that grandiose project turned out to be a financial disaster, he became more cautious with his programming.) Later in 1973 he founded the Jazz Repertory Company, the first company devoted to playing the history of jazz for the purpose of maintaining the

music "as a living thing." Under State Department auspices, the company toured the Soviet Union in 1975, playing the music of Louis Armstrong. Unfortunately, the Jazz Repertory Company did not do well financially, and it disbanded after performing at the Newport Jazz Festival in 1978. The following year, Wein produced his first Munich Jazz Festival, and at the Alexandra Palace on the outskirts of London he initiated the Capital Radio Jazz Festival with a formidable six-day array of talent that included Fats Domino, Lionel Hampton, Dizzy Gillespie, B. B. King, Milt Jackson, and Sonny Stitt.

As the prestige of his festivals grew, Wein was honored with such awards as the French government's Order of Arts and Letters and the Frederick Douglass Award of the New York Urban League (a financial beneficiary of the Newport Jazz Festival). In 1978 President Jimmy Carter honored Wein with a festival on the south lawn of the White House produced by Wein himself. A tribute of another sort was the growing corporate sponsorship of Wein's festivals. Among those coming forward to sponsor individual annual events were *Playboy* magazine (Los Angeles) and the *Boston Globe* (Boston). The Joseph Schlitz Brewing Company was Wein's biggest backer for many years, until the mid-1970s, when the Brown & Williamson Tobacco Company entered the picture, impelled by a ban on broadcast advertising of cigarettes. Brown & Williamson finally offered to underwrite the entire cost of the Newport Jazz Festival in New York, along with nineteen other festivals countrywide, if the festival name were changed to "Kool." Accordingly, the Newport Jazz Festival became the Kool Jazz Festival in 1981. Contributing to the importance of the name change was the fact that there is in competition with Kool cigarettes a mentholated cigarette called Newport, a P. Lorillard product.

When the name of the festival in New York was changed, Wein decided to resume the festival in Newport itself, partly in order to protect his legal right to the Newport name. When the Newport Jazz Festival returned to Newport for two days in August 1981, Mel Lewis, McCoy Tyner, Buddy Rich, and Dick Hyman entertained on the first day and Dave Brubeck, Nancy Wilson, and Lionel Hampton on the second.

The Kool Jazz Festival, staged at Carnegie Hall, Carnegie Recital Hall, and Avery Fisher Hall in New York City in 1984, included "A Salute to Django Reinhardt Featuring Stephan Grapelli," "A Salute to Benny Carter and Illinois Jacquet," "A Salute to Count Basie," piano recitals by Kenny Barron, Denny Zeitlin, Johnny O'Neal, and Oscar Peterson/Cecil Taylor, vocals by Sarah Vaughan and Joe Williams, and performances by the Wynton Marsalis Quintet, Artie Shaw and his band, Miles Davis and his combo, and Lionel Hampton and his.

In reviewing the 1984 festival for the *Village Voice*, Gary Giddins faulted Wein for "having gone the star route instead of sustaining a World Series concept," for not "nurturing modernist and postmodernist jazz," and for paying "only lip service" to "jazz musicians under the age of fifty." Giddins nevertheless acknowledged Wein to be "one of jazz's heartiest and most powerful friends," one who "has used his energy and influence to accomplish much good." "If the under-forty jazz generation had its own Wein," Giddins wrote, "its music would be in much better commercial shape."

Wein produces the George Wein Collection of jazz recordings on the Concord label, and he himself has cut many albums, including *Wein, Women and Song* (Atlantic), *Alive and Well in Mexico* (Columbia), and *The Newport All-Stars* (Impulse). Most of his playing (and singing) is done with his sextet. That combo, originally the Storyville Stompers, has changed its name as well as its personnel over the years, becoming in turn the Newport All-Stars, the Festival All-Stars, and the Newport Jazz Festival All-Stars. Wein and his group, often booked at Michael's Pub and the Plaza Hotel in New York City, tour the United States and Canada for one month annually, playing college towns, performing-arts centers, theatres, and retirement communities each spring.

With the current Newport Jazz Festival All-Stars, Wein has recorded a double LP, released early in 1985. Writing in the *Wall Street Journal* (May 21, 1985), Wein's old friend Nat Hentoff called that album "the most full-bodied, crisply swinging celebration of the joys of jazz in a long time," with "the flowing warmth of the classic jazz groups built according to Mr. [Louis] Armstrong's designs." "It's not that George Wein is a front-ranking jazz pianist," Hentoff observed, "but he so loves the music that he does indeed wail." Wein classifies himself as "a mainstream pianist, swing-oriented," with a "simple" style. Others have described his playing as "incisive," "convincing," and "joyful."

Wein was introduced to his wife, the former Joyce Alexander, by Nat Hentoff in Boston in 1948. "We didn't get married until 1959," Wein told Whitney Balliett of the *New Yorker* (June 24, 1972). "It probably would have been a lot sooner without the racial thing. [Mrs. Wein is black.] My father was dead set against my marrying Joyce." Mrs. Wein interjected: "My mother wasn't all that happy either." Formerly a research biochemist, Joyce Wein now works with her husband as an associate producer. The Weins have three homes: an apartment on New York's Upper West Side, a house in Connecticut, and a villa in Vence on the French Riviera.

Short (five feet seven), rotund, and bald of pate, George Wein was described by Whitney Balliett as "a compact arrangement of spheres." "His round head . . . ," Balliett wrote, "is set directly on a round, perfectly proportioned body that is continually orbited by ball-like hands." Wein is a fast talker with a thundering voice, a ready laugh, and a predilection for superlatives. His chief interests outside of music and the promotion of music are food, photography, and golf.

References: *Guardian* p10 Je 2 '79 por; *Holiday* 40:91+ Jl '65 por; *Los Angeles Times* C p63 N 14 '82 por; *N Y Daily News* p13+ Jl 1 '62 por; *N Y Post* p37 Jl 21 '70 por; *N Y Times* III p6 Je 27 '82 por; *N Y Times* C p8 Je 8 '84 por; Feather, Leonard. *Encyclopedia of Jazz in the Sixties* (1966), *Encyclopedia of Jazz in the Seventies* (1976); Goldblatt, Burt. *Newport Jazz Festival: The Illustrated History* (1960); *Who's Who in America, 1984-85*

## Weiss, Ted

*Sept. 17, 1927– United States Representative from New York. Address: b. Rm. 2442 Rayburn House Office Bldg., Washington, D.C. 20515*

When Ted Weiss, who had been for fourteen years the acknowledged leader of the liberal element of the New York City Council, won election to the United States Congress in 1976, Edward Ranal observed in the *New York Times* (January 2, 1977) that the legislator would be "sorely missed" because he had been "the conscience of the council," the one who "constantly raised questions of principle." On the floor of the House of Representatives, Weiss, a lawyer by training, has continued to raise questions of principle, often in the face of daunting opposition. Occasionally, his passionate idealism has led him to set off on crusades that even his Democratic colleagues have dismissed as "kamikaze missions." But the singleminded determination with which he has espoused such traditional liberal causes as social safety-net programs for the disadvantaged, civil rights, and an end to the nuclear arms race has won him the overwhelming approval of his constituents in New York's 17th Congressional District, who have repeatedly returned him to office by huge majorities.

The son of Joseph and Pearl Weiss, Theodore S. Weiss was born on September 17, 1927 in a village about fifty miles southeast of Budapest, Hungary. When he was about ten years old, he and his mother and sister fled the Nazis, finally immigrating, in March 1938, to the United States. The family settled in South Amboy, New Jersey, where Ted Weiss attended the public schools. Following his graduation from Hoffman High School in 1946, he enlisted in the United States Army and served a tour of duty in Japan working for the Armed Forces Radio Service. Upon his discharge, with the rank of private first class, in 1947, Weiss enrolled at Syracuse University in New York. He earned his B.A. degree, cum laude, in political science in 1951 and his LL.B. degree a year later. In 1953—the year that he became a naturalized United States citizen—he began his legal career, as a volunteer lawyer for the Legal Aid Society. From 1955 to 1959 Weiss served as an assistant district attorney of New York County. Going into private practice, he was a partner in the law firm Gaffin and Weiss for some eight years before he joined Fuchsberg and Fuchsberg as a legal counsel, in 1970.

During the late 1950s, Weiss became increasingly involved in the burgeoning reform movement in Democratic party politics, teaming up with former First Lady Eleanor Roosevelt and other likeminded individuals to organize the Committee for Democratic Voters. In 1961 he won election to the New York City Council, a post he held for the next fifteen years. The representative of Manhattan's liberal Upper West Side, he was repeatedly reelected by increasing margins of victory as voters came to recognize him as a champion of tenants' rights, civil liberties, and environmental protection. Among other things, he helped to write the city's gun-control law, one of the strictest in the country, and, in his capacity as chairman of the council's committee on environmental protection, its stringent noise-control law. Determined to make the council more productive and more responsive to the needs of the city's residents, he joined forces with five other elected officials—United States Representatives Charles Rangel and Bella Abzug, State Senators Fred Ohrenstein and Carl McCall, and State Assemblyman Al Blumenthal—to open a one-stop citizens' service office on Manhattan's West Side. "The constituent gets the benefit of whatever relevance any one of us has," Weiss explained, as quoted in the New York Times (August 16, 1975). "As for us, we deal with constituent problems once, rather than half a dozen times. It used to be that someone with a problem would go to all of us separately." In recognition of his unflagging efforts in behalf of his fellow New Yorkers, the nonpartisan Citizens Union Research Foundation awarded Weiss its highest rating in each of his successive election campaigns for the city council.

An early and vociferous opponent of United States involvement in the Vietnam war, which he repeatedly denounced as "morally indefensible and militarily untenable," Ted Weiss decided, in 1966, to challenge the five-term incumbent Leonard Farbstein, a "paper liberal," in Weiss's words, who unquestioningly supported President Lyndon B. Johnson's policy of military escalation in Indochina, for the Democratic nomination to the 19th Congressional District seat. Running on a "get out of Vietnam" platform, Weiss lost the June primary by only 151 votes. In response to his charge of voting irregularities, the State Supreme Court ordered a new election, in September. Once again, Weiss lost, but this time by more than 900 ballots. Weiss and Farbstein went head to head for the third time in the 1968 Democratic primary. At least partly because of what he called a "dishonest, hand-tailored" redistricting of the Upper West Side that deprived him of the votes of a large block of Reform Democrats, Weiss went down to defeat by a sizable margin.

Over the next few years, Weiss grew increasingly restless and discouraged because the city council was, in his view, "hemmed in by the mayor and [the] state legislature." By the mid-1970s, he was ready to make another bid for the United States Congress, where the potential for progress was "unlimited." His break came in 1976, when Bella Abzug, who had represented Manhattan's liberal 20th Congressional District for six years, decided to seek the Democratic nomination for the United States Senate. Weiss immediately announced his candidacy for her vacated House seat. In what one analyst called "an unusual show of unity for West Side politics," he won the nomination without opposition.

After Mrs. Abzug lost the senatorial primary, however, a few top-level party leaders, among them Lieutenant Governor Mary Anne Krupsak, unsuccessfully tried to persuade Weiss to step aside—according to some reports, in exchange for a judgeship—to allow the former congresswoman to reclaim her office. Weiss refused. Running on the slogan "The city's future is in Washington's hands," Weiss constructed a platform based on increased federal assistance, including loan guarantees to help New York recover its financial stability, additional operating subsidies for mass transit, and perhaps most important, a federal takeover of all welfare expenditures to encourage people to "stay where they have roots." In the general election in November 1976, he overwhelmed his Republican opponent, Denise T. Weiseman, taking 83 percent of the total vote.

Within days of his taking office in January 1977, Weiss began honoring his campaign pledges. Before the month was out, he petitioned the Senate Banking Committee for a five-year extension of the federal emergency loan that had rescued New York City from the brink of bankruptcy. A few weeks later, he secured a place on the special congressional subcommittee set up to scrutinize President Jimmy Carter's planned overhaul of the nation's welfare system. He also made the first of many efforts to persuade government officials to cancel the controversial Westway project, the mammoth, federally funded interstate highway and real-estate–development scheme planned for Manhattan's West Side. Contending that the multi-billion-dollar project was almost unanimously opposed by West Side residents, he urged the Carter administration to scrap the program, which he said was the "unfortunate result" of "back-room, closed-door decision-making," and use the allocated funds for much-needed road and subway repairs. When a Westway appropriations bill came before the House of Representatives on September 11, 1985, Weiss was among the legislators who voted down the proposal, 287 to 132. It was the first time either house had opposed the project.

Even as a freshman representative, Weiss had a considerable impact on Congress. His membership on the House subcommittees dealing with secondary and vocational education, employment opportunities, and manpower and housing—issues of special interest to his constituents—gave him an important voice in the formulation of domestic social and economic policy in the early years of the Carter administration. Generally speaking, he supported President Carter's plans for welfare and tax reform, a comprehensive, mandatory national health plan, and a coherent federal energy program. He was especially concerned about the safety of the growing number of nuclear power plants. "Technology is not infallible," he said, as quoted in the New York Times (November 11, 1977). "Safeguards and protective devices do not always function according to plan." For that reason he advocated the dismantling of the nuclear-fuel reprocessing plant, which he described as "a nuclear time bomb," in Cattaraugus County, New York, called for a ban on the transport of radioactive materials through densely populated urban areas, and launched a drive for the repeal of the 1957 Price-Anderson Act, which set a cap of $560 million on the total amount of payments that can be awarded to victims of nuclear power plant accidents.

On the basis of his first-term voting record, Weiss ranked among the most liberal of the thirty-nine New Yorkers in the House of Representatives. He was one of only eleven congressmen to receive a rating of 100 percent from the liberal political interest group Americans for Democratic Action and one of only three to receive a rating of zero from the Americans for Constitutional Action, its conservative counterpart. His impeccable liberal voting record in that term and the ones that followed virtually guaranteed his reelection in the 20th Congressional District, a bastion of unalloyed liberalism. Regularly returned to office by majorities of more than 80 percent, Weiss faced the possibility of significant opposition only once—in 1982, after Governor Hugh L. Carey approved a reapportionment plan that put Weiss in the same district as Jonathan Bingham, a respected nine-term Democrat from the Bronx. Rather than face Weiss in a primary, Bingham declined to seek reelection. Later in the year, after undergoing single-bypass heart surgery and the implant of a pacemaker, Weiss eas-

ily won election to the 98th Congress from the newly formed 17th Congressional District, which comprised most of lower Manhattan, much of the West Side, Riverdale, and parts of the northeast Bronx. To make himself more accessible to his new constituents, he soon opened two more district offices in New York, bringing the total number to five. (The average number of district offices for a congressman is two.)

Since Ronald Reagan assumed the presidency in January 1981 with a mandate to reduce government expenditures, Weiss has been a leader in the fight to spare vital social services from the budget cutters' ax. As a member of the House Education and Labor Committee, which had been ordered by the House leadership to trim allocations for social programs by some $12 billion, he reluctantly agreed to pare many of the health and welfare programs he had helped to create rather than turn the job over to the Budget Committee. "We were forced to be executioners, with a gun pointed to our heads, with the knowledge that if we didn't do it, somebody else would do it more savagely . . . ," Weiss told Martin Tolchin in an interview for the New York Times (June 7, 1981). "As much as I'm opposed to these cuts, the people who are looking to us expect that we can give them better representation than the Budget Committee, whose only consideration is the bottom line figures."

Congressman Weiss grudgingly approved reductions in funding for some social welfare programs, but he steadfastly refused to consolidate categorical grants for specific programs into no-strings-attached block grants to state and local governments, as the White House preferred, because, in his words, "block grants would have repealed all the programs." He was particularly incensed by President Reagan's proposal to delegate to the states the responsibility for more than forty programs previously administered by the federal government. As he told a reporter for the New York Times (January 26, 1982), Reagan's so-called "new federalism" was, in his view, a "shift and shaft" program—that is, it "shifted the burden and shafted the recipients."

As the chairman of the House subcommittee charged with monitoring health and welfare programs, Weiss kept a watchful eye on the effects of Reagan administration cutbacks on the poor and elderly. Among other things, he strongly opposed the Reagan administration's plan to implement complicated new food-stamp eligibility rules. "The new regulations presume that every poor person who applies for food stamps may be a cheat," Weiss complained, as quoted in the New York Times (October 31, 1983). He also lashed out at the federal government for failing to follow through on its commitments to house and feed the homeless, denouncing in particular the government's dereliction in executing its plan to adapt surplus government buildings for use as shelters. On the House floor, his concern for the elderly was manifested in his efforts to protect the Social Security benefits of millions of retirees and in his outspoken opposition to the administration's plans to pass on a greater share of spiraling health-care costs to Medicare recipients and to ease nursing home regulations. Among the first to perceive the serious implications of the deadly acquired immune deficiency syndrome (AIDS) epidemic, he introduced bills that created an emergency federal fund for research into the disease's cause and cure and made AIDS victims eligible for coverage under Medicare.

A member of the Congressional Caucus for Women's Issues and the National Commission on Working Women, Weiss cosponsored the Economic Equity Act, which guaranteed women economic equality in the workplace, and he was a staunch supporter of the Equal Rights Amendment, maintaining that only a constitutional amendment can insure equality for women "not just in theory, but in the reality of our daily lives." Troubled by the "feminization of poverty" in recent years, he has tried to protect women, particularly poor or elderly women, from what he sees as unwarranted cuts in social programs. Among other things, he pleaded with his fellow congressmen to preserve the federal funding of abortions and not "relegate the poor to the hands of butchers."

In the area of defense and foreign policy, Weiss has from his first days in Congress consistently opposed increased military appropriations, and he has repeatedly voted against funding for the research and development of such technologically sophisticated weapons systems as the B-1 bomber, the MX missile, and the enhanced-radiation neutron bomb. After President Reagan announced in October 1983 his intention to begin deploying first-strike weapons in Europe, Weiss, a longtime supporter of a mutually verifiable freeze on nuclear weapons stockpiling, cosponsored a joint resolution renouncing the first use of nuclear weapons in any future conflict. Arguing that "nuclear war remains an unacceptable and unthinkable response," Weiss told his constituents, in a newsletter dated October 20, 1983, "It is time to bring some sanity to the arms race by declaring we will not be the first to use these weapons."

Named to the House Foreign Affairs Committee in February 1983, Weiss has made humanitarian aid a special concern. Among other things, he submitted legislation providing additional food assistance to drought-stricken areas of Africa and requested the Reagan administration to grant temporary political asylum to Salvadoran and Guatemalan refugees. Regarding President Reagan's hard line toward Communist interference in the western hemisphere, Weiss has often questioned the administration's "lawless" policies toward Nicaragua and has resisted attempts to increase American military involvement there and in other Latin American countries. He has repeatedly demanded, for example, that the United States withdraw its support from the leaders of El Salvador until they "clean up their act," and in September 1983, on the tenth anniversary of General Augusto Pinochet's military takeover of the Chilean government, he

introduced a resolution urging the United States to cut off economic assistance to Chile until the country was returned to democratic rule.

Weiss especially objected to efforts to commit American combat troops to the field in Nicaragua, calling it "a dangerous blueprint for American involvement" similar to the Gulf of Tonkin resolution that legitimized United States military involvement in Vietnam. After President Reagan ordered the invasion of the island of Grenada on October 25, 1983 by United States Marines and Rangers and a small force from six Caribbean nations, Weiss cosponsored a resolution to impeach the president on the grounds that he had usurped the power of Congress to declare war, violated treaty obligations, and disregarded the First Amendment rights of the American people by blocking press coverage. "In ordering the invasion of Grenada," Weiss explained, as quoted in the Wall Street Journal (May 17, 1984), "Ronald Reagan has adopted the tactic of the Japanese attack on Pearl Harbor as the new American standard of behavior."

Despite his occasional public outbursts in defense of liberal causes, Ted Weiss has been described by his associates and friends as having a low-key personal style and a dry sense of humor. He enjoys playing tennis, going to movies, and reading biography and history (his favorite author is Barbara Tuchman), but he has little leisure time for those pleasures. His profound interest in and dedication to his work removes it from the realm of duty. Even when Congress is out of session, Weiss is said to put in long days meeting with constituents in one of his several district offices or inspecting public senior-citizen and day-care facilities. In 1980 Weiss married Sonya M. Hoover, a press officer for the deputy attorney general for Medicaid fraud control for the state of New York. The congressman has two grown sons, Thomas D. and Stephen R., from an earlier marriage that ended in divorce.

References: N Y World-Telegram F 17 '66 por; N Y Times p29+ Ja 10 '77 por; Congressional Directory, 1984; Who's Who in America, 1984–85; Who's Who in American Jewry, 1980; Who's Who in the East, 1985–86

---

## Weizsäcker, Carl Friedrich von

(vīts' ze-kər)

June 28, 1912– West German physicist; philosopher. Address: b. Max-Planck-Institut für Sozialwissenschaften, Mathildenstrasse 16, 8130 Starnberg, West Germany; h. Alpenstrasse 15, 8135 Söcking, West Germany

Scientist and philosopher, peace activist and committed Christian, Carl Friedrich von Weizsäcker is the founder and former director of the Max Planck

*Carl Friedrich Weizsäcker*

Institute for Research into Conditions of Life in the Scientific-Technological World, in Starnberg, West Germany. Culminating a distinguished, multifaceted career, Weizsäcker's work at the Max Planck Institute reflected his concern that science, religion, and philosophy must correlate with the political world, in view of the growing threat of nuclear holocaust. For Weizsäcker, science, religion, philosophy, and political activism are complementary, and he has criticized the compartmentalization and fragmentation of human research as having contributed to the dangerous state of the contemporary world.

Internationally recognized for his seminal contributions to astrophysics, Weizsäcker has in recent years been gaining a global reputation as a philosopher and peace activist as well. In reviewing a volume of his collected essays entitled *Der Garten des Menschlichen: Beiträge zur geschichtlichen Anthropologie* (The Garden of All Things Human; Contributions to Historical Anthropology, 1977), Hans Jürgen Baden wrote in *Die Welt* (February 4, 1978): "These reflections are the work of one of the most universal thinkers of our time, . . . a physicist, . . . cultural critic, philosopher, and mystic. . . . Weizsäcker completely undermines our tendency to think in fixed categories, the mental inflexibility which is at the root of so many misunderstandings."

Carl Friedrich Freiherr von Weizsäcker (the designation "Freiherr" is a German title of lower aristocracy roughly equivalent to "Baron") was born on June 28, 1912 in the north-German port city of Kiel to Ernst Freiherr and Marianne (von Graevenitz) von Weizsäcker. His great-grandfather Karl Heinrich von Weizsäcker was a noted Protestant theologian; his grandfather Carl Freiherr von Weizsäcker served as the last minister president—

or prime minister—of the kingdom of Württemberg, from 1906 to 1918; his uncle Dr. Viktor Freiherr von Weizsäcker was the founder of psychosomatic medicine; and his younger brother, Richard Freiherr von Weizsäcker, became president of the Federal Republic of Germany in June 1984 after serving three years as the governing mayor of West Berlin. Another brother, Heinrich, was killed in World War II. Weizsäcker's father served during the Nazi regime as state secretary in Joachim von Ribbentrop's foreign ministry and as German ambassador to the Vatican. After World War II, Ernst Freiherr von Weizsäcker was convicted of war crimes at the Nuremberg trials and served two years of a seven-year prison term, despite his plea that he had helped Jews to escape persecution and that he had planned to take part in a plot against Hitler. According to Carl Friedrich von Weizsäcker, his father stayed in office during the Hitler regime with the hope of being able to help restore peace, which would require the elimination of Hitler. "If I have inherited my own insistence for peace, it is from my father," Weizsäcker has recalled.

Keenly interested in both religion and science while still a child, Carl Friedrich von Weizsäcker recounted the story of his encounter with Christianity at the age of eleven in his *Der Garten des Menschlichen.* "I read the Sermon on the Mount . . . ," he wrote, "and immediately thought to myself: 'If this is true, then our whole life is wrong, even the life of those I love and respect.'" His embrace of religion stimulated his curiosity about the natural universe, and at the age of twelve he asked for an atlas of the stars and planets that would show their positions at any given day and hour. Enthralled with the idea of seeking the hand of God in the laws of physics, he concluded that religion and science are not opposites but complements of a basic unity.

Weizsäcker attended the University of Berlin in 1929 as an undergraduate, then did graduate work in physics and mathematics at the universities of Göttingen and Copenhagen, and obtained his doctor of philosophy degree from the University of Leipzig in 1933. He considers his studies under Werner Heisenberg and Niels Bohr as seminal in the development of his career as a physicist, and he remembers his nightly discussions with a fellow student of Bohr in Copenhagen, Edward Teller, who like himself later became a renowned and publicly outspoken physicist, but whose advocacy of strong nuclear defense differs from Weizsäcker's insistence on peaceful solutions that might eventually lead to nuclear disarmament.

From 1934 to 1936, Weizsäcker worked as an assistant at the University of Leipzig's Institute of Theoretical Physics, obtaining his *Habilitation,* or formal admission to the faculty, in the latter year. From 1936 to 1942 he taught theoretical physics at the University of Berlin and at the same time worked at Berlin's Kaiser Wilhelm Institute with the nuclear physicists Otto Hahn and Lise Meitner. In 1937 he developed what became known as the

Weizsäcker formula for measuring the energy content of the atomic nucleus. That same year, he published the book *Die Atomkerne* (The Atomic Nuclei).

During the World War II years, Weizsäcker was one of the few on whom devolved the task of attempting to develop an atomic bomb for Germany. He later recalled those years in a May 1958 essay in the *Bulletin of the Atomic Scientists*, writing that German physicists were "spared the last, hard decision," because, fortunately, it was not in their capacity to create an atom bomb. Nonetheless, they were under the illusion that the Americans could not manufacture the bomb either, and they were unaware of strenuous efforts in the United States to develop it, motivated by the fear that the Germans would build it first. "This was a grave error," Weizsäcker observed. "Otherwise we would have probably made a desperate effort to make it known to the West that we in Germany were not making them." From 1942 to 1945, Weizsäcker served as an associate professor of theoretical physics at the University of Strasbourg in German-occupied France. His writings during that period included the book *Zum Weltblick der Physik* (1943), later published in English as *The World View of Physics* (Routledge, 1952).

It was during the war years that Weizsäcker began to outline his holistic philosophy of science in his book *Die Geschichte der Natur* (1948), published in English as *The History of Nature* (Univ. of Chicago Press, 1949). It included chapters on the physical sciences, outlining for the lay reader contemporary findings in nuclear physics, astrophysics, and geology, and examining man in nature and his relationship to it.

Weizsäcker's theme in *The History of Nature*, one that he continued to pursue in his later work, involved the rejection of the dichotomy of nature versus man, of the natural sciences versus the humanities. In it he postulates the reintegration of man in the natural world, recognizing man's dependence on nature as well as the dependence of the concepts of nature on man. Weizsäcker views that as the beginning of the integration of science into a whole that is not separate from either history or religion. The fact that the book was published, in Switzerland, during the war years lends special weight to Weizsäcker's words in his introduction. "The scientist," he wrote, "is never only a scientist. He is at the same time a living human being. . . . He has to ask himself: What is the meaning of my inquiry for the lives of my fellows?—Can I answer for the effects that my work has upon the life of mankind?"

At the end of the war, Weizsäcker was briefly interned by British occupation authorities because of his work on the atom bomb. Then, in 1946, he was appointed a professor of physics at the University of Göttingen and became a department head at the Max Planck Institute for Physics in that city. Over the next few years, he earned an international reputation with his work on the evolution of the earth and his research into nuclear fusion in the interior of stars. Among his publications during his years at Göttingen was the textbook *Physik der Gegenwart* (1952) on which he collaborated with Johannes Julifs. It was published in Great Britain as *Contemporary Physics* (Hutchinson, 1957) and in the United States as *The Rise of Modern Physics* (Braziller, 1957).

In 1957, at the height of his career as one of West Germany's outstanding theoretical physicists, Weizsäcker left the University of Göttingen, to accept a chair at the University of Hamburg in the department of philosophy. To those who knew only of his ground-breaking work in physics, that seemed like an abrupt change of vocation. For Weizsäcker, however, it represented a continuation of the underlying theme of his life's work, the search for an understanding of the meaning, order, and unity of creation.

In a series of Gifford Lectures delivered at the University of Glasgow in 1959-60, Weizsäcker further developed his philosophy of science. The lectures, which were later published as *The Relevance of Science: Creation and Cosmogony* (Harper and Row, 1964), trace the historical development of concepts of cosmogony in the Western world, culminating in modern science and "scientism," which, according to Weizsäcker, has assumed the role of the dominant religion of our time. Weizsäcker is opposed to such a scientism, with its priestly caste of technological experts.

It was also during the late 1950s that Weizsäcker entered the public arena to debate questions of war and peace. The West German government had been considering equipping its army with nuclear weapons, and in March 1957 Weizsäcker declared his opposition to that plan in a national radio broadcast. With his colleague Walther Gerlach, Weizsäcker circulated a manifesto among leading German physicists, of whom sixteen signed, including the Nobel Prize winners Max Born, Otto Hahn, Werner Heisenberg, and Max von Laue. The so-called "manifesto of the eighteen" pledged that the scientists would not participate in any fashion in the production, testing, or use of atomic weapons. In 1959 Weizsäcker was one of the cofounders of the Association of German Scientists, whose aim it was to focus on the danger of nuclear war and the problem of human survival.

Although Weizsäcker did not advocate unilateral Western disarmament and, in fact, acknowledged the deterrent effect of nuclear weapons to war, he noted in the 1958 article for the *Bulletin of the Atomic Scientists* that "the peace of the hydrogen bomb is at best only the incapacity to make war. It freezes conflicts instead of thawing them." In February 1962 he was one of eight prominent members of the German Evangelical Church who signed a memorandum asking the West German government to renounce all claims to the formerly German territory east of the Oder-Neisse line, which had gone to Poland and the Soviet Union at the end of World War II.

Weizsäcker's zeal for digging to the roots of human conflicts, large and small, led him to found in

1970 a "think tank" that was known as the Max-Planck-Institut zur Erforschung der Lebensbedingungen der wissenschaftlich-technischen Welt (Max Planck Institute for Research into Conditions of Life in the Scientific-Technological World). Located in an idyllic Alpine setting, near an old castle on Lake Starnberg, the institute is one of the components of the Max Planck Society for the Advancement of Science, the post–World War II successor to the Kaiser Wilhelm Institute. Named after the originator of the quantum theory of physics, the Max Planck Society operates over fifty separate institutes throughout West Germany.

At the Starnberg institute, Weizsäcker charted a course of investigating the relationship between society and its internal social problems, the economy, and the issues of war and peace. He set up two work groups: the first, headed by himself, to take up political research, philosophy, and science; and the second, under the renowned Frankfurt School sociologist Jürgen Habermas, to study the social and economic dimensions of contemporary society and its conflicts. Research issues tackled by the institute in its first few years included the global population explosion, world hunger, the role of science, and problems of nonindustrialized countries. "For every problem of our society a reasonable solution is possible, provided there is the will to deal with it reasonably," Weizsäcker later declared, during a Christopher Emmet Memorial Lecture that he delivered in New York City.

While the institute assumed the role of an informed, critical public, Weizsäcker had the ear of politicians more directly through his position on the governing board of the German Association for Peace and Conflict Research, an advisory body to the West German government that had been founded by Gustav Heinemann. And throughout the 1970s, Weizsäcker continued to write and speak on the nuclear threat, on the dangers to freedom posed by economic inequities, on the problems of environmental pollution, and the challenge faced by Western capitalist democracy to promote social progress in the developing countries of the third world.

Weizsäcker's published works during those years included his timely Wege in der Gefahr: Eine Studie über Wirtschaft, Gesellschaft, und Kriegsverhütung (1978), translated into English as The Politics of Peril: Economics, Society, and the Prevention of War (Seabury Press, 1978), in which he concluded that humanity was still facing, as it had for thousands of years, the danger of large-scale warfare. To alleviate the peril of nuclear conflict, Weizsäcker pressed publicly for a halt to nuclear proliferation, through the global recognition that nuclear weapons do not guarantee the safety of the world. At the same time, he maintained a sobering view of the causes of armed conflict, focusing on a psychological basis for war in man's attempts to escape self-dissatisfaction through projecting aggression on to others. Ultimately, he argued from a religious viewpoint, "man can find out about himself if he is prepared to open his mind and heart to a power greater than himself," as he put it in an interview with Udo Reiter, published in the German Tribune (May 18, 1980).

The relationship between religion and science dominated many of Weizsäcker's writings in the 1970s. He had not ceased his work as a physicist when he became a professional philosopher. In fact, it was in 1966 that he broke new ground by expanding on Heisenberg's theory on a fundamental field, incorporating a new elementary unit of matter, Ur. Since for Weizsäcker religion and science stand in a mutual relationship with each other, his continued theoretical development as a physicist involved him ever more deeply in the philosophy of religion.

In 1971, Weizsäcker wrote a lengthy introduction to a work by Pandit Gopi Krishna published in English as The Yogi and the Physicist: The Biological Basis of Religion and Genius (Harper & Row, 1971). According to Weizsäcker, it was his meditations on the psychological implications of the quantum theory in physics that led to his interest in Indian thought. He pointed out that modern theoretical physics alters man's conception of the dimensions of space and time and suggests a relationship between matter and energy that is similar to the Indian concept of prana—a form of energy that is simultaneously physical and psychic. In Der Garten des Menschlichen (1977), Weizsäcker further discussed the profound effect on his world view of Indian religious philosophy. Hans Jürgen Baden wrote of the book that "there are passages . . . which sound strange and almost indecent coming from a natural scientist. Yet these passages open up a new dimension which does not contradict scientific thinking, but extends its boundaries by non-rational means." Weizsäcker believes that meditation is a means of "bringing science to its true level" and that its goal is the experience of unity.

Weizsäcker's concept of unity, recurrent throughout his scientific and philosophical writings, is the theme of his twelve-year collection of essays Die Einheit der Natur (1971), published in English as The Unity of Nature (Farrar, Straus, 1980). Some thirty-five years had passed since Weizsäcker first addressed himself to the problem of the unity of science in The History of Nature, and he returned to that theme here, in the context of modern physics, cybernetics, and classical philosophy.

The idea of the unity of nature, Weizsäcker argues, cannot be fully articulated as long as science remains fragmented in specialized disciplines. Philosophy is in his view indispensable for the process of integration of the natural and social sciences because it poses the questions that lead to deeper insights. "If philosophical questioning leads to insights of sufficient depth," Weizsäcker wrote in the introduction to The Unity of Nature, "it will produce a conceptual fusion of the specialized disciplines; i.e., a more highly integrated science." Such an integration of all the disciplines of human understanding has been the vision that has motivated Weizsäcker's life work.

In mid-1980, Weizsäcker stepped down from his post as director of the Max Planck Institute for Research into Conditions of Life in the Scientific-Technological World (now the Max Planck Institute for Social Sciences), but he continued to be associated with the institute in an emeritus capacity. His recent published works include *Deutlichkeit: Beiträge zu politischen und religiösen Gegenwartsfragen* (Clarity: Contributions to Contemporary Political and Religious Questions, 1978); *Der Bedrohte Friede: Politische Aufsätze 1945–1981* (The Threatened Peace: Political Essays 1945–81, 1981); and *Wahrnehmung der Neuzeit* (Observations on Modern Times, 1983).

Weizsäcker is much in demand as a panelist for discussions on such topics as disarmament or nuclear power and as a lay preacher, delivering sermons from the pulpit. The awards and honors he has received testify to his wide-ranging, multifaceted accomplishments. They include the Max Planck medal (1957 and 1966); the Goethe prize of the city of Frankfurt (1958); the grand cross of the Order of Merit of the Federal Republic of Germany, with star (1959); the peace prize of the order Pour le Mérite (1961); the peace prize of the German book trade (1963); the Arnold Reymond prize for physics (1965); the Wilhelm Boelsche gold medal (1965); the Erasmus prize (1969); an honorary doctorate from the University of Tübingen (1977); the Ernst Hell-

mut Vits prize (1980); and the Heine prize of the city of Düsseldorf (1983). In 1979 he turned down a nomination to run as an independent candidate for the presidency of West Germany.

Carl Friedrich von Weizsäcker was married on March 31, 1937 to Gundalena Wille. They have four children: Carl Christian, an economics professor at the University of Bern; Ernst Ulrich, director of the European Institute for Environment Policy in Bonn; Heinrich, a lecturer in mathematics in Munich; and Elisabeth Raiser, who is married to a former deputy secretary general of the World Council of Churches in Geneva, now a professor of ecumenical theology at the University of Bochum. Weizsäcker's recreational activities include walking and playing chess. An intense-looking man with deep-set, piercing eyes and white hair, he was described by Paul Hübner in the *Rheinische Post* (December 8, 1983) as having "personal charm and a power of moral conviction," and as "a skeptical optimist" who "hopes that the tenuous balance of power will hold until better ways of preventing war are found."

*References: German Tribune p4 My 8 '77 por, D 25 '83 por; Reporter 18:15 Ap 3 '58; Scala International 6:18 Je '70 por, no.9 '77 por; Contemporary Authors vol 105 (1982); International Who's Who, 1985–86; Wer ist Wer? (1983)*

---

## Weizsäcker, Richard von

vîts´ze-kər

*Apr. 15, 1920– President of the Federal Republic of Germany. Address: b. "Villa Hammerschmidt," Bonn, Federal Republic of Germany*

On May 23, 1984 a federal assembly elected Richard von Weizsäcker sixth president of the Federal Republic of Germany, succeeding Karl Carstens for a five-year term that began on July 1. A member of a patrician family distinguished for its theologians, educators, statesmen, and scientists, Weizsäcker was a businessman and lawyer, and a lay leader of the Evangelical church, before entering politics as a member of the Christian Democratic Union. Elected to the Bundestag in 1969, Weizsäcker was its vice-president from 1979 to 1981 and then served for three years as West Berlin's governing mayor. Although the West German presidency is largely ceremonial, it remains a post of considerable distinction, since it symbolizes national unity. As a highly respected public figure who has provoked little controversy during his varied career, Weizsäcker seemed to Germany's leading statesmen who selected him an ideal choice for the position. In 1984 a writer for the conservative French newspaper *Le Figaro* called him "the moral conscience of a Germany in uproar."

Richard Freiherr von Weizsäcker ("Freiherr" is the approximate equivalent of "Baron") was born in a castle on the family estate in Stuttgart on April 15, 1920, the youngest of the four children of Ernst Freiherr von Weizsäcker and the former Marianne von Graevenitz. On his father's side, he is a great-grandson of the noted Protestant theologian and chancellor of Tübingen University, Karl Heinrich von Weizsäcker; a grandson of the last minister president of the Kingdom of Württemberg, Carl Freiherr von Weizsäcker; and a nephew of the pioneer of psychosomatic medicine, Dr. Viktor Freiherr von Weizsäcker. His surviving brother is the noted physicist and philosopher Carl Friedrich von Weizsäcker. Another brother, Heinrich, was killed in combat shortly after the outbreak of World War II. Weizsäcker's father, a former naval officer who had begun his career as a diplomat under the Weimar Republic, served as state secretary of the German foreign office and ambassador to the Vatican during the Nazi regime. Convicted of war crimes at the Nuremberg tribunal after World War II because of his position in the government, he served about two years of a seven-year term of imprisonment, despite his claim, reiterated in his *Memoirs* (1951), that he had been an opponent of Hitler. Winston Churchill reportedly regarded the judgment against Ernst von Weizsäcker as a "fatal error."

As a diplomat's son, Richard von Weizsäcker spent his early years at the locations to which his father was assigned, attending schools in Basel, Bern, Copenhagen, and Oslo. After completing his *Abitur* at the Bismarck Gymnasium in Berlin in 1937, he studied law and history for a year, in Grenoble, France and at Oxford University. In 1938 he joined the German Wehrmacht as a member of the ninth Potsdam infantry regiment, which was imbued with the traditions of the Prussian aristocracy. At the outbreak of World War II in 1939 he took part in the invasion of Poland. Later he fought in the Russian campaign and was wounded several times. By that time, Weizsäcker seems to have developed a marked distaste for Nazism, and several of his close friends were implicated in the abortive anti-Hitler plot in 1944.

Demobilized at the end of the war, with the rank of reserve captain, Weizsäcker resumed his law studies in 1945 at the University of Göttingen, taking time out in 1947 to help in the defense of his father at the Nuremberg trials, as an assistant to attorney Helmut Becker. In 1950 Weizsäcker passed his first state legal examination, in 1953 he qualified as an *Assessor*, or assistant judge, and in 1954 he obtained his doctor of jurisprudence degree.

Discouraged by the treatment of his father, Weizsäcker had meanwhile abandoned any intention of entering the civil service of the newly established Federal Republic of Germany and opted instead for private industry. In 1950 he joined the giant steel firm of Mannesman in Düsseldorf as a *Referendar*, or junior barrister, and became director of its economic policy department. In 1958 he was admitted as a partner in the banking house of Waldthausen and Company in Essen. Then, in 1963, he became managing director of the pharmaceutical firm of C. A. Boehringer Sohn in Ingelheim on the Rhine. Weizsäcker's business associations have also included membership on the board of directors of a leading life insurance company. In 1967 he left industry to devote himself full time to church affairs.

In keeping with his family's tradition of liberal Protestantism, Weizsäcker has been involved in church affairs since his youth. In 1962 he was admitted to the presidium of the *Evangelischen Kirchentag*—the standing conference of Evangelical churches— and became active in its synod and its council. Elected in 1964 to succeed Reinhold von Thadden-Trieglaff as president of the *Kirchentag*, he served in that post until August 1970. He also became a member of the executive committee of the World Council of Churches in 1968 and of the council of the Evangelical Church in Germany in 1969. His efforts while president of the *Kirchentag* to forge unity among Christians of East and West Germany brought him occasionally under attack from both left and right. In 1979 Weizsäcker played an important ecumenical role in helping to organize West Germany's first Protestant-Catholic church conference.

According to an article by Joachim Nawrocki in the English edition of *Scala* (no. 7-8, 1984), Weizsäcker's political position is couched in his Christian view of life, but he does not regard the Bible as a manual for political action. He warns against religious fundamentalism, religious impatience, and intolerance. He has often regretted the church's failure throughout German history, and he believes that the reason for that failure lies in ignoring the overriding interests of society as a whole. For this reason he has always advocated cooperation with the Catholic Church.

A relative latecomer to politics, Weizsäcker joined the dominant Christian Democratic Union (CDU) in 1954 because of his commitment to Christianity and to free-market economic policies, but he did not take an active role until more than a decade later. In 1965 Helmut Kohl, then the CDU parliamentary leader in the Rhineland-Palatinate, tried unsuccessfully to persuade him to run as a candidate for the federal Bundestag, but in 1966 Weizsäcker agreed to become a member of the CDU federal executive. When the Federal Republic's president, Heinrich Lübke, announced his forthcoming retirement in November 1968, Weizsäcker was nominated as a CDU candidate for the post, but he was narrowly defeated by Gerhard Schröder, who in turn lost in the final balloting in March 1969 to the Social Democrat Gustav Heinemann.

In the September 1969 parliamentary elections, which brought into power a coalition of Social Democrats and Free Democrats under Chancellor Willy Brandt, Weizsäcker was for the first time elected to the Bundestag, as a CDU candidate from the Rhineland-Palatinate. Since the CDU and its Bavarian affiliate, the Christian Social Union (CSU), were now for the first time excluded from the government of the Federal Republic, Weizsäcker entered the Bundestag as a member of the parliamentary opposition and was reelected in 1972, 1976, and 1980.

As a member of the CDU-CSU executive in the Bundestag beginning in 1969, Weizsäcker was the faction's parliamentary spokesman on questions involving Berlin and relations with East Germany. From 1972 to 1979 he was deputy chairman of the CDU-CSU Bundestag faction. Although he occasionally criticized the Brandt government's policies, he often struck a conciliatory note, and his speeches in the Bundestag debates were usually marked by intellectual distinction. In 1972 he was one of only four members of the opposition to support the nonaggression treaties with the USSR and Poland that highlighted Brandt's *Ostpolitik* of détente with the Soviet bloc. It was largely as a result of his efforts that most CDU-CSU members abstained in the voting on the treaties instead of opposing them outright, thereby making their ratification easier.

In May 1973, following the resignation of the CDU-CSU parliamentary chairman, Rainer Barzel, Weizsäcker was one of three candidates for the post, but he was defeated, along with Gerhard Schröder, by Karl Carstens, who received 131 of the 219 votes cast. A year later, Weizsäcker was once more talked into running for the West German presidency, in view of the impending retirement of Gustav Heinemann, but he was defeated, by a vote of 530 to 498, by the Free Democrat Walter Scheel.

As chairman from 1972 to 1977 of the CDU's commission on basic principles, Weizsäcker played a key role in the drafting of a party manifesto, completed in June 1976, which has remained in force. His own political views are flexible and pragmatic, and he has never been identified with any particular wing of the CDU. Keeping a healthy skepticism toward political parties, whose policies, he once wrote, "are restricted by the election date," Weizsäcker believes that government should take responsibility for legal protection and for such social matters as education, but that the main emphasis should always be on the "self-help and self-responsibility" of the citizen.

In September 1978 Weizsäcker was nominated as the CDU candidate for the post of governing mayor of West Berlin by the party leadership, to challenge the Social Democratic–Free Democratic coalition which had long dominated the city's government. He was elected to the West Berlin legislature in March 1979 but lost out in the mayoral contest, since the CDU polled only 44.4 percent of the vote, while the governing coalition, under the incumbent Social Democratic governing mayor, Dietrich Stobbe, won with a combined vote of 50.8 percent.

On his return to Bonn, Weizsäcker was nominated for the vice-presidency of the Bundestag, but his candidacy was challenged because of his dual mandate as a member of the Bundestag and of the West Berlin legislature. That challenge disappeared when he agreed to give up his Berlin seat. On June 21, 1979 Weizsäcker was elected to the Bundestag vice-presidency, with 272 votes in his favor, 177 against him, and thirty-seven abstentions.

When in January 1981 Dietrich Stobbe was compelled as a result of a financial scandal to step down as governing mayor of West Berlin, Weizsäcker saw a possible opportunity to take over the leadership of that beleaguered city. Elected on March 21, 1981 as chairman of the West Berlin CDU, he resigned as Bundestag vice-president shortly afterwards. Meanwhile, Hans-Jochen Vogel, who had been chosen by the Social Democratic leadership to succeed Stobbe, tried through various reforms to undo some of the damage to his party that had resulted from the scandal, but, unable to keep the Social Democrats in power in West Berlin, he was forced to relinquish his office after less than four months. In the election of May 10, 1981—called two years ahead of schedule at the Christian Democrats' insistence—some 85.7 percent of West Berlin's 1.5 million voters went to the polls, giving the CDU, with Weizsäcker as its standard-bearer, a plurality of 47.9 percent. The Social Democrats, with only 38.4 percent of the vote, lost control of West Berlin's government for the first time since 1954.

On June 11, 1981 the West Berlin legislature formally elected Weizsäcker governing mayor by a vote of sixty-nine to sixty-one, with two abstentions, and on the same day he was sworn in at the head of the ten-member senate, or municipal government. Although he failed to command an absolute majority, Weizsäcker managed to govern effectively with the support of several Free Democrats. In March 1983 the CDU and the Free Democrats formally established a coalition in West Berlin.

As a "man of the middle," Weizsäcker seemed ideally suited to occupy West Berlin's city hall—the Schöneberg Rathaus—at the crossroads of East and West, and he managed to impose some measure of stability on the city's divisive elements, including the often divergent liberal and conservative wings of his own CDU organization. He gained the respect of West Berlin's huge middle class and its army of pensioners, and he maintained amicable relations with the city's Jewish survivors of Nazism. He tried to reduce hostility between native Germans and Turkish migrant workers, and he even achieved some rapport with Berlin's violent and unruly countercultural youth.

During his three years as West Berlin's governing mayor, Weizsäcker introduced reforms in such areas as health, education, child care, traffic control, law enforcement, and combating unemployment; he also involved his administration in high-technology ventures as a means of improving West Berlin's troubled economy. Continuing Vogel's efforts to alleviate the city's shortage of residential housing, Weizsäcker set up an extensive housing construction program and placated a squatters' movement made up of militant youths by not only negotiating with them but also in some cases by granting them rental contracts for the condemned buildings they occupied. The West Berlin correspondent of the weekly *Die Zeit* summed it all up when he wrote that Weizsäcker brought "serenity, magnanimity, and breadth of thought" to his post.

In an unprecedented move for a governing mayor of West Berlin, Weizsäcker visited East Germany's Communist party chief, Erich Honecker, in September 1983 and held cordial negotiations with him on environmental questions and other topics of mutual interest, though he rejected any compromises on basic principles. Weizsäcker does not regard the reunification of Germany as a realistic goal, but he believes that the now sovereign eastern and western sectors are equally German. In his speeches and writings—including his recent book *Die deutsche Geschichte geht weiter* (German History Goes Forward, 1983)—Weizsäcker insists that citizens of the Federal Republic should regard themselves as an integral part of the Western alliance while recognizing that they have special interests in the East. As for relations with the USSR, Weizsäcker said in a speech in early 1983: "We should not blame the Soviet Union for representing its interests in as tough and skillful a way as possible. Our contribution must be to seek an agreement without provocation and with persistent clarity."

In November 1983 CDU leader Helmut Kohl, who had replaced Helmut Schmidt as chancellor of West Germany in October 1982, nominated Weizsäcker for the presidency of the Federal Republic of Germany, to succeed Karl Carstens, who had announced his intention to retire. Kohl saw the need for a person who transcended narrow party concerns to occupy that prestigious post in the interest of national unity, and Hans-Jochen Vogel, now the parliamentary leader of the Social Democrats, agreed that his party would not nominate a candidate of its own to oppose Weizsäcker in the presidential election. Although Weizsäcker had declared in 1981 that he considered Berlin to be his lifetime mission, he agreed to accept his candidacy for the federal presidency.

At the Beethoven Hall in Bonn, on May 23, 1984 a *Bundesversammlung*, or federal assembly, consisting of the 520 members of the Bundestag and the representatives of the parliaments of the ten West German states and West Berlin, elected Weizsäcker with 832 of its 1,017 valid votes. In so doing, it gave him the largest majority attained by a West German presidential candidate since Theodor Heuss was elected to that office in 1954. His sole opponent, the seventy-three-year-old writer Luise Rinser, who received sixty-eight votes as the candidate of the environmentalist and antinuclear Green party, was the first to congratulate him on his victory. On July 1, 1984 he was formally sworn in for a five-year term as the sixth president of the Federal Republic of Germany.

During his first eighteen months in office, while performing his ceremonial duties, Weizsäcker served as host to El Salvador's President José Napoleon Duarte, Romania's Communist party chief Nicolae Ceausescu, Tanzanian President Julius K. Nyerere, and other visiting dignitaries. Countries to which he has made state or semi-official visits include Jordan, Egypt, Finland, the Netherlands, Austria, Italy, Spain, and the United States. On a state visit in November 1984 to France, where he was honored by President François Mitterrand in a reception at the Elysée Palace, Weizsäcker affirmed Franco-German friendship and assured his hosts of his country's commitment to the Atlantic Alliance and the European Community. There would be "no neutral wandering between worlds" for West Germany, he declared.

Weizsäcker won praise for his stirring speech to the Bundestag on May 8, 1985, the fortieth anniversary of Germany's World War II surrender, commemorating the victims of Nazism, which he called "an aberration in German history." In September 1985 Weizsäcker received Richard R. Burt, who succeeded as United States ambassador to West Germany following the retirement of Arthur F. Burns. In October, he became the first West German president to visit Israel.

Richard Freiherr von Weizsäcker and his wife, the former Marianne Kretschmann, whom he married in 1953, have a daughter, Marianne Beatrice, and three sons, Robert, Andreas, and Fritz. According to a 1981 source, the daughter was at the time studying law, one of the sons was a student of mathematics, another was studying medicine, and the third was attending an art academy. White-haired and aristocratic in bearing, Weizsäcker is described in *Scala* as "an excellent speaker and analytical thinker" with a "playful sense of humor." His favorite leisure activities include "family table tennis," "mountain-climbing before dawn," swimming, playing chess, and collecting icons. He listens to the music of Bach and Schubert, reads Shakespeare, Fontane, Kleist, Stendhal, and Tolstoy, and vacations in Scotland or at his summer home in Bavaria. Among his honors are the Federal Republic's Grand Cross of Merit and the honor prize of the city of Solingen. In 1983 he was awarded the Theodor Heuss prize, and in 1984 the New School for Social Research in New York City conferred an honorary doctorate on him.

*References: Christian Sci Mon p15 D 7 '83 por; German Tribune p3 D 18 '83 por, p3+ Je 3 '84 por, p5 Jl 15 '84 por; N Y Times A p3 My 24 '84 por; N Y Times Mag p25+ Je 25 '85 por; Scala p29 no 11 '81 por, p20+ no 7-8 '84 por, p10+ US-Special '84 pors; International Who's Who, 1985–86; Wer ist Wer? (1983)*

---

## Wick, Charles Z.

*Oct. 12, 1917– Director, U.S. Information Agency (USIA). Address: b. USIA, Office of Director, 301 4th St. SW, Washington, D.C. 20547*

One of President Ronald Reagan's most controversial appointees to high office has been Charles Z. Wick, an old crony and a member of his "kitchen cabinet," who raised millions of dollars in behalf

*Charles Z. Wick*

of the Republican ticket in 1980. As director of the United States Information Agency, the former show-business agent and nursing home operator occupies a post once filled by such distinguished broadcast journalists as Edward R. Murrow and John Chancellor. Responsible for the information-al and cultural programs sponsored in foreign countries by the United States government, Wick has won substantial budget increases for the USIA, which employs more than 7,800 persons, and he has begun a much needed modernization of the communications equipment used at its 206 posts in 126 countries around the globe.

Other aspects of Wick's management, however, have overshadowed those accomplishments. His aggressive personality and emphasis on the USIA's potential as an anti-Soviet propaganda tool have alienated many on the agency's staff, and allega-tions that he has used the USIA to advance the par-tisan, domestic interests of conservative Republicans, among other alleged abuses of his po-sition, have led to congressional criticism of his stewardship.

Charles Z. Wick was born Charles Zwick on Oc-tober 12, 1917 in Cleveland, Ohio. His father was a venture capitalist with investments in heavy in-dustry. Wick received his early education in the Cleveland public-school system and graduated in 1940 with a bachelor of music degree from the Uni-versity of Michigan. He then returned to Cleveland to earn a doctor of jurisprudence degree, granted him in 1943, from the law school of Western Re-serve University, now known as Case Western Re-serve University.

During his years as a student Wick helped to support himself by playing the piano and by ar-ranging music for a dance band that he had orga-nized. While still an undergraduate, he caught the

attention of Tommy Dorsey, who brought him to New York City from time to time to do arrange-ments for his orchestra. The plane flights, stays at luxury hotels, and substantial fees were a heady experience for a collegian. "I never had it so good," Wick recalls. "That $250 was more than people do-ing well made in a month then." After Wick gradu-ated from law school, Dorsey brought him to Los Angeles, where, for the next year, he handled the band's business and legal affairs and coached its vocal group. It was during the same period that Wick legally changed his name by dropping the "Z" from Zwick and adopting it as a middle initial. "In show business, in those days particularly," he has explained, "a little easier name was always the thing you did."

In 1944 Charles Z. Wick joined the influential William Morris agency in New York City, where he worked in the radio department for five years before striking out on his own as a personal agent for such clients as Benny Goodman, Pinky Lee, and Ken Murray and as a lawyer with bases in both New York and London. In 1951 another of his cli-ents, the actress Sarah Churchill, introduced him to her father, the then British Prime Minister Wins-ton Churchill, who retained him to handle the American sales of his multivolume *History of the English-Speaking Peoples*.

Among the pioneers in the new field of televi-sion entertainment, Wick sold programs to televi-sion during the early 1950s through his New York firm, Charles Wick Associates, and he founded the Twickenham studios in London. Collaborating with Scotland Yard's famous detective Robert Fa-bian, whom he met through Winston Churchill, he developed and produced the television series *Fabian of the Yard*, which was shown in Great Britain, the United States, and other countries in the early 1950s. Some of its segments were later re-edited into theatrical motion pictures dealing with Fabian's exploits.

Much to his dismay, Charles Z. Wick's best-remembered production remains the movie, *Snow White and the Three Stooges* (1961). "You'd think all I ever did was *Snow White and the Three Stooges*," he once lamented during an interview. According to Wick, he originally wrote the story for his children and then showed it to his friends, the Three Stooges, after he learned that they owned no residual rights to their series of successful films from the 1930s, 1940s, and 1950s. They liked it, he agreed to put up $400,000 for its production, and Twentieth Century-Fox eventually spent $4 mil-lion on the venture. Although critics refused to take *Snow White and the Three Stooges* very seriously, Wick remembers it as "a very beautiful picture."

In the mid-1950s Charles Z. Wick returned to California, where he was soon involved in new en-terprises with his partner, Ralph Evinrude, the suc-cessful manufacturer of boat motors. The pair had met through Evinrude's wife, Frances Langford, the popular singer, who had formerly employed Wick as her agent. Together, Charles Z. Wick and Ralph Evinrude founded United Convalescent

Hospitals, which eventually became one of the largest chains of nursing homes in the United States.

In 1978 Charles Z. Wick sold his chain of nursing homes for $1.8 million and cut down on his other business activities, though he remained president of his investment firm, Mapleton Enterprises. His declared intention was to take life easier, but motivated by personal and political loyalties, he quickly became involved in raising $15 million for the presidential campaign of Ronald Reagan. (Before 1980, he had registered as an Independent.) Wick's wife, the former Mary Jane Woods, whom he married on December 27, 1947, had become friends with Nancy Reagan when their children attended the same private school in the mid-1950s. Sharing common parental concerns led over the years to the development of an intimate friendship between the Wicks and the Reagans, who regularly observe the holidays, including Christmas Eve, together.

After his victory in the 1980 election, Ronald Reagan named Charles Z. Wick to serve as cochairman of the inaugural committee, along with Robert Gray, a Washington, D.C., public relations executive. Under their aegis, the $8-million inaugural turned out to be the most expensive in American history, including fireworks, band concerts, the traditional parade, and an entertainment gala presided over by Frank Sinatra. The festivities, which would have gladdened the heart of Louis XIV, culminated with nine balls in Washington, D.C., and 100 more across the nation, all connected by closed-circuit television. As invitation coordinator, Mrs. Wick had the difficult and delicate responsibility of getting approximately 150,000 guests ticketed for the various functions.

In the meantime, Charles Z. Wick hoped that President Reagan would recognize his talents and his considerable contributions both during and after the campaign by appointing him director of the International Communication Agency, which had been known as the United States Information Agency (USIA) between its founding in August 1953 and its merger with the Department of State's Bureau of Educational and Cultural Affairs in April 1978. An independent organization within the executive branch, the agency returned to its original name in August 1982. When some of the president's advisers seemed wary of placing Wick, who had no governmental experience, in charge of such sensitive USIA activities as the Fulbright scholarship program and the Voice of America, Reagan allegedly told them, "Charles Wick has worked his ass off for me. He can have anything he wants." On March 6, 1981 the president nominated Wick, and on June 8 the Senate confirmed the choice by voice vote. Attorney General William French Smith swore in Wick on the following day.

Supported by a president who is both an old friend and a veteran of the glitzy world of show business, Wick has thus far won a 42-percent increase in the USIA budget and a commitment for a $1-billion modernization by 1990 of the Voice of America's equipment. His introduction of Worldnet, a satellite system that provides direct video communications between the United States and American embassies around the globe, has been an impressive technical accomplishment that has made possible press conferences between newspersons abroad and American officials in Washington, among other achievements. Wick has also proved adept at raising money in the private sector to make substantial increases in youth and educational exchanges, and he has streamlined some Voice of America programming to make it more attractive to younger audiences.

Another significant contribution of Charles Z. Wick has been his moving of the USIA back from the fringe toward the center of the foreign-policy establishment. Because he attends meetings of the National Security Council and Secretary of State George P. Shultz's morning briefings of senior aides, he is "totally aware of what are the nuances of what's developing, what the emphasis should be, what we should be alert for," as he puts it. Wick believes that his immediate access to policy-making circles became critically important when the USIA was able quickly to produce for Ambassador Jeane Kirkpatrick's use at the United Nations a dramatic ten-minute video presentation documenting, from intercepted Soviet communications, the last minutes of Korean Airlines Flight 7, which was shot down over Soviet territory on September 1, 1983.

Under Charles Z. Wick the USIA has become more aggressive in pursuing what he sees as its roles of explaining American policy and of "refuting the massive Soviet campaign of disinformation and misinformation spread about us and our intentions in the world." Through a Wick initiative known as "Project Truth," the USIA, with support from the State and Defense Departments and the Central Intelligence Agency, has begun producing a monthly publication, "Soviet Propaganda Alert," and provides American posts abroad with quick responses to false rumors about U.S. activities. Likewise, Wick was a driving force behind "Let Poland Be Poland," a major television tribute to that country's resistance to Soviet influence. Thanks to a special waiver from Congress of the regulation that bans the domestic distribution of USIA programs to protect the American people from the propaganda efforts of its own government, "Let Poland Be Poland" was seen in the United States as well as around the globe. The production, which Wick describes as "probably the biggest show in the history of the world," may have reached as many as 385 million people on television and another 165 million on radio.

Despite those impressive accomplishments, Wick's tenure at the USIA has been troubled at times. The director's volatile temper, which he sometimes unleashes at erring subordinates, and such actions as distributing a six-page list of things to do and not to do when dealing with him have alienated many agency employees. But Wick retorts, "As you deal with people, you learn that you can't be just a little bit pregnant. Being nice, you can't operate. You've got to blast through." Some in the government have also taken offense at Wick's prodigal lifestyle. The director, who spent something like 177 days abroad in his first two years in office, flies first-class or by supersonic transport, stays in $300-a-day hotel suites, and moves about by limousine in the company of three or four bodyguards. Wick contends, however, that his practices are consistent with those of chief executive officers in the private sector and that he himself makes up the difference between his actual travel expenses and those normally allowed by the government. He also maintains that the take-home pay from his $69,800 salary does not meet the $4,000-a-month rent that he pays for his Washington residence and that he has spent as much as $20,000 a year out of his own pocket for official entertaining.

According to one associate, Charles Z. Wick suffers from "the awful habit of speaking before he thinks." Aides once sidetracked a Wick proposal to include anti-Soviet jokes, including one about General Secretary Leonid Brezhnev's death, in the compendium of news analyses and newspaper editorials regularly distributed to American embassies. Among other unfortunate public statements, he has charged that the Russians entered World War II late and were saved by the United States, and he has suggested that Prime Minister Margaret Thatcher, who committed British forces to war in the Falkland Islands, opposed American intervention in Grenada because she is a woman. According to Wick, the wealth and ostentation flaunted by some members of the Reagan administration are actually a comfort to the nation's poor, just as glamorous Hollywood films produced in the 1930s were to impoverished Americans during the Depression.

The most serious complaints lodged against Wick, however, have been professional rather than personal in nature. Critics admit that the director has not tampered with the news carried on the Voice of America, except perhaps to make the reports shorter and lighter. Nevertheless, the independent United States Advisory Commission on Public Diplomacy has warned that the increasing stridency of the editorial attacks on Soviet activities may undermine the organization's credibility. His critics also object to the apparent politicization of the supposedly nonpartisan USIA, including his selection for coordinator of news analysis of Philip Nicolaides, a conservative radio commentator who conceives, in his words, of the Voice of America as a "propaganda agency." Nicolaides' departure eased some tension, but a flurry of USIA grants to conservative organizations at the end of fiscal 1982 and the handpicking by Wick's office of more than two dozen senior White House officials, Republican party leaders, and conservative spokesmen for expense-paid speaking engagements abroad reactivated resentment in some quarters.

When the anti-Castro Radio Marti was inaugurated by the Voice of America on May 20, 1985, the eighty-third anniversary of Cuban independence, some news commentators felt that it cast yet another chill on the long Cold War between Cuba and the United States at a time when it had shown some signs of thawing. In immediate retaliation, Fidel Castro responded by suspending—but not revoking—the recent United States–Cuban immigration agreement and by placing a ban on visits to Cuba by Cuban-Americans. Established in response to the lobbying pressures of Castrophobic Cubans living in the United States and named after Jose Marti, the anti-imperialist hero of Cuban independence, the daily broadcasts of Radio Marti purvey an innocuous mixture of news, soap operas, sports, and salsa, rock, and pop. Since it operates under a mandate from Congress to "serve as a consistently reliable and authoritative source of accurate, objective, and comprehensive news," Radio Marti broadcasts very little propaganda in the programs that it beams for almost fifteen hours a day to Cuba.

Wick's personal foibles and his mix of partisan politics with public business have occasionally discomfited the Reagan administration. When the director, who has speculated that he may be a target of the KGB, or Soviet secret police, had a $32,000 security system installed at his home, White House aides saved the president from possible embarrassment by persuading Wick to reimburse the government for $22,000 of that cost. Likewise, Wick's persistent efforts in behalf of a Committee for a New Beginning, which would sponsor programs to support Ronald Reagan's policies, caused so many complaints from businesses pressured to give money that the White House put a stop to the project. Moreover, Wick created a furore with his admission in 1983 that the USIA had hired children of leading figures in the administration, including former Secretary of State Alexander M. Haig Jr. and Secretary of Defense Caspar W. Weinberger, and with his acknowledgment early in 1984 that the USIA, often for partisan or ideological reasons, had excluded from government-sponsored speaking trips ninety-five prominent Americans, including authors James Baldwin and Betty Friedan, former Secretary of Defense James Schlesinger, Senator Gary Hart, and former CIA director Stansfield Turner. Although Wick received much of the blame for "Kiddiegate" and the blacklist, investigations revealed that he was only partly involved in the misdeeds of his zealous underlings, and congressmen praised his efforts to correct the problems.

On December 28, 1983 the New York Times charged that Wick had been taping his own telephone conversations without obtaining the consent of the people with whom he happened to be talking. In the weeks that followed, William Safire, the paper's conservative columnist and a staunch foe of clandestine recording since the days when he worked for the Nixon White House and fell prey to Henry Kissinger's practice of tapping phones to catch those who were passing information to the press, kept up the attack. According to some sources, Safire may have been settling a score with Wick, who had put the blame for the "Kiddiegate" scandal on an old friend of the columnist, dismissed the man, and later obstructed his appointment to a post in the State Department. In any event, Safire and the *Times* had ample proof for their allegations, because transcripts of some taped conversations had been leaked to them.

In his first interview with William Safire and Jane Perlex, a reporter from the *New York Times*, Wick had denied making tapes, but a day later he admitted to taping conversations in 1983 and to forgetting, in a few cases, to ask the permission of the person with whom he was talking. On January 9, 1984 Wick publicly apologized for "doing a very dumb thing." "I now understand," he confessed, "that taping of others without their consent is unfair, invades their privacy, and can lead to other, more dangerous practices." Although Safire later contended that Wick hoped to use the tapes to write his memoirs, the director insisted that he had recorded conversations "solely to insure accuracy and facilitate appropriate follow-through on the topics discussed."

Safire's revelations led to investigations of the director's practices by congressional committees and by the General Services Administration. Reviews of tapes, of approximately 175 transcripts of phone conversations, and of a large volume of Wick's daily notes and instructions eventually showed that he had made recordings from January 1982 until December 1983 and that among those taped without their being aware of it were former president Jimmy Carter, newscaster Walter Cronkite, film actor Kirk Douglas, and the Reagan aides James Baker and Edwin Meese. The investigators discovered, in addition, that Wick's action directly violated the advice given him in 1981 by John W. Sloat, the general counsel of the USIA, and that the transcripts of the conversations included no occasion in which Wick revealed he was taping.

The Foreign Affairs Committee of the House of Representatives recommended that Wick be reprimanded for "a serious lapse in judgment" and the General Services Administration concluded that, although the laws of the District of Columbia did not make such taping illegal, the director had violated a federal regulation for which there was no specific penalty. On the other hand, the Senate Foreign Relations Committee found that Wick acted without malicious intent. Likewise, the state of Florida, where Wick made recordings from a hotel phone, decided that the director acted in ignorance of its law against surreptitious recording and declined to prosecute him. Perhaps most important, Ronald Reagan stood loyally behind Wick, whom he described as doing "a splendid job." "I don't think that Charles Wick is a dishonorable man in any way," the president said. "I can understand his forgetting sometimes when he was talking to people, particularly people that he knew."

Charles Z. Wick is a small, stout man who dresses in custom-made $1,000 suits from London's Savile Row, as befits a multimillionaire who earned more than $500,000 from his investments in 1981 alone and whose family income exceeded $1 million in 1984. Although he was raised as a Jew,

he says that he never gave religion "any more thought than math or science," adding that he does not feel "any empathy with organized religion." His wife, however, is a Protestant who once taught Sunday school in California. The Wicks, who formerly lived in the Holmby Hills district of Los Angeles, currently occupy a twelve-room house in Washington, D.C. Their five grown children are Charles Jr., Douglas, Pamela, Cynthia, and Kimberly.

*References: Broadcasting* p81 D 21 '81 por; *Nations Bsns* 71:64+ Ap '83 pors; *People* 15:85+ Ja 26 '81 pors; *Rolling Stone* p33+ F 2 '84 por; *Washington Post* B p1+ My 11 '82 por, A p2 Ja 1 '84 por, C p1 F 20 '85 por; *Who's Who in America*, 1984–85

## Williams, Joe

*Dec. 12, 1918– Musician. Address: b. Willard Alexander, Inc., 600 Madison Ave., New York City, N.Y. 10021*

After struggling for eighteen years to make a name for himself as a singer, Joe Williams became an "overnight" success in 1955 when he recorded "Everyday I Have the Blues" with Count Basie and his orchestra, the first in a long string of their joint hits. With a style that David Weiss described in the *Chicago Tribune* (August 28, 1983) as "an amalgam of uptown class and downtown sass," Williams has been equally well received since he struck out on his own in 1961 with his repertoire of blues, jazz, ballads, and popular songs. Although the sexagenarian vocalist no longer needs to perform to support himself, he continues to tour widely, appear regularly on television, and record extensively. "People's problems are assuaged a little bit when a performance touches them," Williams has explained. "And that's what our business and our music is all about."

Christened Joseph Goreed, Joe Williams was born in Cordele, Georgia on December 12, 1918 and raised by his mother, Anne, and his grandmother. When he was about three, the family moved to Chicago, where his mother found work as a domestic. A few years later, he began attending the Austin Otis Sexton Elementary School. For recreation, he played baseball, tennis, handball, and soccer, but from the age of ten he spent most of his free time working, selling newspapers or fruits and vegetables or earning fifty cents from the iceman for carrying ice to the upper floors of buildings.

An only child, Williams entertained himself when at home by playing the piano, by reading voraciously ("everything from Reader's Digest to technical medical journals"), and by singing the music he heard at the Methodist church where his mother was the organist and both she and his aunt were choir members. "Even as a child," he once recalled, "that music was in my head—the choir, the harmonies, the dynamics, the beauty of the Negro spirituals, the marvelous voices of the singers." But he also enjoyed listening to the radio, especially Saturday afternoon broadcasts from the Metropolitan Opera in New York; programs featuring the contralto Marian Anderson, the baritones Paul Robeson and Lawrence Tibbett, and the tenor Roland Hayes; and jazz and blues concerts from the Cotton Club in Harlem that were given by such big names as Duke Ellington and Ethel Waters, a singer whose "sophisticated phrasing" influenced Williams.

During the 1930s, Williams, who even as a teenager had a rich baritone voice, founded the singing group The Jubilee Boys, which performed at churches in Chicago. He landed his first regular solo spot at the downtown club Kitty Davis's and was soon earning twenty to thirty dollars a night, mostly in tips, for singing and for cleaning there. As a result, at sixteen Williams felt so confident of his ability to make a living as a singer that he dropped out of Englewood High School after his junior year. "I suddenly felt that I was helping out . . . ," he told Leslie Gourse in an interview for Louis' Children (1984). "Thirty dollars a night! It was fun to bring it home."

The streets and bars of Chicago provided an immediate and vital source of musical inspiration for Williams and other musicians and singers. At that time, the traditional blues, which blacks migrating from the South had brought with them, was quickly evolving into a more sophisticated idiom—urban blues—that was strongly dramatic and very rhythmic. In the vanguard of the movement were a number of singers to whom Williams listened: Pha Terrell, Herb Jeffries, Dan Grissom, Count Basie's vocalist Jimmy Rushing, and perhaps most impor-

tant, Big Joe Turner, who in 1938 interested Williams in and "opened [him] up to" the blues.

Williams was also interested in popular music, and often, at his request, bandleaders performing at the local night spots would let him sing a song or two with them. He had begun to make a name for himself by the time the black trumpet player Johnny Long hired him to sing with his dance band four nights a week. With his repertoire of such standards as "Moonlight and Shadows," "Nagasaki," and "I Got Rhythm," Williams performed with Long's band, among others, at local theaters, clubs, ballrooms, and even skating rinks. In 1937 Jimmie Noone, the New Orleans jazz clarinetist par excellence, took Williams on as a soloist with his band, and soon afterwards Williams was singing ballads for the sophisticated jazz orchestra of Erskine Tate. (During one period, Williams was performing with all three bands.) Through regular broadcasts on the CBS and NBC radio networks in 1938 and 1939 with Tate, Noone, and others, he first gained an audience outside of the Chicago area. His radio experience helped to shape his style, which like that of Big Joe Turner, who influenced him greatly, emphasizes a clean sound, precise articulation of lyrics, and sophisticated and variable phrasing rather than gimmickry or theatrics.

During the late 1930s and early 1940s, Williams sang at the Savoy Ballroom in Chicago, performed with the Les Hite Band on a dance-engagement tour, and joined Coleman Hawkins, the preeminent jazz tenor saxophonist, and his big band for dates at Chicago's Cafe Society and other sites. Leaving Hawkins, he struck out on his own in 1941 to tour the Midwest. Since his singing engagements were not always steady, he took on odd jobs, including selling cosmetics door-to-door, to support himself. One such job, guarding the stage entrance of the Regal Theater in 1943, led to one of his big breaks. He not only met there such jazz luminaries as Duke Ellington, Buddy Rich, Charlie Barnet, and Count Basie, but one day was sent by the theatre manager to join Lionel Hampton, the outstanding jazz percussionist, vibraphonist, and composer, and his band at the Tick Tock club in Boston. Williams stayed on to tour with Hampton that year. Performing with the band at that time were several notable sidemen as well as some promising but virtually unknown musicians: Dinah Washington, who would become one of the most influential blues and jazz singers of that era; pianist Milt Buckner, who later became Hampton's arranger; and trumpet player Joe Newman, who had left college to join the band.

Continuing to sing ballads through the 1940s, he also toured with the Andy Kirk Band and often worked with the Red Saunders Band in Chicago. But the constant stress of not knowing when or where he would be singing next and trying to scrape by in the meantime by working as a porter, scrubbing floors, tending bar, delivering newspapers, or running errands took its toll. In 1947 Williams suffered a nervous breakdown that kept him confined to a Chicago hospital for a year, and though he worked for a while around 1949 with the Jay Burkhardt Orchestra at the Blue Note Club in Chicago and occasionally appeared with the Red Saunders Band, by 1950 he was, by his own admission, "out of music" and was selling Fuller Brush Company products door-to-door.

Nevertheless, Williams still enjoyed listening to the great musicians featured at the Chicago clubs, so when the renowned pianist and bandleader Count Basie began appearing with his sextet at the Brass Rail in 1950, Williams went to hear him every night. To the best of Williams' knowledge, Basie had never heard him sing, but one night he called Williams out of the audience to sit in with his band, perhaps at the suggestion of some of his sidemen who knew him. As the Count laid down the first notes of Duke Ellington's moody ballad "Solitude," Williams began to sing, and he then gave his interpretations of such classics as "Ain't Misbehavin'" and "Honeysuckle Rose." After that appearance, Basie summoned Williams to the stage nightly and at the end of the week handed him fifty dollars out of his own pocket.

Williams performed with Count Basie's Band for the remainder of its ten-week engagement at the Brass Rail, a stint that gave him the motivation to get back into the music business. While Basie continued his tour, Williams remained in Chicago for a nine-month engagement at the Club DeLisa. For the next four years, he performed on his own throughout Chicago, but he kept in touch with Basie and jammed with him whenever he returned to that city. After a joint performance at the Trianon Ballroom in Chicago in late 1954, Basie made a vague offer to Williams to join his big band, but since it was so tentative Williams thought no more about it until a week before Christmas of that year, when he received from the Count a telegraphed money order with a message asking him to join the band in New York City.

Williams did, bringing with him his repertoire of ballads, jazz numbers, and blues classics. During the periods he worked with the bands of Coleman Hawkins, Andy Kirk, and Lionel Hampton, blues songs had been reserved for the bands' female vocalists, and Williams was usually restricted to ballads, but when he struck out on his own again in 1950, he added to his act such blues numbers as "Roll 'Em, Pete," "Shake, Rattle and Roll," and "Cherry Red." "I thought these blues things would fit the Basie band," he recalled in an interview with John S. Wilson for the New York Times (May 23, 1980). "As a matter of fact, Basie asked me to sing some blues that [Jimmy] Rushing had sung with him. But I didn't know them. I really didn't."

As a result, for his first recording session with the band in July 1955 Williams sang the blues tunes with which he was most familiar: "Everyday I Have the Blues," "The Comeback," "In the Evening," and "All Right, Okay, You Win." When a single featuring the first two of those songs (both written by Memphis Slim) was released, it soared up the charts, giving Basie his first big hit in fifteen years and Williams the wide recognition for which

he had worked for so long. In Down Beat's annual poll for 1955, readers named Williams the best male band singer, an honor he would recapture in 1956, and the international critics acclaimed him the best new male singer. The following year, he also won top honors from Rhythm and Blues magazine, and in 1959 he placed first in Billboard magazine's DJ poll.

Quick to give Basie the credit for their success, Williams insisted during his interview with Leslie Gourse for Louis' Children that "Basie was the leader. . . . He called the tunes. He set the tempos, the pacing. Actually he was the catalyst of the presentation, and I was just part of it, just one of eighteen voices." But some jazz critics disagree. "So great was his success with Basie," Gary Giddins claimed in New York magazine (October 6, 1976), "that the band itself attained its greatest period of popularity."

Whether Basie "made" Williams or vice versa, their combination produced a kind of alchemy: Basie's band caught fire once again and emerged as one of the hottest jazz groups of the decade. During the mid- and late 1950s, they often performed at Birdland and the Apollo Theater in New York and at the Newport (Rhode Island), Stratford (Ontario, Canada), and New York jazz festivals; toured extensively in the United States and, in 1956, in England and Europe; appeared on the Perry Como, Fred Astaire, and Ed Sullivan television shows, among others; gave a concert at Carnegie Hall in 1957; and played at the Waldorf's elite Starlight Room, the first black group to appear there. In the Nation (November 11, 1978), Nat Hentoff recalled one of Joe Williams' performances with Basie in the 1950s: "Standing there, tall, limber, as self-assured as the sly Count himself, Joe would cannonade the blues against the walls, against the band, against the customers. And he never seemed to make any particular effort to prevent his sound from being swallowed by the band. It just loomed out, clear and penetrating as the brass section." With the Count Basie Orchestra, Williams recorded several albums, including Back to Basie and the Blues (for the Roul label) and Joe Williams Sings Standards, and appeared in two films: Jamboree (Warner Brothers, 1957), which featured Jerry Lee Lewis and Frankie Avalon, and Jerry Lewis' comedy Cinderfella (Paramount, 1960).

After six years with Count Basie, Williams had confidence enough and a large enough following to strike out on his own again. Basie encouraged him in that move, even producing his first solo engagement at the Storyville in Boston in January 1961, and Willard Alexander, the band's manager, lined up a solid six months of bookings for him before he even left the Count. Backed at first by Harry ("Sweets") Edison, a trumpeter who had played with Basie, and his quintet and later by the Junior Mance Trio, Williams performed at such important venues as Birdland in New York, the Tivoli in Chicago, and Club Neve and the Cloisters in Los Angeles. Having spent a total of forty-six weeks on the road, Williams closed that very successful first year with New Year's Eve performances at the Mocambo in Hollywood, California. Until Basie's death in August 1984, however, he and the Count often performed together at reunions of Basie alumni and jazz festivals, for tours and recordings, and on television. As a token of his gratitude, Williams always dedicates "You Are So Beautiful" to Basie.

As Williams gained self-assurance, he added the popular songs and compositions most singers chose to ignore to his repertoire of blues, jazz, and ballads. His straightforward singing style and sincerity won him a large popular following, and for five consecutive years, from 1974 through 1978, Williams carried away the top award in *Down Beat's* annual poll of international critics. Moreover, in 1983 he was honored with a star in the Hollywood Walk of Fame and was given the Los Angeles Governors Award from the National Academy of Recording Arts and Sciences.

For the past two decades, Williams has appeared in major cities in the United States and Europe, and in 1978 and 1979 toured Asia and Africa under the aegis of the State Department. Moreover, he performs regularly at the Newport, Kool, and New York jazz festivals; he is a frequent guest on Johnny Carson's *Tonight Show*, on awards ceremonies, and other television programs; and he has been a featured performer on televised tributes to Duke Ellington, Count Basie, and Eubie Blake. He also had a small role in the unsuccessful Depression-era melodrama *The Moonshine War* (MGM/Filmways, 1970).

Continuing to record, Williams has added more than a dozen albums to his discography since leaving Basie, including *The Song is You, Me & the Blues*, and others for RCA Victor; *That Kind of Woman* for Roulette-Forum; Julian "Cannonball" Adderley's folk opera, *Big Man* (Fantasy), in which Williams sang the role of John Henry; and, more recently, the sound track for the 1981 Burt Reynolds film, *Sharky's Machine* (Warner Brothers Records). For his recording *Nothin' but the Blues*, he was named best jazz vocalist of 1984 at the twenty-seventh annual Grammy Awards.

Joe Williams, who stands about six feet tall, shares his Las Vegas home with his fourth wife, Jillean, a British fan whom he met after a 1957 appearance at the Waldorf and married two years later. By his third wife, he has two children, Joe and Anne. Williams finds time for an occasional round of golf, but he still spends twenty to forty weeks a year on the road, earning $3,000 to $7,000 a night, and frequently gives benefit performances. Although the lean years are now far behind him, Williams maintains that he is no less effective a blues singer: "Today I have security and peace of mind. . . . And tomorrow, God willing, will be the best day we've ever had. But the blues—well, the blues will always be something that a man who has lived them will never forget."

References: *Chicago Tribune* XII p23 Ag 28 '83 por; *N Y Times* C p1+ My 23 '80 por; *Reporter Dispatch* p30 Mr 14 '74; Gourse, Leslie.

*Everyday: The Story of Joe Williams* (1985) and *Louis' Children* (1984); Harris, Sheldon. *Blues Who's Who* (1979); Kinkle, Roger D. *The Complete Encyclopedia of Popular Music and Jazz, 1900–1950* (1974); *Who's Who in America, 1984–1985*

## Woodhouse, Barbara (Blackburn)

*May 9, 1910– British animal trainer; author.*
*Address: h. "Campions," Croxley Green, Rickmansworth, Hertfordshire, England*

"Life for me began at seventy," Barbara Woodhouse, the doyenne of British dog trainers, said recently, referring to the year 1980, when her BBC television series *Training Dogs the Woodhouse Way* became, in the words of a writer for the *London Daily Mail*, "the first genuine hoot of the Eighties." That popular series, later syndicated in the United States and other English-speaking countries, gave a quantum boost to a public career dating back to the 1930s, when Mrs. Woodhouse was chiefly occupied with the training of horses. Later she trained animals, mostly dogs, for motion pictures, and finally she launched the eccentric but effective obedience classes for which she is known to millions of television viewers—"fun" sessions in which she seems to train the dogs by bringing the owners to heel. The *Guinness Book of Records* lists Mrs. Woodhouse as the world's most successful and fastest dog trainer, crediting her with having taught 17,136 dogs to obey the basic commands in the thirty-one-year period ending March 25, 1982.

Mrs. Woodhouse followed up *Training Dogs the Woodhouse Way* with the BBC series *Barbara's*

World of Horses and Ponies (1981) and The Woodhouse Road Show (1983) and, in the United States, with the PBS special Barbara Woodhouse Goes to Beverly Hills (1983). Her television success quickened the sales of her numerous books on dog and horse care and training (many of which had originally been self-published), especially No Bad Dogs: The Woodhouse Way, which was the seventh best-selling hardcover book on the general American lists in 1982. Aside from her firm, distinctive voice, her take-charge manner, her fearlessness, and her vibrant nature ("my wagging tail"), Mrs. Woodhouse attributes her effectiveness at what is known in the trade as "obedience prep" to a "God-given" gift of "telepathy with human beings and animals."

Barbara Woodhouse is the married name of Barbara Blackburn, who was born on May 9, 1910 at St. Columba's College in Rathfarnham, County Dublin, Ireland to William Blackburn, a Protestant clergyman who was headmaster of the college, and Leilah (Masterman) Blackburn. As she recounts in her autobiography, Talking to Animals (Faber, 1954; Norton, 1955; Stein & Day, 1974), what she regards as her seemingly instinctive rapport with animals goes back to infancy, when she "already lived in [her] mind in the world of animals," talking "sweet nothings" to the many deer who roamed the park and woods adjoining the college.

At the beginning of World War I, when Barbara was four, soldiers were billeted at St. Columba's College, and their horses were turned out to graze in the park. "My Nannie tells me that I perpetually escaped from her watchful eye and was often to be found surrounded by enormous horses eating tidbits of grass that I picked for them . . . ," Mrs. Woodhouse wrote in Talking to Animals. "But one day when they missed me I was found sitting on the back of the pony that was kept for the governess's cart . . . trying vainly to put its collar on." By the age of five she was allowed to drive the pony cart alone to pick up the governess at the railroad station in Dundrum, five miles away.

Barbara's mother, who "loved all birds and animals," raised fantail pigeons and rabbits for a hobby. At an early age, Barbara was given two Dutch rabbits for her own, and she would spend hours each day brushing their fur and cleaning their hutch. After William Blackburn died, when Barbara was nine, Mrs. Blackburn moved with her children first to Brighton, England and then to Oxford, where she raised Alsatians as a source of income. Barbara handled and trained the dogs along with her mother, who would often call on her to take a disconsolately barking dog aside and talk to it in her "little" voice. (Mrs. Woodhouse still refers to her low-keyed animal-talk voice as her "little" voice.) On her own, she raised goats, and with the money she earned from the sale of goat milk and kids and from a magazine article on goat-keeping for children she was able to realize her long dream, the purchase of a horse, when she was fourteen. The horse was actually a pony, Tommy, a bad-tempered twenty-seven-year-old carnival veteran, whom she gentled and taught new tricks.

Disdaining conventional schooling because it had nothing to do with her consuming interest, Barbara perplexed her mother when, without consulting her, she enrolled in the Harper Adams Agricultural College in 1927, becoming its only female student. In 1930 she received her certificate in agriculture and went to work as a researcher in the British Ministry of Agriculture, where she remained for six months. Returning to Oxford, she opened a horse-riding school for children. Soon she had a stable of fifteen horses, which she hired out to university undergraduates. Summers, when the horses were out to grass, she enterprisingly boarded dogs in the empty horse boxes.

Invited to Argentina by friends, Barbara Blackburn, as she was then known, sold her riding school in 1934 and sailed to Buenos Aires. In Argentina, demonstrating a natural flair for breaking the wild horses used in the herding of the cattle, she became the chief horse-breaker on the Liebigs Company's estancia. She perfected her techniques of horse riding and training under the tutelage of Guarani Indians, who, as she points out in Barbara's World of Horses and Ponies; Their Care and Training the Woodhouse Way (Summit Books, 1984), develop a "perfection of ease and movement" in their partnership with their mounts because they live "not only with . . . but on" them "for the greatest part of their lives." From the Indians she learned to establish an immediate bond of trust with any horse or pony by breathing down her nose at it—the natural "breathing greeting" that horses themselves exchange when they meet. "You simply put your hands behind your back and breathe gently down your nose," she explained to Diane Caselberry Manuel of the Christian Science Monitor (May 13, 1982). "The horse will then come up and breathe down your nose. That's horse language, you see, for 'How do you do?'" (She has also used the "breathing greeting" successfully with giraffes.)

Having fallen ill, Barbara Blackburn returned to Oxford in 1937. As she regained her health, she began dealing in horses, buying raw or poorly trained animals and grooming and breaking or rebreaking them into mounts that could be sold at a profit. Soon she was financially able to import ponies from Argentina, which she turned into polo ponies, chiefly for the Oxford University Polo Club. She herself often rode with the Oxford polo men.

On August 7, 1940 Barbara Blackburn married Michael Woodhouse, a physician. During World War II Mrs. Woodhouse, partly out of concern for her growing family's nourishment under wartime conditions, bought some cows and launched a dairy business in the small town where her husband engaged in general practice. After the war Dr. Woodhouse went on to become a specialist and the family moved into a succession of country homes with ever ampler acreage for gardening, dairy farming, and cattle dealing. Eventually they settled into Campions, the thirty-acre estate in Rickmansworth, Hertfordshire where Dr. and Mrs. Woodhouse still live.

Mrs. Woodhouse first came to national attention in Britain for her expertise at cattle husbandry. Discovering that she could increase the milk yield of her seventeen-odd cows without increasing their food ration, by covering the animals with rugs, she reported on her success in farm journals, and the story was carried to the general public in Pathé newsreel film.

In addition to cows, the Woodhouse menagerie usually included horses, dogs, and other pets, often runts, sick animals, and other discards whom Barbara nurtured and trained into excellence. One such was Jyntee, a Great Dane whose show value to its previous owners had been lost when it broke its tail. To amuse her younger daughter when she was sick abed, Mrs. Woodhouse wrote her first book, *Jyntee, the Tale of a Dog with a Broken Tail*, illustrated with photographs of the Great Dane, which she self-published in 1950. In seeking publicity for the book, Mrs. Woodhouse made several visits to the offices of the British Broadcasting Company. The visits led to an audition and Mrs. Woodhouse's first broadcast, on the kind way to break horses.

For juveniles Mrs. Woodhouse also wrote *Chica; The Story of a Very Little Dog* (Faber, 1955) and *Wendy: The Story of a Horse* (Parrish, 1959). After the death of Jyntee, Mrs. Woodhouse acquired in turn two other Great Danes, whom she made into film stars. Over a period of twenty-one years, the dogs, under Mrs. Woodhouse's supervision, appeared in some 100 motion pictures, including feature films starring Roger Moore, Peter Finch, and Clark Gable. The dogs and the Woodhouse children starred in a series of "Lassie" type short movies written, produced, and directed by Mrs. Woodhouse and filmed for the most part on the Woodhouse estate. They included *Juno Helps Out*, *Trouble for Juno*, *Juno Makes Friends*, *Juno and the Home Help*, and *Trouble with Junia*. Mrs. Woodhouse also did film work with other animals, including cows and giraffes.

While working in film, Mrs. Woodhouse began to give demonstrations of dog training in schools and before interested organizations. The popularity of her demonstrations led to the establishment of training clubs, and for her growing audience of dog trainers and would-be trainers Mrs. Woodhouse cut a phonograph record of training exercises, made the instructional film *Love Me, Love My Dog*, and wrote the manuals *Dog Training My Way* (Faber, 1955), *Difficult Dogs* (Faber, 1956), *The A to Z of Dogs* (Parrish, 1958), and *The A to Z of Puppies* (Parrish, 1982). When an automobile-accident injury forced her to quit horseback riding, she poured her full energies into canine obedience prep. The keystone of that work became a regular $25 weekend course in dog training at her Hertfordshire home.

In 1972 Stein & Day published the American edition of *Dog Training My Way* and brought together Mrs. Woodhouse's two A-to-Z canine books under the title *The A to Z of Dogs and Puppies*. Some of the cognoscenti in the kennel world thought that the author was too sweeping, especially in health areas calling for veterinary precision, and too "emotional in her derogations of establishment practice on the Obedience Trial circuit," but the books were generally acknowledged to be well-written primers for amateur trainers. On publicity tours of the United States in 1973 Mrs. Woodhouse was seen and heard on television and radio stations across the country, and she set her record of eighty dogs trained in a single day in a demonstration in Denver, Colorado in June 1973. After her first tour of the United States, a correspondent for *Time* (March 12, 1973) described Mrs. Woodhouse putting dogs and their owners through their paces during a training weekend at her estate in Hertfordshire: "She stands sternly, an energetic, graying Englishwoman in tweed skirt and sensible shoes. 'No, no, no! You must not say "Condor, come here," in that weak voice. . . . Stand up and say, "Condor, COME!"' As her voice booms across the lawn . . . owners and dogs tremble involuntarily. . . . The atmosphere is all business. Most of her attention, surprisingly enough, is concentrated not on the dogs but on their owners." The *Time* correspondent quoted her as saying: "I can train any dog in five minutes. It's training the owners that takes longer."

Throughout the 1970s Mrs. Woodhouse sent letter after letter to the BBC, importuning the broadcasting corporation to give her a dog-training television show. The answer was always a polite no—until 1979. One morning in 1979 Mrs. Woodhouse, irate at a TV program containing endless "sheep runs," wrote another letter to the BBC, saying, "I've just seen your *One Man and His Dog*, which is about a dog chasing after sheep. Now, I spend my life teaching dogs how *not* to chase sheep. How about coming down to see me about a series?" This time, the BBC responded positively, dispatching a producer to Campions with the offer of a ten-part series for which Mrs. Woodhouse would be paid £1,700 (then about $3,750) for world rights.

The television series *Training Dogs the Woodhouse Way* consisted of ten training sessions, filmed at Campions on shoestring budgets and showing Mrs. Woodhouse snapping dog owners and their pets into line. Aired weekly by the BBC beginning in January 1980, the series became the surprise hit of the television year in Britain. Describing it as "the most absorbing series on the air," Clive James, the television critic of the London *Observer* (March 9, 1980), wrote, "It's no use trying not to watch it, because perfect strangers come up to you on the street and start telling you about it." What James found most entertaining was Mrs. Woodhouse's method of training a dog "by breaking the spirit of the owner." "If the dog has declined to go walkies," James reported, "the owner is in the cart. 'Your trouble is you're *looking* at her. . . . Move! Move! Run! WALKIES!' The recalcitrant dog who finally agrees to go walkies finds itself the object of as much affection as the one sheep that strayed. . . . 'Now love her! Get down on your knees and love her!'"

*Training Dogs the Woodhouse Way* brought Mrs. Woodhouse the Pye television manufacturing company's 1980 award for outstanding female television personality. By the end of 1981 the series had been rerun twice in Britain and been sold to English-language stations worldwide, including public and commercial stations in the United States. "Now being syndicated on seventy-eight stations throughout the U.S.," Gerald Clarke wrote in *Time* (December 7, 1981), "it should prove equally irresistible to millions of Americans, who will discover in Woodhouse . . . the most original—and unintentionally funny—female TV personality since Julia Child. . . . The dogs appear to be enjoying themselves; the owners, a dozen or so terror-stricken men and women, do not. That, of course, is where all the fun lies for the viewer, in the comic reversal of the customary roles of man and beast." Clarke quoted Mrs. Woodhouse admonishing one Mr. Chambers, the ineffectual owner of an unruly Doberman: "That's not a very creditable performance. You're rather fidgety. Can you calm yourself?"

Mrs. Woodhouse's 1981 BBC television series *Barbara's World of Horses and Ponies* claimed 10 million viewers. For the 1983 BBC series *The Woodhouse Road Show* Mrs. Woodhouse went to five towns and challenged people to bring their problem dogs to be trained in less then six minutes. In 1982 and early 1983 she spent nine months touring the United States, Canada, Australia, South Africa, and Japan (where, in accordance with her conviction that dogs respond to hard consonant sounds, especially the "t," she taught the Japanese to say "Sittt," "Waittt," and "Walkies").

In the United States on April 27, 1983 the Public Broadcasting Service television network broadcast *Barbara Woodhouse Goes to Beverly Hills*, in which Mrs. Woodhouse was seen interviewing such show-business celebrities as Lorne Greene, Britt Eklund, and Dorothy Lamour and helping them discipline their dogs. She told reporters that she disciplined William Shatner's Doberman pinscher "in about two minutes," that Zsa-Zsa Gabor was "very good" with her pets, although "a bit sentimental perhaps"; that ostentatiously expensive pet accessories, while "ridiculous," do no "actual harm"; that to her, a "strong" believer in "a life hereafter" for pets as well as humans, the pet cemetery in Los Angeles was "very touching"; and that, aside from some cruel dog collars, "the only thing [she] found rather difficult" in America was seeing police dogs in Beverly Hills being trained to kill (granted release of their muzzles) even stationary, submissive criminals.

In *No Bad Dogs* (Summit Books, 1982), Mrs. Woodhouse drew from her large and comprehensive casebook of common canine behavioral problems to show right and wrong training techniques and emphasize the importance of tone of voice and immediate and firm action, followed up by affection, in correcting faults or disobedience. The book was an American best-seller for eight months in 1982. Some critics thought that its advice on specific problems was "sound" but "too general" and "oversimplified." "This is an English trainer talking to her fellow pet lovers, reflecting their charming national attitude toward dogs," the reviewer for *Publishers Weekly* (February 19, 1982) observed. Others considered *No Bad Dogs* a well-expressed application of Mrs. Woodhouse's philosophy that "there is no such thing as a difficult dog, only an inexperienced owner." *Walkies: Dog Training and Care the Woodhouse Way* (Benn, 1982; Summit Books, 1983) is a large-scale juvenile picture book, eye-catchingly drawn by Angus Scott in comic-strip style, with Mrs. Woodhouse's text lettered in the form of captions to the cartoon panels.

Mrs. Woodhouse abbreviates her methods as the "the three T's" and the "three F's." The F's are firmness (the dog "needs to know you're in control"; she "longs to obey and respect you"), friendliness ("she needs to be praised"), and fun. The T's are touch ("the great love and empathy that you have for your dog goes through your fingers; there's no doubt about it"), tone ("you must speak clearly . . . so that dogs understand the change in tone," from "severe if they do wrong to fun if they do right"), and, of course, telepathy. The basic physical tool in all of this is a properly weighted choke chain; she uses one that makes a loud click—"and the dogs adore you from that minute." "It all comes down to a few good jerks on the chain, and lots of love," Mrs. Woodhouse explained to a *New Yorker* (November 14, 1983) "Talk of the Town" interviewer. "And you must spit out those commands, especially the 't' sounds—'Si-tuh.' You can't argue with a 't.'"

Some dogs, such as German shepherds, poodles, and Great Danes, are easier to train than others; terriers are the most difficult to train, according to Mrs. Woodhouse. She can train a normal dog in basic obedience (walking, heeling, sitting, staying, and coming on command) in approximately six minutes or less, and she can bring around even most problem dogs within an hour. Believing that most "mental" dogs are the allergic victims of a protein-rich diet, she asserts that schizophrenic and psychopathic dogs will usually become normal in personality if changed to a low-protein diet.

By voice alone, Mrs. Woodhouse has on many occasions effectively given commands to dogs via telephone and radio. After dogs and horses, she most enjoys training pigs ("the cleanest and most intelligent of animals") and she loves spiders (one used to sit on her lap "and watch the telly"). She likes cats, but "they are difficult to train"; the only creatures she abhors are snakes—"horrible cold things."

The *New Yorker* interviewer described Barbara Woodhouse as "charming, all right," with "a musical laugh, a casual, winning manner, a friendly touch on the arm." Easily recognizable in her familiar shetland sweater, pleated skirt, and walking loafers, wherever she walks or drives in and around Rickmansworth she is greeted with shouts of "Walkies!" or accosted by people offering photographs of their pet dogs. According to Claudia Dreyfus, writing in *Dial* (May 1984) about a visit to

Campions, she is "a demon driver on country roads." Mrs. Woodhouse has confessed to a weakness for sweets, especially chocolate and cake. Politically, she is a Conservative and an admirer of Prime Minister Margaret Thatcher.

Dr. and Mrs. Woodhouse have three grown children, Pamela, Judith, and Patrick, and eight grandchildren. Because she believes in treating animals like members of the family, and therefore not leaving them alone for long periods of time, she kept no personal pets after celebrity brought with it a busy international schedule. That may change now that she has been forced to suspend much of her activity, including her dog training, by a stroke that she suffered in May 1984. According to an Associated Press report in October 1984, her physician told her that she would recover her mobility completely, but she still complained of "a frozen shoulder" and "a tremendously painful stiffening of the arm joint."

References: Christian Sci Mon p15 My 13 '82 por, p15 Ap 25 '83 por; Dial 5:34+ My 84 pors; People 17:62+ F 15 '82 pors; Washington Post B p5 Ap 27 '82 por; Contemporary Authors 1st rev vols 5-8 (1969); Woodhouse, Barbara. Talking to Animals (1974)

---

## Photo Credits

Courtesy ACA Galleries, N.Y., Fritz Scholder; AP/Wide World Photos, Boy George, Ben Crenshaw, William C. DeVries, Ellen V. Futter, Gordon P. Getty, W. Wilson Goode, Scott Hamilton, Václav Havel, Gregory Hines, Lena Horne, Kim Dae Jung, Bill Murray, Paul Newman, John S. Reed, Ernesto Sabato, Arthur Scargill, George B. Schaller, Elizabeth Taylor, Desmond Tutu, Sam Waterston, George Wein; © 1985 Brian Aris/Outline, Sting; Erich Auerbach, Charles Mackerras; Bachrach, George Rochberg; Hélène Bamberger, Marguerite Duras; © Joyce Baronio, William Kennedy; Jerry Bauer, Fernand Braudel; John Bellissimo, Cyndi Lauper; Jim Brandenberg, Garrison Keillor; © 1980 Jane Brown, Francis Bacon; Sean Byrnes, 1984, Francesco Scavullo; Robert Campbell/National Geographic Society, Dian Fossey; Stephanie Chernikowski, David Byrne; Deutsche Grammophon/Reinhart Wolf, Gidon Kremer; Sandor Domonohon, Eva Marton; Sigrid Estrada, Michael Korda, Ben J. Wattenberg; Betsy Frampton, Harold H. Greene; French Embassy, Press & Information Division, Laurent Fabius; Courtesy Galerie Maeght, Eduardo Chillida; German Information Center, Richard von Weizsäcker; Michael Germana, Tony Schwartz; Mark Gerson, Michael Frayn; Glogau Studio, Arkady N. Shevchenko; Alex Gottfryd, Oliver Sacks; Paul Harter, Caryl Churchill; Gregory Heisler, Marianna Tcherkassky; Michael Kienitz, Nabih Berri; Walter Kranl, Meredith Monk; Kingdon Lane, Joseph Nathan Kane; Joan Leonard, Elmore Leonard; Jose R. Lopez/New York Times, Stella Adler; © 1983 Arnaud Maggs, Alex Colville; Marbeth, Virginia Johnson; © 1985 Fred W. McDarragh, James Cleveland; Jack Mitchell, Agnes de Mille; Inge Morath, Kate Reid; New York Daily News/Deirdre Drohan, Jonathan Borofsky; Irving Penn, courtesy Vogue, © 1983 Condé Nast, Richard Meier; Donald S. Ross, Reuben Nakian; Ann Sager, Will Barnet; Philip Sayer, Philip Larkin; Richard Leslie Schulman, Richard Serra; Arthur Steel, Barbara Woodhouse; Charles Steinbrunner/Dayton Newspapers, Inc., Helen Hooven Santmyer; Christian Steiner, Christopher Hogwood; W. Suschitzky, Gerald Durrell; Martha Swope, Whoopi Goldberg; © Thomas Victor, Ann Beattie; Barbra Walz, Susan Rothenberg; Delta Willis, Mary Leakey; Joe Wrinn, Carlo Rubbia.

---

# OBITUARIES

**AIKEN, GEORGE D(AVID)** Aug. 30, 1892–Nov. 19, 1984 Liberal Republican U.S. senator from Vermont (1941–75); farmer; before election to Senate, was state representative, lieutenant governor, and governor of Vermont; in Senate, was a maverick, often championed liberal legislation opposed by his own party; as member of Agriculture Committee, preferred flexible price supports on crops to outright subsidies to farmers but led fights for rural electrification and flood control, crop insurance, distribution of food surplus to poor through food stamps (his idea), and creation of St. Lawrence Seaway; on Foreign Relations Committee, was bipartisan internationalist; died in Montpelier, Vt. See Current Biography (June) 1947.

Obituary N Y Times B p10 N 20 '84

**ALEIXANDRE (Y MERLO), VICENTE** Apr. 26, 1898–Dec. 1984 Spanish poet; rooted in Spanish lyric and mystical traditions but receptive to modernism; wrote powerful and original free verse on themes of love, death, and eternity, often using metaphors drawn from nature; received 1977 Nobel Prize for Literature for illuminating "man's condition in the cosmos and in present-day society"; as member of Generation of 1927 movement, especially in poems of La destrucción o el amor (1935), abandoned poesía pura for subjective, sometimes surreal vision of love and destruction as natural, infernal twins; an invalid from age twenty-seven, was the only member of movement not fit enough to die fighting or go into exile during civil war (1936–39); exerted a dominant influence on young postwar poets; in later work, such as in volume *En un vasto dominio* (1962), tied love not to nature but to human solidarity, or the difficulty thereof; died in Madrid. See *Current Biography* (Mar.) 1978.

Obituary *Time* 124:66 D 24 '84

**ARENDS, LESLIE C(ORNELIUS)** Sept. 27, 1895–July 16, 1985 U.S. congressman from Illinois (1935–75); farmer; former president of Commercial State Bank of Melvin, Illinois; House Republican whip from 1943 until retirement in 1975; a politically conservative, stalwart party partisan and advocate of states' rights; as ranking Republican on House Armed Services Committee, consistently fought proposed closing of Air Force's Chanute Technical Training Center in Illinois; U.S. delegate to North Atlantic Assembly (1961–70); named by President Gerald Ford in 1976 to Foreign Intelligence Advisory Board; died in Naples, Fla. See *Current Biography* (Feb.) 1948.

Obituary *N Y Times* A p21 Jl 17 '85

**BAILEY, SIR DONALD COLEMAN** Sept. 15, 1901–May 5, 1985 As a civil engineer with British ministry of supply during WW II, invented Bailey Bridge; constructed of prefabricated sections and used to transport troops, tanks, and weapons across rivers and gorges in European, African, and Asian campaigns, it played a key role in Allied victory; knighted in 1946; died in Bournemouth, England. See *Current Biography* (Oct.) 1945.

Obituary *N Y Times* B p10 My 6 '85

**BARNES, WENDELL B(URTON)** Aug. 23, 1909–June 11, 1985 U.S. government official; lawyer; businessman; Republican member of Oklahoma house of representatives (1950–52); administrator of Small Business Administration, established by President Dwight D. Eisenhower to protect interests of some four million small businesses in U.S. (1953–59); later served in executive posts with Shearson, Hammill & Company, and other firms; died in Walnut Creek, Calif. See *Current Biography* (June) 1957.

Obituary *N Y Times* A p16 Je 17 '85

**BEARD, JAMES (ANDREWS)** May 5, 1903–Jan. 23, 1985 Gastronome; best-selling author of cookbooks; consultant to restaurateurs and food suppliers; although expert in international *haute cuisine*, eschewed gourmet jargon and expounded honest "good cooking," with emphasis on American tradition; during career of almost half a century, wrote twenty-three books, including *Cook It Outdoors, The James Beard Cookbook* (with Isabel E. Callvert), and autobiography *Delights and Prejudices*; in *The New James Beard* (1981), offered low-calorie, salt-free recipes developed for his own dietary needs in his later years; taught culinary arts in his Greenwich Village townhouse; died in New York City. See *Current Biography* (Dec.) 1964.

Obituary *N Y Times* B p6 Ja 24 '85

**BLACKWELL, BETSY TALBOT** 1905(?)–Feb. 5, 1985 Women's magazine editor; fashion expert; began editorial career as assistant at *Charm* in 1923; joined *Mademoiselle* as charter fashion editor in 1935; as editor-in-chief (1937–71) of *Mademoiselle*, bridged gap between world of high fashion and that of mass readership of young women with good taste but limited pocketbooks; in addition, helped raise social consciousness and literary standards of women's magazines; died in Norwalk, Conn. See *Current Biography* (June) 1954.

Obituary *N Y Times* B p6 F 5 '85

**BLAKE, EUGENE CARSON** Nov. 7, 1906–July 31, 1985 Clergyman; influential figure in American Protestantism during 1950s and 1960s; stated clerk, or executive director, of Presbyterian Church in the U.S.A. (1951–66); president of National Council of Churches (1954–57); general secretary of World Council of Churches from 1966 until his retirement in 1972; championed peace, civil rights, and church unity; died in Stamford, Conn. See *Current Biography* (Sept.) 1955.

Obituary *N Y Times* A p16 Ag 1 '85

**BLANDING, SARAH GIBSON** Nov. 22, 1898–Mar. 3, 1985 First woman president of Vassar College (1946–64); social scientist; began career at Univ. of Kentucky, where she was professor of political science and dean of women; was appointed first dean of Cornell University's College of Home Economics in 1941; oversaw home front welfare committees during World War II; at Vassar, directed growth of school's investment portfolio and, as ardent feminist, encouraged women's involvement in public affairs; died in Newton, Pa. See *Current Biography* (June) 1946.

Obituary *N Y Times* B p6 Mr 4 '85

**BÖLL, HEINRICH (THEODOR)** Dec. 21, 1917–July 17, 1985 German author; in chronicling effect of WW II and its aftermath on German life in such widely praised novels as *Billiards at Half Past Nine* (1959) and *Group Portrait With Lady* (1971) and in short stories and plays, examined absurdity of war, victimization of innocent by powerful, and corruption of Christianity by ecclesiastical hierarchies, among other themes; with wife, translated into German works of J. D. Salinger, George Bernard Shaw, Bernard Malamud, and other English-language writers; one of most popular writers in Europe, received 1972 Nobel Prize for Literature; died near Bonn, West Germany. See *Current Biography* (July) 1972.

Obituary *N Y Times* A p20 Jl 17 '85

**BOYLE, W(ILLIAM) A(NTHONY)** Dec. 1, 1904–May 31, 1985 Labor union official; protégé of John L. Lewis; president of United Mine Workers of America from 1963 until his defeat by insurgent leader Arnold Miller in 1972; convicted on charges of embezzlement of union funds (1972); convicted in 1974 on first-degree murder charges in deaths on New Year's Eve 1969 of his union rival Joseph A. Yablonski and members of his family and sentenced to life imprisonment; convicted again in retrial in 1978 and returned to prison; died in Wilkes-Barre, Pa. See *Current Biography* (July) 1970.

Obituary *N Y Times* p29 Je 1 '85

**BROOKS, LOUISE** Nov. 14, 1906–Aug. 8, 1985 Actress; personified erotic image of flapper of the 1920s silent film era; after early career as chorus girl and model, appeared in twenty-four films in Europe and Hollywood (1925–38); was chosen over several German actresses, including Marlene Dietrich, to play the temptress Lulu in G. W. Pabst's *Die Büchse der Pandora/Pandora's Box* (1929); after settling in Rochester, N.Y. in 1956, studied films at Eastman House museum and wrote for film journals; gained renewed attention with Kenneth Tynan's *New Yorker* magazine profile of her (1979) and with retrospective showings of her films and publication of her memoir *Lulu in Hollywood* (1982); died at her Rochester apartment. See *Current Biography* (Apr.) 1984.

Obituary *N Y Times* p29 Ag 10 '85

**BROWN, GEORGE (ALFRED)** Sept. 2, 1914–June 2, 1985 British government official and political leader; outspoken, often controversial Labour party spokesman; member of Parliament (1945–70); deputy leader of Labour party (1960–70), succeeding Aneurin Bevan; secretary of state for economic affairs (1964–66); secretary of state for foreign affairs and deputy prime minister (1966–68); took part in British effort to mediate Vietnam conflict; helped to draft UN security council resolution 242, designed to attain peaceful solution in Middle East; was created a baron in 1970, becoming Lord George-Brown; president of newly formed, centrist Social Democratic Alliance (from 1981); author of *In My Way* (1971) and *The Voice of History* (1979). See *Current Biography* (Dec.) 1963.

Obituary *N Y Times* B p5 Je 4 '85

**BRYNNER, YUL** July 11, 1920(?)–Oct. 10, 1985 Japanese-born actor of Mongolian and Gypsy parentage; best-known for his Tony award-winning portrayal of Siamese monarch in Rodgers and Hammerstein's Broadway hit musical *The King and I* (1951–54) and its film version (1956), which earned him an Academy Award; received special Tony for his performance in its 1985 Broadway revival; appeared in over three-dozen films, including *The Ten Commandments* (1956), *Anastasia* (1956), *The Buccaneer* (1958), *The Brothers Karamazov* (1958), *The Magnificent Seven* (1960), and *Taras Bulba* (1962); directed television plays for CBS in late 1940s; died in New York City. See *Current Biography* (Sept.) 1956.

Obituary *N Y Times* B p7 O 11 '85

**BURNET, SIR (FRANK) MACFARLANE** Sept. 3, 1899–Aug. 31, 1985 Australian virologist; was noted for pioneering work on immune systems of human body and nature of viruses; received Nobel Prize in Medicine (1960) for immunology research; professor of experimental medicine at Melbourne Univ. (1944–65); president of Australian Academy of Sciences (1965–69); author of sixteen books on science and medicine; was knighted in 1951. See *Current Biography* (May) 1954.

Obituary *N Y Times* D p21 S 3 '85

**BURNHAM, (LINDEN) FORBES (SAMPSON)** Feb. 20, 1923–Aug. 6, 1985 Guyanese statesman; cofounder and chairman (1949–55) of People's Progressive party of British Guiana; founder and leader (1957–64) of People's National Congress; after defeat of Marxist government of Cheddi B. Jagan, served as prime minister of British Guiana (1964–66) and of newly independent nation of Guyana (1966–80); president since 1980; was frustrated by economic and political instability in his pursuit of self-sufficient "cooperative socialist" state; remained free from alignments with foreign nations; author of book *A Destiny to Mould* (1970); died in Guyanese hospital after throat surgery. See *Current Biography* (Nov.) 1966.

Obituary *N Y Times* A p9 Ag 7 '85

**BURROWS, ABE** Dec. 18, 1910–May 17, 1985 Writer; director; producer; comedian; on Broadway, collaborated with Frank Loesser on *Guys and Dolls* (1950) and *How to Succeed in Business Without Really Trying* (1961), and with Cole Porter on *Can-Can* (1953) and *Silk Stockings* (1955); directed *Two on the Aisle* (1951), *Forty Carats* (1968), and other plays; wrote screenplay for *Solid Gold Cadillac* (1956); helped to create *Duffy's Tavern* radio show; wrote radio dialogue for Dinah Shore, Fred Allen, and own *Abe Burrows Show* (1947–48); created comic material for Joan Davis television show (1946); composed songs, including "The Girl With the Three Blue Eyes"; published *Abe Burrows Song Book* (1955) and autobiographical *Honest Abe* (1979); died in New York City. See *Current Biography* (Nov.) 1951.

Obituary *N Y Times* p40 My 19 '85

**BYRNES, JOHN W(ILLIAM)** June 12, 1913–Jan. 12, 1985 U.S. representative from Wisconsin (1945–72); Wisconsin state senator (1940–44); served on House Ways and Means Committee for twenty-eight years, becoming ranking member in 1963; as an expert in tax law, was instrumental in passage of Tax Reform Act of 1969; House Republican Policy Committee chairman (1959–65); advocated limited federal spending and voluntary senior-citizen health-insurance program, but opposed President Richard Nixon's revenue-sharing plan; on retiring from House, joined Washington, D.C., law firm; died in Marshfield, Wis. See *Current Biography* (Oct.) 1960.

Obituary *N Y Times* A p16 Ja 14 '85

**CALDWELL, MILLARD F(ILLMORE)** Feb. 6, 1897–Oct. 23, 1984 Governor of Florida (1945–49); lawyer; U.S. Democratic representative from Florida (1933–41); first U.S. Civil Defense Administrator (1950–52); justice (1962–66) and then chief justice (1966–69) of Florida Supreme Court; died at his home in Tallahasee, Fla. See *Current Biography* (Nov.) 1948.

Obituary *N Y Times* B p22 O 25 '84

**CALDWELL, TAYLOR** Sept. 7, 1900–Aug. 30, 1985 English-born author; one of world's most prolific and popular writers, whose subject matter ranged from family epics to historical fiction, religious novels, and antiliberal political commentary; published over thirty books, among them the novels *Dynasty of Death* (1938), *The Eagles Gather* (1940), *The Earth Is the Lord's* (1940), *The Wide House* (1945), *Dear and Glorious Physician* (1959), *Great Lion of God* (1970),

*Captains and Kings* (1972), *Answer as a Man* (1981), and the nonfictional *On Growing Up Tough* (1971); was a founding sponsor of New York State Conservative party; died at her home in Greenwich, Conn. See *Current Biography* (Jan.-Feb.) 1940.

Obituary *N Y Times* p20 S 2 '85

**CALVINO, ITALO** Oct. 15, 1923-Sept. 19, 1985 Italian novelist and short-story writer; a technical virtuoso, wrote cleverly intricate and often comic tales, neo-realistic or surreal or a combination of both, in which he departed from conventional, linear development; "took fiction into new places . . . and back to the fabulous and ancient sources of narrative," as John Updike observed; inspired by folk tales, which he regarded as "true," looked for fantastic and unexpected in the familiar, everyday world; imbued even his relatively straightforward politically-leftist early stories, including *The Path to the Nest of Spiders* (1947), with fairy-tale quality; was best known in U.S. for *If on a Winter's Night a Traveler* (1979), a skewed allegorical fantasy examining the relation of literature to reality through a protagonist who writes parodies of literary styles; died in Siena, Italy. See *Current Biography* (Feb.) 1984.

Obituary *N Y Times* A p20 S 20 '85

**CANADY, JOHN (EDWIN)** Feb. 1, 1907-July 19, 1985 Art critic; author; director of educational activities at Philadelphia Museum of Art (1953-59); from 1959 to 1977, was controversial art news editor for *New York Times*, bluntly attacking much contemporary painting, especially abstract expressionism, while earning praise for enlightening and accessible writing about earlier schools; his many art books include twenty-four-portfolio series *Metropolitan Seminars in Art* (1958-60), four-volume *Lives of the Painters* (1972), and now-standard textbook *Mainstreams of Modern Art* (1959); also wrote seven mystery novels under pseudonym of Matthew Head; died at home in Manhattan. See *Current Biography* (May) 1962.

Obituary *N Y Times* p28 Jl 21 '85

**CHAGALL, MARC** July 7, 1887-Mar. 28, 1985 Russian-born artist; in his magical-looking, almost naive narrative art, showed combined influence of Hasidic legends and European modernism; best known for such paintings as *I and the Village* and *The Rabbi of Vitebsk*, but internationally recognized as master of many media, including etching, mosaic, stained glass, clay, stone, and tapestry; illustrated, among other books, his autobiographical *My Life* (1957) and a 105-plate Old Testament series; in idiosyncratic, usually joyous style, and with vibrant palette, created universe of free-floating figures, human, angelic, animal, and inanimate; is proudly represented in most major museums around the world; died at home in Vence, France. See *Current Biography* (November) 1960.

Obituary *N Y Times* A p1+ Mr 29 '85

**CHARLOTTE, GRAND DUCHESS OF LUXEMBOURG** Jan. 23, 1896-July 9, 1985 Constitutional monarch of her small western European nation from 1919 until 1964, when she retired in favor of her older son, Prince Jean; from her exile during German occupation in WW II, broadcast inspirational messages to her people; was married to the late Prince Félix of Bourbon-Parma; died at Fischbach Castle, near national capital. See *Current Biography* (Apr.) 1949.

Obituary *N Y Times* B p5 Jl 10 '85

**CHERNENKO, KONSTANTIN U(STINOVICH)** Sept. 24, 1911-Mar. 10, 1985 Soviet leader; general secretary of Communist party, chairman of Supreme Soviet of USSR, and chairman of Defense Council (1984-85); under sponsorship of Leonid I. Brezhnev, rose through party ranks beginning in 1950s; during Brezhnev's rule (1960-78), became full member of Central Committee and Politburo; elected general secretary on death of Yuri Andropov in 1984, was seen as caretaker choice pending ascension to power of younger generation; during regime, oversaw escalation of Cold War with U.S., negotiation of trade pact with China, and continuation of some of Andropov's reforms; died in Moscow. See *Current Biography* (Aug.) 1984.

Obituary *N Y Times* A p14 Mr 10 '85

**CLAIRE, INA** Oct. 15, 1892-Feb. 21, 1985 Effervescent "high comedienne" of American theatre, whose witty, sophisticated portrayals lent sparkle and vitality to such Broadway productions as *The Awful Truth* (1922); *The Last of Mrs. Cheyney* (1925); and S.N. Behrman's *Biography* (1932), *End of Summer* (1936), and *The Talley Method* (1941); began career as impersonator of stage luminaries, first in vaudeville and later in Ziegfeld *Follies*; appeared in nine films; made her final radiant Broadway appearance in T. S. Eliot's *The Confidential Clerk* (1954); died in San Francisco. See *Current Biography* (May) 1954.

Obituary *N Y Times* p9 F 23 '85

**CLEMENTS, EARLE C.** Oct. 22, 1896-Mar. 12, 1985 Governor of Kentucky (1947-50); two-term Democratic U.S. congressman (1944-47); as U.S. senator (1950-56), was Democratic whip under majority leader Lyndon B. Johnson and served on committees on Appropriations and on Agriculture and Forestry; as governor, expanded Kentucky's educational system and created state police, state parks, and road-building programs; in later years lobbied for tobacco industry and headed Tobacco Institute; died in Morganfield, Ky. See *Current Biography* (Sept.) 1955.

Obituary *N Y Times* D p27 Mr 14 '85

**COLLINGWOOD, CHARLES (CUMMINGS)** June 4, 1917-Oct. 3, 1985 News correspondent; reporter for United Press in London (1939-41); as correspondent on Edward R. Murrow's CBS staff (1941-46), covered campaigns in North Africa and Europe; first UN correspondent for CBS News (1946-47); White House correspondent (1948-51); chief of CBS London bureau (1957-59); as chief foreign correspondent for CBS News (1964-75), covered Indochina war and such events as President Nixon's visit to China, Arab-Israeli war, and Soviet occupation of Prague; served as host of such series as *Person to Person* and *Chronicle*; retired from CBS News in 1982; received Peabody Award and other journalism honors; commander in Order of the British Empire and Chevalier of French Legion of Honor; died in New York City. See *Current Biography* (June) 1943.

Obituary *N Y Times* D p19 O 4 '85

**CORI, CARL F(ERDINAND)** Dec. 5, 1896–Oct. 19, 1984 Biochemist; educator; with first wife, Gerty T. (Radnitz) Cori, shared one-half of 1947 Nobel Prize in medicine for discovering process by which animal starch glycogen is converted into utilizable sugar and for isolating phosphorylase, the enzyme that begins the process—achievements important in study of diabetes; taught on faculty of Washington Univ. School of Medicine for thirty-five years; after retiring as head of department of biochemistry at Washington Univ., was visiting professor at Massachusetts General Hospital and Harvard Univ. School of Medicine; died in Cambridge, Mass. See *Current Biography* (Oct.) 1947.

Obituary *N Y Times* A p19 O 22 '84

**CORSON, FRED PIERCE** Apr. 11, 1896–Feb. 16, 1985 Methodist bishop; president (1961–66) of World Methodist Council, a fellowship and advisory group to member churches around the world; president (1934–44) of Methodist-affiliated Dickinson College in Carlisle, Pennsylvania; as bishop of United Methodist Church's Philadelphia Area from 1944 to 1968, sought unity among regional conferences under his care; founded "Bishop's Crusaders," a worldwide youth movement, in 1952; was a delegate-observer at Second Vatican Council of Roman Catholic church (1962–65); died in St. Petersburg, Fla. See *Current Biography* (May) 1961.

Obituary *N Y Times* D p17 F 19 '85

**COWLES, GARDNER, JR.** Jan. 31, 1903–July 8, 1985 Publisher; joined *Des Moines Register and Tribune* as city editor (1925) and served as its president (1943–71) and board chairman (1971–73); board chairman of Cowles Communications (1937–71); as founder (1937) and publisher of *Look*, built it into one of most popular mass-circulation, general-interest magazines; founded *San Juan Star*, Puerto Rico's first English-language newspaper, which won Pulitzer prize for editorial writing (1959); a liberal Republican, who championed civil rights and helped to inspire Wendell L. Willkie's book *One World* (1943); deputy director of Office of War Information (1942–43); died at Southampton, N.Y. See *Current Biography* (June) 1943.

Obituary *N Y Times* B p6 Jl 9 '85

**CROSSLEY, ARCHIBALD M(ADDOCK)** Dec. 7, 1896–May 1, 1985 Public opinion analyst; pioneered, with Elmo Roper and George Gallup, in public opinion polling techniques, using scientifically selected random samples; founded market research company Crossley Inc. (1926), which later merged with Stewart, Dougall & Associates to form Crossley Surveys (1954); correctly predicted Franklin D. Roosevelt's victory in 1936 but erroneously forecast victory for Thomas E. Dewey in 1948; continued to conduct presidential polls until 1952; founder and past president of Market Research Council; former president of American Association for Public Opinion Research; died in Princeton, N.J. See *Current Biography* (Dec.) 1941.

Obituary *N Y Times* D p23 My 3 '85

**CUSHMAN, ROBERT E(VERTON), JR.** Dec. 24, 1914–Jan. 2, 1985 Marine Corps general; won several decorations for heroism in combat in Pacific in WW II; was chief adviser on national security affairs to Vice-President Richard Nixon in 1950s; in Vietnam in late 1960s, commanded 162,000 troops, largest battlefront command in Marine history; appointed by President Nixon, served as deputy director of Central Intelligence Agency (1969–72) and commandant of Marine Corps (1972–75); died in Fort Washington, Md. See *Current Biography* (Nov.) 1972.

Obituary *N Y Times* p26 Ja 5 '85

**DIETZ, DAVID** Oct. 6, 1897–Dec. 9, 1984 Journalist; longtime science writer and editor with Scripps-Howard newspapers; won Pulitzer Prize in 1937; from 1940 to 1950 was a science correspondent for NBC News; wrote nine books, including *The Story of Science* (1931) and *Medical Magic* (1937); died in Cleveland Heights, O. See *Current Biography* (Oct.) 1940.

Obituary *N Y Times* B p14 D 11 '84

**DUBUFFET, JEAN** July 31, 1901–May 12, 1985 French painter; sculptor; lithographer; one of most esteemed and influential post-WW II artists; began career in 1942; executed paintings in primitive style, inspired by the "*art brut* of the child, the madman, and the savage" and designed to "bring all disparaged values into the limelight"; used such media as sand, pebbles, and tar to enrich surface texture of paintings; created large-scale representational sculptures, including *Group of Four Trees*, in New York City, and *Monument to the Standing Beast*, in Chicago; died in Paris, France. See *Current Biography* (July) 1962.

Obituary *N Y Times* A p1+ My 15 '85

**EHRICKE, KRAFFT A.** Mar. 24, 1917–Dec. 11, 1984 German-born physicist; rocketry engineer and space-travel theorist; as member of German V-2 rocket team, surrendered to U.S. Army at close of WW II; worked for U.S. Army missile program (1947–52); in private sector, was a major designer of Atlas and Centaur rockets for Convair division of General Dynamics Corp. and scientific adviser to Rockwell International Corp., which built Apollo spacecraft and space shuttle; in later years headed own consulting firm, Space Global; successfully urged formation of civilian space agency, prototype of NASA, in 1950s; author of articles and books on potential of interplanetary exploration; died in La Jolla, Cal. See *Current Biography* (June) 1958.

Obituary *N Y Times* D p30 D 13 '84

**EISENHOWER, MILTON S(TOVER)** Sept. 15, 1899–May 2, 1985 U. S. government official; educator; closest adviser to his older brother, Dwight D. Eisenhower; consultant to other presidents, including Franklin D. Roosevelt, Harry S. Truman, Lyndon B. Johnson, and Richard Nixon; held various government posts, including director of War Relocation Authority (1942–43) and personal representative of president on Latin American affairs; president of Kansas State College (1943–50), Pennsylvania State Univ. (1950–56), and Johns Hopkins Univ. (1956–67,

1970-71); author of book *The President Is Calling* (1974); died in Baltimore, Md. See *Current Biography* (Dec.) 1946.

Obituary *N Y Times* D p23 My 3 '85

**ENGSTROM, E(LMER) W(ILLIAM)** Aug. 25, 1901–Oct. 30, 1984 Electronics engineer; corporation executive; during thirty-nine years with RCA Corp., was responsible for progressive refinements in radar and motion-picture sound as well as radio and television studio apparatus and receivers; directed development of RCA compatible color television system, which became standard American system in 1950s; was president of RCA from 1961 to 1965; remained chief executive officer until 1968 and chairman of executive committee until 1969, when he retired; died in Hightstown, N.J. See *Current Biography* (Dec.) 1951.

Obituary *N Y Times* D p18 N 2 '84

**ERLANDER, TAGE (FRITIOF)** June 13, 1901–June 21, 1985 Swedish statesman; parliamentary leader of Social Democratic Labor party; held various cabinet posts before serving as prime minister (1946–69); enhanced Sweden's socialist welfare state through reforms in education, health care, and security for aged and unemployed; maintained Sweden's neutrality in international affairs and championed UN; wrote several books, including four volumes of memoirs; died in village of Huddinge, near Stockholm. See *Current Biography* (Oct.) 1947.

Obituary *N Y Times* p33 Je 22 '85

**ERVIN, SAM(UEL) J(AMES), JR.** Sept. 17, 1896–Apr. 23, 1985 U.S. Democratic senator from North Carolina (1954–74); served in U.S. House of Representatives (1946–47) and in judicial posts before his appointment to succeed the late Senator Clyde Hoey; an old-fashioned conservative Democrat, was noted for his expertise on U.S. Constitution and for colorful, homespun rhetoric; served on special Senate committee that recommended censure of Senator Joseph R. McCarthy (1954); presided over Senate select committee on presidential campaign activities, investigating Watergate affair, that led to resignation of President Richard Nixon in 1974; author of *The Whole Truth* (1980) and *Preserving the Constitution* (1985); died in Winston-Salem, N.C. See *Current Biography* (Oct.) 1973.

Obituary *N Y Times* B p12 Ap 24 '85

**FISHBACK, MARGARET** Mar. 10, 1904–Sept. 25, 1985 Writer; in late 1920s and early 1930s was chief advertising copywriter for R. H. Macy & Co., the New York City department store; while writing breezy and clever ad copy, also turned her wit to light verse, which appeared piecemeal in such magazines as *Mademoiselle* and *Harper's Bazaar* and was collected in several volumes, including *One to a Customer* (1937) and *Time for a Quick One* (1940); died in Camden, Me. See *Current Biography* (Apr.) 1941.

Obituary *N Y Times* p34 S 28 '85

**FITZGERALD, ROBERT (STUART)** Oct. 12, 1910–Jan. 16, 1985 Poet; translator; critic; emeritus Boylston professor of rhetoric and oratory, Harvard Univ.; influ-enced a generation of scholars with his free, masterly idiomatic translations of Greek classics, especially *The Odyssey* (1961) and *The Iliad* (1974); writing in unrhymed iambic pentameter with spiritual empathy, metrical integrity, and forceful diction, imbued Homer with voice that spoke afresh to our time and place; with Dudley Fitts, translated plays of Sophocles and Euripides; also translated, among others, Dante, Paul Valéry, and St.-John Perse; edited works of Flannery O'Connor and James Agee; produced four volumes of his own finely crafted poetry, including *In the Rose of Time* (1957) and *Spring Shades* (1971); died in Hamden, Conn. See *Current Biography* (Sept.) 1976.

Obituary *N Y Times* B p8 Ja 17 '85

**FLORY, PAUL J(OHN)** June 19, 1910–Sept. 9, 1985 Chemist; professor emeritus at Stanford Univ.; was the leading researcher in advancement of macronuclear chemistry; received Nobel Prize in 1974 for his discovery of a way to compare and study behavior of polymers linked together in repeating sequences, a development making possible the use of new polymeric compounds in plastics, fibers, and other man-made products; used Nobel stipend in cause of human rights, especially protection of Soviet scientists from political persecution; wrote *Principles of Polymer Chemistry* (1953), a classic in its field; died in Big Sur, Calif. See *Current Biography* (Mar.) 1975.

Obituary *N Y Times* B p12 S 12 '85

**FUJIYAMA, AIICHIRO** May 22, 1897–Feb. 22, 1985 Japanese government official; business executive; in 1930s headed sugar-processing and other industrial companies; during WW II, helped bring about fall of Prime Minister Hideki Tojo; was imprisoned by U.S. occupation forces for three years after Japanese surrender; as foreign minister (1957–60), headed Japan's first delegation to the UN (1957), helped revise U.S.-Japanese security treaty (1960), and sought restored diplomatic ties with China; later directed Japan's Economic Planning Agency; died in Tokyo. See *Current Biography* (Apr.) 1958.

Obituary *N Y Times* p9 F 23 '85

**GANDHI, INDIRA (PRIYADARSHINI NEHRU)** Nov. 19, 1917–Oct. 31, 1984 Prime Minister of India (1966–77, 1980–84); dominant Indian political figure for about two decades; joined all-India Congress party in 1938; served as its president in 1959–60; formed breakaway Indian National Congress (I) in 1978; official hostess for her father, Prime Minister Jawaharlal Nehru (1947–64); as prime minister, instituted major reforms, including strong population-control program; was criticized for authoritarian rule, especially under state of emergency (1975–77), and for such acts as raid on Sikh Golden Temple in Amritsar (1984); was assassinated near her home in New Delhi, reportedly by Sikh extremist members of her own security guard. See *Current Biography* (June) 1966.

Obituary *N Y Times* A p1+, B p9 O 31 '84

**GERNREICH, RUDI** Aug. 8, 1922–Apr. 21, 1985 Austrian-born fashion designer; leading American avant-garde designer of 1950s and 1960s; sought to liberate women from restraints of haute couture by creating youthful, free-flowing garments that followed natural form of female body; pioneered in designs of topless swimsuits, miniskirts, patterned hosiery, and see-through blouses, and in use of psychedelic colors; was elected to Coty Hall of Fame (1967); died in Los Angeles, Calif. See *Current Biography* (Dec.) 1968.

Obituary *N Y Times* B p12 Ap 22 '85

**GIDEONSE, HARRY DAVID** May 17, 1901–Mar. 12, 1985 Educator; economist; as president of Brooklyn College (1939–66), oversaw school's growth and enhanced its reputation as a leading liberal-arts institution; was chancellor of New School for Social Research from 1966 to 1975; served on the Chicago and New York councils on foreign relations and as chairman of board of Freedom House; lectured at Columbia and Rutgers universities, among others; wrote widely on international economics and political economy; died in Port Jefferson, N.Y. See *Current Biography* (May) 1940.

Obituary *N Y Times* D p27 Mr 14 '85

**GORDON, RUTH** Oct. 30, 1896–Aug. 28, 1985 Actress; writer; during career spanning some seventy years, performed on Broadway and London stages in such roles as Nora in *A Doll's House* (1937), Natasha in *The Three Sisters* (1942), and Dolly Gallagher Levi, a part that Thornton Wilder had written for her, in *The Matchmaker* (1954–57); appeared on screen as Mary Todd in *Abe Lincoln in Illinois* (1940) and in eccentric roles in such films as *Where's Poppa?* (1970) and *Harold and Maude* (1971); received Oscar for performance in *Rosemary's Baby* (1968) and 1979 Emmy for her role in segment of television situation comedy *Taxi*; with Garson Kanin, whom she married in 1942, wrote screenplays for *A Double Life* (1948), *Adam's Rib* (1949), and other films; also wrote two books and three plays; died in Edgartown, Mass. See *Current Biography* (Apr.) 1972.

Obituary *N Y Times* D p22 Ag 29 '85

**GOULD, CHESTER** Nov. 20, 1900–May 11, 1985 Cartoonist; creator of *Dick Tracy*, the first comic strip not primarily intended to be humorous; featuring granite-jawed detective with message that crime does not pay, it was carried at one time by nearly 1,000 newspapers and read by some 65 million persons a day; created a gallery of bizarre criminal types like Flattop, Pruneface, and the Mole, as well as more benign characters such as Gravel Gertie, B. O. Plenty, and Diet Smith; also conceived of technological innovations, including two-way wrist radio; wrote and drew *Dick Tracy* strip continually from its inception in 1931 until his retirement in 1977; died in Woodstock, Ill. See *Current Biography* (Sept.) 1971.

Obituary *N Y Times* p34 My 12 '85

**GREY, J(AMES) D(AVID)** Dec. 18, 1906–July 26, 1985 Clergyman; was pastor of First Baptist Church in New Orleans for thirty-five years, beginning in 1937; served as president of Southern Baptist Convention from 1951 to 1953; died in New Orleans. See *Current Biography* (Sept.) 1952.

Obituary *N Y Times* B p5 Jl 29 '85

**HADDON, WILLIAM, JR.** May 24, 1926–Mar. 4, 1985 U.S. government official; Harvard-trained physician; expert on automobile-accident research; as director of National Safety Bureau of Dept. of Transportation, issued first overall federal safety regulations for manufacture of 1968-model cars, provoking ire of both auto industry and consumer advocate Ralph Nader; resigned in 1969 to head the private Insurance Institute for Highway Safety; since 1972, headed the Highway Loss Data Institute; championed inflatable airbags in automobiles; died in Washington, D.C. See *Current Biography* (Feb.) 1969.

Obituary *N Y Times* D p27 Mr 5 '85

**HAMILTON, MARGARET** Dec. 9, 1902–May 16, 1985 Actress; appeared in some seventy-five motion pictures, often as irascible spinsters, stern schoolteachers, and other waspish types; was best known for her portrayal of the sinister Wicked Witch of the West in the classic film *The Wizard of Oz* (1939) and, more recently, for her appearance in Maxwell House coffee television commercials; also appeared in many stage plays and in television and radio dramas; died in Salisbury, Conn. See *Current Biography* (April) 1979.

Obituary *N Y Times* D p20 My 17 '85

**HARDEN, CECIL M(URRAY)** Nov. 21, 1894–Dec. 5, 1984 U.S. government official; five-term Republican U.S. representative from Indiana (1948–58); as an early women's-rights advocate, decried "male dominance" in her party and in 1957 proposed federal bill assuring equal pay for women; Republican national committeewoman from Indiana (1944; 1948); special assistant for women's affairs to postmaster general (1959–61); served on national advisory committee for White House Conference on Aging (1970); died in Lafayette, Ind. See *Current Biography* (Feb.) 1949.

Obituary *N Y Times* p17 D 8 '84

**HARRIS, PATRICIA ROBERTS** May 31, 1924–Mar. 23, 1985 U.S. government official; was first black woman to hold cabinet positions, as secretary of Housing and Urban Development (1977–79) and of Health, Education, and Welfare (1979–81; renamed Dept. of Health and Human Services in 1980) under President Carter; in similar feminist breakthrough, achieved highest diplomatic rank, as ambassador to Luxembourg under President Lyndon B. Johnson; was professor and dean of law school at Howard Univ. in 1960s; chaired numerous civil-rights and social-welfare commissions; made unsuccessful mayoral bid in Washington, D.C. in 1982; died in Washington, D.C. See *Current Biography* (Dec.) 1965.

Obituary *N Y Times* p36 Mr 24 '85

**HAUSER, (BENJAMIN) GAYELORD** 1895(?)–Dec. 26, 1984 German-born nutritionist; advocate of natural foods for general health, weight reduction, and curative effects; as lecturer since 1920s and as columnist and television personality in 1950s, gained popularity with American public and with film stars and European nobility; his many books include *Eat and Grow Beautiful* (1936) and best-seller *Look Younger, Live Longer* (1950); founder and editor of journal *Diet Digest* in 1950s; died in North Hollywood, Cal. See

Current Biography (June) 1955.

Obituary N Y Times p26 D 29 '84

**HELSTEIN, RALPH** Dec. 11, 1908–Feb. 14, 1985 Labor-union official; lawyer; elected president of CIO-affiliated United Packinghouse Workers in 1946; led semi-successful, volatile national strike of meatworkers in 1948, resulting in 9-cent hourly wage increase; in 1968 stepped down to vice-presidency of union, which had merged with United Food and Commercial Workers; retired, as president emeritus, in 1972; an antipoverty and pro–civil-rights partisan, was one of few labor leaders to march with Dr. Martin Luther King Jr.; died in Chicago. See Current Biography (June) 1948.

Obituary N Y Times p28 F 16 '85

**HERBSTER, BEN M(OHR)** Aug. 26, 1904–Dec. 16, 1984 Clergyman; first president of United Church of Christ, formed in 1961 through merger of Congregational Christian churches and with Evangelical and Reformed Church; as member of general council of latter, was decisive leader in movement for merger; kept high political profile, speaking out for civil rights and against federal aid to parochial schools; died in Dayton, O. See Current Biography (July) 1962.

Obituary N Y Times p22 D 23 '84

**HILL, LISTER** Dec. 29, 1894–Dec. 20, 1984 U.S. congressman; generally progressive Southern Democrat from Alabama whose forty-five-year career took on a special brilliance during New Deal era; in House of Representatives (1923-37) wrote Tennessee Valley Authority Act in 1933; as senator (1938-68) sponsored GI Bill of Rights for veterans of WW II and Korean conflict, Hill-Burton Hospital Act (1946) extending medical facilities in impoverished and rural areas, and important education legislation; oversaw creation of National Institutes of Health; chairman (1955-68) of Senate Labor and Public Welfare Committee; supported Medicare and Social Security programs; opposed Civil Rights Act of 1965 but later apologized for that stance; hailed in his death as one of his state's great men; died in Montgomery, Ala. See Current Biography (Oct.) 1943.

Obituary N Y Times p29 D 22 '84

**HOLLOMON, J(OHN) HERBERT** Mar. 12, 1919–May 8, 1985 Metallurgist; U.S. government official; educator; served with General Electric Co. in research and managerial posts (from 1946); general manager of its general engineering laboratory (1960-62); assistant secretary of commerce for science and technology (1962-67); president of Univ. of Oklahoma (1968-70); served on advisory panels for federal government; took part in U.S.-USSR metallurgical exchange program; director of Center for Technology and Policy at Boston Univ. at time of his death. See Current Biography (Mar.) 1964.

Obituary N Y Times p17 My 11 '85

**HOLT, JOHN (CALDWELL)** Apr. 14, 1923–Sept. 14, 1985 Educational reformer; foe of "miseducation" and advocate of a "de-schooled society"; began career as staff member of United World Federalists; as private

elementary-school teacher in Carbondale, Col. and Cambridge, Mass. in 1950s and 1960s, became convinced that the prevailing "authoritarian and dangerous" educational system stifled inquisitiveness and natural process of learning and that many children "did poorly because they expected to do poorly"; ignited national debate on quality of American schooling and contributed to alternative-school movement with his controversial teacher's journal How Children Fail (1964) and its sequel How Children Learn (1967); later published newsletter Growing Without Schools and wrote, among other books, Instead of Education: Helping People To Do Things Better (1976) and Never Too Late: My Musical Life Story (1978); in latter, used his lively passion for music and his joys and travails in playing various instruments to document his radical educational ideas; died in Boston, Mass. See Current Biography (June) 1981.

Obituary N Y Times B p8 S 16 '85

**HORNE, JOHN E(LMER)** Mar. 4, 1908–Jan. 8, 1985 U.S. government official; lawyer; longtime advocate of government contracts to small businesses; was assistant to Senator John J. Sparkman of Arkansas in late 1940s; headed Small Defense Plants Administration in 1950s and Small Business Administration from 1961 to 1963; chaired Federal Home Loan Bank Board from 1965 to 1968; died in Alexandria, Va. See Current Biography (Dec.) 1952.

Obituary N Y Times D p23 Ja 10 '85

**HORROCKS, SIR B(RIAN) G(WYNNE)** Sept. 7, 1895–Jan. 6, 1985 British army officer; as lieutenant general in Egypt in 1942, contributed to rout of General Erwin Rommel's desert forces, which secured Middle East for Allies in WW II; considered annihilation of his men at Arnhem in the Netherlands in 1944 (recounted in movie A Bridge Too Far) "the blackest moment" of his life; after war, hosted BBC television series Men in Battle; wrote autobiography A Full Life; knighted by King George VI in 1949; died in Fishbourne, England. See Current Biography (Jan.) 1945.

Obituary N Y Times B p6 Ja 9 '85

**HOXHA, ENVER** Oct. 16, 1908–Apr. 11, 1985 Albanian political leader; wielded virtually absolute political power during four decades of orthodox Stalinist rule; founded Albanian Communist party (1941) as member of underground during Italian occupation; led national liberation campaign (1939-44); prime minister of Albania (1944-54); secretary general (1948-54) and first secretary of Politburo of central committee (from 1954) of Albanian Workers (Communist) party; kept country internationally isolated, breaking ties with USSR in 1961 and with Communist China in 1976; repressed religion and ethnic minorities, but was credited with having eliminated illiteracy; died in Tirana. See Current Biography (Jan.) 1950.

Obituary N Y Times A p1+ Ap 12 '85

**HUDSON, ROCK** Nov. 17, 1925–Oct. 2, 1985 Actor; ruggedly handsome screen idol; appeared in sixty-two films; was perhaps best known for performances in such fluffy romantic comedies, costarring Doris Day, as Pillow Talk (1959), Lover Come Back (1962), and

*Send Me No Flowers* (1964), but also starred in more ambitious films, including *The Magnificent Obsession* (1954) and *A Farewell to Arms* (1958); received Academy Award nomination for portrayal of Texas rancher in epic film *Giant* (1956); starred in recent years in television series *McMillan and Wife* and *The Devlin Connection* and had a recurring role in *Dynasty* series; died in Los Angeles, after suffering for over a year from acquired immune deficiency syndrome (AIDS). See *Current Biography* (Oct.) 1961.

Obituary *N Y Times* D p23 O 3 '85

**HUGHES, SARAH T(ILGHMAN)** Aug. 2, 1896–Apr. 23, 1985 Jurist; women's rights activist; member of Texas state legislature (1931–35); state district judge of Dallas county (1935–61); appointed federal district judge for northern district of Texas by President John F. Kennedy (1961); administered presidential oath of office to Lyndon B. Johnson after Kennedy's assassination (1963); president of National Federation of Business and Professional Women's Clubs (1950–52); died in Dallas, Tex. See *Current Biography* (Nov.) 1950.

Obituary *N Y Times* D p27 Ap 25 '85

**HUNTER, ALBERTA** Apr. 1, 1895–Oct. 17, 1984 Singer; songwriter; relict of the "golden age of jazz"; a leading blues singer in Chicago, New York, and Europe during 1920s and 1930s; played Queenie in London production of *Show Boat* (1928), and on Broadway appeared as Dolly in *Mamba's Daughters* (1939); toured abroad as star of USO shows during WW II and Korean conflict; composed such standards as "Workin' Man" and "Downhearted Blues"; after working for some twenty years as a hospital nurse, resumed her singing career in 1977, performing regularly at the Cookery in New York's Greenwich Village; died at her home on Roosevelt Island, New York City. See *Current Biography* (May) 1979.

Obituary *N Y Times* B p5 O 19 '84

**HUSSEIN, AHMED** Nov. 1, 1902–Dec. 1, 1984 Egyptian ambassador to U.S. (1953–58); expert on rural economy; as undersecretary (1948–50) and minister (1951–1953) of social affairs under King Farouk I, encouraged agrarian reform and progressive social organization; appointed ambassador after 1952 military coup led by Gamal A. Nasser, presented to U.S. his country's view in disputes with Israel and on Egyptian claims to Suez Canal; claiming Egyptian neutrality in Cold War, defended controversial arms purchase from Czechoslovakia; unsuccessfully attempted negotiation of U.S. funding for Aswan High Dam on Nile River; held professorship in agricultural economics at Cairo Univ.; died in Cairo, Egypt. See *Current Biography* (Mar.) 1956.

Obituary *N Y Times* D p31 D 6 '84

**INGERSOLL, RALPH (McALLISTER)** Dec. 8, 1900–Mar. 8, 1985 Journalist; publisher; author; a mover and shaker of mid-twentieth-century American press; best known as founder of innovative, controversial, and short-lived (1940–48) New York City daily *PM*, an ad-less, Rooseveltian liberal tabloid that lambasted isolationists and thumped for U.S. intervention in WW II before any other major newspaper; previously, had been managing editor of *New Yorker* and *Fortune* magazines, general manager of Time Inc., and publisher of *Time*; later owned and ran string of papers in Northeast; wrote, among other books, *Top Secret* (1946), assessment of Allied military leadership in victory over Hitler that was regarded by admirers of Eisenhower and Montgomery as pro–Omar Bradley polemic; died in Miami Beach, Fla. See *Current Biography* (July) 1940.

Obituary *N Y Times* p16 Mr 9 '85

**JENNER, WILLIAM E(ZRA)** July 21, 1908–Mar. 9, 1985 Republican U.S. senator from Indiana (1944–45, 1947–59); was ultraconservative cohort of anti-Communist witchhunter Senator Joseph R. McCarthy; opposed all foreign aid, including Marshall Plan, and foreign entanglements, including NATO; rose to prominence on Senate Judiciary Committee; as chair of Judiciary Subcommittee on Internal Security, investigated allegations of Communist infiltration of teaching profession in mid-1950s; died in Bedford, Ind. See *Current Biography* (June) 1951.

Obituary *N Y Times* B p6 Mr 11 '85

**JOHNSON, (THOMAS) WALTER** June 27, 1915–June 14, 1985 Historian; instructor of history (1940–43) and later full professor and department chairman (1950–61) at Univ. of Chicago; as cochairman of National Stevenson for President Committee, helped engineer Democratic party's draft of Adlai E. Stevenson in 1952; among other works, wrote *The Battle Against Isolationism* (1944), *William Allen White's America* (1947), and, with Avery Craven, *The United States: Experiment in Democracy* (1947); edited eight-volume *The Papers of Adlai Stevenson* (1972–79) and *The Selected Letters of William Allen White, 1899–1943* (1943); chaired Fulbright scholarship selection committee (1950–53); died in Ludington, Mich. See *Current Biography* (Apr.) 1957.

Obituary *N Y Times* p29 Je 15 '85

**KELLY, JOHN B(RENDEN), JR.** May 24, 1927–Mar. 2, 1985 Athletic organization official; amateur sculling champion; winner of 1947 Sullivan award as outstanding nonprofessional athlete in U.S.; recipient of bronze medal for oarsmanship at 1956 Olympic games; as vice-president, in 1960s, and president, in 1970, of AAU, helped modernize international regulations for amateur athletes; as president of U.S. Olympic Committee since 1984, advocated more events for women athletes, among other policies; was brother of late Princess Grace of Monaco; died while jogging in Philadelphia. See *Current Biography* (June) 1971.

Obituary *N Y Times* B p6 Mr 4 '85

**KERTÉSZ, ANDRÉ** July 2, 1894–Sept. 27, 1985 Hungarian-born American photographer; pioneered and refined use of hand-held 35-millimeter camera in magazine photojournalism; first in Paris and then in United States, produced for picture-oriented magazines rich, dreamlike, and sometimes humorous photographs that captured decisive moments in life, that "said everything"; helped open art-museum doors to photography collections; was, in the words of Henri

Cartier-Bresson, "the poetic wellspring" of the medium's development into fine art; died in New York City. See *Current Biography* (Aug.) 1979.

Obituary *N Y Times* B p10 S 30 '85

**KLEIN, EDWARD E(LKAN)** May 25, 1913–July 14, 1985 Rabbi; liberal community activist; served as senior rabbi (1949-81) and rabbi emeritus (1981-85) at Manhattan's Stephen Wise Free Synagogue, a center of Reform Judaism; beginning in 1945, taught religion, philosophy, and education at Hebrew Union College's School of Education in New York; supported Planned Parenthood, NAACP, and Supreme Court's ban on school prayer; cofounded in 1952 interfaith League of West Side Organizations to fight Manhattan's West Side urban blight; national sponsor of Committee for a Sane Nuclear Policy; died at home in Manhattan. See *Current Biography* (Sept.) 1966.

Obituary *N Y Times* A p16 Jl 15 '85

**KOTSCHNIG, WALTER M(ARIA)** Apr. 9, 1901–June 23, 1985 Austrian-born U.S. government official; helped resettle refugees as staff member of League of Nations (1934-36); after moving to U.S. in 1936, taught comparative education at Smith and Mount Holyoke colleges; joined State Department in 1944, becoming chief of Division of International Organizational Affairs in 1947; in 1944-45, took part in conferences establishing UN; as permanent member of U.S. delegation to UN, belonged to General Assembly, UNESCO, ILO, and other UN bodies; deputy assistant secretary of state from 1965 until retirement in 1971; died near Newton, Pa. See *Current Biography* (Oct.) 1952.

Obituary *N Y Times* B p6 Je 25 '85

**KRASNA, NORMAN** Nov. 7, 1909–Nov. 1, 1984 Motion-picture writer, producer, director; playwright; known for comic touch in plots often premised on mistaken or hidden identities and resulting in unexpected denouements; not counting screen adaptations of his plays, such as the Broadway hits *Dear Ruth* (1944-45) and *John Loves Mary* (1947-48), was connected as story or screenplay writer to dozens of films, including *Richest Girl in the World* (1934), *Fury* (1936), and *The Devil and Miss Jones* (1941); won Academy Award for best original screenplay for *Princess O'Rourke* (1943), his first directorial assignment; in early 1950s ran own production company, Wald-Krasna Productions, with Jerry Wald; died in Los Angeles. See *Current Biography* (May) 1952.

Obituary *N Y Times* B p8 N 7 '84

**KUZNETS, SIMON** Apr. 30, 1901–July 8, 1985 Russian-born economist; won 1971 Nobel Prize in Economics for originating concept of gross national product as measure of national income and economic growth; taught economics at Univ. of Pennsylvania (1930-54), Johns Hopkins Univ. (1954-60), and Harvard Univ. (1960-71); throughout career, studied business cycles for National Bureau of Economics; books include *National Income and Its Composition, 1919 to 1938* (1941) and *Economic Growth of Nations* (1971); served as president of American Economic Association, among other societies; received many honorary degrees; died at home in Cambridge, Mass. See *Current Biography* (May) 1972.

Obituary *N Y Times* B p6 Jl 11 '85

**KYSER, KAY** June 18, 1906–July 23, 1985 Band leader; an amiable and energetic showman with little musical training, he was antic "old perfesser" of Kollege of Musical Knowledge, a popular swing "corn" orchestra that used facetious quiz-show format as audience-participation gimmick; beginning at Univ. of North Carolina, his alma mater, in late 1920s, toured campuses and dance halls nationally; through 1940s, hosted radio show that made his Southern-accented voice a familiar American sound; took novelty musical program to television in 1949-50 and was consultant to 1954 summer TV show based on his music/quiz/comedy concept; made hit recordings of "Three Little Fishies" and "Praise the Lord and Pass the Ammunition," among other songs; with his band, starred in several screen comedies, including the self-spoofing *That's Right, You're Wrong* (1939); died in Chapel Hill, N.C. See *Current Biography* (Apr.) 1941.

Obituary *N Y Times* B p5 Jl 24 '85

**LANGER, SUSANNE K(ATHERINA KNAUTH)** Dec. 20, 1895–July 17, 1985 Philosopher; aesthetician; writer; tutor in philosophy at Radcliffe College (1927-42); influenced by philosophers Alfred North Whitehead and Ernst Cassirer, propounded own philosophy of aesthetics, maintaining that artists seek to portray nature of human feeling through symbols rather than arouse or convey emotion and that religion, science, art, and myth, among other fields, are expressions of symbolic thought; presented her theories in several books, including now-classic *Philosophy in a New Key* (1942) and, most recently, three-volume *Mind: An Essay on Human Feeling* (1967-82); member of American Academy of Arts and Sciences; died at home in Old Lyme, Conn. See *Current Biography* (Nov.) 1963.

Obituary *N Y Times* A p12 Jl 19 '85

**LENGYEL, EMIL** Apr. 26, 1895–Feb. 12, 1985 Hungarian-born historian specializing in modern European politics; authority on rise of Nazism; as Austro-Hungarian soldier in WW I, was taken as prisoner of war to Siberia, where he mastered English and other languages; came to U.S. as correspondent for postwar Disarmament Conference in 1921 and stayed on as Central European specialist for *N. Y. Times* and other periodicals; wrote, among other books, *Hitler* (1932); *The Cauldron Boils* (1932); *Millions of Dictators* (1936); and *Siberia* (1943); taught at New York Univ. (1942-1960); died in Manhattan. See *Current Biography* (Feb.) 1942.

Obituary *N Y Times* A p24 F 15 '85

**LODGE, HENRY CABOT (JR.)** July 5, 1902–Feb. 27, 1985 American statesman; scion of patrician Massachusetts family; began political career as isolationist, a position he later repudiated; was elected to first of three terms as Republican senator in 1936; was army combat officer in WW II; served as ambassador to UN from 1953 to 1960, when he became Richard Nixon's running mate in Nixon's unsuccessful first campaign for the presidency; was ambassador to South Vietnam

(1963–64, 1965–67) when war there was escalating; later, was one of succession of U.S. representatives at protracted peace talks in Paris, among other diplomatic posts; wrote autobiography *The Storm Has Many Eyes* (1973); died in Beverly, Mass. See *Current Biography* (May) 1954.

Obituary *N Y Times* A p1+ F 28 '85

**LONDON, GEORGE** May 30, 1921–Mar. 24, 1985 Canadian-born singer; one of great dramatic bass-baritones of opera; won distinction in world's leading opera houses in such roles as Amonasro in *Aïda*, Almaviva in *Marriage of Figaro*, Scarpia in *Tosca*, and in title roles of *Don Giovanni* and *Boris Godunov*; first American to sing on stage of Bolshoi Theater in Moscow; after paralysis of vocal cords ended his singing career, in 1967, served as artistic administrator of John F. Kennedy Center for the Performing Arts (1968–71), executive director of National Opera Institute (1971–77) and, from 1975 until his retirement in 1980, as general director of Opera Society of Washington; died at his home in Armonk, N.Y. See *Current Biography* (Nov.) 1953.

Obituary *Washington Post* B p7 Mr 26 '85

**LONERGAN, BERNARD J(OSEPH) F(RANCIS)** Dec. 17, 1904–Nov. 26, 1984 Canadian-born Jesuit priest; leading Roman Catholic philosopher and theologian; beginning with doctoral thesis (1941–42, published as *Grace and Freedom*, 1971) and essay series "The Concept of *Verbum* in the Writings of St. Thomas" (1946–49), applied philosophical method of Thomas Aquinas to contemporary issues, thereby helping to modernize his church's thought; sought unity of scientific, artistic, and "common sense" cognition through emphasis on preconceptual intellect, especially in his epistemological masterpiece, *Insight; A Study of Human Understanding* (1957); taught at Gregorian Univ. in Rome, Regis College in Toronto, Boston College, and Jesuit seminaries; died in Pickering, Ontario. See *Current Biography* (Jan.) 1972.

Obituary *N Y Times* B p20 N 29 '84

**LÓPEZ BRAVO, GREGORIO** Dec. 19, 1923–Feb. 19, 1985 Spanish government official; marine engineer; served as minister of industry under Generalissimo Francisco Franco beginning in 1963; was appointed foreign minister in the 1969 cabinet shakeup calculated to modernize policy in anticipation of Franco's death; during four years in foreign ministry, improved relations between his country and Common Market nations, Soviet Union, Middle East, and other areas; after Franco's death (1976), was elected parliamentary representative for Madrid and headed commission on fundamental laws of parliament; in 1980s returned to private enterprise as consultant; died in airplane crash near Bilbao, Spain. See *Current Biography* (July) 1971.

Obituary *El País* (Spain) p13 F 20 '85

**LYONS, EUGENE** Jul. 1, 1898–Jan. 7, 1985 Russian-born journalist; author; editor; became naturalized U.S. citizen in 1919; edited *Soviet Russia Pictorial*, (1922–23), first American magazine about USSR; as Moscow correspondent for UPI, was one of first Americans to report from within Soviet Union; at first staunchly supported Stalinism and socialism, but denounced both soon after return to U.S. in articles and books, including autobiography *Assignment in Utopia* (1937); edited *American Mercury* (1939–44) and *Pageant* (1944–45); roving editor (1946–52) and later senior editor (1952–68) for *Reader's Digest*; died in Manhattan. See *Current Biography* (Jan.) 1944.

Obituary *N Y Times* D p23 Jan 10 '85

**MACINNES, HELEN (CLARK)** Oct. 7, 1907–Sept. 30, 1985 Author; the doyenne of international suspense fiction; beginning with *Above Suspicion* (1941) and ending with *Ride a Pale Horse* (1985), wrote twenty-one highly literate novels, most of them exciting spy stories, set against backgrounds of contemporary world events; created heroes pitted against agents of authoritarian or totalitarian regimes—usually Nazis in the 1940s and Communists thereafter; although her cardinal rule was never to write with an eye on sales, enjoyed sales of 23 million in U.S. alone; was translated into twenty-two languages; died in New York City. See *Current Biography* (Nov.) 1967.

Obituary *N Y Times* B p6 O 1 '85

**MALTZ, ALBERT** Oct. 28, 1908–Apr. 26, 1985 Screenwriter; novelist; playwright; one of "Hollywood Ten," jailed in 1950 and blacklisted for refusing to cooperate with House Committee on Un-American Activities in investigation of alleged Communist influence in film industry; won Academy Awards for documentary films *Moscow Strikes Back* (1943) and *The House I Live In* (1945) and O. Henry Memorial Award for short story "The Happiest Man on Earth" (1938); wrote screenplays for such films as *This Gun for Hire* (1942), *Destination Tokyo* (1944), *Pride of the Marines* (1945), *Naked City* (1948), and *Two Mules for Sister Sara* (1970); also wrote plays and novels, including *The Cross and the Arrow* (1944); died in Los Angeles, Calif. See *Current Biography* (Jan.–Feb.) 1940.

Obituary *N Y Times* D p10 Ap 29 '85

**MARRIOTT, J(OHN) WILLARD** Sept. 17, 1900–Aug. 13, 1985 Hotel and restaurant chain executive; parlayed a root-beer stand that he set up in Washington, D.C. (1927) into $3.5-billion Marriott Corporation, with 140,000 employees in twenty-six countries, operating some 1,400 restaurants, 143 hotels and resorts in ninety-five cities, and ninety flight kitchens serving over 150 airlines; president (1928–64) and then board chairman of Marriott Corporation (known until late 1960s as Hot Shoppes, Inc.); a leader in Latter Day Saints church; supporter of philanthropic enterprises and Republican political causes; died in Wolfeboro, N.H. See *Current Biography* (June) 1972.

Obituary *N Y Times* D p23 Ag 15 '85

**MILGRAM, STANLEY** Aug. 15, 1933–Dec. 20, 1984 Social psychologist; educator; professor at Graduate Center of City Univ. of New York since 1966; drew national attention for experiments on obedience, conducted at Yale Univ. in early 1960s, that showed subjects willing to administer painful shocks to others on orders of authority figure and raised political issues about mindless complicity in atrocities or corruption; studied influence of urban living on social interactions and antisocial anomie; applied inventive approaches to social psychology in studies of television violence and photography; produced six scientific films, including award-winning *The City and the Self* (1972); died in New York City. See *Current Biography* (Aug.) 1979.

Obituary *N Y Times* p29 D 22 '84

**MILLER, ARNOLD (RAY)** Apr. 25, 1923–July 13, 1985 President of United Mine Workers of America (1972-79); victim of black-lung disease and founding member of Black Lung Association, he helped to lobby West Virginia legislature successfully for first black-lung compensation bill; with grassroots support of Miners for Democracy faction of UMWA, fought for greater voice for miners in union affairs and won court-ordered election in 1972 for union presidency after conducting bitter campaign against autocratic and corrupt incumbent W. A. Boyle; as president, used strikes and walkouts to win higher wages, better mine safety standards, and greater benefits for UMWA; after 111-day strike in 1978 ended with unfavorable contract, retired to avoid almost certain ouster; died in Charleston, W.Va. See *Current Biography* (Nov.) 1974.

Obituary *N Y Times* p27 Jl 13 '85

**MOCH, JULES (SALVADOR)** Mar. 15, 1893–Aug. 1, 1985 French cabinet minister; Socialist politician; was first elected to chamber of deputies in 1928; rose in government under Premier Léon Blum in 1930s; going underground during WW II, served on Free French general staff under General Charles de Gaulle; as minister of interior in four successive governments (1947-50), created Compagnie Républicaine de Sécurité, a national army-police security force, to suppress Communist-led strikes; when Socialists and Communists formed alliance, resigned from Socialist party, in 1974; died in Grasse, France. See *Current Biography* (Oct.) 1950.

Obituary *N Y Times* D p15 Ag 2 '85

**MONTAGU, EWEN (EDWARD SAMUEL)** Mar. 29, 1901–July 19, 1985 British barrister; author; judge advocate of the fleet (1945-73); as officer in British naval intelligence during WW II, was largely responsible for "Operation Mincemeat," which successfully deceived German high command about Allied invasion of Sicily; detailed operation in his book *The Man Who Never Was* (1953), a film version of which was released in 1956; also wrote *The Archer-Shee Case* (1974) and *Beyond "Top Secret U"* (1977); for his role in "Mincemeat," received Military Order of the British Empire (1944); made Commander of the Order of the British Empire in 1950; died at home in London, England. See *Current Biography* (June) 1956.

Obituary *N Y Times* p28 Jl 21 '85

**MORSE, PHILIP M(CCORD)** Aug. 6, 1903–Sept. 5, 1985 Physicist; educator; a pioneer in atomic, electromagnetic, and electroacoustical theory and its military application; taught at Massachusetts Institute of Technology from 1931 until his death, except for leaves of absence; was first director of Atomic Energy Commission's Brookhaven National Laboratory (1946-49);

wrote *Vibration and Sound* (1936) and, with Edward U. Condon, *Quantum Mechanics* (1929); died in Concord, Mass. See *Current Biography* (June) 1948.

Obituary *N Y Times* D p18 S 13 '85

**NEEL, ALICE (HARTLEY)** Jan. 28, 1900–Oct. 13, 1984 Painter; a representational artist whose unconventional lifestyle once led her to be called the "quintessential bohemian"; noted in particular for her portraits, which tried to capture the inner essence of the subject; also executed landscapes, seascapes, still lifes, interiors, and abstractions; received belated recognition with retrospective exhibition at Whitney Museum of American Art in New York City (1974); first living American artist to have a major retrospective of her work in Moscow (1981); died at her home in New York City. See *Current Biography* (Aug.) 1976.

Obituary *N Y Times* B p8 O 15 '84

**NOLAN, LLOYD** Aug. 11, 1902–Sept. 27, 1985 Actor; appeared in over seventy films, often as a gangster, policeman, or soldier, including *Bataan* (1943), *A Tree Grows in Brooklyn* (1944), *The House on 92d Street* (1945), *Peyton Place* (1957), *Ice Station Zebra* (1968), and *Airport* (1969); won New York Drama Critics award for performance as Captain Philip Queeg in Broadway production of *The Caine Mutiny Court Martial* (1954) and Emmy award for same portrayal in its television adaptation (1955); also starred on television in series *Martin Kane, Private Eye* (1951-52) and *Julia* (1968-71); was chairman of annual Autistic Children's Telethon; died in Los Angeles. See *Current Biography* (Nov.) 1956.

Obituary *N Y Times* p44 S 29 '85

**NORTH, JOHN RINGLING** Aug. 14, 1903–June 4, 1985 President, chairman, and impresario of Ringling Brothers and Barnum & Bailey Circus, billed as the "Greatest Show on Earth"; occupied its presidency intermittently from 1937 until it was sold to Irvin Feld in 1967; transformed it from traditional tented "big top" into lavish indoor extravaganza, staged in large arenas like New York's Madison Square Garden; traveled extensively in search of talent; was noted for flamboyant lifestyle; died in Brussels, Belgium. See *Current Biography* (June) 1951.

Obituary *N Y Times* B p18 Je 6 '85

**ORMANDY, EUGENE** Nov. 18, 1899–Mar. 12, 1985 Symphony conductor; was music director of Philadelphia Orchestra for forty-four years; with roots in nineteenth-century Romantic tradition, produced purely crafted, elegant renditions of repertoire from Beethoven to Shostakovich, with occasional attention to contemporary masters; made Philadelphia debut in 1931 and co-directed orchestra with Leopold Stokowski in the late 1930s, assuming leadership in 1938; led orchestra on world tours, including historic trip to China in 1973; as laureate guest, conducted last concert in 1984; died in Philadelphia. See *Current Biography* (Jan.) 1941.

Obituary *N Y Times* A p1+ Mr 13 '85

**ORMSBY-GORE, (WILLIAM) DAVID** May 20, 1918–Jan. 26, 1985 British ambassador to U.S.

(1961-65); as Conservative member of Parliament for Orwestry, Shropshire (1950-61), held various posts in international relations; as minister of state for foreign affairs (1957-61), gained fame as skilled negotiator in disarmament talks with Soviet bloc; deputy-leader of opposition in House of Lords (1966-67); chairman of Harlech Television since 1967; knighted in 1961; on father's death, succeeded him as fifth Baron Harlech; died in Shrewsbury, England, as result of automobile accident. See *Current Biography* (Mar.) 1961.

Obituary *N Y Times* p22 Ja 27 '85

**PARSONS, ROSE PEABODY** Oct. 11, 1891-Mar. 28, 1985 Organization official; administrator of American Red Cross in North Atlantic area (1942-45); founder and chairman (1946-53) of Women United for the UN; vice-president of International Council of Women (1954-63); president of National Council of Women (1956-59); died in Glen Cove, N.Y. See *Current Biography* (Dec.) 1959.

Obituary *N Y Times* p26 Ap 6 '85

**PECKINPAH, SAM** Feb. 21, 1925-Dec. 28, 1984 Motion-picture director; technically brillant, controversial master of new genre of "dirty westerns" and other film elegies to anti-heroes who defy fate in dramatic rituals of carnage; from TV scriptwriting (*Gunsmoke, Broken Arrow*) and directing (*The Westerner*), graduated into cinema with direction of *The Deadly Companions* (1961) and *Ride the High Country* (1962); achieved wide recognition with *The Wild Bunch* (1969) and *Straw Dogs* (1971), among other films; answered castigations of his work as morally dubious, gratuitously gory, and "fascist" with contention that it represented cathartic evocation of primal courage; died in Inglewood, Cal. See *Current Biography* (May) 1973.

Obituary *N Y Times* p26 D 29 '84

**PEERCE, JAN** June 3(?), 1904-Dec. 15, 1984 Tenor; cantorial singer; in sixty-year career on stage, records, radio, and television thrilled audiences with even scale, stylistic versatility, and rhythmic élan; made singing debut at Radio City Music Hall in 1932; under conductor Arturo Toscanini, made early radio operatic broadcasts and recordings of *La Bohème, La Traviata*, and other works; at Metropolitan Opera (1941-68) took leading tenor roles, including those in *Rigoletto, Tosca, Faust*, and *Madama Butterfly*; a specialist in Italian repertory, retained impeccable poise and enunciatory technique throughout career; died in New York City. See *Current Biography* (May) 1942.

Obituary *N Y Times* A pl+ D 17 '84

**PETRILLO, JAMES CAESAR** Mar. 16, 1892-Oct. 23, 1984 Labor union official; as president of American Federation of Musicians (1940-58), was one of most controversial and colorful leaders in American labor movement; joined AFM in 1918, and after becoming president of its Local 10 in 1922, built it into powerful, well-disciplined organization; clashed with President Franklin D. Roosevelt in 1942, when he called strike to compel recording companies to pay royalties to musicians and union; succeeded after twenty-seven-month strike in obtaining historic royal-ty agreement with studios and establishing Music Performance Trust Fund; after retirement, fought against racial segregation in unions; died in Chicago. See *Current Biography* (Yearbook) 1940.

Obituary *N Y Times* B p22 O 25 '84

**POLLACK, JACK H(ARRISON)** Dec. 4, 1914-Sept. 30, 1984 Author; contributed some thousand articles to newspapers and such popular magazines as *Reader's Digest, Collier's, True*, and *Good Housekeeping*; wrote three books: *Croiset the Clairvoyant* (1964), a study of extrasensory perception, *Dr. Sam: An American Tragedy* (1972), about the murder trial of Dr. Sam Sheppard, and *Earl Warren* (1979), a biography of the Chief Justice of the U.S.; died in New York City. See *Current Biography* (Dec.) 1957.

Obituary *N Y Times* A p29 O 2 '84

**PRESTOPINO, GREGORIO** June 21, 1907-Dec. 16, 1984 Painter; beginning in 1930s, combined style and subject matter of social realism with robust expressionism in brashly colored oil paintings and watercolors and drawings; after 1940, often used his native Manhattan as subject, most successfully in his carefully designed Harlem Series, combining fantasy and urban detail; later turned to impressionistic rural landscapes peopled with nude figures; also created lithographs and seriographs; lectured at Museum of Modern Art and Brooklyn Museum; died in Princeton, N.J. See *Current Biography* (June) 1964.

Obituary *N Y Times* D p22 D 19 '84

**PRICE, GWILYM A(LEXANDER)** June 20, 1895-June 1, 1985 Corporation executive; lawyer; banker; president and chief executive officer (1946-60) and board chairman (1960-63) of Westinghouse Electric Corp. where he promoted pioneer work in atomic energy; as chairman of Univ. of Pittsburgh board of trustees (1959-70), helped to transform it into state-related institution and to restore its solvency; trustee of Carnegie Corporation of New York; national chairman of Crusade for Freedom (1957-59). See *Current Biography* (May) 1949.

Obituary *N Y Times* B p8 Je 3 '85

**QUAY, JAN EDUARD DE** Aug. 26, 1901-July 4, 1985 As Prime Minister of the Netherlands (1959-63), headed center-right coalition government dominated by his Catholic People's party; one of founders, in 1940, of Dutch Union, which sought accommodation with German occupation authorities but was banned by Nazis in 1941; Queen's commissioner of North Brabant province (1946-59); transport minister (1966-67); died in Beers, in the southern Netherlands. See *Current Biography* (May) 1963.

Obituary *N Y Times* p26 Jl 6 '85

**RASKIN, JUDITH** June 21, 1928-Dec. 21, 1984 Soprano; in a score of operatic roles, from Nanetta in Verdi's *Falstaff*, to Adele in Strauss's *Fledermaus* and Sister Constance in Poulenc's *Dialogues des Carmélites*, won acclaim for musicianship, poetic approach, and pure tone as among finest artists of her time; a leading singer with New York City Opera (1959-62) and Metropolitan Opera (1962-72), was most admired for her

Mozart performances (Despina in *Così fan tutte*, Zerlina in *Don Giovanni*); in recent years taught voice at City College (New York) and Manhattan School of Music; died in New York City after long struggle with cancer. See *Current Biography* (Apr.) 1964.

Obituary *N Y Times* p29 D 22 '84

**REDGRAVE, SIR MICHAEL** Mar. 20, 1908–Mar. 21, 1985 British actor; distinguished member of Redgrave theatrical dynasty; in four-decade career on stage and screen, won audiences with his aristocratic bearing, sonorous voice, expressive face, and air of tormented sensibility; began meteoric rise at Old Vic in *Love's Labour's Lost* (1936); performed with John Gielgud's company (1938); made New York stage debut as Macbeth (1948); began screen career as hero in *The Lady Vanishes* (1938), which was followed by roles in, among other films, *Dead of Night* (1946), *Mourning Becomes Electra* (1947), *The Browning Version* (1951), and *Nicholas and Alexandra* (1971), his last picture; wrote two plays and autobiography *In My Mind's Eye* (1983); died in Denham, England. See *Current Biography* (Feb.) 1950.

Obituary *N Y Times* B p5 Mr 22 '85

**RICHTER, CHARLES FRANCIS** Apr. 26, 1900–Sept. 30, 1985 Physicist; geologist; with his colleague Beno Gutenberg at the California Institute of Technology Seismological Laboratory in Pasadena beginning in 1927, created the Richter scale for measuring the magnitude of earthquakes, perfected in 1935; with Gutenberg, wrote *Seismicity of the Earth* (1941; revised and expanded, 1954); after retirement, in 1970, continued to visit Cal Tech lab almost daily while working as consultant with Lindvall, Richter & Associates in Los Angeles; died in Pasadena. See *Current Biography* (May) 1975.

Obituary *N Y Times* B p7 O 1 '85

**ROCK, JOHN** Mar. 24, 1890–Dec. 4, 1984 Gynecologist; obstetrician; with Dr. Gregory Pincus and Dr. M. C. Chang, developed first effective oral contraceptive pill, which went on the market in 1960; founder and director (1926–56) of Fertility and Endocrine Clinic at the Free Hospital for Women in Brookline, Massachusetts; clinical professor of gynecology at Harvard Medical School (1947–56); director of Rock Reproductive Clinic at Brookline (from 1956); as a devout Roman Catholic, failed in his efforts to break down church's prohibition against contraception; died at Peterborough, N.H. See *Current Biography* (Dec.) 1964.

Obituary *N Y Times* A p29 D 5 '84

**ROMANO, EMANUEL** Sept. 23, 1904–Nov. 11, 1984 Italian-born artist; a painter noted for delicacy of line combined with heroic emotion in depictions of common life, also created engravings, murals, and silverpoint drawings; produced woodcut illustrations for special editions of T. S. Eliot's *The Wasteland* and Samuel Beckett's *Waiting for Godot*, among other publications; works housed in Metropolitan Museum of Art, Boston Museum of Fine Arts, and other collections; died in New York City. See *Current Biography* (Mar.) 1940.

Obituary *N Y Times* A p26 N 16 '84

**ROSE, LEONARD** July 27, 1918–Nov. 16, 1984 Violoncellist; noted for his grandeur of style, resonance, and flawless technique; specialized in music of Romantic era; principal cellist with Cleveland Orchestra (1939–43) and New York Philharmonic Orchestra (1943–51); after making final appearance with Philharmonic at Edinburgh festival (1951), pursued career as solo performer; during 1960s and early 1970s, toured world in chamber ensemble with pianist Eugene Istomin and violinist Isaac Stern; also won renown as teacher of cello, at Curtis Institute (1952–62) and Juilliard School of Music (1947–84); died at White Plains (N.Y.) Hospital. See *Current Biography* (January) 1977.

Obituary *N Y Times* D p14 N 19 '84

**RYLE, SIR MARTIN** Sept. 27, 1918–Oct. 14, 1984 British astronomer; noted for his discoveries in radio astronomy; shared 1974 Nobel Prize in physics for development of aperture synthesis technique, combining sensitive radio telescopes with elaborate computers to permit surveying and mapping of cosmic regions beyond the range of optical telescopes; proponent of "big bang" theory of explosive origin of universe; professor of radio astronomy at Cambridge Univ. (1959–82); director of Mullard Radio Astronomy Observatory at Cambridge (1958–82); Great Britain's Astronomer Royal (1972–82); was knighted in 1966; died at his home in Cambridge. See *Current Biography* (Sept.) 1973.

Obituary *N Y Times* D p7 O 17 '84

**SARKIS, ELIAS** July 20, 1924–June 27, 1985 Lebanese statesman; member of dominant Maronite Christian community; governor of Central Bank of Lebanon (1968–76); as president of Lebanon (1976–82), tried but failed to restore peace to his strife-torn country; died at his home in Paris, France. See *Current Biography* (Mar.) 1979.

Obituary *N Y Times* D p16 Je 28 '85

**SCOTT, MICHAEL (GUTHRIE)** July 30, 1907–Sept. 14, 1983 Anglican clergyman; social activist; served church in Britain, India, and South Africa; in South Africa, was jailed for opposing apartheid, in 1946, and declared prohibited person, in 1950; tirelessly lobbied UN in behalf of oppressed Herero, Berg, Damara, and Nama tribes of Namibia; in England in late 1950s, helped Bertrand Russell to found Committee of 100, which agitated for unilateral nuclear disarmament; in 1959, was imprisoned for civil disobedience in ban-the-bomb cause; died in London. See *Current Biography* (Apr.) 1953.

Obituary *Christian Century* 100:930 O 19 '83

**SCOURBY, ALEXANDER** Nov. 13, 1913–Feb. 22, 1985 Actor; narrator; best known for emotive depth his resonant bass voice added to radio and television documentaries, dramas, musical-show and opera commentaries, and commercials; widened world of the blind with hundreds of Talking Books recordings for Library of Congress; on stage, had numerous roles, often as suave villain, in plays by Shakespeare, Sartre, Garcia Lorca, Shaw, Brecht, and others; on screen, was most memorable as Polo, Mexican ranch foreman in *Giant* (1956); died in Boston, Mass. See *Current Biography* (July) 1965.

Obituary *N Y Times* B p6 F 25 '85

**SESSIONS, ROGER (HUNTINGTON)** Dec. 28, 1896–Mar. 16, 1985 Composer; a masterful technician whose complex and intellectual but emotionally textured scores won more esteem from colleagues than from public; during long career, shifted from neoclassic style of suite *The Black Maskers* (1923) to twelve-tone serialism of Symphony No. 3 (1957); composed operas *Trial of Lucullus* and *Montezuma* in 1940s; taught composition at Boston Conservatory, Juilliard School of Music, Princeton Univ., and elsewhere; won two Pulitzer prizes, in 1974 for body of work and in 1982 for Concerto for Orchestra; died in Princeton, N.J. See *Current Biography* (Jan.) 1975.

Obituary *N Y Times* B p6 Mr 18 '85

**SHIVERS, ALLAN** Oct. 5, 1907–Jan. 14, 1985 Governor of Texas (1949–57); partner in law firm of Shivers, Clayton, and Kirkland (1931–49); Texas state senator (1935–47); lieutenant governor (1947–49); became governor on death in office of Beauford H. Jester and was reelected to two more terms; as governor, expanded mental health, educational, and prison administration services; throughout political career, fought for state's claims to oil-rich offshore areas; operated Western Pipe Line, Inc.; member of board of directors of several corporations, Texas banks, and civic organizations; died in Austin. See *Current Biography* (Oct.) 1951.

Obituary *N Y Times* B p5 Ja 16 '85

**SIGNORET, SIMONE** Mar. 25, 1921–Sept. 30, 1985 French actress; an icon of French cinema for four decades; after playing sensuous *femmes fatales* and other glamorous roles, grew old gracefully on screen, refusing "to cling to an appearance that would have been artificial"; starred in some forty films, including *La Ronde* (1950), *Casque d'or* (1951), *Diabolique* (1955), *Ship of Fools* (1965), *Madame Rosa* (1977), and *L'Etoile du Nord* (1982); won Academy Award as best actress for her portrayal of mistress in *Room at the Top* (1958); was also television *vedette*; with husband, Yves Montand, was leftist political activist; wrote novel *Adieu, Volodia* (1985) and three books of nonfiction, including 1977 autobiography; died in Normandy, France. See *Current Biography* (Dec.) 1960.

Obituary *N Y Times* B p6 O 1 '85

**SIMPSON, GEORGE GAYLORD** June 16, 1902–Oct. 6, 1984 Vertebrate paleontologist; was a curator at American Museum of Natural History in New York City for thirty-five years; taught at Columbia and Harvard universities and, since 1967, at Univ. of Arizona; led numerous scientific expeditions, some of which resulted in important fossil finds, including "dawn horse" skulls and bones; developed synthetic theory of evolution integrating Mendelian genetics, paleontological evidence, and modern biology with Darwin's historical theory; contributed several hundred articles to professional journals; wrote some two-score books, from taxonomy, zoology, and biology textbooks to *Concession to the Improbable: An Unconventional Autobiography* (1978); died in Tucson, Ariz. See

*Current Biography* (December) 1964.

Obituary *N Y Times* D p10 O 8 '84

**SIMPSON, HOWARD E(DWARD)** Mar. 15, 1896–Feb. 10, 1985 Railroad executive; rose through ranks, from passenger agent to president (1953–61) of Baltimore & Ohio Railroad; headed B & O during period when, with passenger traffic declining, railroad was becoming dependent on freight traffic for its financial solvency; retired as chairman and chief executive officer in 1963; died in Baltimore, Md. See *Current Biography* (May) 1958.

Obituary *N Y Times* D p27 F 13 '85

**SLOANE, ERIC** 1910(?)–Mar. 6, 1985 Artist; writer; celebrated preindustrial America in wistful, powerfully realized paintings of landscapes, cloudscapes, covered bridges, and farm structures and implements; was influenced equally by Hudson River and Ashcan schools; wrote and illustrated *Folklore of American Weather* (1963) and *I Remember America* (1971), among other books; a meteorology expert, built hall of weather phenomena for American Museum of Natural History; died in New York City. See *Current Biography* (Sept.) 1972.

Obituary *N Y Times* B p6 Mr 8 '85

**SPEIDEL, HANS** Oct. 28, 1897–Nov. 28, 1984 German military expert; officer in German regular army (1914–1945); during WW II, held Wehrmacht command posts and served as chief of staff to Field Marshal Erwin Rommel; took part in abortive plot to assassinate Adolf Hitler (1944); after war, taught modern history at Tübingen Univ. and helped to plan German Federal Republic's new army; commander in chief of West German armed forces (1955–57); commander of Allied land forces in Central Europe, a key NATO post (1957–63); president of Stiftung Wissenschaft und Politik, a research foundation (1964–78); died at his home in Bad Honnef, West Germany. See *Current Biography* (Apr.) 1952.

Obituary *N Y Times* B p20 N 29 '84

**SPRINGER, AXEL (CAESAR)** May 2, 1912–Sept. 22, 1985 West German publisher; in decade following WW II built Axel Springer Verlag, conglomerate employing more than 11,000 people in variety of mostly related enterprises, from paper mills and printing plants to book-publishing companies, magazines, and newspapers, including sensational *Bild Zeitung*, Western Europe's largest-circulation daily, and prestigious *Die Welt*; exerted enormous influence on public opinion with his editorial policies; anti-Nazi, pro-Israel, and pro-Jewish, he became increasingly strident in his cold-war nationalism; died in Berlin. See *Current Biography* (Dec.) 1968.

Obituary *N Y Times* D p15 S 23 '85

**STARR, MARK** Apr. 27, 1894–Apr. 24, 1985 Labor union official; educator; one of pioneers in field of adult education; as education director of International Ladies' Garment Workers Union (1935–60), supervised program offering hundreds of courses in variety of fields to members in U.S. and Canada; served in official posts with American Federation of Teachers and

New York State Liberal party, and with various government commissions and civic organizations; consultant to Office of War Information during WW II; author of several books, including (with Harold U. Faulkner) *Labor in America* (1944); died in Sunnyside, N.Y. See *Current Biography* (July) 1946.

Obituary *N Y Times* D p10 Ap 29 '85

**STERLING, J(OHN) E(WART) WALLACE** Aug. 6, 1906–July 1, 1985 Canadian-born educator; as fifth president of Stanford Univ. (1949–68), brought that institution into top ranks of research universities and greatly expanded its faculty and student body; established new medical center, high-energy research laboratory, and overseas studies centers, among other facilities; had previously served as history professor and department chairman at California Institute of Technology; CBS radio news commentator (1942–48); director of Huntington Library and Art Gallery (1948–49); after retirement as Stanford president, continued to serve university as trustee and fund-raiser; received honorary knighthood from Queen Elizabeth II (1976); died in Woodside, Calif. See *Current Biography* (Jan.) 1951.

Obituary *N Y Times* D p19 Jl 3 '85

**STEVENSON, WILLIAM E(DWARDS)** Oct. 25, 1900–Apr. 2, 1985 U.S. diplomat; educator; a lawyer with talent for organization, established noted law partnership firm of Stevenson and Debevoise in 1930s and set up Red Cross operations in England and North Africa during WW II; was president of Oberlin College from late 1940s through 1950s; was named ambassador to Philippines (1961–64) by President John F. Kennedy; headed Aspen Institute of Humanistic Studies in late 1960s; as young athlete, had been member of record-setting U.S. track team at 1924 Olympic Games in Paris; died in Fort Myers, Fla. See *Current Biography* (Nov.) 1943.

Obituary *N Y Times* D p30 Ap 4 '85

**STRAUS, JACK I(SIDOR)** Jan. 13, 1900–Sept. 19, 1985 Retail executive; civic leader; philanthropist; scion of Straus merchandising family, which bought control of R. H. Macy & Co., "the world's largest store," in 1896; as president and chief executive officer of Macy's during three decades beginning in 1940, oversaw company's expansion into nationwide chain with ninety-three department stores in fourteen states; died in New York City. See *Current Biography* (Mar.) 1952.

Obituary *N Y Times* A p20 S 20 '85

**SWING, JOSEPH M(AY)** Feb. 28, 1894–Dec. 9, 1984 U.S. government official; career military officer and commander in WW II; a West Point graduate, joined U.S. forces in Mexico under Gen. John J. Pershing (1916); served as field artillery captain in France in WW I; as major general in WW II activated 11th Airborne Division and conducted mass landings of parachute and glider troops in New Guinea and Philippines; 11th Airborne first U.S. unit to occupy Japan after its surrender; commandant (1950–51) of Army War College at Ft. Leavenworth, Kan.; served as commissioner of Immigration and Naturalization Service (1954–62); died in San Francisco. See *Current*

*Biography* (Apr.) 1959.

Obituary *N Y Times* A p27 D 12 '84

**TERRY, LUTHER L(EONIDAS)** Sept. 15, 1911–Mar. 29, 1985 Public-health official; physician; as surgeon general of U.S. (1961–65), prepared 1964 report linking cigarette smoking to lung cancer and other diseases; entered Public Health Service in 1942; at National Heart Institute (1953–61), did research on hypertension; was a professor of medicine at Univ. of Pennsylvania from 1965 until retirement in 1982; in later years, campaigned nationally for control of smoking in workplace; died in Philadelphia. See *Current Biography* (Oct.) 1961.

Obituary *N Y Times* p38 Mr 31 '85

**TRUFFAUT, FRANÇOIS** Feb. 6, 1932–Oct. 21, 1984 French motion-picture director; actor; producer; writer; a leading *auteur* of "New Wave" group of French filmmakers, emphasizing individuality and spontaneity; made twenty-one features, beginning with partly autobiographical *The 400 Blows* (1959) and including such classics as *Shoot the Piano Player* (1960), *Jules and Jim* (1961), *Stolen Kisses* (1968), *The Story of Adele H.* (1975), and *The Man Who Loved Women* (1977); received Oscar for best foreign film for his *Day for Night* (1973) and ten César awards from French film industry for *The Last Metro* (1980); author of *Hitchcock* (1967) and other books on cinema; died in Neuilly-sur-Seine, France. See *Current Biography* (Jan.) 1969.

Obituary *N Y Times* A p1 O 22 '84

**VISSER 'T HOOFT, WILLEM A(DOLF)** Sept. 20, 1900–July 4, 1985 Dutch clergyman; world religious organization leader; ordained a minister of Reformed Church (1936); helped to found World Council of Churches, and as its general secretary (1948–66), presided over its growth from 147 denominations in forty countries to some 300 in ninety countries; promoted inclusion of churches in Communist countries, and greater role for Third World and Eastern Orthodox churches, in council, but failed in efforts to bring in Roman Catholic churches; worked with Dutch underground and exile government during WW II; author of *Rembrandt and the Gospel* (1957) and other books; died in Geneva, Switzerland. See *Current Biography* (May) 1949.

Obituary *N Y Times* D p6 Jl 5 '85

**WALLOP, (JOHN) DOUGLASS** Mar. 8, 1920–Apr. 1, 1985 Author; wrote book *The Year the Yankees Lost the Pennant* (1954), on which the hit musical *Damn Yankees* (1955) was based; also wrote *Night Light* (1953), *The Good Life* (1969), *Mixed Singles* (1977), *The Other Side of the River* (1984), and other novels; early in his career, served as amanuensis to Dwight D. Eisenhower for book *Crusade in Europe* (1948); died in Georgetown, Md. See *Current Biography* (Yrbk) 1956.

Obituary *N Y Times* A p16 Ap 5 '85

**WELCH, ROBERT (HENRY WINBORNE, JR.)** Dec. 1, 1899–Jan. 6, 1985 Political ideologue; in such books as *May God Forgive Us* (1952) and *The Politician* (1958) and in his magazine *American Opinion*, warned of "conspiracy" to subvert U.S. republic in name of spurious "democracy" and to subordinate patriotism to international collectivism; after thirty-six years as candy manufacturer, in 1957 left business to devote all of his energies to crusade against Communists and "Comsymps" in government; to spread his "Americanist" message, in 1958 founded John Birch Society, which claimed 100,000 members at its peak, in mid-1960s; eventually came to believe that Communism is only a "front" for, and that Communists are among the pawns of, a secret "inner circle . . . running the show" in both East and West, a centuries-old cabal rooted in or related to the Bavarian Illuminati; died in Winchester, Mass. See *Current Biography* (Nov.) 1976.

Obituary *N Y Times* B p6 Ja 8 '85

**WELLES, (GEORGE) ORSON** May 6, 1915–Oct. 10, 1985 Director; writer; actor; a pivotal and seminal figure in motion pictures, theatre, and the broadcast media; as co-producer of Mercury Theatre of the Air, caused nationwide panic, in 1938, with the verisimilitude of his radio broadcast of H. G. Wells's *War of the Worlds*; produced, directed, and starred in *Citizen Kane* (1941), one of the great innovative film classics of all time; produced and directed *The Magnificent Ambersons* (1942); starred under his own direction in screen adaptations of Shakespeare, including *Macbeth* (1948) and *Othello* (1955), and in such other films as *The Stranger* (1946), *The Lady From Shanghai* (1948), and *Touch of Evil* (1958); acted in dozens of films under other directors, including Carol Reed's *The Third Man* (1949); died in Los Angeles. See *Current Biography* (Feb.) 1965.

Obituary *N Y Times* A p1+ O 11 '85

**WERNER, OSKAR** Nov. 13, 1922–Oct. 23, 1984 Austrian-born actor; director; sensitive, vulnerable hero of European and American motion pictures; began acting career at eighteen with Vienna Burgtheater; made Hollywood debut as anti-Nazi German war prisoner in *Decision Before Dawn* (1951); received Oscar nomination for portrayal of ship's doctor in *Ship of Fools* (1965); also appeared in Max Ophüls' *Lola Montez* (1955), in François Truffaut's *Jules and Jim* (1961) and *Fahrenheit 451* (1966), and in such films as *The Spy Who Came in from the Cold* (1965), *Interlude* (1968), *The Shoes of the Fisherman* (1968), and *Voyage of the Damned* (1976); portrayed Hamlet, Henry V, and other roles on German-language stage; spent his last years as a virtual recluse at his home in Liechtenstein; died in Marburg, West Germany. See *Current Biography* (June) 1966.

Obituary *N Y Times* D p27 O 24 '84

**WHITE, E(LWYN) B(ROOKS)** July 11, 1899–Oct. 1, 1985 Author; editor; dissected vagaries of modern life in witty essays, in "Talk of the Town" section of *New Yorker* (1926–38) and "One Man's Meat" column in *Harper's*, and in such books as *Ho Hum* (1931), *Quo Vadimus?* (1939), and *The Points of My Compass* (1962); collaborated with James Thurber on volume *Is Sex Necessary?* (1929); also wrote poetry, and such classic children's books as *Stuart Little* (1945) and *Charlotte's Web* (1952); earned reputation as an expert on American English usage with his 1959 updating of William Strunk Jr.'s 1918 book *The Elements of Style*, now a standard text; received Presidential Medal of Freedom (1963), special Pulitzer Prize (1978), and other honors; died in North Brooklin, Me. See *Current Biography* (Oct.) 1960.

Obituary *N Y Times* A p1+ O 2 '85

**WHITE, KATHARINE ELKUS** Nov. 25, 1906–Apr. 24, 1985 U.S. ambassador to Denmark (1964–68); Democratic mayor of Red Bank, N.J. (1951–56); chairman of New Jersey Highway Authority (1955–64); died in Red Bank, N.J. See *Current Biography* (Feb.) 1965.

Obituary *N Y Times* p29 Ap 27 '85

**WHITTEMORE, ARTHUR** Oct. 23, 1916–Oct. 23, 1984 Pianist; as collaborator since 1935 with Jack Lowe in two-piano team, Whittemore and Lowe, devised programs of popular and classical selections transcribed for two pianos that achieved nationwide success through live concert tours, recordings, and television appearances in 1940s and 1950s; as naval enlistee in WW II, toured Pacific region with Lowe as first U.S. Navy entertainment unit; appeared with major U.S. symphony orchestras; considered technically brilliant and innovative musical popularizer; died in Southampton, N.Y. See *Current Biography* (Jan.) 1954.

Obituary *N Y Times* B p5 O 26 '84

**WILCOX, FRANCIS O(RLANDO)** Apr. 9, 1908–Feb. 20, 1985 U.S. government official; dean emeritus of Johns Hopkins University's School of Advanced International Studies; beginning in 1942, served in a variety of State Department posts, including assistant secretary of state for international organization affairs (1955–60); since 1975, was director general of Atlantic Council, which promoted closer NATO ties; died in Washington, D.C. See *Current Biography* (Apr.) 1962.

Obituary *N Y Times* p10 F 23 '85

**WILDE, FRAZAR B(ULLARD)** Jan. 26, 1895–May 28, 1985 Insurance executive; joined Connecticut General Life Insurance Co. (now part of Cigna Corp.) as clerk in 1914; served as its fourth president (1936–61) and as board chairman (from 1960); chairman of U.S. Commission on Money and Credit (1961); was appointed to Advisory Committee on International Monetary Arrangements in 1965; served as consultant to board of governors of Federal Reserve Board; died in West Hartford, Conn. See *Current Biography* (May) 1959.

Obituary *N Y Times* D p27 My 29 '85

**WOLFENDEN, SIR JOHN (FREDERICK)** June 26, 1906–Jan. 18, 1985 British educator; director of British Museum (1969–73); began career as philosophy teacher and headmaster; was vice-chancellor of Univ. of Reading (1950–63); chaired several royal committees; became household name as chairman of so-called Wolfenden Committee, whose recommendations were incorporated into Sexual Offences Act (1967), which relaxed laws against homosexuality while outlawing open solicitation for prostitution; became life peer in 1974; died in London. See *Current Biography* (Oct.) 1970.

Obituary *N Y Times* p29 Ja 20 '85

**WOODHOUSE, (MARGARET) CHASE GOING**
1890–Dec. 12, 1984 Two-term U.S. representative from
Connecticut (1944-46, 1948-50); professor of political
economy; Connecticut secretary of state (1940-42); in
Congress, worked for sane, equitable transition to
peacetime economy after WW II; headed Service Bureau for Women's Organizations in Hartford
(1952-80); in 1970s, chaired Connecticut Committee on
Status of Women; taught at Smith College, Univ. of
North Carolina, and Connecticut College; throughout
career, promoted women's professional career development; died in New Canaan, Conn. See *Current
Biography* (Mar.) 1945.

Obituary *N Y Times* D p30 D 13 '84

**YOUNG, STEPHEN M(ARVIN)** May 4, 1890–Dec. 1,
1984 U.S. Democratic senator from Ohio (1959-71);
lawyer; served four terms, intermittently from 1932 to
1951, as member at large of U.S. House of Representatives from Ohio; was noted for his liberal, pro-labor
policies and colorful rhetoric; as member of Senate
Armed Services Committee, was an early opponent of
U.S. military involvement in Vietnam; died at the
Washington Home Hospice in Washington, D.C. See
*Current Biography* (Oct.) 1959.

Obituary *N Y Times* B p12 D 3 '84

**ZEVIN, B(ENJAMIN) D(AVID)** May 16, 1901(?)-Dec.
27, 1984 Publisher; innovative marketing strategist; as
advertising director (1934-36), vice-president
(1939-45), and president (1945-62) of World Publishing
Co., encouraged production of attractive, inexpensive
editions of dictionaries and Bibles; on founding Tower
Books (1939), issued series of nonfiction best-sellers
for forty-nine cents each, including *Roget's Thesaurus*
and Clement Wood's *Complete History of the United
States*, and low-cost fiction by Sherwood Anderson,
John Steinbeck, Richard Wright, and others; chairman
of board for World Publishing Co. (1963-66); died in
Miami Beach, Fla. See *Current Biography* (Sept.)
1943.

Obituary *N Y Times* p26 D 29 '84

**ZIMBALIST, EFREM** Apr. 1889–Feb. 22, 1985 Russian-born violinist; conservatory director; composer of
chamber music and opera *Landara*; came to U.S. in
1911; with symphony orchestras and with his first
wife, soprano Alma Gluck, performed works by
Strauss, Sibelius, Ravel, Beethoven, and Bach, among
others, conveying a clear liquid timbre and sure interpretive sense that Virgil Thomson called "the most
human" of contemporary violin tones; was head of violin department (1928-41) and school director
(1941-68) at Curtis Institute in Philadelphia, conservatory founded by his second wife, Mary L. Curtis Bok;
died in Reno, Nev. See *Current Biography* (Mar.)
1949.

Obituary *N Y Times* p9 F 23 '85

# BIOGRAPHICAL REFERENCES

Almanac of American Politics, 1986

Almanac of Canada (1979)

American Architects Directory, 1970

American Catholic Who's Who, 1978

American Medical Directory, 1979

American Men and Women of Science (1982)

Asia Who's Who (1960)

Biographical Directory of Librarians in the United States and Canada (1970)

Biographical Directory of the American Congress, 1774–1971 (1971)

Biographical Directory of the USSR (1958)

Biographical Encyclopaedia & Who's Who of the American Theatre (1966)

Biographical Encyclopedia of Pakistan, 1971–72

Biographical Encyclopedia of Scientists (1981)

Burke's Peerage, Baronetage, and Knightage, 1970

Canadian Who's Who, 1982

Celebrity Register (1973)

Chi è? (1961)

China Yearbook, 1982

Chujoy, A., and Manchester, P. W., eds. Dance Encyclopedia (1967)

Concise Biographical Dictionary of Singers (1969)

Concise Oxford Dictionary of Ballet (1982)

Congressional Directory, 1960–1981

Congressional Quarterly Almanac, 1960–1984

Contemporary Artists (1983)

Contemporary Authors (1962–84)

Contemporary Dramatists (1982)

Contemporary Foreign Language Writers (1985)

Contemporary Literary Criticism, 1973–82

Contemporary Literary Critics (1982)

Contemporary Novelists (1982)

Contemporary Poets (1980)

Contemporary Poets of the English Language (1970)

Debrett's Peerage and Baronetage (1980)

Dictionary of Contemporary American Artists (1982)

Dictionary of International Biography (1975–84)

Dictionary of Latin American and Caribbean Biography (1971)

Dictionnaire de biographie française (1972)

Directory of American Judges (1955)

Directory of American Scholars (1974)

Directory of British Scientists, 1966–67

Directory of Medical Specialists, 1983–84

Encyclopedia of Pop, Rock and Soul (1977)

Ewen, D., ed, Composers of Today (1936); Living Musicians (1940; First Supplement 1957); Men and Women Who Make Music (1949); American Composers (1982); European Composers Today (1954); The New Book of Modern Composers (1961); Popular American Composers (1962; First Supplement, 1972); Composers Since 1900 (1969); Musicians Since 1900 (1978)

Far East and Australasia, 1984–85

Feather, L. Encyclopedia of Jazz (1984); Encyclopedia of Jazz in the Sixties (1967)

Filmgoer's Companion (1978)

Football Register, 1984

Foremost Women in Communications (1970)

Grove's Dictionary of Music and Musicians (1955)

Hindustan Year Book and Who's Who, 1963

Hvem er Hvem? 1973

International Authors and Writers Who's Who, 1982

International Motion Picture Almanac, 1984

International Television Almanac, 1984

International Who's Who, 1985–86

International Who's Who in Art and Antiques, 1976

International Who's Who in Music, 1980

International Who's Who in Poetry, 1977

International Who's Who of the Arab World (1978)

International Year Book and Statesmen's Who's Who, 1985

Japan Biographical Encyclopedia & Who's Who, 1964–65

Jews in the World of Science (1956)

Junior Book of Authors (1951)

Katz, E. Film Encyclopedia (1982)

Kelly's Handbook to the Titled, Landed and Official Classes, 1964

Kleine Slavische Biographie (1958)

Kraks Bla Bog, 1964

Kürschners Deutscher Gelehrten-Kalender, 1970

Leaders in Education (1974)

Leaders in Electronics (1979)

Leaders in Profile (1975)

Martindale-Hubbell Law Directory, 1979

McGraw-Hill Encyclopedia of World Biography (1973)

McGraw-Hill Encyclopedia of World Drama (1984)

McGraw-Hill Modern Scientists and Engineers (1980)

Middle East and North Africa, 1984–85

More Junior Authors (1963)

Nalanda Year-Book and Who's Who in India and Pakistan, 1958

National Cyclopaedia of American Biography (1926–84)

New Century Cyclopedia of Names (1954)

New Grove Dictionary of Music and Musicians (1980)

Nordness, L., ed. Art USA Now (1963)

Notable Australians (1978)

Notable Names in American Theatre (1976)

Nouveau Dictionnaire National des Contemporains (1968)

Official Baseball Register, 1984

Official Catholic Directory, 1976

Oxford Companion to Film (1976)

Panorama Biografico degli Italiani d'Oggi (1956)

Political Profiles (1976–79)

Politics in America (1986)

Poor's Register of Directors and Executives, 1974

Prominent Personalities in the USSR (1968)

Quién es Quién en la Argentina, 1968–69

Quién es Quién en Venezuela, Panama, Ecuador, Colombia, 1956

Robinson, D. 100 Most Important People in the World Today (1972)

Slonimsky, N. Baker's Biographical Dictionary of Musicians (1978)

Something About the Author (1971–84)

Third Book of Junior Authors (1972)

Thomas, S. Men of Space (1960–68)

Thompson, K. A. Dictionary of Twentieth-Century Composers (1973)

Thompson, O., ed. International Cyclopedia of Music and Musicians, 1975

Thomson, D. Biographical Dictionary of Film (1981)

Twentieth Century Authors (1942; First Supplement, 1955)

Two Hundred Contemporary Authors (1969)

Vem är Det, 1973

Webster's Biographical Dictionary (1971)

Wer ist Wer? (1984)

Who is Who in Music (1951)

Who's Who, 1985–86

Who's Who among Black Americans, 1980–81

Who's Who in Advertising (1963)

Who's Who in Africa, 1973

Who's Who in America, 1984–85

Who's Who in American Art (1984)

Who's Who in American Education, 1967–68

Who's Who in American Politics, 1983–84

Who's Who in Art (1982–83)

Who's Who in Australia, 1980

Who's Who in Austria, 1971–72

Who's Who in Baseball, 1971

Who's Who in Belgium (1962)

Who's Who in California, 1983

Who's Who in Canada, 1984–85

Who's Who in Chicago and Illinois (1950)

Who's Who in Colored America, 1950

Who's Who in Communist China (1969)

Who's Who in Engineering, 1982

Who's Who in Finance and Industry, 1983–84

Who's Who in France, 1983–84

Who's Who in France (Paris), 1953–54

Who's Who in Germany (1980)

Who's Who in Hollywood, 1900–1976

Who's Who in Israel, 1981–82

Who's Who in Italy, 1957–58

Who's Who in Labor, 1976

Who's Who in Latin America (1971)

Who's Who in Library and Information Services (1982)

Who's Who in Malaysia, 1983

Who's Who in Music, 1969

Who's Who in New York State, 1982

Who's Who in New Zealand (1968)

Who's Who in Opera, 1976

Who's Who in Philosophy (1969)

Who's Who in Professional Baseball (1973)

Who's Who in Publishing (1971)

Who's Who in Railroading in North America (1959)

Who's Who in Rock Music (1982)

Who's Who in Saudi Arabia, 1984

Who's Who in Space, 1966–67

Who's Who in Spain, 1965

Who's Who in Switzerland, 1982–83

Who's Who in the Arab World, 1984

Who's Who in the East, 1983–84

Who's Who in the Midwest, 1984–85

Who's Who in the Netherlands, 1962–63

Who's Who in the People's Republic of China (1981)

Who's Who in the South and Southwest, 1984–85

Who's Who in the Soviet Union, 1984

Who's Who in the Theatre (1981)

Who's Who in the United Nations (1975)

Who's Who in the West, 1984–85

Who's Who in Western Europe (1981)

Who's Who in the World, 1984–85

Who's Who in World Aviation and Astronautics (1958)

Who's Who in World Jewry (1978)

Who's Who of American Women, 1983–84

Who's Who of British Engineers, 1980–81

Who's Who of British Scientists, 1980–81

Who's Who of Jazz (1985)

Who's Who of Rhodesia, Mauritius, Central and East Africa, 1965

Who's Who of Southern Africa, 1982

Who's Who on Television (1983)

Wie is Dat? (1956)

Women Lawyers in the United States (1957)

World Artists 1950–1980 (1984)

World Authors 1950–1970 (1975)

World Authors 1970–75 (1980)

World Authors 1975–80 (1985)

World Biography (1954)

World Who's Who in Science (1968)

World's Who's Who of Women (1983)

Writers Directory (1984–86)

# PERIODICALS AND NEWSPAPERS CONSULTED

**ALA Bul**—American Library Association Bulletin
**After Dark**
**Am Artist**—American Artist
**Am Libs**—American Libraries
**Am Scholar**—American Scholar
**Am Sociol R**—American Sociological Review
**America**
**Américas**
**Arch Rec**—Architectural Record
**Archaeology**
**Art & Artists**
**Artforum**
**Artnews**
**Arts**
**Arts & Arch**—Arts & Architecture
**Atlan**—Atlantic Monthly
**Aviation W**—Aviation Week and Space Technology

**Ballet N**—Ballet News
**Barron's**
**Biog N**—Biography News (disc.)
**Book-of-the-Month Club N**—Book-of-the-Month Club News
**Book World**
**Broadcasting**
**Bsns W**—Business Week

**Cath World**—Catholic World
**Chicago Tribune**
**Christian Sci Mon**—Christian Science Monitor
**Columbia J R**—Columbia Journalism Review
**Commonweal**
**Cong Digest**—Congressional Digest
**Cong Q**—Congressional Quarterly Weekly Report
**Cosmo**—Cosmopolitan
**Crawdaddy**
**Cue** (now incorporated into New York)
**Cur Hist**—Current History
**Cur World Leaders**—Current World Leaders

**Dance & Dancers**
**Dance Mag**—Dance Magazine
**Discover**

**Ebony**
**Economist**
**Ed & Pub**—Editor & Publisher
**Encounter**
**Esquire**

**Facts on File**
**Family Circle**
**Films & Filming**
**For Affairs**—Foreign Affairs

**For Policy Bul**—Foreign Policy Bulletin
**Forbes**
**Fortune**

**Geo**
**German Tribune**
**Good H**—Good Housekeeping
**Guardian**

**Harper's**
**Hi Fi**—High Fidelity
**Hi Fi/Stereo R**—Hi/Fi Stereo Review
**Holiday**
**Horizon**

**Illus Lond N**—Illustrated London News
**India News**
**International Herald Tribune**

**Ladies Home J**—Ladies' Home Journal
**Le Monde**
**Lib J**—Library Journal
**Life**
**London Observer**
**London R of Bks**—London Review of Books
**Look**—(disc.)
**Los Angeles Times**

**McCall's**
**Maclean's**
**Mlle**—Mademoiselle
**Modern Maturity**
**Ms**—Ms.
**Mus Am**—Musical America
**Mus Mod Art**—Museum of Modern Art Bulletin

**N Y Daily News**
**N Y Herald Tribune Bk R**—New York Herald Tribune Book Review (disc.)
**N Y Post**
**N Y Rev of Bks**—New York Review of Books
**N Y Sunday News**
**N Y Times**
**N Y Times Bk R**—New York Times Book Review
**N Y Times Mag**—New York Times Magazine
**N Y World-Telegram**—New York World-Telegram and Sun (disc.)
**N Y World Journal Tribune**—(disc.)
**Nat Geog Mag**—National Geographic Magazine
**Nat R**—National Review
**Nation**
**Nations Bsns**—Nation's Business
**Nature**

**New Leader**
**New Repub**—New Republic
**New Statesm**—New Statesman
**New York**
**New Yorker**
**Newsday**
**Newsweek**

**Omni**
**Opera N**—Opera News

**Parade**
**Penthouse**
**People**
**Philadelphia Inquirer**
**Playbill**
**Playboy**
**Plays & Players**
**Pop Sci**—Popular Science Monthly
**Psych Today**—Psychology Today
**Pub W**—Publishers Weekly

**Read Digest**—Reader's Digest
**Redbook**
**Rolling Stone**

**Sat Eve Post**—Saturday Evening Post
**Sat R**—Saturday Review
**Scala** (English edition)
**Sci Am**—Scientific American
**Sci Mo**—Scientific Monthly
**Sci N L**—Science News Letter
**Science**
**Smithsonian**
**Spec**—Spectator
**Spiegel**—Der Spiegel
**Sport**
**Sports Illus**—Sports Illustrated
**Sr Schol**—Senior Scholastic

**Time**
**Times**—London Times
**Times Lit Sup**—London Times Literary Supplement
**Toronto Globe and Mail**
**TV Guide**

**U N Rev**—United Nations Review
**U S News**—U.S. News & World Report

**Variety**
**Village Voice**
**Vogue**

**Wall St J**—Wall Street Journal
**Washington M**—Washington Monthly
**Washington Post**
**Wilson Lib Bul**—Wilson Library Bulletin

**Yale R**—Yale Review

# CLASSIFICATION BY PROFESSION—1985

ARCHITECTURE
Meier, Richard

ART
Bacon, Francis
Barnet, Will
Bartlett, Jennifer
Borofsky, Jonathan
Chillida, Eduardo
Colville, Alex
Nakian, Reuben
Rothenberg, Susan
Scholder, Fritz
Serra, Richard
Slade, Roy

ASTRONAUTICS
Garn, Jake

AVIATION
Gandhi, Rajiv

BUSINESS
Davis, Al
Getty, Gordon P.
Helmsley, Harry B.
Heseltine, Michael
Jarvik, Robert K.
Lehman, John F., Jr.
McEwen, Terence A.
Newman, Paul
Pickens, T. Boone
Schwartz, Tony
Stavropoulos, George
Ueberroth, Peter V.
Wein, George
Wick, Charles Z.

DANCE
De Mille, Agnes
Hines, Gregory
Johnson, Virginia
Monk, Meredith
Tcherkassky, Marianna

DIPLOMACY
Betancur, Belisario

EDUCATION
Adler, Stella
Barnet, Will
Bennett, William J.
Braudel, Fernand
Eco, Umberto
Eliade, Mircea
Futter, Ellen V.
Gregorian, Vartan
Himmelfarb, Gertrude
Johnson, Sonia
Lasch, Christopher
Mikulski, Barbara A.
Rochberg, George
Rubbia, Carlo
Santmyer, Helen Hooven
Schwartz, Tony
Slade, Roy
Weizsäcker, Carl
 Friedrich von

FASHION
Scavullo, Francesco
Stavropoulos, George

FINANCE
Reed, John S.

GOVERNMENT AND
 POLITICS, FOREIGN
Berri, Nabih
Fabius, Laurent
Gandhi, Rajiv
Garcia Pérez, Alan
Gorbachev, Mikhail
Heseltine, Michael
Kim Dae Jung
Lange, David
Özal, Turgut
Shevchenko, Arkady N.
Siles Zuazo, Hernán
Weizsäcker, Richard von

GOVERNMENT AND
 POLITICS, U.S.
Adelman, Kenneth L.
Ariyoshi, George R.
Buchanan, Patrick J.
Garn, Jake
Goode, W. Wilson
Greene, Harold H.
Hawkins, Paula
Johnson, Sonia
Kean, Thomas H.
Lamm, Richard D.
Lehman, John F., Jr.
Mikulski, Barbara A.
O'Neill, William A.
Schwartz, Tony
Shevchenko, Arkady N.
Speakes, Larry
Wattenberg, Ben J.
Weiss, Ted
Wick, Charles Z.

INTERNATIONAL
 RELATIONS
Adelman, Kenneth L.
Shevchenko, Arkady N.

JOURNALISM
Buchanan, Patrick J.
Evans, Harold
Frayn, Michael
Kane, Joseph Nathan
Kennedy, William
King, Larry
Sawyer, Diane
Speakes, Larry
Wattenberg, Ben J.

LABOR
Scargill, Arthur

LAW
Futter, Ellen V.
Greene, Harold H.
Lange, David
Weiss, Ted

Davis, Al
Flutie, Doug
Hamilton, Scott
Madden, John
Payton, Walter
Trottier, Bryan
Ueberroth, Peter
Walker, Herschel
Woodhouse, Barbara

TECHNOLOGY
Jarvik, Robert K.

TELEVISION
Conti, Tom
Frayn, Michael
Horne, Lena
Kane, Joseph Nathan
King, Larry

Lauper, Cyndi
Leonard, Elmore
Madden, John
Moreno, Rita
Murray, Bill
Newman, Paul
Reid, Kate
Sawyer, Diane
Scavullo, Francesco
Schwartz, Tony
Taylor, Elizabeth
Waterston, Sam
Wattenberg, Ben J.
Williams, Joe
Woodhouse, Barbara

THEATRE
Adler, Stella
Churchill, Caryl

Conti, Tom
De Mille, Agnes
Duras, Marguerite
Frayn, Michael
Goldberg, Whoopi
Havel, Václav
Hines, Gregory
Horne, Lena
Lortel, Lucille
Monk, Meredith
Moreno, Rita
Murray, Bill
Newman, Paul
Reid, Kate
Taylor, Elizabeth
Waterston, Sam

# CUMULATED INDEX—1981–1985

For the index to 1940–1985 biographies, see
Current Biography Cumulative Index 1940–1985.

Abdullah, Mohammad obit
Jan 83
Ace, Goodman obit May 82
Adair, Frank E(arl) obit Feb 82
Adams, Ansel (Easton) obit
Jun 84
Adelman, Kenneth L(ee) Jul 85
Adkins, Bertha S(heppard) obit
Mar 83
Adler, Renata Jun 84
Adler, Stella Aug 85
Agam, Yaacov Apr 81
Agar, Herbert (Sebastian) obit
Jan 81
Aiken, George D(avid) obit
Feb 85
Albertson, Jack obit Jan 82
Albion, Robert Greenhalgh
obit Oct 83
Albright, Ivan (Le Lorraine)
obit Jan 84
Aleixandre (Y Merlo), Vicente
obit Mar 85
Alemán, Miguel obit Jul 83
Alfonsín, Raúl Jul 84
Allen, Peter Mar 83
Allen, Steve Mar 82
Alsop, Mary See O'Hara,
Mary obit
Alston, Walter (Emmons) obit
Nov 84
Amalrik, Andrei (Alek-
seyevich) obit Jan 81
Amdahl, Gene M(yron) Aug 82
Ameling, Elly Oct 82
Amerasinghe, Hamilton Shir-
ley obit Feb 81
Ammons, A(rchie) R(andolph)
Feb 82
Andersen, Ib Aug 84
Anderson, Laurie Jul 83
Anderson, Robert O(rville)
Sep 82
Anderson, Roy A(rnold) Aug
83
Andrews, Cicily Isabel (Fair-
field) See West, Dame Re-
becca obit
Andropov, Yuri
(Vladimirovich) May 83 obit
Apr 84
Appel, James Z(iegler) obit Oct
81
Arends, Leslie C(ornelius) obit
Sep 85
Ariyoshi, George R. Jan 85
Armani, Giorgio Jan 83
Armour, Norman obit Nov 82

Aroldingen, Karin von Jan 83
Aron, Raymond (Claude Fer-
dinand) obit Jan 84
Ashbrook, John M(ilan) obit
Jun 82
Ashley, Merrill Nov 81
Aspinall, Wayne (Norviel) obit
Nov 83
Astin, Allen V(arley) obit Apr
84
Atkinson, (Justin) Brooks obit
Mar 84
Attenborough, David (Freder-
ick) Apr 83
Attenborough, Richard May 84
Atwood, Margaret (Eleanor)
May 84
Auchinleck, Sir Claude (John
Eyre) obit May 81
Austin, Tracy May 81
Ax, Emanuel Mar 84

Backman, Jules obit Jun 82
Bacon, Francis Aug 85
Bagnold, Enid (Algerine) obit
May 81
Bagramian, Ivan
C(hristoforovich) obit Jan 83
Bailey, Sir Donald Coleman
obit Jul 85
Bainton, Roland H(erbert) obit
Jun 84
Baker, James A(ddison), 3d
Feb 82
Balanchine, George obit Jun
83
Balderston, William obit Oct
83
Baldrige, (Howard) Malcolm
Aug 82
Baldwin, Roger Nash obit Oct
81
Balmain, Pierre (Alexandre)
obit Aug 82
Baltimore, David Jul 83
Bani-Sadr, Abolhassan Feb 81
Banning, Margaret Culkin obit
Feb 82
Barber, Samuel obit Mar 81
Barnes, Wendell B(urton) obit
Aug 85
Barnet, Will Jun 85
Barr, Alfred H(amilton), Jr.
obit Oct 81
Barr, (Frank) Stringfellow obit
Apr 82
Barrett, William (C.) Aug 82
Bartlett, Jennifer Nov 85

Barzini, Luigi (Giorgio, Jr.) obit
May 84
Basie, Count obit Jun 84
Basie, William See Basie,
Count obit
Battle, Kathleen Nov 84
Beard, Charles E(dmund) obit
Oct 82
Beard, James (Andrews) obit
Mar 85
Beatrix, Queen of the Nether-
lands May 81
Beattie, Ann Oct 85
Behrens, Hildegard Jan 85
Bell, Elliott V(allance) obit
Mar 83
Belushi, John obit Apr 82
Benchley, Nathaniel (God-
dard) obit Feb 82
Benelli, Giovanni Cardinal
obit Jan 83
Benn, Anthony (Neil) Wedg-
wood See Benn, Tony
Benn, Tony Nov 82
Bennett, Michael Mar 81
Bennett, Robert Russell obit
Oct 81
Bennett, William J(ohn) Sep 85
Bergen, John J(oseph) obit Feb
81
Berger, Peter L(udwig) Mar 83
Bergman, (Ernst) Ingmar Oct
81
Bergman, Ingrid obit Oct 82
Berlinguer, Enrico obit Aug 84
Berman, Emile Zola obit Aug
81
Bernardin, Joseph L(ouis) Oct
82
Bernbach, William obit Nov
82
Berri, Nabih Nov 85
Betancourt, Rómulo obit Nov
81
Betancur (Cuartas), Belisario
Apr 85
Betjeman, Sir John obit Jul 84
Bettis, Valerie obit Nov 82
Bhave, Vinoba obit Jan 83
Bidault, Georges obit Mar 83
Biddle, Katherine Garrison
Chapin obit Jan 84
Binns, Joseph Patterson obit
Mar 81
Bird, Larry June 82
Bird, Rose E(lizabeth) May 84
Black, William obit May 83

Blackwell, Betsy Talbot obit Apr 85

Blake, Eubie obit Apr 83

Blake, Eugene Carson obit Oct 85

Blanding, Sarah Gibson obit Apr 85

Bliss, Ray C(harles) obit Oct 81

Bloch, Felix obit Nov 83

Block, John R(usling) Apr 82

Bluford, Guion S(tewart), Jr. Sep 84

Bly, Robert (Elwood) Mar 84

Böhm, Karl obit Oct 81

Boles, Paul Darcy obit Jun 84

Böll, Heinrich (Theodor) obit Sep 85

Bolotowsky, Ilya obit Jan 82

Bonynge, Richard Feb 81

Boone, Richard obit Mar 81

Boorstin, Daniel J(oseph) Jan 84

Borofsky, Jonathan Jul 85

Bossy, Mike Jun 81

Botha, Roelof F(rederik) May 84

Boult, Sir Adrian (Cedric) obit Apr 83

Bourgeois, Louise Oct 83

Boyer, Ken(ton Lloyd) obit Oct 82

Boyer, M(arion) W(illard) obit Jan 83

Boy George Oct 85

Boyle, W(illiam) A(nthony) obit Jul 85

Boylston, Helen Dore obit Nov 84

Bradbury, Ray Jul 82

Bradford, Robert F(iske) obit May 83

Bradley, Bill Sep 82

Bradley, Omar N(elson) obit May 81

Bradley, William W(arren) See Bradley, Bill

Bradshaw, Thornton F(rederick) Jun 82

Brady, William T(homas) obit Jul 84

Brandt, Bill Aug 81 obit Feb 84

Braudel, Fernand (Paul) Apr 85

Brett, George Jul 81

Brett, George P(latt), Jr. obit May 84

Breuer, Marcel (Lajos) obit Aug 81

Brezhnev, Leonid I(lyich) obit Jan 83

Brinton, Howard H(aines) obit Yrbk 84 (died Apr 73)

Bristow, Gwen obit Yrbk 84 (died Aug 80)

Brodsky, Joseph (Alexandrovich) Jul 82

Brokaw, Tom May 81

Brooks, Louise Apr 84 obit Oct 85

Brower, Charles (Hendrickson) obit Nov 84

Brown, Charles L(ee, Jr.) Sep 81

Brown, George obit Jul 85

Brown, Sterling (Allen) Aug 82

Brundtland, Gro Harlem Nov 81

Bruner, Jerome (Seymour) Oct 84

Bryant, Paul W(illiam) obit Mar 83

Brynner, Yul obit Nov 85

Buchanan, Patrick J(oseph) Aug 85

Buckley, William F(rank) Jr. Oct 82

Buckmaster, Henrietta obit Jun 83

Bugas, John S(tephen) obit Feb 83

Bunker, Ellsworth obit Nov 84

Buñuel, Luis obit Sep 83

Burnet, Sir (Frank) Macfarlane obit Oct 85

Burnham, (Linden) Forbes (Sampson) obit Oct 85

Burrows, Abe obit Jul 85

Burton, Richard obit Sep 84

Buscaglia, (Felice) Leo(nardo) Oct 83

Bush, George (Herbert Walker) Sep 83

Butler, Richard Austen See Butler of Saffron Walden, R.A.B., Baron obit

Butler of Saffron Walden, Richard Austen Butler, Baron obit May 82

Byrne, David Jun 85

Byrne, John Keyes See Leonard, Hugh

Byrnes, John W(illiam) obit Mar 85

Cabot, John M(oors) obit Apr 81

Caetano, Marcello (José) obit Jan 81

Caldicott, Helen Oct 83

Caldwell, Millard F(illmore) obit Feb 85

Caldwell, Taylor obit Oct 85

Callahan, Harry M(orey) Nov 84

Calvino, Italo Feb 84 obit Nov 85

Calvo Sotelo (y Bustelo), Leopoldo Aug 81

Campbell, Earl Apr 83

Campbell, Joseph Jun 84

Cámpora, Héctor José obit Feb 81

Canady, John (Edwin) obit Sep 85

Canetti, Elias Jan 83

Canham, Erwin D(ain) obit Feb 82

Capote, Truman obit Oct 84

Carlino, Lewis John May 83

Carlisle, Kitty See Hart, Kitty Carlisle

Carlucci, Frank (Charles 3d) Oct 81

Carmichael, Hoagy obit Feb 82

Caro, Anthony Nov 81

Caro, Robert A. Jan 84

Carroll, John A(lbert) obit Oct 83

Carroll, Vinnette Sep 83

Carson, Johnny Apr 82

Carter, Betty Mar 82

Carter, (William) Hodding 3d Aug 81

Carter, (Bessie) Lillian obit Jan 84

Carver, Raymond Feb 84

Cary, William L(ucius) obit Apr 83

Case, Clifford P(hilip) obit Apr 82

Castelli, Leo Aug 84

Catledge, Turner obit Jul 83

Celler, Emanuel obit Mar 81

Chagall, Marc obit May 85

Chagla, Mahomed Ali Currim obit Jan 84

Chaikin, Joseph Jul 81

Chapin, Katherine Garrison See Biddle, K. G. C. obit

Chapman, Albert K(inkade) obit Yrbk 84

Chapman, Charles F(rederic) obit Yrbk 84 (died Mar 76)

Charles, Prince of Belgium obit Jul 83

Charlot, Jean obit Yrbk 84 (died Mar 79)

Charlotte, Grand Duchess of Luxembourg obit Aug 85

Chase, Mary (Coyle) obit Jan 82

Chayefsky, Paddy obit Sep 81

Cheever, John obit Aug 82

Chernenko, Konstantin U(stinovich) Aug 84 obit May 85

Chicago, Judy Feb 81

Childs, Lucinda Apr 84

Chillida, Eduardo Sep 85

Christopher, Warren M(inor) Jun 81

Chuikov, Vasili (Ivanovitch) obit May 82

Chun Doo Hwan Mar 81

Church, Frank (Forrester) obit May 84

Church, Sam(uel Morgan), Jr. Oct 81

Churchill, Caryl Jun 85

Churchill, Sarah obit Jan 83

Cimino, Michael Jan 81

Citrine of Wembley, Walter McLennan Citrine, 1st Baron obit Apr 83
Clair, René obit May 81
Claire, Ina obit Apr 85
Clark, Lord Kenneth (Mackenzie) obit Jul 83
Clark, Mark W(ayne) obit Jun 84
Clark, William P(atrick) Jul 82
Clausen, A(lden) W(inship) Nov 81
Clavell, James Oct 81
Cleese, John Jan 84
Clements, Earle C. obit May 85
Cleveland, James Aug 85
Close, Charles See Close, Chuck
Close, Chuck Jul 83
Close, Glenn Nov 84
Cody, John Patrick Cardinal obit Jun 82
Cohen, Benjamin V(ictor) obit Oct 83
Cohen, William S(ebastian) Apr 82
Coleman, Lonnie (William) obit Oct 82
Collingwood, Charles (Cummings) obit Nov 85
Collins, Joan Jan 84
Colville, Alex Mar 85
Conable, Barber B., Jr. Jul 84
Conley, Eugene obit Feb 82
Connelly, Marc obit Feb 81
Conti, Tom Jun 85
Conway, Tim Apr 81
Cook, Donald C(larence) obit Feb 82
Cooke, Terence J(ames) Cardinal obit Nov 83
Coon, Carleton S(tevens) obit Jul 81
Corcoran, Thomas Gardiner obit Feb 82
Cori, Carl F(erdinand) obit Feb 85
Corman, Roger Feb 83
Corson, Fred Pierce obit Apr 85
Cortázar, Julio obit Apr 84
Cossiga, Francesco Jan 81
Costello, Elvis Sep 83
Cotrubas, Ileana Oct 81
Cowles, Gardner, Jr. obit Aug 85
Cowles, John obit Apr 83
Cowles, Virginia (Spencer) obit Nov 83
Cox, Allyn obit Jan 83
Cox, William Trevor See Trevor, William
Craft, Robert Mar 84
Craxi, Bettino Feb 84
Crenshaw, Ben Sep 85
Crick, Francis Mar 83
Crisler, Herbert Orin obit Oct 82

Cronin, A(rchibald) J(oseph) obit Mar 81
Cronin, Joe obit Nov 84
Crosby, John (O'Hea) Nov 81
Cross, Ben Aug 84
Crossley, Archibald M(addock) obit Jul 85
Crowther, (F.) Bosley obit Apr 81
Cruyff, Johan Nov 81
Cruz, Celia Jul 83
Cukor, George obit Mar 83
Cullberg, Birgit Nov 82
Cunningham, Sir Alan (Gordon) obit Apr 83
Cunningham, Mary (Elizabeth) Nov 84
Cuomo, Mario (Matthew) Aug 83
Curran, Joseph E(dwin) obit Oct 81
Curzon, Clifford obit Oct 82
Cushman, Robert E(verton), Jr. obit Apr 85

Dacre of Glanton, Baron, See Trevor-Roper, H. R.
Dalai Lama Jun 82
Dale, Jim Jul 81
D'Amato, Alfonse Sep 83
Daniels, Jonathan (Worth) obit Jan 82
Dannay, Frederic obit Oct 82
Danner, Blythe Jan 81
Dart, Justin W(hitlock) obit Mar 84
D'Aubuisson, Roberto Jul 83
Dausset, Jean May 81
Davis, Al(len) Jul 85
Davis, Andrew May 83
Davis, James C(urran) obit Feb 82
Davis, Peter (Frank) Feb 83
Day, Dorothy obit Jan 81
Dayan, Moshe obit Jan 82
Dean, William F(rishe) obit Oct 81
Debray, (Jules) Régis Jun 82
Debus, Kurt H(einrich) obit Nov 83
Decker, Mary Oct 83
Decter, Midge Apr 82
Deighton, Len Sep 84
De Kooning, Elaine (Marie Catharine) Jul 82
De Kooning, Willem Sep 84
De La Madrid (Hurtado), Miguel Apr 83
Del Tredici, David Mar 83
De Mille, Agnes Jan 85
Demme, Jonathan Apr 85
De Montebello, (Guy-)Philippe (Lannes) Apr 81
Dempsey, Jack obit Jul 83
Dempsey, William Harrison See Dempsey, Jack obit
Densen-Gerber, Judianne Nov 83

Denton, Jeremiah A(ndrew) Jr. May 82
De Palma, Brian Sep 82
De Rochemont, Richard (Guertis) obit Sept 82
Deukmejian, (Courken) George, Jr. Jun 83
DeVries, William C(astle) Jan 85
Dewey, Charles S(chuveldt) obit Feb 81
Dial, Morse G(rant) obit Jan 83
Diamond, Neil May 81
Diana, Princess of Wales Jan 83
Dickinson, Angie Feb 81
Dietz, David obit Apr 85
Dietz, Howard obit Sep 83
Dillard, Annie Jan 83
Dillon, Matt May 85
Dingell, John D(avid) Jr. Aug 83
DiSalle, Michael V(incent) obit Nov 81
Dodds, Harold W(illis) obit Jan 81
Dodge, Cleveland E(arl) obit Feb 83
Doe, Samuel K(anyon) May 81
Doenitz, Karl obit Feb 81
Dohnányi, Christoph von Oct 85
Dole, Elizabeth Hanford Jun 83
Dolin, Anton obit Jan 84
Domenici, Pete V(ichi) Jun 82
Donovan, Raymond J(ames) Jan 82
Dorticós (Torrado), Osvaldo obit Aug 83
Douglas, Donald W(ills) obit Mar 81
Douglas, Melvyn obit Sep 81
Drabble, Margaret May 81
Drew, George A(lexander) obit May 84
Druckman, Jacob May 81
Drummond, (James) Roscoe obit Nov 83
Duarte (Fuentes), José Napoleón Sep 81
Dubinsky, David obit Jan 83
Dubos, René J(ules) obit Apr 82
Dubuffet, Jean obit Jul 85
Dunne, John Gregory Jun 83
Durant, Will(iam James) obit Jan 82
Duras, Marguerite Nov 85
Durrell, Gerald May 85

Eckstein, Gustav obit Nov 81
Eckstein, Otto obit May 84
Eco, Umberto Apr 85
Edwards, Blake Jan 83
Edwards, (W.) Don(lon) Mar 83

Edwards, James B(urrows) Nov 82
Edwards, Joan obit Oct 81
Egan, William Allen obit Jul 84
Ehricke, Krafft A. obit Feb 85
Eisenhower, Milton S(tover) obit Jul 85
Eliade, Mircea Nov 85
Elizabeth, Queen Mother of Great Britain Aug 81
Emerson, Faye obit May 83
Engstrom, E(lmer) W(illiam) obit Feb 85
Erlander, Tage (Fritiof) obit Aug 85
Ernst, Jimmy obit Apr 84
Ershad, Hussain Muhammad Nov 84
Ervin, Sam(uel) J(ames), Jr. obit Jun 85
Ethridge, Mark (Foster) obit Jun 81
Evans, Harold (Matthew) Apr 85
Evans, Luther H(arris) obit Feb 82
Evren, Kenan Apr 84

Fabius, Laurent Feb 85
Fagerholm, Karl-August obit Jul 84
Fagg, Fred D(ow) Jr. obit Jan 82
Falwell, Jerry Jan 81
Farrar, Margaret (Petherbridge) obit Aug 84
Farrington, (Mary) Elizabeth Pruett obit Sep 84
Fassbinder, Rainer Werner obit Aug 82
Feinsinger, Nathan P(aul) obit Jan 84
Feld, Irvin obit Nov 84
Feldstein, Martin (Stuart) May 83
Ferguson, Homer obit Mar 83
Ferraro, Geraldine A(nne) Sep 84
Fielding, Temple (Hornaday) obit Jul 83
Fierstein, Harvey Feb 84
Fishback, Margaret obit Nov 85
Fisher, M(ary) F(rances) K(ennedy) Sep 83
Fisher, Welthy (Blakesley Honsinger) obit Feb 81
Fisk, James Brown obit Oct 81
Fitzgerald, Albert J. obit Jul 82
Fitzgerald, Ed obit Jun 82
FitzGerald, Garret Aug 84
Fitzgerald, Robert (Stuart) obit Mar 85
Fitzsimmons, Frank E(dward) obit Jul 81
Florinsky, Michael T(imofeevich) obit Jan 82

Flory, Paul J(ohn) obit Nov 85
Flutie, Doug Oct 85
Folon, Jean-Michel Feb 81
Fonda, Henry obit Sep 82
Fontanne, Lynn obit Sep 83
Foot, Michael (Mackintosh) May 81
Ford, Harrison Sep 84
Fortas, Abe obit May 82
Fossey, Dian May 85
Foster, Jodie Jun 81
Fox, Carol obit Sep 81
Fox, Robert J(ohn) obit Jun 84
Fox, Virgil (Keel) obit Jan 81
Francis, Dick Aug 81
Fraser of North Cape, Bruce Austin Fraser, 1st Baron obit Apr 81
Frayn, Michael Jan 85
Frederika (Louise), Consort of Paul I, King of the Hellenes obit Apr 81
Frei (Montalva), Eduardo obit Mar 82
Freud, Anna obit Mar 83
Frings, Ketti (Hartley) obit Apr 81
Frisch, Karl von obit Yrbk 83 (died Jun 82)
Frye, (Herman) Northrop Aug 83
Fujiyama, Aiichiro obit May 85
Fuller, R(ichard) Buckminster (Jr.) obit Aug 83
Futter, Ellen V(ictoria) Oct 85

Gajdusek, D(aniel) Carleton Jun 81
Gallup, George (Horace) obit Sep 84
Galtieri, Leopoldo (Fortunato) Aug 82
Gandhi, Indira (Priyadarshini Nehru) obit Yrbk 84 Jan 85
Gandhi, Rajiv (Ratna) Apr 85
Garcia Pérez, Alan Nov 85
Gardner, John (Champlin, Jr.) obit Nov 82
Garn, Edwin (Jacob) See Garn, J.
Garn, Jake Aug 85
Garroway, Dave obit Sep 82
Garth, David Jan 81
Gates, Thomas S(overeign), Jr. obit May 83
Gemayel, Amin Mar 83
George, Boy See Boy George
George-Brown, Baron See Brown, G. obit
Gerbner, George Aug 83
Gernreich, Rudi obit Jun 85
Gershwin, Ira obit Oct 83
Getty, Gordon P(eter) Feb 85
Giauque, William F(rancis) obit May 82
Gibb, Barry Sep 81
Gibson, Mel Apr 84

Gibson, William Jul 83
Gideonse, Harry David obit May 85
Gielgud, John Feb 84
Gilder, George Oct 81
Giles, Barney McKinney obit Aug 84
Gimbel, Peter (Robin) Jan 82
Giroux, Robert Nov 82
Glass, Philip Mar 81
Glemp, Jozef Sep 82
Gobbi, Tito obit May 84
Godfrey, Arthur obit May 83
Godunov, Alexander Feb 83
Goldberg, Whoopi Mar 85
Golden, Harry (Lewis) obit Nov 81
Goldmann, Nahum obit Oct 82
Golub, Leon (Albert) Aug 84
Gomulka, Wladyslaw obit Oct 82
Goode, W(illie) Wilson Oct 85
Goodrich, Frances obit Apr 84
Gorbachev, Mikhail (Sergeyevich) Aug 85
Gordon, Mary (Catherine) Nov 81
Gordon, Ruth obit Oct 85
Gorin, Igor obit Jun 82
Gorsuch, Anne (McGill) Sep 82
Gosden, Freeman F(isher) obit Feb 83
Gossage, Rich Aug 84
Goudge, Elizabeth obit Aug 84
Gould, Chester obit Jul 85
Gould, Glenn obit Nov 82
Gould, Stephen Jay Sep 82
Grace, Princess of Monaco obit Nov 82
Gramm, Donald obit Jul 83
Grass, Günter (Wilhelm) Jul 83
Grasso, Ella T(ambussi) obit Mar 81
Graves, Nancy (Stevenson) May 81
Gray, Gordon obit Feb 83
Gray, Simon (James Holliday) Jun 83
Greene, Harold H(erman) Aug 85
Gregorian, Vartan Oct 85
Gretzky, Wayne, Feb 82
Grey, J(ames) D(avid) obit Sep 85
Gribble, Harry Wagstaff (Graham-) obit Apr 81
Griffin, (Samuel) Marvin obit Aug 82
Grillo, Frank Raúl See Machito
Grosvenor, Melville Bell obit Jun 82
Gruenther, Alfred M(aximilian) obit Jul 83
Grumman, Leroy R(andle) obit Jan 83
Guare, John Aug 82
Guinness, Alec Mar 81

Guthrie, Arlo Feb 82

Habib, Philip C(harles) Sep 81
Haddon, William, Jr. obit Apr 85
Hagegard, Hakan May 85
Hagerty, James C. obit Jun 81
Hale, Clara Jul 85
Hall, Donald (Andrew) May 84
Hall, Joyce C(lyde) obit Jan 83
Hallstein, Walter obit May 82
Hamilton, Margaret obit Jul 85
Hamilton, Scott Apr 85
Handler, Philip obit Feb 82
Handy, Thomas T(roy) obit Jun 82
Hanks, Nancy obit Mar 83
Hanna, William Jul 83
Hanson, Duane (Elwood) Oct 83
Hanson, Howard obit Apr 81
Harburg, E(dgar) Y(ipsel) obit Apr 81
Harden, Cecil M(urray) obit Feb 85
Hardwick, Elizabeth Feb 81
Hare, David Aug 83
Harkness, Rebekah (West) obit Sep 82
Harlech, Fifth Baron See Ormsby-Gore, (W.) D. obit
Harrar, J(acob) George obit Jun 82
Harrell, Lynn Feb 83
Harris, Sir Arthur Travers obit May 84
Harris, Patricia Roberts obit May 85
Harrison, Wallace K(irkman) obit Jan 82
Harry, Debbie Nov 81
Hart, Kitty Carlisle Oct 82
Hartman, David Jun 81
Hatch, Orrin G(rant) Aug 82
Hatfield, Mark O(dom) Mar 84
Hauge, Gabriel (Sylfest) obit Sep 81
Haughey, Charles J(ames) Feb 81
Hauser, (Benjamin) Gayelord Feb 85
Havel, Václav Mar 85
Hawke, Bob Aug 83
Hawke, Robert James Lee See Hawke, Bob
Hawking, Stephen W(illiam) May 84
Hawkins, Augustus F(reeman) Feb 83
Hawkins, Paula (Fickes) Sep 85
Hays, (Lawrence) Brooks obit Jan 82
Head, Edith obit Jan 82
Heaney, Seamus (Justin) Jan 82
Hearns, Thomas Mar 83

Hearst, Patricia (Campbell) Aug 82
Heckler, Margaret M(ary O'Shaughnessy) Aug 83
Heinz, (Henry) John, (3d) Apr 81
Hellman, Lillian obit Aug 84
Helmsley, Harry B(rakmann) Jun 85
Helstein, Ralph obit May 85
Henley, Beth Feb 83
Herbster, Ben M(ohr) obit Mar 85
Hersh, Seymour (Myron) Mar 84
Hesburgh, Theodore M(artin) Jul 82
Heseltine, Michael (Ray Dibdin) Jun 85
Hicks, Granville obit Aug 82
Hildebrand, Joel H(enry) obit Jul 83
Hill, Benny Feb 83
Hill, Lister obit Feb 85
Hillenkoetter, Roscoe H(enry) obit Aug 82
Himmelfarb, Gertrude May 85
Hines, Earl (Kenneth) obit Jun 83
Hines, Fatha See Hines, Earl (Kenneth) obit
Hines, Gregory Jul 85
Hirsch, John (Stephen) Apr 84
Hirsch, Judd Mar 84
Hirshhorn, Joseph H(erman) obit Oct 81
Hoagland, Edward (Morley) Sept 82
Hoffa, James R(iddle) obit Mar 83
Hoffer, Eric obit Jul 83
Hoffman, Abbie Apr 81
Hoffman, Anna M(arie) Rosenberg obit Jul 83
Hogben, Lancelot (Thomas) obit Jan 84
Hogwood, Christopher Jul 85
Holden, William obit Jan 82
Holliday, Jennifer Jun 83
Hollings, Ernest F(rederick) Jul 82
Hollomon, J(ohn) Herbert obit Aug 85
Holloway, Stanley obit Mar 82
Holmes, Larry Aug 81
Holt, John (Caldwell) Jun 81 obit Nov 85
Holyoake, Keith J(acka) obit Feb 84
Hope, Stanley C. obit Oct 82
Horne, John E(lmer) obit Apr 85
Horne, Lena Nov 85
Horner, H(orace) Mansfield obit Jul 83
Horrocks, Sir B(rian) G(wynne) obit Mar 85
Hosmer, (Chester) Craig obit Mar 83

Houghton, Amory obit Apr 81
Houseman, John Apr 84
Howard, Elston (Gene) obit Feb 81
Hoxha, Enver obit Jun 85
Hu Yaobang Nov 83
Hudson, Rock obit Nov 85
Hughes, Barnard Sep 81
Hughes, Emmet John obit Nov 82
Hughes, Sarah T(ilghman) obit Jul 85
Hunsaker, Jerome C(larke) obit Nov 84
Hunter, Alberta obit Jan 85
Huppert, Isabelle Nov 81
Hurd, Peter obit Sep 84
Hurt, John Jan 82
Hussein, Ahmed obit Feb 85
Hussein, Saddam (al-Tikriti) Sep 81
Huston, John Mar 81

Idris Senussi I, King of Libya obit Jul 83
Idriss Senussi I, King of Libya See Idris Senussi I, King of Libya obit
Iglesias, Julio Jun 84
Ilg, Frances L(illian) obit Sep 81
Illia, Arturo (Umberto) obit Mar 83
Ingersoll, Ralph (McAllister) obit May 85
Irons, Jeremy Aug 84
Ivory, James Jul 81

Jackson, Henry M(artin) obit Oct 83
Jackson, Michael Nov 83
Jacobi, Derek May 81
James, Clive (Vivian Leopold) Nov 84
James, Harry obit Aug 83
Jarrett, Keith May 85
Jaruzelski, Wojciech (Witold) Mar 82
Jarvik, Robert K(offler) Jul 85
Jaworski, Leon obit Feb 83
Jayewardene, J(unius) R(ichard) Jan 84
Jenkins, Ray H(oward) obit Feb 81
Jenkins, Roy (Harris) Oct 82
Jenner, William E(zra) obit May 85
Jennings, Peter (Charles) Nov 83
Jennings, Waylon Apr 82
Jensen, Jackie obit Oct 82
Jessel, George (Albert) obit Jul 81
Jobs, Steven (Paul) Mar 83
Johanson, Donald C(arl) Feb 84
John, Tommy Oct 81
Johnson, Crockett obit Jan 84

Johnson, Earvin Jan 82
Johnson, Harold K(eith) obit Nov 83
Johnson, Magic See Johnson, Earvin Jan 82
Johnson, Pamela Hansford obit Aug 81
Johnson, Sonia Feb 85
Johnson, Virginia May 85
Johnson, (Thomas) Walter obit Sep 85
Jones, Carolyn obit Sep 83
Jones, David C(harles) Jul 82
Jones, James R(obert) Oct 81
Jones, Marvin obit Jan 84
Julia, Raul Sep 82

Kahn, Herman obit Aug 83
Kaiser, Edgar F(osburgh) obit Feb 82
Kane, Harnett T(homas) obit Yrbk 84
Kane, Joseph Nathan Nov 85
Kania, Stanislaw Jun 81
Kapitsa, Pyotr L(eonidovich) obit May 84
Kapitza, Peter L(eonidovich) See Kapitsa, P. L. obit
Karmal, Babrak Mar 81
Kassebaum, Nancy Landon Feb 82
Kastler, Alfred obit Mar 84
Kaufman, Henry Aug 81
Kay, Hershy obit Feb 82
Kean, Thomas H(oward) Jul 85
Keighley, William obit Aug 84
Keillor, Garrison Aug 85
Kelly, Grace See Grace, Princess of Monaco obit
Kelly, John B(renden), Jr. obit Apr 85
Kelly, Petra (Karin) Mar 84
Kelman, Charles D(avid) Jun 84
Kemper, James S(cott) obit Nov 81
Kennedy, Donald Jul 84
Kennedy, William May 85
Kertész, André obit Nov 85
Khalid, King of Saudi Arabia obit Aug 82
Kieran, John (Francis) obit Feb 82
Kim Dae Jung Sep 85
King, Don Jun 84
King, Larry May 85
King, Stephen Oct 81
Kingman, Dave Mar 82
Kingsley, Ben Nov 83
Kinnock, Neil (Gordon) Apr 84
Kinski, Nastassja Jun 84
Kintner, Robert E(dmonds) obit Feb 81
Kirkpatrick, Jeane (Duane) J(ordan) Jul 81
Kirkpatrick, Ralph obit Aug 84
Kistiakowsky, George B(ogdan) obit Feb 83

Kitaj, R(onald) B(rooks) Apr 82
Kitchell, Iva obit Jan 84
Klein, Edward E(lkan) obit Sep 85
Klein, Julius obit May 84
Kline, Nathan S(chellenberg) obit May 83
Knight, John S(hively) obit Aug 81
Knopf, Alfred A. obit Oct 84
Koestler, Arthur obit Apr 83
Koivisto, Mauno (Henrik) Sep 82
Kolff, Willem Johan May 83
Kolvenbach, Peter-Hans May 84
Komar, Vitaly, and Melamid, Aleksandr Oct 84
Koop, C(harles) Everett Sep 83
Koppel, Ted Jul 84
Korda, Michael (Vincent) Aug 85
Kosygin, Aleksei N(ikolayevich) obit Feb 81
Kotschnig, Walter M(aria) obit Sep 85
Krantz, Judith May 82
Krasna, Norman obit Feb 85
Krasner, Lee obit Aug 84
Krebs, Sir Hans obit Feb 82
Kremer, Gidon Mar 85
Kroc, Ray(mond) A. obit Mar 84
Kucuk, Fazil See Kutchuk, (M.) F. obit
Kundera, Milan Mar 83
Kuralt, Charles Jul 81
Kutchuk, (Mustafa) Fazil obit Mar 84
Kuznets, Simon obit Sep 85
Kylian, Jiri Sep 82
Kyser, Kay obit Sep 85

Ladurie, Emmanuel Le Roy See Le Roy Ladurie, E.
Laffer, Arthur (Betz) Feb 82
Lagerfeld, Karl Jan 82
LaMarsh, Judy obit Jan 81
Lamm, Richard D(ouglas) May 85
Land, Edwin H(erbert) Mar 81
Lang, Jack Aug 83
Lange, David Sep 85
Lange, Jessica May 83
Langer, Susanne K(atharina Knauth) obit Sep 85
Lansing, Sherry (Lee) May 81
Larkin, Philip (Arthur) Jan 85
Lasch, Christopher Mar 85
Laughlin, James May 82
Lauper, Cyndi Aug 85
Laurents, Arthur Nov 84
Lawe, John (Edward) Jan 84
Leakey, Mary (Douglas) Apr 85
Lebowitz, Fran(ces Ann) Mar 82
Leboyer, Frédérick Jul 82

Léger, Jules obit Jan 81
Le Guin, Ursula K(roeber) Jan 83
Lehman, John F(rancis), Jr. Nov 85
Lehrer, Tom Jul 82
Lelouch, Claude Nov 82
Lendl, Ivan Sep 84
Lengyel, Emil obit Apr 85
Lennon, John obit Feb 81
Lennox-Boyd, Lord Alan T(indal) obit May 83
Lenya, Lotte obit Jan 82
Leonard, Elmore Sep 85
Leonard, Hugh Apr 83
Leonard, Ray See Leonard, Sugar Ray
Leonard, Sugar Ray Feb 81
Leopold III, King of the Belgians obit Nov 83
Le Roy Ladurie, Emmanuel (Bernard) Jul 84
Lesage, Jean obit Feb 81
LeSourd, Catherine Marshall See Marshall, S.C.W. obit
Levi, Julian (Edwin) obit Apr 82
Levin, Meyer obit Sep 81
Lewis, Carl Nov 84
Lewis, Drew Feb 82
Liberman, Evseï (Grigorevich) obit May 83
Liebman, Max obit Sep 81
Lilienthal, David E(li) obit Mar 81
Limann, Hilla Jun 81
Link, Edwin (Albert) obit Yrbk 83 (died Sep 81)
Littlejohn, Robert McG(owan) obit Jul 82
Llewellyn, Richard obit Jan 84
Lloyd Webber, Andrew Jun 82
Lockridge, Richard obit Oct 82
Lodge, Henry Cabot (Jr.) obit Apr 85
Loeb, William obit Nov 81
London, George obit Jun 85
Lonergan, Bernard J(oseph) F(rancis) obit Feb 85
Longo, Luigi obit Jan 81
Loos, Anita obit Oct 81
López Bravo, Gregorio obit Apr 85
Loquasto, Santo Jun 81
Loring, Eugene obit Oct 82
Lortel, Lucille Feb 85
Losey, Joseph obit Aug 84
Loudon, Dorothy Jun 84
Louganis, Greg Oct 84
Louis, Joe obit Jun 81
Love, Iris (Cornelia) Aug 82
Lowery, Joseph E. Nov 82
Lucas, Martha B. See Pate, M. B. L. obit
Ludlum, Robert Nov 82
Luns, Joseph M(arie) A(ntoine) H(ubert) Apr 82
Lustiger, Jean-Marie Feb 84

Lynd, Staughton (Craig) May 83

Lynde, Paul (Edward) obit Feb 82

Lyons, Eugene obit Mar 85

Ma, Yo-Yo Jul 82

MacDermot, Galt Jul 84

Macdonald, Dwight obit Mar 83

MacDonald, Malcolm (John) obit Mar 81

Macdonald, Ross obit Sep 83

MacEachen, Allan J(oseph) Apr 83

Machel, Samora Moises Mar 84

Machito Feb 83 obit Jun 84

MacInnes, Helen (Clark) obit Nov 85

Mackay, John A(lexander) obit Aug 83

Mackerras, Sir Charles Feb 85

MacLeish, Archibald obit Jun 82

Madden, John Aug 85

Malik, Adam obit Nov 84

Maltz, Albert obit Jul 85

Mandela, Nelson (Rolihlahla) Jan 84

Mandrell, Barbara Aug 82

Marriott, J. Willard obit Oct 85

Marsalis, Wynton Oct 84

Marshall, (Sarah) Catherine (Wood) obit May 83

Marton, Eva Apr 85

Mason, James obit Sep 84

Mason, Marsha Apr 81

Massey, Raymond obit Sep 83

Mauroy, Pierre Jun 82

Mayr, Ernst Nov 84

Mays, Benjamin E(lijah) obit May 84

Mazey, Emil obit Nov 83

McBride, Lloyd obit Jan 84

McCabe, Thomas B(ayard) obit Jul 82

McCain, John S(idney), Jr. obit Jun 81

McCall, Tom (Lawson) obit Mar 83

McClintock, Barbara Mar 84

McColough, C(harles) Peter Jan 81

McCormack, John W(illiam) obit Jan 81

McCullough, Colleen Apr 82

McEwen, Terence A(lexander) Jul 85

McFadden, Mary Apr 83

McFarland, Ernest W(illiam) obit Aug 84

McFarlane, Robert C(arl) May 84

McGannon, Donald H(enry) obit Jul 84

McGinniss, Joe Jan 84

McKellen, Ian Jan 84

McLean, Robert obit Feb 81

McLuhan, (Herbert) Marshall obit Feb 81

McMurtry, Larry (Jeff) Jun 84

McPhee, John (Angus) Oct 82

McQueen, Steve obit Jan 81

McRae, Carmen Apr 83

Mearns, David C(hambers) obit Jul 81

Medeiros, Humberto S(ousa) obit Nov 83

Medvedev, Roy (Aleksandr) Sep 84

Meese, Edwin, 3d Sep 81

Meier, Richard Jan 85

Melamid, Aleksandr See Komar, V.

Mendès-France, Pierre obit Jan 83

Mengistu Haile Mariam Jul 81

Mennin, Peter obit Aug 83

Menon, K(umara) P(admanbha) S(ivasankara) obit Yrbk 83 (died Nov 82)

Mercer, Mabel obit Jun 84

Merman, Ethel obit Apr 84

Merrifield, R(obert) Bruce Mar 85

Merrill, James (Ingram) Aug 81

Michals, Duane (Steven) Apr 81

Michel, Robert H(enry) Sep 81

Mifune, Toshiro Jun 81

Mikulski, Barbara A(nn) Nov 85

Milgram, Stanley obit Mar 85

Millar, Kenneth See Macdonald, R. obit

Miller, Arnold (Ray) obit Sep 85

Miller, Irving obit Feb 81

Miller, William E(dward) obit Aug 83

Milosz, Czeslaw Oct 81

Miner, Worthington (C.) obit Mar 83

Mintoff, Dom Mar 84

Miró, Joan obit Feb 84

Mitterrand, François (Maurice) Oct 82

Moch, Jules (Salvador) obit Nov 85

Monaco, Mario del obit Jan 83

Monk, Meredith Feb 85

Monk, Thelonious obit Apr 82

Montagu, Ewen (Edward Samuel) obit Sep 85

Montale, Eugenio obit Nov 81

Montana, Joe Sep 83

Montebello, (Guy-)Philippe (Lannes) de See De Montebello, Philippe

Montgomery, Robert obit Nov 81

Moody, Joseph E(ugene) obit Jul 84

Moon, Sun Myung Mar 83

Moore, Dudley Jun 82

Moreno, Rita Sep 85

Morgan, Joe Sep 84

Morganfield, McKinley See Waters, Muddy

Morley, Malcolm A. Jun 84

Morris, Wright (Marion) May 82

Morrison, Philip Jul 81

Morse, Philip M(cCord) obit Nov 85

Mortimer, John (Clifford) Apr 83

Morton, Thruston B(allard) obit Oct 82

Moses, Robert obit Sep 81

Mosley, Sir Oswald (Ernald) obit Feb 81

Motley, Arthur H(arrison) obit Jul 84

Mubarak, (Mohamed) Hosni Apr 82

Mudd, Roger (Harrison) Jan 81

Mueller, R(euben) H(erbert) obit Sep 82

Mulroney, (Martin) Brian Apr 84

Mumford, L(awrence) Quincy obit Jan 83

Murphy, Charles S(prings) obit Oct 83

Murphy, Eddie Nov 83

Murray, Anne Jan 82

Murray, Bill Jan 85

Myer, Dillon S(eymour) obit Jan 83

Naisbitt, John Nov 84

Nakasone, Yasuhiro Jun 83

Nakian, Reuben Feb 85

Navon, Yitzhak May 82

Nearing, Scott obit Oct 83

Neel, Alice (Hartley) obit Jan 85

Nelligan, Kate Jul 83

Nesbitt, Cathleen (Mary) obit Sep 82

Nettles, Graig Jul 84

Neumann, Emanuel obit Jan 81

Newell, Homer E(dward), Jr. obit Sep 83

Newman, Paul May 85

Newman, Randy Oct 82

Nicholson, Ben obit Apr 82

Nicolson, Marjorie Hope obit Jun 81

Niemöller, (Friedrich Gustav Emil) Martin obit May 84

Niven, David obit Sep 83

Noel-Baker, Philip J(ohn) obit Mar 83

Nofziger, Lyn Jan 83

Nolan, Lloyd obit Nov 85

Norman, Marsha May 84

North, John Ringling obit Jul 85

Northrop, John K(nudsen) obit Apr 81

Novak, Michael Feb 85
Nozick, Robert Jun 82

Obote, (Apollo) Milton Apr 81
Obraztsova, Elena Feb 83
O'Brien, Leo W(illiam) obit Jul
82
O'Brien, Pat obit Jan 84
Ochsner, (Edward William)
Alton obit Nov 81
O'Connor, John J(oseph) Jun
84
O'Connor, Sandra Day Jan 82
Odishaw, Hugh obit Jun 84
O'Dowd, George A. See Boy
George
O'Hara, Mary obit Jan 81
Oliver, James A(rthur) obit
May 82
Olson, Harry F(erdinand) obit
Jun 82
O'Neil, James F(rancis) obit
Sep 81
O'Neill, William A(tchison)
Feb 85
Orff, Carl obit May 82
Ormandy, Eugene obit May 85
Ormsby-Gore, (William) David
obit Mar 85
Ortega, Daniel Oct 84
Osborn, Frederick (Henry) obit
Mar 81
O'Shea, Milo Jun 82
Ovandia Candia, Alfredo obit
Mar 82
Owings, Nathaniel
A(lexander) obit Aug 84
Oz, Amos Jul 83

Özal, Turgut Jun 85

Ozick, Cynthia Aug 83

Packwood, Bob Jan 81
Padover, Saul K(ussiel) obit
Apr 81
Paige, Leroy (Robert) obit Aug
82
Paik, Nam June Mar 83
Papandreou, Andreas (George)
Apr 83
Parker, Buddy obit Jun 82
Parsons, Harriet (Oettinger)
obit Mar 83
Parsons, Rose Peabody obit
Jun 85
Parsons, Mrs. William Barclay
See Parsons, R. P. obit
Partch, Virgil F(ranklin) obit
Oct 84
Pate, Martha B. Lucas obit Jul
83
Paterno, Joe Feb 84
Pauley, Edwin W(endell) obit
Sep 81
Paxton, Tom Sep 82

Payne, (Pierre Stephen) Robert
obit Apr 83
Payton, Walter Nov 85
Peckinpah, Sam obit Feb 85
Peerce, Jan obit Feb 85
Pella, Giuseppe obit Aug 81
Pelletier, Wilfrid obit Jun 82
Pelli, Cesar Apr 83
Peltz, Mary Ellis (Opdycke)
obit Jan 82
Pendleton, Clarence
M(cLane), Jr. Sep 84
Penzias, Arno A(llan) Sep 85
Pepper, Claude (Denson) Jan
83
Perahia, Murray Mar 82
Pérez de Cuéllar, Javier Aug
82
Pérez Esquivel, Adolfo Mar 81
Perkins, Carl D(ewey) obit Sep
84
Perkins, Dexter obit Jul 84
Perlman, Alfred E(dward) obit
Jul 83
Perry, Gaylord Nov 82
Peters, Bernadette Sep 84
Peterson, Oscar Oct 83
Peterson, (Frederick)
Val(demar Erastus) obit Jan
84
Petrillo, James Caesar obit Jan
85
Phillips, William Oct 84
Pickens, T(homas) Boone (Jr.)
Jul 85
Pidgeon, Walter obit Nov 84
Pierce, Samuel Riley, Jr. Nov
82
Piñero, Miguel Nov 83
Plunkett, Jim Feb 82
Podgorny, Nikolai (Vik-
torovich) obit Mar 83
Pollack, Jack H(arrison) obit
Feb 85
Ponnamperuma, Cyril (An-
drew) Apr 84
Ponnelle, Jean-Pierre Mar 83
Popkin, Zelda obit Jul 83
Potok, Chaim May 83
Powell, William obit May 84
Presser, Jackie Sep 83
Pressler, Larry Oct 83
Prestopino, Gregorio obit Apr
85
Price, Byron obit Sep 81
Price, George (Cadle) Aug 84
Price, Gwilym A(lexander)
obit Aug 85
Priestley, J(ohn) B(oynton) obit
Oct 84
Primrose, William obit July 82
Putnam, Ashley Mar 82
Pym, Francis (Leslie) Sep 82

Quay, Jan Eduard de obit Aug
85
Quennell, Peter (Courtney)
May 84

Quimby, Edith H(inkley) obit
Mar 83

Rafferty, Max(well Lewis, Jr.)
obit Aug 82
Rahner, Karl obit May 84
Rambert, Marie Feb 81 obit
Aug 82
Ramey, Samuel Jul 81
Rand, Ayn May 82 obit May
82
Rangel, Charles B(ernard) Mar
84
Raskin, Judith obit Feb 85
Rauschning, Hermann obit
Apr 83
Rawlings, Jerry (John) Jun 82
Rawls, Lou Mar 84
Reagan, Nancy May 82
Reagan, Ronald (Wilson) Nov
82
Reddy, N(eelam) Sanjiva Mar
81
Redford, Robert Mar 82
Redgrave, Sir Michael obit
May 85
Redpath, Jean Feb 84
Reed, John S(hepard) Jan 85
Reeve, Christopher May 82
Regan, Donald T(homas) Nov
81
Reichelderfer, F(rancis)
W(ilton) obit Mar 83
Reid, Kate Mar 85
Renault, Mary obit Feb 84
Rexroth, Kenneth Apr 81 obit
Aug 82
Richardson, Sir Ralph obit
Nov 83
Richie, Lionel Jul 84
Richter, Charles Francis obit
Nov 85
Riddleberger, James W(illiams)
obit Jan 83
Ride, Sally K(risten) Oct 83
Riley, Bridget (Louise) Sep 81
Ríos Montt, José Efraín May
83
Ritter, Bruce Jun 83
Rivera, Chita Oct 84
Rivlin, Alice M(itchell) Oct 82
Roa (y García), Raúl obit Sep
82
Robarts, John P(armenter) obit
Jan 83
Robinson, John (Arthur Thom-
as) obit Feb 84
Robinson, M(aurice) R(ichard)
obit May 82
Robison, Paula May 82
Robitzek, Edward H(einrich)
obit May 84
Robson, Dame Flora obit Sep
84
Rochberg, George Sep 85
Rock, John obit Jan 85
Rodgers, Bill Aug 82

Rogers, Bernard W(illiam) Oct 84
Rogers, Kenny Jan 81
Rogers, Roy Oct 83
Rogge, O(etje) John obit Jun 81
Romano, Emanuel obit Feb 85
Romano, Umberto obit Nov 82
Rooney, Andy Jul 82
Root, Waverley (Lewis) obit Jan 83
Rose, George Sep 84
Rose, Leonard obit Jan 85
Rosen, Samuel obit Jan 82
Rosenberg, Anna M(arie) See Hoffman, A.M.R. obit
Rostenkowski, Dan(iel D.) Jan 82
Roszak, Theodore obit Oct 81
Roszak, Theodore Apr 82
Roth, William V(ictor), Jr. Apr 83
Rotha, Paul obit May 84
Rothenberg, Susan Mar 85
Rothschild, Louis S(amuel) obit Oct 84
Rouse, James W(ilson) Feb 82
Rubbia, Carlo Jun 85
Rubinstein, Artur obit Mar 83
Rukeyser, Louis Feb 83
Russell, Mark Mar 81
Ryan, T(ubal) Claude obit Nov 82
Ryle, Sir Martin obit Jan 85

Sabato, Ernesto Oct 85
Sacks, Oliver (Wolf) Feb 85
Sadat, Anwar (el-) obit Nov 81
St. George, Katharine (Delano Price Collier) obit Jul 83
Salazar, Alberto May 83
Salisbury, Harrison E(vans) Jan 82
Sananikone, Phoui obit Feb 84
Sanders, Harland obit Feb 81
Sanders, Marlene Feb 81
Sanger, Frederick Jul 81
Santmyer, Helen Hooven Feb 85
Sargeant, Howland H(ill) obit Apr 84
Sarkis, Elias obit Aug 85
Saroyan, William obit Jul 81
Sarton, May May 82
Sauvé, Jeanne Aug 84
Savitch, Jessica Jan 83 obit Mar 84
Sawyer, Diane Oct 85
Sayles, John Feb 84
Scargill, Arthur Jan 85
Scavullo, Francesco May 85
Schacht, Al(exander) obit Sep 84
Schaller, George B(eals) Aug 85
Schapiro, Meyer Jul 84
Schaufuss, Peter May 82
Schillebeeckx, Edward Jun 83
Schlöndorff, Volker Aug 83

Schnabel, Julian Nov 83
Schneerson, Menachem Mendel Sep 83
Schneider, Alan obit Jun 84
Schneider, Romy obit Jul 82
Scholder, Fritz Apr 85
Schrader, Paul Aug 81
Schreyer, Edward Richard Feb 81
Schwartz, Arthur obit Oct 84
Schwartz, Tony Jul 85
Schygulla, Hanna Jul 84
Scott, Hazel (Dorothy) obit Nov 81
Scott, Michael (Guthrie) obit Apr 85
Scourby, Alexander obit Apr 85
Seaga, Edward (Phillip George) Apr 81
Seghers, Anna obit Jul 83
Seifert, Elizabeth obit Oct 83
Selleck, Tom Nov 83
Selye, Hans (Hugo Bruno) Jan 81 obit Jan 83
Serra, Richard (Antony) Jan 85
Sert, José Luis obit May 83
Sert, Josep Lluis See Sert, José Luis obit
Sessions, Roger obit May 85
Seymour, Whitney North obit Jul 83
Shamir, Yitzhak Feb 83
Sharon, Ariel Apr 81
Shaw, Irwin obit Jul 84
Sheed, Frank (Joseph) Sep 81 obit Jan 82
Sheed, Wilfrid Aug 81
Shehan, Lawrence (Joseph), Cardinal obit Oct 84
Shehu, Mehmet obit Feb 82
Shepherd, Jean (Parker) Apr 84
Shera, Jesse H(auk) obit Jun 82
Shevchenko, Arkady N(ikolayevich) Sep 85
Shields, Brooke Oct 82
Shivers, Allan obit Mar 85
Sholokhov, Mikhail A(leksandrovich) obit Apr 84
Shoup, David M(onroe) obit Mar 83
Sidney, Sylvia Oct 81
Signoret, Simone obit Nov 85
Silber, John R(obert) Feb 84
Siles Zuazo, Hernán Jun 85
Sills, Beverly Feb 82
Simmons, Richard May 82
Simpson, George Gaylord obit Jan 85
Simpson, Howard E(dward) obit Apr 85
Sinclair, Adelaide Helen Grant Macdonald See Sinclair, Mrs. D. B. obit
Sinclair, Mrs. D. B. obit Jan 83
Slade, Roy Jun 85
Slezak, Walter obit Jun 83

Slick, Grace Apr 82
Sliwa, Curtis Feb 83
Sloane, Eric obit May 85
Smith, Carleton obit Jul 84
Smith, James H(opkins), Jr. obit Feb 83
Smith, Red obit Feb 82
Smith, William French Jan 82
Smuin, Michael Oct 84
Sneider, Vern obit Jun 81
Soames, (Arthur) Christopher (John), Baron of Fletching Aug 81
Sobhuza II, King of Swaziland Mar 82 obit Oct 82
Söderström, Elisabeth Nov 85
Soong Ching-ling. See Sun Yat-sen, Mme. obit
Souvanna Phouma, Prince of Laos obit Mar 84
Sovern, Michael I(ra) Feb 81
Sowell, Thomas Jul 81
Soyer, Isaac obit Sep 81
Speakes, Larry Mar 85
Speer, Albert obit Oct 81
Speidel, Hans obit Feb 85
Spiegelman, Sol(omon) obit Mar 83
Spillane, Mickey Sep 81
Springer, Axel (Caesar) obit Nov 85
Stankiewicz, Richard (Peter) obit May 83
Starr, Mark obit Jul 85
Stavropoulos, George (Peter) Mar 85
Stein, Jules (Caesar) obit Jun 81
Steiner, (Francis) George Oct 83
Stenmark, Ingemar Apr 82
Sterling, J(ohn) E(wart) Wallace obit Aug 85
Stevens, Robert T(en Broeck) obit Mar 83
Stevenson, William E(dwards) obit May 85
Stever, H(orton) Guyford Jan 81
Stigler, George J(oseph) Jul 83
Sting Jul 85
Stockman, David (Alan) Aug 81
Stoddard, George D(insmore) obit Feb 82
Strasberg, Lee obit Apr 82
Straus, Jack I(sidor) obit Nov 85
Strawberry, Darryl Jun 84
Stroessner, Alfredo Mar 81
Struble, Arthur D(ewey) obit Jul 83
Stuart, Jesse obit Apr 84
Stutz, Geraldine (Veronica) May 83
Styne, Jule May 83
Sullivan, John L(awrence) obit Oct 82
Sumner, Gordon See Sting

Sun Myung Moon See Moon, S. M.
Sun Yat-sen, Mme. obit Jul 81
Sunay, Cevdet obit Aug 82
Suslov, Mikhail A(ndreyevich) obit Mar 82
Sutherland, Donald Feb 81
Suzuki, Zenko Jan 81
Swanson, Gloria obit May 83
Swing, Joseph M(ay) obit Feb 85
Syberberg, Hans Jürgen Apr 83

Tabb, Mary Decker See Decker, Mary
Taft, Charles P(helps, 2d) obit Aug 83
Talvela, Martti Oct 83
Tandy, Jessica Aug 84
Tati, Jacques obit Jan 83
Taylor, A(lan) J(ohn) P(ercivale) Nov 83
Taylor, Elizabeth Oct 85
Taylor, Glen H(earst) obit Jul 84
Tcherkassky, Marianna Nov 85
Teague, Olin E(arl) obit Apr 81
Teale, Edwin Way obit Jan 81
Teller, Edward Nov 83
Tennstedt, Klaus Sep 83
Terry, Luther L(eonidas) obit May 85
Theorell, (Axel) Hugo (Teodor) obit Oct 82
Thomas, Charles Allen obit May 82
Thomas, Charles S(parks) obit Jan 84
Thomas, D(onald) M(ichael) Nov 83
Thomas, Franklin A(ugustine) Oct 81
Thomas, Lowell (Jackson) obit Oct 81
Thompson, Hunter S(tockton) Mar 81
Thompson, Paul See Rotha, Paul obit
Thornton, Charles B(ates) obit Jan 82
Thurman, Howard obit Jun 81
Tiegs, Cheryl Nov 82
Tiger, Lionel Jan 81
Timerman, Jacobo Nov 81
Tinker, Grant A. Mar 82
Tobin, James Oct 84
Todd, Richard May 82
Tomasson, Helgi Apr 82
Tormé, Mel Mar 83
Torrijos Herrera, Omar obit Sep 81
Tors, Ivan (Lawrence) obit Aug 83
Touré, (Ahmed) Sekou obit May 84
Townshend, Peter Aug 83

Trevor, William Sep 84
Trevor-Roper, H(ugh) R(edwald) Sep 83
Trippe, Juan T(erry) obit May 81
Trottier, Bryan Jun 85
Truffaut, François obit Jan 85
Truman, Bess (Wallace) See Truman, Mrs. Harry S obit
Truman, Mrs. Harry S obit Jan 83
Trump, Donald J(ohn) Feb 84
Tsarapkin, Semyon K(onstantinovich) obit Nov 84
Tsongas, Paul E(fthemios) Jul 81
Tubb, Ernest Oct 83 obit Oct 84
Tuck, William M(unford) obit Aug 83
Tully, Alice Jan 84
Tune, Tommy Jan 83
Turner, John (Napier) Nov 84
Turner, Tina Nov 84
Tutu, Desmond (Mpilo) Jan 85
Twining, Nathan F(arragut) obit May 82
Tworkov, Jack obit Oct 82
Tyler, Anne Jun 81

Ueberroth, Peter V(ictor) Apr 85
Umberto II, King of Italy obit May 83
Underhill, Ruth M(urray) obit Oct 84
Updike, John (Hoyer) Oct 84
Urey, Harold C(layton) obit Mar 81
Urrutia Lleo, Manuel obit Aug 81

Vadim, Roger Jan 84
Vagnozzi, Egidio Cardinal obit Feb 81
Valenzuela, Fernando Oct 82
Van den Haag, Ernest Oct 83
Vaughan, Harry H(awkins) obit Jul 81
Vera-Ellen obit Oct 81
Vidal, Gore Jun 83
Vidor, King obit Jan 83
Viguerie, Richard A(rt) Jan 83
Vinson, Carl obit Jul 81
Visser 't Hooft, Willem A(dolf) obit Aug 85
Vogel, Hans-Jochen Jan 84
Von Zell, Harry obit Jan 82
Voorhis, (Horace) Jerry obit Nov 84
Vorster, Balthazar Johannes obit Nov 83

Wadsworth, James J(eremiah) obit May 84
Wagner, Robert Jun 84
Waitz, Grete Apr 81

Wajda, Andrzej Jul 82
Walcott, Derek (Alton) Apr 84
Walesa, Lech Apr 81
Walker, Alice Mar 84
Walker, Herschel Mar 85
Wallace, DeWitt obit May 81
Wallace, Lila (Bell) Acheson obit Jul 84
Wallenstein, Alfred obit Mar 83
Wallop, (John) Douglass obit Jun 85
Walton, Sir William Turner obit May 83
Wang Shih-chieh obit Jun 81
Ward, Barbara (Mary) obit Jul 81
Waring, Fred obit Sep 84
Warren, Harry obit Nov 81
Washington, Harold Feb 84
Waters, Muddy May 81 obit Jun 83
Waterston, Sam Sep 85
Watt, James G(aius) Jan 82
Wattenberg, Ben J. Jun 85
Watts, Heather May 83
Weaver, Earl Feb 83
Webb, Jack obit Mar 83
Webber, Andrew Lloyd See Lloyd Webber, A.
Wechsberg, Joseph obit Jun 83
Weidenbaum, Murray L(ew) Mar 82
Weidlein, Edward R(ay) obit Nov 83
Wein, George (Theodore) Oct 85
Weinberg, Robert A(llan) Jun 83
Weir, Peter Aug 84
Weiss, Peter obit Jul 82
Weiss, Ted Oct 85
Weizsäcker, Carl Friedrich von Jan 85
Weizsäcker, Richard von Mar 85
Welch, Robert (Henry Winborne Jr.) obit Mar 85
Welles, (George) Orson obit Nov 85
Wenders, Wim Jul 84
Werner, Oskar obit Jan 85
Wertham, Fredric obit Jan 82
West, Jessamyn obit Apr 84
West, Mae obit Jan 81
West, Dame Rebecca obit May 83
Weston, (Theodore) Brett Feb 82
White, E(lwyn) B(rooks) obit Nov 85
White, Katharine Elkus obit Jun 85
White, Robert E(dward) May 84
Whitehead, Don(ald Ford) obit Mar 81
Whitney, John Hay obit Apr 82

Whittemore, Arthur obit Feb 85

Wick, Charles Z. Mar 85

Wilcox, Francis O(rlando) obit Apr 85

Wilde, Frazar B(ullard) obit Aug 85

Wilder, Alec obit Feb 81

Wilder, Billy Oct 84

Wilkins, Roy obit Oct 81

Will, George F(rederick) Sep 81

Williams, Billy Dee Apr 84

Williams, Eric (Eustace) obit May 81

Williams, Gluyas obit Apr 82

Williams, Joe Apr 85

Williams, John Jul 83

Williams, John Bell obit May 83

Williams, Mary Lou obit Jul 81

Williams, Paul Jun 83

Williams, Tennessee obit Apr 83

Williams, Vanessa May 84

Wills, Garry Jun 82

Willson, Meredith obit Aug 84

Wilson, Carroll Louis obit Mar 83

Wilson, Kenneth G(eddes) Sep 83

Wilson, Peter (Cecil) obit Aug 84

Winchell, Constance M(abel) obit Sep 84

Winfield, Dave Jan 84

Winger, Debra Jul 84

Wise, James DeCamp obit Apr 84

Wolfenden, Lord See Wolfenden, Sir John obit

Wolfenden, Sir John (Frederick) obit Mar 85

Wood, John Apr 83

Wood, Natalie obit Jan 82

Woodhouse, Barbara (Blackburn) Feb 85

Woodhouse, (Margaret) Chase Going obit Apr 85

Woods, Donald Feb 82

Woods, George D(avid) obit Oct 82

Woodson, Carter G(odwin) obit Yrbk 84 (died Apr 50)

Wright, Louis B(ooker) obit Jun 84

Wu, K(uo) C(heng) obit Aug 84

Wurf, Jerry obit Feb 82

Wyeth, Andrew (Newell) Nov 81

Wyler, William obit Sep 81

Wyman, Thomas H(unt) Jun 83

Wyszynski, Stefan Cardinal obit Jul 81

Yadin, Yigael obit Aug 84

Yankelovich, Daniel Mar 82

Yeh, George K(ung-)C(hao) obit Jan 82

Yost, Charles W(oodruff) obit Jul 81

Young, Milton R(uben) obit Jul 83

Young, Stephen M(arvin) obit Feb 85

Yourcenar, Maguerite Nov 82

Yukawa, Hideki obit Nov 81

Zablocki, Clement J(ohn) Jun 83 obit Jan 84

Zevin, B(enjamin) D(avid) obit Feb 85

Zhao Ziyang Jun 84

Ziaur Rahman Jun 81 obit Jul 81

Zimbalist, Efrem obit Apr 85

Zulli, Floyd, Jr. obit Jan 81

Zworykin, Vladimir K(osma) obit Sep 82